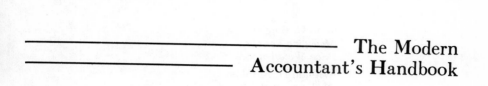

The Modern
Accountant's Handbook

The Modern Accountant's Handbook

edited by

James Don Edwards
J. M. Tull Professor of Accounting
University of Georgia

Homer A. Black
Professor of Accounting
Florida State University

Dow Jones-Irwin   Homewood, Illinois   60430

2 3 4 5 6 7 8 9 0 MP 5 4 3 2 1 0 9 8

ISBN 0-87094-121-6
Library of Congress Catalog Card No. 76–2112
Printed in the United States of America

Dedicated to Dick Irwin
for his contributions to
professional education for business,
and for his personal friendship,
encouragement, and support
for this project.

Preface

Executives and their professional accounting and financial advisers face exceedingly complex responsibilities in formulating and carrying out accounting policy for the economic enterprise of today. *The Modern Accountant's Handbook* is designed as a unique, practical guide to assist them in fulfilling these responsibilities.

The impact of accounting policy on the ability of an enterprise to attract capital and to operate effectively and profitably has increased enormously in the last 25 years, primarily as a result of:

1. The increasing comprehensiveness of public financial reporting requirements.
2. The extended use of sophisticated management concepts and analytical techniques in planning and controlling enterprise activity.
3. The accelerating use of high-speed, high-capacity data processing systems.
4. The growing demands for more and better information by the Internal Revenue Service, the Securities and Exchange Commission, the stock exchanges, and other public agencies.

The expanding scope of enterprise accountability and the intensifying need for more and better accounting information demand new and more comprehensive knowledge on the part of executives and their professional advisers. Previously the executive had to obtain this knowledge mainly by spending great amounts of time in reading many different publications. The objective of *The Modern Accountant's Handbook* is to fill a void in accounting literature by providing in one convenient volume practical guidance for solving a wide variety of accounting and reporting problems of the modern enterprise. The *Handbook* is an accurate, up-to-date compendium of current knowledge on accounting policies that have proved to be practically effective, written by individuals who have been involved extensively and significantly in formulating and implementing accounting policy. Most of the contributing authors are professional accounting executives from industry, but there is also significant input from leading public accountants and accounting educators.

The authors include executives in a broad range of industries including aircraft, automotive, banking, chemicals, communications, consumer goods, food, petroleum, steel, and public utilities. Professional firms and organizations represented among the authors include accountants, appraisers, attorneys, and investment analysts.

The Editorial Advisory Board consists of top-level executives in professional accounting, investment banking, and industry.

Part 1 of the *Handbook* examines the objectives of financial accounting with great weight of authority, reflecting the viewpoints of the business executive, the independent public accountant, the financial analyst, and public policy.

Parts 2 and 3 pertain to establishing and carrying out management objectives in controlling the enterprise's assets and in realizing and measuring its income. Part 4 deals with special accounting-related problems in administering the enterprise, including reporting return on investment, segment reporting, accounting for human resources and social costs, reporting changes in price levels and current values, and accounting for businesses in financial difficulty. Part 5 examines in depth the problems of preparing interim and annual financial reports and of coordinating the firm's accounting and reporting with the independent auditor.

Part 6 addresses some special accounting policy questions of the enterprise which result particularly from the requirements of governmental agencies and the public interest. Part 7 deals with the diverse accounting standards for selected industries and not-for-profit enterprises; Part 8, with planning and control.

A detailed, comprehensive index is included in order to make the *Handbook* a more useful tool to the reader.

In summary, *The Modern Accountant's Handbook* is current, theoretically and professionally sound, and operational. It is a relevant, dependable, and useful guide for those who must make the accounting, reporting, and related managerial decisions for economic enterprises.

We especially wish to acknowledge the significant contribution made by the members of our editorial advisory board, John C. Biegler, William H. Franklin, Donald R. Hibbert, Charles Hornbostel, Archie M. Long, Russell E. Palmer, Thomas C. Pryor, Robert D. Rowan, Howard O. Wagner, and Alva O. Way; Richard F. Vancil, Harvard University, Editor-in-Chief of the Dow Jones-Irwin Handbook series; and, for her outstanding typing assistance, Isabel L. Barnes.

August 1976   **James Don Edwards**
Homer A. Black

Contributing authors

ANDERSON, H. R. (Chapter 44*)—Professor of Accounting, California State University, Fullerton

BAHIN, JAMES M. (Chapter 24*)—Controller, Fuqua Industries, Inc.

BARDEN, RONALD S. (Chapter 5*)—Associate Professor of Accounting, Florida State University

BENTZEL, C. H. (Chapter 30)—Vice President and Comptroller, ITT Rayonier Inc.

BRAUWEILER, CARL (Chapter 32*)—Director Accounting Research, Sears, Roebuck and Co.

CALHOUN, CHARLES H., III (Chapter 42*)—Department of Accounting, University of South Carolina

CAMPBELL, J. B. (Chapter 44*)—Vice President and Controller, Northrop Corporation

CHAMBERLIN, GEORGE L. (Chapter 5*)—Vice President and Controller, Scott Paper Company

CHETKOVICH, MICHAEL N. (Chapter 31*)—Managing Partner, Haskins & Sells

COLLINS, DANIEL W. (Chapter 23*)—Associate Professor of Accounting, Michigan State University

COOPER, ALAN B. (Chapter 11*)—Director of Personnel, Armco Enterprise Group (formerly Assistant Controller and Director–General Accounting, Armco Steel Corporation)

CRANE, ALLAN (Chapter 29)—Vice President and Controller, A. O. Smith Corporation

CROOCH, G. MICHAEL (Chapter 12*)—Oklahoma State University

DAVIS, THEODORE H. (Chapter 24*)—Vice President–Operations, Fuqua Industries, Inc.

DEFLIESE, PHILIP L. (Chapter 10)—Managing Partner, Coopers & Lybrand

DILLINGHAM, PAUL L. (Chapter 39)—Vice President–Director of Taxes, The Coca-Cola Company

---

* Denotes coauthor.

DISNEY, DONALD G. (Chapter 34*)—Manager, Office Methods & Procedures, Caterpillar Tractor Co.

ERICKSON, JOHN (Chapter 13)—Vice President—Controller, First National Bank of Minneapolis

EVANS, CHARLES (Chapter 42*)—Treasurer, ServAmerica, Inc.

FISHBACK, J. KARL (Chapter 14*)—Corporate Controller (retired), City Stores Company

GRAHAM, ERWIN H. (Chapter 8)—Vice President and General Auditor, Chrysler Corporation

GUTTRY, HARVEY V., JR. (Chapter 18*)—Vice President and Controller, The Times Mirror Company

HANMER, A. PHILIP (Chapter 15)—Controller, The Dow Chemical Company

HARPER, WILLIAM K. (Chapter 18*)—Chairman, Department of Accounting, School of Business Administration, University of Southern California

HARRIS, EDWARD C. (Chapter 41*)—Partner, Price Waterhouse & Co.

HINSDALE, BEN (Chapter 32*)—Director Shareholder Relations, Sears, Roebuck and Co.

HORNE, WILLIAM M., JR. (Chapter 14*)—Senior Vice President and General Tax Counsel, Citicorp

KAPNICK, HARVEY (Chapter 2)—Chairman, Arthur Andersen & Co.

KESSELMAN, JEROME J. (Chapter 19*)—School of Accountancy, University of Denver

KINCANNON, JACK (Chapter 32*)—Senior Vice President, Finance, Sears, Roebuck and Co.

KING, ALFRED M. (Chapter 9)—Vice President–Finance, American Appraisal Associates, Inc.

KLINK, JAMES J. (Chapter 41*)—Partner, Price Waterhouse & Co.

KOONS, ROBERT (Chapter 26*)—Project Director, Financial Accounting Standards Board

LAMDEN, CHARLES W. (Chapter 43)—Partner, Peat, Marwick, Mitchell & Co.

LANDEKICH, STEPHEN (Chapter 25)—Research Director, National Association of Accountants

LAYTON, LEROY (Chapter 36)—Senior Partner, Main Lafrentz & Co. (retired). Chairman of the Board, McLintock Main Lafrentz—International

LONG, A. M. (Chapter 22)—Comptroller, General Motors Corporation

LOVE, WILLIAM R. (Chapter 17)—Vice President and Comptroller, Texaco Inc.

McGOUGH, THOMAS P. (Chapter 31*)—Manager, Haskins & Sells

MARAFINO, VINCENT N. (Chapter 12*)—Vice President and Controller, Lockheed Aircraft Corporation

MAUTZ, ROBERT K. (Chapter 38)—Partner, Ernst & Ernst

MILLER, GIBBES ULMER (Chapter 27)—Florida State University

MORGAN, ROBERT A. (Chapter 34*)—Controller, Caterpillar Tractor Co.

NICHOLSON, JOHN W. (Chapter 37)—Director of SEC Practice & Research, Arthur Young & Company

---

* Denotes coauthor.

NORBY, WILLIAM C. (Chapter 3°)—Senior Vice President, Duff and Phelps, Inc.

NORTHROP, C. A. (Chapter 47)—Controller, IBM Corporation

PARKER, C. REED (Chapter 3°)—Executive Vice President, Duff and Phelps, Inc.

PLUM, CHARLES W. (Chapter 23°)—Vice President–Accounting and Management Systems, Standard Oil Company (Ohio)

REINHART, ANDREW J. (Chapter 28)—Vice President–Systems and Administration, The Singer Company, Inc.

RICE, ROBERT M. (Chapter 45)—Vice President–Finance, and Chief Financial Officer, Rockwell International

SACK, ROBERT J. (Chapter 33)—Partner, Touche Ross & Co.

SAVOIE, LEONARD M. (Chapter 1)—Vice President and Controller, Clark Equipment Company

SCHULTZ, GLENN V. (Chapter 34°)—Manager, Office Systems & Procedures, Caterpillar Tractor Co.

SECORD, DEAN H. (Chapter 34°)—Partner, Price Waterhouse & Co.

SELLECK, DONALD P. (Chapter 20)—Vice President–Controller, 3-M Company

SILVERSTEIN, ADOLPH T. (Chapter 7)—Controller, Freuhauf Corporation

SPILBERG, JOSEPH F. (Chapter 16)—Executive Partner, Laventhol & Horwath, Los Angeles

STERN, JOEL M. (Chapter 21)—Vice President, Chase Manhattan Bank

THOMPSON, R. C. (Chapter 26°)—Controller, Shell Oil Company

VAN PELT, JOHN V., III (Chapter 35)—Vice President–Finance (retired), Vulcan Materials Company

WEEKS, L. G. (Chapter 11°)— Assistant Vice President–Finance, and Corporate Controller, Armco Steel Corporation

WHEAT, FRANCIS M. (Chapter 4)—Gibson, Dunn & Crutcher

WHITMAN, ROBERT O. (Chapter 40)—Senior Executive Vice President, Treasurer, and Chief Accounting Officer, American Electric Power Service Corporation (Management Arm of AEP System)

WILLIAMS, GEORGE E. (Chapter 46)—Senior Vice President, Finance, Otis Elevator Company

WINDAL, FLOYD W. (Chapter 6)—Head, Department of Accounting and Business Law, University of Georgia

---

° Denotes coauthor.

Contents

and the disclosure of financial information. Public policy and the implementation of improved standards. Public policy and the elimination of regulatory conflicts. Public policy and practical limitations on political influence. Public policy and the education of investors. Public policy and the enlargement of accounting. Conclusion.

Part 2   Realization and measurement of earnings

Purpose and outline of the chapter. A look at the defining and measurement processes and one definition of income. User-oriented definitions of income: *The shareholder. Taxing authorities and management. The economist and the average citizen. Summary example.* Summary. A look at the future. Appendix: *Cost of capital formulas and a numerical example.*

The nature of revenue: *Definition. Main versus ancillary operations. Gross versus net. Gains from the sale or exchange of assets. The earning of revenue.* The recognition of revenue: *The concept of realization. The sale as a test for realization. Departures from the sales basis.* Installment sales illustration. Long-term construction illustration: *Percentage of completion method. Completed contract method.* Other departures from the sales basis. The valuation of receivables: *Trade discounts. Cash discounts. Returns and allowances. Freight. Uncollectible accounts. Interest.* Summary.

Inventory systems. Planning the physical inventory. Valuation. Inventory valuation methods. *Fifo. Lifo. Average cost.* Other components of inventory: *Labor. Burden. Freight. Tooling.* Obsolescence and market value: *Lower of cost or market. Obsolescence.* Interim statements.

Definitions of subject. Types of products offering warranties and warranty terms. Method of accruing for warranty costs. Appraisal of the adequacy of the accrued warranty liability account: *Percent of cost of sales. Average of past incurred costs. Estimated lifetime cost (ELTC). Months-in-service basis.* Summary of testing methods. Methods of deferring service contract income.

Part 3   Special problems in accounting measurement

certain marketable securities under FASB Statement No. 12. Valuation of other investments. Individual, group, or portfolio valuation. Changes after the balance sheet date. Write-ups following write-downs. Market value disclosure. Advances to investees. Components of cost: *Costs to be included. Other costs associated with purchase and maintenance of securities. Apportionment of costs among securities acquired for a lump sum. Advances. Identification of costs for purposes of sale.* Debt securities: *Short-term securities. Bonds. Recognition of interest income. Discount or premium. Nonamortization for temporary investments. Accrued interest at purchase or sale. Call premiums. Serial bonds. Multiple coupon rates. Mortgages.* Equity securities: *Preferred stock. Dividends. Premium or discount. Call or redemption provisions. Common stock. Consolidation. Equity method. Intercompany profits. Cost method. Property dividends. Liquidating dividends. Stock dividends and splits. Changes in ownership interest.* Warrants and rights. Convertible securities: *Nature of convertibles. Discount or premium amortization. Income recognition before conversion. Conversion.*

Financial statement disclosure of dividends. Establishing a dividend policy. Accounting for stock options: *Nature. Qualified stock options. Methods of accounting for stock options. Measurement of compensation. Disclosure of options and warrants. Conclusion.*

Part 4 Special problems in administering corporate resources

The need for forecasts. The practice of corporate forecasting. Organization for forecasting. Short-term forecasting cycle. Forecasting by responsibility center. Aids in forecasting. Developments in forecast disclosure. Ability to forecast. Advantages and disadvantages of public forecasting. Presentation. Distribution. Legal liability. Summary. Appendix.

Human resource accounting: *The basic conceptual approaches. Methods
and techniques. Implementation. Conclusion.* Social cost accounting:
*Areas of corporate social performance. Public reporting of corporate social
performance. Social costing versus conventional costing. Measurement and
reporting of social costs. Nonmonetary indicators of corporate social performance. Conclusion.*

Background. Possible alternatives to historical cost. Reporting the effect
of price-level changes. Preparation of general price-level adjusted financial statements: *Step 1. Select index and compute conversion factors.
Step 2. Identify monetary and nonmonetary items. Step 3. Restate nonmonetary items. Step 4. Restate monetary items in the balance sheet at
the beginning of the first year. Step 5. Analyze income–expense items
and all dividends or other changes in retained earnings and determine
when amounts originated. Step 6. Apply the "cost or market" rule to restated assets and liabilities where such rule would be applied in historical
cost financial statements. Step 7. Compute the general purchasing power
gain or loss on monetary items. Step 8. Roll forward restated statements
of the prior year to units of current purchasing power.* Short-cut or alternative procedures. Current value: *Current replacement cost. Exit, liquidation, or market value. Present value of future cash flow.* Current value
accounting. Conclusion.

Purpose of chapter. Introduction to the bankruptcy act: *History of the
bankruptcy act. Meaning and significance of insolvency. Basis of accountability under the act. General nature of the proceedings.* Establishing judicial control: *Commencement of proceedings. Hearing for adjudication or dismissal. First meeting of creditors. Election and qualification
of trustee.* Accounting and reporting requirements. Administration of the

estate: *Financial and management audit. Operation and rehabilitation of the business. Submission of plan.* Summary.

Part 5 Publication of financial information

interim reports. SEC Rule 10b-5. Guidelines for interim financial reporting. Opinion No. 28. Unsettled areas. What should interim reports include? The future.

Part 6 Accounting policy and corporate liability

39. **Corporate tax management,** *Paul L. Dillingham* **898**

Why a corporate tax department? Tax compliance: *Sales tax of vendors. Sales tax of purchaser. Information for income tax returns.* Tax planning: *Use of computers in tax compliance and planning. When should a tax department be formed? How should a tax department be structured? Acquiring and training professional tax staff. Tax library. Sources of tax department personnel. Continuing education. Some operating guidelines. Relationships within and outside the company.* Summary.

Part 7 **Accounting standards for special profit and nonprofit enterprises**

40. **Current problems and practical solutions of accounting and reporting for regulated electric and gas utilities,**
Robert O. Whitman **917**

Changed economic and sociological environments. Public utility accounting: Special considerations: *Impact of rate making on application of generally accepted accounting principles to utility accounting. Public utility accounting regulation.* Eroding interest coverage: A critical situation for utilities and their customers: *What is coverage? The problem. The result. Possible solutions.* Allowance for funds used during construction (AFDC): *Factors to be considered in computing the allowance for funds used during construction. SEC disclosure requirements. Example of AFDC calculation. An accounting mechanism to meet changed conditions. Compensating for the recovery lag.* Flow through versus normalization accounting: Two acceptable methods for accounting for federal income tax reductions depending upon method adopted in establishing rates: *Normalization accounting. Flow-through accounting.* The cost of improving the environment: Adding to the financial burden: *Industrial development bonds and tax incentives: Helping to lighten the burden. The need for environmental quality protection (EQP) clauses in electric utility rate schedules.* Lease capitalization: What will be the implications? *Why public utilities lease. The captalization controversy.* Rate making: The key to problems: *An era gone by. A changed climate. Rate regulation responsibility: Fair treatment for both consumer and investor. The necessity for changes in rate making. Compensate for regulatory lag. Increase the use of automatic escalation clauses. Use projected test years.*

Include construction work in progress in rate base. Increase the usage of normalization accounting. Provide for a return on efficiency. Recognize appropriate differentials between rate of return for equity capital and interests costs for long-term debt. The management accounting approach and utility accounting.

Part 8 Planning and control

The traditional costing systems: *Job order costing system. Process costing system. Hybrid costing systems.* Fundamental purposes of a cost system: *Cost control for financial target realization. Cost analysis for pricing and contract negotiation. Records supporting inventory valuation. Performance measurement. Accurate and timely reports. Historical records and documentation. Accumulation of data for special studies. Audit support detail.* Operational aspects of a costing system: *Support records, documents, and files. Internal analysis and reporting. Controlling change orders. Cost control through systems management.* Federal cost accounting standards: *CAS No. 401—Consistency in Estimating, Accumulating, and Reporting Costs. CAS No. 402—Consistency in Allocating Costs Incurred for the Same Purpose. CAS No. 403—Allocation of Home Office Expenses to Segments. CAS No. 404—Capitalization of Tangible Assets. CAS No. 405—Accounting for Unallowable Costs. CAS No. 406—Cost Accounting Period. CAS No. 407—Use of Standard Costs for Direct Material and Direct Labor. CAS No. 408—Accounting for Costs of Compensated Personal Absence. CAS No. 409—Depreciation of Tangible Capital Assets. CAS No. 410—Allocation of Business Unit General and Administrative Expense to Final Cost Objectives. CAS No. 411—Accounting for the Acquisition Costs of Material. CAS No. 412—Composition and Measurement of Pension Cost.* The controller's function: *Organization. Responsibilities.* Appendix.

Control of operations. Motivation of people. Use of standard cost data by the general manager: *Business plans. Organizational structure. Motivating subordinates. Goals and objectives. Decisions regarding alternative actions.* Use of standard cost data by the finance function: *Reporting and analyzing operating results. Estimating costs of new products. Pricing decisions. Plans and forecasts. Alternative courses of action.* Use of standard cost data by the production function: *Direct labor performance variance. Direct labor rate variance. Direct material usage variance. Overhead variances.* Use of standard cost data by the purchasing function: *Purchase price variance. Direct material usage variance. Direct labor performance variance.* Use of standard cost data by the materials control function: *Material scheduling. Inventory level. Direct labor performance and direct material usage variances.* Use of standard cost data by the production scheduling function. Use of standard cost data by the personnel function: *Direct labor rate variance. Direct labor performance variance.* Use of standard cost data by the industrial engineering function: *Checking validity of engineered standards. BWS / CWS variance. Selection of production method.* Use of standard cost data by the plant engineering function: *Plant maintenance. Capital expenditures.* Use of standard cost data by the marketing function. Additional uses of standard cost data common to all staffs: *Planning staff requirements. Performance measurement.* Summary.

PART 1

The objectives of corporate financial accounting

Chapter 1

The objectives of corporate financial accounting— The firm's view

Discussions of the objectives of financial accounting often are limited only to the objectives of financial statements issued to the public. Financial accounting includes much more than external reporting, for it is absolutely necessary to manage a business.

This is recognized in a basic policy statement approved by the Council of the American Institute of Certified Public Accountants in 1966. It states in part:

> Accounting is a discipline which provides financial and other information essential to the efficient conduct and evaluation of the activities of any organization.
>
> The information which accounting provides is essential for (1) effective planning, control and decision making by management, and (2) discharging the accountability of organizations to investors, creditors, government agencies, taxing authorities, association members, contributors to welfare institutions, and others.

Accounting information measures the progress of a commercial enterprise in reaching its primary goal, which is to use cash to make a profit and to generate a maximum amount of cash to return to its owners.

* Vice President and Controller, Clark Equipment Company.

3

INTERNAL USES OF ACCOUNTING

It is pointless to argue the relative importance of internal and external reporting. Both kinds of reporting are needed, and both emanate from a single system of accounting. Although internal and external reports may differ in scope, detail, and relative emphasis, the requirements for public reporting result in management reports which are essentially consistent with those same requirements.

Accounting is used by management for control, planning, and decision making. Management is concerned with accounting information primarily for the present and the future. Information is reported at least monthly, and some of it even weekly or daily.

Control

The management of a company must control the business. It must have a system that provides a basis for carrying out its plans. That system is accounting.

Accounting, using centuries-old double-entry bookkeeping, is still the nearly universal system for providing financial control of business. Its balancing requirements build in an important check on accuracy. Of course, vast technical improvements have been made in accumulating, processing, and reporting information; and significant additional internal checks and controls have been developed to provide integrity of financial information and to safeguard assets. Many companies, for example, use a standard cost accounting system integrated with the basic accounting system as a further means of providing financial control over the operations of the business.

Accounting reports are among the most important means of communicating management's plans, policies, and accomplishments. Properly used, they can assist in the motivation of managers. Appraisal of management's performance is often based in part on accounting information, frequently resulting in a salary increase or decrease, a promotion or demotion, or other appropriate action.

Planning

Management must plan business actions of the future. Historical accounting information is helpful in this process, but assumptions about the future are necessary. Although forecasts of future conditions must be made, a plan is much more than a forecast. It is a blueprint of how to make things happen.

Plans must be stated in accounting terms consistent with the reporting system in use to produce actual results, which will be compared to the plans. A budgeting system for a period, usually of a year, is often followed as part of the plan.

Management plans are frequently called profit plans in order to stress the importance of profits to business. It is necessary in planning, however, to consider also the resources that will be required to achieve a profit plan. For example, a plan to increase production and shipments of a product may require additional plant facilities, inventory, and other working capital, thus calling for additional financing. Plans must integrate all facets of financial management.

Decision making

Accounting information is used in decision making. The decision may be to enter a new market, develop a new product, buy or rent a piece of equipment, discontinue a product line, acquire another company, or take other actions to increase profits or solve problems. Often alternative solutions to a problem are available. Sometimes financial or other constraints may force comparisons and selection of a single course of action from among otherwise unrelated and dissimilar alternatives.

EFFECT OF EXTERNAL REPORTING ON INTERNAL REPORTING

The foregoing brief discussion is intended to reveal the primary uses of accounting information by management. Management also must discharge its public reporting obligations. In doing so, management is bound by a vast array of rules emanating from several regulatory bodies. A change in those rules may have a significant effect on internal reporting. For example, our company made two changes in its financial reporting to the public in 1974.

Our finance subsidiaries changed their method of accounting for finance revenue to comply with a new pronouncement of the American Institute of Certified Public Accountants. The pronouncement requires the new method to be applied retroactively by restating prior period financial statements. Therefore, we restated appropriate balance sheet and income statement items for internal purposes for the prior 4 years and for external purposes for the prior 14 years. Because the income of the finance subsidiaries is included in consolidated income of the company, its statements were also restated for the prior 14 years. This extensive restatement was necessary because we present a 15-year table of financial information in our annual report to stockholders. In addition, our long-range profit plans were restated for the next five years.

Also in 1974, the company changed its method of pricing domestic inventories from the first-in, first-out (Fifo) method previously used to the last-in, first-out (Lifo) method. Although we were not required to make this change, the income tax savings under Lifo made it highly desirable for us to do so. Prior periods cannot be restated under Lifo, but for internal purposes we restated our five-year profit plans to attempt to recognize the anticipated Lifo effect.

Changes which have a profound effect on management's use of information to manage the business should not be imposed upon industry without a full consideration of this effect.

DEVELOPMENTS IN EXTERNAL REPORTING

While accounting for internal purposes has been progressing satisfactorily and quietly, external financial reporting for decades has been developing in tumultuous and controversial surroundings. As a result, American business today is highly regulated in the way it must report financial information to investors, government agencies, and others. This regulation is imposed upon business by several rule-making bodies, which have begun to issue conflicting rules.

No one can deny that great progress has been made in corporate financial reporting in the first three quarters of the 20th century. Yet today we continue to be faced with criticism of financial reporting because of our failure to arrive at fundamental goals, together with an orderly set of guidelines for implementing the goals and a suitable organizational structure for issuing and enforcing the guidelines.

Progress in financial reporting has been influenced by many groups and sectors, but it has been brought about largely by the Securities and Exchange Commission, corporate financial executives, and the public accounting profession. Financial reporting has also been influenced significantly by the U.S. Treasury Department, its Internal Revenue Service, and the U.S. Congress.

A brief history may help in understanding why accounting progress is developing the way it is used and how we might expect it to develop in the future.

Early conditions

In 1926 William Z. Ripley, a professor of economics at Harvard, caused a stir with a bristling attack in *The Atlantic Monthly* on the inadequacy of corporate financial reporting of that era. To illustrate the attitude of some managements, Ripley cited a paragraph from the annual report of a company he did not identify:

> The settled plan of the directors has been to withhold information from the stockholders and others that is not called for by the stockholders in a body. So far no request for information has been made in the manner prescribed by the directors. Distribution of stock has not meant distribution of control.

After describing deficiencies in other annual reports, resulting presumably from the same sort of thinking, Ripley wrote: "Stockholders are entitled to adequate information and the State and the general public have a right to the same privilege." Others shared Ripley's concern about the "limitless obfuscation" of financial reporting in the 20s. Among them were some leading certified public accountants, who suggested to the New York Stock Exchange that the accounting profession and the Exchange collaborate in drawing up reporting standards for listed companies.

The proposal brought no action at the time. But with the Great Depression, attitudes changed; and discussions between the Exchange and the accounting profession, begun in 1932, culminated in 1934 in the publication of *Audits of Corporate Accounts*.

This proved to be a seminal document. Not only did it set forth principles to be followed in financial reporting but it also led to the first standard form of auditor's report and to a requirement that the financial statements of companies applying for listing with the Exchange be independently audited.

The securities acts

Meanwhile, Congress passed the Securities Act of 1933 and the Securities Exchange Act of 1934, which provided for federal regulation of securities sales. The function was undertaken by the Federal Trade Commission in 1933 but was soon transferred to the new Securities and Exchange Commission (SEC) set up by the 1934 act. In line with the arrangement being worked out by the CPAs and the Exchange, companies subject to reporting under the securities acts were required to be audited by independent public accountants.

While the securities acts empowered the Commission to prescribe accounting practices for publicly held companies, the Commission made known that it expected the accounting profession itself to assume the main burden of rule setting. Yet the SEC in 1937 began a program, through its *Accounting Series Releases,* to publish opinions on accounting principles for the purpose of contributing to the development of uniform accounting standards and practices. It wasn't until two years later, in 1939, that the American Institute of Certified Public Accountants (AICPA) formed a Committee on Accounting Procedure, which was authorized to issue formal pronouncements on accounting principles and practices.

During the next two decades, many *Releases* were issued by the Commission and many *Accounting Research Bulletins* were issued by the AICPA Committee. Generally, the SEC was concerned primarily with disclosure, while the AICPA concentrated on accounting methods.

Growing criticism

Despite the substantial progress that was made under these arrangements there was a growing criticism of the state of the art and the mechanism for making improvements. Arguments arose between those who favored uniformity of accounting principles in order to provide comparability of financial statements among companies and those who favored flexibility of principles in order to accommodate the unique needs of individual companies. The words "uniformity" and "flexibility" became charged with emotion. Also at issue was whether general acceptance should be achieved by compulsion or persuasion.

Criticism was heaped on the ill-defined term "generally accepted accounting principles." In response to mounting complaints, the AICPA in 1959 formed the Accounting Principles Board (APB) to carry on the work of the former Committee on Accounting Procedure more intensively and with greater research resources.

The Accounting Principles Board

While over several decades principles of accounting had been studied, analyzed, organized, articulated, and presented by many respected scholars, there had not emerged a conceptual framework from which solutions to individual problems could be drawn in a logical and consistent manner. Therefore the APB directed its research arm's initial effort to the search for basic postulates, from which principles would be derived, and these principles in turn would lead to rules of practice that would overcome all of the ills of financial reporting.

Although highly regarded scholars did a commendable job in finding basic postulates and broad principles of accounting, the APB promptly rejected the studies as being "too radically different from present generally accepted accounting principles for acceptance at this time." The APB then set about to issue *Opinions*, which primarily constituted detailed rules concerning various accounting problem areas.

Throughout the life of the APB, many business scandals occurred in which fraud and bad business judgment were involved. These scandals named management and public accounting firms as defendants, and the latter often sought as a defense their adherence to generally accepted accounting principles. This kind of situation heaped additional criticism on accounting principles and the organizational structure for determining them.

Under the APB, rule making became more of a participative activity, with industry and others being given an opportunity to voice their needs and concerns.

The APB approach to detailed rule making brought forth a further controversy over whether companies and their accountants had to follow the *Opinions* or were free to depart from them if they wished. The argument brought clearly into focus a condition which had long prevailed but suddenly had become critical: The AICPA, most recently through its APB, had assumed a regulatory responsibility which it had no authority to carry out.

Valiant efforts were made by the accounting profession to seek, through the AICPA *Code of Professional Ethics*, the sanctions many felt were necessary to enforce *APB Opinions*. Meanwhile, it was becoming more and more apparent to more and more people that the only enforcer was the SEC.

In fact, the SEC assumed a dominant position in determining

accounting rules and the APB a subordinate one. The SEC used the APB for doing research and detailed rule making within parameters set by the SEC. This was a convenient arrangement for the SEC. It permitted the SEC to function wih a relatively small accounting staff while enjoying the extensive expert services of a private sector board. This arrangement diverted almost all criticism and some pressures to the APB.

The decline of the APB

While this arrangement was fine for the SEC, it was intolerable for the APB, which faced a number of crises in 1969 and 1970 that indicated its remaining life would be short. After taking an initial unequivocal position on accounting for business combinations based on principle, which would have ruled out pooling-of-interests accounting, the APB was hit by intense pressures to modify that position. As the months went by and pressures mounted, the APB backed down step by step to a weak position under which poolings remain alive and well and living in the United States today. Industry and the accounting profession joined in fighting the APB. Some groups wrote to key congressional committees suggesting that this subject should more appropriately be left to the legislative and regulatory functions of the federal government. Others threatened to sue the APB if the *Opinion* was issued.

Some of the APB's opponents were not satisfied with defeating the APB on business combinations. Once again the call was for a renewed search for a conceptual base for accounting and a new organizational structure. Perhaps it is of passing interest now to note that the event which, for all practical purposes committed the AICPA to ultimate abandonment of the APB and its responsibility for accounting principles, took place on January 7 and 8, 1971, at the Watergate—at a meeting of managing partners of 21 public accounting firms, clandestinely arranged but later publicized as a major achievement in determination of accounting standards in the private sector.

Two study groups

From this meeting emerged studies of the objectives of financial statements and of the organizational structure for setting accounting principles.

In both studies the terminology had changed, but not the issues. The prospectus of the structure study, to become known as the Wheat Committee, called for finding "ways for the AICPA to improve its function of establishing accounting principles." The final report, however, changed the terminology to "establishing financial accounting standards," and recommended removing the function from the AICPA and placing it in a new Financial Accounting Standards Board (FASB) independent of all other groups.

The charter of the objectives study, to become known as the Trueblood Committee, rejected the terms postulates and principles and stated the purpose of the study as being to refine the objectives of financial statements, which "should facilitate establishment of guidelines and criteria for improving accounting and financial reporting."

Both study groups were composed of eminent men who approached their studies in a professional manner. Both final reports were quickly accepted and highly praised as representing substantial progress in improving the corporate financial reporting process.

The report on objectives is an excellent document. Who can quarrel with "The basic objective of financial statements is to provide information useful for making economic decisions"? The study does become more specific than this, and its conclusions are backed by reasoned discussion.

The difficulty, however, will come as the FASB considers the objectives study and attempts to draw guidelines from it. This process may prove to be as elusive as earlier attempts to draw practices and methods from fundamental accounting principles. Perhaps it is too much to expect guidelines to flow from objectives in an orderly fashion when we are dealing with a practical art, which is already enmeshed in laws and rules emanating from several regulatory bodies.

The end of the APB

While the study to set standards was progressing in 1971, several more events transpired which had a bearing on the study group's recommendation to remove the function from the AICPA. One concerned the investment tax credit, which had embroiled the APB in controversy since the credit first appeared in 1962. This time, however, the APB had a strong majority in favor of a single accounting method—reducing cost over the life of the asset which gives rise to the credit. They also had the backing of the SEC. Business executives and professional accountants went directly to members of Congress with the story that the APB was trying to remove an economic incentive granted by Congress. No amount of accounting logic about matching costs and revenues could overcome this economic argument—and legislative challenge. Congress responded by writing into law that no taxpayer shall be required to use any particular method of accounting for the credit. Here was a display of raw power that should forever be a lesson to those who wish to set rules without having authority to do so. SEC support of the APB was not enough to make a difference—nor was it enough to attract blame for the debacle. The APB seemed to get all the blame.

In 1971 the APB was moving toward a position of carrying marketable securities at market value, with changes in market value included in income currently. Chief executives of several fire and casualty insurance companies opposed this position, took the issue to the SEC, and effectively forced the APB to drop the project.

In 1971 the APB was also considering full cost accounting versus successful effort cost accounting in the petroleum industry. The APB expressed a tentative preference for successful effort accounting. On the other hand, the Federal Power Commission had already issued a regulation, in accordance with a petition from an accounting firm, requiring full cost accounting by natural gas pipeline companies. The industry was divided, and opposing positions were drawn up. Once again industry, together with accounting firms, took the issue before the SEC and forced an impasse, thus assuring the status quo for some time to come.

Along about the same time, the APB was considering accounting for leases. Although no position had been formed, leasing companies began lobbying in Congress to head off any possibility of an *APB Opinion* which would require capitalization of leases. The APB tabled the matter, but the lobbying continues today. Arguments at the congressional level turn on social and economic issues, not on technical niceties of accounting principle.

These setbacks during the course of the study on establishment of standards contributed heavily to the conclusion of the study group that the function should be removed from the APB and AICPA. These episodes are proof of the fundamental weakness of a private sector group attempting to carry out a regulatory function without the authority to do so.

The Financial Accounting Standards Board

The FASB is structured with that same infirmity. It has assumed responsibility without authority. This frailty was brought to the attention of the study group, but they apparently wished it away by pointing to good features of the FASB. Now amid evidence of increased SEC activism, even the FASB seems to be recognizing its precarious position. The FASB speaks wanly of a policy between it and the SEC of "mutual nonsurprise." Apparently this translates into a request for the SEC to get instructions out early enough for the FASB to be responsive in an acceptable manner.

The success of the FASB will depend on the willingness of the SEC to support it on controversial issues.

Finally, the FASB seems to be recognizing that it is involved in a political process that transcends even the SEC. The Board has announced that it is commencing a program to communicate with members of Congress. When the FASB was being appointed, I suggested that some of the positions should be granted to skilled lobbyists rather than skilled accountants. That suggestion was ignored.

Since its formation in early 1973, the FASB has made some progress, issuing ten *Statements of Financial Accounting Standards*, six *Interpretations*, exposure drafts of additional statements, and discussion memoranda on still other topics. The completed *Standards* and *Interpretations* are relatively noncontroversial, whereas the work in process concerns some highly controversial matters, such as price-level accounting, reporting for segments of a business, and accounting for leases. The FASB's handling of these subjects will be a real test of its ability to survive.

Meanwhile, during the short lifetime of the FASB, the SEC has issued some 40 *Releases* affecting financial accounting and reporting. And, after years of saying it does not want to dictate the content of annual reports to stockholders, the SEC in 1974 amended its proxy rules to do just that. As a result, we increased space in our annual report devoted to financial information from 12 pages in 1973 to 17 pages in 1974.

According to an old saying, there are two ways to deceive the public: one is to tell them nothing and the other is to tell them everything. In the 1926 case cited by Ripley, the company told stockholders nothing. Now, nearly 50 years later, the SEC seems determined to force companies to tell stockholders everything. We are happy to comply with full disclosure, but there are times when we wonder if disclosure of massive financial details may be confusing to some stockholders.

New rules by the FASB and SEC have greatly increased the technical accounting and reporting compliance requirements for 1975, and we are certain to encounter more rules in 1976.

The Lifo method of valuing inventories

But the most significant current development in accounting stems not from new FASB and SEC rules but from the Revenue Acts of 1938 and 1939, which introduced the last-in, first-out (Lifo) method of valuing inventories.

While innumerable economic events made front-page headlines in 1974, hundreds of major companies were quietly adopting the Lifo method of valuing inventories. The reasons were many: double-digit inflation, tight money, high interest rates, and a stock market which did not respond to earnings per share increases. The potential tax and related interest savings from Lifo simply loomed too large to be ignored.

The Lifo method first emerged during the 1930s when it was adopted by some oil companies. The Revenue Act of 1938 authorized the use of Lifo for income tax purposes, but only for specified raw materials used by leather tanners and producers and processors of certain nonferrous metals. The Revenue Act of 1939 permitted any taxpayer to use Lifo, but restrictive Treasury Department regulations made it impractical except for companies dealing in uniform physical units such as oil, steel, and meat. Finally, in 1948 the dollar-value method was approved in a tax court case, and the use of Lifo spread to a wide variety of companies.

In pleadings with Congress for extension of the elective use of Lifo to any taxpayer, public accountants and business executives stated that Lifo was a "generally accepted accounting principle," and therefore should be approved as a method for determining taxable income. Noting very little use of the method, a skeptical Congress decided to limit its application for tax purposes to those companies that used it in other financial reports. Consequently, since 1939 there has been a statutory requirement that if Lifo is used for tax purposes, no other method can be used for determining income in reports to stockholders and creditors.

The legislative history indicates that the purpose of this conformity requirement was to give assurance that with respect to a particular taxpayer, the Lifo method clearly reflects income. However, Richard B. Barker, a Washington attorney who was influential in establishing Lifo, says: "Perhaps the best answer is that the outside report requirement was put into the law as a deterrent to the use of the Lifo method of inventory valuation." Until the 1970s this was the only time the revenue laws were used to control private accounting.

The conformity requirement has been so influential that only in recent years, after SEC intervention with the Internal Revenue Service (IRS), have companies felt comfortable in disclosing the amount of the Lifo reserve—that is, the difference between Lifo and Fifo.

As recently as January 23, 1975, the IRS was still tinkering with the Lifo disclosures it would permit companies to make in order to comply with requirements of the APB, FASB, and SEC. An IRS release on that day allows companies adopting Lifo to adhere to APB and FASB requirements by stating the reason Lifo is preferable, and by reporting the effect of the change on income for the year of the change only. The release also permits companies to follow the SEC requirement to disclose the excess of replacement or current cost of inventories over the stated value. Without the dispensation provided in the release, Lifo companies would have been forced to violate APB, FASB, and SEC disclosure rules.

Companies must continue to be very careful to limit the Lifo information they give in order to avoid termination of the Lifo method for tax purposes. For example, Clark Equipment Company will not disclose the Lifo effect on inventories by lines of business.

Without the requirement for financial statement conformity, most companies would probably adopt Lifo for tax purposes and use Fifo in reporting to stockholders. The conformity requirement makes a harsh choice between Lifo and Fifo. One may save taxes and report lower earnings under Lifo, or pay more taxes and report higher earnings under Fifo.

Although there are some respected accountants who argue eloquently about the conceptual superiority of Lifo for determining income, business executives and the accounting profession seem to regard Lifo primarily as a tax-saving device. This is borne out in an AICPA survey of inventory valuation methods disclosed in 600 stockholders reports for 1973. Only 150 of the companies used Lifo and, of those companies, only 8 applied it to all inventory classes; and the trend for several years had been toward fewer companies using Lifo. Of course, this trend was dramatically reversed in 1974.

Nevertheless, most Lifo companies use Fifo for running the business and merely superimpose a Lifo reserve adjustment on Fifo results. In fact, most large manufacturing companies, whether on Lifo or Fifo, value inventories at standard costs for management control purposes.

The Lifo method is seldom used for financial reporting overseas, and is not recognized by most countries for income tax purposes. Therefore, until 1974, few Lifo companies used Lifo for foreign inventories because they received no tax benefit. Lifo companies could have applied a Lifo adjustment to foreign inventories in consolidation, but apparently they did not believe it was necessary to have internal consistency in inventory methods.

In 1974, however, a few more companies did adopt Lifo for foreign inventories, perhaps because they now think it is a better method in inflationary times, or perhaps because they now wish internal consistency in methods. Then, too, some companies may be adjusting foreign inventories to Lifo for computing foreign tax credits or the amount of minimum distribution, and they believe that consolidated financial statements should be presented on the same basis. There may even be some companies using Lifo for foreign inventories to hide excessively high profits which would be reported under Fifo.

Aside from the few permitted disclosures discussed earlier, Lifo techniques lie entirely in the domain of the IRS, and not that of any other regulatory body. In fact, the Cost Accounting Standards Board has proposed a standard that prohibits the use of Lifo in determining costs for defense contract purposes.

Although Lifo is considered to be a "generally accepted accounting principle," it is primarily an instrument for tax reduction and is inconsistent with almost all other accounting theories and concepts. It is incompatible with traditional historical cost accounting principles, and also with price-level, fair-value, and replacement-cost concepts which receive attention in inflationary periods.

The FASB has proposed to require that companies report income in terms of units of general purchasing power of the U.S. dollar as measured by a general price index. (The SEC staff seems to favor instead a replacement cost concept.) But it seems unlikely that the FASB proposal will become final because of the Lifo financial statement conformity requirement. Unless the law is changed, the IRS is required to terminate Lifo if a company reports its income on any other basis. Given the choice of terminating Lifo or following the FASB standard, most companies would probably ignore the FASB standard.

This situation also means that the FASB is unlikely to bring about uniformity in accounting for inventories under traditional historical cost accounting. The FASB will probably not recommend Lifo as the preferred method for all companies, and the SEC requirement for disclosure of current or replacement cost of Lifo inventories implies a preference for other methods. Attempts to eliminate Lifo in financial reporting would run afoul of the conformity law. Very likely, companies enjoying the benefits of Lifo would strongly oppose efforts by the FASB, SEC, or anyone else to delete the conformity clause in the law, for fear that Congress would remove the very right to use Lifo. Furthermore, companies resisting attempts to change the law would probably successfully enlist their public accounting firms in support of their resistance.

Although statistics are not available as to the popularity of Lifo today, the many Lifo adoptions reported in 1974 probably make it the method predominantly used now by large industrial companies for valuing domestic inventories. The support of a long-established law by a majority of U.S. industrial companies would be hard to overcome. There is little reason to believe the FASB and SEC would be any more successful in an attack on the Lifo law than the APB and SEC were in their attempt to avert congressional involvement in accounting for the investment credit.

Accounting for tax purposes

In other respects, accounting for tax purposes has had a more significant effect on financial reporting than is frequently acknowledged. Private companies typically use accounting methods that produce the lowest income tax, and they use these methods for financial reporting purposes as well as for income tax purposes. When a private company goes public, accounting methods sometimes must be changed, but many of the methods used for tax purposes are continued.

In addition, in recent years direct action by the U.S. Treasury Department is affecting financial reporting to stockholders.

Since about 1970 the U.S. Treasury Department selectively has been putting a financial statement conformity requirement in regulations on accounting for income tax purposes. The language used in the regulations is similar to the Lifo conformity language used in the Revenue Act of 1939. When two or more alternative accounting methods are available, one of which produces maximum tax benefits and the other produces better financial reports to investors, the U.S. Treasury Department has required that a method may be used for tax purposes only if it is used in financial reports to stockholders and creditors. Notable examples of this requirement are in IRS regulations on full cost accounting for inventories and proposed but later withdrawn regulations on construction contract accounting. If this movement continues, it will further impinge upon the accounting rule-making function of the FASB and SEC.

A ranking of authorities

Where does this leave the beleaguered accounting officer in his or her attempts to comply with an ever-increasing welter of rules emanating from several sources? We look first at the most authoritative sources for guidance. They are in this order:

1. U.S. Congress.
2. U.S. Treasury Department.
3. Securities and Exchange Commission.
4. Financial Accounting Standards Board.

Congress has not spoken often on accounting matters, but when it has, it has become the absolute authority. Treasury Department rules have the effect of law; and where conformity in financial reporting is the price to be paid for tax savings, these rules are authoritative. Tax savings produce cash flow, and this is usually more important to a company than defense of a specific principle of accounting.

Third in line of authorities is the SEC. Its rules also have the effect of law.

Fourth in line is the FASB. Its pronouncements have been either

ordered by the SEC or at least approved by the SEC, and they will
be enforced by the SEC.

Some industries are affected by still more rule-making bodies,
such as the Federal Power Commission, Interstate Commerce Commission, and Civil Aeronautics Board. And there are other agencies
which make rules for special-purpose reporting, like the Federal
Trade Commission and the Cost Accounting Standards Board.
These agencies may have an effect on public financial reporting in
the future.

Several international groups are issuing statements on accounting. These groups include the Accountants International Study
Group and the International Accounting Standards Committee. The
AICPA is still issuing auditing standards in which accounting matters are intricately entwined, and the AICPA has commenced issuing
accounting position papers.

An obvious answer to the problem of too many rule-making
bodies is a single agency. Such an agency would be viable only if
it were an independent government agency. Even this arrangement
would be effective only if Congress gave the agency powers that
could not be infringed on by any other agency and only if Congress
itself kept hands off. An all-powerful agency does not appear to be
likely in the near future; and if we had one, we might wish we
were back in the hands of the overlapping rule makers.

There remains room for the FASB to perform a constructive role
in the accounting rule-making function. But we should recognize its
limitations. We should be aware that the FASB has been legally
foreclosed from dealing with some subjects, and that its pronouncements are limited in scope and subject to approval of others. The
FASB is not writing on a clean slate; it must deal with rules that
exist in the present environment.

As rules proliferate, the role of the independent accounting firm
is changing from advocate of preferable accounting methods selected from among several available, to advisor as to the specific accounting method which is applicable in compliance with the rules.

Progress can still be made

Further progress may be made in establishing the objectives of
financial reporting. But progress to the most strident voices often
calls for a complete change from the historical cost basis of account-

ing. For example, it is fashionable to talk in terms of introducing "economic reality" into financial reporting. The trouble is that few can agree on what constitutes economic reality and how it should be measured.

Presumably, economic reality requires reporting in terms of current values or fair values. But this would lead accounting information farther away from the commercial enterprise goal of using cash to make a profit and generate more cash to return to its owners. Nevertheless, debate on issues like this is healthy and ultimately leads to changing basic objectives of corporate financial accounting.

Meanwhile, further progress *will* be made in accounting rule making, and somehow industry will survive the plethora of rules. Management will find a way to run its business under any accounting regulations imposed on it. Even with our peculiar overlapping rule-making structure, I see hope for cooperation among rule makers in moving toward a more coherent conceptual basis for accounting. But to expect a neat set of basic objectives, broad standards, and detailed rules, all totally consistent with each other, is expecting too much of a practical art. If that could be accomplished to the general satisfaction of all concerned, it would have been done long ago. Accounting progress will continue to be accomplished in a practical, political way through debates and confrontations, which are lively, spirited, controversial, and sometimes painful.

We should accept these conditions and be happy with them. History has shown that too many economic considerations are at stake for too many interested groups to permit progress in financial reporting to be simple and harmonious.

Chapter 2

The objectives of corporate financial accounting—The independent auditor's view

*Harvey Kapnick**

OBJECTIVES ARE GOALS

Any serious effort directed toward obtaining agreement on the objectives of corporate financial accounting must view these objectives as goals. Goals need not be achievable to serve a useful purpose. However, they need to provide clear guidelines in order to facilitate progress. Enough accept/reject criteria must be supplied so that those working on the resolution of accounting controversies will be assisted when they refer to the objectives.

Although the environment in which accounting exists is complicated and intricate, it will probably strike some as being naive to take a position that accounting objectives need to be simple and easily comprehended. Without these features, those concerned with financial reporting will fail to perceive a clear direction in which to move to improve financial statements.

In no way is there an intention here to imply that for objectives to be excellent they must be easy to implement. Neither is there an intention to suggest that one of the tests for excellence for objectives is whether their attainment can be quickly achieved. Accountants may never attain the goal set forth by their objectives,

* Chairman, Arthur Andersen & Co.

but, if their objectives are to generate progress, they will need to be reasonably specific and easily comprehended by the business community.

Accountants have been tortoise slow in facing up to the goal specification issue, and its resolution even now cannot be predicted with great confidence. This difficulty with goal specification for accounting is to some extent a consequence to be expected given that several groups with varying interests have some rights, responsibilities, and powers—partially conflicting and overlapping and unclearly specified—in connection with financial reporting. Management, regulators, investors, and independent auditors are parties that readily come to mind. Even so, such a confusing environment hardly justifies the past inability to give sufficient priority to goal setting. One would think that all parties involved with financial reporting would sooner or later—at least by now—have put a proper and realistic priority on goal determination.

However, a recital of the difficulties and lack of progress in obtaining agreement on the objectives of corporate financial accounting is not the purpose of this chapter. It will be assumed that some progress is underway in this matter as a result of the recent attention by the accounting profession to the objectives of financial statements. A point still worth making is that unless financial statements report and reflect economic reality as perceived by members of the business community, including investors, the ultimate goal will not have been achieved, regardless of the words used to state it or the efforts made to attain it. Only if financial statements give a reasonable indication of economic reality will there be some assurance that the present arrangement under which the financial reporting function is implemented will continue to be acceptable to society. There is nothing sacred or permanent about the present arrangement whereby management is given the privilege and responsibility of initiating the financial statements and the independent auditor is relied upon to add credibility thereto.

"Economic reality" is a nebulous, complex concept. Whether an attempt at its definition here would prove helpful is questionable. Also acknowledged is the unlikelihood of obtaining complete agreement on the kinds of accounting information that are useful for the portrayal of economic reality. However, I believe that a consensus of sorts exists, though presently unstated, about the kinds of information that if presented in financial statements would probably cause them not to achieve a very effective portrayal of economic reality. For instance, I suspect that many knowledgeable statement users give low "economic reality" ratings to historical-cost data and those balance sheet amounts that are the result of applying the matching concept—at least when that concept is broadly applied.

A GROWING CONCERN

Since historical cost and matching are the principal ingredients of generally accepted accounting principles (GAAP), there is some basis for doubt whether financial statements currently are portraying even a reasonable approximation of economic reality. This is an age when many traditional, longstanding customs and beliefs are being challenged. Many heretofore accepted truths have been overturned. In recent years, accounting has not escaped critical reexamination, but to date cost and matching remain firmly entrenched as the twin cornerstones of GAAP.

Of course, cost has some strengths that serve it well as a basic accounting concept. First of all, cost is an excellent indicator of value, at least at the time of initial recording. Under conditions of stable prices and a modest rate of technological change, cost can provide a continuing indication of value, and hence economic reality, without significant erosion. However, present conditions, in fact those prevailing since World War II, do not fit the stable-price, modest-rate-of-technological-change model by a wide margin.

Second, cost is generally given credit for adding objectivity to the accounting process. Accountants assign great importance to objectivity. Obviously, objectivity is a desirable feature, but objectivity associated with an initial recording of cost does not necessarily result in a number that has continuing relevance. An ancient cost may remain "perfectly" objective, yet be almost meaningless for purposes of reporting economic reality. It seems at times that objectivity has been accorded greater stature than has professional judgment, which should be a cause for worry.

THE PERVASIVE MATCHING CONCEPT

These briefly mentioned problems associated with cost have been discussed many times. Perhaps less frequently noted is the relationship between cost and matching and the arbitrariness that matching introduces to the accounting process, particularly if matching is broadly applied.

When cost is used as the basis for both the initial recording and the subsequent carrying value, modified only by occasional write-downs as a result of applying a broad recoverability test, matching becomes a necessary feature of the income determination process. In contrast, a thorough-going, value-based approach to financial accounting would eliminate the need for such great reliance on the matching concept.

Even under cost-based accounting, matching can be applied broadly or narrowly. If narrowly applied, then a direct relationship between revenue and expense is required. If broadly applied, then whenever an outlay is made with the expectation or hope that it will generate future revenue, a case can be made for deferral. The latter alternative results in the inclusion of many intangibles on the balance sheet as well as the deferral of certain types of cost. A casual review of annual reports will reveal the fact that the matching concept is being broadly applied. A consequence of such matching is that many asset balances are nothing more than residuals awaiting future assignment to expense. Such residual balances have a low "economic reality" rating in my view.

The widespread reliance placed on matching and the endorsement accorded it by the present generation of career accountants can be traced, at least in part, to the fact that accounting educators have generally subscribed to and taught the merits of matching for at least a generation. My impression is that during this period accounting textbooks as a general rule viewed accounting's main concern as being with income measurement via matching rather than by periodic asset valuation. Thus, accounting students were taught the merits of matching. Current practice suggests that they believed what they were taught.

OBJECTIVES ADVOCATED

The unlikelihood that GAAP, given today's business environment, will result in a reasonable portrayal of economic reality has led me to conclude that the objectives of corporate financial accounting should be value based rather than cost based. This coincides with the position taken by my firm. In its book, *Objectives of Financial Statements for Business Enterprises*,[1] the position advocated is that

---

[1] *Objectives of Financial Statements for Business Enterprises* (Chicago: Arthur Andersen & Co.), 1972.

the overall purpose of financial statements is to communicate information concerning the nature and value of the economic resources of a business enterprise, the interests of creditors and the equity of owners in the economic resources, and the changes in the nature and value of those resources from period to period.

Economic resources are defined as those elements of wealth that possess the three basic characteristics of utility, scarcity, and exchangeability, which in combination give the resources economic value. *Exchangeability,* as the term is used, is not intended to suggest that an economic resource is necessarily immediately marketable or that it is being held for immediate sale. Rather, exchangeability means that an economic resource is something that is separable from a business as a whole and that has value in and of itself—that it is not solely dependent on the fortunes of the particular business enterprise to which the resource is attached.

The basic characteristics prescribed for economic resources tend to exclude the wide assortment of unidentifiable intangibles or attributes of a business enterprise that may give it an advantage over others in a relatively free, competitive system and, hence, enable it to achieve earnings beyond a normal rate of return on capital. These attributes or unidentifiable intangibles may be extremely valuable—they may arise through deliberate effort or accidentally—but information about their quality and potential value should be conveyed primarily by information on earnings rather than through direct measurement and inclusion in the balance sheet as assets.

The value approach advocated also determines the related earnings concept. If earnings are to be considered a result of the measurement of economic resources, then the periodic earnings will be determined by the change in the owners' equity shown by comparative balance sheets, after a provision for the maintenance of owners' capital to reflect the effects of inflation and after recognizing additional investments by owners and distributions to owners. In other words, the earnings concept is ultimately based on changes in value of economic resources.

AN IMPORTANT DISTINCTION

An important distinction implicit in this position on objectives concerns the difference between valuing individual assets and valuing the enterprise. The position taken holds that the function of financial accounting is not to convey information about the value of the business as a whole but rather to convey value information about the economic resources of a business.

This distinction recognizes the need to segregate the accounting function from the investor function. The evaluations and interpretations made by investors based in part on information provided by financial statements should not be allowed to affect or to be introduced directly into those financial statements. For example, the total market value of a company's securities represents the market's spot valuation of the enterprise at a particular time, but such valuation has no place in the enterprise's financial statements. Failure to observe this segregation of functions in the past has introduced a circularity that has reduced the usefulness of financial information and has resulted in great confusion in the resolution of individual accounting problems (e.g., goodwill) and in growing confusion over responsibilities of financial forecasts.

Segregation of these functions demands that a careful distinction be made between presenting financial information and predicting the future. While financial statements should be presented in a manner that will assist as much as possible in assessing the future and its risks, the role of accounting and the resulting financial statements is not to predict or to interpret the future. Making predictions and reaching economic decisions are the responsibilities of management in operating the enterprise, and of the investors and other users of financial statements for their various purposes.

Human beings have always wanted to know about the future so that the very uncertainty of their existence can be overcome. Therefore, an interest in every type of financial information about the future is understandable, since investors are more interested in the future—the uncertainty of the investment—than in the past performance. However, predicting the future is the very essence of the investor function, and the investor who guesses correctly will reap rewards, whereas the investor who guesses incorrectly may incur substantial losses.

VALUE CONCEPTS

The accountant should use that value concept which offers the prospect of indicating the closest approximation of an asset's value, taking into consideration such factors as relevance, feasibility, and verifiability. Obviously, some trade-off among these factors is an inevitable feature of accounting. Of course, verifiability is particularly important to the independent auditor. Because accounting has made such little use of value data, the practicing accountant has not been really challenged to search for evidence about values. It is my view that more verifiable support for value information exists than is generally believed.

The value of an economic resource is the price it commands in exchange. This may be indicated by its cost, by a market price, by a cost to reproduce a similar product or service, or by reference to values of other economic resources that would provide comparable services. In a relatively free economy, determinations of value are made every day by those engaged in business activity; therefore, information about value is available to those who might use it for measurement and communication purposes. The question of the most appropriate values to be used in various circumstances will always involve difficult areas of judgment, but these difficulties must be faced if financial information is to be made more relevant and useful.

Accounting should be concerned primarily with market-determined value concepts for asset-measurement purposes rather than value concepts of an aesthetic or philosophical origin. Market-determined value concepts are those that can be identified with business transactions—either past transactions (historical cost), present transactions (replacement cost), or future transactions (recoverable cost).

Historical cost, being a realistic measure of value at the time of asset acquisition (assuming free market conditions and rational parties in a transaction), is and will continue to be a useful approach to the accounting for many economic resources and would not necessarily be abandoned on a wide scale even if agreement were reached that the proper goal for corporate financial accounting is value reporting. For a wide variety of assets, particularly in areas such as inventories and plant and equipment, cost not only will be the best initial valuation but will probably be a suitable continuing valuation in most cases if the purchasing power of the dollar, which is primarily controlled by government action, is kept reasonably stable. However, when there is an obvious and significant divergence between historical cost and current value, accountants should address themselves to that problem to determine if more current and relevant value data are available for recognition.

The concept of realizable value will be useful when plant and equipment suffer obvious losses in economic value, when inventory disposal will not support historical or reproduction costs, and in the valuation of receivables and other claims. Receivables that do not bear a reasonable market rate of interest should be appropriately discounted for an interest factor so that their current values are properly stated. Write-downs of long-term assets, such as plant and equipment, to realizable values should take into account the business risks of the estimated period of recovery so that write-downs are in fact made to estimated current value and not merely to estimated gross amounts ultimately recoverable.

Realizable value or net selling price is also appropriate in accounting for goods manufactured to specific order. The cost concept would appear irrelevant in those cases, since the selling effort will have been completed in advance. Such goods should not be accounted for by the same method, for example, as retail inventories or goods manufactured for stock, which are prudently not valued at selling price.

In certain cases, such as security investments and inventories of fungible commodities, quoted market prices are available and will often provide useful approaches to asset valuation. Such market price data will be relevant with respect to both value increments and losses in value. The best method of applying quoted market prices in asset valuation will vary with circumstances. Consideration should be given to such factors as blockage, extent of trading, and volatility of prices.

Where current value differs obviously and significantly from historical cost, the accountant should feel compelled to modify the recorded amount. Replacement cost may prove to be the most meaningful basis for modification of inventory and plant and equipment under some circumstances, but not in every case. For instance, when significant differences between historical cost and current value of inventory and plant and equipment develop, it will often be that the current value is below historical cost, in which event the accountant might properly turn to realizable value rather than replacement cost as the valuation basis. In addition, with respect to inventory, the turnover will usually be sufficiently rapid to keep the difference between recorded cost and replacement cost small.

However, where the depreciated cost of plant and equipment constitutes a clear and major understatement in relation to current value, the most appropriate and useful value concept to be employed will often be current replacement cost less estimated depreciation. In the long run, the value of things that are replaceable cannot greatly exceed their replacement cost because prospective purchasers would tend to elect to construct or purchase new assets when values for existing assets exceeded replacement costs. The additional supply thus induced would serve to reduce the value of existing assets. Because of such potential market forces, replacement costs can provide a meaningful ceiling for purposes of estimating current values.

Alternatively, exit values—that is, realizable values—for plant and equipment are generally not pertinent for recognition of increments in value except in rare circumstances, since immediate exit values are not available to a company not trading in plant or equipment. The company does not have an established organization for disposing of plant and equipment. Thus, replacement cost determined on a reasonable basis and reflecting estimated accumulated depreciation will often be the best method.

Absent other changes in the particular circumstances of an industry, the application of an appropriate price-level index to plant and equipment may provide a useful indicator of replacement cost without appraisal. However, circumstances of individual companies may vary drastically from those reflected in price-level indexes; when such is the case, a reasonable appraisal method should be used.

Technological developments sometimes produce different kinds of assets that provide the same services as those rendered by existing plant and equipment. Under these circumstances, replacement cost should not be determined by reference to the identical existing facility or existing equipment. The value of the existing plant or equipment should be estimated by reference to the estimated remaining services available from such plant and equipment, translated into the equivalent depreciated replacement cost of the new type of facility or equipment.

These measurements will often be very difficult, but they must be made on occasion if meaningful information is to be provided about the value of plant and equipment where original cost becomes clearly and materially inadequate as a means of valuation.

Discounted cash flows may be appropriate for the valuation of certain kinds of economic resources. For example, for recognition of the value of mineral and timber reserves, the discounted cash flow approach may be meaningful and useful in some cases.

At this time, it would be premature to identify one particular value approach as the best for all or certain kinds of assets. Experience is needed. Further, different or nontraditional ways of accounting for cost can also move accounting information in the direction of the goal advocated here.

RELATION OF PRICE-LEVEL ACCOUNTING TO OBJECTIVES

Recent inflationary conditions have served to revive an interest in price-level accounting. Accounting uses the dollar as its unit of measurement and assumes that fluctuations in the dollar's purchasing power will be so insignificant as not to undermine its usefulness for such purpose. During certain periods, this assumption has squared substantially with reality. In an inflationary period, however, it is difficult to justify the continued reliance on the assumption.

By the use of a general index of purchasing power, price-level accounting adjusts the recorded amounts to restate them in dollars of equal size, generally in terms of current dollars. Price-level accounting also undertakes to measure, and reflect in the financial statements, the gains and losses in purchasing power from holding monetary assets and liabilities. Given inflationary conditions, price-level accounting has appeal when the alternative is conventional accounting.

However, because a general price index is advocated if price-level accounting is adopted, the restated financial statements will not usually reflect the impact of inflation on the particular business firm. Likewise, as a general rule the price-level adjusted amounts will not closely approximate current values. Because price-level accounting follows the same ground rules as those specified by GAAP, it is evident that the objectives advocated herein cannot be achieved by price-level accounting.

My position, and that of my firm, has been that, so long as continued reliance is placed on cost and matching and realization, price-level accounting would be an improvement. We have considered price-level accounting to be desirable, even necessary, in the absence of value-based accounting, but we don't consider price-level accounting as a logical first step toward the goal advocated in this chapter.

A BASIS FOR MAKING CHOICES

A useful objective should provide a basis for making choices. Accountants rely on and make use of a variety of principles and procedures in their implementation of the accounting process. Thus, whenever alternative accounting principles or procedures are being evaluated, there is a need to refer to the purpose or objective of the accounting process. If value is the goal, a basis for making choices exists. The accounting alternative believed to have the capability of producing the closest approximation of value or the best indicator of value should be preferred, subject, of course, to reasonable levels of feasibility and verifiability.

Adoption of value as the objective provides a basis for progress—not instant success. Some of the amounts shown in the financial statements would be closer to value than other financial statement data. Accountants should endeavor, through various disclosure devices, to provide some indication to the statement user of those areas where value attainment has been reasonably achieved and those areas where considerable improvement is required. To acknowledge imperfections and to be forthright about the basis for temporarily continuing deficient practices should enhance public confidence in financial reporting.

THE BIAS IN FAVOR OF OBJECTIVITY

Perhaps the basic problem in moving forward to more economic realism in corporate financial accounting has been the concern of accountants with objectivity. Apparently, objectivity is equated with placing a minimum of reliance on judgment. Presumably, if an account balance has been determined objectively, several accountants working independently would find themselves in close agreement about the correctness of the number. This is the condition commonly associated with cost, but not with value.

Also, there is a strong implication that cost can be verified and that value cannot. Of course, at the time of initial recording, cost generally equals value, or at least closely approximates it. So, initially, cost and value should be equally verifiable, and there should be no significant differences of opinion about what cost is, or what value is.

What happens with the passage of time? As costs are assigned, allocated, amortized, or matched against revenue, they become subjective because judgment has been employed. The identification of costs as attaching to particular transactions, operations, product lines, or assets, or as matchable with present or future revenue, involves philosophy, assumptions, conventions, tradition, and judgment as much as fact determination. As time passes, there is less agreement among several accountants working independently about what is the correct balance for such adjusted, amortized, depreciated, partially assigned cost balances. The cluster of agreement and verifiability associated with cost at the time of initial recording does not necessarily persist indefinitely. The basic question is whether the kind of judgment used in matching costs with revenue is of a different and higher quality than that needed to make value determinations. In practice, might not there be as much evidence available to support a value estimate as a cost estimate?

Because I suspect that for some kinds of accounts value determinations would prove to be capable of meeting the objectivity criteria as satisfactorily as would determinations based on the matching or spreading of cost, and because I believe more economic reality attaches to value-based information than old cost information, I believe that accountants should lessen their commitment to matching. I propose that, henceforth, matching be labeled as subjective. In the same vein, let us acknowledge that subjectivity is not bad, per se, any more than is the use of judgment in the accounting process.

Judgment is at the heart of the accounting process, and it is this element that makes accounting a profession. Judgment demands competence and honesty. Given these conditions, why the tenacious clinging to the cost basis? Accountants continue to present irrelevant information because they can "prove" it with a document, rather than to approximate something that would be useful.

Financial statement users need relevant information, not irrelevant information that can be "proved." Somehow, accountants have come to think of themselves as precise "fact finders," ignoring the need for judgment. There should be open acknowledgment of the fact that the portrayal of the financial status and results of operations of a complex organization, whether domestic or international, by a few numbers depends on a great many estimates and much judgment.

THE VALUE APPROACH

Without doubt, transactions will continue as the major criterion for value-change recognition for financial reporting. Transactions translate values into cost that under many circumstances will be a continuously dependable and reliable means of conveying value information about economic resources.

What is being advocated is a basic change in attitude that will acknowledge value as a goal so that cost will be regarded as a means of conveying information about value, rather than being viewed as an end or objective in itself. Presentation of value-based information concerning economic resources in financial statements should be of great relevance to investors, creditors, and others who use financial statements. This information indicates the economic strength of a business enterprise and, together with the historical record of accomplishment, should provide an important basis upon which to judge the capacity of the enterprise to produce and enhance its economic resources in the future.

Substantially all economic decisions that are derived from financial information concern the future. Financial statement users make assessments of the future that are based in part on information about current economic strength and past performance displayed by the financial statements. This central role of financial statements will obviously be served best if the information is based on current data concerning values and changes therein.

Current-value information concerning economic resources enables investors to make a more meaningful comparison of the market price of the stock of the company with those values, thus providing a better measure of the current premium an investor would pay in anticipation of future earnings. Similarly, creditors are concerned with values in relation to their interests. It is difficult to see how any debt-asset or debt-equity ratios can be significant or be other than misleading unless amounts assigned to economic resources provide some reasonable measure of value.

The value objective is sensible, not radical. There is reason to believe that this objective is intuitively held by a wide range of users of financial statements, including business management, and by accountants who prepare statements. Much accounting literature has denied value as an objective, but the resolution of day-to-day accounting problems belies such literature. There is, for example, a continuous concern in accounting practice with one aspect of value. Is the asset at least worth its carrying value? Is its carrying value recoverable from future operations? Business executives, accountants, and knowledgeable users consider many balance sheets to be almost worthless in the sense of conveying meaningful information. Why is this true? They do not regard the information as indicative of the value of the assets. Isn't this attitude really a subtle acknowledgment of what the objectives of corporate financial accounting are or should be?

A FINAL CONSIDERATION

The main theme of this chapter has been that unless financial statements do a reasonably good job of portraying economic reality, as that concept is perceived by the business community, corporate financial accounting will not have been responsive to the needs of users of such information and that, in general, value-based financial statements are better suited for that purpose than are cost-based financial statements that conform to present-day GAAP.

Although advocating value for financial accounting purposes is neither new nor rare, perhaps the most significant obstacle to change in this regard is the notion that cost-based corporate financial accounting is better because it is supported by objectivity while value relies on subjectivity. Such a categorization treats the matching concept as an objective concept, when in reality it is based as much on hopes, expectations, custom, and judgment as are value concepts. Something needs to be done to dislodge this fallacy.

The independent auditor's primary function in the financial reporting process is to add credibility to the financial statements. Such credibility is signified by an expression of opinion in the auditors' report. When the standard wording is used, the auditor represents that the "financial statements present fairly . . . in conformity with generally accepted accounting principles applied on a consistent basis."

In spite of recent and continuing efforts by the accounting profession to establish a special meaning for the words used in the auditors' report, some uncertainty remains as to whether these words imply that financial statements prepared in conformity with GAAP will present fairly or whether they make a dual representation that the financial statements (1) present fairly and (2) were prepared in compliance with GAAP. Given the fact that from time to time financial reporting is carried on under inflationary conditions, it is risky to expect that conventional accounting, given its emphasis on historical cost and matching and realization, will result in a fair presentation, as statement users interpret these words. Such risk is accentuated by a lack of agreement on objectives.

The above uncertainty might be taken as ample reason why the independent auditor should revise the wording of his or her opinion if the intention is to continue being faithful to present-day GAAP rather than persist in an effort to attach a special meaning to the words "present fairly." However, the message contained in some recent court cases is clearly to the effect that, in the final analysis, no matter whether the standards followed by the independent auditor were enunciated by the profession, supported by conventional wisdom, or in compliance with well-established practices, the financial statements must have presented fairly, as the words are interpreted by a judge or jury—even though such a conclusion may have been reached with the help of some 20-20 hindsight. This suggests that any attention given to a revision of the wording used in the standard opinion might be misdirected effort.

With the courts' viewpoint so clearly evident, all accountants, and particularly practicing CPAs, must turn their attention to the adoption of objectives for corporate financial accounting that will minimize the likelihood that the financial statements will unfairly present. Such objectives must not be so broad, intricate, complex, or comprehensive that a clear direction for progress will be lacking.

The chances for financial statements to present fairly will be enhanced as accountants become willing to acknowledge that the measurement, accumulation, and summarization of the vast array of economic data about a business enterprise are highly subjective processes. It is inevitable that financial statements will be based on opinion and judgment. Indisputable financial facts are scarce in the world of business.

Forceful acknowledgment of this condition would be helpful. Rather than clinging to the hope of being able to present completely "objective" data, accountants should strive for that which is most meaningful and most likely to result in a fair presentation— yet permit the attainment of sufficient verifiability standards to enable the independent auditor to add credibility to the financial statements. Such an attitude would support current value as an excellent, understandable goal toward which to strive.

Chapter 3

The investment analyst's view

C. Reed Parker, C.F.A.*
William C. Norby, C.F.A.†

The investment analyst is a primary user of corporate financial statements acting on behalf of investors. The analyst is often one or more steps removed from buy-sell-hold decisions on specific securities. Analysts may be members of an institutional investor's staff, or they may be employed by a broker or advisor providing advice to investors. In the early part of this chapter, we list some general characteristics of investment analysts and briefly describe their role in the investment process. Somewhat more detail is presented in summarizing investment analytical methodology as it relates to analysis of individual companies and industries. The last part of the chapter discusses what the analyst looks for in corporate financial statements.

THE INVESTMENT ANALYST

The investment or securities analyst is one who analyzes securities and makes recommendations thereon. Thus, an investment analyst is one who (1) analyzes companies and industries and makes recommendations thereon, or (2) as a principal or advisor selects securities for purchase or sale in an investment portfolio to achieve

---

* Executive Vice President, Duff and Phelps, Inc.
† Senior Vice President, Duff and Phelps, Inc.

the objectives of the fund, or (3) manages all or part of the organization responsible for those functions.

These functions have been a part of the investment process since the beginning, but they have become increasingly specialized and institutionalized in the past 30 years coincident with the expansion of savings intermediaries, increased capital investment in a growing economy, and growth in confidence in common stocks as a medium of investment. These developments stimulated a rapid growth in the emerging profession of financial analysis. Analysts usually have extensive formal education and have typically moved up in their organization fairly quickly. Their mean age is now in the early 40s, but some one third are under 35. A high educational attainment is indicated by the fact that over 90 percent have college degrees and half have one or more graduate degrees. The average experience in investments approaches 15 years. More than 40 percent of financial analysts have attained a high organizational level—either vice president or above in the corporate sector, or partner in the noncorporate sector. As to numbers of active financial analysts today the membership of the U.S.–Canadian Financial Analysts Federation provides a good measure. Membership of the Federation is now around 14,000 with all members having at least three years of experience.

The major employers of investment analysts are:

1. Trust departments of commercial banks.
2. Insurance companies.
3. Investment bankers and brokers.
4. Mutual fund managers.
5. Pension funds.
6. Endowment funds.
7. Investment counselors.

As can be surmised from this list, the largest group of investment analysts are employed by institutions engaged in both major areas of investment—research and portfolio management. Furthermore, the same person often has a role in both developing advice based on research and security selection/portfolio surveillance. Adding to the interrelationship of function and personnel, analysts employed by brokers not only develop a large portion of the investment advice reaching individuals but also provide extensive services to the large group of analysts employed by institutions. Lastly, analysts employed by some institutions (notably some of the larger bank trust departments) and by such a firm as the authors' employer provide investment research and advice to other investment analysts.

Financial analysis is an exciting occupation. Its subject matter encompasses not only business and finance but also science, government, and society around the world. Its perspective is both broad and deep. It is future oriented. It has a strong influence on the direction of capital investment and hence on the shape of business and industry. It employs a wide diversity of analytical techniques including economics, mathematics, accounting, and psychology. Financial analysis thus holds fascination for many able people.

The term "financial analyst" has broad usage throughout business and/or external purposes such as capital expenditure programs, current operating budgets, or long-term financial plans. Here we are concerned with financial analysis as related to security investments. In this context "financial analyst" is synonymous with "security analyst" or "investment analyst."

Even within the field of investment, financial analysis is sometimes used to describe the entire field of investment management but at other times is confined to the narrower function of company and industry analysis. Continuing the definition then, the authors use the term financial analysis as comprehending the entire function of securities investment management, including both analysis of companies and industries and the management of investment portfolios.

Investment analysis is relatively young as a profession and is still developing the identifiable body of knowledge, ethical standards, and disciplinary procedures that have long marked such established business professions as law and accounting. Leading investment analysts, however, now meet other professional leaders on equal ground. Also, investment analysts have by now often risen to the chief executive level of financial institutions and, in a few instances, of other businesses as well. Nevertheless, there is still a wide range of skills, experience, and standards among investment analysts and probably lower average levels of all three than for lawyers and accountants.

THE INVESTMENT PROCESS

The investment decision process may be thought of as a three-legged stool. One leg is the analysis of the company and its securities and of the industry in which it operates. The second is the assessment of the economic environment which includes the business outlook, financial markets and interest rates, and international trade and finance. The third is the portfolio decision in which these two streams of information are integrated into an investment appraisal related to the objectives of the fund. Portfolio decisions sort out expected rates of return (income and appreciation) relative to risk, as the portfolio manager seeks that combination of securities which will produce the highest total return available within the risk constraints selected for the fund. In this continual winnowing process, investment funds tend to flow toward the most favorably situated companies and industries and away from the weaker and less promising areas. Economic theory tells us that this free market direction of investment capital leads to the most efficient employment of scarce economic resources.

Investment analysts play a key role in this capital allocation process. As security analysts they study and select industries and companies, gathering from the discipline of economics the general economic assumptions for their work. As portfolio managers they appraise and integrate the outlook for business and the financial markets with the securities recommendations of the analysts to make portfolio selections. These roles are interdependent; each contributes a necessary element to the investment decision.

Always the job of the investment analyst (combining research and portfolio management) is to (*a*) determine the purpose of the fund or portfolio; (*b*) decide the appropriate and tolerable levels of risk appropriate in seeking to achieve the fund's purpose; (*c*) select the strategy (types and proportions of investment vehicles) and tactics (individual securities) for the fund; and (*d*) administer the execution of strategy and tactics and monitor the results.

In all of these functions the common element is *comparison* in order to determine the most attractive (greatest) returns in relation to levels of risk. Accordingly, a prime need for analysts is breadth of knowledge and especially of different types of investment vehicles and of different issuers of securities. In addition to common stocks and fixed income securities (plus their hybrids—convertible securities) they may well have use for familiarity with the competitive merits of such vehicles as warrants, options, and interests in commingled funds (e.g., real estate investment trusts, oil drilling participations, and the like). Among issuers they must know and compare corporations and governmental units (plus with each passing year they find that foreign issuers are growing in ability to compete with domestic companies and governments).

Further, the comparison required between individual securities is itself multifaceted. Degree of predictability is a pervading comparative requirement. How sure can one be (what are the odds) that time and unforeseen events will not prevent the expected range of performance for a given security from occurring? More specifically, what are the characteristics of each security as regards magnitude and predictability of current return versus capital appreciation over time? Also, what are the taxation consequences of holding and selling each security in the portfolio?

Thus, as the discussion moves toward the narrower topic of how the analyst uses financial statements, it should be clear that "the figures" are only the base underlying the investment decision-making process. The purpose in using financial statements is to learn what one can about the past so as to help forecast the future *and* to provide quantitative comparisons among companies and individual securities.

COMPANY AND INDUSTRY ANALYSIS

It is useful, having defined the functions of the financial analyst, to put the methodology of securities analysis in broad perspective. The primary objective of any security analysis is the determination of future earning power because earning power is the source of cash flow to the investor (interest or dividends). Capitalized earning power is the primary basis of wealth. In the long run, the quality of any security rests on earning power; and so the essentials of analysis are the same for all types of securities, although the areas of emphasis may differ. Investment analysis concentrates largely on common stocks because they represent the residual claim on the business and the security whose changes in value and risk are greatest.

The methodology of investment analysis is directed to identifying change, and change in the rate of change, in the earning power and financial position of a company. A typical analysis begins with a review of the company's history, products, markets, operations, earnings, and financial position. Data for the firm are then related to information about the industry in which it operates, to its competitors within that industry, and to the general economy in order to determine the dynamic relationships between the firm and its environment. Analysis of the individual firm must also encompass management and its decision-making philosophy, product development and marketing capabilities, production facilities, and changes in all of these as they have occurred over time.

The many elements of an investment analysis must be summarized and expressed in quantitative terms. Investors generally consider net earnings as the best measure of a company's performance and the indicator of value in most continuing enterprises. The *quality of earnings* is tested by the concepts of normality (i.e., what a company might earn under normal economic conditions absent strikes, floods, wars, and the like); extraordinary earnings from special nonrecurring events in the company; the trend over a five- or ten-year period or a succession of business cycles; and stability or variability from year to year around the trend line.

All these facets of earnings add up to the concept of *earning power*, which may be defined as the ability of the company to produce continuing earnings from the operating assets of the business over a period of years. It encompasses the foregoing concepts of normality, stability, and growth. It is not fixed but will change with changes in management, the life cycle of industries, and other long-term factors. Investors are constantly on the alert to catch incipient shifts in the direction of earning power; consequently, even small variations in earnings, depending upon their cause, can have a magnified impact on investor expectations.

Underlying the interest of the analyst in earning power is the relationship of earnings and cash payments by the company to owners of its debt and equity securities. As stated in the AICPA's "Trueblood Report" on Objectives of Financial Statements:

> Enterprise earning power has as its essence the notion of ability to generate cash in the future. Cash generating ability and earnings are closely related and the longer the period, the closer the relationship. For a relatively short period like a month, a quarter, or even a year, net cash flows (other than capital changes) will differ from earnings because of changes in such items as receivables, payables, inventories, and plant. For such relatively short periods, the accrual basis provides a more useful measure of enterprise progress than the cash basis. Over longer periods, cash generation and earnings come closer together. Over the entire life of an enterprise,

they are the same. That is, earnings can only come from cash generated by operations; cash generating ability and earning power are equivalent.

Thus, the overall concept of earning power represents the enterprise's ability to achieve its ultimate goal of providing maximum cash to its owners.

The historical record is the basis for an evaluation of management's ability to plan and to take advantage of economic opportunity or defend against economic adversity. It also is the basis for the analyst's estimate of earning power over future periods—one, three, and perhaps five years. The estimating process moves from the general to the particular, starting with the outlook for the economy and the industry. Detailed analysis of new markets, new capital investment, new technology, regulatory changes, price trends, and many other factors follow. Their impact on the company is measured through the financial statements. The analytical conclusion usually is cast in the form of a forecast of earnings, dividends, and financial requirements for the period ahead. In a dynamic economy the margin of error in such forecasts is bound to be considerable, but nevertheless investors can only base their decisions on expectations of the future.

This kind of future-oriented information is not readily available to the analyst in convenient brochures or corporate plans. Much of it must be pieced together from various sources, making inferences based on past experience. Projective information is subject to considerable error and must be checked against other information. Thus, the task of the analyst is difficult and strenuous. Ingenuity is required to collect and organize all of this data. Yet these analytical procedures must be repeated many times since the investor is faced with continually shifting investment alternatives. Investment analysis is comparative between companies in the same industry, between different industries, and over time.

As part of the analysis of earning power, the analyst studies a company's financial position. With the increase in volume of debt securities available to investors and the now advanced trend toward extensively leveraged capital structures, increasing attention is being given to balance sheet analysis. *Cost of capital*—especially as it will impact future earnings—is an important element in forecasting future earning power. Also, the degree of leeway available to management for financing planned future growth must be evaluated. For example, an analyst may see a danger signal in the process of projecting future earning power prospects of a company by discovering that historical profit margins and dividend payout ratios do not square with the amount of new capital to finance the expected growth, and that the debt ratio has already been pushed to or beyond practicably sustainable limits.

Finally, we must stress once more the importance of integrating general economic assumptions into analytical projections of earning power and financial position. The experience of recent years is a poignant reminder of the enormous distortion of normal expectations that can occur when rates of inflation change drastically or when an enormous change in petroleum prices occurs suddenly. This is a problem shared by company managements and investment analysts. Shifts in economic trends are the cause of many of the analysts' worst forecasting errors just as they are for management. Hence the analyst's interest in 10, 20, and more years of financial statements based on reasonably consistent accounting policies. Hence, also, the analyst's natural conclusion that a company and/or an industry that has coped well with double-digit inflation both in the late 1940s and in the mid-1970s has a better chance of doing so should the condition recur than would be the case without so extensive a record.

WHAT THE INVESTMENT ANALYST LOOKS FOR IN CORPORATE FINANCIAL STATEMENTS

In this section the term "corporate financial statements" will most usually refer to the formal statements regularly reported to shareholders—income statement, balance sheet, sources and uses of funds—as well as normal supporting exhibits and footnotes. In addition, however, reference will be made to the numerical and textual material most closely associated with the financial statements themselves as they appear in formal reports to shareholders and to regulatory authorities. Most prominent among these are the annual report to shareholders and such reports to the Securities and Exchange Commission as the "10-K" and "S-7" (in connection with public offerings of securities).

The analyst's search for comparability and consistency

As stated earlier, investment analysis is comparative between companies and over time. In the analyst's search for comparability and consistency of quantitative data the following are the major factors considered:

1. *Explanation of the company's accounting policies.* Generally accepted accounting principles, or GAAP, continue to encompass significant alternatives for accounting for similar transactions. Examples are Lifo and Fifo among inventory accounting alternatives and "flow through" versus "spread the benefit" for the investment tax credit; but the list is long, and the variant effect of the alternatives is often very large. Thus, at the outset, the analyst seeks a readable explanation of the set of accounting policies used by the company. Formerly this involved a laborious search through formal footnotes to financial statements, and often required specific inquiry to management before an understanding of even the major accounting policies could be developed. More often now, the annual report presents in logical text format brief explanations of all the major accounting policies used.

2. *Accounting for income tax versus for shareholder reporting.* With the extensive codification of acceptable accounting for income tax calculation plus the universal and powerful desire to minimize tax payments, greater comparability and consistency appears in companies' tax accounting than in their reporting to shareholders. Hence, a normal analytical procedure is to compare a given company's accounting policy differences between tax and shareholder reporting and, often, to compare tax and book figures of one company with another. The purpose is diagnostic and part of the search for comparability. For any two or more companies, a comparison of tax and shareholder net earnings-per-share figures signals the size of the differential and indicates the degree of need for a more detailed analysis of the differences in accounting policies among the companies being compared.

The SEC requirement for a reconciliation of tax-book and stockholder income has simplified the task and improved accuracy in this type of analysis. Formerly, the financial statements themselves failed to yield all the data needed, and specific inquiries to management were required to determine tax-book income.

3. *Changing accounting policies.* Year-to-year changes in accounting policies by a company sometimes are an improvement, sometimes are mandated by accounting or governmental authorities, but are always an impediment in the analyst's search for comparability and consistency. Naturally the analyst seeks an explanation for the change. Also, pro forma data (using the new policy) for at least one earlier year and preferably for five are most useful.

Accounting policy changes do, however, often provide the analyst valuable qualitative insight as to management and its hopes and fears concerning future earnings trends. Management's strong desire to maintain or improve upon established earnings growth trends (or avoid declines) is natural, as is the related desire to "smooth" year-to-year fluctuations of earnings. Sadly, it has often been apparent that the main reason for an accounting policy shift is a desire to "improve" or "smooth" earnings rather than anything relating to the economics of the business. Some notorious examples are:

a. U.S. Steel—charging more for depreciation on shareholder's books than allowed for tax purposes during the high earnings years of the late 1940s and early 1950s; drastically reducing pension funding in the sharp recession of 1958; shifting from accelerated to straight-line depreciation on shareholders' books during the recession year 1970.

b. International Harvester—changing from straight-line to accelerated depreciation for shareholder reporting in bonanza earnings year 1966 and reversing the procedure in the poor farm equipment year of 1969.

c. Ford Motor—changing investment tax credit accounting from spread the benefit to flow through in recession year 1975, thereby including in reported earnings the entire balance of prior accruals.

d. Lockheed—changing to capitalize more research and development costs the year it began its L-1011 aircraft program.

e. Chrysler—shifting from Lifo to Fifo inventory accounting in recession year 1970.

The analyst's search for normal earnings

Analysts seek to quantify normal earnings, as indicated earlier, in order to have a cleaner base for forecasting potential future earnings. In the search for normal earnings they seek to adjust current and past results, not only for nonrecurring developments but also for the recurring effects of the ups and downs of the business cycle. The following are the major areas of use of financial statements and related material in this search for normal earnings:

1. *Extraordinary items.* Under *APB Opinion No. 30* many cash transactions considered by most investment analysts to fall outside the definition of normal earnings are reported as part of net earnings. These items that seem extraordinary to the analyst are not always consistent across industry lines. For example, gains and losses from sale of securities would be considered part of normal earnings for an insurance company or a bank but not for such companies as Allied Chemical, Newmont, or Owens-Illinois—all of which hold significant amounts of common stock of other companies salable in the market at any time. The analyst's test: Is the transaction a normal part of the company's business?

    Also, analysts are likely to want to exclude most nonrecurring noncash items from their calculation of normal earnings. An example is the debit (or charge) to income to reverse past accruals when an accounting policy change is effected.

    The authors' firm typically calculates an additional earnings-per-share figure to exclude items that seem not to be part of normal earnings whenever the amount of such items exceeds 3 percent of reported earnings, and this restated figure is used in calculation of such ratios as dividend payout and price/earnings.

2. *Comparative historical data.* Annual reports now commonly present ten-year comparisons of key income statement and balance sheet data. The analyst makes extensive use of these tables and often develops two or more decades of such data. Cross comparison of many years of company data with similar records of macroeconomic data is one way to observe business cycle effects on the individual company.

3. *Quantitative data in addition to the financial statements.* Com-

pany annual reports and/or prospectuses more and more often
include quantitative data such as the following:

a. Calculation of ratios typically used by analysts, such as cur-
    rent assets to current liabilities, inventory turnover, fixed
    assets to sales, return on equity and total capital, and break-
    down of capitalization.
b. Prices of company products either for specific items or a
    weighted index for a number of products.
c. Order backlog totals.
d. Production, sales, and/or fixed plant measures in physical
    terms (e.g., tons of shipments, number of retail stores, tons
    of capacity).
e. Number of common shares outstanding.
f. Price record of the company's common stock and other
    securities.

A number of companies have developed statistical supplements
to incorporate multiyear presentations of both financial statements and other quantitative data useful to the analyst.

4. *Text explanation of year-to-year financial statement changes.*
    The analyst is naturally keenly interested in management's in-
    terpretation of the major factors affecting a given year's sales
    and earnings. The SEC requirement for "management's discus-
    sion and analysis of the statements of consolidated earnings" is
    typically viewed by analysts as a significant stimulus to im-
    proved management communication of this type of information.
5. *Pro forma data on business combinations.* By comparing finan-
    cial statements as actually reported for prior years with current
    statements on a combined basis and statements for earlier years
    on a pro forma basis for the combination, the analyst seeks to
    determine the effect of the combination on the company's earn-
    ing power.
6. *Segment reporting.* Line-of-business and geographic (e.g. do-
    mestic versus foreign) breakdowns of financial statement data
    are another aid in the search for normal earnings. The impact
    on total companywide results of exceptional developments af-
    fecting one area of the business can be seen much more clearly.
    An example is Monsanto Company, whose textile fiber and agri-
    cultural chemical businesses exhibited large and extremely dis-
    parate results as general economic activity peaked, fell into
    recession, and began to recover during 1973–75. The SEC has

taken the lead in regulating segment reporting, but the Financial Accounting Standards Board is also considering action in this area at the time of this writing.

Quarterly financial statements

Just as management finds interim reports useful to identify changes in business trends affecting earnings, so does the analyst. Also, the trend over the years toward more detailed annual financial statements for shareholders has a counterpart in quarterly reporting. The SEC's new requirements for reporting interim earnings has long been advocated by analysts, and it is hoped that managements will now provide this information directly and promptly to the shareholders. The progress of companies is really a continuum; there is nothing especially important about the year-end except to provide a bench mark for interim periods.

Forecasting

Along with increased management disclosure and interpretation of past data, the issuance of forecasts of the future has begun to receive widespread attention. Analysts have always sought and used management forecasts wherever and whenever available. In the end, however, analysts must "second-guess" management and test their own economic and other underlying assumptions against those of management. Accordingly, the forecasting issue seems to be primarily one of disclosure—of finding the fairest and most effective methods of communicating management thinking to shareholders and their advisors.

"Inflation" and "social" accounting

For decades proposals have been made for restatement of accounting statements based on historical cost to reflect changes in purchasing power, replacement cost, and other indications of the phenomenon generally referred to as inflation. Also, there have been proposals to amplify the financial statement reflection of the effects on companies of other economic, social, or political developments such as pollution, safety, and minority hiring regulation. All of these proposals have been controversial, and every shade of opinion on these issues can be found in the investment community, just as among accountants. Indeed, financial analysts presently use a wide variety of techniques in seeking to evaluate the impact on companies of inflation and "social" costs and benefits. For the financial analyst, however, since principal, interest, dividends, and securities prices are all measured in actual units of currency at the time of each transaction, transaction-oriented accounting based on historical costs seems certain to have continuing relevance. The potential usefulness of alternative accounting methods seems therefore to be in improving the ability to forecast future "historical cost" results.

Chapter 4

The objectives of corporate financial accounting—The public policy view

*Francis M. Wheat**

This chapter regrettably presumes upon the reader from the out-set. Its author is neither prophet nor politician. There will always be enough prophets and politicians to assail us with their views on public policy, and doubtless the world would be better off if the rest of us kept out of the fray.

The subject of public policy is a difficult one for another reason. In free societies, public policy has no other valid source than the felt needs of the people. Much of the time those needs are far from obvious. There is no single authoritative speaker for the public. Instead, a welter of voices arises, some loud and clamorous, others more difficult to hear and yet perhaps more authentic in the long run. The case of financial accounting is no exception. Beyond the proposition that it should be as informative as practicable, where does one go to ascertain the public need?

The possible sources are many. The SEC, the courts, the institutions and leaders of the accounting profession, the academic community, the Cost Accounting Standards Board, the news media, the financial analysts, the major securities exchanges, and the markets themselves, all have something to say. Each trumpet sounds a some-

---

* Gibson, Dunn & Crutcher.

what different note. To any serious question, the risk is great that one's answer might well be proved wrong.

Yet sound public policy in financial accounting is of immediate and compelling importance. Our American capital markets have been, until recently, the envy of the developed world. As Professor James H. Lorie recently observed: "Some informed observers feel that the relative vitality of the American economy has been fostered to an important degree by our system of capital markets."[1] As is true of any markets, the capital markets are sustained by information. The success they have achieved has resulted from the relative confidence of investors in the reliability of that information. The vital core of the information flowing to investors in the capital markets is provided by financial accounting.

Public confidence in our capital markets has recently been shaken. Only part of the loss of confidence has to do with corporate financial accounting, but it is an important part. Improvements in accounting which will help to reverse this loss of confidence are surely an important goal of public policy. Only an active and healthy capital market can serve the function of allocating available capital to the most productive uses. This is at once the hoped-for result and the acid test of the relative degree of economic freedom we enjoy.

PUBLIC POLICY AND MECHANISMS FOR IMPROVING ACCOUNTING STANDARDS

What sort of improvements are needed in financial accounting? As has been mentioned, the answers are elusive at best. For this reason, public policy must concern itself as much with the *process* by which those answers are developed as with the answers themselves. In the long run, a well-founded process may turn out to be our most important public policy objective.

An intensive study of this process was commissioned by the AICPA in 1971. The report of that study, published in the spring of 1972, concluded with strong emphasis that public policy would best be served by a process heavily emphasizing the role of the so-called private sector. Its recommendations were accepted; and

[1] "Public Policy for American Capital Markets," a report to the Secretary of the Treasury, February 7, 1974.

the present full-time Financial Accounting Standards Board, popularly termed the FASB, came into being in 1973.

Marking the advent of the FASB with expressions of approval and the promise of cooperation, the SEC confirmed a unique public-private relationship initiated many years previously. Although possessed of statutory authority to preempt the work of the FASB or its predecessor, the Accounting Principles Board, the SEC long ago recognized the value of encouraging the accounting profession to take the initiative in developing accounting and reporting standards. That initiative is now shared by the AICPA with other concerned groups, all of which contribute to the financial support of the private foundation which, in turn, supports the FASB.

This process is pregnant with the opportunity for constructive results. The magnitude of the financial commitment which has been made and the resulting scope of the FASB's effort reflect a widely shared concern that if the FASB had not been organized, governmental institutions might well have had to take over the entire job. The output of the FASB is a challenge and stimulus to the SEC and its accounting staff. A certain degree of tension between the two bodies is both inevitable and desirable. Each knows that its product will be reviewed with a critical eye by the other. Through this means, each should be called to account for errors that might otherwise escape adequate attention. Moreover, the likelihood that errors can be avoided is enhanced by the procedures adopted by the FASB. Its stress on "due process" ensures everyone, including the public, an ample opportunity to comment on issues raised by the Board and to criticize its draft pronouncements.

During its first two years, the FASB has swung into action with commendable vigor. Will the process succeed? No one can tell for sure at this juncture. The real test will come when the Board publishes its first highly controversial statement of an accounting standard. The importance of this test was highlighted by Reginald Jones, chairman of the board of the General Electric Company, on the day the FASB was launched:

> We must recognize that with its first decision, the new Board is going to gore somebody's ox and that will be the time for us to pull together and not to splinter apart. If we falter, government stands ready to do for us what we cannot do for ourselves.[2]

---

[2] Address to the AICPA dinner in New York City, March 28, 1973.

PUBLIC POLICY AND THE OBJECTIVES OF
FINANCIAL ACCOUNTING

It may seem strange to those who have come lately on the scene, but the principal objectives and goals of financial accounting have been the subject of both doubt and dispute over the years. Once again, in 1971 the AICPA brought its resources to bear when the need for definition became compelling. Its massive study of "The Objectives of Financial Statements," reflecting the views of a diverse and distinguished body of individuals, was concluded shortly after the organization of the FASB. The timing was fortunate. The report of the Objectives Study can be a fruitful source of policy guidance for the FASB as that body undertakes the task of writing specific standards.

Possibly the most important thrust of the Objectives Study in this writer's view is its emphasis on the need to develop financial accounting standards which permit a more accurate assessment of the ability of a business enterprise to generate cash. This is no easy task, given the "single figure" syndrome—the tendency of investors, the media, and corporations themselves to overemphasize the earnings figure. In more than one highly publicized recent case, deterioration of cash-generating ability was masked by published reports of high earnings; when the enterprise collapsed, the results in terms of public confidence were disastrous indeed. It is to be hoped that the FASB will lay heavy stress on a broader concept of earnings measurement or, in the words of the Objectives Study, "enterprise earning power," which more closely reflects the ability of the enterprise to generate cash flows to creditors and investors.

PUBLIC POLICY AND THE DISCLOSURE OF
FINANCIAL INFORMATION

For many years, the most peaceful concept in the field of securities regulation was that of disclosure. Everyone assumed its necessity. It was viewed by the most conservative as a shield against demands for more substantive regulation. Its general focus was well established in the SEC's forms. It had approached the status of a sacred cow.

One might say that yesterday's cow is today's rampaging bull.

No longer is disclosure a matter of concern only when a periodic report must be filed or a prospectus for an offering prepared. The expanding scope of the SEC's Rule 10b-5 has made an omission or inadequacy in any corporate press release dealing with financial matters a source of potential liability. The specter of a securities fraud charge awaits those who fail to make careful attention to disclosure a daily concern.

Meanwhile, an activist SEC has substantially increased the financial disclosure requirements of the old forms and has added new ones. Such a regulatory response to the financial disasters of the late 1960s and early 1970s was, of course, inevitable. At the same time the Commission has been confronted by something of a philosophical dilemma. The traditional SEC view has been that required disclosures are designed for the benefit of all investors. Thus, disclosures should be simplified. For many years, financial statements in prospectuses have been required to be presented in summary form. Registrants have been asked to summarize the essential financial data on the opening page. Pie charts and bar graphs were recently made mandatory for some prospectuses. The SEC's traditional view received support from the Objectives Study, which concluded that financial statements should serve primarily those users who have limited "clout" and must rely on such statements as their principal sources of information.

On the other hand, recent events have impelled the SEC to develop requirements for significant new data bearing on the quality of reported earnings and the liquidity of the corporate enterprise. Much of this data would be difficult if not impossible for the ordinary investor to understand, much less evaluate. The need for data of this sort has caused some observers to ask the question: shouldn't the SEC's traditional emphasis on providing information to the ordinary investor be discarded as anachronistic? In "The Myth of the Informed Layman" (*The Business Lawyer*, January 1973), Professor Homer Kripke writes:

> This myth that it is the layman to whom the prospectus is addressed permeates the SEC's concept of disclosure. It limits the usefulness of disclosure to those who should be its proper objective, the sophisticated investor and professional through whom information ought to filter down to the layman. . . .
>
> Disclosure should be oriented to disclosing what the informed investor may think is important . . . value estimates, earnings pro-

jections, probable and potential minerals—not exclusively what is in the past and not limited to what the layman can handle. . . .

How does this concept affect accounting, the present principal repository for financial information? I think that we may have been on the wrong track in trying to reduce accounting to single numbers. . . . Perhaps accounting should move backwards somewhat in the direction of disclosing more detail, more information, and letting the analyst or the informed investor make his own decisions as to what is significant.

In the attempt to escape from its philosophical dilemma, the SEC recently invented a policy of "differential disclosure." Public investors and sophisticated financial analysts have different capacities and different needs. Those documents sent to public investors, notably the annual report to shareholders and the prospectus, will contain information of a general nature. Other documents will be expressly designed for the sophisticated and will contain details as to compensating balances, tax allocations, "as if" disclosure of the results of following accounting alternatives, repayment schedules for borrowings, data as to lines of credit, and the like.

There would seem to be at least three potential difficulties with such a concept of "differential disclosure" from a public policy standpoint.

The first is that in practice, the tendency may well be for "differential disclosure" to amount simply to "added disclosure." Accountants are faced with heavy potential liabilities if the statements they prepare omit to state some material fact necessary to make the statements not misleading. If detailed disclosures of the sort designed for the sophisticated are thought to be important enough to be mandated by the SEC, can an accountant safely omit them from any published set of financial statements?

Secondly, accounting disclosure and accounting principle are hopelessly enmeshed. Separated, they tend to lose significance. The current SEC view that disclosure in relation to financial accounting matters is somehow the agency's responsibility, perhaps even its exclusive province, has some unfortunate implications. FASB standards will be useful only as they incorporate whatever disclosures are deemed essential by that body with the responsibility for developing them. In fact, the requirement of a separate set of disclosures mandated by the SEC might be thought (perhaps by the FASB itself) to lessen or possibly substitute for the need to develop comprehensive new financial accounting standards. Further confusion and complexity would be the inevitable result.

Fortunately, there are signs that the SEC recognizes this problem. Some of its recent requirements (as, for example, those pertaining to accounting for leases) are designed to be lifted when and if the FASB concludes its work and announces a single standard in the area. Such a policy is to be welcomed, for it will permit and even encourage a degree of simplification at a future date.

Finally, "differential disclosure" tends to remove those restraints which operated under the old philosophy to inhibit excessive complexity. We are all experts at adding new requirements. Few of us have the courage to undertake the difficult process of simplification. The SEC should not overestimate the skills of so-called professionals or their willingness to analyze effectively an increasingly complex set of financial materials. Disclosure, like anything else, is subject to the law of diminishing returns. As new requirements are added, the likelihood that careful attention will be paid to the more important points of disclosure is reduced. Institutions go through cycles of complexity. It is hoped that we are near the height of complexity in our disclosure system for the present cycle. Much will depend on the vigor of the FASB and how well it responds to the challenge to make basic financial statements more meaningful.

PUBLIC POLICY AND THE IMPLEMENTATION OF IMPROVED STANDARDS

The vast effort expended on improving financial accounting standards would be futile indeed if new standards, once adopted, were not widely implemented. Financial accounting standards are not mere mechanical rules. They reflect broad policies as well as more detailed requirements and necessarily call for the exercise of discretion and judgment. It must be so, for if accounting is to be fostered as a true profession its hallmark, like that of other professions, will be the need for applying informed and educated judgment.

Whether or not financial accounting standards are effectively implemented depends to a great degree on the attitude of accountants in the exercise of such professional judgment. What is obviously essential is a sense of independence—independence that will enable accountants, in applying their judgment, to resist pressures inimical to the spirit of high standards of financial accounting.

How is a sense of independence to be encouraged? As with so many public policy concerns, there is no obvious or easy answer. The importance of the question from a public policy standpoint was perceived many years ago. Indeed, it is stressed in the language of the earliest of the federal securities laws. But the process of strengthening the independence of public accountants will undoubtedly be a continuing one. There are several fronts on which challenge and response can be anticipated.

At the outset, reference should be made to the involvement of the SEC. Decades ago, the SEC adopted its first rules on the independence of public accountants. These have been followed by a string of pronouncements and interpretations over the years. At this writing, new proposals to require increased disclosure of relationships between registrants and public accountants have just been published for comment. Yet the commitment of the SEC to reliance upon independent accountants as a foundation stone of the system for regulation of the securities markets remains unaltered. In the opening paragraphs of its release (Securities Act of 1933 Release 5534) the Commission said:

> The decision that the Commission and investors should rely on independent public accountants for the audit of financial statements was made by Congress when it enacted the Securities Acts forty years ago, and in the judgment of the Commission this system has worked effectively in the interests of investors. The independence of these professionals both in fact and appearance is an essential ingredient in the system, and the Commission has taken a number of steps to strengthen this independence. The amendments proposed herein are a further effort in this direction.

Questions will doubtless arise as to the necessity or practicability of some of the proposed new requirements relating to the ventilation of disagreements between the independent accountant and the registrant. However, there is little doubt in the writer's mind that most of the proposals will be adopted. In the recent past, several major corporate enterprises have gone into liquidation to the accompaniment of charges that their financial statements in prior periods presented a false picture to the public. In several of these cases, management was accustomed to discharge the independent accountants at will, without prior consideration of the matter by the board of directors. The Commission's newest proposals will inhibit but not limit the discretion of the corporation in effecting a change of independent accountants. They represent a conservative approach. More radical ideas have been suggested by others, including the proposal that independent accountants be immune from discharge for a period of years after their engagement.

Secondly, potential changes are afoot on the legislative front. The American Law Institute's Federal Securities Code Project has focused careful and detailed attention on the issue of the independence of accountants. Tentative Draft No. 3 of the Code, published by the Institute in April 1974, includes a provision (Section 1503(d)) authorizing the SEC to prescribe rules for all registered companies which would require (a) the selection of independent accountants within 30 days before or after the beginning of the fiscal year, or before the annual meeting of stockholders in that year, (b) the submission of the selection to the stockholders, (c) the attendance by the independent accountants at all meetings of the stockholders, with the right to be heard and to respond to questions, (d) the addressing of the accountants' report to both the directors and the shareholders, and (e) a procedure for terminating the employment of the accountants which would require the vote of the shareholders, in which event the vacancy could only be filled by the vote of the shareholders. Commenting on these provisions in the Tentative Draft, Professor Louis Loss, the reporter for the project, observed:

> All this may smack more of symbol than of substance. But symbolism, too, is important. And the same thing is essentially true of the whole concept of management responsibility to shareholders in the case of the great publicly held companies—indeed, of the disclosure philosophy generally.

Thirdly, perhaps it could be said that the most powerful factor in the recent past tending to strengthen the independent exercise of judgment by public accountants has been the threat of civil liability. However, in our litigious age it has become commonplace for lawyers representing injured shareholder groups to include the independent accounting firm as a prime "deep-pocket" defendant in almost every case. Huge judgments are demanded in litigation of this sort, conducive more to fear of potentially disastrous consequences if an error should escape notice than to the exercise of wise and balanced judgment. Good public policy is not furthered by such an atmosphere.

Fortunately, a significant aspect of the proposed new Federal Securities Code being drafted under the auspices of the American Law Institute will be a limitation on liability. In the case of independent public accountants who are unaware of the falsity of the data which gives rise to the claim, *Tentative Draft No. 2* (published in March of 1973) generally prescribes a liability limit of $100,000 or 1 percent of the firm's gross income (to a maximum of $1,000,000), whichever is greater, if the action relates to a registration statement, other filing with the SEC, report to shareholders, or public release by the company (Sections 1403 [g] [2] and 1406 [c]). It is hoped that the impetus behind the new Code will remain strong so that its early introduction in the form of a congressional bill can be expected.

Fourthly, many have recognized the importance of using communication between the public accountant and outside directors of a corporate enterprise to strengthen the sense of indepedence of the accountant. Although lacking general power to prescribe the use by public companies of audit committees composed of independent directors, the SEC has strongly urged registrants to employ them. On occasion, in settlement of administrative or judicial proceedings alleging the publication of misleading financial statements, the Commission has successfully sought to have the settlement order or injunctive decree require the registrant to institute and maintain such a committee. (See, for example, Mattel, Inc., and Lum's Inc.). The New York Stock Exchange has urged listed companies to institute audit committees, preferably composed of outside directors ("Recommendations and Comments on Financial Reporting to Shareholders and Related Matters," 1973). Although the Exchange could have mandated the audit committee, it contented itself (regrettably, in the writer's view) with an admonition. Leading accountants and accounting firms have urged the establishment of audit committees and have authored useful pamphlets concerning practical procedures for their use.

How can the value of the audit committee as an aid to independence and critical judgment on the part of public accountants be measured? There is no accurate way to do so, but one cannot help but be impressed by the diversity of support which this device has engendered. Already, a number of able people who serve as outside directors of corporations have made the existence of such a committee a condition of their service. It can be hoped, and in the writer's view expected, that as time passes more will do so.

PUBLIC POLICY AND THE ELIMINATION OF REGULATORY CONFLICTS

Financial accounting ought to employ the best standards regardless of the nature of a company's business or the existence of federal or state regulation over aspects of that business.

This seems obvious enough. Yet the law presents a patchwork of authority over the accounting practices of regulated companies. Many agencies insist that they have the power under their statutes to require reports to shareholders to conform to their own accounting procedures—procedures designed to meet their particular needs in rate making, the awarding of franchises, and the like rather than aimed at producing the most informative reports to investors.

This state of affairs is far from healthy even though a number of agencies have exercised a wise restraint. Thus, the FCC and the CAB have, in general, permitted companies under their jurisdiction to follow generally accepted accounting principles in reporting to shareholders even though their own accounting procedures and rules (applicable to reports designed for agency use) are not always consistent with those principles. Since 1962, the ICC has also permitted carriers under its jurisdiction to publish financial statements based on generally accepted accounting principles even though many railroads still report to their shareholders according to the ICC's rules. The recent policy of the U.S. Treasury Department has tended to minimize the earlier "booking" controversy.

Inflation may, however, create new pressures adverse to the development of improved financial accounting in regulated industries. The tendency of regulatory bodies, eager to minimize pressures for rate increases, has been to favor accounting practices which enhance current reported income and, conversely, to forbid the use of practices which reduce or defer income. Should new standards be found necessary in order more accurately to reflect the financial progress of an enterprise in an inflationary era (including price-level or replacement cost adjustments) the result could well bring about a steep reduction in the income that would otherwise be reported. If both the FASB and SEC lack power to require such new standards to be followed in the case of regulated companies (after allowing for proper exceptions), confusion among investors and a weakening of the process of improving financial accounting standards could result.

From the viewpoint of public policy it makes sense that there should be but one regulatory agency with ultimate authority over financial reporting to public investors. That agency should be the SEC, which has as its prime objective the protection of investors. It is to be hoped that legislative progress in this direction will not be too long delayed.

PUBLIC POLICY AND PRACTICAL LIMITATIONS ON POLITICAL INFLUENCE

As indicated at the outset of this chapter, the discernment of public needs in the area of financial accounting is no easy task. Opinions differ and always will. Hence, the integrity of the process by which standards of financial accounting are established becomes doubly important. If that process can be kept free of deleterious influences, we can feel reasonably assured that its results will approach, as near as may be, the public policy ideal.

Conversely, if the exercise of political power is permitted to supersede a process so laboriously constructed and set in motion, the worst possible results can be confidently anticipated.

One is reminded of an episode of political intervention in the establishment of financial accounting principles which ought not to be forgotten. That episode involved the question of accounting for the investment credit. Among several alternatives, two were at opposite ends of the spectrum: flow through, and deferral of the credit over the life of the improvement. In 1963, shortly after the investment credit was first enacted into law, the SEC, with a bow to expediency, fatally undercut the APB's effort of the previous year to arrive at a single standard of accounting for the credit. The APB had no real choice but to adopt its *Opinion No. 4*, rescinding its *Opinion No. 2* and permitting either accounting treatment to be used at the option of management.

In 1971 an investment credit was again permitted by law. This time, the SEC stood behind the controversial effort of the APB to eliminate alternative methods of accounting for the credit. A clearer case for elimination of alternatives could hardly be conceived: the new credit was broadly available, was calculated the same way in each instance and, whatever the amount, operated in similar fashion to reduce the immediate outflow of cash to pay federal income taxes. However, heavy political pressures were laid upon powerful congressional figures by those managements which wanted the reporting benefits of flow through. Despite the efforts of the SEC and the APB, these pressures were sufficient to secure passage of a federal law forbidding either the APB or the SEC to interfere with management's choice in accounting for the credit.

This regrettable episode of political interference in the establishment of financial accounting standards can be partially accounted for by two factors. One is the fact that the APB was entirely the creature of the accounting profession and, specifically, of the AIPCA. Business management did not consider itself a participant in the processes of the APB. Secondly, and perhaps even more importantly, neither the APB nor the institutions of the accounting profession had solid lines of communication with important congressional figures. When the APB became conscious of the need to secure both a hearing and a ready understanding of its concerns, it was already too late.

Fortunately, these two factors have been somewhat ameliorated. The FASB is broadly supported by groups interested in the financial reporting process. Such groups include the Financial Executives Institute, strongly aligned with corporate management. Today, important elements of management are more likely to come to the aid of the FASB than was the case of the APB in its last years. Moreover, the FASB has embarked on a regular procedure for communicating with Congress. This procedure, it is hoped, will enable the FASB to convey the purposes of its efforts to important committee chairmen and staff members. The process of educating those in positions of ultimate power, once neglected, has at last begun.

PUBLIC POLICY AND THE EDUCATION OF INVESTORS

Education of investors in the limitations of financial accounting is a continuing requirement of sound public policy.

Commissioners and leading staff members of the SEC appear to be alive to this need. As Commissioner Loomis put it in June 1974 before the Machinery and Allied Products Institute: "I would suspect unsophisticated investors tend to think of accounting as essentially a mathematical exercise." A more graphic illustration of the problem was provided by the Commission's Chief Accountant, John C. Burton, in a speech given for the Dean's Forum at the UCLA Graduate School of Management in January 1974:

> One of my favorite stories in this respect came from a former dean at Columbia who once explained to me his view of accountants. He said that it was substantially influenced by an experience he had when he was flying down to Argentina. He was sitting on the plane next to a man who identified himself as a CPA. As the plane passed over Brazil, the CPA tapped him on the shoulder, pointed out the window, and said, "There's the Amazon river. That river is one billion and two years old." The dean said, "That's very interesting. How did you know that?" And the accountant answered, "It's easy. Two years ago, I was flying down with a geologist, and he told me it was a billion years old." What we really need is a search for imprecision, not for precision.

The FASB can do more in this vein. When its statements are issued, it should emphasize that the measurements which they relate are of necessity imprecise to the extent they are based on allocations and similar estimates.

Beyond this, it may be possible to develop techniques for expressing accounting measurements in ranges rather than in terms of single numbers. The Objectives Study observed:

> Many economic decision-makers would prefer simple, not complex, answers, but simple answers may not serve them as well as complex ones. Single numbers supplemented by ranges and investments grouped by relative risk may be more complex, but they may also communicate more accurately the imprecision involved in making judgments.

Another method which might prove useful in this educational venture is the use of multiple-column statements. Should price-level adjusted statements or statements adjusted to reflect replacement cost of productive assets and inventories be mandated as supplementary information (as seems probable at this writing), the most useful way to portray the differences between the cost-based and the adjusted figures would appear to be in two adjacent columns. It has been suggested that in enterprises of particular complexity where, for example, inventory values depend heavily on estimates of future sales, a two-column approach, utilizing estimates at the top and bottom of the possible range, could perhaps enable the reader to grasp the significance of the statements more readily.

If public investors can be persuaded to view the results of financial accounting more realistically, one result will be a reduction of emphasis on the earnings per share figure and a growth of interest in other kinds of measurements, no one of which can be regarded as all-important in determining the value of an enterprise.

Realistic confidence in the relevance of available accounting information need not be destroyed by the occasional grand fraud which escapes detection by the independent auditor. Public investors should be brought to understand that no amount of effort or refinement of technique will enable the auditor to expose every episode of management dishonesty. Nor need confidence be impaired when standards are changed, hopefully for the better. In this process, however, care should be exercised by the FASB lest it unwittingly cast doubt on the validity of past practice or permit the unintended inference that prior financial statements were somehow misleading. A part of each FASB statement should reemphasize that the Board is dealing with matters of convention and tradition which can and must be changed with the progress of events.

PUBLIC POLICY AND THE ENLARGEMENT OF ACCOUNTING

The profession of accounting has expanded in recent years along with a growing awareness of the value, indeed the necessity, of the role of the accountant in a complex society. No other group possesses a similar tradition of independent judgment. Areas calling for the exercise of such a judgment outside the sphere of governmental sanction have multiplied. There is little doubt that strong considerations of public policy will enlarge the scope of activity of independent accounting firms.

An entire chapter could be written on the subject of the coming enlargement of accounting. Space will permit only brief mention of a few of the areas in which this writer expects independent accountants to take on wider responsibilities.

Much adverse comment on the competence of corporate management has been inspired by recent financial failures. Thoughtful chief executives are as concerned as shareholders over the availability of reliable techniques for evaluating important management personnel. Independent accountants will increasingly be called upon to develop such techniques and to attest their results. Eventually, as the mechanisms are developed, they may well be applied to top management itself.

Authorization by the SEC for voluntary use of financial forecasts in statements filed with the Commission appears imminent, despite the controversy which has surrounded this subject for many years. It is inevitable that independent accountants will become involved in preparing these forecasts, attesting the consistency of the assumptions used, and providing assurance that such assumptions conform to a standard of reasonableness.

The influence of interim financial reports in the market for securities is widely recognized, as is the relative absence of any independent review of such reports. A degree of involvement by independent accountants in the preparation of interim reports, short of a full audit, is certain to come about, along with refinement of standards of accounting applicable to such reports.

The large, diversified corporate enterprise is a fixture on the contemporary scene, and the need for disaggregated financial data about such enterprises is now widely recognized. A period of experimentation with unaudited line-of-business reporting by these enterprises is coming to an end. It can be expected that new standards, and the requirement of an audit of the figures by independent accountants, will apply in the near future to line-of-business data.

As time passes, more corporations and independent accountants have come to consider a careful "management letter" on the adequacy of the internal controls and accounting procedures of a client corporation to be an essential part of the annual audit procedure. The posture of the independent accountant inevitably calls for the exercise of similar objective judgment on the employment of those accounting standards which are most useful and least likely to mislead when there is a choice of alternatives. Along with this growing obligation may come the requirement of an independent commentary on significant aspects of the financial statements. As the Objectives Study observed:

> The basic objective of financial statements is to provide information useful for making economic decisions. To accomplish this basic objective, it may be that financial statements should not be limited

solely to quantified information. Amplification, in narrative form, of data included in statements may be required.

Finally, measurement of social costs and benefits, presently in its infant stage, is too important from the viewpoint of long-range public policy to be left a founding. The accounting profession will be expected to apply its energies and experience to find solutions. If the degradation of our environment is to be slowed without the massive involvement of government in the allocation of available resources, some mechanism must be found to identify and measure the cost to society of cleaning up the damage which inevitably flows from the operations of certain manufacturing and utility enterprises. That cost can then be charged through the tax system to the specific enterprises and passed on by them to the consumers of their products, rather than being shouldered as it is today by all taxpayers.

Though hesitant and doubtful on specifics, the Objectives Study reached a conclusion which is at least philosophically in accord:

> An objective of financial statements is to report on those activities of the enterprise affecting society which can be determined and described or measured and which are important to the role of the enterprise in its social environment.

CONCLUSION

The consumer movement in the United States has made dissatisfaction with old norms and practices in the business world a potent force for change. Far from escaping the whirlwind are old norms and practices of financial accounting. The beleaguered public accountant has felt the sting of criticism and the lash of litigation. Fortunately, conditions are ripe for constructive response. An experienced FASB, well funded and assisted by an able staff, is ready to play an active role in the improvement of accounting standards. Is American business prepared to accept the new standards which are surely coming? Frank Weston, a lucid commentator on the accounting scene, reflected a hopeful view in his article in the September–October 1974 issue of the *Harvard Business Review:*

> Corporate managers in the United States are about to encounter an exciting challenge: a significant revolution in financial accounting and reporting in a relatively short period of time. They would be well advised to respond to this revolution in a positive and orderly manner.

PART 2

Realization and measurement of earnings

Chapter 5

Income and the objectives of its measurement

*George L. Chamberlin**
Ronald S. Barden†

Corporations are a major factor in society with the power to direct and utilize vast amounts of resources toward the accomplishment of corporate objectives. The accountant must design an information system with sufficient feedback to enable prompt and effective corrective actions based upon actual results of these corporate efforts. There are a variety of overlapping special-interest groups which have a desire—and in some cases a right—to know how effective, efficient, and economical the corporate entity has been in this goal-directed activity which has deprived others of the use of the particular resources committed.

One can imagine a strong desire for some way of aggregating the results of various efforts into a single criterion for evaluation purposes. Such a key success factor for corporate performance is "income" and/or some ratio which includes "income." The process of income measurement and reporting has an extremely significant impact on the resource allocation decision in our society.

* Vice President and Controller, Scott Paper Company.
† Associate Professor of Accounting, Florida State University.

PURPOSE AND OUTLINE OF THE CHAPTER

The purpose of this chapter is to provide an overview of the concept of income and the objectives of its measurement. The chapter begins with a brief discussion of the defining and measurement processes. As a part of this discussion, three kinds of definitions are described. A single definition of income is then provided as a point of departure. After a brief review of the role of income in financial reporting throughout history, the important accounting information criterion of *relevance* is discussed. Since relevance is user-oriented, several different user groups and their particular concepts of income are described and discussed. In addition to relevance, each of these income concepts exhibits to some extent *measurement* problems such as quantifiability, freedom from bias, and verifiability.

As a summary of the discussion of the various user groups, a simplified numerical example of the concept of income from different points of view is presented as Exhibit 1 on page 82. A further written summary of the parameters of income definition and measurement is provided.

The chapter concludes with a look at possible future income concepts and measurement methodologies which might alleviate some of the problems identified in the users section. In some cases, specific topic areas are the subject of later chapters in this Handbook. When this is true, as in the case of forecasts and social accounting, specific reference to these later chapters is made in the text of the current chapter.

A LOOK AT THE DEFINING AND MEASUREMENT PROCESSES AND ONE DEFINITION OF INCOME

Accounting has been called the "language of business." Today it is viewed by nearly everyone as an information discipline. One of the essential requirements of a language is a set of terms or symbols to represent the phenomena and/or properties of those phenomena which are of interest to the constituency the information discipline serves. The phenomena or symbols used to represent other phenomena are called "surrogates," and the phenomena that are represented by surrogates are called "principals." For example, the portion of the earth's surface is a principal for which a map is a surrogate. The financial position, operating results, and changes in financial position of a firm are the principal for which the financial statements of the firms are a surrogate.[1]

Not all phenomena are of interest to an information discipline. It is the goal or objective of the information discipline which determines where the appropriate boundaries are drawn. One could argue that these boundaries should be determined by the users of the outputs of the information system based upon their particular information needs. Since users' objectives vary, the boundaries of their information system will vary, leading to different definitions or principal-surrogate relationships. This point will be examined in detail in a later section.

For the moment, it shall be assumed that the users of the information system are known and are enough alike in their information needs that a particular set of principals has been identified for the defining process. The defining process is an attempt to convey meaning through surrogates which show some relationship to the principals they represent. There are various kinds of definitions. This discussion will be limited to three.

1. One of the most important kinds of definition is "real" definition. A *real definition* is "conceived of as a statement of the 'essential characteristics' of some entity, as when man is defined as a rational animal or a chair as a separate movable seat for one person."[2]

2. Another kind of definition which is frequent in accounting is the "nominal" definition. A *nominal definition* is "a convention which merely introduces an alternative—and usually abbreviatory—notation for a given linguistic expression, in the manner of the stipulation."[3] In other words, a nominal definition is a stipulation to the effect that a specified expression is synonymous with a certain other expression whose meaning is already determined. Nominal definitions may be used for specifying class membership.

---

[1] Yuji Ijiri, *The Foundations of Accounting Measurement: A Mathematical, Economic, and Behavioral Inquiry* (Englewood Cliffs, N.J.: Prentice-Hall, Inc., 1967), pp. 4–5.

[2] Carl G. Hempel, *Fundamentals of Concept Formation in Empirical Science* (Chicago: The University of Chicago Press, 1952), p. 2.

[3] Ibid., p. 2.

3. In between, and perhaps even including some of the essence of
    real and nominal definitions, is the "operational" definition. An
    operational definition is basically a description which includes
    appropriate rules for the measurement of the term being
    defined.[4]

The term "measurement" which is included in the concept of
operational definition should also be defined for purposes of this
discussion. Measurement has been characterized in the following
ways:

> . . . the assignment of numerals to objects or events according to
> rules.[5]

> . . . the organization of experiences in such a way that they code-
> termine purposive decisions in a wide variety of contexts—where
> the organization is subject to control.[6]

> . . . the assignment of particular mathematical characteristics to
> conceptual entities in such a way as to permit (1) an unambiguous
> mathematical description of every situation involving the entity and
> (2) the arrangement of all occurrences of it in a quasi-serial order.[7]

The latter definition comes the closest to fulfilling the strict requirements of measurement theory.

Do accountants measure income? Is income operationally defined? Accounting contains many nominal definitions. The specification of rules for manipulation of components to arrive at "net
income" is really pseudo-measurement and would thus have to be
called a "pseudo-operational definition."[8]

Both nominal and pseudo-operational definitions are limited in
a theoretical sense. Thus, a look to a "real" definition is a logical
point of departure.

One of the best overall definitions of income, which also
approaches a real definition, comes from a well-known economist,

---

[4] Ibid., pp. 39–50.

[5] R. L. Ackoff, *Scientific Method: Optimizing Applied Research Decisions* (New York: John Wiley & Sons, Inc., 1962), p. 677.

[6] C. West Churchman, *Prediction and Optimal Decision: Philosophical Issues of a Science of Values* (Englewood Cliffs, N.J.: Prentice-Hall, Inc., 1961), p. 101.

[7] Peter Caws, "Definition and Measurement in Physics," in C. West Churchman and Philburn Ratoosh, eds., *Measurement, Definitions and Theories* (New York: John Wiley & Sons, Inc., 1959), p. 5.

[8] See Don W. Vickrey, "Is Accounting a Measurement Discipline?" *The Account-ing Review*, October 1970, pp. 731–42.

J. R. Hicks. Hicks defines income as "the amount that a person can consume during a period of time and be as well off at the end of that time as he was at the beginning."[9]

This definition could be better explained and/or modified. For example, the term "person" could be replaced very easily by "entity." The entity could be a corporation, a partnership, a not-for-profit institution, or even society as a whole. Certainly, there are varied opinions as to the meaning of "well-offness." However, with this brief introduction to what approaches a real definition of income, the chapter will now consider the role of income in accounting over the years and possible clarifications of the definition above.

USER-ORIENTED DEFINITIONS OF INCOME

From the earliest concepts of accounting in history until the late 1920s and early 1930s, emphasis was placed on the balance sheet as a primary source of information. This emphasis also led to a static measurement approach as of the balance sheet date as opposed to a transactions approach throughout the accounting period. In the early 1930s with the *Securities Act of 1933* and the *Securities Exchange Act of 1934,* a shift in emphasis to the income statement and the transactions approach was noted. In recent years, there has been an increased interest in funds or cash flow. This was formalized as a recommendation in *Accounting Principles Board Opinion No. 3* of October 1963 and more recently as a requirement in *Accounting Principles Board Opinion No. 19* of March 1971. Furthermore, accountants and others have come to realize that accounting is a very broad interdisciplinary art of providing useful information to resource allocation decision makers. Various writers and even authoritative bodies have pondered the nature of appropriate accounting information criteria.[10] A common thread in all of these writings is a concern for "relevance."

Relevance is indeed a key for selection of a particular item of information in an accounting information system. A little reflection

---

[9] J. R. Hicks, *Value and Capital* (Oxford: Clarendon Press, 1946), p. 172.

[10] For example, see Howard J. Snavely, "Accounting Information Criteria," *The Accounting Review* (April 1967), pp. 223–32; *A Statement of Basic Accounting Theory,* Committee to Prepare a Statement of Basic Accounting Theory, American Accounting Association, 1966; or AICPA, *Objectives of Financial Statements,* Report of the Study Group on the Objectives of Financial Statements (New York, 1973).

by the reader will lead him or her to the conclusion that *relevance requires specification of to whom accounting information will be directed* before detailed content questions, such as "What is well-offness?" may be answered.

According to *APB Statement No. 4*,[11] those persons with a direct interest in accounting information include owners; creditors and suppliers; potential owners, creditors, and suppliers; management (including directors and officers); taxing authorities; employees; and customers. Those users with indirect interests are financial analysts and advisors, stock exchanges, lawyers, regulatory or registration authorities, financial press and reporting agencies, trade associations, and labor unions. The nature and extent of the interest of each of these users of accounting information vary greatly and depend upon the kinds of resource allocation decisions particular to such information users. This difference in objectives for accounting information leads each group to have a different concept of what should be included in income.

The accountant is faced with the problem of providing useful information to these resource allocation decision makers who have different decision models. If the accountant could be even partially aware of the structure and content of the users' decision models, the problem of relevance would be simplified. Therefore, the next step in this analysis is a consideration of possible decision models of several users of accounting information.

The shareholder

The most commonly identified user of published accounting information is the shareholder or the potential shareholder. For the shareholder, the accountant has been charged with providing aggregations of results which may be "verified" by the professional opinion of the external auditor to "present fairly . . . in accordance with generally accepted accounting principles applied on a basis consistent with the preceding year." As mentioned earlier, generally accepted accounting principles have evolved from a period of emphasis on the balance sheet, through a period of concern for the income statement, and now to a time of explicit attention to cash

---

[11] AICPA, Accounting Principles Board, *Statement of the Accounting Principles Board No. 4,* "Basic Concepts and Accounting Principles Underlying Financial Statements of Business Enterprises" (New York, October 1970), pp. 18–19.

flow. The AICPA's "Report of the Study Group on the Objectives of Financial Statements" has identified investors and creditors as the principal users of financial statements. This Study Group suggests that "an objective of financial statements is to provide users with information for predicting, comparing, and evaluating enterprise earning power." This is in part based upon the assumption that "users of financial statements seek to predict, compare, and evaluate the cash consequences of their economic decisions." Thus the emphasis on cash consequences is reflected in the definition of enterprise earning power as the ability to generate cash in the future." The distinction between cash generated by operations as earnings versus cash provided to the firm as capital is important.[12] However, the Study Group feels that information about periodic income according to generally accepted accounting principles (largely accrual accounting) is more useful than information about current cash flows for predicting those future cash flows that evidence the earning power of the enterprise.[13]

Taxing authorities and management

Nearly all of the users identified earlier are concerned to some degree with the investor's definition of income. A major additional facet of income which is particularly relevant to users other than shareholders is some form of current and/or future cash flow.

Taxing authorities. The tax collector's concept of taxable income is likely to differ from any other accounting definition of income. These differences stem from the objectives of the taxing authority. These objectives are (1) to raise funds sufficient to support government operations and services and (2) to accomplish this taxation in an equitable manner. To accomplish these objectives, the Congress and various legislatures have provided a definition of income which differs from the investor's concept of income due largely to timing differences and special allowances, deductions, exemptions, and exclusions.

1. The timing differences include recognizing taxable income when unearned revenue is received as cash in advance. This is an

---

[12] For an outstanding evaluation of the Study Group Report discussed above see Hector R. Anton, "Objectives of Financial Accounting: Review and Analysis," *The Journal of Accountancy,* January 1976, pp. 40–51.

[13] Ibid., p. 46.

attempt to be equitable based upon ability to pay with cash on hand.

2. Other differences, such as the oil depletion allowance or the investment credit, are based upon an attempt to achieve specific economic goals through the tax laws.[14]

3. One of the major differences in income for financial statement purposes and income for tax purposes is the use of accelerated depreciation for tax purposes and straight-line depreciation for book purposes. This timing difference leads to interperiod income tax allocation.[15]

Management.   Management is another major user of accounting information. While being cognizant and concerned for traditional external financial reporting, the principal income concept for management is cash flow. Management's resource allocation decisions include both long-run and short-run decisions.

Some of the short-run decisions might involve fiscal planning to manage inventories of goods and cash. Cash flow projections are vital here.

Long-run decisions, such as capital budgeting investment decisions which can take the form of new plant and equipment or even new product lines, are concerned primarily with incremental cash flows. These incremental cash flows are different between alternative courses of action. Furthermore, in capital budgeting decisions, proposals should be evaluated at the firm's weighted average cost of capital.[16] Thus mangement's primary concept of income is some form of after-tax cash flow.

The economist and the average citizen

The last two users of accounting information to be discussed in this chapter are the economist and the average citizen. The reason for grouping these two together is that both desire income concepts which present significant measurement problems in the real world. Therefore, the discussions of the economist's and the average

---

[14] For further discussion, see Eldon S. Hendriksen, *Accounting Theory* (Homewood, Ill.: Richard D. Irwin, Inc., 1965), pp. 122–24.

[15] For further discussion, see Homer A. Black, "Interperiod Allocation of Corporate Income Taxes," *Accounting Research Study, No. 9* (New York: AICPA, 1966).

[16] The concept of a firm's weighted average cost of capital is extremely important to managerial decision making. An Appendix to this chapter, showing the various formulas and a numerical example, is provided for the interested reader.

citizen's income concepts might be aptly called "measuring the unmeasurable."

The economist's view of income is the increase in wealth over time not provided by newly invested capital. The economist's balance sheet consists of opportunity cost values for assets and liabilities. The opportunity cost concept recognizes the highest value for assets and liabilities in any alternative use or its current use, whichever is larger. Income is deemed to be realized when changes in opportunity cost values take place even though an actual exchange or transaction has not taken place. Accordingly, the economist's income statement includes holding gains and losses representing these changes in opportunity cost values. For example, if a firm's land rises in current appraised value by $1,000, the economist's balance sheet figure for that land would increase by $1,000; and a $1,000 holding gain—that is, the increase in the opportunity cost value while holding ownership and control of that asset—is recognized in his or her income statement as income. The accountant reporting to shareholders will not recognize this $1,000 holding gain or any other holding gain or loss in the financial statements until a transaction, such as sale of that land, occurs. Thus, to a large extent, differences in the economist's and the accountant's concepts of income are due to the differences in their respective definitions of income realization (see Chapter 6).

A final user of accounting information who does not usually appear among traditional lists of users of accounting information is the ordinary citizen. The principal reason for listing him or her in this discussion is to highlight a potential need for a societal view of income measurement and reporting. What are the costs to society of pollution? Unless a company pays fines, the accountant normally reports the costs as zero. Therefore, an argument may be made that accountants contribute to pollution by fostering an accounting system which encourages postponement, perhaps indefinitely, of expenditures to prevent or repair the effects of water, air, and land pollution. Earnings per share of a socially responsible company will be less than that of a socially irresponsible company, all other things being equal, since social costs, which are presumably greater than actual pollution abatement costs (the latter expended by the socially responsible company only), are not recorded in the traditional accounting model.[17]

---

[17] Floyd A. Beams and Paul E. Fertig, "Pollution Control Through Social Cost Conversion," *The Journal of Accountancy*, November, 1971, p. 38.

Summary example

To illustrate more clearly how the concept of income varies with the different users discussed in the preceding paragraphs, Exhibit 1 is provided. Exhibit 1 is a simplified numerical example showing that for a given set of data, income ranges from $85 for the shareholder to a $55 net loss for the average citizen. These differences are due to the inclusion or exclusion of various items relevant to the decision systems of the particular users. Assumptions and simplifications are clearly labeled.

SUMMARY

Accountants have always thought they were measuring economic phenomena and processing some properties about those phenomena into useful reports. They assigned numbers to events called *transactions* or *exchanges* using the best evidence available, and they then aggregated this batch of current and historical (sometimes ancient) exchange data to form income statements, balance sheets, and more recently statements of changes in financial position.

One of these aggregations is called *income*. To have meaning, this measurement must not only be relevant in terms of its content as discussed in the previous sections but it must also appear with other income figures against which a comparison may be made. There are several choices for this comparison base.

1. One comparison base is *income figures for the same entity for prior periods*. Income measurement is imprecise to say the least. Therefore, while one recognizes that current income measurement is nothing more than a "dip-stick" approach (in the sense that true income cannot be measured except from the beginning to the end of an entity), a comparison of such imprecise figures in the form of trend analysis might reveal important patterns in resource allocation relative to stated corporate goals.
2. Another possible comparison base is the net assets used as a basis for generating such income. This is a *return on investment* computation.
3. Another possible comparison base is the *industry-wide average income*.
4. A final refinement of the comparison exercise is the recognition

of the *stage the corporation has reached in its life* cycle. Industries and corporations within industries follow growth patterns similar to new products. There is introduction, rapid growth, maturity, and finally decline. The length of any of these periods will vary, depending upon the subject entity. However, recognition of these considerations can be useful input to resource allocation decisions with respect to future earning power.

A LOOK AT THE FUTURE

One of the most significant problems which must be resolved in the future is the quantification of the nonquantifiable elements of income. Already accountants are beginning to develop an area called *social accounting* in which the entity concept has been expanded to include costs to society. *Human resource accounting*, a branch of social accounting, is moving into areas of costs in terms of morale and creativity (see Chapter 25). Behavioral accounting research and the subset called "human information processing" are looking at the ways in which various elements and products of the accounting information system are used by and affect people in various roles inside and outside the organization.

Another vital area of research is the notion of *forecasts* (see Chapter 24). It is likely that forecasts will be requested by more and more user groups in the future. The concept of some form of *current values* as opposed to historical costs has received heightened interest due to the rampant inflation in the last 20 years. The simplest approach toward current values or the economist's opportunity cost values is price-level adjusted historical costs. Such "updated historical costs" are easy to "measure," but have little relevance. Other more relevant alternatives might be (1) current entry price or replacement cost[18] or current exit price or liquidation sales price.[19] These important areas of research will lead to better income measurement (see Chapter 26). Use of some form of current value or purchasing power could possibly cause income determination to become true measurement.[20] Indeed, an overall goal for income

---

[18] See Edgar O. Edwards and Phillip W. Bell, *The Theory and Measurement of Business Income* (Berkeley, Calif.: University of California Press, 1961).

[19] See Raymond J. Chambers, *Accounting, Evaluation and Economic Behavior* (Englewood Cliffs, N.J.: Prentice-Hall, Inc., 1966).

[20] Vickrey, "Is Accounting a Measurement Discipline?" p. 741.

EXHIBIT 1
A simplified numerical example of the concept of income from different points of view

	Item value	Share-holder	Tax collector	Economist	General manager investment decision	Fiscal planner cash flow	Average citizen
Values received for production:							
Sales(a)	$200	$200	$200	$200	$200	$200	$200
Interest, dividends, other(b)	10	10	10	10		10	10
Change in equity in affiliates measured by:							
(1) Historical cost	45	45					
(2) Current value	70	$255	$210	$280	$200	$210	$280
Costs of production:							
Labor, materials, services:							
Direct—incremental(c)	60	$60	$60	$60	$60	$60	$60
Indirect—fixed	40	40	40	40		40	40
Capital consumed:							
Depreciation—regular	20	20	20	20			20
—additional accelerated	10		10				
Cost for use of capital:	45			45	45*		45
Includes: Interest 10		10	10			10(f)	
Dividends.... 30						30	
Expected annual growth rate of dividends 5(d)							
Taxes on income (50% assumed):							
Current	35	35	35	35	50(e)	35	35
Deferred	5	5					
Pollution costs to society	135						135
		$170	$140	$200	$155	$175	$335
Income		$85	$70	$80	$45	$35	$(55) net loss

* See taxes below.

(a) Reported sales figures could differ between cash basis and accrual basis accounting, but for this example the differences are assumed to be minimal.

(b) Some items in this category, such as interest on municipal bonds, might not be taxable. However, for this example these differences have been assumed away.

(c) It is definitely true that direct costs may be variable or fixed, and indirect costs may be variable or fixed. It is further true that incremental costs may be variable or fixed. However, for purposes of this illustration, all direct costs are assumed to be incremental and all indirect costs are nonincremental.

(d) This amount represents the "g" in the cost of capital for common stock which is not paid out currently. See the Appendix to this chapter for an explanation of the various cost of capital formulas.

(e) Tax on sales minus incremental production costs is $(50\% \times (\$200 - \$60)) = \$70$. However, the interest payments in this capital structure are tax deductible. This is also true of the depreciation which in early years will be higher and in later years lower than straight line. Thus the taxes are $(\$70 - (50\% \times (10 + 30))) = \$50$.

(f) In this example, bonds are assumed to be selling at par, so the nominal and effective rates of interest are the same.

measurement will be production of valid signals of the degree of real productivity within an entity. When there is increased productivity, then wages and dividends may properly rise without adversely affecting prices in terms of needless inflation.

Business executives must assist authoritative accounting bodies in defining proper accounting measurement principles which consider the actual day-to-day decisions necessary to manage the corporation properly. The accounting profession must define new concepts and educate constituents as to their proper use. The consequence of failure to participate in the policy formulation of accounting theory and practice could be the downfall of our entire economic system. This is a challenge to us all.

APPENDIX

Cost of capital formulas and a numerical example

The major elements of most corporations' capital structures are bonds, preferred stock, and common stock. Each of these three elements has a specific cost of capital formula. These will be presented below. However, it is the weighted average cost of capital—that is, the sum of the products of the specific costs of capital for each of these three elements times their respective percentage of the total market value for all debt and capital stock outstanding—that is useful in capital budgeting decision making. The weighted average cost of capital represents the long-run breakeven for all projects of a capital nature.

The formulas for the three items discussed above are as follows:

$$\text{Bonds:} \quad k = \frac{(1 - t)\left[R + \left(\dfrac{P - M}{n}\right)\right]}{\frac{1}{2}(P + M)}$$

where

k = the specific cost of debt capital.
t = the applicable income tax rate.
R = the nominal interest rate on the debt multiplied by the par or face value (P) of the outstanding debt.
P = the par or face value of the outstanding debt.
M = the market value of the outstanding debt.
n = the number of years to maturity of the debt.

$$\text{Preferred stock:} \quad k = \frac{D}{M}$$

where

k = the specific cost of preferred equity capital.
D = the current dividend per share of preferred stock.
M = the current market price per share of preferred stock.

$$\text{Common stock:} \quad k = \frac{D}{M} + g$$

where

k = the specific cost of common equity capital.
D = the current dividend per share of common stock.
M = the current market price per share of common stock.
g = the expected average annual rate of growth in dividends.

Using the above formulas and the data in the table below, the reader can see the steps necessary to compute a firm's average cost of capital.[21]

TABLE 1
Computation of average cost of capital

		Source of capital		
	Bonds*	Preferred stock	Common stock	Total
Maturity value.	$100,000			
Nominal interest rate	8%			
Years to maturity	18			
Annual interest or dividend	$ 8,000	$ 1,200	$ 2,000	
Market value of capital.	$ 88,000	$20,000	$40,000	$148,000
Specific cost of capital:				
Preliminary	9.2%	6.0%	5.0%	
Growth factor.	–	–	7.0%	
After tax at 46%	5.0%	6.0%	12.0%	
Percentage of total market value	59.5%	13.5%	27.0%	
Average cost of capital	2.98%	0.81%	3.24%	7.03%

* Only one kind and issue of bonds was assumed in this simple example.

[21] For a further discussion, see James M. Fremgen, *Accounting for Managerial Analysis*, 3d ed. (Homewood, Illinois: Richard D. Irwin, Inc., 1976), pp. 451–54.

Chapter 6

Revenue recognition and receivable valuation

*Floyd W. Windal**

THE NATURE OF REVENUE

Definition

Revenue is sometimes defined as the amount of assets received or liabilities liquidated by an enterprise in return for services rendered or products produced and delivered. The Committee on Terminology of the American Institute of Certified Public Accountants takes a broader view, however, and includes within the concept gains from the sale or exchange of assets (other than stock in trade), and any other increases in the owners' equity except those arising from capital contributions and capital adjustments.[1] The Accounting Principles Board differs slightly from the Committee on Terminology in that it defines the gross inflow from the sale or exchange of assets as revenue, rather than including only the gain thereon.[2]

Main versus ancillary operations

The distinction is frequently made between revenue generated by the main operations of the enterprise and that resulting from such

---

* Head, Department of Accounting and Business Law, University of Georgia.

[1] Committee on Terminology, AICPA, *Accounting Terminology Bulletin No. 2* (New York, 1955), par. 5.

[2] AICPA, "Basic Concepts and Accounting Principles Underlying Financial Statements of Business Enterprises," *Statement of the Accounting Principles Board No. 4* (New York, 1970), par. 134, p. 51.

items as rent, royalties, interest, dividends, and from the sale or exchange of assets not held as stock in trade. Revenue arising from main operations is usually shown separately on the income statement from the inflows arising from these ancillary sources.

Gross versus net

Contrasted with the concept of income, revenue is normally a gross concept. That is, the entire sales price of goods delivered is considered revenue, even though a portion of that sales price is required to cover the cost of producing and selling the item. On an income statement, the revenue is shown first and all related expenses are deducted from it to arrive at income.

An exception to the gross concept is found in such minor revenue producers as by-products and scrap. Revenue from by-product sales is often recorded and shown in the income statement net of any expenses incurred to sell or complete the by-product. Likewise, any costs incurred to remove or dispose of scrap would typically be deducted from the sales price and the revenue would be shown net. The inclusion of gain on the sale or exchange of assets would also represent an exception to the gross concept.

Gains from the sale or exchange of assets

One of the ancillary sources of inflow is a gain on the sale or exchange of assets, when such assets are not stock in trade. Such gains result when the book value of the asset (cost less accumulated depreciation) is less than the amount received. Such a gain may be caused by any or a combination of several factors, including incorrect prior depreciation, an increase in the value of the specific asset, and a general price level increase. The reader is referred to Chapters 9 and 26 for a discussion of problems associated with this special kind of transaction. The whole problem of increases in the value of assets is also discussed in these chapters.

The earning of revenue

Revenue does not suddenly come into existence at a single point in time. The majority viewpoint is that revenue comes into being gradually as it is *earned*. The embryo stage of revenue might be viewed as beginning when the decision is first made to produce a product for resale or to render a service, or perhaps when the buyer and seller first meet if that event precedes the decision to produce. Maturity would arrive when the buyer pays for the product or service sold. In between these two points, many things may take place. An agreement may be reached between the buyer and seller, a product may be produced or a service rendered, delivery may be made, and a bill may be sent to the buyer.

Both *effort* and *return* are involved in this continuum. On the effort or earning side, many actions take place. Stated in dollar terms, costs are incurred in the sales effort, the production effort, the delivery effort, and perhaps in a servicing effort. On the return or inflow side, an obligation from seller to buyer becomes more firm as the efforts of the seller are taking place, until at length the buyer remits a cash payment.

In the case of ancillary revenues such as rent, royalties, interest, and dividends, the effort or earning takes a different form. The seller is in effect selling the use of its assets over a period of time, and as time passes this utilization takes place and the revenue is earned.

It should be noted that the process of earning is a condition precedent to the existence of revenue. An asset received from a buyer prior to any effort being expended by the seller would be in the nature of a deposit rather than a revenue. As stated in the definition of revenue given earlier, revenue is the amount of assets received *in return for* services rendered or products produced and delivered.

THE RECOGNITION OF REVENUE

The concept of realization

Faced with the previously described continuum wherein effort and return move from an embryo to a maturity stage, the accountant needs some guidelines as to when revenue should be recognized in the accounts.

Before the accountant can even consider recognition, revenue must *exist*. There must not only be an inflow but it must be properly classifiable as revenue. Thus, some earning process must have taken place. Some effort must have been expended. But how much earning is required? Are the efforts incurred to generate the order sufficient? Should the purchase of raw materials and the actual production have taken place? In a retail situation, is the purchase and placement of items on the shelf sufficient? Or should the delivery have first been made? How about servicing commitments?

On the return side, what evidence should be required to satisfy the accountant that an inflow exists? Is the existence of a sales contract sufficient justification? Or should acceptance of the merchandise by the buyer be considered a condition precedent? Should the receipt of cash be required?

The conceptual answer to these questions is found in the accountant's concept of *realization*. This concept sets forth two conditions which must be met prior to the time revenue can be recognized in the accounts, that is, prior to its being considered "realized." Meeting these two conditions is also normally considered *prima facie* evidence that sufficient earning has taken place to bring revenue into existence.

1.   The revenue must be measurable.
2.   The revenue must be certain.

These two conditions relate well to the definition of realization formulated by a committee of the American Accounting Association: "The essential meaning of realization is that a change in an asset or liability has become sufficiently definite and objective to warrant recognition in the accounts."[3]

Measurability.   The requirement of measurability results from the very nature of the accounting process. Accounting is basically a process of quantitative description, and if an item is not measurable it cannot be described quantitatively.

Measurability relates closely to the notion of *objectivity* stated in the American Accounting Association definition above. Objective is, of course, the opposite of subjective. Therefore, in order for an item to be sufficiently objective for recognition, it must appear substantially the same to all those examining it. It must not be subject to different interpretations by different people. If an item can be measured with reasonable accuracy, it assumes a large degree of objectivity.

The accountant's judgment necessarily enters into the application of this factor. Although some reasonable degree of accuracy is all

---

[3] American Accounting Association, *Accounting and Reporting Standards for Corporate Financial Statements and Preceding Statements and Supplements* (Columbus, 1957), p. 3.

that is required, a decision must be made in each case. Although in the past accountants have not used statistical or mathematical techniques to guide them, there is some evidence that they will be asked to do so in the future. Normally, their past experience with like items and their technical background give them a good basis for arriving at a sound conclusion.

Certainty. To be sufficiently definite, an item must appear unlikely to be reversed. It must appear to have a degree of certainty about it. Questions such as the following come to mind when considering this condition. Will the sales contract ever be fulfilled, even though the sales price and costs can be estimated with reasonable accuracy? Can the product be sold even though it may already have been produced and its sales price is fixed by the market? How certain are we of servicing requirements, even though their costs might be capable of estimation?

It should be noted that the condition of certainty relates to the effort as well as to the return, to the outflow as well as to the inflow. If this criterion cannot be met for the outflow, for example, the revenue connot be considered earned, and any inflow must be treated merely as a deposit.

Some authors consider the quality of certainty to be a part of the measurability criterion. That is, an item is not measurable in their eyes unless it is also certain. The position taken here is that an item might be quantitatively measurable but not certain enough to warrant recognition in the accounts.[4]

The sale as a test for realization

In the vast majority of cases, the *sale* is used as the practical signal that the conditions of realization have been met, and that the revenue can be recognized in the accounts. In lieu of the legal passing of title, the shipment of goods is usually the signal for recognition. In the case of services, the performance of the service is the signal.

The time of sale has been so closely associated with realization over the years that it is often viewed as being synonymous with

[4] The Accounting Principles Board definition of realization incorporates notions of earning, certainty, and measurement. *Statement No. 4* states: "Revenue is generally recognized when both the following conditions are met: (1) the earning process is complete or virtually complete, and (2) an exchange has taken place." See par. 150, p. 59.

realization. In actuality, however, it is only a convenient bench mark which serves very well in most cases as a guide to when the revenue is both measurable and certain enough for recognition.

Usually, the exchange transaction agreed to in the sale sets a definite price, thereby satisfying the requirement of measurability for the inflow. Usually also, the costs and expenses associated with the sale have already been determined by that time, or are capable of reasonable estimation. Thus, the earning process is substantially complete and the outflows are measurable.

The sale constitutes a contract between the buyer and the seller, thus lending certainty to the transaction. The delivery of the goods further increases the certainty that the transaction will not be reversed. In most cases, the amount of sales which will prove uncollectible or which will be canceled can be estimated with reasonable accuracy and offset against the related total sales revenue.

Departures from the sales basis

There are a number of circumstances in which the sales basis is not a reliable indicator that the conditions of realization have been met. In some cases, realization does not take place until after cash has been received. In others, the completion of a portion or all of the production process may be what is required. Sometimes, where a very high degree of risk is involved, no revenue is to be realized until after all costs have been recovered. Some of the circumstances under which these departures from the sales basis would be justified will now be discussed.

Installment sales. Although the normal procedure in connection with installment sales is to recognize all revenue at the time of sale, there may be circumstances where the collection of the sale price is not reasonably assured and where there is no reasonable basis for estimating the degree of collectibility. In such cases, the realization requirement for certainty is violated and a cash collection basis may be utilized.[5] That is, the recognition of revenue will be deferred until cash is received.

When this is done, a departure is made from the gross basis of recording revenue, and except in the year of sale the revenue is reported net of related costs. In the year of sale, the usual treatment is to show gross sales less cost of goods sold equaling gross margin,

---

[5] AICPA, "Omnibus Opinion–1966," AICPA, *Accounting Principles Board, Opinion No. 10* (New York, 1966), par. 12, p. 149.

and then to deduct gross margin unrealized either because of default or because the receivables are uncollected at year-end.

It may be desirable to elect the installment sales method for income tax purposes whether or not there is a reasonable basis for estimating the degree of collectibility, because it results in postponing the recognition of taxable income. For this reason the installment sales method is of importance to many businesses.

INSTALLMENT SALES ILLUSTRATION

The Blake Corporation sells most of its merchandise on an installment basis, with 19xx installment sales totaling $2,540,000. The cost of these goods was $2,032,000. Down payments amounted to $254,000, and collections on account during the year were $762,000. The following summary entries indicate how these sales are treated under the installment method.

```
Cash .............................................        254,000
   Installments Receivable ........................      2,286,000
      Installment Sales ............................                  2,540,000
      To record the total amount of installment sales during 19xx
      and the related down payments.

Cost of Installment Sales.........................      2,032,000
   Merchandise Inventory...........................                  2,032,000
      To record the cost of all 19xx installment sales.

Cash .............................................        762,000
   Installments Receivable ........................                    762,000
      To record collections on account during 19xx.

Installment Sales ................................      2,540,000
   Deferred Gross Margin on Installment Sales .......                    508,000
   Cost of Installment Sales.......................                  2,032,000
      To close cost and sales accounts relative to installment sales
      and set up a Deferred Gross Margin account.

Deferred Gross Margin on Installment Sales .........      203,200
   Realized Margin on Installment Sales............                    203,200
      To recognize that portion of the deferred gross margin which
      has been realized from cash receipts.
```

$$\text{Cash received } (\$254,000 + \$762,000) \quad \frac{\$1,016,000}{\$2,540,000} = 40\%$$
$$40\% \times \$508,000 = \$203,200$$

or

$$\text{Gross margin} \quad \frac{\$508,000}{\$2,540,000} = 20\% \text{ gross margin percentage}$$
Collections, $1,016,000 \times 20\% = \$203,200$

Because gross margin percentages may differ in different years, it is necessary when using this method to account separately for the receivables and collections which result from each year's sales. There will normally also be a separate Deferred Gross Margin account for each year.

Defaults on these installment contracts and subsequent repossession of merchandise require careful accounting treatment. The fair market value of the repossessed goods at date of repossession is recorded in an inventory account, the related uncollected receivable balance is removed from the Installments Receivable account, the related amount of Deferred Gross Margin is debited to that account, and the resulting difference is taken to a Gain or Loss account.

Utilizing the figures from the preceding example, assume that in the subsequent year merchandise with a fair market value of $700 was repossessed. Its original selling price was $1,270, and $200 of the original receivable had been collected. The entry at the time of repossession would be as follows:

Repossessed Merchandise 700
Deferred Gross Margin on Installment Sales 214
Loss on Repossession. 156
    Installments Receivable   1,070
    Uncollectible receivable $1,070 times 20 percent gross margin percentage equals $214 unrealized gross margin.

Additional factors entering into the accounting for installment sales are service charges and interest. Interest should be allowed to flow into the income statement only as time passes, even though the total interest charge may have been included in the original Installments Receivable entry. The preferable method of computing interest income would involve an allocation of interest in such a way that it results in a constant rate on the unpaid balance. A straight-line method of allocating interest to periods may be used if the results are not materially different from those under the "interest" method. Service charges are either treated as an additional revenue item in the period of the charge to match properly with the related costs of acquiring the account, or they are allocated to revenue over the life of the contract.

Long-term construction contracts. Difficulty in meeting either or both of the conditions of measurability and certainty are appropriate causes for departing from the sales basis of recognizing revenue in the case of long-term construction contracts. The long period over which such production takes place often makes it difficult (1) to estimate the total amount of costs with reasonable accuracy or (2) to know whether the project will in fact be completed. In addition to these difficulties, the spreading of the earning process over more than one accounting period raises the question of whether or not all of the revenue is truly in existence at the time of sale.

Where it is possible to estimate reasonably the percentage of completion, and to estimate the ultimate sales price and ultimate total costs, revenue should be recognized proportionately with the progress of the work. As the work progresses, a portion of the earning process takes place, a portion of the costs becomes measurable and certain, and often a portion of the revenue is collected. Likewise, a portion of estimated income can be recorded.

When total sales price, total costs, and progress toward completion cannot be reasonably estimated, the completed-contract method should be used. Under this method revenue and related costs are recognized in the period when the project is completed, or substantially completed.

LONG-TERM CONSTRUCTION ILLUSTRATION

Percentage of completion method

The Jodie Construction Company has a contract to build a manufacturing facility at a total contract price of $15,000,000. Costs are estimated to run $13,500,000. The Jodie Corporation will bill the purchases on a percentage of completion basis for 95 percent of the earned revenue, pending satisfactory completion of the project.

Construction in Progress	2,025,000	
Various Credits		2,025,000

To record the incurrence of costs on the contract during 19xx.

Accounts Receivable–Unbilled	112,500	
Accounts Receivable–Billed	2,137,500	
Construction Revenue		2,250,000

To record the revenues earned and billed for 19xx:

$$\text{Cost incurred to date} \quad \frac{\$2,025,000}{\$13,500,000} = 15\%$$

$15\% \times \$15,000,000 = \$2,250,000 \times 95\% = \$2,137,500$

Construction in Progress	225,000	
Income from Construction Contracts		225,000

To record realized gross margin on construction contract:

Contract price	$15,000,000
Estimated total costs	13,500,000
Estimated gross margin	$ 1,500,000
Percentage of costs incurred to date	15%
Realized gross margin (15% × $1,500,000)	$ 225,000

An additional complication is introduced when the percentage of completion of the contract cannot be reasonably measured by the percentage of costs incurred. In that event, engineering estimates need to be made as a basis for computation. When utilizing costs to compute the percentage of completion, care should be taken in the early stages of a contract not to include costs of such items as materials which have merely been acquired but not used.

Completed contract method

Had the completed contract method been used because estimates of total sales price, total costs, or progress toward completion were not dependable, the following entries would have been made.

Construction in Progress	2,025,000	
Various Credits		2,025,000
To record the incurrence of costs on the contract during 19xx.		
Accounts Receivable	2,137,500	
Construction Revenue Billed		2,137,500
To record revenues billed during 19xx.		

No income would be recorded on the contract until it is completed, or substantially so. A contract may be regarded as substantially completed if remaining costs are not significant in amount.

The difference between the billings to date of $2,137,500 and the costs incurred of $2,025,000 would be shown in the 19xx balance sheet as a current liability. Should there be an excess of costs over billings, it would be shown as a current asset. The current liability item would be described as "billings on uncompleted contracts in excess of related costs."

In addition to basing income recognition on finally determined results rather than on estimates, the completed contract method results in postponing the recognition of taxable income. Its principal disadvantage is that it distorts the income picture by recognizing all of the gain in the year of completion, and none during the years of construction.

OTHER DEPARTURES FROM THE
SALES BASIS

Two other situations where a departure from the sales basis may be justified are in land development companies and in franchise sales companies. The reader is referred to Chapters 41 and 42 for a discussion of revenue recognition by these types of companies.

The sales basis may also be departed from in the case of gold and silver production. When there is an effective government-controlled market at a fixed monetary value, such products may be valued in the inventory at selling price, less estimated direct costs of disposal. The result is to report revenues in the period in which production is essentially complete. A similar treatment applies to inventories representing agricultural, mineral, and other products where units are interchangeable, there is immediate marketability at quoted prices, and appropriate costs may be difficult to obtain.[6] Accretion is not in itself a sufficient basis for realization, but it must be accompanied by these preconditions.

In addition to those situations where companies on an accrual basis require the receipt of cash as a precondition for revenue recognition or for the recognition of taxable income, some relatively small businesses keep their books completely on a cash basis. That is, expenses and revenue are recorded only when cash is received or paid out. This cash basis of accounting is generally considered acceptable only in those situations where it yields approximately the same results as the accrual basis.

THE VALUATION OF RECEIVABLES

Closely allied to the recognition of revenue is the valuation of the receivables with which those revenues are often associated. Not only will the proper valuation of receivables insure an accurate balance sheet presentation, but it will also insure a correct statement of net income. Of primary concern are the following valuation items: trade and cash discounts, returns and allowances, freight, uncollectible accounts, and interest.

Trade discounts

In some industries, it is common practice to quote prices to various classes of customers in terms of some base or list price, which is reduced by one or more trade discounts. This procedure provides an easy method of quoting different prices to different cus-

---

[6] AICPA, *Accounting Research Bulletin No. 43* (New York, 1953), chap. 4, par 9.

tomers and also does away with the requirement of frequently re-printing the price catalog.

Sequential *trade discounts* of 10, 20, and 5 percent applied to a list price of $500 would result in the following gross price. (It is a gross price in the sense that it is before deducting any *cash discount.*)

List price.	$500
Less 10%.	50
	$450
Less 20%.	90
	$360
Less 5%.	18
Gross Price.	$342

The receivable should be recorded at $342, rather than at the list price. The basis for any cash discount would also be $342, as discussed in the next section.

Cash discounts

In order to induce customers to promptly remit balances due, many companies allow a cash discount for payments within a certain time span after the billing date or after the date of shipment.

For example, an invoice for $1,000 might have terms of 3/10, n/30, meaning that a 3 percent cash discount would be granted for payment within 10 days, with the amount becoming past due after 30 days.

Method 1. One way of accounting for this type of sale is to record the receivable and the *revenue at the gross amount,* and to account for the discount as it is taken.

Accounts Receivable	1,000	
Sales		1,000
To record the sale at gross.		
Cash	970	
Cash Discounts on Sales	30	
Accounts Receivable.		1,000
To record the payment of the receivable within the discount period and the taking of the discount.		

When utilizing this method, an adjustment is necessary at the end of any accounting period to record any material amount of discount that is likely to be taken on outstanding accounts receivable.

Cash Discounts on Sales XX
   Allowance for Cash Discounts XX
    To record estimated cash discounts on outstanding Accounts Receivable.

The estimated cash discount figure which is debited in the preceding entry serves to adjust the period's net income, and the Allowance for Cash Discounts is deducted from Accounts Receivable on the balance sheet. Cash Discounts on Sales is normally either deducted from sales on the income statement, or the sales are shown net. Sometimes these discounts are treated as an expense. The effects of all three disclosure methods on income are the same.

Method 2. A second approach to the treatment of cash discount is to record the *revenue net of the discount,* either recording the receivable at the net figure also or setting it up gross, with a valuation contra account containing the discount. If an allowance account is set up, it would be reduced as the discounts are actually taken.

Accounts Receivable 1,000
   Allowance for Cash Discounts 30
   Sales 970
    To record the revenue net of the discount and the receivable at gross.

Cash 970
Allowance for Cash Discount 30
   Accounts Receivable 1,000
    To record the collection of cash within the discount period.

When revenue is recorded net of available cash discounts, those discounts not taken would be removed from the allowance account and added to net income. If no allowance account has been set up at the time of sale, any cash receipts in excess of net would be taken to a separate income account.

Returns and allowances

Customers often either return goods or receive an allowance for damaged or unsatisfactory merchandise. Returns and allowances are recorded when they occur. In addition, returns and allowances expected on outstanding sales at the end of the period, if material, should be estimated in order to properly state the income for the period, and to properly value the receivables at the end of the period.

```
Sales Returns and Allowances...........................  XX
    Accounts Receivable. ...............................      XX
    To record returns or allowances made to specific customers.

Sales Returns and Allowances...........................  XX
    Estimated Sales Returns and Allowances ..................      XX
    To record estimates of returns and allowances related to outstanding
    receivables.
```

The Sales Returns and Allowances balance may be deducted from sales revenue on the income statement, or sales revenue may be shown net of Sales Returns and Allowances. Similarly, the Accounts Receivable may be shown net of the Estimated Returns and Allowances amount, or the estimate may be shown as a deduction from Accounts Receivable.

Freight

In circumstances where the terms of sale are f.o.b. destination, but the customer is to pay the freight bill, the receivables should be set up at the net figure and the sale should be recorded gross.

```
Accounts Receivable............................. 5,000
Transportation-Out.............................   500
    Sales ....................................        5,500
    To record $5,500 sale and estimated freight payment by customer of
    $500.
```

An alternative treatment, should the freight amount be difficult to determine, is to record the receivable and the sale at gross, leaving the freight entry until after the customer reports the amount of the freight bill. At the end of a fiscal period, an estimate of such freight bills needs to be made and booked if the amount is material.

Uncollectible accounts

Some portion of accounts receivable will never be collected. It is desirable, therefore, to reduce the net income in each fiscal period for the portion of that period's revenue which is estimated to be uncollectible. At the same time, consideration needs to be given to the net receivable balance to insure that the balance sheet figure is correctly stated.

The several possible methods of providing for uncollectible receivables focus either on the income statement or on the balance sheet, with consequent slighting of the one not emphasized.

Direct charge-off. The simplest method, and usually the least desirable one, is to simply write off accounts as they go bad, removing the specific balance from Accounts Receivable and charging it to a Bad Debts Expense account. This reduces the income of the period in which accounts are determined to be uncollectible.

One obvious disadvantage of this method is that the charge-off is not likely to occur in the period in which the sale is made, thus overstating the income in that period and understating it in the later period when the charge-off is made. There would also be a serious question of whether the receivable balance at any one time is overstated because it contains accounts which may go bad in the future.

Allowance account based on analysis of receivables. A second approach, still emphasizing the proper statement of receivables on the balance sheet, involves a periodic analysis of the accounts comprising the receivables balance. Typically, this analysis begins with an aging of the receivables. That is, the receivables are divided according to the number of days they have been outstanding.

SEELEY CORPORATION
Aging of Accounts Receivable
December 31, 19xx

	Amount	Percent
Current (not yet due)	$400,000	80%
Up to 30 days past due.	50,000	10
31–60 days past due	25,000	5
61–90 days past due	15,000	3
Over 90 days past due	10,000	2
	$500,000	100%

An analysis of past company experience would show the likely percentage of receivables in each of these categories which will go bad. For example, experience may show that only 2 percent of receivables in the current category are likely to prove uncollectible, whereas 10 percent of those in the 61–90 days past-due category will prove bad. When accounts reach the over 90 days past-due category, it may be necessary to analyze them individually to estimate their collectibility.

As a result of this kind of analysis, an amount can be determined which represents the desired balance in an Allowance for Doubtful Accounts, which will be deducted from the receivables balance in the balance sheet. The difference between the desired balance and the amount already in the allowance account from prior years will be the amount of the current period's entry.

Bad Debts Expense XX
    Allowance for Doubtful Accounts   XX

To increase the Allowance for Doubtful Accounts to reflect the estimated amount of uncollectibles.

As with the direct charge-off method, this method is unlikely to result in a correct matching of the bad debts expense with the revenue related to them. Given a consistent pattern of uncollectibles over time, however, the misstatement may not prove to be material.

Allowance based on sales. The method which best matches cause and effect, or revenue and related deductions, is that which charges each period's income with an estimated percentage of the credit sales of that period, based on past bad debt loss experience. In this way, the revenue from total sales made is offset by a charge for estimated uncollectible accounts. If the company's experience shows that the relationship between credit and cash sales is fairly constant, the percentage of uncollectibles may be stated in relation to *total sales* rather than credit sales.

Under both of the methods utilizing an Allowance for Doubtful Accounts, actual write-offs are charged against the allowance account. Thus, income is reduced in the period of sale rather than in the period of write-off.

When utilizing this method, it is still desirable to prepare an aging schedule for the receivables in order to test the reasonableness of the Allowance for Doubtful Accounts balance. If the aging analysis shows that the balance is materially over- or understated, an adjustment and a reevaluation of the percentages being used is in order. This combination of methods is necessary in order to provide good matching and at the same time to assure that the collectible value of accounts receivable is properly stated.

Interest

Whenever there is a difference between the face amount of a receivable and the present value of the consideration given in exchange, interest is presumed to exist. This is true even though there is no stated provision for interest. The difference between the face amount of the receivable and the present value of the consideration given should be treated as interest and amortized over the period of collection. This rule does not apply to receivables arising from transactions with customers in the normal course of business which are due in customary trade terms not exceeding approximately one year.

As indicated in the discussion of installment receivables, the preferable method of handling interest is to amortize it in such a way as to result in a constant rate when applied to the amount outstanding at the beginning of any given period. Other methods of amortization such as straight line may be used if the results are not materially different from those under the "interest" method.

In the absence of an established price for goods or services exchanged for the receivable, the present value of the consideration given should be determined by discounting all future payments on the receivable using an imputed rate of interest. In determining an appropriate imputed interest rate, the objective is to approximate the rate which would have resulted if an independent borrower and an independent lender had negotiated a similar transaction under comparable terms and conditions with the option to pay the cash price upon purchase or to give a note for the amount of the purchase which bears the prevailing rate of interest to maturity.[7]

The reader is referred to Chapter 13, "Accounting for Bonds, Notes, and Interest," for a further discussion of interest on receivables.

SUMMARY

Revenue is sometimes defined as the amount of assets received or liabilities liquidated by an enterprise in return for service rendered or products produced and delivered. Sometimes the concept is broadened to include such things as a gain on the sale or exchange of assets or the gross inflow from such sale or exchange.

Revenue comes into being as it is *earned*. The concept of *realization* is used to determine when revenue should be recognized in the accounts. The concept sets forth two conditions which must be met prior to the time of recognition: (1) the revenue must be measurable, and (2) the revenue must be certain.

---

[7] AICPA, *Accounting Principles Board Opinion No. 21* (New York, 1971).

The *sale* is a convenient bench mark which serves well in most cases as a guide to when the revenue is both measurable and certain enough for recognition. There are a number of circumstances, however, in which the sale is not a reliable indicator that the conditions of realization have been met, and in which such bases as the receipt of cash, production, and the recovery of cost are utilized. Some circumstances which may call for a deviation from the sales basis are installment sales, long-term construction contracts, and the production of gold or silver.

Closely allied to the recognition of revenue is the valuation of the receivables with which those revenues are often associated. Of primary concern are such items as trade and cash discounts, returns and allowances, freight, uncollectible accounts, and interest.

Trade discounts provide an easy method of quoting different prices to different customers. *Cash discounts* are offered to induce customers to promptly remit balances due. A combination of methods is necessary in the handling of *uncollectible accounts* in order to insure a good matching of revenue with expense, and to assure that the collectible value of receivables is properly stated on the balance sheet. Possible methods are direct charge-off, allowance account based on analysis of receivables, and allowances based on sales. Any interest charge included in receivables must be separately accounted for, and allowed to flow into the income statement only as time passes.

Chapter 7

Cost of sales, pricing, and inventories

*Adolph T. Silverstein**

The reader may be surprised at the inclusion of "pricing" in the chapter title. The method of inventory valuation elected by a corporation will depend in surprisingly large measure on the company's method of product pricing. Any controller or practicing CPA would advise a pricing procedure predicated at least in part upon book inventory values—adjusted for cost trends, current and projected. The need for pricing information and meaningful interim statements has dictated simple, short-cut inventory systems. The cost accounting system must be useful in developing an accurate interpretation of the *reasons* for the results actually achieved as well as generating the results themselves.

Accounting in the United States has undergone a complete redirection in the last few years insofar as the allocation of costs between cost of sales and inventory is concerned. A combination of double-digit inflation, cash shortages, high interest rates, and increasing emphasis on the earnings statement has made the adoption of the Lifo method of inventory valuation the most pervasive non-mandated change in our history. One inescapable side effect of the extensive adoption of Lifo will be a reduction over a period of years

---

* Controller, Fruehauf Corporation.

in the integrity of the balance sheet. The current market value of a Lifo valued inventory can only be determined by simultaneous reference to the balance sheet and a footnote which delineates the amount of "Lifo reserve." This is in sharp contrast to earlier years when the balance sheet was generally considered the most signifi-cant financial statement.

If severe inflation continues rampant in our land, we should an-ticipate ever-increasing attention to some form of price-level ac-counting with special emphasis on inventories and properties.

There are several facets of inventory (and cost of sales) that merit discussion, including the inventory systems, physical inven-tory, valuation methods, obsolescence and market value, and in-terim reporting. Federal income tax regulations covering the use of Lifo are included in Section 1.472, and other inventory related regulations are in Section 1.471.

In all of these areas, *consistency* is considered of major impor-tance.[1] The AICPA requires that a change in inventory method be disclosed in the accountant's certificate in the year of change if the effect is material in relation to the financial statements.[2] Internal Revenue Service income tax forms contain a space to indicate whether any change in inventory method has been effected during the year. Certain changes in accounting method require IRS ap-proval, for which a request must be filed not later than 180 days after the start of the year of change.[3] Changes in inventory method often create a need for changes in loan agreements, indentures, profit-sharing plans, and financial reporting formats. The areas of impact can be numerous; thus when a change in method is being considered, the chief financial officer should immediately obtain the involvement of the company's CPA, controller, treasurer, and legal counsel. It is not uncommon to see a four-month period re-quired to obtain rulings involving changes in inventory method from the Internal Revenue Service. If agency approval is not granted immediately, negotiations could further extend the time required. Thus, inventory planning should be completed before the beginning of the year of change; all too often it is not. Hasty elec-tions may be made which cannot be readily revoked.

---

[1] Section 1.471-2(b) of the Treasury Regulations.

[2] *APB Opinion No. 20*, par. 27 and 28; *ARB No. 43*, Statement 8.

[3] Rev. Proc. 70-27. With good cause, up to nine months is permitted.

INVENTORY SYSTEMS

Controllers should participate in the design and development of inventory-related systems used by departments other than their own. The primary areas requiring such involvement would include economic order quantity, lead times, the basic management information system controlling inventories, forecasting (as it relates to inventory planning), and the general planning function. All departments involved except the controller's department tend to develop inventory systems which avoid stockout conditions at the expense of controlled inventory levels. The primary pressure for reduced inventories must come from the controllership function; and in order to properly exert such pressure, the controller must be aware of and exert some influence over the underlying systems.

Management will constantly want to have as much information available to it as possible. In the event that inventories are increasing, the controller would be expected to report on the areas of increase, as would the planning department. This will inevitably lead the planning department to want to have information on very minute subdivisions of the inventory. The controller has to deal with this request very carefully, because while the inventory input can be charged to these subdivisions with relatively complete accuracy and ease, the relief of the inventory is not always this straightforward. It is the ability to accurately and easily cost out the product and generate the inventory relief which should dictate the level of subdivision of the inventory.

Most major companies on a standard cost system with a wide range of products are on what is called a "four-wall inventory." This means that there is no distinction between material in process and material on hand awaiting input to the production cycle. The alternative practice involves a raw material and/or stores inventory with a requisition system to charge items to work in process as used. The use of the requisition system involves a great deal of additional paperwork that often cannot be cost justified on the basis of the value of the additional information generated.

The book-to-physical adjustment arises from two causes, *differences in quantities* and *differences in prices*. It is important to know the difference exclusive of the effect of changes in prices from one physical inventory to the next. Only this comparison can assure the controller of the efficacy of the inventory accounting system and its implementation. With the advent of computers, it has become economically feasible to compute the extended value of the physical inventory using both the current (new) price standards and the standards applicable to the previous physical inventory. This permits measurement of the impact of inflation on the book-to-physical adjustment. If the cost system is designed to overcost by a small percentage, the accumulated overcosting should similarly be deducted from the book-to-physical pickup. When double pricing the inventory, care should be taken that the computer program gives proper effect to items that are in the present inventory that were not in the prior inventory. The most common practice is to value such items at the current standard cost for the inventory compilation of each year.

PLANNING THE PHYSICAL INVENTORY

Any method of inventory valuation requires periodic determination of the physical quantities on hand. This determination is called a "physical inventory." The success of a physical inventory depends in large measure upon proper planning, an integral part of which is the development and use of a *Physical Inventory Instruction Manual*. Preparation of this manual should involve, as a minimum, senior representation from the purchasing, manufacturing, planning, material control, computer, and controller's functions. Once this manual is prepared by management it should be reviewed by the certified public accountants if the financial statements are to be covered by an auditor's certificate. The manual should include an up-to-date map of the facility being inventoried. Responsibility for each area should be definitely assigned to someone familiar with work done in that area. Such assignments should be indicated on the map, preferably by color coding. The manual should be annotated extensively so that people taking the inventory can quickly find answers to almost any question. Too often the preparation of the manual and the responsibility for the taking of the inventory are assigned to the manufacturing department, with the controller's department getting involved only after the quantities have been compiled.

There are a great many steps involved in planning the physical inventory. The most important aspect of planning involves maximizing the *preidentification* by part number. There have been cases where an entire plant was closed for an additional day because of the time consumed in identifying a relatively small number of obsolete or seldom used parts. This problem can be aggravated when such parts are removed to a central storage area remote from the place where they were manufactured and/or installed. Often parts are assigned a "base number," and minor engineering changes thereafter are assigned the base number plus a suffix. Care must be taken that part numbers reflect the appropriate engineering changes so that the part may be properly costed.

Inventory planning should be designed to minimize costs, which include the *opportunity cost of not producing*—as much an element of the cost of the taking of the inventory as the wages paid to the people involved in the inventory taking. Many companies unduly restrict the number of people or use of overtime in the taking of the inventory, thereby prolonging the time required and delaying the resumption of normal production.

The first thing to be established is the *date of taking the inventory*. The inventory should be taken at the time when the loss of production can best be afforded. This will generally coincide with the period of lowest inventory levels. If there is outdoor storage, care should be taken lest inclement weather force a postponement or increase the cost of taking the inventory. The benefit of pre-identification and pretagging of inventories stored outside is often lost because the tags are ruined due to wind, rain, or snow. The accuracy of the inventories of materials stored outside can be ruined because of the lack of willingness of people to work outside in the weather.

Traditionally, inventories have been taken at the end of the fiscal year. This practice is often ill-advised. Many times it is cheaper to take an inventory as much as three months before the end of the fiscal year, which allows a great deal of time for review and pricing. The objection is often raised that early inventories require the extra task of reviewing inventory transactions from the physical inventory date to the end of the fiscal year. This is true, but given a reliable cost accounting system, the cost and complexity of this step is minimal.

The financial people should be deeply involved in a review of shipping and receiving "cutoff" procedures to insure that "before inventory" and "after inventory" shipments and receipts are properly included in or excluded from both physical and book inventory totals.

If there is a major error in the compilation of the physical inventory, it often involves *unit of measure*. Great care must be taken that the inventory tickets provide clearly for this information. The manual should contain a specific reference to the fact that the checkers as well as the ticket writers are responsible for the use of the proper unit of measure. The inventory ticket should also provide space for an indication of *condition*. Properly used, this can be a clue for unreported obsolescence. Representatives of the controller's department should review the tickets in each area prior to the time when the tickets are physically removed from the inventory for further processing. They should be specifically advised to watch for such indications of excess or obsolete inventory as dust, rust, prior year inventory tags, and cobwebs.

Data processing personnel will often recommend use of *pre-printed cards* containing descriptive information (but not quantities). Unless each part has a relatively fixed location within an area, it is possible to spend an excess amount of time placing the inventory card at the physical location of the part. The last step in the compilation of physical inventory, exclusive of pricing, is a comparison of the physical inventory cards to the planning records. This should be done for all major items as soon as possible after the inventory is taken. Major discrepancies should be investigated.

A vital step in any physical inventory is *tag control*. Tags must be prenumbered and should be properly designed. Consecutive groups of tags should be assigned to each area, and a master record should be maintained showing the numbers assigned. In the event that a tag is found to be missing, you at least know the area from which it should have been returned to the control area. The first step in compilation should be a determination that all tag numbers have been accounted for. A control count should be established as to the total number of tags used.

Consigned inventory should be confirmed with the consignee; and if a substantial amount is involved, consideration should be given to the actual observation of the consigned inventory. Controllers often have been undone professionally by improper utilization of this inventory by consignees.

If your financial statements are to be certified, you can expect that the auditors will insist upon being present at the taking of the physical inventory. Properly utilized, they can be of great assistance; however, their attendance is not required at every physical inventory, and not every inventory need be the subject of a physical every year. Generally accepted auditing standards permit reliance on inventory records where appropriate. The failure to take a physical inventory of an insignificant portion of the total should not result in a qualified opinion.

VALUATION

Once the quantities in inventory are ascertained, the inventory must be priced. There are certain considerations involved in pricing that are independent of the method of valuation followed. The starting point for any of the valuation methods is the underlying documentation showing the history of purchases individually for each item of inventory, both as to price and quantity. It must be stressed that when an inventory is valued at cost, there must be enough purchases at the cost used to cover the quantity of the item in inventory.

Standard cost systems are most prevalent in industries involved in the repetitive production of similar items. Standards are established at least annually, usually at the time of physical inventory, for each item of inventory. Wherever possible the standards should not be changed during the inventory year, for such changes often complicate development of interim statements (see Chapter 35). An interim change in standards does not present a problem if planning (or accounting) records permit an accurate determination of the effect of the change on the inventory at time of change. Unfortunately, records adequate for this purpose are the exception rather than the rule.

Actual cost systems are most often encountered in government contracting, building construction, and heavy equipment manufacturing. Sales prices in such industries are often predicated at least in part on costs. Use of an actual cost system avoids potential arguments over the allocation of variances (differences between actual costs and standard costs).

INVENTORY VALUATION METHODS

The three most generally accepted methods of inventory valuation are: (1) first-in, first-out (Fifo); (2) last-in, first-out (Lifo); and (3) average cost. The methods of inventory valuation are usually similarly applied to all categories of cost within a single inventory. We shall discuss the valuation methods in the context of raw material and/or purchased parts and then proceed to a discussion of the peculiarities of other elements of inventory, such as labor, burden, freight, and tooling.

Fifo

The first-in, first-out (Fifo) method assumes that the flow of costs is identical with the (assumed) flow of material, that is, the first acquired is the first used. This is the traditional method of valuing inventories and is used to keep the basic accounting records, even when Lifo is used for ultimate inventory valuation. An example follows.

	Units	Unit cost	Total
Beginning of month inventory.	100	$5.00	$500.00
Purchases:			
1st	60	4.50	270.00
2d	80	4.75	380.00
3d	75	5.25	393.75
End of month inventory	125	5.05	631.25

The procedure used to determine the value of the ending inventory involves use of the price of the most recent purchases until sufficient quantities are accumulated to match the ending inventory. In the example this is applied as follows:

3d purchase	75	$5.25	$393.75
2d purchase	50	4.75	237.50
	125	$5.05	$631.25

Observe that the ending inventory is valued at a per unit cost which does not match any individual purchase. This "artificial" unit cost would customarily be carried forward as the unit cost of the beginning inventory for the next month rather than the unit cost of individual acquisitions. However, either unit costing procedure would be correct if consistently applied.

The primary problem encountered while using Fifo in a standard cost environment is that revised standards are often established late in the year, when there may not be sufficient purchases at the new standard by year-end to accumulate the quantity in the ending inventory. This problem is aggravated during periods of inflation when prices increase at a more rapid rate and new standards tend to be set somewhat high to provide a level of "cost protection" during the ensuing period.

Lifo

In our economy, prices have historically tended to increase. The last-in, first-out (Lifo) method of inventory valuation in periods of rising prices will reduce the illusory impact upon earnings of inventory gains from inflation and result in lower amounts of income taxes payable to the government. Paragraph 16 of *APB Opinion No. 20* requires justification for the change to Lifo *other than* tax consequences. The justification usually offered is a variation of the concept, "Lifo better matches current costs with current revenues."

Use of Lifo for income tax purposes is not permitted in Canada, which has inhibited its use in that country.

Lifo has its own jargon and a matrix of decisions that must be made when Lifo is initially adopted. The decision to adopt Lifo must be made before the tax return is filed for the year of adoption, and it can be made without obtaining prior Internal Revenue Service approval by filing Form 970, Application to Use LIFO Inventory Method, as a part of the federal income tax return. However, all external financial reporting for the *year of adoption* and thereafter must be on the Lifo basis. Practically that means that publicly held companies must make the election before year-end financial results are announced so that the year-end results are stated on a Lifo basis. Publication of results for three quarters of the year of change using Fifo would not prevent a year-end decision to adopt Lifo retroactive to the first of that year. A change from Lifo back to Fifo does require IRS approval, which must be requested within 180 days after the start of the year of reversion. When the change from Lifo to Fifo is approved, the taxpayer is required to pay the tax on the income resulting from the change ratably over the lesser of ten years or twice the period Lifo was employed.

Once having adopted and abandoned Lifo, a second election to use Lifo requires prior IRS approval, which may be difficult to obtain. Prior IRS approval is *not* required when the use of Lifo is being extended to an additional group of items.

There are several considerations that must be evaluated in reaching a decision on the adoption of Lifo. These include the potential impact on the market price and price/earnings ratio of the company's stock, the impact on the company's ability to raise debt or equity capital, the effect on dividends, the impact on salary practices including incentive bonus plans, and, often overlooked, the effect on working capital and debt-to-equity covenants. In addition to the foregoing, one should be aware of the added accounting (which will be addressed in detail later), and the potential reduction in the tax timing benefit from the use of Lifo caused by the inability to deduct for tax purposes any write-down of inventory from cost to market.

Lifo techniques. After it has been decided to adopt Lifo, there are four basic decision areas that must be addressed:

1. The composition of the Lifo "pool" or "pools."
2. Use of dollar-value or unit method of valuing inventory.
3. Method of calculating dollar-value index (if dollar-value method is used).
4. Method of building "layers."

Exhibit 1 shows the basic procedure for calculating the Lifo adjustment.

Let me summarize this example. During 1973 the change in inventory was caused only by inflation; at base cost beginning and ending inventory were the same. The total effect of inflation is the difference between Fifo and Lifo values (Lifo difference).

In 1974 there was no cost inflation, but the inventory expressed in terms of base cost rose $3,000. This $3,000 becomes a "layer" with an index of 1.2. Observe that with no cost inflation and an increased base cost of inventory, the Lifo difference is unchanged and Lifo earnings are the same as Fifo earnings for the period. With no inflation and a reduction in inventory quantities expressed in terms of base cost, the Lifo reserve would decrease, resulting in Lifo earnings being greater than Fifo. Try the example using 12/31/74 inventory at $4,000 in terms of base cost. You will get a Lifo difference of only $800—thus Lifo pretax income would be $200 higher than Fifo.

In 1975 there was cost inflation, but a reduction in the inventory expressed in terms of base cost. Notice that the most recently created "layer" is the first to be eroded. Also, the Lifo

EXHIBIT 1
Example of Lifo calculations

	At current cost (Fifo)	At base cost	Index	Incre- ment (liqui- dation)	Layer	Index	Lifo inven- tory	Differ- ence between Fifo and Lifo
1/1/73 (effective date of adoption)......	$ 5,000	$ 5,000	1.00		$5,000	1.00	$ 5,000	
12/31/73..........	6,000	5,000	1.20	None	5,000	1.00	$ 5,000	$1,000
12/31/74..........	9,600	8,000	1.20	$ 3,000	5,000	1.00	$ 5,000	
					3,000	1.20	3,600	
							$ 8,600	1,000
12/31/75..........	9,000	6,000	1.50	(2,000)	5,000	1.00	$ 5,000	
					1,000	1.20	1,200	
							$ 6,200	2,800
12/31/76..........	15,000	7,500	2.00	1,500	5,000	1.00	$ 5,000	
					1,000	1.20	1,200	
					1,500	1.50	2,250	
							$ 8,450	6,550
12/31/77..........	21,000	14,000	1.50	6,500	5,000	1.00	$ 5,000	
					1,000	1.20	1,200	
					1,500	1.50	2,250	
					6,500	2.00	13,000	
							$21,450	(450)

difference ($2,800) is less than the difference between ending inventory valued at current cost and at base cost ($9,000 — $6,000 = $3,000).

In 1976 there was both inflation and an increase in inventory expressed in terms of base cost. Easy. A layer is built or liquidated, measured by the change in inventory expressed in base cost. Observe that the layer which was liquidated in 1975 is never restored—the 1976 layer is valued at 1975 index (see later discussion of "Lifo layers").

In 1977 there was cost deflation accompanied by a sizable increase in inventory expressed in terms of base cost. Observe that the Lifo inventory ($21,450) is higher than Fifo ($21,000). While this is an extreme example, it does show the variation in results which could occur. With deflation but no change in inventory expressed in terms of base cost, the Lifo reserve is only liquidated in part. In the 1977 example, using an unchanged inventory at base

cost ($7,500), current cost would be $11,250 and the Lifo difference would be $2,800 ($11,250 — $8,450).

Pools. One of the most important decisions to make when
adopting the Lifo method is how the various components of inventory are to be allocated into Lifo "groups" or "pools" for the
purpose of comparing the relative quantity of goods on hand at the
end of each year.

There are some caveats as to the pool options available. Internal
Revenue Service regulations do not permit a single pool to include
inventory of more than one corporation. Before an election as to
pool content is made, Section 1.472 of the Treasury Regulations
should be carefully reviewed.

To maximize the Lifo/Fifo difference, as few pools as possible
should be utilized. By using fewer pools, liquidation of one item
within a pool can be offset by an increase in another item within
the *same* pool. This is clearly shown in Exhibit 2, which assumes
two items with identical cost trends.

While Exhibit 2 shows only decreases in the inventory expressed
in terms of base cost, a similar advantage results for the single pool
as compared to two pools when the inventories increase fairly
steadily or merely fluctuate. If there is never a decrease in either
pool (and therefore no liquidation of layers), it makes no difference whether there is one pool or many.

Unit method or dollar value. By using the *unit method* (specific
goods method) to value inventory, a separate Lifo history is developed for each item in the inventory.[4] Practically, this makes
each item a separate pool. When using the *dollar-value method*
the number of dollars of inventory in a given pool is considered an
item.

The rationale previously used, which dictates a minimum number
of pools, leads inevitably to the selection of the dollar-value method
rather than the unit method. The sheer clerical effort of the unit
method can be frightening unless the inventory consists of very
few items. Use of the unit method results in the loss of the favorable base when an item is deleted from the inventory. Similarly,
if a new item is added to the inventory some years after the adoption of Lifo, the beginning valuation point for that item is the cost
at the time it first becomes a part of the inventory.

Calculation of dollar-value index. There are four generally ac-

---

[4] Section 1.472-1 of the Treasury Regulations.

EXHIBIT 2
Lifo pools

	Item I	Item II
1/1/73 (year of adoption)	$5,000	$5,000
12/31/73	2,500	7,500
12/31/74	7,500	2,400
12/31/75	5,000	5,000

	At current cost	At base cost	Index	Increment (liquidation)	Lifo layers	Index	Lifo value
Pool—Item I:							
1/1/73	$ 5,000	$ 5,000	1.00	None	$ 5,000	1.00	$ 5,000
12/31/73	2,500	2,000	1.25	$(3,000)	2,000	1.00	2,000
12/31/74	7,500	5,000	1.50	3,000	2,000	1.00	2,000
					3,000	1.25	3,750
							$ 5,750
12/31/75	5,000	2,500	2.00	(2,500)	2,000	1.00	$ 2,000
					500	1.25	625
							$ 2,625
Pool—Item II:							
1/1/73	$ 5,000	$ 5,000	1.00	None	$ 5,000	1.00	$ 5,000
12/31/73	7,500	6,000	1.25	$ 1,000	5,000	1.00	$ 5,000
					1,000	1.00	1,000
							$ 6,000
12/31/74	2,400	1,600	1.50	(4,400)	1,600	1.00	$ 1,600
12/31/75	5,000	2,500	2.00	900	1,600	1.00	$ 1,600
					900	1.50	1,350
							$ 2,950
Pool—Combine Items I and II:							
1/1/73	$10,000	$10,000	1.00	None	$10,000	1.00	$10,000
12/31/73	10,000	8,000	1.25	$(2,000)	8,000	1.00	8,000
12/31/74	9,900	6,600	1.50	(1,400)	6,600	1.00	6,600
12/31/75	10,000	5,000	2.00	(1,600)	5,000	1.00	5,000

Comparison of Lifo value

	Pool—Item I	Pool—Item II	Total two pools	Single pool
12/31/73	$2,000	$6,000	$8,000	$8,000
12/31/74	5,750	1,600	7,350	6,600
12/31/75	2,625	2,950	5,575	5,000

cepted methods of developing indices that can be used in computing the inventory under the dollar-value method. The election of an index method must be reported as Item 8(c) on Form 970 and cannot be changed thereafter without prior Internal Revenue Service approval. The four methods are:

1. Double extension.
2. Direct index.
3. Link-chain index.
4. External index.

The procedure for applying the index to develop layers, and ultimately to value the Lifo inventory, is the same regardless of the index method used.

The double-extension method is the most direct method used, and is expressly preferred by the Internal Revenue Service, perhaps because it is the easiest to audit. Under this method the ending inventory is priced at current costs and completely repriced at base period costs (costs of the year Lifo was initially adopted). This method indisputably gives the most accurate answer, but if there is significant change in the items comprising the inventory, reconstruction of a base period cost for new items can be time consuming and difficult. Internal Revenue Service regulations permit the use of base-year price lists, catalogs, current-year cost, or a reasonably reconstructed base-period cost (Sec. 1.472-8 [e] [2] [iii]), but the more time that passes after the adoption of Lifo, the more difficult these techniques become to apply.

The direct-index method is the same as the double-extention method, except that only a representative sample of the current inventory is repriced to develop the index. The sample may be judgmental or statistical; if judgmental, one should expect challenge from the Internal Revenue Service. The advantage of the direct-index method is the reduction in number of items to be handled.

The link-chain method utilizes an index computed by using the ending inventory priced at current costs and at beginning of year costs. This index is then applied to the prior year's index to develop the cumulative index. The current year-end inventory dollars are divided by the cumulative index to restate that inventory at base cost. The Lifo value is then computed as in the examples in Exhibit 2, Lifo pools.

The advantage of the link-chain method is that (1) there inevitably is much less change in the items constituting the inventory on an annual basis than on a cumulative basis since the base period, and (2) the year earlier costs should be much more accessible than base-period costs when a new item is added to the inventory.

The primary disadvantage inherent in the link-chain method is that changes in inventory mix and prices can generate inaccurate results. To prevent such an occurrence, periodic reviews of major items should be made on a direct-index basis.

Exhibit 3 is a simplified example of the problem that results

EXHIBIT 3
Comparison of dollar-value LIFO indexes

				Link-chain index				Double-extension index		
Year	Part	Quan-tity	Unit cost	End of year	Beginning of year	Cur-rent index	Cumula-tive index	Current cost	Base cost	Index
Base	A	5	$ 1							
	B	8	5							
	C	20	10							
1	A	5	2	$ 10	$ 5			$ 10	$ 5	
	B	9	10	90	45			90	45	
	C	25	11	275	250			275	250	
				$ 375	$ 300	1.25	1.25	$ 375	$ 300	1.25
2	A	15	4	$ 60	$ 30			$ 60	$ 15	
	B	25	12	300	250		1.25	300	125	
	C	20	8	160	220	1.04	× 1.04	160	200	
				$ 520	$ 500	1.04	1.30	$ 520	$ 340	1.53
3	A	15	1	$ 15	$ 60			$ 15	$ 15	
	B	10	5	50	120		1.30	50	50	
	C	110	10	1,100	880		× 1.10	1,100	1,100	
				$1,165	$1,060	1.10	1.43	$1,165	$1,165	1.00

when beginning and ending costs by item are the same, generating a double extension (or direct index) of 1.00, whereas the cumulative link-chain index for the identical inventory at the end of year 3 would be 1.43.

The use of external indices is prevalent in the retailing industry. The advantage is the ready availability of the index and the resultant ease of application. The primary disadvantage is that the external index, even if developed for a specific industry, may not reflect the quantities or prices of the company using the index.

Lifo layers. Inventory layers under the Lifo method of accounting represent increments to inventory, or quantity increases, and should be included in the year-end inventories at current year costs. The presence of a new layer is determined by comparing end-of-year inventory levels, in terms of units of inventory items (unit method) or in terms of base period costs (dollar-value method), to beginning-of-year levels.

Internal Revenue Service regulations pertaining to the pricing of inventory increments (layers) are identical for both the unit method and the dollar-value methods.[5] They generally provide for four optional methods for determining current year costs:

1. Most recent purchases or production.
2. Earliest purchases or production during the year in the order of acquisition.
3. Average of all goods purchased or produced during the year.
4. Any other proper method which, in the opinion of the Commissioner, clearly reflects income.

Method 2 above appears to be most consistent with the Lifo principle. In periods of rising prices, the "earliest cost" method will result in inventory increments being priced at lower costs than those computed under other methods. Another advantage of the "earliest cost" approach is that the current year unit costs under the unit method may be computed in the early part of the year, while the development of unit costs under the other approaches cannot begin until all inventory transactions for the year are completed.

Average cost

In addition to the Fifo and Lifo methods most common in manufacturing environments, use of an average cost method is often encountered in process or extractive industries. There are two basic average cost methods currently utilized, and both are based on weighted averages: use of a period average cost (the more prevalent method) and use of a moving average cost. Examples of each method are given in Exhibit 4.

Notice that in using the period average method, any usage is removed from the inventory after the period average cost is determined. As a practical matter, it is often necessary to cost out usage based on the average cost at the *beginning* of the period. Use

---

[5] Regs. par. 1.472-2 (d) (1), 1,472-2 (d) (2), and 1.472-8 (e) (2) (ii).

EXHIBIT 4
Examples of average cost methods

	Period average				Moving average			
	Units	Unit cost	Extended	Average cost	Units	Unit cost	Extended	Average cost
Beginning inventory	1,000	$40.00	$40,000 ÷ 1,000	$40.00	1,000	$40.00	$40,000 ÷ 1,000	$40.00
1st purchase	250	39.00	9,750		250	39.00	9,750	
							$49,750 ÷ 1,250	39.80
2nd purchase	500	38.00	19,000		500	38.00	19,000	
							$68,750 ÷ 1,750	39.286
Usage					600	39.286	23,572	
							$45,178 ÷ 1,150	39.285
3rd purchase	500	38.50	19,250		500	38.50	19,250	
							$64,428 ÷ 1,650	39.05
Total Receipts	2,250		$88,000 ÷ 2,250	39.11				
Usage	600		23,466					
Ending inventory	1,650		$64,534 ÷ 1,650	39.11			$64,428 ÷ 1,650	$39.05

of this practice *consistently* should yield reasonably accurate results. Use of a moving average can be very time consuming if there are frequent inventory transactions. As in most areas of inventory, consistency of application from period to period is very important.

OTHER COMPONENTS OF INVENTORY

All of the foregoing methodologies have been described as if applicable to material, although they are equally applicable to other components of inventory. Each of the components has peculiarities; therefore, we will include a short discussion of each major component.

Labor

Problems in accounting for labor fall into two groups: those related to quantity and those related to cost. Standards should be used both for quantity and cost. In order to control the Direct Labor Inventory account, records should be maintained in both standard hours and dollars. Controllers should be careful to avoid the buildup of nonexistent hours in inventory. They should make frequent trips through their plant to get the "feel" of the level of business. Fluctuations in the hours in inventory should be carefully analyzed. Wherever possible, standard labor should be entered on the books ("paid" is the term commonly used) only on the basis of end product produced. This is commonly referred to as the "*single pay point*" method. It is common practice to have a single pay point with distribution to multiple departments of the total standard hour content of a given end product.

In many industries the production cycle is so prolonged that the single pay point would distort reported departmental and plant efficiency; the efficiency report is the single most important measurement of line management in a plant. Primarily to improve the accuracy of departmental efficiency reports, there can be *multiple pay points*—usually when a product leaves a department or a building, although there can even be *operational pay points* within a department. But remember that more pay points increase the opportunity for error.

Do not succumb to the fallacy that multiple departments automatically dictate multiple pay points. This is particularly true in an

environment that combines parts fabrication and assembly operations. There is a tendency for the parts fabrication department to
overstate piece production, particularly if piecework compensation
or incentive is involved. (Such overreporting can also hamper
production of the end product because of the automatic distortion
of planning records.) In any time period, departmental and plant
efficiency is affected only by the *change* in labor hours in process
in each department or plant. The *single pay point* method is recommended whenever feasible.

Once the hours in inventory are properly controlled, the cost of
each hour must be determined. Wherever possible a single *plantwide
labor rate* (standard) should be used, based on a projection of the
weighted average of the mix of hours projected to be acquired
during the ensuing inventory year. If the product has a high labor
content and a wide variance in the cost of the various skills involved, use of multiple labor rates is dictated.

The cost of as many fringe benefits as possible should be included
in the standard hourly labor rate. Many of these items could just
as easily be considered burden. Their inclusion as direct labor has
a double-dip impact on the burden rate. It decreases the dollar
amount of burden while increasing the dollar amount of labor, which
is the base customarily used for burden absorption. This is significant because in many pricing negotiations the starting point is
standard cost, and it is usually easier to sell a *higher dollar amount
of direct labor* in conjunction with a *lower burden rate* rather than
a lower direct labor content with a higher burden rate. Obviously,
the total dollar cost of labor and burden would be identical; it is
just a matter of customer reaction.

Another reason to include fringes as an element of direct labor
is the attention it directs to the cost of the fringes during union
contract negotiation.

Burden

Historically, several methods have been used to apply manufacturing expenses to the cost of inventories. The methods can be
generally grouped as follows:

1. *Prime costing,* in which no overhead costs are included in
   inventory.

2. *Direct costing,* in which no fixed overhead costs are included in inventory, but in which variable overhead costs are included. In other words, fixed factory costs are treated as a period cost rather than as a product cost.
3. *Absorption costing,* in which all manufacturing overhead costs, including fixed factory costs, are regarded as product costs.

In September 1973 the Internal Revenue Service adopted regulations[6] on inventory costing for manufacturing and production companies which require full absorption accounting and effectively disallow the prime costing[7] and direct-costing methods.[8] The thrust of the regulations was to conform tax practice with generally accepted accounting procedures. The rules require that all direct costs must be inventoried—the definition of direct cost follows traditional accounting. The treatment accorded indirect costs depends on which of the following three categories they are included in:

1. All items in the first category, which includes repairs and maintenance, indirect labor and fringes, tools and supplies, and quality control and inspection, must be inventoried for tax purposes whether or not they are inventoried for book purposes.
2. Items in the second category, which includes selling expenses, interest, research and development expenses, and general and administrative expenses, need not be included in inventory for tax purposes even if inventoried for book purposes.
3. Expenses in the third category, which includes depreciation, pension costs, scrap, spoilage, factory administration, and insurance costs, must be handled consistently for book and tax purposes. If any of these expenses are inventoried for book purposes they must be inventoried for tax purposes, and vice versa.

Production overhead costs can be charged to units of inventory by using many different techniques. Basically the formula for allocation is:

$$\frac{\text{Overhead Cost Pool}}{\text{Basis of Application}} = \text{Burden Application Rate}$$

---

[6] Section 1.471-11 of the Treasury Regulations.
[7] Section 1.471-2 (F) (7) of the Treasury Regulations.
[8] Section 1.471-2 (F) (6) of the Treasury Regulations.

The overhead pool used can be either of the following:

1. *Actual.* Using actual costs for a period for burden application has the obvious major disadvantage of requiring a constant calculation of burden rates and the lack of ability to perform "forward costing."
2. *Projected.* Production overhead costs can be estimated at the beginning of a period, and this estimate will be used as the overhead pool for that period. An average of historical costs, adjusted for anticipated inflation, is usually the basis for this estimate. This has the advantage of a "forward costing" technique but suffers from the same pitfalls as all other forecasts.

The basis of application requires setting a level of activity during a given period and also selecting the proper unit of measure. *Levels of activity* which may be used are the following:

1. Actual.
2. Expected.
3. Normal.
4. Practical capacity.
5. Theoretical capacity.

The *actual activity* method uses actual production and can only be computed after the close of the period in which the activity took place.

When the *expected activity* level is used, both the production and the overhead amount are estimated in advance for each accounting period. Any variances (over- or underabsorbed overhead) are closed out to cost of sales. When financial statements are prepared, variances should be reviewed; and if material in amount, appropriate adjustment should be made to the book inventory (for methodology of calculation see section on "Interim Statements" at the end of this chapter).

The *normal activity* method uses that level of production which will satisfy average demand over a span of time that takes into account seasonal, cyclical, and trend factors. The use of the normal activity method assumes that total production over a period of years can be estimated with reasonable accuracy and either (*a*) overhead amounts will be consistent or (*b*) the total overhead amount for the entire period of years can be estimated so that a constant overhead rate per unit can be applied. As a practical matter these conditions rarely exist; therefore, the applicability of the normal method is limited.

The *practical capacity* method allows for estimated delays due to such things as normal maintenance, relief time, occasional unpredictable breakdown, and so on. This determination is often based upon actual output achieved during a sustained period of prior experience.

Theoretical capacity is the method of determining levels of production output that may be expected under conditions that fully utilize the plant operating facilities on an ideal schedule for the company or industry. This is calculated to reflect the normal operating characteristics of the company; that is, it gives allowance for periodic shutdown, normal vacations, holidays, and so on.

The *basis of application* should be tailored to the particular industry and plant. The following are the primary units of measure used to express the basis of application:

1. Labor dollars.
2. Labor hours.
3. Machine-hours.
4. Units of production.

Direct labor hours or dollars are more commonly used in the more labor-intensive industries. With an increasing emphasis in the use of automated equipment and attendant reduced direct labor input, there is an increasing trend in many industries to use machine-hours or units of production as the basis for allocating burden.

Freight

An element of inventory often overlooked is inbound freight. Again a determination must be made whether to establish a separate freight rate for each product or to use a plantwide freight rate. Some material is purchased freight prepaid; most is not. The sole criterion as to whether to develop a separate freight rate for different products should be the impact on the end-product cost.

The controller should watch the balance in the inbound freight account as a percentage of inventory. This relationship should not tend to change dramatically from month to month, unless there is a change in product mix. The controller should scrutinize the debits to this account periodically because in most operations it does not receive the same care that is used to set material standards or to review variances incurred. Care should be taken to insure that outbound freight does not inadvertently get charged to this account.

Tooling

Tooling costs are a proper element of product cost. These items can be charged to the product based on amortization of a specific number of units, or as a percentage of material or total product cost. It is also proper to treat tooling as an element of burden, in which case it would usually be spread to end products based on direct labor content.

The primary concern with tooling costs is to insure that the amortization period is reasonable. Often tooling is acquired for a specific product, and then demand for that product falls short of the sales volume anticipated at the time unit tooling cost was developed. If the demand for the product is too low, an entry should be made charging cost of sales and crediting the tooling inventory account for the lack of absorption caused by the difference between the planned production rate and the actual production rate. The controller should anticipate a challenge from the Internal Revenue Service in the event that the period selected for amortization falls significantly short of the expected useful life of the tooling. Remember, by the time the Internal Revenue agents make their examination, they will have the benefit of "20/20 hindsight."

A related problem occurs in a multiplant environment where the tooling is not on site but is at a vendor who makes the same part for more than one plant of the same company. The decision is often left with the purchasing department as to whether the vendor is to pay for the tooling and amortize the cost in the piece price, or whether the customer pays for the tooling. If the customer pays for the tooling, the internal accounting system should provide for amortization in the piece price to each using plant. This can best be accomplished by requiring the vendor to give the corporate accounting department a credit which should be compared periodically to a report of purchases by the using plants.

The purchasing department will usually suggest that the vendor acquire the tooling because it is the simplest method. However, if this is done the vendor will tend to use an amortization period or quantity which is relatively low and often will thereby benefit through overabsorption. If the vendor has been a supplier for a reasonable period of time, you can be sure that the vendor knows as much about your estimates of production as does your own management. Do not expect a profit from the vendor's overestimation of the size of production orders. One caveat—if the tooling can be used to make parts used by others, the vendor should buy the tooling because there is no way of restricting its usage to your parts. In an extreme case, you could wind up paying for the tooling; and the vendor, if unscrupulous, could be using it to provide parts for your competitors, free to them of any tooling cost.

OBSOLESCENCE AND MARKET VALUE

Lower of cost or market

Inventories are generally stated at the lower of cost or market. There is a great deal of discussion as to what constitutes market for purposes of inventory valuation.[9] Closely intertwined with market value is obsolescence. From a practical standpoint, the problem involved in establishing market value differs as between a finished product and raw materials or purchased parts.

The Internal Revenue regulations require that in order to get a deduction in the current year, obsolete material must be disposed of within 30 days after the year-end. (Bear in mind that Lifo regulations do not allow the use of "the lower of cost or market"; use of *cost* is mandatory.) This can often be done for raw material or purchased parts where there may be a relatively ready market, but what do you do with a finished product of your own manufacture? The distinction between slow moving, obsolete, and overvalued becomes rather blurred in real life unless the product has been removed from the marketplace. In any case, the ability to dispose of the product within 30 days after the end of the year presents an often insurmountable problem unless the problem has been addressed well ahead of year-end.

Quite often the product cannot be moved at any cost within this time period. Query: In such a case, what is market? One very

---

[9] *ARB No. 43*, chap. 4, Statements 5–7, par. 8–11 and Sections 1.471-2 (c) and 1.471-4 of the Treasury Regulations.

definite recommendation is that when attempting to effectuate a tax deductible revaluation of finished goods, the ability to negotiate with the Internal Revenue Service is significantly improved if the revaluation is specifically applied in the inventory compilation to specific units. It is very difficult to obtain a current tax deduction for a percentage or round dollar reserve.

A related problem involves outstanding purchase commitments at a price above current market. A reserve should be established for the excess cost and this amount should be charged to cost of sales currently.[10]

Obsolescence

Another consideration at time of pricing is obsolescence. In a one-plant environment, it is relatively easy for the controller to assist in the taking of the physical inventory and thereby develop a subjective opinion of the approximate quantity of obsolete material on hand. This becomes increasingly difficult as the number of plants proliferates. The planning department records are a logical source for determination of obsolescence, and the planning supervisor should be given some definition as to obsolescence and also as to excess inventory. In a multiplant environment, the planning managers may be reluctant to indicate the true level of obsolescence lest it be viewed as a criticism of their own performance.

Query: How do corporate controllers determine the accuracy of the reported obsolescence? They must rely heavily on their resident controller at each plant. For this purpose (and many others) plant controllers should report directly to division or corporate controllers, not plant managers.

If the same material is used in more than one plant, as soon as the determination of obsolete and excess material is completed, a detailed listing should be circulated to all plants so that any plant with requirements for such material can then acquire the material from the plant that has no further use for it. To create motivation, the accounting system should be such that there is a *slight* price advantage to the plant using material from the excess and obsolete listing. Since an interplant transfer should not affect the consolidated carrying value of the inventory, some companies require the trans-

---

[10] *ARB No. 43*, chap. 4, Statement 10, par. 17.

ferring plant to grant an allowance (say 5 or 10 percent) from standard and give the transferee plant an identical allowance. Both the transferor and the transferree should reflect this allowance in results of operations, not as an adjustment of inventory value.

Excess inventory should be defined as the inventory in excess of a particular number of months' requirements, based on planned production levels. Certainly the maximum should not exceed six months unless there are very unusual circumstances.

INTERIM STATEMENTS

Although the subject of interim statements is dealt with separately in this volume in Chapter 35, the impact on the interim statements of the inflation in inventory is potentially great enough to require inclusion herein. The objective should be to treat each interim period ". . . as an integral part of an annual period."[11] The effect of this pronouncement is to indicate that each interim period should contain a proportionate share of the year-end adjustments. Suffice it to say that this concept is easier to espouse than to comply with—especially as it affects inventory.

If there is no inflation, the Fifo or Lifo statements can be prepared directly from the accounts. However, in the event of significant inflation, the interim statements should treat the effect of variances on the inventory at the end of the period as a component of ending inventory value. The practice most generally followed is to capitalize the amount of purchase price variance incurred on the most recent volume of purchases required to equal the end-of-period inventory. The calculation is based on the assumption that the mix of purchases is the same as the mix of end-of-period inventory.

Obviously, this assumption does not yield a precise calculation as turnover rates will vary significantly among different elements of inventory. However, there is no preferable method available. The amount capitalized should be set up in a separate inventory account and adjusted at the time of the next succeeding interim statement. If a multiplant or multicorporation environment is involved, there is little value in spreading these adjustments back to the individual operations. A sample calculation follows.

---

[11] *APB Opinion No. 28*, par. 9.

Facts

Ending inventory at standard cost = $2,000,000

Purchases

	Actual cost	Standard cost	Variance
Most recent month	$1,200,000	$1,100,000	$100,000
Second preceding month.	600,000	560,000	40,000
Third preceding month.	500,000	475,000	25,000
	$2,300,000	$2,135,000	$165,000
Most recent month	$1,200,000	$1,100,000	$100,000
Second preceding month.	600,000	560,000	40,000
Third preceding month.	357,895*	340,000	17,895
	$2,157,895	$2,000,000	
Variance to be capitalized			$157,895

$$* \frac{\$500,000}{\$475,000} \times \$340,000 = \$357,895$$

In the example notice that the accumulation of purchases is based on *standard cost,* not *actual cost.* Also observe that the average variance for the period of accumulation (165,000/2,135,000) is not used; rather, a Fifo assumption is made as to the flow of costs.

The problem of inventory valuation for interim statements is greatly accentuated if the company has adopted the Lifo method. The first step involves a calculation of the Lifo adjustment determined as if the interim period was a full fiscal year. However, once the related Lifo calculations are completed, the accounting treatment is vastly different from that which would prevail for a full fiscal year.

The treatment for interim statements can be summarized as follows:

a. *Changes in price levels.* The effect of a change in price levels during a period should be recorded at the end of that period so long as the index is free from temporary statistical aberrations. Where an increase in the price level results in additional cost of goods sold in that period, that cost should be recognized; where a decrease in the price level results in an indicated reduction, it should not be recognized in the interim period but should be deferred until it is "realized" in the year-end inventory. This is consistent with the fundamental accounting tenet which requires that losses be anticipated but that gains be deferred until realized.

b.   Changes in inventory levels.   i.   The income effect of a *temporary* (within the fiscal year) variation in the inventory levels, either up or down, should not be recognized in the interim statements.

ii.   The income effect of a planned *permanent* (for the fiscal year) change in inventory levels should be allocated over the year on the basis of projected total cost of sales.[12] To the extent that "income" actually results from a change in inventory level, it is not appropriate to identify that income with any particular period except—

iii.   When a change in inventory levels can be identified with a specific event, such as the closing of a location or a similar unusual or extraordinary event, the income effect of that change should be reported in the period of the related event, and identified as an effect of that event.

In practice, it is often very difficult to compute a Lifo adjustment on an actual basis at the end of each interim period. Many companies do not take a physical inventory on a quarterly basis, and lacking a reliable perpetual inventory system, are not in a position to perform the detailed "double extension" necessary to compute an index of inflation for the period. These companies often compute an "estimated index" by double extending a representative sample of the more significant inventory items. By using this "estimated index" and assuming no change in inventory mix, a reasonable approximation of the required interim Lifo adjustment can be made.

I have discussed the problem of interim reporting in terms of a single Lifo inventory pool involving material. The same concepts apply for all other inventory components. Similar calculations must be made for each pool; and it is not unlikely that if a company has several pools, the results could differ substantially between pools.

Due to the increased use of Lifo and the added attention currently directed toward interim statements, it is reasonable to expect considerable writings on the subject in the near future.

---

[12] *APB Opinion No. 28*, par. 17.

Chapter 8

Accounting for product warranty and service contract costs

*Erwin H. Graham**

DEFINITION OF SUBJECT

Warranty has been defined in *A Dictionary for Accountants*[1] as "a promise by a seller to . . . make good on a deficiency as to quantity, quality, or performance of a product. The character of the deficiency and the period covered are usually attached to the bill of sale or to the product itself." Warranty has also been defined in *Industrial Accountants' Encyclopedia Dictionary*[2] as "a promise or representation of fact by the seller relating to and forming part of the contract of sale with the buyer."

The manufacturer normally provides this warranty through a dealer; but there are many products that are sold and serviced direct, in which case the manufacturer will provide the service directly. Undoubtedly, the decision to provide a warranty was originally formulated by the powerful forces of competition that required a high degree of consumer satisfaction. For this reason,

---

* Vice President and General Auditor, Chrysler Corporation.

[1] Eric L. Kohler, *A Dictionary for Accountants* (Englewood Cliffs, N.J.: Prentice-Hall, Inc., 1970).

[2] Prentice-Hall Editorial Staff, *Industrial Accountants' Encyclopedia Dictionary* (Englewood Cliffs, N.J.: Prentice-Hall, Inc., 1964).

most warranty policies consist of stated and unstated conditions, the former covering rather precise terms and the latter being discretionary adjustments. While the original decision to provide a guarantee may have been prompted by competitive forces, more recently a new force has had a profound effect on this area—consumerism. Consumerism is a political force that has left its impression in both the legislative and judicial areas. New and tougher laws have been and are still being promulgated that require adherence to stated conditions, and courts of law have been inclined to find in favor of the consumer with respect to suits brought against manufacturers or dealers.

Despite the existence of product warranties for many years and their increasing importance due to consumerism, accounting literature usually covers the subject in a general way. The discussions are mostly directed towards the alternative methods of accounting to achieve a proper matching of revenue and expense: revenue deferral or expense accrual. It is recognized that either method accomplishes the intended objective. It is usually theorized, however, that since revenue should not be recognized until substantially all services are performed, deferral of revenue is the more logical accounting. It is also acknowledged, however, that a more frequent practice of accountants is to accrue expense.

A contributing factor to the discord is that a clear distinction is not drawn between a product warranty and a service contract. Also contributing to the discord is the fact that similar analytical techniques form the basis for either accounting treatment.

It is proffered that the *basic consideration* involved in a contract is the major determinant of the most logical accounting treatment. For example, product warranty is by definition an integral part of a product *sales contract*. It is, therefore, one of many marketing considerations used by a seller to induce a buyer to purchase his or her product. As such, warranty is considered just one of the many costs and expenses incurred in consummating a product sale, and not as a specific source of revenue. It is more logical to account for warranty as an obligation which will result in a future cost; that is, an accrued expense.

In contrast to a product warranty incorporated within a product sales contract, the basic consideration in a *service contract* (by whatever name it may be called) is that for a fixed fee, the seller of a *service function* agrees to provide a defined type of service over a definite future period of time. A service contract may be written by a manufacturer or a distributor and is common in the appliance field as well as television sets. The contract can be written to cover items, such as labor, that may not be covered by the warranty terms; or it may be written to cover service calls covering both parts and labor after the warranty period has expired. In either case it is most logical that the revenue obtained from a service contract be deferred and recognized over the period covered by the contract in which the applicable costs will be incurred.

In the following pages, some more precise analytical techniques will be outlined that can be used to record accurately the cost of warranted products, as well as to maintain an accrual which adequately covers the cost associated with products sold that are covered by the terms of the warranty. Also outlined are analytical techniques that can be used to defer revenue accurately under a service contract.

TYPES OF PRODUCTS OFFERING WARRANTIES AND WARRANTY TERMS

It is difficult to conceive of a product that is either sold directly to a consumer, or to a producer for assembly or manufacture into a consumer product, that is not covered by some form of guarantee or warranty. Certain products will have more complex warranties than others. Automobile warranties, for example, are more complex and therefore more difficult to administer than a warranty for, say, a hand tool. Likewise, those products that are sold to a producer for assembly or further manufacture will have a different type of warranty than a complete product, since in the first case the product is transferred into something else and in the second it is sold for use by the consumer. A typical warranty is one that stipulates that the product is free from defects occasioned by the manufacturer and that it will be replaced within a certain time frame if it is found defective, fails, breaks, or otherwise cannot perform the job for which it was designed. The product usually is replaced completely during the stated time period, and it may be replaced on a pro rata basis for a longer period of time. Certain household products would be in this category. In some products the warranty covers parts only, in which case the consumer must pay for installation charges. Appliances and television sets are generally warranted in this manner. Some products, such as automobile tires, are warranted by the original manufacturer, although a part of an end product. An automobile may have numerous parts that are warranted by the original manufacturer, although the automobile manufacturer warrants the complete vehicle (generally, except tires) for a certain length of time or mileage, whichever occurs first. The automobile manufacturer may then have a claim against the supplier of component parts.

Terms of warranty may vary from a simple 30-, 60-, or 90-day guarantee during which time the product will be replaced, to a complex one which may cover both parts and labor or parts only. Everyone is familiar with the guarantees included with most household products. These guarantees are usually simply stated, and the consumer is required to send in a coupon indicating date of purchase and the dealer from whom purchased. Without covering the legal aspects of these warranties, it can be stated that they are generally easily understood by both parties, therefore requiring a minimum of administration and written procedures. On the other hand, more complex warranties such as those for automobiles and other complicated machines, including electronic equipment, will require detailed procedures to outline what is covered and how claims are to be prepared, and probably will include the requirement to send defective parts back to the manufacturer so that corrective action can be taken to reduce or eliminate future problems. If the terms of the warranty require a dealer to perform the service and then make a claim on the manufacturer, the procedures must detail how a claim is to be prepared, what parts are returnable, and how costs are to be substantiated for both parts and labor. As important as a statement of what is warranted is a clear statement of what is not warranted and under what conditions the warranty will not apply. Warranties by manufacturers of like products will often vary in certain terms and conditions. The following would be a general statement for an automobile manufacturer and could also apply to other products:

The warranty will not apply to—

1. Any vehicle on which the odometer mileage has been altered.
2. Normal maintenance services (as outlined in the *Operator's Manual* supplied with vehicle) and the parts used in connection with such services.

3. Normal deterioration due to wear or exposure.
4. Repairs caused by failure of the owner to have maintenance services performed as specified in the owners manual.
5. Repairs necessitated by accident, abuse, negligence, racing, or use of parts not approved by the manufacturer.
6. Loss of use of the vehicle, loss of time, inconvenience, or other consequential damages.
7. Any component parts (including special equipment items) that fail as a result of improper installation by other than the manufacturer.

METHOD OF ACCRUING FOR WARRANTY COSTS

The fact that warranty costs should be accrued is well founded in accounting theory and practice. APB *Statement No. 4* issued in October 1970 by the Accounting Principles Board of the American Institute of Certified Public Accountants states in paragraph 35, Accrual, that "the effects of transactions and other events on the assets and liabilities of a business enterprise are recognized and reported in the time periods to which they relate rather than only when cash is received or paid." More recently, an Exposure Draft dated October 21, 1974, entitled *Accounting for Contingencies*, issued by the Financial Accounting Standards Board, states that warranty obligations are an example of a loss contingency requiring an accrual since they represent a contractual obligation with reasonable expectation of future customer claims, and the amount of loss can be reasonably estimated even though the particular parties that will make claims may not be identifiable.

It is further recognized that as warranty costs are costs to be incurred in a future period from the time of manufacture or sale, a reasonable estimate predicated upon the manufacturer's past experience is required. This estimate should be periodically updated so that the accrual will reflect the most recent experience. The accrual preferably should be made at time of sale to match costs with related revenue and usually is a period charge in the year of sale.

In some cases warranty expense may be an insignificant expense and therefore may be accounted for on a modified cash basis. In an article entitled "Accounting for Warranty (Product Guarantee)

Expense" in the July 1964 issue of *The Arthur Young Journal* the following is stated:

> Some companies, of course, may omit warranty provisions because they would not be material. In other cases, the absence of a provision for warranty costs may be due to particular circumstances. As an example, consider a company whose major product problems typically relate only to new models and whose new models are introduced early in each fiscal year. For such a company, the major portion of warranty costs applicable to the sales for a given fiscal year would ordinarily develop by the end of the year and would be recognized in expense on either the modified cash-basis method or the accrual method. (In interim financial statements of such a company, however, an accrual provision for warranty costs might be required.) Another company might carry replacement parts for prior years' models in inventory at a fairly low amount, so that use of such parts for warranty purposes would not normally result in significant costs, particularly if labor charges were billed at some profit margin. In the absence of such special circumstances, however, the accrual method should be used.[3]

On the other hand, the SEC has outlined the following position:

> Warranty expense was a factor *In The Matter of Drayer-Hanson, Incorporated* (*SEC Accounting Series Release No. 64, March 1948*). Drayer-Hanson guaranteed heating and cooling units, which it manufactured, against defects in materials, parts or workmanship for one year after installation. Sales began in March 1946; at the end of August 1946 it was apparent that there were numerous mechanical difficulties in the units. In ASR 64, the SEC held that the company's registration statement, which became effective in December 1946, contained misstatements and omissions. Among other matters, the Release expressed the SEC's opinion that ". . . the summary of earnings for the six months ended October 31, 1946, which included sales of . . . [the heating and cooling] units, . . . [was] materially misleading by reason of the failure to include a provision for unrecoverable costs which might arise under the company's guarantee of its product."[4]

---

[3] Accounting for Warranty (Product Guarantee) Expense, *The Arthur Young Journal*, vol. 12, July 1964, pp. 40–41.

[4] *Accounting Series Release No. 64, Securities Act Release No. 3277, In The Matter of Drayer-Hanson, Inc., Federal Securities Law Report,* Commerce Clearing House, Inc., March 18, 1948, pp. 62, 161.

The method of accrual will depend upon the warranty policy established by the manufacturer. An example of such a policy might be stated as follows:

Policy Statement

Estimated lifetime costs for warranty against inherent product defects are accrued and charged to income at the time of sale.

Implementation of Policy

The estimated lifetime costs are determined by year and series, using statistical, graphical, and judgmental projections based upon actual costs incurred to date.

The unit amounts are multiplied by the number of units in the applicable year and series on which sales to the public have been recognized in order to obtain the total estimated warranty to be paid for the year.

Financial Statement Presentation

Warranty liabilities estimated to be payable within one year are included in current liabilities. Amounts estimated to be payable more than one year from the balance sheet date are included in other noncurrent liabilities. The expense is included in costs of products sold.

The estimated lifetime costs would be made by each group or division of the company that had an end product, and these unit rates would be segregated by years, product lines, or units, as appropriate. For each new model the rates would be based on current comparable model experience adjusted for known product changes, anticipated changes in quality, changes in the warranty policy, and changes in economic conditions.

The accrual rates normally would be developed by manufacturing divisions and would be reviewed and approved by the central staff prior to use. In a company that uses the profit center concept, the accruals would be made by the operating divisions on a monthly basis. The monthly accrual would be based on shipments, and the provision would be charged to Warranty and Policy Expense and credited to Accrued Warranty Claims and Policy Adjustments. The accrual accounts would be subdivided by model series (year), product lines, or units for which separate accrual rates have been provided. Separate contra accounts for warranty and policy adjustments would also be established to charge the payment of approved claims and to credit the recovery from vendors. The following journal entries of a sales division will illustrate the above method.

(*a*)

Warranty and Policy Expense	1,000,000	
Accrued Warranty and Policy Adjustments		1,000,000

To establish accrual for sales of 20,000 units in June of
product A at anticipated lifetime cost of $50 per unit.

(*b*)

Accrued Warranty Adjustment—Contra	500,000	
Accrued Policy Adjustments—Contra.	100,000	
Accounts Payable		600,000

To record payment of warranty claims in the month of June.

(*c*)

Accounts Receivable	100,000	
Accrued Warranty Adjustments—Contra.		80,000
Accrued Policy Adjustments—Contra		20,000

To record recoveries of warranty claims paid from vendors in
the month of June.

The total company position would be the consolidation of all
divisions. On the basis of the one division in the foregoing example,
the warranty expense for the month was $1,000,000 and the warranty
liability was increased $500,000. As previously stated, the expense
will be reflected in cost of sales and the accrual will be shown as a
current liability if it is expected that it will be payable within one
year; otherwise the accrual will be reflected as a noncurrent liability.
The liability should provide for all costs expected to be incurred so
that it will be adequate at the end of the accounting period, but
its adequacy must be appraised periodically and at year-end.

As a further analytical tool, a portion of the $1,000,000 will be
charged to other divisions which may have been responsible for the
expense. The charges retained by the sales division, for example, may
be a portion of the claims that are expected to be policy-type
adjustments, and the balance charged to other divisions may be
based on an analysis of claims by responsibility.

It should be noted that warranty expense is not deductible for
tax purposes until incurred. Therefore, the provision for warranty
expense should ordinarily be accompanied by a corresponding allocation of income taxes. Using the $500,000 increase in warranty
liability above, and assuming an income tax rate of 50 percent, the
entry would be:

Income Tax Allocable to the Following Year*	250,000	
Income Tax Expense.		250,000

To record income tax allocable to the following year on the
increase in warranty liability for the month of June.

* Alternative title: Deferred Charge for Income Tax.

APPRAISAL OF THE ADEQUACY OF THE ACCRUED
WARRANTY LIABILITY ACCOUNT

An appraisal of the adequacy of the warranty accrual is required at periodic intervals but is essential at year-end in order to present the financial statements correctly. The appraisal will depend upon the method used in the original accrual and will necessarily vary depending upon the type of information the system provides. There will always be a certain amount of judgment exercised in the evaluation process, but care should be taken to ensure that all relevant data is used in the review process.

The evaluation process can take the form of analyzing actual cost data and carefully reviewing it with the quality assurance department, which can assist in spotting either good or bad trends, and using its knowledge of programs established to eliminate or reduce the high cost defects. Other areas, such as product engineering, can also provide valuable input in the form of design changes which could result in mandatory modifications of the product. The effect of special recall campaigns, such as occur in the automobile industry, must also be taken into account. After utilizing all available information, the final test will normally include the use of some type of formula. This can either be a simple application of a percentage to the current year's sales or cost of sales, an average of past incurred costs, an estimated lifetime cost based upon a mathematical formula empirically derived from a standard probability formula, or an analysis of costs on a months-in-service basis. These four methods will be discussed briefly.

Percent of cost of sales

1. Calculate a moving average cost percentage of warranty costs incurred, after first eliminating unusual items, to total cost of sales for five years—the current and four previous years—for each class of product that has different characteristics or a different warranty period. If the warranty costs accumulated indicate a definite trend, then a projected cost may be used in arriving at these percentages.
2. To "test" the adequacy of the accrual apply these percentages to the cost of sales of various products reported for the current year. Add this amount to the amount calculated for the previous

two years and arrive at an estimated annual average dollar value by dividing the total by three. Compare the sum of these product line calculations with the accrual presently on the books. The following shows the calculation for one product line.

Calculation of five-year moving average percentage

	Warranty cost	Product line "A" cost of sales	Percent
Current year.	$ 7,500	$ 500,000	1.50
1st prior year	7,000	479,000	1.46
2d prior year.	6,500	450,000	1.44
3d prior year.	6,000	400,000	1.50
4th prior year	6,200	375,000	1.65
	$33,200	$2,204,000	1.51

Calculation of three-year average values

	Product line cost of sales	Five-year moving average	Value (Col. 1 × Col. 2)
Current year.	$500,000	1.51%	$ 7,550
1st prior year	479,000	1.51	7,233
2d prior year.	450,000	1.51	6,795
			$21,578
Divided by 3			$ 7,193

In this illustration an accrual of $7,193 is required for product line "A," which will be added to other product line calculations for comparison with the accrued liability on the books.

Average of past incurred costs

A different formula will be used for each product line, depending upon the warranty period. The following is a suggested review of the accrual for products with a one-year and a five-year warranty.

1. *One-year warranty products*
    a. Expenditures will be segregated by product line, and the charges for a four-year period—the current year plus the prior three—will be averaged. The accrual required will be at least one half of this amount. If the expenditures during the four-year period indicate a definite trend, then the pro-

jected amount should be used instead of the average, and one half of this amount will be the accrual required. Also, if there are known liabilities which are in excess of this amount, the accrual will need to be adjusted.

b. This formula is a very simple approach to determining the adequacy of the accrual but requires an analysis of known events. It does not take actual production or sales into account except as to the possible effect they may have on establishing a trend. The theory is that warranty expenditures for any one year relate approximately one half to the current year and one half to prior years' sales. Averaging four years will smooth out unusual distortions, and an accrual for one half this amount should be sufficient. The following illustrates this approach:

	Charges to the accrual account
Current year.	$10,000
1st prior year	18,000
2d prior year	15,000
3d prior year.	20,000
	$63,000
Average—divide by 4	$15,750
Accrual required—one half.	$ 7,875

2. *Products with warranties in excess of one year*

a. Expenditures will also be segregated by product line, and two significant figures will be developed, based on past experience. One of these is the per unit cost to replace or repair the product, and the other is the number or percentage of units expected to fail in each year after sale until the expiration of the full warranty period. At the end of any particular year the year's sales outstanding still within full warranty will be determined and valued by year of sale for each such year. The cost determined for the last full warranty year of each year's sales will be reduced to half. Here the key is the accurate determination of cost per unit to repair or replace, as well as expected failures. The past experience may not be a good indication of the future, so due recognition needs to be given to changes in design, known defects, and economic conditions. For new products, failure frequency and cost will have to be estimated.

b. The theory of this formula is similar to the one covering products warranted for one year, that is, that the expenditures for the last year of the full warranty period will apply one half to one year and one half to the next. The following illustrates this method for a product with a four-year warranty period.

Year of sale	Percent failure by year	Units sold	Total units to be accrued	Unit cost	Total
Current year	Next year. 16%				
	1st subsequent year. 10				
	2d subsequent year 6				
	3d subsequent year 1/2. 8				
	Total. 40%	10,000	4,000	$4	$16,000
1st prior year	1st subsequent year. 10%				
	2d subsequent year 6				
	3d subsequent year 8				
	Total. 24%	12,000	2,880	4	11,520
2d prior year	2d subsequent year 6%				
	3d subsequent year 1/2. 8				
	Total. 14%	8,000	1,120	4	4,480
3d prior year	3d subsequent year 1/2. . . . . . 8%	9,000	720	4	2,880
	Total Accrual Required . .				$34,880

Estimated lifetime cost (ELTC)

The use of an estimated lifetime cost (ELTC) for developing the warranty accrual will provide the most accurate amount and at the earliest possible point in time. Expenditures will need to be segregated by product or model and by year (series). Any warranty period can be used, but for simplicity it is assumed that the product has a 12-month warranty. The compilation of costs will eventually tell when a lifetime cost has been reached, but this could be many months after the end of the calendar year for which an accrual is required. Several techniques will provide an estimate on a timely basis as to the required accrual. For example, by plotting costs by month for each product and series on a graph, it is possible to extrapolate a reasonably accurate cost of a recent series at an early point in the cost cycle by referring to the cost curve generated by earlier series. Exhibit 1 illustrates this technique.

Exhibit 1 shows the cost per unit curves of three separate series. Series 1 has cost experience throughout a 36-month period after

EXHIBIT 1
Cost per unit curves

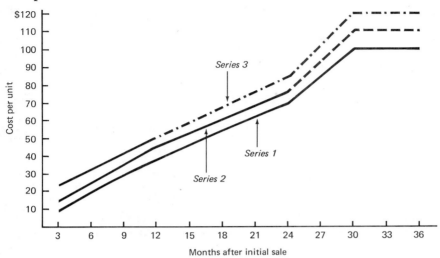

initial sale, and therefore the cost per unit may be considered final; while series 2 and 3 have attained costs for only 24 and 12 months after initial sale, respectively. An updated estimated lifetime cost per unit can be obtained for series 2 and 3 by using a five-point analysis. For example, the known points on the graph are as follows:

3 series @ 12 months ($50)
2 series @ 12 months ($45) and 24 months ($77)
1 series @   24 months ($70) and
                                          36 months ($100)

Therefore,

2 series @ 36 months = 1 series @ 36 months

$$\times \frac{2 \text{ series @ 24 months}}{1 \text{ series @ 24 months}}$$

and

3 series @ 36 months =

1 series @ 36 months $\times \dfrac{2 \text{ series @ 24 months}}{1 \text{ series @ 24 months}}$

$$\times \frac{3 \text{ series @ 12 months}}{2 \text{ series @ 12 months}}$$

or

$$2 \text{ series @ 36 months} = \$100 \times \frac{\$77}{\$70} = \$110$$

and

$$3 \text{ series @ 36 months} = \$100 \times \frac{\$77}{\$70} \times \frac{\$50}{\$45} = \$122$$

The estimated lifetime costs for series 2 and 3 are, therefore, $110 and $122 as compared to $100 for series 1.

Months-in-service basis

A more precise and timely method is possible by analyzing costs on a months-in-service basis. By use of data processing equipment, it is possible to segregate warranty costs by the time in service (i.e., months after date of sale) of the product at the time of failure. Similarly, the quantity of production which has attained each time-in-service age can be determined. Thus, an expense per unit for each month in service can be calculated based on that portion of production which has attained each age level.

Assuming that these products are representative of the remainder of production, we can total the expense per unit for each month of service for which we have experience from one up to a maximum of 12 (at which time the warranty expires), and the result will be the total warranty accumulation through as many months in service as the current age of the first unit sold. Twelve months after the initial sale we have a total through 12 months of service and this represents the lifetime expense per unit.

Prior to 12 months after the initial sale, no units will have attained 12 months in service. But it is possible to *forecast* the expense per unit for intervals in which we have no *actual* data, since a curve based on probability theory and adjusted empirically to the product in question can be fitted to the pattern of expense per unit in each month.

For instance, the expense per unit generated in "months in service" might be shown empirically for certain products to follow the formula $r_t = Ae^{-B^{t^k}}$, which is based on the theory of probability failure.[5] In this formula,

[5] A. M. Neville and J. B. Kennedy, *Basic Statistical Methods* (Scranton, Pa.: International Textbook Co., 1964), pp. 171–202.

t = months in service.

r_t = increment of expense per unit for months in service t.

A = a constant which measures the most likely first month expense per unit.

B = a constant which measures how the expense per unit changes during the warranty lifetime.

k = a constant which defines the shape of the expense per unit curve over the warranty lifetime.

e = the base of natural logarithms (2.718281).

By analysis of actual data, the cost per unit for each month in service is measured and can be plotted (x) as shown in Exhibit 2.

EXHIBIT 2
Cost per unit for each month in service

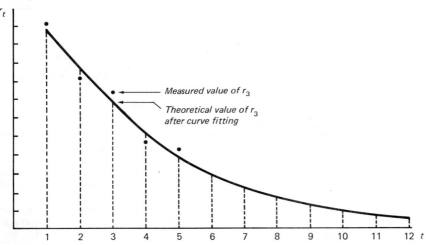

During the year following the initial sale year we will have measured values of r_1, r_2, r_3, and so on, up to the time in service of the first units sold. We then use a curve-fitting technique (least squares) to fit the formula $r_t = Ae^{-B^{t^k}}$ to the measured values of r_t. This gives us the constants A and B, and we can recalculate the theoretical values of r_1, r_2 up to r_{12}. By adding the theoretical r_1, r_2, . . . , r_{12}, as in Exhibit 3, we obtain $r_{L/T}$, the estimated lifetime cost per unit.

After obtaining the estimated lifetime cost per unit by product and series, these amounts will be multiplied by units sold and com-

EXHIBIT 3
Estimated lifetime cost per unit

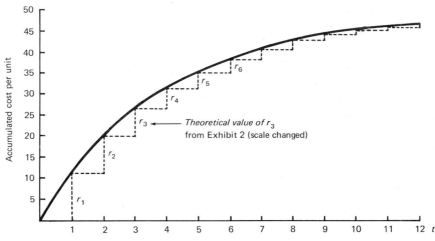

pared to the amount of warranty cost provided for, under the method of accruing, to determine whether the accrual is adequate. The procedure is shown in the following table:

Warranty accrual as of December 31, 197—

Year (series or product)	Units sold	Amounts provided	Estimated lifetime cost Per unit	Total	Provision over (under) ELTC
3	25,000	$3,000,000	$122	$3,050,000	$(50,000)
2	30,000	3,100,000	110	3,300,000	(200,000)
1	22,000	2,300,000	100	2,200,000	100,000
					$(150,000)

The accrual in this illustration is underaccrued by $150,000, which will require a year-end adjustment. Before making the adjustment, due regard should be taken for special campaigns or other unusual situations previously discussed.

SUMMARY OF TESTING METHODS

Although four formulas or tests of the adequacy of the Accrued Warranty Liability account have been stated, it should be understood that there may be a variety of acceptable ways of approaching the problem. The systems used will determine the approach and will vary depending upon the complexity of the problem and the cost impact of warranty expense. A highly sophisticated system can be costly and may be unjustified. However, it must also be realized that providing a guarantee for a product which ultimately involves a cost is not without its benefits. While many warranty policies are dictated by the need to provide a guarantee by law, there are others that evolve from an analysis of marketing conditions wherein it is felt that a more favorable policy will result in a competitive advantage. It may be difficult to measure these advantages or benefits, just as it is in the case of certain advertising or sales promotion programs, but there is no doubt that sales benefits can be derived from a well-conceived and well-executed warranty policy.

In addition to benefits of a marketing nature, the analysis of warranty costs can be beneficial in other areas. Quality control programs can be assisted by warranty cost analysis. For example, the warranty claim forms can provide for coding so that a periodic compilation will produce information as to the top ten or so defects, as well as indicate the manufacturing plant responsible. The review of this information will assist in determining whether the defects resulted from a poor design, or whether it is purely a manufacturing problem and corrective action can be taken. These points must be considered, therefore, in determining the warranty system to use, which will then determine the appropriate formula to use in appraising the adequacy of the accrued liability account.

METHODS OF DEFERRING SERVICE
CONTRACT INCOME

In some respects the method of deferring service contract income is similar to accruing for expected warranty costs. The difference is that in the case of service contracts a set fee has been determined for which it is necessary to determine how the income is to be earned, and in the warranty the sale of a product with warranty attached establishes an obligation which will result in a future cost. The revenue obtained from a service contract should be deferred and written off over the period covered by the contract. The write-off can best be accomplished by establishing a "call rate" which has been developed from past experience, the "call rate" being the average number of service calls the product will require over the life of the contract. This experience rate will be determined on a moving average basis and will be expressed by a percentage for each month's expected calls. The intent is to match, as nearly as possible, revenues with costs; so the rate should be periodically adjusted, possibly quarterly, but in any event annually.

If the volume of contracts is large, the development of the "call rate" will probably be most easily obtained by computer analysis of service calls; but a manual method may be more suitable for smaller volume. It is necessary, of course, to develop rates for products with similar characteristics. For example, refrigerators may exhibit a different "call rate" than washing machines. Similarly, it is possible that more intricate or more automatic equipment will have a different "call rate," such as refrigerators with an icemaker feature as compared to an ordinary refrigerator. After the "call rate" has been developed for each product line, a schedule is prepared to write off, or amortize, the service contract revenue over the months in which the expense is expected to be incurred.

Schedule A indicates one method of deferring service contract revenue after the "call rate" has been determined. Only one product line is shown, which indicates an upward trend from the 1st to the 12th month. As stated, the "call rate" should be based on actual experience, and there should be one for each product line. It also

SCHEDULE A
Accrual and deferral of service contract revenue

		Percent to total	
Month after service contract is written	*Average number of service calls*	*Monthly revenue accrual*	*Cumulative deferred revenue (beginning of month)*
12 36		14.45%	14.45%
11 35		14.06	28.51
10 30		12.05	40.56
9 26		10.44	51.00
8 24		9.64	60.64
7 22		8.84	69.48
6 20		8.03	77.51
5 16		6.43	83.94
4 15		6.02	89.96
3 11		4.42	94.38
2 09		3.61	97.99
1 05		2.01	100.00
Total Calls Expected 2.49			

must be reviewed periodically as the trend line will not always be the same. It may, for instance, be more of a straight line or resemble a bell curve, rather than as indicated.

In order to defer the revenue correctly, it is necessary to multiply the average revenue for each service contract by the above per-centages. For example, if each contract is sold for $100, the amount to be recorded in revenue will be $2.01 in the first month after the contract is written, $3.61 in the second, and so on. If this method is used, all revenue is first credited to a deferral account and then amortized each month by setting up a schedule similar to the above with the sales contracts added. The average number of service calls has been set up to show the 12th month first, and so on, in order to facilitate a year-end, or more frequent, review to check the accuracy of the deferred account. This can be done as shown in Schedule B, which is the position of one product line at the end of the fiscal year.

SCHEDULE B
Balance of deferred service revenue at year-end

Contracts written		Total revenue	Months unexpired at year-end	Amount unexpired for each contract	Total amount to be deferred
Month	Number				
January.	10,000	$ 1,000,000	1	$ 14.45	$ 144,500
February	15,000	1,500,000	2	28.51	427,650
March.	12,000	1,200,000	3	40.56	486,720
April	9,000	900,000	4	51.00	459,000
May.	11,000	1,100,000	5	60.64	667,040
June	12,000	1,200,000	6	69.48	833,760
July	16,000	1,600,000	7	77.51	1,240,160
August	17,000	1,700,000	8	83.94	1,426,980
September	15,000	1,500,000	9	89.96	1,349,400
October	8,000	800,000	10	94.38	755,040
November	7,000	700,000	11	97.99	685,930
December	6,000	600,000	12	100.00	600,000
Total.	138,000	$13,800,000			$9,076,180

As indicated, Schedule B shows the deferred amount at the end of the year. A schedule similar to this one can also be prepared each month. Then, by adding the most recent month's activity and drop-ping the one on which all revenue has been earned the total amount deferred is correctly stated. In this case the total revenue is credited as contracts are written, and a month-end entry is made to reduce revenue by the deferred amount.

In using either of the methods described it is not necessary to relate the actual service contract costs to the deferred revenue account, since the revenue and related costs will be correctly stated if the "call rate" is accurately stated. Therefore, costs will be charged off as incurred.

It should also be noted that in accordance with provisions of the Internal Revenue Code, income on service contracts can be deferred if the contract written covers a period no longer than the end of the following year. Otherwise, the revenue is considered to be income in the year in which it is received.

SELECTED REFERENCES

"Accounting for Warranty (Product Guarantee) Expense." *Arthur Young Journal,* vol. 12, July 1964, pp. 40–41.

Accounting Series Release No. 64, Securities Act Release No. 3277. In *The Matter of Drayer-Hanson, Inc.,* Federal Securities Law Report, Commerce Clearing House, Inc., March 18, 1948, pp. 62, 161.

AICPA. "Basic Concepts and Accounting Principles Underlying Financial Statements of Business Enterprises." *Statement of the Accounting Principles Board No. 4.* New York, 1970.

Anderson, H. M. *Basic Accounting Concepts,* pp. 268–69. Pacific Palisades, Calif.: Goodyear Publishing Co., Inc., 1974.

Financial Accounting Standards Board. *Statement of Financial Accounting Standards No. 5,* "Accounting for Contingencies," March, 1975.

Heck, W. R. "Accounting for Warranty Costs." *Accounting Review,* vol. 28, July 1963, pp. 577–78.

Menke, Warren W. "Call Out the Reserves—Warranty That Is." *Management Services,* vol. 7, January–February 1970, pp. 47–54.

——— "Determination of Warranty Reserves." *Management Science,* vol. 15, June 1969, pp. B-542–49.

Neville, A. M., and Kennedy, J. B. *Basic Statistical Methods,* pp. 171–202. Scranton, Pa.: International Textbook Co., 1964.

Prentice-Hall Editorial Staff. *Industrial Accountants' Encyclopedia Dictionary.* Englewood Cliffs, N.J., Prentice-Hall, Inc., 1964.

Rados, David L. "Product Liability: Tougher Ground Rules." *Harvard Business Review,* vol. 47, July–August 1969, pp. 144–52.

Chapter 9

Valuation and expiration of long-lived tangible assets

Alfred M. King[*]

Investment in long-lived assets, often referred to as *fixed assets,* represents well over half of all invested funds for most industrial companies. Large firms usually have formal procedures for determining capital budgets and monitoring capital expenditures. After the acquisition, when it comes to *control* of those same assets—for financial reporting as well as physical custody—far less management attention is usually given than might be anticipated based on the importance and magnitude of the dollars involved. Financial managers, in response to pressures in other areas, pay attention to monitoring, reporting, analyzing, and controlling cash balances, accounts receivable, and inventories. Because physical assets are considered "fixed," there is an assumption that the items will not go away—therefore, fixed assets do not *need* much attention. In a self-fulfilling prophecy, fixed asset accounting then receives little attention.

Every specialist maintains that his or her area of expertise should receive more corporate attention and resources. Those responsible for control over fixed assets make the same plea. In the final analysis, however, when measured by actual performance, company management usually puts control over long-lived tangible assets near

[*] Vice President–Finance, American Appraisal Associates, Inc.

the bottom of its list of priorities in terms of resources devoted to the task. Auditors do not require periodic inventories of fixed assets such as are taken for raw materials, work in process, and finished goods. Independent accountants do not require confirmation that fixed assets exist, comparable to the procedures whereby customers are circulated for confirmation of receivable balances.

The reasons for this lack of effort to control fixed assets lie in the fact that determination of depreciation expense need be done only once a year for purposes of audited financial statements. It is also felt that the required level of precision and accuracy in calculating depreciation is low, since "it's only a bookkeeping entry." Depreciation calculations do involve a great deal of judgment and subjectivity; consequently financial managers often feel that a corresponding lack of precision in controlling the physical assets is somehow inherent in the task—and thus, not worth any extra effort.

Finally, a company which has been in business a number of years, and which has not paid attention to fixed asset accounting and control, will often consider it an almost hopeless task to get on top of the problem at any point in time. An unstated assumption then is made, "as long as we have managed to get along for 20 years with inadequate records, if we just compare this year to last year, it is immaterial if we have 21 years of bad records."

The situation is not hopeless. Control can be exercised over fixed assets. Companies can institute modern control systems at any point in time and, at a minimum, begin to apply them to new asset additions from there forward. Over a period of time, as older assets are retired control can gradually be built up over the entire fixed asset category. Alternatively, a "once-and-for-all" physical inventory of fixed assets can be taken. Following reconciliation to the books, an up-to-date record-keeping system can be developed from that inventory. Control policies can be instituted and ongoing procedures installed which will provide the benefits which control of fixed assets can give corporate management.

OBJECTIVES OF FIXED ASSET CONTROL

What are the tangible benefits provided by proper control of fixed assets? Put another way, what areas of corporate decision making suffer from inadequate control?

1. *Cash flow.* For profitable companies paying taxes, optimum cash flows can only be developed by claiming the maximum depreciation allowed for income tax purposes. Investment tax credits also can be maximized only with supportable records.

2. *Product pricing.* In an inflationary period the prices at which products are sold must cover all costs of production, including expiration of fixed assets. Today's selling prices must include a proportionate element for the replacement of the capital invested in fixed assets currently being used in the production process; thus, it is important to know what assets are involved in producing each product line, whether realistic economic lives have been assigned to existing assets, and what is the current replacement cost of those assets. Special analyses for pricing purposes can then be made to adjust depreciation based on historical cost for the presumably higher price involved today in replacing those assets. In the absence of this knowledge a company can pay out in taxes and dividends more than 100 percent of "real" earnings and end up "decapitalizing" itself.

3. *Return on investment.* In large organizations corporate management usually measures individual unit or division performance on the basis of return on assets employed, or return on net investment. It is important for each general manager to be aware of what assets he or she is being charged for, on which a return must be earned. Idle assets can be disposed of. Similarly, corporate management, in the absence of good records, may make erroneous decisions as to individual unit performance. Ideally, for purposes of evaluating return on investment, assets would be valued at current value rather than depreciated historical cost.

4. *Insurance.* One of the primary responsibilities of financial management is to safeguard corporate assets. This is usually accomplished through purchase of insurance. It is necessary in placing insurance to have an idea as to the cost of reproduction of assets at risk. Further, in the event of loss, it is essential to provide the insurance carrier with proof of loss. Adequate property records go a long way both in meeting insurance requirements for proof of loss and in helping arrive at insurable values. Proper determination of the cost of reproduction is necessary to prevent overpayment of insurance premiums through assuming too high a value for insurance purposes.

Undervaluing assets, however, while it may temporarily save on insurance premiums, may mean that an insurance carrier will fight a subsequent claim because the usual coinsurance requirement was not met.

5. *Property taxes.* Whether it is equitable or not, corporations are considered "fair game" for property tax assessors in local communities. Corporations do not have voting power; given the political nature of property tax assessments and collections, the burden of proof is usually on a corporation to sustain its position as to the value of assets the company has in each taxing district. Accurate property records, detailing the physical location of assets, are an essential first step in reviewing whether property tax assessments are equitable. Age, cost, and condition of the assets are additional information useful in evaluating tax assessments.

6. *Asset retirement and replacement.* A combination of good asset records plus an analysis of maintenance and repair expenditures enables financial and production managers to determine optimum replacement schedules for fixed assets. Typically, operating managers always want the "latest" equipment. Elaborate presentations can be made to "justify" replacement. But with good historical records detailing actual useful life, financial analyses can be performed which will confirm or disprove allegations that "we can't afford to keep this equipment any longer." Most capital expenditure decisions involve a combination of both replacement and expansion of productive capacity. It is desirable to separate these two functions in making capital expenditure decisions; good property records go a long way in providing factual support for replacement decisions.

PHYSICAL CONTROL OF PROPERTY

Control over fixed assets involves two major ingredients: physical control over the tangible assets themselves, plus a good accounting system which captures the significant data in a form where it can be used for a multiplicity of purposes. In the real world, "fixed" assets are just the opposite of fixed. In most companies they turn out to be highly movable. This is why it is so difficult to take a physical inventory of fixed assets and to reconcile the data to existing records.

Manufacturing and engineering managers, when facing a production problem, are often not particularly concerned about the niceties of "control." If the solution to a production emergency requires removing a motor from an inactively used piece of equipment and replacing it on a critically needed machine, they have no hesitation in doing it. If this is done frequently without proper paperwork, either before or after the event, financial managers soon find that their records differ from what is out on the shop floor. Emergencies are not the only cause of such actions. Growth in a company's product line requires changes and rearrangements in the production process; innovative process engineers will often cannibalize existing equipment and rebuild it to meet current requirements. Once again records and reality can soon part company.

Systems and controls can be set up requiring management approval, plus proper paperwork, for all changes involving fixed assets. But no control system for fixed assets is any better than how well it is monitored and managed. Unless individual managers feel the same responsibility toward custody of fixed assets that they do toward cash, customer receivables, or a physical inventory of raw materials, the best paperwork system in the world will not work. With management insistence, it can be made to work. It is reasonable for management to expect adherence to policies and procedures if management itself is convinced of the benefits.

CAPITALIZATION POLICY AND TAGGING

In order to make any system work, it must be relevant to the real needs of the organization. Those designing a property control system often think in terms of control over fixed assets the same way they view control over petty cash. Every penny must be accounted for in cash management; therefore, fixed asset expenditures should be controlled to the penny. In the mistaken belief that more detail results in better control, very detailed records are often set up. Operating supervisors who later are assigned responsibility for living within the guidelines begin to say to themselves that the rules are ridiculously tight. Soon, because the effort in maintaining the system appears disproportionately high, nothing is accomplished.

The answer is to start with a realistic assessment as to what can and should be controlled. In practice, this means consciously disregarding any attempts to control minor assets. A capitalization policy should be established under which only items which can be identified—assets which retain their identity over a period of years—

are even defined as fixed assets and capitalized. Sometimes, in an effort to boost reported net income for the year, there is a tendency for a company to capitalize items which more properly should be expensed. This quickly will destroy the integrity of an asset control system.

A general rule should be that every asset which is capitalized should be identifiable with a property record tag; any asset so identified should then be assigned as the responsibility of some individual operating manager. Given a reasonable number of assets under control, transfers—within a plant or between plants—of capitalized assets can then reasonably be expected to be reflected in subsequent paperwork which flows to the property record section of the accounting department.

If experience indicates that a particular class of assets is not controllable, yet the unit acquisition cost exceeds the corporate capitalization guideline, it should be placed in a group or composite account and no attempt made *subsequently* to control the asset physically. As an example, in the category of office equipment a firm may have a capitalization policy which says that all assets with a unit cost of over $200 have to be capitalized. Regardless of cost it is not practicable to try to control individual desks, chairs, or file cabinets. If a chair is purchased for $225 and capitalized as a fixed asset, it does not make sense to attempt to put a property tag on the item and attempt to follow its physical location for the next 10, 15, or 20 years.

No general guidelines can be set up which apply to all companies in all industries. Each company should determine for itself what types of assets fall into the minor equipment category. A conscious decision should then be reached that management time and effort simply will not be spent in attempting to keep track of those assets; instead, the accounting resources will be devoted to controlling the much smaller number of items which have a major dollar impact on the company.

Generally speaking, then, any asset which is capitalized and will be put into the control system should be tagged or identified with a property asset number and a separate unit asset record prepared for subsequent maintenance in the accounting system. In instances where a very large asset is built up from several discrete components, consideration should be given to separately identifying each of the major elements. This provides better control through permitting varying lives and depreciation rates to be applied to the separate components, which individually may not have the same life as the composite total asset.

PROPERTY RECORD SYSTEM

Whether a property record system will be maintained manually or on a computer is not particularly significant. Given a wide range of inexpensive software programs specifically designed to handle property record accounting, and the availability for smaller companies of computer resources at service bureaus, this discussion assumes use of a computerized property control system. Nevertheless, it should be emphasized that the computer only processes data faster and more accurately; it permits various classifications and reports to be prepared which might be difficult to obtain manually. The end product is the same. The control concepts are identical.

Shown in Exhibit 1 is a sample of a typical input record for a

EXHIBIT 1
Uni-group property record

ASSET NO. BASE	SUF	TC
1-8	9-10	11

TC:
1 ☐ Delete
2 ☐ Addition
3 ☐ Transfer - Complete
4 ☐ Transfer - Partial
5 ☐ Adjustment
6 ☐ Change

	LOCATIONAL DATA								DESCRIPTIVE DATA		
CARD CODE	DIVISN CODE	PLANT/ BRANCH	COST CENTER	DEPT	ACCT NO.	BLDG.	FLR.	TAX DISTRICT	MANUFACTURER'S NAME	MODEL NO	SERIAL NO.
12-15	16 - 19	20-23	24-27	28-31	32-35	36-39	40-1	42-46	47 - 61	62-69	70 - 79
PM01											

															DESCRIPTIVE DATA	
CARD CODE	CLASS CODE BASE SUF	OWNERSHIP	GUIDE LINE CLASS	CS	STATUS	INS	BOOK	TAX	ITC	P/R	N/U	NEG	ADR	QTY.	STANDARD DESCRIPTION	SUPPLEMENTAL DESCRIPTION (VOUCHER #)
12-15	16 - 21	22-3	24-27	28	29	30	31	32	33	34	35	36	37	38-40	41 - 70	71-80
PM02																

		BOOK DATA						TAX DATA						
CARD CODE	CALENDAR DATE OF ACQUISITION	ORIGINAL COST	SALV. %	DEPR. BEGIN	TOTAL LIFE	DM	CONV	ORIGINAL COST	SALV %	DEPR. BEGIN	TOTAL LIFE	DM	CONV	ITC AMOUNT
12-15	16-21	22-30	31- 3	34-39	40-44	45	46	47-55	56- 8	59-64	65-69	70	71	72 - 79
PM03														

	BOOK DATA		TAX DATA		PHYSICAL CONTROL			
CARD CODE	DEPRECIATION RESERVE	YEAR-TO-DATE RESERVE	DEPRECIATION RESERVE	YEAR-TO-DATE RESERVE	COST OF REPRODUCTION	INSURABLE VALUE	PHYS. DEPR %	MAINTENANCE COST
12-15	16-24	25-33	34-42	43 - 51	52 - 56	59 - 65	66 8	69-74
PM04								

	ANNUAL PROVISION	
CARD CODE	BOOK	TAX
12-15	16-24	25-33
PM05		

computerized property record system. The key information which should be captured initially would include at least the following:

1. Asset number or tag number.
2. Locational data, including plant, cost center, building floor, and general ledger account number.
3. Geographical location—specific tax district for property tax analyses.
4. Descriptive data including manufacturer's name, model number, and the serial number of the unit if it carries one.
5. Miscellaneous information, such as whether the asset was acquired new or used, is personal or real property, is eligible for investment tax credit; whether the value should or should not be included in an insurable value report; and whether the item is owned or leased.
6. A standard description, which can be input through a class code or a specific description written out for the asset.
7. Date of acquisition.
8. Original cost.
9. Estimated salvage value.
10. Estimated economic life.
11. Depreciation method, convention, and starting date for depreciation calculation.
12. Tax information, which in some cases will differ from book purposes for items 7–11 above. Different depreciation methods or lives may, where appropriate, be used for tax purposes.
13. Where appropriate, an estimate of cost of reproduction can be provided.
14. Insurable values, which may be less than cost of reproduction because of depreciation.
15. Maintenance cost, where maintenance is a significant factor in operating expense.

Almost all the data described above is available at the time of acquisition of the asset or, if it is part of a major construction program, when the unit is put into service and capitalized.

Most computerized software systems for property record control will automatically calculate depreciation expense for books and taxes, make investment tax credit calculations, determine gain or loss upon retirement, investment tax credit recapture if appropriate, and so forth. Further, the basic data base can be sorted by geographical location, plant, or local tax district. Projections of future depreciation expense for budgeting and pricing are usually available. Depending upon requirements of the company's insurance policies, special runs can be generated to show insurable values or cost of reproduction if this information has been inputted specifically. Alternatively, specially developed index numbers can be applied to various classes of assets based on year of acquisition, and the original cost thus trended. In short, a good computerized property record system has almost unlimited flexibility in manipulating whatever data has been captured.

The heart of any fixed asset control system, however, is in keeping track of changes subsequent to the original acquisition. There are no easy solutions to the problem. Forms, approval requirements, and documentation are of little value if individuals in the production and maintenance area face no penalty in not following corporate guidelines. Yet without good record keeping regarding transfers, retirements, and trade-ins, information captured in the property record system will soon lose its value. The fixed asset information maintained in the accounting department will be no more than a theoretical record, useful only for purposes of computing depreciation on what "should" be present. For this reason it is better to exclude all minor assets from the detailed record-keeping requirements; management effort can then be brought to bear effectively to control major pieces of equipment where, using the 80/20 rule, significant dollars are involved.

INSURANCE COVERAGE

This chapter cannot cover all ramifications of insurance placement and proof of loss. One should keep in mind insurance requirements in designing a property record system and control of fixed assets. Classification of property is essential. It is well known that land does not depreciate and is excluded from insurance (on the premise that if a building burned down the land would still be available for the replacement building). Items such as below-ground excavations and foundations are also excluded from insurance policies and must be identified and classified in the property record system. Various types of assets often carry different insurance rates; and, where worthwhile, classification of assets by insurance rate category can be advantageous. Assets may be fully depreciated both for financial statement purposes and tax records but nevertheless remain economically useful. In this instance insurable values have to be maintained because, in case of loss, the physical assets would still have to be replaced.

While it is not a substitute for a detailed appraisal, maintaining property records on a unit basis with specific asset identification can facilitate proof of loss. That is, in case of fire the property record, assuming it has been kept up to date, can be sorted to provide a printout of all assets in the geographical area at which the loss occurred. Independent verification periodically as to the existence of the assets shown on the property record will enhance the value of the property record in providing proof of loss. This is often accomplished through the use of independent appraisals. Proper determination of insurable values is important. Insurance coverage is usually placed on the basis of cost of reproduction new or cost of reproduction new less depreciation. Since the purpose of insurance is to make the insured whole in case of a loss, it is irrelevant what the assets cost originally. Both the insured and the insurance company are interested, at the time of loss, in knowing what is the reproduction cost. The insurance company, therefore, has a prime interest in making sure that assets are fully insured based on current reproduction costs. Insurance premiums which are based on current value will be higher, and should be sufficient to pay the losses actually incurred. If insurance premiums were based on original cost and payments under the policy were to be based on current costs—which are higher resulting from inflation—insurance companies would soon go out of business. Thus, insurance companies insist that insurable values be maintained by policy owners.

Some insurance companies specializing in coverage of private residences have recently gone to a procedure of automatically increasing the insurable value (and premium) on the basis of generalized indexes of home construction costs. It is unlikely that a single index number can be developed to apply to corporate assets. Specific indexes for various types of corporate assets, including buildings, machinery, and equipment, can be utilized in determining insurable values for a period of time. Periodically a verification of insurable values through a specific appraisal designed for that purpose is probably necessary, but a discussion of that subject is beyond the scope of this chapter.

PROPERTY TAXES

In most communities a substantial amount of revenue is raised through taxes on real and personal property. These are often referred to as *ad valorem* taxes, because the amount of tax paid by each property owner is proportionate to the value of his or her property. Sound property records are required to minimize the tax burden. It is usually impractical for the local assessor, or other official with the responsibility for determining values, to make a detailed appraisal of industrial property. A description of the property against which taxes are levied is usually supplied by the taxpayer. Regardless of how the values are determined, the starting point always is the basic record as to what property is located within the geographical boundaries of the taxing district. In many communities there are overlapping taxing districts; a particular factory and affiliated warehouse facilities might be in separate school districts, sanitary districts, drainage districts, townships, or even counties. If a company's properties are spread throughout a community, say with a factory in one location and a parts warehouse several miles away, it might well be that the factory and parts warehouse pay taxes at quite different rates because they are in different combinations of taxing districts. Proper input at time of acquisition as to geographical location, followed by scrupulous attention to recording physical transfers, can lead to a computer printout showing the specific assets geographically located in each tax district. A lack of records often subjects property to taxes unnecessarily.

The basis of most property tax assessments therefore starts with company records of property at each location. Determining the values against which the tax rate applies may result in figures different from book value. Many communities establish standard lives or depreciation percentages which the taxpayer applies to the historical cost of property located within the specific jurisdiction. Other localities provide their own indexes to apply to original cost. A company might own a computer and depreciate it over seven years on its books, but the property tax authorities may permit only ten-year depreciation. Regardless of method, accurate company property records are needed.

Many companies have found, on taking a physical inventory of fixed assets, that a substantial amount of assets cannot be located. These "unrecorded retirements" had been previously traded in, scrapped, stolen, or cannibalized without proper record keeping. Irrespective of the reason for disappearance, continuing to carry such assets on the books of account almost invariably subjects a company to unnecessary property taxes as well as excess insurance premiums. This is a good argument to justify the cost of an appraisal, which includes a physical inventory of assets on hand.

A slightly more difficult situation arises in the case of assets still physically present but fully depreciated on the books. Whereas for determining insurable values it is desirable to keep track of the asset even if it has a zero book value, just the opposite incentive exists relative to property taxes. While there is no easy solution, perhaps a good practical approach to the problem would be to identify, through a physical inventory, those items which become fully depreciated each year. Those which cannot be found or which have no economic value should be immediately retired from the property record system. Significant assets which still have a useful economic life should be retained on the basic property record even though fully depreciated.

CASH FLOW AND DEPRECIATION

There is no direct relationship between cash flow and depreciation charged on the books. Those who argue that depreciation and cash flow are the same should answer the question, "Can you meet a payroll with depreciation?" The answer is self-evident. Cash flows out of a business when an asset is purchased. Cash flows into a business from customer receipts, derived by selling products and services.

To identify a bookkeeping entry for depreciation expense as having some effect of its own relative to cash flow totally distorts reality. Most companies must replace assets each year. Given a desire for growth, combined with an inflationary bias in the economy, most companies spend more cash on new capital expenditures each year than they charge off as depreciation expense for previously acquired assets. Depreciation is not a source of funds; it is not a cash flow. Only if a company is shrinking, and not replacing assets, will the charge for depreciation be equivalent to the availability of funds for purposes such as dividends or loan repayments.

FIXED ASSET ACCOUNTING FOR
FINANCIAL STATEMENTS

There are few topics in accounting which have brought forth more discussion than the subject of depreciation. Aside from measuring their effect on cash flow, which is related only to the corporate income tax, depreciation calculations for financial statements still would involve some complexities. There still would be a problem of reconciling the conflicting objectives of proper matching of revenue and expense and the goals involving levels of reported income.

The original rationale for charging depreciation was to recognize that a portion of the cost of every long-lived asset had to be recovered through the revenue stream before any income emerged. The initial dollar expenditure, rather than being written off as an expense in the period acquired, was to be matched with the future revenues generated by use of the asset over the period of time during which the asset was productive.

The basic accounting model for depreciation assumes a static company in a noninflationary environment. If a punch press will perform 1 million cycles, at the rate of 100,000 per year, and the press will be retired ten years later, proper matching of costs and revenues requires charging one tenth of the original cost of the press (less estimated salvage) ratably to inventory and cost of goods sold each year. Ideally, if one could determine, as in the case of the punch press, how much utilization each asset would provide, depreciation could be calculated on a unit-of-production basis and spread over the actual useful life. However, for almost all assets the physical life cannot be accurately determined in advance, nor can accurate estimates be made of specific production volume. Further, future changes in technology are almost impossible to predict, which makes calculation of the *economic* life even more difficult.

Asset life

It is at this point that complexity begins. However arbitrary, *some* assumption must be made as to the period of time over which an asset will be used. Any projection into the future involves uncertainties; those responsible for anticipating expected useful lives necessarily use judgment. In some cases this determination can routinely be based directly on past experience with like kinds of assets. In other cases, individual professional judgment must be used. Appraisers, trained in the field of estimating useful lives by using engineering and other technical data, can usually do a better job than accountants, who may have little knowledge of property or production economics. However accomplished, the goal is to make the best estimate possible of the physical or economic life, whichever is shorter. Consideration should be given to segregating and identifying various functional and operational components of large complex assets made up of numerous components, such as a building or a large integrated production line, rather than capital- izing the entire amount as a single item and identifying it with a single tag number. Instead of having one line entry on the fixed asset records for a $600,000 building, one might end up with different entries for each functional system, such as elevators, wiring, air con- ditioning, and so on. Separate economic lives can then be assigned to each functional unit and a shorter weighted average life estab- lished than would be possible by taking the entire asset as a unit. A balance has to be struck between the cost of maintaining sepa- rate records and the benefits from physical control, better analysis of depreciation expense, and better review of subsequent mainte- nance expenditures.

Even if there were perfect foresight and the actual useful life could be determined in advance, a company might consciously choose to use a different life for accounting purposes because of financial and tax policies. Thus, some companies have established policies under which assets in various categories will be assigned more or less arbitrary lives for financial reporting purposes. While this practice can perhaps be justified on the bases of ease of admin- istration and of being in the interest of some overriding financial goal (such as to minimize reported earnings), the effect of depre- ciating assets over a time frame different from that in which the asset is expected to be economically useful creates potentially serious problems.

In summary, to the extent that depreciation expense is utilized in the application of pricing policies or measuring divisional return on assets, incorrect decisions and evaluations may be made if arti- ficial lives, rather than the best estimate of anticipated useful lives, are utilized. There is no answer to this problem. In the final analysis the corporate financial officer must choose between having the best possible information available for management purposes and trying to achieve some financial or cash management goal.

Depreciation method

A second controversy revolves around how best to allocate the total cost of the asset over the estimated life. That is, should one assume that an equal portion of the asset will be expended each year? Alternatively, on the assumption that as a machine gets older more maintenance expense will be incurred, an argument is often advanced that a greater portion of the original cost should be charged off early so that in later years—when maintenance expense climbs, or the asset is technologically out of date—depreciation charges will be less.

There are also advocates of using an *annuity* or *compound interest* approach similar to a return on investment calculation. These would recover the original cost and a return on that outlay in the same manner as a bank calculates a level monthly mortgage, involving a constantly changing mix between interest and principal. Under this concept each asset has an opportunity cost of capital. While perhaps soundest theoretically, at least in terms of financial analysis, the annuity approach is seldom used in practice, other than in full payout financing-type leases. There the lessee's monthly payment is the equivalent of depreciation, interest, and a return on the original investment.

While properly based on physical expectations and economic or technological analysis, in practice the choices of asset life and depreciation method for financial statements are based on financial policy considerations more often than not.

Financial policy

Financial policy considerations must be addressed openly. To the extent that depreciation expense is an element in computing net income on a periodic basis, assignment of short lives combined with use of an accelerated depreciation method will have the effect of reporting *lower* profits initially. The reverse, setting long lives and use of straight-line depreciation, tends to *increase* reported profit. Since financial statements are utilized by shareholders in evaluating the reasonableness of dividends and by employees arguing for higher wages, management may have an incentive to reduce reported profits. This can, in large measure, be accomplished by higher depreciation charges. The other side of the coin is that if management wishes to report higher earnings, perhaps in an attempt to raise the price of its stock, then reducing depreciation charges will show higher book income.

These considerations are real and cannot be overlooked. From the point of view from someone outside the business community, however, "playing games" with depreciation expense to affect reported income is viewed suspiciously. To solve this problem the Accounting Principles Board issued *Opinion No. 20,* which made it much harder for a company arbitrarily to *change* lives of assets, or depreciation method, solely to affect net income in a particular year. According to this *Opinion,* an entity may change an accounting principle only if the alternative principle is preferable. Further, the SEC requires consistency from year to year. But the initial choice of lives and depreciation still is—and should be—a management prerogative.

While changing the amount of depreciation charged in a year will affect reported net income, it will *not* affect *cash flow* (aside from its tax effect), which many financial managers are coming to believe is the key measure of economic success. Under a cash flow approach, therefore, proper choice of lives and depreciation method (straight-line versus accelerated) can be based on the best estimate of the *economic life* pattern of that specific asset for the company. Only on grounds of conservatism should one err on the side of using shorter lives or accelerated depreciation methods. Accrual accounting, with an emphasis on reported net income, may place a premium on substituting policy considerations for economic consideration. If cash flow is the predominant determinant of financial and accounting policies, however, management can base its depreciation policies solely on economic criteria. The financial statements produced by using depreciation expense figures will be relevant for decision making only if good judgment is used in setting lives and choosing an appropriate depreciation method. Decisions on product pricing, product line profitability, and divisional return on investment will otherwise be distorted. Letting a desire to maximize or minimize short-term reported earnings determine depreciation policy can be self-defeating. Once a decision is made regarding capitalization policy, depreciation method, and useful lives, the factors underlying that decision are soon lost sight of. The resulting financial statements are then looked at as "correct," even if there was positive intent to "slant" them one way or the other. Too much stress cannot be placed on the desirability of not sacrificing realistic fixed asset accounting policies to some other goal regarding reported income.

Depreciation for tax accounting

There is one area in which depreciation expense affects cash flows of a company. In determining taxable income—as compared to book income used in financial reports to shareholders—the amount charged for depreciation expense results in an immediate change in cash outflow for taxes. It is well known that financial statements prepared for the Internal Revenue Service can differ widely from those published as representing the results of operations. The IRS asks for a reconciliation of tax and book income. But for tax purposes depreciation charges, like everything else, must be reported in conformity with tax laws and regulations, not on the basis of generally accepted accounting principles or of what provides for good management control.

The differences between book income and tax income follow directly from policy decisions made by Congress, which permit tax liabilities to be determined from specific definitions of taxable income. Further, Congress has often acted in the belief that tax laws should have economic or social consequences. There is a strong bias in reporting taxable income, because all parties recognize that it is to a company's advantage to report the *lowest* possible taxable income, thus minimizing cash outflows for taxes. Meanwhile, the government wishes to maximize taxable income so as to maximize tax revenue.

In short, there is nothing wrong for a company to try to minimize reported taxable income. The courts have been clear on this. For a profitable company paying taxes, an area where taxable income can easily be minimized is depreciation. Claiming the maximum depreciation as early as possible results, on a present value basis, in maximizing cash flow. A deduction for depreciation taken today is more valuable than one taken five years from now. The following table shows an example.

Assume that an asset cost $15,000 and has a useful life of five years:

Year	*Straight line*			*Accelerated (sum of year's digits)*		
	Depre-ciation	*P.V. factor (8%)*	*Present value Year 1*	*Depre-ciation*	*P.V. factor (8%)*	*Present value Year 1*
1	$ 3,000	.926	$ 2,778	$ 5,000	.926	$ 4,630
2	3,000	.857	2,571	4,000	.857	3,428
3	3,000	.794	2,382	3,000	.794	2,382
4	3,000	.735	2,205	2,000	.735	1,470
5	3,000	.681	2,043	1,000	.681	681
Total	$15,000		$11,979	$15,000		$12,591

While it is obvious that both depreciation methods end up with $15,000 being deducted from taxable income over the five-year period, most analysts would agree that it is usually better to take the maximum as soon as possible. In this example the accelerated approach provides deductions with a present worth of $12,591, or $612 more than straight line. Only if a company is operating in a net loss position is it desirable to retard depreciation.

It is well known that a company can choose a *different depreciation method* for tax reporting compared to financial reporting. *Differing economic lives* can also often be utilized for the two purposes. The burden of proof would be on the taxpayer if he or she utilized much shorter lives for taxes than for financial statements. Since the scope of this chapter does not include the subject of taxation, it is sufficient here to remind the corporate financial officer to be aware of the tax impact of depreciation expense on cash outflows and to attempt, with good tax advice, to maximize deductions for depreciation.

Investment tax credit

The investment tax credit was originally instituted by Congress as an effort, on a short-term basis, to stimulate expenditures on capital assets—expenditures which are thought by many economists, politicians, and others, to increase employment. The subsequent history of the Investment Tax Credit (ITC) indicates that politicians have utilized it as a device to try to stimulate or slow down the economy. Others have argued for ITC, saying there is a bias in the tax system against the formation of capital. ITC is viewed in this way as an effort to redress the balance, to lower effective taxes for those companies which are capital intensive. Regardless of why it was developed or for what ultimate political or social purposes it is maintained, the availability of the investment tax credit cannot be overlooked.

Under present ITC rules, a company is allowed to take a percentage of eligible investments directly as a credit in determining taxes payable. Thus, for example, if $100,000 of eligible investment has been made and the ITC rate is 10 percent, a company is allowed to deduct 10 percent, or $10,000, from its tax bill. Effectively, then, a dollar of investment tax credit is worth as much as $2 of expense deductions if the effective tax rate is near 50 percent. Conversely, for a company operating at a loss and paying no taxes, the investment tax credit today provides no financial incentive for investment.

The laws and regulations defining what is an eligible investment have been subject to change. Basically, investments in machinery, equipment, and production processes are eligible, whereas investments in buildings and structures are not. However, since a significant portion of the cost of many buildings involves components built in for the production process, and the latter are eligible, it is at times difficult to determine the amount of eligible investment. Because of the substantial financial impact of the ITC, it is desirable for a company to obtain professional consultation regarding the determination, on an engineering basis, of building components which qualify for ITC.

As the investment tax credit is presently structured, a higher rate is applicable to assets which have a longer useful life. For example, at the beginning of 1976 the schedule was as follows:

Useful life years	Investment tax credit
0–2	–0–
3–5	$3\frac{1}{3}\%$
5–7	$6\frac{2}{3}\%$
7–over	10%

Earlier it was stated that one can optimize cash flow by using short lives to claim the maximum depreciation expense. There are cases, however, where using a shorter economic life will place the asset in a different and lower ITC category. In the choice of lives, fairly precise calculations must be made as to the proper tradeoff between maximizing current depreciation expense and obtaining a lower rate of investment tax credit.

Depreciation recapture

If tax rates are at the 50 percent level each dollar of depreciation saves 50 cents in taxes, because depreciation expense is a deduction in calculating taxable income. The tax laws in the United States are set up so that capital gains, as distinguished from ordinary income, are taxed at a lower rate. If one is able to take an asset with an original cost of $15,000 and write it off to zero in five years, there will be a tax savings of $7,500. If the asset can be sold subsequently for $6,000, and a capital gains tax of 25 percent is levied on the full $6,000 sale price (because the basis was zero after fully depreciating the asset), it would mean that when the original cost of the asset was taken as a deduction, taxes were saved at a 50 percent rate; but when the asset is sold at a higher amount, taxes are payable at only half the *rate* on the gain.

Essentially this procedure was stopped through a change in the tax law which provided that capital gains treatment would only apply on the amount for which the asset was sold in excess of its original cost. Meanwhile, any gain attributable to depreciation deductions taken in excess of the sales price was "recaptured"—in practice, the previous depreciation deduction was reversed.

As a result of the depreciation recapture regulations it is now necessary, whenever an asset is sold, to calculate the amount of depreciation taken if the asset is sold at anything above book value (tax book value, not financial statement book value). When a part of a business is sold, such calculations are complex. The first requirement is to allocate the sale price among each of the assets disposed of. This procedure usually requires outside professional help. Then the sale price of each individual asset is reconciled to the depreciation already taken, based on original acquisition price, in order to calculate the taxable gain or loss. Recognition that depreciation recapture calculations may have to be made at some point in the future is essential in setting up and maintaining a fixed asset accounting system.

Corrections and restatements

The thrust of this chapter has been that the essence of a good fixed asset accounting system is a *detailed factual property record* for each asset under control. Knowing what assets are owned and where they are utilized provides information of maximum value. Estimates and judgment, however, are constantly being applied in areas such as choice of life, choice of depreciation method, and capitalization policy. What should be done if it is determined that previous estimates are later found wrong, that assets will be disposed of earlier or later than anticipated? What about the effect of technological change on salvage value?

Generally speaking, if previous estimates change the resulting effect has to be recognized prospectively. If at acquisition a life of ten years was established, and after five years it was determined that the item would be disposed of in two years, the remaining undepreciated cost would be spread over the new remaining shorter useful life. While a theoretical argument could be made for restating the reported income of prior years for the higher depreciation charges which should have been taken, the accounting profession has chosen to eliminate or drastically restrict such prior period adjustments. For practical purposes GAAP require spreading the undepreciated cost over the new remaining life. The same holds true in accounting for changes in estimated salvage value.

How should situations be handled where the estimated useful life, and perhaps even the salvage value, are considered accurate, but because of changes in technology or market place the real market value of the asset is significantly below the current undepreciated cost on the company's books?

Assume that a general-purpose office building is owned in a deteriorating neighborhood. If the current market value is below the historical cost book value, conservatism might suggest that the asset be written down to market. However, this is not usually considered acceptable unless a discontinuance of operations in that geographical area is contemplated and the building is going to be placed on the market for sale. The rationale is that since assets are not written up if market value increases, depreciation charges should continue to be based on historical cost when market value declines, in the absence of a decision to dispose of the asset, irrespective of outside market influences.

Historical cost and current values

Given a combination of a relatively rapid inflation rate and a society that is changing, both technologically and socially, soon

after acquisition of an asset it becomes impossible to utilize historical cost information for determining current asset values. Somewhat ironically, the only time asset values are changed to market
is when an entire business is acquired and the accounting is handled as a purchase transaction. Then the purchase price is allocated
over all assets acquired on the basis of current values. The acquisition cost of what is then secondhand or used equipment reflects
market values at that date. Future depreciation charges will be determined from the new market values; subsequent revaluations
are precluded unless the business is once again sold.

Many business executives have questioned the usefulness of
sticking to historical costs when business decisions are usually
based on current estimates of value. There are substantial difficulties—both in theory and in practice—in attempting to revalue
assets on a recurring basis for financial statements. Different concepts of value would be needed even for a particular operating
division, depending on the type of decision being taken. A corporate manager might want to know the liquidation value of
individual machine tools, the market value as a going concern
for the division as a whole, or the current cost to replace existing facilities with the most up-to-date technologically advanced
equivalents.

No one definition of value can be utilized for the myriad decisions made in a business. Determining the cost of reproduction,
which is necessary for insurance purposes, is irrelevant in deciding
whether to dispose of an asset or business segment. Determining
the current market value of an acreage of forest owned by a paper
company is not necessary if the land is going to be retained by the
company and the trees used as raw materials. Only if a decision to
sell is contemplated are market values relevant. In short, corporate books of account are likely to be maintained on the basis of
historical cost for some time. Where it is necessary to make specific
decisions, various concepts of value can be determined for the purpose at hand.

Chapter 10

Capitalization and amortization of leases

*Philip L. Defliese**

NATURE OF THE PROBLEM

Lease accounting has been surrounded by controversy for many years, particularly during the postwar period and the 60's when leasing became more popular. It is estimated that $100 billion of assets are on lease in 1975. The issues involved have settled into a gray zone between economic reality and fundamental accounting rules—*substance versus form.* Business decisions concerning the use of assets to produce revenue are founded on economic reality. How the assets are obtained would appear to be of lesser significance. One might suppose that two companies using similar assets to produce similar revenue would report results that look alike. However, this is not true when one acquires its assets through purchase and the other through leasing. Present accounting rules prescribe a meticulous examination of the rights involved in and the form of transactions. While authoritative pronouncements attempt to recognize substance, accounting practice has emphasized form, and has created a motive for basing economic decisions, in part, on how accounting rules will make transactions appear.

At present, an Exposure Draft of a proposed accounting standard on *Accounting for Leases* issued by the Financial Accounting

---

* Managing Partner, Coopers & Lybrand.

Standards Board (FASB) is under consideration. Much comment was elicited by the FASB from the accounting profession, regulatory bodies, and the financial and investing community, and a public hearing was held on the subject before the draft was issued. While significant changes in existing accounting rules for leasing may result from its adoption, the present status leaves management with considerable leeway. This results in part from the nature of leasing itself and in part from the somewhat inconclusive state of present accounting rules. This chapter will deal with the status quo (with appropriate caveats), but will also provide an outline of the proposed new standard.[1]

A *lease* is a legal instrument that transfers certain property rights and obligations from lessor to lessee. It resembles a sale-and-purchase agreement in the kind of rights and obligations that change hands, but differs in the extent to which control is transferred. Because the lessor retains some *control* (e.g., title), accounting for leases as sales is often not appropriate. Further, *performance,* that is, delivery and payment, required for a sale is not completed at the time a lease is transacted, as the lessor continues to make the property available and the lessee pays only as the property is used. Yet many leases do give the lessee the same effective use of property as would be obtained in a purchase.

The effective use of property without ownership and a reduced initial cash demand are the economic bases for leasing. While these economic realities have been given proper legal form, the accounting transition from simple sales reporting to a reflection of this new package of rights and obligations remains incomplete at present.

The development of more definitive accounting rules has lagged behind the economic use of leases. Leasing was originally confined primarily to land, but its use has expanded substantially in the last 20 years to other types of assets. Since business attitudes towards ownership of machinery are different from attitudes towards ownership of land, business has been able to sidestep the legal strictures of ownership in its pursuit of the economic benefits of leasing. Economics and law have helped to create a gap, and accountants are still in the middle.

The impact on financial statements of the distinction between

---

[1] Copies may be obtained from Financial Accounting Standards Board, High Ridge Park, Stamford, Connecticut 06905. Copies of a Discussion Memorandum on the subject, previously published by the FASB, may also be obtained.

owning and leasing is significant. "Accounting" assets appear on the balance sheet along with the debt obligations incurred to obtain those assets. If leased property is judged not to be an accounting asset, the balance sheet of a lessee is not directly affected. That decision will also create different costs in the income statement and different disclosure requirements in the notes. Thus, two companies doing the same work, with the same physical plant, will seem to perform quite differently if one capitalizes property and the other does not. Some would agree that they are in fact not exactly alike and should therefore not appear to be; others disagree. The dispute centers around measuring the similarities and differences accurately and reflecting the economic substance appropriately within the present conceptual framework of accounting[2] and the needs of financial statement users.

Since the lessee's degree of control over assets need not always be absolute or for their entire physical life, leasing is an attractive way to produce the same revenue as by purchasing assets and simultaneously to advance other goals. These goals include the exercise of some influence over the following: the income statement, by allowing a choice as to the pace of cost recognition; the balance sheet, through options for the recording of assets and liabilities; tax planning; and impact on performance ratios.

Uniform lease/purchase accounting treatment, however, will not necessarily cause two companies using similar assets to produce similar revenue to report results that look alike. Among factors, other than lease accounting, that produce these differences are: (1) ancillary accounting issues, such as deferral of preopening costs (a major retailer who primarily leases charges off preopening costs as incurred, while a very similar retailer who owns stores capitalizes such costs); (2) timing of acquisitions (although indexing of costs can mitigate this problem); and (3) operating philosophy (one supermarket chain leases stores on a 15- or 20-year term in order to sell its groceries, while another chain sells groceries in order to acquire real estate under long-term leases which it believes will appreciate in value).

Accounting rules have also affected the financial statements of *lessors*. These rules determine whether a lease is a *financing arrangement* (where a lending institution is involved) or a *sale* (in

---

[2] The FASB has on its agenda a proposed standard on the *Conceptual Framework of Accounting*.

the case of a manufacturer or dealer). Still other leases, in which the lessor will reacquire the property to be leased again, are strictly of an *operating* nature. Each type of lease requires different accounting treatment, and a careful examination of the contract terms and circumstances must be made to determine which treatment is appropriate. The outcome of this analysis is critical to the pace at which manufacturing profit, if any, is recognized, and to the timing and nature of income items for financing institutions.

OVERVIEW

This chapter will explore the economic issues that affect leasing decisions, as well as the pertinent present and proposed authoritative accounting pronouncements. The impact that the alternative decisions have on financial statements will be discussed. The principal accounting questions involve the determination of which leases are to be capitalized by the lessee, and how income is to be recognized by the lessor. Corollary issues are symmetry, that is, whether the accounting determinations of lessee and lessor should be consistent with one another, and whether certain types of leases, such as leveraged leases, leases between related parties, and leases by manufacturer or dealer lessors, require special rules.

The economic decision to acquire assets occurs before the decision as to the method of obtaining them. The "lease or buy" decision, viewed from the point of economic alternatives, focuses on the pragmatic questions of the tax impact of accelerated depreciation and the investment tax credit, possible obsolescence, asset life and period of need, available credit, and, of course, cost measured by the discounted cash flow technique. These questions concern the substance of real needs and available resources, as well as the impact that the alternative decisions will have on daily operations and efficiency. To the extent that no universally accepted technique for measuring cost is available and subjective judgment is a very important feature (such as in determining an appropriate discount rate), the determination of economic impact in arriving at a lease or buy decision can be very difficult.

Authoritative accounting pronouncements have sought to eliminate the advantages that have arisen due solely to choice of *form*. While allowing "true" leases to be accounted for as such, accounting rules have attempted to require transactions that are in substance purchases or sales, but take the form of leases, to be recorded as purchases or sales. The first of these pronouncements, still in effect, *Accounting Principles Board (APB) Opinion No. 5,* "Reporting of Leases in Financial Statements of Lessee" (September 1964), set criteria for a lessee's recognition of a purchase where the substance of the transaction so indicates. *APB Opinion No. 7,* "Accounting for Leases in Financial Statements of Lessors" (May 1966), prescribed somewhat different criteria for a financing arrangement or sale recognition by a lessor. *APB Opinion No. 27,* "Accounting for Lease Transactions by Manufacturer or Dealer Lessors" (November 1972), deals with the special circumstances of manufacturer-dealer lessors, as contrasted with financing institutions. *APB Opinion No. 31,* "Disclosure of Lease Commitments by Lessees" (July 1973), is the profession's most recent pronouncement on the subject, and deals exclusively with disclosure requirements for lessees. The Securities and Exchange Commission (SEC), in *Accounting Series Release (ASR) No. 147* (October 1973), set SEC disclosure requirements. These extend considerably beyond, and effectively supersede, *APB Opinion No. 31* for public companies. The proposed FASB standard, if adopted in present or slightly modified form, would supersede all previous AICPA pronouncements, and may supersede the SEC's[3] as well.

THE LEASE OR BUY DECISION

Leasing has distinct advantages and disadvantages, which can be identified and evaluated in specific circumstances. Some aspects of the question of whether to lease are subjective, leaving room for more than one answer. Most importantly, leasing is an alternative worth considering even if it is ultimately rejected.

Advantages of leasing

To the lessee

Economic issues:

1. *Limited commitment in case of property obsolescence.*
2. *Entire cost of property is financed* (including interest during and after construction).
3. *Restrictive loan provisions* barring new debt may be overcome in some instances.

---

[3] Full texts of all pronouncements should be consulted.

4. *Period of need* may be considerably shorter than property's useful life.
5. *Tax deductibility* even for property that is not normally depreciable (e.g., land).
6. *Possible avoidance of some local taxes* where these are based on property values.
7. *Ability to share tax advantages* of ownership where these cannot be used directly by the lessee (see later section, "The Economic Issues").

Accounting issues:

1. *Off-balance sheet accounting treatment:* no recorded assets or liabilities provided the transaction meets certain accounting requirements (see later section, "Criteria for Capitalization").
2. *Improved income statement performance in early years:* level lease payments will generally be less than the combined interest and depreciation expense resulting from ownership accounting (this reverses in later years).

To the lessor

Economic issues:

1. *Secured interest in property* (but limited general creditor rights in bankruptcy as to rentals for remaining lease term).
2. *Right to residual value of property at end of lease.*
3. *Rate of return greater* than on the loan of an equivalent sum.

Accounting issues:

1. *Sales accounting* may be available under certain conditions.

Disadvantages of leasing

To the lessee

Economic issues:

1. *Higher total cost of discounted cash flows* (see Exhibit 1).
2. *No interest in residual property value* where recovery is reasonably certain.

EXHIBIT 1
Buying versus leasing: Comparison of cash flows ($100,000 asset)

	Buy								Lease			
Period	Debt service(a)	Principal repayment	Interest payment	Depreciation(b)	Interest plus depreciation	Tax benefit at 50%	After-tax cash cost	Present value	Rental(c)	Tax benefit at 50%	After-tax cash cost	Present value
1	$ 11,507	$ 3,614	$ 7,893	$ 12,500	$ 20,393	$10,197	$ 1,310	$ 1,213	$ 10,990	$ 5,495	$ 5,495	$ 5,088
2	11,507	3,912	7,595	11,667	19,262	9,631	1,876	1,608	10,990	5,495	5,495	4,711
3	11,507	4,234	7,273	10,833	18,106	9,053	2,454	1,948	10,990	5,495	5,495	4,362
4	11,507	4,583	6,924	10,000	16,924	8,462	3,045	2,238	10,990	5,495	5,495	4,038
5	11,507	4,961	6,546	9,167	15,713	7,856	3,651	2,485	10,990	5,495	5,495	3,740
6	11,507	5,370	6,137	8,333	14,470	7,235	4,272	2,692	10,990	5,495	5,495	3,463
7	11,507	5,813	5,694	7,500	13,194	6,597	4,910	2,865	10,990	5,495	5,495	3,206
8	11,507	6,292	5,215	6,667	11,882	5,941	5,566	3,007	10,990	5,495	5,495	2,969
9	11,507	6,810	4,697	5,833	10,530	5,265	6,242	2,622	10,990	5,495	5,495	2,749
10	11,507	7,372	4,135	5,000	9,135	4,567	6,940	3,214	10,990	5,495	5,495	2,545
11	11,507	7,979	3,528	4,167	7,695	3,848	7,659	3,285	10,990	5,495	5,495	2,358
12	11,507	8,637	2,870	3,333	6,203	3,101	8,406	3,338	10,990	5,495	5,495	2,182
13	11,507	9,349	2,158	2,500	4,658	2,329	9,178	3,375	10,990	5,495	5,495	2,020
14	11,507	10,120	1,387	1,667	3,054	1,527	9,980	3,398	10,990	5,495	5,495	1,871
15	11,507	10,954	553	833	1,386	693	10,814	3,409	10,990	5,495	5,495	1,732
	$172,605	$100,000	$72,605	$100,000	$172,605	$86,302	$86,303(d)	$40,697	$164,850	$82,425	$82,425(e)	$47,034

(a) $100,000 of debt borrowed at 8 percent. The debt service, payable quarterly in arrears, will be sufficient to amortize the loan fully over 15 years.

(b) Asset cost of $100,000 will be depreciated over 15 years using the sum-of-the-years'-digits method. It was assumed that the asset had no salvage value.

(c) Rental on a 15-year lease will be payable quarterly in arrears. The rental was based on an interest factor of 7¼ percent. It was assumed that the lessee's credit would require 8 percent interest. Since the lessor retains the depreciation benefits of the asset, he or she can charge a rent based on 7¼ percent even though the acquisition has been financed at 8 percent.

(d) Present worth of $86,303 cost of buying, at 8 percent, is $40,697.

(e) Present worth of $82,425 cost of leasing, at 8 percent, is $47,034.

Comment on Notes (d) and (e): When comparing the cumulative after-tax cash costs, buying is the more expensive alternative by about $4,000. However, present valuing the annual outflows results in buying being the more economical alternative by approximately $6,000.

3. *Loss of tax advantages* of investment tax credit and accelerated depreciation. Exhibit 1 does not give recognition to the investment tax credit the purchaser could obtain in the first year. This effect would be neutralized if the lessor arranges either to pass through the credit to the lessee or appropriately reduce the rental payments.

To the lessor

Economic issues:

1. *Obsolescence* may impair recovery of residual value or ability to re-lease after first lease term.
2. *Profit is dependent* on viability of lessee.
3. *Reversal of tax advantages* in later years of lease.

THE ECONOMIC ISSUES

Answering the substantive question, should a company lease or buy, involves several factors:

Cost: The costs related to each alternative may be compared on the basis of their associated cash flows, discounted to present values at an appropriate rate. Generally the rate that measures the *opportunity cost*[4] of funds is used. The tax effects that attend these choices are critical elements in this comparison and are discussed below.

Tax impact: For the lessee, lease payments for business purposes are tax deductible even though the asset might not be depreciable if bought, for example, land. Accelerated depreciation and the investment tax credit are major considerations in the cash flows used to determine relative cost. If these cannot be used by a would-be purchaser (e.g., because of insufficient taxable income), their use in the analysis must be adjusted accordingly. For the lessor, positive cash flows are generated from these tax advantages when he retains them. Alternatively, if a lessor cannot use the investment tax credit, he or she may under certain conditions pass it through to the lessee.

The foregoing tax impact must be tempered with the caution that the Internal Revenue Service, upon examining the

---

[4] The rate of return obtainable from equivalent funds in investments of the same risk.

terms of lease transactions, may require that a lease be treated as a purchase and sale, with the concomitant tax changes. Its rules of thumb for issuance of an advance ruling that a lessor (particularly in a leveraged lease transaction) may use the operating method are set forth in Rev. Proc. 75.21 and are generally as follows:

1. The lessor's minimum investment in the property must be equal to 20 percent of the property's cost, and this minimum must be maintained throughout the life of the lease. At the end of the lease, the value of the property must be at least 20 percent of the original property cost. (Compliance with this condition is difficult to establish where the property, at the expiration of the lease, is of the special-purpose type—that is, usable only by the lessee. The Revenue Service has not yet determined whether it will issue rulings in this circumstance.) Only the amount of consideration paid or personal liability incurred by the lessor to buy the property will count toward this minimum. The lessor's net worth must be sufficient to satisfy any personal liability the lessor assumes.

2. The lessor must show that at the end of the lease term, the useful life remaining to the property is one year, or 20 percent of the originally estimated useful life, whichever is greater. In applying these conditions, the IRS will deem the lease term to include all renewals and extensions except when they are negotiated (1) at the option of the lessee and (2) for fair rental value at the time of the renewal or extension.

3. Where the lessee has an option to purchase the property, he or she cannot also have a contractual right to pay less than the value of the property as determined at the time the option is exercised. There cannot be a contractual agreement whereby the lessor can compel the lessee or any other party to buy the property, nor can the lessor have any intention to negotiate such an agreement. This prohibition applies to provisions allowing the lessor to abandon the property to any party.

4. The lessee may not furnish any part of the cost of the property (with minor exceptions), or make loans to, or guar-

antee loans on behalf of, the lessor to enable the latter to acquire the property. However, loans or loan guarantees may be permissible under certain conditions if repaid or rescinded before the property is placed in service.

5. The lessor must show a reasonable expectation of profit from the transaction, apart from tax deductions, allowances, credits, and other tax benefits.

6. If rent payments fluctuate more than 10 percent above or below the level calculated evenly over the lease term, the Service has the right to determine what, if any, part of the excess or deficiency is prepaid or deferred rent, respectively.

Failure to meet the tax ruling criteria does not automatically result in capitalization for tax purposes. Subjective criteria similar to the accounting criteria are considered for this purpose.

It should be noted that some lessees prefer capitalization for tax purposes (but not necessarily for accounting purposes), and so elect if they can justify the result in accordance with the applicable accounting and tax criteria.

Period of need: If the asset is not needed for a major portion of its economic life, leasing is a convenient way to obtain its use only for the period needed.

Obsolescence: Where flexibility to replace existing assets quickly and easily is important—for example, because of changing technology or erratic competition—leasing may be preferred.

Existing debenture or other covenants: If a company is specifically precluded from incurring additional debt to purchase assets, a lease may provide asset use without indenture violation; however, many lenders are now restricting lease obligations.

Available credit: Purchase requires larger credit at inception, and may be more difficult to finance, than a lease.

Accounting effect: Leasing that provides off-balance sheet financing of the facility to the lessee and level lease charges to income that are generally lower than combined depreciation and interest charges in the early years may result in economic advantages in the capital market. In addition to a better debt-equity ratio, a young growing company will show better earnings during this period.

At one extreme, if the need for an asset is quite short and the asset's useful life is relatively long, a lease provides use without ownership, financing of debt, risk of recovery of residual value, or expense of selling when the asset is no longer needed. (The use of a car for two months for a visiting executive is an example.) At the other extreme, a company with cash or available credit facilities (at a low rate) can buy more inexpensively than lease, assuming that it can use the cash flow benefits of accelerated depreciation and the investment tax credit. Even in those circumstances, however, more subjective factors, such as obsolescence, may result in a decision to lease.

Clear-cut examples make good textbook reading, but rarely seem to fit business reality. Among the elements affecting the decision are some having a subjective impact whose importance may vary from situation to situation. In addition, not all quantifiable data can be relied on to remain static, so today's correct decision may become incorrect in tomorrow's world. Nonetheless, decisions must be made on the basis of available facts.

The most interesting examples from the business executive's point of view are those where alternatives are available and an optimum answer is required. Weighing the impact of a substantial asset acquisition in terms of a lease or buy decision can be reduced to a simple economic model of discounted cash flows. But if the asset has a high obsolescence potential (e.g., a computer, or heavy equipment for a product in a volatile market, such as double-knit fabric machinery), a decision that purchasing is less expensive, based on discounted cash flows, will be disregarded for a way to minimize losses if conditions change. Potential obsolescence is one of the most cogent reasons to incur a higher total lease cost. To the extent that possible business reversals can be anticipated, this higher cost can be predetermined and identified as a form of insurance.

In most cases, the asset will cost the lessor who buys and then leases it a sum equivalent to what a would-be lessee would pay for it. Since the lessor's cost of financing the purchase is included in the lease payments, the lessee can usually be assured that he or she will be paying the lessor at least what would have been paid had the lessee bought the asset, assuming the lessor cannot obtain credit at a lower cost than the lessee. Should the prospective lessee not be able to make use of the tax advantages of ownership, especially accelerated depreciation and the investment tax credit, leasing may provide a vehicle whereby those benefits may be at least partially passed through to the lessee in the form of reduced lease payments.

In summary, dollar cost will generally be lower in buying provided that full use of tax advantages (depending on effective tax rate) can be made. However, the individual circumstances of each situation should be weighed carefully in reaching a decision.

THE ACCOUNTING ISSUES

The accounting treatments for purchases and sales, and for financing and operating leases, are clear-cut. Unfortunately, many lease transactions do not fit neatly into these categories. In theory, if a lease transaction is in substance a sale or purchase, then the lessee is required to capitalize the asset and to record the related debt. The lessee depreciates the asset and pays off the debt; the lessor removes the asset from the plant or inventory accounts and replaces it with a receivable. For a financing institution, the excess of total payments to be received over the asset cost represents income to be recognized in decreasing amounts over the term of the lease (generally as a percentage of the remaining investment). Where a manufacturer or dealer profit is involved, accounting for a lease as equivalent to a sale will also allow early recognition of the manufacturing profit. If there is no sale or purchase, the accounting is even simpler: the lessee pays and records lease costs as they come due, making appropriate accruals when payments and accounting periods do not coincide; the lessor records an operating lease, taking rent revenue into income as it accrues and depreciating the asset, which stays on the books.

The lessee

Criteria for capitalization. *APB Opinion No. 5* requires capitalization if the transaction is "clearly in substance" a purchase. It expressed this concept by utilizing the term "material equity." If a lessee has such an interest in the leased property or the lease payments create one, capitalization is called for. Evidence of material equity, discussed at length in the next section includes the following:

1. The lease is noncancelable by either party, except upon a remote contingency, and
2. The initial term and renewal options cover the property's useful life, and the rental at renewal is substantially less than the fair rental value (bargain renewal option), or
3. A purchase option exists at a price that appears to be at the inception of the lease substantially less than the probable fair value at the time of exercise of the option (bargain purchase option).

The following circumstances are indicative of a purchase in all circumstances, *except where it is clear that no material equity exists:*

1. The property is for special-purpose use of the lessee.
2. The lease term is substantially equal to the life of the property, and lessee pays costs incidental to ownership, for example, taxes, insurance.
3. The lessee guarantees the lessor's obligations.
4. The lease is capitalized for tax purposes.

The practical effect of the application of *APB Opinion No. 5* has been to require capitalization of few long-term leases. Most lessees have been able to structure their leases so that no "material equity" builds up. Generally, a level payment lease with fair value options to purchase or renew, even though the lease term is substantially equivalent to economic life, will not result in the buildup of equity, and will hence be treated as a lease.

The above criteria do not apply, however, if the parties are related (discussed below). Recently, the SEC has invoked this section of *APB Opinion No. 5* where an intermediary lessor has been created for the purpose of holding and financing a lease, and such lessor is in the nature of a sham or of no economic substance.

Effectively, *APB Opinion No. 5* requires capitalization of all leases between related parties. Paragraph 12 states as follows:

> 12. In cases in which the lessee and the lessor are related, leases should often be treated as purchases even though they do not meet the criteria set forth [above], i.e., even though no direct equity is being built up by the lessee. In these cases, a lease should be recorded as a purchase if a primary purpose of ownership of the property by the lessor is to lease it to the lessee and (1) the lease

payments are pledged to secure the debts of the lessor or (2) the lessee is able, directly or indirectly, to control or influence significantly the actions of the lessor with respect to the lease. The following illustrate situations in which these conditions are frequently present:

a. The lessor is an unconsolidated subsidiary of the lessee, or the lessee and the lessor are subsidiaries of the same parent and either is unconsolidated.

b. The lessee and the lessor have common officers, directors, or shareholders to a significant degree.

c. The lessor has been created, directly or indirectly, by the lessee and is substantially dependent on the lessee for its operations.

d. The lessee (or its parent) has the right, through options or otherwise, to acquire control of the lessor.

Disclosure.   As the leasing movement grew, increased emphasis was given to greater disclosure of the terms of noncapitalized long-term leases so that users could draw therefrom any conclusions they considered pertinent. *APB Opinion No. 31,* Disclosure of Lease Commitments by Lessees (1973), superseded previous requirements. It requires the following disclosures (paragraphs 8, 9, and 10) as an integral part of the financial statements:

Total Rental Expense

8. Total rental expense (reduced by rentals from subleases, with disclosure of such amounts) entering into the determination of results of operations for each period for which an income statement is presented should be disclosed. Rental payments under short-term leases for a month or less which are not expected to be renewed need not be included. Contingent rentals, such as those based upon usage or sales, should be reported separately from the basic or minimum rentals.

Minimum Rental Commitments

9. The minimum rental commitments[1] under all noncancelable leases[2] should be disclosed, as of the date of the latest balance sheet presented, in the aggregate for:

a.   Each of the five succeeding fiscal years,

b.   Each of the next three five-year periods, and

c.   The remainder as a single amount.

The amounts so determined should be reduced by rentals to be received from existing noncancelable subleases (with disclosure of the amounts of such rentals). The total of the amounts included in (*a*), (*b*), and (*c*) should also be classified by major categories of properties, such as real estate, aircraft, truck fleets, and other equipment.

Additional Disclosures

10. Additional disclosures should be made to report in general terms:

a. The basis for calculating rental payments if dependent upon factors other than the lapse of time.

b. Existence and terms of renewal or purchase options, escalation clauses, etc.

c. The nature and amount of related guarantees made or obligations assumed.

d. Restrictions on paying dividends, incurring additional debt, further leasing, etc.

e. Any other information necessary to assess the effect of lease commitments upon the financial position, results of operations, and changes in financial position of the lessee. (For example, in instances where significant changes in lease arrangements are likely it may be desirable to state that the information given is for existing leases only and is not a forecast of future rental expense. A statement could also be made that the amounts given may not necessarily represent the amounts payable in the event of default.)

[1] The minimum rental commitments are not necessarily indicative of the values of the property rights vested in the lessee.

[2] For purposes of this Opinion a noncancelable lease is defined as one that has an initial or remaining term of more than one year and is noncancelable, or is cancelable only upon the occurrence of some remote contingency or upon the payment of a substantial penalty.

The *Opinion* recommended, but did not require, disclosure of the present value of net fixed minimum rentals (by major categories of assets), based on interest rates implicit when negotiated.

The SEC's disclosure requirements set forth in *Accounting Series Release No. 147* are more extensive and more stringent. Specific measures of materiality are set forth for the disclosures enumerated above (i.e., 1 percent of revenue). If other measures of materiality are met (5 percent of total long-term debt and equity, 3 percent effect on net income), then disclosure is required of present value of minimum lease commitments, average interest rate used, and the impact on net income of capitalizing all financing leases and recording straight-line depreciation and interest expense. For this purpose, "financing leases" are defined as those with noncancelable terms equal to 75 percent or more of the property's economic life, or those that assure the lessor of a recovery of his or her investment plus a reasonable return. The data collection and computation required for those disclosures can be extensive.

The lessor[5]

Capitalization does not pose the same problems for lessors. The lease is always recorded—as property if it is an operating lease or as a receivable (or investment) if it is a financing lease. The main difference is in the manner of recording income. Under the "operating method" rent revenue is recognized as it is received; if a lease is accounted for as having the substance of financing the sale of the leased property, the "financing method" is used. A simple example shows the major characteristics of the two different methods. The assumed facts illustrated are:

Company A manufactures a piece of equipment at a cost of $35,000 and has it available for sale or lease at January 1, 19x1.

The equipment has an estimated useful life of five years and has no scrap value.

Operating method. On January 1, 19x1, Company A leases the equipment to Company B for five years, beginning January 1, 19x1, and ending December 31, 19x5, for $10,000 annually payable each year in advance. Company A uses the operating method; it recognizes revenue as the rent is earned and depreciates the asset by a straight-line method based on the five-year estimated life, resulting in a profit in each of the five years as follows:

Rent revenue	$10,000
Depreciation of equipment	7,000
Income from Leased Property	$ 3,000

Company A's profit for the five years totals $15,000.

Financing method. Company A uses the financing method, which acounts for the lease as equivalent to the sale of the property, resulting in a long-term receivable from Company B. Company A recognizes an immediate gross profit of $6,700, representing the difference between cost ($35,000) and the present value of the

---

[5] Portions of this section have been extracted from Philip L. Defliese, Kenneth P. Johnson, and Roderick K. Macleod, *Montgomery's Auditing*, 9th ed. (New York: The Ronald Press Co., 1975), with permission.

five payments ($41,700) using a rate of 10 percent as the rate of discount. This is equivalent to the normal selling price. Interest on the receivable is then recorded as follows:

Year	Uncollected receivable at December 31	Interest earned
19x1	$34,870	$3,170
19x2	27,356	2,486
19x3	19,019	1,735
19x4	10,000	909
19x5	-0-	-0-
Total Interest		$8,300

The total income is the same under the financing (sales) method ($6,700 plus $8,300 interest = $15,000) as under the operating method, but it is recognized in a different pattern—more in the earlier and less in the later years of the lease period.

Lease transaction variations. The preceding example illustrates the two basic methods. However, they may appear in combination depending upon possible variations in the transactions. For example:

1. Company A might have leased the equipment to Company B and then assigned the lease (not the property) to Company C for $41,700. Company A could recognize the gross profit immediately by treating the transactions as a sale and an assignment of a receivable. Company C would recognize the interest earned from the long-term receivable as it is earned.
2. Company A might have sold the equipment for $41,700 to Company C (a finance or leasing company), which in turn would lease the equipment to Company B under the same terms, producing the same aggregate accounting result.
3. If Company C borrowed the purchase price (or a portion of it) at an effective rate of less than 10 percent, a transaction known as a "leveraged lease" would result (see below).

Choice of method. The methods of accounting for lease revenue and their combinations cannot be applied indiscriminately. *APB Opinions Nos.* 7 and 27 describe the circumstances in which each type of accounting is appropriate.

In general, revenue should be recognized by the operating method if a lessor retains significant risks or rewards of ownership or is unable to estimate reasonably the collectibility of amounts due or amounts of future costs under the terms of the lease. Many leases obligate the lessor to service the equipment. Accounting for leases as equivalent to sales, that is, by the financing method, is an example of accounting for the substance of a transaction rather than its form when it appears that a sale by a manufacturer or dealer has really taken place, or when the manufacturer is assured the receipt of normal selling price under the terms of the lease, appropriately discounted. That often requires dividing a transaction into its elements —an element of sale and an element of long-term financing—and accounting for the elements separately. Banks and financing and leasing companies that purchase property for the purpose of financing a long-term lessee normally use the financing method for accounting purposes, but might use the operating method for income tax purposes (including accelerated depreciation). That combination would give rise to deferred income taxes.

The *APB Opinions* referred to above are complicated; and a reader should consult them, particularly to understand fully the accounting for leases as financing or sale transactions. For example, a manufacturer- or dealer-lessor must account for a lease transaction with an independent lessee as a sale if at the time of entering into the transaction (1) collectibility of the payments required from the lessee is reasonably assured, (2) no important uncertainties exist concerning the amount of costs yet to be incurred under the lease, and (3) any *one* of the following conditions is present:

a. The lease transfers title to the property to the lessee by the end of its fixed, noncancelable term; or

b. The lease gives the lessee the option to obtain title to the property without cost or at a nominal cost by the end of the fixed, noncancelable term of the lease; or

c. The leased property, or like property, is available for sale, and the sum of (1) the present value of the required rental payments by the lessee under the lease during the fixed, noncancelable term of the lease (excluding any renewal or other option) and (2) any related investment tax credit retained by the lessor (if realization of such credit is assured beyond any reasonable doubt) is equal to or greater than the normal selling price or, in the absence thereof, the fair value (either of which may be less than cost) of the leased property or like property; or

d. The fixed, noncancelable term of the lease (excluding any renewal option) is substantially equal to the remaining economic life of the property. (This test cannot be complied with (1) by estimating an economic life substantially equal to the noncancelable term if this is unrealistic or (2) if a material contingent residual interest is retained in the property.) [*APB Opinion No. 27,* par. 4.]

Leveraged leases

A leveraged lease is a refinement of the leasing vehicle in which three parties instead of two play a role. The lessor, often referred to as the *equity participant,* is the owner of the property but may have contributed as little as 20 percent or less toward its acquisition. A lender provides long-term credit on a nonrecourse (mortgage) basis for the bulk of the acquisition cost. The leveraged lease is a carefully balanced package of cash flows and tax benefits for the lessor. They result in a return of his or her initial investment very quickly, followed by cash accumulation, net outflow, and finally net proceeds from sale of the asset. The ultimate profitability of such an arrangement to the lessor is heavily dependent on the effective use of the temporarily excess funds arising from the investment tax credit and accelerated depreciation. The availability of the anticipated tax benefits must be substantially assured before the actual yield rate can be safely computed.

The accounting for this seemingly precarious balance is very much at issue. The long-term lender has recourse only through the leased property and the lessee; consequently, it is acceptable (in this case only) to record the investment on a net basis, with excess tax credits accounted for as deferred credits. The real issue is the allocation of overall income to proper periods. Some would apply existing (*APB Opinion No. 7*) standards to leveraged leases, while others propose that new standards be developed. It is argued that the lessor should recognize revenue from the transaction by applying an overall yield percentage, mathematically computed, in proportion to the unrecovered net investment, since that investment is the lessor's only economic contribution to the transaction and there is no direct liability. In many cases, however, that theory must be substantially qualified or negated by the test of collectibility, because sometimes full utilization of the tax benefits and the projected cash flow sufficient to completely recover the investment cannot be considered reasonably assured in the early years of a lease.

The question of overall yield is also at issue. Some believe that an imputed yield during the period of the negative investment (when realized tax benefits exceed net investment) should be anticipated in determining overall yield. Many variations are found in practice, and there are no authoritative pronouncements on the subject at present. The standard proposed by the FASB's Exposure Draft requires calculating the overall yield without any yield imputation on negative investment and spreading income over only those periods in which a positive investment exists. (Earnings on the excess cash during the negative years would flow through to income on a realized basis.) Exhibit 2, taken from the FASB's

EXHIBIT 2
Leveraged lease example—terms and assumptions

Cost of leased asset (equipment)	$1,000,000
Lease term.	15 years, dating from December 31, 1974
Lease rental payments	$90,000 per year (payable last day of each year)
Residual value.	$200,000 estimated to be realized one year after lease termination
Financing:	
Equity investment by lessor.	$400,000
Long-term nonrecourse debt	$600,000, bearing interest at 9% and repayable in annual installments (on last day of each year) of $74,435.30
Depreciation allowable to lessor for income tax purposes	7-year ADR life using double-declining balance method for the first two years; sum-of-the-years'-digits method for remaining life, depreciated to $100,000 salvage value
Lessor's income tax rate (federal and state)	50.4% (assumed to continue in existence throughout the term of the lease)
Investment tax credit.	7% of equipment cost or $70,000 (realized by the lessor on last day of first year of lease)

Exposure Draft (with permission) and modified slightly, demonstrates this method. (It should be noted that the investment tax credit is spread over all positive periods—the preferred method. Alternatively, it may be taken into income immediately when realized as provided by the Revenue Act of 1971.)

Third parties

Lessors are motivated by, among other things, the need to secure financing and the desire to promote the early recognition of profit. Where a manufacturer—or dealer—lessor can transfer all the risks

EXHIBIT 2 (continued)
Cash flow analysis by years

Year	(1) Gross lease rentals and residual value	(2) Depreciation (for income tax purposes)*	(3) Loan interest payments	(4) Taxable income (loss) (col. 1 − 2 − 3)	(5) Income tax credits (charges) (col. 4 × 50.4%)	(6) Loan principal payments	(7) Investment tax credit realized	(8) Annual cash flow (col. 1 − 3 + 5 − 6 + 7)	(9) Cumulative cash flow
Initial investment	—			—				$(400,000)	$(400,000)
1	$ 90,000	$ 137,222	$ 54,000	$(101,222)	$ 51,016	$ 20,435	$70,000	136,581	(263,419)
2	90,000	243,628	52,161	(205,789)	103,717	22,274	—	119,282	(144,137)
3	90,000	203,303	50,156	(163,459)	82,383	24,279	—	97,948	(46,189)
4	90,000	162,978	47,971	(120,949)	60,959	26,464	—	76,524	30,335
5	90,000	122,654	45,589	(78,243)	39,435	28,846	—	55,000	85,335
6	90,000	30,215	42,993	16,792	(8,463)	31,442	—	7,102	92,437
7	90,000	—	40,163	49,837	(25,118)	34,272	—	(9,553)	82,884
8	90,000	—	37,079	52,921	(26,672)	37,357	—	(11,108)	71,776
9	90,000	—	33,717	56,283	(28,367)	40,719	—	(12,803)	58,973
10	90,000	—	30,052	59,948	(30,214)	44,383	—	(14,649)	44,324
11	90,000	—	26,058	63,942	(32,227)	48,378	—	(16,663)	27,661
12	90,000	—	21,704	68,296	(34,421)	52,732	—	(18,857)	8,804
13	90,000	—	16,957	73,043	(36,813)	57,478	—	(21,248)	(12,444)
14	90,000	—	11,785	78,215	(39,421)	62,651	—	(23,857)	(36,301)
15	90,000	—	6,145	83,855	(42,262)	68,290	—	(26,697)	(62,998)
16	200,000	100,000	—	100,000	(50,400)	—	—	149,600	86,602
Totals	$1,550,000	$1,000,000	$516,530	$ 33,470	$ (16,868)	$600,000	$70,000	$ 86,602	

* Due to computer error, the annual depreciation amounts vary from those that would have appeared on the tax return.

EXHIBIT 2 (*concluded*)
Allocation of annual cash flow to investment and income

	(1)	(2)	(3)	(4)	(5)	(6)	(7)
			Annual cash flow			Components of income*	
Year	Lessor's net investment at beginning of year	Total (from cash flow analysis, col. 8)	Allocated to investment	Allocated to income†	Pretax income	Tax effect of pretax income	Investment tax credit
1.	$400,000	$136,581	$112,436	$24,145	$ 9,331	$ (4,703)	$19,517
2.	287,564	119,282	101,924	17,358	6,709	(3,381)	14,030
3.	185,640	97,948	86,742	11,206	4,331	(2,183)	9,058
4.	98,898	76,524	70,554	5,970	2,307	(1,163)	4,826
5.	28,344	55,000	53,288	1,712	662	(334)	1,384
6.	(24,944)	7,102	7,102	–	–	–	–
7.	(32,046)	(9,553)	(9,553)	–	–	–	–
8.	(22,493)	(11,108)	(11,108)	–	–	–	–
9.	(11,385)	(12,803)	(12,803)	–	–	. .	–
10.	1,418	(14,649)	(14,735)	86	33	(16)	69
11.	16,153	(16,663)	(17,637)	974	377	(190)	787
12.	33,790	(18,857)	(20,896)	2,039	788	(397)	1,648
13.	54,686	(21,248)	(24,550)	3,302	1,276	(643)	2,669
14.	79,236	(23,857)	(28,639)	4,782	1,848	(931)	3,865
15.	107,875	(26,697)	(33,209)	6,512	2,517	(1,268)	5,263
16.	141,084	149,600	141,084	8,516	3,291	(1,659)	6,884
Totals		$486,602	$400,000	$86,602	$33,470	$(16,868)	$70,000

* Each component is allocated among the years of positive net investment in proportion to the allocation of net income in Column 4.

† Lease income is recognized as 6.036 percent of the unrecovered investment at the beginning of each year in which the net investment is positive. The rate is the implicit rate which when applied to the net investment in the years in which the net investment is positive will distribute the net income to those years.

and rewards of ownership to a financing institution and receive a full payout of the investment, both objectives may be accomplished. *APB Opinion No. 27* addresses this area and basically prescribes that if the original lease agreement between lessor and lessee is not a sale, then the subsequent transfer of the lease to a third party is also not a sale unless the risk/reward/payment criteria noted above are met.

Symmetry

The symmetry issue arises from the inconsistent accounting definitions and standards set for lessees vis-à-vis those for lessors. *APB Opinion No. 5* set narrow, though sometimes difficult, criteria for lessees, while *APB Opinion No. 7* set comparatively broad standards for lessors. Further, the thrust of the lessee requirements is toward balance sheet recognition (capitalization) and the resultant effect on income, while the lessor standards are mainly concerned with income recognition. As applied to lease accounting, symmetry would require that what is a sale for the lessor is a purchase for the lessee. Conversely, what is not sold by the lessor cannot have been bought by the lessee. The problem has been that because of the unequal criteria set for lessees and lessors, property considered as sold by a lessor has been viewed by a lessee as an operating lease and has not been capitalized on the balance sheet. Some feel strongly that as a matter of pure theoretical substance symmetry is essential. Others disagree on the basis that each company must account for transactions in accordance with its own circumstances. The proposed standard in the FASB's Exposure Draft (discussed below) implicitly requires symmetry.

Sale and leaseback

There is generally no dispute concerning the proper accounting for sales of property with a concurrent long-term lease of the property from the purchaser back to the original owner. *APB Opinion No. 5* (paragraphs 21 and 22) settled the matter. All profits and losses (after taxes) on such transactions must ordinarily be *deferred and amortized* proportionally over the lease term as a modification of rent (or depreciation if the lease is required to be capitalized). One exception was granted to construction companies that both build and operate commercial properties, permitting them to reflect a reasonable profit on completion of construction. Losses must be recognized immediately if the fair value of the property at the time of the sale and leaseback is less than the depreciated cost.

The proposed standard in the FASB's Exposure Draft adheres to this general concept, with the following modifications:

1. The exemption for construction companies is eliminated.
2. The deferment of profit is not required if the lease does not qualify as a "capital" lease (as defined below) that is required to be capitalized, and the rental is equal to or greater than a "fair rental" determined for the property.

This proposal appears to be a liberalization of the current rule to the extent that some profits may be recognized immediately.

Proposed FASB standard on accounting for leases

The Exposure Draft issued by the FASB on August 26, 1975, has previously been referred to. While its adoption in present form cannot be assured, readers should be aware of the indicated trend, recognizing that the proposed standard, which is the most comprehensive ever issued on the subject by an authoritative body, comes after long study and research and a history of considerable controversy over the issue of lease capitalization.

Some aspects of the proposal have been referred to in previous sections on "Leveraged Leases" and "Sale and Leaseback." The other major points, including changes from present standards (*APB Opinions Nos.* 5, 7, 27, and 31), would be as discussed in the following paragraphs.

From the lessee's standpoint. Leases must be capitalized if they qualify as "capital leases" (a new term for financing leases). A *capital lease* is one meeting any *one* of the following criteria:

1. Title passes to lessee at end of lease term (no change).
2. The lease contains bargain purchase options (no change).
3. The lease term (which includes bargain renewal option periods) is equal to 75 percent or more of the estimated economic life of the property (new).
4. The estimated residual value at the end of lease term is less than 25 percent of the property's fair value at the inception of the lease (new).
5. The property is special purpose to the lessee, that is, it cannot be used by others except with excessive (uneconomic) cost (new).

All other leases are classified as *operating leases.*

As at present, capitalization results in recording debt at its present value and allocating rental payments to interest and principal. Depreciation of the resultant asset is required "consistent with the lessee's normal depreciation policy." The meaning of the latter term is unclear; as a minimum, straight-line depreciation would be required.

From the standpoint of the lessor. The financing method currently in use by lessors qualifying under *APB Opinion Nos.* 7 and 27 would generally remain in effect. Such leases would be classified as "sales type" when held by a manufacturer or dealer and "direct financing" when held by others (usually financial institutions), and (as at present) unearned income would be amortized to income over the lease term in proportion to the remaining balance of the receivable. However, the proposal does liberalize the criteria to some extent. Whereas *APB Opinion No. 27* requires that the discounted payments must equal normal selling price or fair value, the proposed standard requires only that the lease qualify as a "capital lease," as defined above.

Disclosure.   Since the capitalization criteria would be effective only for leases entered into after December 31, 1975, the proposal provides for disclosing the present value of all existing and subsequently transacted noncapitalized leases (including operating leases) in the balance sheet (on both sides), with the amounts shown short, that is, not included in the totals. With respect to both capitalized and noncapitalized leases, the disclosures presently required by *APB Opinion No. 31*, previously discussed, are generally retained and somewhat expanded. The SEC requirement of providing an alternative net income figure "as if" all noncapitalized finance-type (capital) leases were capitalized retrospectively has not been proposed.

There are many other finer point variations of disclosure between the proposed standard and present practice which need not be covered here since they may be changed before final adoption. The entire text of the Exposure Draft should be consulted.[6]

SUMMARY

The objective of accounting in general, and lease accounting in particular, is to enable users of financial data to better understand events and their impact on the condition of a business entity. Users necessarily view lease accounting not as an argument about technicalities, but rather as a pragmatic decision-making vehicle. This much is elementary; however, the identity of these would-be users, the information they are seeking, and the decisions they want to make are often unclear and sometimes unknown. Nevertheless, users have a common interest in the events that take place and their effects, but the different uses to which they would put this information require that accounting not allow misleading inferences. The

---

[6] As of April 1, 1976 the FASB has not yet acted on the proposed standard.

data that appear in the financial statements must be correct, identifiable, and complete. It is often argued that at some point more information adds no more to understanding and may actually be counterproductive. Since there is no way to anticipate the use to which any accounting data may be put, the balance of reporting swings toward more complete disclosure.

As leasing continues to be discussed and the alternatives in lease accounting continue to be studied, we approach a consensus position on what presentation of the facts is most appropriate. Adoption of the FASB Exposure Draft in present or modified form may put an end to much of this discussion. But use of a facility to generate revenue is acknowledged to be an economic cornerstone. The costs associated with the use of a facility over its useful life can be estimated and matched with revenue as it is earned. One of the most pervasive disputes concerns the speed and regularity with which costs are charged against revenue. Alternatives vary from that of conservatives who would accelerate the charges, claiming that future revenue production is uncertain, to concepts that combine total anticipated costs (including interest on unrecovered capital employed) and tax benefits and allocate them over the life of the facilities on a level basis.[7] The leveling bears witness to the widespread desirability of a level income impact. There is certainly a good argument for using the sinking-fund depreciation method (not permitted in the United States by the SEC) to counterbalance high interest costs in early years and achieve this leveling.

The possibility of implementing a far-reaching change to present accounting practice by bringing several problem areas together for simultaneous resolution has been addressed before and will continue to receive the attention of the accounting profession.

---

[7] Philip L. Defliese, *Should Accountants Capitalize Leases?* (Coopers & Lybrand, 1973).

Chapter 11

Measurement of pension and other labor fringe benefits

*Alan B. Cooper** *
L. G. Weeks†

THE BENEFIT PLAN

Measurement of pension and other labor fringe costs known as employee benefit cost must begin earlier than most financial managers realize. Measurement of these costs should begin far in advance of even the development, much less the negotiation, of a new employee benefit or change in an ongoing plan. Each financial manager needs to ask a very important question: "How much is my function involved in the initial stage of benefit program development?"

Let's address ourselves to programs that result from negotiated contracts with employees represented by some form of labor union. First, prenegotiation involvement by finance is required to establish the areas in which finance can render a valuable service to the industrial relations people charged with arriving at an agreed-upon contract. We are in no way suggesting that finance personnel actually negotiate a contract. This must be left to "industrial relations,"

* Director of Personnel, Armco Enterprise Group (formerly Assistant Controller and Director—General Accounting, Armco Steel Corporation).

† Assistant Vice President–Finance, and Corporate Controller, Armco Steel Corporation.

a field requiring highly specialized managers with years of experience, in order to reach a final agreement successfully. Career financial officers do not generally have the training or expertise required to inject themselves into the line negotiating process. Therefore, we are outlining the role of finance in the negotiation process wherein finance acts in a staff capacity, providing advice and counsel to the negotiating team.

Long before negotiations begin, the financial manager must be fully equipped with facts. For example, you must:

1. Know your current cost of employee benefits.
2. Project your future cost of employee benefits considering scheduled, agreed-upon increases.
3. Keep abreast of trends in contract settlements as they relate to possible changes in your benefits.
4. Assess these trends in light of current cost.
5. Search for alternative benefit plans and financing arrangements.
6. Isolate and accumulate employee benefit administrative costs.
7. Develop a data base large enough so that during the negotiating period the cost of various alternatives can be readily determined.

During the negotiating process, your primary responsibility calls for developing cost data covering the types of improvements or new plans being considered by the negotiating team. Equally important, you will also have a responsibility to search for acceptable alternatives to the type of plan being considered, as well as to seek the least costly financing arrangement for the plans under study. Each plan must be studied by the finance function, giving consideration to items such as tax consequences; vesting dates; reporting requirements; administrative costs; contract clarity; recording problems arising from rules of the FASB, CASB, SEC, and other regulative agencies; and the timing of cost recognition. During these examinations, you can frequently offer suggestions that in no way alter the value of the benefit being sought for the employee, but which reduce the cost to the company.

After a basic agreement is reached, and during the period that the detailed contract language is being written, the financial representative continues to be of valuable assistance to the industrial relations staff. Since you have been present throughout the negotiating process, you will have firsthand knowledge of what was agreed upon. You are thus in a position to be certain that the financing language of the plan meets the intent of the parties. Moreover, since you have been involved throughout this entire period, you will have a more complete comprehension of the technical aspects of the plan and will be better able to administer it from the financial aspect.

Several other important factors have a bearing on the subject of the role of finance in the development of employee benefit plans. First, finance's responsibility to act in a staff capacity to industrial relations is a permanent, ongoing responsibility. You are not fulfilling your obligation in this regard if your services are only offered, or sought, during those periods when negotiations are in process. Second, the finance function will not be the only function that is advising the industrial relations group. It is vital to that group that there is accord with respect to all staff recommendations. Industrial relations is placed in a most difficult position whenever the groups providing advice and counsel cannot arrive at a consensus.

Despite these obvious reasons for early involvement by finance, all too often the measurement of employee benefit cost begins too late. The entire process must take place before a benefit plan can be agreed upon, and must be handled with finance expertise. Yet how often have we all seen a plan developed, given to the employees and made effective—and then the measurement of cost takes place. In addition, we think the finance function in most companies needs to meet two problems head on: the cost of nonproductive labor and the timing of cost recognition.

THE COST OF NONPRODUCTIVE LABOR (TERMINATIONS AND LAYOFFS)

For the purpose of this discussion, we shall identify nonproductive labor as being work which might otherwise have been performed by qualified employees except that they have been temporarily or permanently separated by company action. Layoffs and terminations are cost-affecting actions, but all too often only the apparent cost savings are utilized as the basis for management action. The offsets of cost incursion must be considered.

Termination may be either the direct or indirect result of management action. Very little has been done to evaluate the future costs of recruiting, orientation, training, and so on, of replacements for qualified employees who may be unnecessarily lost. It should be a challenge to the profession to identify the attained skills and knowledge as assets lost on termination. These assets must be repurchased to regain the same operational competence. Also, very little has been done to evaluate the value/cost ratio of productive effort for the employment cost of an individual offset by the cost of termination.

It should be obvious to all managers that the cost of employees on layoff is becoming so excessive that better ways must be found to schedule and utilize our work forces. Not too many years ago, an employee on layoff had no income, save that which was secured through odd jobs, and there was little or no cost effect on the company. Certainly the employee had no employee benefit continuation. This is no longer true. The cost of an employee on layoff today can include unemployment compensation, supplemental unemployment benefits (SUB), pensions, insurance, and vacations.

Not only does this coverage exist during layoff, but the cost of such coverage is also continually increasing. Each time a serious layoff occurs and a company's SUB plan becomes depleted, later contract negotiations generally result in a more expensive SUB plan and corresponding increases in benefit payments. Many contracts call for extension of company-paid insurance (i.e., medical and life) during periods of layoff. Pension plans involve significant costs that have increased substantially in recent years. Pension plans may provide benefits attributable to periods of layoff.

All of these costs are incurred on nonproductive labor, and in the overwhelming majority of cases they are spent for employees who would prefer to be in constructive pursuit of their trade instead of being idled.

We believe each company must recognize that determining the costs of people on layoff is not only necessary, but critical. This analysis should encompass the determination of these costs in prior periods, today, and as forecasted for the future under like conditions. We believe this information will convince management to make a concerted effort to attempt to smooth out these high cost employment cycles.

THE TIMING OF COST RECOGNITION

Over the past 25 years, the ever-increasing cost attributable to layoff may have resulted in a significant distortion in the matching of revenue and expense. The magnitude of this problem has not yet been recognized in its truest sense. However, we believe it has now reached such a proportion that industry must fully consider its impact and develop the alternatives necessary to begin to bring this situation back within its proper perspective.

Let's consider first what is happening. One of the more easily understood examples is in the area of insurance (i.e., hospitalization and surgical coverage), where coverage is continued during layoff at company cost, partially or totally. This cost is generally recognized during the period of layoff, as well as certain costs attributable to other types of insurance, pensions, and vacation expense.

The cost of SUB plans follows this theory, but on a more complex basis. The initial SUB plans provided for accruals generally based upon cents per hour worked by covered employees, and allowed for an extensive period of time to build up a fund before benefits were paid. In the case of the steel industry, the first plan called for 5 cents per hour worked. This rate has now increased to 10.5 cents per hour worked, more than double. How does the plan work insofar as the recognition of cost of benefits?

History shows that high cost occurs during periods of heavy layoff and the lowest cost occurs during periods of full employment. Exhibit 1 covers a period of time depicting one economic cycle. The

EXHIBIT 1

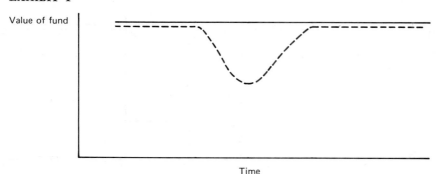

solid lines represent maximum value of the fund that is required by the plan. The dotted line represents the amount actually in the fund and/or owed to the fund by the company. Because of the mechanics of financing most SUB plans, the dotted line also happens to represent one other factor—employment. If we now superimpose upon this chart the phases of the economic cycle, it would appear as shown in Exhibit 2.

EXHIBIT 2

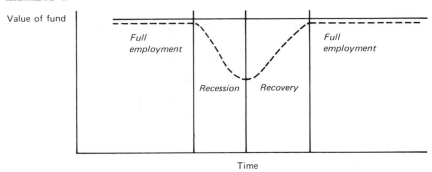

As you can see from Exhibit 2, the fund is fully financed during full employment, is drained during the heavy layoff period, begins to recover as employees are being recalled, and then fully recovers during the subsequent full employment period. If we take this one step further and look at the profit and loss effect, we will find it tracks as shown in Exhibit 3.

EXHIBIT 3

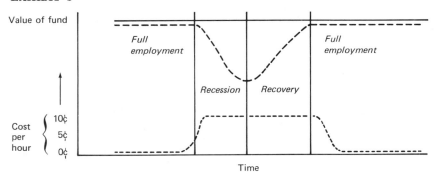

Here we find that the cost per hour is either minimal or zero during periods of full employment, reaches its peak during the heavy layoff periods, and continues at this high level during the recovery period. Granted, this doesn't answer the question of whether or not these costs should be incurred during full employment prior to a layoff or during full employment after a layoff. But it does raise the very obvious question of whether or not the recognition of cost is coming at the right time.

When does a company actually incur the cost of protecting employees through a SUB plan? In our opinion, this protection is undoubtedly provided prior to a layoff. Every pertinent provision in our SUB plan points in that direction. For example, most SUB plans, after inception, provided for lengthy accruals to the plan over periods of time before they provided any entitlement to benefits. In other words, there was a period of time during which the fund was permitted to build up in order to provide benefits for employees on layoff at some subsequent period in time. In addition, these types of plans always have continuous service connotations: employees are not eligible for the benefits until they have been employees for some period of time.

Generally an employee benefit plan provides that employees will be paid benefits for specified periods of time, once they have earned the right to benefits by working for a specified period of time. We conclude that the payment of an employee benefit during layoff is a cost which was incurred *prior* to the layoff, not during or after the layoff. Generally, employee benefit plans are neither financed nor costed on this basis.

We have been studying this problem for several years and have developed the mechanics for one resolution to the problem. A company's SUB plans can be financed under provisions that provide higher costs during full employment and lower costs during recessionary periods. In addition, the plan can be modified to cover other benefit payments for employees on layoff (i.e., insurance premiums). Under this concept the plan truly becomes an "unemployment benefit" plan.

COST ANALYSIS

A discussion of specifics on the measurement of employees' benefit cost is rather difficult because of the wide variety of types of coverage throughout business. This problem is compounded by the fact that there are differences in the degree of employee participation in the cost of the benefits that have been extended. In some cases, the company merely administers a benefit plan which otherwise is paid for entirely by its employees. Other plan provisions range from partial payment by employees to a benefit fully paid for by the company.

The information we are providing regarding our method of measuring these costs relates to employee benefits which are fully paid by the company. Exhibit 4 is a copy of a report prepared by each unit of the company on a monthly basis. On the following page you will find the reporting instructions for such report.

EXHIBIT 4

								MONTH	

ITEM	EMPLOYMENT AND HOURS	CURRENT MONTH			YEAR-TO-DATE		
		Wage A	Salaried B	Total C	Wage D	Salaried E	Total F
1. No. of Employees Rec. Pay					XXXXXX	XXXXXX	XXXXXX
2. No. of Separations					XXXXXX	XXXXXX	XXXXXX
3. No. of Additions					XXXXXX	XXXXXX	XXXXXX
4. Net No. of Employees							
5. Total Hours Worked							
6. Avg. Hrs. Per Week Per Emp.							

EMPLOYMENT COST—WAGE EMPLOYEES	PER MAN-HOUR WORKED		AGGREGATE AMOUNT (WHOLE DOLLARS)	
	Current Month A	Year-To-Date B	Current Month C	Year-To-Date D
7. Straight Time Earnings — Base				
8. " " " — Incentive				
9. " " " — Shift Differential				
10. " " " — Sunday Premium				
11. Cost of Living Adjustment				
12. Overtime Premium				
13. Holiday Provision				
14. Vacation Provision — Regular				
15. " " — Savings and Vacation Plan				
16. " " — Vacation Bonus				
17. Earnings Protection Plan Payments				
18. Allowances				
19. Nonincentive Bonus				
20. Other (Specify)				
21. Total Payroll — Wage Employees				
22. Payroll Taxes — Federal Insurance Contributions Act				
23. " " — Unemployment Compensation-State and Federal				
24. Supplemental Unemployment Benefits				
25. Savings and Vacation Plan (Exclusive of Item 15)				
26. Pensions				
27. Insurance				
28. Workmen's Compensation				
29. Other (Specify)				
30. Total Benefits — Wage Employees				
31. Total Employment Cost — Wage Employees				
EMPLOYMENT COST—SALARIED EMPLOYEES				
32. Total Payroll — Salaried Employees				
33. Total Benefits — Salaried Employees				
34. Total Employment Cost — Salaried Employees				
EMPLOYMENT COST—ALL EMPLOYEES				
35. Total Payroll — All Employees				
36. Total Benefits — All Employees				
37. Total Employment Cost — All Employees				

MEMO—SALARIED EMPLOYEES	EXEMPT A	NON-EXEMPT B	TOTAL C
38. Total Payroll — Year-To-Date (Item 32 Column D)			
39. Hours Worked — Year-To-Date (Item 5 Column E)			

MEMO—WAGE EMPLOYEES	PREMIUM FOR WORK	PAY FOR NOT WORKED	TOTAL
40. Actual Holiday Cost — December Report — Year-To-Date			

EXHIBIT 4 (*continued*)

REPORTING INSTRUCTIONS

ITEM NO.	DETAIL
1	**NO. OF EMPLOYEES RECEIVING PAY**—Wage employees—Include number who received pay for time worked or were on vacation (including SVP) during the month—Exclude Apprentices Special Training. Do not count employees receiving vacation pay while on lay-off. Salaried employees—include number who received pay for time worked, vacation taken (including SVP) or sick leave during the month.
2	**NO. OF SEPARATIONS**—Include quits, discharges, death, retirements, enlisted or drafted for military service, leave of absence, layoffs, termination during probationary period, terminated with severance allowance, illness or injury (including Workmen's Compensation cases).
3	**NO. OF ADDITIONS**—Include newly hired employees and employees reinstated without a break in service such as recall from layoff, return from military service, leave of absence or physical disability.
4	**NET NUMBER OF EMPLOYEES**—Item 1 minus 1/2 of (Items 2 + 3). The purpose of Item 4 is to eliminate the effects of Labor Turnover from Item 1, and thus avoid the deflation of derived Average Hours per Week and Average Weekly Earnings which would otherwise occur.
5	**TOTAL HOURS WORKED**—Wage employees—Represents hours actually worked—Exclude Apprentice Special Training Hours. Non-exempt salaried employees—include hours actually worked, i.e., exclude unworked hours paid for holidays, vacations taken or paid in lieu, sick leave, etc. Exempt salaried employees—include at 173 hours per month plus overtime hours paid for less unworked unpaid hours by reason of employees hired after month-beginning, quit before month-end, etc. Combine non-exempt and exempt salaried.
6	**AVERAGE HOURS PER WEEK PER EMPLOYEE**—Total hours worked (Item 5), divided by Net Number of Employees (Item 4); result divided by number of weeks in the month or year-to-date
7	**STRAIGHT TIME EARNINGS**—**BASE**—Represents payment at Job Class rates including hourly additive for Incentive jobs where standard scales are in effect and at occupational rates where standard scales do not apply (include out of line differentials where applicable) (Exclude Apprentice Special Training Payments).
8	**STRAIGHT TIME EARNINGS**—**INCENTIVE**—Amount earned in excess of base earnings due to favorable performance under incentive plans.
9	**STRAIGHT TIME EARNINGS**—**SHIFT DIFFERENTIAL**—Direct Cost only. Exclude such overtime, Sunday or Holiday premium as may be attributable to basic shift differential pay.
10	**STRAIGHT TIME EARNINGS**—**SUNDAY PREMIUM**—Premium portion only of pay for work performed on Sunday, as such. Include Sunday premium attributable to base pay, incentives, shift differentials, etc. Exclude overtime premium applicable to Sunday work.
11	**COST OF LIVING ADJUSTMENT**—Amount of adjustment applicable to hours worked, overtime premium, premium for holiday work, and reporting allowance.
12	**OVERTIME PREMIUM**—Premium pay for hours worked in excess of the established hours per day or per week under overtime provisions of labor agreements or company policy relating to overtime. Include overtime premium attributable to base pay, incentive, and shift differential.
13	**HOLIDAY PROVISION**—Month—Include that portion of the estimated annual cost of payments to employees for holidays not worked and premium pay for work performed on holiday applicable to the current month. Adjustments made in the current month applicable to prior months should be reported in the year-to-date columns only.
14	**VACATION PROVISION**—**REGULAR**—Month—Include that portion of the estimated annual cost of regular vacations applicable to the current month. Adjustments made in the current month applicable to prior periods should be reported in the year-to-date columns only.
15	**VACATION PROVISION**—**SAVINGS AND VACATION PLAN**—Include that portion of the estimated annual cost of vacation time-off and weeks paid in lieu of vacation time-off under SVP applicable to the current month. Adjustments made in the current month applicable to prior periods should be reported in the year-to-date columns only. Note instructions for Item No. 25.
16	**VACATION PROVISION**—**VACATION BONUS**—Month—Include that portion of the estimated annual vacation bonus applicable to the current month. Adjustments made in the current month should be reported in the year-to-date columns only.
17	**EARNINGS PROTECTION PLAN PAYMENTS**—Month—Include that portion of the current quarter EPP payments applicable to the current month and adjust to actual at the end of each quarter. Adjustments made in the current month applicable to prior periods should be reported in the year-to-date columns only.
18	**ALLOWANCES**—Include allowances paid to employees such as reporting allowance, allowance for participation in military and naval training programs, jury duty, witness pay, funeral leave, rate consent decree and similar actions, severance pay, etc. Do not include special items such as suggestion awards, educational assistance, etc.
19	**NONINCENTIVE BONUS**—Represents 10¢ per hour worked bonus paid to employees with 5 or more years service working on a nonincentive job. (Includes associated overtime premium and premium for holiday worked).
20	**OTHER**—Include in this item all retroactive payments applicable to previous years. When such payments are applicable to prior months of the current year, they should be reported in the year-to-date column opposite the appropriate title (Item 7 through Item 19). Thus, the total reported opposite Item 20 in the year-to-date column will include only payments which apply to previous years. This item is also reserved for reporting any unusual payroll items which may be designated for special handling
21	**TOTAL PAYROLL**—The sum of Items 7 through 20.
22 & 23	**PAYROLL TAXES**—**F.I.C.A. and U.C.**—Include the employer's portion of this contribution equally proportioned over the entire calendar year, i.e., the cents per hour amount should be the same for the first 11 months with December adjusted so that the year-to-date for December will agree with the total accrual for the year.
24	**SUPPLEMENTAL UNEMPLOYMENT BENEFITS**—Include the amount required to maintain maximum financing of the plan reduced by EPP payments (Item No. 17) and compounding. Rate Retention payments and compounding (not to exceed the reduction permitted by the plan), Vacation Bonus payments and compounding (until ACL account is liquidated), compounding of Apprentice Special Training payments.
25	**SAVINGS AND VACATION PLAN**—Include that portion of the estimated annual cost of vacation benefits deferred to retirement, retirement benefits (EVRB), death benefits and benefits payable on discontinuance of employment applicable to the current month. Adjustments made in the current month applicable to prior periods should be reported in the year-to-date columns only.
26	**PENSIONS**—Accrual toward the cost of pension plans and associated expense (include cost of payments to Pension Benefit Guaranty Corporation).
27	**INSURANCE**—Company contribution toward the cost of employee insurance programs (include cost of payments for State Disability Benefit Taxes).
28	**WORKMEN'S COMPENSATION**—Report accruals and/or payments for Workmen's Compensation including insurance and related expenses.
29	**OTHER (SPECIFY)**—This item is reserved for reporting any unusual employee benefits which may be designated for special handling
30	**TOTAL BENEFITS**—**WAGE EMPLOYEES**—The sum of Items 22 through 29.
31	**TOTAL EMPLOYMENT COST**—**WAGE EMPLOYEES**—Total of Items 21 and 30.
32	**TOTAL PAYROLL**—**SALARIED EMPLOYEES**—Accrued payroll for salaried employees consistent with above definitions for wage employees.
33	**TOTAL BENEFITS**—**SALARIED EMPLOYEES**—Employee benefits for salaried employees consistent with above definitions for wage employees.
34	**TOTAL EMPLOYMENT COST**—**SALARIED EMPLOYEES**—Total of Items 32 and 33.
35	**TOTAL PAYROLL**—**ALL EMPLOYEES**—The sum of Items 21 and 32.
36	**TOTAL BENEFITS**—**ALL EMPLOYEES**—Total of Items 30 and 33.
37	**TOTAL EMPLOYMENT COST**—**ALL EMPLOYEES**—Total of Items 35 and 36.
NOTE	Cost per man-hour for Items 7 through 37 is obtained by dividing aggregate amounts reported in Columns C or D by total hours worked Item 5 Columns A or D.
38	**TOTAL PAYROLL YEAR-TO-DATE**—The split of salaried payroll, reported on Item 32 Column D, between Non-exempt Salaried and Exempt Salaried. These data should be entered on each monthly report.
39	**SALARIED HOURS WORKED**—**YEAR-TO-DATE**—The split of the sum of salaried hours reported on Item 5 Column E between Non-exempt Salaried and Exempt Salaried. These data should be entered on each monthly report.
40	**HOLIDAY COST (WAGE EMPLOYEES)**—On the December report show the actual holiday premium cost for the year for holidays worked and the annual amount paid for holidays not worked. Item 40 Column C should equal Item 13 Column D.

We find that the amount of detail developed through this reporting method is necessary for proper management control. The report provides us with an up-to-date status of the cost per man-hour worked for wages as well as employee benefits. This represents a consistent basis for trending cost elements and is invaluable in providing the basic data needed for forecasting. This information also serves as the foundation for cost analysis of proposed changes in employee benefits as well as wages. While the format we use relates to the specific types of benefits in our company, it still serves as a guide for any company with a variety of employee benefits or differing employee benefit/cost relationships. This report can be adapted to fit any enterprise. When it is reviewed on a companywide basis, this report provides an excellent overview of a wide variety of items which require monitoring on the part of management.

The trend picturing the number of employees, both hourly paid and salaried, and the average hours per week provides some insight when related to prior, present, and forecasted volume of the company. It also helps trigger studies judging whether or not additional overtime, as opposed to force addition, is in the best interest of the employee as well as the company. The information supplies indicators of the additions of extra shifts or movement into Sunday production in order to meet demand. It provides a clear indication of the cost of vacations and other wage payments.

The report's benefit portion relates benefit costs to hours worked, while at the same time supplying the total cost of each benefit. This section of the report could, for management convenience, be broken down into far more detail. For example, there are several different types of insurance coverage which have been consolidated into one category. These could be reported by type of insurance coverage.

The biggest shortcoming of this report is the fact that it does not disclose the cost of administering the employee benefit programs. We believe it is extremely important for management to monitor the administrative costs on an ongoing basis. Earlier in this chapter, we pointed out that top priority should be given to the assessment of administrative costs during the developmental stage of any employee benefit plan.

Over the years these administrative costs have grown substantially. We are concerned that too little regard has been given to this cost impact in benefit plan development. To the extent that these costs are excessive, they are certainly nonproductive costs. The one area of the greatest cost savings potential, without altering the value of the benefit to the employee, rests in a reduction of employee benefits administrative cost. We suggest that each and every company isolate its administrative costs and maintain them in a separate cost center. You may even consider consolidating the applicable cost centers in order to determine the total cost impact. It appears to us that American ingenuity needs to be put to work in this area in order to find the methods by which these costs can be reduced. Another shortcoming of the calculated benefit cost is the effect, whether deliberate or not, of policies' timing, funding, reserves, interest assumptions, actuarial assumptions, and so on. Those variables should be evaluated in order to interpret the calculated cost data properly.

FORECASTING

Another management problem we think needs to be addressed relates to the interrelationship of various employee benefits and wages in forecasting total cost increases. One cannot assume that an increase in a basic wage rate of a certain percentage is the total increase in employment cost. There frequently are compounding factors involved in increases of this type. For example, an increase in wages will more often than not result in increases in a variety of employee benefits. Generally, such an increase results in higher vacation payments, higher SUB payments, and higher payments for time off such as military duty and reporting allowances. Such an increase will also frequently affect pension cost, and in some cases may affect insurance cost. At the same time, there are some employee benefits that would not be affected by a general wage increase.

Each item in the total compensation package can have some effect on the other items in the package. Therefore, it is imperative that you prepare a chart reflecting the interrelationship of every item, and from these interrelationships you can determine the total effect of any isolated change. From this chart or table, a company may find that a change in the base rate of 5 percent has a compounding factor equal to some percentage of the basic wage rate changes, say 20 percent on other benefits. You can then interpolate that the 5 percent basic wage change, coupled with a 20 percent compounding factor (or 20 percent × 5 percent = 1 percent), means the proposed basic wage change will result in an effective increase in the wage rate of 6 percent for forecasting purposes.

While a basic wage change may affect pension costs, increases in other portions of the wage package may not. For example, cost of living allowances may not be considered for pension purposes; therefore, in determining a compounding factor for cost of living, it would not include an effect on pension cost. Overtime premium may not affect payments for time off such as jury duty. It would not be expected that premiums for shift differential or Sunday premiums would affect payment for time off. However, overtime premiums will in most cases have some effect on pensions.

If you can see that in a complex wage and benefit package there is an equally complex arrangement as to which wage items and benefit items have a relationship to each other, you can also see how important it is for this relationship to be clearly defined for management control purposes. Moreover, you can also see how imperative it is that a basis of interpolation be maintained if you are to determine quickly the true cost of proposed changes.

IMPACT OF COST ACCOUNTING STANDARDS

As an agency of Congress charged with the responsibility for developing cost accounting standards applicable to negotiated defense contracts, the Cost Accounting Standards Board (CASB) is addressing itself to standards covering employee benefit cost. As these standards are promulgated, they must be adhered to by companies with covered contracts.

To date (July 1975) the CASB has issued one standard which is applicable to costing of employee benefits (Standard 408—Accounting for Costs of Compensated Personnel Absences). The board has also published a proposed standard on the Composition and Measurement of Pension Cost, and is conducting research on the subject of composition, measurement, and allocability of deferred compensation cost.

Initially, it was believed that only those companies with negotiated defense contracts need be concerned with standards promulgated by the CASB. Based on the standards being adopted, we now recognize the necessity of more widespread involvement.

First, companies not now engaged in defense business, but which have products or services that might be sought by government defense agencies, must follow the pronouncements and adopt some standards. This will be necessary in order to be in a ready position to take a future contract.

Second, government agencies other than defense agencies have given notice that their suppliers must utilize CASB standards.

Third, late in 1974 the Renegotiation Board issued a proposed change in its regulations that would have required the use of these standards for all renegotiable sales. This would have resulted in a tremendous increase in the number of companies subject to the standards. The Renegotiation Board subsequently restated this position and required compliance only in those cases where companies were subject to CASB standards.

It is not possible to predict the ultimate full extent of the required use of CASB standards. Individual companies must determine the extent to which they plan to keep abreast of CASB activities. Few companies, however, are really in a position to ignore the standards, because the future requirements are not known.

PENSIONS

It is almost impossible to discuss pension cost so soon after the enactment of the Employee Retirement Income Security Act of 1974 (ERISA), and before the receipt of regulations arising from this act. There are still so many unknown factors relating to every aspect of pension plans. Although much has already been written, most of it is merely a long list of unanswered questions. Volumes will be written once the answers have been supplied.

We interviewed the manager of employee benefit accounting of a large corporation and these are his broad generalizations regarding the present status of pension plans, cost of pensions, and administration.

ERISA is more than a pension law. ERISA encompasses virtually every facet of employee pension and benefit plans with directions, restrictions, and mandates. The law is an entanglement which has left financial executives, attorneys, tax experts, accountants, and investment advisers in a quagmire of ambiguity. ERISA exists complete with deadlines and strict penalties for failure to comply. It is also the greatest source of perplexing questions yet concocted by government regulation. From its birth, experts sardonically nick-named it the "Lawyers' and Accountants' Perpetual Employment Act."

The bounds of ERISA have not yet been comprehended, but one thing is certain—ERISA will be expensive: expensive in the new involvement demanded of financial executives, expensive in man-hours to comprehend the act, expensive in the required changes and related penalities, expensive in administration, expensive in the systems which must monitor the administration, expensive in the additional cash requirement, and expensive in the income state-ment. Financial executives *must* review their new pension responsi-bilities. They must look at controls and assess their adequacy to meet the expanded demands of ERISA. Record retention must be examined in light of the act.

Administrative costs

Underlying these new responsibilities are increasing demands for administrative dollars. Expanded employee records, longer re-tention requirements, and more frequent access to files will greatly increase these costs. We estimate that the additional annual cost to cover this administrative burden will range from $2 to $10 per employee. Forthcoming regulations could further increase this expense. One expert is quoting administrative cost increases of 50 percent to 100 percent and says this is already causing plan termi-nations by some smaller companies.

Accounting, payroll, tax, and personnel staffs are faced with the problem of gathering and maintaining detailed employment records. As a result of ERISA, these records must be retained long after employees terminate employment because they may be rehired and thereby "bridge" their service with that prior to the break. In addi-tion to the longer retention period, the data maintained must be expanded to be able to inform the employees of both their accrued and vested benefits.

ERISA has expanded the scope of involvement into nearly all areas of the organization. Our team working to meet the demands of ERISA is comprised of personnel compensation and benefits, in-dustrial relations, cash management, investment management, legal, systems, employee benefit accounting, and actuarial consultants. It is a team of specialists whose goal is converting the uncertainty

ERISA has spawned into a comprehensible program of pension administration. The role of each member is well defined in a *Financial Executive* article by Ernest L. Hicks, partner, Arthur Young & Company, in which he included the following summary:

Organizing the employer's responses

The makeup of a team to respond to ERISA will differ from employer to employer, and so will the tasks assigned to members representing specific functions. This example shows how a team might be structured and tasks assigned.

Personnel

Review compensation practices; identify and evaluate alternatives.

Review reasonableness of actuarial assumptions with regard to employment matters.

Draft description booklet and other communications with employees.

Draft nonfinancial section of annual report to Secretary of Labor.

Arrange to obtain required actuarial reports and certification.

Tax

Analyze legislation and (as they become available) regulations and interpretations.

Identify aspects of plans that must or may be changed in order to retain qualified status for plans.

Assure that all available tax benefits are obtained.

Consider updating plans for revisions bypassed in prior years.

Finance

Determine impact of necessary changes in plan terms or funding practices on earnings and cash flow.

Review pension cost accounting methods for continued applicability.

Review fund investment policy and performance.

Review reasonableness of actuarial assumptions with regard to financial matters.

Revise financial plans to reflect changes made.

Draft format of financial segments of required reports.

Arrange for required certification of plan financial information.

Legal

Draft required amendments to plans.

Assure conformity with fiduciary standards.

Prepare or revise agreements with fiduciaries.

Obtain annual representations from fiduciaries regarding compliance with standards.

Systems

Revise internal systems to generate data required for new reports.

Operations

Advise as to future operating levels and anticipated changes in numbers and classification of employees.

Only a fortune teller could predict the extent of involvement of these company task forces and the ultimate answers they will find to the myriad of ERISA questions. No doubt even the initial answers may be altered by forthcoming regulations and pronouncements.

Besides confusion, ambiguity, and questions generated by ERISA, a new dimension in the cost of pensions has emerged which is of equal significance in its effect on the financial statements. The new rules on participation, coverage, vesting, and funding will not only be troublesome administratively. For most plans, the new rules will have a significant effect on the corporate profit and loss. Failure to comply with all of ERISA's requirements could prove even more costly in the long run.

Before ERISA, many plans did not provide vesting prior to retirement eligibility. Since all participants must now be vested after no more than 15 years of service, many pension funds incurred a new liability overnight.

Actuarial assumptions must be reviewed and may have to be altered. Of particular concern are the wage progression and inflation assumptions. Historically, the IRS has not permitted deductions for anticipated wage increases. However, under ERISA the emphasis has shifted from the concern for tax deduction to concern for the employee and for providing adequate benefits. Consequently, assumptions must be structured to provide sufficient assets for the payments of benefits when they are due. The effect of inflation comprehended in the pension estimates could have the largest single impact on pension expense.

Another dimension of increased costs occurs in the amortization of the past service liability. *Accounting Principles Board Opinion No. 8* requires the minimum expense to include normal cost plus interest on the past service liability. ERISA requires that in addition to normal cost, the past service liability must be amortized over 30 or 40 years and experience gains and losses amortized over not more than 15 years.

ERISA has created a need for improved communications. One of the major objectives of ERISA is to provide employees with a better understanding of their benefits. This means that in most cases significant improvement in communications will be required to fulfill the responsibilities under the new regulations. Developing a sophisticated communications system to meet this need will require a special expertise. Our company has been providing its employees with a statement of benefits on an annual basis. A typical statement of benefits is depicted in Exhibit 5.

The composite effect of all the new costs of ERISA may place severe strains on the financial health of some companies. Every

EXHIBIT 5
Statement of benefits

IN 1974 YOUR TOTAL EARNINGS WERE $16,429. IN 1975
YOUR REGULAR VACATION ENTITLEMENT IS 4 WEEKS
(PLUS EXTRA VACATION PAY)
AND THERE ARE 9 SCHEDULED HOLIDAYS. IN ADDITION
YOUR BENEFITS AT THE PRESENT TIME ARE AS FOLLOWS:

Family Security Now...for you and your eligible dependents

HOSPITAL-BLUE CROSS

100% OF THE EXPENSES INCURRED FOR SEMI-PRIVATE ROOM ACCOMMODATIONS AND OTHER ELIGIBLE HOSPITAL CHARGES FOR UP TO 730 DAYS.

PHYSICIAN SERVICES-BLUE SHIELD

100% OF THE PREVAILING FEE FOR SERVICES PERFORMED IN THE HOSPITAL AND CERTAIN OTHER ELIGIBLE COVERED PROCEDURES.

MAJOR MEDICAL EXPENSE

80% OF COVERED MEDICAL EXPENSES IN EXCESS OF A CASH DEDUCTIBLE ($50 PER PERSON BUT NOT MORE THAN $100 PER FAMILY PER CALENDAR YEAR).

$250,000 LIFETIME MAXIMUM BENEFIT FOR YOU AND FOR EACH OF YOUR ELIGIBLE DEPENDENTS.

DENTAL EXPENSE

85-100% OF COVERED DENTAL EXPENSE - NO CASH DEDUCTIBLE MAXIMUM BENEFIT
$750 FOR YOU AND FOR EACH OF YOUR ELIGIBLE DEPENDENTS PER CALENDAR YEAR ON DENTAL SERVICES AND SUPPLIES EXCLUDING ORTHODONTICS.
$500 MAXIMUM BENEFITS PER INDIVIDUAL PER CALENDAR YEAR FOR ORTHODONTICS.

VISION CARE EXPENSE

85% OF COVERED VISION CARE EXPENSE FOR EXAMINATIONS, EYE GLASS LENSES AND FRAMES AND CONTACT LENSES.
$100 MAXIMUM BENEFIT FOR YOU AND FOR EACH OF YOUR ELIGIBLE DEPENDENTS PER CALENDAR YEAR.

INCOME PROTECTION

IF YOU BECOME DISABLED DUE TO SICKNESS OR INJURY AND ARE UNABLE TO WORK, YOU WILL BE ELIGIBLE TO RECEIVE:
FULL PAY, INCLUDING BONUS, FOR 3 MONTHS AND FULL BASE PAY FOR AN ADDITIONAL 7.0 MONTH(S).

$624 PER MONTH FOR 2.0 MONTH(S), YOUR SICKNESS AND ACCIDENT BENEFIT, INCLUSIVE OF SOCIAL SECURITY DISABILITY BENEFITS.
IF YOUR DISABILITY CONTINUES AND IS PERMANENT, YOU WILL RECEIVE LONG TERM DISABILITY BENEFITS OF:

$725 PER MONTH UNTIL AGE 62.
$362 PER MONTH AFTER AGE 62.

THESE LONG TERM DISABILITY BENEFITS INCLUDE ANY COMPANY-PROVIDED REGULAR OR SPECIAL PENSION. HOSPITAL, PHYSICIAN SERVICES AND MAJOR MEDICAL EXPENSE BENEFITS WILL BE EXTENDED TO YOU AND YOUR ELIGIBLE DEPENDENTS DURING DISABILITY.

$316 SOCIAL SECURITY DISABILITY BENEFITS IF FULLY COVERED AT MAXIMUM EARNING RATES. (IN ADDITION TO THE ABOVE COMPANY-PROVIDED BENEFITS).
YOU WILL ALSO RECEIVE THE TOTAL VALUE OF THE THRIFT PLAN UPON RETIREMENT DUE TO DISABILITY.

DEATH BENEFITS

IN CASE OF YOUR DEATH WHILE AN ACTIVE EMPLOYEE YOUR CURRENT PROTECTION INCLUDES:

$39,000 GROUP LIFE INSURANCE.

$4,676 TOTAL VALUE OF THRIFT PLAN IS PAYABLE UPON YOUR DEATH.

$255 SOCIAL SECURITY DEATH BENEFIT

$43,931 TOTAL LUMP SUM

ADDITIONAL ACCIDENTAL DEATH BENEFITS

$25,000 ACCIDENTAL DEATH AND DISMEMBERMENT INSURANCE

MONTHLY FAMILY INCOME BENEFITS

$573 MONTHLY MAXIMUM BENEFIT FROM SOCIAL SECURITY FOR A FAMILY WITH CHILDREN UNDER AGE 18.

$158 THIS AMOUNT WILL BE PAID TO YOUR SURVIVING SPOUSE UNTIL ELIGIBLE FOR WIDOW OR WIDOWER BENEFITS, AT WHICH TIME IT WILL BE REDUCED BY 50% OF THE SOCIAL SECURITY WIDOW OR WIDOWER BENEFIT.

$50 WILL BE PAID TO YOUR SURVIVING SPOUSE FOR LIFE FOLLOWING THE REDUCTION.

$316 SOCIAL SECURITY BENEFITS TO YOUR SURVIVING SPOUSE AT AGE 65 IF FULLY INSURED AT MAXIMUM EARNINGS RATES. (REDUCED AMOUNTS ARE AVAILABLE STARTING AT AGE 60)

HOSPITAL, PHYSICIAN SERVICES AND MAJOR MEDICAL EXPENSE BENEFITS EXTENDED TO YOUR SPOUSE AND ELIGIBLE DEPENDENTS UNTIL SPOUSE REMARRIES.

DEPENDENT DEATH BENEFITS

$3,000 DEPENDENT DEATH BENEFIT WILL BE PAID TO YOU IN THE EVENT OF YOUR SPOUSE'S DEATH.

$1,000 WILL BE PAID TO YOU IN THE EVENT OF THE DEATH OF A DEPENDENT CHILD.

$4,676 IS THE TOTAL VALUE OF YOUR THRIFT PLAN, BASED ON MARKET VALUE OF THE SECURITIES 12/31/74.

Because of the wide variety of benefits that are payable in the event of your death it's a good idea to make sure that *all* your beneficiary designations are up to date.

EXHIBIT 5 (*continued*)

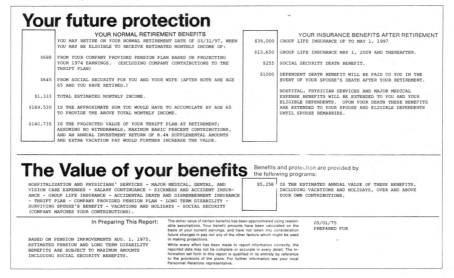

company is trying to answer the question: "How do we cope with all of ERISA's ramifications?" Answers in the form of regulations must be the starting point. We must look to the FASB, AICPA, and Washington for guidance and interpretation.

Our concern, however, is in the timeliness of such pronouncements. Systems design doesn't result from the push of a computer switch. Time will be required in order to develop and design the systems so that information can be provided in the many forms required. We need help to meet our obligations under ERISA, and we also need understanding. The lawmakers must realize our plight and move quickly, yet thoroughly, to resolve the growing list of questions. The long-term effects of ERISA won't be realized fully for years.

We believe ERISA may have turned the labor contract negotiating table into a new arena. With the enormous financial responsibilities ERISA has imposed, improvements in the wages which affect pensions or pension plans now must be carefully evaluated to determine their true cost impact. Of particular concern are wage increases and cost of living adjustments which will further escalate the inflation factors in pension funding. In any event, ERISA means a greater portion of the cost of each succeeding contract settlement will be in the form of pension cost.

All companies with a pension plan should currently have ERISA research as a top priority. We recommend the June 1975 and July 1975 issues of the *Financial Executive* as excellent resource material. These entire issues are devoted to pensions, with separate articles covering each important aspect of ERISA.

THE AUDIT

Employee benefit costs are increasing at a rate most people consider astounding. We have discussed a number of concerns and hopefully have offered food for thought. We believe there is one more important management tool required to adequately control employee benefit cost. That is an audit approach.

We can safely say that if you have multiunits in your company, have decentralized the eligibility determination or the payment points, and are not auditing for consistent application, you are absorbing excessive cost for your employee benefit program. Each and every employee benefit plan is highly technical, very complex, and subject to interpretation. Decentralization will always result in more than one interpreter. Only through an audit can you determine what interpretations have been made and how the plans are being applied, along with the resulting cost of the benefits.

The development of a uniform audit program is an absolute must for cost control. Any management that fails to do so is failing to fulfill its role as managers. While this point is being made from the standpoint of effect on the company, our comment should not be construed to mean that we do not share an equal concern for the rights of the employee. The employee is fully entitled to whatever benefits have been agreed upon. Through the audits you not only control the cost of benefits but you also assure equal treatment of all employees and fairness in the application of the provisions of the benefit plan.

Chapter 12

Accounting for research and development costs

*Vincent N. Marafino**
G. Michael Crooch†

Recognizing the significance of research and development expenditures and the alternative accounting and reporting practices that were being followed, the Financial Accounting Standards Board released *Statement of Financial Accounting Standards No. 2*, "Accounting for Research and Development Costs," in October 1974. This *Statement* specifies (1) the activities to be identified as research and development for financial accounting and reporting purposes, (2) the elements of costs to be identified with research and development activities, (3) the accounting for research and development costs, and (4) the financial statement disclosures related to research and development costs. On the surface, at least, the accounting for research and development is a closed question with its proper accounting and reporting fully delineated; however, many questions remain unanswered concerning the *Statement* and various problems that may result from its application.

This chapter discusses research and development in three sections. The first section describes the requirements of *Statement No. 2* and *Interpretations 4, 5,* and *6* which deal with the applicability of

---

* Vice President & Controller, Lockheed Aircraft Corporation.
† Oklahoma State University.

Standard No. 2 to business combinations accounted for by the purchase method, to enterprises in the development stage, and to computer software. The second section discusses the theoretical and practical problems which underlie the accounting and reporting for research and development as required by the Standard. The third section contains a critique of some of the conclusions reached in *Statement No. 2*.

STANDARD NO. 2—ACCOUNTING FOR
RESEARCH AND DEVELOPMENT COSTS

Standard No. 2 requires only one sentence to specify the proper accounting for research and development costs. "All research and development costs encompassed by this Statement shall be charged to expense when incurred."[1] The remainder of the *Statement* specifies research and development activities, elements of research and development costs, and financial statement disclosures related to research and development. This section outlines and demonstrates the *Statement's* requirements.

Applicability

Statement No. 2 does not specifically identify the financial reporting situations to which it is applicable. However, the applicability of all FASB *Statements* and *Interpretations* has been discussed and decided by both the American Institute of Certified Public Accountants (AICPA) and the Securities and Exchange Commission (SEC). Rule 203 of the Code of Professional Ethics of the AICPA says, in part, that no member shall express an opinion that financial statements are presented in conformity with generally accepted accounting principles if such statements contain any departure from an accounting principle promulgated by the body designated by Council to establish such principles which has a material effect on the statements taken as a whole unless the member can demonstrate that due to the unusual circumstances the financial statements would have been misleading.[2] In the spring of 1973, the Council of the AICPA designated the FASB as the body to establish accounting principles pursuant to Rule 203. As a

[1] *Statement of Financial Accounting Standards No. 2,* "Accounting for Research and Development Costs," par. 12.

[2] Rule 203, Revised Code of Professional Ethics.

result, all externally distributed financial statements which purport to report the results of operations in conformity with generally accepted accounting principles fall within the purview of *Statement No. 2.*

The SEC sets forth in *Accounting Series Release No. 150* that the pronouncements of the FASB will be considered to constitute substantial authoritative support for accounting and reporting procedures and practices used in preparing financial statements to be filed with the Commission. Further, in SEC *Release 33-5541* the SEC indicated that Regulation S-X will be amended to eliminate differences between the SEC requirements for accounting for research and development costs and those of *Statement No. 2.* When Regulation S-X is so amended all filings with the SEC must conform to *Statement No. 2.*

Items specifically excluded

Two categories of research and development are specifically excluded from the scope of the *Statement.* They are:

1. Research and development costs (including reimbursable indirect costs) incurred for others under a contractual agreement, and
2. Costs incurred in activities unique to the extractive industries such as prospecting, acquisition of mineral rights, drilling, mining, and so on.

Reimbursable research and development costs were excluded from the *Statement* because the Board felt these costs should be accounted for in the same manner as other contractual arrangements. Any change in the proper accounting for contracts should not come on a piecemeal basis but should be the subject of a full investigation. The same philosophy applies to activities unique to the extractive industries. These activities and costs were believed sufficiently different from the research and development considered in the *Statement* that they required separate treatment by the Board.

Official pronouncements amended by the Statement

Two *APB Opinions* are amended by the *Statement.* Research and development cost are removed from the scope of *APB Opinion*

No. 17, "Intangible Assets," and paragraph 13 of *APB Opinion No. 22,* "Disclosure of Accounting Policies," is amended to remove research and development and its basis of amortization as an example of those disclosures "commonly required" with respect to accounting policies.

Research and development defined

Research and development may have as many definitions as there are people attempting to define it. Consequently, one of the most difficult tasks faced by the Board was that of defining research and development in a manner which was both mutually exclusive and exhaustive. The task proved impossible. As a result, the Board adopted a guidelines approach which includes both definitions of research and development and specific examples of items included and excluded from the scope of the *Statement.* Using this approach, the *Statement* defines research and development as follows:

> *a.* *Research* is planned search or critical investigation aimed at discovery of new knowledge with the hope that such knowledge will be useful in developing a new product or service or a new process or technique or in bringing about a significant improvement to an existing product or process.
>
> *b.* *Development* is the translation of research findings or other knowledge into a plan or design for a new product or process or for a significant improvement to an existing product or process whether intended for sale or use. It includes the conceptual formulation, designing, and testing of product alternatives, construction of prototypes, and operation of pilot plants. It does not include routine or periodic alterations to existing products, production lines, manufacturing processes, and other on-going operations even though those alterations may represent improvements and it does not include market research or market testing activities.

The *Statement* then goes on to list examples of those items which are and are not research and development. Those items which *are* research and development include:

1. Laboratory research aimed at discovery of new knowledge.
2. Searching for applications of new research findings or other knowledge.

3. Conceptual formulation and design of possible product or process alternatives.
4. Testing in search for or evaluation of product or process alternatives.
5. Modification of the formulation or design of a product or process.
6. Design, construction, and testing of pre-production prototypes and models.
7. Design of tools, jigs, molds, and dies involving new technology.
8. Design, construction, and operation of a pilot plant that is not of a scale economically feasible to the enterprise for commercial production.
9. Engineering activity required to advance the design of a product to the point that it meets specific functional and economic requirements and is ready for manufacture.

Those items which *are not* research and development include:

1. Engineering follow-through in an early phase of commercial production.
2. Quality control during commercial production including routine testing of products.
3. Trouble-shooting in connection with breakdowns during commercial production.
4. Routine, ongoing efforts to define, enrich, or otherwise improve upon the qualities of an existing product.
5. Adaptation of an existing capability to a particular requirement or customer's need as part of a continuing commercial activity.
6. Seasonal or other periodic design changes to existing products.
7. Routine design of tools, jigs, molds, and dies.
8. Activity, including design and construction engineering, related to the construction, relocation, rearrangement, or start-up of facilities or equipment other than (1) pilot plants (see paragraph 9[h] and (2) facilities or equipment whose sole use is for a particular research and development project (see paragraph 11[a]).
9. Legal work in connection with patent applications or litigation, and the sale or licensing of patents.

Clearly, even with these lengthy definitions and extensive lists of examples, the determination of whether a particular activity is or is not a research and development activity will continue to require professional judgment. A given activity might be research and development in one instance and not in another. Each activity must be evaluated in light of the particular surrounding circumstances. Notice, also, that the definition of development includes items being developed for *sale or use*. The item of concern need not be intended for sale to an outside party to qualify within the *Statement's* definition of research and development. The second section discusses some problems with applying the *Statement's* definition of research and development.

Costs included in research and development

The *Statement* basically divides the costs identified with research and development activities into those items which have alternative uses and those which do not. Materials, equipment, facilities, and intangibles purchased from others that *have* alternative future uses (whether in other research and development projects or otherwise) should be capitalized and charged to research and development as they are consumed, depreciated, or amortized following existing generally accepted accounting principles. Materials, equipment, facilities, or intangibles purchased from others which *do not have* alternative uses should be expensed as incurred.[3] The cost of wages, salaries, other related personnel costs, and services performed by others (known as contract services) must be expensed through research and development as incurred. Also, research and development must contain "a reasonable allocation of indirect costs" but should not include general and administrative costs not clearly related to research and development.

Disclosure

The *Statement* requires only a minimum disclosure in financial statements. "Disclosure shall be made in the financial statements of the total research and development costs charged to expense in each period for which an income statement is presented."[4] On the other hand, government-regulated companies may be required to

---

[3] Note that this requirement changes the accounting for research and development outlined in *APB Opinion No. 17*.

[4] FASB *Statement of Financial Accounting Standards No. 2*, par. 13.

capitalize and amortize certain research and development costs for rate-making purposes and financial accounting purposes in accordance with the Addendum to *APB Opinion No. 2,* "Accounting for the 'Investment Credit.'" In these regulated instances, companies must disclose the following additional information concerning research and development costs:

    a. Accounting policy, including basis for amortization.

    b. Total research and development costs incurred in each period for which an income statement is presented and the amount of those costs that has been capitalized or deferred in each period.[5]

None of these disclosures are required for periods prior to the effective date of the *Statement,* although such disclosures are encouraged. However, when financial information for periods before the effective date are presented, they must be restated to reflect the prior period adjustment as explained in the next paragraph.

Effective date and transition

Statement No. 2 applies to all periods beginning on or after January 1, 1975, although earlier application was encouraged. Transition from previously applied methods of accounting for research and development to the requirements of *Statement No. 2* must include the following items:

1. The requirements of *Statement No. 2* shall be applied retroactively as a prior period adjustment as described by *APB Opinion No. 9.*
2. Financial summaries or statements for periods beginning prior to January 1, 1975, must be restated to reflect the prior period adjustment if these summaries or statements are presented.
3. The prior period adjustment must be made net of applicable tax effects.
4. In the period of the change, the company must disclose—
    a. The nature of the change.
    b. In each period presented, the effect of the change on—
        (1) Income before extraordinary items.
        (2) Net income.
        (3) Related per share amounts.

---

[5] *Ibid.,* par. 14.

FASB Interpretation No. 4—Applicability of FASB Statement No. 2 to business combinations accounted for by the purchase method

Accounting Principles Board Opinion No. 16 requires that "all identifiable assets acquired, either individually or by type, and liabilities assumed in a business combination, *whether or not shown on the financial statements of the acquired company,* should be assigned a portion of the costs of the acquired company, normally equal to their fair values at date of acquisition" (emphasis added).[6] *Statement No. 2* specifically states in paragraph 34 that its provisions are not intended to alter the conclusions of *APB Opinion No. 16* with regard to the allocation of cost to assets acquired in a business combination accounted for as a purchase. As a result of these requirements, any portion of the purchase price of an acquired company which is attributable to research and development should be recorded on the books of the acquiring company at its fair value. This requirement, itself, does not cause too much difficulty other than that caused by the problem of valuing an intangible which was a "hidden asset" on the books of the acquired company. The problem arises with determining the disposition of the acquired research and development after it has been valued. Under *APB Opinion No. 17,* "Intangible Assets," an intangible must be amortized by systematic charges to income over the period believed to be benefited. But *Statement No. 2* specifically excludes from the scope of *APB Opinion No. 17* all costs included within the scope of the *Statement.* The question then becomes: What should be the disposition of the capitalized research and development?

FASB *Interpretation No. 4* was issued to answer that question and essentially extends the logic of *Statement No. 2* to research and development acquired in a business combination accounted for as a purchase. That is, costs allocated to assets to be used in research and development activities which have no alternative use must be expensed at the date of consummation of the combination. Costs allocated to assets to be used in research and development activities which do have alternative uses must be capitalized and amortized to research and development on a basis consistent with generally accepted accounting principles. Therefore, the accounting for the cost of an asset to be used in research and development

---

[6] *Accounting Principles Board Opinion No. 16,* par. 87.

is the same under *Statement No. 2* whether the item is purchased individually, as part of a group of assets, or as part of a business combination accounted for as a purchase.

Application of *Interpretation No. 4* to business combinations accounted for as a purchase is:

1. Required for combinations initiated after March 31, 1975.
2. Encouraged but not required for combinations initiated prior to April 1, 1975, and consummated after March 31, 1975, and may be applied selectively to these combinations.
3. Encouraged but not required for combinations initiated and consummated prior to April 1, 1975, but if an enterprise decides to apply the interpretation, it must be applied retroactively as a prior period adjustment to *all* combinations accounted for as a purchase and consummated prior to April 1, 1975.

FASB Interpretation No. 5—Applicability of FASB Statement No. 2 to development stage enterprises

A question arose subsequent to *Statement No. 2's* issuance as to whether the *Statement* applies to the reports of development stage companies.[7] The problem exists because some development stage companies have adopted accounting and reporting practices which do not conform with those of operating companies. For example, some development stage companies defer preoperating costs (sometimes including general and administrative costs and interest cost), do not assign dollar values to shares issued for other than cash, and offset revenue against deferred costs. Further, some development stage companies have adopted reporting formats which do not include statements of financial position, changes in financial position, and operating results prepared in accordance with generally accepted accounting principles. The Board concluded in *Interpretation No. 5* that the requirements of *Statement No. 2* apply to the accounting and reporting by development stage

_____

[7] In June 1975 the FASB issued *Statement No. 7*, "Accounting and Reporting by Development Stage Companies," which requires enterprises that are defined as being in the development stage to present financial position, changes in financial position, and results of operations in conformity with the generally accepted accounting principles that apply to operating enterprises, with required additional disclosures. The special reporting formats described in *FASB Interpretation No. 5* are no longer acceptable.

companies only if the financial reports of the companies present financial position, changes in financial position, and operating results in conformity with generally accepted accounting principles. *Statement No. 2* also applies if the development stage company's results are included by consolidation or the equity method in the statements of a company which issues reports in conformity with generally accepted accounting principles. *Statement No. 2* does not apply to development stage companies which issue special statements or otherwise do not purport to report in accordance with generally accepted accounting principles. However, if the development stage company adopts a format in conformity with generally accepted accounting principles then the requirements of *Statement No. 2* must be applied retroactively as a prior period adjustment in conformity with *APB Opinion No. 9*.

Interpretation No. 5 became effective March 31, 1975, for fiscal years beginning on or after January 1, 1975, although earlier application was encouraged.

FASB Interpretation No. 6—Applicability of FASB Statement No. 2 to computer software

Paragraph 8(a) of *Statement No. 2* defines development in part as follows: "*Development* is the translation of research findings or other knowledge into a plan or design for a new product or process or for a significant improvement to an existing product or process whether intended *for sale or use*" (emphasis added).[8] By its wording, the *Statement* does not exclude a research and development project if it is being created for internal use only and not intended for sale as such. Unfortunately, the computer software example used to illustrate whether the creation of a software package was a research and development activity contained only efforts to create a new or higher level package which fit the guidelines of the *Statement* and *was intended for sale*. Some accountants argued that since the example did not encompass software packages that were being created for internal use only, the Board did not consider their creation a research and development activity. The solution of this question has a great impact on many companies' financial statements. Consider the cost, for example, of creating the software package used by airlines for reservations or the cost of an inventory

---
[8] *Statement No. 2*, par. 8(b).

control package for a large manufacturing firm. Expensing these items in accordance with the *Statement* could have significant effects on the financial statements of some large companies. As a result of these problems the Board issued FASB *Interpretation No. 6* which contains the following points concerning the applicability of *Statement No. 2* to computer software:

1. Costs incurred to acquire or develop computer software used in selling and administrative activities are not research and development costs. (Airline reservation systems and management information systems development are specifically defined as selling and administrative activities.)
2. Costs to develop software internally for research and development activities are research and development costs.
3. If software is developed internally in an effort to create a new or significantly improved product or process or if the internally developed software itself is a marketable product or process, costs incurred for conceptual formulation or the translation of knowledge into a design would be research and development costs.
4. Accounting for the cost of developing computer software under contractual arrangement is beyond the scope of *Statement No. 2*.
5. Costs to purchase or lease software developed by others are not research and development costs if the software is not used in research and development activities.

The requirements of the *Interpretation* became effective for fiscal periods beginning on or after April 1, 1975, although earlier application was encouraged.

THEORETICAL AND PRACTICAL PROBLEMS OF APPLYING *STATEMENT NO. 2*

Statements of Financial Accounting Standards are not intended to be step-by-step rulebooks of the accounting and reporting of the subject discussed. Instead, these *Statements* are written to be guides to proper accounting and reporting, and the application of these Standards will require continual interpretation by corporate and public accountants. As new problems of application arise, each must be evaluated in light of the intended purpose and stated requirements of the *Statement*. *Statement No. 2* has not been required accounting and reporting for a sufficient length of time for a great number of problems to arise; however, the problems which have arisen point out the difficulty of interpreting and applying what might be thought of as a relatively simple requirement. The following paragraphs discuss some of the interpretative problems which have arisen concerning *Statement No. 2.*

What is an alternative use?

Paragraph 11(a) of the *Statement* requires that the costs of materials, equipment, or facilities that are acquired or constructed for research and development activities and that have alternative uses must be capitalized as tangible assets and amortized to research and development on the basis of existing generally accepted accounting principles. On the other hand, materials, equipment, or constructed facilities acquired for research and development purposes that do not have alternative uses must be expensed in the year acquired or constructed. Two problems arise from this requirement. First, what characteristics constitute an alternative use and second, once the item is determined to have an alternative use, what dollar amount must be capitalized?

The *Statement* gives little or no help in determining what is to be considered an alternative use. As a result, each time a new category of item is acquired for research and development purposes a decision must be made as to whether the item does or does not have an alternative use and separate economic value. A strict interpretation of the *Statement* results in the determination that *any* alternative use or separate economic value means the item should be capitalized and amortized to the project over time. Such interpretations, however, would in many cases violate the spirit of the *Statement.* For example, a nominal scrap value is a separate use and economic value but obviously does not fit the intention of the Board. On the other hand, not so clear cases arise when special-purpose items are purchased from outside suppliers. Some have argued that the fact that the item has a sales price (it must have since the company just purchased the item) means that there is a market for the item and an alternative use exists—namely the alternative of a sale. The solution here is not yet settled. Apparently, if the item in fact has a market value and could be sold, then an alternative use and economic value exists. However, evidence of a *past sale* does not mean that other parties would be willing to buy the item. Therefore, the authors believe that only if verifiable evidence exists that *outside parties* are willing to buy the item should the item be capitalized and amortized. Otherwise, evidence of a sale does not constitute an alternative use.[9]

On the other hand, the proper accounting treatment of a research and development item which has an alternative use but whose value in that alternative use is less (or conceivably more) than the original cost is not entirely clear. Suppose, for example, that a research and development item cost $100,000 and, with only slight modification, could be used in production process A; however, items normally purchased for that particular use in process A only cost $50,000. The item obviously has an alternative use. The only question is the proper amount to capitalize and amortize. Again, the *Statement* does not consider such a problem. If literally interpreted, the *Statement* would only allow either complete expensing or complete capitalization. The more theoretically correct third alternative of part-expensing, part-capitalization is not considered. The authors believe that if the value of the item in the alternative use is material, verifiable, and materially different from its cost, the value of the item in the alternative use is the proper value to capitalize. The remaining cost should be expensed in the period of acquisition. This approach, we believe, best recognizes the possible future benefits which could be derived from the item and expenses that portion of the item's cost which is currently attributable to the research and development project.

Research and development partially covered by contractual agreement

Paragraph 2 of *Statement No. 2* states that "accounting for the costs of research and development activities conducted for others under a contractual arrangement is a part of accounting for contracts in general and is beyond the scope of this Statement."[10] This straightforward requirement causes little difficulty until a situation arises where only part of a significant development project is covered by a contractual agreement. Perhaps an example will

---

[9] At least one international public accounting firm has determined that the ability to sell does not constitute an alternative use. Should this position be taken by other firms, then generally accepted accounting principles may not allow this alternative.

[10] *Statement No. 2*, par. 2.

clarify the difficulty. Suppose your firm has an operational aircraft that it has been marketing for several months. A prospective buyer approaches you and indicates that he or she would be willing to buy an aircraft if you would add an additional cargo door. You agree to do so and spend $25 million developing the cargo door. Further, you believe the additional cargo door is a significant improvement in the aircraft and will generate additional sales beyond that to the prospective buyer. As a result, you decide that only 10 percent if any, of the development cost should be included in the contract. The question then is: How much, if any, of the cost of developing the cargo door for the aircraft is chargeable to the cost of the aircraft sold to the prospective buyer and how much is development as defined by *Statement No. 2* and should be expensed in the year incurred?

No clear solution to the difficulty exists short of an FASB *Interpretation*. Clearly (assuming the contract is properly worded) a portion of the development cost falls under the contractual agreement section of the *Statement* and is a product cost, and that portion not covered by the contract should be expensed as incurred. However, unless the contract specifically states the portion of the development costs which are includible in the sales price of the aircraft sold, the determination of the percentage of development cost to be capitalized becomes arbitrary and subject to abuse— clearly a situation which violates the spirit of *Statement No. 2*. Therefore, the authors believe that, in the absence of a specific statement as to the portion of research and development covered by the contract, the entire amount of the development costs incurred should be considered to fall within the scope of *Statement No. 2* and be expensed as incurred.

Transition and the prior period adjustment

The *Statement* requires that any comparative statements presented for periods prior to the effective date be restated to reflect the *Statement's* requirements and requires that all research and development be accounted for as an expense through a prior period adjustment on a net-of-tax basis. The following example illustrates the procedures necessary to satisfy this requirement.

Suppose Firm X has engaged in research and development activities for only the past three years and has followed the procedure of capitalizing all research and development expenditures.[11] To calculate the required prior period adjustment one must find the net change (net of tax) that would have occurred if instead of capitalizing and amortizing research and development, the company had expensed research and development in the year incurred. Table 1 demonstrates the calculation.

TABLE 1

Year 4 calculation of the prior period adjustment for research and development of years 1, 2, 3

Description	Effect on income—increase (decrease)		
	Year 1	Year 2	Year 3
Research and development originally capitalized, now expensed.	$(50,000)	$(75,000)	$(100,000)
Add amounts already expensed:			
Amortization* Year 1	5,000	5,000	5,000
Amortization* Year 2		7,500	7,500
Amortization* Year 3			10,000
Net change before tax	$(45,000)	$(62,500)	$ (77,500)
Tax effect (48% marginal rate)	21,600	30,000	37,200
Prior Period Adjustment, After Tax	$(23,400)	$(32,500)	$ (40,300)

* Assumes straight-line amortization over ten years with no salvage and a full year's amortization in year acquired.

The calculation points out that the prior period adjustment is the net-of-tax amount that results from expensing all capitalized research and development, after allowing for amounts already expensed. In Year 2, for example, the $75,000 research and development cost was capitalized but is now expensed. However, $12,500 amortization ($5,000 in Year 1 and $7,500 in Year 2) was actually taken in Year 2. Therefore, the net change before tax in Year 2 income is $75,000 less $12,500, or $62,500. After tax considerations, the prior period adjustment for Year 2 is $32,500.

The actual entry to book the adjustment is:

	Debit	Credit
Retained Earnings.	96,200	
Deferred Tax Credit	88,800	
Deferred R&D Costs		185,000

The Retained Earnings adjustment is the decrease in net income that would have occurred if research and development had been

---

[11] The example assumes that the firm's past definition of research and development coincides with the current FASB definition. Should this not be the case, additional adjustments would be required to be sure that the costs subject to the prior period adjustment conform to the FASB definition.

expensed instead of capitalized. The Deferred Tax Credit arose because research and development expenditures are deductible in the year incurred for tax purposes and the company's policy of capitalization created a Deferred Tax Credit. Since the research and development is no longer capitalized, the Deferred Tax Credit no longer exists. Of course, the credit to Deferred Research and Development Costs merely writes off the unamortized amount of capitalized research and development.

CRITIQUE

If anything had been learned about the formulation of accounting policy in the last 30 years, it is that no statement of accounting policy is going to please all interested parties. Each special interest group feels that its best interests are those which should be protected. *Statement No. 2* will probably prove to be no exception to the rule. Already certain criticisms have been aimed at the *Statement*. The purpose of this section is to voice these criticisms and examine the Board's justification for its decisions.

Is research and development never an asset?

Although many definitions of an asset have been suggested, almost all contain some reference to items having future benefit to the entity.[12] To the degree that research and development expenditures create new products or services, improve old products or services, or reduce future operating costs, they are expected to benefit future periods and not just the current period. If, in fact, future periods are to be benefited, then the results of research and development activities are an asset to the firm, or an increase in existing assets, or an increase in the value of the firm as a whole.[13] Since it is ridiculous to assume that industry would invest resources in research and development projects which do not contain at least the *expectation* of future benefits, the critical question appears to be, "When are the expected future benefits from research and development expenditures of sufficient probability to justify their entrance on the balance sheet as assets?" The answer put forth by

---

[12] For a review of these definitions see FASB *Exposure Draft* "Accounting for Research and Development and Similar Costs," Appendix B.

[13] Eldon S. Hendriksen, *Accounting Theory,* rev. ed. (Homewood, Ill.: Richard D. Irwin, Inc., 1970), p. 431.

the FASB in *Statement No. 2* is "Never." That is, by requiring that all research and development costs be expensed in the year of their incurrence the Board implies that the future benefits to be derived from research and development activities are never sufficiently probable to justify asset status. The Board based this decision on the following reasons:[14]

1. *Uncertainty of future benefits.* The failure rate for research and development projects is very high. One research study indicates that an average of less than 2 percent of all new product ideas and less than 15 percent of product development projects are commercially successful.
2. *Lack of causal relationship between expenditures and benefits.* Empirical research can find no direct relationship between research and development expenditures and specific future revenues.
3. *Accounting recognition of economic resources.* Current financial statements do not recognize all economic resources of the firm, and no definitive criteria have been established for choosing those to be recognized. Two criteria, measurability and exchangeability, have been suggested for this choice. However, the Board concluded that although the future benefits of a research and development project may be foreseen, they cannot be measured with a reasonable degree of certainty. Further, the Board did not consider exchangeability as a criterion and neither accepted nor rejected its use.
4. *Expense recognition and matching.* Since no causal relationship can be found between research and development expenditures and future revenues and because so many research and development projects fail, the Board believed that matching—when used to refer to the process of recognizing costs as expenses on any sort of cause-and-effect basis—cannot be applied to research and development costs.
5. *Usefulness of resulting information.* The Board believed (for several reasons) that capitalization of research and development expenditures does not enhance the ability to predict the return on investment and the variability of that return and, therefore, is of questionable usefulness.

---

[14] Readers are urged to refer to Appendix B of *Statement No. 2* for a full narrative of the Board's reasoning.

6. *Capitalization of all costs when incurred.* The Board also rejected the argument that research and development projects taken as a whole will yield future benefits; and, therefore, all research and development expenditures should be capitalized without regard to future benefits. Their reasoning included (1) future benefits should be judged on an individual project basis and not on broad categories, (2) meaningful amortization of a firm's total program of research and development is not possible because of the inability to determine a period of benefit, and (3) research shows that over 90 percent of firms responding intend for research and development expenditures to be recovered by current revenues.

7. *Selective capitalization.* The Board rejected capitalizing research and development expenditures when certain criteria are fulfilled and expensing all others because (1) no set of conditions could be established which could be objectively and comparably applied to all firms, and (2) selective capitalization would not indicate total costs incurred to produce benefits and "matching" would not be achieved.

8. *Accumulation of costs in a special category.* The Board rejected accumulating all research and development expenditures in a special category and subsequently transferring to assets those with reasonably assured future benefits and expensing those with no significant future benefits because (1) such a category would not be useful in assessing the future earning power of the company, and (2) such a category would complicate the computation of ratios and other financial data.

No purpose would be served by arguing each of the reasons for the Board's decision. These arguments are well documented in other sources and need not be repeated here. However, one point concerning the Board's decision process needs to be aired. The Board has defined an asset by implication. That is, research and development expenditures should not be capitalized as assets because their future economic benefits are uncertain or, if they can be foreseen, cannot be measured with a reasonable degree of certainty, and because there is no relationship between the amount of an expenditure and its future benefits. No fault is found with the Board's decision to define an asset by implication and implementation. Accountants employ other terms which have not been rigorously defined. (For example, "generally accepted accounting principles" lacks rigorous definition.) Our criticism centers on the fact that the Board's implied definition cannot be applied to other expenditures normally considered to be assets without drastically (and ridiculously) changing the makeup of the balance sheet. For example, almost every expenditure for a capital asset involves uncertain future benefits which are not measurable with a reasonable degree of certainty. The unpredictable frailties of the economic environment may make a sound investment unsound overnight. If the additional requirement of a relationship between the size of the expenditure and the expected return is imposed, capital expenditures are even more difficult to fit within the definition of an asset. The same type of analysis applies to virtually every item currently considered an asset except perhaps trade accounts receivable and cash.[15] Undoubtedly, the Board will not impose these criteria on other assets. To do so would be ludicrous. The end result then must be that the Board has made a decision concerning the accounting for an expenditure on the basis of criteria which it will not be able to apply universally in additional circumstances—a result we find unfortunate. We would have much preferred that the Board admit that any alternative other than the one chosen created as many problems as it solved and, therefore, the only practical solution was to expense research and development as incurred.

Expensing research and development items acquired in a business combination accounted for as a purchase

A second criticism concerns the Board's decision to require immediate expensing of research and development assets which are acquired in a business combination accounted for as a purchase, and which have no alternative use. This requirement, which has little support in accounting theory, forces the accountant to write off immediately an asset which was deemed to constitute part of the value of the acquired company. Immediate write-off implies that the acquiring company was willing to purchase an item which has no value from an accounting standpoint even though a value could be determined for the item at the date of acquisition.

---

[15] This argument was put forth by Sidney Davidson in a speech before the 1974 American Accounting Association Convention.

The authors believe that research and development acquired in a business combination accounted for as a purchase should be capitalized and amortized as any other acquired intangible according to the rules supplied by *APB Opinion No. 17*. If the intangible research and development with no alternative use has a value at the date of acquisition that the acquiring company is willing to pay for, then the acquiring company must believe it is buying an asset which will at least return its purchase price at some point in the future. Proper accounting then would dictate capitalizing the asset and amortizing its cost against the future revenues it generates. Unfortunately, however, the alternative of capitalization and amortization does not exist under the *Statement*. We believe the Board needs to reconsider this situation.

Before leaving this argument a discussion of one further alternative is appropriate. That is, an argument can be made that the acquired research and development should not be valued on the books at the date of acquisition. This argument centers on the point that the incidence of an acquisition does not change research and development from an item not worthy of capitalization on the acquired company's books to a capitalizable item on the acquiring company's books. This argument, however, does not have much backing in accounting theory. Traditionally, realization through sale has been the best evidence of value of any asset. All other evidence of asset values is considered inferior. In addition, if followed, this method would serve only to increase the amount of the purchase price attributed to goodwill and would force the capitalization and amortization of the unrecognized value of the acquired research and development under the guise of goodwill. The final result, of course, coincides with the authors' bias toward capitalization and amortization but accomplishes this end for the wrong reason, and under an improper label.

Does one method of accounting apply to all research and development expenditures?

A third critical shortcoming of the *Statement* is the Board's decision to require only one method of accounting for research and development expenditures. There is a significant body of literature which supports the theory that given sufficient information, the market can accurately interpret the implications of accounting data on security prices.[16] An implication of this research is that many accounting and reporting issues are trivial. That is, if (1) there is essentially no difference in cost to the firm of reporting by any particular method, and (2) there is essentially no cost to the user of adjusting from one reporting method to another, then there is a simple solution. Report under one method and require sufficient additional disclosure to allow users of financial statements to adjust from that method to any other.

Had the Board followed the results of these research findings they would not have been placed in the untenable position of trying to argue that research and development expenditures never have sufficiently identifiable future benefits to warrant asset status. Corporate accountants realize that the nature of the activities encompassed by research and development vary significantly. To enforce a single method of accounting on this broad category of costs and at the same time not require sufficient additional disclosure to interpret the resulting numbers does not allow accounting statements to reflect economic reality.

SUMMARY AND CONCLUSION

This chapter attempts to (1) present the requirements of *Statement of Financial Accounting Standard No. 2,* "Accounting for Research and Development Costs," (2) discuss some early implementation problems which must be faced when applying the *Statement,* and (3) critique the accounting requirements of the *Statement* on both theoretical and practical grounds. As with all other attempts to set accounting policy, *Statement No. 2* does not completely alleviate the problems which must be faced in accounting for research and development expenditures. Much professional judgment must still be brought to bear on the topic. However, a visible sigh of relief occurred on the part of many corporate and public accountants and financial analysts when the *Statement* required the removal of an obviously "soft" asset from the balance sheet. We can only hope that this attempt at establishing accounting policy accomplishes its goal with less difficulty than its predecessors.

---

[16] For a very readable review of this literature see William H. Beaver, "What Should Be the FASB's Objectives?" *The Journal of Accountancy,* August 1973, pp. 49–56.

Chapter 13

Accounting for bonds, notes, and interest

*John Erickson**

Two common forms of long-term liabilities are promissory notes and bonds. Some authors include mortgages as a third form of long-term liability, but because a mortgage is a special type of long-term promissory note that has been given greater protection by the pledging of certain pieces of property as security, this chapter will deal with notes and bonds only.

When a corporation determines that it should use debt financing, its management should conduct a thorough, objective evaluation of the company's financial position and earnings prospects, keeping these points in mind:

1. Consider past experience and the vulnerability of the business to its own business cycle.
2. Evaluate the industry's long-term trend within its own life cycle. Most industries go through various stages of promotion, expansion and development, maturity, and decline. A corporation should be hesitant to arrange long-term debt financing when the industry is in the later stages of maturity or in the declining sales stage.
3. Consider the number of times that earnings cover debt interest charges. The higher the coverage of earnings over fixed interest

---

* Vice President and Controller, First National Bank of Minneapolis.

charges, the greater the ability of the corporation to utilize borrowings as a means of financing.

4. Consider the ability of a corporation to meet its debt obligations. Experience has proven that it is wise to provide for debt retirement through use of a sinking fund. A sinking fund constitutes an annual payment to the trustee required under the trust indenture, in cash and/or outstanding debentures, either to be held for maturity or to be used for immediate retirement of certain bonds outstanding.

PROMISSORY NOTES

A promissory note is a written promise to repay money borrowed and usually has a maturity ranging from 30 days to 10 or more years. Notes issued by a corporation can be offered publicly but are usually negotiated with one or several commercial banks. When a note is offered publicly it is issued under a corporate trust indenture with the same formalities as a long-term bond issue. When bond interest rates are temporarily unfavorable and funds are available from other sources, long-term notes maturing in two, three, or five years have been issued instead of bonds. There are also instances when long-term notes are issued in order to avoid the cost of issuing bonds and dealing with numerous bondholders.

Long-term notes are often secured by mortgages or collateral trust bonds. Those maturing in ten or more years may provide for a sinking fund. Thus, long-term notes often take on the characteristics of bonds and differ only in that they are placed with a few lenders. Accounting for such notes follows the same general principles as those applied to bonds and hence will not be given special accounting treatment in this chapter.

BONDS

Corporations have made extensive use of bonds as a means of financing. Bond issues are elaborate, formal, subdivided, long-term promissory notes usually coupled with some form of physical security. They are subdivided to offer many different people the opportunity to furnish funds as creditors. Bonds are usually negotiable and are made out in standard denominations. Bond maturities are usually longer than those of promissory notes, generally ten years or more after issuance. The following are advantages and disadvantages in selecting bond financing as an alternative to equity financing.

Advantages of bond financing

1. Bondholders are creditors and therefore have no vote and do not partake in management, whereas stockholders are owners of the corporation and share in the control of management.
2. Borrowed funds can usually be obtained at a lower rate because bonds are usually secured by a mortgage or lien, and the interest payments are in fixed amounts.
3. Without a public offering of bonds it is not necessary for management to disclose the affairs of the business, whereas with stock offerings it is necessary for corporations to file a statement under the Securities Act of 1933. Many small companies take advantage of not having to disclose the affairs of the business by using nonpublic bond offerings.
4. Bond financing is trading on equity. Many businesses find it profitable to borrow a part of the capital needed because the rate of return from the use of borrowed funds exceeds the interest rate paid for the use of borrowed funds. Frequently, the amount of bonds authorized will be larger than presently needed. This is done to avoid additional costs of authorizing more bonds at a later date when the need arises.

Disadvantages of bond financing

1. Interest expense is a fixed charge and must be paid on specified dates.
2. The need to meet interest requirements and sinking fund requirements can weaken the financial position of a company.
3. A sudden decline in earnings could bring about default and force reorganization of the business.
4. Borrowing now may undermine the ability to borrow in the future when the need could be greater. Some corporations have found it to their advantage to preserve their borrowing power.

Other considerations of bond financing

Federal income tax is often the most important factor in a decision between issuing preferred stocks or bonds. Bond interest is a deductible expense in calculating income subject to taxes, while dividends are a sharing of income and are not a deductible expense. The alternative tax effects can be seen on the following chart using three plans: the issuing of (1) common stock, (2) preferred stock, and (3) bonds.

The estimated amount of future earnings and the probable stability of income can also be significant determining factors in issuing additional stocks or bonds (refer to Table 1). If the earning rate per dollar invested is expected to be greater than the bond interest rate or the rate of dividends on preferred stock, and is expected to be stable, it is usually to the advantage of the common stockholder for the corporation to issue either bonds or preferred stock. On the other hand, if the expected earnings rate is less than the bond interest rate or rate of dividend on preferred stock, the common stockholder will receive a greater return if additional common stock is issued rather than preferred stocks or bonds.

Types of bonds

There are two general classifications of bonds with respect to the method of paying interest: *coupon bonds* and *registered bonds*. Coupon bonds are negotiable to bearer and are therefore sometimes referred to as *bearer bonds*. The coupons represent periodic interest payments payable to bearer. The bearer presents these coupons to the trustee for the interest payments. Most corporations issue coupon bonds due to the ease of administering the interest and principal payments and the ease of transferring ownership. Registered bonds are recorded as being owned by a specific party whose name appears on the face of the bond. They are transferable only by the issuing company or its duly authorized transfer agent, and only after the transfer has been made on the face of the bond and in the bond register. Registered bonds may be registered only as to principal; the interest coupons will be payable to bearer. If they are fully registered, there are no coupons to present and the interest payment is routinely mailed to the registered bondholder.

There is difficulty in classifying bonds, because over the years corporation lawyers and financiers have created wide varieties of bonds, each with slightly different combinations of characteristics. Basically, however, bonds can be classified in two ways: (1) as to the nature of business or obligor, that is, federal or state government, municipals, and public utilities; or (2) as to the nature of underlying collateral, that is, mortgage or income. Within the

TABLE 1
Income tax effect (bonds versus common and preferred stock)

	Operating income of $400,000			Operating income of $30,000		
	Plan 1 (common)	Plan 2 (preferred)	Plan 3 (bonds)	Plan 1 (common)	Plan 2 (preferred)	Plan 3 (bonds)
Common stock, $100 par (20,000 shares)	$2,000,000	$2,000,000	$2,000,000	$2,000,000	$2,000,000	$2,000,000
Additional common stock, $100 par (10,000 shares)	1,000,000			1,000,000		
Preferred stock, 6% cumulative		1,000,000			1,000,000	
5% bonds			1,000,000			1,000,000
Total Capitalization	$3,000,000	$3,000,000	$3,000,000	$3,000,000	$3,000,000	$3,000,000
Operating income before federal income tax	$ 400,000	$ 400,000	$ 400,000	$ 30,000	$ 30,000	$ 30,000
Deduct: Bond interest expense	-0-	-0-	50,000	-0-	-0-	50,000
Income (or loss) after bond interest expense	$ 400,000	$ 400,000	$ 350,000	$ 30,000	$ 30,000	$ (20,000)
Deduct: Federal and state income taxes of 50%	200,000	200,000	175,000	15,000	15,000	-0-*
Net income (or loss) after federal taxes	$ 200,000	$ 200,000	$ 175,000	$ 15,000	$ 15,000	$ (20,000)
Preferred dividends	-0-	60,000	-0-	-0-	60,000	-0-
Income (or loss) to Common Stock Equity	$ 200,000	$ 140,000	$ 175,000	$ 15,000	$ (45,000)	$ (20,000)
Income (or loss) per share of common stock	$6.67	$7.00	$8.75	$.50	$(2.25)	$(1.00)

* Excluding possibility of utilizing a loss carryover.

above classifications, bonds may have various features such as serial maturities, a call feature, or a convertibility option.

Serial bonds. Bond issues can have variable maturities instead of having one fixed, single maturity. Bond issues which have a portion of the issue maturing periodically are called *serial bonds.* There are two distinct advantages to the issue of serial bonds as opposed to single maturity bonds:

1. The issuer of serial bonds periodically retires a part of its long-term debt obligation and consequently does not have to establish a sinking fund or similar provision for repayment. This is of particular importance if the interest expense on the outstanding bonds is greater than the interest that might be earned on a sinking fund.

2. When short-term interest rates are lower than long-term rates, the issuer can attach a lower coupon rate to the shorter term serial bonds.

Callable bonds. The call feature requires the holder to surrender the bonds in return for the contractual call price at the option of the debtor corporation.

Convertibility option. Convertible bonds extend to the holder the privilege of converting the bonds into another security of the issuing corporation under specific terms and conditions. The convertibility feature gives the holder a more assured income and secured principal during the development period of the issuing company than the holder might have as a stockholder, with the right to become a stockholder if the company is successful.

Convertible bonds are issued at an interest rate that is lower than the issuer would generally pay for a similar nonconvertible bond. The initial conversion price is greater than the market value of the common stock at the time of issuance, and the conversion price does not usually decrease. Convertible bonds are an attractive debt instrument for both the issuer and the purchaser. For the issuer, convertible bonds are issued at a lower interest rate and the issuer can view convertible bonds as a source of equity capital; that is, if the market value of its common stock increases sufficiently in the future, the issuer can force conversion into common stock by calling the issue for redemption. If, on the other hand, the market value of the stock does not increase sufficiently, the issuer will have received the benefit of the cash proceeds to the scheduled maturity date at a lower interest cost than could be obtained by nonconvertible bonds. The purchaser benefits in that if the market value of the stock increases sufficiently the bonds can be converted to stock at below market cost. If the market value of the stock does not increase sufficiently, the purchaser has the protection of debt security. A possible disadvantage to the corporation in issuing convertible bonds is that a substantial conversion into common stock could shift the control of the company away from the management.

Bonds classified by nature of underlying collateral

1. *Mortgage bonds* are secured by a mortgage deed of trust which contains a conditional conveyance or pledge of property. By securing a bond by a mortgage, the holder's position is strengthened. Generally, the use of secured bonds by a corporation will tend to lower its cost of funds as compared with the use of unsecured bonds.
2. *Collateral trust bonds* are secured solely, or for the most part, by the pledge of stocks or bonds, or both, as collateral with the trustee under a collateral trust indenture. The indenture empowers the trustee to sell the pledged securities in case of default, and from the proceeds to recover the sum due on the books.
3. *Guaranteed bonds* are bonds whose payment is contractually assured by a company other than the issuing company. Oftentimes a holding company makes such a guarantee for one of its subsidiaries. The use of a guaranteed bond or any secured bond improves the credit risk of a weaker subsidiary. The guaranty may apply to the payment of both the principal and interest, or to interest alone. The value of the guaranty depends on (1) the financial position of the guarantor, (2) the interest of the guarantor in the business and assets of the debtor corporation, and (3) the strategic importance of the business and assets of the debtor corporation to the guarantor.
4. *Debenture bonds* are unsecured bonds. Assurance that the bond payments will be made rests solely upon the corporation's general credit, without a specific mortgage, pledge, or assignment of property.
5. *Income bonds* have a peculiar feature in that the payment of interest is dependent upon the net profits of the issuing corporation. The principal of the bond is payable like that of other bonds, and may be secured or unsecured. The issuance of in-

come bonds has been chiefly used in connection with the reorganization of corporations.

6. *Participating bonds* receive interest in excess of a minimum stipulated amount, generally when earnings exceed certain levels, as defined in the trust indenture. As a result, they have sometimes been referred to as "profit-sharing bonds." The issuance of these bonds has usually been by corporations handicapped by poor credit or reorganization.

ACCOUNTING FOR BONDS PAYABLE

Issuance of bonds at par

To illustrate the accounting necessary for bonds payable issued at par, assume that the Abbott Corporation voted to issue a $500,000 bond issue at a coupon rate of 6 percent payable on January 1 and July 1 of each year. The bonds were issued at par on July 1, 1976, with a maturity of ten years from that date. The entries used to record this long-term debt on the general ledger of the Abbott Corporation are as follows:

July 1, 1976

Cash	500,000	
Bonds Payable		500,000

Bond interest expense—Par

On December 31, 1976, the end of Abbott's fiscal year, the corporation records the accrued interest expense of $15,000 ($500,000 \times$ .06 $\times$ 6/12) from July 1, 1976, through December 31, 1976.

December 31, 1976

Bond Interest Expense	15,000	
Bond Interest Payable		15,000

On January 1, 1977, the Abbott Corporation remits the coupon interest payment to the trustee for bondholder distribution. The entries to record this payment on January 1, 1977, are as follows:

January 1, 1977

Bond Interest Payable	15,000	
Cash		15,000

Bonds payable issued at a discount

Cash interest payments on a bond issue are at a fixed rate; that is, a percent of the par value is to be paid to the holder at stated intervals over the life of the bond, usually annually or semiannually. A bondholder who had a $1,000 par value bond with a coupon rate of 6 percent would receive $30 ($1,000 \times .06 \times 6/12$) every six months, or $60 annually. The coupon rate is fixed prior to the issue date, however, and may not reflect the current market rate that investors are demanding on similar investments of equal risk. When the coupon rate is less than the market rate, the bonds are sold at something less than the par value. The deficiency between the amount received and the par value is known as a *discount*. Conversely, when the coupon rate is higher than the market rate, investors are willing to pay more than the par value in return for the future streams of interest payments and the payment of the face amount of the bonds at maturity. The excess of the selling price over the par value is referred to as a *premium*.

To illustrate the accounting for bonds sold at a discount, assume that the Abbott Corporation authorized a bond issue of $500,000 par value with a coupon rate of 6 percent. On June 25, 1976, when the issue was sold to an underwriter, the market rate of interest for similar securities was 7 percent. The underwriter will discount the future stream of interest payments and the maturity value to yield slightly more than 7 percent return on the bond investment. The underwriter intends to sell these bonds to individual investors to yield 7 percent, but will discount them at slightly more than 7 percent in order to provide for the underwriter fee. However, for simplicity a discount rate of 7 percent is used in the following illustration.

Computation of issue price

Present value of $500,000 due in 10 years discounted at 7% per year	$251,283
Present value of $15,000 every 6 months for 10 years at 7% (3½% semiannually)	213,186
Proceeds of Bond Issue	$464,469

The Abbott Corporation would receive $464,469 from the underwriter for its promise to pay $15,000 semiannually for the next ten years plus $500,000 at maturity. The $35,531 difference between the face value of $500,000 and the issue price of $464,469 is called a *discount* and would be recorded on the Abbott Corporation's general ledger on the sale date as follows:

July 1, 1976

```
Cash  . . . . . . . . . . . . . . . . . . . . . . . . . . . . . . . . . . .  464,469
Discount on Bonds Payable . . . . . . . . . . . . . . . . . . . . . .   35,531
    Bonds Payable  . . . . . . . . . . . . . . . . . . . . . . . . . . .         500,000
```

The price an investor is willing to pay for a bond is normally stated as a percent of par value. In the case of the Abbott Corporation, the bonds were sold for 92.88 percent of par. The bond discount of $35,531 is amortized from the date of sale until the maturity date because it represents additional interest expense over the life of the bonds.

There are two methods commonly used to amortize the discount or premium over the life of the bond: the *straight-line method* and the *effective interest method.* It should be noted, however, that both methods are acceptable and yield approximately the same results, and that the degree of difference depends on the amount of the discount or premium and the length of time until maturity.

Straight-line method of amortizing discount

If the straight-line method of amortization is used, a constant portion of the discount is amortized each month and the $35,531 would be amortized at $1,776.55 ($35,531/10 × 6/12) semiannually. The entries used to record these transactions are:

December 31, 1976

```
Bond Interest Expense . . . . . . . . . . . . . . . . . . . . . . . . 16,776.55
    Discount on Bonds Payable . . . . . . . . . . . . . . . . .          1,776.55
    Bond Interest Payable . . . . . . . . . . . . . . . . . . . . .         15,000.00
```

A portion of the discount is amortized into expense as time passes and hence the carrying value of the bonds at subsequent dates will increase until they equal par value at maturity.

Bond discount amortized under straight-line method

Semiannual interest period	Nominal interest	Amortization of discount — Frac-tion	Amortization of discount — Amount	Effective interest	Carrying value of bonds at end of period
Original issue price					$464,469.00
1.	$15,000	6/120	$1,776.55	$16,776.55	466,245.55
2.	15,000	6/120	1,776.55	16,776.55	468,022.10
3.	15,000	6/120	1,776.55	16,776.55	469,798.65
.	.	.	.	.	.
18.	15,000	6/120	1,776.55	16,776.55	496,446.90
19.	15,000	6/120	1,776.55	16,776.55	498,223.45
20.	15,000	6/120	1,776.55	16,776.55	500,000.00

Effective interest method of amortizing discount

An alternative method is to amortize the bond discount in a manner to yield a constant effective rate of interest on the principal balance at the beginning of each interest period. The amount of discount amortized each period will vary, and is determined by subtracting the nominal interest from the effective interest.

First six-month period:
Effective interest ($464,469 × 7% × 6/12) = $16,256.41
Nominal interest ($500,000 × 6% × 6/12) =   15,000.00
Discount to be amortized . . . . $ 1,256.41

Bond discount amortized under effective interest method

Semiannual interest period	Effective interest	Nominal interest	Discount amortized	Carrying value of bonds at end of period
Original issue price				$464,469.00
1.	$16,256.41	$15,000	$1,256.41	465,725.41
2.	16,300.39	15,000	1,300.39	467,025.80
3.	16,345.90	15,000	1,345.90	468,371.70
.	.	.	.	.
.	.	.	.	.
18.	17,254.86	15,000	2,254.86	495,250.76
19.	17,333.78	15,000	2,333.78	497,584.54
20.	17,415.46	15,000	2,415.46	500,000.00

It should be emphasized that the cash outlay for interest expense will always be the stated coupon rate times the par value, whereas the amount of interest expense charged through the income statement will be the sum of the coupon interest and the amortization of the discount.

Bonds payable issued at a premium

To illustrate the accounting for bonds issued at a premium, assume that the Abbott Corporation issued $500,000 par value, 20-year, 6 percent bonds at 112.55 for a total price of $562,750. This price results in an effective yield of approximately 5 percent. The entries to record this transaction are:

July 1, 1976

Cash 562,750
  Bonds Payable   500,000
  Premium on Bonds Payable   62,750

The premium of $62,750 will be amortized over the next 20 years as a reduction in interest expense from the coupon rate. Each amortization period will reduce the balance in the Premium on Bonds Payable account, and consequently the carrying value of the bonds, until they exactly equal par at maturity. Again the two commonly used methods for amortizing the premium on bonds are the straight-line method and the effective interest method.

Straight-line method of amortizing premium

Using the straight-line method, the amount to be amortized each period is computed the same way as the discount ($62,750 ÷ 20 years = $3,137.50), which was discussed in the section "Straight-Line Method of Amortizing Discount."

On December 31, 1976, the Abbott Corporation records the interest accrual and the amortization of premium for the six-month period as follows:

December 31, 1976

Bond Interest Expense	13,431.25	
Premium on Bonds Payable	1,568.75	
Bond Interest Payable		15,000.00

The bond interest expense for the period is $13,431.25 ($15,000.00 − $1,568.75).

Effective interest method of amortizing premium

The effective interest method for amortizing the premium on bonds payable is essentially the same as for amortizing the discount on bonds payable as previously discussed. The amount of premium to amortize each period is determined by applying the effective rate of interest to the carrying value of the bonds payable at the beginning of each interest period, and then subtracting this amount of interest from the coupon interest.

First period:
Nominal interest ($500,000 × 6% × 6/12)	$15,000.00
Less effective interest ($562,750 × 5% × 6/12)	14,068.75
Premium to Be Amortized	$ 931.25

The effective interest method is a more accurate measure of the true interest cost and hence is the preferred method of expense recognition from a theoretical point of view. From a practical point of view, the straight-line method is easier to compute since a constant amount of premium or discount is amortized each period. Also, since the straight-line method does not significantly alter the effective yield, it is the most commonly used form of amortization. The unamortized premium or discount associated with bonds payable should be reported in the balance sheet as a direct addition to or reduction of the face amount of the bonds. The face amount and the effective rate should be disclosed (refer to *APB Opinions No. 12* and *No. 21*).

Bond issue costs

Costs often associated with a bond issue are legal fees, registration costs, and printing costs. Because a bond issue is a borrowing for a specified period of time, these bond issuance costs should be amortized over the life of the bond issue. If these charges are used to reduce the carrying value of the bonds payable, the result will not accurately reflect the yield demanded by investors at the issue date. Therefore, these bond issuance costs should be recorded as deferred charges and amortized.

Bonds payable issued between interest dates

We have assumed in preceding illustrations that all bonds are issued at the beginning of an interest period. In many instances, however, bonds are issued during an interest period. For example, assume that the Abbott Corporation issues an additional $100,000 of bonds on April 1, 1978, bearing an interest coupon at 6 percent with interest payable on January 1 and July 1 until maturity on June 30, 1986. The bonds were sold for 102.3 percent of par plus accrued interest for three months. Bonds are sold with accrued interest because at the next contractual interest date the buyer will receive interest from the last interest date (six months). The buyer always pays the seller for any accrued interest, because the debtor corporation is obligated to pay the full amount of interest to the holder of the bond on the payment date irrespective of duration of ownership. The bonds were sold for $103,800. Of this amount, $1,500 ($100,000 × .06 × 3/12) is accrued interest and $2,300 is a premium paid by the buyer. The entry is:

April 1, 1978

Cash 103,800
      Bonds Payable   100,000
      Premium on Bonds Payable   2,300
      Bond Interest Expense.   1,500

This entry records the sale of $100,000 par value bonds at 6 percent interest, sold at 102.3 plus accrued interest for three months. The credit to Bond Interest Expense is a partial offset to the debit which will be made to Bond Interest Expense on the next semiannual interest payment date.

On July 1, 1978, the corporation records the six months of accrued interest. The accrued interest of $3,000 ($100,000 \times .06 \times 1/2$) is recorded as follows:

July 1, 1978

Bond Interest Expense 3,000
      Cash   3,000

Also on July 1, 1978, the corporation amortizes the premium for three months. The premium is always amortized from issue date until maturity because the discount or premium is an adjustment to the interest paid to the investor. The amortized premium of $69.70 ($2,300 \times 3/99$) using the straight-line method would be recorded as follows:

July 1, 1978

Premium on Bonds Payable 69.70
      Bond Interest Expense. 69.70

On December 31, the corporation will record the interest accrual and premium amortization for the second half of 1978 as follows:

December 31, 1978

Bond Interest Expense 3,000.00
Premium on Bonds Payable 139.39
      Cash 3,000.00
      Bond Interest Expense. 139.39

Two points to remember regarding bonds sold between interest dates are that interest at the coupon rate is sold from the last interest date until the sale date, and the discount or premium is amortized from sale date until maturity.

Reacquisition and redemption of term bonds

Bonds are sometimes acquired by the issuing corporation prior to maturity. These bonds may be permanently retired or they may be held in the corporate treasury as part of a sinking fund. A gain or a loss is realized if there is a difference between the purchase price and the current book value (par value, plus unamortized premium, or less unamortized discount) plus any unamortized issuing costs. The bond premium or discount amortization should be updated from the last interest date to the date of sale. To illustrate, assume that on March 31, 1978, the Abbott Corporation purchases $20,000 par value of a $100,000 par value bond issue with a 5 percent coupon rate for $20,200. The bonds were issued on January 1, 1975, with a six-year maturity. The bonds were originally sold at 102.5, or a $2,500 premium. The premium has been amortized semiannually up to December 31, 1977.

Three months of the $2,500 premium on $20,000 par value, or $20.83 ($2,500 × $20,000/$100,000 × 3/72), is charged to Bond Interest Expense for the first three months of 1978. The remaining premium of $229.17 ($2,500 × $20,000/$100,000 × 33/72) which is applicable to the bond purchase is charged off on the same day the bonds are purchased.

March 31, 1978

Bonds Payable.	20,000.00	
Premium on Bonds Payable	229.17	
Cash		20,200.00
Gain on Bond Acquisition.		29.17

In this example, the corporation realized a gain on the purchase of its outstanding bonds. Some bonds are originally issued with a call feature, which means they can be reacquired at the option of the corporation at a stated price after the expiration of some specified time period. The stated price is normally higher than the issue price; consequently, when bonds are reacquired by using the call feature the corporation normally realizes a loss from the purchase.

If the bonds are acquired but not retired, treasury bonds may be debited for the par value of the acquired bonds. The treasury bonds are not an asset but should be deducted from bonds payable on the balance sheet. Interest should not be paid on reacquired bonds unless they are held as an investment by a company-sponsored fund.

Accounting for serial bonds

Serial bonds may sell for a premium or discount. If possible, one should determine the premium or discount applicable to each of the various maturities; in effect, it would be as though each maturity was a unique bond issue. Many times, however, it is not possible to determine the discount or premium on each maturity directly, because the underwriter offers a bid for the entire block of serial bonds and does not distinguish the yield rate for each maturity.

If the effective-interest method is used for amortizing premium or discount on serial bonds, the procedure and accuracy will be similar to the effective interest method employed for single maturity issues. If the straight-line method were used for amortization, the result would be an unduly large distortion in the bond interest expense rate due to the decline in the outstanding balance of the liability. To eliminate the distortion, there is a modified straight-line method known as the bonds outstanding method which does reflect interest expense very close to that under the effective yield method.

To illustrate the calculation of interest expense for the effective interest and bonds outstanding methods, assume that the Abbott Corporation issued $100,000, five-year, 5 percent serial bonds. The bonds are repayable in amounts of $20,000 at the end of each year. Assume that the interest payments are annual and the bonds are sold to yield 6 percent. The proceeds from this bond issue would be approximately $97,375, using present value computation.

Bonds outstanding method

Year	Maturity value of bonds outstanding	Portion of total bonds outstanding	Amortization of discount	Coupon payment	Interest expense
1	$100,000	10/30	$ 875	$ 5,000	$ 5,875
2	80,000	8/30	700	4,000	4,700
3	60,000	6/30	525	3,000	3,525
4	40,000	4/30	350	2,000	2,350
5	20,000	2/30	175	1,000	1,175
Total	$300,000	30/30	$2,625	$15,000	$17,625

Effective interest method

Year	Book value of bonds outstanding	Effective interest expense	Coupon payment	Discount amortized	Bond discount balance	Principal payment
Issue	$97,375				$2,625	
1	78,217	$5,842	$ 5,000	$ 842	1,783	$ 20,000
2	58,910	4,693	4,000	693	1,090	20,000
3	39,444	3,534	3,000	534	556	20,000
4	19,811	2,367	2,000	367	189	20,000
5	–0–	1,189	1,000	189	–0–	20,000
			$15,000	$2,625		$100,000

The bonds outstanding method is similar to the straight-line method in that it results in a constant amortization of discount or premium per $1,000 of maturity value of bonds outstanding ($2,625 ÷ $300 = $8.75). Thus, interest expense is 5.875 percent of the face of the bonds outstanding in any year under this method. Under the effective method, the interest expense for each year is 6 percent of the book value of the bonds at the beginning of the year.

Accounting for convertible bonds

There are differences of opinion as to whether convertible bonds should be treated solely as a debt or whether the convertible feature should require a special accounting treatment. Those who contend that convertible bonds should be treated solely as debt argue that the debt and the conversion option are inseparable. The holder cannot sell the conversion option and retain the bond, and likewise the holder cannot sell the bond and retain his or her right to buy stock at a fixed price. The two choices are mutually exclusive; they cannot both be exercised.

Another reason for accounting for convertible bonds solely as debt is that a totally objective value cannot be placed on either of the options separately. A convertible bond is usually less restrictive than a nonconvertible bond; hence it is difficult to compare a convertible bond to a similar nonconvertible bond.

The alternative view is that the convertible bond should be accounted for on both the debt aspects and on the convertibility aspects. Holders of this view believe that a portion of the proceeds attributable to the conversion feature should be accounted for as paid-in capital and an amortized bond discount (or reduced premium) should be recorded.

Opinion No. 14 of the Accounting Principles Board states in paragraph 12 that

> the Board is of the opinion that no portion of the proceeds from the issuance of the type of convertible debt securities described in paragraph 3 should be accounted for as attributable to the conversion feature. In reaching the conclusion, the Board places greater weight on the inseparability of the debt and the conversion option (as described in paragraph 7) and less weight on practical difficulties.

The securities described were convertible bonds where there were no separate stock purchase warrants.

Bonds issued with warrants attached

Unlike convertible debt, debt with detachable stock purchase warrants is normally issued with the expectation that the bonds will remain outstanding until maturity. The provisions of the bond indenture are usually more restrictive to the issuer and more protective for the holder. In this type of financing the warrant to buy stock can be detached and sold; in other words, it stands alone and may have its own value. A bond issue with attached warrants for the purchase of stock results in a lower cash interest cost to the issuer than would otherwise be possible. Normally the issuer cannot force the holder of the warrant to exercise his or her option to buy stock. The bonds would mature or be prematurely redeemed irrespective of whether the warrants are exercised. There is general agreement among accountants that the proceeds from this type of bond issue should be allocated to both the bond issue and the stock purchase warrants. This agreement stems from the separability of the bonds and the warrants. The allocation should be based on the relative fair values of the bond issue without the warrants and of the warrants themselves at the time of issue. The portion of the proceeds so allocated to the warrants should be accounted for as paid-in capital. *Opinion No. 14* of the Accounting Principles Board states in paragraph 16 that

> The Board is of the opinion that the portion of the proceeds of debt securities issued with detachable stock purchase warrants which is allocable to the warrants should be accounted for as paid-in capital. The allocation should be based on the relative fair values of the two securities at time of issuance. Any resulting discount or premium on the debt securities should be accounted for as such. The same accounting treatment applies to issues of debt securities (issued with detachable warrants) which may be surrendered in settlement of the exercise price of the warrant. However, when stock purchase warrants are not detachable from the debt and the debt security must be surrendered in order to exercise the warrant, the two securities taken together are substantially equivalent to convertible debt and the accounting specified in paragraph 12 should apply.

Statement presentation for notes and bonds payable

Long-term debt is usually presented on the balance sheet as one total, less the current portion of the liability, accompanied by an explanatory note. The current portion of the long-term liability is that portion which matures within one year, and should be shown as a current liability. In the presentation, the valuation of the bond should be shown at book value; the market value may be disclosed in a parenthetical note.

The following example is intended to clarify the discussion.

Liabilities and Shareholder's Equity	*1979*	*1978*
Current Liabilities:		
Notes payable to banks	$ 3,000,000	$ 2,000,000
Current portion of long-term debt	80,000	80,000
Accounts payable	2,500,000	1,400,000
Accrued expenses	2,700,000	1,800,000
Income taxes	2,200,000	520,000
Total Current Liabilities	$10,480,000	$ 5,800,000
Long-term debt, less current portion above (Note D)	$ 6,500,000	$ 8,400,000
Shareholders' equity (Notes E and F)		
Common stock, $1 par value, authorized 3,000,000 shares, 2,480,000 and 1,550,000 shares outstanding, respectively	$ 2,480,000	$ 1,550,000
Additional paid-in capital	76,000	60,000
Retained earnings	14,100,000	12,000,000
Total Capital	$16,656,000	$13,610,000
Total Liabilities and Capital	$33,636,000	$27,810,000

The explanatory note supports the long-term debt with supplementary schedules showing pertinent details. The recommended guidelines for reporting long-term debt by the *Opinions* of the Accounting Principles Board and Regulation S-X issued by the Securities and Exchange Commission are that the following should be shown:

1. General characteristics of each type of debt including interest rate.
2. Date of maturity or dates if maturing serially, that is, 1970–80.
3. The basis of convertibility, if applicable.
4. Brief indication of priority.
5. The aggregate amount of maturing securities and sinking fund requirements each year for the five years following date of the balance sheet.

6.   If payment of principal or interest is contingent, an appropriate indication of such contingency.

Notes to Consolidated Financial Statements	*1979*
D—Long-term debt	
Promissory note, ¼% above prime rate; converting to a term loan on December 31, 1976, payable in 16 equal quarterly installments with interest at ½% above prime rate	$ 1,180,000
7% mortgage—Secured by land and building in varying annual amounts	200,000
4⅝% sinking fund debentures, due August 1, 1990	1,500,000
Two 20-year 3½% promissory notes of $1,000,000 each due May 1, 1981 and May 1, 1982	2,000,000
Unsecured 8% note, payable quarterly through 1991, prepayable from cash throw-off of campground operation	1,700,000
	$ 6,580,000
Less current portion	80,000
	$ 6,500,000

Aggregate annual maturities of long-term debt for the next five years are as follows: 1980, $93,000; 1981, $700,512; 1982, $987,405; 1983, $1,829,686; 1984, $571,723.

Also stated within the note should be the amount of unused commitments and the terms, including fees and conditions, under which the commitments may be withdrawn. A description of all significant accounting policies relating to long-term debt should be stated, including the disclosure of the method and period of amortization.

Reacquired debt should not be reported as an asset, but rather as a deduction from total authorized issues. In the event of a default under a credit agreement, it is necessary to state the nature and amount of default. Any gains or losses on the securities should be identified in the income statement as a separate item.

LONG-TERM INVESTMENT IN BONDS

Purchase of bonds

Many businesses make long-term investments in government and corporate bonds. Banks, insurance companies, and trust companies frequently make large block purchases of bonds. These corporations are often regulated by various government agencies as to the extent and type of investments they make, although there is seldom any restriction placed on the extent of U.S. government and government agency bonds that these corporations may have.

The accounting treatment used for the purchase of bonds, bond interest revenue, and bonds purchased between interest dates is essentially the same as that employed by the bond issuer. The brokerage fees associated with the purchase of a bond investment are treated as an addition to the bond premium or a reduction of the bond discount and are amortized in the same manner as the premium or discount. The discount or premium may be amortized using either the straight-line method or the effective-interest method; both of these methods were discussed previously in this chapter. The accuracy and computational disadvantage aspects outlined previously are the same when accounting for bonds from the investor's viewpoint.

To illustrate the complete accounting treatment necessary for bonds purchased as an investment, assume that on June 1, 1976, the Abbott Corporation purchases $60,000 par value, 5 percent bonds of Unico Corporation at 98 plus accrued interest and a broker's fee of $90. The bonds are due to mature on October 1, 1979. Interest is paid semiannually on April 1 and October 1.

Bond purchase price	$58,800
Broker's fee	90
Total Bond Cost	$58,890
Accrued interest ($60,000 × .05 × $^2/_{12}$)	500
Total Cash Outlay	$59,390

The discount or premium associated with bonds receivable should be reported in the balance sheet as a direct addition to or reduction from the face amount of the item. The face amount and effective interest rate should also be disclosed. (Refer to *APB Opinion No. 12* and *No. 21.*) The entry to record the purchase is:

June 1, 1976

Long-Term Investment—5% Bonds of Unico.	58,890	
Bond Interest Revenue.	500	
Cash		59,390

Two months of accrued interest is purchased at the coupon rate.

On October 1, 1976, the Abbott Corporation receives the semi-annual interest payment of $1,500 ($60,000 × .05 × 6/12). The entry for the collection is:

October 1, 1976

Cash	1,500	
Bond Interest Revenue.		1,500

The bonds were purchased at a discount of $1,110 ($60,000 —

$58,890). The corporation elected to amortize this discount on the straight-line basis over the 40 months to maturity. Each month the Abbott Corporation will amortize $27.75 ($1,110 ÷ 40). The entry on October 1, 1976, is:

October 1, 1976

Long-Term Investment—5% Bonds of Unico. 111.00
    Bond Interest Revenue. 111.00
    To record amortization of discount from June 1 through September 30, 1976.

On December 31, 1976, the corporation records the accrued interest of $750 from October 1 to December 31, 1976, and amortizes the appropriate discount.

December 31, 1976

Bond Interest Receivable. 750.00
Long-Term Investment—5% Bonds of Unico. 83.25
    Bond Interest Revenue. 833.25

The Bond Interest Revenue account balance will reflect the total bond interest earned for the year from both the coupon interest and the amortization of discount. The Long-Term Investment— 5 percent Bonds of Unico acount will reflect the year-to-date amortization of discount and the current book value of the bond investment.

Long-term investment—5 percent bonds of Unico

Date	Description	Dr.	Cr.	Balance
June 1, 1976	$60,000 bonds purchased at 98	$58,890.00		$58,890.00
October 1, 1976	Amortized discount (June 1–September 30)	111.00		59,001.00
December 31, 1976	Amortized discount (October 1–December 31)	83.25		59,084.25

If the bonds were purchased at a premium, the same accounting principles would apply for the periodic recognition of interest revenue and a periodic amortization of premium. In the case of a premium, however, there would be periodic debits (reductions) to the Bond Interest Revenue account and periodic credits (decreases) to the Long-Term Investment—5 percent Bonds of Unico account. Some accountants prefer to amortize the premium or discount on bonds once annually, at the end of each fiscal year.

Chapter 14

Recognition and measurement of corporate income taxes

William M. Horne, Jr. [*]
J. Karl Fishbach

HISTORICAL BACKGROUND

The reporting of income taxes on financial statements has been a problem as far back as the early years of corporate federal income taxes. The rates of these taxes increased from 1 percent at their inception in 1913 to 10 percent and 11 percent in the 1920s, to 12 percent to 19 percent in the 1930s, to 40 percent for most of the World War II years (1942–45) (excluding war excess profits taxes), and then up to the 48 percent to 52 percent corporate tax rate prevailing in recent years. With such tax rate increases, the federal income tax became a significant factor in the determination of net income.

Even in the 1920s and 1930s, companies were faced with the problem that tax accounting differed from financial accounting. For example, certain large retail companies made provision in their financial reports for deferred income taxes on installment sales.

Application of the statutory rate of income tax to the financial

---

[*] Senior Vice President and General Tax Counsel, Citicorp.
[†] Corporate Controller (Retired), City Stores Company.

accounting income results in a theoretical amount of tax. Invariably, the amount of tax so calculated varies from the actual tax per the tax return for two reasons, namely, *timing* differences and *permanent* differences.

Timing differences arise because certain income and expense items are reported in the tax return after they are reported for financial accounting purposes, while certain other income and expense items are reported in the tax return before they are reported for financial accounting purposes. These variations exist because financial accounting is governed by generally accepted accounting principles using the accrual method, whereas tax accounting is governed by statutes and regulations determining, with respect to many items of taxable income and allowable deductions, taxability on an occurrence basis. This, in effect, treats such items on a cash receipts or disbursements basis. Major attention will be placed on these timing differences.

Permanent differences arise when other income and expense items do not enter into the tax calculation on the income tax return because they constitute nontaxable income, or special and/or unallowable deductions. These items cause the ratio of income tax to financial accounting income before tax to be more or less than one would expect to result from the tax rate schedule. Unlike timing differences, permanent differences do not cause any variation between income tax reported in financial accounting income and the income tax in the income tax return. In addition, certain classes of income may be subject to special tax rates and the income tax may be reduced by certain statutory tax credits, thus constituting further income tax reductions or abnormal relationships between tax and income before tax.

The permanent differences are covered in detail later in this chapter and in Exhibits 2, 3, and 4.

NATURE OF INCOME TAX

There has been considerable controversy among public accountants, financial executives in industry, financial analysts, and academicians as to the precise nature of the income tax charge. It has been characterized as an expense, a profit distribution, a loss, or an anomalous item. Although the Accounting Principles Board in *APB Opinion No. 11* treats income tax as an expense and the

Securities and Exchange Commission (SEC) in its *Accounting Series Release (ASR) No. 149* does likewise, the characterization is still not free from doubt. For example, Wheeler and Galliart, who recently completed a research study, "An Appraisal of Interperiod Income Tax Allocation," characterized the income tax as an anomalous (hybrid) item.[1]

RELATIVE INCOME TAX BURDENS

Because income taxes are based on income before such taxes, it is customary to show each of the following on income statements:

1. Income before income taxes.
2. Income tax (federal, state, and foreign).
3. Net income.

(*Note:* State income taxes are deemed to include local income taxes and franchise taxes based on income.)

The above form of presentation puts these factors into perspective and thus facilitates the analysis of the magnitude of income taxes in relation to income before tax. If there were no timing differences and no permanent differences, the expense for federal income tax would be the product of income before tax and the current statutory rate of 48 percent.[2] If all of the income were subject to state income taxes of 12 percent (the highest prevailing corporate state income tax rate), the total tax would be determined as follows:

Income before income taxes.	$1,000,000	100.00%
Federal income tax:		
Income before tax of $1,000,000 less state income tax of $120,000 equals $880,000, which multiplied by 48% equals	422,400	42.24
State income tax—12% of $1,000,000	120,000	12.00
Total Income Tax	$ 542,400	54.24%

---

[1] Wheeler and Galliart, "An Appraisal of Interperiod Income Tax Allocation," Financial Executives Research Foundation (1974). The Trustees of the Financial Executives Research Foundation "believe that this study [Wheeler and Galliart] will become a major piece of original research and will serve as a solid theoretical basis for the resolution of many of the controversial accounting problems associated with the concept of comprehensive interperiod income tax allocation."

[2] The statutory rate of 48 percent, of course, does not take into account the surtax exemption and tax rates for special classes of income (such as the special rate on capital gains).

This is the customary method of reporting such taxes in published financial statements. Note that the same income (except for the federal deduction of state income taxes) is subject to each of the two taxes. If there is a city or other local income tax, then there would be three tiers of tax on the same income.

For internal management reporting purposes, the federal income tax may be shown without regard to the tax benefit from the state income tax, and the state income tax shown net of the federal income tax benefit it produces, as follows:

Federal income tax at 48% on $1,000,000.	$480,000	48.00%
State income tax at 12% less federal tax benefit of 48% thereof or 5.76% leaving a net of 6.24% or.	62,400	6.24
Total Income Taxes	$542,400	54.24%

In illustrating the reconciliation between a theoretical federal income tax of 48 percent with various components causing variations including state income taxes, the SEC employed this type of analysis in *ASR No. 149.*

Since, as indicated above, federal and state taxes apply to the same income subject to the interaction between the two taxes, the total tax is equal to the sum of the two rates less the effect of the interaction.

For companies operating exclusively in a domestic market, there could be wide variations in the effect of state income taxes because:

1. Certain states have no income tax.
2. The remaining states have rates ranging from 2.5 percent to 12 percent.

The total state tax would depend on the relative amount of income earned in the respective states of operation. Recently there has been a distinct rising trend in state income tax rates.

The corporate financial executive usually has little basis for evaluating or projecting the composition of state income taxes of other companies in comparative analyses, but must rely on the aggregate amount reported for such taxes. Professional analysts face similar problems in projecting state income tax levels. In the typical case of a company operating in most or all states, the level of such taxes does not change significantly from year to year. For companies which operate in a relatively small number of states, however, shifts in location of states in which principal operations are conducted may cause more significant variations in the level of state income taxes.

INCOME TAXES OF DOMESTIC COMPANIES
OPERATING ABROAD

When a domestic corporation (and/or its domestic subsidiaries) operates abroad, the foreign income is tentatively subject to the usual 48 percent federal income tax (excluding certain special-purpose corporations having special income taxes). This tentative tax is then reduced by the foreign tax credit for income taxes paid to foreign countries with two alternative limitations generally being allowed, namely, the "per country" and the "overall" limitation.[3]

Under the *per country* limitation, the credit for taxes paid to *each country* is limited to that percentage of income tax before credits owed to the United States which taxable income from that country is of total taxable income.

Under the *overall limitation,* the amount of credit is based on the total tax paid to all foreign countries (and U.S. possessions). The credit may not exceed the same proportion of the tax against which the credit is taken as the taxpayer's taxable income from sources outside the United States bears to its entire taxable income.

The taxpayer has the option of electing either limitation subject, however, to certain restrictive rules in the case of the overall limitation.

With respect to election of the overall limitation, consideration must be given to (*a*) the proportion of foreign income subject to foreign tax rates in excess of 48 percent versus the amount of foreign income subject to rates lower than the federal rate of 48 percent, and (*b*) foreign loss operations. These factors will be the principal determinants as to whether the overall or per country limitation is more favorable.

Foreign taxes represent another area in which the corporate financial executive or professional analyst faces great difficulty in evaluating or projecting the foreign income taxes and the additional federal income taxes in excess of foreign tax credits paid by a company on its foreign operations. Excluding foreign subsidiaries, the combination of the foreign income taxes and the federal income

---

[3] Legislative proposals were pending in the Congress to repeal the "per country" limitation as an elective alternative at the time this chapter was written.

taxes on foreign operations should generally approximate the federal rate (except for permanent tax differences), so long as the average effective foreign tax rate does not exceed the U.S. statutory rate. Subject to the same limitations, the benefit of permanent foreign tax differences is generally lost to the extent that they diminish the foreign tax credit applicable to the federal income tax.

INCOME TAXES OF FOREIGN SUBSIDIARIES OPERATING ABROAD

When a foreign subsidiary of a domestic corporation operates abroad (but not in the United States), it pays foreign income taxes at the rates prevailing in the countries in which it operates. To the extent that the foreign subsidiary pays dividends to its domestic parent, such dividends are includible in gross income and do not qualify for the special deduction available for dividends received from domestic corporations. The domestic parent, however, is allowed a "deemed paid" credit for foreign income taxes on earnings from which the dividends are distributed. This credit is subject to technical rules for determination of earnings and profits for federal income tax purposes, and for the "gross up" of the foreign income taxes when calculating the foreign tax credit on dividends from a foreign subsidiary in a developed country (but not from a less developed country).[4]

Under the present federal income tax law, earnings of a foreign subsidiary which are not paid as dividends to its U.S. parent are ordinarily not subject to federal income tax. The question arises, therefore, as to whether any provision should be made for possible future tax on repatriation of these earnings or dividends. If the U.S. company determines that the foreign earnings are reinvested in the business of the foreign subsidiary and will remain so reinvested for the indefinite future, then no provision is necessary for federal income tax on possible future dividend payments of these reinvested earnings. *APB Opinion No. 23* sets forth the criteria for determining whether or not to accrue domestic income taxes on the reinvested earnings of foreign subsidiaries.[5] With respect to tax provisions of

---

[4] For a discussion of these technical rules, see for example, E. Owens, *The Foreign Tax Credit* (1961); B. Bittker and J. Eustice, *Federal Income Taxation of Corporations and Shareholders* (1971); Geen, 5–3rd, Tax Management Portfolio, *Foreign Tax Credit* (1971).

undistributed earnings of 20 percent to 50 percent owned foreign affiliates, the generally accepted accounting principles are set forth in *APB Opinion No. 24.*

The above describes the general rules involving taxation of foreign operations. There are also special classes of corporations which have special tax benefits, such as special deductions and postponement of taxes, which are too complex and are of too limited interest for inclusion here.

The new SEC rules in *ARS No. 149*, discussed later in this chapter, require certain disclosures on foreign income taxes. These disclosure rules require a reconciliation showing dollar amount or percentages of the underlying causes for the differences between the effective income tax indicated by the income statement and a theoretical amount obtained by multiplying the income before tax by the 48 percent federal income tax rate. The result, among other causes, is the net variation from the theoretical federal rate of the foreign income taxes paid. While this now provides considerably more information than previously, the professional analyst does not generally have available means for determining the extent to which foreign income is subject to federal income tax. However, with the additional information required by the new SEC disclosure rules, the analyst will be in a better position to evaluate and project the impact of foreign income taxes on the basis of patterns and trends.

FINANCIAL ACCOUNTING INCOME VERSUS TAXABLE INCOME

In the illustrations given in the earlier sections, it was generally assumed that there was no difference between financial accounting income and taxable income. The first section of this chapter points out that significant differences can arise between financial accounting income and taxable income. With the growth in complexity of federal, state, and foreign taxes and the current high level of tax

---

[5] In AICPA, *Accounting Trends and Techniques* (New York, 1974), Table 3-19, it is indicated that of 600 companies surveyed in 1973, 41 disclosed that taxes were accrued on all undistributed earnings, 142 reported that taxes were accrued on a portion of undistributed earnings, 189 stated that taxes were *not* accrued on undistributed earnings, and 228 did not mention undistributed earnings in their statements of accounting policies.

An example of a typical statement in this respect would be as follows: "United States income taxes have not been provided on the undistributed earnings of foreign subsidiaries since the company considers such earnings to be permanently invested abroad. The cumulative amount of such undistributed earnings as of xxx is approximately $xxx."

rates, these variations take on increasing importance in financial reporting. The real problem, therefore, is to determine the extent to which recognition should be given in the income statement for the income tax effect applicable to the difference between financial accounting income and taxable income.

The earlier section indicates that permanent tax differences do not require any adjustment of the income tax expense. However, in accordance with *APB Opinion No. 11*,[6] provision should be made for the tax effects applicable to the timing differences between financial accounting income and taxable income. These timing differences stem from the fact that (*a*) certain revenue and gains and (*b*) certain expenses and losses are included or deducted earlier for financial accounting purposes than for taxable income while (*c*) certain other classes of revenue and gains and (*d*) certain expenses and losses are included or deducted later for financial accounting purposes than they are for taxable income.[7] The following table summarizes these categories, together with their treatment in the federal income tax return reconciliation of net income with taxable

TABLE 1
Treatment of tax timing differences

Class of transaction	Earlier or later reporting		As reported in Schedule M-1 of income tax return— adjustments to net income per books		Income tax journal entries	
	Financial accounting	Tax return	Addi- tions	Deduc- tions	Income tax provision	Balance sheet deferred tax accounts
A. Revenues and gains	E	L		Line 7	Debit	Credit
B. Expenses and losses	E	L	Line 5		Credit	Debit
C. Revenues and gains	L	E	Line 4		Credit	Debit
D. Expenses and losses	L	E		Line 8	Debit	Credit

income and the journal entries made recording the income and balance sheet effects.

Typical transactions subject to the above financial accounting and tax treatments are listed in Exhibit 1.

---

[6] *APB Opinion No. 11* adopted only in part the recommendations in *Accounting Research Study No. 9* of the American Institute of Certified Public Accountants (AICPA) by Homer Black.

[7] If expenses and losses create an operating loss carryover for income tax purposes, there must be proof beyond a reasonable doubt that the tax benefit will be utilized before it can be recognized currently. See later discussion.

EXHIBIT 1
Illustration of differences: Financial accounting income versus Taxable income

Classes of transactions	Earlier or later reporting — Financial accounting	Tax return	Per Schedule M-1 – Federal Income Tax Return – Form 1120* Reconciliation of income per books with income per return — Additions	Deductions
A. Revenues and gains				Line 7–Income reported on books this year, not included on this return
1. Installment sales—gross profit	Earlier	Later		Included when accounts are collected
2. Revenues on long-term contracts—using percentage of completion method	Earlier	Later		Included when contracts are completed
B. Expenses and losses			Line 5–Expenses reported on books this year, not deducted in this return	
1. Guaranties and warranties—estimated cost	Earlier	Later	Deducted when later paid	
2. Pending lawsuits and claims—estimated cost of settling	Earlier	Later	Deducted when later paid	
3. Provision for maintenance and repairs	Earlier	Later	Deducted later when incurred	
C. Revenues and gains			Line 4–Taxable income not reported on books this year	
1. Rents and royalties—received in advance	Later	Earlier	Reported in years earned	
2. Gain on sale and leaseback of property	Later	Earlier	Reported ratably during period of lease	

EXHIBIT 1 (*continued*)

D. *Expenses and losses*

			Line 8–Deductions in this tax return–not charged against book income this year
1. Depreciation–early years of acceleration method or shorter lives for tax return; also, amortization of emergency facilities under certificates of necessity.	Later	Earlier	Charged against book income in later years
2. Research and development costs deferred and amortized for financial accounting.	Later	Earlier	Charged against book income during period of amortization
3. Pre-operating expenses deferred and amortized for financial accounting	Later	Earlier	Charged against book income during period of amortization

Note: The Financial Accounting Standards Board outlawed such deferral commencing with years beginning in 1975.

* Schedule M-1 also provides for:

Line 2 – Federal income tax
Line 3　Excess of capital losses over capital gains

which items are not significant in this exhibit.

Source: This exhibit is adopted from "Interperiod Allocation of Corporate Income Taxes" by Homer A. Black (*Accounting Research Study No. 9*, AICPA, 1966).

TAX PROVISIONS AND RELATED BALANCE SHEET ACCOUNTS

The debit and credit balance sheet tax accounts shown in the preceding section are defined in *APB Opinion No. 11* as *deferred* tax accounts. In Table 1, Class C transactions, representing earlier recognition in the tax return of revenue and gains, and Class B transactions, representing earlier recognition of expenses and losses for financial accounting, give rise to *balance sheet debit* accounts. These are *deferred charges* to income tax expense of the future years in which the effect of timing differences reverses, with the credit being made to the current year's income tax expense.

Conversely, Class A transactions, involving the later recognition in the tax return of revenue and gains, and Class D transactions, involving the later recognition of expenses and losses for financial accounting, give rise to *balance sheet credit* accounts. These are *deferred credits* to income tax expense of the future years in which the effect of timing differences reverses, with the contra debit being made to the current year's income tax expense. The rationale of deferments of credits or charges to income tax expense of future years stems from the so-called "deferred concept," as defined in the following section.

DEFERRED METHOD AND COMPREHENSIVE ALLOCATION

The deferred method places the emphasis of the effect of timing differences on the income of the period in which the timing difference originates. Therefore, income tax expense is a function of pretax financial accounting income and includes the tax effect of the timing difference. The deferred balance sheet debit accounts are, in effect, amortized in future years as additions to income tax expense (debit); and the deferred balance sheet credit accounts are, in effect, amortized in future years as reductions of income tax expense (credit). Both of these tax deferments are based on the nature of the transactions producing the tax effects and on the manner in which these transactions enter into the determination of pretax financial accounting income in relation to the taxable income, as portrayed in Table 1. It should be noted that the deferred tax accounts are carried on the balance sheet until such time as the timing differences reverse themselves in future years. Furthermore, they are carried at the tax rates used at their inception with no adjustment for possible changes in income tax rates during the period that they are deferred.

The net effect is that, with respect to financial accounting income for a particular year, the income tax expense includes not only income tax reported for that year but also provision (at current tax rates) for any additional income taxes, or deductions for tax credits, that may be reported in tax returns of future years. The practice of making these tax deferments is known as *interperiod allocation* of income taxes, as distinguished from *intraperiod* allocation. (See the later section, "Income Taxes in the Income Statement.")

Comprehensive allocation is the practice of recording the tax effect of all timing differences in the year in which the timing differences occur. When there is a rollover of a transaction involving comprehensive allocation of deferred taxes, the rollover is viewed as a liquidation of the previous transaction and its deferred tax is then viewed as a new transaction with its resultant tax deferral. Comprehensive allocation is differentiated from "partial allocation" that is advocated by many financial people from industry and by some public accountants. Partial allocation will be covered later in this chapter.

BALANCE SHEET TAX ACCOUNTS

Table 1 indicates that Class A and D transactions give rise to balance sheet credit tax accounts and Class B and C transactions to balance sheet debit tax accounts. *APB Opinion No. 11* requires that these accounts be separated into their *current* and *noncurrent* elements, and that the balance sheet report the net current amount, debit or credit, and the net noncurrent amount, debit or credit, as follows:

Class of tax deferment transactions	Balance sheet account	Current accounts	or	Non-current accounts
A	Credit	X		X
B	Debit	X		X
C	Debit	X		X
D	Credit	X		X
Net Current Accounts (Debit or Credit)		X		
Net Noncurrent Accounts (Debit or Credit)				X

The current and noncurrent classifications of the balance sheet tax accounts follow the transactions from which they stem. For example, the deferred tax credit account based on a Class A transaction involving the tax deferral of gross profit on short-term installment receivables is classified as a current credit item. Conversely, the deferred tax debit account based on a Class C transaction involving the next year's rental income received, and taxed, in advance is classified as a current debit item.

Prior to the requirement of *APB Opinion No. 11,* the SEC had ruled in *ASR No. 102* that the deferred income taxes with respect to current installment receivables should be classified under liabilities, notwithstanding the fact that on a going-concern basis the level of tax credits from transactions may be constantly increasing so that, in effect, the deferred tax may be viewed as permanently postponed. A few astute professional analysts recognize the realism of this concept in their determination of projected cash flows by eliminating the impact of treating such deferred tax credit accounts as current liabilities.

In this vein, it is significant to note that certain state tax agencies reclassify such tax credit accounts from current liabilities to stockholders' equity and impose franchise or net worth taxes on such equity values. In addition, certain companies with large installment receivables, that report gross profit on the installment basis in their income tax returns, modify their funds flow statements to show "working funds" in addition to working capital. *Working funds* are defined as the excess of current assets over current liabilities, excluding the deferred tax on installment receivables. These practices raise a doubt as to the realism of the rigid APB and SEC rules requiring the classification of these deferred tax credits in the current liability section, with a resultant decrease in working capital. The alternative of treating such deferred taxes as noncurrent is, in the authors' opinion, more realistic.

INCOME TAXES ON THE INCOME STATEMENT

The SEC regulation *ASR No. 149,* effective for 1973 and later years, imposes more stringent requirements for reporting income taxes on the income statement than does *APB Opinion No. 11.* In reports to the SEC, total income tax must now be reported under *ASR No. 149* as follows:

(i)   Taxes currently payable
(ii) Net tax effects, as applicable, of
    (a)   Timing differences
    (b)   Operating losses
(iii) Net deferred investment tax credits.

These requirements differ from those of *APB Opinion No. 11* in the following respects:

(i)   *APB Opinion No. 11* requires "Total estimated to be payable." In the practical sense, most companies will need to estimate such taxes notwithstanding the rigidity of *ASR No. 149* because they usually cannot complete the federal, state, and foreign tax returns at the time of preparing their annual financial reports.

(ii)(a) *APB Opinion No. 11* requires a statement of the reasons for significant variations in the customary relationships between income tax expenses and pretax financial accounting income if they are not otherwise apparent from the financial statements or from the nature of the business. It also recommends the disclosure of the nature of significant differences between financial accounting income and taxable income.

The regulations, however, require elaborate disclosure of each major component of timing differences analyzed by federal, state, and other taxes, as well as a reconciliation in dollars or percentages of each of the underlying causes for the difference between reported income tax expense and the "expected" tax expense, determined by multiplying the income before tax by the current statutory federal rate of 48 percent. This will be covered further in the next section.

Income taxes are usually shown immediately after income before tax so that the relative tax burden is self-evident. Under certain circumstances, the income statement is divided into the following sections:

1. Income before items below.
2. Income or loss from discontinued operations.
3. Extraordinary items.

The total income tax expense indicated earlier in this section should be allocated among the above items so that each will have its own tax provision. Usually, the tax effects of (2) and (3) are reported parenthetically in the income statement or in a supporting note. Allocation of income tax in this manner as required by *APB Opinion No. 11* is known as *intraperiod income tax allocation.*

With rare exceptions, *APB Opinion No. 11* requires that the tax benefit of an *operating loss carryforward* ("net operating loss carryovers" in Internal Revenue Code language) not utilized as a carryback to any prior period not be reported as an income tax credit in the year in which the loss is incurred. Instead, it must be carried forward and applied to the year or years in which it may be deductible for income tax purposes. When the loss carryforward is utilized, the tax benefit cannot be applied as a reduction of the basic tax provision on current operations but must instead be treated as an extraordinary income tax credit in the year or years realized.

Recognition of the tax benefit of a loss carryforward in the year of loss is a rare occurrence and can only be accomplished when realization of the tax benefit appears to be assured beyond a reasonable doubt. That would occur when *both* of the following conditions exist: (*a*) the loss results from an identifiable isolated and nonrecurring cause and the company either has been continuously profitable over a long period, or has suffered occasional losses which were more than offset by taxable income in subsequent years; and (*b*) future taxable income is virtually certain to be large enough to offset the loss carryforward and will occur soon enough to provide realization during the carryforward period. Anticipated reductions of future income taxes arising fom recognition of the tax effects of operating loss carryforwards should be classified as current or noncurrent, determined by the period over which realization is expected.

When a company incurs a net operating loss and the tax effects of an operating loss carryback can be utilized against taxable income of prior years, the refund so determined can be set up as a current asset (or noncurrent in unusual cases) with a credit to income tax expense for the loss year.

With respect to the relatively unusual case of prior period adjustments, the applicable tax effects should be treated as adjustments of such period results. Similar application should be made to the opening balances of retained earnings as well as to direct entries to other stockholders' equity accounts. The amounts of such applicable tax effects should be disclosed.

OTHER SEC INCOME TAX DISCLOSURES

With respect to the tax effects of timing differences, *ASR No. 149* further requires disclosure of the estimated tax effect of each of the various types of timing differences, for example:

1. Depreciation.
2. Research and development costs.[8]
3. Warranty costs.

Individual types of timing differences may be combined if their applicable taxes are each less than 15 percent of the deferred tax amount in the income statement. Another test for the necessity of disclosing timing differences involves multiplying income before tax by the statutory federal tax rate (currently 48 percent in most cases). If the taxes applicable to the aggregate amount of timing differences are less than 5 percent of such computed amount, then no disclosure is required of each of the types of timing differences.

For each of the major components of income tax expense, *ASR No. 149* further requires disclosure of (*a*) federal income taxes, (*b*) foreign income taxes, and (*c*) other income taxes, unless the amounts applicable to either foreign or other income taxes do not exceed 5 percent of the total for the components. With respect to other income taxes—that is, state and local income taxes—the SEC reconciliation requirements apparently pertain to their gross amounts before deducting the federal income tax benefits that they produce.

The SEC is concerned with any possible impact of taxes on cash requirements within the next three years. Thus, the SEC also requires reporting of the appropriate amount of any substantial expected cash requirement in excess of income tax expense for each of such years and the reasons for such impact. Such a situation could arise, for example, where a company made an installment sale of a nonrecurring nature. While it may have enjoyed the benefit in the year of sale of having elected the installment method of tax reporting, the tax payable in the year or years of collection could be substantial in relation to income tax for the year. (The tax payment, in effect, would be charged against the deferred tax liability account.) In reporting the cash impact of taxes in such a transac-

---

[8] Under new FASB accounting rules, research and development costs are no longer deferrable commencing in 1975 (FASB *Statement of Financial Accounting Standards No. 2*, October 1974).

tion, the company may be in a position to point out that the tax to be disbursed will not be a burden because it had collected the deferred receivable on a gross basis, as opposed to income tax applicable to the gross profit on such sale. However, if it had invested the proceeds in fixed assets or to retire long-term debt, it would then need to raise current funds to meet the tax imposed.

In the foreword to *ASR No. 149*, the SEC has stated its perceived obligation to fulfill the needs of professional financial analysts who seek to develop an understanding in depth of corporate results far beyond the understanding of the average investor. This is evident not only in the requirements already indicated above but also in the additional requirement to disclose the reasons for significant variations in the customary relationship between income tax expense and pretax financial accounting income, if they are not otherwise apparent from the financial statements or from the nature of the entity's business.

ASR No. 149 requires a reconciliation in dollar amounts or percentages of each of the underlying causes for the differences between reported income tax expense and the "expected" tax expense, based on the current statutory tax rate of 48 percent for domestic corporations. Small items aggregating less than 5 percent of the computed amount may be excluded from the reconciliation. These differences represent permanent tax differences, for which we will present our own version in the next section before reviewing the example furnished in *ASR No. 149*.

It has been suggested that the effect of the disclosure requirements of *ASR No. 149* is to create generally accepted accounting principles, not only for companies subject to SEC jurisdiction but also for companies not so subject. This accentuates the controversy as to whether accounting principles should be set in the public or private sector.[9]

PERMANENT INCOME TAX DIFFERENCES—FEDERAL

If income before tax on a financial accounting basis agreed with taxable income, and if the income was subject solely to the statutory federal income tax rate of 48 percent, then the income tax expense would be the same as the income tax payable per the tax return.

---

[9] Ducray, "Tax Disclosure under the SEC's ASR No. 149," *Financial Executive,* October 1974.

The first section of this chapter indicated briefly the broad reasons for permanent income tax differences which cause reported income tax expenses to differ from "expected" income tax expense based on the current statutory rate of 48 percent. Exhibit 2 covers more specifically the following five classes of transactions that create permanent tax differences:

Reference to
Exhibit 2

I.   Certain items may be nontaxable . . . . (A)
II. Certain deductions may be unallowable . . . . (B)
III. Capital gains are taxed at different rates . . . . (D)
IV. Special deductions are allowable for
     certain dividends received . . . . (D)
V.   Tax credits are available . . . . (F)

As a result of assumed amounts for the above items, income before tax of $100,000 in Exhibit 2 is reduced to $74,550 with resultant federal and foreign income taxes of $31,564. Compared with a statutory tax rate of 48 percent, these taxes amount to 31.564 percent of income before tax. Compared with taxable income of $74,550, these taxes result in an effective rate of 42.339 percent and are less than the statutory federal rate of 48 percent because of the items classified as III, IV, and V above.

For sake of simplicity, state income taxes are omitted and it is assumed that there are no permanent tax differences applicable to the foreign income taxes.

At the end of the preceding section, reference was made to the reconciliation of the underlying causes for the differences between reported income tax expense and the "expected" income tax expense based on the statutory rate of 48 percent. Exhibit 3 includes a verbatim copy of the illustrative note given in *ASR No. 149*. Because this illustrative note commingles, in one column, the various elements included with respect to federal income taxes, foreign income taxes on foreign subsidiaries, and other income taxes (state and local), the illustrative note in Exhibit 4 has been extended to show, in addition, the data with respect to each of these separate classes of income taxes in separate columns. This brings the illustrative note into sharper focus and also highlights how state and local income taxes are treated net of federal income tax benefit.

In the authors' view, the treatment of the state taxes of $208 net of federal income tax benefit is misleading in that it is in conflict with prevalent practices of reporting state taxes gross and applying

EXHIBIT 2

Illustration of permanent tax differences including tax rate differences, special deductions, and tax credits (in 000s)

	Income before tax	Income tax
Income before tax and income tax	$100,000	$ 48,000*
A. Nontaxable income (deduct):		
1. Income on tax-exempt state and municipal obligations. . .	(2,000)	(960)
2. Percentage depletion in excess of cost depletion.	(15,000)	(7,200)
3. Proceeds of life insurance on officer	(500)	(240)
4. Income of foreign subsidiary—permanently invested outside United States	(10,500)	(5,040)
	$ (28,000)	$(13,440)
B. Unallowable deductions (add):		
1. Amortization of goodwill	$ 5,000	$ 2,400
2. Penalty for late filing of certain returns.	25	12
3. Fines, etc.	25	12
4. Excess contributions not utilized by carryforwards	50	24
	$ 5,100	$ 2,448
C. Subtotals	$ 77,100	$ 37,008
D. Tax rate differences and special deductions:		
1. Capital gain of $4,000—taxable at 30%, difference 18% . .	–	(720)
2. Dividend on unconsolidated subsidiaries of $3,000 subject to reduction of 85%, or $2,550 at 48%	(2,550)	(1,224)
	$ (2,550)	$ (1,944)
E. Taxable income and income tax before tax credits	$ 74,550	$ 35,064
F. Tax credits:		
1. Foreign tax credit†—based on $20,000 foreign income included in taxable income and 48% federal income tax of $9,600; foreign income tax of 38% or $7,600 leaves $2,000 federal tax on foreign income.	–	(7,600)
2. Investment tax credit—7% on qualified property of $50,000; flow-through method	–	(3,500)
	–	(11,100)
G. Taxable income and federal income tax.	$ 74,550	$ 23,964
H. Foreign income tax	–	7,600
I. Taxable income and federal and foreign income taxes.	$ 74,550	$ 31,564
J.	*Summary*	
Domestic taxable income and federal income tax	$ 54,550	$ 21,964
Foreign income.	$ 20,000	–
Federal tax on foreign income	–	$ 2,000
Foreign tax on foreign income	–	7,600
	$ 20,000	$ 9,600
Combined income and tax	$ 74,550	$ 31,564

(Total taxes equal 42.339% of taxable income)

* Ignoring surtax credit of $6.5.

† Limited to lower of foreign tax paid, $7,600, or such portion of U.S. income tax (before credits), $35,064, as foreign income, $20,000, bears to total taxable income, $74,550.

$$\frac{\$20,000}{\$74,550} = 27\% \times \$35,064 = \$9,467; \text{ therefore, use } \$7,600$$

Note: Where a company is unable to use part or all of an operating loss carryforward, such unused loss has the effect of a tentative permanent timing difference (adverse). If it expires, it becomes permanent; if utilized in part or full the timing difference is reduced accordingly.

EXHIBIT 3
Extract from SEC Accounting Series Release No. 149

ILLUSTRATIVE NOTE

Note—Income tax expense (all data in thousands).

Income tax expense is made up of the following components:

	U.S. federal	Foreign	State and local	Total
Current tax expense	$2,312	$360	$400	$3,072
Deferred tax expense	2,328	420	–0–	2,748
	$4,640	$780	$400	$5,820

Deferred tax expense results from timing differences in the recognition of revenue and expense for tax and financial statement purposes. The sources of these differences in 1973 and the tax effect of each were as follows:

	Tax effects
Excess of tax over book depreciation.	$ 600
Research and development costs expensed on tax return and deferred on books	1,440
Revenue recognized on completed contract basis on tax return and on percentage of completion basis on books	960
Tax deductible inventory reserve provided in foreign tax jurisdiction	420
Warranty cost charged to expense on books but not deductible until paid	(672)
	$2,748

Total tax expense amounted to $5,820 (an effective rate of 38.8%), a total less than the amount of $7,200 computed by applying the U.S. federal income tax rate of 48% to income before tax. The reasons for this difference are as follows:

	Amount	% of pretax income
Computed "expected" tax expense.	$7,200	48.0%
Increases (reductions) in taxes resulting from:		
Foreign income subject to foreign income tax but not expected to be subject to U.S. tax in foreseeable future ($2,400 × 48%) – $780 = $372.	(372)	(2.5)
Tax-exempt municipal bond income	(720)	(4.8)
Investment tax credit on assets purchased in 1973	(700)	(4.7)
Goodwill amortization not deductible for tax purposes	384	2.6
State and local income taxes, net of federal income tax benefit*	208	1.4
Benefit from income taxes at capital gains rate (1,000 × 48%) – (1,000 × 30%) = $180*	(180)	(1.2)
Actual Tax Expense	$5,820	38.8%

Based upon currently anticipated expenditures and operations, it is expected that the deferred income tax balance will be substantially reduced in 1976 and the cash outlay for taxes associated with that year will exceed tax expense by approximately $4,000, primarily due to the book amortization in that year of research and development expense previously deducted for tax purposes.

* Since these amounts are less than 5 percent of the computed "expected" tax expense, they could be combined with any other items less than $360 into an aggregate total. For example, these items could be disclosed as follows: "Miscellaneous items . . . $28 . . . 0.2%."

If no single item had exceeded $360 in this case and the total net difference of all items was also less than $360, this reconciliation would not have been required.

EXHIBIT 4
Accountability for income taxes, adapted from ASR No. 149 (in 000s)

	Total	Federal tax	Foreign tax*	State and local tax
Income before tax	$15,000	$12,600	$2,400	[$5,000]†
				(included in federal)
Income tax expense:				
Current.	$ 3,072	$ 2,312	$ 360	$ 400
Deferred	2,748	2,328	420	—
	$ 5,820	$ 4,640	$ 780	$ 400
Reconciliation—Income tax expense with computed "expected" tax expense				
Theoretical income tax at 48%	$ 7,200	$ 6,048	$1,152	—
Increases (reductions) in taxes resulting from: Foreign income subject to foreign income tax but not expected to be subject to U.S. tax [($2,400 × .48) = $1,152 less $780]	(372)		(372)	
Tax-exempt municipal bond income ($1,500 × .48)	(720)	(720)		
Investment tax credit on assets purchased in 1973.	(700)	(700)		
Goodwill amortization not deductible for tax ($800 × .48)	384	384		
State and local taxes net of federal income tax benefit of $192	208			208
Reclassify federal tax benefit on state and local tax	—	(192)		192
Benefit from income taxed at capital gains rate ($1,000 × [.48 − .30]).	(180)	(180)		
Net decrease	$ (1,380)	$ (1,408)	$ (372)	$ 400
Actual Tax Expense	$ 5,820	$ 4,640	$ 780	$ 400
	38.8%		[32.5% of $2,400]	[8% of $5,000]

* While not so indicated, these deferred income taxes would have to be applicable to income of foreign subsidiaries.

† As indicated in Section 3, the same income is subject to both federal and state income taxes.

the federal tax benefit as a reduction of federal income taxes. (See the earlier section, "Relative Income Tax Burdens.") Accordingly, in Exhibit 4 the tax credit on state and local income taxes has been reclassified so as to add it to the "net of tax" amount in the SEC example, thus restoring the state income tax to a gross amount.

Note that Exhibit 4 covers income of foreign subsidiaries, foreign income tax payable currently, and deferred taxes on foreign income, whereas our earlier example in Exhibit 2 covers income of foreign divisions, its inclusion in federal taxable income, and the foreign tax credit. Exhibit 2 does not provide for deferred income from foreign subsidiaries.

INCOME TAX ACCOUNTING FOR
INTERIM PERIODS

Since income taxes are deferred on the basis of a statutory year, it may not be realistic to base determinations of taxes payable currently or taxes deferred on interim periods that reflect seasonal variations within the year.

Lifo accounting for inventory[10] is an illustration in which an interim report may reflect a large temporary or seasonal liquidation of Lifo inventory layers, with the result that income tax is apparently currently payable, followed by replacement of such layers by the end of the year and reduction of the tentative tax liability. In order to avoid such provision for current taxes and recoupment, the Lifo calculation should be made on the basis that the temporary liquidation of inventory did not occur.

Accounting for installment receivables is another illustration in which a large temporary or seasonal liquidation of receivables reported for taxes on the installment basis may cause a temporary tax liability, offset before the end of the year by recoupment of such taxes. Accordingly, in splitting the tax provision between the amounts payable currently and those deferred, the seasonal liquidation of the receivables expected to be replaced by year-end should be ignored. Thus, in setting up the tax provision and its split be-

---

[10] The Lifo method of inventory is unusual because of the Internal Revenue Code requirement that Lifo taxpayers use the Lifo method in their annual reports to stockholders, creditors, and so on. Because of this conformity, no interperiod allocation of income taxes is appropriate.

In view of the extremely strict technical Internal Revenue Service requirements imposed on Lifo taxpayers, it is interesting to note recent developments of conflict between the SEC and the IRS which were accentuated by the recent double digit inflation and the accompanying adoption of Lifo by many taxpayers.

The SEC requires that management's analysis of operations include a description of the change in accounting principles upon adoption of Lifo and the effect of the change on the earnings and the earnings per share for the year of change. This is required in addition to a similar note to the related financial statements.

While the use of the note for this purpose had previously been recognized by the IRS, any other reference to the change to Lifo was precluded in prior IRS rulings. As a result of consultation between the IRS and the SEC, the IRS now recognizes (IRS *Technical Information Release 1339*, January 23, 1975) the indicated reporting requirement of the SEC but still forbids such reference for years other than the year of adoption of Lifo.

tween current and deferred, similar recognition should be given on an annual basis to various other seasonal timing differences.

Where a company with a strong record of annual earnings incurs seasonal losses in the earlier parts of the fiscal year, such losses may be carried back to income of prior years for purposes of setting up an interim provision for income tax creditable to the loss operation. Application of the above principles should result in realistic income tax accounting for interim periods. (See *APB Opinion No. 28*, May 1973.)

LIABILITY METHOD AND PARTIAL ALLOCATION

The earlier section entitled "Deferred Method and Comprehensive Allocation" indicated that by recording the full tax effects of timing differences at their inception, the deferred tax accounts are carried at rates set up initially, without any adjustment for subsequent changes in tax rates.

Under the *liability method* (which is not recognized as a generally accepted accounting principle under *APB Opinion No. 11*), the tax effects of timing differences are recorded as part of the income tax provision (debit or credit) at the tax rates prevailing when the timing differences originate, and are adjusted subsequently when and as tax rates change.

The practice of *partial allocation* under the liability method would involve recording deferred tax balance sheet accounts (credit or debit), with the contra entry to tax provision, only if the transactions are expected to turn around (or liquidate themselves) without replacement. If, however, management expects to continue to replace liquidations for the foreseeable future, then no deferred tax liability (or asset) account would be recorded.

The two most important transactions that would lend themselves to partial allocation by management are:

1. The use of accelerated depreciation or short lives for tax purposes but not for financial accounting purposes, and
2. The use of the installment method for tax reporting coupled with use of the accrual method (as required) for financial accounting purposes.

If partial allocation were not prohibited, tax liabilities would be recorded in the year in which such transactions reverse themselves (no liability having been set up initially). The reversal in the current period, and a tax liability increase, could result from a management decision to shift from purchase of equipment to leasing such equipment, or a decision to reduce the credit period on installment sales.

Since *APB Opinion No. 11* requires the use of comprehensive allocation under the deferred method and forbids the use of partial allocation, the balance sheets of American corporations include substantial deferred tax amounts, both in current liabilities related to installment accounts receivable and in noncurrent liabilities for deferred taxes attributable to such items as machinery and equipment. For growth companies, these deferred tax accounts are carried virtually in perpetuity. This treatment is sometimes not well understood by professional analysts, with the result that cash flow evaluations may not properly reflect the absence of cash demands to discharge these (deferred) liability accounts.

Furthermore, prohibition of partial tax allocation for equipment purchases has a retarding effect on maintaining plants at optimum efficiency and productivity. The income tax laws provide tax incentives in the form of the investment tax credit and various forms of more rapid depreciation by accelerated methods or shorter lives. Although the immediate effect of the investment tax credit is reflected in the financial accounts by the "flow-through" method,[11] no similar benefit is available for investment in equipment. This benefit would result from partial allocation, as illustrated above by the examples of accelerated depreciation and installment sales. Since partial allocation is recognized by some accounting authorities[12] and also has management support, correction of the present anomaly (failure to accept partial allocation) would bring financial statements of American industry back to the world of reality. The authors

---

[11] For a discussion of the controversy that has raged over the "flow-through" versus the amortization method of accounting for the investment tax credit, see Wheeler and Galliart, *An Appraisal of Interperiod Income Tax Allocation,* Financial Executives Research Foundation (1974), pp. 30–37.

[12] See, for example, Wheeler and Galliart, pp. 208–10; *Is Generally Acceptable Accounting for Income Taxes Possibly Misleading Investors?* A Statement of Position on Income Tax Allocation (Price Waterhouse & Co., July 1967), 27 pp. plus Appendix; Herman W. Bevis, "Measuring Federal Income Tax Cost," *Corporate Financial Reporting in a Competitive Economy,* (New York: Columbia University and The MacMillan Co., 1965), pp. 122–25; H. W. Bevis, "Contingencies and Probabilities in Financial Statements," *The Journal of Accountancy,* October 1968, pp. 37–45; David F. Hawkins; "Deferred Taxes: Source of Non-Operating Funds," *Financial Executive,* February 1969, pp. 35–37, 40–42, and 44.

suggest that this is an important area for the Financial Accounting Standards Board to consider.

NEED FOR TAX RELIEF

When one recognizes the inhibiting effect of the recent double digit inflation in the light of the inadequacies of accounting for machinery and equipment on the basis of historical cost, the need for more drastic tax relief comes into focus. This relief could include depreciation allowances based on monetary factors (as in Brazil), or a similar variation of price-level accounting. This would help prevent the taxation of illusory profits inherent in inflation and would help improve the competitive position of U.S. companies, particularly in comparison with their counterparts in other industrial countries.

PART 3

Special problems in accounting measurement

Chapter 15

Accounting for contingencies

*A. Philip Hanmer**

The title of this chapter presents a contradiction in terms for a fairly large body of qualified and informed accountants. They would contend that many, if not most, contingencies are to be *disclosed* rather than *accounted for*. The difficulty arises over the interpretation of a "contingency." Thus, it is essential at the outset that the word be defined in order for the reader to comprehend fully the views on individual issues which follow.

CONTINGENCIES DEFINED

Webster's dictionary defines contingency as ". . . a possible or unforeseen occurrence; something liable to happen as an adjunct to something else."

Accounting Research Bulletin No. 43, Chapter 6, without providing a definition,[1] dealt with contingency reserves in a very narrow sense in that the only examples of contingency conditions related to inventory valuation. *Accounting Research Bulletin No. 50* covering contingencies had this explanation: "In accounting a contingency is an existing condition, situation or set of circumstances, involving

---

* Controller, The Dow Chemical Company.

[1] Committee on Accounting Procedure, AICPA, "Restatement and Revision of Accounting Research Bulletins," *Accounting Research Bulletin No. 43* (New York, 1953).

a considerable degree of uncertainty, which may, through a related future event, result in the acquisition or loss of an asset, or the incurrence or avoidance of a liability, usually with concurrence of a gain or loss. A commitment which is not dependent upon some significant intervening factor or decision should not be described as a contingency."[2]

Statement of Financial Accounting Standards No. 5, "Accounting for Contingencies," issued in March 1975 defined a contingency as:

> . . . an existing condition, situation, or set of circumstances involving uncertainty as to possible gain (hereinafter a "gain contingency") or loss[3] (hereinafter a "loss contingency") to an enterprise that will ultimately be resolved when one or more future events occur or fail to occur. Resolution of the uncertainty may confirm the acquisition of an asset or the reduction of a liability or the loss or impairment of an asset or the incurrence of a liability.

CONTINGENT GAINS AND LOSSES

It is important to recognize that contingencies can involve contingent assets and contingent gains as well as contingent asset reductions and contingent losses, in addition to the more familiar contingent liabilities and contingent losses. Examples of *contingent assets* include tax operating loss and investment credit carryforwards and claims against debtors primarily as the result of legal action. Examples of *contingent asset reductions* are anticipated uncollectible accounts receivable and estimated obsolescence or deterioration of inventories.

RECOGNIZING CONTINGENT ASSETS

The principles of accounting for gain contingencies, which were stated in paragraphs 3 and 5 of *ARB No. 50,* remain in effect. They are:

> (a) Contingencies that might result in gains usually are not reflected in the accounts since to do so might be to recognize revenue prior to its realization.

---

[2] Committee on Accounting Procedure, AICPA, "Contingencies," *Accounting Research Bulletin No. 50* (New York, 1958).

[3] The term *loss* is used for convenience to include many charges against income that are commonly referred to as *expenses* and others that are commonly referred to as *losses.*

(*b*)   Adequate disclosure shall be made of contingencies that might result in gains, but care shall be exercised to avoid misleading implications as to the likelihood of realization.

There is almost no condition under which an asset whose realization is dependent upon some significant future event can be recorded in the accounts. Rather, the accepted practice is to divulge all of the pertinent facts through footnote disclosure. An example of such disclosure can be found in the Annual Report to Stockholders issued by Boise Cascade Corporation for the year ended December 31, 1972. Note 7 reads in part as follows:

> A subsidiary of the Company, Shanghai Power Co., formerly owned and operated an electric utility serving Shanghai, China. Its properties were taken over by the People's Republic of China in 1950. Pursuant to the China Claims Act, the U.S. Foreign Claims Settlement Commission has certified a claim against the People's Republic of $55,600,000 plus interest at 6% from 1950 for the expropriated properties. The Company has been informed that as part of the efforts to normalize relations between the United States and the People's Republic, negotiations will be undertaken during 1973 between the two governments seeking to settle this and similar claims against the People's Republic by other American nationals aggregating approximately $200,000,000. It is not possible, of course, to predict the outcome of those negotiations and therefore the claim is not reflected in the Company's assets.

RECOGNIZING CONTINGENT LOSSES

In FASB *Standard No. 5* the Board pointed out that not all uncertainties inherent in the accounting process give rise to contingencies. The fact that an estimate is involved does not by itself constitute the type of uncertainty referred to in the Board's definition of contingency.

In establishing principles for accounting for loss contingencies the Board recognized that the likelihood that future events will confirm the loss or impairment of an asset, or the incurrence of a liability, can range from probable to remote. The degrees of probability were defined as follows:

(*a*)   *Probable.* The future event or events are likely to occur.
(*b*)   *Reasonably possible.* The chance of the future event or events occurring is more than remote but less than likely.

(*c*)   *Remote.* The chance of the future event or events occurring is slight.

The FASB required the *accrual of an estimated loss* from a loss contingency, reflected as a charge to income, if the loss is *probable* and its amount can be *reasonably estimated.* In circumstances described in paragraphs 23–24 of *APB Opinion No. 9,* "Reporting the Results of Operations," a prior period adjustment may be appropriate. The FASB explained the first criterion as follows:

> Information available prior to issuance of the financial statements indicates that it is probable that an asset had been impaired or a liability had been incurred at the date of the financial statements. It is implicit in this condition that one or more future events will occur confirming the fact of the loss.

It may be necessary to disclose the nature of the accrual, and in some circumstances the amount accrued, in order that the financial statements will not be misleading.

DISCLOSURE OF LOSS CONTINGENCIES

FASB *Standard No. 5,* paragraph 10, required disclosure in cases where no accrual was made for a loss contingency because one or both of the criteria for accrual are not met, or because an exposure to loss exists greater than the amount of loss accrued, where there is at least a *reasonable possibility* that a loss or an additional loss may have been incurred. The disclosure in these cases must either (*a*) indicate the nature of the contingency and give an estimate of the amount of the possible loss or range of loss, or (*b*) state that such an estimate cannot be made.

After the date of the financial statements but before they are issued information may become available indicating that an asset was impaired or a liability was incurred *after* the statement date, or that there was at least a reasonable possibility of asset impairment or liability incurrence. This information may relate to a loss contingency that existed at the date of the statements, such as an asset that was not insured. On the other hand, it may deal with a loss contingency that did not exist at statement date, such as threat of expropriation of assets after the statement date. In these types of cases accrual of a loss was not required because there was no asset impairment nor liability incurrence at the date of the statements. However, it may be necessary to disclose such losses or loss contingencies to keep the financial statements from being misleading. If such disclosure is considered necessary, it should either (*a*) indicate the nature of the loss or loss contingency and the amount or range of loss or possible loss, or (*b*) state that such an estimate cannot be made.

Occasionally when a loss arises after statement date the amount of the loss can be reasonably estimated, and it may be best to disclose the situation by supplementing the historical statements with pro forma financial data giving effect to the loss as if it had occurred at the date of the statements. (FASB *Standard No. 5*, paragraph 11.)

FASB *Statement No. 5* recommended continuing to disclose certain loss contingencies that are now being disclosed in financial statements even though the possibility of loss may be remote. A common characteristic of these losses is a guarantee, usually with a right to proceed against an outside party if the guarantor is required to satisfy the guarantee. The Statement recommends that consideration be given to disclosing, if it can be estimated, the value of any recovery that could be expected by proceeding against an outside party.

OPPOSING VIEWPOINTS FOR RECOGNIZING CONTINGENT LOSSES

The crux of the issue in accounting for contingencies is the *degree of certainty* needed in order to recognize the potential event in the financial statements. So-called accounting purists adopt the view that most situations lack sufficient predictability and measurability to permit current recognition. They believe, basically, that financial statements should present information about events that have taken place. The position to be taken herein is that good accounting practice requires full recognition of events whose timing and magnitude lacks certainty but can, nevertheless, be reasonably estimated.

The accounting principles which are brought into sharp focus by the opposing viewpoints are the proper *timing of costs* in the income statement and the determination of *when a contingency qualifies as a liability.* In presenting the two points of view, it must be realized that they are held with different degrees of intensity depending on the individual situation under consideration.

It is conceded that the matching of costs with revenues is an important criterion. Those who embrace the view that an event should not be recognized prior to finalization of incurred costs place a high priority on accuracy, and at the same time express concern over the ability of companies to manipulate or manage income between fiscal periods by the use of questionable estimates of contingent costs. The opposite view is that the whole process of accounting, from concept to practice, is founded on informed judgment which is no less effective when applied to contingencies than to any other area of uncertainty. It maintains that a reasonable estimate of such costs provides a better matching of costs with revenues than does waiting until precisely measurable amounts are available.

When an accrual is made for a contingent cost, the credit appears in the balance sheet in one of several ways. It may be deducted from an asset as a valuation account or it may be shown as a liability, either current or noncurrent. There are a number of instances in which the accrual would not meet the classical definition of a liability as being an amount owed by a debtor to a creditor and payable in cash or noncash assets. Many accountants would cite this reason to support their view that some contingent costs should not be recognized prior to the final determination of incurrence. They maintain that the absence of a legitimate, identifiable creditor prevents recognition currently.

Those holding the opposing view would concede that the credit may not be a liability in the narrow legal sense; but to them, the impact on income is the overriding issue. They cite *Accounting Principles Board Opinion No. 11,* "Accounting for Income Taxes," as a precedent for giving primacy to income statement considerations. In that opinion, the Board concluded that comprehensive interperiod tax allocation is an integral part of the determination of income tax expense and that "deferred charges and deferred credits relating to timing differences represent the cumulative recognition given to their tax effects and, as such, do not represent receivables or payables in the usual sense."[4]

---

[4] AICPA, "Accounting for Income Taxes," *Accounting Principles Board Opinion No. 11* (New York, 1967).

TYPES OF CONTINGENCIES

The contingencies to be discussed in some detail in this chapter are listed below:

1. Uncollectible accounts and notes receivable.
2. Inventory obsolescence.
3. Losses on long-term construction contracts.
4. Loss on investments.
5. Foreign expropriation.
6. Future maintenance and repair of equipment.
7. Lease bonus amortization.
8. Mining restoration costs.
9. Product liability claims.
10. Workmen's compensation.
11. Probable tax assessments.
12. Pension expense.
13. Industrial diseases.
14. Patent violations.
15. Lawsuits.
16. Future penalty costs for nondelivery.
17. Catastrophe losses.
18. Self-insured losses.

Uncollectible accounts and notes receivable

This probably typifies contingency accounting as well as any situation, but it is likely to be recognized as contingency accounting by fewer accountants than many other situations to be discussed. The reason probably is the frequency with which it is encountered. It is accepted, if not required, practice today for a company to set aside out of current income a provision for future nonpayment by debtors of accounts and notes receivable. The amount of such provision must, of necessity, be based upon management's judgment of the condition of the accounts and notes supported by aging and analysis.

Experience is beneficial in drawing conclusions, but it should be remembered that none of the accounts covered by the allowance have been finalized as uncollectible. In every case, the realization of the bad debt is contingent upon a subsequent final determination of the debtor's inability to pay accounts due.

Inventory obsolescence

Obsolescence is discussed briefly here to bring attention to the contingent nature of the provision.

Whenever products priced in accordance with regular and accepted practices are subject to conditions which require a lower value to be placed on them to recognize obsolescence, it is usually accomplished by providing an allowance which is deducted from the related asset in the balance sheet.

The true value is not a matter of fact, so the valuation must be judged by management pending final realization. The contingent aspects of full realization do not preclude recognizing the loss by means of an allowance provision.

An example of this accounting treatment can be seen in the Annual Report of Continental Airlines for 1973. The balance sheet caption reads as follows: "Spare parts and supplies, less reserve for obsolescence of $6,761,847 in 1973 and $3,450,868 in 1972 (note 12)." Note 12 stated the following:

> In 1971, the Company began an extensive aircraft fleet modernization program providing for the disposition of all its Boeing 320C, Boeing 720B and McDonnell Douglas DC-9C aircraft and related spare parts. During 1973, the Company expanded this program to include the planned disposition of its four Boeing 747 aircraft and related spare parts. On January 10, 1974, the Company removed from service its Boeing 747 aircraft. Although the market and future prices for aircraft of this type are not presently determinable, based on recent purchase inquiries, management believes that no material gain or loss will result from their disposition.
>
> In connection with this program, the Company, in 1973, increased the reserves for expendable and spare parts obsolesence and depreciation, respectively, by $2,939,000 and $2,872,000, to adjust the net book values to estimated realizable values.

Losses on long-term construction contracts

Because of the length of time required to complete some construction contracts, the contractor must constantly assess cost escalations, construction efficiency, and price escalation potentials to determine the probabilities of an ultimate loss upon completion. Each of these factors frequently has different degrees of contingent potential about it. This does not relieve management of its responsibility to assess all conditions and to provide such an allowance as it deems appropriate.

Loss on investments

In establishing an allowance for some investments, such as marketable securities, management usually relies on factual market quotations which remove the contingency element from the decision at the date of the balance sheet. However, on more permanent investments which are not subject to the equity method of valuation, management is obliged to recognize any permanent loss in value by establishing an allowance for loss. Such a determination frequently requires the assessment of many contingencies in order to arrive at a reasonable allowance. The absence of fact does not preclude making such a determination.

Foreign expropriation

Many companies today are heavily involved and invested in multinational operations. The political climate in some countries is such that the risk of expropriation of assets or the diminutions in value of assets by virtue of the use of force or by the promulgation of restrictive laws, which accomplish the same result, makes the occurrence of a loss imminent. Under such conditions, the management should recognize the probable loss by providing an appropriate allowance. In all probability, the allowance should be classified as a reduction of the related asset in the balance sheet.

General Motors Corporation has maintained such an account for several years. It was described in note 1 of Notes to Financial Statements in the 1973 Annual Report as follows:

> The general reserve applicable to foreign operations was established in 1954 and is available to absorb extraordinary losses, such as losses from discontinuing foreign operations in any locality, either voluntarily or because of conditions beyond the Corporation's control. There has been no change in this reserve since its establishment.

The FASB statement, "Accounting for Contingencies," appears to require the reversal of this account unless it can be demonstrated that the losses are imminent.

Future maintenance and repair of equipment

Some companies have adopted the practice of providing a reserve out of current earnings to cover the estimated cost of repairs of equipment in future periods. It is not a common practice, and those that use it apply it to special-purpose equipment, such as aircraft overhaul and steel furnace rebuilding, which can be anticipated with some degree of certainty even though the repair has not been performed. Regularly recurring general maintenance is considered to be a charge to income as completed.

Several United States airlines follow the practice of accruing for maintenance. Note 1c of Notes to Financial Statements of the 1973 Annual Report of Western Airlines described that company's practice as follows:

> Reserves for Overhauls of Flight Equipment: The estimated future costs of airframe and engine overhauls are provided for by charges to maintenance expense based on hours flown.

Lease bonus amortization

While this procedure is limited to companies prospecting below the earth's surface for minerals, the total of such amortization is substantial for the economy. Such companies pay landowners cash known as a "lease bonus" for the right to subsurface gas, oil, and so on. Because the success rate in finding the mineral through drilling operations is so low, many companies commence an amortization program immediately after the payment is made to recognize the contingent loss. Using this method, the cost of lease bonuses is usually charged to expense in advance of the date when dry holes have established with certainty the absence of the sought-after mineral and the need to relinquish all interest in the leased property. The amortization is usually treated as a direct reduction of the asset value as opposed to a contra account.

Mining restoration costs

In the present-day concern for ecology, companies engaged in mining operations are faced with huge costs at the conclusion of their efforts to restore the surface and/or subsurface conditions to a state acceptable to the public, both as to appearance and use.

Likewise, oil companies conducting offshore drilling operations have similar restoration demands on them. This contingent expenditure usually appears to have enough certainty about it, and should be satisfactorily quantifiable, to permit an appropriate accrual of the future cost against the current income stream.

Product liability claims

Chapter 8 deals with accounting for product warranty and service contract costs. The purpose in including it here is to remind the reader that in establishing a liability for product claims and warranties, one must deal with uncompleted transactions or contingent events. The imprecision of such conditions does not preclude recognition of such liabilities in the accounts.

The 1973 Annual Report of G. D. Searle & Company did not show the amount of liability accrued, but its Summary of Significant Accounting Policies included the following:

> The company purchases product liability insurance coverage, but assumes the risk for deductible amounts specified in the policies. Reserves are set up each year which, in the company's judgment, adequately provide for the cost of losses which, if sustained, would not be covered by insurance policies.

Workmen's compensation

Companies that assume the full risk of this liability without purchased insurance coverage must rely in part on contingent developments. After a compensable accident has occurred and before the determination of benefits has been made, the company should accrue the expense or loss and the related liability on the basis of best estimates.

Probable tax assessments

It is the responsibility of every management to provide fully for all taxes which may be reasonably assessed against the company as a result of past events. The need to recognize an income tax liability may arise from several sources. The company may have a report from an examining agent to which it intends to agree in whole or in part. Determining the amount and timing of such liability is reasonably factual and should be recognized as soon as the conditions support it.

Somewhat more difficult, but just as demanding of recognition, is the liability for certain income tax issues which may or may not be specifically identifiable. It is common practice to file a tax return which treats controversial tax issues in the most favorable light and thus produces the lowest tax on the return. Prudence requires recognition in the books of the tax liability that may be ultimately assessed on such issues. Beyond that, it is acceptable and common practice to recognize in the accounts audit disallowances that have already been made and to accrue tax liability on unidentified and thus contingent issues.

Pension expense

The accrual of pension liability is charged against earnings based on many actuarial assumptions which dictate both the amount and timing of payments under the pension plan. Pension accounting is a very complicated subject, and the purpose in including it here is simply to cite it as another example of contingency accounting.

Industrial diseases

A number of companies are faced with the potential liability to employees to compensate them for diseases such as black lung and cancer allegedly incurred during employment activity. To the extent that a reasonable determination can be made of the certainty of the exposure and the amount thereof, a liability should be provided in the accounts.

Patent violations

In the event that a company faces a liability for violation of patent rights, it should be recognized in the accounts to the extent that the exposure can be measured. Such liability could be based upon information arising from either discussion with the company's attorney or lawsuits filed. In any event, the contingent nature of the circumstances should not forestall the recognition of the liability.

Lawsuits

Liabilities under general lawsuits are not unlike those discussed in the preceding paragraph in that the liability should be recognized where it can be quantified reasonably. In both cases, managements are frequently reluctant to provide a reserve to cover the contingent liability because where important amounts are involved, the disclosure might provide a clue to the plaintiff. However, a prudent stance requires recognition as soon as there are clear indications that liability of measurable proportions exists.

Many companies are understandably reluctant to disclose the amounts provided for exposure under lawsuits. One method of indicating that recognition has been given to the contingent liability can be seen in this excerpt from The Dow Chemical Company 1973 Annual Report—Notes to Financial Statements:

> Note K. Contingent Liabilities and Commitments. Suits have been started against the Company and certain subsidiaries because of alleged product damages and other claims. All suits are being contested and the amount of uninsured liability thereunder is considered adequately covered by provisions made.

Future penalty costs for nondelivery

During times of material shortages, it occasionally happens that companies committed under long-term supply contracts to furnish stipulated quantities in certain time segments must pay a cash penalty in the event of noncompliance. When the probability of such a penalty can be foreseen with clarity and the amount can be measured, it does not matter that the event has not yet taken place. The liability should be recorded. It is argued in support of this practice that the current income stream should be burdened with the expense in order to provide a better revenue/cost match.

Catastrophe losses

The insurance industry is about equally divided in its views on the need for and the propriety of a catastrophe loss reserve for property and casualty companies. It is an immensely complex problem, and one which may not have much interest for those outside the insurance industry. However, many companies have organized captive insurance subsidiaries which will have to consider the alternatives.

Briefly stated, when an insurance company establishes its premium rate schedule, recognition is presumably given and an amount is factored in to cover so-called catastrophes which are significant in amount and do not necessarily occur with regular frequency. It has been argued that the catastrophe premium should be deferred over an extended period, and catastrophe losses charged against it. The rebuttal to this position is that the amount of the premium element related to catastrophes is not always known. This is particularly true when the official rate structure is discounted in competitive situations.

On the other hand, rate-making specialists contend that their statistical data provide a sufficiently reliable basis for establishing the amount of such catastrophes which will occur over an extended period of time. Their uncertainty relates to the amount to be associated with annual time segments. Thus, those who support the provision of an allowance out of current earnings rely on this position. Various formulas have been devised to calculate the amount of the allowance requirements on a regular and consistent basis.

In a sense, this allowance and the one discussed next in this chapter differ significantly from all of the others mentioned in that the provision is not rooted in an event that has already happened. In this case, no event has occurred. Any provision must, of necessity, be made in anticipation of something happening.

The following excerpt from FASB *Statement of Financial Accounting Standards No. 5,* "Accounting for Contingencies," sets forth the reasons advanced by the proponents of catastrophe loss accrual and the FASB reactions to them:

(a) *Catastrophes certain to occur.* Over the long term, catastrophes are certain to occur; therefore, they are not contingencies.

(b) *Predictability of catastrophe losses.* On the basis of experience and by application of appropriate statistical techniques, catastrophe losses can be predicted over the long term with reasonable accuracy.

(c) *Matching.* Some portion of property and casualty insurance premiums is intended to cover losses that usually occur infrequently and at intervals longer than both the terms of the policies in force and the financial accounting and reporting period. Catastrophe losses should, therefore, be accrued when the revenue is recognized (or premiums should be deferred beyond the terms of policies in force to periods in which the catastrophes occur) to match catastrophe losses with the related revenue.

(d)   *Stabilization of reported income.* Catastrophe reserve accounting stabilizes reported income and avoids erratic variations caused by irregularly occurring catastrophes.

(e)   *Comparability.* Reinsurance premiums paid by a prime insurer are said to be similar to accrual of catastrophe losses prior to their occurrence because the reinsurance premiums paid reduce income before a catastrophe loss occurs.

(f)   *Non-accrual would force purchase of reinsurance.* Nonaccrual of catastrophe losses will force property and casualty companies to purchase reinsurance.

(g)   *Generations of policyholders.* Periodic accrual of estimated catastrophe losses charges each generation of policyholders with its share of the losses through the premium structure.

The Board does not find those arguments persuasive. The fact that over the long term catastrophes are certain to occur does not justify accrual before the catastrophes occur. As stated in paragraph 59, the purpose of the conditions for accrual in paragraph 8 is to require accrual of losses if they are reasonably estimable *and relate to the current or a prior period.* . . . As indicated in paragraphs 67–68, financial accounting and reporting reflects primarily the effects of past transactions and existing conditions, not future transactions or conditions; accrual for losses from catastrophes that are expected to occur *beyond the terms of insurance policies in force* would amount to accrual of a liability before one has been incurred. Existing policyholders are insured only during the period covered by their insurance contracts; an insurance company is not presently obligated to policyholders for catastrophes that may occur after expiration of their policies. Accrual for those catastrophe losses would record a liability that is inconsistent with the concept of a liability discussed in paragraphs 69–73.

Thus, FASB *Standard No. 5* effectively bars recognition of catastrophe losses by property and casualty insurance companies.

Self-insured losses

The loss experience of many companies has caused them to drop outside insurance coverage in whole or in part in favor of a self-assumption of such risks. Other companies have found coverage for certain of their high risk situations unavailable at any cost, which automatically places them in the position of assuming full responsibility for such incurred losses.

Strong differences of opinion have developed over the proper method and timing for recognizing losses not insured by an outside carrier. On the one hand, it is held that since no casualty loss has occurred and no premium has been paid, there is no basis for recording an expense. The credit side of any such entry would have to be classified in the balance sheet as a liability, and proponents of nonrecognition maintain that there is no creditor and thus no cause for the entry.

The opposing view is that a priority should be placed on the consistency of income determination. The payment of premiums to an insurer represents recognition of losses in advance of occurrence. The absence of the cash outflow should not prohibit the recording of the expense. Those who hold this view would concede that it is essential to support the amount of the annual allowance provision with consistent and reliable evidence.

The FASB also discussed the problem of accounting for uninsured risks in *Standard No. 5*, paragraphs 29 and 30, as follows:

> An enterprise may choose not to purchase insurance against risk of loss that may result from injury to others, damage to the property of others, or interruption of its business operations. Exposure to risks of those types constitutes an existing condition involving uncertainty about the amount and timing of any losses that may occur, in which case a contingency exists as defined in paragraph 1.
>
> Mere exposure to risks of those types, however, does not mean that an asset has been impaired or a liability has been incurred. The condition for accrual in paragraph 8(*a*) is not met with respect to loss that may result from injury to others, damage to the property of others, or business interruption that may occur after the date of an enterprise's financial statements. Losses of those types do not relate to the current or a prior period but rather to the *future* period in which they occur. Thus, for example, an enterprise with a fleet of vehicles should not accrue for injury to others or damage to the property of others that may be caused by those vehicles in the future even if the amount of those losses may be reasonably estimable. On the other hand, the conditions in paragraph 8 would be met with respect to uninsured losses resulting from injury to others or damage to the property of others that took place prior to the

date of the financial statements, even though the enterprise may not become aware of those matters until after that date, if the experience of the enterprise or other information enables it to make a reasonable estimate of the loss that was incurred prior to the date of its financial statements.

SUMMARY

FASB *Statement No. 5,* "Accounting for Contingencies," contained these key points:

1. Loss contingencies can be accrued by a charge to income if an asset's impairment or the incurrence of a liability is *probable;* one or more events will likely occur to confirm the fact and amount of loss; and the loss can be reasonably estimated.
2. Gain contingencies (the acquisition of assets or the reductions of liabilities) should be recognized in the accounts prior to realization only in rare instances.
3. Disclosure of the nature and amount of an accrual may be necessary if material. Disclosure of the nature and amount (if possible) of significant loss and gain contingencies not recorded should be made when there is a *reasonable possibility* that they will be incurred or realized.
4. Recognition of losses which may arise from uninsured risks and catastrophe losses of property and casualty insurance companies is prohibited prior to realization.

The FASB statement on contingencies, while in large measure a reaffirmation of previous rules on the subject, will nevertheless provide useful guidelines in determining the proper recording and disclosure requirement for events of a contingent nature. Management will always be charged with the responsibility for making a full determination and prudent and conservative evaluation of all facts related to the contingency prior to taking any action.

Chapter 16

Domestic investments: Earnings and classification

Joseph F. Spilberg[*]

Purpose of investment

A corporation invests cash in domestic securities for various reasons. Idle cash is usually invested to provide a return otherwise unavailable and, in periods of inflation, to minimize losses in purchasing power. Investments may be made, therefore, in order to maximize return on corporate assets. Investments in securities may also be made to establish a relationship between the investor and the investee. This relationship may be for the purpose of controlling or influencing the investee, which could be a supplier or major customer, or the securities may be held to participate in earnings of the investee resulting from business transactions between the investor and the investee.

General content of this chapter

In periods when the rate of inflation is high and economic uncertainties exist, prudent investment of available cash becomes more important. Risks also increase, however, and the accounting for income or loss from the investments becomes more complex and more significant. This chapter discusses many of the more dif-

---

[*] Executive Partner, Laventhol & Horwath.

ficult aspects of accounting for investments, their acquisition, retention, and disposition. Some of the more significant topics covered include balance sheet classification as current or noncurrent assets, write-downs, write-ups, determination of cost, accrual of income, use of the equity method versus the cost method, and conversions.

These matters are addressed from the corporate viewpoint and are confined primarily to investments represented by securities. The types of investments covered include those generally categorized as debt securities (notes, certificates of deposit, bonds and mortgages), those generally classified as equity securities (preferred and common stocks), warrants and rights, and convertible securities.

BALANCE SHEET CLASSIFICATION AND VALUATION

Current versus noncurrent

Classification of investments within the current assets section or within the noncurrent section of the balance sheet is significant to the determination of the amount of working capital of the investor. It is also important in accounting for changes in market value, as discussed later.

Accounting Research Bulletin No. 43 defines working capital as identifying "the relatively liquid portion of total enterprise capital which constitutes a margin or buffer for meeting obligations within the ordinary operating cycle of the business."[1] In line with this general definition of working capital, it describes current assets as including "cash available for current operations and items which are the equivalent of cash," and "marketable securities representing the investment of cash available for current operations."[2] This discussion clearly provides for including in current assets investments in marketable securities which can easily be converted into cash for operations. Hence, marketable securities must truly have a ready market to establish their immediate liquidity in order to provide the necessary "margin or buffer" which is contemplated in the measurement of working capital.

---

[1] AICPA, "Restatement and Revision of Accounting Research Bulletins," *Accounting Research Bulletin No. 43*, (New York, 1953), chap. 3, sec. A, par. 3.

[2] Ibid., par. 4.

ARB No. 43 describes assets which are not part of current assets, including "investments in securities (whether marketable or not) or advances which have been made for the purpose of control, affiliation, or other continuing business advantage."[3] Investments of this type are not temporary investments of cash otherwise available for current operations. The purposes of these investments are such that liquidation is not normally expected in the immediate future. In fact, liquidation may be difficult and may cause a substantial hardship for the corporation if required. Therefore, investments which establish business relationships should not be included in current assets even if they are in the form of traded securities which have a ready market.

ARB No. 43 also contemplates that cash restricted or earmarked for investment in long-term assets should not be included in current assets. Correspondingly, even though investments in marketable securities might not be for the purpose of a continuing business relationship, if it is intended that the marketable securities will not be available to meet current cash needs if required, such marketable securities would be excluded from current assets. This does not mean, however, that simply because a marketable security is not expected to be sold within, say, one year, it must be excluded from current assets. The test is whether or not it is reasonably available, on the basis of intent, to meet current cash needs.

Valuation of certain marketable securities under FASB Statement No. 12

In December 1975 the FASB issued its *Statement No. 12,* "Accounting for Certain Marketable Securities," in which it adopted new accounting rules for the recognition of changes in the value of investments in marketable equity securities.[4] *Statement No. 12,* and any interpretations thereof, should be read for details of the accounting and disclosure rules. Marketable equity securities are defined for the purpose of *Statement No. 12* as those "representing ownership shares (e.g., common, preferred, and other capital stock), or the right to acquire (e.g., warrants, rights, and call

---

[3] Ibid., par. 6.

[4] FASB, "Accounting for Certain Marketable Securities," *Statement of Financial Accounting Standards No. 12,* (Stamford, Conn., December 1975).

options) or dispose of (e.g., put options) ownership shares in an enterprise at fixed or determinable prices. The term does not encompass preferred stock that by its terms either must be redeemed by the issuing enterprise or is redeemable at the option of the investor, nor does it include treasury stock or convertible bonds."[5] The security is considered marketable if prices are currently available on a national securities exchange or are reported in the over-the-counter market by the National Association of Securities Dealers Automatic Quotations (NASDAQ) system or by the National Quotations Bureau, Inc. (provided quotations are available from at least three dealers). Restricted stock which will not qualify for sale within one year is not considered to be a marketable security.

The marketable equity securities included on the balance sheet as current assets are considered as one portfolio for valuation purposes and those classified as noncurrent assets are considered as another portfolio (excluding investments accounted for by the equity method in accordance with *APB Opinion No. 18*, discussed later in this chapter). Each portfolio is to be carried on the balance sheet at the lower of its aggregate cost or market value at the balance sheet date. Write-downs to market value (unrealized losses) are accounted for through a valuation allowance.

If, in a subsequent period, the aggregate market value of either portfolio increases (an unrealized gain), the increase is recognized in that period as a reduction in the valuation allowance previously established. However, a write-up above cost is not acceptable.

Changes in the *current asset* valuation allowance are to be included in the determination of *net income* for the period in which the changes occur. However, changes in the *noncurrent asset* valuation allowance are included in *shareholders' equity* and are not part of the determination of net income. If an unclassified balance sheet is used, changes in the valuation allowance are accounted for in the same manner as though the securities were classified as a noncurrent asset. Realized gains or losses are included in income.

When there is a decline in value of a marketable equity security carried as a noncurrent asset, an evaluation must be made as to whether the decline is other than temporary (that is, a permanent impairment in value). If the decline is considered to be a permanent impairment, the cost basis of that individual security is to be

---

[5] Ibid., par. 7.

written down and a new cost basis established. The write-down is accounted for as a realized loss. Any increase in market value above the new cost basis is not recognized until realized through disposal of the security. (The determination of whether a loss is permanent or temporary is reviewed in the next section.)

If there is a change in classification of a marketable equity security between current and noncurrent, the transfer is made at the lower of cost or market at the date of transfer. If market value is less than cost, the difference is to be treated as a realized loss and included in the income statement for the period.

Unrealized gains and losses are considered income tax timing differences and the provisions of *APB Opinion No. 11*, "Accounting for Income Taxes," are to be applied. However, a tax effect of an unrealized capital loss may be recognized only when there is assurance beyond a reasonable doubt that the loss will be offset against capital gains.

Statement No. 12 recognizes that specialized accounting practices are applied to marketable securities by companies in certain industries, such as investment companies, brokers and dealers in securities, stock life insurance companies, and fire and casualty insurance companies. *Statement No. 12* has not altered these specialized industry practices, with two exceptions. If marketable equity securities have been carried at cost, they are to be carried at the lower of aggregate cost or market value (or accounted for at market value, if an accepted industry practice). Further, a permanent impairment in the value of an individual security must be accounted for as a realized loss, with a new cost basis established.

In consolidated financial statements, all of the marketable equity securities owned by the consolidated entities are included in the groupings of current and noncurrent portfolios. However, if portfolios of certain of the consolidated entities follow the same specialized industry accounting practices, and these are different from the practices followed by the remaining entities in the consolidated group, such portfolios are treated separately. The portfolios of nonconsolidated subsidiaries and other investees are not combined with those of the reporting entity.

The method of accounting for marketable equity securities by a consolidated subsidiary or a nonconsolidated subsidiary or other investee is not changed or adjusted in consolidation or by the investor in accounting for its equity in the income or loss of such subsidiary or investee, with one exception. If it is the practice of the parent or investor to include realized gains and losses in the determination of net income, that practice is also to be followed in reporting (in consolidation or through the equity method) any realized gains or losses on marketable securities of the subsidiary or investee.

Statement No. 12 requires that the following disclosures be made by companies which do not follow specialized industry accounting practices:

(a) As of the date of each balance sheet presented, aggregate cost and market value (each segregated between current and noncurrent portfolios when a classified balance sheet is presented) with identification as to which is the carrying amount.

(b) As of the date of the latest balance sheet presented, the following, segregated between current and noncurrent portfolios when a classified balance sheet is presented:

 (1) Gross unrealized gains representing the excess of market value over cost for all marketable equity securities in the portfolio having such an excess.

 (2) Gross unrealized losses representing the excess of cost over market value for all marketable equity securities in the portfolio having such an excess.

(c) For each period for which an income statement is presented:

 (1) Net realized gain or loss included in the determination of net income.

 (2) The basis on which cost was determined in computing realized gain or loss (i.e., average cost or other method used).

 (3) The change in the valuation allowance(s) that has been included in the equity section of the balance sheet during the period and, when a classified balance sheet is presented, the amount of such change included in the determination of net income.[6]

Companies following specialized industry practices that do not include unrealized gains and losses in net income are required to disclose, with respect to all marketable securities (as that term is used in the industry), the amounts of gross unrealized gains and losses as of the latest balance sheet date, and the amount by which net unrealized gain or loss included in equity has been increased or

---

[6] *Ibid.*, par. 12.

decreased for each period for which an income statement is presented.

Valuation of other investments

Investments are normally stated at cost, possibly adjusted for amortization of discount or premium, or accrued interest when appropriate. When the market value of securities held as investments, which are not covered by FASB *Statement No. 12*, falls below the amount carried in the financial statements, it becomes necessary to decide whether to record a write-down to the lower market value. *ARB No. 43* has the following to say about this matter (emphasis added):

> The amounts at which various *current assets* are carried do not always represent their present realizable cash values. Accounts receivable . . . are effectively stated at the amount of cash estimated as realizable. However, practice varies with respect to the carrying basis for current assets such as marketable securities and inventories. In the case of marketable securities where market value is less than cost by a *substantial* amount and it is evident that the decline in market value is *not due to a mere temporary condition,* the amount to be included as a current asset should not exceed the market value.[7]

Accounting Principles Board Statement No. 4, of much more recent vintage, says (emphasis added):

> If market price of marketable securities classified as current assets is less than cost, and it is evident that the decline is *not due to a temporary condition* a loss is recorded when the price declines.[8]

Observe that the word "substantial" appearing in *ARB No. 43* was not included in *Statement No. 4.* The concern is whether or not a decline in value is "temporary." This must be determined within a frame of reference.

One approach to determining whether or not a market value impairment is temporary is to determine the expected time of disposal of the security. *ARB No. 43* states this principle with respect to inventory pricing (emphasis added):

---

[7] *ARB No. 43,* chap. 3, sec. A, par. 9.

[8] AICPA, "Basic Concepts and Accounting Principles Underlying Financial Statements of Business Enterprises," *Accounting Principles Board Statement No. 4* (New York, October 1970), par. 183 (S-5B).

Where there is evidence that the utility of goods, *in their disposal in the ordinary course of business,* will be less than cost, whether due to physical deterioration, obsolescence, changes in price levels, or other causes, the difference should be recognized as a loss of the current period.[9]

Regarding noncurrent assets, *APB Statement No. 4* states the following (emphasis added):

Reductions in the market prices of noncurrent assets are generally not recorded until the assets are disposed of or are determined to be worthless. . . . In unusual circumstances a reduction in the market price of securities classified as noncurrent assets may provide persuasive evidence of an *inability to recover cost* although the securities have not become worthless. The amount at which those securities are carried is sometimes reduced and a loss recognized prior to disposition of the securities.[10]

Common stock investments are subject to frequent wide fluctuations in market value. Often it is not possible to predict just how long a certain market value will continue for a particular common stock. There are two factors to be evaluated. One is the general movement of the market in which the stock is traded and the second is a change in the value underlying the particular common stock, that is, a change in the value of the corporation which issued the common stock. One might recover, but the other might not. A significant downturn in the general market might be viewed as temporary, but if the business in which the investment has been made is experiencing considerable difficulty, the market value decline might not be temporary.

In 1975 the Auditing Standards Executive Committee of the AICPA issued an auditing interpretation discussing the nature of the evidential matter that the auditor should obtain in support of the classification and carrying amount of marketable securities. Regarding marketable securities classified as current assets, the interpretation states:

When marketable securities classified as a current asset have a market value lower than cost, retention of the cost basis requires persuasive evidence that indicates a recovery in the market value

---

[9] *ARB No. 43,* chap. 4, Statement 5.
[10] *APB Statement No. 4,* par. 183 (S-5E).

will occur before the earlier of the scheduled maturity or sale date of the securities or within a one-year period from the balance sheet date. Generally, such evidence would be limited to substantial recovery subsequent to the year-end.[11]

With respect to investments in marketable securities classified as noncurrent assets, the interpretation states:

> If there has been a decline in the market value of those investments, the auditor should obtain evidence concerning the nature of the decline. In making that determination, he should consider the ability to ultimately recover the carrying amount of the investments.

> When the market decline is attributable to specific adverse conditions for a particular security, stocks or bonds, a write-down in carrying amount is necessary unless persuasive evidence exists to support the carrying amount.

> The value of investments in marketable securities classified as noncurrent assets may decline because of general market conditions that reflect prospects of the economy as a whole or prospects of a particular industry. Such declines may or may not be indicative of the ability to ultimately recover the carrying amount of investments. The auditor should consider all available evidence to evaluate the carrying amount of the securities. For investments in bonds and other investments with fixed maturity amounts, market declines may be considered temporary unless the evidence indicates that such investments will be disposed of before they mature or that they may not be realizable."[12]

Individual, group, or portfolio valuation

In applying the lower of cost or market rule to securities not covered by FASB *Statement No. 12*, write-downs to market can be made for individual securities, groups of securities, or for entire portfolios. However, if write-downs are made for some individual securities which are part of a larger portfolio, the amount at which the portfolio is stated on the balance sheet will be less than its aggregate market value. Since appreciation is usually not recognized, it may be unduly conservative to write down indi-

---

[11] AICPA, *Journal of Accountancy*, April 1975, p. 70.
[12] Ibid.

vidual securities except for those whose value is deemed to be permanently impaired.

Investments may include securities which are intended to be held for long periods, including bonds to be held to maturity, and also may include short-term investments. In evaluating the securities, they may be grouped according to the expected holding period, and the lower of cost or market rule applied to each group (which may consist of one or more securities).

Changes after the balance sheet date

Valuation of investments should be based primarily on facts at the balance sheet date. Quoted market prices or other data at that date would be used. A subsequent decline in market value would not be recorded unless (with respect to securities not covered by FASB *Statement No. 12*) the change is indicative of conditions existing at the balance sheet date.[13] Increases in market value occurring after the balance sheet date but before the securities are sold should be considered in determining the extent to which impairments of market value at the balance sheet date may be temporary.

Write-ups following write-downs

Subsequent to the period in which a write-down is made, market value might increase before disposal of a security. The question which arises is whether a write-up of the security would be appropriate in instances where FASB *Statement No. 12* does not apply. Generally, write-ups to higher market value are not recognized in accounting until realized. *APB Statement No. 4* states, "External events other than transfers that increase market prices or utility of assets . . . are generally not recorded when they occur. Instead their effects are usually reflected at the time of later exchanges. . . . Examples of the few exceptions . . . are (1) increases in market prices of marketable securities held by investment companies. . . ."[14]

---

[13] AICPA, "Codification of Auditing Standards and Procedures," *Statement on Auditing Standards No. 1* (New York, 1973), sec. 560.

[14] *APB Statement No. 4*, par. 183 (S-4 and S-4A). *Statement No. 4* is primarily a description of generally accepted accounting principles in existence in 1970, when the *Statement* was published. It is considered authoritative, but it is not as authoritative as APB *Opinions* or FASB *Statements*.

Concerning inventory pricing, *ARB No. 43* states, "In the case of goods which have been written down below cost at the close of a fiscal period, such reduced amount is to be considered the cost for subsequent accounting purposes."[15] Until the issuance of FASB *Statement No. 12*, there had been no authoritative pronouncement concerning the treatment of write-ups following write-downs with respect to marketable securities or investments, and a practice similar to that used in inventory pricing usually had been followed. As described earlier in this chapter, *Statement No. 12* permits write-ups, to the extent of cost, for certain marketable securities. The author is of the opinion that ultimately other securities and investments will be accorded similar treatment.

Market value disclosure

Since the currently realizable value of a current asset is of more importance than cost when measuring the amount and liquidity of working capital, information concerning market value should be disclosed.[16] As discussed previously, FASB *Statement No. 12* requires various disclosures for marketable equity securities. *APB Opinion No. 18* requires disclosing the value of common stock investments for which the equity method is used if quoted market prices are available, except for investments in subsidiaries.[17] Disclosure of the market value of other long-term investments, such as bonds, is usually desirable if the market value is significantly different from the amount at which the investments are stated on the balance sheet.

Advances to investees

An investor may have a receivable from an investee resulting from cash advances or other transactions. Sometimes these amounts receivable are included with the investment on the balance sheet as one amount, perhaps termed "investments and advances." This treatment is usually followed if the receivable is not expected to be collected within a short time, and is not, therefore, a current asset. Recoverability of advances must be taken into con-

---

[15] *ARB No. 43,* chap. 4, fn. 2.

[16] *ARB No. 43*, chap. 3, sec. A, par. 9.

[17] AICPA, "The Equity Method of Accounting for Investments in Common Stock," *Accounting Principles Board Opinion No. 18* (New York, March 1971), par. 20.

sideration in determining market value and disclosing market value information.

If an investee is having financial difficulty, the valuation of both the advances and the investment must be considered carefully. Conditions necessitating a write-down or write-off of an advance often suggest similar treatment for the investment account.

COMPONENTS OF COST

The cost of a security is either its original cost or a new cost basis assigned as the result of impairment in its value deemed to be other than temporary. The elements which are includable in "cost" and the apportionment of cost when securities are purchased and sold in varying lots are discussed in this section.

Costs to be included

Certain costs are obviously includable in the value to be assigned to securities. The price paid, including the broker's commission or fee, for the securities purchased is clearly to be included in the cost of the securities. Other direct costs associated with the purchase are also ordinarily included. Such costs could include attorneys' and accountants' fees in negotiating and arranging the purchase, appraisal fees, costs of market surveys, and any other direct costs which might be necessary to consummate the purchase.

Other costs associated with purchase and maintenance of securities

Other costs may be incurred which are only indirectly related to the purchase of securities. It is not general practice to include such indirect costs in the cost of securities. An example is the cost of an investment department, which may devote its time to locating and evaluating potential investments. It is often difficult to associate time spent by an investment department with specific securities purchases. It may be possible to allocate the cost of the department among investments made during a specific period. The basis for allocation may be the time spent on specific investment projects, the costs of investments, or the expected return on investments. A similar procedure could be employed to allocate the compensation cost of employees who spend all or only part of their time evaluating investments.

Even if a rational method of assigning the costs of an investment department to specific investment activities can be devised, there is still the question of whether or not such costs should be included in the cost of securities. One may argue that if the efforts of the investment department produce a superior return, there may be a basis for capitalization of some of the costs. However, in practice such costs are usually not included in the carrying value of investments.[18] The costs of maintaining investments, such as the cost of a safe-deposit box, safe, guard, or custodian, should be charged to expense immediately and should not be capitalized. Such costs merely provide for the safety of investments during the period in which the costs are incurred and are more properly associated with investment revenue for the period.

Apportionment of costs among securities acquired for a lump sum

When a group containing more than one type of security is acquired, it is necessary to allocate a portion of the cost to each type of security. This situation arises most frequently when either debt or equity securities are purchased together with warrants to purchase additional securities. These securities packages are often referred to as "units."

In cases where there is a known market value for each type of security purchased, allocation may be made based on the relative market values. For example, assume units of common stock and warrants were purchased for a total of $48,000. Allocation would be as follows:

| | | Market price | | % of | Allocated |
Security	Quantity	Per security	Total	total	cost
Warrants	10,000	$1.00	$10,000	20%	$ 9,600
Common stock	10,000	4.00	40,000	80	38,400
			$50,000	100%	$48,000

---

[18] If the investment is a business combination, *APB Opinion No. 16*, paragraph 76, requires recording "indirect and general expenses related to acquisitions" as current expenses rather than as part of the cost of the company acquired.

It is also possible to know the market value of all but one of the securities purchased. In such cases, if the results are not unreasonable, it is acceptable to assign cost on the basis of the known market price and to assign the remaining amount to the security for which no market price exists. Using the example above, if only the value of common stock were known, which is $40,000, that amount would be assigned to the common stock and the remainder, $8,000, would be allocated to the warrants.

A third possible situation is that there is no market price for any of the individual securities. Ordinarily, in such cases, it is necessary to obtain appraisals, perhaps from investment advisers, for each of the securities involved. If the market price will become established by trading in one or more of the types of securities involved (for example, a new issue of stock with warrants attached) shortly after the purchase is made, the assignment of cost to the securities may be based on the market price subsequently established. This may not be appropriate, however, if the circumstances surrounding the purchase are significantly different from those which are related to the establishment of a market price; for example, a "private placement" preceding a public offering.

Advances

The cost of an investment should not include advances to investees, unless in substance the advances are part of the investment. Such advances should be accounted for as receivables, although the advances may be combined with the investment and shown as one amount on the balance sheet.

Identification of costs for purposes of sale

When identical securities have been purchased over a period of time at varying prices, a problem may arise regarding the costs to be identified with securities which are sold at a later date. This situation, similar to the one in costing inventory, requires an assumption regarding the "flow of costs." The following is a discussion of possible cost-flow assumptions which may be employed.

Specific identification. Since most security certificates are identified with a number, it is possible to keep a record of the cost of individual securities. The historical cost of a specific security may be used in recording a sale. One deficiency inherent in this method is the possibility of manipulation. Since securities purchased at different dates may have varying costs, the amount of income or loss which would be recognized when securities are sold could be manipulated in the selection of securities. This method is acceptable for income tax purposes and is frequently seen in practice.

First-in, first-out. Using the first-in, first-out assumption, records of the costs of individual securities need not be kept by certificate number. When securities are sold, the cost used in recording the transaction is based upon the oldest cost of the securities on hand. It would not matter which specific certificates were given up in the sale. This method is acceptable for tax purposes and is frequently seen in practice.

Weighted average. The weighted average method does not identify the actual cost of the securities sold. Instead, for a specific type of security investment, the cost per share of each group of securities purchased is multiplied times the number of shares in that group. The results of each of these multiplications are then added together and divided by the total number of shares owned to determine the weighted average cost of the securities. This method is not acceptable for tax purposes but is found in practice.

Last-in, first-out. The last-in, first-out assumption, like the first-in, first-out assumption, is based upon the actual cost of securities purchased. In the last-in, first-out assumption, however, the cost assigned to securities sold is the cost of the most recently acquired securities. This method is not acceptable for tax purposes and is not usually found in practice.

DEBT SECURITIES

Short-term securities

Corporations often invest available cash in short-term debt securities such as bonds and notes issued by agencies of the U.S. government, commercial paper, and certificates of deposit. These investments frequently provide a good combination of high yield, liquidity, and low risk.

The most popular U.S. government security held for short-term investment purposes is the U.S. Treasury Bill. Treasury Bills are issued at a discount instead of at par, with 3-, 6-, 9-, and 12-month maturities. Investment income is realized on the difference between the discount price and either the sales price if sold prior to maturity, or par at maturity. Bills are usually issued at a variety of denominations beginning with $10,000. Lower denominations have sometimes been made available.

Commercial paper are notes issued by large corporations. Maturities may be from 1 day to 270 days. Commercial paper is usually issued at a discount, and the return may be a fraction of 1 percent greater than on U.S. Treasury Bills. Denominations are usually $100,000 or more.

Certificates of deposit are issued by banks with maturities ranging from 90 days to 5 or more years.

Bonds

U.S. Treasury Bonds, the most popular long-term government obligation, are usually issued with maturities of more than 5 years, although they may be issued for shorter periods. As with Treasury Bills, Treasury Bonds are readily marketable and thus represent a very liquid investment. Unlike Treasury Bills, Treasury Bonds bear interest.

Bonds issued by states and municipalities are attractive because the interest income is not subject to federal income taxes. Interest income on corporate and U.S. government obligations, however, is subject to federal income taxes.

Recognition of interest income

When a bond or note which pays interest is purchased at its face or par amount, interest income is equivalent to the cash payments received periodically. When financial statements are prepared as of dates in between the interest payment dates, interest income must be accrued. The accrual can be computed at the rate of interest stated in the contract for the period of time which has elapsed since the last interest payment or since the date bonds were purchased. Alternatively, instead of using the interest rate, a simpler method would be to multiply the amount of periodic interest payment by a fraction based on the period which has elapsed since the last interest payment date.

The second approach can be applied to a short-term security

acquired on a discount basis, for which the investment return is realized by a redemption at par on maturity, such as a Treasury Bill. The amount of discount earned for the period can be calculated by applying a fraction representing the portion of the total investment holding period which has elapsed, as illustrated in the following example:

Purchase price, $95,000
Par, $100,000
Discount, $5,000
Period to maturity, 9 months
Time elapsed, 6 months

$$\text{Accrual} = \$5,000 \times \frac{6}{9} = \$3,333$$

An accrual using this approach will recognize interest income at the effective yield rate for the investment. Using the same example, the yield rate and accrual are calculated as follows:

$$\text{Yield} = \frac{5}{95} \times \frac{12}{9} = .070175$$

$$\text{Accrual} = \$95,000 \times .070175 \times \frac{6}{12} = \$3,333$$

Since the accrual is the same in this approach as in the one preceding, it proves that the apportionment of interest between payment dates on the basis of a simple fraction applied to the discount will result in accruing interest income on a yield basis.

Discount or premium

If the stated or coupon interest rate for a bond does not reflect the market rate of interest for the investment, the purchase price will be at a discount or premium with respect to the face amount of the bond. When held to maturity, the investment will yield to the investor the rate of return expected at the time the bond was purchased.

To arrive at the purchase price, a determination must be made of the present value of the bond at the purchase date. The present value of a bond is the sum of the present value of the face amount and the present value of the series of interest payments. Formulas for these calculations are:

$$VM = \frac{M}{(1 + i)^n}$$

$$VI = I \left[\frac{1 - \dfrac{1}{(1 + i)^n}}{i} \right]$$

VM = present value of amount at maturity.
VI = present value of interest payments.
i = interest yield rate per period.
n = number of interest periods.
M = amount payable at maturity.
I = amount of each interest payment.

For example, assume bonds mature in 10 years at a face amount of $100,000 and have semiannual interest payments of $4,000. Assuming the investor desires a yield of 10 percent per year, with interest compounded semiannually, applying the formulas results in the following determination of present value:

$$VM = \frac{\$100,000}{(1 + .05)^{20}} = \$37,690$$

$$VI = \$4,000 \left[\frac{1 - \dfrac{1}{(1 + .05)^{20}}}{.05} \right] = \$49,848$$

The present value of the investment is $87,538, the sum of $37,690 and $49,848.

It is easier to use compound interest tables, which are generally available, than to go through the above calculations. Using these tables, the approach would be:

Factors from tables (5% compounded semiannually):

Present value of 1: .376889
Present value of 1 per period: 12.462210

Applying factors:

$$
\begin{aligned}
VM &= \$100,000 \times .376889 = \$37,689 \\
VI &= \$4,000 \times 12.462210 = \underline{49,849} \\
&\qquad\qquad\qquad\qquad\qquad \underline{\underline{\$87,538}}
\end{aligned}
$$

Note that in this example the present value of the interest payments (*VI*) exceeds the present value of the amount to be received at maturity (*VM*). This is often true for long-term bonds which pay interest periodically.

To reflect properly the amount of interest earned in each period, the discount or premium must be amortized. One method is to amortize the discount or premium on a straight-line basis over the life of the investment. Equal amounts are credited or charged to income in each period. The result will be to reflect the same amount of interest income in each period. This may appear to be correct, but it does not reflect economic reality if interest is received periodically.

Since the cash interest payment is different from the amount which would be recognized as interest income, the amount invested is actually changing over the period of time it is held. If a discount is amortized, cash receipts are less than interest income recognized. The difference is an increase in the investment. This increase in investment may be understood by imagining that cash receipts equal total interest income including discount amortization, and that cash in an amount equivalent to the discount amortization is reinvested. This "reinvested cash" increases the net investment upon which a yield is expected. The reverse is true if the bond is purchased at a premium.

If the amount invested is changing, the amount of interest earned on that investment should also change, assuming a constant rate of return. The "effective yield" method provides for a constant rate of return, and is therefore more acceptable today in practice. However, frequently the straight-line method is used where the effect is not material. This may be the case with a highly diversified portfolio.

Using the effective yield method, the yield rate is applied to the investment balance as of the beginning of the current interest period (or date of acquisition, if later). The result is the amount of interest income for the period. Any difference between that amount and cash received is added to or subtracted from the investment balance.

For example, the illustration of present value above assumes a yield of 10 percent per year, compounded semiannually. The amount invested at the beginning is $87,538. Interest income for the first semiannual interest period should be 5 percent thereof, or $4,377. The amount of cash received on collection of the interest coupons is $4,000. The difference of $377 represents "discount amortization" and is added to the investment balance, increasing the investment to $87,915. In the second interest period, the interest income should be 5 percent of $87,915, or $4,396. Subtracting the $4,000 cash receipt, the difference of $396 represents "discount amortization," to be added to the investment balance, arriving at a new total of $88,311, and so on. The adjustment to the investment account can be made only on interest payment dates, as it represents a compounding of interest.

The journal entries to record the purchase of this bond and the two subsequent interest receipts are illustrated as follows:

```
Investment. . . . . . . . . . . . . . . . . . . . . . . . . . . . . . . . . . . . . .  87,538
    Cash . . . . . . . . . . . . . . . . . . . . . . . . . . . . . . . . . . . . . .              87,538
        To record bond purchase.

Cash . . . . . . . . . . . . . . . . . . . . . . . . . . . . . . . . . . . . . .   4,000
Investment. . . . . . . . . . . . . . . . . . . . . . . . . . . . . . . . . .        377
    Interest Income. . . . . . . . . . . . . . . . . . . . . . . . . . . . .                 4,377
        To record first period interest income and investment adjustment.

Cash . . . . . . . . . . . . . . . . . . . . . . . . . . . . . . . . . . . . . .   4,000
Investment. . . . . . . . . . . . . . . . . . . . . . . . . . . . . . . . . .        396
    Interest Income. . . . . . . . . . . . . . . . . . . . . . . . . . . . .                 4,396
        To record second period interest income and investment adjustment.
```

Note that the amount of interest income in the second semiannual period exceeds the amount in the first period. This is due to an increase in the investment. In the last year the investment is held, the investment will have grown toward the maturity amount of $100,000 and interest income will be close to $10,000 for the year, reflecting the 10 percent yield.

The same approach would be used if a bond is purchased at a premium. Periodic interest income will be less than cash receipts and the amount at which the investment is carried will be decreased to the face amount at maturity.

In order to apply the effective yield method, the yield on the investment must be known. The broker or dealer should be able to supply the exact yield rate. If not, the yield rate must be calculated. It should be noted that a discount rate used in quoting the price of Treasury Bills and some other securities sold on a "bank discount" basis differs from the yield rate. The discount rate is a percentage of face amount; the yield rate is based on the amount invested.

Nonamortization for temporary investments

Some accountants believe it is appropriate to ignore amortization if the investment is to be held on a temporary basis, that is, not retained to maturity. Nonamortization prevents reflecting interest income at the true yield amount. Further, if there is no change in the market rate of interest, the market value of the investment will change exactly as the investment balance would change using the effective yield method. Nonamortization will result in a gradual departure from market value which will have to be reflected at the time of disposition as a gain or loss. Amortization would appear to be appropriate even for temporary holdings for most bond investments. The premium on convertible bonds, discussed later, might not be amortized.

Accrued interest at purchase or sale

If a bond is purchased or sold between interest payment dates, the price will be based on the present value of the bond determined at the market rate of interest or expected yield, the same as if a purchase is made on an interest payment date or at the original issue date. The present value of future interest payments will include the present value of the next interest payment. As the purchase date moves closer to the next interest payment date, the present value of the interest payments will increase (as will the present value of the maturity amount). Immediately after passing the interest payment date, the present value will decrease by the amount of the interest payment and then will start to build up again toward the next interest payment date.

It is a customary practice in bond sales to calculate an amount of "accrued interest," reflecting the accrual of interest at the stated or coupon rate between interest payment dates. This "accrued interest" is deducted from the present value of the investment to arrive at the "purchase price" and then is added back to arrive at the total price.

The calculation of accrued interest is a simple and appropriate way to determine purchase price if a bond is trading at its stated interest rate. However, if the total price is determined on a present value yield basis, which takes into consideration the "accrual" of interest to the date of sale, the separate calculation of accrued interest is an unnecessary complication. Further, a distortion in income accounting results if "accrued interest" is recorded separately for bonds purchased on a yield basis, since the "accrued interest" is calculated using the stated or coupon rate of interest, instead of at the yield rate.

If the effective yield method is used, the total amount paid to acquire the bond should be set up as the carrying amount for the investment. The effective yield method will appropriately account for the amortization of the discount or premium to the date of maturity and will properly reflect interest income at the yield rate implicit in the investment. For example, assume that the investment illustrated above is made 1 day before the first interest payment date. The present value would have increased from $87,538, the present value at the beginning of the 10 year period, to $91,891 because of the growth of $4,353, calculated as follows:

$$\$87,538 \times .05 \times \frac{179}{180} = \$4,353$$

On the next day, interest of $4,000 will be received and the journal entry will be as follows:

```
Cash . . . . . . . . . . . . . . . . . . . . . . . . . . . . . . . . . . .  4,000
    Interest Income. . . . . . . . . . . . . . . . . . . . . . . . . . . .            26
    Investment  . . . . . . . . . . . . . . . . . . . . . . . . . . . . .         3,974
       To record first period interest income and investment adjustment.
```

The $3,974 credit to the investment account represents a partial return of investment, reducing the investment from $91,891 to $87,917. The use of the effective yield method as in this example makes the computation of interest and related adjustments to investment account fairly simple compared to calculating separately the amortization of a discount or premium and accounting for "accrued interest." Further, this technique lends itself easily to computer application, in which the speed and accuracy of calculations are at an optimum.

Despite the simplicity of the effective yield approach, tradition results in a widespread practice of recording "accrued interest" at the time bonds are purchased, with a subsequent credit to that account at the amount at which it was established when the first coupon payment is received. The result of this accounting practice is similar to that shown above, but the amounts are different. In many cases, the difference between these two methods will be immaterial. Using the above example, accrued interest would be calculated on the date of purchase as:

$$\$4,000 \times \frac{179}{180} = \$3,978$$

The journal entries to record the transactions are:

```
Accrued Interest Receivable. . . . . . . . . . . . . . . . . . . . . . . .   3,978
Investment. . . . . . . . . . . . . . . . . . . . . . . . . . . . . . . . .  88,821
    Cash . . . . . . . . . . . . . . . . . . . . . . . . . . . . . . . . .           92,799
        To record purchase of bond.

Cash . . . . . . . . . . . . . . . . . . . . . . . . . . . . . . . . . . .   4,000
    Interest Income. . . . . . . . . . . . . . . . . . . . . . . . . . . .               22
    Accrued Interest Receivable. . . . . . . . . . . . . . . . . . . . .            3,978
        To record first period interest income and accrued interest.
```

The same concepts apply when a bond is sold prior to maturity. At that time no special accounting is required for "accrued interest," although it may be used. Assuming it has been adjusted to the date of sale using the effective yield method, the bond investment represents the proper basis for determining any gain or loss on the disposition. For example, assume the same facts as in the immediately preceding example when the bond was purchased 1 day prior to the next interest payment date with the exception that instead, the bond had been purchased when its value was $88,403 (10 years before maturity) and then was sold 1 day prior to the next interest payment date. The investment account would have been adjusted to $92,799, representing its present value at that time. The gain or loss on sale would be measured simply by the difference between the proceeds and the carrying amount of $92,799. Assuming a selling price of $95,000, the following journal entries would be made at the date of sale:

```
Investment. . . . . . . . . . . . . . . . . . . . . . . . . . . . . . . . .   4,396
    Interest Income. . . . . . . . . . . . . . . . . . . . . . . . . . . .            4,396
        To record interest income accrued on investment to date of sale.

Cash . . . . . . . . . . . . . . . . . . . . . . . . . . . . . . . . . . .  95,000
    Investment  . . . . . . . . . . . . . . . . . . . . . . . . . . . . .           92,799
    Gain on Sale of Investment . . . . . . . . . . . . . . . . . . . . .            2,201
        To record sale of investment.
```

Call premiums

Sometimes a bond is callable at a premium by the issuer at a specified future date or dates. The call provisions must be considered in accounting for the bond. It is often not possible to know whether a bond will be called because it is not possible to predict the market rate of interest at the time the call option may be exercised by the issuer. The decision to be made by the issuer will depend upon whether or not it will be to the issuer's advantage economically to either refinance the bonds with new debt bearing different interest rates, or pay off the outstanding debt with cash.

Bonds are purchased at a discount because the market rate of interest is higher than the stated or coupon rate. If the market rate of interest continues to exceed the stated rate, it is doubtful that in most instances the issuer would call the bonds. In such cases the issuer might be able to purchase the bonds at the market price on the open market instead of calling them at a higher price. In such circumstances it is not ordinarily appropriate to amortize a discount so that the investment will be equal to the call price at the date the bond is callable.

On the other hand, bonds may be trading currently at a premium, indicating conditions which are likely to result in a call by the issuer at a future date. In such cases it would be undesirable to adopt an amortization scheme which would result in the investment account being stated at amounts in excess of the call amount at the date callable.

If the effective yield method would result in carrying the investment at an amount exceeding the call price at the call date, the method may be modified. An assumption may be made that the bond will be called, and a yield rate determined on that basis. Applying this yield rate using the effective yield method should make the investment account equal the call price at the call date.

Serial bonds

Serial bonds can be considered a multiplicity of individual bonds with varying maturities. These can be accounted for using the effective yield method either for a series of separate investments or as a single investment, with the same results. Because of its inherent simplicity and accuracy, applying the effective yield method to the entire investment is recommended. As portions of the serial bond mature, the investment account is credited with the excess of proceeds over interest income recognized. No gain or loss is recognized.

If desired the straight-line method of amortizing a discount or premium may be used for the individual maturity segments of the bond. This requires knowing the amount of discount or premium for each segment.

Alternatively, the "bonds outstanding" method may be used, which is essentially a weighted average straight-line method of amortization. This method is useful if the straight-line method is desired, and the discount or premium is known only for the total bond, not according to its segments. The portion of discount or premium recognized for a period is based on the total amount of bonds outstanding for the period in relation to the sum for all periods of bonds outstanding during each period. For example, assume a bond matures $100,000 per year over 5 years, and was purchased for $470,000, representing a discount of $30,000. The amortization of discount for each year is based on the ratio of the sum of the bonds outstanding during each year to the sum for all years, calculated as follows:

Year		*Bonds outstanding*
1	$100,000 × 5 =	$ 500,000
2	100,000 × 4 =	400,000
3	100,000 × 3 =	300,000
4	100,000 × 2 =	200,000
5	100,000 × 1 =	100,000
	Total	$1,500,000

For each year, the amortization is:

Year		*Amortization*
1	$\dfrac{500,000}{1,500,000} \times \$30,000$	$10,000
2	$\dfrac{400,000}{1,500,000} \times \$30,000$	8,000
3	$\dfrac{300,000}{1,500,000} \times \$30,000$	6,000
4	$\dfrac{200,000}{1,500,000} \times \$30,000$	4,000
5	$\dfrac{100,000}{1,500,000} \times \$30,000$	2,000
	Total.	$30,000

Multiple coupon rates

Sometimes a bond has coupons with interest rates which change over the period of time in which the bond is outstanding. For example, coupons may bear interest at a rate of 5 percent for the first 5 years, and at 7 percent for the remaining life of the bond. The effective yield method will be appropriate for these types of investments, as it reflects the single yield rate implicit in the initial investment decision. Coupon changes reflect cash flow changes, which are taken into consideration in calculating the present value of the investment at the date of purchase.

Mortgages

Mortgages are often purchased as investments. Generally, the underlying mortgaged real estate has a value significantly higher than the amount of the mortgage. This helps to minimize the risk of loss. Most mortgages are "self-amortizing" loans, with each payment part principal and part interest. This provides a continuous level cash flow over the period of payment.

Sometimes the investor is able to purchase a mortgage at a discount. The discount may take the form of a "fee" or "points." Regardless of how described, these amounts which are in substance discounts should be recognized as part of interest income over the period of the contract, using the effective yield method described for bond investments.

Valuation of mortgage receivables is a critical problem if the underlying real estate is in a depressed area, or represents a new development or real estate project which is not producing the amount of periodic income as originally projected. When the value of real estate has been impaired, the impairment is less likely to be temporary than it might be for investments in common stocks or bonds. In such cases, write-downs to the amount realizable on the mortgage is appropriate, recognizing amounts which may be recovered through other collateral or recourse to guarantors.

EQUITY SECURITIES

A common form of investments is equity securities. The two common types of equity securities are preferred stock and common stock. Investments in preferred stock are normally made primarily for a cash return in the form of dividends, or possibly because of a convertibility feature which may be associated with the preferred stock. Common stock may be held for appreciation or dividends, or both, or for business operating purposes.

Preferred stock

Accounting for investments in preferred stock depends upon the provisions which may be a part of the preferred stock certificate. Of particular consequence are provisions regarding cumulative or noncumulative dividend rights, participating or nonparticipating status, and call, redemption, or conversion provisions.

Dividends

Preferred stockholders generally have preference over common shareholders with regard to liquidation and dividends. However, preferred shareholders are not entitled to receive dividends until such dividends have been declared by the board of directors. The preferred shareholders must be paid before dividends can be paid to common shareholders, but the preferred shareholders usually cannot demand payment of dividends. Dividend income should be recognized when dividends have been declared or, in unusual cases, when actually received by the investor.

In many instances, the preferred stock certificate contains a provision which requires accumulation of dividends which were not paid in the past. This "cumulative" provision requires that a corporation which has not paid dividends to preferred shareholders in past years must pay all such accumulated dividends before it may pay any dividend to common shareholders. Undeclared accumulated preferred stock dividends should not be shown as a receivable by the investor. The existence of such accumulated but undeclared dividends may be disclosed in the notes to the investor's financial statements.[19]

Occasionally a preferred stock issue may include participating provisions. In such cases, in addition to the normal preferred dividend, preferred shareholders may receive a greater dividend based upon the results of operations for the period. Hence, they "participate" in the earnings with common shareholders.

Premium or discount

Preferred stock values are generally equivalent to the present value of the future stream of dividend payments. In most instances,

---

[19] FASB, "Accounting for Contingencies," *Statement of Financial Accounting Standards No. 5*, (Stamford, Conn.: March 1975), par. 17.

this stream of payments will continue indefinitely because the preferred stock has no fixed maturity. It is not uncommon for preferred stock to trade at a premium or discount from par. Generally, amortization of the premium or discount would not be appropriate, because of the absence of a maturity and because the yield will be reflected in the recorded dividend payments without amortization.

Call or redemption provisions

In many instances, preferred stock is callable at a specified price by the issuing corporation or, in some cases, redeemable by the holder. The inclusion of a call provision is made to allow flexibility for the issuing corporation in its equity structure. If the corporation generates sufficient cash to pay off the preferred stockholders or if the market for additional financing makes a favorable change, a corporation may wish to call its preferred stock and possibly replace it with some other form of equity or debt financing. Before an issue of preferred stock may be called, accumulated preferred dividends must be paid. The existence of call, redemption, and cumulative provisions gives preferred stock many of the characteristics of debt. However, unlike debt, preferred stock usually has no contractual provisions requiring the payment of dividends or the call or redemption price at any specific point in time. In most circumstances, preferred stock should be accounted for by an investor in the same manner as any other equity investment. Call or redemption of the preferred stock is accounted for the same as a sale of preferred stock and any gain or loss is recognized by the investor at such time as the call or redemption is effected.

The existence of call provisions should not affect the accounting for premiums or discounts paid for preferred stock. If the amount at which the preferred stock may be called is less than the amount at which it is carried on the balance sheet, the call amount should be disclosed in the financial statements or notes thereto. If preferred stock is redeemable by the holder, amortization of a premium or a discount may be appropriate if it is reasonably expected that redemption will occur.

Common stock

Investments in common stock are relatively more risky than investments in preferred stock or bonds. Upon liquidation of a business, the common shareholders are last in line, after secured debt holders, creditors, preferred shareholders, and to receive liquidation distributions. On the other hand, common shareholders usually receive a greater share, or perhaps all, of residual profits. The return on an investment in common stock is realized through dividends, and appreciation in value is reflected in proceeds upon disposal.

In most instances, only common shareholders have voting rights regarding election of directors and other shareholder decisions. Voting power is of particular significance if the common stock is held in order to establish or maintain a business relationship.

There are three methods of accounting for investments in common stock: the cost method, the equity method, and consolidation. Using the *cost* method, income is recognized only by the amount of dividends to be received, when declared by the investee. Under the *equity* method, the investor recognizes a percentage (based upon the ownership interest in the investee) of the investee's income or loss, regardless of the payment of dividends by the investee. In *consolidation* accounting, the financial statements of the investee are combined with those of the investor.

The method to be employed depends upon whether or not the investor may exert significant influence or control over the investee. Ownership of a substantial voting interest allows an investor to influence the operating policies of an investee. The degree of ownership may be large enough to enable the investor to control the investee.

Consolidation

In determining the appropriate method, the initial presumption should be made that if the investor owns a controlling interest in the investee, consolidated financial statements should be presented. *ARB No. 51* states:

> There is a presumption that consolidated statements are more meaningful than separate statements and that they are usually necessary for a fair presentation when one of the companies in the group directly or indirectly has a controlling financial interest in the other companies.[20]

---

[20] AICPA, "Consolidated Financial Statements," *Accounting Research Bulletin No. 51* (New York, August 1959), par. 1. This statement is quoted and supported in *APB Opinion No. 18*, par. 4.

Control usually exists when the investor owns, directly or indirectly, more than 50 percent of the outstanding voting stock of the investee. Control may exist with less than a majority of the voting stock. Consolidation is not appropriate, however, in cases in which control is temporary or rests with a party other than the majority owners. It is also suggested that:

> . . . separate statements or combined statements would be preferable for a subsidiary or group of subsidiaries if the presentation of financial information concerning the particular activities of such subsidiaries would be more informative to shareholders and creditors of the parent company than would the inclusion of such subsidiaries in the consolidation. For example, separate statements may be required for a subsidiary which is a bank or an insurance company and may be preferable for a finance company where the parent and the other subsidiaries are engaged in manufacturing operations.[21]

A discussion of consolidated financial statements appears elsewhere in this book.

Equity method

In situations in which the investor does not own a controlling interest in the investee, but where the "investment in voting stock gives it (the investor) the ability to exercise *significant influence* over operating and financing policies of an investee . . . ,"[22] the equity method of accounting for the investment is appropriate (emphasis added). In addition, the equity method is used for investments in corporate joint ventures.[23] Because the investor has the ability to influence the results of operations of the investee, it is appropriate to include a part of these results in the results of operations of the investor. The ability of the investor to influence the investee may not be easily determinable. Such influence may often be subtle or unexercised.

The Accounting Principles Board provided guidelines in *Opinion No. 18* to assist in making judgments about "significant influence."

> In order to achieve a reasonable degree of uniformity in application, the Board concludes that an investment (direct or indirect)

---

[21] Ibid., par. 3.

[22] *APB Opinion No. 18,* op. cit., par. 17.

[23] Ibid., par. 16.

of 20% or more of the voting stock of an investee should lead to a
presumption that in the absence of evidence to the contrary an
investor has the ability to exercise significant influence over an
investee. Conversely, an investment of less than 20% of the voting
stock of an investee should lead to a presumption that an investor
does not have the ability to exercise significant influence unless
such ability can be demonstrated.[24]

Recognition of profit under the equity method is almost identical
to profit recognition in consolidation. Profit under the equity method
is recognized by the investor as a percentage of the investee's profit.
This percentage is based upon the relationship of the investor's
voting common shares to all outstanding voting common shares.
One difference in profit recognition between consolidation accounting and the equity method occurs when the investor's share of losses
of the investee exceeds the total of the investor's investment and
any advances to the investee. Application of the equity method
should normally cease at this point. Continued application would
occur only if the imminent return to profitable operations by the
investee is assured or if the investor is committed to further financial
support.[25] Another difference is in the amount of intercompany profit
elimination. A third difference is in determining the contents of
portfolios of marketable equity securities in accounting for changes
in market value, as described in the section "Valuation of Certain
Marketable Securities under FASB Statement No. 12" appearing
earlier in this chapter.

The investment should be carried as a single amount in the financial statements and should be adjusted by the investor's share of
the income or loss of the investee. Such income or loss should be
reported as a single item on the income statement except for extraordinary gains or losses, results of discontinued operations, and the
cumulative effect of a change in accounting principle, if such items
are material to the investor's income statement. Intercompany
profits should be eliminated, as discussed below.

A difference between the cost of investment and underlying net
equity should be accounted for as in consolidated financial statements. This difference should be allocated among identifiable assets
to the extent possible, and any remainder should be treated as good-

[24] Ibid., par. 17.
[25] Ibid., par. 19 and fn. 10.

will and amortized over a period not to exceed 40 years.[26] Dividends are treated as a return of invested capital and reduce the amount of the investment.

Intercompany profits

Investors often engage in business transactions with investees. In fact, the reason for many investments may be to ensure continuing business relationships. Because of the relationship between the investor and the investee in situations in which the equity method is used, a portion of the profit on intercompany transactions may have to be eliminated. *APB Opinion No. 18* states: "Intercompany profits and losses should be eliminated until realized by the investor or investee as if a subsidiary, corporate joint venture or investee company were consolidated."[27]

An interpretation of *Opinion No. 18* provides guidance in determining the circumstances in which intercompany profit should be eliminated, and the amount to eliminate. In general, to the extent profit remains in assets (e.g., inventory, fixed assets, etc.) on the balance sheet of either party, profit elimination is required. The amount to be eliminated is based on the percentage of common stock owned by the investor. If, for example, an investor which owns a 25 percent interest in an investee records profits of $100,000 on a sale of merchandise to the investee, and the cost of the merchandise is in inventory on the investee's balance sheet, 25 percent of the profit ($25,000) must be eliminated from the investor's income. Similarly, part of the profit recorded by the investee on transactions with the investor should be eliminated if the cost to the investor is on the investor's balance sheet. For example, if the investee had recorded $100,000 profit on a sale of merchandise to the investor which is held by the investor at the balance sheet date, the investor would exclude the entire $100,000 from the investee's income for purposes of computing the amount of investee income to be recognized under the equity method. Since the investor would recognize 25 percent of the investee's income, the investor's income would be reduced by $25,000. If the investor controls the investee through ownership of a majority voting interest or otherwise, no profit

---

[26] Ibid., par. 19n.
[27] Ibid., par. 19a.

should be recognized until realized through transactions with third parties.[28] If the investment is accounted for under the cost method, profits on transactions with investees may be recognized currently.

Cost method

If the investor is unable to exert significant influence upon the investee, the investor should use the cost method in accounting for the investment. As quoted above, *APB Opinion No. 18* states that lack of significant influence should be assumed if the investor owns less than 20 percent of the outstanding stock of the investor.

In applying the cost method, income is recognized as dividends are declared. The investment is carried at cost unless:

1. There is a circumstance which causes a decline in the value of the investment which is not merely temporary, or
2. Dividends are received in excess of the earnings of the investee since the date of purchase of the investment.[29]

The cost of the investment should be written down if either of the above situations exists. If dividends exceed earnings, the investment should be written down only by an amount equal to the excess of the dividends received over total earnings since acquisition. If, for example, during the first two years of ownership by an investor the investee had paid dividends equal in amount to its earnings and during the third year paid the investor dividends which exceeded its share of net income in that year by $20,000, the cost of the investment should be written down by $20,000 in the third year.

Property dividends

The receipt of cash dividends by the investor seldom poses an accounting problem. As previously discussed, dividends are normally accounted for as a reduction in investment under the equity method and as income under the cost method. Occasionally, however, an investor may receive a dividend in the form of property. *APB Opinion No. 29* requires recording such transactions at the

[28] AICPA, "1. Intercompany Profit Eliminations under Equity Method," *Accounting Interpretations of APB Opinion No. 18* (New York, November 1971).
[29] *APB Opinion No. 18*, par. 6a.

fair market value of the property, except in the following circumstances:

1. The fair value is not objectively measurable or would not clearly be realizable to the investee in an outright sale.
2. The property is distributed in a spin-off, reorganization, liquidation, or rescission of a business combination.
3. The property is stock of another corporation consolidated with the investee or is an investment accounted for by the investee under the equity method.[30]

In these circumstances, the transactions should be recorded on the basis of the amount at which the property was recorded on the books of the investee.

Liquidating dividends

Another problem may arise if the dividend distributed to the investor represents a partial or complete liquidation of the investee. If the investor accounts for its investment in the investee under the equity method, all dividends are applied to reduce the investment account. It is necessary, however, to reassess the remaining equity in the investee following a partial liquidation to determine whether the remaining balance in the investment account is justifiable. If it is not, a loss should be taken at the time of partial liquidation. In the case of complete liquidation, the investment account should be closed and the resulting gain or loss recorded.

If the investment is accounted for under the cost method, dividends paid in excess of earnings since the date of purchase are treated as reductions in the investment account. Liquidating dividends would be treated similarly, and, as with the equity method, the remaining balance in the investment account should be evaluated and a gain or loss should be recognized when appropriate.

Stock dividends and splits

In order to encourage wider ownership of stock or to reduce market price per share, corporations sometimes issue stock dividends or declare stock splits. Such occurrences should have no impact on

---

[30] AICPA, "Accounting for Nonmonetary Transactions," *Accounting Principles Board Opinion No. 29* (New York, May 1973), par. 23.

the carrying value of investments by investors. The equity interest in the investee is not changed by such distributions; the interest is merely distributed over a greater number of shares. Such distributions would only affect the cost to be assigned to individual shares which are sold subsequent to the distribution of the stock dividend or the stock split. The cost to be assigned to the distributed shares should be based upon the number of shares on hand which have been purchased at each different price. If, for example, the investor owns 100 shares of the investee which were purchased at $50 per share and 200 shares of the investee which were purchased at $100 per share, the declaration of a two-for-one stock split would result in carrying 200 shares at $25 and 400 shares at $50.

Changes in ownership interest

The ownership interest of the investor in the investee may change over a period of time. Such changes may result from the disposition or acquisition of additional shares by the investor, the sale of additional shares by the investee, or exercise of rights, warrants, options, or conversion of other securities to acquire common stock of the investee. The change in ownership may cause the investor's share of the investee's common stock to drop below or move above the 20 percent ownership test for the equity method. If the ownership falls below and significant influence cannot be exercised by the investor, application of the equity method should cease. The amount at which the investment is carried at the date of cessation of the equity method should be treated as cost for application of the cost method. Dividends received subsequent to the change in method which are in excess of earnings subsequent to the change should be treated as a reduction in investment. If the ownership interest in the investee increases to a point where the investor may exert significant influence (usually a 20 percent or more interest) the equity method should be applied retroactively " . . . in a manner consistent with the accounting for a step-by-step acquisition of a subsidiary."[31] Under this method, the investor retroactively recognizes its share of investee earnings on the basis of the ownership interest prior to attaining the ability to exert significant influence.

The investor's ownership interest in the equity of the investee will also change if shares are purchased or sold by the investee at

---

[31] *APB Opinion No. 18,* par. 19m.

prices other than book value. For example, if an investor owned one share of stock in an investee with only five shares outstanding and total equity of $50, the equity per share would be $10 ($50/5 shares). If a sixth share of stock was sold by the investee for $16, the new equity would be $66 ($50 + $16) and equity per share would be $11 ($66/6 shares). Similarly, the repurchase by the investee of a share of stock at a price of $14 would cause total equity to be $36 ($50 − $14) and equity per share to be $9 ($36/4 shares). Transactions by the investee which change the equity of the investor should be recognized by the investor as gains or losses and the carrying value of the investment should be adjusted if the investment is accounted for under the equity method. If the cost method is used only losses should be recognized. Some argue, however, that the gain or loss in equity should be credited or charged directly to the capital accounts of the investor. The Securities and Exchange Commission has followed a policy of requiring that a gain be credited to consolidated capital when the gain arises from a sale by a consolidated subsidiary of the stock.[32] However, if the parent sells all or part of its holdings of subsidiary stock, the gain may be credited to consolidated income. Since income recognition and financial statement presentation follows primarily a proprietary concept, under which net income is the residual available to the equity owners of the parent company, a credit (or charge if a loss) to income would appear to be appropriate in most instances.

WARRANTS AND RIGHTS

Both warrants and rights represent contracts from the issuer offering common stock at a specific price for a specific period of time. Rights are generally distributed to existing shareholders in proportion to their individual holdings. Warrants may be acquired individually or received in conjunction with other securities.

Accounting for the purchase of warrants is much like accounting for the purchase of any other security. They should be originally recorded and carried at cost. (The problem of apportioning cost between warrants and other securities purchased as a lump sum is discussed in a previous section in this chapter.) If the warrants are sold, a gain or loss should be recognized on the transaction. War-

---

[32] H. L. Kellogg and N. Poloway, *Accountants SEC Practice Manual* (Chicago: Commerce Clearing House, Inc., 1971), par. 4384.

rants which lapse should be written off and a loss should be recognized equal to the cost of the warrants. When warrants are exercised, the accepted practice has been to add the cost of the warrants to the exercise price to determine the cost of the stock so acquired.

When rights are received in connection with shares owned by the investor, the original cost of the shares must be apportioned between the shares and the new rights. Since the rights usually allow for purchase of stock at below the current market price, a market generally develops for the rights on the day when the rights can be sold separately from the stock. On this day, the stock is sold without rights (ex-rights) and the cost apportionment should be made between the two securities. The ratio between the market value of a right and the sum of the market value of both securities may be used to determine the cost to be allocated to the rights. For example, if the cost of one thousand shares of stock when originally purchased was $100,000 and, subsequent to the issuance of rights, the stock was trading at an aggregate of $136,000 (ex-rights) and the rights were trading at $4,000, the portion of cost to be assigned to the rights would be computed as follows:

$$\frac{\$4,000}{\$136,000 + \$4,000} = \frac{x}{\$100,000}$$

$$x = \$2,857$$

The cost to be allocated to the right would be $2,857 leaving a cost of $97,143 assigned to the stock. If the rights are later sold, any gain or loss should be computed based upon the cost assigned to the rights. If the rights lapse without exercise, a loss should be recognized equal to the cost assigned to the rights. When rights are exercised, the cost assigned to the rights should be added to the cash paid to determine the cost of securities acquired by the exercise.

CONVERTIBLE SECURITIES

Nature of convertibles

Convertibles are securities which may be exchanged at the option of the holder for another security; one investment may be converted to another investment. Normally, convertible securities are issued only by corporations, and are usually debt instruments or preferred stock convertible into common stock. A convertible gives the holder some protection against the risk of a decline in value to which a common stockholder is exposed, and also gives the holder the opportunity to share in appreciation in the value of common stock.

A convertible may be trading in the marketplace on the basis of the characteristics of one of the inherent securities but not the other. For example, a convertible debt may be trading at a substantial premium because the common stock into which it is convertible has risen greatly in value, giving the convertible debt holder greater value through the conversion privilege than that which attaches to the debt. In this case the convertible security is trading on its common stock value. If the common stock price does not exceed the conversion price, a premium would reflect primarily the current market rate of interest on the debt, in which case the convertible security is trading on its debt characteristics. A convertible debt selling at a substantial discount is usually trading only on its debt characteristics, due to a coupon rate lower than the current market rate of interest for the debt.

A convertible may be considered as being a combination of the primary security and an option to purchase another security. The value of the option feature will be, as in the case of all options, equal to the sum of the value of the conversion right and the conversion premium. The conversion premium is the excess of the value of the security which may be purchased over the exercise or conversion price. If the common stock is currently trading at an amount which exceeds the conversion price, a premium will be included in the value of the option feature, and hence will be reflected in the price of the convertible security. If common stock is not trading at such an excess, the value of the option feature will be limited to the value of the right. If the common stock is trading at a very low price in comparison to the conversion price, the value of the right will also be very low. In either case, the value of the option feature will be included in the price of the convertible security, even if it is trading on the basis of its debt or preferred stock value.

Conceivably, the value of the option feature could be measured as the difference between the price at which the convertible is trading and the price at which the underlying debt or preferred stock would trade without the conversion option.[33] The determination of the present value of a debt or preferred stock is affected by the ex-

---

[33] AICPA, "Omnibus Opinion," *Accounting Principles Board Opinion No. 10* (New York, December 1966), par. 9.

pected disposal date and disposal price. It is possible to assume that the preferred stock or debt will be converted in making this calculation. But the nature of a convertible security does not permit such an assumption, as it leaves this decision to the holder to be made at a later date.[34] One can assume neither conversion nor absence of conversion. If it were not for this complexity, one could easily value the option feature inherent in a convertible security and account for it separate from the accounting for the underlying debt or preferred stock. Therefore, under present practice, the convertible is accounted for as a single investment.

Discount or premium amortization

As indicated in the earlier discussion of preferred stock, amortization of a premium or discount is usually not required for preferred stock because it has no fixed maturity. The same would be true for convertible preferred stock. In addition, if a convertible preferred premium reflects common stock value, there should be no need to amortize the premium.

When convertible debt is purchased at a discount or premium, a slight modification in the approach is necessary. To the extent that a premium is attributable to common stock value, amortization would not be required. However, if the premium or discount is related primarily to the market rate of interest differing from the interest on the debt, the premium or discount should be amortized on the basis of the maturity or perhaps the call provisions of the debt.

Income recognition before conversion

A question which sometimes arises is whether income should be recognized on the basis of the nature of the investment into which the convertible security could be converted or on the basis of the underlying security. For example, if the holder of a convertible debt

---

[34] AICPA, "Accounting for Convertible Debt and Debt Issued with Stock Purchase Warrants," *Accounting Principles Board Opinion No. 14* (New York, March 1969). This opinion reversed the conclusion in *APB Opinion No. 10* regarding convertible debt and expressed the conclusion that separate accounting by an issuer for the two segments of a convertible debt is not acceptable because of the inseparability of the debt and conversion option (par. 7 and 12). See also AICPA, "Early Extinguishment of Debt," *Accounting Principles Board Opinion No. 26* (New York, October 1972), par. 11–15.

exercises significant influence with respect to the investee and anticipates converting the debt into common stock at some future date,
should the investor recognize equity in the earnings of the common
stock into which the debt could be converted? If the earnings of the
investee available for common stockholders are distributed in the
form of dividends, such earnings are not available for the convertible
security holder. If the earnings are not distributed, they accrue to the
benefit of the holder only upon conversion and until then have not
been realized. For these reasons and perhaps others, ordinarily it
would not be appropriate to recognize income on a basis other than
that attributable to the underlying security held.[35]

Conversion

Two alternative methods of accounting have been used in practice
when a convertible security is converted. Under one method, the
cost of the convertible security carries over and becomes the cost of
the security received in exchange. Under the other method, the
security received in exchange is recorded at the fair market value at
the date of exchange and a gain or loss is recognized on conversion.
Arguments in favor of carryover of cost are usually on the basis that
the initial investment was made for the purpose of its ultimate determination and thus the cost of the securities ultimately acquired is
represented by the initial cost and not the values at the date of exchange. Another reason is that the convertible security represents an
option and gains are not usually recognized when an option holder
exercises the option. A third reason is that the market value of the
securities received in exchange may not reflect the value ascribed to
the security by the investor making the conversion. The investor
may believe that the security into which the conversion is made is
worth less than its market value, but the value the investor ascribes
to that security may still be sufficiently high to induce conversion.
Finally, conversion may be forced by the issuer through a call of the
convertible security. In such forced conversion cases, the holder of
the security has no choice but to convert if the value of the securities
to be received exceeds the call price. But in such situations, the investor may not have been willing to acquire the securities at their
market value.

Arguments in favor of recognizing a gain or loss upon conversion

---

[35] *APB Opinion No. 18*, par. 18.

include the fact that the conversion is a transaction similar to other sales and purchases in which one asset is disposed of so that another can be acquired. Usually in these transactions, a market value is established for both the convertible security and the security received in exchange. If market values clearly exist for both securities, many maintain that these market values represent objective evidence of values realized. Further, the amount at which the convertible security could be sold on the market represents an opportunity cost and thus a measure of the cost of the securities acquired in exchange. Finally, *APB Opinion No. 29* requires recognizing fair values and hence gain or loss in most nonmonetary exchanges. If the exchange of a convertible debt or convertible preferred stock for common stock is a nonmonetary transaction, *APB Opinion No. 29* applies.[36]

SELECTED REFERENCES

AICPA. Industry Audit Guides, *Audits of Brokers and Dealers in Securities, Audits of Savings and Loan Associations, Audits of Banks, Audits of Fire and Casualty Insurance Companies, Audits of Stock Life Insurance Companies.* New York.

Gushee, C. H., ed. *Financial Compound Interest and Annuity Tables.* 5th ed. Boston: Financial Publishing Co., 1970.

Hendriksen, E. S. *Accounting Theory.* Homewood, Ill.: Richard D. Irwin, Inc., Revised ed., 1970.

Meigs, W. B.; Mosich, A. N.; Johnson, C. E.; and Keller, T. F. *Intermediate Accounting.* 3rd ed. New York: McGraw-Hill Book Co., 1974, chap. 21.

Mosich, A. N.; Larsen, E. J. *Modern Advanced Accounting.* New York: McGraw-Hill Book Co., 1975.

Moonitz, M., and Jordan, L. H. *Accounting—An Analysis of Its Problems.* New York: Holt, Rinehart and Winston, Inc., 1964.

---

[36] *APB Opinion No. 29* applies to exchanges and nonreciprocal transfers of nonmonetary items, with reference in footnote 2 to AICPA, "Financial Statements Restated for General Price-Level Changes," *Accounting Principles Board Statement No. 3*(New York, June 1969), for an explanation of monetary and nonmonetary items. *Statement No. 3* describes in Appendix B "investments in convertible bonds" as being nonmonetary if "held for price speculation or with expectation of converting into common stock." *APB Opinion No. 29* also refers, in footnote 3, to *APB Statement No. 4* for an explanation of exchanges and nonreciprocal transfers. Paragraph 182 of *Statement No. 4* gives several examples of nonreciprocal transfers, including "conversion of convertible debt." *APB Opinion No. 29* amends *Statement No. 4* "to the extent it relates to measuring transfers of certain nonmonetary assets" (see par. 4). Paragraph 18 specifies that "a nonmonetary asset received in a nonreciprocal transfer should be recorded at the fair value of the asset received."

Securities and Exchange Commission. Regulation S-X, Accounting Series Releases, and Staff Accounting Bulletins.

Simons, H. *Intermediate Accounting.* 5th ed. Cincinnati, Ohio: South-Western Publishing Co., 1972.

Skinner, R. M. *Accounting Principles.* Toronto: The Canadian Institute of Chartered Accountants, 1972, chaps. 16 and 17.

Chapter 17

Accounting for foreign operations

*William R. Love**

The post–World War II period of economic development has been marked by substantial increase in investment by U.S. companies throughout most of the free world. The steadily and rapidly developing growth in the amount and scope of investments by U.S. companies has brought on the need for sound management controls and well understood communications between U.S. parent companies and their affiliates operating abroad. Achievement of these management objectives must rest to a substantial degree on establishment of mutually understood and effective accounting and reporting standards and practices. The resulting accounting and information systems must be able to accommodate the differences that have developed over the years between accounting and reporting philosophies in the United States and in many areas abroad. This accommodation must span many elements beyond the purely technical aspects of accounting and reporting, such as differences in educational training for business subjects, the effect of varying tax and other legislation, and similar factors.

The establishment of accounting and reporting practices to meet local needs as well as overall consolidated financial and operating requirements requires a many-faceted and well-coordinated

---

* Vice President and Comptroller, Texaco Inc.

approach. Careful planning and execution on a continuing basis at all operating and reporting levels is necessary.

BACKGROUND OF DIFFERENCES
BETWEEN COUNTRIES

In reporting on operations of subsidiary and nonsubsidiary companies abroad, U.S. companies must make provision for dealing with the divergence of accounting policies and practices among the many different countries. There are also wide differences in the scope and amount of academic or on-the-job training in accounting and related business subjects and in formal professional qualifications. The more highly industrialized nations have well-established standards for accounting and reporting policies and adequate provision for education and qualification of personnel. In other countries these matters are in various stages of development and progress is being made. It should be stressed that standards are set and facilities and capabilities are in existence and are being further developed to meet the local requirements. The additional dimension that is necessary is the proper combining of the local needs with the overall consolidated requirements.

(In addition to the effect of educational resources, the development of an overall staff capability is also influenced by the laws and regulations established by governments.) In many countries there have been over the years restrictions on the number of non-nationals allowed to work in a country. Requirements of this type have grown substantially in recent years, prompted by the legitimate desire of local governments to advance the status of their nationals more rapidly, and the trend appears to be increasingly toward 100 percent staffing by nationals.

(Local governmental regulations normally set the requirements for accounting and reporting standards and practices in the countries involved. In many instances these local requirements differ from the policies followed by the parent company, and the accounting and reporting must be set up so that both the local requirements and the consolidation requirements of the parent company are met.)

The record-keeping and procedural mechanism for accomplishing this can take one of two forms. In addition to the books and records required to be maintained in accordance with the local requirements, supplemental records may also be maintained locally to permit conformance to consolidated requirements at the local level. In some instances this may not be permissible or desirable. An alternative approach is to maintain additional records, such as home office books or consolidating entries, in which accounting entries are made to conform the local accounting and reporting to that employed for purposes of the consolidated financial statements.

The fact that differing accounting standards are in use throughout the world, and that there is a resulting need for some means of arriving at a better basis for a commonality of understanding and interpretation, has been recognized by accounting and professional groups. One such group is the International Accounting Standards Committee, which has as its objective "to formulate and publish in the public interest, basic standards to be observed in the presentation of audited accounts and financial statements and to promote their worldwide acceptance and observance." Another such group is the European Economic Community, which has begun work towards establishment of minimum accounting and reporting standards for its member countries.

Accounting and reporting for operations in a foreign area have thus far been discussed in general terms as an introduction to a more detailed presentation of some of the more important matters to be dealt with in accounting for the operations abroad of subsidiaries and affiliates of a U.S. parent company. While it would be impracticable to cover every facet, the following paragraphs will afford some insight into the ramifications of the differences between consolidated accounting and reporting requirements and local office accounting practices.

EXAMPLES OF DIFFERENT ACCOUNTING PRACTICES

Local accounting practices may differ from generally accepted accounting practices in the United States in a number of ways, as exemplified by the following illustrations.

Some European countries permit corporate directorates wider latitude than U.S. practice allows in establishing reserves out of current earnings. For example, reserves may be created in the accounts through such measures as depreciation charges which reflect a rate faster than that used for purposes of the consolidated financial statements. Adjustments in the carrying value of inventories and accrual of additional provisions for expenses may be permitted by local regulations.

Investment grants or subsidies are used by many foreign countries to stimulate investment in specified long-term assets. The accounting methods used to record these subsidies vary among countries, and optional treatments may be allowed within a country. Generally the methods employed record the amount of the cash subsidy either as current income, as deferred income, or as a reduction in the carrying value of the related assets. For example, in Great Britain, government-prescribed accounting practices provide that investment grants may be recorded either as a reduction in the asset values of the related assets or as deferred credits. In Germany, however, the subsidy may be recorded as a reduction of the cost of the assets or it may be recorded as income in the period the cash subsidy is received. In France, a company may elect to recognize a cash subsidy as income in the year received or over a period of years.

Reductions or write-downs in inventory values are permissible in several countries. Normally these write-downs must be recorded in the books of account if they are to become available for tax purposes. In Denmark, the maximum reduction that can be taken in inventory cost is 35 percent under current regulations. This maximum may be applied to inventory values computed either at historical cost or at replacement cost. Under Swedish practices, inventories must generally be valued on a first-in, first-out (Fifo) basis. Amounts so determined may then be reduced by 5 percent for possible obsolescence, and thereafter by no more than 60 percent of the remaining amount for general inventory reserve purposes. Accordingly, the aggregate possible reduction in inventory carrying value amounts to 62 percent of Fifo historical cost.

Interperiod income tax allocation is still another area in which accounting practices in foreign countries may differ from those followed in the United States. Accordingly, it may be necessary in some instances to establish tax allocation accounting practices for local reporting purposes, and then to conform those practices to the requirements of the accounting practices that must be observed in the final consolidated accounting. In the absence of local requirements, appropriate provision must nevertheless be made for tax allocation accounting in order to conform to the consolidated reporting needs of the parent company.

In the United States, comprehensive income tax allocation on a deferral basis for all material timing differences is required under the provisions of Accounting Principles Board Opinions. Similarly, the practice of income tax allocation accounting in varying degrees is either required or has been recommended by professional societies in other countries such as Canada, Germany, the United Kingdom, and Australia. The principle of income tax allocation is also followed in varying degrees in other countries. However, even among countries where income tax allocation accounting is recognized, it may be carried out by differing methods, as for example the deferral method, the liability method, or the net-of-tax method. The extent of application may also vary. For example, comprehensive tax allocation may be required for all material timing differences or, alternatively, may be applied on the basis of a limited treatment of those timing differences which are not continually recurring.

In addition to the basic need for conforming varying tax allocation accounting methods, there are other conforming adjustments that may be involved in defining the timing differences for which deferred taxes are to be provided. For example, depreciation rates used in the accounts of the foreign company may be required to be the same for book and tax purposes, with no need for tax allocation accounting at the local level. Under such circumstances, the local book depreciation rate may differ from that reflecting the estimated useful life used for consolidated reporting purposes, and the depreciation method would also probably be different. Conformance of the local treatment to the overall corporate depreciation rate and method for purposes of the parent company's consolidated accounting and reporting would be necessary. In such instances the appropriate book depreciation amount to be utilized for determining tax allocation must be considered. The treatment can vary depending on the circumstances, including the matter of identifying the income tax rate that is applicable.

There are instances in which the taxes of more than one national taxing jurisdiction may be applicable, making it necessary to determine which is the appropriate income tax rate to be used in accounting for the deferred tax effect. For a subsidiary incorporated in a foreign country and subject only to local income taxes, the local rate should be used. However, if the subsidiary is incorporated in the United States or is a branch of such a subsidiary operating in a foreign area, the subsidiary or branch will normally be subject to both foreign and U.S. income taxes. In such circumstances, when determining the appropriate rate to be used consideration must be given to the effect of any credit for foreign income tax that may be allowed against the U.S. income tax liability. For example, in foreign countries where the local income tax rates are higher than the U.S. income tax rate, the U.S. tax liability may be eliminated by the foreign tax credit; in such cases deferred taxes applicable to timing differences would be provided at the prevailing foreign income tax rate. Conversely, in situations in which the foreign tax rate is lower than the U.S. tax rate, the U.S. income tax liability ordinarily would not be eliminated by the foreign tax credit. In these situations it would be appropriate to provide deferred taxes at the prevailing U.S. rate.

In situations in which incorporated subsidiaries or branches of U.S. companies operate in a number of foreign countries, the determination of whether the U.S. income tax rate or the foreign rates should be used can become further complicated by the manner in which the U.S. parent company files its income tax return (either on a single company or consolidated basis) and by its choice of the method of calculating the foreign tax credit application to its U.S. income tax liability (per country or global method). (See Chapter 14 for more detailed information on this topic.) However, the basic premise outlined above still applies; that is, deferred taxes applicable to timing differences in foreign operations should be provided on the basis of the effective income tax rate that is in fact applicable, either United States or foreign, but not on both rates.

As illustrated in the foregoing paragraghs, general guidelines can be stated for application of income tax allocation accounting. However, because of the interplay of the various factors that may be involved, the treatment to be followed must be determined for each individual situation. Once determined, the circumstances need to be kept under continuing review because of the changes that can occur, and frequently do, in the various factors involved.

FOREIGN CURRENCY TRANSLATION

Until recently, translation principles and methods had been developed over the years more through evolution and usage than through a body of well-defined, formalized standards. With the adoption of *Financial Accounting Standards Board Statement No. 8* in October, 1975, comprehensive principles have been formally established.

Selection of the appropriate exchange rate to be utilized for a particular type of transaction will be the subject of much of the subsequent discussion in this section. An exchange rate can be described as a ratio expressed in terms of the amount of one currency that can be purchased by a unit of another currency at a particular time. A variety of rates exists, such as the buying rate of dollars, selling rate of dollars, buying or selling rate of the local currency, or an average rate for a period. In general, the exchange rate to be utilized to translate foreign currency financial statements to U.S. dollars is the rate for buying U.S. dollars at which remittances may legally be made.

In certain instances, a specific rate of exchange may be established for commercial purposes by a foreign government, such as an "oil rate" or other commodity rate. Such rates would also normally be appropriate for use by a company for its internal accounting purposes. If a special rate is set by the government for imports of merchandise, that rate would normally be applied to transactions involving merchandise imports.

In addition to describing which of various types of rates might be utilized for financial reporting purposes, it is also necessary to decide whether *current* or *historical* exchange rates should be utilized to translate individual accounts. The current rate of exchange is defined as the rate in effect at the balance sheet date. The historical rate is the exchange rate at which the foreign currency was or could have been exchanged for U.S. dollars at the time of a particular transaction in the past.

An exchange gain or loss will arise from a change in the rate of exchange. The gain or loss is determined by comparing the dollar equivalent of a local currency amount at the new and old exchange rate. The exchange gain or loss may be either *realized* or *unrealized*. Such gains or losses are realized when a receipt or transfer of funds occurs. Unrealized gains or losses result from the translation of balance sheet accounts at changing exchange rates.

Exchange gains and losses should be included in determining net income for the period in which the rate changes in accordance with *Financial Accounting Standards Board Statement No. 8* dated

October, 1975. Present disclosure requirements concerning exchange gains or losses are also contained in *Financial Accounting Standards Board Statement No. 8.*

To the extent that exchange gains or losses are included in different periods for financial statement purposes than for tax purposes, deferred tax accounting should be practiced where applicable.

Prior to the adoption of *Financial Accounting Standards Board Statement No. 8* there were various acceptable methods of translation which had been developed over the years for use in expressing foreign financial statements in U.S. dollars. These methods and a brief description of their use are outlined below. The principles to be followed under the provisions of *FASB No. 8* are generally comparable to those described below under the *temporal* method.

Monetary-nonmonetary method

The monetary-nonmonetary method generally translates *monetary* assets and liabilities at the current rate and *nonmonetary* assets and liabilities at applicable historical rates. Monetary assets and liabilities are cash, claims to cash, and those assets that can be converted directly into cash without an interim transaction involving either a credit or charge to the income account. Balance sheet accounts not falling in these classifications are termed nonmonetary, and consist of accounts such as inventories, property, plant and equipment, and capital accounts. The other account affected when a monetary account is debited or credited, that is, cash or accounts payable or receivable, would normally be a nonmonetary account such as property, plant, and equipment or inventory.

Current-noncurrent method

The current-noncurrent method generally translates *current* assets and liabilities at the current rate, and *noncurrent* assets and liabilities at the applicable historical rate. Current assets can be defined as unrestricted cash and other assets held for conversion within one year (or operating cycle, if longer) into cash or other similar assets, or useful goods or services. Current liabilities are those that are payable within one year (or operating cycle, if longer) from the balance sheet date.

Current rate method

The *current rate* method translates all assets and liabilities at the current rate of exchange. The use of the current rate method continually revalues all assets, including property, plant, and equipment and inventories, at the current rate of exchange. As a result the relationship of the accounts to each other as stated at the historical acquisition cost in foreign currency is not maintained.

Temporal method

Leonard Lorensen, in *Accounting Research Study No. 12* published in 1972 by the American Institute of Certified Public Accountants, advocated the *temporal* approach, described as follows:

> The nature of translation as a measurement conversion process requires that the assets and liabilities of foreign subsidiaries be translated in a manner that retains the accounting principles used to measure them in the foreign money financial statements; that is, that the attributes of the assets and liabilities measured be the same after translation as before. . . . The attributes measured—for example, historical cost, current replacement price, or current selling price—are thus retained. . . .

The temporal method is similar to the monetary-nonmonetary method. Under the temporal method, those accounts such as cash, receivables, and payables, which are realizable or payable in the foreign currency at the amounts stated, should be translated using the exchange rate in effect at the balance sheet date. Other assets and liabilities should be translated at the historical rate of exchange.

A discussion of the translation process utilizing the temporal method as applied to specific accounts is outlined below.

Fixed assets. The translation of fixed assets into U.S. dollars would be made at the exchange rate in effect at the date of acquisition. The related depreciation, depletion, and amortization charges and credits applicable to these fixed assets, and book values applicable to retirements, would be translated at those rates used to translate the related property, plant, and equipment into U.S. dollars (historical rates). Thus, the total gross cost and the accumulated extinguishment allowances would be stated at comparable weighted average translation rates.

Current assets and liabilities (excluding inventories). Cash, current receivables, and liabilities are accounts which are recorded at their current values and are realizable or payable at the amounts stated. For this reason, under the temporal method the current exchange rate would be used for translation.

Inventories. The temporal method requires the use of acquisition rates (historical) in translating inventories carried at cost. However, inventories carried at current replacement or market values are to be translated at the current exchange rate, unless the translated market value exceeds the historical dollar costs.

Revenue, costs, and expenses. The temporal method provides for the translation of revenue, costs, and expenses at average rates for the reporting period, except for those accounts (such as depreciation) which are related to balance sheet accounts which have been translated at historical rates.

Long-term debt. Long-term debt denominated in a foreign currency will be repaid in the future when exchange rates can be expected to be different from those prevailing at the time the debt was incurred. Such liabilities should be translated at the current rate. This treatment results in expressing the amount of debt in the amount of U.S. dollars that would be currently required to repay the debt. In translating the debt in this manner, a translation gain or loss will be recorded, dependent upon the change in exchange rates from the initial rates and rates subsequently used. However, until such time as the debt is retired these are unrealized gains or losses.

Remittances. Remittances from foreign operations usually relate to the transfer of current or prior period earnings to the parent. In the case of a company incorporated in a country other than the United States, the transfer would be made by means of a dividend. The dollar equivalent of prior period retained earnings on the local company's books is normally considered to be fixed at the historical dollar equivalent, and not translatable at the current rate of exchange. Therefore, a realized exchange gain or loss will occur when a dividend is paid which is translatable at the current rate. The payment of the dividend results in the realization of previously recognized exchange gains or losses that were recorded at the date the rates changed.

ACCOUNTING TREATMENT OF
FOREIGN INVESTMENTS

Consolidation of the accounts of affiliates is permitted under U.S. accounting principles but only for majority-owned subsidiaries. However, *Accounting Research Bulletin No. 43* of June 1953, also makes provision for not consolidating the accounts of subsidiary companies under some circumstances. Paragraph B in Chapter 12 of *Accounting Research Bulletin No. 43* states:

> In view of the uncertain values and availability of the assets and net income of foreign subsidiaries subject to controls and exchange restrictions and the consequent unrealistic statements of income that may result from translation of many foreign currencies into dollars, careful consideration should be given to the fundamental question of whether it is proper to consolidate the statements of foreign subsidiaries with the statements of United States companies.

When the rate of inflation in a country is of such a magnitude that the results of operations if consolidated might result in reporting misleading information, consideration should be given to not consolidating the subsidiary but rather recording the investment as an investment at cost. Similar consideration should be given to non-consolidation when funds cannot be repatriated and must be reinvested.

When a foreign entity is owned 50 percent or less, the investment may be accounted for under either the equity or cost method, based upon the guidelines set forth below.

Accounting Principles Board Opinion No. 18 established criteria for accounting for an affiliate under the equity basis. The basic principle embodied in the criteria is that when an investor has the ability to exercise significant influence over an investee, the investment in the affiliate should be accounted for under the equity method. In the *Opinion* the presumption is stated that an investment of 20 percent or more of the voting stock of an investee would require accounting for the entity under the equity method. However, this presumption can be overcome by evidence to the contrary. Moreover, the method can be used for less than 20 percent if significant influence is demonstrated.

Under the *cost method* the investment in the investee company is reflected in the investor's balance sheet at cost, except in situations in which the underlying equity is below such cost (and this condition is expected to continue). In the latter case, a write-down of carrying value from cost to underlying equity would be appropriate. When the investment is accounted for on the cost basis, earnings from the investment are reflected in the investor's income statement only on the basis of declaration or receipt of dividends.

Under the *equity method,* earnings or losses from the investment are reflected in the income statement on the basis of the investor's equity in the current earnings of the investee. The cost to the investor company of the investment in the investee is adjusted upward or downward to reflect, respectively, equity in earnings or losses of the investee. The investor company's investment is therefore carried at an amount equal to cost, plus or minus the change in the investee's underlying net assets since the investment was acquired, rather than at cost. Under the equity method, dividends receivable from an investee are applied to reduce the carrying value of the investment. (See *Accounting Principles Board Opinion No. 18* covering the equity method of accounting for investment in common stock.)

When the investment in an investee company is accounted for on the equity method, the same principles that govern the translation of foreign currencies in the case of a consolidated subsidiary company are applicable. Similarly, the principles governing conformance of accounting and reporting practices to consolidated requirements should be followed. In actual practice it may not always be possible to apply these principles to the extent desirable, because of inability to obtain the necessary information from the investee company, or to obtain it on the schedule or with the frequency called for by the timetable of the consolidated reporting requirements.

Chapter 18

Accounting for business combinations and goodwill

*Harvey V. Guttry, Jr.**
William K. Harper†

A hallowed tradition of business is the philosophy of growth, change, and expansion. The subject of business combinations (acquisitions and mergers) is related to overall corporate growth strategy. When we speak of corporate growth strategy, we refer to new products, new markets (geographical or customer), new distribution systems, additional productive capacity, and new management. Acquisitions are one way of accomplishing many growth objectives. With few exceptions (such as patents which cannot be circumvented), growth may be accomplished either through the internal expenditure of resources by the firm to develop internally new products, markets, and so on, *or* through the external expenditure of resources for the acquisition of a firm which has already made progress toward the objective sought. This theme of alternative strategies for growth will be carried throughout this chapter as it relates to accounting for business combinations and goodwill.

It is difficult to determine the exact extent of business acquisition activity that has taken place in the United States. Table 1

Vice President and Controller, The Times Mirror Company.

† Chairman, Department of Accounting, School of Business Administration, University of Southern California.

provides some approximation of acquisition activity in the past ten years.

As can be seen from Table 1, a sharp decline in the number of acquisitions occurred after 1969. It is difficult to determine the

TABLE 1
Acquisition and merger activity

Year	Number of acquisitions
1975 (9 months)	1,732*
1974	2,861
1973	4,040
1972	4,801
1971	4,608
1970	5,152
1969	6,107
1968	4,462
1967	2,975
1966	2,377

* Twenty-five percent below the nine-month figures for 1974.
Source: W. T. Grimm & Co., a Chicago-based consulting firm.

causes. *APB Opinions* (APBO) *No. 16* ("Business Combinations") and *No. 17* ("Intangible Assets") became effective October 31, 1970; the 1970s brought a sharp decline in the economic environment; and the stock market peaked in May 1973. One could speculate that the new *APB Opinions* might have been the most important factors and that the decline was due to fewer pooling-of-interests business combinations because of more restrictive accounting requirements. One empirical study would suggest that the previous statement is not true, since approximately 81 percent of the mergers sampled both before and after *APB Opinions No. 16* and *17* were accounted for as poolings.[1]

Prior to the 1960s it was common to think in terms of product-market strategies. During the expansionary period of the 1960s, the development of financial strategy as a key element of corporate strategy became an important consideration.

Any business combination requires careful advance planning and consideration of numerous factors, including the legal, tax, accounting, and operating considerations. Two alternative accounting

[1] Frank R. Rayburn, "Another Look at the Impact of Accounting Principles Board Opinion No. 16—An Empirical Study," *Mergers and Acquisitions* (Spring 1975), pp. 7–9.

treatments are available which may result in the reporting of significantly different financial results (e.g., earnings per share, total assets, and return on investment). Because of the potential materiality of the different accounting treatments, they may affect the negotiations and terms of the combination.

Provisions of the Internal Revenue Code (Section 368) provide the opportunity to defer taxes on the exchange of shares in certain so-called "tax-free" business combinations. In essence, the stock acquired by the seller assumes the cost basis attached to the stock tendered. Thus, the capital gain or loss for tax purposes does not occur with the business combination transaction, but at a subsequent date when the stock received from the buying corporation in the exchange is sold. Several technical characteristics must be met for the various types of "tax-free" business combinations. A common characteristic is the encouragement provided by tax law to use voting securities to accomplish business combinations. In a "tax-free" combination the assets acquired cannot be written up for tax-purposes even if the acquisition is accounted for as a "purchase" for financial reporting purposes.

The crux of accounting for the business combination issue has been, and continues to be, the theoretical validity of pooling-of-interests business combinations and how to account for goodwill in purchase accounting. If evidence is needed that the accounting profession has yet to resolve this issue satisfactorily, we only need to look at Table 2, which summarizes key publications of the

TABLE 2
Accounting Research Bulletins (ARB), Accounting Research Studies (ARS), and Accounting Principles Board Opinions (APBO) related to business combinations and goodwill

Date

1944	*ARB No. 24:*	"Accounting for Intangible Assets"
1950	*ARB No. 40:*	"Business Combinations"
1953	*ARB No. 43:*	"Restatement and Revision of Accounting Research Bulletins." Summarized previous 42 ARBs (Chapter 5 and 7c).
1957	*ARB No. 48:*	"Business Combinations"
1963	*ARS No. 5:*	"A Critical Study of Accounting for Business Combinations"
1965	*APBO No. 6:*	"Status of Accounting Research Bulletins. Essentially reconfirmed *ARB No. 48.*
1966	*APBO No. 10:*	"Omnibus Opinion–1966." Amended paragraph 12 of *ARB No. 48* on financial statement presentation of business combinations.
1968	*ARS No. 10:*	"Accounting for Goodwill"
1970	*APBO No. 16:*	"Business Combinations"
1970	*APBO No. 17:*	"Intangible Assets"
1975	*FASB Interpretation No. 4:*	"Applicability of FASB Statement No. 2 to Business Combinations Accounted for by the Purchase Method"

American Institute of Certified Public Accounts (AICPA) and Financial Accounting Standards Board (FASB) on the business combination issue. In May 1974, the FASB announced that it would reconsider criteria for accounting for business combinations as pooling of interests. Two months later, the FASB announced that a total review of accounting for business combinations and purchased intangibles would be made. At this writing, the project has been assigned to an FASB member, staff has been assembled, and an advisory task force has been formed. It is anticipated that a discussion memorandum will be issued during the first half of 1976.

ACCOUNTING PRONOUNCEMENTS

Accounting Research Bulletin (ARB) No. 40

From the beginning the AICPA, through its Committee on Accounting Procedure, took the position that the *economic substance* of a transaction should determine the appropriate accounting treatment. In other words, accounting procedures and financial reports were to reflect economic (substance), not legal (form), events. This was confirmed with *ARB No. 40*.

Pooling-of-interests accounting was considered appropriate when there was a continuation of ownership, management, and control subsequent to the combination transaction, similar to that which had existed in each separate company prior to the business combination. *ARB No. 40* contemplated that pooling accounting would be used only in those situations where the combining firms were of approximately the same size and in the same or related businesses.

Purchase accounting was determined to be appropriate in all cases where pooling-of-interests accounting was not. No one criterion was considered essential for either type of accounting. Perhaps the only exception was that if a substantial proportion of the price consisted of cash, then the cash was presumptive evidence that a purchase, not pooling, had taken place. Management and the independent auditor were expected to review all pertinent factors in reaching a conclusion as to the proper accounting method in each case.

This first attempt at defining the concepts in support of two significantly different accounting treatments, and the accounting procedures to be followed, clarified a number of issues but left several unresolved. Table 3 summarizes several key differences.

TABLE 3
Accounting for business combinations under *ARB No. 40*

	Purchase	*Pooling of interests*
Carrying value of acquired assets and liabilities	Fair market value	Book value
Goodwill of acquired company	Excess of purchase price over FMV of net assets	Not allowed
Goodwill amortization	Optional	Not applicable
Income statement—period covered	Not specified	Not specified
Treatment of acquired retained earnings	Not allowed	May be carried forward

In 1953 *ARB No. 43* was issued, summarizing the previous 42 bulletins. *ARB No. 43* did not make any significant changes in the accounting for business combinations with the exception of paragraph 7 of Chapter 7(c), which said that if the retained earnings of the acquired company are carried forward, a consolidated statement of income should be presented for all periods reported.

ARB No. 48

Seven years after the issuance of *ARB No. 40*, *ARB No. 48* was issued to update and revise the accounting treatment for business combinations to reflect new thinking on the subject and evaluations of the results of applying *ARB No. 40* from 1950 to 1957.

Major changes from *ARB No. 40* to *ARB No. 48* included: (1) clarification of the size criterion, (2) treatment of retained earnings of the acquired company, (3) reporting of operating results, and (4) combined subsidiaries.

The criterion that companies should be similar in size had proven to be such an ambiguous term that specific rules were adopted in *ARB No. 48*. Under some pressure, the Committee on Accounting Procedure defined similarity of size as meaning that the acquired company must be at least equal to 5 to 10 percent of the combined company in voting rights or other relevant size criteria. Even this generous definition of similarity of size was quickly eroded in practice, due in no small part to the acquiescence of the Securities and Exchange Commission (SEC) and the fact that the size criterion was only suggestive. The size criterion rapidly became a noncriterion for pooling versus purchase accounting. Thus, the attempt of *ARB No. 48* to enforce a concept from *ARB No. 40* more rigidly was not successful.

With further development of the "marriage" concept of poolings and the idea that the combined firms should be viewed as though they had always been a single business entity, it was necessary to establish standards for the time period covered for reporting operations of the combined entity and the attendant treatment of retained earnings. The concept of oneness for the time prior to the date of combination resulted in operations of the combined entity being presented for the entire accounting period during which the combination was effected, without regard to the date of combination. Under purchase accounting, operations for the acquired entity are only included for the time subsequent to the combination.

To also be consistent with the concept of oneness even prior to the business combination, the retained earnings of the separate entities were also combined. This practice was permitted and evolved prior to the issuance of *ARB No. 48*; thus *ARB No. 48* reflected: (1) existing practice by saying the practice *should* be followed, (2) a more complete extension of the pooling concept, and (3) a better understanding of the nature and derivation of amounts reported as retained earnings.

The continuation of one of the constituent companies as a legal subsidiary subsequent to the business combination had caused some concern as to the appropriateness of pooling-of-interests accounting in those situations. To some this was concern over the legal status and whether it reflected a oneness. To others, however, it was a question as to whether a true combination and continuation of the sharing of ownership risks had prevailed. Obviously, there are valid business reasons for the legal separation of entities. *ARB No. 48* confirmed that separate legal status was not sufficient, by itself, to reject pooling-of-interests accounting.

Accounting Principles Board Opinion No. 10

APBO No. 10, issued in 1967, did not result in a comprehensive reevaluation of the business combination issue or come to grips in any significant way with the abuses taking place in the interpretation and application of existing pronouncements. Examples of business combination abuses that occurred during the 1960s were: retroactive poolings, retrospective poolings, part pooling–part purchase accounting, treasury stock issuances, issuance of unusual securities, creation of "instant earnings," contingent payouts, and "burying" the costs of pooling combinations.[2] The only significant change resulting from *APBO No. 10* was the attempt to bring some restraint to the reporting of business combinations, accounted for as poolings of interests, which took place subsequent to the end of the accounting period as though such combinations had occurred prior to the end of the period.

Accounting Research Studies Nos. 5 and 10

ARS No. 5, "A Critical Study of Accounting for Business Combinations," by Arthur R. Wyatt, was published in June 1963. The primary recommendations and conclusions of the study were:

1. A business combination is essentially an exchange transaction similar to other types of exchange transactions between independent parties and should be accounted for in a similar manner; that is, a purchase should be recorded at the value indicated by consideration or values exchanged.
2. No theoretical justification exists for pooling-of-interests accounting if the business combination results in an exchange of assets and/or equities between independent parties.

Accounting Research Studies do not represent official positions of the AICPA or APB. *Research Studies* are designed to promote discussion and understanding of significant accounting issues. The Director of Accounting Research of the AICPA commented on *ARS No. 5* in part as follows:

> ". . . some members (of the project advisory committee) feel that its conclusions and recommendations are not realistic and do not give adequate recognition to other points of view. . . . The committee feels that the distinction between poolings and purchases should be continued, but with some modifications. . . ."

ARS No. 10, "Accounting for Goodwill," was published in 1968. With regard to business combinations, the conclusion of *ARS No. 10* was similar to the position taken in *ARS No. 5*. Catlett and Olson (coauthors of *ARS No. 10*) concluded:

---

[2] Meigs, Mosich, and Larsen, *Modern Advanced Accounting* (New York: McGraw-Hill Book Co. 1975), p. 138.

Most business combinations, whether effected by payment in cash or other property or by the issuance of stock, are purchase transactions and should be accounted for the same as other purchases. Wyatt reached the same conclusion in Accounting Research Study No. 5. . . .

No logical basis exists for the two (pooling and purchase) radically different approaches to accounting for business combinations. . . .

Pooling of interests accounting is not a valid method of accounting for business combinations.

There was considerable disagreement by the project advisory committee with some of the conclusions of *ARS No. 10* and with each other. The primary recommendations and conclusions of *ARS No. 10* on goodwill were:

1. Goodwill is not a separable resource or property right, and after assigning a value to it in a business combination it should be written off against retained earnings.
2. Such a treatment brings consistency to internally generated goodwill and externally purchased goodwill for balance sheet and income statement presentation.
3. Most business combinations are purchases and should be accounted for accordingly. The inference appears to be that "most" is not 51 percent of all business combinations, but more like 99-plus percent.

American Accounting Association (AAA)

In 1966, on page 33 of its "Statement of Basic Accounting Theory," the AAA concluded:

. . . It is more than questionable that such a (pooling of interest) treatment, which essentially ignores the new exchange values created by a significant market transaction such as the combination of two companies, can be said to be relevant for investment decisions. . . . The committee feels that in most instances, in such a transaction enough evidence exists to provide verifiability and freedom from bias, and that relevant exchange values resulting from such transactions should be recognized and thus recommends that the pooling of interest techniques be disallowed.

The AAA has not discussed the problem of accounting for goodwill.

APBO Nos. 16 and 17

With the background of two research studies, increased merger activity in the late 1960s, and severe criticism from the financial, business, government, and academic communities, the Accounting Principles Board undertook a major reevaluation of accounting for business combinations and goodwill and issued *APBO No. 16*, "Business Combinations," and *APBO No. 17*, "Intangible Assets," in 1970. To indicate that *APBO Nos. 16* and *17* were controversial is more than a mild understatement. The Accounting Principles Board consisted of between 17 and 21 members during the period in which it issued opinions from 1962 to 1973. Adoption of an opinion required the assenting votes of two thirds of the members. Of the 31 APBOs issued, only four received the minimum vote (including *APBO No. 16*) and three received one more than the minimum vote (including *APBO No. 17*). Of the 18 members serving on the APB in 1970, 3 dissented to both opinions and 5 dissented to one of the opinions. Initially, business combinations were considered together for one opinion by the Board. When it became apparent that a two-thirds affirmative vote was not present, it became necessary to split the opinion into the two parts in order to gain passage. Many observers are skeptical of the results of *APBO Nos. 16* and *17*. Five years of implementation and approximately 40 interpretations of the opinions by the APB suggest that the results include:

1. Clarification of some aspects of accounting for business combinations and goodwill.
2. Curtailment or elimination of some abuses (e.g., part-pooling/part-purchase).
3. New inequities created (e.g., treasury stock restrictions and price contingencies).
4. Arbitrary and regulatory criteria (e.g., 90 percent of voting stock rule; combination effected by a single transaction).
5. Confusion by many business executives regarding the appropriate accounting treatment.
6. Nature of the criteria invite efforts by business to structure the

business combination in a manner which may be contrary to good business concepts.

7. Continued dissatisfaction that the opinions have not resolved the fundamental accounting issues surrounding business combinations.

Prior to *APBO No. 16,* it was possible to interpret the circumstances of a business combination to be either a pooling or a purchase. While *APBO No. 16* retained both purchase and pooling as acceptable accounting methods, an extensive list of criteria had to be met. If *all* criteria were met, the business combination *must* be accounted for as a pooling of interests. If *any* of the criteria are *not* met, the business combination *must* be accounted for as a purchase. It is a relatively simple matter to structure the circumstances so that purchase accounting will be required. It is possible, but more difficult, to insure that all criteria are met if pooling-of-interests accounting is desired. Exhibit 1 presents a chart of the accounting criteria and accounting treatment for business combinations specified in *APBO No. 16.* The criteria which must be met in order to qualify for pooling-of-interests accounting are:

A. Attributes of the combining companies:
1. Each of the combining companies is autonomous and has not been a subsidiary or division of another corporation within two years before the plan of combination is initiated.
2. Each of the combining companies is independent of the other combining companies.
B. Combining of interests:
1. The combination is effected in a single transaction or is completed in accordance with a specific plan within one year after the plan is initiated.
2. A corporation offers and issues only common stock with rights identical to those of the majority of its outstanding voting common stock in exchange for substantially all of the voting common stock interest of another company at the date the plan of combination is consummated.
3. None of the combining companies changes the equity interest of the voting common stock in contemplation of effecting the combination either within two years before

EXHIBIT 1
Accounting (planning) for business combinations—A decision chart

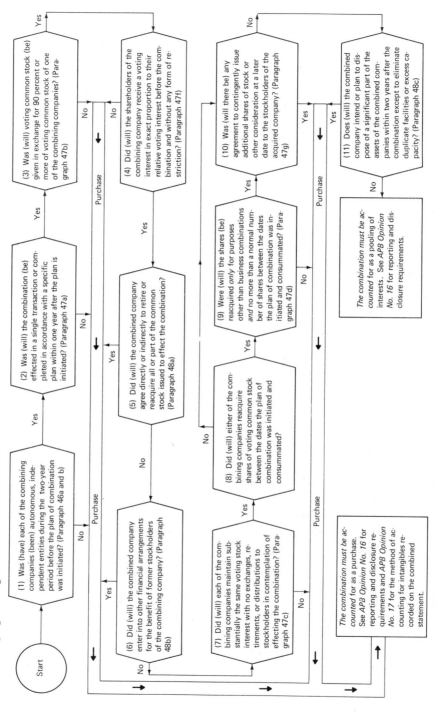

Source: Robert E. Hamilton and James W. Pratt, "Accounting (Planning) for Business Combinations," Practitioners Forum, *The Journal of Accountancy*, January 1972, p. 83.

the plan of combination is initiated or between the dates the combination is initiated and consummated; changes in contemplation of effecting the combination may include distributions to stockholders and additional issuances, exchanges, and retirements of securities.

4. Each of the combining companies reacquires shares of voting common stock only for purposes other than business combinations, and no company reacquires more than a normal number of shares between the dates the plan of combination is initiated and consummated.

5. The ratio of the interest of an individual common stockholder to those of other common stockholders in a combining company remains the same as a result of the exchange of stock to effect the combination.

6. The voting rights to which the common stock ownership interests in the resulting combined corporation are entitled are exercisable by the stockholders; the stockholders are neither deprived of nor restricted in exercising those rights for a period.

7. The combination is resolved at the date the plan is consummated, and no provisions of the plan relating to the issue of securities or other consideration are pending.

C. Absence of planned transactions.

1. The combined corporation does not agree directly or indirectly to retire or reacquire all or part of the common stock issued to effect the combination.

2. The combined corporation does not enter into other financial arrangements for the benefit of the former stockholders of a combining company, such as a guaranty of loans secured by stock issued in the combination, which in effect negates the exchange of equity securities.

3. The combined corporation does not intend or plan to dispose of a significant part of the assets of the combining companies within two years after the combination, other than disposals in the ordinary course of business of the formerly separate companies and to eliminate duplicate facilities or excess capacity.

Purchased goodwill arises as a result of a business combination in which the purchase price exceeds the fair market value of the identifiable intangible and tangible assets, minus liabilities. The accounting literature has developed two classes, identifiable and unidentifiable, of intangible assets for accounting purposes.

The primary conclusions of *APBO Nos. 16* and *17* related to goodwill are:

1. The cost of purchased goodwill should be recorded as an asset.
2. The costs of developing, maintaining, or restoring enterprise goodwill should be deducted from income when incurred.
3. Goodwill is not defined, but the measurement process, deductive in nature, is described.
4. The useful life of goodwill is indeterminate but limited, and therefore goodwill must be amortized.
5. The amortization period must not exceed 40 years.
6. The method of amortization is straight-line unless a company can demonstrate a more appropriate systematic method.

CONCEPTUAL ISSUES OF BUSINESS COMBINATIONS

At this time there is still no unanimous agreement on the theoretical merits of purchase accounting or pooling accounting. We will attempt to summarize in this section the key conceptual arguments which favor and oppose each method.

The following are arguments *in favor of purchase accounting:*

1. An acquisition has taken place. In most, if not all, business combinations, one company acquires another. It is usually obvious which company is doing the acquiring, which is clearly dominant, and which is the continuing entity which has control.
2. A business combination is a significant economic event reflecting a bargained transaction between independent parties. The agreed terms primarily reflect bargained values, not book costs.
3. The nature of consideration in effecting the combination, whether distribution of cash or other assets, assumption of liabilities, or issuance of stock, reflects agreed-upon values which should not alter the basic accounting procedures for recording the event.
4. To report the economic consequence of acquiring assets by a business combination requires that those assets be recorded according to the accounting procedures followed in accounting

for other types of purchased assets. The costs of the previous owner are not relevant to the exchange values reflected by the event which should be recorded by the purchaser.

Some of the key arguments *against purchase accounting* or defects attributed to it include:

1. When stock is used, the fair value of the consideration given may be difficult to measure.
2. Direct measurement of intangible assets (particularly goodwill) acquired is often difficult or impossible, making the process of allocation of the purchase price to the components arbitrary and suspect.
3. Even if it is assumed that goodwill and other assets are directly measurable, it is contended that business combinations effected with stock are based on the market prices of the securities involved, which in turn are influenced by anticipated earnings rather than evaluations of assets.
4. Only fair values and goodwill of the *acquired* company are included. When the business combination involves stock and companies of similar size, the managements and stockholders of both companies are evaluating the "fair" values of the other. Thus, either book value for both or new enterprise accounting (fair value for both) is more appropriate than purchase accounting.

The following are arguments *in favor of pooling-of-interests accounting:*

1. The use of common stock does not result in the disbursement of any corporate assets to stockholders.
2. Equity is used to effect the transaction and net equity increases by the amount of the net equity of the acquired business. There is no newly invested capital.
3. Stockholder groups remain intact, but are combined. It is a transaction among stockholders, not between entities or between an entity and stockholders. A sharing of combined assets and risks is created.
4. Pooling is compatible with historical-cost accounting and the going-concern concept.
5. Financial reporting which combines the companies for the

accounting period and restates previous periods satisfies users' needs for comparability over time.

Arguments offered *opposing pooling-of-interests accounting* include:

1. Pooling fails to recognize a significant economic event and bargained transaction, and thus the economic substance of the event is ignored.
2. Effective criteria for identifying a pooling do not exist because the concept itself is unsound.
3. Criteria which have been proposed sometimes contradict the concept—for example, only the stockholders receiving new stock are prohibited from disposing of their stock within some limited time period. Restrictions on only one group of stockholders tends to support the conclusion that a purchase has taken place.
4. The amounts recorded for assets and liabilities in a pooling are constant regardless of the number of shares issued. Such treatment does not reflect the assumption that stock is issued only for value received.

Although it was stated earlier that there is no agreement on the merits of the two alternatives, there is evidence to suggest that: (1) support for the pooling concept has diminished over time; and (2) in spite of attempts to reinforce the conceptual nature of pooling and establish more regulatory type of criteria, the use of pooling is still abused.[3]

CONCEPTUAL ISSUES OF GOODWILL

It is perhaps only a modest overstatement to say that if unidentified intangibles acquired in a business combination were tax deductible, a substantial majority of accountants and business executives would not mourn the demise of pooling-of-interests accounting. This section will describe the different concepts of goodwill and the related accounting treatment. The selection and use of the term "goodwill" is one of the most unfortunate terminology choices in accounting. There is no generally accepted definition, no gen-

---

[3] Rayburn, "Another Look;" and Arthur B. Wyatt, "Inequities in Accounting for Business Combinations," *Financial Executive*, 1972.

erally accepted explanation of its derivation, and no generally accepted method of valuation. We will not concern ourselves with various aspects of the legal concepts of goodwill.

From the writings of various academicians and practitioners, we might develop four possible concepts of purchased goodwill.

1. "Superior" earning power.
2. Going-concern value.
3. Master valuation account.
4. Unrecorded assets.

"Superior" earning power. Superior or excess earning power is obviously a "relative" concept. Superior to what?

Some alternative definitions of "superior" would be:

1. Earnings superior to a risk-free return on an investment of the same amount.
2. Earnings superior to the next best alternative investment to the acquisition selected.
3. Earnings superior to the sum of earnings which could be earned from the individual assets.
4. Earnings superior to the average earned by businesses of a similar size and in the same or a similar industry.

It is the last of these definitions (No. 4) that is most generally implied. The fallacies of the concept of excess or superior future earnings are twofold:

1. Empirical evidence exists of companies which operate at losses and are acquired for more than net book value.
2. If a company is expected to have superior earnings as defined in No. 4 above, the excess is likely to be due to certain specific intangibles which may or may not be easily identified and measured.

Going-concern value. Again we have a term which is not easily defined. Some writers refer to this as the value of synergism. Other writers consider it to be the value of the organization, without further explanation. Perhaps the most rational approach would be the "start-up" value. In theory, start-up value would be the present value of future net income and losses to bring a new business into existence and develop it to the stage of the acquired business. Said another way, it is the fair market value of expenditures treated as period costs by the acquired company, for example, costs for which future benefits will be derived but which were not, or could not, be measured at the time of the expenditure. Examples would include training costs, advertising, and certain R&D expenditures.

Master valuation account. Two views of this concept of goodwill exist. The first is the "gap" method, which defines the measurement process more than the nature of what is measured. Thus, the valuation is the difference between the purchase price of a company and the fair value of the identifiable net assets (tangible and intangible).

A second approach to this concept is to define it as the difference between the value in use versus the market value of individual assets. Assuming the asset exists to be purchased separately, a company would not pay more than the market value.

Unrecorded assets. Unrecorded assets may be viewed as assets valued at zero. In concept this is not significantly different from the going-concern valuation concept.

Summary. Only three of the methods attempt to deal effectively with the nature of goodwill: superior earning power, going-concern value, and unrecorded assets. In fact, all three could be considered the same. If we define "superior earning power" in an operational sense as being superior *cash flows* compared to the specific alternative capital investment of internal development, we have the typical make-buy decision which attempts to value the same factors as the going-concern concept and the unrecorded asset concept. In addition, there is some empirical evidence that this concept does describe management's analysis in making such a decision. The going-concern start-up concept also explains why a company operating at a loss may be purchased for more than the fair market value of the net assets. In evaluating merger-acquisition candidates, management uses discounted cash flow techniques to value expected future earnings, specifically values assets and liabilities, evaluates the impact of the merger on earnings per share, considers the significance and materiality of the merger from both a short-run and long-run viewpoint, and looks at the relative market values of the stock of each company. All these factors may be taken into account in determining the purchase price or exchange ratios.

Tearney reported the results of analyzing 209 New York Stock Exchange listing applications for 1969 in which business combinations were accounted for by the purchase method.[4] The analysis was made according to the reason for the acquisition. The results were:

1. Achieving product diversification. 40.1%
2. Achieving integration 33.2
3. Achieving a particular market objective 9.8
4. Acquiring management and/or technical skills 5.6
5. Saving time in expanding into a new area 4.3
6. Other or not indicated 7.0

    100.0%

Items 1–4 are alternatives to internal development; an indication of a make-or-buy decision. The above findings should not be surprising since the usual primary reasons cited for deciding on growth via acquisition as opposed to internal development are timing and risk. When related to capital investment decision making, this translates into higher present values of cash flows for external versus internal growth. Timing is probably the single most significant reason.

Further analysis would then lead to the conclusion that going-concern values such as established products, work force, brand recognition, management, established financial sources, distribution systems, and so on, are the intangibles purchased. By acquiring a going concern, these "start-up" costs are avoided. The going-concern concept itself is of value in focusing on the identification of the intangibles acquired and an approach to measurement. Vaughan suggested a possible classification of intangibles by ascertainable and unascertainable lives:[5]

Intangible assets considered in terms of useful life

Ascertainable life	*Unascertainable life (goodwill)*
Patents	Copyrights
Patent applications	Trademarks and brand names
Franchises	Technical "know-how"
License agreements	Personnel
Noncompetition agreements	Market acceptance
Royalty agreements	Reputation
Employment contracts	Established location
Purchase contracts	Secret processes and formulas
Lease agreements	
Design rights	
Technical libraries	
Pending contracts	
Water rights	

[4] Michael G. Tearney, "Accounting for Goodwill: A Realistic Approach," *The Journal of Accountancy,* July 1973, p. 42.
[5] John L. Vaughan, Jr., "Give Intangible Assets Useful Life," *Harvard Business Review,* September–October 1972, p. 128.

There is no need to quarrel with Vaughan's classifications except to indicate that experience may indeed allow many of the unascertainable lives to be reasonably estimated. For example, many of those listed are closely related to product life cycles: many copyrights, many brand names, technical "know-how," market acceptance, secret processes and formulas. Personnel can be related to employee turnover. Given our perpetuity or indefinite life concept of the entity, some copyrights, trademarks, and brand names may be similar to organizational expenses and Vaughan's basic premise related to tax matters, which will be discussed in more detail later. The prevailing accounting concept remains one of *avoidable costs*— that is, by acquiring a firm, we avoid the incurrence of similar costs to reach the same stage of business development either internally or via an alternative acquisition. For effective accounting and disclosure to occur, greater efforts must be made to identify intangibles.

Copeland and Wojdak examined 169 pooling-of-interests business combinations by 26 firms in the one-year period from July 1, 1966, to June 30, 1967.[6] The results are staggering:

Purchase price paid	$2,257,949,000	100.0%
Book values recorded	652,956,000	28.9
Unrecorded asset values	$1,604,993,000	71.1%

The total unrecorded asset values of $1.6 billion was about 2½ times the total values recorded. Seventy-one percent of the assets acquired were not recorded by the acquiring company—and this was for a one-year period only!

ACCOUNTING TREATMENT OF PURCHASED GOODWILL

Five suggested accounting treatments for purchased goodwill are:

1. Purchased goodwill is not an asset and therefore should be recorded and immediately written off to stockholders' equity at the time of its acquisition.
2. Purchased goodwill is a "permanent" asset. The recorded value of goodwill should not be reduced in the absence of specific circumstances which indicate a diminution in value.

---

[6] Ronald M. Copeland and Joseph F. Wojdak, "Valuation of Unrecorded Goodwill in Merger-Minded Firms," *Financial Analysts Journal,* September–October 1969, p. 60.

3. Purchased goodwill is an asset which should be written off in accordance with an established method and schedule.
4. The individual components of purchased goodwill can be identified and valued separately, and an appropriate amortization method and time period can be determined.
5. Purchased goodwill should not be classified as an operating asset but should be set forth in a separate section of the balance sheet.

A study of the preferences of three groups was conducted by Nelson and Strawser.[7] The exposure draft of what was to become *APBO Nos. 16* and *17* was out at that time. The authors asked respondents to consider three alternatives:

1. Arthur Andersen & Co. proposal: virtually eliminate pooling-of-interests accounting; goodwill recorded and written off against stockholders' equity; and when the acquiring company cannot be identified account for the combination as a new entity.
2. Current practice: *ARB Nos. 43* and *48*.
3. Exposure draft on business combinations and intangibles.

The following research results were obtained:

	Preparer/user group*		
	CPAs	Accounting educators	Financial analysts
Most preferable	1	1	1
Middle	2	2	2
Least preferable	3	3	3

* Numbers relate to alternative practices listed above.

Within all responding groups, the most preferred alternative was the Arthur Andersen & Co. proposal and the alternative with the least support by each group was the exposure draft. At this point, we will consider the arguments for each of the five proposed methods.

Write off immediately. The primary thrust of the argument in favor of an immediate write off of purchased goodwill to stockholders' equity is related to the contention that it is not an asset, at least in the accounting sense. Proponents of this treatment argue

[7] Kenneth Nelson and Robert H. Strawser, "A Note on APB Opinion No. 16," *Journal of Accounting Research,* Autumn, 1970, p. 286.

that an asset (economic resource) must have the following characteristics: utility, scarcity, and exchangeability. Exchangeability means that the resource is separable from the business as a whole and has value in and of itself. One can wonder if that means that special-purpose capital additions—such as certain equipment, signs, perhaps even plant—should be expensed on purchase and carried at scrap value. Further, implicit in the inclusion of separability as a criterion is negation of the going-concern assumption underlying the accounting for all economic resources in financial statements.

Additional arguments for the immediate write-off of purchased goodwill include:

1. It is not an economic resource used or consumed in the process of generating future revenues, and thus amortization violates the matching of revenues and expenses.
2. Such treatment provides for consistency in accounting for externally purchased and internally purchased (generated) goodwill. Many of the factors claimed to represent purchased goodwill are charged off to income as expense in the period incurred for similar internal activities (e.g., advertising). However, most proposals for the immediate write-off of purchased goodwill call for the charge to be to retained earnings, rather than income.
3. Goodwill is not a "producing" asset. This argument basically relies on the "gap" method of measurement to justify such a conclusion, rather than a going-concern approach.
4. Immediate write-off avoids the "double" charge to income occurring from amortization. Amortization charges future income for internal expenditures to "maintain" an asset that is being amortized.
5. The superior earnings which justify a purchase price in excess of fair market value are distorted and penalized by amortization. This is a very specious argument. A very close analogy would be to the purchase of a corporate bond at a premium. If a 10 percent coupon bond is purchased to yield 8 percent, a premium is involved. The premium is not separable from the bond, so it is immediately written off to stockholders' equity—in essence a "loss" is incurred but not charged to income. Finally, as interest is received, a 10 percent return is reported on an asset which was purchased to yield an 8 percent return. Consequently, an

investment which an investor was willing to make because it had an 8 percent return will now be recorded as a 10 percent return.

Permanent asset. The basic argument in favor of recording purchased goodwill as an asset without any amortization is that a reduction in carrying value of an asset should occur only when it is based on evidence that the value of the acquired asset has become less than its cost. If goodwill is considered to derive from superior earnings, then a decline in earnings would be an indication of an impairment of the asset. Land and inventories are good examples of current applications of this concept. Proponents of this point of view argue that purchased goodwill is different from consumable assets like plant and equipment.

Some opponents would argue that goodwill attaches to the organization as an on-going entity, and is thus not like land or inventory. Organizations have limited but indeterminate lives, and therefore such assets as goodwill must be amortized over some period of time.

Amortize by plan. This particular alternative rests, somewhat precariously, on the previous assertion that goodwill has a limited but indeterminate life. The theoretical underpinnings may be weak, but the practical compromise is strong. By setting minimum and maximum (arbitrary) amortization periods, those who insist that the cost of goodwill be charged against future revenue are at least somewhat satisfied. Those concerned with the impact on reported earnings are somewhat satisfied by the small annual impact resulting from the very long amortization periods. The advocates who remain totally dissatisfied are those who believe that goodwill is not an asset and should not be charged against revenue, and those who believe that the component parts of goodwill can be identified, valued, and amortized separately.

Component amortization. This position is obviously tied to the concept of goodwill which argues that the various components of goodwill can be identified and valued, and that reasonable estimates of useful lives can be made. If that is true, then such differences should be recognized in the accounting process and a homogeneous class of assets does not exist. Opponents naturally argue either that the concept (i.e., the definition of goodwill) is in error, or that even if true, the identification and measurement problems are insurmountable.

Separate asset and stockholders' equity accounts. Those favoring this treatment believe that the asset created by the cost paid in excess of asset value is fundamentally different from other assets because "it is based on future earning power rather than being the cause of it."[8] Goodwill should not be classified as an operating asset but should be set forth in a separate section of the balance sheet as "Cost of Future Earning Power Acquired in Business Combination." A new account entitled "Equity Representing Future Earning Power Acquired in Business Combination" should be created in the following manner when a business combination takes place. When equity securities or warrants are issued in a combination, the amount attributed to future earning power should be segregated in the stockholders' equity section of the balance sheet. When cash or debt are given, the amount to be segregated should be deducted from retained earnings. These new accounts would be systematically reduced by direct charges to them based on a percentage of earnings of the acquired entity or on some other basis, with full disclosure and reasoning therefor rather than by amortization to the income statement.

An advantage of this approach is that the goodwill created in a business combination would be recognized as an asset and treated as a stockholder investment in the acquisition of future earning power, but operations and stockholders' equity would not be distorted. A disadvantage is that new asset and stockholders' equity accounts would be created with the resultant difficulties of understanding and comparability, and the significance of retained earnings might be eroded for combined enterprises which enter into cash acquisitions resulting in significant goodwill.

Summary. It might be assumed in a business combination using stock that the purchase price is greater than the fair market value of net assets, which in turn is greater than the book value of net assets. The effects of each of five alternative accounting methods for business combinations can be ranked in terms of resulting dollar amounts for total assets, stockholders' equity, and net income. Similarly, the effects of each business combination method can be ranked in terms of such performance measures as return on investment and return on equity. The five business combination accounting methods are:

---

[8] John C. Burton, "Accounting for Business Combinations" (a publication of the Research Foundation of Financial Executives Institute), 1970, pp. 88 and 89.

1. Pooling of interests (tax-free)
2. Purchase (taxable)—Immediate write-off of goodwill (P_1)
3. Purchase (taxable)—No amortization of goodwill (P_2)
4. Purchase (taxable)—Writeoff over long period (40 years) (P_3)
5. Purchase (taxable)—Specific identification and amortization (P_4)

	Accounting method				
	Pooling	P_1	P_2	P_3	P_4
Total assets	5	4	1*	2*	3*
Stockholders' equity	5	4	1*	2*	3*
Net income	1	2	2	4	5
Return on assets.	1	2	3	4	5
Return on equity	1	2	3	4	5
Cash flow	2	2	2	2	1

1 = Highest percent or largest dollar amounts.
5 = Lowest percent or smallest dollar amounts.
* All equal at time of business combination. Rankings indicate "short-term" results.

As shown in the table above, pooling generally will be most desirable from a financial statement point of view, and (P_4) purchase—specific identification and amortization of intangibles, the least desirable from a financial statement point of view but most desirable from a cash flow standpoint. It should be pointed out that the taxable status of the combination could add additional columns. The table assumes a taxable purchase combination or tax-free pooling of interests. Existing accounting procedures and tax laws make it possible to have taxable poolings and tax-free purchases.

ACCOUNTING AND BUSINESS IMPLICATIONS

Possible income effects. In the substantial majority of business combinations, the economic purchase price (fair market value of consideration given or received) will exceed the book value of the net assets acquired. That being the case, the use of purchase accounting will result in lower reported earnings than pooling. The reasons for this are twofold:

1. Assets will be written up from book value, resulting in larger charges against income in future periods than if book values had been carried forward.
2. Goodwill must be carried as an asset and charged against income of future periods. Since goodwill is not deductible for

tax purposes, the effect on earnings after taxes could be significant. In fact, a company could show a profit for tax purposes and show an after-tax loss for financial reporting purposes.

Example

	Financial reporting	Tax reporting
Income before amortization of goodwill*	150	150
Goodwill amortization	(100)	—
Income before taxes	50	150
Income taxes (50%)*	(75)	(75)
Net income (loss)	(25)	75

* Assumed no timing differences requiring interperiod tax allocation, and that fair market values equal book values on assets acquired.

Return on investment and return on equity. Since the net income figure under pooling will normally exceed net income from purchase accounting, it is obvious that return on assets will be higher under pooling than purchase, where ROA = Net Income/ Total Assets. When you combine the higher net income of pooling with a lower asset basis (no goodwill and no increase of book values to fair market value), return on assets may be significantly better with pooling accounting than with purchase accounting. The exception would occur if the purchase price was less than the book value of net assets and the assets were written down.

Return on equity is also enhanced by pooling-of-interest accounting. If ROE = Net Income/Stockholders' Equity, we have a higher net income figure for a business combination accounted for as a pooling and a lower stockholders' equity. Under pooling, the stockholders' equity will not reflect the goodwill implied by the purchase price or the fair market values of the assets which exceed book values.

Example of effects on stockholders' equity. Pooling-of-interests accounting may be considered to have the effect of reporting as income a portion of the proceeds from the issuance of stock. To provide a simplified and exaggerated example, assume that Company A acquired 100 percent of Company B for 10,000,000 shares of $1 par common stock. The fair market value of the stock issued and the stock received was $20 per share for a total of $200 million. The only asset of Company B consisted of inventory with a book value of $100 million. Company B had no liabilities and its owners' equity consisted of $10 million in common stock and $90 million of retained earnings. The inventory is sold during the accounting period immediately subsequent to the business combination for $200 million.

Purchase accounting. Assuming that the acquisition did not qualify for pooling-of-interests accounting because it failed to meet one of the criteria established in *APBO No. 16*, the following would be required in *consolidated* statements:

1. Assets (inventory) of Company B written up by $100 million to fair market value.
2. Company A common stock increased by $10 million and additional paid-in capital increased by $190 million.
3. In the subsequent year, no income is recognized on the sale of the inventory.

Pooling-of-interests accounting. If the transaction could be accounted for as a pooling-of-interests business combination, the results would have been different, as follows:

1. Carrying value of Company B inventory unchanged and carried at $100 million.
2. Company A common stock increased by $10 million and consolidated retained earnings increased by $90 million.
3. In the subsequent year when the inventory is sold for $200 million, a profit before 50 percent income taxes of $100 million is reported and retained earnings is increased by $50 million. In effect, a portion of the value received from the issuance of $200 million of common stock appears as income on the income statement and is added to retained earnings.

Valuation considerations. APBO No. 17 may encourage management to undervalue tangible assets and not identify intangible assets from a financial reporting viewpoint. Very few identifiable assets (tangible or intangible) have estimated lives as long as 40 years. The assignment of a large portion of the difference between the purchase price and the book value of the net assets acquired to goodwill will spread the charges against income over more periods and reduce the impact on any one period.

Debt capacity considerations. Purchase accounting may be helpful to a company needing additional capital and wishing to acquire such capital through borrowing. The reason for this is that purchase accounting (providing stock is used for the acquisition) will result in a larger addition to equity (as a result of capitalizing goodwill and assets at fair market value) than pooling, thus improving the debt/equity ratio of the firm. The opposite conclusion would be reached if the purchase were to be made with cash. However, some analysts deduct intangibles from the assets and reduce equity in making credit decisions.

Some tax considerations of intangibles. Careful consideration of specific identifiable intangibles may prove to be a key factor in merger strategy. Certain intangibles in some specific situations have been accepted by the Internal Revenue Services and/or the courts as deductible for tax purposes.[9]

1. Finance company's loan balances.
2. Rights to service insurance company's mortgage loans.
3. Rights to utilize mortgage escrow funds and other intangibles.
4. Rights-of-way for transmission lines.
5. Pipeline easements.
6. Fuel oil customers.
7. TV license and single-network affiliation contracts.
8. *TV Guide* franchise.
9. Secondary, not primary, network affiliation contracts.

The reader should be aware that the tax-deductible nature of intangibles varies from one court's jurisdiction to the next and under very limited factual situations. At times, the intangible may not be amortized for tax purposes, but may qualify as an ordinary loss under rules and regulations governing abandonment. Generally, the Internal Revenue Service will not permit amortization of intangibles for tax purposes. Management should work closely with their tax advisers in drafting business combination agreements.

Summary. In most cases, it appears that pooling-of-interests accounting is most desirable for management from a financial statement presentation viewpoint. However, what management gains in higher reported earnings, it tends to lose in cash flow. From a cash flow point of view, management wants to increase the amount and accelerate the timing of taxable deductions. Management *permanently* sacrifices cash flow by *not* revaluing acquired assets to fair market value and by *not* attempting to isolate as many specific identifiable intangibles as possible in a taxable exchange. If management

---

[9] D. Spencer Yohe, "Allocation and Amortization of Intangibles," *The Arthur Andersen Chronicle,* January 1974, p. 55.

fails to recognize the cash flow consequences of selected accounting treatments and the potential distortion of accounting information in business combinations, it is possible corporate strategy selections may be improperly made between internal and external growth.

Further, it is possible to infer that the availability of pooling-of-interests accounting could distort the capital budgeting type of make-versus-buy decision implicit in acquisition analysis. It is possible that internal development could be most attractive from a net present value cash flow analysis whereas a business combination accounted for as a pooling of interests would be most attractive on a reported earnings basis. If that should be the case, it could be argued that the accounting policies operate to the long-term disadvantage of stockholders and result in an inefficient allocation of economic resources on both a microeconomic and a macroeconomic basis.

CONCLUSIONS

In spite of much attention, the business combination-goodwill controversy continues. Many are hopeful that the FASB will be able to finally resolve a 25-year-old controversy that was little closer to settlement after *APBO Nos. 16* and *17* in 1970 than it was with the issuance of *ARB No. 40* in 1950. The extreme dissatisfaction that remains with the current practices of accounting for business combinations must be eliminated by development of a conceptually sound approach to the issues, rather than arbitrary rules or compromises.

Chapter 19

Paid-in capital

*Jerome J. Kesselman**

Since the corporate entity is a creature of statute, it exists and must operate in contemplation of the laws under which it came into being. Thus, there are 50 jurisdictions and 50 statutes regulating the corporation. In addition, several administrative bodies at the federal level—the Securities and Exchange Commission, in particular—have extensive powers related to the financial reporting procedures pursued by corporations subject to their jurisdiction. As one studies these laws and regulations, a considerable number of threads can be found which are common to all, or at least most, jurisdictions. It is also obvious that there are many differences and variations in the statutory requirements among the states. In general, the discussion following attempts to highlight the "general rules" wherever possible, and some attention is given to various exceptions to the rule.

NET WORTH—IN GENERAL

A corporation can accumulate, or enhance, its stockholders' equity by only two processes; namely, *contribution* and the *accumulation and retention of earnings.*

Contributed capital, also identified as *paid-in capital,* must be identified, valued, and separated from retained earnings in accounting for and reporting on the stockholders' equity in the enterprise.

---

* School of Accountancy, University of Denver.

390

The paid-in capital originates by contributions from several sources. Principal classifications of these categories are:

1. Legal stated capital.
2. Premiums on capital stock.
3. Donated capital.
4. Miscellaneous.

In the process of creating the corporate entity, the promoters must prepare and file a series of legal documents with the appropriate state agency. One of these instruments is the articles of incorporation (often called the charter). Although the articles must enumerate a great number of other matters, one of the most important relates to the number, type, and characteristics of the capital shares to be authorized for possible future issuance. These provisions spell out in considerable detail the rights, privileges, and immunities of each class of capital stock and also indicate the number of shares of each class which may be issued to raise the capital required by the enterprise for its operations.

Where only a single class of shares of stock is authorized, the shares are *common shares*. Basically, this merely means that the owners of these shares are the *residual owners* of the corporation. In terms of creditor rights, all legitimate interests of creditors have a prior claim on the assets of the firm and are entitled to both a stipulated rate of return during the term of the advance as well as a predetermined liquidation value at the stated due date. Conversely, the common stock has no stated due date, nor does it have any assurance of a stipulated rate of return. The common stockholder takes the full risk of all losses, but is entitled to the benefit of profits, however large or small they may be. Similarly, the common equityholder has a claim on the assets of the company only after all prior claims have been fully satisfied. However, as residual owners, this class of stock is entitled to share in all the assets of the enterprise after prior claims have been liquidated. It is apparent, then, that as the residual owners, the risks are greater but the potential for income and incremental growth is also greater.

The basic rights of the common stockholder usually include (1) the right to exercise control over the board of directors and the affairs of the company through the right to vote at all stockholder meetings; (2) the right to share prorata in any distributions of dividends; (3) the right to preemption, which is a protective device afforded the stockholder from an involuntary dilution of his or her equity; and (4) the privilege of sharing in a prorata distribution of assets, whether in partial or complete liquidation of the firm.

Frequently, the articles of incorporation may provide for more than one class of stock. When such a provision exists, it is evident that the various rights of a stockholder of each class must contain some differences. If this were not the case, the attempt to distinguish between the classes becomes an inane effort. Where more than one class of stock is authorized, certain priorities, or preferences, are provided for in respect to one class as compared to the other. In this event, the class which has these special privileges is the *preferred* stock, while the class with the residual privileges becomes the *common* stock. Although there is an almost endless variety of cases, the typical preferences identified with the "preferred" class are:

1. A prior right to share in any dividend distribution before the common stock is entitled to any part of it.
2. A right to cumulative dividends.
3. A right to participation in distributions of unusual amount.
4. A preferential claim on assets in the event of liquidation.

On the other hand, it is customary to deny the preferred class any voting rights, although such rights may become operative in the event specified conditions occur, such as a failure to distribute a dividend after a given number of years.

The classes of stock may also be assigned a *par value* or be *no-par value* shares. The par value assigned may be any dollar amount determined by the promoters and provided for in the articles of incorporation. Although historically $100 was a very popular number to use, the amount designated could be any figure, for example $2, or 10 cents, or 1 mill. In general, the par value of a share has primary meaning only at the time of the original issuance of a share of the class. The par ordinarily sets a *legal minimum* value for which the shares may be issued. Although a share may be initially issued for more value than the par multiplied by the number of shares involved, it is not legally acceptable to issue shares for a lesser value.

As an alternative to par, a class may be authorized as a no-par class. Typically this means that the shares may initially be issued in exchange for whatever value the marketplace determines and still be fully paid shares. The basic requirement is that the various prices at which a share is issued must be determined by an arm's-length transaction between the parties. In some cases, a *minimum stated value* may be assigned to a no-par class. In general, where this is done, the value assigned is somewhat similar to a par value in that the minimum stated value would determine the minimum price for which shares might be legally issued.

Preferential classes of stock are customarily assigned a designated dividend rate, or a formula is stipulated by which the amount of dividend entitlement can be determined. A common class is not assigned a stipulated dividend rate, since it represents the residual equity and is, therefore, entitled to whatever remaining amount is to be distributed.

ISSUANCE OF SHARES

Once a set of articles of incorporation is submitted and approved by the appropriate agency of the state, the entity is in existence as a "de facto" corporation. However, in order to evolve a "de jure" entity, at least one or more shares of stock must be issued for value.

Usually, shares are issued in exchange for—

1. Money,
2. Noncash assets,
3. Services, or on a
4. Subscription contract.

The basic principles apply in substantially an identical manner to all classes of stock, although differences in accounting recognition may arise, depending on whether the class of stock is a par or a no-par class.

Few measurement questions arise when the issuance is for money, since the value received by the corporation in exchange for the shares is self-measurable by count and summation. Journal entries for various transactions involving the issuance of stock are shown in the following paragraphs.

1. If cash equal to the par (or the minimum stated value) is received:

  Cash xx
    Capital Stock xx

The Capital Stock account may include such descriptive adjectives as "issued" or "outstanding." However, when not otherwise modified, it is intended to reflect shares that have been fully paid and are issued and outstanding.

2. If cash received exceeds the number of shares issued times the par (or minimum stated value):

```
Cash . . . . . . . . . . . . . . . . . . . . . . . . . . . . . . . . . . . . . . . . . XXX
        Capital Stock . . . . . . . . . . . . . . . . . . . . . . . . . . . . . . . .      XX
        Premium on Capital Stock. . . . . . . . . . . . . . . . . . . . . . . .           X
```

The premium account represents the value received on initial issuance in excess of the "legal stated capital" and is a paid-in capital account. It is a part of the contributed capital of the entity, and separate accounts are usually accumulated for each class of stock.

3. For a no-par class without minimum stated value, the cash proceeds automatically determine the credit to the Capital Stock account:

```
Cash . . . . . . . . . . . . . . . . . . . . . . . . . . . . . . . . . . . . . . . . . XX
        Capital Stock . . . . . . . . . . . . . . . . . . . . . . . . . . . . . . . .      XX
```

The major problem which must be resolved when shares are issued in exchange for noncash assets or services is the valuation of the assets or services received. The value assigned should reflect the market, or fair value, of the stock or the fair market value of the consideration received, whichever is more clearly evident. The value must approximate that of an arm's-length transaction in an open competitive market exchange. Such a value may be determined by reference to quoted market prices (as in the case of traded shares) or to appraisals (as may be necessary where real estate or machinery or other similar items are involved). Similar valuation must be made for services received in exchange for shares.

A critical problem which might arise is the "watering" of the stock. This occurs when, either intentionally or not, the values assigned the assets received exceed their fair market value and the equity accounts credited in the issuing event reflect an inflated number of dollars.

SUBSCRIPTIONS TO SHARES

Although the sale of shares on a subscription contract is not a commonplace event, when it does occur the parties stipulate an issue price for the shares. The investor usually will make a partial payment and promise the corporation to pay the balance on call.

The subscription agreement generally contains no predetermined due date for the balance, and thus the board of directors would have to issue a call for the payment on or before the announced due date. Several problems may arise in these situations relating to:

1. The physical issuance of the shares.
2. The rights of the subscriber.
3. The presentation of the accounts on interim financial statements.
4. The call and payment.
5. The call and failure to pay.

Illustrative entries and description might best explain the above. Assume a par of $10 per share, a subscription contract for $12 per share, initial payment of $3 per share, and that 100 shares are involved.

1. *The initial contract is made:*

Cash	300	
Subscriptions Receivable	900	
Capital Stock Subscribed		1,000
Premium on Capital Stock Subscribed		200

The shares are not issued to the subscriber, and the Capital Stock Subscribed account reflects the status of the contract at any reporting date.

A subscriber generally is entitled to all the rights of a stockholder even though he or she does not have physical possession of the shares.

The preferable balance sheet treatment of the above is to show the subscriptions receivable balance as a deduction from the equity accounts in the net worth section. When a call is made, many accountants will then report the subscriptions receivable as an asset, since there is now an established due date for the promise to pay. Others will continue to report the unpaid subscription receivable as a contra-account as earlier indicated.

2. *The call is made:*

No entry necessary.

3. *Payment occurs:*

Cash	900	
Capital Stock Subscribed	1,000	
Premium on Capital Stock Subscribed	200	
Subscriptions Receivable		900
Capital Stock		1,000
Premium on Capital Stock		200

The shares are issued in the normal course and the record is modified to reflect the transaction.

4. *Forfeiture occurs as the call is not met by the subscribers:*

Capital Stock Subscribed.	1,000	
Premium on Capital Stock Subscribed	200	
Subscriptions Receivable		900
Paid-In Capital—Subscriptions Forfeited.		300

Although state statutes vary, the above entry reflects a typical case. The deposit is forfeited, and the shares revert to an authorized status with no restrictions attaching to them.

TREASURY STOCK

Capital stock may be classified in many ways to indicate its *status*. Among the most common designations are:

1. Authorized shares.
2. Issued shares.
3. Outstanding shares.
4. Treasury shares.

The articles of incorporation stipulate the maximum number of shares of each class which may be sold. This number is the *authorization,* which permits the promoters of the enterprise to issue the shares for value if they can attract the necessary investors who are willing to buy them.

Shares are *issued* when the company has received adequate value and the certificates, representing the shares, are delivered to the investor. Shares are *outstanding* as long as they are owned by third party investors. Generally, the number of shares issued and outstanding are synonymous. However, if for some reason the company reacquires some of its own shares, whether through purchase or other procedure, they may either be canceled or be held alive in the treasury. If canceled, these shares become relegated to the category of authorized but unissued shares and may be reissued at some future date as in an initial sale.

When shares are reacquired and held in the treasury as *treasury stock,* various considerations become operative. First, under a legal fiction, the shares in the treasury are still considered to be issued though they are not outstanding. The board of directors may ultimately decide to cancel them or to resell them. Since the resale is not considered to be an initial issuance, the constraints that customarily operate in an original issue transaction do not apply. Given an arm's-length transaction, these shares may be sold at any price without regard to the limitation imposed by a par value and may be offered to anyone whomsoever, whether a stockholder at the time or not. In other words, if the shares are subject to the right of preemption, the preemptive privilege may be disregarded. This concept will be discussed below in more detail. The principal uses of such treasury shares are to satisfy the needs of employee stock option and stock bonus plans or other similar compensation arrangements. However, it is not uncommon to utilize treasury shares to raise working capital in highly speculative ventures and for any other legitimate purpose a management may determine.

Accounting for treasury shares and balance sheet reporting practices also pose significant problems. Treasury shares acquired might be accounted for—

1. At par,
2. At cost, or
3. At a prorata part of the class of stock.

Balance sheet presentation is modified somewhat to accommodate each of the above procedures.

To illustrate:

1. If at *par*, the entry to record the purchase is:

Treasury Stock	At Par
Premium on Treasury Shares	X
Cash	At Cost
Discount on Treasury Shares	X

The preferable balance sheet presentation is to show the treasury stock as a deduction from the legal stated capital account of the class and the balance in the premium or discount account as a positive or negative element in the contributed capital section of net worth.

When resold, a typical entry would reflect the following:

Cash	Sale Price
Discount on Treasury Shares	X
Treasury Stock	At Par
Premium on Treasury Shares	X

The premium or discount account may be aggregated and shown at the net dollar balance, taking into account all the transactions involving treasury shares.

2. If at *cost*, the purchase entry might be:

    Treasury Stock . . . . At Cost
    Cash . . . .   At Cost

The Treasury Stock account should be reported on a balance sheet as a deduction from the total net worth to measure the balance after the contraction in the stockholder equity resulting from the purchase of the shares.

When resold, the entry would reflect the event as follows:

    Cash . . . . Sale Price
    Discount on Treasury Stock.   X
    Treasury Stock . . . .   At Cost
    Premium on Treasury Stock.   X

Here, too, the net of all the entries in the premium or discount account would be a positive or negative contributed capital element.

3. If recorded on a *pro rata* basis:

    Treasury Stock. . . . . At Par
    Premium on Capital Stock. . . . . Pro Rata
    Cash . . . .   Cost

Where the purchase price is less than the average issue price of each share of the class, the *debit to the premium* account is for the excess of cost over par. If the purchase price exceeds the pro rata, the excess cost over the pro rata would be used to *reduce the retained earnings* balance. The balance sheet presentation follows essentially the same concepts as the par case above.

When resold, the record might reflect:

    Cash . . . . Proceeds
    Treasury Stock . . . .   At Par
    Premium/Discount on Capital Stock.   X

The sale entry follows the same principles as though an original issue were involved.

While in the treasury, the shares are not entitled to any distribution nor are they entitled to vote. They are, however, treated otherwise as though they were issued shares.

STOCK RIGHTS

Many statutes governing corporate enterprise provide that an existing stockholder is entitled to protection from an *involuntary dilution* of his or her equity. The dilution test is customarily applied to the percentage of interest, calculated by dividing the number of shares the corporation has outstanding into the number of shares held by the investor. This right is commonly identified as the *preemptive right,* or the right to preemption. Even in those states where the preemptive right is inherent, it can be contracted away by appropriate denial of the right in the articles of incorporation.

Whenever a corporation, through appropriate action by the stockholders, decides to issue additional shares of stock, it may elect to offer them to existing shareholders in their pro rata share of ownership, or it may be compelled to do so because the prior shares issued and outstanding are protected under the right of preemption. In either case, the usual process of achieving this goal is to use a *stock right* procedure.

In such a case, the corporation will issue the same number of rights as it has shares outstanding. Each shareholder will then be mailed the same number of rights as there are shares in his or her investment portfolio. The rights extend to the shareholder the first opportunity to buy a stipulated number of shares in the new issue, which will permit the shareholder to retain his or her percentage interest in the company. The rights are customarily transferable, which means the owner can accept the offer to buy (exercise), buy additional rights, or sell all or a part of the rights.

The rights contain three basic elements other than procedural information as to the process by which they may be exercised or transferred. The principal items are:

1. The ratio,
2. The subscription price, and
3. The date of forfeiture.

The *ratio* is determined by relating the number of additional shares to be issued to the number of shares then outstanding. For example, if the number outstanding is to be doubled, the ratio would be one right for one share. If the number of new shares is to increase the total number after the issuance by 50 percent, the ratio would be two rights for one share. The *subscription price* is the cost per share which the investor will have to pay for each one the investor buys. This price cannot be less than par, as previously indicated, and is usually somewhat below the then market price of the share. This makes the exercise attractive and, obviously, gives value to the rights. After the expiration of the *date of forfeiture*, the company may offer the unissued shares to any purchaser willing to buy them. Generally, forfeiture will not occur because the rights have value and will be disposed of by sale to someone interested in exercising them. If it does occur, it is through oversight or neglect.

Since the rights are transferable, once issued they may be bought or sold separately from the shares which produced them. The shares also can be bought or sold separately from the rights, or they could be transferred together as a unit.

On the date of issue of the rights, the *theoretical value* of the right is determined by an allocation process, as follows:

Assume:

1. Market price of the share—ex-rights, $132.
2. Subscription price for a new share, $120.
3. Ratio—two rights for a new share.

$$\text{Theoretical value of right} = \frac{132 - 120}{2} = \$6$$

The rights will typically start trading at about $6 each and, like the shares themselves, will then fluctuate with the market.

The effects on the investor of receiving stock rights will depend on his or her reaction to the offer to buy.

If the investor *exercises*, the appropriate number of dollars will be remitted, related to the subscription price and the number of new shares to which he or she is entitled, together with the rights. Although this additional cost increases the total investment the investor now has in the shares, the per share cost by lots must be recomputed. This is accomplished by a relative sales price allocation, as illustrated below. Despite the fact that the investor was able to buy the new shares at an advantageous price, there is no gain for either financial reporting or for taxation purposes.

Assume:

1. The investor owns 200 shares, originally purchased in one lot, for $90 each.
2. The investor receives 200 rights, as above.
3. On the date of issue, the market price of a share ex-rights is $132.

4. On the date of issue, the market price of the rights is quoted as $6.

If the investor exercises, 100 new shares will be bought and a check remitted for $12,000 ($120 × 100). The investment will change as follows:

Before exercise:
200 shares @ $90 each = $18,000
After exercise:
200 shares @ $86.09* = $17,218
100 shares @ $127.82† = 12,782
Total cost of 300 shares. $30,000

* Original cost of $90.00 × 132/138 = $86.09.
† New share cost = $120 + 2(6/138 × 90) or $127.82.

Relative sales price computation:
Market price of share—ex-rights. $132
Market price of right—right 6
Market price—share with right on. $138

It should be noted that the owners' equity of the corporation is not affected by the above allocation of part of the cost to rights, but merely will reflect a $120 increase for each new share sold.

If the shareholder sells his or her rights, the recomputed per share cost of the interest retained is the same as above, namely $86.09. The shareholder must recognize gain or loss by comparing the per right cost, $3.91, with the sale price per right.

OPTIONS AND WARRANTS

The corporation may wish to give various groups of persons an opportunity to buy shares of stock at some future date.

Typically, the company would give existing *employees* such an opportunity by granting them *stock options*. From the point of view of the enterprise, the privilege of buying shares requires that a waiting period elapse, and generally stipulates a purchase price (or a method of determining it subsequently) on the date the option was granted. Other than the limitations that might exist because of par values and preemptive rights, for every share issued the company merely records the event like any other initial sale. If the limitations are applicable, treasury shares permit the corporation to circumvent the problem. Options are normally *nontrans-*

ferable and exercisable only by the grantee once all conditions precedent to their issue are satisfied.

Warrants are usually granted to *other groups,* giving them the opportunity to buy shares of stock within a stated interval and at a predetermined price. They are *transferable* in most cases, and thus may be bought and sold on the marketplace. Once a warrant is exercised, the corporate treatment is identical to the sale of shares in the normal course, except that any sum the corporation previously received when the warrants were issued is reclassified as a part of the credit to the capital stock or additional paid-in capital accounts.

STOCK SPLITS AND REVERSE STOCK SPLITS

There are many reasons why a management would suggest that the stockholders entertain a *stock split.* Ordinarily, it is to make the shares more widely tradeable, because the consequence of a split is to reduce the market price of a share of the stock. Stockholder approval is traditionally required, particularly if the articles of incorporation must be amended to permit the split to be accomplished. Such amendment would be essential if the number of shares authorized must be increased or if the par value per share must be changed.

A stock split is effected by issuing more shares on a pro rata basis to existing stockholders without changing the dollar balance of either the legal stated capital accounts or of any other component of stockholder equity. This is achieved by increasing the number of shares but decreasing the per share par value in a compensatory manner. For example, assume:

```
Common stock—$50 par—5,000 shares. . . . . . . $250,000
Retained earnings. . . . . . . . . . . . . . . . . . .   175,000
        Total. . . . . . . . . . . . . . . . . . . . . . . $425,000
```

If the decision is made to issue an additional 45,000 shares (a 10-for-1 split), the par would have to be reduced to $5 per share. The result, after the completion of the event, would be:

```
Common stock—$5 par—50,000 shares. . . . . . . $250,000
Retained earnings. . . . . . . . . . . . . . . . . . .   175,000
        Total. . . . . . . . . . . . . . . . . . . . . . . $425,000
```

Obviously the 10-for-1 split merely means that the shareholder will ultimately have ten shares for every one share previously owned.

The number of new shares to be issued will typically be determined by the market price the management wishes to attain. Theoretically, the above split should reduce the trading price to 10 percent of what it was prior to the transaction. It is critical to observe that the split does not alter any of the component elements of the stockholder equity.

A *reverse split* accomplishes the exact opposite result. By decreasing the number of shares and making a compensatory modification in the par value, the components of the net worth remain unchanged, but the market price of a share would move proportionately upward.

DIVIDENDS

In cases where the corporation has only a single class of stock outstanding, it represents the residual equity and is described as the *common* class. Since dividends represent the distribution of accumulated earnings to the stockholders, it is evident that each share of the common class is entitled to identical treatment. Therefore, the amount of the distribution would be divided by the number of shares outstanding and each share would be entitled to receive a pro rata share of the dividend.

Problems arise when there is a *stock dividend* and where there are two or more classes of stock outstanding.

Unlike the cases of cash, scrip, or property dividends, which do actually reduce the net worth (the retained earnings) of the corporation, when a dividend is declared payable in the *corporation's own shares* the *total net worth remains unchanged*. A stock dividend ultimately causes the elements of the net worth to change, but they change in a compensatory manner so as to leave the total net worth the same after, as it was before, the declaration and distribution.

In effect, a stock dividend capitalizes retained earnings. This merely means that the paid-in capital of the corporation increases by the same amount as the retained earnings decreases. The corporation will distribute to each stockholder the appropriate number of additional shares of stock commensurate with a pro rata procedure.

For example, assume that before a stock dividend is declared the net worth of the corporation is:

```
Common stock—$100 par—5,000 shares
    authorized—4,000 shares issued . . . . . . . . . . . . $400,000
Premium on above . . . . . . . . . . . . . . . . . . . . .    20,000
Retained earnings . . . . . . . . . . . . . . . . . . . . .   130,000
        Total Net Worth . . . . . . . . . . . . . . . . . . $550,000
```

Assume further that a 5 percent stock dividend is declared. This means that the board of directors will issue 200 additional shares of the 1,000 authorized and unissued. It also means that each stockholder is entitled to receive 1 new share for every 20 previously owned. Many corporations will issue fractional shares where necessary. Thus if a stockholder holds ten shares, he or she would be entitled to receive one-half share in the distribution. Other corporations refuse to issue fractional shares and, as an alternative, will pay out cash equal to the value of the fractional share or will permit a stockholder to buy, and pay for, the fractional share necessary to give him or her a whole share of stock. These procedures result in some minor mechanical adjustments, depending on the circumstances.

Generally, however, a basic element which must be resolved is the dollar value to assign to the declaration. Three different bases of valuation which are sometimes found in accounting practice are:

1. Par,
2. Market value, or
3. Pro rata value.

If *par* is selected, the retained earnings would be diminished by $20,000 (200 shares at $100 each) and the legal stated capital balance would increase by a like amount.

If a *pro rata* value is used ($420,000 divided by 4,000 or $105), the retained earnings is reduced by $21,000 (200 × $105), the legal stated capital would increase by $20,000 (200 × $100), and the premium on capital stock issued would increase by $1,000.

Market value may be used, provided it is at least equal to par. Thus, if the market were at least $100, the amount of retained earnings being transferred to paid-in capital would be determined by the market value of the dividend shares, and the results would follow the same patterns as those already illustrated. If the shares were selling for less than $100, the discount limitation on initial issue would apply and the shares could not be capitalized at that dollar amount.

The AICPA Committee on Accounting Procedure recognized that, while a stock dividend is not a distribution of corporate earnings, many recipients of such dividends mistakenly view them as income, usually equal to the fair value of the additional shares received.[1] The committee felt that such views are strengthened in the many cases where the issuances are so small in relation to shares previously outstanding that they have no apparent effect on the share market price. Under these circumstances the committee recommended that retained earnings be capitalized in an amount equal to the fair value of the additional shares issued.

On the other hand, where the number of dividend shares is great it probably has the effect of materially reducing the market value per share. In these cases the recipient is not likely to misinterpret the dividend as income; it is more like a stock split-up. In such cases it is only necessary for the company to capitalize retained earnings sufficient to meet legal requirements. The use of the word "dividend" should be avoided if possible in such cases.

While the point at which the relative size of the dividend becomes large enough to materially influence unit market price will vary with the circumstances, usually a dividend of less than 20 percent or 25 percent of the previously outstanding shares would require capitalizing the fair value of the dividend shares.

There is probably no danger of misinterpreting stock dividends of closely-held companies; and it should be sufficient for them to capitalize only enough retained earnings to meet legal requirements.

The effect of a stock dividend is to "lock in" the retained earnings in the business and to convert it to a legal status where distribution can no longer be validly made. It permits the corporation to retain the earnings in the business and, generally, makes the investor an involuntary party to the transaction. Involuntary here means that no attempt was made to get the investor's agreement or permission to the transaction.

It is also important to note that the declaration of a dividend, payable in cash, in scrip, or in property, creates a liability automatically. The liability is liquidated by the eventual distribution of the appropriate means of payment. A stock dividend creates no such liability at declaration. It merely requires that there be a limitation, or restriction, imposed on the balance of the retained

---

[1] AICPA, *Accounting Research Bulletin No. 43*, "Stock Dividends and Stock Split-Ups" (New York: AICPA, 1953), Chapter 7B, pars. 10–13.

earnings still available for further distribution. This could be disclosed by a parenthetical note or by a footnote comment if financial statements are published after declaration and before the shares are actually distributed.

If more than one class of stock is outstanding, for example a preferred class and a common class, a dividend must be allocated properly between the classes. As indicated earlier, the preferred class is almost invariably entitled to a dividend preference. This may take the form of—

1. Being entitled to a distribution *before* the common class receives anything,
2. Being *cumulative*, which is no guarantee that a dividend will be paid but is an assurance that the preferred class will receive its stipulated return on an annual basis before common gets anything, or
3. Being *participating*, which means the preferred class is permitted to share with the common in an unusually large distribution, or
4. A combination of the above.

The application of these differences has been developed elsewhere and is merely referred to here to make certain that the concepts are recognized.

BOOK VALUE

A computation that is sometimes used relates to the *book value of a share* of stock. Book value only has meaning when applied to a share of common stock. If there are two or more classes outstanding, the book value calculation refers to the common, or residual, class whether or not it so stipulates.

Book value is a *liquidating concept*. Basically it computes what the per share, pro rata, distribution of assets would be if the firm were liquidating and were able to dispose of its noncash assets at neither gain nor loss. Although these assumptions might be contrary to fact, and although the recorded value (book value) of the assets may not necessarily reflect a fair market amount, the computation nevertheless does communicate another bit of useful information to third party users of the financial statements.

The principle involved in the computation is simple:

$$\text{Book Value} = \frac{\text{Net Worth Allocable to the Residual Class}}{\text{Number of Shares of That Class Outstanding}}$$

In most cases, the denominator poses no great problem as it is objectively determinable on any reporting date.

The numerator is the area where complexities might arise. Where there is only a single class of stock outstanding, the numerator is the total net worth as it appears on the balance sheet. This is so since a no-gain, no-loss conversion of all noncash property will yield an amount of cash exactly equal to the book value (carrying value) of the assets. Thus, an amount of money is available exactly equal to all the equities. Creditor interests have the first claim on this stockpile of cash. Once creditors have been paid in full, the balance of cash still remaining must, of necessity, equal the total recorded owners' equity. The numerator, then, is the same dollar amount as the net worth and is entirely allocable to the single class of shares over which it is to be divided.

Where more than one class is outstanding, a more complicated situation develops. After all liabilities are satisfied, the remaining available stockpile of assets is still equal to the net equity of the stockholders. However, there are two classes, a preferred and a common class, and the preferred class virtually always has a prior claim on the assets of a company in the event of distribution or liquidation. Thus, from the viewpoint of the common stockholders, the preferred class of shareholders has a prior claim on the remaining balance of money available to distribute. This must be computed first before the residual number of dollars available to the common (residual) class can be determined.

Assume the following net worth at a given year-end date:

Preferred stock—$50 par—3,000 shares issued.	$150,000
Premium on above	15,000
Common stock—$10 par—10,000 shares issued	100,000
Retained earnings.	75,000
Total Net Worth	$340,000

To compute the book value of the common stock, the prior claim of the preferential class must be calculated first. The general rule in the United States would be as follows in a step-by-step calculation:

1. The minimum dollar amount the preferred would be entitled to receive is the *par* times the number of shares issued and outstanding.

2. If the class were a *no-par* class, the articles of incorporation, the bylaws of the entity, and the certificate of stock itself would stipulate a liquidation value. This per share amount times the number of shares issued and outstanding would be substituted for No. 1 above.

3. If the par class has a predetermined stated *call,* or *liquidation, value* assigned, that value would be substituted for No. 1 above. Such a stated dollar amount is not abnormal and generally reflects an amount somewhat greater than par. For example, there could be a stated liquidation value of $57 per share.

4. A determination has to be made as to the stated dividend rate and as to the *dividend preferences* to which the preferred class is entitled. For example, the preferred class might be a 6 percent class, noncumulative and nonparticipating. In such a case, the dividend position of the preferred class is immaterial and the book value would be determined by reference to Nos. 1, 2, and 3 above, as applicable.

5. If the shares of the preferred class were *cumulative,* a further determination must be made regarding the arrearage, if any. If there is no dividend arrearage from prior years, the cumulative provision can be disregarded. If, however, the preferred class is in arrears, because it has not received its stipulated dividend on an annual basis through the computation date, then the total arrearage for the class must be computed and must be added to the previously calculated amount in No. 4. Liquidation cannot legally be used as a procedure to circumvent the statutory or contractual cumulative provisions of the preferential class.

6. The general rule in this country is to *disregard a participation clause,* although there is some argument on the other side of the issue. The idea is that a participation clause relates to the distribution of earnings by a going concern in the form of a dividend. It is not applicable in the distribution of assets in a liquidating concern. Since book value takes a liquidation viewpoint, it appears that most accountants would not consider a participation clause in the computation of book value.

To illustrate further, assume in the set of figures above that the preferred class has a liquidation value of $57, is an 8 percent class, is cumulative, and dividends are 3 years in arrears at the computation date. The following allocation would be made:

Total net worth		$340,000
Allocable to the preferred class:		
Par—$50 × 3,000 shares	$150,000	
Liquidation premium—$7 × 3,000	21,000	
Dividend arrearage—$12 × 3,000	36,000	207,000
Allocable to residual class		$133,000

$$\text{Book Value of Common} = \frac{\$133,000}{10,000} = \underline{\$13.30} \text{ per Share}$$

It is critical to reemphasize that although the book value of a share is frequently computed and reported upon in the financial statements, its meaningfulness is subject to question. Among the reasons that one must interpret book value in a critical way is that the result need have no necessary relationship to fair value, intrinsic value, or actual liquidating value. This is the case since the assets are recorded on a basis of incurred historical cost, less depreciation, and this may have no relevancy in terms of a present market value. It does communicate a hypothetical value based on some arbitrary assumptions, indicated earlier.

QUASI-REORGANIZATIONS

Another situation in which paid-in capital is involved is the *quasi-reorganization*. Briefly such an event occurs when, with the approval of the stockholders, the articles of incorporation are amended and the legal stated capital is thereby reduced. To the extent of the reduction, a deficit might be eliminated or assets might be written down, or both may occur. If the legal stated capital is reduced by an amount greater than is needed to write down assets and to eliminate the deficit, such excess is disclosed on the balance sheet as a part of paid-in capital. The balance sheet should disclose that retained earnings have been accumulated only since the quasi-reorganization. This dating continues until there appears to be no useful purpose served by doing so further. At that time, the disclosure need not be made on subsequent statements.

OTHER CHANGES IN PAID-IN CAPITAL

There is a great variety of other events which may occur and which might affect the paid-in capital accounts. Among such events are receivership, liquidation, reorganization under the bankruptcy statutes, and other legal devices to assist the corporation in getting a new lease on life and, hopefully, to perpetuate its activities.

Among the less commonplace events are donations and the whole area of acquisitions, mergers, other combinations, and divestitures. The latter problem areas are too extensive to be developed in this section.

As to *donations* of assets, the fair value of the asset received should be reflected for reporting purposes as the amount by which the contributed net worth was increased. Similarly, where donative intent exists on the part of the creditor, a reduction of indebtedness is the measure by which the net worth of the corporation is augmented. When variations in the above items occur, each should be evaluated on an individual basis.

SUMMARY

Accounting for, and reporting upon, the net worth of a corporate entity is governed by statutory requirements and by accounting and reporting principles and conventions.

Unquestionably clear is the mandate that contributed net worth and accumulated earnings be carefully distinguished and separately accounted for. The principal elements of accounting for transactions which commonly affect the paid-in capital (contributed net worth) have been set forth above. In all cases, generalizations reflecting popular interpretations and practices have been discussed. It is vital to keep in mind that variations will occur, either because of a peculiar practice in an industry or because of statutory differences. It is critical, if in doubt, to have the statutes of the state of incorporation researched so as to be certain to conform with their provisions.

Chapter 20

Accounting for dividends and stock options

Donald P. Selleck[*]

Special problems in accounting measurement for dividends and stock options are directly related to management objectives in controlling the firm's assets and in realizing and measuring its income. As the information of this chapter is developed, you will see that a dividend payment is generally a distribution of the corporate assets, and the granting of a stock option will generally change the earnings per share.

The problems associated with accounting for dividends and stock options have many common characteristics. For example:

1. The granting of dividends or stock options requires definite action by the corporate board of directors.
2. The granting of dividends or stock options may be restricted by the corporate bylaws, by restrictions placed upon the corporation under borrowing arrangements, or by other legal restrictions.
3. The granting of dividends and stock options is generally restricted to companies that are incorporated or have a similar legal entity.

The accounting pattern for measuring dividends or stock options is normally established by the company that grants the dividend or

* Vice President—Controller, 3-M Company.

411

stock option. Therefore, the grantor of dividends or stock options must be thoroughly familiar with the accounting treatment accorded the recipient, since it is important that both parties receive the maximum benefit from the transaction.

ACCOUNTING FOR DIVIDENDS

Generally a business corporation is operated for a profit. In the normal course of events, these profits accumulate and corporate assets increase. Although these assets belong to the corporation, the shareholders or owners of the corporation normally expect some type of return for their investment. The return can be an appreciation in the market value of their investment or it can be in the form of a dividend, which is a distribution of the corporate assets. A specific and positive action by the board of directors is required to declare a dividend distribution. Since this declaration results in a legal debt, it should be recognized by recording a liability for dividends payable. This reduces the corporate net worth. Generally a corporation pays only a portion of its profits to its shareholders and reinvests the remainder in the business. Sometimes it is possible that a dividend may include a partial return of capital to the shareholder. This is especially true in companies that develop natural resources.

When declaring a dividend, the board of directors must be certain that the proposed dividend is legal and that the distribution is financially sound. For example, a dividend declaration may be restricted by the laws of the state in which the corporation is incorporated. These restrictions are placed on dividends for the protection of creditors against unwarranted distribution of corporate assets to shareholders and for the protection of shareholders against informal liquidation of their investment in the enterprise.

Also, dividends may be restricted under borrowing arrangements. When financial institutions loan money to a corporation, it is not unusual for them to place restrictions on dividend declarations so that their loan may be protected from distribution to the shareholders. The bylaws of the corporation may place restrictions on dividends to protect the rights of the various classes of shareholders.

Generally, a degree of conservatism with respect to profit distribution is considered desirable. If there is any danger that the distribution of funds as dividends will impair the strength of the enterprise, directors may decide that a dividend is not in the best interest of a company. For example, borrowing is seldom justified solely for the purpose of making dividend payments to the shareholders.

Procedure to be used when paying dividends

After the board of directors has declared a dividend, this declaration should be included in the minutes of the board meeting. The date that the board of directors declares a dividend is the date the company incurs a legal liability to make a dividend payment. However, the amount that the corporation is legally bound to pay is not determined until the record date. The record date is the date established to determine the actual shareholders of the company who are entitled to receive the dividend. At that date, the individual or firm responsible for maintaining shareholder records will review shareholder transactions to determine that an appropriate cutoff has been established. Normally, the record date is approximately one month after the declaration date. After the dividend distribution has been completed, the legal liability is discharged.

When the outstanding stock of a corporation is listed on the New York Stock Exchange, a dividend declaration or a decision to pass a dividend requires prompt notification to both the New York Stock Exchange and to the news services. This notification is required so that an informed shareholder may not capitalize on this information before the dividend declaration is made available to the public.

As a practical matter, most large corporations have a transfer agent and a registrar. The transfer agent is responsible for maintaining a list of shareholders and, in some instances, for paying dividends. The registrar is responsible for issuing stock certificates and seeing that certificates being returned to the corporation are properly canceled. U.S. stock exchanges require that publicly held companies have an independent registrar. Some publicly held companies have chosen to be their own transfer agent. This so-called "in-house" transfer agent function is becoming more popular as the cost of an independent transfer agent increases and as large corporations transact sufficient activity to justify in-house services. The existence of an independent registrar and transfer agent may reduce the requirement for a careful review of internal control and the legal requirements associated with publicly held stock, since these agencies will assist corporations in maintaining adequate records required under the laws of the various states and regulations of the exchanges. The cost of maintaining an independent transfer agent and registrar differs, depending upon the number of shareholders an individual corporation has, the amount of activity which a corporation has with its shareholders, and the types of service performed by the independent registrar or transfer agent.

TYPES OF DIVIDENDS

Dividends are usually paid in cash, but occasionally other types of dividend payments are made. Decisions relating to the type of dividend payment are made by the board of directors at the time the dividend is declared. Comments relating to specific types of dividends follow.

Cash dividends

Cash dividends are normally made by using dividend checks drawn on special dividend bank accounts. It is important to recognize that a distribution of a dividend check to shareholders constitutes the final payment. Therefore, the liability is satisfied when the dividend check clears the bank. Most large publicly held companies issue one check for the total amount of dividends and deposit that check in a separate bank account. Then the transfer agent or dividend paying agent writes individual checks to the shareholders against that account. In some cases, a separate account is established for each individual dividend declared so that at any one time the amount remaining in the account is supported by a list of outstanding dividend checks. Unclaimed dividends should be returned to retained earnings after an appropriate period of time has elapsed, provided that the laws of the state permit and legal counsel so advises.

Cash dividends are not normally paid on treasury stock. If dividends are paid on treasury stock, the dividend received should be subtracted from the dividend paid and should not be taken into income.

Stock dividends

A corporation may elect to distribute stock dividends in lieu of, or in some cases in addition to, cash dividends. A stock dividend is a realignment of corporate shareholders' equity and is accomplished merely by a bookkeeping entry transferring retained earnings to the capital accounts and, in some instances, capital in excess of par (or stated) value. Although the state statutes may specify only one method, from an accounting viewpoint the corporation should transfer to permanent capital an amount equal to the fair value of stock distributed. The fair value amount in excess of par (or stated) value is considered to be capital in excess of par (or stated) value and is classified accordingly. The amount transferred to the capital accounts is a legal transfer to capital and precludes the payment of these amounts as dividends from retained earnings. The advantage of a stock dividend to a corporation is that it permits a corporation to retain cash required for corporate operations while at the same time increasing the number of shares available to be traded and continuing a policy of regular dividend distribution to its shareholders.

A stock dividend is different from a stock split. A *stock split-up* is "an issuance by a corporation of its own common shares to its common shareholders without consideration and under conditions indicating that such action is prompted mainly by a desire to increase the number of outstanding shares for the purpose of effecting a reduction in their unit market price and, thereby, of obtaining wider distribution and improved marketability of the shares."[1] In the case of a stock split-up, there is no transfer of retained earnings to the capital account of the corporation. Total capital is unchanged while the number of shares is increased; thus, the pro rata value of shares is reduced.

When stock dividends are distributed, it is generally desirable for the distributing corporation to adjust the number of treasury shares and shares under option if such shares exist. This adjustment permits all existing shareholders and potential shareholders to share equally the benefits of a stock dividend. However, this may not be permitted by some states, and it is essential that the statutes be reviewed carefully to determine the treatment that is acceptable under the law in the state of domicile.

In the hands of the shareholder, a stock dividend or a stock split generally does not result in income to the shareholder. Rather, it reduces the cost basis per share. The Internal Revenue Service (IRS) has indicated that taxable income does not result from a

---

[1] AICPA, *Accounting Research Bulletin No. 43*, Chapter 7B.

stock dividend unless the shareholder can elect to receive either a cash or stock dividend.

The company which issues a stock dividend discloses it within the financial statements as well as in the footnotes. The balance sheet reflects the ending balances after giving effect to the dividend distribution in the net worth accounts. The statement of retained earnings, together with the footnotes, must provide enough information so that the changes in the net worth accounts can be reconciled. An example of this is shown below:

	19x6	19x5
Stockholders' Equity:		
Common stock—$5 par value authorized 5,000,000 shares; issued and outstanding 19x6, 4,200,000; 19x5, 4,000,000.	$ 21,000,000	$ 20,000,000
Additional paid-in capital	10,000,000	9,000,000
Retained earnings	109,180,000	89,600,000
Total Stockholders' Equity	$140,180,000	$118,600,000
Additional Paid-In Capital:		
Beginning balance	$ 9,000,000	$ 9,000,000
Excess of fair market value over par value of common stock issued as a stock dividend	1,000,000	—
Ending Balance	$ 10,000,000	$ 9,000,000
Retained Earnings:		
Beginning balance	$ 89,600,000	$ 75,000,000
Net earnings for year	22,000,000	15,000,000
Less dividends paid: cash dividend, $.10 per share in 19x6 and 19x5	(420,000)	(400,000)
Stock dividend: 5%, at fair market value on date of declaration in 1974	(2,000,000)	—
	$109,180,000	$ 89,600,000

Dividends payable in kind

Dividends paid in kind fall into a number of different categories. For example, the company may give inventory items to its shareholders or it may distribute some of its other assets to shareholders. Each of these types of dividends involves a problem of pro rata distribution and an additional problem of determining the proper value of the dividend to be distributed. These problems do not arise when the company distributes cash.

To determine the pro rata distribution to the shareholders, it is necessary first to establish a value of the dividend being distributed, which is normally the original cost of the property to the distributing corporation. However, in certain cases where a market is readily available, the corporation may choose to write up the value of the distribution to market value. When this is done, it is necessary that the corporation making the distribution recognize the difference between cost and market as income in the year the distribution is made.

The person receiving the property dividend must determine its value for income measurement. As a general rule, the Internal Revenue Service (IRS) has determined that the market value shall be considered dividend income for tax purposes.

As a practical matter, because of the difficulties of valuation and pro rata distribution, dividends in kind are seldom used by large publicly held companies.

Liquidating or wasting asset dividends

While dividends ordinarily represent distributions of earnings, a liquidating dividend or a wasting asset dividend represents a return of part or all of the shareholder's investment. When the distribution is made, the declaring company will normally reduce its capital stock for a pro rata portion of the dividend that is being disbursed. In the hands of the recipient, the pro rata portion of these dividends is considered a return of capital and it should be used to reduce the cost basis of the investment. Although liquidating and wasting asset dividends are generally accepted under most laws, a corporation that is considering declaring these dividends should carefully review the corporate bylaws and the laws of the states in which it operates, since it may find that these dividend payments are restricted in certain cases.

Constructive dividends

A determination that a constructive dividend has been distributed is sometimes made under IRS regulations for closely held corporations. When distributions are made to shareholders of small, closely held corporations, the IRS may choose to call the distribution a constructive dividend, although the corporation may have meant to pay its shareholders a salary or other payment for services rendered to the corporation. Some of the criteria used by the IRS in making its determination as to whether the distribution is a dividend are:

1. The intention at the time of payment.
2. The documentation supporting the payment—for example, a promissory note—and whether interest is charged or paid.
3. History of repaying loans.
4. The total number of shareholders. The more closely a corporation is held, the more support will be required to evaluate the nature of the payment.

Since constructive dividends are not generally recognized for accounting purposes, they are commented on here only for general information.

Financial statement disclosure of dividends

For financial reporting purposes, dividends per share should be shown within the dividend caption on the financial statements. (See the example on page 416.) Declared but unpaid cash dividends are obligations of the declaring company and represent current liabilities. Declared but unpaid stock dividends are not liabilities, but should be reflected as an addition to capital stock and perhaps additional paid-in capital, with an appropriate explanation.

Cumulative dividends in arrears on preferred stock are shown in a footnote or parenthetically only, since no liability exists until declaration. The amount of the arrearage per share and in total must be disclosed.

ESTABLISHING A DIVIDEND POLICY

It is the responsibility of the board of directors to develop a corporate dividend policy. The board will probably consider both the corporation's requirements for operating funds and also the needs and expectations of its shareholders for a present source of income. While the board directs its efforts to maximizing the value of the firm to shareholders, it will find few clearly established and proven rules that describe an "ideal" dividend policy. The lack of definitive studies on the effectiveness and financial impact of various dividend policies means that management will often rely on intuitive judgment in determining dividend policy.

The board will look at dividend policy partially as a financing decision. Under this financing criterion, the firm would be guided by the availability of profitable investment opportunities. The firm is theoretically justified in retaining funds for reinvestment as long as management is able to invest funds more profitably than the shareholder can invest them elsewhere. The corporation with abundant profitable investment opportunities would pay no dividends, and only the company with limited ability to successfully reinvest funds would pay cash dividends. Thus, the company that treated dividends solely as a financing decision would treat the dividend decision only as a method of distributing unused funds. However, in practical terms, the directors must also consider whether the company's shareholders expect a certain level of dividends to be paid, and whether the absence of dividends would harm the market value of the company's common stock.

Whatever the theoretical justification for retaining earnings, most managements recognize that shareholders expect some participation in the current earnings of the firm and that the stock market places a value on the payment of dividends. While there is some debate over the "information content of dividends" (the idea that present dividends convey information about future earnings), management is usually sensitive to how the stock market will evaluate dividend actions. Management may often be reluctant to make any changes from past dividend policy since this might be interpreted as an indication of changes in prospects for future earnings.

There are basically three types of dividend policies a firm may follow:

1. It may follow a constant payout ratio, with dividends fluctuating along with earnings. Many shareholders will object to the uncertain source of income provided by such a policy.
2. A firm may pay a low regular dividend that is supplemented with *extra* dividends as earnings change. While this does provide a more stable source of minimum income to the shareholder, total income is still volatile.
3. The company interested in establishing a stable dividend policy will pay a stable dollar amount per share. The dividend size would be increased slowly and methodically as earnings increase. Dividend changes would lag behind earnings increases as management cautiously evaluates whether increased earnings

are supportable. This type of stable dividend policy is popular with many corporate managements who believe that stable dividends and stable earnings are positively evaluated in the stock market.

A stable dividend policy is basically attractive as a method of increasing the market value of a company's stock. Stable dividends are seen by shareholders as being less risky than fluctuating dividends. Many shareholders are willing to pay a premium price for a lower risk stock. A stock with a stable dividend is attractive to the substantial number of investors who live on current income from dividends, and thus the stock is able to be sold to a larger number of shareholders. Finally, a stable dividend stock is more likely to be included on the "legal list" of securities in which pension funds, insurance companies, mutual savings banks, and other fiduciary institutions are allowed to invest.

There are other considerations management should evaluate in setting a dividend policy. These include the following:

1. Dividend policies of other companies in the same industry.
2. The dividend payment restrictions in the company's various debt contracts.
3. The liquidity of the company and the relative shortage/excess of operating cash.
4. The company's ability to borrow from outside sources.
5. The nature of the shareholder. If there are few shareholders and they are in higher tax brackets, low dividends may be preferred over a higher current income.
6. The provision for depreciation may be inadequate to replace existing equipment due to inflation or changes in requirements. In such a case, the company may wish to retain more earnings to compensate for the inadequate depreciation provisions.

ACCOUNTING FOR STOCK OPTIONS

Nature

Stock options represent the right given to a bondholder, stockholder, underwriter, officer, or employee to purchase stock of the corporation at a specified price, during a certain period, and in accordance with conditions set forth in the option. Options, or warrants as they are often called, may be attached to stock to increase the marketability of the issue. The options may be detachable or nondetachable. If detachable, the purchaser of the stock may sell the warrant, exercise it, or permit it to expire. If nondetachable, the purchaser must either exercise it, sell it with the security to which it is attached, or let it lapse at the expiration date.

Qualified stock options

Stock options may be qualified or nonqualified. A qualified option gives the holder of an option certain advantages under tax regulations. In order for an option to be qualified under tax regulations, it must meet the following conditions:

1. The option must be granted to an individual after 1963 (other than a restricted stock option granted under a binding, written contract entered into before 1974) for reasons connected with his or her employment, if granted by the employer corporation or its parent or subsidiary corporation to purchase stock of any such corporation.
2. The option price must not be less than the fair market value of the stock when the option is granted. There is one minor exception to this rule which will be explained later.
3. The plan under which the option is granted must be approved by stockholders within 12 months before or after adoption by the corporation. It must be in writing and indicate the total shares issuable under the options and the employees or classes of employees eligible to receive options.
4. The option must be granted within ten years after the earlier of the date of stockholder approval or of corporate adoption.
5. The option must be exercisable after a period expiring five years from the date it is granted.
6. The option must not be exercisable while any qualified stock option granted to the employee at an earlier time and with a higher option price is outstanding. (If an option is modified, it is considered to be outstanding according to its original terms.)
7. The option must not be transferrable, other than by will or by laws of inheritance, and must be exercisable during the employee's life only by the employee to whom it is granted.
8. The employee receiving the option must not, immediately after the option is granted, own over 5 percent of the voting power

or value of all classes of stock of the corporation or its subsidiaries or parent. However, where the equity capital of a corporation is less than $1 million, the percentage is 10 percent. Where equity capital is between $1 million and $2 million, the percentage decreases proportionately down to 5 percent as equity capital rises to $2 million.

The tax advantages to an employee who receives stock options are effective only if the employee holds the stock for a certain period of time and meets other specific qualifications under tax regulations. In addition, in certain cases employee stock purchase plans qualify if the option price is as low as 85 percent of the market value of the stock at the time the option is granted or at the time the option is exercised. If stock acquired under such a plan is disposed of after being held for the required period, the employee will realize ordinary income to the extent of the excess of the fair market value of the stock at the time the option is granted.

Methods of accounting for stock options

Accounting for stock options can be divided into two broad categories. The first type of stock option is involved in a plan whereby the corporation attempts to get *wide distribution of its stock,* and it is an important means of raising capital. This type of stock option plan does not involve compensation, and the accounting is relatively simple. The value received for the stock option is credited to capital stock, and the debit is to cash.

The second type of stock option is more complicated, since it involves an inducement for employees, officers, or others to perform services for the corporation. The cost of these services must be recorded as *compensation* expense on the books of the company issuing the stock. Normally, the person receiving these stock options has the right to purchase the stock of the issuing corporation at a cost which is less than the fair market value. However, no element of compensation need be considered if the purchase price is not lower than is reasonably required to interest employees generally.

Measurement of compensation

In the case of stock options involving compensation, the measurement of the compensation is the difference between the fair market value and the option price at the date the option is granted. Five other dates which have been considered for measurement purposes, but have been determined not to be appropriate, are:

1. The date of the adoption of an option plan.
2. The date on which the grantee has performed any condition precedent to exercise of the option.
3. The date on which the grantee can first exercise the option.
4. The date on which the option is exercised by the grantee.
5. The date on which the grantee disposes of the stock acquired.

When the option is variable and the final price determination cannot be made until the occurrence of some future event, the compensation is the difference between the fair market price and the option price at the time that the event has occurred. This situation exists, for example, when the option price is reduced if the company exceeds a preestablished profit level. An estimate of the compensation cost of these plans should be made and the expense adjusted as the estimated cost changes.

Disclosure of options and warrants

Terms of stock warrants and options granted should be adequately disclosed on the balance sheet so that the stockholders may know to what extent potential purchasers have options on stock which otherwise would be available for sale or issue. When option rights have been issued to officers and employees as compensation for services but have not been satisfied as yet by the issuance of shares, an amount equivalent to such compensation (to the extent it can be measured) should be shown in the capital section of the balance sheet in a manner similar to that for proceeds from subscriptions for capital stock. As the options are exercised, this amount will be relieved by transfer of appropriate amounts to a capital stock account and possibly to an additional paid-in capital account, adequately described.

As to disclosure in financial statements with respect to stock option plans, *Accounting Research Bulletin No. 43*, chap. 13, sec. B, states:

> In connection with financial statements, disclosure should be made as to the status of the option or plan at the end of the period of

report, including the number of shares under option, the option price, and the number of shares as to which options were exercisable. As to options exercised during the period, disclosure should be made of the number of shares involved and the option price thereof.

Disclosure of stock options for SEC purposes goes beyond generally accepted accounting principles as expressed in *ARB No. 43*, chap. 13, sec. B. The information required under Rule 3–16 (n) is as follows:

A brief description of the terms of each option arrangement, including (i) the title and amount of securities subject to option; (ii) the year or years during which the options are granted; and (iii) the year or years during which the optionees became, or will become, entitled to exercise the options.

A statement of (i) the number of shares under option at the balance sheet date, and the option price and the fair value thereof, per share and in total, at the date the options were granted; (ii) the number of shares with respect to which options became exercisable during each period presented, and the option price and the fair value thereof, per share and in total, at the dates the options became exercisable; (iii) the number of shares with respect to which options were exercised during each period, and the option price and the fair value thereof, per share and in total, at the dates the options were exercised; and (iv) the number of unoptioned shares available at the beginning and at the close of the latest period presented for granting options under an option plan.

A brief description of the terms of each arrangement covering shares sold or offered for sale to only officers, directors and key employees, including the number of shares, and the offered price and the fair value thereof, per share and in total, at the dates of sale or offer to sell, as appropriate.

The required information must be appropriately summarized and tabulated for all option plans as a group, as well as for plans under which shares are sold or offered for sale as a group. The basis of accounting for such option plans and the amount of the related charges to income must be disclosed.

If the financial statements are filed as part of a prospectus or proxy statement which contains information regarding stock options in the narrative section, cross-reference may be made in the notes to financial statements to such information and thereby avoid needless repetition.

The following is a suggested form of a note to financial statements dealing with a stock option plan only, which complies with the requirements of Rule 3–16 (n).

> At (balance sheet date), (number) shares of common stock of the Company were reserved for sale to officers and employees under a stock option plan approved by stockholders on (date). The plan provides that the option price shall be fixed by a committee of the Board of Directors, but shall not be less than ____% of the market value of the stock at date of grant. Options are exercisable ____ months after grant and may not be exercised after ____ years. Options were granted for (number) shares in 19____, (number) shares in 19____, and (number) shares in 19____.
>
> Information as of (balance sheet date) and for the year 19____ through 19____ with respect to options granted under the plan is as follows:

	Number of shares	Option price Per share	Option price Total	Market price Per share	Market price Total
Shares under option at (balance sheet date)	____	$____ to $____	$____	$____ to $____ (a)	$____
Options which became exercisable during:					
19__	____	$____ to $____	$____	$____ to $____ (b)	$____
19__	____	$____ to $____	$____	$____ to $____ (b)	$____
19__	____	$____ to $____	$____	$____ to $____ (b)	$____
Options exercised during:					
19__	____	$____ to $____	$____	$____ to $____ (c)	$____
19__	____	$____ to $____	$____	$____ to $____ (c)	$____
19__	____	$____ to $____	$____	$____ to $____ (c)	$____

(a) At the dates options were granted.
(b) At the dates options become exercisable.
(c) At the dates options were exercised.

> At the beginning of (period), there were (number) unoptioned shares available for the granting of options under the plan; at the end of such period there were (number) unoptioned shares available.
>
> The company makes no charges to income in connection with the plan.

On the other hand, for a company that has securities listed for trading on the New York Stock Exchange, there are additional requirements which, in some respects, differ from those in the SEC rule.

The Exchange's current requirements for listing contain a provision with regard to the information to be disclosed in annual reports to security holders concerning the operation of stock option plans. The applicable portion of the listing agreement follows:

> The corporation will disclose in its annual report to shareholders, for the year covered by the report, (1) the number of shares of its stock issuable under outstanding options at the beginning of the year; separate totals of changes in the number of shares of its stock under option resulting from issuance, exercise, expiration or cancellation of options; and the number of shares issuable under outstanding options at the close of the year, (2) the number of unoptioned shares available at the beginning and at the close of the year for the granting of options under an option plan, and (3) any changes in the exercise price of outstanding options, through cancellation and reissuance or otherwise, except price changes resulting from the normal operation of anti-dilution provisions of the options.

It may be noted that the Exchange's requirement is for the disclosure of the information in question—but not necessarily as a part of the financial statements. Some companies do, in fact, furnish the required information in the text portion of their annual reports; others, however, include it in their financial statements and combine it with the information otherwise required to be furnished in respect of stock options.

Conclusion

Accounting for dividends and stock options involves many specific legal and financial disclosure questions as well as accounting issues. Although this chapter has identified the general concepts involved, the official pronouncements issued by the American Institute of Certified Public Accountants, the Financial Accounting Standards Board, the New York Stock Exchange, and the Securities and Exchange Commission should be reviewed carefully when dividends or stock options are considered. These pronouncements include detailed procedures and instructions which must be followed if the corporation is to treat these transactions correctly.

PART 4

Special problems in administering corporate resources

Chapter 21

Free cash flow as a measure of corporate performance

*Joel M. Stern**

Management needs an effective measure of corporate performance so that resources are properly allocated to their most productive uses. The common shareholders require an accurate measure of performance in order to ascertain if they are being adequately rewarded for the business and financial risks they bear. If management attempts to undertake investments and employ financing policies that serve the best interest of the common shareholders, the measure of corporate performance should be identical for both parties.

EVALUATION OF EARNINGS PER SHARE

Earnings per share (EPS) is a misleading indicator of performance that almost always results in a severe misallocation of resources. Substandard projects are likely to be undertaken and erroneous financing policies implemented that will shortchange the common shareholders, thereby causing an erosion in the market price of the common shares. Because EPS is simple to calculate and easy to understand are poor reasons for its use as an objective

* Vice President, Chase Manhattan Bank.

performance indicator, when an alternative measure is available that avoids its shortcomings.

Weaknesses of EPS

EPS is bad for four principal reasons, which will be elaborated on later in this chapter:

1. *EPS confuses investment decisions with financing policy.* Consequently, substandard projects that management expects will provide insufficient benefits may be undertaken because they can appear desirable in terms of their impact on EPS simply by evaluating the expenditures and their financing requirements simultaneously. Utilize sufficient financial leverage and a predetermined desired amount of EPS will usually result. This error is most obvious in the evaluation of prospective mergers and acquisitions.

2. *EPS can convince management to employ debt because leverage usually increases EPS, even though the benefits of debt to the common shareholders have nothing to do with EPS. And, for extraordinarily successful companies that sell at high price/earnings ratios, focusing on EPS can convince management to employ a debt-free policy that reduces the common share price.* Paradoxically, achieving a maximum share price and maximum price/earnings ratio (P/E) is impossible when companies command high P/E's.

3. *EPS is not a primary, nontransitory determinant of share price.* That is, EPS and share price are only spuriously and occasionally correlated. As is often the case when EPS is increasing rapidly and the company's share price is falling, management can erroneously conclude that investors are irrational or poorly informed, when the reverse is true.

4. *Because investors emphasize free cash flow in measuring corporate performance, focusing on EPS wastes management's time.* Decisions that appear to be important are trivial, such as capitalizing versus expensing research and development costs, and expensing goodwill that results from purchase accounting of acquisitions. Crucial decisions are improperly studied, including switching from Fifo to Lifo inventory accounting.

All four reasons for abandoning EPS are based on a key assumption, namely, that the stock market is dominated by financially sophisticated investors and that share prices therefore reflect basic underlying economic values. There is considerable published evidence to substantiate this theoretical view of market behavior, which will be briefly presented. First, however, EPS must be clearly defined and each of its four shortcomings should be carefully examined. It is essential to establish the nature and implications of investor sophistication, which results in an optimal measure of corporate performance.

Definition of earnings per share (EPS)

Bottom-line profit, net profit after taxes (NPAT) is equal to revenue minus all operating expenses, financing costs, and corporate income taxes. Dividing NPAT by the weighted number of common shares and common share equivalents outstanding results in "primary" EPS.

If convertible preferred stock or convertible debentures which are not common stock equivalents are outstanding, a more conservative measure of EPS is called "fully diluted," which assumes that conversion has occurred at the conversion price. This latter calculation omits the convertible security's dividend obligation or interest expense (after income tax) from the numerator, increasing NPAT, but it also increases the assumed number of outstanding common shares used in the denominator.

Thus, if the percentage increase in NPAT exceeds the percentage increase in the number of outstanding common shares, the magnitude of fully diluted EPS will be greater than the amount of primary EPS. The reverse is also true.

Problems in defining EPS meaningfully

Two problems are immediately obvious. First, since all corporate income taxes are subtracted from revenues in calculating either primary or fully diluted EPS, the common shareholders' need for an economic measure of performance is overlooked. That is, corporate income taxes usually consists of two components—currently payable and deferred—but prudent investors can often expect that the deferred income tax will never be paid in the aggregate. As long as capital expenditures for new plant and equipment are at least as large as the current depreciation expense, a reasonable investor expectation, in virtually all cases the deferred tax is equivalent to a noninterest-bearing perpetual loan from the government. (This is also the case for deferred taxes arising from installment receivable accounting.) Hence, subtracting the deferred income tax from revenue to calculate EPS understates true corporate performance. On a company's tax accounts, this deferred item does not appear since, in effect, it is a part of shareholders' equity, where it properly belongs.

Second, both the theory and evidence regarding the primary determinants of share prices indicate that fully diluted EPS is rarely, if ever, important to investors.[1] The reason is that since share prices are based on expectations of average future corporate performance, and because a company's ratio of debt to equity is important (debt is cheaper than equity), it is the average expected future debt ratio that matters, not short-run fluctuations in the ratio that are occasionally due to the conversion of outstanding debentures.

Clearly, these problems indicate that specifying a meaningful calculation of EPS is difficult. However, the four major shortcomings are considerably more serious than the problems associated with the calculation of EPS, beginning with the confounding of investment decisions and financing policy.

MAJOR SHORTCOMINGS OF EPS

1. EPS confuses investment with financing

A key principle in corporate finance is that specific sources of financing cannot be identified with specific investment projects. Yet, when evaluating individual investment proposals, the calculation of EPS violates this principle by subtracting the interest cost and cash dividends on preferred stock from net operating profit before the resulting NPAT is divided by the number of common shares. The significance of this shortcoming can be appreciated most easily in acquisition analysis.

---

[1] Joel M. Stern, "Earnings per Share Don't Count," *Financial Analysts Journal*, July–August 1974, p. 39.

Too often, we are told that companies should make acquisitions because of the "earnings leverage" that will result. As an example, assume that Company A sells at a P/E of 20 and that Company B sells at a P/E of 10. Frequently, we are told that Company A can offer B's shareholders of P/E of, say, 15—a 50 percent premium—and that A can still increase its EPS. For each dollar of earnings A is buying, A has to give up shares earning only 75 cents. Thus, if A uses its shares to acquire B and form a new company AB (pro forma A), the new company's EPS will always exceed A's. Hence, we are told that the acquisition of B is good for A's shareholders, even in the absence of operating or financial synergism (i.e., direct or indirect savings that result from the acquisition). And, apparently, it is good for B's shareholders since they obtain a 50 percent premium above the market price of their shares.

However, if the example is turned around, the danger of using EPS becomes obvious. If B acquires A to form BA, B will pay at least A's P/E of 20. But now BA's EPS will be less than B's because the company with the lower P/E must offer more shares per dollar of acquired earnings. The same people who tell us that AB is good for A's and B's shareholders tell us that BA is bad for B's shareholders, even though AB and BA are the same company, most often with the same assets and earnings expectations and even the same management. Should we therefore expect AB and BA to sell at different market prices when they are really the same company?

A's acquisition of B or B's acquisition of A is in fact good for the buyer's shareholders only if synergism is expected. And the synergism must be large enough to justify the premium paid above the seller's current share price.

Thus, it is illogical to claim that IBM, for instance, can afford to pay more for B than could the Chase Manhattan Bank simply because IBM sells at a much higher P/E than the Chase. Furthermore, if IBM (or any company selling at a high P/E) were to acquire firms for which it paid full value (i.e., for which there were no added benefits to the buyer's shareholders), all the evidence on stock market behavior suggests that IBM's P/E would fall to offset the gain in EPS.

"The AB-BA fallacy" lies in the unsubstantiated assumption that the pro forma EPS determines the pro forma share price. Because share prices are not in fact determined so simply, relying on EPS to evaluate alternative acquisition candidates often results in costly decisions.

Therefore, it is foolish to conclude that the maximum price a buyer can afford to pay for a seller is a function of the buyer's current P/E, or that a seller's demanded price that was formerly considered excessive now is fair because the buyer's P/E increased relative to the seller's P/E.

Confusing investment with financing can take another popular form in acquisition analysis. In a recent case, the president of a well-diversified manufacturer selling at 16 times earnings wanted to acquire a small, but exceptionally profitable, pharmaceutical company for a P/E of 25. Since an equity swap would "dilute" the pro forma EPS, we suggested, somewhat facetiously, that it sell itself to the pharmaceutical company, even though the latter was only a tenth of the size of the manufacturer, so that the EPS would rise.

The president of the manufacturer suggested an alternative: use debt to finance the acquisition. The anticipated increase in profits from the acquisition would more than cover the out-of-pocket cost of interest on debt, and hence the company's earnings would rise, while the number of outstanding shares would remain unchanged. The president was correct; the pro forma EPS would rise. However, there was a conceptual problem with the president's suggestion. Since EPS can be enhanced simply by employing debt (or preferred stock), a bad investment often can be made to appear good merely by levering the firm sufficiently to increase the EPS at the time the investment is undertaken. Of course, if the leverage idea is sound—the firm is overcapitalized and management believes a larger ratio of debt to equity is prudent and desirable—management can increase EPS without making any investment whatever, simply by borrowing to retire common shares. (However, share repurchase is only rarely permitted outside the United States.)

Although there are many ways financing decisions can affect EPS, they cannot alter the intrinsic desirability of an acquisition or any capital expenditure decision. This means that investment decisions must be made independently of financing decisions, or, in other words, on the basis of considerations other than the effect on EPS. Since EPS is calculated by dividing NPAT by the number of shares outstanding, basing investment decisions on EPS unfortunately implies that a specific source of funds finances a specific use of funds, which conceptually is wrong.

If a company borrows at the same time it builds a plant, how can the lender be sure the borrower will not use a portion of the funds to pay dividends or build inventories? Do we ever see arrows identifying specific sources and uses of funds on statements of change in financial position (funds statements)? Clearly, such identification would be erroneous.

Consequently, the investment-financing shortcoming of employing EPS as a measure of corporate performance is that, other things remaining the same, (*a*) the desirability of acquisitions is determined by the existing P/E's of the buyer and seller, so that synergism may be excluded from consideration: and (*b*) EPS can lead the decision maker to believe that bad investments are good investments; levering the firm sufficiently at the time an investment is undertaken can enhance EPS to any desired level.

2. EPS obscures the real benefits of debt

An emphasis on EPS not only misdirects management in pricing acquisitions and selecting investments; it also leads to ridiculous conclusions about the desirable proportions of debt and equity in a company's financial structure. Depending on the P/E multiple, mechanical reliance on EPS can encourage expansion of debt to cover dubious projects, or the elimination of all debt by issuing common shares. Even though in most cases an increase in the amount of debt in relation to equity will enhance EPS, the benefits to a company's share price derived from its financing policies have nothing to do with EPS. This conclusion is based on both the following discussion and the evidence cited later on the efficiency of the stock market.

A company can use debt to increase its EPS as long as its after-tax return on total capital (i.e., all interest-bearing debt and equity) is larger than its after-tax interest costs. Today high-grade bonds usually cost the firm less than 5 percent after taxes. Thus, corporate investments in new plant and equipment and working capital that yield more than 5 percent after taxes would appear desirable to analysts emphasizing EPS.

It is certainly not difficult to imagine the likely direction of

IBM's share price if projects were undertaken earning a mere 6 percent on total capital, even if EPS were rising.

The market will not ignore the fact that an increase in debt forces the common shareholder to assume greater financial risk, as a result of higher interest costs. Unless some other factor offsets part of this new risk, the P/E will decline. The price of the common shares would remain unchanged despite the added EPS.

On the other hand, using the EPS criterion alone would dictate that high P/E firms should issue shares to retire debt. It works out mathematically that EPS can be increased by issuing shares to retire debt so long as the P/E is larger than the reciprocal of the after-tax borrowing rate. If a company's after-tax cost of borrowed funds is 5 percent, the reciprocal is one divided by 5 percent, or 20. Whenever the P/E exceeds 20, management can increase EPS simply by issuing equity to retire debt. Hence supporters of EPS maximization would recommend that companies selling at very high P/E's be debt-free, a policy hardly beneficial to the common shareholders.

Actually there is considerable evidence that debt financing does add to the market price of a firm's common shares. The reason is that part of the increase in relative risk due to the fixed interest expense is borne by the federal government—up to 48 percent, the corporate income tax rate, as long as net operating profit before interest expense is as large as the interest cost, or tax loss carryovers can be sold to a profitable company. The deductibility of interest expense in calculating taxable income means that a company's earnings are reduced by only 52 percent of the cost of debt.

A large body of empirical evidence confirms our intuition about borrowed capital—namely, that investors do not expect management to reduce debt.[2] As it comes due, they expect management to refinance, hence to maintain a particular target debt ratio. A target debt ratio implies that sophisticated investors expect the annual tax saving to continue forever. The present value of this perpetual stream is simply the corporate income tax rate multiplied by the amount of interest-bearing debt that the market expects to be in the target capital structure. As long as the level of debt does not exceed prudent limits, the aggregate market price of a com-

---

[2] Robert Litzenberger and Cherukuri U. Rao, "Estimates of the Marginal Rate of Time Preference and Average Risk Aversion of Investors in Electric Utility Shares: 1960–66." *Bell Journal of Economics*, vol. 2, No. 1 (Spring 1971).

pany's common shares will rise 48 cents for each dollar of interest-bearing debt in its target capital structure. The real benefit of debt financing to the common shareholders is not the added EPS; it is the government tax saving.

3. EPS doesn't count

Clearly, from Sections 1 and 2, an EPS criterion frequently misallocates valuable corporate resources and shortchanges the shareholders. Nor, to judge by market behavior, is EPS the criterion that impresses investors, especially the sophisticated investors who really determine share prices. What do these investors look for in evaluating a company's overall performance?

Investors do not discount earnings per se. Consider two companies, X and Y. Assume that, from all we know, they are the same in every way and that their profits are expected to increase at identical annual rates of 15 percent. At this stage, a foolish question would be: Which company should sell at a higher price, X or Y? Obviously, we would expect X and Y to sell at an identical price since, in the absence of additional information, X and Y are the same company!

However, with the addition of one other piece of information about the two companies, we must conclude that X would command the greater market price. Assume that we learn that X requires almost no investment in new capital to increase its profits 15 percent annually, whereas Y requires a dollar of additional capital for each incremental dollar of sales. X should sell at the higher price and P/E because it requires less capital than Y to grow at a given rate, despite the fact that X and Y are expected to have identical future profits. This is because X has a larger expected rate of return on incremental capital. The key determinant of market price in this case is the expected rate of return on incremental capital invested.

The implication of this example is that investors do not simply discount expected earnings; rather, they discount anticipated earnings net of the amount of capital required to be invested in order to maintain an expected rate of growth in profits. I refer to the latter stream as the expected future "free cash flow," the expected future stream of operating cash flows that remain after deducting the anticipated future capital requirements of the business. It is free cash flow (FCF) that is important to the market. EPS is immaterial.

4. EPS wastes management's time

Focusing on EPS, rather than on free cash flow (FCF), misdirects management's decision-making process. The next section explains how this occurs.

FREE CASH FLOW: AN ALTERNATIVE TO EPS

Free cash flow defined

Free cash flow (FCF) is equal to net operating profit after taxes to be paid (NOPAT) minus net new capital investment (I). NOPAT is the profit before financing costs but after taxes that are expected to be paid: that is, NOPAT ignores deferred income taxes. I is equal to capital expenditures on land, plant, and equipment, and other long-term investments minus depreciation and other noncash expenses (e.g., depletion, amortization), plus the increase in working capital. An alternative and equivalent definition of net new capital investment is the increase in total assets minus the increase in non-interest-bearing current liabilities.[3]

FCF can also be calculated as NOPAT plus depreciation and other noncash expenses—net operating cash flow—minus gross capital expenditures and additions to working capital.

FCF illustrated

In Table 1, the numerical example illustrates the calculation of NOPAT, I, and FCF and compares NOPAT with NPAT and FCF with the popular concept, net cash flow. The difference between NOPAT ($2,100) and NPAT ($1,880) is $220, the sum of the after-tax financing cost ($120), assuming a corporate income tax rate of 50 percent, and the year-to-year increase in deferred income taxes ($100), which investors expect will not be paid.

---

[3] Because investors expect short-term interest-bearing debt to be refinanced in order for the company to maintain a long-run average, or target ratio of interest-bearing debt to total capital, net new capital investment includes increases in short-term interest-bearing debt. Thus, working capital is current assets minus non-interest-bearing current liabilities.

TABLE 1
Comparison of NOPAT and NPAT, and FCF and NCF

	Balance sheets		Operating statement year ending 12/31/78	
	12/31/77	*12/31/78*		
Current assets	$ 3,000	$ 4,000	Revenues.	$15,000
Net plant.	5,000	6,000	Cost of goods sold*.	7,000
Other assets	2,000	3,000	Gross profit	$ 8,000
Total Assets.	$10,000	$13,000	Selling, general, and administrative	
			expenses	4,000
Current Liabilities:			Net operating profit	$ 4,000
Accruals and accounts payable.	$ 1,000	$ 1,500	Interest expense.	240
Current portion of long-term debt	1,000	1,000	Net profit before tax	$ 3,760
	$ 2,000	$ 2,500	Provision for income tax:	
Long-term debt	2,000	2,900	Current.	$ 1,730
Deferred income taxes	500	600	Deferred†.	150
Shareholders' equity	5,500	7,000		$ 1,880
Liabilities and Equity	$10,000	$13,000	Net Profit after Taxes (NPAT)	$ 1,880

NOPAT = NPAT plus interest expense after taxes plus increases in deferred tax on balance sheet
     = $1,880 + $120 + $100
     = $2,100

   I = increase in total assets minus increase in noninterest-bearing liabilities
     = $3,000 – $500
     = $2,500

 FCF = NOPAT minus I
     = $2,100 – $2,500
     = –$ 400

Net Cash Flow = NPAT plus Depreciation
         = $1,889 + $400
         = $2,280

   * Including depreciation of $400.
   † The current allocation to deferred income taxes of $150 on the operating statement is less than the year-to-year change on the balance sheets because retirement or sale of plant and equipment has been assumed. The purpose of this assumption is to show that it is the change in the balance sheet item that is the noninterest-bearing perpetual loan from the government, not the amount on the operating statement.

Net new capital investment, I, is $2,500, equal to the increase in total assets ($3,000) minus the increase in noninterest bearing current liabilities ($500). FCF is equal to $400, because gross new capital (I plus noncash expenses) of $2,900 exceeds by $400 the net operating cash flow of $2,500 (NOPAT, $2,100, plus noncash expenses, $400).

Net cash flow is bottom-line profit, NPAT, of $1,880, plus noncash expenses of $400, a total of $2,280.

How FCF influences investors' decisions

An important question for management is: Do stock market investors prefer that current FCF be positive, zero, or negative? In the illustration, current FCF is negative.

If the current amounts of NOPAT and I reflect a company's normal and anticipated performance (i.e., a constant rate of new investment, I divided by NOPAT), a positive current FCF means that the company possesses a relatively small magnitude of investment opportunities. A negative FCF indicates the reverse. Consequently, the question can be restated: Do investors prefer a small I (positive current FCF), or a large I (negative current FCF); that is, under which condition will a company's market value be greater—current FCF is positive, or current FCF is negative?

Examining the determinants of a company's market value provides the answer. A company's market value is equal to the discounted value of current and expected future FCF, where the discount rate is the weighted average cost of debt and equity capital. Thus, the answer depends on the amount of FCF investors expect management to generate in the years after projects are undertaken. If current and anticipated projects are expected to result in a relatively large amount of FCF in future years, the expected rate of return on these projects will be high. If the expected rate of return exceeds the cost of capital, investors will prefer a negative current FCF because a large magnitude of investments will generate a greater amount of future FCF, and hence, a higher market value.

Because FCF is the true indicator of corporate performance, managements who believe EPS is relevant often are confused about the functioning of the stock market during periods of rapidly accelerating inflation. Underdepreciation of plant and equipment on a historical cost basis and the utilization of first-in, first-out (Fifo) inventory accounting, rather than replacement cost accounting (i.e., an "indexation" of corporate profits), overstate real profits. However, during such periods, FCF usually does not increase. Normally, FCF declines—profit increases usually are more than offset by a dramatic rise in needed capital investment (I), greater expenditures for the replacement of plant and equipment and working capital. Furthermore, inflation increases the cost of debt and equity capital. Thus, if share prices reflect underlying economic value, as the evidence indicates, increases in EPS and a precipitous decline in share prices should be expected during periods of rapid inflation because FCF is eroded and the cost of capital is greater.

How FCF improves management decisions

Focusing on EPS, rather than FCF, misdirects management's decision-making process. A belief that EPS is a proper indicator of performance results in a considerable waste of time. Issues that are trivial, because the outcome of management's decision does not affect underlying economic value (i.e., FCF), are considered at great length, whereas issues that are crucial, because they impact on FCF, are incorrectly resolved. For example, how should management account for research and development costs? If R&D is capitalized, and thus expensed slowly over the useful life of a project, reported EPS will be larger in the year the project is undertaken than if the R&D cost is expensed in its entirety in the year in which it is incurred.

If EPS is the proper measure of performance, a prudent management will favor the capitalization of R&D outlays. If FCF matters, the accounting procedure for reporting to shareholders is irrelevant, because only the tax treatment is important; that is, R&D outlays only affect FCF as a result of the tax treatment. Consequently, expensing, rather than capitalizing, R&D costs as incurred on the company's tax books produces greater FCF.

This line of reasoning is applicable to many other issues, too, most notably in recent years to the treatment of goodwill in the analysis of mergers and acquisitions. Offering cash or debentures in the past (and now even preferred stock) for prospective acquisition candidates requires the buyer to establish a goodwill account on the balance sheet and to expense this item over a period not to exceed 40 years. The amount of goodwill recorded is equal to the difference between the seller's "fair value" and the acquisition price paid by the buyer. Since expensing goodwill reduces EPS, many managements conclude that acquisitions which are otherwise justifiable on economic grounds are undesirable.

An FCF criterion leads to the opposite conclusion. Because the amortization of goodwill is a noncash, nontax–deductible charge, expensing goodwill has no effect on FCF. Therefore, the accounting treatment of goodwill never should dissuade management from consummating desirable acquisitions. In many instances, such acquisitions are made more attractive because the fair value of the net assets acquired exceeds the seller's book value and a portion of the difference is depreciable on the buyer's tax books, thereby increasing the buyer's FCF. If anything, the accounting procedure that creates goodwill on a company's books is good, not bad, for the shareholders, even though EPS is reduced, not because of the goodwill item itself, but because the accounting procedure that creates goodwill can permit a write-up of plant and equipment.

Focusing on EPS also can result in reduced FCF and lower share prices. Inventory accounting is a prime example. Attempting to maximize current EPS during periods of inflation leads management to employ Fifo rather than last-in, first-out (Lifo), because Fifo enables the company to report the increase in the value of inventory—from the time it is purchased until it is sold—as income on the operating statement. But because this income is taxed, after-tax cash flow (and, thus, FCF) is less with Fifo than with Lifo.

Intuitively, management must be aware that FCF is the accurate measure of performance, because numerous companies switch from Fifo to Lifo inventory accounting during the periods of rapid inflation.

Unfortunately, the financial press is to blame for part of management's delay. In almost every reported conversion from Fifo to Lifo, the press has announced the extent to which EPS will be reduced, when proper reporting would also have stated *and emphasized* the degree to which after-tax cash flow would be enhanced. Hence, the press must believe that it is EPS that is important, not FCF.

SOPHISTICATED INVESTORS AND THE EFFICIENT MARKET

EPS versus FCF

If the press places importance on EPS and if investors read such reports and behave in the stock market as if EPS is the crucial measure of corporate success, should we not suggest that it would be sensible for management to focus on EPS if a principal corporate goal is to assure that the company's share price be "fair"? That is, we must differentiate between normative statements about how investors *should* behave, and positive statements that conclude how investors in the real world *do* behave. Stating that FCF, not EPS, should be the measure of corporate performance may be interesting, but its relevance in the real world clearly depends on the degree to which financially sophisticated investors dominate the stock market, and thus determine share prices.

One may argue intuitively or theoretically that sophisticated investors sort out the distortions created by EPS. Yet, there is plenty of room to wonder whether the market really is as omniscient as this conception suggests. Observance of market behavior could convince some that share prices are affected by fads appearing to have little to do with market efficiency and FCF. Perhaps these are merely random errors of an ultimately efficient mechanism, but then again, perhaps not. An intuitive conception of market behavior could lead one to believe that the market is merely a psychological game, and to concentrate on spotting the next fad a week earlier than the rest. To accept the view that sophistication in the real world is an appreciation of underlying economic values based on FCF one has to understand the "efficient markets" concept and the nature of the empirical evidence supporting it.

Fortunately for managements who wish to discharge their responsibility on the basis of underlying economic values (FCF), there is overwhelming and persuasive published evidence that share prices on the stock market are determined by astute investors. The nature of this investor behavior and the evidence in support of a sophisticated market are crucial in abandoning EPS and accepting FCF as the best measure of corporate performance. A summary of this evidence is presented in the next section.

Characteristics of an efficient market

A financially sophisticated stock market, also called an "efficient" market, has two essential characteristics. First, share price must fully reflect all available relevant information regarding current and expected future FCF. This means that as new information (e.g., backlogs, new product developments, sales, changes in government regulation, etc.) becomes available to astute investors, it is quickly disseminated and evaluated, and if it affects investor estimates of current or future FCF, it is translated virtually instantaneously into new share prices.

On an efficient market, clearly, sophisticated investors perform an extremely useful function. Their activities assure that fair prices and market prices are almost always the same. By attempting to estimate a company's current and expected future FCF, they often pursue information in the hope that they will be the first to learn, and thus benefit from, it. Transacting on the basis of their belief that they can identify overvalued or undervalued securities, they become the mechanism by which new information is translated into new market prices, causing market prices to make once-and-for-all adjustments to new information. This information gathering and evaluation process results in an exceptionally rapid price change because only by being first to obtain new relevant information can the investor generate superior investment results.

The second characteristic of an efficient market is that no single investor, or group of investors, may have monopoly access to new relevant information. That is, if one or a few investors could consistently obtain important price-sensitive information first, they would consistently outperform other less fortunate investors. The latter would cease their search for new information, and hence efficiency would break down.

Consequently, for a market to be efficient, prices must fully reflect all available relevant information regarding current and expected future FCF and no investor, or group of investors, may possess monopoly access to this information.

EVIDENCE ON MARKET EFFICIENCY

There are three distinct forms of market efficiency, the "weak form," the "semistrong form," and the "strong form."

Weak form

If share prices fully reflect all available relevant information, successive changes in share prices should not follow a discernible or predictable pattern. Future share prices would be based on unpredictable information not yet known. The key word, unpredictable, means that changes in share price also would be unpredictable. Thus, a graph of historical share prices would be expected to follow no particular pattern. This is the so-called weak form of efficiency. Only if the stock market were dominated by highly sophisticated investors would share prices conform to the weak form of market efficiency. The evidence on this point is bountiful.

Among the many studies of share price behavior, the most prominent include the work performed on the London stock market in 1953 by Maurice Kendall and on the New York stock market by Harry Roberts and M. F. M. Osborne in 1959, Arnold B. Moore in 1962, Eugene Fama in 1965, and Marshall Blume in 1966. All of these concluded that price patterns are virtually absent, substantiation of at least weak-form efficiency.

Semistrong form

The semistrong form states that public information about specific companies' financial data is fully reflected in the firm's current share prices. That is, by the time management issues financial statements quarterly and annually, this information already has been detected and evaluated by security analysts through other sources, such as interviews with management, company and trade association releases of production and shipment figures, press reports, and inquiries made with competitors, suppliers, and customers.

Ray Ball and Philip Brown in 1968 examined the extent to which earnings announcements are anticipated by investors. Their study covered the period 1946–66 on the New York Stock Exchange. They concluded that earnings announcements were fully anticipated well in advance of management's announcements.

Since management often signals its expectations about prospective profitability by splitting the company common shares, Eugene Fama, Lawrence Fisher, Michael Jensen, and Richard Roll in 1969 evaluated the extent to which such announcements altered investors' expectations and the speed with which share prices reflected this new information. In this second study of the semistrong form, the conclusion was that share prices of the 622 companies in the sample from the New York Stock Exchange, spanning the years 1927 through 1969, did not rise or fall more than would have been expected after abstracting general movements in the market as a whole during the months surrounding the announcement of the stock split.

Thus, it is likely that the market becomes aware of improved expected corporate performance well in advance of management's announcements.

Strong form

The strong form is the greatest degree of efficiency. This form requires that share prices reflect not only information known to investors through public announcements but also information that may not be generally known. The performance of professionally managed portfolios, managed by groups that might have monopoly access to important information (e.g., mutual funds), have been analyzed to test the existence of the strong form.

It is important to note that even if half of the professional money managers outperform the market as a whole, a market conforms to the strong form of efficiency as long as they do not generate superior results consistently.

Five comprehensive studies of mutual fund performance present considerable support for the existence of the strong form of market efficiency. The evidence indicates that mutual funds have not outperformed a simple buy-and-hold investment strategy.

Empirical studies of market performance

The 1962 Wharton Business School study conducted by a team headed by Irwin Friend covered the performance of 189 funds for the period December 1952 to September 1958. Its major conclusion was that on the average these funds performed no better than an unmanaged portfolio. Although approximately half of the funds performed better than an unmanaged portfolio and about half performed worse, none demonstrated results that were consistently superior to the market as a whole. Only a handful of funds performed better than they would have had they fully invested their resources in the shares of the Standard and Poor's 500-share Index.

In 1966, William F. Sharpe added an important improvement to the technique of measuring fund performance. He measured the riskiness of the portfolio as well as its rate of return. This can be crucial because large portfolio rates of return may simply be the result of investments in highly risky securities which outperform the market as a whole during periods of rising share prices, and generate inferior performance during periods of declining share prices. Since share prices rise over time to compensate investors for the corporate business and financial risks they bear, on the average high risk portfolios outperform market indices. By adjusting actual rates of return for the specific portfolio risks, Sharpe calculated the portfolios' true rates of return. Measured in this manner, fund managers' performance reflected their ability to identify undervalued and overvalued securities. His study examined the performance of 34 mutual funds for the period 1954–63. After adjusting for risk, and ignoring the fund's expenses, 19 funds inconsistently[4] outperformed the Dow Jones Industrial Average (DJIA). Including their expenses, only 11 funds inconsistently outperformed the DJIA.

Michael Jensen's 1968 study of 115 mutual funds for the period 1955–64 was more comprehensive than Sharpe's. Jensen employed Sharpe's risk measure, but compared actual mutual funds' performance with the rates of return that would have been achieved in randomly selected portfolios of equal risk.

His major conclusions were that—

1. On average, for the ten years 1955–64, the terminal value of the 115 funds in his study (assuming reinvestment of dividends) was 9 percent less than the terminal value of randomly selected, identically risky portfolios. When load charges were taken into account, the funds' terminal value was 15 percent less than the identically risky, random portfolios.
2. If a fund's results were superior to an identically risky random portfolio in any one year, the likelihood of duplicating this performance in a subsequent year was only about 50 percent. That is, in the subsequent year the fund's performance was inferior to the random portfolio about half the time.

CONCLUSION

In view of the four principal shortcomings inherent in EPS as an indicator of corporate performance—confusing investment decisions with financing policy, confounding the real benefit of debt financing, failing to focus on the indicator investors employ to evaluate performance, and wasting management's time by directing attention to trivial corporate planning issues while failing to consider the consequences of more crucial matters—management should abandon EPS as a measure of performance. FCF is not only more

---

[4] "Inconsistently" means that the performance was unpredictable from year to year. A fund that was superior, or inferior, in one year was no more likely to be superior, or inferior, the next year than a fund selected totally at random from the sample.

intuitively appealing because it avoids all of the problems associated with EPS, but there is considerable evidence that in highly
efficient stock markets (e.g., New York, London) investors focus
on FCF in calculating market values and evaluating corporate
performance.

If one of management's principal objectives is to have the company's market value and the fair value of the common shares be
identical, the only proper measure of corporate performance is FCF.
Earnings per share don't count!

Chapter 22

Return on investment as a measure of financial responsibility

A. M. Long*

GENERAL

Return on investment (ROI), or more properly rate of return on investment, is the relationship, generally expressed as a percentage, between the net income of an enterprise and the investment (or capital commitment) required to earn that net income.

Probably no term in finance is so widely used or subject to so many interpretations as ROI. The application that we will be analyzing in this chapter is often called the "accounting method" or the "mercantile rate of return." This application is used by analysts and stockholders to evaluate the effectiveness of an enterprise's management and, with some modifications, by top management to evaluate the performance of divisional (or subsidiary) management.

Another application of ROI is its use to aid in the selection of investment alternatives and capital expenditures in new products and facilities. However, in this application other analytical techniques, such as the "discounted cash flow method" or the "payback period method," are also widely used; thus, we limit this chapter to the discussion of the use of ROI as a measure of performance. In the

---

* Comptroller, General Motors Corporation.

following pages then, we will examine the relationship of the various elements involved in the calculation of an ROI and of how an analysis of these elements can give a full measure of the performance of a company at the corporate level. We will also consider the application of an ROI analysis at the divisional (or subsidiary) level.

Every business is constantly being evaluated and judged. If the activity is a small, one-owner business, the evaluation is done by the owner; if the activity is a larger concern, the evaluation is done by current management who in turn are being evaluated by current and prospective stockholders. What, then, is the best measure of the performance of a business, be it small or large? Some would use the quality of the firm's product or service; some would use the relationship of the owner/manager with the employees; and some would refer to the stature of the business in the local and national community. All of these are factors, of course, but they are only necessary parts of what is probably the ultimate measure of a commercial venture's performance—the return on the owner/stockholder's investment over the long run. To be sure, if a firm doesn't generally satisfy its customers, employees, and the community it will not be able to produce a satisfactory return to its owners over the long run; but on the other hand, it may do all of these things and still not be able to produce a satisfactory return, in which case it will eventually go out of business.

NEW VERSUS EXISTING ENTERPRISES AND SPECULATOR VERSUS PERMANENT INVESTOR

We should, at this point, distinguish (1) between starting a new business and an existing business and (2) between the speculator and the permanent investor. In starting a new enterprise, prospective owners will have studied the probable market for the planned product or service, evaluated the management/employee team, and reviewed projections of the capital requirements and the anticipated return thereon. If the projected return is competitive with alternative investments, considering intangibles such as the desire to own a business and the risk factor involved, the prospective investors will go ahead and make the investment. However, once they have committed their funds, they are "locked-in" to the extent that they must now either make the business a success, so that new investors would be interested in either adding new capital or buying out the initial investors, or lose their investment if the business fails.

Naturally, the business may just struggle along and only break even, in which case the initial investors would not be receiving a satisfactory return and would not be able to attract new investors nor sell their interest, except at a loss large enough to make it possible for succeeding investors to believe they could earn a satisfactory return on *their* investment. (This course is often forced on a business through bankruptcy.) Profit, then, is the enabling factor that attracts risk capital and supports debt capability. In the absence of profits, or at least the potential for profits, there are no sources of capital other than public (government) assistance or charity.

In contrast to the permanent investor, however, there is the speculator and/or professional investor. The definition of a speculator, or professional investor, which we prefer in this context is that given by John Maynard Keynes in his book, *The General Theory of Employment, Interest, and Money:*

> For most of these persons are, in fact, largely concerned, not with making superior long-term forecasts of the probable field of an investment over its whole life, but with foreseeing changes in the conventional basis of valuation a short time ahead of the general public. They are concerned, not with what an investment is really worth to a man who buys it "for keeps," but with what the market will value it at, under the influence of mass psychology, three months or a year hence.[1]

This definition, of course, includes a goal in the evaluation of a business that is outside the scope of our comments. The following discussion is aimed at the permanent investor and will be restricted to the systematic evaluation of the performance of a business over the long run.

EARNINGS PER SHARE

At this point, let's consider the use of a firm's earnings per share (EPS) as a measurement of performance. The popularity of the use

---

[1] John Maynard Keynes, *The General Theory of Employment, Interest, and Money* (New York: Harcourt Brace & Co., 1960), pp. 154–55.

of a company's EPS for this purpose, since World War II, stems principally from the relationship of EPS to the rate of ROI, coupled with the simplicity of the EPS figure compared to the rate of return calculation. A company's ability to show a steady growth rate in its annual earnings per share is considered to be an indication of management's ability to maintain a steady (and presumably satisfactory) rate of return on the stockholders' investment.

Of course, this is a broad generalization, since EPS can be affected by many factors including the dividend payout, the use of interest-bearing debt instead of equity capital, changes in the number of shares of common stock outstanding, the effect of a merger accomplished by a pooling of interests, and by inflation. Nevertheless, the most common factor contributing to an increase in the EPS of a company is generally the reinvestment of earnings, with the consequent increase in the asset base, coupled with management's ability to continue to earn at least the same rate of return on the increased investment base.

Thus, while we certainly recognize the importance of the EPS as a measure of performance, we believe the ROI to be a more complete tool. In short, we agree with the conclusion of the *Report of the Study Group on the Objectives of Financial Statements* to the effect that the primary goal of an enterprise is "returning, over time, the maximum amount of cash to its owners (investors)."[2]

OPTIMUM RETURN

This conclusion, of course, raises the question, "What is the maximum amount of cash, that is, the optimum return?" While there is no definitive answer to this question, it is not necessarily the highest attainable rate of return in the short run, but rather the highest return consistent with a sustainable volume, with care being exercised to assure that the profit on each increment of volume will at least equal the economic cost of the additional capital required. Therefore, we can state that the minimum acceptable return must be at least equal to the cost of capital, that is, the rate which a company must earn in order to attract investment funds. However, the cost of capital cannot be stated in the form of a simple formula because of the risk factor. This is a subjective factor which does not

[2] AICPA, *Report of the Study Group on the Objectives of Financial Statements* (New York, October, 1973), p. 63.

easily lend itself to mathematical expression. We can, however, make some observations which will give a fairly narrow range for an acceptable rate of return.

First of all, we can assume that the minimum rate an investor would accept in either debt or equity securities would be the prevailing rate on high-quality government obligations, except for the speculative investor who might choose stock which is considered to be undervalued. Since government obligations carry a minimum risk and are generally salable, they would always be available as an alternative and thus set the "floor" for an acceptable rate. The high point is not quite so easy to determine. It certainly would be in excess of the rate paid on prime, short-term commercial paper; otherwise, the investor would choose the less risky commercial paper. Thus, the range during 1974, for example, would be at least in excess of a Series "E" Bond rate of about 6 percent up to something greater than the maximum prime rate in that year of 12 percent, depending on the risk involved.

With this range in mind, it is interesting to review the schedule shown in Exhibit 1. The schedule was compiled from the *Forbes 26th Annual Report on American Industry* and contains the median return for 30 industry classifications for the 5-year period 1969 through the latest reported 12 months as of January 1, 1974. It is interesting to note that the median return on common stockholders' equity is only 11.4 percent and the median return on total capital employed is just 8.2 percent. The general behavior of the stock market during 1974 relative to the prime interest rate and the rate on government securities was a graphic demonstration of the validity of the earlier statement that the minimum acceptable return must be at least a rate which will attract investment risk funds.

VARIOUS ANALYTICAL METHODS

Although there is general acceptance regarding the use of some form of return on investment as a measure of management performance, there is not the same agreement as to the exact method to be used in calculating the rate of return.

In the analysis shown in Exhibit 1, *Forbes* has employed two commonly used methods for calculating the rate of return. The first column is a return computed by stating net income as a percentage of stockholders' equity at the beginning of the year. The

EXHIBIT 1
Five-year industry median (1969–1974)

Industry	Return on equity (%)	Return on total capital (%)
Health care (drugs, etc.)	17.2	15.1
Personal products	14.5	13.3
Financial	14.3	7.3
Leisure and education	13.9	10.2
Construction and drilling	13.1	8.2
Food and drink	12.9	9.5
Retailers	12.8	9.7
Banks	12.6	10.9
Natural gas	12.6	6.9
Household goods	12.2	9.2
Wholesalers	12.1	10.0
Nonferrous metals	11.8	8.7
Insurance	11.7	11.6
Electronics	11.7	10.0
Information processing	11.4	8.8
Conglomerates	11.2	7.7
Electric and telephone	11.1	5.8
Industrial equipment	11.0	7.8
Automotive	11.0	8.6
Energy	11.0	8.2
Aerospace and defense	10.9	7.7
Building materials	10.7	8.8
Chemicals	10.5	7.8
Supermarkets	10.4	7.9
Apparel	9.6	7.2
Multi-industry	9.5	7.9
Forest products	9.4	7.1
Metals	6.1	5.1
Surface transportation	5.4	4.7
Airlines	4.8	3.1

second column is based upon return on total capital, which means that capital from all sources—preferred stock, long-term debt, deferred tax credits, and so on—is included in the denominator.

Another approach is used by *Fortune* magazine in its annual compilation and analysis of the "500" largest industrial companies. *Fortune* utilizes a very complex computation termed "total return to investors," which includes the effect of stock market fluctuations of the company's dividend yield. The inclusion of these factors has resulted in some startling statistics: for example, the median total return on the top "500" for 1973 was a *minus* 25.49 percent as a result of the sharp decline in the stock market during that year!

The Report of the Federal Trade Commission on Rates of Return in Selected Manufacturing Industries, which has been published periodically since 1947, is based upon the average of stock-holders' investment at the beginning and end of each year. The stockholders' investment in this computation consists of ". . . capital stock outstanding, paid in or other capital surplus, earned surplus, surplus reserves, and minority interest in capital stock and surplus, less any reported appreciation."[3] Net income (*after income taxes*) is used in the FTC calculation.

Another widely used method is the so-called "Du Pont method," named after the company which pioneered its use. The "Du Pont method" uses gross assets as the investment base for the calculation of the ROI, rather than stockholders' equity. The effect of this method can best be illustrated in an example (Exhibit 2). As the reader will note, the return on gross investment (total assets) is less than the return on net investment (equity). The choice between the use of these bases depends entirely on the user's purpose. Assets are generally used as the measurement base when the goal is to measure the performance of a management group in utilizing the total investment entrusted to it. On the other hand, if the goal is to measure the effectiveness of management in employing non-equity type financing, as well as asset management, then the use of stockholders' equity as the measurement base is more appropriate. Since managements of divisions of a company generally do not have the authority or responsibility to obtain capital, the "Du Pont method" is widely used to compute the rate of return on investment at the divisional level. This analysis will be more fully explored later in the chapter.

PREFERRED METHOD

In considering the use of ROI as a measurement of corporate management, however, we prefer the use of *stockholders' equity* as the base in order to include a factor for leverage. As the reader will note from a review of Exhibit 2, there are three basic factors involved in the calculation of ROI: the *return on sales* (net profit margin), the *asset turnover,* and the *leverage factor.* It is possible to compute the rate of return by simply dividing the net income (after taxes) by (1) the stockholders' equity at the beginning of the year, which is the calculation shown in column 1 of Exhibit 1; or

---

[3] *Report of the Federal Trade Commission on Rates of Return in Selected Manufacturing Industries 1962–1971* (Washington, D.C.: U.S. Government Printing Office), p. 2.

EXHIBIT 2
Return on investment: Comparison of asset base with equity base

	Company A	Company B
Sales	$1,000,000	$10,000,000
Net income (after taxes)	$ 40,000	$ 500,000
Return on sales	4.0%	5.0%
Total assets—beginning of year	$ 250,000	$ 3,333,333
Asset turnover (sales ÷ assets)	4.0	3.0
Return on gross investment (assets)	16.0%	15.0%
Stockholders' equity—beginning of year	$ 166,667	$ 1,666,667
Leverage factor (assets ÷ equity)	1.5	2.0
Return on net investment (equity)	24.0%	30.0%

(2) the average stockholders' equity for the year, which is the method employed in the FTC Report.

However, the simplicity of the calculation conceals the influence that the three factors named above have on ROI. The first, return on sales or net profit margin, of course, is a common measurement of a company's performance. This ratio generally reflects the efficiency of the company's production and distribution efforts, as well as the pricing policies. The second factor, asset turnover, is affected by the sales volume, the efficiency of inventory control policies, the cash sale/credit sale (receivable) mix; and by the property and equipment requirements and capacity utilization.

While the return on sales and asset turnover ratios are clearly a reflection of management's ability to manage, the third factor, leverage, is not quite so clear-cut. The use of leverage—that is, the use of debt, particularly of the long-term type, or preferred stock (which is excluded from the common stockholders' equity)—as a source of capital will generally increase the rate of return, and thus is widespread. The leverage factor then provides the means to measure management's ability to make money on borrowed money.

If the leverage factor (computed by *dividing the rate of return on equity by the rate of return on assets*) is greater than one, the stockholders have probably benefited through the use of funds supplied by creditors at a rate lower than the rate of return earned on the income-producing assets acquired with the funds; otherwise, the rate of return on equity would be less than the rate of return on assets. However, to evaluate fully the effect of leverage, it is necessary to assess the increased risk to which the company is exposed as the result of using debt (and the accompanying fixed interest and principal payments) rather than equity capital. While a high debt-to-equity ratio may be easy to sustain during prosperous times, the fixed nature of debt payments can prove to be a serious burden in hard times.

In preparing the analysis shown in Exhibit 2, we have used various bases for which there is no general agreement, although they are probably the most widely used because they are readily available and understandable. First of all, we have used net income (after taxes) in calculating the return on sales. Although this is the popular base, some people prefer to use income before income taxes in order to avoid any distortion that varying tax incentives and policies may have on the calculation. Certainly this has been less of a problem since the adoption of *Accounting Principles Board Opinion No. 11* requiring allocation of income taxes. Another alternative base is in the use of total assets per the balance sheet, in which the property and other assets are stated at net book value. Many prefer to use property values at original cost, excluding accumulated depreciation, to avoid the distortion that varying depreciation policies among companies will cause in any comparisons being made. Of course, some people, particularly in an inflationary period, may use some estimation of current value of property in the calculation.

Finally, a leverage factor based on all liabilities, deferred credits, and reserves has been utilized to determine the return on common stockholders' equity. Many people would calculate the rate of return based on total capital employed, which would generally be defined as including only long-term debt and preferred and common stock. *Forbes* also includes deferred tax credits, if any.

NEED FOR CONSISTENT APPLICATION

Although a variety of methods and definitions are utilized in calculating a rate of return, the significant point is that in evaluating the performance of a company's management, all of the comparisons being reviewed should be on a consistent and comparable basis and the method and definitions used should be clearly understood.

The fundamental point, then, is not the precise method upon which the calculation of the rate of return is based, but the consistent use of one method to measure management's ability to run the company. In the case of judging a single company's performance over a period of time, consistency from period to period is necessary. In comparing one firm's performance to that of another, consistency of method between firms is important.

ROI IS AN OVERALL MEASUREMENT

ROI reflects all phases of a company's operations. The general influence of the marketing and research policies is demonstrated by the sales volume, while the profit margin reflects the effect of cost control methods and the pricing policy on volume, as well. The production group's effectiveness in producing a quality product efficiently is reflected in the profit margin. The impact on the customer of product quality, in relation to price, is also seen as another factor which will eventually effect sales volume. Finally, the influence of the financial policies can be seen by the effect the judicious use of long-term debt will have on the rate of return.

Of course, many other factors influence each phase of the business, and thus a detailed analysis by factor would be necessary to determine which are favorable and which are unfavorable. For example, assume that the sales volume is rising. This could be due to a combination of several factors:

1. Pricing policy—have the prices of products been adjusted to the point that volume is being achieved without any profit?
2. Advertising—perhaps an expensive advertising program has been undertaken which may not raise volume enough to offset its expense.
3. Research—has a new product been placed on the market and gained quick acceptance?
4. Engineering—has product quality been improved to the point that customer acceptance is growing?

The list could go on and on: Have new territories been opened? Have more salespersons been placed in the field? Are general economic conditions quite favorable to the company's line of products? Has a significant competitor changed its marketing strategy? Is the increase simply due to wider acceptance of the existing products? And so on.

To summarize, the rate of return on investment is the most popular overall basis by which to judge a management's performance. It is preferred to earnings per share because it reflects not only net income (after taxes), as does EPS, but all the other factors of a business—total assets, sales, and leverage.

DIVISIONAL (OR SUBSIDIARY) MEASUREMENT

Thus far we have concerned ourselves with the development and use of the rate of return as a means of evaluating the overall performance of a company. Such an evaluation is, of course, made periodically by a company's board of directors, by stockholders, by security analysts, by prospective investors and creditors, and by management itself.

We will now turn to an analysis of the use of the rate of return on a regular, month-to-month basis by top management as a means of evaluating the performance of the various divisions, branches, or subsidiaries of the firm. As in the case of an entire company, consistency in the method between periods and/or between operating segments is essential.

Profit center versus cost center

The initial question which must be answered, before we discuss the appropriateness of the use of ROI as a measure of divisional (or subsidiary) performance, is whether the divisions are operated as *profit centers* or as *cost centers*. Usually subsidiaries are operated on a profit center basis, while divisions will vary according to the desires of company management. It is not the purpose of this discussion to evaluate the pros and cons of a profit center concept compared to a cost center concept. However, the use of ROI is obviously ruled out as a measurement standard for those companies in which the divisions (or subsidiaries) are not expected to earn a profit on their operations.

Restrictions on ROI for a segment

Even in those instances in which divisions are operated as profit centers, considerable caution must be exercised in using ROI as a measurement of performance, because a division is only a *segment* of a company. A basic question we need to determine is the degree of decentralization. Are the segments actually separate corporations, owned by a holding company, with boards of directors which exercise only broad policy control? In such a case, the use of ROI as a measurement of the subsidiaries' management would be almost as appropriate as for the entire company. Or, at the other extreme, are the segments only divisions of a multidivision, highly integrated company, all of which is closely managed by a headquarters (executive office) group? In that case, it is doubtful that a particular division's ROI would be a fair gauge of the divisional management's performance. This would be particularly true if the headquarters group established the capital budget, directed product planning and marketing activities, and set the prices at which the divisions transferred their products to other divisions. Probably the more typical case, however, is somewhere between these two extremes, in which case the use of ROI must be tempered by the degree of autonomy the division (or subsidiary) actually has.

Naturally, the more a division or subsidiary operates in an independent company manner, the more appropriate will be the use of ROI as a measurement of that performance. Nevertheless, the use of ROI in those situations where there is only a moderate degree of autonomy can be valuable if the divisions (or subsidiaries) are comparable in the degree of autonomy and if there is a consistency in this respect from year to year.

In using ROI as a performance measurement for divisions (or subsidiaries) we must keep in mind that while the concept of delegation of authority and responsibility which underlies all decentralized organizations is certainly a proven, valid concept, there is a point at which it conflicts with the simple fact that top company management must optimize the company's total profits. If too much emphasis is placed on ROI at the divisional (or subsidiary) level, the pressure may be strong for the divisional management to maximize their profits at the expense of overall profits. The fact that segments of a company are not independent firms also results in the consideration of three other factors in utilizing a ROI calculation: first, the *definition of the investment base;* second, the *allocation of the expenses* associated with shared corporate activities; and third, the effect on a segment's profits of what is termed the *"transfer price"* problem.

Investment base

In considering the problem of how the investment base should be established, we must recognize that a segment of a company is different from the total company, inasmuch as a segment does not have stockholders' equity or long-term debt (unless the segment is a subsidiary of the parent corporation). Thus, the investment base must be measured from the "uses" side, rather than the "sources" side of the balance sheet. In addition components, both controllable and noncontrollable by the segment management, must be considered.

In computing the investment base for a segment of a company, the following alternatives need to be considered. (Note that some of these alternatives are the same as those which must be considered in evaluating the entire company.)

1. Should the investment in the segment be defined as total assets, net assets, or just property and equipment?
2. Should the property and equipment be valued at acquisition cost, at depreciated value, at estimated replacement cost, or at current appraised value?
3. Should shared corporate assets, such as research laboratories, executives offices, and so on, be reflected in a division's investment or only at the corporate level?
4. Should consideration be given to activities which may be centralized, such as cash control, receivables, investment portfolios, purchasing, or corporate long-term debt, or should they be ignored?

In considering these alternatives, it is clear that there is no definitive answer. Basically, the most important factors are (1) that all of the segments be on the same base so that comparable data can be compiled and (2) that there be a consistent application of the base. A fundamental concept to keep in mind in choosing a base is that it seems most reasonable to hold people responsible for only those things over which they have some *control*. Thus, allocation of shared corporate assets might not be desirable. Any basis of such an allocation, be it sales, payrolls, property, a combination of these factors, or some other basis, would be arbitrary and would be difficult to apply to the segments on a fair and equitable basis.

With regard to the first question (i.e., the use of total assets, net assets, or property and equipment as an investment base for a segment), the predominant practice is to use total assets as the investment base by which divisional management will be judged. The popularity of this method seems reasonable because, as mentioned earlier, it is not practicable to use the "sources" side to measure the divisional management. Instead, divisional management is held accountable for only the assets that it is using. There are variations to this approach which are also understandable. In those companies where certain activities (such as cash or receivables control) are centralized, the assets involved may be excluded from the divisional investment base because divisional management is not accountable for those assets. Nevertheless, many companies do allocate a specific amount of cash to the divisions in order to reflect the anticipated cash requirements of the division.

In those instances where the segment is, in fact, a separate subsidiary which negotiates its own long-term debt, we believe that the "uses" approach to the investment base is not appropriate and, instead, the customary "sources"—that is, stockholders' equity and long-term debt approach—should be used.

Insofar as the valuation of property and equipment is concerned, there is merit in each of the suggested methods—acquisition cost, depreciated value, estimated replacement cost, and current appraised value. Most companies, however, use *depreciated value based on acquisition cost,* probably, in part at least, because this is the basis used in reporting these same assets in the balance sheet. Some companies use the *gross acquisition cost* to avoid the favorable effect a declining asset (investment) base would have on the ROI. However, those favoring the use of depreciated value argue that the depreciation policy of a company, if properly determined, aids in the growth of a company; thus, the ROI should reflect both sides of the effect of depreciation. In addition, if depreciation expense is reflected in the net income used in the ROI calculation, there seems to be considerable merit in reflecting it in the asset base as well.

The most serious problem that can result from the use of depreciated value for property and equipment at the divisional level is the *conflict of interest* that it creates for divisional management. If corporate management places too strong an emphasis on divisional ROI as a performance measurement, a divisional manager may tend to postpone recommendations for capital improvements until the payback period is quite short—that is, the ROI is abnormally high. This condition can be eased by using gross value of the property and equipment in the investment base or by establishing broad corporate control of capital improvement and expansion programs. (To some degree, this conflict would also exist for corporate management.)

Neither the *estimated replacement cost* nor the *current appraised value* methods for valuing property and equipment has gained wide acceptance, probably because of the difficulty in preparing or obtaining such valuations, coupled with the fact that the most important point in the evaluation process is not the method but rather *consistency* in the application of the method used. This same point applies to the third and fourth alternatives—handling shared corporate assets such as research laboratories and centralized activities such as cash control. As mentioned earlier, divisional management should generally be held accountable only for those items over which they have some control. Although some companies allocate all corporate assets to their divisions on the precept that all corporate assets should be included in the ROI base, there really doesn't seem to be much value in allocating general corporate assets to those units. The principal exception to this is cash.

To summarize, we believe that the *preferred approach* for determining the investment base of a division is to use the *total assets under the control of the division plus a fixed ratio of sales for the cash requirements* of a division. Furthermore, property and equipment should be included at depreciated value. This approach has gained wide acceptance and is often called the "Du Pont method," referred to earlier. The various factors which influence the ROI in this method are shown by element in Exhibit 3. As the reader will note, this method places strong emphasis on volume of sales, control of costs and expenses, and on the maximum utilization of receivables, inventories, and net property, plant, and equipment (i.e., the elements divisional management are expected to control). By calculating and reviewing these ratios each month, management can determine the causes of a decline in the ROI and take corrective action, if possible.

Allocation of shared corporate expenses

Another major problem area in the use of ROI as a measurement of divisional performance is the allocation of the expense of corporate (shared) activities. Regardless of the degree of decentralization, there is almost certain to be some corporate headquarters group with accompanying expenses that must be shared by the divisions or subsidiaries of the company. As implied earlier in the chapter, in regard to the calculation of the divisional investment base there is no "best" way to handle headquarters expense.

EXHIBIT 3
Factors affecting return on investment ("Du Pont method")

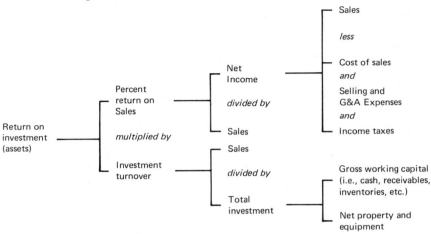

Whether the expenses are allocated based on the ratio of divisional sales to total company sales, property, or payroll, or a combination of all three (called the "Massachusetts formula" because it was first used by that state in taxation), or by some other method, the basis selected is purely arbitrary and will probably bear little relationship to the headquarters effort expended for a given division.

Nevertheless, we believe that all of the expense of the head-quarters activities and shared assets should be allocated to the divisions (or subsidiaries), on whatever basis is believed to be the most equitable in a particular company's circumstances. This will result in the divisions' (or subsidiaries') revenue-producing efforts being charged for all of the costs and expenses incurred in the production of revenue and the divisional ROI will be more comparable to the overall corporate rate.

Transfer price problem

We turn now to perhaps the most difficult problem in the accounting for divisions as profit centers—the "transfer price" problem. Of course, if the divisions of a company produce and sell non-complementary products and thus do not have dealings with one another, there is no "transfer price" problem. This may be true in widely diversified companies where the divisions (or subsidiaries) operate practically as separate entities and can be judged accordingly. In the majority of companies, however, there exist varying degrees of interdependency, in which case some basis must be established for pricing the goods and/or services which are transferred.

Ideally, the transfer price will be based on as much of an "arm's-length" basis as possible, so that the profits of the selling division and the costs of the acquiring division are reasonable. It may seem unimportant whether or not the price is reasonable since, on a corporate basis, costs are simply moving from "one pocket to another." Nevertheless, the effect of an unreasonable price is to cause a conflict of interest at the receiving division. Since the receiving (buying) division's profits and return on investment will be adversely affected by an unfair price, the division will, to the extent possible, tend to reduce its use of that product, or attempt to switch to another source of supply. If that source is outside the corporate group and the price is lower than the unfair price sought by the selling division (but higher than the cost of that division), on an overall corporate basis the company will experience lower profits even though the selling division is improving its profits. Furthermore, the selling division's capacity will be underutilized by the amount of production lost, which would adversely affect both that division's and the corporate profits. In short, that is the "transfer price" problem.

There are many methods employed to establish the transfer price, such as:

1. *Comparison with an independent, outside market price.* Obviously, if an established independent price for the product exists, it is an ideal basis for setting the price at which divisional transfers are made. That is the only price which we can safely say avoids any distortion in the use of return on investment as a measurement of a division's performance.
2. *Wholesale or retail price, less a stated discount.* Here again, the existence of an outside market price establishes an independent basis from which a reasonable discount can be negotiated by the divisions.
3. *Cost plus a negotiated markup* where no independent price is established. This method is much less desirable from the standpoint of measuring divisional return on investment, although

the reasonableness of the various divisions' costs will ultimately be determined by the overall profitability (or lack of same) of the corporate group. However, that doesn't preclude the possibility of the existence of an inefficient division whose inefficiencies are offset by other divisions within the group.

4. *Arbitrary prices set by corporate headquarters management.* This method is quite undesirable from the standpoint of measuring divisional return on investment since, in effect, the profitability of a division is determined by a central control group. In such cases it would seem more reasonable to evaluate the divisions as cost centers, that is, on the basis of their performance against a predetermined budget.

To summarize, in order to measure divisional performance effectively by the use of return on investment, the transfer price system must be established on as near an "arm's-length" basis as possible (assuming transfers between divisions occur). The further the pricing system varies from an "arm's-length" relationship, the less satisfactory the use of ROI will be as a measure of performance.

Residual income measurement base

One modification of the use of ROI as a measurement of divisional performance is called the "residual income" approach. This approach overcomes the conflict of interest often caused by requiring divisional management to maximize divisional ROI *and* corporate profits. Basically, residual income is defined as being the *net income earned in excess of the cost of capital required to earn any income.* Such income varies, of course, with the cost of capital, as is best illustrated by the following example:

	Division "Y"	*Division "Z"*
Investment base	$10,000	$15,000
Net income	2,500	3,000
Residual income when cost of capital is:		
6%	1,900	2,100
8%	1,700	1,800
10%	1,500	1,500
12%	1,300	1,200

As can be seen, the residual income approach reflects the greater effect of an increase in the cost of capital on a division that is more capital intensive than another division. The principal merit of this approach, however, is that it encourages divisional management to consider capital improvements, since they can increase their residual income by any investment that will yield a profit higher than the cost of capital. This would not be the case under a simple ROI approach. Thus, one of the big objections to the use of ROI to measure divisional performance can be overcome. Naturally, if divisional management has no voice in establishing their capital budget, then there isn't much point in employing the residual income variation of ROI.

Conclusion

Although the residual income variation can be used to overcome the tendency of divisional management to avoid new capital investment until the payback period is quite short, there is no entirely satisfactory approach to the resolution of the transfer price problem. In spite of the transfer price problem, the use of ROI as a measurement of divisional performance is preferred subject to the following conditions:

1. The divisional manager should also either hold an executive position at corporate headquarters or be represented by an executive who has the responsibility for several divisions with similar operations. In this capacity, the divisional manager or a representative should serve on one or more of the corporate operating committees and thus retain the overall company perspective.
2. The basic long-range planning for products and facilities should be under the general control of top management to alleviate the possible conflict of interest for the divisional manager.

SUMMARY

1. Every business is constantly being evaluated and judged. There are many bases for such an evaluation, such as the quality of the firm's product or service, the relationship of management with the employees, or the stature of the business in the community. However, if a business doesn't produce a satisfactory return to its owners over the long run, it will not be able to fulfill any of the other possible goals.

2. Earnings per share is an excellent general measure of performance because of its simplicity, but it lacks the overall measurement characteristics that return on investment has.

3. There are variations in the establishment of the base upon which a rate of return for a business can be calculated, but the use of stockholders' equity as the base is preferred. This, then, will result in a calculation which includes the three basic measurement factors:

   a. The return on sales (net profit margin).

   b. The asset turnover rate.

   c. The leverage factor.

4. The use of ROI on a segmental basis must be employed with caution, because the segments of a business are not truly independent entities. Moreover, the concept would not apply to segments operated as cost centers.

5. The segment's ROI generally cannot be based upon stockholders' equity. Instead, it should be based upon the assets for which the segment is held accountable by management, including any shared assets, such as cash, that management chooses to include.

6. Since there are variations in the calculation of ROI, it is essential that whichever method is used be applied on a consistent basis, so that the period results and trends of performance being measured are comparable.

7. Shared corporate expenses should be allocated to the segments on a consistent, reasonable basis.

8. The transfer price of goods or services "sold" among segments in a vertically integrated company can cause a problem because of the lack of a true "arm's-length" price.

9. The use of a residual income approach in the calculation of the income to be used in the ROI calculation for a segment encourages the segment's management to consider capital improvements on a timely basis and alleviates the tendency to maximize a segment's income by deferring such expenditures.

10. Managers of the segments should be represented at corporate headquarters in order to maintain the overall company view.

11. Properly understood and applied on a consistent basis, the rate of return on investment is a comprehensive, reasonable measurement of the performance of management, both at the corporate and divisional, or subsidiary, level.

Chapter 23

Business segment reporting

*Charles W. Plum**
Daniel W. Collins†

The issue of *segment reporting* has received considerable attention in the past decade due primarily to increased diversification of firms through internal development, mergers, and acquisitions. The growing complexity and diversity of many corporations has brought with it demands for increased financial disclosure. Investors, creditors, and security analysts have expressed concern that consolidated financial statements are of limited usefulness in assessing the future prospects of diversified firms. They argue that individual segments or areas of economic activity within a diversified company respond differently to changing economic conditions and have different rates of growth, profitability, and risk. Accordingly, to appraise properly the investment and credit worth of such a company requires some measure of each *segment's contribution* to the revenues and profits of the total enterprise.

Despite the seemingly overwhelming support for segment reporting voiced by the investment community, considerable resistance to such extended disclosure continues to exist. Opponents of segment reporting cite dysfunctional consequences for the firm and its shareholders, together with various implementation problems

---

* Vice President-Accounting and Management Systems, Standard Oil Company (Ohio).

† Associate Professor of Accounting, Michigan State University.

which, it is alleged, severely limit the reliability and usefulness of segment data.

The objective in this chapter is to identify the major implementation problems and the alternative solutions which have been proposed with respect to segment reporting. The sequence of events and developments with respect to segment disclosure is reviewed, and the conclusions and recommendations of studies sponsored by various professional organizations are summarized. The positions of accounting policy-making bodies including the Accounting Principles Board and its successor, the Financial Accounting Standards Board, are considered together with current rules and regulations as set forth by the Securities and Exchange Commission and the Federal Trade Commission. Finally, several current examples in annual shareholder reports and SEC 10-K filings are provided. This chapter provides an awareness of the many challenges that face the corporate accountant in this emerging, highly controversial area of financial reporting.

HISTORICAL PERSPECTIVE OF THE SEGMENT REPORTING ISSUE[1]

One of the first to suggest that diversified firms should report their operating results on a segmented basis was Professor Joel Dirlam of Rhode Island University. In testimony presented in 1965 before the Subcommittee on Anti-Trust and Monopoly of the Senate Committee on the Judiciary, Professor Dirlam asserted that disclosure of "the relative profitability of different divisions and product lines" was essential to antitrust authorities and to the average investor in making informed investment decisions.[2] Subsequently, the Subcommittee asked Chairman Manuel Cohen of the SEC to comment on the Dirlam proposal. Cohen responded with a detailed memorandum in which he set forth existing regulations of the SEC and pointed out some of the practical difficulties in implementing Dirlam's recommendations.[3] He further indicated that, due to those implementation difficulties, the Commission was re-

---

[1] The basis for much of this historical perspective comes from Alfred Rappaport and Eugene Lerner, *A Framework for Financial Reporting by Diversified Companies* (New York: National Association of Accountants, 1969), Appendix A.

[2] Hearings before the Subcommittee on Anti-Trust and Monopoly, Committee on the Judiciary, U.S. Senate, 89th Cong. 1st sess., p. 769.

[3] Ibid., pp. 1069–71.

luctant to require disclosure of profitability by segments at that time.

Nevertheless, the wheels had been set in motion, and within a year Cohen was urging the financial community to give serious consideration to potential "change(s) in financial reporting requirements to provide the kind of information needed to evaluate the experience and prospects of conglomerate companies."[4]

Potential SEC involvement in reporting requirements for diversified companies apparently prompted the Accounting Principles Board (APB) of the American Institute of Certified Public Accountants to issue *Statement No. 2* in September 1967 entitled "Disclosure of Supplemental Financial Information by Diversified Companies." The Board stated that "disclosure of financial data relating to separable industry activities of a diversified company has *not* been considered essential for fair presentation of financial position and results of operations in conformity with generally accepted accounting principles."[5] However, the Board noted the increasing trend towards segment disclosure and urged ". . . diversified companies to review their own circumstances carefully and objectively with a view toward disclosing voluntarily supplemental financial information as to industry segments of the business."[6] It should be noted that the Board refrained, at this time, from requiring any form of segment disclosure or from recommending any specific reporting guidelines.

Shortly after the APB issued its statement encouraging segment disclosure, a seminar on the subject of public reporting by conglomerates was convened at Tulane University. Representatives from the legal profession, investment community, SEC, management, public accounting profession, and academia were invited to discuss the various issues associated with segment disclosure.[7]

While there was general agreement among those participating in the conference that segment disclosure was needed, critical implementation problems were cited which tempered the enthusiasm

---

[4] Address before the Nineteenth Annual Conference of the Financial Analysts Federation, New York, May 24, 1966, p. 6.

[5] AICPA, "Disclosure of Supplemental Financial Information by Diversified Companies," *Statement of the Accounting Principles Board No. 2* (New York, September 1967), p. 1.

[6] Ibid., p. 4.

[7] Alfred Rappaport, Peter Firmin, and Stephen Zeff, *Public Reporting by Conglomerates: The Issues, the Problems, and Some Possible Solutions* (Englewood Cliffs, N.J.: Prentice-Hall, Inc., 1968).

for such reporting. One of the primary concerns was the basis used to segment the firm for reporting purposes. In addition, allocation of joint costs among segments and pricing of intersegment transfers were identified as particularly troublesome areas. As might be expected, there was considerable diversity of opinion among the participants as to the proper way to resolve these implementation issues. Several of the alternative solutions which were proposed are discussed in a subsequent section of this chapter.

THE FEI AND NAA STUDIES

Motivated by the SEC concern over the reporting practices of diversified companies, the Financial Executives Institute (FEI) and the National Association of Accountants (NAA) sponsored separate research studies on segment reporting.[8] Published in 1968, the objectives of these studies were very similar: (1) to evaluate the need and desirability of segment reporting by diversified companies; (2) to identify the kinds of segment financial information that can best serve the needs of creditors and investors; and (3) to ascertain the major limitations and inherent disadvantages of such reporting.

In both the NAA and FEI studies, comments with respect to these issues were sought from a broad cross section of professional financial analysts and corporate management.[9] In addition, commercial bankers were surveyed in the NAA study to ascertain the potential usefulness of segment data in making short- and long-run credit decisions. In the interest of brevity, the alternative methodologies employed in these studies are not discussed, nor are the many findings of each of these studies detailed. Rather, what follows is a compilation of the primary advantages and limitations of segment reporting, together with alternative proposals for dealing with the implementation issues which, collectively, were re-

---

[8] Robert K. Mautz, *Financial Reporting by Diversified Companies* (New York: Financial Executives Research Foundation, 1968); and Morton Backer and Walter B. MacFarland, *External Reporting for Segments of a Business* (New York: National Association of Accountants, 1968).

[9] In the NAA study, interviews were conducted with 72 financial analysts, 71 commercial bankers, and 70 executives from large industrial corporations. In the FEI study, 218 financial analysts responded to the investor questionnaire and 412 companies responded to the corporate questionnaire. Among the companies responding were 66 of the 100 largest industrial corporations listed in the "Fortune 500" and 26 of "Fortune's" 46 most diversified companies.

vealed through these two major surveys.[10] Where appropriate, salient points from other sources are included to supplement the discussion of the various issues and recommendations that arose from the FEI and NAA studies.

THE NEED FOR SEGMENT REPORTING

The results of both the NAA and FEI studies revealed that knowledge of segment operating results is considered by members of the investment community as being essential to making sound investment and credit decisions with respect to companies whose component activities differ significantly in rates of growth, profitability, and risk. Analysts and bankers indicated that one of the major factors in their assessment of the investment and credit worth of a company is its future earnings potential. There was general agreement that to judge the future earnings prospects of a diversified company, information descriptive of its various activities and share of the market on an industry-by-industry basis is needed. According to those analysts surveyed, knowledge of the economic outlook for each industry or market segment within a diversified company, together with historical relationships between segment sales and earnings contributions, would greatly enhance their ability to project future consolidated earnings.

In a more recent study conducted by the Financial Analysts Federation, some 270 professional analysts were asked to evaluate the usefulness of various financial disclosures, including segment revenue and profitability data. Nearly two thirds of the analysts surveyed indicated that segment data were used extensively in their evaluation of diversified companies and improved their earnings projections in at least some cases.[11] Moreover, recent empirical evidence presented in studies conducted by Kinney[12] and Collins[13] suggests that segment-based forecasts are significantly more accurate than consolidated-based forecasts of the future earnings of multibusiness firms.

---

[10] The reader is referred to the individual studies for details of the methodology and specific findings of each.

[11] Financial Analysts Federation, *Evaluation of Corporate Financial Reporting in Selected Industries for the Year 1971* (New York: Financial Analysts Federation, 1972).

[12] William R. Kinney, "Predicting Earnings: Entity versus Subentity Data," *Journal of Accounting Research*, Spring 1971, pp. 127–36.

[13] Daniel W. Collins, "Predicting Earnings with Sub-Entity Data: Some Further Evidence," forthcoming, *Journal of Accounting Research*.

In addition to providing a better basis for assessing the future earnings potential of diversified companies, analysts in the FEI and NAA studies alleged that information concerning the component activities of diversified companies is useful to an investor in seeking a desired balance in the investor's portfolio. Just as the company seeks to diversify its risk by producing several different products, the investor seeks to diversify his or her portfolio by holding securities from different industries or markets. Accordingly, without segment disclosure an investor may unknowingly maintain too large a commitment in a particular market or industry, or the investor may pass up investment opportunities that might otherwise improve the portfolio diversification.

Another component of the relative risk of a diversified company is measured by its response to changes in general economic activity. If the component activities of a diversified company are distributed broadly among both leading and lagging economic sectors, then it would be considered to have a low economic risk, whereas another company not diversified across economic sectors might have a high risk. Thus, it is argued that reporting the results of operations of diversified companies on a segmented basis enhances one's ability to assess the potential reaction of a firm to changes in general economic activity and, hence, the riskiness of the firm.

From the bank credit analyst's viewpoint, primary consideration is given to the financial strength of a company, particularly the source of funds for paying principal and interest on loan commitments. According to the bankers surveyed in the NAA study, segment data can provide creditors with a better basis for estimating the overall cash generating potential of the company by signaling out areas of weakness, such as unprofitable products or markets that absorb rather than produce funds.

These are but a few of the many reasons that investors and creditors cite in support of segment disclosure. However, producing the type of segment information they desire presents the corporate accountant with several difficult implementation problems.

CHOOSING A BASIS FOR SEGMENTING THE FIRM

A critical factor in producing segment information to satisfy the needs of investors and creditors is the basis used to segment the firm for external reporting purposes. Ideally, the reported segments of diversified companies should reflect areas of reasonably homogeneous economic activity within the firm, differentiated from one another in terms of growth, profitability, and risk. From a practical standpoint, however, this ideal has proven most difficult to achieve.

A frequently recommended basis for segmenting the operations of diversified companies is according to *product lines*. In general, a product line may be defined as a group of closely related goods or services. It was suggested by many in the FEI and NAA studies that segmentation by product lines would most likely differentiate areas of economic activity within the firm according to their prospects for growth, profitability, and risk. However, quite different results can be obtained depending upon how narrowly or broadly one defines a product line. Also, there is the question of how to classify new products and of what to do with an item that is sold individually, as well as being used as a component part of several other dissimilar products sold by the company.

One suggestion for achieving some degree of consistency across firms in product-line reporting is to identify products according to the *Standard Industrial Classification.*[14] This classification is prepared by the Technical Committee on Industrial Classification under the general supervision of the Office of Statistical Standards of the Bureau of the Budget, primarily for collecting and disseminating information concerning major industrial sectors within our economy. In addition to promoting some degree of consistency, some argue that segmentation according to SIC codes would provide investors with individual firm operating data that are reasonably compatible with various sources of both historical and projected industry data which are periodically reported by the U.S. Department of Commerce.[15] As Rappaport and Lerner note in a recent NAA study, compatibility of external data with the information released by the firm is of obvious importance to the shareholder or potential investor who is attempting to integrate the two sources of data to arrive at an estimate of the

[14] U.S. Executive Office of the President, Office of Management and Budget, *Standard Industrial Classification Manual* (Washington, D.C.: U.S. Government Printing Office, 1972).

[15] Among the sources of industry data collected and reported according to SIC code are the following: U.S. Department of Commerce, *U.S. Industrial Outlook,* Washington, D.C., U.S. Government Printing Office; U.S. Department of Commerce, *Industry Profiles 1958–1969,* Washington, D.C., U.S. Government Printing Office; U.S. Department of Commerce, *Current Industrial Reports,* Washington, D.C., U.S. Government Printing Office.

future earnings of the diversified company.[16] However, many have rejected this alternative on the grounds that it is unlikely that any single uniform classification of segments based on industry characteristics can in any way reduce unlike companies to comparable terms. Moreover, it was noted that internal accounting systems are typically designed to measure financial performance according to areas of managerial responsibility. Therefore, to require a diversified company to report according to a rigid industry classification would not only be very costly but might well result in financial statements not fully representative of the company's natural components.

Accordingly, several of those surveyed in the NAA and FEI studies suggested that diversified companies segment their operations for external reporting purposes along organizational lines or according to *areas of managerial responsibility*. A major argument in favor of this sort of divisional reporting is that such data would probably be available at little or no additional cost, since it would already be reported internally for control and planning purposes. Moreover, it is suggested that the way in which management organizes the activities of a diversified company would take into consideration the most significant distinctions within the company's operations and ignore those of little importance.

Although the way in which the company is organized may indicate significant distinctions within the firm from the standpoint of management, there are those who question whether the same distinctions will provide meaningful information for investment and credit decisions by outsiders. The following excerpt from the FEI study summarizes the major concern with respect to segmenting the operations of diversified companies along organizational lines for external reporting purposes.

> However well prepared the divisional reports may be, their usefulness to outsiders depends on the ease with which they can be understood by a reader unfamiliar with the technical and economic problems involved in the divisional operations and with the format and terminology of reports prepared primarily for a technically and financially sophisticated management. Although much can be done through careful selection and interpretive presentation to make data understandable, the basis on which the information is accumulated may provide fundamental difficulty.[17]

---

[16] Alfred Rappaport and Eugene Lerner, *Segment Reporting for Managers and Investors* (New York: National Association of Accountants, 1972), p. 10.

[17] Mautz, *Financial Reporting*, p. 47.

Markets served is yet another basis suggested by those surveyed in the FEI and NAA studies for segmenting the diversified firm for reporting purposes. Various methods have been proposed for identifying important market segments. For example, markets may be distinguished on a geographical basis, such as foreign versus domestic sales. Alternatively, markets could be defined in terms of the type of customer served. Here, an important distinction might be the proportion of sales and profits attributable to government contracts versus those made to private enterprises. Each of these bases of market segmentation could provide useful indications of the risk and potential for growth within the diversified company.

In summary, it should be obvious from this brief discussion that one of the most critical problems in segment disclosure is the determination of a basis for defining and reporting the varied activities of a diversified company. After considering the many alternative solutions to this problem, the FEI and NAA studies reached similar conclusions: namely, that there is no single basis which would be most appropriate in all circumstances and for all firms. Accordingly, it was recommended that a flexible approach be adopted, leaving the decision as to the most appropriate basis for segmenting the firm to the discretion of management, who is in the best position to separate the company into realistic and meaningful components for external reporting purposes.

MEASURING SEGMENT SALES AND THE TRANSFER PRICING PROBLEM

Once the basis of segmentation has been determined, the next logical step in the reporting process is the measurement of segment sales. Here the major issue centers around the treatment of intracompany transfers. When reporting on a consolidated basis, intracompany transactions are typically eliminated on the grounds that they lack the necessary degree of objectivity associated with an arm's-length transaction between unrelated parties. When the operations of a diversified company are broken down and reported on a segment basis, however, some persons contend that intersegment transfers should be included in segment sales. They argue that inclusion of intersegment transfers more realistically portrays the level of segment activity, and enhances the comparability of segments whose sales are primarily internal with segments that operate independently of the remainder of the company or have no significant intracompany transactions.

If intersegment transfers are included in reported segment sales, a second question concerns the most appropriate method of pricing such transfers. Several alternatives have been identified in practice that may be grouped into the following broad classifications: (1) *cost* or *cost plus markup;* (2) *market;* and (3) *negotiated price.*

Recording intersegment transfers at *full cost,* including overhead, possesses the virtues of being well understood and easy to apply. However, in terms of assessing the relative profitability of segments within a diversified company, some argue that it is of limited usefulness since it guarantees the selling affiliate recovery of its cost. Moreover, there is the problem of interfirm comparability since not all enterprises compute full cost in the same manner.

Under *full cost plus markup* the transfer price is established at an amount to provide for the recovery of all costs plus a "reasonable" return to the selling affiliate. This method is said to approximate a market value transfer price where reliable external market prices are not available. Those who support this method argue that it produces a segment sales figure which is comparable to that of segments selling only to parties outside the firm. The major shortcoming of this technique is that it allows the selling affiliate to report a profit that has not been realized through an arm's-length transaction. Moreover, some contend that it encourages "controlled earnings" through management manipulation of the level of intersegment transfers.

The basic notion underlying the use of *market price* is that transfers should be priced at whatever would be realized or paid in an arm's-length transaction occurring in the "open market," thus producing results as if the reporting segment were operated as an independent and distinct legal entity. It is argued that using the market price established in transactions between unrelated parties results in relatively objective revenue and profit figures and reduces the potential for management manipulation of reported segment operating results. However, the applicability of this method is severely limited by the absence of dependable market price quotations for many products. Also, like the cost-plus-markup method, using market prices to record intracompany transfers results in unrealized profit being included in segment sales.

In the event that market prices are not readily available, some persons suggest that intersegment transfers be priced at an *amount negotiated between the managers of the segments* involved in the transfer. Because each manager is assumed to be motivated by economic self-interest, the resultant negotiated price is felt to be more realistic than that obtained via an arbitrary cost-plus formula. Obviously, this technique will produce meaningful results only where the reporting segments within a company operate as independent profit centers, are charged with the responsibility of earning a reasonable return on investment, and are given the authority to make decisions which affect that return.

The major limitation of this technique is that the resultant prices may be so dependent upon the relative bargaining abilities of the segment managers involved that the results may not be meaningful. Moreover, it tends to divert the efforts of key personnel from promoting overall company welfare to those affecting the economic well-being of their own individual segments.

It should be obvious that each method of transfer pricing has certain advantages over the others, depending upon the attendant circumstances and the particular purpose to be served. Accordingly, no single transfer pricing scheme is likely to serve all possible situations equally well. Despite this fact, some have urged that a single method of pricing intersegment transfers should be established in order to enhance the comparability of segment information among enterprises. Furthermore, it is suggested that adoption of this approach would reduce the possibility of management manipulation of reported segment sales and income by selection of the most favorable transfer pricing method in the particular circumstances.

This proposal was rejected, however, in the FEI study. Based on the survey of analysts and management, it was concluded that the choice of the most appropriate method of pricing intracompany transfers should be left to the discretion of management. The justification for this conclusion is that management is intimately familiar with the nature and extent of segment operations, and therefore is in the best position to judge the relative merits of alternative transfer pricing methods. However, it was recommended that if the method of pricing intracompany transfers significantly affects the reported income contribution of the reporting components, the method used should be fully disclosed. Analysts indicated that intracompany transactions in excess of 10 percent of the reported transactions of a segment should be considered significant enough to warrant the indicated disclosure.[18]

THE PROBLEM OF COMMON COSTS

When disaggregating the activities of a diversified company for reporting purposes, certain costs are inevitably encountered that are common to two or more of the reporting segments. Examples of such costs might include various general and administrative expenses, institutional advertising, research and development costs, interest expense, pensions, and executive bonuses and other compensation. How to handle such costs presents a major dilemma in measuring segment profitability.

Common or *joint* costs may be allocated among the reporting segments in a variety of ways: for example, on the basis of sales or other gross revenue, assets employed, net income before joint costs, or on the basis of some other measure of benefits received. All of these procedures, however, are essentially arbitary. It is generally impossible to verify any of the assumptions upon which a particular allocation is based. Consequently, the best guides available for choosing among alternative allocation schemes are subjective tests of "equity" and "reasonableness." But an allocation method that may appear entirely equitable and reasonable for internal reporting purposes may, in fact, result in segment profitability figures that are misleading to outsiders who are not familiar with the underlying circumstances. This concern is reflected in the following comments made by corporate management surveyed in the FEI study.

> The public is not cognizant of how certain allocation decisions are made. . . . Without this awareness, false or misleading conclusions will be made.[19]

> Allocations of costs are at best matters of opinion and it is quite possible that the most conscientious of allocations might result in erroneous conclusions, re[garding] a particular division, that would not come about from full company reporting.[20]

---

[18] Ibid., p. 39.

[19] Ibid., p. 32.

[20] Ibid.

The cost accounting expense which would have to be incurred to develop an accurate statement of earnings by products or product lines would be prohibitive. Consequently, we adopt simple, practical rules for prorating these costs. These rules are under constant review and discussion and unless the reader of these results is aware of the numerous bases of allocation, the statement would be misleading.[21]

The fact that the alternative allocation schemes can have a substantial differential effect on reported segment profitability (and thus be potentially misleading to outside users) was forcefully demonstrated in a study by Mautz and Skousen.[22] They intensively investigated the allocation practices of six diversified companies representing a broad cross section of American industry. The companies studied had varying levels of common costs and followed significantly different methods in allocating these costs for purposes of reporting segment profitability. For each company they developed segment earnings figures under several alternative allocation schemes. Their analysis led them to the following conclusions:

1. The choice of the method to be used for allocating noninventoriable common costs may influence significantly the burden of charges among the several segments of a company.
2. The influence on segment net income of selecting one basis of allocating noninventoriable common costs rather than another may change the rank order of reported segment net income and the rank order of rates of return on investment by segment.

Because of the sensitivity of reported segment profits to the particular allocation basis chosen to apportion common costs, some of those surveyed in the FEI and NAA studies proposed that a single method of allocation should be required of all firms. In general, they argued that this approach would provide for comparability among enterprises and would reduce the potential of management manipulation of reported segment income via selection of the most favorable method of allocation in varying circumstances. However, Mautz rejected this proposal in the following terms:

[21] Ibid.
[22] Robert K. Mautz and K. Fred Skousen, "Common Cost Allocation in Diversified Companies," *Financial Executive*, June 1968, pp. 15–17, 19–25.

In view of the variety of industries and companies concerned with the common cost allocation problem, it appears unlikely that any such requirements could produce useful results in all cases.[23]

Similarly, in the NAA study, Backer and MacFarland concluded:

The problem raised by joint costs cannot be solved by establishing uniform allocation methods to be used by all companies because this would not avoid the arbitrary determination of costs which causes segment margin to be invalid as measures of segment contributions to company profit.[24]

As an alternative to arbitrarily allocating joint costs among segments, some have proposed that such costs be omitted from the determination of segment profitability.[25] Labeled the *"defined profit"* or *"contribution margin"* approach, this procedure calls for separating all costs into two groups: (1) those incurred solely by or for, or directly identified with, an individual segment (separable costs); and (2) those not directly attributable to individual segments (common or joint costs). Separable costs, which may vary considerably from firm to firm, are subtracted directly from segment sales, giving rise to a "defined profit" or "contribution margin." No attempt is made to assign the common costs to the various segments; rather, they are deducted from the total of the defined profits or contribution margins of all segments. An example of the reporting format under the contribution margin approach to segment reporting is presented in Exhibit 1.

In general, the reaction of security analysts and investment bankers to this type of segment profit disclosure seems to be quite favorable. For example, analysts surveyed in the NAA study had the following comments when asked to evaluate the contribution margin form of segment reporting:

This would be very valuable. It would throw light on companies and divisions with high operating leverages.[26]

Contribution margin reporting would provide a much more significant tool. If corporations reported line contribution margins,

---

[23] Robert K. Mautz, "Conglomerate Reporting and Data Reliability," *Financial Executive*, September 1967, p. 31.

[24] Backer and MacFarland, *External Reporting*, p. 23.

[25] See, for example, Mautz, *Financial Reporting*; Backer and MacFarland, *External Reporting*; and Rappaport and Lerner, *Segment Reporting*.

[26] Backer and MacFarland, *External Reporting*, p. 35.

EXHIBIT 1
Segment contributions to company profit* (000 omitted)

	Segment A	Segment B	Segment C	Totals
Sales	$300,000	$200,000	$500,000	$1,000,000
Separable segment costs:				
Materials, supplies, and services.				
Wages, salaries, employee benefits		(Details omitted)		
Insurance, property taxes				
Depreciation.				
Advertising and selling expenses.				
Totals	$245,000	$187,500	$407,500	$ 840,000
Segment contribution to corporate common costs and profit	$ 55,000	$ 12,500	$ 92,500	$ 160,000
Corporate common costs:				
Administration				
Research and development.		(Details omitted)		
Interest on borrowed funds				
Income tax				
Total				$ 80,000
Net Profit				$ 80,000

* Adapted from MacFarland, *Concepts for Management Accounting* (New York: National Association of Accountants, 1966), p. 69.

security analysts would be able to achieve a level of sophistication not now possible. . . .[27]

Similarly, bankers endorsed contribution margin reporting, as witnessed by the following representative comments:

> We certainly could do a better job of analysis with this type of income statement. It would facilitate the preparation of cash flow projections and permit more sophisticated analysis of the reasons for profit fluctuations.[28]

> Contribution margin reporting would greatly assist us in substantiating management's profit and cash flow forecasts. We use this type of data now, but it is largely derived by preparing rough statements based on information obtained in conversation with customers.[29]

[27] Ibid., p. 37.
[28] Ibid.
[29] Ibid.

The apparent enthusiasm on the part of investors and creditors for disclosing segment profitability on a *defined profit* or *contribution margin* basis was not shared by the majority of the corporate executives participating in the NAA study. One important question raised was whether the several categories of costs can be distinguished with sufficient clarity to warrant application of the contribution margin approach in external reporting. Also, management expressed concern that certain users, namely, regulatory agencies, legislators, and unions may misinterpret "defined profits" to be actual profits. There is a fear that this would trigger accusations that the firm was making unusually large profits, which would have numerous dysfunctional consequences for the firm and its shareholders.

Clearly, management is in the best position to weigh the relative advantages of the alternative ways of dealing with the common cost problem which has been briefly reviewed above. It would seem, however, that regardless of whether common costs are fully allocated or the contribution margin (defined profit) approach is used, the emphasis should be on *full disclosure* of the procedures used. In this way users can better evaluate the inherent limitations of the reported segment profit figures and avoid unwarranted interpretations.

OTHER ISSUES

In addition to the major problems discussed above, there are a number of other implementation issues which, although often relegated to a lesser role, are nevertheless important and must be resolved when preparing segmented reports. Space does not permit a discussion of each of these in detail. Therefore, some of these additional problem areas, together with a few of the proposed solutions, are identified briefly. A more complete discussion can be found in the sources referenced in the footnotes.

Judging the significance of a segment

Regardless of the basis used to segment a business, the corporate accountant is faced with a decision as to how significant the operations of a particular segment or area of economic activity should be before being given separate disclosure. Obviously, this problem breaks down into choosing an appropriate measure of economic activity and establishing a test measured in terms of this activity (either in percentage or dollar amounts) by which to relate the segment operations to the operations of the total enterprise. Since the accounting profession is currently considering the broader issue of materiality in financial reporting, hopefully some guidance will be available in the near future for resolving materiality questions in segment reporting.[30]

Currently, under the line-of-business reporting requirements of the SEC, a line of business is deemed significant if it accounts for 10 percent or more of the revenues or income before taxes and extraordinary items of the total entity. For companies with revenues of $50 million or less, the applicable percentage test is 15 percent rather than 10 percent.[31]

The 15 percent of gross revenue test was also recommended by Mautz in the FEI study.[32] However, he noted that where the gross revenue of a segment was significantly disproportionate to the amounts of income from, or assets employed in, the segment as compared to other components of the company, a more representative test using some other basis should be applied.

Treatment of income taxes

Because income taxes (local, state, federal, and foreign) are levied against the total enterprise and not against individual segments, some have proposed that taxes be treated as a corporate deduction and not allocated among segments. They argue that this treatment is most consistent with the underlying aspects of tax administration of a diversified company, in which tax credits and deductions arising from the operations of one segment may be used to offset the tax liability arising from the operations of another segment.

Rappaport and Lerner note, however, that since taxes are a major component of total corporate expenses (which also constitute a major use of funds), investors need and desire information

---

[30] Financial Accounting Standards Board, Discussion Memorandum, "An Analysis of Issues Related to Criteria for Determining Materiality" (Stamford, Conn., 1975).

[31] Securities and Exchange Commission, "Adoption of Amendments to Forms S-1, S-7, and 10-K," *Securities Exchange Act of 1934 Release No. 8650* (Washington, D.C.: U.S. Government Printing Office, July 14, 1969).

[32] Mautz, *Financial Reporting*, p. 158.

to differentiate those activities that attract special tax benefits from those that do not.[33] Accordingly, they believe that to the extent taxes are traceable to the operations of a specific segment they should be deducted in computing the earnings contribution of that segment.

If taxes are to be allocated to the segments, a question arises as to the treatment of a tax benefit resulting from the operating loss of a particular segment. Allocation of taxes is a complex area with the potential to significantly affect segmented earnings depending upon the method used. Among the reporting alternatives that have been proposed are the following:

1. Allocate the tax benefit on a pro rata basis to each segment which has taxable income.
2. Allocate the tax benefit entirely to the segment incurring the loss.
3. Do not allocate the tax benefit in the year of the loss but treat it as a deferred corporate item. Then in future years, if and when the segment that incurred the loss realizes taxable income, the tax benefit should be credited to the income of that segment. If the carryforward period expires before all of the deferred tax benefit is allocated to the loss segment, the unallocated loss would then be allocated to the other segments or treated as a corporate item.

Treatment of extraordinary items

Some controversy exists over whether segment income should be reported before or after extraordinary items. One argument for associating extraordinary items with individual segments is that it may provide useful insights into certain risks peculiar to a segment's particular industry. On the other hand, Rappaport and Lerner rationalize the opposite position in the following manner:

> Since extraordinary items by definition are not expected to recur frequently and since the investor wishes to use historical earnings growth rates as a basis for projecting future growth, it seems clear that an investor is better able to develop estimates if the earnings

---

[33] Alfred Rappaport and Eugene Lerner, *A Framework for Financial Reporting by Diversified Companies* (New York: National Association for Accountants, 1969), p. 32.

contribution of "basic activities" are calculated before extraordinary items.[34]

If extraordinary items are to be associated with individual segments, an additional question concerns whether extraordinary items should be judged from the standpoint of the total enterprise or from the perspective of each segment as an "autonomous entity." Taking the latter approach may necessitate a reclassification of an item for segment reporting purposes because it is material to the segment, but not from the standpoint of the total enterprise. Also, an item may be judged to be both unusual and infrequent when viewed from the perspective of the individual segment, and yet not meet these tests from the standpoint of the total enterprise. Many argue that to reclassify certain items as being extraordinary for segment reporting purposes can only lead to confusion on the part of the user. Accordingly, they suggest that the extraordinary nature of an item be judged from the standpoint of the total enterprise.

Treatment of investee earnings and minority interests

According to *APB Opinion No. 18,* "The Equity Method of Accounting for Investments in Common Stock," an investor company is required to use the equity method of accounting for all unconsolidated subsidiaries and for all investee corporations over which the investor exercises significant influence.[35] This raises a question of how to disclose investee earnings when reporting on a segment basis. Some argue that where the investment holdings can be directly identified with a segment, the reported earnings of that segment would be more meaningful if the proportionate equity in investee earnings were included. Others contend, however, that inclusion of investee earnings may distort the relationship between reported segment sales and profitability.

One approach to resolving this dilemma is to give separate disclosure to the amount of investee earnings included in the reported profits of a particular segment. Another approach employed by some companies is to include a proportionate share of investee sales in the reported sales of an individual segment, in addition to

---

[34] Ibid., p. 33.

[35] Paragraph 17 of *APB Opinion No. 18* states that an investor company is considered to exercise significant influence if it holds 20 percent or more (either directly or indirectly) of the voting stock of the investee.

its equity in the reported profits of the investee. The justification for this treatment is that it creates a more reasonable relationship between segment sales and segment income than would otherwise exist. Also, it is believed that inclusion of these amounts best portrays the level of segment operations.

The question of how to treat the *minority share* of subsidiary income when reporting the results of a consolidated entity on a segment basis presents problems similar to those discussed above. On the one hand, the argument is made that the minority share of income should be deducted from the segment's results of operations to which it is attributable in order to portray more meaningful segment earnings. Others contend, however, that the relationship between segment sales and earnings would be distorted if such minority interests were deducted without separate disclosure. One apparent way to resolve this issue is to show as a separate line item any minority interest deduction made in the computation of segment earnings.

OTHER SEGMENT DISCLOSURES

To this point attention has been focused on the income statement and the various problems associated with disclosure of segment revenue and profitability data. Members of the investment community have also expressed a need for segment *balance sheet data.* They argue that segment profitability figures may be misleading unless information concerning the asset base used in generating such profits is presented. In addition to providing a basis for computing return on investment, disclosure of segment asset data provides an indication of management's financial commitment to a particular area of economic activity. Such data are needed to assess a segment's ability to continue as a "going concern."

Segment information related to the *statement of changes in financial position* has also been strongly advocated. For example, Rappaport and Lerner argue that unless capital expenditures are segmented by areas of economic activity, it may be quite difficult for an investor to assess a firm's ability to sustain its present growth rate.[36] In addition, it is alleged that investors' concern over corporate liquidity necessitates the presentation of information as to which segments are *net sources of funds* and which are *net users.*

[36] Rappaport and Lerner, *Segment Reporting*, pp. 16–18.

The major problem encountered when attempting to present segment balance sheet data or segment information related to the statement of changes in financial position is the difficulty in identifying a major portion of the entity's assets and liabilities with individual segments. Some have proposed that only those assets and liabilities (and associated sources and uses of funds) which are *directly identifiable* with a particular segment should be disclosed. Others argue that such partial disclosure is inadequate and that an attempt should be made to allocate all of an entity's assets and liabilities to individual segments. However, any allocation would necessarily be arbitrary, and without adequate disclosure could be misleading to users. Clearly, the corporate accountant faces many challenges in attempting to satisfy the demands for segment balance sheet data and segment information related to the statement of changes in financial position.

REGULATORY REQUIREMENTS—SEC
LINE-OF-BUSINESS REPORTING

After considering the growing demand from the investment community for segment disclosure, together with the associated implementation problems which have been outlined above, the Securities and Exchange Commission (SEC) issued a proposal in September 1968 for extending the disclosure requirements of diversified companies. The line-of-business reporting guidelines were released in final form on July 14, 1969, effective for all registration statements filed on or after August 14, 1969.[37] In October 1970, these reporting requirements were extended to annual Form 10-K reports covering periods ending on or after December 31, 1970.[38] In a further move to increase the dissemination of segment information, the SEC proposed in January 1974 to amend its proxy rules to require such disclosures in annual reports sent to shareholders.[39] Subsequently, in

---

[37] Securities and Exchange Commission, *Securities Exchange Act of 1934 Release No. 8650.*

[38] Securities and Exchange Commission, "Adoption of Revised Form 10-K," *Securities Act of 1934 Release No. 9000* (Washington, D.C.: U.S. Government Printing Office, October 21, 1970).

[39] Securities and Exchange Commission, "Notice of Proposed Amendments to Rules 14-a and 14c-3 under the Securities Exchange Act of 1934 to Improve Disclosure in Annual Reports Furnished to Security Holders Pursuant to Those Rules, and to Improve Dissemination of Annual Reports to Security Holders and of Annual Reports on Form 10-K; and Adoption of Amendments to Item 7 of Schedule 14a under the Act," *Securities Exchange Act of 1934 Release No. 10591* (Washington, D.C.: U.S. Government Printing Office, January 10, 1974).

October 1974, the Commission adopted the proposed rules and, in addition, ruled that management must provide its shareholders with copies of the 10-K report upon request.[40]

The specific line-of-business disclosure requirements set forth by the SEC are as follows:

> If the registrant and its subsidiaries are engaged in more than one line of business, state, for each of the registrant's last five fiscal years, or for each fiscal year ending after December 31, 1966, or for each fiscal year the registrant has been engaged in business, whichever period is less, the approximate amount or percentage of (1) total sales and revenues, and (2) income (or loss) before income taxes and extraordinary items, attributable to each line of business which during either of the last two fiscal years accounted for:
>
> (A)   10 percent or more of the total sales and revenues
>
> (B)   10 percent or more of income before income taxes and extraordinary items computed without deduction of loss resulting from operations of any line of business, or
>
> (C)   a loss which equalled or exceeded 10 percent of the amount of income specified in (B) above
>
> However, if total sales and revenues did not exceed $50,000,000 during either of the last two fiscal years, the percentages specified in (A), (B) and (C) above shall be 15 percent, instead of 10 percent.
>
> If it is impracticable to state the contribution to income (or loss) before income taxes and extraordinary items for any line of business, state the contribution thereof to the results of operations most closely approaching such income, together with a brief explanation of the reasons why it is not practicable to state the contribution to such income or loss.

In addition to these line-of-business disclosures, the registrant is required to disclose:

1.   Revenues (in dollars or percentages) by class of similar products and services with the same materiality tests as for "line-of-business" information.

---

[40] Securities and Exchange Commission, "Notice of Adoption of Amendments to Rules 14-a, 14c-3, and 14c-7 under the Securities Exchange Act of 1934 ("Exchange Act") to Improve the Disclosure in, and the Dissemination of, Annual Reports to Security Holders and to Improve the Dissemination of Annual Reports on Form 10-K or 12-K Filed with the Commission under the Exchange Act," *Release 34-11079* (Washington, D.C.: U.S. Government Printing Office, October 31, 1974).

2. Information concerning the identity and importance of any single customer or group of customers on whose business the registrant is materially dependent.
3. Information about the nature, risks, and (if practicable) volume and relative profitability of foreign operations.

As an aid to the registrant in implementing these disclosure requirements, the SEC issued the following guidelines. It should be noted that in general these guidelines are quite broad and flexible, allowing management considerable discretion in dealing with the major implementation problems discussed earlier. However, emphasis is on full disclosure where the particular method of transfer pricing or common cost allocation significantly affects segment profitability.

1. If the number of lines of business for which information is required exceeds ten, the registrant may, at its option, furnish the required information only for the ten lines of business deemed most important to an understanding of the business. In such event, a statement to that effect shall be set forth.
2. In grouping products or services as lines of business, appropriate consideration shall be given to all relevant factors, including rates of profitability of operations, degrees of risk, and opportunity for growth. The basis for grouping such products or services and any material changes between periods in such groupings shall be briefly described.
3. Where material amounts of products or services are transferred from one line of business to another, the receiving and transferring lines may be considered a single line of business for the purpose of reporting the operating results thereof.
4. If the method of pricing intracompany transfers of products or services or the method of allocation of common or corporate costs materially affects the reported contribution to income of a line of business, such methods and any material changes between periods in such methods and the effect thereof shall be described briefly.

As an example of the type of segment disclosure presently being provided under the SEC line-of-business and product-line reporting guidelines, relevant portions of the 1974 10-K report of W. R. Grace & Company are presented in Appendix A at the end of the chapter.

REGULATORY REQUIREMENTS—FEDERAL
TRADE COMMISSION LINE-OF-BUSINESS
(LB) REPORTING

One of the more recent, and certainly one of the most contro-versial developments in the area of segment disclosure is the Federal Trade Commission's (FTC) Line-of-Business (LB) re-porting program. The first draft proposal of the LB report was developed in 1970 in an attempt to fulfill the FTC's obligation to collect and disseminate information on the financial performance and competitive conditions within various sectors of American busi-ness.[41] After major revisions, the LB report form and collection of data were approved for the 1973 and 1974 report years.

Under the LB program, the FTC intends to require, at most, the 500 largest manufacturing corporations (measured in terms of sales) to file annually with the FTC figures relating to assets, sales, profits, advertising expenses, other selling and promotional ex-penses, research and development costs, and intracompany transfers on some 219 manufacturing lines of business identified by three- and four-digit SIC codes.[42] The objective in specifying this rather rigid basis of segmentation is, allegedly, to achieve a degree of con-sistency and comparability among firms so that the data can be aggregated and reported in a meaningful way.

The FTC claims that the LB reports will enable them to guide better the efficient allocation of resources within our economy by providing investors with valuable information to consider in select-ing investment opportunities. In addition, they believe that the information generated from the LB reports will enable firms to judge better their own organization's performance against industrywide averages, and will permit the FTC to allocate its enforcement re-sources in the most effective manner.[43]

Despite the many advantages claimed by the FTC for its LB program, there has been, and continues to be, overwhelming resis-

---

[41] For a review of the developments in FTC Line-of-Business reporting see R. T. McNamar, "FTC Line-of-Business Reporting: Fact and Fiction," *Financial Executive*, August 1974, pp. 20–27.

[42] For report details see Federal Trade Commission, "Annual Line-of-Business Report Program" (Washington D.C.: U.S. Government Printing Office, 1974).

[43] For a complete discussion of the alleged advantages of LB reporting, see Bureau of Economics' Staff Report, "The FTC Line-of-Business Reporting Program" (Washington, D.C.: U.S. Government Printing Office, 1974).

tance from the industrial community. This resistance has even taken the route of court suits challenging both the FTC's authority to require the LB reports and the validity of the General Accounting Office's approval under the Administrative Procedures Act.[44] The main arguments of those who oppose the LB reporting are, among other things, that the LB program is conceptually unsound, that it will not provide meaningful aggregate data, that the confidentiality of individual company data is not assured, and that the burden of compliance far exceeds any benefits to be derived.

The experience of those companies which filed the LB report for 1973 data has confirmed the reporting difficulty and distortions that result when attempts are made to combine individual corporate accounting systems into standard statistical categories. Further, the shift of the FTC from an original objective to define "line of business" as product markets to a manufacturing industry concept, and now to a hybrid approach of either establishments, product lines, profit centers, or other organizational units, has proved the conclusions reached in the earlier studies of segment reporting; namely, that it is unlikely that any single uniform classification of segments based on industry characteristics could reduce unlike companies to comparable terms.

In summary, there appears to be substantial support for the collection and dissemination of data concerning the financial performance and competitive conditions of various industrial sectors within our economy. Whether the present LB reports can fill this need is certainly questionable. At present, all indications point to a long debate between the FTC and industry over this particular aspect of the segment disclosure issue.

FINANCIAL ACCOUNTING STANDARDS
BOARD AND SEGMENT DISCLOSURE

The positive action taken by the SEC and FTC in advancing the cause of segment disclosure has prompted the accounting profession to give serious consideration to establishing official reporting standards in this area. In April 1973 when the Financial Accounting Standards Board took over the policy-making duties of the Account-

---

[44] Shirley Scheibla, "Illegal Search and Seizure—Industry Has Balked at Disclosing Line-of-Business Data," *Barrons*, February 17, 1975, pp. 5, 17–18.

ing Principles Board, the subject of segment reporting by diversified companies was identified as one of seven original agenda items.

In May 1974 the FASB, with the counsel of a special Task Force, issued a Discussion Memorandum (DM) entitled, "Financial Reporting for Segments of a Business Enterprise." Eleven issues were identified and discussed in this neutral document. The first and primary issue identified in the DM is whether information about segments of a business enterprise should be included in financial statements. Assuming that this issue is decided in the affirmative, the remaining ten issues are concerned with identifying what segment information should be included and how it should be presented.

The written and verbal response to this DM was impressive. In total, 144 position papers were received from various interested parties. In addition, oral testimony was presented by 21 representatives from business, financial, and professional groups during the public hearings in August 1974. Although there was a diversity of opinion among those who responded to the DM, there seemed to be general agreement in the following areas:

1. Segment reporting provides useful information to investors.
2. Management should determine the segments that are to be reported.
3. The FASB should limit its statement to broad guidelines and should not establish detailed rules for identifying segments to be reported.[45]

After careful evaluation of the many recommendations received in response to the DM, the FASB issued a proposed statement of financial accounting standards on September 30, 1975, entitled "Financial Reporting for Segments of a Business Enterprise." In this exposure draft, the Board expressed its belief that segment disclosure is needed to "permit a better appraisal of the enterprise's past performance and future risks and prospects."[46] To accomplish this objective the Board proposed that annual or interim financial statements prepared in accordance with generally accepted accounting principles should include segmented data relating to (1)

---

[45] "Business Segment Reports Recommended by Institute," news report section, *Journal of Accountancy,* September 1974.

[46] Financial Accounting Standards Board, Proposed Statement of Financial Accounting Standards, "Financial Reporting for Segments of a Business Enterprise" (Stamford, Conn., September 30, 1975), par. 5.

an enterprise's operations in different industries, (2) its foreign operations, (3) its major customers, and (4) its export sales.

In proposing disclosure of enterprise operations in different industries, the Board left to management's judgment the selection of an appropriate basis of segmenting the firm for external reporting purposes. However, the Board did suggest that an enterprise's existing profit centers (areas of activity within the firm for which revenue and expense information is accumulated for internal planning and control purposes) could be used as a logical starting point for determining reportable industry segments. The Standard Industrial Classification (SIC) and Enterprise Standard Industrial Classification (ESIC) were also suggested as systems that may be helpful in grouping an enterprise's products and services by industry lines. However, the Board cautioned against relying totally on these classification systems. The nature of the product, production process, markets, and marketing methods were cited as important factors that should be considered in determining whether products or services are related or unrelated.

For each reportable industry segment, the Board proposed the following disclosures:

1. *Total revenue* with separate disclosure of sales of goods and services to both unaffiliated customers and to other segments within the enterprise. The Board did *not* suggest any single method of pricing intersegment sales, but rather proposed that transfers of goods and services should be accounted for at amounts which would allow for a realistic determination of a reportable segment's profit or loss contribution and operating profit or loss (see below).

2. *Profit or loss contribution* determined by subtracting directly traceable costs and expenses (those costs incurred directly by or for or are otherwise directly identifiable with the industry segment) from industry segment revenue. The Board specifically stated that the following items should be *excluded* in determining the profit and loss contribution of each reportable segment: operating costs and expenses not directly traceable to it; revenue earned and general and administrative expenses incurred at the enterprise's central administrative office; interest expense; domestic and foreign income taxes; gain or loss on discontinued operations; extraordinary items; minority interest; and the cumulative effect of a change in accounting principle

as per *APB Opinion No. 20.* Income from investments in common stock accounted for by the equity method are to be included in computing the profit or loss contribution of an industry segment only if the investee is in the same industry as the segment.

3. *Operating profit and loss* which is to be determined by subtracting from a segment's profit and loss contribution those costs not directly traceable to it, but which can be allocated to that segment on a reasonable basis. Again, the Board left the determination of a "reasonable allocation basis" to the discretion of management. With the exception of these allocable costs, those items specifically excluded in determining a segment's profit and loss contribution (listed in the previous paragraph) are also to be excluded in determining a segment's operating profit or loss.

4. *Identifiable assets* which are defined as those tangible and intangible assets that are used by or are directly associable with the industry segment. Such assets are to include those used exclusively by that industry segment and an appropriate portion of assets whose use is shared with other industry segments if there is a reasonable basis for allocating such usage among segments.

An example of the proposed disclosure by industry segments is presented in Exhibit 2.

The Board proposed that disclosure similar to that presented in Exhibit 2 should be provided for each industry segment that is "significant" to the enterprise as a whole. To be deemed "significant" one or more of the following tests must be met:

(a) The industry segment's revenue is 10 percent or more of the combined revenue of all of the enterprise's industry segments.

(b) The industry segment's operating profit or operating loss is 10 percent or more of the greater, in absolute amount, of:
   (1) The combined operating profit of all industry segments that did not incur a loss, or
   (2) The combined operating loss of all industry segments that did incur a loss.

(c) The industry segment's identifiable assets are 10 percent or more of the combined identifiable assets of all industry segments.[47]

---
[47] Ibid., par. 18.

EXHIBIT 2

X COMPANY
Information about the Company's Operations in
Different Industries
Year Ended December 31, 1976

	Industry A	Industry B	Industry C	Other	Elimi-nations	Consoli-dated
Sales to unaffiliated customers	$1,000	$2,000	$1,500	$ 200		$ 4,700
Intersegment sales.	200		500		$(700)	
Total revenue	$1,200	$2,000	$2,000	$ 200	$(700)	$ 4,700
Directly traceable costs and expenses	(800)	(1,560)	(1,200)	(100)	660	(3,000)
Equity in net income of Z Co. (25% owned)	100					100
Profit contribution.	$ 500	$ 440	$ 800	$ 100	$ (40)	$ 1,800
Allocated operating costs and expenses	(200)	(150)	(200)	(50)		(600)
Operating profit	$ 300	$ 290	$ 600	$ 50	$ (40)	$ 1,200
Expenses of central administrative office.	(20)	(40)	(30)	(10)		(100)
Interest expense.	(30)	(50)	(100)	(20)		(200)
Income from continuing opera-tions before income taxes.	$ 250	$ 200	$ 470	$ 20	$ (40)	$ 900
Income taxes	(110)	(70)	(230)	(10)	20	(400)
Income from continuing operations.	$ 140	$ 130	$ 240	$ 10	(20)	500
Loss on discontinued operations		(200)				(200)
Income (loss) before extraor-dinary gain and before cumulative effect of change in accounting principle	$ 140	$ (70)	$ 240	$ 10	$ (20)	$ 300
Extraordinary gain	90					90
Cumulative effect on prior years of change from straight line to acceler-ated depreciation	(30)	(10)	(20)			(60)
Net income (loss)	$ 200	$ (80)	$ 220	$ 10	$ (20)	$ 330
Identifiable assets at December 31, 1976	$2,400	$4,050	$6,000	$1,000	$ (50)	$13,400
Assets employed at the Company's central administrative office.						$ 1,600
Total Assets at December 31, 1976.						$15,000

Source: Appendix E, FASB Proposed Statement of Financial Accounting Standards, "Financial Reporting for Segments of a Business Enterprise."

In addition to these materiality guidelines, the reportable industry segment information must meet an aggregate test. Specifically, the Board proposed that at least 75 percent of the sales to unaffiliated customers of all industry segments must be represented by the defined reportable industry segments. If the aggregated defined reportable segments do not meet this test, then the Board proposes that additional reportable segments should be identified until the 75 percent test is met.

In addition to the proposed disclosures for industry segments, the exposure draft calls for disclosure of revenues, profit or loss contribution, operating profit or loss, and identifiable assets for an enterprise's foreign operations in the aggregate and for its domestic operations. Moreover, significant revenue derived from export sales to unaffiliated foreign customers is to be disclosed. Finally, individual customers on whose business the enterprise or any reportable industry segment depends significantly are to be identified.

In summary, if the proposals set forth in this FASB exposure draft are adopted, much more information from a great many more companies will be presented than is presently called for under the existing requirements which were reviewed earlier. Exhibit 3 provides a summary comparison of the proposed FASB requirements with existing SEC and FTC requirements.

SUMMARY AND CONCLUSIONS

Few areas of financial reporting have attracted the attention given to the issue of segment disclosure by diversified companies. The demands from the financial community together with growing government involvement in the area have greatly increased the extent of segment disclosure in the past decade. As an indication of the dramatic growth and importance of this area of financial reporting, Table 1 presents a summary of segment disclosure practices among 600 companies surveyed annually by the AICPA and reported in *Accounting Trends and Techniques*.

The demands for segmental disclosure present several very real and difficult problems of implementation. In this chapter the major problems have been identified together with some of the alternative solutions proposed by investors, management, various professional organizations, regulatory agencies, and the public accounting profession. In summary, it appears that the resolution of such problems as transfer pricing, joint cost allocation, and segmentation of the firm are best left to the discretion of management, with the help of the corporate accountant. These parties are in the best position to choose among those alternatives which will result in a realistic and meaningful portrayal of segment operations within their firm.

EXHIBIT 3

Comparison of FASB, SEC, and FTC segment reporting requirements

The SEC has had its present line-of-business reporting regulations in effect since 1969. In 1974 the Federal Trade Commission imposed limited line-of-business reporting for fiscal years ended prior to July 31, 1974, and extended its requirement in 1975. A comparison of the requirements of these authorities with the FASB proposal follows:

	Line-of-business/segment reporting programs		
Requirements	*FASB*	*SEC*	*FTC*
Does the program apply to all companies issuing financial statements based upon GAAP?	Yes (for all profit-seeking companies)	No (registrants only)	No (selected manufacturing companies only)
Are worldwide operations to be reported?	Yes	Yes	No (domestic activities only)
Is there a formal list of categories which must be used in developing industry segments?	No* (SIC codes mentioned)	No*	Yes–SIC codes
How often must the information be reported?	Included in any GAAP financial statements	Annually	As ordered
Test to determine if a segment is significant and reportable?	Essentially 10% of enterprise revenues, or identifiable assets, or profits	Segment equals 10% or more of consolidated revenues†	Segment revenues over $10 million
Is the following information required by segment:			
Operating revenues?	Yes	Yes	Yes
Operating expenses?	Yes	Yes	Yes
Allocation of indirect expenses?	Some	No	Yes
Assets?	Yes	No	Yes
Is information required on a geographic basis as well as industry segmentation?	Yes	No	No
Are major customers disclosed?	Yes	Yes	No
Are export sales disclosed?	Yes	No	No

* The existing SEC guidelines for determining a segment appear to permit much wider latitude for management judgment than those proposed by the FASB.

† Fifteen percent for companies with less than $50 million in sales.

Source: Reprinted from Financial Reporting Developments Series file retrieval No. 38396 with permission of Ernst & Ernst.

In Appendix B at the end of the chapter, portions of several recent annual reports are provided in an attempt to demonstrate the variety of segment reporting formats and to illustrate how diversified companies are coping with the problems of segmentation, common cost allocation, and transfer pricing. These examples, together with the previous discussion, should provide corporate accountants with a brief background and awareness of the many challenges which they face in this very important area of financial disclosure.

TABLE 1

Summary of segment disclosure practices among 600 companies surveyed annually in *Accounting Trends and Techniques**

Presentation of Revenue Information							
Information presented	*1973*	*1972*	*1971*	*1970*	*1969*	*1968*	*1967*
By product line	250	218	176	162	152	140⎫	154
By division or subsidiary	130	140	144	139	117	65⎭	
Total foreign sales.	119	115	139	116	103	53	NA
Sales to government	38	33	44	53	61	35	NA
Sales to particular industry or type of customer.	44	45	29	54	58	46	NA
By geographic areas.	27	30	20	17	19	32	NA
Total Presentations	608	581	552	541	510	371	NA
Number of companies:							
Revenue information presented.	384	382	358	335	319	264	NA
Revenue information not presented	216	218	242	265	281	336	NA
Total.	600	600	600	600	600	600	600

Presentation of Income Information							
Information presented	*1973*	*1972*	*1971*	*1970*	*1969*	*1968*	*1967*
By product line	149	114	83	59	30	27⎫	93
By division or subsidiary	91	98	88	70	53	26⎭	
Total foreign income	79	71	97	96	87	37	NA
Income attributable to business with government, particular industry, or type of customer.	20	19	13	17	12	3	NA
By geographical areas.	11	16	12	16	12	13	NA
Subtotal	350	318	293	258	194	106	NA
Separate financial statements or summaries for subsidiaries or groups of subsidiaries. .	58	68	65	79	65	44	41
Segment of reporting entity operating at a loss	13	28	14	55	50	20	18
Total Presentations	421	414	372	392	309	170	NA
Number of companies:							
Income information presented	280	281	280	270	225	131	NA
Income information not presented	320	319	320	330	375	469	NA
Total.	600	600	600	600	600	600	600

* AICPA, *Accounting Trends and Techniques* (New York, 1970–73).
NA = not available.

APPENDIX A

Line-of-business disclosure

W. R. GRACE COMPANY

1974 10-K Report

Lines of Business and Classes of Services (in millions of dollars restated for poolings of interests and changes in accounting principles)

The following table gives the consolidated sales and operating revenues of the Company and its subsidiaries for each line of business for the five years ended December 31, 1974.

CONSOLIDATED SALES AND OPERATING REVENUES

	1970	1971	1972	1973	1974	1970	1971	1972	1973	1974
Chemical										
Industrial & Specialty	$ 479	$ 518	$ 591	$ 700	$ 908	25%	25%	25%	25%	26%
Packaging & Plastics	195	212	242	290	347	10	10	10	10	10
Agricultural	272	266	283	363	504	15	13	12	13	15
Total Chemical ...	946	996	1,116	1,353	1,759	50	48	47	48	51
Natural Resources	84	73	77	79	145	4	4	3	3	4
Consumer										
Fashion & Leisure	289	329	390	447	467	15	16	17	16	13
Consumer Services	151	197	261	369	449	8	10	11	13	13
Packaged Foods	445	457	518	585	652	23	22	22	20	19
Total Consumer ..	885	983	1,169	1,401	1,568	46	48	50	49	45
Total(1)	$1,915	$2,052	$2,362	$2,833	$3,472	100%	100%	100%	100%	100%
Foreign (non-U.S.)										
Operations Included Above	$ 771	$ 726	$ 818	$1,038	$1,306	40%	35%	35%	37%	38%

(1) Does not include sales and operating revenues of Peruvian and other Latin American operations divested as follows: 1970—$141; 1971—$41; 1972—$6; 1973—$2.

The following table gives the consolidated operating income after taxes of the Company and its subsidiaries for each line of business, computed before extraordinary items and allocation of general corporate overhead and general corporate interest (as these expenses are attributable to all lines of business and cannot reasonably be allocated to specific lines), for the five years ended December 31, 1974. For this table, taxes are computed substantially on a separate return basis for each subsidiary and each division of the Company. In the case of each U. S. subsidiary and division, benefits for all generated investment tax credits and operating losses, if any, are recognized currently.

CONSOLIDATED OPERATING INCOME AFTER TAXES

	1970	1971	1972	1973	1974	1970	1971	1972	1973	1974
Chemical										
Industrial & Specialty	$26.8	$29.2	$37.9	$ 47.1	$ 55.4(1)	39%	43%	43%	39%	28%
Packaging & Plastics	6.6	6.3	10.1	15.8	25.9(1)	10	9	12	13	13
Agricultural	6.9	7.6	13.6	27.4	87.6	10	11	15	23	45
Total Chemical ...	40.3	43.1	61.6	90.3	168.9(2)	59	63	70	75	86
Natural Resources	6.2	1.6	2.3	5.4	11.4	9	3	3	5	6
Consumer										
Fashion & Leisure	10.2	8.7	9.4	9.9	10.4	15	13	11	8	5
Consumer Services	4.6	6.8	8.6	11.8	8.6	7	10	9	10	4
Packaged Foods	6.8	7.9	6.2	3.0	(1.6)	10	11	7	2	(1)
Total Consumer ..	21.6	23.4	24.2	24.7	17.4	32	34	27	20	8
Total	$68.1	$68.1	$88.1	$120.4	$197.7	100%	100%	100%	100%	100%
Foreign (non-U.S.)										
Operations Included Above	$27.9	$26.8	$29.0	$ 43.8	$ 54.2	41%	39%	33%	36%	27%

(1) Before deducting $7.4 for Industrial & Speciality and $3.9 for Packaging & Plastics representing provisions recorded in 1974 for settlement of litigation and certain foreign tax matters relating to prior periods.

(2) After a reduction of $14.0 resulting from the adoption of the last-in, first-out method of inventory valuation for substantially all chemical operations in the United States.

6

APPENDIX B

Examples of segment disclosure in annual reports issued to shareholders

STANDARD BRANDS

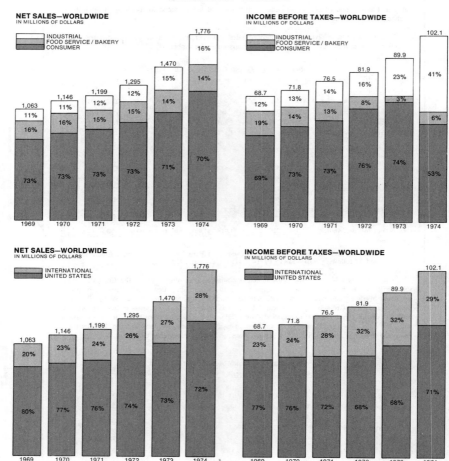

NET SALES—WORLDWIDE
IN MILLIONS OF DOLLARS

INDUSTRIAL
FOOD SERVICE / BAKERY
CONSUMER

INCOME BEFORE TAXES—WORLDWIDE
IN MILLIONS OF DOLLARS

INDUSTRIAL
FOOD SERVICE / BAKERY
CONSUMER

NET SALES—WORLDWIDE
IN MILLIONS OF DOLLARS

INTERNATIONAL
UNITED STATES

INCOME BEFORE TAXES—WORLDWIDE
IN MILLIONS OF DOLLARS

INTERNATIONAL
UNITED STATES

CLARK EQUIPMENT COMPANY

Clark is a highly integrated manufacturer and a distributor of capital goods. More than 90% of Clark's present business is axles, transmissions and related components, material handling equipment and construction machinery. Approximately one-half of Clark's output of axles, transmissions and related components is transferred to other product plants and used in the production primarily of material handling equipment and construction machinery, where it is estimated that such axles, transmissions and components represent between 20% and 30% of manufacturing costs. The rental of its products and the sale of replacement parts are important phases of Clark's operations. Sales to the United States Government in 1974 accounted for less than 2% of Clark's sales.

The following table sets forth sales and income before income taxes by lines of business for the five years ended December 31, 1974 (amounts in millions of dollars):

	1974		1973		1972		1971		1970	
	Amount	%	Amount	%	Amount	%	Amount	%	Amount	%
Sales:										
Axles and transmissions	$ 222.0	16	$ 169.3	15	$135.3	15	$111.0	15	$108.0	16
Material handling equipment	480.3	35	409.7	36	321.5	36	273.0	37	280.9	42
Construction machinery	506.2	37	389.9	35	299.6	33	241.8	32	181.3	27
Truck trailers **	81.2	6	87.7	8	76.0	8	57.7	8	51.2	8
Refrigeration and food service equipment	80.8	6	71.2	6	68.7	8	58.7	8	49.6	7
Total net sales	$1,370.5	100	$1,127.8	100	$901.1	100	$742.2	100	$671.0	100
Income before income taxes:										
Axles and transmissions	$ 16.3*	20	$ 19.7	21	$ 9.9	14	$ 7.6	14	$ 9.0	13
Material handling equipment	30.3*	38	55.9	59	43.3	62	33.9	62	40.2	60
Construction machinery	24.1*	30	17.4	18	13.2	19	10.6	20	19.1	29
Truck trailers**	(1.9)*	(2)	1.3	1	.2	—	(1.0)	(2)	(.9)	(1)
Refrigeration and food service equipment	2.5*	3	.4	—	3.2	5	3.3	6	2.9	4
Other	8.4	11	1.3	1	.6	—	(.3)	—	(3.4)	(5)
Total income before income taxes........	$ 79.7	100	$ 96.0	100	$ 70.4	100	$ 54.1	100	$ 66.9	100

* Income before income taxes reflects a change in 1974 to the Lifo method of valuing domestic inventories. See discussion on page 8.

** In November 1974, Clark began to implement a plan to withdraw entirely from the truck trailer business. See discussion on page 8.

Clark has numerous competitors in all its lines of business. Axle and transmission sales and income shown in the table relate to outside customers only and sales and income of such components produced for Clark end products are included in material handling equipment and construction machinery. Corporate general and administrative expenses and interest expense are allocated to lines of business on a consistent basis for the years shown.

Clark's organizational structure has been changing over the last five years and today its operations are organized on a product line basis world-wide. These operations are described in the operations review section on pages 24 to 36. Because of significant inter-company transactions involved in sales of products overseas, it is not practicable to determine precisely the share of consolidated net income attributable to sources outside the United States.

Clark Equipment Credit Corporation, a wholly-owned, non-consolidated domestic subsidiary of Clark, finances retail time sales of new Clark products to ultimate consumers through Clark's independent dealers and retail branches, sales at wholesale to dealers and retail branches, and rental fleets held by dealers and branches. Clark Credit also finances some export sales and some used products. Wholly-owned manufacturing subsidiaries of Clark in West Germany, England, France, Canada and Australia have subsidiaries which assist in the financing of the sales of its manufacturing subsidiaries. These non-U.S. finance subsidiaries are combined with Clark Credit for administration and reporting purposes.

REVLON

Management Review
Years ended December 31, 1974 and 1973

Sales

Sales for 1974 were a record $605,937,000 representing a 19.7% increase over $506,085,000 in 1973. Comparative sales for each of the quarters were:

	1974	1973	% Increase
	(000's omitted)		
First	$127,000	$110,000	15.5
Second	138,000	116,000	19.0
Third	148,000	122,000	21.3
Fourth	192,937	158,085	22.0
	$605,937	$506,085	19.7

Sales and Operating Profit

Sales and operating profit (which excludes interest expense, other deductions—net, and the provision for taxes on income) for 1974 and 1973 were as follows:

1974 Division	Sales	Operating Profit	Operating Profit Margin
	(000's omitted)		
Cosmetics—			
United States	$282,627	$41,683	14.7%
International	169,414	24,316	14.4
Pharmaceuticals—			
United States	56,260	15,151	26.9
International	47,125	5,665	12.0
Health Services	23,190	5,086	21.9
Proprietary Drug and Toiletries	27,321	3,655	13.4
	$605,937	$95,556	15.8%

1973 Division	Sales	Operating Profit	Operating Profit Margin
	(000's omitted)		
Cosmetics—			
United States	$230,610	$34,265	14.9%
International	140,818	22,978	16.3
Pharmaceuticals—			
United States	52,181	13,954	26.7
International	41,187	6,310	15.3
Health Services	16,708	2,460	14.7
Proprietary Drug and Toiletries	24,581	2,650	10.8
	$506,085	$82,617	16.3%

The following table provides a percentage breakdown of sales and operating profit between beauty and health products:

Sales	1974	1973	1972	1971	1970
Beauty products	78	77	75	74	77
Health products	22	23	25	26	23

Operating Profit	1974	1973	1972	1971	1970
Beauty products	73	72	68	58	61
Health products	27	28	32	42	39

Sales by Major Market Area

Sales on a geographic basis in 1974 and 1973 were as follows:

	1974	1973	% Increase
	(000's omitted)		
North America	$420,276	$345,935	21.5
Europe	90,321	78,117	15.6
Africa, Asia, Australia and Far East	68,186	57,228	19.1
Latin America and all other	27,154	24,805	9.5
Total	$605,937	$506,085	19.7

Earnings

Earnings before taxes, net earnings and earnings per share for 1974 were records for the Company. Comparisons with 1973 on a quarterly basis are:

Earnings Before Taxes	1974	1973	% Increase
	(000's omitted)		
First	$20,000	$17,200	16.3
Second	23,500	20,300	15.8
Third	20,600	18,100	13.8
Fourth	26,557	23,149	14.7
	$90,657	$78,749	15.1

Net Earnings	1974	1973	% Increase
	(000's omitted)		
First	$10,800	$ 9,300	16.1
Second	13,000	11,200	16.1
Third	11,700	10,300	13.6
Fourth	14,304	12,642	13.1
	$49,804	$43,442	14.6

Earnings Per Share	1974	1973	% Increase
First	$ .82	$ .71	15.5
Second	.98	.85	15.3
Third	.88	.78	12.8
Fourth	1.08	.96	12.5
	$3.76	$3.30	13.9

WALTER KIDDE & COMPANY, INC.

Product Line Results, 1973 and 1974

	Net Sales (thousands)		Operating Profit* (thousands)	
	1974	1973	**1974**	1973
Safety, security and protection				
Fire and intrusion protection equipment	**$ 151,448**	$116,192	**$ 14,469**	$ 3,948
Bank security equipment and locks	**115,319**	100,092	**12,982†**	11,799
Testing and engineering equipment and services	**69,943**	63,029	**5,749**	5,308
Security guard services	**50,696**	50,609	**3,649**	3,714
	$ 387,406	$329,922	**$ 36,849**	$24,769
Consumer and commercial products				
Consumer durable products	**$ 284,404**	$281,145	**$ 21,441†**	$37,785
Commercial fixtures and products	**44,215**	44,290	**1,794†**	2,441
	$ 328,619	$325,435	**$ 23,235**	$40,226
Industrial equipment				
Hydraulic cranes and materials handling equipment	**$ 251,319**	$179,209	**$ 27,452†**	$22,296
Automotive and truck components	**69,328**	74,530	**8,065†**	8,167
Aircraft equipment	**43,346**	40,607	**1,655**	1,435
Office supplies and equipment	**22,126**	17,493	**2,717**	1,434
	$ 386,119	$311,839	**$ 39,889**	$33,332
Total continuing operations	**$1,102,144**	$967,196	**$ 99,973†**	$98,327
Discontinued operations	**5,023**	10,592	**100**	678
Total operations	**$1,107,167**	$977,788	**$100,073†**	$99,005

*Operating profit is determined before general and administrative expenses common to all divisions, interest, taxes on income and other nonoperating items.

†1974 results were reduced for a change to the LIFO method of accounting for inventories. See note to consolidated financial statements on page 29.

DAYCO CORPORATION

Dayco's divisions and subsidiaries are organized into four product groups.
The 1974 sales and profits* are indicated by each group's contribution.

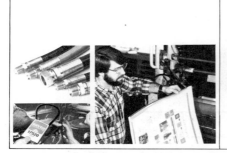

Dayco Rubber Products Co.
is the world's largest manufacturer of V-belts for industrial applications. It also produces hydraulic and industrial hose, fittings and power transmission flexible couplings for all industries. Manufacturers of agricultural equipment and other heavy-duty off-the-road vehicles are major customers of the division. Other industries using its products are appliance, chemical, construction, lawn and garden, petroleum, mining, and railroad.
J. O. Quamme, *President*
J. T. Dempsey, *V.P.*
D. E. Ross, *V.P.*

Dayco Automotive Aftermarket Co.
manufactures and markets automotive products including V-belts, hose clamps and radiator and heater hose. It also services the fleet and heavy-duty markets with a full-range of belts and hose. All products are sold through automotive wholesalers, mass merchandising outlets and major oil companies.
U. H. Bauske, *President*
K. Mitchell, *V.P.*

Flexible Metal Hose Manufacturing Co.
specializes in the manufacture of engineered products conveying high pressure gasses and corrosive

Cadillac Plastic & Chemical Co.
is the world's largest manufacturer/distributor of plastic sheets, rods, tubes and film, as well as the largest distributor of safety products in the United States. Its OSHA-SPEC trademarked safety products are marketed through service centers located in major metropolitan areas.
W. D. Benkelman, *President*
G. C. Barber, *Executive V.P.*

Plastics Div.
(Dayflex Co.)
manufactures engineered flexible plastic hoses for appliance, industrial, construction, marine, mining and medical applications. The division also manufactures ventilating hose for commercial and residential use and engineered products for the meat processing industry.
P. J. Neroni, *President*
D. L. Kleykamp, *Sales Manager*

Allen Industries, Inc.
is a leading supplier of automotive original equipment, providing components such as carpet, crash pads, molded door panels, seat covers, polyurethane seat cushioning and trunk liners. A major area of growth for Allen's automotive division is the manufacture of sound-absorbing material for automotive interiors.
R. D. Kemp, *President*

Automotive Original Equipment Div.
(Dayco Rubber Products Co.)
is the world's largest supplier of V-belts to original equipment manufacturers of passenger cars, trucks and tractors. The V-belts are used on alternator and fan applications, power steering, air-condi-

Dayco Carpet Cushion Co.
manufactures a complete line of carpet cushion which enables it to meet virtually every residential and commercial carpet application. The broad selection includes sponge rubber, latex foam, bonded urethane and rubberized fiber-center carpet cushion.
H. D. Albert, *President*

Seward Luggage Co.
is the world's leading manufacturer of foot lockers and trunks and a major producer of contemporarily designed hard and soft-sided luggage. The luggage line is sold under the Seward®, Mutual® and Travel Wise® brand names. Private brand lines are supplied to major department, chain and variety

DAYCO CORPORATION *(continued)*

*Profits represent earnings before federal income taxes, interest on debentures used to make acquisitions, certain other minor expenses and inventory is priced on Last-in/First-out inventory method.

---

liquids. These products include metal hose, bellows, expansion joints and ducting systems.
E. C. Hallett, *Chairman*
T. Hallett, *President*

Colonial Rubber Works, Inc.
is the world's largest independent custom compounder and formulator of rubber and plastic. Specialty compounds for virtually all American industries are continuously developed and mixed in large quantities at the company's two plants. Principal customers include members of the appliance, agricultural, energy and automotive industries.
D. L. Hotaling, *President*
W. M. Heathcott, *Executive V.P.*

Printing Products Div.
(Dayflex Co.)
is a leading manufacturer of graphic arts supplies for the printing industry, including lithographic blankets, inking rollers and equipment to split colors on press runs. Included in its numerous product lines are pre-inked business machine rollers for print-out applications and large conveying and squeezing rolls for various industries. Products range from tiny credit-card roller-imprinters to huge magnetic cylinders for commercial, corrugated board and business forms printers.
P. J. Neroni, *President*
K. A. Hines, *V.P.*

Textile Products Div.
(Dayflex Co.)
manufactures replaceable component parts for the textile industry's production machinery. The division's cots and aprons are used in drafting and spinning operations. Its loom supplies help in the weaving of cloth and its texturizing aprons help add bulk and resilience to synthetic fibers.
P. J. Neroni, *President*
K. K. Karns, *V.P.*

	$	%
Sales		
	$185.8	42.8%
Profits		
	$8.5	47.2%

Star Textile and Research, Inc.
is a producer of nylon staple fiber and processes other man-made fibers for a wide variety of applications. Its non-woven division supplies insulating material for garments and home furnishings and fabrics for shape retention and certain filtration uses.
P. G. Casabonne, *Chairman*
H. E. Gabriels, *President*

TFE, Inc.
manufactures a diversified range of plastic products using fluorocarbon technology. Products include fabricated parts, shapes, bearings, automatic molded parts, high temperature class "H" insulating film and pressure sensitive tapes utilizing Teflon* and other fluorocarbon materials.
E. W. Dennison, Jr., *President*
*Registered trademark of duPont

	$	%
Sales		
	$113.2	26.0%
Profits		
	$7.8	43.5%

---

tioning, air pollution control pumps and water pumps. It also supplies Synchro-Cog® belts, used on overhead camshaft engines in small automobiles.
J. O. Quamme, *President*
B. Ambrosini, *V. P.*

	$	%
Sales		
	$77.2	17.8%
Profits		
	$ .8	4.6%

---

stores. A complete line of briefcases is manufactured and distributed under the Mutual name.
G. F. Liebscher, *President*
P. E. Dayton, *Executive V.P., Marketing*

L. E. Carpenter and Co.
is the world's foremost manufacturer of high style wall coverings for commercial and public use. Its Vicracoustic® noise reduction systems are the standard by which architects and interior designers measure versatility and attractiveness in acoustical applications.
F. J. Singleton, *President*
K. W. Hanlon, *Executive V.P.*

	$	%
Sales		
	$58.1	13.4%
Profits		
	$ .9	4.7%

NORTHROP CORPORATION

It should be recognized, of course, that construction and service product lines, while achieving a lower percent of net income to sales than aircraft, do have a relatively high rate of return on investment since they are not capital intensive. The net income by product lines is set forth below:

Net income (loss) by product line

	1974		1973	
$ in thousands	Amount	%	Amount	%
Aircraft	$15,004	82.8	$14,294	123.1
Electronics/communications	1,240	6.8	1,669	14.4
Construction	548	3.0	(1,972)	(17.0)
Services	1,179	6.5	830	7.2
Other	165	.9	(3,213)	(27.7)
	$18,136	100.0	$11,608	100.0

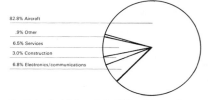

82.8% Aircraft

.9% Other

6.5% Services

3.0% Construction

6.8% Electronics/communications

Considering the inflation spiral in 1974 and the overall economic environment, the improved operating margins and resultant net income reflect, among other factors, management's concentration on better cost controls and efficiency. Significant net losses, aggregating $5.2 million in construction and other product lines in 1973, were eliminated in 1974. Net income of the "Other" category in 1974 was profitable despite the inclusion of a write-off of approximately $2.0 million for inventory of unsold LASH barges and phasedown costs.

In reviewing the product line data it should be noted that net income improved in all activities except electronics-communications. It should be recalled that the company has booked sales on a long-term contract with the Imperial Government of Iran, without recording profits, since 1971; hence the rate of return in the electronics-communications business is less than expected overall. It is anticipated that this contract will be completed in 1975.

Management believes that, in 1975, with certain loss areas eliminated, and continued improvement in operating margins and increasing volume, the earnings of the company should improve—although to a lesser degree than was evidenced in 1974 relative to 1973.

The factors contributing to the increase in net income in 1974 over 1973 are as follows:

Net income for 1974	$18,136,000
Net income for 1973	11,608,000
Increase in net income	**$ 6,528,000**
Factors increasing income	
Increase (decrease) in operating margins:	
Aircraft	$ 5,377,000
Electronics/communications	(2,393,000)
Construction	1,913,000
Services	682,000
Other	6,660,000
Net increase in margins	12,239,000
Decrease in interest expense	3,358,000
Increase in interest income & other changes (net)	1,497,000
Total increases	**17,094,000**
Factors decreasing income	
Decreased profit on purchase of debt at a discount	2,485,000
Reduced royalty income	1,277,000
Total decreases	**3,762,000**
Net increase in income before taxes	13,332,000
Higher income taxes on increased income	6,804,000
Increase in net income—1974 over 1973	**$ 6,528,000**

The 1973 annual report to shareholders provided this analysis of changes in net income for 1973 over 1972:

Net income for 1973	$11,608,000
Net income for 1972	11,136,000
Increase in net income	**$ 472,000**
Factors increasing income	
Increase in electronics/communications operating margins—volume and rate	$ 3,600,000
Increase in aircraft operating margins— volume, net of rate	700,000
Higher profit on purchase of subordinated debt	2,581,000
Reduction in federal and foreign income taxes	997,000
All other changes—net	1,104,000
Total increases	**8,982,000**
Factors decreasing income	
Increased operating writeoff for the "other" product line	3,900,000
Higher interest expense	2,481,000
Increased other deductions	2,129,000
Total decreases	**8,510,000**
Increase in net income—1973 and 1972	**$ 472,000**

Dividends

Northrop shareholders received $5,373,000 in dividends in 1974. During the year the company twice increased its dividends—from $.25 per share (paid since 1962) to $.28 per share in March and to $.40 per share in September.

31

SELECTED REFERENCES

AICPA   "Disclosure of Supplemental Financial Information by Diversified Companies," *Accounting Principles Board Statement No. 2.* New York, September 1967.

————   *Accounting Trends and Techniques.* 26th and 27th ed. New York, 1972–73.

Backer, Morton, and MacFarland, Walter B.   *External Reporting for Segments of a Business.* New York: National Association of Accountants, 1968.

Bureau of Economics Staff Report "The Federal Trade Commission Line-of-Business Reporting Program." Washington, D.C., 1974.

Collins, Daniel W. "Predicting Earnings with Sub-Entity Data: Some Further Evidence," forthcoming, *Journal of Accounting Research.*

Federal Trade Commission "Annual Line-of-Business Report Program." Washington, D.C., March 27, 1974.

Financial Accounting Standards Board Discussion Memorandum, "An Analysis of Issues Related to Financial Reporting for Segments of a Business Enterprise." Stamford, Conn., May 22, 1974.

———— Position papers submitted in response to "Discussion Memorandum on Financial Reporting for Segments of a Business Enterprise," Part 1, Sections A and B, November 1974.

Financial Analysts Federation *Evaluation of Corporate Financial Reporting in Selected Industries for the Year 1971.* New York, November 15, 1972.

Financial Executives Institute "Line-of-Business Reporting in Annual Reports," *FEI Policy Statement.* New York, May 13, 1971.

Kinney, William R. "Predicting Earnings: Entity versus Subentity Data." *Journal of Accounting Research,* Spring 1971, pp. 127–36.

McNamar, R. T. "FTC Line-of-Business Reporting: Fact and Fiction." *Financial Executive,* August 1974, pp. 20–27.

Mautz, Robert K. "Bases for More Detailed Reporting by Diversified Companies." *Financial Executive,* November 1967, pp. 52–54, 56–58, 60.

———— "Conglomerate Reporting and Data Reliability." *Financial Executive,* September 1967, pp. 25–26, 31, 33–35.

———— *Financial Reporting by Diversified Companies.* New York: Financial Executives Research Foundation, 1968.

———— "Financial Reporting by Conglomerate Companies." *Financial Executive,* February 1968, pp. 52–53, 55–56, 59–60, 63–65.

————, **and Skousen, K. Fred** "Common Cost Allocation in Diversified Companies." *Financial Executive,* June 1968, pp. 15–17, 19–25.

National Association of Accountants Committee on Management Accounting Practices, "Financial Reporting by Diversified Companies," *Statement on Management Accounting Practices No. 3.* New York, June 1972.

Pacter, Paul "Line-of-Business Earnings Disclosure in Recent SEC Filings." *The Journal of Accountancy,* October 1970, pp. 56–63.

———— "Some Recent Examples of Earnings Reports by Division." *The Journal of Accountancy,* December 1968, pp. 40–51.

Rappaport, A.; Firmin, P.; and Zeff, S., eds. *Public Reporting by Conglomerates: The Issues, the Problems and Some Possible Solutions,* Englewood Cliffs, N.J.: Prentice-Hall, Inc., 1968.

———, **and Lerner, Eugene** *A Framework for Financial Reporting by Diversified Companies.* New York: National Association of Accountants, 1969.

———, **and Lerner, E.** *Segment Reporting for Managers and Investors.* New York: National Association of Accountants, 1972.

Scheibla, Shirley "Illegal Search and Seizure—Industry Has Balked at Disclosing Line-of-Business Data." *Barrons,* February 17, 1975, pp. 5, 17–18.

Securities and Exchange Commission "Adoption of Amendments to Forms S-1, S-7, and 10," *Securities Exchange Act of 1934 Release No. 8650.* Washington, D.C., July 14, 1969.

——— "Adoption of Revised Form 10-K," *Securities Exchange Act of 1934 Release No. 9000.* Washington, D.C., October 21, 1970.

——— "Notice of Proposed Amendments to Rules 14a-3 and 14c-3 under the Securities Exchange Act of 1934 to Improve Disclosure in Annual Reports Furnished to Security Holders Pursuant to Those Rules, and to Improve Dissemination of Annual Reports to Security Holders and of Annual Reports on Form 10-K; and Adoption of Amendments to Item 7 of Schedule 14A under that Act," *Securities Exchange Act of 1934 Release No. 10591.* Washington, D.C., January 10, 1974.

——— *SEC Release 34-11079.* Washington, D.C., October 31, 1974.

Skousen, Fred "Chronicle of Events Surrounding the Segment Reporting Issue." *Journal of Accounting Research,* Autumn 1970, pp. 293–99.

——— "A Format for Reporting Segment Profits." *Management Accounting,* June 1971, pp. 15–20.

——— "Standards for Reporting by Lines of Business." *The Journal of Accountancy,* February 1970, pp. 39–46.

Sprouse, Robert T. "Diversified Views about Diversified Companies." *Journal of Accounting Research,* Spring 1969, pp. 137–59.

U.S. Executive Office of the President, Office of Management and Budget *Standard Industrial Classification Manual.* Washington, D.C., U.S. Government Printing Office, 1972.

U.S. House Committee on the Judiciary, Subcommittee on Anti-trust *Investigation of Conglomerate Corporations: A Report by the Staff,* 92d Cong., 1st sess., 1971.

U.S. Senate Committee on the Judiciary, Subcommittee on Anti-trust and Monopoly *Hearings on Economic Concentration: Part 1. Overall and Conglomerate Aspects,* 88th Cong., 2d sess., 1964.

———— *Hearings on Economic Concentration: Part 2. Mergers and Other Factors Affecting Industry Concentration; Part 3. Concentration, Invention and Innovation; Part 4. Concentration and Efficiency,* 89th Cong., 1st sess., 1965.

———— *Hearings on Economic Concentrations: Part 5. Concentration: and Divisional Reporting,* 89th Cong., 2d sess., and 90th Cong., 1st sess., 1966.

Chapter 24

_____ Forecasting for today's corporation

*Theodore H. Davis**
James M. Bahin†

THE NEED FOR FORECASTS

The history books may not have recorded the first business venture, but in the beginning of that venture was a forecast, a forecast in which the proprietor thought about how much money would have to be invested in order to begin the venture, how much product could be sold, how much it would cost for the goods sold, and subsequently what the reward would be for risking time, energy, and, of course, money. Some determination of future earnings and future cash flows thus accompanied the earliest business venture.

Over the years of history of business enterprise, the basic use of these forecasts has not changed. The scope of the forecast, however, has expanded dramatically. With the evolution of the modern complex corporation, professional managers and stockholders have discovered that forecasts are an integral part of business planning and investing.

While the use of forecasts by management in evaluating the future impact of current business decisions is well known, the desire of stockholders to know what results management expects from the course of action that has been chosen has only recently received

---

* Vice President Operations, Fuqua Industries, Inc.
† Controller, Fuqua Industries, Inc.

widespread attention. Stockholders, like a proprietor, are the owners of a business; therefore, they can realistically be expected to want all the relevant facts concerning the business. Future expectations should be the single most important information that any business owner could have. The means by which management can be evaluated by investors is not only by past performance but also by comparison of future plans and actual performance.

The recent emphasis on forecasting has been for use by top management, lenders, and stockholders. Management at all levels is finding the well-prepared forecast to be a vital management tool, as actual performance can be compared to forecasted data on a monthly basis. The variances from forecast then become the exceptions for management action.

THE PRACTICE OF CORPORATE FORECASTING

Corporate forecasting encompasses both long-term forecasts of several years and short-term forecasts of the current year. Long-term forecasts are prepared most frequently to evaluate alternative business strategies, considering different combinations of alternative plans for acquisitions, new products, new markets, or new facilities.

The *long-term forecast* enables management to determine which course of action it wishes to pursue and what assets it needs to acquire in order to achieve the desired goals. In this planning process the size of the expenditure and the productive results (efficiency, increased capacity, new design, etc.) are estimated and weighed against each other to determine the possible effect on the business. Alternative amounts of assets and expenditures can also be analyzed in the search for the best possible course of action. The long-term forecast is a necessary management tool to determine the need for future financing, human and physical resources, and competitive strategy. The long-term forecast is flexible and should always be subject to modification.

Once a corporate strategy encompassing a set of objectives is adopted it becomes the framework for management's *one-year operating plan (budget)*. This 1-year plan can either be based on the company's fiscal year or based on a rolling 12 months. The one-year plan can then be translated quantitatively into a set of expected financial statements. This operating plan ties planned operating results into planned financial position, as receivables are based on expected sales and collection levels, inventories are based on expected production and sales levels, and other asset and liability accounts are based on the expected overall activity of the firm. Actual results can then be compared with the planned activity to determine if any variances have occurred. Analysis of the variances in both balance sheet and operating accounts will identify the conditions that are different from those forecasted. Some of these variances may warrant management action. Many companies operate on a "management by exception" basis in which only exceptional variances (those which vary by more or less than a predetermined percentage or dollar amount) are used to determine further management action. This same type of analysis can provide the basis for evaluating management performance at all levels of the organization. The annual forecast, properly prepared and maintained, enables management to view decisions and their execution in terms of the ultimate financial results—the attainment of planned objectives. This exercise coordinates all phases of planning and control in a manner designed to generate performance consistent with desired results.

ORGANIZATION FOR FORECASTING

To be effective, managers of forecasting must thoroughly understand the company, its people, and its industry. A financial background is usually necessary. In addition, they must have an understanding of the key business and economic indicators which affect the firm. They must have the confidence of and access to all levels of management, as forecasting will become a self-defeating exercise if it is not properly managed and provided with top-management support. The forecasting function deserves a full-time manager in all but the simplest business organizations.

SHORT-TERM FORECASTING CYCLE

The annual forecast should be updated at least quarterly during the year. A typical cycle of forecasting is as follows:

Forecast prepared	*Data submitted for quarter ending—*			
	March 31	*June 30*	*September 30*	*December 31*
April	Actual	Forecast	Forecast	Forecast
July.	Actual	Actual	Forecast	Forecast
October	Actual	Actual	Actual	Forecast

The quarterly forecast revisions should be prepared in the month following the end of each quarter. This update will allow management to review its original assumptions, considering the actual results to date and new economic, market, and resource knowledge. The latest information available for all of the key indicators and factors used in the original forecast should be used in the revised forecast. Simply adding year-to-date actual to the original forecast for the remainder of the year is usually unsatisfactory. The revised forecast will provide the latest outlook for the year, but the original forecast (budget) should be maintained, as well, for year-to-date comparisons to the original operating plan.

FORECASTING BY RESPONSIBILITY CENTER

Complete financial statement forecasts should be consolidated from the budgets of each responsibility center, whether a cost center or a profit center. The manager of each responsibility center should play a major role in the development of the center's budget. Budgeting at this level will provide for the later comparison of actual results to forecast results. Variances can then be easily identified and acted upon at the responsibility center level. The consolidation of all responsibility center budgets will result in the forecast for the organization. Each responsibility center manager must understand the forecasting process and devote the necessary time to the forecasting exercise. This will be an important factor in motivating the responsibility center manager to strive to fulfill the plan.

A major task of the manager of forecasting is to educate each responsibility center manager on the preparation and use of forecasts. This usually requires group meetings as well as individual counseling sessions. While each responsibility center budget must be reasonable and generally compatible with the goals of the organization, rigid guidelines dictated by top management (such as a 15 percent sales increase or a 15 percent cut in expenses) will discourage the initiative of the individual manager.

AIDS IN FORECASTING

Many government and industry statistical publications are available to assist in forecasting. Trends in economic statistics affecting the company's customers or reflecting economic activity which has an ultimate effect on materials, labor, financing, or other resources must be considered in forecasting. Of the mass of statistics and other information available, a few key indicators can usually be found that will best reflect the business environment of any one company. Examples of these key indicators might be the nation's Gross National Product, trends in purchasing power and discretionary spending, automobile sales (even for nonautomobile related companies), industrial production, and so on.

Computer applications for forecasting are today highly developed and in use in many large companies. These are available for smaller organizations from many service bureaus. These applications are mainly for a twofold purpose. The first is to analyze the trends of a business or product line against key indicators or external variables. The sales of any product line are determined by the combination of many factors. The major factors are the economic environment, factors controlled internally by management, the action of competitors, and random events.

Relevant economic factors may include the general state of the economy, the cost of money, the level of production in the market in which the product is sold, and so on. Sophisticated computer statistical packages can help identify relevant data and their effects on product lines. With these effects known, an econometric model can be formulated to show the historical relationship between the relevant economic factors and the performance of the product line. This model can then be used, varying either expected macroeconomic data or alternative management strategies to forecast the expected outcome.

The second purpose would be a similar use of the computer using smaller company-defined models to examine the effects of varying business decisions. The model would be a definition of the company's fixed and variable expenses. By examining expected sales and the numerous decisions on expenditures, as well as the variable costs, expected profit levels could be determined. The effect on profits of higher or lower sales and/or different variable cost relationships can be seen by using such a model. Management can determine the probable outcome of different decisions before they occur, thus enabling it to determine if the results are congruous with corporate goals.

DEVELOPMENTS IN FORECAST DISCLOSURE

Public companies are now facing an unprecedented trend in financial reporting requirements toward greatly increased disclosures. In 1973 the AICPA, SEC, and FASB issued 16 opinions, interpretations, and releases, all of which dealt with increased disclosure of financial data. The flow of additional requirements and proposals has continued into 1976. One of the primary reasons given for this trend is the contention that the average investor has not been provided with the same information concerning managements' expectations of future operations as have professional analysts and large investors.

In February of 1973 the SEC issued a statement on "The Disclosure of Projections of Future Economic Performance." In this release the Commission reversed a long-standing position and provided that public companies may, but are not required to, include forecasts in reports filed with the SEC. The reason cited for this reversal of position is as follows:

> The Commission recognizes that projections are currently widespread in the securities markets and are relied upon in the investment process. Persons invest with the future in mind and the market value of a security reflects the judgments of investors about the future economic performance of the issuer. Thus projections are sought by all investors, whether institutional or individual. The Commission is concerned, however, that all investors do not have equal access to this material information. . . . Information gathered at the hearings reinforced the Commission's observation that management's assessment of a company's future performance is information of significant importance to the investor, that such assessment should be able to be understood in light of the assumptions made, and that such information should be available, if at all, on an equitable basis to all investors.[1]

The Commission, although making the disclosure of forecasts voluntary, did stipulate that issuers of forecasts using "the financial media, financial analysts or otherwise" for dissemination of the projections be required to file such projections with the SEC. Other determinations of the Commission are as follows:

---

[1] *Securities Act Release No. 5362. Exchange Act Release No. 9984*, February 2, 1973.

1. Issuers of forecasts who are public companies and who meet certain standards (to be developed) relating to their earnings histories and budgeting experience should be permitted to include projections in Commission filings.
2. Any issuer who files projections should be required to update the filed projection on a regular basis and whenever the issuer materially changes its projections.
3. A company filing projections should be permitted to stop filing such information if it discloses its decision and the reasons therefor.
4. No statement verification or certification by a third party should be permitted.

The SEC further stated that it would issue a release at a later date which would include, among other things, standards for preparation, dissemination of projections, and the Commission's comments concerning the adverse consequences of issuing projections, that is, legal liability.[2] To date, a new release by the SEC has not been issued on the subject. The American Institute of Certified Public Accountants has, however, issued an exposure draft proposing standards for a forecast preparation.[3]

ABILITY TO FORECAST

The door clearly has been opened for businesses to make public their internal projections. One must, however, weigh the positive and negative aspects of making such a decision and determine if the particular company is in a position to forecast accurately. The ability to produce a relatively reliable forecast encompasses the following questions:

1. Is the industry in which the company operates subject to significant swings in its activity?
2. Is the company a significant part of its industry?
3. Is the company involved in more than one line of business and, if so, how related are they?
4. What is the company's track record with internal forecasting?

---

[2] Ibid.

[3] AICPA, *Standards for Systems for the Preparation of Financial Forecasts*, Exposure Draft, Forecasting Task Force, Management Advisory Services Division (New York, March 28, 1974).

If the answer to the first question is positive, the safest approach would be to keep projections for internal use only. Regardless of the company's expertise and experience, if its industry is volatile, the chances of maintaining any consistent success in forecasting are considerably lessened. Any advantages to be gained by public disclosure are lost if reliability cannot be demonstrated.

If the company commands a significant position in its industry, then two points must be considered. The larger the market share the more vulnerable the company is to industry swings. On the other hand, because of its size the company may be able to maintain greater control over what happens in the industry.

Involvement in more than one nonrelated line of business is a definite advantage in making financial projections. Even in periods of general economic decline, some lines of businesses and product lines can outperform others, and thus declines in one area of business may be offset by improvement in other areas. A company's involvement in more than one nonrelated product line is a definite stabilizing factor in helping to produce more consistent results. Going even further, a planned line of complementary products could help to reduce seasonal swings in business activity and aid in developing more reliable data.

ADVANTAGES AND DISADVANTAGES
OF PUBLIC FORECASTING

The positive and negative aspects of public disclosure of financial projections can be related to the three groups affected by the decision, that is, stockholders, management, and professional security analysts. For management there are few advantages. Assuming that a good internal budgeting system already exists, which must be the case if public disclosure is made, there would be relatively nothing gained. The so-called outsiders, however, would benefit significantly. Shareholders and potential investors would receive a statement of management's expectations with which to compare the security analysts' projections. These expectations should be more reliable since they are based on a greater amount of information from within the business and should provide some continuity between the various projections made by outside analysts. They also should, if presented in such a manner, help in the analysis of complicated businesses such as many of today's con-

glomerates. Many companies are involved in several different industries, and industry specialization by today's professional analysts
limits their ability to cope with such operations.

What could be the most significant *positive factor* in consideration of public disclosure of forecasts is the equal dissemination of
information. For many years professional analysts and large shareholders, mostly institutions, have been receiving a greater volume
of data regarding "public" companies' operations than have the
average individual shareholders. Many analysts communicate frequently with corporate executives, and with this communication
comes a significantly greater knowledge of a company's operations.
This is knowledge to which every shareholder is entitled. The analyst obtains information for the purpose of preparing projections
and making recommendations regarding investment in certain companies. Every shareholder should have the right to make his or her
own determination, and equal dissemination of management's projections would facilitate this.

To management the *negative aspects,* or disadvantages, of public forecasting are perhaps more numerous than the positive aspects
but they do not necessarily outweigh them. These disadvantages
include legal liability, extraordinary pressure, and additional reporting requirements. Undoubtedly the legal question is the most
important factor to consider, and thus will be covered in greater
detail at the end of the chapter.

An additional disadvantage of public disclosure of forecasts is
the obvious added pressure on management to see that its forecasts
do materialize. It is important to management that it maintain a
credible position with shareholders and analysts. This credibility
could be weakened by a badly missed forecast, and management knows this. If a company's management places a great enough
emphasis on its public image, the pressures are significant to make
business decisions which would benefit the short-term results for
the sake of the forecast while not being particularly beneficial to
the long-term operation. The solution to this would be the immediate disclosure of significant and material variances of the basic assumptions when they become known to management.

A lesser but more practical problem is that almost continuous
analysis of actual results compared to forecast is required in order
to determine if public disclosure of these deviations is required.

As a result, additional manpower and perhaps changes in the normal internal reporting systems may be required.

Another negative factor which management must consider is that the disclosure of both the estimated figures for future periods and the assumptions upon which the projections are based might be a competitive disadvantage. An example might be the disclosure of the intentions to open a new plant or to expand the product line. Information such as this could destroy any competitive advantage to be gained by the move. Similarly, disclosure of expected future earnings might well affect labor negotiations or other contract agreements.

An additional deterrent would be the possibility of overreliance on management's estimates by the less sophisticated investor. This factor, however, reemphasizes the importance of future expectations on the shareholder's investment decision. Generally, anything detrimental to management and its attempts to improve the company's and ultimately its shareholder's position is a disadvantage of public forecasting from the shareholder's viewpoint.

PRESENTATION

Once the decision has been reached to make public the company's expected results, the format of presentation becomes an important consideration. The SEC in its guidelines "contemplated that there would be certain restrictions on the type of projection that could be filed . . . that it relate at a minimum to sales and earnings, that it be expressed as an exact figure or within a reasonable range, that the underlying assumptions be set forth, and that it be for a reasonable period, such as a fiscal year."[4] Consideration should be given to forecast presentation incorporated with several other years' historical data. A five-year presentation might include four years' historical data, including the most recent actual results compared to that year's forecast. In the discussion of the legal question it could be concluded that the investor should be given a company's track record so that the investor can make the determination as to how much reliance can be placed on a published forecast. The following is an example of how income statement data could be presented (product line data will be discussed later):

---

[4] *Securities Act Release No. 5362.*

Table used for both sales and earnings

| | *Actual* | | | *1977* | | *1978* |
	1974	1975	1976	*Forecast*	*Actual*	*forecast*
Product A						
Product B						
Product C						
Total.						
EPS						

Results of the recent legal cases indicate the importance of disclosure of significant assumptions associated with the published forecast for the reason stated above. Not only should the basic assumptions be disclosed but also other data, such as product-line information (if the company is a multiproduct or multi-industry business), should be provided in sufficient detail for the investor to draw his or her own conclusions as to the prediction's accuracy. As a minimum the following information relating to operations should be disclosed:

1. General expectations of economic outlook.
2. The company's expectations for its particular industry or industries.
3. Change in effective tax rate, if applicable.
4. Reasons for changes in profit percentages, if applicable.
5. Reasons why the company's outlook does not coincide with outlook for the economy or the company's industry, if applicable.
6. Assumptions regarding foreign operations, if applicable.

Key balance sheet data is also necessary from an analytical standpoint. Since one of the positive aspects of forecast disclosure is to aid the professional analyst, balance sheet data is needed to complete the package. This information should include the following:

1. Anticipated capital expenditures (plant expansion).
2. Financing of large expenditures by debt or equity and any changes in outstanding shares.
3. Anticipated debt levels and expectations as to levels of working capital.

DISTRIBUTION

To accomplish the previously stated objective of equal dissemination of information the forecast should be distributed, if not actually in the annual and quarterly reports to the stockholders, at least to the same individuals and organizations that receive annual and quarterly reports. If forecast data is presented in these regular reports to shareholders, this information should be displayed clearly and separately from the historical financial statements. This should be done so that the reader is not misled as to applicability and the amount of reliance to be placed on the data. It should be made clear that the accountant's letter and report on the company do not cover any forecast.

LEGAL LIABILITY

The legal basis of forecasting has two aspects: first, the preparation of a forecast which satisfies the requirements of applicable law, or guidelines; and second, the development of sufficient documentation to demonstrate the care that was exercised in preparing the forecast. The Securities and Exchange Commission has ruled that a forecast should be of sales and earnings and should be expressed as a reasonably definite figure—for a reasonable period of time. The Commission has emphasized, however, that a forecast is not a promise.[5]

The way to a proper forecast is proper method and adequate publication. The courts and the Securities and Exchange Commission uniformly recognize that if the right procedures are used in the preparation of the forecast, the forecast is legally acceptable in the sense that no liability will attach to the company or management which publishes the forecast. One description says that a proper forecast is one which is comprehensive, accurate, and believed by management. Another description says that a proper forecast is one which is reasonably based on fact, prepared with reasonable care, and carefully reviewed. Both these descriptions boil down to a practical requirement that in preparing the forecast the most capable and qualified people in the company must be assigned to making the calculations that go into the forecast, whether they be assessments of the expected general economic climate in the forecast period, marketing or sales expectations, or anticipated costs. The forecast team must then consider and weigh all the facts which are significant with respect to the forecast and must make the assumptions which are necessary to the forecast.

---

[5] Ibid.

The calculations which result from this activity must be carefully reviewed and approved by people with the maximum expertise in the area.

In the event of an ultimate test through litigation of the diligence with which the forecast was prepared, the determination will be based upon whether or not the activity was carried on with due care, that is, without negligence. The courts and the Securities and Exchange Commission all speak in terms of "reasonableness" and "care," and require that the forecast be expressed as a "reasonably definite figure" for a "reasonable period of time." In litigation, management will have to show through testimony, including expert testimony, that the forecast team, the reviewers, and top management used all the thoroughness, experience, and knowledge in preparing the forecast that an ordinary prudent person engaged in an activity as important as forecasting could be expected to use in performing that activity. This means that a forecast must be the product of a carefully constructed program set up by management for its production. The program is important for two reasons: first, because it helps to insure that the forecast is comprehensive and consistent; and second, because it acts as the basis for producing evidence of due care in the event of litigation. This means that not only must the program be carefully constructed but the facts gathered and assumptions made in following the program (and the activities performed in gathering the facts and making the assumptions) must be carefully recorded and preserved.

Once the forecast has been made it must be published. In addition to the projected figures for sales and earnings, certain of the assumptions underlying the forecast should also be disclosed. Undoubtedly the forecast will be based in part on assumptions about the general economy in the forecast period. These should be disclosed, as should any other assumptions about matters which are subject to varied interpretation. It is particularly important to disclose any unresolved, substantial dissent expressed within the forecast team upon review as a part of the forecast procedure.

To illustrate the problems facing management in regard to legal liability, the two best known court cases are compared below.

Prior to any specific guidelines being issued by the SEC on potential liability, management must look to the leading court cases which are the *SEC* v. *Texas Gulf Sulphur*,[6] *Dolgow* v. *Anderson* involving Monsanto,[7] and *Beecher* v. *Able* involving Douglas Aircraft,[8] the last two illustrating the judicial attitude toward application of rule 10B-5 of the 1934 Act to forecasts. Both of the later cases involved major corporations who had made forecasts that failed to materialize. The *Monsanto* case came first and is the most satisfactory case for a management in favor of public forecasting. Many felt that this case relieved management of undue liability in regard to forecasts which do not materialize. However, the *Douglas Aircraft* case is the latest case, and it set much higher standards for disclosure and guidelines for management development of forecasts. For example, the court, in *Monsanto*, did not insist on disclosure of underlying assumptions and seemed to indicate that it was sufficient for public forecasts to be a fair and accurate reflection of carefully prepared forecasts which are the best estimates and are believed by management. In the *Douglas Aircraft* case, however, the court suggested that the forecast be one that the reasonably prudent investor would agree was "highly probable." Another important difference in these two cases was that while the court indicated its concern that Douglas executives were not sincere in their optimism, in the *Monsanto* case the court stated that investors should exercise some judgment regarding executive psychology.

SUMMARY

Forecasting has become an integral part of today's corporations and of the job of the people who run them. Recent emphasis on public disclosure of forecasts has broadened the usefulness of this form of business planning. The increased desire to know and the inherent right of stockholders as owners have provided substantial impetus in the movement towards greater disclosure of management's expectations of future results. Before a corporation undertakes this effort, however, serious consideration must be given to the advantages and disadvantages of such disclosure, and care-

---

[6] *S.E.C.* v. *Texas Gulf Sulphur*, 401 F. 2d 833 (2d Cir. 1968).

[7] *Dolgow* v. *Anderson*, 53 F.R.D. 664 (E.D.N.Y. 1971), aff'd, 464 F. 2d 437 (2d Cir. 1972).

[8] *Beecher* v. *Able*, CCH Fed. Sec. L. Rep. ¶94,450 (S.D.N.Y. 1974).

ful evaluation must be made of the organization, its systems, its structure, and its people.

APPENDIX

In December 1972, Fuqua Industries, Inc., produced a "Preliminary Annual Report—A Look Ahead to 1973." In this publication Fuqua Chairman J. B. Fuqua stated that the company felt that "the Securities and Exchange Commission will shortly require public companies to make forecasts of future operations." Fuqua further urged the readers "to understand that forecasts of future operations are based on business factors as evaluated by management at the time such forecasts are made."

The presentation of the forecast was done by product line for sales and earnings. Five-year history was given to put the forecast in perspective (Exhibit 1).

The 1973 annual report reported a continuation of the efforts to publicly disclose the company's forecast, even though no ruling requiring them came from the SEC. Actual results for 1973 were compared to the original forecast as adjusted for the sale of some businesses not anticipated in the forecast. In addition, the results for 1974 were forecast. Enclosed in the six months' interim report for each of these years were updates of the original forecast if adjustments were necessary (Exhibit 2).

During 1974, however, the art of corporate budgeting started to become a key concern in the executive suites. The world economy had become caught up in a whirlwind of galloping inflation, record-high interest rates, and material shortages. Forecast revisions became the rule rather than the exception as critical assumptions and situations developed.[9] In early 1975, Fuqua Industries announced that the company would "reluctantly discontinue its former practice of making a forecast of future earnings." Citing that the company would continue with its internal budgets, Mr. Fuqua stated that "this year (1975) there is so much uncertainty in the economic outlook that we would have to qualify any forecast as little more than an educated guess." The company stated, however, that this was temporary; and when the conditions stabilized, public disclosures of forecasts might continue.[10]

---

[9] *Business Week,* July 20, 1974, pp. 22–23.

[10] Fuqua Industries, Inc. Press Release, February 21, 1975.

EXHIBIT 1

FUQUA INDUSTRIES, INC.
Summary of Operations
Years Ended December 31
($ millions)

Sales and revenues	1967	1968	1969	1970	1971	Esti-mated 1972	Fore-cast 1973
Leisure time:							
Snowmobiles and lawnmowers	$ 13.9	$ 21.4	$ 30.9	$ 36.9	$ 56.0	$ 56.0	$ 68.0
Sporting goods	15.9	19.8	24.1	28.3	31.4	37.0	39.0
Marine products.	38.4	49.7	49.5	29.7	34.0	41.0	48.0
Entertainment.	24.6	24.5	25.0	26.9	27.1	38.0	45.0
Photographic finishing	14.1	17.0	19.6	18.1	17.9	21.0	23.0
Total Leisure	$106.9	$132.4	$149.1	$139.9	$166.4	$193.0	$223.0
Transportation	66.5	72.0	97.5	113.2	131.0	140.0	147.0
Shelter*	26.0	29.7	37.3	39.4	41.6	60.1	74.0
Agribusiness	18.1	20.9	21.0	28.9	33.0	36.0	40.0
Total Continuing Operations†	$217.5	$255.0	$304.9	$321.4	$372.0	$430.1	$484.0
Add: Discontinued operations.	42.4	40.8	43.7	28.5	6.1	–	–
Less: Restatements of business purchased .	36.7	40.8	11.0	5.5	1.3	–	–
Total Sales and Revenues	$223.2	$255.0	$337.6	$344.4	$376.8	$430.1	$484.0

Earnings	1967	1968	1969	1970	1971	Esti-mated 1972	% of total	Compound annual growth rate %	Fore-cast 1973
Leisure time:									
Snowmobiles and lawnmowers . . .	$ 2.4	$ 4.7	$ 5.8	$ 6.2	$ 7.3	$ 9.7	22%	32%	$11.4
Sporting goods	1.1	2.0	2.9	3.2	3.1	4.1	9	30	4.1
Boats and boat trailers	1.0	3.6	3.3	0.3	0.6	3.3	7	27	4.5
Entertainment.	2.5	3.2	4.5	4.2	4.5	6.4	14	16	6.8
Photographic finishing	1.6	1.8	1.4	1.0	1.7	2.5	6	9	2.9
Total Leisure	$ 8.6	$15.3	$17.9	$14.9	$17.2	$26.0	58%	24%	$29.7
Transportation	3.6	4.3	6.0	4.5	9.2	10.0	22	23	10.0
Shelter*	0.3	2.0	5.9	6.2	4.7	2.8	5	56	5.5
Agribusiness	3.1	3.0	1.5	3.1	5.3	6.7	15	17	6.9
Total Continuing Operations† . .	$15.6	$24.6	$31.3	$28.7	$36.4	$45.5	100%	23%	$52.1
Add: Discontinued operations.	1.7	1.6	0.5	1.6	(.8)	(.1)			–
Less: Unallocated corporate expenses and corporate interest	0.9	1.7	3.9	6.2	7.9	9.7			9.7
Less: Restatements of business purchased	1.2	2.7	0.3	1.0	0.2	–			–
Income before income taxes . . .	$15.2	$21.8	$27.6	$23.1	$27.5	$35.7		19%	$42.4
Income taxes	7.0	11.0	13.6	11.5	13.5	17.7			21.0
Net Operating Income	$ 8.2	$10.8	$14.0	$11.6	$14.0	$18.0		17%	$21.4

* Does not include Brigadier Industries since acquisition had not been completed.
† Includes all continuing companies for all periods regardless of date of acquisition except that Gulf States Theatres is included only for the periods since June 1, 1972. Gulf States Theatres was only a part of a business complex, and accurate data for prior periods on the theatres is not available.

EXHIBIT 2

FUQUA INDUSTRIES, INC.
Performance Review
Summary of Operations
($ millions)

Sales and revenues	1970	1971	1972	1973 Dec. 1972 forecast	1973 Actual	1974 forecast
Recreation:						
Lawn and garden equipment	$ 22.2	$ 26.3	$ 36.0	$ 42.0[b]	$ 54.9	$ 65.0
Sporting goods	22.7	30.1	39.1	39.0	54.7	84.0
Marine products.	29.6	34.0	42.4	48.0	49.8	43.0
Entertainment.	26.4	25.9	37.2	45.0	46.5	47.0
Photofinishing.	17.9	17.8	21.8	23.0	26.2	29.0
Total Recreation	$118.8	$134.1	$176.5	$197.0	$232.1	$268.0
Transportation	112.6	130.5	140.7	147.0	156.6	182.0
Shelter[c]	42.7	45.1	69.2	85.0[b]	90.5	91.0
Total Sales[a]	$274.1	$309.7	$386.4	$429.0[b]	$479.2	$541.0

Earnings	1970	1971	1972	1973 Dec. 1972 forecast	1973 Actual	1974 forecast
Recreation:						
Lawn and garden equipment	$ 5.3	$ 5.9	$ 8.9	$ 9.4[b]	$13.2	$14.2
Sporting goods	2.2	3.0	4.0	4.1	4.1	7.6
Marine products.	0.3	0.6	3.3	4.5	4.2	2.7
Entertainment.	4.2	4.5	6.2	6.8	6.4	7.0
Photofinishing.	1.0	1.7	2.4	2.9	3.3	3.9
Total Recreation	$13.0	$15.7	$24.8	$27.7	$31.2	$35.4
Transportation	4.5	9.2	10.0	10.0	9.8	9.8
Shelter[c]	6.4	5.1	5.6	7.9[b]	10.9	13.
Total Operations[a]	$23.9	$30.0	$40.4	$45.6	$51.9	$58.
Unallocated corporate expenses and interest	(6.2)	(8.3)	(9.9)	(9.7)	(12.1)	(11.
Income before taxes—continuing operations	$17.7	$21.7	$30.5	$35.9	$39.8	$47
Income taxes	8.8	10.6	14.6	17.8	19.5	23
Income from Continuing Operations[a].	$ 8.9	$11.1	$15.9	$18.1[b]	$20.3	$24

(a) Includes purchased businesses from date of acquisition; restated for discontinued operations.
(b) Restated for discontinued businesses; original forecasts, which included discontinued business
were $484.0 for total sales and $21.4 for income from continuing operations.
(c) Stormor division moved from discontinued "Agribusiness" group to "Shelter."

Chapter 25

Accounting for human resources and social costs

*Stephen Landekich**

This chapter deals with an area which is rather new to accounting practice, though it has been given considerable attention in the recent accounting literature. Discussions in this area tend to focus either on human resources or social costs. For the reader's convenience, we will follow suit, with only an occasional reminder, here and there, that the underlying concepts and basic goals are common to both of these subjects, as are many of the issues and problems involved.

As an accounting topic, accounting for human resources preceded accounting for social costs. Alternatively, it may also be said that accounting for human resources is a part of accounting for social costs.

Discussions related to human resources usually refer to "human resource accounting" or "human asset accounting." The former seems preferable.

Discussions related to social costs (and social benefits) appear under the captions of "social accounting" or "social audit" or, less frequently, "accounting for corporate social performance."

Accounting for human resources and social costs can be viewed as a proposition, still in the experimental stage, to extend the accounting model so as to accommodate and reflect the recently

---

* Research Director, National Association of Accountants.

expanded notion of the activities and goals pursued by business enterprises. There is no doubt that those activities and goals now run over a wider spectrum than ever before. Accounting for human resources and social costs is an attempt to apply accounting techniques to these new areas of managerial concern and to use the specialized abilities of the accountant in the process of discharging these new responsibilities. This presents, therefore, an important challenge to the accounting profession and an opportunity to contribute in resolving a variety of urgent problems facing contemporary society.

In order to provide adequate information on human resources and social costs, it will be necessary to consider not only new applications of the conventional accounting approaches but also to develop new means of measuring and reporting. Moreover, it is a question of involvement and attitude on the part of the accountant. In addition to technical competence in the traditional sense, the accountant will have to acquire an understanding of the related behavioral, organizational, and societal aspects to a much greater extent than was needed for accounting while it was oriented exclusively to recording and interpreting economic data. These data will have to be treated in reference to a broader framework so as to analyze multiple effects of given economic events and establish a meaningful relationship among the various concerns and points of view as they apply to the factual information which is being reported.

HUMAN RESOURCE ACCOUNTING

Human resource accounting has been defined by the American Accounting Association's Committee on Human Resource Accounting, in the Committee's report published in 1973, as "the process of identifying and measuring data about human resources and communicating this information to interested parties." It may be noted here that this definition does not exclude nonmonetary measurements.

The primary purpose is to help business management by generating reports suitable for use in planning, acquiring, developing, and managing the firm's human resources. A good part of the literature on human resource accounting deals specifically with the potential management uses of the resulting information.

It is also deemed desirable to issue some accounting information on human resources for disclosure to interested parties. Use of this information in external reporting would subject it to the various procedural constraints, such as external reporting standards, and would require consideration of the factors, such as tax effects, which are largely extraneous to the basic conceptual approaches involved in human resource accounting. Hence, our treatment of the subject will be focused on the decision-making impact of human resource accounting.

The basic conceptual approaches

The impact of increases in productivity. The overall performance of the economy is commonly viewed in terms of economic growth. A major factor is increase in productivity.

As economists attempt to explain productivity changes, they realize that the conventional measures do not adequately reflect the impact of the changing labor characteristics—a factor of growing relative importance. The relationship between increases in productivity and changes in value of human resources is a prominent issue in the following considerations related to the need for human resource accounting:

1. Human resource accounting may be instrumental in resolving productivity problems both at the individual level and at the organizational level. Problems of the former type are associated with competence, motivation, and other factors which affect the performance of different individuals in varying degrees. Problems of the latter type are associated with the organization as a social system; they tend to affect the performance of all employees.
2. Measures used in human resource accounting are based largely on productivity changes. Flamholtz (1972), for example, places productivity in the central position among the postulated elements of the individual's conditional value to the firm. Likert and Bowers (1973) propose the use of productivity data for obtaining estimates of changes in the value of the human organization.

Investments in human beings. To develop the analytical means for inclusion of the human factor in economic analyses, economists have introduced the concept of investments in human beings. Some economists go beyond the shift in emphasis from physical means to human resources. They maintain that investments in human beings are of central importance to the economy and society.

The concept of investments in human beings has considerable bearing on the resolution of similar problems within a human resource accounting system. For example, firms spend sizable amounts to finance on-the-job training, but accounting data on such costs are rarely available. The costs typically borne by the firms comprise the following categories:

1. Direct outlays, including the time spent by employees in teaching activities.
2. Indirect costs, including the expense brought about by substandard performance of the trainee.
3. Depreciation of human capital—write-offs due to labor turnover and so on.

Cost versus value of investments in human beings. The cost of investments in human beings cannot be readily obtained from the conventional accounting system. Analyses are, therefore, necessarily based on various cost estimates.

Many economists reject the use of "cost." They favor a valuation approach which takes as the point of departure the data showing the earnings differentials that are attributed to investments in human beings. The value of the investment is then determined by calculating the present worth of the respective future earnings stream.

These two approaches underlie most of the systems of human resource accounting presented in the accounting literature. They are based either on cost measurements or on value measurements, or on some combination of both the cost and value measurements, such as those employing replacement costs and opportunity costs.

Behavioral concepts: Value of the human organization. A different approach has been advocated by the organizational and behavioral theorists and practitioners, particularly by Rensis Likert, whose research work has had a seminal role in the development of human resource accounting. He demonstrated the need for human resource accounting through his study of management styles and the related effects on performance.

Likert's research findings show that the typical accounting measures which are used for evaluating performance are biased in favor of the less effective management styles. Accordingly, present-day accounting systems represent a barrier to achieving the most effective and efficient functioning of organizations. In order to remedy this defect in accounting, it is necessary to expand the scope of accounting to include measurements of the value of human resources and changes in that value over time.

The case for human resource accounting was thus established by Likert in terms of its behavioral impact. Not only did Likert document the need for accounting reports which would show the human organizational effects of different management styles, he also brought within the realm of feasibility a human resource model based on behavioral measurement.

It may be appropriate to observe here that the human behavior dimension underlies all of the approaches to human resource accounting. Moreover, the human behavior dimension is also a critical factor in determining the potential usefulness of the information generated by human resource accounting.

Managerial use of human resource accounting. The rationale for human resource accounting rests on the premise that accounting data have a significant behavioral impact on the people who rely on accounting information in the conduct of their business affairs and particularly on the people whose performance is measured in accounting terms. This behavioral impact may be expected to take place as long as the information on human resources retains the requisite characteristics that are associated with accounting information. Hence, human resource accounting should be compatible with the conventional accounting systems so as to be perceived as part of the accounting system.

Analyses of business practice indicate that there has been gradual evolution in patterns of organization and management. The changes reflect primarily the evolving attitudes toward employees in accordance with the changing managerial views of motivation and behavior.

The cause-effect relationship between motivation and behavior has long been recognized by business managers who must, by definition, get things done through or by other people. As a rule, managers realize that the present-day employees are not responsive to highly structured directive leadership styles. Instead of the traditional carrot-and-stick approach, contemporary managerial thinking is increasingly oriented toward participative forms of management designed to help the employees develop their abilities in a self-directed and creative working environment. It is this style of leadership and management that brings to the fore the concern for people and the demand for information on human resources.

On the other hand, as long as the firm's management does not view its responsibilities in terms of maximizing the human value of the organization, one may argue that in such a firm there is no place for human resource accounting. Indiscriminate introduction of a human resource accounting system is likely to fall short of the desired objectives. Moreover, there is no need or justification for information which is irrelevant for management purposes.

Methods and techniques

Many a question has been raised in the literature regarding the conceptual side of human resource accounting. These questions are usually stated with reference to the traditional historical cost model rather than within a broad framework of accounting theory which embodies various other models as well. As we will demonstrate, human resource accounting can be developed on the basis of historical cost alone. It appears, however, that such a system would not fully meet the objectives of human resource accounting.

The methods and techniques presented below have been selected for illustrative purposes only. The interested reader will find more comprehensive coverage in the sources listed at the end of this chapter.

Capitalization of human resource costs. Human resource accounting has been closely associated with the notion of human assets. Accountants have been reluctant to accept this notion for several reasons related to accounting conventions. The critical question is whether human assets constitute "the rights to receive future economic benefits," that is, whether the notion of human assets meets the criteria of accounting assets as they are defined in conventional accounting theory.

It is not necessary to follow this line of reasoning. The question is more appropriately stated in terms of the investment-expense dilemma. The argument, developed in more detail by this writer in Caplan and Landekich (1974), is that costs incurred to develop human resources in an organization have the requisite characteristics of unexpired costs, that is, the costs incurred in one accounting period that apply to subsequent accounting periods. These costs should, therefore, be accounted for in a manner comparable to that applied to costs incurred to develop the physical capacity of the organization.

As far as the recording of the cost is concerned, the difference between the two alternative treatments—capitalization or expensing—of human resource costs is one of timing, that is, of determining the amounts to be expensed in each of the subsequent years until all the capitalized amount has been expensed. This is conveniently done by constructing an amortization (depreciation) schedule.

In the system developed by the R. G. Barry Corporation, the costs that qualify as investments are recorded for each individual on a separate account form which is designed to show seven cost categories: (1) recruiting, (2) acquisition, (3) orientation, (4) training, (5) familiarization, (6) informal development, and (7) formal development. The beginning balances were established on the basis of standard amounts developed for various levels and positions of employees. These standards are continually (annually) updated to reflect changes due to inflation and other factors.

Exhibit 1 shows the standard amounts, computed on the basis of replacement costs, and the initial amortization adjustment. The

EXHIBIT 1
Resource acquisition and developmental information (replacement investment of managerial personnel at the R. G. Barry Corporation, January 1, 1968)

	A first-line supervisor	A middle manager	A high-level manager	85 managers	% of total
Recruiting costs	$ 600	$ 2,000	$ 6,700	$154,100	(16)
Acquisition costs	200	1,700	3,500	103,500	(10)
Formal training and orientation	100	500	1,000	22,300	(2)
On-the-job training	1,000	3,000	5,100	204,100	(21)
Familiarization	1,900	6,800	10,200	399,000	(40)
Development	200	1,400	2,000	103,600	(11)
Total	$4,000	$15,400	$28,500	$986,600	(100)
Initial amortization adjustment				458,300 (−)	
"Book value"—January 1, 1968				$528,300	

Source: William C. Pyle, "Implementation of Human Resource Accounting in Industry," in *Human Resource Accounting: Development and Implementation in Industry*, edited by R. Lee Brummet, Eric G. Flamholtz, and William C. Pyle (Ann Arbor, Mich.: Foundation for Research on Human Behavior, 1969), p. 45.

net amount indicates the initial "book value" of investments in 85 managers.

The R. G. Barry Corporation project calls for gradual development and implementation of human resource accounting. In the subsequent stages, the system can be extended not only to all personnel as individuals but also to include two additional forms of investments, that is, the investments in (*a*) the interaction-influence system on a group or social system basis and (*b*) the customer relations (goodwill).

Amortization reflects expirations of investments (costs) as the expected benefits are realized over time, that is, the amortization schedule is determined in accordance with the expected useful life of the respective investment. The investments that decline in usefulness over time, such as development costs, are subject to amortization over a predetermined period of time which is, as a rule, of shorter duration than the individual's expected working period ("working life"). The expected useful life of certain investment (cost) categories, such as recruiting and acquisition costs, is equal to the expected working life of the respective individual.

The length of the working life is calculated as the maximum working life weighted by the probability of continued tenure. This probability is, of course, inversely related to the probability of turnover, which is calculated by taking into account the following three factors: (1) age, (2) existing tenure, and (3) level of the position in the company.

The system described above illustrates capitalization of human resource costs through the use of two methods: (1) replacement costs, with adjustments for price-level changes; and (2) outlay (original, historical) costs. According to the model shown in Exhibit 2, additional methods will be introduced subsequently in order to establish the total economic value of human resources. The applicable methods are presented in the next two sections of this chapter.

Human resource valuation of individuals. The commonly used methods of investment valuation can be readily applied to valuation of individuals. One such method is to compute the present worth of the expected future earnings stream attributable to an individual. The pattern of the stream is calculated on the basis of the expected earnings differentials on the present job, taking also into account the differentials related to the expected mobility of the individual. In calculating the present worth for the purposes of human re-

EXHIBIT 2
Model of a human resource accounting system

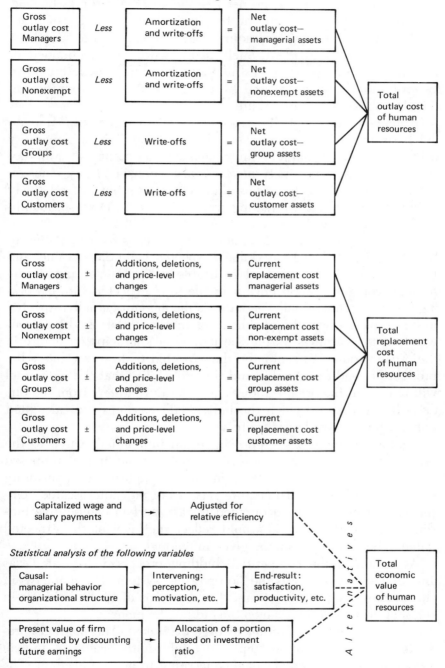

Source: Robert L. Woodruff, Jr., and Robert G. Whitman, *The Behavioral Aspects of Accounting Data for Performance Evaluation,* edited by Thomas J. Burns (Columbus: The Ohio State University, College of Administrative Science, 1970), p. 12.

source accounting there is no need to include the earnings beyond the expected future length of the individual's service (employment) with the firm. This requires an estimate of the length of service for each individual. Such an estimate can be obtained in several ways. An applicable estimating procedure was described in the preceding section, as used by the R. G. Barry Corporation to calculate the expected useful life.

In general, the length of expected service can be estimated on the basis of (1) age and (2) mobility. An individual's mobility within the firm is largely under management control. Mobility among the firms, that is, turnover, is also controllable by management through various policies that affect retention. A relatively simple procedure for estimating transition and turnover probabilities is described by Vroom and MacCrimmon (1972).

A model developed by Flamholtz (1974) calls for calculation of two variables: (1) the individual's expected conditional value, and (2) the individual's expected realizable value. The former is the present worth of the earnings over the total expected future working life of the individual. The latter is the amount actually expected to be derived, given the likelihood of turnover, that is, the present worth of the earnings during the individual's anticipated tenure in the organization. Conceptually, the expected realizable value is the product of conditional value and the probability that the individual will remain in the organization. This procedure differs from the one described earlier in which the individual's earnings are calculated only for the expected service life.

Another method is to approximate an individual's value to the organization through a process of competitive bidding, as proposed by Hekimian and Jones (1967) in order to determine opportunity cost of an individual. To acquire services of valuable (scarce) employees, managers are encouraged to take part in competitive bidding. Each manager's bid would reflect the level of the expected value to be received from the given individual.

A version of the competitive bidding process, in use at Texas Instruments, is known as the "job-posting" system. The emphasis in this system is on the involvement and actions of the individuals in quest of growth rather than on the bidding by managers.

Human resource valuation of organizations. The methods presented here represent attempts to establish the value of human resources on the basis of benefits accruing to an organization. The amounts of such benefits are derived from the value differentials attributable to investments in human resources. These value differentials may be computed for a firm or by groups of employees.

An obvious method is to calculate the total value by adding up the amounts obtained in valuation of individuals, which was covered in the preceding section. The value thus obtained would not include the benefits attributable to interactions among individuals or groups and their relationships with the system, and the benefits attributable to the relationships between the system and its environment.

A business firm may be viewed as a social system. It functions through the purposive and continually changing interrelationships. The nature and direction of these behavioral processes determine the effectiveness of the human resources in an organization which, in turn, is a primary determinant of organizational performance.

Exhibit 3 depicts the relationship of the goals of two groups (management and subordinates) to the goals of the organization. Varying levels of accomplishment are associated with the degrees of compatibility (closeness) among these goals.

In order to capture the value of human resources working in cooperative teams, groups, and systems, it is necessary to extend measurements beyond valuation of individuals. There is no doubt that valuation of individuals reflects the value of their contributions to the group and system. We are concerned here with the values inherent in these groups and systems which are not directly attributable to their members as individuals.

The methods proposed and/or developed with the purpose of valuing human resources in terms of working groups or organizational and social systems may be classified as *economic* or *behavioral*. The methods of economic valuation derive the value of human resources from the value of the firm. The methods of behavioral valuation attempt to establish the value or, rather, the changes in the value of human resources directly, by analyzing and measuring various behavioral indicators which underlie the human value of organizations. Economic valuation is covered in this section, and behavioral valuation is covered in the next section.

One method is to apply the economic valuation by calculating the present worth of the expected future earnings stream attributable to the firm's human resources. Conceptually, this is the same approach as the one discussed under valuation of individuals in

EXHIBIT 3
Relationships of goals of management and subordinates to goals of the organization

Directions of goals of management,
subordinates, and the organization—
moderate organizational accomplishment.

Little organizational accomplishment.

No positive organizational accomplishment.

An integration of the goals of
management, subordinates, and
the organization—*high* organizational accomplishment.

Source: Paul Hersey and Kenneth H. Blanchard, *Management of Organizational Behavior: Utilizing Human Reources* (Englewood Cliffs, N.J.: Prentice-Hall, Inc., 1969), pp. 116–118.

the preceding section. In its application to valuation of "human assets," first proposed by Hermanson (1964), the present worth of the firm, based on the expected earnings, is allocated to human resources according to the ratio of human to total assets. The value of human assets depends on the adjustment of the present value of the future wage (salary) payments to reflect the average efficiency. The average efficiency ratio is computed to show the firm's relative earnings performance and thus indicates the "excess worth created by relatively efficient human resources." A ratio of less than 1 would call for the recognition of a decrease in the value of the firm to reflect future human resource inefficiency.

Hermanson (1964) also proposed "the unpurchased goodwill method," which attributes the differential earnings of a firm to human resources. The differential earnings equal the excess of a firm's current rate of return over the applicable average rate of return.

Changes in the human value of an organization. There is considerable analytical evidence that behavioral dimensions are causal factors of organizational effectiveness and performance. It has also been documented that the *expected* changes in performance can be assessed by measuring the *current* changes in selected behavioral indicators.

Likert (1967 and 1973) uses a relatively small number of key variables:

1. Managerial leadership behavior.
2. Organizational climate.
3. Subordinate (peer) leadership behavior.
4. Group processes.
5. Satisfaction.
6. Performance or effectiveness.

According to Likert, these variables fall into three classes: (*a*) causal (under 1 and 2 above); (*b*) intervening or intermediate (under 3, 4, and 5 above); and (*c*) end result (under 6 above). When trends over time are examined, favorable scores on the causal variables are associated quite consistently with favorable scores on the intervening variables and, in turn, with favorable scores on the end-result variables.

These relationships have been documented by the findings of numerous studies conducted by Likert and other researchers, particularly those associated with the Institute for Social Research of the University of Michigan (see, for example, Taylor and Bowers, 1972). The Institute is also a sponsor of the University's Human Resource Accounting Program, directed by Dr. William A. Pyle who earlier developed initial measurements for the R. G. Barry Corporation (see Exhibit 1) and also coauthored with Brummet and Flamholtz (1968 and 1969) several articles on human resource accounting.

Exhibit 4 shows a model designed by Likert to generate a dollar estimate of the change in value of the productive capability of the human organization from one reporting period to the next. This

EXHIBIT 4

Relationships among human organizational dimensions and to performance

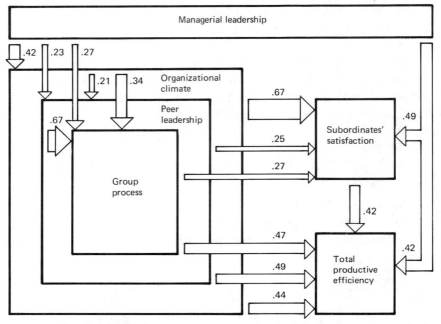

Source: Rensis Likert, "Human resource accounting: Building and assessing productive organizations," *Personnel,* May/June 1973, p. 12.

dollar estimate can be capitalized to reflect the change that has occurred in asset value. The term, "total productive efficiency," stands for the combined data on several performance dimensions such as productivity, costs, and earnings. The width of each arrow signifies approximately the magnitude of the respective relationship. The numerical values are shown in terms of the statistical measure of correlation (the variance) between the variables. Thus, for example, the .42 next to the arrow pointing from managerial leadership to organizational climate means that 42 percent of the variance in organizational climate is accounted for by managerial leadership.

The required behavior indicators are derived from behavioral analyses based on periodic measurements of the key variables. In order to obtain these measurements, Likert uses a questionnaire, "Profile of organizational characteristics," designed to show the condition of each listed item along a scale divided into four segments, each of which comprises five points. The Likert scale corresponds to the four major systems of management style identified in his studies: System 1 ("exploitive-authoritative"), System 2 ("benevolent-authoritative"), System 3 ("consultative"), and System 4 ("science-based"). The basic thesis is that the closer to System 4 an organization's causal and intervening variables appear to be on the scale, the more favorable will be the end-result variables of that organization.

Implementation

In this section we will briefly cover several characteristics of human resource accounting as they pertain to the implementation decisions and procedures. Here we deal with the process of converting available knowledge into a serviceable system.

The reasoning of the type that leads to recognition of human resource accounting as a potential service to corporate management, as presented earlier in this chapter, should enable a corporate accountant to decide whether such a service would be of interest to his or her company. We have also described some of the methods and techniques which could be used for this purpose. Both types of decisions—whether to introduce human resource accounting and, if so, which method(s) to apply—will require a considerable amount of professional judgment in order to evaluate the practical implications of developing a human resource accounting system in a given firm. In the relatively well-established areas, the choice is rather limited. Usually, there are only two alternatives available, and it is likely that there is more authoritative support in favor of one of them. In the areas of human resource accounting, the choice encompasses several approaches and a set of alternative methods within each of these approaches. It is suggested that the interested reader consult additional sources on the subject, such as those listed at the end of this chapter, before deciding on the method to be used in his or her company, since it is always possible that a method which has not been included here may be the most practicable one for a specific set of circumstances and needs.

Exhibit 5 shows a design and implementation model. It depicts five phases and lists the related activities.

Our discussion is organized in two parts. We believe that the first stage should consist of a thorough analysis of the firm. The second

EXHIBIT 5
Generalized model of process design and implementation of a human resource accounting system

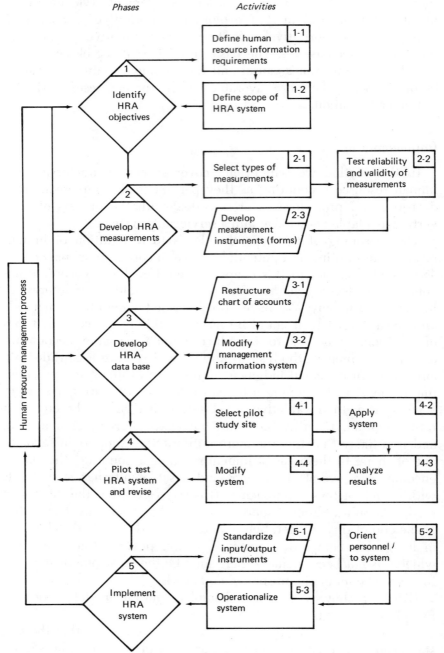

Source: Eric Flamholtz, *Human Resource Accounting* (Encino, Calif.: Dickenson Publishing Co., Inc., 1974), p. 278.

stage would then focus on the design and implementation of the model as selected, at least in broad terms, on the basis of the analytical conclusions obtained in the first stage.

Human-resource profile of the firm.   The objective is to acquire a clear understanding of the organizational and behavioral factors as they relate to the contemplated development of human resource accounting. More specifically, the question is whether a new type of accounting services will meet any existing needs, though not yet fully recognized, for additional information.

The proponents of human resource accounting believe that managers would make good use of accounting information on human resources if it were available. They also argue that it is up to the accountant to take the initiative and introduce such information into the accounting reporting system.

In general, the best candidates for human resource accounting will be the firms with "science-type" management styles, or however else we may designate those firms whose managements not only accept in theory but also follow in practice the thinking associated with a "human resource approach." Among the other likely candidates are the firms whose primary "assets" are their employees, the firms which invest heavily in training and development programs or even the firms experiencing a shortage of qualified personnel due to turnover problems. The least likely candidates will be the firms practicing "exploitive-authoritative" management styles, for even a well-designed system could not be expected to become fully operational in a behavioral sense under the conditions prevailing in such firms. Sooner or later, the system would turn out to be yet another tool of the exploitive policies.

The corporate accountant should, therefore, carefully analyze the organizational and behavioral aspects of human resource accounting as they relate to his or her firm. This analysis should refer to the anticipated effects in the future rather than be restricted to the initial stages only. In other words, implementation of a system should not be undertaken even if it is considered acceptable, unless there are reasonable expectations that it will yield useful results over a period of time extending at least several years into the future.

The next step is to test the analytical conclusions by conducting a test, or a series of tests. The testing should be focused on a few factors which appear to be of critical importance in the light of the initial analysis. A related goal is to acquaint the people in the organization with the functions and objectives of the system under consideration. The testing procedure may consist of informal consultations, or it may also include a formal survey administered through a brief questionnaire. In either case, it is important to contact a representative sample of employees, including nonmanagerial personnel.

System design and development. Once a decision has been made to go ahead with the project, we should proceed on the basis of the conclusions made in the preceding stage. The human resource profile of the firm should serve as the document governing all the subsequent considerations. This seems fairly obvious, except for the observed tendency to give more weight to the new problems which arise as the project is progressing. For example, selection of the appropriate methods and techniques should be made in accordance with the scope and objectives of the system rather than only in terms of the related accounting procedural problems.

A system based on historical (outlay) costs is a likely candidate at the outset. One may assume that capitalization of human resources is a method readily understood by accountants and managers, and also probably more acceptable than any other method.

If at all feasible, a system involving multiple methods should be installed from the very beginning rather than have an inadequate system developed initially, with a plan to add various improvements in the later stages. Our suggestion is to view the initial project as an experimental phase in the design and development of a human resource accounting system. We may even want to test more methods than we expect to use in the system, so as to verify our selection of the methods applicable to our project.

The extent of the experiment is a completely different matter. Here it may be advisable to start out on a small scale by including just a few variables or by directing the project toward a special-purpose objective, such as developing human resource data for capital expenditure decisions.

Some methods appear to be difficult because they include calculations which are not customarily needed in conventional accounting. One example would be the individual's expected conditional value weighted by the probability of continued tenure. This calculation could be considerably simplified, if need be, and still retain its usefulness. Even when adopted in its most elaborate mathematical form, each of these mathematical expressions can and should be transformed into a set (program) of procedural steps involving nothing more than the four basic arithmetic operations.

There is no doubt, however, that methods of behavior measurement present relatively complicated problems. Still, behavior measurement should be made a part of the experiment, if only for the critical role of behavior variables in any system of human resource accounting. The main implementation problem is in computation of monetary measures for behavior variables. However, the nonmonetary measures are admissible, relevant, and usable for the purposes of a human resource accounting system. Moreover, the nonmonetary measures seem preferable until more reliable (accurate) monetary measures have been developed.

Conclusion

In the human resource model of management, which is suggested by modern organizational and managerial concepts, human and organizational objectives complement one another. Accomplishment of organizational objectives is largely attributed to successful human resource management which, in turn, is defined as the process of developing people. To assist management in fulfilling this task, the corporate accountant should acquire the capability of providing appropriate information by developing human resource data for inclusion in the accounting reporting system.

The human resource reports should be consistent with the overall reporting systems, and the information should be generated by methods and techniques having the requisite characteristics associated with accounting measurements. On the other hand, the human resource reports must be designed in accordance with the specific nature of human resource accounting, which in some important respects differs from accounting for physical and financial resources. To illustrate, let us point out a few properties of the human resource information which may require recognition in the reporting system:

1. It takes considerable time to develop human resources in a firm. Cumulative reporting emphasizing long-term patterns and trends will be needed to a greater extent.
2. The human resource changes do not, as a rule, have an immediate effect on organizational performance. Reporting should be designed to relate costs and benefits several years apart in

order to yield meaningful numerical relationships, ratios, and so on.

3. The information on human resources will not lend itself readily to presentation in the form of a single summary indicator. A set of statistics will more appropriately reflect the process and results as they pertain to teams or groups or performance categories of personnel, while the breakdown in terms of organizational units may be relegated to a secondary reporting format.

4. Quantitative measures expressed in nonmonetary terms will serve an important function, particulary with respect to the short-term behavioral impact of human resource management as contrasted to the longer term organizational performance impact.

The reader has undoubtedly noted that our presentation has not included an attempt to construct a model. The focus has been on illustrating rather than evaluating the relevant views and propositions. The explanatory comments have been designed to promote the understanding rather than to advocate the acceptance of human resource accounting. It is our hope that the interested reader will continue to inquire until satisfied to the degree needed to pass a personal professional judgment on the subject matter.

SOCIAL COST ACCOUNTING

A business may be viewed as a social system. It functions through the purposive and continuing activities which involve a number of individuals or groups. This social aspect of business activities was the subject of the preceding section. Much of the discussion under human resource accounting pertains as well to the interaction of the business firm with its social and physical environment.

There is a growing consensus in our society that business managers are responsible for the social and environmental effects of business activities. In order to discharge this social responsibility effectively, business managers need a set of social performance criteria comparable to the criteria used in assessing their economic performance, as well as a system of social measurement comparable to the system of economic measurement provided for by conventional accounting. To this purpose, several attempts have been made to design a suitable information system on social performance, but the subject area is still in the exploratory stage. Considerable research efforts are presently underway, and it is expected that an acceptable system of accounting for corporate social performance will be developed in the near future. Such a system will presumably generate information on social benefits as well as costs. In our presentation we will discuss some of the relevant considerations, report briefly on some proposed approaches to the problem, and outline a rudimentary technique for extending conventional costing to cover the area of social costing.

Areas of corporate social performance

Accounting for corporate social performance requires a broadened concept of entity in order to include the various "constituencies" of the corporation, that is, those groups that are affected by the corporation's social performance, such as employees, stockholders, creditors, suppliers, dealers, competitors, communities, public, and government. It is interesting to note here that the R. G. Barry Corporation project, illustrated in the preceding section, provides for information on the customer relations.

Another way of breaking down corporate social performance into analytically manageable categories is to identify and classify the areas of corporate social impact. A listing compiled by the National Association of Accountants (The Committee on Accounting for Corporate Social Performance, "Accounting for Corporate Social Performance," *Management Accounting*, February 1974) is given below:

 A. *Community Involvement*
  1. General philanthropy
  2. Public and private transportation
  3. Health services
  4. Housing
  5. Aid in personal and business problems
  6. Community planning and improvement
  7. Volunteer activities
  8. Specialized food programs
  9. Education
 B. *Human Resources*
  1. Employment practices
  2. Training programs
  3. Promotion policies
  4. Employment continuity

     5. Remuneration
     6. Working conditions
     7. Drugs and alcohol
     8. Job enrichment
     9. Communications
  C. *Physical Resources and Environmental Contributions*
     1. Air
     2. Water
     3. Sound
     4. Solid waste
     5. Use of scarce resources
     6. Aesthetics
  D. *Product or Service Contributions*
     1. Completeness and clarity of labeling, packaging, and marketing representation
     2. Warranty provisions
     3. Responsiveness to consumer complaints
     4. Consumer education
     5. Product quality
     6. Product safety
     7. Content and frequency of advertising
     8. Constructive research

According to a survey of annual reports of the Fortune 500 Industrials conducted by the CPA firm of Ernst & Ernst, the number of companies making social measurement disclosures has increased from 239 in 1971 to 286 in 1972 and to 298 in 1973. The major categories adopted for this survey are: (1) environmental controls, (2) minority employment and aid to the disadvantaged, (3) responsibility to personnel, (4) community activities, (5) product improvement, and (6) other disclosures on social measurement. (For further information, see D. R. Beresford, "How Companies Are Reporting Social Performance," *Management Accounting*, August 1974.)

Public reporting of corporate social performance

The most prevalent methods of reporting corporate social performance to the public are descriptive reports, though quantified information is sometimes provided. The quantified information is presented in dollar terms and/or in terms of other indices of performance. In most cases, the monetary measurements show the amounts spent rather than both costs and benefits.

Bauer and Fenn (1972) proposed "the process audit" approach as a beginning effort toward assessment of the corporate social programs. D. Linowes (1973) proposed an audit system that would generate a "socioeconomic operating statement." C. Abt (1972) proposed a social audit approach resulting in an integrated social/financial set of balance sheets and income statements. The 1973 annual report of Abt Associates, Inc., also includes an estimate of the financial return on social investment. Dilley and Weygandt (1973) described a cost outlay approach resulting in a social responsibility annual report.

Charnes, Colantoni, and Cooper (1974) made an attempt to present a "social report" within the usual income statement by adding the data for effects on physical and social environment (Exhibit 6).

The extension labeled "external payments" indicates the amounts of money disbursed by the corporation and thus introduced into the economy to be respent with further contributions to GNP. Each column under social effects is stated in the units customarily used in reference to the respective activity or condition, but each column is also related to the monetary figure and, hence, expressed in common units of measurement. As the firm transits through the various stages of social performance, the respective columns are incorporated (closed into) the appropriate financial accounts.

Social costing versus conventional costing

The notion of social costs refers to a new cost dimension which is not explicitly recognized in the measurement and reporting systems within conventional management accounting. The first problem is to decide whether the firm's social costs warrant explicit recognition in the corporate accounting system. In addition to the usual considerations, such as the magnitude of the amounts involved, which are applicable to any cost category, there are three attributes specific to many social costs which are relevant here—social costs are incremental, discretionary, and transitory. Social costs are added to the regular business costs at the management's discretion for the time being so as to participate in or contribute to the social programs which are currently considered important by one or more of the corporate social constituencies.

Some social costs are incurred in response to external pressure in

EXHIBIT 6

A hypothetical multidimensional extension of income and expense statements for corporate social reporting

	Traditional income statement (in million $)		*Extension* *External payments (in million $)*
Net sales		$4,600	
Less cost of goods sold:			
Beginning inventory	$ 840		
Plus manufacturing costs:			
Labor:			
Wages	$1,440		$1,440
Benefits	360		360
Materials	1,725		1,725
Depreciation	225		452*
Total Manufacturing		3,750	
Goods available		$4,590	
Less ending inventory		923	
Total Cost of Goods Sold		$3,667	
Gross margin		933	
Less selling and administrative:			
Salaries	$ 352		$ 352
Benefits	88		88
Materials and supplies	420		420
Depreciation	56	916	
Net operating income		$ 17	
Plus other income		360	
Income before distributions		$ 377	
Less distributions:			
Interest	$ 74		$ 74
Taxes	149		149
Dividends	97	320	97
Net Income Transferred to Accumulated Undistributed Earnings		$ 57	$5,157

* Net purchases of plant and equipment.

Source: A. Charnes, C. Colantoni, and W. W. Cooper, "A Futurological Justification for Historical Cost and Multi-Dimensional Accounting" (Pittsburgh: Carnegie-Mellon University, November 1, 19740, p. 13.

order to placate the groups requesting the firm's involvement and action. As Cohn (1971, p. 18) commented,

> Sometimes the givers do not choose to achieve anything more than ingratiating themselves with recipients, or pacifying a pressuring public. A corporate gift can be a bribe, paid in return for a gadfly

Physical environment			Social environment					
Sulfur emissions (million lbs.)	Sulfur removal (million $)	Particulate emissions (million lbs.)	Employment: # workers (in thousands)	OSHA Index (worker accident days lost)	Participation rates — Black %	Participation rates — Female %	Manpower training (in workers)	Corporate owned housing (in dwelling units)
	24.1							
	6.0							
	1.2		144	216	9.1%	1.2%	1,600	2,100
	16.9							
	28.9							(75)
50		35						
1		2						
			36	2	0.9	10.3	400	150
								35
	22.8							
	(24.1)							
51	(27.6)	37	180	218	7.5%	3.8%	2,000	2,210

group's promise to keep still and refrain from criticism of corporate policies. Just as a mayor will grease the wheel that squeaks, so will a corporation president.

Nevertheless, such expenditures are social costs rather than economic costs, as long as they are related primarily to the social rather than the economic performance of the firm.

It is not the task of the corporate accountant to define social priorities for the managers, but only to facilitate their decisions by

providing the information obtained through the systematic accounting for social costs as distinct from economic costs. To this purpose,
it seems appropriate to include all social costs, even those that do
not appear to have any constructive social value and those that are
not meaningfully related to the continuing interests of any of the
corporate constituencies. For it is only on the basis of complete information on all types of social costs that the managers could improve their decision making regarding the allocation of the corporate
resources intended for achievement of the corporate social performance objectives. Moreover, such a complete accounting for past
costs provides a basis for reevaluation of the respective policies and
for planning of corporate social activities to be undertaken in the
future.

The complete information approach may be implemented from
the very beginning to provide a basis for the initial decisions regarding the introduction and development of social costing. The corporate accountant will have to compile an up-to-date inventory of the
firm's social activities as a reference in the cost data collection process. These data will not be readily available, but an effort should
be made to establish the aggregate amount of all social costs incurred
by the firm in the recent past. In addition to the costs of the firm's
social activities, it will be necessary, of course, to obtain data on the
magnitude of the social costs which appear as incremental costs of
the business decisions in the areas that are not closely related to the
firm's social programs. The incremental social costs can be obtained
by adopting an experimental procedure for segregating the costs
attributable to the firm's social awareness and commitment to social
performance from the total costs of the respective business activities.

A breakdown of the costs by corporate social constituencies and
by areas of social performance, such as the ones illustrated above,
will be useful at this stage. Further analysis will be needed, however, in order to segregate the social costs in the areas which include
both business and social cost elements.

As to the differentiation between the two cost categories, there
are several alternatives, depending on the views as to what constitutes social cost to a firm. In our discussion, we will treat this problem as an issue of accounting policy which is to be resolved in a
manner consistent with the managerial concepts prevailing in the
firm, as evidenced by management's decision making with respect to

the matters of the firm's social policy. Consequently, all the costs associated by the managers with the firm's social performance should be taken into account and carefully scrutinized. Such decisions are not necessarily made within the confines of various social programs; any managerial decision may have been affected by the firm's social performance considerations. As a matter of accounting policy, the incremental costs voluntarily incurred by the managers on account of the desired social effects would all qualify for consideration in social costing. Determination of the actual amounts to be accounted for as social costs is a problem of measurement rather than of policy.

It is recognized that many a voluntary social action of today will become a standard and compulsory requirement at some point in the future. It may be assumed, furthermore, that expectations of this type sometimes motivate the managers to undertake such social actions at the present time. As mentioned earlier, many of the current social costs are transitory in the sense that they tend to become business costs or to be supplemented by other social activities. There is no doubt, however, that they are social costs as long as the managers act voluntarily.

Measurement and reporting of social costs

Adoption of the accounting policy described above should enable the corporate accountant to identify social costs under two broad classification categories: (*a*) costs of the firm's social activities, and (*b*) social costs incremental to business costs in the firm's business activities. An example taken from human resource accounting may be appropriate here. The costs borne by the firm to provide for general on-the-job training are social costs, for the firm stands to lose any potential benefits whenever trained workers are bid away by other firms. The costs of completely specific training that has no potential effect on earnings of the trainee in any other firm are business costs, or business investments in human resources. On the other hand, unavoidable costs of on-the-job training as an economical substitute for the costs of hiring new employees for the given jobs are not training costs at all; the potential benefits to the trainees are generated at no incremental cost to the firm. A similar situation exists with respect to the voluntary social activities of the employees which are performed at no cost to the firm. According to the accounting policy based on actual costs to the firm, such employee activities are not accounted for as the firm's social costs. An alternative policy of including these costs simply because of the encouragement provided by the firm to the employees to participate on their own time in social activities would result in a measurement system which enables the firm to appropriate the social benefits that cannot be meaningfully traced back to the costs incurred by the firm.

In the same vein, if an extension of social costing is contemplated so as to include external effects, we would suggest that it be first applied to social costs rather than social benefits. Such an extension would provide for systematic data on the costs incurred by the firm to society, where the firm appropriates the benefits even though the related costs are not borne by the firm. On the basis of the information derived from these data the managers could plan the amounts needed to offset the respective external costs in order to establish and maintain a sound social balance in the future.

The social costing approach outlined here presents no measurement or reporting difficulties which could not be resolved through the application of the appropriate techniques currently used in conventional management accounting. The only major difference is in the process of matching costs with revenues. Social costs are not traceable to economic gains. Hence, there are no revenues in an accounting sense.

There are numerous fairly reliable and relatively easy-to-implement methods available for use in computing social benefits resulting from corporate social performance. We do not anticipate, however, widespread utilization of these methods in accounting for corporate social performance, since they have not as yet been widely used in conventional management accounting.

Calculations of the expected benefits could be used to advantage, for example, on a project basis for resource allocation decisions, just as the expected money flows are calculated (discounted) in order to select capital expenditure projects. The use of these calculations, or other relevant methods such as shadow prices, for the purpose of establishing a monetary input for reports to management would not be consistent with the present state of technology in management accounting. Furthermore, accounting for social costs seems to be sufficiently informative in terms of the current managerial decision techniques.

Nonmonetary indicators of corporate social performance

Many corporate social performance activities do not lend themselves readily to measurement in monetary terms.[1] In general, monetary measures of the input (costs) are more likely to be both practicable and satisfactory than are monetary measures of the output (benefits).

The input originates largely in monetary terms as cash outlay (donations, grants, etc.) or cost borne by the firm which is already determined, or is easily determinable, in monetary units. The output, on the other hand, often takes the form of intangible benefits affecting in varying degrees a number of people over an unspecified period of time.

Monetary measures of "internalized" benefits, such as improvements in corporate human organizational dimensions, may be quantified and even converted into dollars with reference to the benefits to be appropriated by the firm in the future through the impact of such improvements on corporate economic performance. The benefits of this type are, however, economic as well as social. Monetary measures of the benefits which appear as external societal, including environmental, effects cannot be readily calculated in monetary terms. What is perhaps equally important, calculations of this type would not yield information meaningful to most of the beneficiaries or interested constituencies. Consequently, information on the benefits external to the firm should preferably be stated in the units appropriate to the respective benefits, as illustrated in Exhibit 6. Such nonmonetary indicators may alternatively be used to portray the magnitude and type of the input elements, along with the monetary data on the costs involved.

Conclusion

Accounting for social costs adds another dimension to the information provided for management. It seems reasonable to expect that such information would be of considerable assistance to management

---

[1] The term "social performance activities" is introduced here advisedly to denote the activities toward social performance goals as distinguished from the activities toward economic performance goals. Corporate activities of both types may be termed "social activities."

in an important and sensitive area of corporate performance where methodical decision making could yield substantial benefits, both economic and social.

The effort required on the part of the corporate accountant is not likely to be material, not even in the initial stage. Most of the data are accessible; and once the appropriate procedure has been made operational, social costing will yield useful information generated at a nominal cost to the corporation.

We have not explicitly dealt with the matters of external reporting of the information on social costs. There is no doubt, however, that this information would be suitable for release to the various corporate social constituencies, including the stockholders.

SELECTED REFERENCES

Abt, Clark "Managing to Save Money While Doing Good." *Innovation,* January 1972.

Bauer, Raymond A., and Dan Fenn, Jr. *The Corporate Social Audit,* New York: Russell Sage Foundation, 1972.

Brummet, R. Lee; Flamholtz, Eric G.; and Pyle, William C. "Human Resource Accounting: A Tool to Increase Managerial Effectiveness." *Management Accounting,* August 1969.

———— "Human Resource Measurement—A Challenge for Accountants," *The Accounting Review,* April 1968.

Caplan, Edwin H., and Landekich, Stephen *Human Resource Accounting: Past, Present and Future.* New York: National Association of Accountants, 1974.

Charnes, A.; Colantoni, C.; and Cooper, W. W. "A Futurological Justification for Historical Cost and Multi-Dimensional Accounting." Pittsburgh: Carnegie-Mellon University, November 1, 1974.

Cohn, Jules *The Conscience of the Corporations.* Baltimore, Md.: The Johns Hopkins Press, 1971.

Dilley, Steven C., and Weygandt, Jerry J. "Measuring Social Responsibility: An Empirical Test." *Journal of Accountancy,* September 1973.

Flamholtz, Eric *Human Resource Accounting.* Encino, Calif.: Dickenson Publishing Company, Inc., 1974.

———— "Toward a Theory of Human Resource Value in Formal Organization." *The Accounting Review,* October 1972.

Hekimian, James S., and Jones, Curtis H. "Put People on Your Balance Sheet." *Harvard Business Review,* January–February 1967.

Hermanson, Roger H. *Accounting for Human Assets.* East Lansing, Mich.: Michigan State University, 1964.

Likert, Rensis *The Human Organizations: Its Management and Value.* New York: McGraw-Hill Book Co., 1967.

————, **and Bowers, David G.** "Improving the Accuracy of P/L Reports by Estimating the Change in Dollar Value of the Human Organization," *Michigan Business Review,* March 1973.

Linowes, David F. "The Accounting Profession and Social Progress." *The Journal of Accountancy,* July 1973.

Taylor, James C., and Bowers, David G. *Survey of Organizations.* Ann Arbor, Mich.: The University of Michigan, 1972.

Vroom, V. H., and MacCrimmon, K. R. "Toward a Stochastic Model of Managerial Careers," *Administrative Science Quarterly,* June 1968, reprinted in *Manpower Planning and Programming,* edited by E. H. Burack and J. W. Walker. New York: Allyn & Bacon, Inc., 1972.

Chapter 26

Accounting for changes in general price levels and current values

*R. C. Thompson**
Robert Koons†

BACKGROUND

Since World War II, inflation has had a fluctuating but persistent impact on the U.S. economy. Initially, price levels rose rapidly after wartime price controls were removed. This was followed by some 25 years of modest but stubborn inflation. Meantime, while gradually rising price levels diminished the usefulness of traditional measures of income and financial condition, consideration for modifying financial reports was generally limited to academic writing and theory. Then, the accelerating rate of inflation in the early 1970s aggravated the problem and raised more persistent questions as to the usefulness of the historical cost accounting model to present relevant financial statements.

The central problem with historical cost in a period of inflation is that assets are recorded at cost but the dollars expended and recouped over time have different values. As assets are consumed, charges to income via depreciation or amortization of other prior

---

* Controller, Shell Oil Company.
† Project director, Financial Accounting Standards Board.

period costs do not reflect current cost of those assets. Therefore, in real terms, the provision is generally inadequate to replace the assets consumed, and income tends to be overstated. While this is the general consequence, there may be offsetting factors such as gains from repaying past obligations in currently cheaper dollars.

The historical cost system is quite effective in producing consistently comparable results when the monetary unit is stable or is changing by very nominal amounts. However, the dollar's command over goods and services—its purchasing power—is not constant since its ability to command goods and services in the marketplace is always changing. Although monetary units occasionally increase in value, most of history reflects the diminution in monetary value known as inflation. When inflation is relatively mild its effects may be little noticed, but a significant increase quickly causes national concern. Aside from its adverse impact on individuals and business, inflation also reduces the usefulness of financial statements based upon historical cost.

Financial statements of going business concerns invariably contain items of mixed vintage and/or purchasing power. Assets purchased years ago, when the dollar would buy twice the goods and services it does today, are combined into accounts with new assets without recognition that the dollars involved were unlike units of measurement. The depreciation provision for fixed assets, therefore, is a hybrid resulting from the averaging of unlike terms. It could be said that adding such varying units of measure is like adding dollars, francs, and guilders without regard to the different monetary symbols. This questionable procedure, then, is the basis for the concern that historical cost statements fail to provide a true and fair view of financial position or the results of operations over a period of time.

Some of the defects of historical cost accounting during a period of even nominal or moderate inflation are:

1. Reported profits generally tend to be overstated.
2. Investment in fixed assets and shareholders' equity are understated.
3. Taxation takes a greater portion of real income than reported.
4. Dividends paid to shareholders represent a larger portion of earnings than indicated. (It is quite possible that dividends might exceed earnings if both were expressed in current dollars.)

5. Employees, or their bargaining agents, believe they are receiving a lesser share of the value added than is the true case.
6. Losses and gains which arise from holding monetary assets and liabilities are not recognized.
7. Conventional ratios used to gauge the health of the enterprise are distorted. Ratios such as debt/equity, net income/equity, dividends/earnings, and so on, may cause misleading financial decisions.
8. The impact of inflation by no means affects all commodities, transactions, or financial reports in the same way. On the contrary, the effects can be significantly different. Therefore, conclusions or impressions as to relative conditions or financial performance can be incorrect.

During a period of sustained inflation, net income and dividends may be reported to be level or rising. However, in terms of purchasing power, or dollars of current vintage, net income and dividends may well be declining. Failure to measure and disclose this possibility can be considered a failure of the conventional model to perform fairly the stewardship reporting function. Economists who have a different concept of profit than accountants frequently object to the historical cost model for reasons other than its failure to remove the effect of inflation. In considering what, if any, change or supplement is to be made in the basic accounting model, it seems essential to keep in mind why a change is being sought. Is it merely to remove the effects of inflation from the conventional model, or is it to change from an accounting to an economic concept of profit? In the first instance a supplemental general price-level adjustment appears to accomplish the change desired. If the reason for change is a different concept of profit, new disciplines are required.

POSSIBLE ALTERNATIVES TO HISTORICAL COST

Numerous businesses have adopted last-in, first-out inventory valuation procedures and accelerated methods of depreciation to partially counter the impact of inflation. While these are generally accepted accounting principles, they have provided only partial solutions. Many other methods of correcting the defects in the present accounting model have been proposed, but basic alteration of accepted custom and practice can be accomplished only at great cost and effort. Furthermore, while a desire for some change is growing, the nature of the change to be made is by no means self-evident or generally accepted.

In general, the alternatives to historical cost may be divided into two broad categories:

1. Price-level adjusted reporting (general purchasing power re-statements), which adjusts for the changing value of the currency.
2. Current value reporting, which adjusts for the changing worth of specific assets based on many economic variables.

At this time only price-level reporting has authoritative support, including methodology, and therefore most of the chapter is devoted to this technique, followed by a brief description of the major current value accounting methods currently advocated.

Price-level adjusted financial statements are simply historical cost statements expressed in dollars of constant purchasing power rather than in historical cost dollars—that is, financial statements are prepared exactly as they are now, and then adjusted to reflect a constant, as opposed to a variable, monetary unit. The adjustment does not purport to produce current value of particular assets or liabilities held but does adjust for the value of the currency used for measurement over various time periods.

A definition of *current value* is both vaguer and more controversial. It may be variously defined as the present value of the future net cash flows to be derived from an asset, or the current replacement cost, exit value, liquidation value, or market value. Although information on these values would be useful if it could be obtained, there is a wide diversity of opinion as to how such accounting could be accomplished, and serious doubt exists that such a system could be implemented on an ongoing basis. These methods are described later in the chapter.

REPORTING THE EFFECT OF
PRICE-LEVEL CHANGES

Several ways have been suggested for using a price-level adjustment to eliminate the distorting effects of inflation on the financial reports. The adjustment can be made once, at a specific point in time, after which subsequent transactions are accounted for in the conventional manner of historical cost. Alternatively, the adjustment can be a continuing process.[1]

The specific moment-in-time adjustment has been employed on occasion in several foreign countries for both book and tax purposes. The principal merit lies in the ability to restate uniformly the assets of all companies after a period of severe inflation. However, with continuing inflation the adjustment soon becomes obsolete. This type of adjustment for inflation is not an alternative being considered in the United States.

Two different approaches have been suggested for making the ongoing or continuing adjustment for inflation. The first method adjusts for changes in the general price level, and the second adjusts for specific price changes of individual items.

The general price-level system applies an index, which approximates changes in the value of money, to the historical cost amounts. It is generally agreed that the Gross National Product (GNP) Implicit Price Deflator is the best general index to measure the change in the value of the U.S. dollar. This is also the index recommended by the Accounting Principles Board and the Financial Accounting Standards Board. Some advocate the use of the Consumer Price Index or Wholesale Price Index; but generally these are regarded as too narrow and specific in scope for general price-level adjustments.

The GNP Deflator Index is based upon year 1958 as 100. If one were interested only in results in constant 1958 dollars, they could readily be obtained by using the deflator directly. However, since most users would have difficulty in relating to the dollar's value in the past, the preferred practice is to convert the current GNP Deflator to 100, thus stating the price-level results in current dollars. This latter practice has the disadvantage of requiring revision of all prior periods with each new restatement. However, understanding the roll-forward adjustment should not be particularly difficult for those who understand the concept of constant dollars.

Use of the GNP Deflator isolates effects of changes in purchasing power of money from the accounts but not changes in individual prices or values. The following example demonstrates the difference between historical cost and general price-level adjusted accounts.

A depreciable asset was purchased for $1,000 on January 1, 1968.

---

[1] Morton Backer, *Current Value Accounting* (Financial Executive Research Foundation, 1973), pp. 118–22.

Physical and economic life was ten years. Salvage was zero. The GNP Price Deflator was 121.8 for 1968 and 158.4 for fourth quarter 1973. The restatement factor is therefore 158.4/121.8, or 1.3004, and the 1973 accounts would be reported as follows:

	Historical cost	12/31/73 dollars
Fixed asset 12/31/73	$1,000	$1,300
Accumulated depreciation	600	780
Net fixed asset 12/31/73	400	520
Depreciation for year 1973	100	130

The price-level adjusted data indicates that the $1,000 invested in 1968 is the same as 1,300 year-end 1973 dollars. In current dollars, depreciation on the investment is $130 instead of the historical depreciation of $100. Obviously, the replacement cost or the current value of this asset may be quite different from either of the above sets of data. The current price may actually be less than $400 or more than the $520 depreciated cost in current dollars, or, in extreme cases, even more than the original $1,000.

Advocates of specific indices favor the use of measures which more nearly depict the cost and price levels of the goods and services utilized by the enterprise. They favor use of a specific price index on individual items, or groups of similar items, to restate the financial reports in order to approximate replacement value more nearly. The multiplicity of available indices which measure prices within a given industry is one of the major deterrents in obtaining general acceptance of the principle. Also, many believe that results can be influenced or managed by the index selection.

Proponents of general price-level reporting generally claim the following advantages:

1. Historical costs that are adjusted for changes in the price level provide a proper matching of costs and revenues since both are expressed in current purchasing power dollars.
2. General price-level adjustment provides more meaningful intercompany and interperiod comparisons.
3. General price-level adjustments are not a deviation from historical cost concepts and are compatible with generally accepted accounting principles.
4. Monetary gains or losses can be significant in certain firms and industries, and therefore should be reported in financial statements.

5. General price-level reporting removes the impact of inflation on measurements of income.

Opponents of general price-level reporting frequently cite two weaknesses. First, doubt is expressed that a general index can be applied to individual amounts to create meaningful figures in the financial statements. This doubt is based on two considerations:

1. A true index for the purchasing power of the dollar cannot be accurately determined; the only reason that the index, such as the GNP, is called a general index is because it has a broad base.[2]
2. The general index does not reflect the change in value of assets, which opponents feel would be more useful information.

Secondly, opponents question statement utility since researchers have found that the business community generally does not understand such reports.[3]

In 1969, with the issuance of *Statement No. 3*, the APB recommended adoption of comprehensive price-level adjusted statements as supplements to historical cost statements, and provided guidelines for their preparation. Its recommendation was based on the conclusion that statements adjusted for general price-level changes presented useful information not available from historical dollar statements. Through 1973, the recommendation was generally ignored in published reports.

In 1974 the Financial Accounting Standards Board issued an exposure draft for public comment which, if adopted, will require the reporting of supplemental price-level adjusted data. Many firms began testing or attempting to apply the APB/FASB methodology. Although few have adopted this method of dealing with inflation, it is the only comprehensive system currently available which has been fully tested and is capable of immediate implementation.

PREPARATION OF GENERAL PRICE-LEVEL ADJUSTED FINANCIAL STATEMENTS

The full impact of inflation can be measured only by a comprehensive restatement of all elements of the financial statements,

---

[2] Ibid., p. 144.

[3] Ibid., p. 146.

Partial restatements such as adjustments of only depreciation expense or inventory profits may provide misleading and biased results, since there are positive as well as negative effects from inflation. The age of assets held by a firm, the composition of working capital, and the proportion of debt to equity will determine the impact of a change in the general price level. Holders of monetary assets such as cash lose purchasing power during a period of inflation, whereas investments in nonmonetary items are not similarly affected. Conversely, holders of liabilities payable in a fixed number of dollars realize a gain during such periods since obligations can be satisfied with dollars of reduced purchasing power.

Large corporations or multidivisional companies can generally develop sufficiently accurate price-level adjusted statements from consolidated financial information. However, in the event significant partially owned subsidiaries which are accounted for on an equity basis are involved, the statements of the subsidiary should first be price-level adjusted to determine the proper adjustment on the parent's reports. In restating results from consolidated data rather than individual transactions, particular care must be exercised to insure that all adjustments are consistently reflected in both the income statement and the balance sheet. Ideally, the change in restated shareholders' equity for the period should exactly equal the restated income less dividends plus new equity issues. Nominal differences should be expected in practice because of rounding restatement factors and amounts, changes in GNP indicators, and short-cut procedures employed.

The major steps in preparing comprehensive price-level adjusted financial statements are as follows:

1. Select a price-level index and calculate restatement factors to state prior period transactions in terms of their current monetary equivalents.
2. Identify monetary and nonmonetary assets and liabilities, and determine the date nonmonetary components originated.
3. Restate nonmonetary items.
4. Restate monetary items in the balance sheet at the beginning of the first year for which price-level adjusted statements were prepared.
5. Analyze and determine the age of all revenue and expense transactions in the income statement for the current year and

all dividends and other changes in retained earnings during
the year.
6. Apply the "cost or market" rule to restated assets and liabilities
   where that rule would be applied to historical cost financial
   statements.
7. Compute the general purchasing power gain or loss for the
   current year.
8. Roll forward restated statements of the prior year to units of
   current general purchasing power.

These steps generally conform with methods suggested in *Accounting Principles Board Statement No. 3* and with the Financial
Accounting Standards Board exposure draft. Some of the logic and
basic principles involved in each step are discussed below. This is
followed by illustrative statements and worksheets for the complete
restatement procedure in Schedules R-1 through R-12, as well as
alternative methods and procedures for estimating the age of fixed
assets, restating depreciation, and calculating monetary gains and
losses.

Step 1. Select index and compute conversion factors

The Financial Accounting Standards Board and the former Accounting Principles Board, as previously mentioned, have recommended use of the Gross National Product Implicit Price Deflator
as the appropriate measure for general price-level adjustments.

The GNP Deflator is issued quarterly by the Bureau of Economic Analysis of the U.S. Department of Commerce approximately
45 days after the end of each quarter. However, an early estimate
of the index is released approximately 15 days after the quarter
which, if necessary, can be used for statement preparation. Initial
announcements of the Deflator are by press release, with subsequent
publication in *Survey of Current Business*.[4] Because of technological changes in goods and services and technical problems in developing the index, the year 1945 is suggested as the earliest date for
which the index is sufficiently comparable. The average annual
index may be used for transactions occurring uniformly throughout
a given year and the most recently published quarterly GNP De-

---

[4] Social and Economic Statistical Administration, Bureau of Economic Analysis,
U.S. Department of Commerce.

flator should be used as an approximation of the index of general purchasing power of the dollar at the balance sheet date.

The GNP Deflators and the factors used for restating amounts into units of 12/31/74 purchasing power are shown in Schedule R-1.

Step 2. Identify monetary and nonmonetary items

In measuring the effects of general price-level changes it is necessary to distinguish between monetary and nonmonetary items. *Monetary items* are cash and claims to cash, as well as obligations that have balances which are fixed as to number of dollars regardless of changes in the general price level—that is, value of the dollar. All other items are *nonmonetary.*

Examples of monetary assets are cash, accounts and notes receivable, refundable deposits, and cash surrender value of life insurance. Marketable securities may also be monetary, depending upon the securities involved. For example, short-term investments in commercial paper and certificates of deposit which will be redeemed for a fixed number of dollars are monetary, while equity investments which will not be liquidated by a fixed number of dollars are nonmonetary. Most liabilities are monetary since they will be settled by payment of fixed amounts. Preferred stock may also be monetary if it is carried in the balance sheet at an amount equal to its fixed liquidation or redemption price.

The principal nonmonetary assets are property, plant, and equipment, inventories, prepaid expenses, and deferred charges. Examples of nonmonetary liabilities include debt payable in foreign currency (although this is still being debated) and advances received on sales contracts or other obligations for future delivery of nonmonetary goods and services.

There is conflicting opinion on whether deferred income tax credits are monetary or nonmonetary. *Accounting Principles Board Statement No. 3* and the Financial Accounting Standards Board's exposure draft have selected nonmonetary treatment on the basis that the balances represent a past cost saving which will be amortized in future periods. Also cited is the fact that amounts ultimately paid may differ because of changes in tax rates and tax laws and that payment is dependent upon future taxable income. Conversely, while proponents of the monetary classification of deferred taxes agree that the amounts involved are estimates and may vary, they conclude that these variations are in no way related to changes in price levels. They also emphasize the characteristics of future obligations rather than past cost savings. When timing differences reverse, the result is taxes payable in current dollars, and unless a company expects to pay such amounts in the future the basic purpose and principle of tax allocation is not justified. The monetary treatment is supported by AICPA *Accounting Research Study No. 6* and has been followed in all exhibits in this chapter.

Step 3. Restate nonmonetary items

After monetary items are identified, the remaining items in the balance sheet are classified as nonmonetary and must be analyzed to determine the age of the amounts retained in the balance sheet as well as of items that have passed through to the income statement.

Retained earnings in the first balance sheet for which general purchasing power restatements are prepared may be computed as the balancing amount. This avoids the restatement of all prior financial statements. Retained earnings in subsequent restated balance sheets is determined by adding restated income and subtracting restated dividends from the opening retained earnings balance (which must be rolled forward to reflect the price level at the end of the current year).

Step 4. Restate monetary items in the balance sheet at the beginning of the first year

Monetary items at the beginning of the first year for which price-level adjusted statements are prepared are expressed in prior year dollars and must be restated to the general purchasing power of the dollar at the end of the current year. Monetary balances at the end of the current year are already expressed in current purchasing power and no restatement is necessary.

Step 5. Analyze income–expense items and all dividends or other changes in retained earnings and determine when amounts originated

For many companies revenues are received and expenses incurred fairly evenly during the year. In those instances, the amounts can be restated at the average general purchasing power index for the year. If revenues or expenses are not spread evenly throughout the year, quarterly amounts should be restated by using appropriate quarterly indices.

Much of the information needed for income and expense restatement is derived from balance sheet restatements and frequently both can be restated in a single computation. For example, the analysis and aging of prepayments and deferrals will also reveal the amortization of such items and the age of amounts flowing into the income statement. Similarly the restatement of inventories is an essential element in adjusting cost of goods sold. On the other hand, a review of purchases, production costs, or cost flows is needed to age inventories properly.

Problems may be encountered in restating inventories and cost of goods sold since amounts contained in inventory valuations are not readily identifiable. Generally, the amounts involved do not warrant the time-consuming analysis needed for precise aging, and sufficient accuracy is achieved by estimating the weighted average age of total inventory. If inventories are valued on a first-in, first-out basis, all of the component amounts may have originated in the most recent quarter and are therefore expressed in current purchasing power dollars. If so, no restatement is necessary. Lifo inventories usually can be segregated into annual layers and each layer restated by the average general price-level index for the year involved. Inventories valued by averaging methods present a greater problem because they will retain the effects of changing costs since inception of the enterprise. One method of estimating the age of such inventories is to compare the average carrying value per unit with the unit purchase or production costs that prevailed in previous periods. The weighted average age will be the point in time at which such costs per unit were similar to current average carrying values.

Step 6. Apply the "cost or market" rule to restated assets and liabilities where such rule would be applied in historical cost financial statements

Nonmonetary assets which are expressed at the lower of cost or market should not be restated to amounts exceeding market value in price-level adjusted statements. For example, restated costs of inventories or securities may exceed the current market value. In this event the restated amounts should be written down to market just as would be done in historical dollar statements.

Similarly, nonmonetary liabilities should not be restated to amounts in excess of those required to discharge the obligations, but they may require a write-down. This same constraint should also apply to deferred tax credits in the event they are classified as nonmonetary items.

Step 7. Compute the general purchasing power gain or loss on monetary items

The gain or loss that arises from holding monetary items during a period of inflation or deflation is reported in price-level adjusted income statements. The procedure recommended by the Financial Accounting Standards Board for calculating such gains or losses is shown in Schedule R-12 and is based on an analysis of transactions which cause changes in the monetary items.

A simplified method of calculating purchasing power gain or loss is presented following the basic illustrations.

Step 8. Roll forward restated statements of the prior year to units of current purchasing power

Once financial statements or components have been restated to the purchasing power at a given point in time they can be rolled forward (or backward if desired) to the purchasing power at other times by applying the ratio of purchasing power indexes for the two periods. Prior year restatements are rolled forward to dollars of the current year by multiplying each amount by the prior year's fourth-quarter restatement factor. For example, an amount which had been restated to $100 at end of year 1973 is rolled forward to 12/31/74 dollars as $112 by applying the 1.118 factor shown in Schedule R-1. This roll forward of the prior year statements is not only useful for comparative purposes, but also provides the opening retained earnings balance in current dollars which is needed for the statement of income and retained earnings.

As indicated earlier, the government's initial estimate of the GNP Implicit Price Deflator is usually revised at a later date, and the revision will frequently occur after price-level statements have been prepared and published. In this event, the roll forward to a subsequent year's dollars should be based on the amount of change that has occurred from the index actually used in preparing the statements of the prior period, regardless of what the index was subsequently determined to be.

The total restatement procedure is illustrated in the following Schedules, R-1 through R-12.

SCHEDULE R-1

KJ&B INC.
General Purchasing Power Restatement—1974
Gross National Product Implicit Price Deflators and Restatement Factors

	Annual average			Quarterly average	
Year	GNP deflator	Restatement factor	Year	GNP deflator	Restatement factor
1945	59.7	2.976	1972		
1946	66.7	2.664	1st qtr.	144.85	1.227
1947	74.6	2.382	2d.	145.42	1.222
1948	79.6	2.232	3d.	146.42	1.213
1949	79.1	2.246	4th	147.63	1.204
1950	80.2	2.215			
1951	85.6	2.076	1973		
1952	87.5	2.031	1st qtr.	149.95	1.185
1953	88.3	2.012	2d.	152.61	1.164
1954	89.6	1.983	3d.	155.67	1.141
1955	90.9	1.955	4th	158.93	1.118
1956	94.0	1.890			
1957	97.5	1.822	1974		
1958	100.0	1.777	1st qtr.	163.61	1.086
1959	101.6	1.749	2d.	167.31	1.062
1960	103.3	1.720	3d.	172.04	1.033
1961	104.6	1.699	4th	177.68*	1.000
1962	105.8	1.679			
1963	107.2	1.657			
1964	108.8	1.633			
1965	110.9	1.602			
1966	113.9	1.560			
1967	117.6	1.511			
1968	122.3	1.453			
1969	128.2	1.386			
1970	135.2	1.314			
1971	141.6	1.255			
1972	146.1	1.216			
1973	154.3	1.152			
1974	170.16	1.044			

$$\text{Restatement Factor} = \frac{\text{4th Quarter 1974 Deflator}}{\text{Deflator for Period Involved}}$$

* Based upon preliminary index issued in January 1975 by the U.S. Department of Commerce, Bureau of Economic Analysis.

SCHEDULE R-2

KJ&B INC.
General Purchasing Power Restatement—1974
Working Balance Sheets—12/31/73 and 12/31/74
(in thousands)

	12/31/73			12/31/74		
	Historical dollars	*Restatement factor or source*	*Restated to 12/31/74 dollars*	*Historical dollars*	*Restatement factor or source*	*Restated to 12/31/74 dollars*
Assets:						
Cash	600	(1) 1.118	671	208	(2)	208
Marketable securities	3,800	(3) 1.118	4,248	5,992	(3)	5,992
Receivables—net	9,000	(1) 1.118	10,062	9,630	(2)	9,630
Inventories:						
Finished goods (Lifo)	3,200	R-4	4,717	3,900	R-4	5,420
Materials and supplies (Fifo) . . .	400	(4) 1.118	447	960	(4)	960
Prepaid expenses	500	R-5	608	380	R-5	439
Total Current Assets	17,500		20,753	21,070		22,649
Property, plant, and equipment						
(at cost)	68,300	R-6	94,638	74,625	R-6	99,798
Less: Accumulated depreciation .	33,100	R-7	49,164	36,605	R-7	53,175
	35,200		45,474	38,020		46,623
	52,700		66,227	59,090		69,272
Liabilities and deferred credits:						
Accounts payable	8,700	(1) 1.118	9,727	11,630	(2)	11,630
Deferred income—payments						
received in advance	110	R-8	127	90	R-8	93
Long-term debt	10,200	(1) 1.118	11,404	9,900	(2)	9,900
Deferred income taxes	3,030	(1) 1.118	3,388	3,200	(2)	3,200
	22,040		24,646	24,820		24,823
Shareholders' equity:						
Capital stock—common	2,340	R-9	3,580	2,360	R-9	3,601
Additional paid-in capital	5,830	R-9	8,783	5,870	R-9	8,824
Retained earnings	22,490	(5)	29,218	26,040	R-3	32,024
	30,660		41,581	34,270		44,449
	52,700		66,227	59,090		69,272

(1) 12/31/73 monetary items are stated in 12/31/73 dollars and the restatement factor for the fourth quarter 1973 is used to restate them to 12/31/74 dollars.
(2) 12/31/74 monetary items are stated in 12/31/74 dollars, and no restatement is necessary.
(3) Securities in this illustration are certificates of deposit, a monetary item, and reported as in notes (1) and (2). Nonmonetary securities carried at cost must be analyzed in a manner similar to the illustration shown for Lifo inventories in Schedule R-4.
(4) Assumes all significant costs of materials and supplies inventory were incurred in last quarter of year.
(5) In a company's first general purchasing power restatement of the balance sheet, retained earnings is restated to the amount necessary to make the balance sheet balance.

SCHEDULE R-3

KJ&B INC.
General Purchasing Power Restatement—1974
Working Statement of Income and Retained Earnings
(in thousands)

	Historical dollars	Restatement factor or source	Restated to 12/31/74 dollars
Sales	84,930	R–10	88,680
Operating expenses:			
Cost of sales (except depreciation)	62,350	R–10	65,193
Depreciation	5,945	R–7	7,869
Selling and administrative expenses	5,200	R–11	5,474
	73,495		78,536
Operating profit	11,435		10,144
Loss on sale of equipment	(135)		(287)
Net general purchasing power gain		R–12	1,040
Income before federal income taxes	11,300		10,897
Federal income taxes	5,400	(1) 1.044	5,638
Net income	5,900		5,259
Retained earnings 12/31/73	22,490		29,218
	28,390		34,477
Dividends paid	2,350	(2) 1.044	2,453
Retained earnings 12/31/74	26,040		32,024

(1) Assumed to have accrued ratably throughout the year.
(2) Uniform quarterly distribution of dividends.

SCHEDULE R-4

KJ&B INC.
General Purchasing Power Restatement—1974
Analysis of Finished Goods Inventory
(in thousands)

Year acquired	Factor to restate to 12/31/74 dollars	Historical dollars	Restated to 12/31/74 dollars	Market value
1965	1.602	1,100	1,762	
1967	1.511	800	1,209	
1968	1.453	50	73	
1969	1.386	940	1,303	
1971	1.255	120	151	
1973	1.152	190	219	
Balances 12/31/73		3,200	4,717	4,740
1974	1.044	700	731	
Balances 12/31/74		3,900	5,448 (1)	5,420

(1) In this illustration inventories are valued at the lower of cost or market in historical dollar statements. The same principle must therefore be followed in general purchasing power restatements.

SCHEDULE R-5

KJ&B INC.
General Purchasing Power Restatement–1974
Analysis of Prepaid Expenses
(in thousands)

Year acquired	Factor to restate to 12/31/74 dollars	Historical dollars				Restated to 12/31/74 dollars			
		Balance 12/31/73	Additions	Amortizations	Balance 12/31/74	Balance 12/31/73	Additions	Amortizations	Balance 12/31/74
1970	1.314	80		80		105		105	
1971	1.255	110		55	55	138		69	69
1972	1.216	130		32	98	158		39	119
1973	1.152	180		60	120	207		69	138
1974:									
1st qtr.	1.086		67		67		73		73
2d qtr.	1.062								
3d qtr.	1.033								
4th qtr.	1.000		40		40		40		40
		500	107	227	380	608	113	282	439

SCHEDULE R-6

KJ&B INC.
General Purchasing Power Restatement–1974
Analysis of Property, Plant, and Equipment
(in thousands)

Year acquired	Factor to restate to 12/31/74 dollars	Historical dollars				Restated to 12/31/74 dollars			
		Balance 12/31/73	Additions	Retirements	Balance 12/31/74	Balance 12/31/73	Additions	Retirements	Balance 12/31/74
1965	1.602	12,200		2,100	10,100	19,544		3,364	16,180
1966	1.560	4,000			4,000	6,240			6,240
1967	1.511	6,500			6,500	9,822			9,822
1968	1.453	3,400		675	2,725	4,940		981	3,959
1969	1.386	16,100			16,100	22,315			22,315
1970	1.314	5,200			5,200	6,833			6,833
1971	1.255	6,000			6,000	7,530			7,530
1972	1.216	3,900			3,900	4,742			4,742
1973	1.152	11,000			11,000	12,672			12,672
1974:									
1st qtr.	1.086		2,200		2,200		2,389		2,389
2d qtr.	1.062		2,300		2,300		2,443		2,443
3d qtr.	1.033		2,200		2,200		2,273		2,273
4th qtr.	1.000		2,400		2,400		2,400		2,400
		68,300	9,100	2,775	74,625	94,638	9,505	4,345	99,798

SCHEDULE R-7

KJ&B INC.
General Purchasing Power Restatement—1974
Analysis of Accumulated Depreciation
(in thousands)

Year assets acquired	Factor to restate to 12/31/74 dollars	Historical dollars				Restated to 12/31/74 dollars			
		Balance 12/31/73	Depreciation	Retirements	Balance 12/31/74	Balance 12/31/73	Depreciation	Retirements	Balance 12/31/74
1965	1.602	12,200		2,100	10,100	19,544		3,364	16,180
1966	1.560	3,200	400		3,600	4,992	624		5,616
1967	1.511	4,300	650		4,950	6,497	982		7,479
1968	1.453	1,700	380	340	1,740	2,470	552	494	2,528
1969	1.386	7,245	1,570		8,815	10,042	2,176		12,218
1970	1.314	1,820	520		2,340	2,391	683		3,074
1971	1.255	1,500	600		2,100	1,883	753		2,636
1972	1.216	585	390		975	711	474		1,185
1973	1.152	550	1,100		1,650	634	1,267		1,901
1974:									
1st qtr.	1.086		165		165		179		179
2d qtr.	1.062		115		115		122		122
3d qtr.	1.033		55		55		57		57
4th qtr.	1.000								
		33,100	5,945	2,440	36,605	49,164	7,869	3,858	53,175

SCHEDULE R-8

KJ&B INC.
General Purchasing Power Restatement—1974
Analysis of Deferred Income
(in thousands)

Year acquired	Factor to restate to 12/31/74 dollars	Historical dollars				Restated to 12/31/74 dollars			
		Balance 12/31/73	Additions	Realized	Balance 12/31/74	Balance 12/31/73	Additions	Realized	Balance 12/31/74
1973	1.152	110		110		127		127	
1974:									
1st qtr.	1.086		50	20	30		54	22	32
2d qtr.	1.062		40	15	25		42	16	26
3d qtr.	1.033		15		15		15		15
4th qtr.	1.000		20		20		20		20
		110	125	145	90	127	131	165	93

SHORT-CUT OR ALTERNATIVE PROCEDURES

One of the more difficult and time-consuming parts of purchasing power restatements is the aging of property, plant, and equipment and related depreciation. Generally, these are the largest adjustments in the restatement process and therefore likely the most important. Unfortunately, the majority of companies have not

SCHEDULE R-9

KJ&B INC.
General Purchasing Power Restatement—1974
Analysis of Capital Stock and Additional Paid-In Capital
(in thousands)

Year issued	Factor to restate to 12/31/74 dollars	Capital stock—common		Additional paid-in capital	
		Historical dollars	Restated to 12/31/74 dollars	Historical dollars	Restated to 12/31/74 dollars
1964	1.633	860	1,404	1,800	2,939
1965	1.602	580	929	1,200	1,922
1969	1.386	900	1,247	2,830	3,922
Balances 1973		2,340	3,580	5,830	8,783
1974:					
3d qtr.	1.033	20	21	40	41
Balances 12/31/74		2,360	3,601	5,870	8,824

SCHEDULE R-10

KJ&B INC.
General Purchasing Power Restatement—1974
Analysis of Sales and Cost of Sales
(in thousands)

	Historical dollars	Restatement factor or source	Restated to 12/31/74 dollars
Sales:			
Current sales.	84,785	(1) 1.044	88,515
Deferred sales realized	145	R–8	165
Total Sales	84,930		88,680
Cost of sales (except depreciation):			
Inventories—12/31/73:			
Finished goods	3,200	R–2	4,717
Materials and supplies	400	R–2	447
Purchases, production, and other costs.	63,610	(1) 1.044	66,409
	67,210		71,573
Inventories—12/31/74:			
Finished goods	3,900	R–2	5,420
Materials and supplies	960	R–2	960
	4,860		6,380
	62,350		65,193

(1) Spread evenly throughout year.

maintained property and equipment records by year of acquisition, and to reconstruct them may be impossible or require an inordinate amount of time. In these instances, the age must be estimated for price-level adjusted statements.

The information available within a company's records will usually suggest various means of estimating the age of assets. One

SCHEDULE R-11

KJ&B INC.
General Purchasing Power Restatement—1974
Analysis of Expenses
(in thousands)

	Historical dollars	Restatement factor or source	Restated to 12/31/74 dollars
Selling and administrative expenses:			
Amortization of prepaid expenses	227	R-5	282
Other.	4,973	1.044	5,192
	5,200		5,474
Loss on sale of equipment:			
Cost	2,775	R-6	4,345
Accumulated depreciation.	2,440	R-7	3,858
	335		487
Proceeds, November 1974	200	1.000	200
Loss	135		287

method frequently proposed is to compare the total accumulated provision with the annual depreciation provision. For example, in the previous illustration the accumulated depreciation at the end of 1974 was $36,605 in historical dollars and the current year's provision was $5,945. The weighted average age of the assets is calculated as $36,605/$5,945, or 6.2 years. The opening property, plant, and equipment balance is restated by applying the factor for the sixth year prior to 12/31/74 to the entire balance, that is $68,300 × 1.386 = $94,664. This happens to be abnormally close to the $94,638 that was determined by individual aging in Schedule R-6. The closing balance can be developed from this starting point by adding current year additions at current restatement rates and deducting retirements at the rate appropriate for the composite weighted average age. Using amounts shown in the previous illustration the restatement would be as follows:

	Historical dollars	Restatement factor	Restated to 12/31/74 dollars
Balance 12/31/73	$68,300	1.386	$ 94,664
Additions:			
1st qtr.	2,200	1.086	2,389
2d qtr.	2,300	1.062	2,443
3d qtr.	2,200	1.033	2,273
4th qtr.	2,400	1.000	2,400
Less retirements.	(2,775)	1.386	(3,846)
Balance 12/31/74	$74,625		$100,323

SCHEDULE R-12

KJ&B INC.
General Purchasing Power Restatement—1974
Net General Purchasing Power Gain or Loss
(in thousands)

| | 12/31/73 | | 12/31/74 |
	Historical dollars	Restated to 12/31/74 dollars	historical dollars
Net monetary items:			
Cash	600	671	208
Marketable securities	3,800	4,248	5,992
Receivables	9,000	10,062	9,630
Current liabilities	(8,700)	(9,727)	(11,630)
Long-term debt	(10,200)	(11,404)	(9,900)
Deferred income taxes	(3,030)	(3,388)	(3,200)
	(8,530)	(9,538)	(8,900)

	Historical dollars	Source	Restated to 12/31/74 dollars
Net monetary items 12/31/73	(8,530)	As above	(9,538)
Add:			
Current sales	84,785	R–10	88,515
Additions to deferred income	125	R–8	131
Proceeds—sale of equipment	200	R–11	200
Issuance of company shares	60	R–9	62
	76,640		79,370
Deduct:			
Purchases and production costs	63,610	R–10	66,409
Selling and administrative expenses—current	4,973	R–11	5,192
Federal income taxes	5,400	R–3	5,638
Dividends paid	2,350	R–3	2,453
Additions to prepaid expenses	107	R–5	113
Purchases of property, plant, and equipment	9,100	R–6	9,505
	85,540		89,310
Net monetary items—historical dollars 12/31/74	(8,900)		
Net monetary items—restated—12/31/74			(9,940)
Net monetary items—12/31/74 historical dollars			(8,900)
Net General Purchasing Power Gain			1,040

The depreciation provision and accumulated reserve balances are similarly restated by applying the same weighted average age restatement factor.

The estimating process may also be refined by first identifying major expansions or additions for which the amount and timing are known, and also by excluding from the ratio calculation the accumulated depreciation balances which pertain to fully depreciated assets. The estimate can then be confined to the residual amounts. For established companies the estimate is also improved by basing the calculation on the average depreciation provision over a longer period of time, such as the last five years, rather than the current year's provision. Eventually, it would be desirable to maintain all gross and net fixed asset records by year of acquisition.

Another simplification which is appropriate for many companies is in the calculation of the net general purchasing power gain or loss. When income and expenses are spread fairly uniformly throughout the year, a reasonably accurate monetary gain or loss can be calculated on the basis of the average balance of monetary items rather than the transactions which created them. For example, using amounts shown in Schedule R-12, the net balance of monetary items at 12/31/73 and 12/31/74 were ($8,530) and ($8,900), for an average net monetary liability of ($8,715). Applying the rate of inflation that occurred over the full year (1.118 − 1.000) to the average monetary liability indicates a gain of $1,028. This closely approximates the $1,040 gain that was determined by analyzing all transactions affecting monetary items.

CURRENT VALUE

Since there is no one accepted definition for an item's current value and there have been no pronouncements on the subject by authoritative bodies, current value means different things to different people. This controversy has produced a number of proposed valuation models but none have gained general acceptance. Most of the proposals are based on one or a combination of the following valuation theories:

1. Current replacement costs.
2. Exit, liquidation, or market value.
3. Present value of future cash flows.

Each of these theories is discussed below, together with an illustration of a current value accounting system which encompasses all of the methods described.

Current replacement cost

Current replacement cost may be defined as either (1) the *current cost of an identical asset* or (2) the *current cost of an asset which is equivalent in capacity and service.* The identical asset definition provides a more objective assessment of value since it is a direct measurement of an existing asset. However, it does not recognize technological changes that have taken place since the original asset was acquired, and therefore the second definition will frequently provide a more appropriate measure of value. Under either definition, values can be based on current prices if the assets are readily obtainable in the marketplace. When a market price is not available, the current value must be estimated. Generally, this is accomplished by adjusting the original cost on the basis of an appropriate cost index. The index may be one which simply measures the change in similar costs, such as the Engineering News Record Cost Index, or it may be one which is corrected for changing technology, such as the Chemical Engineering Plant Cost Index. Each of these measures provides costs or values for new assets and should be further adjusted for the age and condition of the assets involved.

Current replacement cost measurement may aid the investor's decision process, but the subjective nature of the information detracts from its practicability. Different assumptions about the assets can be employed and different current replacement cost methods can be used in determining current replacement costs. This could cause companies with similar assets to report completely different replacement costs in their financial statements.

There are some assets, such as mineral resources and intangibles, which cannot be replaced. For example, it is not possible to replace the East Texas Oil Field or the Mesabi Range. While some combination of properties might have a similar unmined reserve in barrels or tons, they would not have the same production cost, chemical composition, product yield through a given process unit, location advantage, and so on. For such assets replacement cost under either definition is little more than a highly subjective, theoretical number.

Exit, liquidation, or market value

The *exit value* measurement indicates the expected amount of cash or generalized purchasing power that could be realized at the reporting date by disposing of the firm's assets. The measurement tends to depict a minimum value of the enterprise. Stating the firm's assets at liquidation values permits the stockholders and creditors to determine the firm's value if operations were discontinued, as opposed to its going-concern value. Conceivably, liquidation values can aid the stockholders in appraising the effectiveness of managerial decisions by assessing trends and growth in such values.

Exit or liquidation values are estimates of market values at the reporting date. Some consider this method to be the best measure of value because the assets are restated at current market value and a market exists for all assets. However, in applying this concept, the only assets that can actually reflect a current market value are those traded in the marketplace such as marketable securities. In practice a market value is not determinable for many fixed and intangible assets and an arbitrary value must be assigned. In addition, critics question the usefulness of such values for a going concern for which liquidation is neither contemplated nor economically feasible.

For a firm contemplating liquidation or dissolution, however, the liquidation or exit value is the most appropriate measurement basis. In such specialized or limited cases the services of an appraiser would likely be sought and the relevant information is not the product of an accounting system.

Present value of future cash flow

Present value of future cash flow (sometimes called discounted cash flow) measures the wealth of a firm by discounting its expected net cash flows at a proper discount rate. Discounted cash flow is considered the ideal measurement because financial statements using it would reflect economic values. This valuation measurement enables the financial statement users to make financial decisions concerning the outcome of incomplete business cycles.

In this valuation method proper discount rates and realistic forecasts are essential to obtain meaningful information. Discount rates are a problem, since investors have different time preferences for money and it is not possible to translate directly the present value determined by one discount rate to the present value at a different rate. Forecasting is usually cited as the primary weakness of the system, since the future is so difficult to predict. Another objection relates to financial statement presentations. Related assets and liabilities are usually combined in the balance sheet to facilitate cash flow projections. Many object to this presentation. Less emphasis is also placed on elements of the income statement since profits are measured as the increase in owner's equity from one date to a subsequent date.

For most companies new investments are continually being made and many are intimately related to growth of the existing business. Thus, while the practical problems of forecasting the future cash flow from existing assets are difficult and subjective, it is virtually impossible to segregate the firm's projected cash flow as between existing assets and assets yet to be acquired. The discounted cash flow technique is very useful and widely practiced in evaluating discrete investment projects, even though it is difficult to apply to a total company.

CURRENT VALUE ACCOUNTING

Current value accounting, sometimes called a "multi-measurement system,"[5] attempts to integrate the various methods described in the previous models into an integrated valuation model. This allows the current values to be based on the valuation which is the most appropriate for the item and not on a single valuation method. For example, the selection of a current valuation method for equipment, raw materials, and patents might be as follows:

Equipment: Since equipment covers a wide range of items, various valuation methods may be most appropriate in different situations. Market value would normally be best for equipment which is readily available in the marketplace. When there is not an established market price it will be necessary to use one of the methods for estimating current replacement cost or, if determinable, the present value of future flows. Practical limitations and time constraints may also dictate the method of valuation used.

Raw materials: Raw materials are tangible goods that are obtained directly from the marketplace. Therefore, current replacement cost is generally the most appropriate valuation method.

Patents: Generally, patents' current value cannot be calculated by either the market value method or the current replacement cost method because patents do not have a competitive market price and cannot legally be reproduced unless a specific period of time

---
[5] Backer, pp. 35–37.

has expired. The best measurement method would therefore be the adjusted historical cost.

Similar logic should be applied to each balance sheet item to select the most realistic measurement of value.

CONCLUSION

The various current value accounting models mentioned are unlikely to gain general acceptance as forms of ongoing financial reporting in the foreseeable future. Standards must first be developed for each industry to insure objective and comparable presentations. Until such time applications are likely to be restricted to special situations such as acquisitions and dissolutions, or to specific accounts such as the selective replacement cost data now required by the Securities and Exchange Commission.

On the other hand, some form of supplemental reporting is urgently needed to disclose the full impact of inflation. The price-level method is further developed, conforms with presently accepted accounting standards, and therefore appears to be a logical first step. However, the ultimate solution will probably utilize elements of several methods to satisfy the widely divergent needs of financial statement users.

SELECTED REFERENCES

AICPA "Financial Statements Restated for General Price-Level Changes," *Accounting Principles Board Statement No. 3*. New York, June 1969.

—————— *Objectives of Financial Statements: Study Group's Report*. New York, October 1973.

—————— *Objectives of Financial Statements: Selected Papers*. New York, May 1974.

—————— Staff of the Accounting Research Division, "Reporting the Financial Effects of Price-Level Changes," *Accounting Research Study No. 6*. New York, 1963.

Backer, Morton *Current Value Accounting*. Financial Executive Research Foundation, 1973.

Davidson, Sidney, and Weil, Roman "Inflation Accounting—What Will General Price Level Adjusted Income Statements Show?" *Financial Analysts Journal*, January–February 1975.

Edwards, E. O., and Bell, P. W. *The Theory and Measurement of Business Income.* Berkeley: University of California Press, 1964.

Financial Accounting Standards Board "Financial Reporting in Units of General Purchasing Power," *Proposed Statement of Financial Accounting Standards.* Connecticut, December 31, 1974.

——— "Reporting the Effects of General Price-Level Changes in Financial Statements," *FASB Discussion Memorandum.* Connecticut, February 1974.

Rosen, L. S. *Current Value Accounting and Price-Level Restatements.* Toronto: Canadian Institute of Chartered Accountants, 1972.

Ross, Howard *Financial Statements: A Crusade for Current Value.* New York: Pitman Publishing Co., 1969.

Sterling, Robert "Relevant Financial Reporting in an Age of Price Changes." *The Journal of Accountancy,* February 1975.

———, ed. *Asset Valuation and Income Determination.* Lawrence, Kansas: Scholars Book Co., 1971.

U.S. Department of Commerce *Survey of Current Business.* Social and Economic Statistical Administration, Bureau of Economic Analysis.

Weston, Frank "Adjust Your Accounting for Inflation." *Harvard Business Review,* January–February 1975.

Chapter 27

Some accounting-related implications of corporate reorganization in bankruptcy

*Gibbes Ulmer Miller**

PURPOSE OF CHAPTER

Financial statements of a business corporation are ordinarily prepared in accordance with generally accepted accounting principles, the applicability of which is governed by the "going-concern postulate." Accounting's going-concern postulate rests upon the firm expectation that the financial obligations embodied in the corporation's contracts with customers, employees, creditors, investors, governmental agencies, and others will be substantially fulfilled, and that new contracts will be entered into and executed on a continuing and routine basis. To illustrate, if the collectibility of monies due under sales agreements with customers, or the forthcoming of labor services agreed to in collective bargaining, or the delivery of goods contracted for with outside suppliers is materially in doubt, the potential disruption arising from breach of contract substantially impairs the significance of any income measurement as an index of corporate earning power. Likewise, if payment of the corporation's notes and accounts to outsiders or delivery of goods or

* Florida State University.

services obligated for under contract to others is not performed as agreed, disruptive retaliation is certain to ensue, rendering very uncertain the continued earnings potential.

If the going-concern assumption represents the bedrock of accounting consistency, its absence must signify accounting quicksand. In bankruptcy proceedings an attempt must be made to deal rationally with financial reporting problems in the absence of the going-concern simplification. Although a considerable number of modern business corporations face real possibilities of reorganization in bankruptcy, guidelines of accounting for these out-of-the-ordinary situations are difficult to come by. Unfortunately, it is unlikely that principles of accounting for financially distressed corporations can be reduced to a simplified logical structure. However, it may be useful to review some of the conditions and events of bankruptcy reorganizations as a prelude to development of more specific guiding principles. This chapter attempts such a review.

INTRODUCTION TO THE BANKRUPTCY ACT

History of the bankruptcy act

The Federal Bankruptcy Act was enacted by Congress in 1898 to establish in the judicial system a means to settle in a fair and orderly way the conflicting interests which arise among the creditors of a debtor who is unable to pay his or her debts. Two major objectives were sought by this act:

1. To make a fair distribution of the debtor's assets among all creditors in settlement of their claims and to avoid the favoring of a few informed or aggressive creditors at the expense of others uninformed or less aggressive.
2. To provide a fresh start for the debtor by releasing the debtor from all previous debts after surrendering his or her assets, for what they might be worth, for distribution to those to whom the debtor was indebted.

Although a business corporation could avail itself of relief under the original bankruptcy act, it would likely do so only as a last resort, seeking alternative remedies elsewhere because bankruptcy proceedings could lead only to liquidation. For the same reason, railroads and public utilities were exempted from the act, since their continued services were regarded as essential to the public interest. Ordinarily, the financially distressed corporation would seek an agreement or accommodation with its creditors which would permit a continuation of business activity. The following alternatives were often sought outside the bankruptcy act.

1. *Extension*—a compromise with creditors in which the maturities of the corporation's debts are placed at later dates to allow more time for payment in keeping with the corporation's earning power and cash generating ability.

2. *Composition*—a more drastic compromise with creditors in which they agree among themselves and with the corporation to accept less than the full amount of their claims in full settlement of the debt.

3. *Reorganization under creditors' committee*—an agreement with creditors in which management of the corporation is turned over to a committee of the creditors, which develops a plan for compromising debts or of otherwise modifying the corporation's capital structure. If reorganization and continuation proves impractical, the committee may alternatively liquidate the corporation.

4. *Reorganization in equity receivership*—petition in a court of equity, either federal or state, for appointment of a receiver, placing the property and the affairs of the corporation under the jurisdiction of the court of equity. A reorganization committee elected by the creditors is formed to develop a reorganization plan to be ratified by at least a majority of the creditors. Upon approval of the plan by the court, a public foreclosure sale is held under which the reorganization committee bids in the properties of the corporation, using cash and securities deposited (usually by creditors) with the committee toward the purchase price. The sale price establishes the equity of security holders who do not agree to the plan.

The consent of creditors required for successful compromise or equity receivership settlements is more often than not extremely troublesome, if not impossible, to obtain. Moreover, the economic turmoil of the 1930s brought about the financial failure of many corporate enterprises, a result of far-reaching significance and public concern in a time of high unemployment. Consequently, the Federal Bankruptcy Act was amended many times in the early 1930s and completely revised by the Chandler Act in 1938. One of the most significant objectives of this revision was to provide the protection of the Federal Bankruptcy Act for the rehabilitation and reorganization of business corporations, a protection not available under the original act.

Special chapters of the revised act apply to railroads, public utilities, and municipal corporations. Ordinary business corporations can petition for relief of two kinds under Chapter X or Chapter XI. A Chapter XI petition, called an *arrangement,* is appropriate when the relief being sought can likely be accomplished by a composition in which only the corporation's unsecured debt is likely to be affected or modified. A Chapter X petition, called a *reorganization,* is appropriate in the more complex situations in which both secured and unsecured debt, as well as stockholder interests, are likely to be affected or modified in providing the necessary relief.

Meaning and significance of insolvency

The Federal Bankruptcy Act is primarily a means of dealing with the problem of financial insolvency. Although the act states that a person shall be deemed *insolvent* if the aggregate of his or her property shall not at a fair valuation be sufficient in amount to pay the person's debts, in practice the interpretation of this definition implies a time dimension with alternative meanings.

Alternative definitions of insolvency. "Insolvency" may have one of two meanings in connection with a corporate bankruptcy case. It may mean merely that the company is currently unable to pay its debts as they come due. Either because of management error or by unexpected changes in business conditions, debt maturities may be out of phase with operating cash flows, causing financial embarrassment and distress. It is implied here that the company may have very substantial earning power over the long run if its financial plan can be tailored to facilitate its immediate or short-run cash requirements. For convenience, this definition will herein be referred to as *"constructive" insolvency.*

On the other hand, "insolvency" might mean that the corporation's earning power has been so substantially impaired that liquidation seems imminent. This is the usual meaning when the business is said to be insolvent in the bankruptcy sense if present liquidation value is likely to fall short of total debt. The implication is that even though the company might presently have sufficient cash to pay immediate debt maturities, in the longer term cash requirements are likely to exceed cash receipts. In such a case, no profits will be available to the existing equity, and even existing creditors may have to absorb losses. For further convenience, this definition will be referred to as *"substantive" insolvency* or insolvency in the bankruptcy sense.

The question of insolvency is central to any contemplation of corporate bankruptcy. Indeed, the power of the court to take jurisdiction over corporate affairs depends upon a showing of insolvency; and under the court's jurisdiction, the respective rights of the various classes of creditors and investors depends on both the nature and extent (degree) of the insolvency.

Significance of initiating bankruptcy. Any business corporation can initiate bankruptcy proceedings by filing a petition with the federal district court asserting that the company is unable to pay its debts as they come due. This is called *voluntary bankruptcy.* However, if the company opposes voluntary bankruptcy, proceedings can be initiated by creditors, who may file a petition for *involuntary bankruptcy.* This petition by creditors must allege that the corporate debtor, within four months of the filing, has performed one of six specific acts of bankruptcy, which are:

1. Concealed or disposed of its property with the intent of hindering or defrauding its creditors;
2. While insolvent (in the bankruptcy sense), made a preferential assignment or transfer of its property favoring any creditor over others;
3. While insolvent (in the bankruptcy sense), permitted any creditor to obtain a lien on its property through legal proceedings without a timely discharge of the lien;
4. Made a general assignment of its property for the benefit of its creditors;
5. While insolvent (in the bankruptcy sense) or merely unable to pay its debts as they mature, made or permitted the appointment of a receiver or trustee to take charge of its property;
6. Admitted in writing its inability to pay its debts and its willingness to be adjudged a bankrupt.

Ordinarily, under the Federal Bankruptcy Act creditors can force involuntary bankruptcy proceedings on an unwilling corporate debtor only upon evidence of fraud (usually very difficult to prove) or upon a showing (also difficult to establish definitively) that the corporation is insolvent in the strict bankruptcy sense. As indicated in acts 4–6 above where the debtor has shown willingness to make some accommodation with creditors (although willingness short of its own voluntary petition) creditors can force the proceedings to be brought under the jurisdiction of the federal court by filing an involuntary petition. Otherwise, substantive insolvency or fraud must be established.

Significance in determination of rights in the proceedings. The central issue regarding a corporation's solvency or insolvency is: *who has the right to control* the use and disposition of the corporation's property? If the owner's equity of the corporation is supported by substantial prospective earnings and liquidity is sufficiently maintained to assure timely debt payment, the corporation's stockholders, through their officers and directors, have almost complete freedom to acquire and dispose of corporate assets, to incur debts, and to pledge assets to support the corporate debts. These rights of private property, which in a business corporation inhere to the stockholders, are almost absolute under the United States Constitution so long as the corporation is solvent. However, if the corporation's solvency becomes seriously questioned, the rights of the present officers, directors, and stockholders to control the corporate property become severely restricted, perhaps eliminated. If eliminated by insolvency these rights transfer to others. It is the main purpose of the bankruptcy court to see to it that such a transition of property rights from one group of persons to another is orderly and equitable.

As indicated in the preceding section, when the rights of creditors seem threatened by actual or impending insolvency of a debtor corporation, the creditors may petition the court to take jurisdiction of the corporate affairs, adjudge the corporation a bankrupt, and provide for the creditors eventually to take control of the corporate property.

While evidence of potential insolvency is sufficient to allow the court to take jurisdiction of the affairs of a financially distressed debtor, the court must ultimately determine whether the insolvency is in fact substantive or only constructive in order to dispose of the case. The court may determine that the corporation suffers merely from constructive insolvency, that the corporation's long-run earning power rests on a sound footing economically, and that the financial distress arose primarily from an unfortunate structuring of untimely debt maturities. This means that the expected cash flows from future operations within a longer but reasonable time frame must be more than sufficient to pay operating expenditures and debt service charges, leaving a surplus for existing owners. In that case, existing stockholders retain some measure of their rights, remain parties at interest in the bankruptcy proceedings, and are entitled to participate in resulting distributions, possibly having the corporate affairs returned completely to their control.

Alternatively, the court may determine that the insolvency is substantive—that expected future receipts from operations will be inadequate to provide any excess over debt obligations. In that case, all rights of the existing stockholders are terminated and existing stockholders are eliminated as parties at interest.

The elimination of existing stockholders because of corporate insolvency does not imply that the *rights of ownership,* as distinguished from the rights of existing stockholders, are extinguished, however. The equities of a corporation are of two fundamental classes which for convenience may be called *passive* and *active,* roughly corresponding to the usual distinction between creditor and ownership interests. If the corporation is to be liquidated, this distinction is moot. However, if business continuation is contemplated, the distinction between the passive (creditor) and active (ownership) interests must be determined. That is, someone always occupies the residual equity position in any ongoing business enterprise, and someone must perform the ownership function. Effective at the time the bankruptcy petition is filed, if the debtor corporation proves to be insolvent in the bankruptcy (substantive) sense, the residual equity and ownership position is automatically (by operation of law) occupied by some group of creditor interests. It remains a question of fact to be determined in the proceedings exactly which creditor interests represent the new ownership (active equity) and which creditor interests retain status as debt holders (passive equity). The point is important in determining continuity of ownership in accounting for a corporate merger or combination in the reorganization plan.

Basis of accountability under the act

Perhaps the most significant fact about the Federal Bankruptcy Act is its explicit authorization in the Constitution of the United

States. Private property and related rights of contract are almost sacred to American freedom, and we like to assume that they have absolute protection in the Constitution. Nevertheless, Article 8 of the Constitution restricts this protection by explicitly authorizing Congress, in keeping with the public interest, to enact laws regulating bankruptcies. Thus, under the Federal Bankruptcy Act, the court has powers with far-reaching ramifications for any business enterprise. For emphasis these powers are listed as follows:

1. *Debt instruments.* The terms, including payment dates, interest rates, and nature of liens, might be modified by order of the court.
2. *Executory contracts.* Contracts under which a debtor corporation is obligated to acquire goods or services from others, including leases of real or personal property or contracts under which the debtor is obligated to provide goods or services to others, may be canceled if it is deemed to be in the best interest of the debtor. Moreover, an outside supplier providing goods or services under contract to the debtor corporation may be denied any rights the supplier may have had to terminate the contract, or even to refuse to renew an expiring contract, if the goods or services are deemed to be essential to the continuation of the debtor's business.

The failure of any corporation doing a substantial amount of business usually has far-reaching economic and financial impact involving the public interest. The jobs and careers of a number of employees may be seriously interrupted, with limited opportunity of alternative employment. The total income of a community and the local tax base essential to many public services may be seriously eroded. Capital losses to numerous creditors and investors may have important social consequences if unnecessarily exaggerated or inequitably distributed. The tendency is to consider some degree of public interest to be involved in the failure of any business corporation of substantial size, allowing remedies available under the Federal Bankruptcy Act to be judicially applied. In most cases involving large sums of money, a disinterested trustee or receiver is appointed by the court to administer the property and affairs of the distressed corporation and to advise the court on the nature and causes of the financial distress and appropriate remedial measures. The assumption is that an independent and disinterested trustee or receiver acting in a professional capacity will be diligent and objective in attempting a financially sound and equitable resolution of the conflicting interests which arise among the various groups of creditors and investors, and will avoid shortsighted and one-sided arrangements which unduly compromise some interests in favor of others.

Considerations of the accounting entity.   When a natural person files for bankruptcy, the person's financial affairs in effect cease, his or her property is turned over to a receiver for distribution to creditors, and the person makes a new beginning financially. The estate created on behalf of creditors from the debtor's property constitutes an accounting entity separate and apart from that of the natural person in his or her contracting capacity either before or after bankruptcy. The estate's basis of accountability is *fair market value* of the estate property at the *date of the bankruptcy petition.*

When a business corporation (legal person) files for bankruptcy, the case is not so clear-cut. If the case is one of straight bankruptcy in which *liquidation* of the corporation *is clearly contemplated,* the procedure is similar to that of a natural person: a receiver is appointed to take title to the corporate property, to wind up the affairs of the estate, to liquidate the corporate assets, and to distribute the proceeds to creditors. In cases of this kind, the bankruptcy estate would constitute an accounting entity separate and apart from that of the corporation. Prior to bankruptcy, the corporation would be assumed to have indefinite life with long-run profit maximization as the central motive. The corporate accounts would be governed by the going-concern assumption with historical cost as the basis of accountability. Subsequent to the bankruptcy petition, the estate of the corporation would be assumed to have definite or limited life with the central motive of *maximizing the liquidation value* of the estate, and current market value as the basis of accountability.

However, the constitution of the accounting entity is questionable in the many cases in which *liquidation is sought to be avoided.* In most instances, liquidation will result in the sacrificing of substantial values which might be preserved if the business can be maintained on a going-concern basis. Maintaining these going-concern values is the main purpose of Chapters X and XI of the Federal Bankruptcy Act, which are designed to facilitate rehabilitation and reorganization of financially distressed business corporations. Thus, the trustee or receiver is charged in a fiduciary capacity with title to the corporate property and with responsibility for operating the business. Herein arises an implied conflict in the basis of accountability.

The trustee under Chapter X or XI is *accountable to the court* in his or her private capacity *as a fiduciary.* The trustee must safeguard the corporation's assets, determine equitable interests of various groups of creditors and investors, and make appropriate reports and distributions. These responsibilities imply accountability based upon the fair value of the assets entrusted. Indeed, the trustee is usually instructed by the court to close the debtor's books and to open new accounts for the estate.

On the other hand, the business of the debtor corporation is to be continued in the hope of rehabilitation. For several reasons it should be continued as a distinct accounting entity without an immediate change in the basis of accountability until a clear picture of the reorganizational requirements is obtained. For example, the existing corporation may survive the reorganization with its property and control being returned to present stockholders, to new stockholders, or to some mixture of both. Alternatively, the existing corporation may be merged with another corporation wherein the option of pooling or purchase might be an important consideration. Moreover, current income tax liability, and options regarding recognition of future gains and losses or carry-over privileges, may importantly influence the administration of the estate or the final reorganization plan. In the light of considerations such as these, *an immediate change in the basis of the ongoing business accounts should be avoided.*

The implied conflict in bases of accountability referred to above has a comparatively simple solution. The *primary entity is the estate* under the administration of the trustee. An inventory of all assets entrusted, appraised at fair market value at the date of the trustee's appointment, will establish the primary basis of accountability. The *debtor's business* can be administered on a going-concern basis as a *subdivision of the estate* with the business accounts remaining intact and retaining continuity in the periodic financial statements until such time as a change in basis is clearly needed. However, until the solvency of the corporation is determined by the court, general publication of these statements should be suspended except insofar as they might be included in the trustee's reports to the court with full explanation of their tentative nature. Moreover, the business accounts should be arranged in such a way that the trustee's reports can also be made on a *contribution basis*. The justification for continuing the business stands on the assumption that operating net receipts, properly discounted for interest, are likely to exceed prospective liquidation proceeds. The trustee must constantly monitor this assumption in fulfilling his or her fiduciary responsibility. The periodic operating contribution, computed as the difference between revenues and operating costs (excluding depreciation and amortization on the original assets of the estate), will aid in this monitoring.

Valuation postulates. Two concepts of value have important influence in proceedings for the reorganization of a business corporation under the Federal Bankruptcy Act. These are:

1. Fair market value of the corporation's assets, assuming sale at public auction at the time the bankruptcy proceedings were initiated.
2. Capitalized value of the expected earnings from future operations of the business at the time the reorganization plan is made effective.

The fair market value (*liquidation value*) at the beginning of the proceedings is a reasonable basis for *establishing the fiduciary accountability* and for evaluating the ultimate success of the proceedings. This valuation must be made by appraisal, since the specific market test can never take place. The *capitalized value of future earnings* is the legal basis for determining the manner and extent to which the various claims of creditors and investors will participate in the final reorganization if liquidation or sale to outsiders is avoided. This also is an appraisal not subject to actual market test, but one which is subject to acceptance or rejection by the parties at interest. Of course, if the rehabilitation and reorganization effort is unsuccessful, fair market value represented by actual proceeds of the liquidation sale will determine the amount to be paid to each claim holder.

General nature of the proceedings

Proceedings under the Federal Bankruptcy Act are brought in the federal district court which has jurisdiction of the territory in which the corporation is domiciled or has its principal place of business. The court will usually appoint a *referee* to consider petitions and other matters that need to be heard and ruled upon. Of course, all matters considered by the referee are always subject to review by the judge. A *receiver* or *trustee* is appointed to administer the affairs of the estate and to bring before the referee those matters requiring judicial consideration. Upon recommendation by the trustee, an *attorney* is usually appointed to advise the trustee and to draft documents required for presentation of matters to the court. All *claim holders* or their legal representatives are formally notified of all hearings on matters affecting their interests in order that they might participate in the decisions and judgments to be rendered. Sometimes a *creditor's committee* might be appointed to work with the trustee on behalf of claim holders.

Other aspects of the proceedings and their implications for accounting are considered in more detail in the remaining sections of this chapter.

ESTABLISHING JUDICIAL CONTROL

The initial phase of proceedings under Chapters X or XI of the Federal Bankruptcy Act include the following major events: (1) filing of the petition, (2) hearing on the petition for adjudication or dismissal, (3) first meeting of creditors, and (4) election and qualification of trustee. The major objective of this phase is to determine the merit of establishing judicial control over the affairs of a private enterprise, and if so, to establish a trusteeship over the private estate. The time required to achieve this initial objective may vary from a few days to several weeks, depending on the following:

1. Convenience of scheduling in the court's calendar.
2. The complexity of the case, including the volume of necessary paper work and the number of interested parties and time required for proper notice.
3. Whether the adjudication is to be contested, a probability if the petition is involuntary.
4. Difficulties encountered in obtaining services of a trustee who is acceptable to the court and to the parties at interest.

Commencement of proceedings

Bankruptcy proceedings are initiated by the filing of a petition in the federal court, either voluntary by the debtor corporation or involuntary by creditors, stating that the corporation is insolvent or unable to pay its debts as they mature, and with the expressed intent of having the court to adjudge the corporation a bankrupt. The motivations of the petition are complex. A voluntary petition by the corporation is likely to be regarded by management as a last resort defensive action after having exhausted all options at locating new financing or reaching a mutually advantageous agreement with influential creditors. It is against the nature of the entrepreneur to admit or imply failure, and no responsible person would advocate that a decision to file bankruptcy should be made hastily. However, to exhaust all financial resources, as well as the patience and good-will of accommodating creditors, in unduly postponing the inevitable is wasteful when a timely resort to judicial proceedings with some remaining financial flexibility may measurably improve chances of a successful rehabilitation.

Moreover, creditors may often be reluctant to file an involuntary petition. Without cooperation from management the existence of insolvency, which is required to establish an act of bankruptcy, may be very difficult to prove, and a hasty attempt may invite retaliation for damages. Also, influential creditors may prefer to negotiate for corrective action and for control of management outside the courts, since in bankruptcy their influence is subordinate to extensive discretionary powers of the court. An involuntary petition may be brought by creditors of lesser influence whose interests appear in danger of being circumvented by such out-of-court negotiations.

Hearing for adjudication or dismissal

Once a bankruptcy petition has been filed, the court must hear the issues and decide for adjudication or dismissal. The main issue is whether the financial distress being experienced by the corporation is of a nature to justify the intervention of the court. A *voluntary petition* is tantamount to an admission by the corporation adequate to justify judicial proceedings and to have the effect of a legal adjudication even without a court decree. A possible exception may arise in the unlikely event that management's authority to make the filing is contested by stockholders or dissenting directors. An *involuntary petition* may elicit a contest from any party at interest, including the debtor corporation, who feels that his or her interest is jeopardized. In such a case, the specific act of bankruptcy alleged in the petition must be established. Those objecting to the petition would seek to establish the solvency of the corporation, the absence of fraud against the creditors on the part of the corporation's officers and directors, and the absence of any illegitimate action by the officers or directors to give preferential treatment to some creditors at the expense of others in the light of the existing financial uncertainties.

If the petition appears to the court to have been filed in good faith and no successful objection emerges from the facts presented at the hearing, the court approves the petition and adjudges the corporation a bankrupt. Under Chapters X and XI, the judicial designation is "Debtor" rather than literally "Bankrupt," to avoid the implication of the latter term that liquidation is to be expected and perhaps to mitigate any possibile stigma which might attach.

After the adjudication is made the court sets the date, usually within 10 to 30 days, for the first meeting of creditors. At this time also the court usually issues a temporary stay of all claims against the corporation and enjoins the commencement or continuation of any suit against the debtor estate or any act or proceeding to enforce a lien upon property of the estate.

First meeting of creditors

Although other business may be considered, the first meeting of creditors has three major objectives:

1. To allow or disallow claims which might be presented at the meeting, and to set a date by which all claims should be filed.
2. To publicly examine officers of the corporation by the court and by any creditors desiring to do so on the affairs of the corporation, including the behavior of its officers and directors and the causes of failure.
3. To elect and appoint a trustee(s).

Election and qualification of trustee

During the first phase of the proceedings, until a trustee qualifies, the property usually remains in the possession of the debtor, who acts in a fiduciary capacity strictly accountable to the court.

Under Chapter XI, the debtor seeks an arrangement or composition, which is a compromise settlement with unsecured creditors.

Presumably, the interests of secured creditors and stockholders will not be affected. To expedite the rather limited objective of these cases, the court very frequently will retain the debtor in possession throughout the proceedings, although a disinterested trustee will be appointed upon the insistence of any party at interest. Cases which require a more comprehensive remedy in which the interests of secured creditors and stockholders are likely to be affected are adjudicated under Chapter X. In these cases, if the indebtedness is $250,000 or more, one or more disinterested trustees must be appointed. If indebtedness is less than $250,000, a trustee may be appointed or the debtor may be continued in possession. The creditors attending the first meeting may elect the trustee subject to approval of the court, or if no election is made, the court may make the appointment. The appointed trustee qualifies by filing with the court evidence of having secured a bond in an amount specified by the court.

ACCOUNTING AND REPORTING REQUIREMENTS

A petition to initiate proceedings under Chapter X or Chapter XI of the Federal Bankruptcy Act must allege that the debtor corporation is insolvent or unable to pay its debts as they mature. In making the assertion, the petition raises the demand for a host of accounting information, and must be accompanied by the following data:

1. A description of the nature of the business, including its organizational structure.
2. A statement of financial position at the filing date, supported by detailed schedules of assets, liabilities, and capital stock.
3. A statement providing full disclosure of all pending proceedings and other contingencies affecting the property of the corporation.
4. A description of the nature and status of any plan of liquidation, arrangement, reorganization, or readjustment affecting the property of the corporation proposed by the parties at interest or pending, either in connection with or apart from any other judicial proceeding.
5. A *statement of affairs* given under oath by officers of the corporation and in the form prescribed by law, including a list of

executory contracts and lists of all assets and all creditors and stockholders and their addresses.

In order to sustain a petition for adjudication under Chapter X, it must be shown that the petition was filed in good faith and that a remedy appropriate to the debtor corporation's existing circumstances is not available under Chapter XI. That is, facts must be presented to show that liquidation or a mere composition of unsecured debt would be impracticable or inequitable. The court will be most favorably disposed to grant a Chapter X decree if it finds in the facts and circumstances of the case that proceedings under the chapter will make possible a degree of rehabilitation which is likely to salvage some element of solvency and to preserve values of creditor and stockholder interests which would otherwise be sacrificed. The following additional data should be presented to support such a finding by the court:

1. *Pro forma balance sheet* showing assets appraised at liquidation values.
2. Income and funds flow statements for periods preceding bankruptcy, including any prior history of profitable operations.
3. Projected cash flows and income statements for the current year and for two to five years ahead, assuming a moratorium on interest and debt payments for the immediate future.
4. Pro forma financial position statement showing appraisal increments of assets and owner's equity based on replacement cost.

Detailed accounting records for all transactions of the estate during the proceedings must be kept. A monthly accounting of cash receipts, disbursements, and where practicable, interim earnings will likely be required by the court.

ADMINISTRATION OF THE ESTATE

The remainder of this chapter is primarily concerned with administrative problems especially related to Chapter X reorganizations rather than to Chapter XI arrangements. Chapter XI proceedings are usually more expeditious, seeking an extension of time or reduction in principal amount or in interest rates on unsecured debt. Such compromises are usually worked out with the debtor in possession handling negotiations with major unsecured creditors or a creditor's committee. Any agreed-upon arrangement is subject to the approval of the court, and is usually much less complicated and less time-consuming than the more comprehensive financial reorganizations usually sought under Chapter X.

Chapter X cases are ordinarily administered by a trustee, who usually must obtain a complete restructuring of the corporation's financial plan. Major responsibilities assigned by the court to the trustee include: (1) a comprehensive financial and management audit; (2) operation and, if feasible, rehabilitation of the corporation's business; and (3) preparation and submission of a plan. These responsibilities are elaborated in the following sections.

Financial and management audit

The court order appointing the trustee usually directs the trustee to make a thorough investigation of the acts, conduct, property, liabilities, financial condition, and business operations of the debtor corporation, including (if desirable) an examination of officers and directors and other persons who might have information pertinent to the investigation. This investigation serves several major purposes, which are discussed in the following paragraphs.

1. *To ascertain a complete inventory of the assets of the debtor's estate.* Upon his or her appointment the trustee obtains, by operation of law, title to all assets of the estate, including property rights of all kinds. The date of the bankruptcy petition is the effective date of the trustee's title. A physical inventory and simple audit of the property accounts are not likely to suffice in most instances. Interests in patents, copyrights, and trademarks, including rights in pending applications and royalty contracts, must be ascertained if not already reflected in the accounts. Also, rights of action arising from contracts or torts prior to bankruptcy may afford substantial values to the estate. Especially to be sought are instances in which property might have been unlawfully transferred, concealed, or assigned in the months preceding bankruptcy. Other important unrecorded assets might be allowable tax rebates and tax loss carryforward privileges. The trustee must file with the court a complete listing of the estate assets as a basis for evaluating the interests of all parties at interest.

2. *To determine the nature and validity of all claims against the estate.* At the outset of the proceedings the trustee must file with the court a list of all known claims, and must supplement this list as

new claims become known. Each claim holder must file independently, by a time set by the court, his or her own claim and documentary proofs. The trustee must evaluate the claims and proofs filed and object to any that are not properly substantiated. Moreover, pending litigation against the estate that was temporarily stayed by the court at the outset of the proceedings must be resolved and the related claims liquidated as to amount, either by negotiation between the trustee and the parties to the action or by allowing the legal actions to proceed after the trustee is adequately informed in the facts and circumstances. These liquidated claims are includable in the liabilities of the debtor estate.

3. *To evaluate the desirability of rejecting or accepting any executory contracts.* Leases on personal or real property or other continuing contracts for the purchase or sale of goods or services must be examined and evaluated. Any executory contracts which seem burdensome to the estate may be rejected by the trustee, and resulting damages would be treated as an unsecured claim. Executory contracts which seem beneficial may be accepted by the trustee, and costs accruing under the accepted contracts are treated as administrative costs. Unless the court explicitly extends the time, any executory contract not specifically accepted by 60 days after the adjudication or 30 days after the qualification of the trustee, whichever occurs later, is deemed to be rejected. Automatic rejection after the designated time is a potential hazard demanding the timely attention of the trustee in preserving valuable contractual rights of the estate.

4. *To discover any evidence of fraud, misconduct, mismanagement, or other irregularities.* Acts and conduct of insiders require special scrutiny. It is the trustee's responsibility to determine the existence of any cause of action related to the misappropriation or misplacement of assets by the corporation's management, or any losses arising from gross negligence, dishonesty, or deceit by officers, directors, or other responsible parties. The basis of any claims against the estate filed by officers, directors, or major stockholders should be carefully scrutinized to verify the actual rendering of valuable goods or services and the authenticity of the compensation claimed. Claims based on profit sharing, commissions, or bonuses may be questioned in the light of events leading to bankruptcy. Large debts to major stockholders may sometimes be questioned on the issue of *thin capitalization* if it appears that the debt structure was unbalanced and the debt afforded special protection to the

influential stockholders. Section 167 of the act requires the trustee to make a special report to the court on these matters.

5. *To evaluate the causes of the corporation's financial distress, its prospects for rehabilitation, and the desirability of business continuation.* These matters are also required to be treated in the Section 167 report to the court. Of course, the desirability of business continuation ultimately depends upon a successful rehabilitation effort. Conclusions and recommendations made in the Section 167 report must be regarded as tentative until the trustee has become "seasoned" in the business and is able to test the practical adaptability of the corporation's cost-volume-profit relationships and to project future demand for the corporation's products and services.

6. *To determine the solvency or insolvency of the corporation.* The issue of solvency must be scheduled for hearing and determination by the court, usually prior to submission of the final plan. Rights of stockholders, and possibly of low priority creditors, to participate in the reorganization plan are affected by this determination. If the plan contemplates continuation of the business, solvency depends on whether and to what extent the fair value of the business estimated by capitalizing expected future earnings exceeds the total debts of the estate. If the plan contemplates sale or liquidation of the business, current market value determines the solvency issue.

Operation and rehabilitation of the business

The trustee's major objective in operating and attempting to rehabilitate the business is to restore the sources of valuable goodwill that usually are severely impaired in the course of events leading to bankruptcy. Lost or weakened customer patronage must be regained, and valued customers persuaded of the corporation's continued reliability for quality of products and services. Suppliers must be persuaded to honor purchase commitments and to continue shipments. Key employees must be encouraged about prospects of their continued productive employment. The tasks are monumental, considering the dearth of financial resources inherited by the trustee.

In most instances the financial distress leading to bankruptcy involves overexpansion of the business (extending commitments beyond the limits of the corporation's financial reserves and managerial capacity) and excessive employment. In such instances, a good rule of thumb is for the trustee to quickly err in the opposite direction, reducing employment to the least essential minimum, and substantially contracting the scope of operations. "Too few people for each task" might be a good silent motto. Quick elimination of marginal operations, and even favorable sale of some reasonably profitable ones, may reduce immediate cash needs and provide funds essential to salvation of the foundering enterprise.

Several provisions of the bankruptcy act facilitate the trustee's efforts to finance the continued operations of the debtor corporation's business. These provisions include (1) stay of prepetition debts and claims, (2) priority of administrative costs, (3) trustee's certificates, and (4) sale or lease of property.

Stay of prepetition debts and claims. The order of the court approving the bankruptcy petition suspends payment of any debts, claims, or dividends existing at the date of the petition, and stays temporarily any legal action pending against the debtor to establish new claims or to enforce liens. This moratorium on debt payment allows existing and incoming funds to accumulate for use in the best interests of the estate. If the court approves, these funds can be disbursed, with caution, to pay costs and expenses incurred by the trustee in administering the estate and operating the business. The caution is that the rights of creditors regarding assets pledged as collateral for secured debts must be respected.

A Chapter X case is administered under the rule of *absolute equity*. This means that claims must be paid in the strict order of their priorities. All creditors in a given class, starting with the highest priority, must receive the full equivalence of their claims before any in the class of next lower priority receives anything, and so on in succession. This rule governs the distribution of funds if the estate is liquidated, and it governs the distribution of funds or securities issued pursuant to a reorganization plan. The rule is also affected by interim disbursements for costs and expenses of the estate to the extent that the funds disbursed represent proceeds from the sale or conversion of pledged assets. To that extent the lienholder would suffer a diminution of collateral. As a result, unless otherwise agreed to by the parties at interest, proceeds from a sale or conversion of pledged assets are usually disbursed to lienholders, and proceeds from a sale or conversion of lien-free assets are used to pay costs of interim operations. As a special case, liens on inventories and receivables seriously impair the trustee's financial flexibility, often allowing the lienholder to obtain strong influence in the proceedings.

Often business continuation under Chapter X proceedings is for the benefit of secured creditors, a good example being real estate ventures mortgaged on the basis of capitalized future rentals. In some commercial and industrial cases, business continuation might be in the interests of unsecured creditors or stockholders. The question of which parties at interest are the primary beneficiaries of the business continuation will influence the court in approving fund disbursements that involve risks to other classes of claims.

Priority of administrative costs. The liabilities incurred by the trustee for costs and expenses in the administration of the estate are of a different classification from the prepetition liabilities of the corporation. They are presumed to be incurred for the general benefit of all parties at interest in the estate, and have priority in advance of any payment to creditors for prepetition debts. This provision facilitates efforts of the trustee to obtain needed trade credit. Without this provision business continuation would be impossible, since trade sources could not otherwise afford to share the risks already inherent in the defaulted prepetition debts. Even the administrative cost priority is often an insufficient persuader because of the general uncertainty surrounding bankruptcy proceedings.

The administrative cost priority may also enable the trustee to use as working capital the proceeds from sale or conversion of pledged assets. Secured creditors may be persuaded to release their liens on specific assets and forego their claim to the sale proceeds provided that the court approves converting the related portion of the claim to, and reclassifying it as, administrative cost. This procedure is perfectly in keeping with the nature of the financing transaction. It avoids diminution of, and could possibly improve, the collateral position of the agreeable creditor.

The major creditors who attend hearings and monitor the proceedings in person or through their attorneys will be alert for changes in administrative cost obligations, and will bring pressures to keep these obligations in balance with expected earnings. If the estate is itself to remain solvent (a matter of utmost importance to the court, the trustee, and all parties at interest, including the new post-petition creditors of the estate), expected earnings from business operations must exceed the costs and expenses incurred by the trustee in continuing those operations. Even the new post-petition creditors with administrative cost classification may bear some risk of loss if the estate itself is likely to become insolvent.

Trustee's certificates.   Upon proper notice and justification by the trustee, the court may authorize the trustee to issue certificates of indebtedness for loans, purchases of property, or other consideration. These Trustee Certificates may be issued upon whatever terms, conditions, security, and priority in payment over existing obligations (whether secured or unsecured) is equitable in the particular circumstances. This authority is peculiar to Chapter X proceedings and demonstrates the far-reaching powers attributed to the court in reorganizations deemed to affect the public interest.

Theoretically, the authority to issue certificates of indebtedness, with priority above existing lienholders, secured by specific assets of the estate should give the trustee access to credit from banking and other financial institutions. In practice, institutional lenders are likely to hesitate, either for lack of understanding of these extraordinary bankruptcy features, or because the ambiguities inherent in the public interest aspects and the basis of equitable justification cloud the stipulated security position, unless existing lienholders are willing to give a specific subordination.

Sale or lease of assets.   Upon proper notice and justification by the trustee, the court may authorize the trustee to sell or to lease any of the estate property upon whatever terms may be approved by the court. Under this provision, the trustee may easily obtain approval of ordinary business leases and sales of unneeded equipment and other personal property to provide needed revenues and working capital additions. Possibilities of much larger financial consequence, such as sale and leaseback of real property or the outright sale of unneeded real property, are subject to limitations similar to those referred to in the last paragraph above. Without agreement and specific satisfaction of liens by existing lienholders, titles might be sufficiently clouded to discourage purchasers. Resort to sale at public auction to remedy the title issues would usually discourage the private negotiations and impair the realizable sale price.

Submission of plan

The court order appointing the trustee will likely set an early date for a plan, or plans, to be submitted to the court, a procedure designed to expedite the proceedings with the main goal constantly in sight. However, it is usually necessary to postpone the filing date to allow the trustee time to become knowledgeable in the affairs of the business and to work out practical means of financing. Three to five years is not an unusual requirement to develop a successful plan in Chapter X reorganizations.

Source of plans. Primary responsibility for recommending a reorganization plan to the court rests with the trustee. However, at a time designated by the court, the trustee must notify all parties at interest of their right to submit suggestions to him or her. The trustee is not bound by outside suggestions, but the need to produce a practical plan that is acceptable to a two-thirds majority of every class of creditors or stockholders whose interests are affected will induce the trustee's substantial consideration of any useful recommendations.

In turn, the court is not bound to approve any plan or plans recommended by the trustee. Other parties at interest may recommend alternative plans for the court's consideration.

Classification of claims. A useful first step in developing the reorganization plan requires a classification of claims and interests in order of priority. All claims and interests can be placed in the following three major groupings:

A. *Priority Claims*—all claims given priority by law.
B. *Secured Claims*—all claims supported by specific liens.
C. *Unsecured Claims and Interests*—all claims and interests other than priority and secured claims.

The following list of classes under these general headings, ranked in order of priority or preference, should be useful in most cases. Class I, Administrative Costs, pertains exclusively to obligations arising after the filing of the petition. The other classes pertain to prepetition obligations and debts.

A. *Priority Claims:*

Class I, *Administrative Costs:* The costs and expenses incurred in administering the estate and operating the business subsequent to the filing of the petition, including attorney's fees and other costs approved by the court.

Class II, *Wages and Commissions:* Compensation not to exceed $600 per person earned by employees of the debtor within three months before the date of the petition.

Class III, *Taxes:* Any taxes owed by the debtor corporation to the United States or to any state or any subdivision thereof arising prior to filing the petition.

Class IV, *Obligations Other than Taxes:* Any other debts entitled by law to priority and owed by the debtor to the United States, any state or subdivision thereof, or any other person, except taxes, wages, and administrative costs.

B.   *Secured Claims:*

Class V, *Real Estate Liens:* All claims based on prepetition debts of the debtor secured by mortgages, deeds of trust, or other liens upon real property.

Class VI, *Personal Property Liens:* All claims based on prepetition debts of the debtor secured by chattel mortgages, conditional sales contracts, or other liens upon personal property.

C.   *Unsecured Claims and Interests:*

Class VII, *Unsecured Debt:* All claims based on prepetition debts of the debtor, unsupported by any real or personal property liens.

Class VIII, *Preferred Equity:* Any remaining interests of the corporation's preferred stockholders.

Class IX, *Common Equity:* Any remaining interests of the corporation's common stockholders.

The reorganization plan may include provisions affecting all or any class of claims and interests, either through the issuance of new securities or by otherwise altering or modifying their contractual rights. However, the plan must provide for all claims and interests under the rule of *absolute equity.* That is, the plan must provide for full payment, usually in cash, of all administrative costs and other priority claims ahead of secured creditors. Similarly, the plan must provide that secured creditors shall receive the full equivalence of their claims ahead of unsecured creditors. It must specify which classes of claims or interests are not to be affected by the plan, and what provisions are made for them. It must also provide adequate protection for any class of creditors affected by the plan but not accepting the plan by two-thirds majority.

Valuation of property. The reorganization plan may be developed from the following two major approaches, or from many variations or combinations of them.

1. Sale to one or more successor corporations, either newly formed for the purpose or already established.
2. Recapitalization and survival of the debtor corporation.

Either approach requires a valuation of the estate by capitalizing expected future earnings: in the first instance to determine the basis of a reasonable selling price, and in the second instance to determine a reasonable total of the claims and interests to be included in the recapitalization. Projected statements of income, financial position, and funds flow for five years will be useful in making the capitalization estimate and in testing the financial consequences of the explicit or implicit operating assumptions.

Whether the plan contemplates sale or recapitalization, sufficient cash should be available either in the estate, from a sale of surplus assets or new securities, or from part of a contemplated sale price to pay all priority claims and to pay all accrued interest and past-due installments on any secured claims which are to be continued or assumed under the terms of their original contracts. If new securities are to be exchanged for secured claims, an appraisal of the current fair market value of the assets supporting their respective liens will be required in establishing their necessary equivalency.

Current fair market value appraisal will be useful for other purposes also. The valuation of the estate determined by capitalizing future earnings must be allocated in two ways: (1) between debt and equity securities, and (2) among various individual assets. The basis of individual assets for use in reporting financial position and in measuring periodic income should be determined by fair market value at the effective date of the plan. The current market value of tangible assets should place stringent limits on the total debt included in the new capitalization.

Feasibility of the plan. Any plan recommended by the trustee must provide adequate means for its execution. If the plan is approved by the court and accepted by a two-thirds majority of the affected classes of claims and interests, its practical implementation should be assured. Thus, alternatives should be available in the plan to deal with foreseeable contingencies. The alternatives may include the retention by the debtor corporation of all or any part of its property, or a sale in liquidation of all or any part of the property subject to or free from any liens, or a distribution of all or any part of the property to parties at interest in satisfaction of their claims. It is important that contingencies and the alternative procedures be clearly identified and explained in the plan, so that the parties at interest will be fully aware of the potential consequences of their acceptance.

SUMMARY

This chapter has reviewed some of the conditions and events of proceedings for rehabilitation and reorganization under the Federal Bankruptcy Act. This review indicates a need in the proceedings for guidance in several aspects related to accounting policy and procedure.

The ongoing production and distribution activities performed in large measure by business corporations are vital to the public interest. The Federal Bankruptcy Act of 1898, as revised by the Chandler Act in 1938, recognizes this aspect of the public interest and provides judicial means to rehabilitate and continue the operations of financially insolvent business corporations which otherwise would be discontinued and liquidated.

The main purpose of corporate arrangements and reorganizations under the Federal Bankruptcy Act, as revised, is to reestablish the financial integrity of corporations which, for various reasons of internal or external diseconomy, become insolvent. A business corporation is *constructively insolvent* if the corporation, although economically sound in the long-run, is unable to satisfy its current debt requirements. A business corporation is *substantively insolvent* when the capitalized value of its future earnings is less than the total corporate debt. The boundary between these two types of insolvency in a given case is usually very difficult to determine equitably. Either "constructive" or "substantive" insolvency can lead to bankruptcy proceedings for a judicial determination of the respective rights of the creditors and investors to control and enjoy the benefits of the corporate property. The judicial restructuring of property rights is reflected either in a new capital structure reestablishing corporate solvency when reorganization is feasible, or in the distribution of liquidation proceeds when reorganization is not feasible. Of considerable importance in accounting for corporate mergers and combinations is the fact that an event of substantive insolvency shifts rights of ownership in a corporation from stockholders to a determinable group of creditors, effective at the date of the bankruptcy petition. Although the equity position is not vacated, what particular persons occupy the position is a question of fact to be decided in the circumstances.

Of fundamental importance in evaluating the property rights in a debtor corporation is the constitutional authority of the bankruptcy courts to modify the terms and conditions of corporate contracts and debt instruments in the public interest. When the court approves a bankruptcy petition, title to the corporate property passes to a *trustee,* and all rights of action to establish or enforce liens against the estate are temporarily suspended. The court-appointed trustee is strictly accountable in a fiduciary capacity to all parties at interest for the use and disposition of estate properties. With court approval, the trustee may either reject, or accept and enforce, any executory contracts. The reorganizational plan may affect or modify the rights of any or all parties at interest in a Chapter X proceeding.

The *estate of a debtor corporation* under a trustee in bankruptcy constitutes an *accounting entity* separate and apart from that of the corporate entity. The estate has a limited life, and the trustee's major goal is to maximize the current value of the estate on behalf of all parties at interest, implying a prominence of the balance sheet among the trustee's periodic financial statements. The trustee's continuation of the corporate business is justified on the assumption that net proceeds from operations, properly discounted for interest, will exceed prospective liquidation (current market) values of the estate properties. Periodic financial reports on a contribution basis will aid in monitoring this assumption during the proceedings. It may be advantageous to retain intact the historical cost basis of the business accounts to facilitate the reorganizational plan and for tax purposes.

The accounting principle of *full disclosure* probably finds greatest expression in corporate reorganizational proceedings. Here all matters affecting the interests of creditors and investors must be reported to all parties at interest and heard in court. Here the legal and financial credibility of the reorganization plan hinges upon acceptance by all classes of recognized claim holders. Full disclosure is in complete harmony with the congressional philosophy of the Federal Bankruptcy Act, which seeks *absolute equity* and *business continuation* in the public interest.

Current market value appraisals and *capitalized future earnings* estimates importantly influence the administration of reorganizational proceedings and may affect the rights of various parties at interest. Due care and objectivity can reasonably be cautioned.

The trustee's responsibilities in administering the affairs of the estate can be facilitated by various accounting skills. The comprehensive management and financial audit required by Section 167 of the Federal Bankruptcy Act brings to bear principles of both financial and managerial accounting, as well as auditing techniques. The need to make periodic financial reports requires application of generally accepted accounting principles. The preparation of the plan requires special attention to the nature and the amount of various liabilities and to the nature and values of specific assets. It requires careful attention to anticipating and measuring the practical consequences of alternative procedures for meeting the contingencies which are likely to be encountered in the plan's execution.

SELECTED REFERENCES

Arsdell, Paul M. *Corporate Finance.* New York: The Ronald Press Co., 1968.

Laube, William T., and Herzog, Asa S. *1973 Bankruptcy Act and Rules.* New York: Matthew Bender & Co., 1973.

Moore, James William, and King, Lawrence P., editors-in-chief *Collier on Bankruptcy,* vols. 6, 8, 14th ed. New York: Matthew Bender & Co., 1972.

Tillinghart, David R., and Gardner, Stephen D. "Acquisitive Reorganizations and Chapters X and XI of the Bankruptcy Act." *Tax Law Review,* vol. 26 (1971), pp. 663–723.

PART 5

Publication of financial information

Chapter 28 ————————————————————

————————— The annual financial report
and financial public relations

Andrew J. Reinhart*

Corporations have an obligation to communicate with their investors and their potential investors. This obligation extends from an annual informing of stockholders and creditors as to the company's past performance and plans, via the vehicle of the annual report, to the day-to-day, ongoing report of current developments affecting operations. The latter can be broadly categorized as *financial public relations.* Data selected for public dissemination should aim at providing information useful for assessing the impact of current developments on the earning power of the enterprise.

Although a company's annual report is considered by many to be the single most important element in a financial public relations program, it is, by definition, a document published and distributed only once a year. Effective investor relations cannot be accomplished on a once-a-year basis. Events affecting a company's operations and financial outlook can, and do, occur daily. For most companies, the responsibility for fulfilling their obligation to keep shareholders and the financial community informed on a current basis rests with a separate segment of the organization headed by a public relations executive.

———
* Vice President Systems and Administration, The Singer Company, Inc.

Financial public relations

Financial public relations has emerged as a management function
of major significance. There has been, and continues to be, a tremendous movement towards fuller disclosure by corporations of relevant information needed by investors to make informed investment
decisions. The federal government, through the actions of the Securities and Exchange Commission and other regulatory agencies, is
showing an ever-deepening interest in what companies tell, and do
not tell, the investing public. A company whose securities are publicly listed and traded is expected to release quickly any news or
information which might reasonably be expected to materially affect the market price for those securities. In addition, the company
must act promptly to dispel unfounded rumors which have per-
meated investors' circles, resulting in unusual market activity or
price variations.[1]

The function of financial public relations should never be considered unimportant nor should it be relegated to a middle-manage-
ment position. The function should carry with it the exclusive responsibility for dealing with the public, or at least coordinating the
company's contact with shareholders and the financial community.
Financial public relations entails reflecting and interpreting the
company's corporate character to the public. Projecting the proper
corporate image and theme is of the utmost importance in maintaining a stable and efficient market for the company's securities. In
addition, the function carries with it the responsibility for interpreting and evaluating public opinion and keeping top management
aware of popular feelings. Responsibility for the performance of this
duty should rest with one individual who is adequately versed in
financial affairs. Depending upon the size of the company, the position could warrant a full-time effort. For most companies public relations is best accomplished by a separate department within the
organization.

The public relations department should maintain central control
over day-to-day contacts with shareholders, institutional investors,
and financial analysts. Contacts with principal executives within the
organization are arranged through the department to emphasize the
need for internal coordination in an effort to provide consistent and
unified information. Requests for information directed to operating

---

[1] New York Stock Exchange, Company Manual, p. A-18.

units of the company by analysts or members of the financial press should be referred to the public relations department. The goal is to provide appropriate information promptly in response to legitimate inquiries and to allow the investor or potential investor to make a personal evaluation. One must strive to attain and maintain credibility with the investing public.

The executive entrusted with the responsibility for the company's financial public relations must communicate a clear and accurate picture of the organization's basic objectives and major achievements to all interested parties who may be of importance to, and have an impact on, company operations. The corporate message or theme must be woven, if possible, into all communications with the public.

Implementation of the financial public relations function

To implement effectively the financial public relations function within an organization one should start with a formal, written corporate policy on the matter. Such a policy would enumerate specific guidelines and/or principles of operation which must be followed. The typical policy normally dictates that the company's annual report and Form 10-K (filed annually with the Securities and Exchange Commission) be used as an information base. In addition, earnings estimates or forecasts generally are not provided nor are projections or evaluations made by analysts commented on. Prompt answers to shareholder inquiries should be of primary importance.

The executive responsible for this function should develop and maintain close relationships with key people in the financial press, with financial analysts and investment counselors, and with information services and others in the financial community. An effort should be made through these contacts to develop and place feature articles in business and trade journals that stress the company's positive achievements.

The rapid dissemination of important corporate events to the public is achieved via the press release. Any release of information that could reasonably be expected to have an impact on the market price for a company's securities should be given to the wire service and the press marked "For Immediate Release." Examples of news items that should be handled on an immediate release basis are annual and quarterly earnings, dividend announcements, acquisitions and divestments, and major management changes. In addition, news of major new products, contract awards, patents, and discoveries often fall into the same category.[2] In some circumstances product-related press releases tend to supplement the company's advertising efforts.

Another essential responsibility assigned to the financial public relations area of the company is the coordination of the production and distribution of various shareholder material including (but not limited to) the company's annual report, interim reports, proxy statements, dividend notices, and sundry other publications. In the performance of this function there should be close coordination with the offices of the controller and the treasurer for finance-related matters included in the publication, and with the activities of the operating units for product-oriented information included in the document.

In all financial public relations efforts, close contact should be maintained with legal counsel to avoid embarrassing and costly problems for the company. Counsel should be asked for their guidance in this area. The danger here is that, to assure the avoidance of any trouble, counsel may be quick to recommend a "do nothing" approach. One must be constantly aware that doing nothing can be criticized more severely than doing too much.

The keystone of an information-oriented financial public relations program for any company is the annual report. This document sets forth the bulk of the key information of a factual nature about the company which should be given to all shareholders and other interested parties. The annual report is the fundamental document with which analysts and interested shareowners begin in doing their homework on a company.

EXTERNAL FINANCIAL REPORTING

The most useful form of financial information is a company's financial statements, namely, a balance sheet, an income statement, and a statement of changes in financial position, along with the related footnotes to these statements. Most companies publish and distribute full financial statements including footnotes only once

---

[2] Ibid., p. A-22.

annually. Investment decision makers, however, need continuous information about an enterprise's degree of success or failure in order to make timely and wise determinations. *Interim reports* are an attempt to fill the gap.

Financial statements should be prepared in a manner geared to satisfying the needs of financial statement users. Users of financial statements vary in their degree of expertise and familiarity with company, industry, and general economic factors affecting such financial statements. Some of the more prominent users of financial statements are shareholders, prospective shareholders, security analysts, creditors, and regulatory agencies. With the exception of regulatory agencies, the needs of most users can be broadly categorized as the need to predict, compare, and evaluate the cash consequences of economic decisions based upon available financial information.[3] The needs of regulatory agencies are designed to make certain that the needs of the other financial statement users are adequately fulfilled. In most cases, the regulatory agencies serve as "watch dogs" for the financial community.

The annual financial report is an important document. To most individuals who have limited access to information about a company and are limited in their ability to interpret information, the annual report represents the single most important source of information available about the enterprise. Knowing this, management should strive to make this document its most effective means of financial public relations. Language used in the annual report should be concise, understandable, and not written in a legalistic fashion. Information is only of value if it is communicated effectively. Effective communication is not *what is written* but *how it is interpreted* by the reader.

The annual report should provide information about actual results. Its content, however, should not be restricted just to historical information. Short of giving outright projections and forecasts, management should tell the reader about company and industry trends and the reaction of the company to fluctuations in the economic environment. Such information assists the user in attempting to predict the future for the company. Care must be exercised in the wording of such material to avoid misleading conclusions.

The trend in recent years has been toward fuller disclosure in a

[3] AICPA, *Objectives of Financial Statements—Report of the Study Group* (New York, October 1973), p. 13.

company's annual report. A number of factors have contributed to this trend, namely:

1. Significant influence exerted by the regulatory agencies, most notably the Securities and Exchange Commission.
2. Better accounting and reporting techniques generated by the accounting profession and the Financial Accounting Standards Board.
3. Growing public relations awareness of corporations.

In the past many companies regarded any disclosure as potentially damaging. In addition, they wanted to avoid any appearance of acting to influence the price of their securities in the marketplace. Today, there is growing acceptance of the idea that management has a right and, more importantly, an obligation to take legitimate action to insure that its securities are realistically priced.

The annual report—the primary financial statement

As needs have increased, financial statements have become more elaborate and complex. A review of annual reports published for 1974 as compared with those issued in 1964 reveals vast changes in the same document within a ten-year period. Although the basic size of the document, in terms of the number of pages, is comparable for the two years, the quantity and style of information contained therein has changed dramatically. Type size used has been reduced to permit more words in the same amount of space. The use of photographs has diminished somewhat; and in most instances charts, tables, and graphs appear more frequently.

By far the most noticeable difference in annual reports today compared with those of ten years ago is the increased number of pages devoted to financial statements and footnote information in relation to the total number of pages in the document. For one company whose annual report was composed of 36 pages in both 1964 and 1974, financial statements and related information increased from 8 pages in 1964 to 17 pages in 1974.

Most of the increased information was prompted by new disclosure requirements of the accounting profession and the Securities and Exchange Commission. During that ten-year period of time the Accounting Principles Board of the American Institute of Certified

Public Accountants issued 31 *Opinions* through June of 1973, when it was replaced by the Financial Accounting Standards Board. Since its inception and through April of 1976 the FASB has issued twelve *Statements of Financial Accounting Standards* (comparable to the previous *Opinions*). Commencing with 1971 annual reports, the statement of changes in financial position became a required basic financial statement, along with the balance sheet and the statement of income and retained earnings. In 1972 a description of all *significant accounting policies* of the reporting company became mandatory and was required to be included as an integral part of the financial statements.

Footnote information has expanded greatly in the last decade, prompted by disclosure requirements issued by the Securities and Exchange Commission for companies required to file periodic reports. The SEC has prompted disclosures relating to a company's leasing activities, its compensating balance arrangements with banks, long-term contract activities, and income tax rate reconciliations, to name a few. Late in 1974 the SEC issued a mass of new disclosure rules designed to bring annual reports more closely in line with information rendered to the SEC on the company's Form 10-K. As a result, most companies found that they needed to allocate approximately an additional four pages in their annual report to accommodate all the new required material.[4] There can be no alternative but to conclude that financial statements have become, and will continue to be, more elaborate and complex in each successive year.

To the unsophisticated reader of financial statements, presentation of information in the annual report implies a high degree of precision. These financial statement users, however, fail to realize that what appears on the surface to be precise is not in fact precise. Financial statements are wrought with judgments and subjective estimates based upon those judgments. A close look at a balance sheet reveals that the only precise figure in that statement, not subject to valuation judgment, may be cash. And even there, when foreign operations are involved, currency translation rates can have an effect on the numbers. Receivables, inventories, and fixed assets are all contingent upon a review of their potential realizable value.

Financial statements, where possible, should distinguish fact from interpretation. Both factual and interpretive information are

---

[4] "An Open-Door Policy for Annual Reports," *Business Week,* May 12, 1975, p. 48.

needed by investment decision makers about transactions and other events affecting the company in order to assess the degree of uncertainty and risk involved.

A judgment must always be made as to what information is selected for reporting.[5] Materiality of the transaction or event upon the past or future outlook for the company is always a factor in making this judgment.

Basic components of the annual financial report

The annual financial report should be designed and structured to tell management's story to the varied segments of readership interest, ranging from the sophisticated security analyst to the loyal shareholder who has invested funds in the company. The annual report consists of four basic sections, each serving a different purpose and each intended for different audiences:

1. The president's letter to shareholders.
2. The textual material describing the business.
3. Financial highlights as depicted in charts, tables, and graphs.
4. The financial statements, along with related financial information.

The president's letter is normally addressed to the general shareholder and should be written in a language and style designed to be concise and understandable, using nontechnical terms. The letter is normally one or two pages in length and appears as the very first item after the cover page in the annual report. Topics covered in this area generally include a summary of operations during the year, a general outline of prospects for the upcoming year, any changes in the management of the company during the period, and overall comments as to the general economic climate and the performance of the company in such an environment.

The textual portion of the annual report is designed to educate the shareholder by providing a degree of clarity and meaning to the financial statements. Textual material is usually segmented by product line and embellished with photographs of products or facilities in use by the company. Highlights of achievements and/or failures in various segments of the company's operation, with reasons therefor, are brought forth in the textual material. To illustrate how the textual portion can serve to educate the shareholder by providing

---

[5] AICPA, *Objectives of Financial Statements*, p. 33.

meaning to financial statements one need only look to fluctuations in financial statement components. Financial statements are concise and conform to standards. A fluctuation in say a property, plant, and equipment account in the balance sheet does not, by itself, inform a shareholder that a new plant has been completed with the potential for expanding market areas for the company's products. An explanation of this fact in the text portion of the annual report does so inform the shareholder. An intelligent shareholder or analyst needs this information in order to evaluate the performance management has attained and may attain.

Charts, tables, and graphs are designed to highlight trends and to amplify what is being discussed in the textual portion and what is being reflected in the financial statements. Each of these visual aids should be simple and easy to understand by the unsophisticated reader. In addition, such displays should not be misleading by depicting a more favorable financial picture than the financial statements themselves reveal.

Financial statements and related information in a company's annual report normally encompass the following:

1. Balance sheet, which is a measure of the financial worth of an enterprise at a point in time (or at points in time) as defined by generally accepted accounting principles.
2. Statement of income and retained earnings, which represents the results of operations for the company over a period of time (or over comparable periods of time) and the accumulated results of operations, after deducting dividends paid to shareholders, since the inception of the organization.
3. Statement of changes in financial position, formerly referred to as a statement of source and application of funds, which is designed to reflect transactions in cash or working capital during the period being reported upon.
4. Summary of accounting policies, which represents a brief description of the accounting methods and practices upon which the statements are based.
5. Notes to financial statements, which are an amplification and explanation of the detailed components of the basic financial statements.
6. Auditor's report, which is the independent attestation of the fairness of the company's financial statements.

7. Supplementary information, which is relatively new to annual reports and is the result of the mass of new disclosure requirements instituted by the Securities and Exchange Commission late in 1974. The required information is designed to make the company's annual report comparable with the report rendered to the SEC on the company's Form 10-K.

Under the new SEC rules, public companies are required to give shareholders, via the annual report, the same product-line information that they report in Form 10-K. (See Chapter 37 for more detail concerning SEC requirements.) In addition, a five-year summary of operations is required, accompanied by a narrative analysis by management describing the factors that materially affected the company's results of operations for the past two years. Companies must provide a quarterly breakdown of dividends paid to all voting security holders for the past two years, with comparable quarterly high and low market prices for those securities for the two-year period.

Chapter 29 describes the components of financial statements in more detail and presents illustrations of reporting practices.

Requirements for information included in the annual financial report

The standards for the preparation and presentation of all financial statements is mandated by generally accepted accounting principles as dictated by the Financial Accounting Standards Board. For those companies whose securities are publicly held and traded, the Securities and Exchange Commission plays a dominant role in determining what information is presented in annual reports, and how. Regulation S-X dictates the form and content of financial statements to be filed with the Commission. Publicly held companies, at a minimum, are required to file with the SEC an annual report on Form 10-K.

Under the Securities Exchange Act proxy rules, any solicitation of shareholders on behalf of management, and in relation to an annual meeting at which directors are to be elected, must be accompanied by the company's annual report. In an attempt to assure greater disclosure of important financial and other business information, the Securities and Exchange Commission amended its proxy rules effective December 20, 1974. The amended rules require clearer and more expansive disclosure of the financial condition and business operations of the company to be included in the annual report. Under the amended rules, annual reports to security holders must include the following disclosures:

1. Certified financial statements for the issuer's last two fiscal years.
2. A summary and management's analysis of the issuer's operations for the last five fiscal years.
3. Description of the nature and scope of the issuer's business and that of its subsidiaries.
4. Information on lines of business.
5. Information about the management of the company, including identification of the issuer's executive officers and directors.
6. Market and dividend information.[6]

These new disclosure requirements of the Securities and Exchange Commission reflect the belief that a more effective vehicle for communication between a company's management and its shareholders can be achieved via the annual report to shareholders.

Preparation of the annual financial report

The degree of effort required to prepare a company's annual report to shareholders depends, to a large extent, on the size and diversity of the corporation. For the multinational firm with diverse operations spread throughout the world, a concerted effort must be expended in order to perform a competent job and achieve the end result of a professional-looking annual report.

Review of reporting requirements. The necessary first step in the preparation of the annual financial report is a thorough review of new or revised reporting requirements issued by the Financial Accounting Standards Board and/or the Securities and Exchange Commission. It is imperative for the preparer of the annual reports to know what must be disclosed. A passive, cursory review will not suffice. A perfect example of the need to keep abreast of current developments is the mass of new disclosure rules issued by the Securities and Exchange Commission effective December 20, 1974—just 11 days before most companies had their year-end closing!

Special requests for information. The next step after a review of compliance requirements is to determine what information is

_____
[6] Commerce Clearing House, Inc., *Annual Reports to Security Holders,* (Chicago: 1974), p. 7.

readily available and what information will take time and effort to accumulate. The multinational company with operations spread throughout the world and crossing many product lines and industries has many problems in the information gathering process. For most companies, normal monthly or quarterly management reporting requirements do not encompass the vast spectrum of compliance reporting needs for the annual report. Therefore, prior to the year-end closing, the individuals responsible for the preparation of the annual report must compare information required for inclusion in the annual report with information obtained by management on a periodic basis from operating units throughout the world. Any deficiencies must be compensated for by a special request for the needed information. For many companies this is achieved via the annual reporting package. As the name implies it is a "package" of preprinted forms addressed to all reporting units, requesting the recipient to prepare carefully the information exactly as specified on the form. The recipient is instructed to direct any questions concerning any of the forms to a specific individual or individuals in the corporate office. The keynotes for the annual reporting package are *consistent preparation* of like information by all reporting units and *accuracy* of information. The annual reporting package, once completed, is returned to the corporate office where like information is consolidated and used in its proper place in the annual report.

Not all required information is maintained by all reporting units. Therefore, it may become necessary to supplement the annual reporting package with specialized request letters addressed only to specific sectors of the company. An example of the type of information obtained via a special request letter can be taken from the Securities and Exchange Commission's disclosure requirements relative to a company's long-term contract activities. Unless the multinational company is exclusively in an industry that operates under long-term contracts, this information is highly specialized and limited to those sectors of the company that have this type of activity. To include instructions and forms needed to capture this information in the annual reporting package would be both wasteful and confusing. The special request letter fulfills the purpose.

One of the major problems encountered by anyone using the annual reporting package or the special request letters revolves around effective communication with personnel in the field. Effective communication is mandatory to assure that all of the required disclosure information is obtained in an accurate state. To do this involves the careful preparation of instructions and forms which are readily understandable and easy to complete by the individual in the field who might not be familiar with the particulars of new disclosure requirements.

Method and style of preparation. After information is requested and before it is scheduled to be submitted, thought and effort should be devoted to the method and style of financial statement presentation. One way of accomplishing this task is to review other companies' annual reports for style and format. In addition, the American Institute of Certified Public Accountants publishes annually a book entitled *Accounting Trends and Techniques,* which represents a survey of the accounting aspects of the annual reports of selected industrial and commercial corporations. Both of these tools can assist the annual report preparer with new and popular methods of disclosing various items of information.

The textual portion of the annual report is intended to educate the reader by providing clarity and meaning to the financial statements. Textual material should be prepared by key operating executives responsible for the activities of the specific lines of business being discussed in the annual report. Once prepared, such material is then edited and rewritten by professional communication specialists, with the close scrutiny of financial personnel to assure accuracy of meaning. The revised proxy rules require that the annual report to shareholders contain a description of the company's business, including line-of-business information, in a manner adequate to reflect the general nature and scope of operations. Business information included in the textual material in the annual report should be consistent with what is required to be disclosed in the "Business" section of the company's annual report on Form 10-K filed with the Securities and Exchange Commission.

Key accounting specialists should prepare the financial statements and compose the notes to financial statements. Prior year data and any other historical data should be inserted wherever useful or required. The Securities and Exchange Commission encourages the use of tables, schedules, charts, and graphic illustrations to present the financial information in an understandable fashion. However, such presentations must be consistent with the data in the financial statements contained in the annual report.

Preparation of supplementary information. To assist in the preparation of supplementary information included in the annual report, the "Business" section and the "Summary of Operations" section of the company's Form 10-K should be updated to insure compliance with proxy rules. The "Business" section of Form 10-K requires the reporting company to describe the business done and intended to be done. Such a description should include competitive conditions in the industries in which the company is active, information relative to the company's backlog of orders, sources and availability of essential raw materials, amount of research and development expenditures, and number of employees. The seasonal nature of the company's business cycle should be disclosed if applicable. Information as to sales and income by lines of business should be disclosed if these lines account for 10 percent or more of total sales and income before taxes.

The "Summary of Operations" section of Form 10-K calls for a five-year comparative income statement, which must include a separate section entitled "Management's Discussion and Analysis of the Summary of Operations" for the most current two years of the five-year summary. The major portion of material required by the amended proxy rules is this narrative analysis by management, designed to be written in an understandable fashion, describing the factors that materially affected the company's financial results for the past two years. A line item of the summary of operations is material for purposes of this analysis if it reflects a 10 percent or greater change from the prior year, and if such change is greater than 2 percent of the average of net income for the most recent three-year period.

Circulation of statement drafts. If everything functions according to plan, the annual report should be nearly completed by the time the current year information is available. Once such current information is consolidated, all open items of the annual report can be completed and a first draft can be distributed to interested parties for their comments. Two of the first groups of individuals to be contacted for comments are the independent accountants and legal counsel. Adequacy of disclosure in both an accounting and a legal sense must be assured.

Comments on the annual report draft should be received from key executives of various segments of the company including, but not limited to, the controller's office, the treasurer's office, the secretary's office, key operating executives, and, of course, the chief financial officer and the president of the company. Everyone reviewing the draft of the annual report should do so with diligence and understanding of the importance of the document. Extreme care must be exercised in the review of material described in the president's letter and the textual portion of the annual report. Poor usage of words could seriously impair the meaning and accuracy of the thought being conveyed. Legal ramifications could be the end result of carelessly prepared remarks. A point in time should be established for all substantive comments to be submitted for consideration.

Distribution of the annual financial report

Publicly held companies are guided by the Exchange Act proxy rules which provide that any solicitation of security holders made on behalf of management, and relating to an annual meeting at which directors are to be elected, must be accompanied or preceded by an annual report containing basic financial information regarding the company's operations.[7]

For those companies whose securities are traded on the New York Stock Exchange, the Exchange requires that the annual report be published and submitted to shareholders at least 15 days before the annual meeting, but no later than 3 months after the close of the fiscal year. Therefore, for calendar year companies the annual report must be distributed to shareholders prior to March 31 of each year.[8]

The general publicity practice recommended for all companies is to release annual financial information to the financial media as soon as possible. Information as to sales and earnings normally stipulates that it is subject to the completion of the year-end audit adjustments. Such a release is normally followed by the distribution of the printed annual report some time later. The key point here is that earnings information should be released as soon after year-end as it is available. The company should not wait until the annual report is printed and ready for distribution before it releases earnings data to the public.

Both the New York and American stock exchanges urge broad distribution of the annual report to shareholders. Such distribution should include, but not be limited to, security analysts, statistical

---

[7] Ibid., p. 7.

[8] Robert W. Taft, "Disclosure: Avoiding a Roadmap to Fraud," *The 1974 Conference on Financial Reporting* (New York: AMR International, Inc.), 1974.

services such as Moody's and Standard & Poor's, research departments of institutional investors, and business libraries. A broad distribution is recommended to insure available information for ready public reference.

The printed annual report and appropriate year-end news releases should be carefully checked to insure that they conform to information submitted to the Securities and Exchange Commission on Form 10-K. With new disclosure requirements making the company's annual report virtually a "mirror image" of its Form 10-K, it is imperative that these two documents be consistent as to information disclosed. To highlight the importance of both documents the Securities and Exchange Commission requires that companies inform their shareholders of the fact that they may obtain a copy of the company's Form 10-K without charge and upon written request. Most companies apprise their shareholders of this fact by including a section on the cover page of their annual report instructing the reader to contact the secretary of the company if a copy of the Form 10-K is desired.

The annual meeting of shareholders

The holding of an annual meeting of shareholders is normally required by state law or by the bylaws of the company. The annual meeting can be viewed, on the one hand, as a useful forum in which management justifies and defends its action to ownership interests, or, on the other hand, as a necessary nuisance. If handled properly, the annual meeting of shareholders can serve as still another effective means of financial public relations. The size of the company and the number of shareowners normally dictates the degree of significance placed by the company on its annual meeting. Generally, the greater the company size and ownership distribution, the more likely a company is to attach significance to the annual meeting as a means of informing shareholders.

Shareholder interest in annual meetings tends to bear a converse relationship to the earnings and the amount of dividends paid by the company. Normally if earnings performance is good and dividend payouts are respectable, shareholder interest in the annual meeting is somewhat passive. Should the reverse be true, where earnings are falling and thereby affecting the dividend policy of the company, then shareholder interest and attendance at the annual meeting becomes very active. The encouragement of shareholders to attend the annual meeting, for most companies, generally does not go beyond a cordially worded invitation appearing in the proxy statement and the annual report.

Regardless of the anticipated attendance and the projected mood of those shareholders attending the meeting, management must be adequately prepared to handle inquiries from the floor. For the larger, widely held companies it is almost assured that questions will be generated by very articulate and knowledgeable "professional shareholders." To prepare for the annual meeting management should endeavor, through various channels both inside and outside the company, to obtain a list of questions that may be asked by shareholders at the meeting. The company's independent accountants and legal counsel are a good starting base to obtain information about the type of questions asked at other annual meetings held during the year. In addition, a careful review of the annual report should be performed to determine which areas may raise questions. Management should be equipped at the meeting to provide detail behind any amounts appearing in the annual report.

Security analysts are often invited to the annual meeting. In addition, most larger companies make it a practice to hold a *supplemental news briefing* directly following the meeting for those analysts and members of the financial press who are in attendance. Such a press conference is designed to improve relations with the financial press and the representatives of the securities industry and, hopefully, to achieve favorable press coverage for the annual meeting.

As soon as possible after the annual meeting a *post-meeting report* should be published and distributed to all shareholders. The report is a somewhat detailed account of what transpired at the annual meeting, highlighting significant comments and questions. The principal reason for publishing and distributing a post-meeting report is to inform all shareholders, not just the minority who attended the meeting, of what took place. The post-meeting report is yet another financial public relations tool available for use by the company.

Financial public relations between annual reports

The annual financial report is considered as both the beginning and the end of the financial public relations cycle for a company. Financial public relations and a company's financial reporting program, however, are year-round functions. A company should strive to achieve a strong financial public relations program. A satisfactory effort in this area can be of benefit in a number of ways. It can encourage broader and more loyal share ownership. It can help to stabilize the prices for the company's securities in the marketplace which will, in turn, provide for a fair price/earnings ratio for such stock. A strong financial public relations awareness may add to the corporation's financing capabilities by offering greater receptivity for new security issuances, be they debt or equity securities. Finally, strong financial public relations will improve dealings with security analysts and the financial press.

Security analysts are the most important communication link with the financial community. Although an effective shareholder relations program should be geared to cover all investors, professional investors and analysts have a major impact on formulating the market's opinion as to prospects for investment. If analysts are stymied in their attempts to gain information from a company, their frustration may be translated into a poor recommendation or complete lack of interest as to the investment quality of the company's securities in the marketplace. This, in turn, may result in unstable prices and low price/earnings multiples for the corporation's securities.

An effective financial public relations program involves the issuance of a number of publications during the year. *Interim reports,* usually on a quarterly basis, are the most prevalent form of publication issued by most companies during their fiscal year. (See Chapter 35 for further information.) The typical interim report gives sales and earnings information on a comparative quarter and year-to-date basis. Some companies publish full income statement information, supplemented by comments on operations for the period. The topic of interim reporting and information that should be rendered on a quarterly basis is of extreme interest to the Securities and Exchange Commission. The SEC has recently adopted certain interim reporting requirements for public companies in preparing their quarterly report on Form 10-Q filed with the Commission. In addition to an income statement, the rules require a balance sheet and a statement of changes in financial position, along with a narrative analysis of the results of operations similar to that required for the summary of operations in Form 10-K. The interest in interim reporting on the part of the Securities and Exchange Commission and other organizations emphasizes the need and importance of current information. Financial public relations is a full-time endeavor.

In-house magazines are also a helpful device in promoting good public relations with employee-shareholders. Information about the company and the people who make up the company tends to create an identity between the company and the employee-shareholder.

A financial public relations program takes on many forms, one of which is the *face to face contact* between management and the financial community. This contact is achieved in various ways, from presentations and addresses by company executives to interviews with representatives of the financial community, including analysts and the financial press. The direct contact approach to financial public relations is extremely important. One of the most significant judgments a security analyst makes in evaluating the investment quality of a company's securities is his or her opinion of the management of that company. Much of a company's written material serves as a basis for this opinion, but the personal contact with members of management is a very important element.

Management's approach to financial public relations today must revolve around high-quality company reporting and accessibility of corporate personnel to the financial community. The financial community extends from the small shareholder with the basic question to the sophisticated analyst with the probing inquiry. Management must be prepared to deal effectively with both extremes.

SUMMARY

The annual financial report is the cornerstone of an effective financial public relations program. The annual report should be written in a way that explains management's story to a variety of readership interests. The report should encompass a discussion of *what happened* financially and operationally during the year and, more importantly, *why it happened* and the *anticipated effects* of such events on the future. The company's competitive position within its industry or industries, along with the effects on the company of a fluctuating economic environment, should be brought across in the annual report narrative.

An effort should be made to stimulate readership interest in this most important tool of financial public relations. Clear and simple language should be used at all times. Do not try to avoid explaining adverse developments as they arise. All items should be put in their proper perspective with a discussion of management's plans for corrective action.

Financial public relations is an ongoing responsibility for the dynamic corporation. The function does not cease when the annual report is distributed to shareholders and the financial community. Part of management's responsibility is to protect and increase the value of the ownership interest in its company. Establishing credibility between company management and shareholders is imperative in assuring an adequate price in the marketplace for a company's securities. Maintaining and strengthening this credibility is the function of a financial public relations program.

Chapter 29

The modern annual report— more information, faster!

*Allan Crane**

Almost 6,000 companies whose shares are traded on the New York Stock Exchange, American Exchange, and over the counter annually arrange for the creation, production, and distribution of an annual report. Publicly held companies are spending an estimated $120 million annually for these reports.[1] Why is so much money and time devoted to the publication of a glossy and sometimes colorful company report?

Encouraged by member reporting requirements of the major stock exchanges, all companies view the annual report as a necessary document for disclosure of required financial statements and other pertinent data. Many of these companies tend to disclose the "minimum." More and more companies, however, recognize the value of the annual report as a means of communicating to a large number of publics and tend to disclose an increasing amount of information.

The primary "public" is the company shareholders. They are joined, however, by a broad range of interested readers including:

---

* Vice President and Controller, A. O. Smith Corporation.

[1] According to Lory Roston Associates, a New York public relations company.

Prospective shareholders.   Competitors.
Financial analysts.   Creditors.
Customers.   Labor unions.
Vendors.   Government (federal, state, and local).
Employees.   Educators.
Students.   General public.

Special interest groups concerned with:

Pollution.   Equal employment opportunities.
Safety.   Energy conservation.

Faced with such a varied audience a company must decide whether to prepare an elaborate report or to create a document with minimum content. A very successful Milwaukee, Wisconsin member company of the NYSE issues a brief 14-page report with a minimum of pictures and charts to its 13,535 shareholders. Most companies distribute a two or more color booklet averaging about 40 pages. A few companies will issue unusually elaborate and colorful reports and, occasionally, include separate financial or nonfinancial inserts.

What are some of the factors that cause a company to be modest or elaborate? If a company sells consumer items such as automobiles or food items it will probably issue a colorful report replete with many pictures of tempting products. A company which sells parts to a limited number of other companies for inclusion in a final product may be more modest in its report content.

The interests of the particular audience(s) the reporting company is attempting to reach will frequently dictate the emphasis of report content. An example of varied user interests is illustrated in Exhibit 1.

Other factors to be considered are the number of shareholders (AT&T has over 3 million shareholders); an unusual event such as a "centennial" celebration, recent major acquisition, major product breakthrough, or shortage; and corporate image or the need to change the image.

Improved disclosure of company operations is the key change in the annual reports of the 1970s. The appeal or requirement for added disclosure comes mainly from stock exchanges (such as the New York Stock Exchange), governmental agencies (such as the Securities and Exchange Commission), accounting bodies (Account-

EXHIBIT 1

Interests of various groups of financial statement users

User	Interests
Housewives	New product research, promotional activities that are entertaining and educational, women in management, ecology measures, market position, profit and dividend performance.
Disadvantaged groups	Hiring needs, recruiting plans, educational programs, future plans, aid offered to small businesses, contributions.
General public	Antipollution, crime, and discrimination programs; future plans.
Investment analysts	Relative performance, distinguished performance, potential, public favor, investor enthusiasm and apathy.
Investors (owners)	Profits, dividends, earnings per share (probably placed on a separate page that is bordered in gold leaf), capital gains, future outlook, plans for meeting competition, societal image, employee morale, a listing of "bid" and "ask" prices on several dates during the year for both the company and its close competitors.
Creditors	Ability to repay, potential for future business, societal image.
Management (top)	Expansion of sales volume, curtailment of costs, expansion of company (or perhaps retrenchment—an often overlooked but perhaps desirable alternative), finances, morale, societal image.
Management (middle)	Advancement, status, departmental rather than corporate performance, morale, societal image.
Unions	Employees' shares in monetary rewards, employee recreation, employment, job satisfaction for employees, security.
Employees	Job satisfaction, employee education, employee recompense, job security, profits, dividends, societal image, corporate security and plans.
Uncle Sam, the local mayor, and the state governor	Tax revenues, favorable employment conditions, corporate plans, societal image, environmental problems.
Accountants	Form of the statements, consistency, conservatism, timeliness, fair presentation. (This group should be more concerned with the usefulness of reports and with satisfying the curiosity of *all* statement audiences.)

Source: A. Wayne Corcoran and Wayne E. Leininger, Jr., "Financial Statements, Who Needs Them?" *Financial Executive*, August 1970, pp. 34–38, 45–47.

ing Principles Board and now the Financial Accounting Standards Board), and financial analysts.

REPORTING REQUIREMENTS OF THE STOCK EXCHANGES

The objective of the major stock exchanges' requirements is to provide stockholders with full disclosure of all material facts and figures relating to the status and progress of the business. The requirements of the New York Stock Exchange, which can be found in the company's listing agreement, are most comprehensive. Briefly stated, they are as follows:

1. Publish at least once a year and submit to stockholders at least 15 days prior to annual stockholders' meeting and not later than 3 months after the close of the preceding fiscal year:
    a.   A consolidated balance sheet.
    b.   A consolidated retained earnings statement.
    c.   A consolidated income statement.
    d.   Appropriate footnotes.
2. Published annual financial statements must be audited by independent public accountants.

The New York Stock Exchange, through the issuance of a White Paper entitled "Recommendations and Comments on Financial Reporting to Shareholders and Related Matters," has strongly urged companies to expand their annual report disclosure in the following areas:

1. Quarterly sales and earnings data for each of the quarters compared with prior year's data.
2. Form 10-K (annual report to SEC) data that is material to the financial status of the company.
3. Annual debt maturities for the succeeding five years if debt structure is complicated.
4. Line-of-business data similar to that disclosed in the SEC 10-K report.
5. Computation of federal income tax, if reported tax percentage to income is materially different from the statutory rate.
6. Clarification of the computation of earnings per share.
7. Nature and volume of transactions between the company and affiliated and related parties (in financial statement footnotes).
8. Material deferred charges and provisions for unusual items.
9. Common stock price ranges, price/earnings ratio ranges, dividends, and rate of payout and return, along with book value.
10. Current versus prior year detailed analysis of increase or decrease in earnings, in tabular form, supplemented by descriptive text.
11. An offer to make the 10-K available to stockholders.

REPORTING REQUIREMENTS OF THE SEC

Increasingly in the early 1970s, the Securities and Exchange Commission has pushed for more and more detailed disclosure of financial information in annual statements (Form 10-K) and in registration statements filed with the Commission. Late in 1974 the SEC published amendments to proxy solicitation rules which make mandatory for inclusion in annual reports to shareholders certain disclosures, including some information previously required only in the annual Form 10-K. The new requirements illustrate the Commission's updated views as to what is needed for a more meaningful report to shareholders. Highlights of the SEC annual report requirements include:

1. A description of the business together with information about the company's lines of business for the last five fiscal years.
2. A "Summary of Operations" similar to that required in the SEC Form 10-K and a management analysis thereof.
3. Certified financial statements for the issuer's last two fiscal years.
4. Identification of the issuer's directors and executive officers and the disclosure of each such person's principal occupation or employment and of the name and principal business of any organization by which such person is so employed.
5. The identity of principal market(s) where shares are traded.
6. High and low sales prices or range of bid and ask quotations for securities for each quarterly period within the most recent two years.
7. Dividends paid on securities for those two years.

RECENT TRENDS IN ANNUAL REPORTING

A review of a representative sample of annual reports shows that some of the above proposals have already been accepted by a number of reporting companies. It is to be expected, given the impetus of an active SEC leadership, that the trend of including information recommended by the Commission in the annual report to shareholders will continue.

During 1974 many companies made an offer in their annual reports to provide a copy of SEC Form 10-K to any reader who requested it in writing. Most companies offered the report without cost, but a few made a nominal charge for handling and mailing. A later survey[2] of companies offering copies of the 10-Ks indicated that fewer than 1 percent of all shareholders in each company requested the SEC report.

The Financial Accounting Standards Board will be considering the recommendations of the AICPA Study Group on Objectives of Financial Statements. These recommendations broaden traditional concepts of financial statement purposes to encompass forecasts, social impact reports, and current values. Added disclosure has been or will be considered in other subject areas such as line-of-business (segment) reporting, leases, foreign currency translation, research and development costs, and future losses.

Documentary information about a company is the bread and butter of financial analysts. Their interest in the past and present permits them to make judgments about a company's future prospects. David Norr, past president of the New York Society of Security Analysts, stated,

> There is much that management can do in an annual report beyond mere accounting. The basic elements are 1) meaningful text information, 2) a discussion of variances, and 3) a table of divisional earnings. Beyond that, the specifics may vary in each situation. All this is designed to make the report understandable. It is the obligation of management to provide information adequate to achieve understanding.

In summary, the trend toward greater corporate disclosure is revealed in a *Business Week* analysis of 100 companies (Exhibit 2).

Business Week also noted that the companies tend to respond to current events.

> In 1972 companies went out of their way to display their concern for corporate social responsibility. But in 1973 the issue took a back seat to the energy crisis. Only 22% made prominent mention of social issues in their 1973 annual reports, compared with 64% of a year earlier.

CONTENT OF THE ANNUAL REPORT

The specific content of the annual report is not completely prescribed by any agency except for certain recommendations of the

---

[2] Hill and Knowlton survey, *Wall Street Journal*, July 11, 1974, p. 1.

EXHIBIT 2
What companies are revealing in their annual reports

	Percent			
Sample of 100 companies	*1970*	*1971*	*1972*	*1973*
Sales and earnings by product line	32%	51%	57%	58%
Sales only by product line	24	19	21	22
Financial statistics for 10 years or more	67	63	67	73
Research and development expenditures.	17	24	35	26
Concern for corporate responsibilities	30	60	64	22
Availability of 10-K reports	NA	NA	NA	15
Foreign sales and earnings	NA	NA	NA	38
Currency translation gains and losses	NA	NA	NA	34
Quarterly earnings	NA	NA	NA	26
Inventory profits	NA	NA	NA	26
Effective income tax rates				53*
Compensating bank balances				40*
Capitalization of leases				29*

* Required by the Securities and Exchange Commission for the first time in 10-K reports.
NA = not available.
Source: *Business Week*, April 27, 1974, p. 63.

SEC and certain requirements of the NYSE. All annual reports include certified financial statements. In addition, the following sections appear in most reports:

1. Financial highlights.
2. Chief executive officer's letter.
3. Operational summary.
4. Financial review.
5. Historical financial review.
6. Reference data (plants, officers, registrar, directors, etc.).

As greater disclosure has become the theme for many companies additional sections have appeared in some reports. Examples of the more popular are:

1. Operational highlights.
2. Line-of-business summary.
3. Socioeconomic highlights.

The content of the report will usually be that which most closely meets the objectives of the company. The precise sequence of the material varies from company report to company report, but a journalistic pattern is followed by many. Newspapers identify a story with a headline, highlight the whole story in the first paragraph, and follow up with more detail as more and more paragraphs are added. The reader can stop with the headline, the first paragraph, or go further, depending on his interest in detail.

An annual report can be prepared in the same manner. First to appear may be operational highlights and financial highlights. The reader need not proceed further but will have the whole story in a nutshell. The chief executive's letter may appear next and provide more information. For the reader who needs considerable detail, the operational summary and the financial review will be next in sequence. Financial statements and reference data will complete the report.

Brief comments about each section of the report follow.

Financial highlights

The financial highlights section may vary by company but should include data which will give the shareholders a quick review of the company's financial performance. At a minimum, quarterly net sales, earnings, and dividends per share for the current and prior year should be disclosed. Frequently, the section is expanded to include more years and also more data such as return on net worth, capital expenditures, depreciation, taxes, and working capital. This section is also usually located inside the front cover or on "Page One." (See Exhibit 3.)

Operational highlights

Operational highlights are usually short headliner-type statements placed in chronological sequence depicting the significant occurrences of the year. Formations or acquisitions of subsidiaries or business units, major product introduction, divestments, liquidations, new or refurbished facilities, time or delivery milestones, major financing, industry or internal labor strikes significantly affecting the business, and special awards for safety or equal opportunity activities are a few examples of such a chronology sketch. This section is not specifically required for disclosure purposes, but can serve those who are satisfied in only scanning an annual report for salient happenings, along with financial highlights, without taking valuable time to read longer and more detailed text material. The operational highlights section also provides a ready reference of historical occurrences for the many users of annual reports, including internal management. This section is usually located inside the front cover or on the first page and may be displayed in conjunction with financial highlights (see Exhibit 3).

EXHIBIT 3

FEDERAL–MOGUL CORPORATION

1973 Highlights

FINANCIAL RESULTS IN BRIEF	1973	1972
Net Sales	$341,225,000	$289,862,000
Earnings Before Income Taxes and Extraordinary Item	25,040,000	27,669,000
Income Taxes	10,900,000	13,100,000
Earnings Before Extraordinary Item	14,140,000	14,569,000
As a Percent of Sales	4.1%	5.0%
Per Common and Common Equivalent Share	$2.46	$2.55
Extraordinary Credit	—0—	.12
Net Earnings Per Share	2.46	2.67
Dividends Paid Per Common Share	1.80	1.80
Number of Shareholders of Record	19,350	18,437
Number of Employees	14,482	14,711

Manufacturing
- Production began at a large tapered roller bearing plant in Alabama
- Ground was broken for a major oil seal plant in South Carolina
- Production began at a new oil seal facility in Belgium
- Oil seal manufacturing facilities were added to a plant in Brazil
- Engine bearing plants were expanded in France, Brazil, Argentina and Mexico
- O-ring manufacturing facilities were expanded in California

Marketing
- Ground was broken for Worldwide Distribution Center in Alabama
- New International Distribution Center was completed in Belgium
- New central distribution warehouse was opened in France

- Global sales organization was expanded
- Re-entry made into foreign markets with parts coverage for the majority of foreign vehicles
- Added improvements were made in the extensive U.S. distribution network
- Heavy duty, agricultural and foreign vehicle parts coverage was expanded

Finance
- Successful sale of $30 million of 7½ percent debentures to finance capital additions and for general corporate funds
- Successful sale of $5½ million of industrial revenue bonds to finance the large, new facilities now under construction in South Carolina and Alabama.

Chief executive officer's letter

The chief executive officer's letter is probably the best read text material in the entire annual report. The letter is the only signed portion of the publication (other than the auditor's opinion) and often carries the signatures of both the chairman and president. Most often, the CEO's letter occupies one or two pages near the front of the report. However, there have been reports in which the entire review of operations is signed and this becomes, in effect, a very long CEO letter.

The major purpose of the CEO letter is to provide the shareholders with cogent reasons for the trend of earnings during the past year. The CEO letter should not, in most cases, get too specific in reporting events of the past year since those items should be adequately covered in the operational summary or the financial review.

Another important function of the CEO letter is to provide readers with an indication of how the leaders of the company view the future in terms of impact on sales and earnings. Specific forecasts are almost always avoided, but general statements to the effect that things look good, bad, or flat are usually included, supplemented by supporting reasons. If a specific forecast is desired, the CEO letter is a good vehicle.

The CEO letter is also used by some companies to discuss government policies which may be adversely affecting business, or to urge adoption of other policies which may improve the business climate. Often the CEO letter is used to state or restate company policies relating to equal employment, social responsibilities, or community involvement. Finally, many CEOs like to use the letter to thank shareholders, directors, customers, and employees for their support and loyalty over the past year.

Line-of-business reporting

The Securities and Exchange Commission and the New York Stock Exchange recommend that companies include segment (line-of-business) reporting in annual reports to shareholders on a basis similar to that included in the SEC 10-K report.

In a sample of 100 companies,[3] 58 percent reported both sales and profits while 22 percent reported sales only during 1973. This indicates that some form of product line reporting is being made by about 80 percent of large companies used in the sample.

There are a number of considerations involved in making a line of business report useful and meaningful to the reader of an annual report.

1. *Should all lines of business be shown on a historical basis or should only the current and continuing lines of business be shown with a separate aggregation of "discontinued lines of business"?* Most readers are concerned about the future of the company and the apparent trends of continuing lines of busi-

---

[3] Sample made by *Business Week*, April 27, 1974, pp. 63, 66.

ness and, therefore, would prefer separate aggregation of discontinued lines with notes disclosing which businesses are involved.

2. *What constitutes a "line of business"?* This selection should be at the discretion of the reporting company based on availability of data and vulnerability to revelation of competitive information detrimental to its current market position. Some companies report data by market (see Exhibit 4), some by type of product, some by geography, and some by process. It would

EXHIBIT 4

SALES AND EARNINGS BY LINE OF BUSINESS						A.O. SMITH CORPORATION				
(Millions)		SALES					EARNINGS (LOSS)(1)			
	1975	1974	1973	1972	1971	1975(2)	1974(2)	1973	1972	1971
OEM PRODUCTS Automotive and truck frames, auto components, railroad equipment, hermetic, jet pump and other electric motors	$ 347.3	337.7	383.4	309.8	268.6	4.6	(1.8)	24.2	17.3	14.8
%	73	70	76	76	76	127	(62)	72	65	65
CONSUMER PRODUCTS Water heaters, heating equipment.	$ 59.0	55.9	52.5	46.4	40.3	2.0	.7	3.1	3.7	3.3
%	13	12	10	11	11	56	24	9	14	15
AGRICULTURE Livestock feed storage, handling and feeding systems, finance subsidiary	$ 52.9	73.3	58.7	44.8	38.8	(5.0)	2.2	5.7	5.5	4.3
%	11	15	12	11	11	(139)	76	17	20	19
DIVERSIFIED Computer systems, reinforced plastic pipe, metal powder	$ 14.5	13.8	8.5	7.0	5.6	2.0	1.8	.5	.3	.2
%	3	3	2	2	2	56	62	2	1	1
TOTAL	$ 473.7	480.7	503.1	408.0	353.3	3.6	2.9	33.5	26.8	22.6
%	100	100	100	100	100	100	100	100	100	100
Eliminated Operations(3)	$ —	—	22.4	31.6	49.0	—	—	(1.7)	(1.2)	(.2)
Elimination of Equity in Unconsolidated Affiliates Included Above(4)	$ (21.9)	(22.9)	(16.9)	(21.5)	(27.2)	(4.9)	(4.7)	(1.7)	—	(1.4)
Continuing Operations	$ 451.8	457.8	508.6	418.1	375.1	(1.3)	(1.8)	30.1	25.6	21.0
Discontinued Operations (5)	$ 108.0	109.9	101.9	74.7	81.7	(3.1)	(4.8)	(3.2)	(5.8)	2.3

NOTES

(1) Line of business earnings are before income taxes and extraordinary items and are determined after allocation of certain administrative and interest costs (not actually charged to operating units) which are necessarily arbitrary but which the company believes to be reasonable.

(2) Reflects the company's election to change its method of valuing domestic productive inventories to LIFO from FIFO effective January 1, 1974.

(3) Eliminated operations, which have been segregated in order to better display the history of the continuing operations, include the following:

(a) Electrical control business sold effective January 2, 1974, with the provision for loss made in 1973.

(b) Equity in the affiliate line pipe operation sold effective November 30, 1972.

(c) The vertical turbine pump business sold effective January 1, 1972, with the provision for loss made in 1971.

(d) Irrigation equipment business sold in late 1971.

(e) A 50%-owned affiliate sold its specialty plastic products business effective January 31, 1971.

(4) Equity in sales and earnings of unconsolidated affiliates has been shown by line of business and then deducted in order to reconcile with the consolidated statements.

(5) Sales and earnings before income taxes of discontinued operations are shown as memo data. Further information is included in Note 1 to the financial statements on page 9 and the Financial Review Section on pages 1 and 2.

seem that any consistent reporting which fits the business and improves shareholder understanding is useful. Another categorization concept for line-of-business reporting involves the use of specific Standard Industry (SIC) Codes. The Federal Trade Commission has issued a reporting requirement for sales and earnings by SIC code to a limited number of companies.

3. *How many years of data should be shown?* Five years is reasonable, but a minimum of three years is desirable.

4. *Should both sales and earnings be displayed?* Sales and earnings should be shown except where it might be harmful to the company's competitive position.

5. *Should both dollars and percent of total business be shown?* It is normal and useful to include both dollars and percentages for purposes of analyzing the major sources of revenue and earnings.

6. *Should the report include equity in unconsolidated affiliates?* This is optional; however, it does enhance the value of the report if equity amounts are included.

7. *Should corporate expenses and interest expense be allocated to lines of business?* This is certainly a question that can be discussed from varying points of view. Some will argue that any allocation is arbitrary and, therefore, results can be misleading. Others will argue that earnings before absorption of these expenses will mislead the reader relative to apparent profit margins. Relative earnings of lines of business to the total could also be affected by such allocations if they are not carefully and consistently made.

8. *Should extraordinary items be included in or excluded from line of business reporting?* The very nature of the item seems to dictate that these items should be excluded.

9. *Should earnings be before or after tax?* Earnings by line of business are probably more meaningful on a pretax basis. The tax calculation is frequently influenced by adjustments which do not necessarily relate to particular lines of business.

Notes which adequately disclose the basis of the information reported should be added in order to make the line of business report useful. Many companies use a foldout page, color code, or other means to relate the line of business data to the operations review section of the annual report. This technique provides an area for more explanation and gives the reader a better understanding of the various business lines.

Operational summary

The major purpose of the operational summary is to give readers an overall view of each major line of business so that someone not familiar with the company will have a fairly good understanding of each line of business after reading the report.

The operational summary in most annual reports is designed to report events which appear to influence the results of each major operating unit of the company. Very often this is done on a line-of-business basis—that is, headlines are used to separate the text into separate sections, each one of which discusses a specific line of business. This is the part of the report where some details can be provided about the progress each major segment made during the past year. Usual subjects discussed include new products, new plants, acquisitions, divestitures, market penetration, new sales territories, new markets, research and development breakthroughs, and major capital expenditures.

Negative events such as strikes, plant closings, production cutbacks, and market withdrawals must also be reviewed.

Financial review

In recent years the financial review section of the annual report has taken various forms. With the advent of increased disclosure in financial statement footnotes some companies have deleted the separate financial review section. In most cases these companies have expanded their financial highlights and historical review or included some commentary related to financial matters in the operational summary. Other companies have combined the required financial statement footnotes with the financial review section. This approach necessitates that all commentary in the financial review be certified by the independent accountants.

Most companies choose to have a separate financial review section which includes commentary on material financial occurrences during the current fiscal year. Areas frequently covered include corporate data such as sales, earnings, return on stockholders' equity, working capital, dividends, capital expenditures, depreciation, long-term debt, taxes, pensions, and stock options. This section frequently is supplemented by tabular comparisons with prior years and/or appropriate charts.

The New York Stock Exchange's White Paper recommends that each public company publish a summary of quarterly sales and earnings data for each quarter of the current fiscal year compared to the same periods of the prior year. This information is frequently included in the financial review section.

Financial statements

In the section of the annual report reserved for financial statements the following are normally presented:

1. Balance sheet.
2. Income statement.
3. Stockholders' equity.
4. Statement of changes in financial position.
5. Notes to financial statements.
6. Auditor's report.

While preparation of the financial statements is the responsibility of the management of the company, the title, form, captions, and amount of detail presented are customarily discussed with and agreed upon with the public accountants. Companies incorporating their annual report to shareholders in their report on Form 10-K to the Securities and Exchange Commission will use as a guide the SEC's Regulation S-X. This publication, "Form and Content of Financial Statements," sets forth the requirements for financial statements filed with the Commission. Preparation of the company's financial statements in practical compliance with S-X rules permits the incorporation of the annual report to shareholders in the company's Form 10-K, and reduces the specific effort required to prepare Form 10-K.

The SEC requires financial statements in the annual report to appear in Roman type at least as large and as legible as 8-point modern. Notes to financial statements shall be in Roman type as large and as legible as ten-point modern type. In printer's jargon, such type should be leaded to at least two points.

The recognized source for trends in the use of form, captions, and content of the financial statements is a publication of the

American Institute of Certified Public Accountants, *Accounting Trends and Techniques.* Each annual edition covers a study of the accounting aspects of the financial reports issued by 600 industrial companies to their stockholders. The book has proven an invaluable aid in the preparation of financial statements and is available from the AICPA at 1211 Avenue of the Americas, New York, N.Y. 10036.

Balance sheet

Most companies use the title "balance sheet" to describe the statement of assets, liabilities, and stockholders' equity. Other titles such as "statement of financial position" and "statement of financial condition" appear to be utilized less and less (*Accounting Trends and Techniques,* 1973). In format, a preponderance of companies use the "account form" which shows total assets equal to the sum of liabilities and stockholders' equity.

As an alternative, the "financial position" form shows noncurrent assets added to working capital and noncurrent liabilities deducted, to arrive at a balance equal to stockholders' equity. Use of this form is supported by those accountants who perceive an advantage in displaying working capital as a separate figure on the face of the statement.

Statement of income

"Statement of income" is the most popular title for the statement reflecting the results of operations for the period, although "statement of earnings" and "statement of operations" are also in current use. In form, the statements may be *multiple step* or *single step.*

In the multiple-step form, costs (and sometimes operating expenses) are deducted from gross revenues and a gross margin (or a profit from operations) is shown as a separate net amount to which other charges and credits are applied. In the single-step statement, costs and expenses are aggregated and no margin or profit from operations is separately displayed.

Accounting Trends and Techniques provides guidance in the placement of additional items such as equity in earnings of other companies and operating results of discontinued operations.

Stockholders' equity

This statement presents transactions other than net income which affect the stockholders' equity accounts for the period. Typically, the major transaction is the payment of dividends. Many companies use a combined statement of income and retained earnings. Others prefer separate income and retained earnings statements. When there are numerous transactions affecting the stockholders' equity section, the information is better presented in a separate statement.

Statement of changes in financial position

With the publication of *Accounting Principles Board Opinion No. 19* in March 1971, the statement of chnages in financial position became a basic statement for inclusion in annual reports. Prior to 1971, funds statements in various forms appeared with the financial statements, in the financial review section, or elsewhere in the report. While the precise definition of funds used in the statement is not dictated by the *Opinion*, guidelines are set forth which cover the content of the statement and establish the overall form the statement will take. The statement may be based on the flow of cash, but if so, changes in other elements of working capital which constitute sources and uses of cash must be disclosed in appropriate detail in the body of the statement. Most companies have chosen to show changes in working capital, detailing the increases or decreases in each component.

Financial statements of unconsolidated subsidiaries

Industrial company subsidiaries engaged in financial operations are normally not consolidated with the parent (see *Accounting Research Bulletin No. 51*). Finance, leasing, and insurance companies, as well as banks, are examples. The operating results of these subsidiaries are usually recorded by the parent on an equity in earnings basis. In the interest of good reporting and the most meaningful disclosure, the financial statements of these unconsolidated subsidiaries (where material) should be included in the annual report to shareholders. Customarily, these financial statements are assigned to a section near the end of the report and are prominently labeled to avoid confusion with the parent company statements.

Notes to financial statements

The requirements for disclosure of financial information of Financial Accounting Standards Board Statements, *Opinions* of the Accounting Principles Board, the *Statement of Auditing Standards No. 1*, and the *Accounting Research Bulletins* cannot be adequately satisfied by the financial statements alone. Explanatory notes must be included as an integral part of the reports.

If the annual report is to be included as part of the company's report on Form 10-K to the SEC, reference should be made to the requirements of Regulation S-X and the Accounting Series Releases to be certain disclosure of all required financial information is accomplished.

Summary of significant accounting policies

Effective with the publication of *APB Opinion No. 22* in 1972, a summary of significant accounting policies is required to be included in the financial statement section either just preceding the notes or as the initial note. According to the *Opinion*, the summary must encompass the accounting principles and methods that involve any of the following:

    a. A selection from existing acceptable alternatives;
    b. Principles and methods peculiar to the industry in which the reporting entity operates, even if such principles and methods are predominantly followed in that industry;
    c. Unusual or innovative applications of generally accepted accounting principles (and, as applicable, of principles and methods peculiar to the industry in which the reporting entity operates).

Some examples of policies to be disclosed cited in the *Opinion* include those relating to basis of consolidation, depreciation method, amortization of intangibles, inventory pricing, translation of foreign currencies, recognition of profit on long-term construction contracts, and recognition of revenue from franchising and leasing operations. The SEC has also shown an active interest in the disclosure of accounting policies.

Auditors' opinion

The opinion of the independent accountants as to fairness of the financial statements usually follows all statements and related notes. While this is the most common position, the opinion is also found immediately preceding the statements or elsewhere in the financial statement section. Even though the certification statement is an "opinion" the use of that title has not gained in popularity and most companies refer to the auditor's letter as a "report." "Auditors' Report," "Accountants' Report," and "Report of Independent Accountants" are common titles. The certification letter is most often addressed to the directors and stockholders.

Early disclosure

Careful organization and planning for the preparation of the annual report will be wasted if the audited financial statements are not ready for inclusion when the report is ready for the printer. Actually, many companies have found it advantageous from several points of view to target the certification of their statements for two to three weeks after the end of the year. Among the many benefits of such early year-end closings are the following:

1. Prompt release of audited results for the year to stockholders and to the financial community.
2. Final old-year results are accepted by company management at an early date and managerial attention can more quickly be paid to new year operations.
3. Because it is accepted that there will be little time in January (for calendar year companies) for discussion and decision making, accounting problem areas are forced to the foreground for resolution in November and December or earlier.
4. In order to make the early closing practical, it is mandatory that operating units take unusual charges and credits as soon as they are recognized, that is, that few items are held for resolution at year-end. Thus, December (or January) becomes just another month. Interim reports are more accurate, reflecting as closely as possible the financial position and results of operations through each interim date.
5. There is better control over the audit fee. Targeting a specific

date forces detailed planning and budgeting of time, allowing the company to maintain a closer check on auditors' time and progress.

6. Auditors' adjustments, if any, may be booked in the opening balances of the new year's ledgers, which is not possible if year-end closing is delayed until after the January closing.

Historical financial review

This section usually appears near the financial statements but is normally not included with reports certified by the public accountant. The historical financial review section should not deviate from audited data without full disclosure. When accounting restatements are made as the result of stock dividends or accounting changes, data for all years displayed should be restated in order that proper comparisons can be made and trends observed.

Companies vary in the data included and in the number of years displayed. A sampling of 100 companies indicates 73 percent displayed for ten years or more in 1973.[4] Some companies limit this historical data to five years.

Data included in the section ranges from a few key highlights (see Exhibit 5) to a full balance sheet along with significant elements of the earnings and financial position change reports. Additional information frequently displayed (not shown in Exhibit 5) includes the following:

1. Number of employees.
2. Units shipped.
3. Order backlog.
4. Dividend payout (dividends related to earnings as a percentage).
5. Major elements of working capital.
6. Current ratio (current assets/current liabilities).
7. "Quick" ratio (cash and accounts receivable/current liabilities).
8. Capital expenditures.
9. Depreciation.
10. Long-term debt.
11. Debt to equity ratio.

---

[4] *Business Week* sample published April 27, 1974, pp. 63, 66.

EXHIBIT 5

BLACK & DECKER MANUFACTURING CO.

Growth: Fifteen Consecutive Years

Fiscal 1973 was a milestone which marked our fifteenth year of fast and consistent growth. During this period, sales rose from $43.5 million in 1958 to $427 million in 1973, and net earnings increased more than ten fold from $3.2 million to $33.3 million.

Many benefits have accrued from this kind of growth: For employees, it continually has created new opportunities for advancement. For customers, it has assured a constantly expanding line of quality products at best value prices. For stockholders, it has greatly increased the value of their investment.

The information on these pages illustrates how this growth has been achieved and some of the ways in which it has benefited our employees, customers, and stockholders.

15-Year Comparative Financial Data (thousands of dollars)

| | Net sales | % Increase | Earnings before taxes | % of net sales | % Increase | Taxes on earnings | Net earnings | % Increase | Earnings retained in business | Working capital | Current ratio | Net worth | Return on average investment | PER SHARE** | | |
														Net earnings	Dividends paid	Net worth
1973	427,014	23.5	66,879	15.7	22.5	33,600	33,279	25.1	20,217	128,049	2.0-1	249,344	17.0†	2.60	$1.02	18.63
1972	345,656	20.5	54,610	15.8	21.3	28,000	26,610	20.8	14,610	116,427	2.7-1	183,518	15.7	2.14	96.2¢	14.38
1971	286,733	12.3	45,021	15.7	11.0	23,000	22,021	13.1	11,437	106,942	2.7-1	156,037	16.3	1.84	87.5¢	12.65
1970	255,433	15.2	40,574	15.9	9.1	21,100	19,474	10.8	10,276	79,940	2.3-1	113,991	18.4	1.67	78.8¢	9.72
1969	221,772	16.9	37,205	16.8	13.1	19,625	17,580	14.4	9,054	77,518	2.8-1	97,978	19.0	1.53	74.5¢	8.50
1968	189,720	12.5	32,897	17.3	14.1	17,525	15,372*	7.5	6,838	72,968	3.2-1	87,560	18.4*	1.35*	67.3¢	7.66
1967	168,566	14.8	28,828	17.1	11.8	14,526	14,302	10.1	7,510	68,741	3.0-1	79,768	19.0	1.26	59.8¢	7.00
1966	146,828	20.9	25,787	17.6	18.3	12,800	12,987	17.9	6,220	45,901	2.2-1	71,072	19.2	1.15	59.8¢	6.28
1965	121,462	20.3	21,789	17.9	19.0	10,771	11,018	25.7	5,730	38,134	2.3-1	64,076	18.1	.98	47.0¢	5.69
1964	100,973	18.6	18,309	18.1	19.4	9,543	8,766	19.5	3,974	34,408	2.8-1	57,725	15.8	.78	39.5¢	5.15
1963	85,113	12.3	15,328	18.0	14.1	7,994	7,334	12.3	3,408	32,339	3.2-1	53,197	14.3	.66	35.3¢	4.77
1962	75,816	12.1	13,439	17.7	11.9	6,907	6,532	15.0	2,728	30,797	3.5-1	49,717	13.7	.59	34.2¢	4.47
1961	67,637	11.3	12,005	17.7	7.7	6,326	5,679	3.5	1,976	30,131	4.0-1	45,943	12.7	.52	34.2¢	4.23
1960	60,775	15.2	11,151	18.3	9.9	5,663	5,488	14.4	2,129	29,124	4.3-1	43,686	13.4	.51	32.0¢	4.05
1959	52,771	21.2	10,149	19.2	56.5	5,350	4,799	47.1	2,579	26,118	4.1-1	38,031	13.3	.48	22.4¢	3.77

* Before extraordinary charge of $850,000 from devaluation of foreign currencies — 8¢ per share.
** Based on the average number of shares of common stock outstanding during each year, except net worth which is based on shares outstanding at each year end, adjusted to give effect to the two-for-one stock splits in 1959 and 1964, the three-for-two stock splits in 1967 and 1970, and the 4% stock dividend in 1972.
† Based on net worth before the October 1, 1973 purchase of McCulloch Corporation.

The above constitutes normal historical coverage of financial information. Additional data which will enhance the knowledge and understanding of the shareholder and investing public in a particular company should also be considered.

Reference data

Most annual reports contain certain basic data used for reference by the readers. This includes a listing of officers, directors, plants, and products. This material is normally found toward the end of the report.

Outside directors are nearly always identified with their principal occupation and place of business. Inside directors are identified by job title. More and more companies are providing biographies of both directors and officers and sometimes include photographs and ages.

Plant listings usually include physical location and type of product manufactured. Product listings can be very detailed or very brief, depending upon how much use the sales force makes of the annual report. The purpose of the plant and product listing is to give the reader an idea of the breadth of the company.

Securities data

For years companies have included in their annual reports the names of stock exchanges on which their securities are listed along with the names and addresses of the transfer agents and registrars. This data is frequently revealed in the back of the annual report close to the section covering plants, products, and offices.

The New York Stock Exchange White Paper suggests the inclusion in the annual report of common stock price/earnings ratio ranges, dividends, rate of dividend payout and dividend yield, book values per share, and comparisons with appropriate market indices. This data would cover a two-year period and be published in close proximity to the historical review section.

Social action programs

A growing number of companies now set aside a portion of the report for discussion of social action programs, and some even include actual reports of progress made. Social action covers a wide range of subjects including employment opportunity, environmental control, community involvement, and consumer interests.

Design, photos, artwork, charts, graphs

The design of an annual report is frequently performed by a professional. There are three categories of designers: free lance, in-house, and those employed full time by printers.

All designers perform the same function, that is, they lay out, organize, and illustrate the report. No matter how small or large an annual report is, someone has to select the type face, determine page margins, decide the size of photos, prepare charts, select paper stock, determine how colors are to be used, and perform all other tasks necessary for the competent compilation of the assignment.

The function of design in an annual report is to organize the various segments into a cohesive whole to make the report easy to read and understand, and to highlight various elements by means of graphic devices such as photos, charts, and headlines.

A designer should be brought into the annual report planning program at an early date to offer alternative approaches. The designer should be provided with some measure of the amount of material to be included in the report so that the number of pages required can be estimated. From this point the designer normally prepares several paper "dummies" for presentation to the company. These dummies, often called "pencils," provide an inexpensive way for the company to select the final design. Once this is approved the designer will produce a "comprehensive dummy" complete with color. The comprehensive dummy then becomes the working outline of the final design. Changes in design after the comprehensive dummy is approved are expensive.

Charts, photos, and illustrations are frequently used to focus attention on significant themes or features of the report. The usual purpose of charts is merely to present the trend of various financial results, so charts can be fairly small.

Photos are normally used in the operating review section of the annual report. Since many studies have indicated that the average reader spends very little time on an annual report, good photos can stop a reader and encourage him or her to look further. Large photos attract more attention.

Sketches are frequently used in place of photos and are particularly suited to showing things which are not yet in existence. For instance, new products which are not yet coming off the assembly line can be illustrated to provide the reader with an idea of what the product looks like.

Planning for publication of report

1. *Responsibility.* Because the annual report represents the company before so many "publics" the approval of the very top executive is usually necessary before publication is authorized. This means the chairman of the board and/or the president is

involved. Responsibility for the actual planning and compilation of the report is usually assigned to the vice president–finance, treasurer, or secretary.

2. *Annual report committee.* The first step in the development of an annual report is the establishment of a working committee. Most frequently the committee includes representatives of the public relations function, the accounting and finance functions, and the investor relations area. Representatives of other functions may be included, depending upon the nature of the company and the scope and objectives of the annual report.

3. *Budget.* With ever-increasing costs of paper, printing, and artwork and the growing number of annual report copies published, the cost of publishing an annual report has become a significant expense to many companies. It is essential that a budget for the annual report be prepared. This budget provides the annual report committee with the framework within which they must plan. The development of the budget is not particularly difficult for a company that has been publishing reports for several years. However, for the company about to publish its first report, the task can be most difficult. It is recommended that companies in this situation contact other experienced companies and/or a reputable printing company which has been printing annual reports for many years.

Based on an American Management Association study of annual reports, the size of the report (number of pages) sometimes depends on the size of the company and whether the responsibility for planning is given to a financial or a public relations executive. Public relations directors and larger companies seem to favor larger reports. A random sampling of a modest number of reports indicated that 36 to 40 pages is about average with the range from 14 to 66 pages. The number of pages included covers and foldout pages.

4. *Planning schedule.* The planning process for publication of an annual report must begin many months prior to the expected date of publication. If the annual report is to serve a special purpose, such as anniversary or first report after a major merger, planning must start even earlier.

The actual planning schedule should be developed backwards from the date of mailing. In other words, if the company expects to put the report in the mail on March 1, this should be the first date put in the schedule and everything should be scheduled from there. Many companies and annual report consultants develop PERT charts to help them meet all deadlines. Exhibit 6 is an example of a planning schedule.

EXHIBIT 6

Annual Report to Shareholders
Planning Schedule

Event	*Due date*
Develop and receive approval of theme and tentative format	August 1st
Hire designer, printer, typesetter, and photographer	August 7th
Approve final layout	October 30th
Complete first drafts of nonfinancial material	November 15th
Select final photographs and illustrations	December 1st
Complete final drafts of nonfinancial data and send to printer for typesetting	December 15th
Financial statement certification	January 16th
Deliver all financial data to printer	January 18th
Final approval of all material	February 1st
Final "on press" approval	February 4th
Distribution to shareholders	February 15th

It is very important to allow more time for completing each phase of the report than might normally be estimated. This is to take care of contingencies such as printer's strikes, paper unavailability, delay in getting approvals, and reshooting photos.

Once the planning schedule has been prepared, the next step for the annual report committee is to select a theme and format. Following this, hiring of designers, photographers, printers, writers, and artists can begin. All photography and illustrations for the annual report should be completed two months before date of publication.

Assignments to the writers of various sections of the report should also be made following the selection of the theme and format. The assignment should include some guidance as to length, style, and deadlines. First drafts of nonfinancial material should be written and submitted to the committee approximately two and a half months before printing of the report.

Some companies send prior year financial statement formats to the printer well before current year figures are available. This saves time in typesetting the ten-year summary and other tabular material. However, if the company will be changing the line items in the financial statements, they should not be type-set in advance since it would all have to be redone and this is very expensive.

Allow approximately 30 days from the time current financial material is available until the report comes off the press.

Distribution

Each shareholder is provided with a copy of the report. In addition, many companies distribute copies to employees, customers, bankers, financial analysts, newspaper and magazine financial editors, vendors, and community leaders. Requests are usually received from colleges and libraries. Many companies also reserve a number of reports to be used for college recruiting purposes.

Report grading

While there are several organizations which annually review reports to determine which companies publish the best reports, the

EXHIBIT 7

Financial World annual report evaluation factors

Broad essentials:
President's letter
Highlights (2 years); % change a plus
  factor
Narrative section
Per share earnings, dividends
Balance sheet and income statement with
  prior year's data
Source and application of funds
Adequate and easy-to-read notes to
  financial statement
Auditor's statement
Statistical summary, minimum of five
  years

Desirable information:
Construction and financing data
Late information
Territory development
Outlook
Stockholder data
Sales and earnings breakdown by
  products and/or divisions, quarterly
  sales, earnings
Research and development
Foreign business
Labor relations
Advertising/marketing data
Management

Additional useful information:
New products
Advertising policies
Affiliations of directors
Length of service; officers and directors
Basic data such as address of executive
  office, transfer agent, registrant, etc.
Special feature on industry or related
  subject
Table of contents
Map of territory
Public relations activities
Profile of company
Social/economic problems

Appearance and understandability:
Design and typography:
  Cover
  Inside pages
Useful charts
Appropriate photos and/or illustrations
Material organized logically
Useful subject area headings
Text clear, interesting, easy to read

Financial World Magazine conducts perhaps the most popular evaluation.

Financial World evaluates many specific areas of the annual report (see Exhibit 7) but weights its evaluation 50 percent for content for stockholders, 25 percent for content for analysts and professionals, and 25 percent for general appearance.

SUMMARY

The trend in the 70s is for companies to provide a significant increase in financial information in the annual report. The added information is designed to meet the needs of many types of users, in addition to shareholders, and to satisfy the suggestions and requirements of public bodies such as the SEC and NYSE.

This chapter has described how greater disclosure impacts the traditional as well as new sections of the shareholder's report. In addition, it was noted that an important facet of disclosure is timeliness. Early disclosure can be aided by targeting the certification of financial statements, accompanied by a well-conceived program for early accounting closings. To achieve prompt printing and distribution of the report a planning schedule should be meticulously conceived and followed.

Chapter 30

Reporting on the flow of funds

*C. H. Bentzel**

THE NEED FOR INFORMATION ON THE FLOW OF FUNDS

The *external user* of the funds statement (statement of changes in financial position) will generally be looking for answers to such questions as the firm's probable future ability to maintain (and increase) dividends; its possible need for external financing and how much; and the source of the funds used, or to be used, to finance replacement or expansion.

The *internal user* of the funds statement is interested in the same information as the external user. In addition, he or she needs to understand such things as the reasons for changes in working capital, the major facets of financing and investing, the major features of the operations of autonomous or partly autonomous divisions, and the projection of the firm's ability to pay its debts. An important benefit to be derived from the funds statement is that it provides the user an opportunity to recognize potential difficulties resulting from the composition of the firm's asset structure.

The information made available to the users of these statements enables them to ask pertinent questions concerning operating efficiencies, and provides an additional base to enable them to deter-

---

* Vice President and Comptroller, ITT Rayonier Inc.

mine how well management is doing its job and thereby successfully achieving the objectives of the company.

A "total package" of relevant financial information about an enterprise should include financial information concerning the past, the present, and the future. The income statement satisfies the requirement for "past" information, the balance sheet concerns itself with the present—thus it is the statement of funds to which we must look if we are to gather information applicable to the future (i.e., how dividend policies will be accomplished and expansion plans financed, the viability and desirability of changes in the firm's capital structure, revision of debt/equity ratios, etc.).

If we accept that the "sources" section of the funds statement is basically a recitation of past events, then it is to the "applications" segment that we must look if we are to be best able to form an educated judgment about the future. In order to have the information required, we must appropriately classify, and expand upon, the contents of this section of the funds statement.

Management decisions concerning the future of the company cannot be based solely on the statement of funds flows. Most certainly these decisions must be tested by the unit's income performance and resource accumulation; thus the "total package" concept (interrelationship of the elements comprising the income statement, balance sheet, and funds statement) is critical to the decision-making process.

APB Opinion No. 19, "Reporting Changes in Financial Position," became effective for fiscal periods ending after September 30, 1971, and required that a statement summarizing changes in financial position be presented as a basic financial statement for each period for which an income statement is presented.

In general, accounting is concerned with the measurement of the utilization of economic resources at the enterprise level. Enterprise resources are of two types: *productive* and *financial.*

The balance sheet, being a stopping point in the continuous flow process, consolidates changes of resources; it is not designed to reflect movement of resources. The income statement, being a flow statement, includes only a number of selected transactions resulting from the employment of productive resources; in other words, it purports to describe the productive side of the firm's activity without explaining how production takes place or is financed. Thus, there exists some type of gap between the balance sheet and the income statement. Certain obviously relevant, and vitally required, information is therefore either omitted or not sufficiently presented in those two conventional statements. Accordingly, it is apparent that there is the need for an accounting technique, a tool, which can bridge this gap.

FINANCIAL AND NONFINANCIAL FUNDS FLOWS

While it is essential that we recognize the distinction between the financial and nonfinancial flows of the firm's operations, it is also important to analyze their interplay. Productive activities may be financed internally, externally, or both. A detailed presentation of the financial activities not only shows how additional productive resources are acquired but—in part at least—also provides a basis for analyzing expansion and future income flow.

There can be no doubt that financing is a significant part of the management task. Frequently, adequacy of financing is a deciding factor in the degree of success of the enterprise. From a theoretical point of view, a division of resources into productive and financial is all that is necessary to permit an evaluation of the firm's overall efficiency. The components of resources and their movements are interrelated. Accordingly, the utilization of resources and its end results (changes in values of resources) are best understood under a *total* concept. The funds statement, when properly extended, will substantially provide us with the ability to bridge the gap between the information provided by the income statement and that provided by the balance sheet.

In general, all movements of monetary assets and liabilities are flows of a financial nature. Productive or nonfinancial flows include changes in "real" assets and incomes of factors of production. These flows are associated in part with real output and income (i.e., the value added concept of income). Thus, it can be seen that the sale and purchase of supplies and external services, materials utilized in the manufacturing process, employee salaries and wages, and items of a similar nature are productive or nonfinancial flows. Additionally, *changes* in productive or nonmonetary assets are also examples of nonfinancial flows.

Most nonfinancial flows are related to financial flows. For example, the purchase of a piece of equipment must be matched by a financial flow (i.e., the means of financing), whether by reducing the available cash balance, or by incurring a liability, or by issuing additional shares of capital stock. We might cite several other examples of business transactions which are typical of financial flows: purchase and sale of corporate securities, borrowings through bank loans or the issuance of bonds, and the issuance of stock.

Both types of flows signify movements of resources. The statement showing the changes in financial position reports, in a broad sense, on the utilization of all financial resources of the company, which is a basic goal of accounting.

DISCLOSURE REQUIREMENTS

There are a number of acceptable definitions of funds, of which "all financial resources" is preferred. The Accounting Principles Board, in *Opinion No. 19*, requires companies to include a funds flow statement along with the balance sheet and income statement in published annual reports. In addition, the APB also requires that the funds flow statement be covered by the auditor's opinion.

In addition to its recommendation in *APB Opinion No. 19* that companies use the all financial resources definition, the APB has also stressed the need for disclosing the details of changes in net working capital where appropriate, the presentation of funds statements for all periods covered by the auditor's opinion, and the disclosure of the gross amounts in offsetting or related fund transactions (rather than the net effect).

In addition to working capital or cash provided from operations and changes in the components of working capital, the statement of changes in financial position should also clearly disclose the following:

1. Outlays for the purchase of long-term assets, which should be classified as property, intangibles, or investments.
2. The proceeds, or the amount of working capital or cash provided, by the sale of long-term assets other than in the normal course of business. The assets should be classified according to No. (1), and related expenses involving the current use of cash or working capital should be deducted.
3. Conversion of long-term debt to common stock.
4. Conversion of preference securities to common stock.

5. The issuance, redemption, assumption and/or repayment of long-term debt.
6. The issuance, redemption, or purchase of capital stock for cash and/or other assets.
7. Dividends in cash or in kind, or other distributions to shareholders (except stock dividends and stock split-ups—as defined in *ARB No. 43*, chap. 7B).

It is important to recognize that "internal" transactions are types of nonfund transactions which should not appear in the funds statement. Funds flows occur as a result of external events or transactions.

Financial reporting will be greatly improved by the separate reporting of the operating and nonoperating sources and applications of funds. The effect of extraordinary items should be reported separately from the effects of normal items. Offsetting of transactions, without separate disclosure, should not be permitted.

COMMON MISCONCEPTIONS RELATED TO FUNDS FLOW STATEMENTS

It must be stressed that "cash flow per share" cannot be considered as a substitute for, or an improvement upon, properly determined net income as a measure of management's effectiveness. Accordingly, isolated statistics concerning "cash flow" which are not placed in the proper perspective can result in misleading implications.

It is essential for clarity of presentation that a complete understanding be had of items which, while they are elements of expense and similar items, do not require the utilization of working capital. This point is dealt with at greater length in other sections of this chapter.

PURPOSE AND OBJECTIVE OF THE STATEMENT OF CHANGES IN FINANCIAL POSITION

The funds statement is related to both the income statement and the balance sheet and, as noted earlier, serves as a bridge between those two general-purpose statements. Its purpose is to provide information that can result only partially—or at most in piecemeal form—from the interpretation of those two basic financial statements.

An income statement, together with a statement of retained earnings, reports results of operations but does not show other changes in financial position. Comparative balance sheets can significantly augment that information. And while the statement of changes in financial position cannot replace either the income statement or the balance sheet, its objectives require that all such information be selected, classified, and summarized in meaningful form. Thus, it can be seen that the objectives[1] of a funds statement are (a) to summarize and disclose separately[2] the financing and investing activities of the entity, including the extent to which the enterprise has generated funds from operations during the period, and (b) to complete the disclosure of the changes in financial position during the period.

Information concerning the financing and investing activities of a business enterprise and the resultant changes in its financial position is clearly essential for financial statement users, particularly the owners and creditors, in order to permit them to make optimum economic decisions. Therefore, to be most useful to all parties concerned, the statement summarizing changes in financial position should be based on a broad concept[3] embracing all changes in financial position.

In our rapidly changing economic climate, the organized and skillful analysis of the funds statements over a series of periods, as reflected in balance sheet changes supplemented with material from the income statements, is a necessary—even a vital—tool in arriving at an understanding of the needs of the company and how they have been (or may be) met. Clearly, an understanding of the opposing flows of funds between the various sources and applications can be invaluable in determining whether the company's liquidity and profitability objectives are being met.

No matter by what name we may call it—"source and application of funds," "changes in financial position," "where from, how used"—in its simplest form the funds statement is an analysis de-

---

[1] *APB Opinion No. 19,* par. 4.

[2] *APB Opinion No. 19,* par. 6.

[3] For a detailed review of the different uses of the term "funds" refer to Perry Mason's *Accounting Research Study No. 2* (pp. 51–56) published by the AICPA in November 1961.

rived from the income statement and the balance sheet which is designed to give a concise summary of the major sources and dispositions of funds.

Certainly, contemporary financial accounting is increasingly concerned with maintaining a continuing record of capital invested in an enterprise from a two-sided point of view, the *sources* and *uses* of funds, with funds broadly defined as *all financial resources*. This concern is in line with current financial management theory and practice, which tends to view assets as funds invested within the enterprise, and liabilities and net worth as sources external to the business, from which financial resources were obtained.

It therefore follows that the funds statement is intended to account for both productive and financial activities of the enterprise and, in addition, to show their interrelationship. Again, the objective of the funds statement should be emphasized: summarization of the financing and investing activities of the company during the period due to (*a*) the changes in financial condition and (*b*) operations.

ACCEPTABLE DEFINITIONS OF "FUNDS"

The term "funds" as used in funds flow analysis is somewhat ambiguous, and can be readily defined in at least five different ways. These definitions define funds flow as changes in one of the following:

1. Cash.
2. Sum of cash and marketable securities.
3. Net monetary assets.
4. Working capital.
5. All financial resources.

The "all financial resources" definition is preferred.

A funds flow statement based on either the cash or the working capital concept of funds sometimes excludes certain financing and investing activities because they do not directly affect cash and/or working capital during the period. To meet its objectives fully, however, a funds statement should disclose separately the financing and investing aspects of all significant transactions.

Each of these definitions results in placing emphasis on a different aspect of funds flow. Whether or not a particular transaction is described as a funds flow will depend on the specific definition of funds used. The appropriateness of any definition will depend upon the particular circumstances involved and the purpose for which the statement is to be used. A simple example based on a common management action will serve to illustrate the point being made, and at the same time to emphasize the necessity of carefully choosing the definition which is to be applied.

For example, the *declaration* of dividends changes a firm's net monetary assets, net working capital, and "all financial resources." Thus, in a company that uses one of these three funds definitions, the action would be clearly regarded for accounting purposes as a funds flow. If the funds definition in use relates only to changes in cash, or cash and marketable securities, however, the declaration of dividends would not be recognized as a flow of funds.

On the other hand, the *payment* of the dividends previously declared, and recorded on the books as a dividend payable, would be regarded as a flow of funds by those companies defining funds as changes in either cash or cash and marketable securities.

Perhaps one further example will be helpful. If one of the narrower concepts of funds is used, acquisitions effected by an exchange of stocks, bonds, and/or various convertible securities are not disclosed in the funds statement. Obviously, however, these are extremely important sources of financing for acquisition-minded companies and should be reported in the statement of changes in financial position.

FORMAT OF STATEMENT

The format of statements of changes in financial position may show the changes in working capital or cash and cash equivalents in one of three ways: as a balancing figure, as an addition to a beginning balance to obtain an ending balance, or as the statement's final amount.

Paragraph 10 of *APB Opinion No. 19* clearly states that the funds statement should prominently disclose working capital or cash provided from or used in the operations for the period. This presentation/disclosure is most informative if the effects of extraordinary, unusual and/or nonrecurring items are reported separately from the effects of normal operations.

The statement should fully disclose all important aspects of the unit's financing and investing activities whether or not cash or other elements of working capital are directly affected. The effects of such financing and investing activities should be individually disclosed. Related items should be shown in proximity to contribute to statement clarity. Individual immaterial items may be combined.

Whether or not the working capital concept of funds flow is used in the statement, the net changes in each element of working capital should be appropriately disclosed, at least for the current period. This may be satisfactorily accomplished either in the statement or in a related tabulation. The exhibits at the end of the chapter illustrate acceptable statements incorporating these points.

Just as with the balance sheet and the income statement, the statement of changes in financial position should be read with full adherence to the standard notation seen in published reports— that is, "The accompanying notes to financial statements are an integral part of the above statements." Following this recommendation will improve clarity and help to ensure that maximum utility is provided to the statement user.

THE FUNDS STATEMENT AS A BRIDGE
BETWEEN PAST AND FUTURE

Today there is an ever-increasing pressure to include in the published financial data information pertinent not only to the past and to the present but also to the future. The accountant is subjected to the claim of the user and the critic of published financial data, that the information about the future is really the most relevant and desired of all.

The income statement clearly concerns itself with past financial information; it is designed to show the results of operations for some specific past period. The balance sheet presents the balances of assets, liabilities, and equities as of the most recent date—the present. It is the funds statement, which incorporates carefully selected items from these other two basic statements, that can provide meaningful data, to enable us to chart more effectively the course for the future.

It has often been assumed that both the sources and applications set forth on the statement of funds are the reporting of past events. As to the sources of funds, that assumption is reasonably valid. But, as to the applications of funds, a closer examination reveals that the transactions reported therein are inherently related to the future. The successful future of an enterprise depends upon the astute use of the funds provided. There must be sufficient detailed disclosures within the funds statement to provide the elements necessary, when studied in conjunction with the balance sheet and the income statement, to permit a reasonable judgment to be made with regard to the firm's ability to exist profitably in the future.

By expanding and reclassifying the application of funds section to include details representing those expenditures, we can provide information that will help the statement user arrive at educated conclusions regarding the future of the firm.

THE FUNDS STATEMENT UNDER THE "ALL FINANCIAL RESOURCES" PRESENTATION

Accounting Principles Board Opinion No. 19 requires disclosing in the funds statement all important aspects of the firm's financing and investing activities, regardless of whether cash or other elements of working capital are directly affected. This all financial resources presentation is consistent with all four concepts of funds which are acceptable. Thus, the increase or decrease in funds for the period under the "all financial resources" presentation still equals the increase or decrease in working capital, in net monetary assets, in cash and cash equivalents, or in cash alone, depending on the concept of funds employed.

Opinion No. 19 requires that the funds statement report all major changes in the financial structure of the enterprise. This includes *external* items such as the conversion or refunding of debt and equity issues and all acquisitions of assets, whether by purchase, exchange, gift, or otherwise. On the other hand, *internal* items such as stock dividends, appropriations of retained earnings for special reserves, and asset write-ups and write-downs, are types of nonfund transactions which should not appear in the funds statement. It should be emphasized that funds flow as a result of external transactions or events where payment in the normal course of events is expected in the short term.

Financial reporting has been greatly improved by the requirement for separate reporting of the operating and nonoperating sources and applications of funds and by the prohibition of the offsetting, without separate disclosure, of supposedly related sources and uses of funds. An understanding of the opposing flows of funds among the various sources and applications can be invaluable in determining whether the firm's liquidity and profitability objectives are being met. Carried one step further, inflowing funds from the various sources must be carefully synchronized with the many alternative uses planned. Reporting will also be more informative and useful because the effects of extraordinary items must now be reported separately from the effects of normal items.[4]

IMPACT OF RESTATED RESULTS ON THE FUNDS STATEMENT

Certain requirements of *Accounting Principles Board Opinion No. 20*, "Accounting Changes," alter the income statement and hence may affect the funds statement. These requirements primarily relate to (*a*) changes in accounting principles and (*b*) changes in accounting estimates.

In general, when a change in accounting principle is made, financial statements of prior periods are not restated. Rather, the cumulative effect of the change on retained earnings as of the beginning of the period in which the change took place is included in the net income of the period of change.

Some changes in accounting principle do not affect the funds statement. Changes in accounting principle most commonly affect statement items which do not represent a source or use of working capital or cash. Examples of this type of change are:

1. A change in the method of depreciation and/or amortization, and
2. A change in the method of accounting for research and development costs.

Other changes in accounting principle do affect working capital, and therefore may affect a source or use of working capital provided by operations. Changes which may affect working capital include a change in inventory costing method (e.g., from Lifo to Fifo) and a change in the method of accounting for long-term construction-type contracts. However, the anticipated effect on working capital does not materialize in the current period's funds statement

---

[4] *APB Opinion No. 20*, par. 27; *APB Opinion No. 9*, pars. 21 and 22.

since *Opinion No. 20* affords special treatment to these changes—that is, the financial statements of all affected prior periods should be restated. As a result of this treatment, there will be no item in the income statement of the current period reflecting the cumulative effect of these changes on prior periods' income. Rather, each prior period's restated financial statements, including the funds statements, will reflect the changes as they relate to those periods.

The discussion and related examples provided in *Opinion No. 20* seem to require that prior period financial statements, including the funds statements, be restated as a result of those material changes in accounting principle which do affect working capital. If significant, those prior year adjustments should be identified as separate line items.

Another type of accounting change may occur in situations in which the enterprise wishes to revise certain earlier estimates: for example, the remaining useful life of an asset, or the amount of accounts receivable which is expected to become uncollectible. In these cases, no adjustment is made in the statements of prior periods to reflect the application of the new estimates, nor is any cumulative effect of the revised estimates on prior periods' earnings shown on the current period's income statement. Rather, the effect of new estimates will be incorporated in the determination of the income (loss) from normal operations for the period in which the revised estimates are made, and for future periods, if applicable.

TREATMENT OF DEPRECIATION IN THE FUNDS STATEMENT

To promote accuracy of description and clarity of understanding of funds flows, it is probably worthwhile to comment on those items included in the funds statement which neither use nor provide working capital during a period. Classic examples include depreciation, amortization, and depletion. We will use depreciation as the basis of our explanation.

Depreciation which is charged directly to the expense of a period neither uses nor provides working capital, except through its tax deductibility. For example, depreciation on a fixed asset which is used in selling or administration is an expense, but it is an item of expense which does not require working capital. Depreciation is a reflection of the amount of fixed-asset cost which has been assigned as an expense to the period under review. The working capital was used when the depreciable asset was acquired; the subsequent write-off (i.e., the depreciation) does not affect the working capital balance.

To the extent that revenues cover depreciation expense, working capital obtained from operations includes a partial recovery, through revenues, of those funds previously spent for depreciable fixed assets. The effect of such fixed assets on funds flows is reported as the current expenditures for the renewal and replacement of those assets.

At the point of sale of goods or services, depreciation on fixed assets used in production generates neither cash nor working capital. Only at the point of manufacture does depreciation generate working capital; it does so in the amount of depreciation/amortization of manufacturing facilities that is incorporated in the cost of inventoriable product. Let us stress, however, that this funds effect results from the accounting cost conversion cycle by which a long-lived asset's cost is gradually added to inventory, a component of working capital.

TREATMENT OF INCOME TAXES IN THE FUNDS STATEMENT

A review of the impact of deferring the payment of income taxes on the funds statement of the period is essential to a complete understanding of the problems of preparing and presenting the funds flow statement.

It is not our intention to go into the fundamental question of whether the annual income tax expense reported in the published income statement should be based on the taxable income reported to the Internal Revenue Service, or on the pretax income reported on the financial statements, or some other amount. *Accounting Principles Board Opinions No. 11* and *23* cover this issue.

The income tax allocation controversy is a direct outgrowth of the government's increasing use of income taxes as a positive or negative stimulus in the economy. The use of taxes as a stimulus takes a variety of forms; we are only interested in one of those here, and its resultant impact on the flow of funds: changes in the timing of recognizing taxable revenues or tax-deductible expenses.

Probably among the most common type of tax timing difference encountered is the use of straight-line depreciation in the financial reports but accelerated depreciation in tax returns. The tax deferral thus created due to timing differences is a special source of funds resulting from the postponement of taxes otherwise currently payable.

One might argue that a deferred tax credit is not technically a funds source, but that rather it is similar to depreciation; that is, it is simply a nonfund "bookkeeping" adjustment. But a deferred tax is different in character from depreciation, and it is those differences which make it a genuine source of funds. Deferred tax credits relate to the accounting period in which they occur rather than to some past period, as does depreciation. The funds are obtained in the current period through a postponement of the timing of cash outflows to the taxing authorities *and* a decision by management that the pattern of expenses recognized for tax purposes is not appropriate for book purposes. Both conditions must be present.

Let us explain this in the following way: if one starts with the assumption that management uses for book purposes the most appropriate depreciation policy for its particular business and assets, then its use of another method for tax purposes must be motivated and justified only as a tax strategy to change the flow of funds related to its tax obligations. A company using accelerated depreciation for *both* tax and book purposes can delay the payment of taxes. However, in this case the delayed taxes do not represent a special source of funds, because the company is using for tax purposes the same depreciation method it believes is also most suitable for measuring the results of its operations for financial reporting purposes.

The source of funds is created by a difference between the company's using straight line for book purposes and accelerated depreciation for tax purposes (its "real" versus its tax depreciation policy). In this way it has been able to take advantage of a special concession from the government; namely, to utilize for tax purposes a depreciation method that does not, in the opinion of management, reflect fairly the results of operations. It should be recognized that the funds result from a timing difference between book and tax items, not between the actual tax timing used and some alternative timing of the tax recognition of revenues and costs.

One might well consider that the postponement of tax payments is equivalent in practice to an interest-free loan, and therefore should be clearly includible as a source of funds on the funds flow statement. Also, placing emphasis on the amounts of resources obtained currently from tax deferrals rather than the amount owed removes the need to determine and report the deferrals on a discounted basis.

CASH FLOW PER SHARE

In recent years we have seen increasing emphasis placed on the subject of cash flow per share. The users of such information usually define cash flow per share as net profit after tax plus noncash expenses, such as depreciation. Unfortunately, the impression often given is that cash flow per share is superior to net income as a measure of management performance. In response to this development, the Accounting Principles Board has stressed that the amount of funds derived from operations cannot be considered as a substitute for—or an improvement upon—properly determined net income as a measure of results of operations and the consequent effect on financial position.[5]

Isolated statistics concerning "cash flow" which are not placed in the proper perspective to the net income figures and to a complete analysis of the flow of funds can result in misleading implications being drawn by the user of such information.[6] A complete statement of funds makes it unnecessary to quote isolated statistics on cash flow; over the long term, the best indication of dividend-paying ability and market growth of share price is still the net income of the firm.

Terms referring to "cash" should not be used to describe amounts provided from operations unless all noncash items have been appropriately adjusted. The adjusted amount should be described accurately, in conformity with the nature of the adjustment. For example, "cash provided from operations for the period" or "working capital provided from operations for the period" are appropriate. It is strongly recommended that isolated statistics of working capital or cash provided from operations, especially per-share amounts, not be presented in the annual report to shareholders.

[5] *APB Opinion No. 3.*
[6] Mason, *ARS No. 2.*

INTERNAL USES OF FUNDS STATEMENT

Although our emphasis up to this point has been more on the external aspects and utilization of the statement of changes in financial position, we must also recognize its value for internal reporting and control purposes.

Some of the more important uses which can be made of this statement are:

1. To pinpoint problem areas related to unusual changes in the working capital accounts.
2. To provide data regarding the major facets of the financing and investing activities which have taken place over a period of years.
3. To assist management in evaluating and coordinating the operations of autonomous or semiautonomous components of the organization.
4. To help management in determining the firm's ability to pay its debts and in ascertaining the length of time which any debt financing should cover.

Considering its potential utility, it is worthwhile to elaborate further on the internal utilization of the funds statement. There is frequently a misunderstanding regarding the relationship of an enterprise's net income to its ability to remain solvent and to carry on with its normal operations. Net income represents the increase in net assets resulting from operating activities. However, a substantial portion of that net asset increase may be the result of increases in assets of a highly nonliquid nature. Therefore, a firm may have an outstanding record of profitability and yet encounter financial difficulties because of the composition of its asset structure.

Additionally, net income may include both extraordinary items and the cumulative effect of changes in accounting principles on prior years' earnings. Both of these tend to represent nonrecurring events, and neither may represent a source or use of liquid assets.

If a series of current and projected fund statements is developed using the cash concept, the changes and the causes of changes in cash are clearly disclosed. An evaluation of the probable sufficiency of cash resources in future periods to cover the demands for cash expenditures can be obtained from these statements. Additionally, some insight can be obtained into the pattern which the repayment of credit obligations should take. The result is a facility for better matching cash requirements with the projected cash inflow.

If the current and projected funds statements utilize the working capital concept, interpretation in terms of debt paying ability is less direct. The statements will disclose the projected changes in the relationship between current assets and current liabilities, as opposed to changes in cash alone.

In both cases, since the statements show the sources of either working capital or cash provided (i.e., by operations, by owners, and by creditors), changes in the composition of these various sources may provide important information relevant to planning for future operations.

Unusual changes in the elements of working capital can be directly and dramatically obtained and presented through the medium of the funds statement. Such information generates related questions concerning operating efficiencies: for example, is the change justified in terms of future plans and company objectives, or does it represent some basic problem in management control? In such a manner problem areas in working capital items may be revealed and timely corrective action instituted.

Yet another important use of the funds statement concerns the education of the personnel and coordination of the operations of autonomous and semiautonomous divisions of the enterprise. For instance, several comparable divisions may appear to have quite dissimilar results of operations based on traditional divisional income statements. Yet, upon critical analysis, these differences may not be due to a difference in the level of managerial efficiency but to different depreciation charges resulting from the application of different depreciation methods or rates, or to cost differences arising soley from the timing of the acquisition of depreciable assets.

Coordination of activities of the various organizational components of the firm will be facilitated through the preparation of current and projected funds statements. The prospects for future profitability and the wisdom of financial management decisions may also be better assessed through the use of comprehensive, properly prepared, and skillfully presented statements of changes in financial position.

Another important use of the funds statement is to evaluate performance in a historical perspective to determine if the established objectives have been achieved. The statement will disclose the manner in which working capital or cash has been used. These actual uses, together with the sources of the funds, may be compared with prior projections to determine whether, and how well, the plans have been achieved.

FORMAT OF THE FUNDS STATEMENT

Provided that the guidelines set forth in *APB Opinion No. 19* are met, the statement may take whatever form gives the most useful portrayal of the financing and investing activities, and the changes in financial position, of the reporting entity. The statement should disclose all important changes in financial position for the period covered. Obviously, the types of transactions reported may, of necessity, vary substantially in relative importance from period to period and from company to company.[7]

The statement for the period should begin with income or loss before extraordinary items, if any, and add back (or deduct) items recognized in determining that income (loss) which neither provided nor used working capital or cash during the period. As emphasized earlier, these items are not sources or uses of working capital or cash, and the related captions should make this clear.

An acceptable alternative procedure is to begin with the total revenue that provided working capital or cash during the period, and deduct the operating costs and expenses which required the outlay of working capital or cash. In either case the resulting amount of working capital or cash should be appropriately described: for example, "working capital provided from (used in) operations for the period, exclusive of extraordinary items." This total should be immediately followed by working capital or cash provided or used by the income (loss) from extraordinary items, if any. The extraordinary income (loss) should also be adjusted for those items recognized as neither providing nor using working capital or cash during the period.

Abbreviated examples of the several acceptable presentations are included at the end of this chapter.

HISTORICAL SUMMARY

The statement of funds has waited in the wings for a long time to receive its official recognition and the high degree of acceptance which it has only rather recently been accorded. Its origin probably

---

[7] *APB Opinion No. 19*, par. 11.

antedates 1920; over the intervening years, enthusiasm concerning it has fluctuated up and down the scale.[8]

In retrospect, it is difficult to understand fully the apparent reluctance of the accounting profession on the one hand, and the business community on the other, to utilize this tool more fully.

Today, the statement of source and application of funds (statement of changes in financial position), is undoubtedly one of the most useful tools in the financial managers' kit of diagnostic techniques. During the past 15 years the statement of funds has been used with increasing frequency. This use has certainly been stimulated in part by the issuance in 1963 of the *Accounting Principles Board Opinion No. 3*, "The Statement of Source and Application of Funds." Although *APB Opinion No. 3* encouraged the use of a funds statement, it did not require its presentation. Nevertheless, support of that *Opinion* by the principal stock exchanges and acceptance by the business community in general did result in a significant increase in the number of companies that presented a statement of source and application of funds in published annual financial reports to their shareholders. Accordingly, and in view of the growing and widespread recognition of the usefulness of information on the sources and uses of funds, the Accounting Principles Board began to consider whether presentation of such a statement should be required to complement the income statement and the balance sheet. In addition, since *APB Opinion No. 3* also permitted considerable latitude as to the form and content of the funds statement, and practice had varied widely, the Accounting Principles Board also examined the necessity to establish guides for methods of presenting such statements in published financial reports.

The broadening interest in the funds statement, no doubt significantly reinforced by the expanding awareness of the "bridge" thus provided between the income statement and the balance sheet, resulted in the issuance in March 1971, of *APB Opinion No. 19* "Reporting Changes in Financial Position."[9] The statement of funds

---

[8] For an excellent background review of the history of funds statements and their development into the 1940s, see Rosen and DeCoster, "Funds Statements: A Historical Perspective," *The Accounting Review,* January 1969, pp. 124–36.

[9] *APB Opinion No. 19* supersedes *APB Opinion No. 3*, "The Statement of Source and Application of Funds", and in view of the broadened concept of the funds statement adopted in *Opinion No. 19,* the title of the statement was changed to "Statement of Changes in Financial Position." This latter *Opinion* (*No. 19*), also amends *APB Statement No. 4* ("Basic Concepts and Accounting Principles Underlying Financial Statements of Business Enterprises") to the extent that it relates to reporting changes in financial position.

has finally been officially admitted to the family of general-purpose financial statements.

It is generally acknowledged in current practice that background data which results in a better understanding of a firm's sources and uses of funds is most useful for a variety of purposes, and that it can affect both operating and investment decisions.

THE STATEMENT OF CHANGES IN
FINANCIAL POSITION IN
CURRENT PRACTICE

The author has reviewed more than two hundred published annual reports which set forth the story, in financial and other terms, of publicly owned companies for 1973. The companies represented in this random sample run the entire spectrum of size, ranging from the giant conglomerates to the smaller enterprises. These companies were engaged in a variety of activities: manufacturing, real estate, construction, merchandising, and financial and other services. In some cases their financial reports were audited by one of the "Big 8" firms; in others the auditor was from one of the smaller, more localized public accounting firms.

It was interesting to note that there was no reference to "cash flow" per share in any of these reports or in the financial statements included therein. Furthermore, while there were differences in the format and content of the statement of changes in financial position, these differences were relatively minor or even immaterial. Those differences which were noted arose primarily in comparing the presentation of the financial results of companies in different industries, rather than in comparing the reports of entities within the same industrial classification.

Finally, while each of the annual reports reviewed did present a comparative statement of changes in financial position for the current and immediately prior year (i.e., 1973 and 1972), only one presented a ten years' comparative statement of changes in financial position. It also included a percentage analysis, thus presenting to the readers of its annual report a most complete and concise picture of the events which occurred.

In the financial statements of one company we found a specific line item labeled "Cash Flow—Net Income Plus Depreciation," which had no single reference point on the consolidated statement of changes in financial position. From the all financial resources point of view this presentation is potentially misleading.

SOME QUESTIONS WHICH THE FUNDS STATEMENT SHOULD BE ABLE TO ANSWER

A properly constructed funds statement can be expected to facilitate the answers to questions such as the following:

1. Are there major low-growth activities which constitute a significant drain on the company's funds?
2. Is the company committing its available funds primarily to potential high-growth activities, or are the funds being diverted to support lower growth programs?
3. What is the productivity of the funds invested in the various segments of the enterprise?
4. Is it probable that the company will require external financing over the near term? If so, how much?
5. Based upon the facts disclosed, what changes (if any) in the dividend rate can be expected?
6. What has become of the profits of the period? Why were dividends or wages not larger?
7. What were the major financial policies applied, and what changes in them were made during the period?
8. Were funds for replacement or expansion generated internally, or were outside sources relied on?
9. What detailed form did the major sources and uses of funds take?

To provide the answers to these and similar questions, a funds flow statement segregating different basic activities, and showing their growth rates, can be developed.[10] A segmented funds flow statement provides the user with some guidance as to the future direction and emphasis of the firm.

ILLUSTRATIONS OF THE STATEMENT OF CHANGES IN FINANCIAL POSITION

The several illustrations which follow are not intended to be all-inclusive—their purpose is to demonstrate the acceptable alter-

---

[10] See "A Framework for Financial Reporting by Diversified Companies," pp. 39–44, published by the NAA, 1969.

natives in format and scope of presentation. The details of the individual statements have been compressed in order to illustrate more clearly the specific point which each is designed to present. The basic quality sought is clarity of information, presented fairly and objectively. (The figures used have no significance and are presented only to facilitate an understanding of the examples.)

TYPE I
Cash plus marketable securities concept; sources equal uses

	1974	*1973*
Funds Provided by:		
Operations:		
Net income	45,000	40,000
Depreciation	22,000	20,000
Increase in deferred liabilities	15,000	10,000
Total funds provided by operations	82,000	70,000
Retirement or sale of plant and equipment	2,000	3,000
Issuance of new long-term debt	10,000	1,000
(Increase) decrease in receivables	3,000	(1,000)
Increase in accounts payable	15,000	3,000
Increase (decrease) in other accrued current liabilities net of prepaid income taxes	10,000	(8,000)
Increase in accrued U.S. and foreign income taxes	5,000	10,000
Increases—other liabilities	1,000	2,000
Total	128,000	80,000
Funds Used for:		
Dividends declared	25,000	15,000
Additions to plant and equipment	40,000	30,000
Repayment of long-term debt	10,000	5,000
Acquisition of treasury stock	5,000	5,000
Decrease of bank loans—foreign subsidiaries	10,000	5,000
Increase in inventories	10,000	7,000
Increase (decrease) in cash and marketable securities	28,000	13,000
Total	128,000	80,000

TYPE II
Increase (decrease) in working capital

	1974	1973
Sources of Funds:		
Net earnings	100,000	85,000
Expenses not requiring outlay of working capital:		
Depreciation and amortization, property, plant, and equipment . . .	35,000	30,000
Other charges against net earnings	6,000	3,000
Provided from operations	141,000	118,000
Proceeds from sale of capital stock under options	7,000	5,000
Proceeds from sales of property, plant, and equipment	2,000	3,000
Total.	150,000	126,000
Use of Funds:		
Additions to property, plant, and equipment	70,000	50,000
Cash dividends paid.	20,000	16,000
Reduction in long-term debt.	5,000	2,000
Other items—net	3,000	1,000
	98,000	69,000
Increase in working capital	52,000	57,000

TYPE III
End of year working capital (or cash) (thousands of dollars)

	1974	1973
Sources of Working Capital:		
Net income	55,000	33,000
Charges not requiring current outlay of funds:		
Depreciation.	10,000	7,000
Deferred income taxes	2,000	1,000
Working capital provided from operations.	67,000	41,000
Long-term borrowing.	7,000	4,000
Common stock issued to purchase assets.	3,000	5,000
Other sources	2,000	1,000
Total.	79,000	51,000
Uses of Working Capital:		
Purchase of plant and equipment	27,000	12,000
Excess of investment cost over equity in acquired companies	1,000	3,000
Reduction of long-term debt.	5,000	6,000
Purchase of minority stockholders' interest in subsidiaries.	4,000	1,000
Purchase of preferred stock for retirement.	4,000	4,000
Cash dividends.	20,000	15,000
Other uses	4,000	1,000
Total.	65,000	42,000
Increase in working capital.	14,000	9,000
Working capital—beginning of year	30,000	21,000
Working Capital—End of Year	44,000	30,000

TYPE IV

Increase (decrease) in working capital—Extraordinary items (thousands of dollars)

	1974	*1973*
Sources of Working Capital:		
Operations:		
Earnings (loss) before extraordinary items.	40,000	(10,000)
Costs and expenses not requiring the use of working capital:		
Depreciation, depletion, and amortization of property,		
plant, and equipment	60,000	50,000
Provisions for deferred income taxes—noncurrent	6,000	10,000
Amortization of equipment on lease	1,000	1,000
Minority shareholders' equity in net earnings of subsidiaries		
before extraordinary items, less dividends.	2,000	1,000
Increase in equity in unconsolidated subsidiaries	(1,000)	(1,000)
Total Provided by Operations before Extraordinary Items . . .	108,000	51,000
Extraordinary gains.	–	4,000
Charges against proceeds from extraordinary items not requiring		
the use of working capital:		
Minority shareholders' equity in extraordinary items	–	2,000
Other.	–	1,000
Total provided by extraordinary items	–	7,000
Increase in long-term debt	20,000	30,000
Borrowings from unconsolidated finance subsidiaries	3,000	5,000
Other sources—net	2,000	(1,000)
Total Funds from Other Sources	25,000	34,000
Total.	133,000	92,000
Use of Working Capital:		
Expenditures for property, plant, and equipment.	80,000	65,000
Current maturities on long-term debt.	10,000	15,000
Repayment of borrowings from unconsolidated finance		
subsidiaries	2,000	4,000
Manufactured products placed on long-term lease	10,000	10,000
Total.	102,000	94,000
Increase (Decrease) in Working Capital for the Year	31,000	(2,000)

TYPE V

Change in working capital—Analysis included as part of statement (thousands of dollars)

	1974	1973
Financial Resources Were Provided by:		
Net income	200,000	150,000
Income charges (credits) not affecting working capital in the period:		
Depreciation.	90,000	80,000
Deferred income taxes	30,000	35,000
Minority interest in net income of subsidiaries	15,000	12,000
Income from nonconsolidated subsidiaries	(20,000)	(10,000)
Working capital provided by operations for the period.	315,000	267,000
Increase in long-term debt	60,000	90,000
Issuance of 10,000,000 shares of common stock	250,000	—
Issuance of common stock under options	25,000	20,000
Total.	650,000	377,000
Financial Resources Were Used for:		
Expenditures for facilities	300,000	190,000
Dividend payments	100,000	75,000
Reduction in long-term debt.	45,000	60,000
Increase in investment in subsidiaries.	90,000	25,000
Other—net	8,000	3,000
Total.	543,000	353,000
Changes in Working Capital:		
Current assets—increase (decrease):		
Cash and marketable securities	40,000	44,000
Customer receivables.	42,000	24,000
Inventories.	55,000	28,000
Prepaid expenses	10,000	4,000
Current liabilities—decrease (increase):		
Short-term loans and current portion of long-term debt	(22,000)	(50,000)
Accounts payable—trade.	7,000	(10,000)
Federal and foreign income taxes.	(20,000)	(12,000)
All other current liabilities.	(5,000)	(4,000)
Working capital increase	107,000	24,000
Total.	650,000	377,000

Chapter 31

Footnotes; reporting accounting policies and accounting changes

*Michael N. Chetkovich**
Thomas P. McGough†

Financial statements are the primary means of conveying to interested parties information about the financial position and operations of an enterprise. Footnotes are an integral part of such statements and are essential to the reader in providing information as to the accounting policies of the enterprise and other vital disclosures.

As to disclosure, the Accounting Principles Board has stated[1] ". . . in general, information that might affect the conclusions formed by a reasonably informed reader of the financial statements should be disclosed." This chapter reviews some of the more common footnote disclosures and the manner of reporting accounting policies and accounting changes.

Specific disclosures are required by pronouncements of the Financial Accounting Standards Board (FASB) and the Accounting Prin-

---

* Managing Partner, Haskins & Sells.

† Manager, Haskins & Sells.

[1] AICPA, "Basic Concepts and Accounting Principles Underlying Financial Statements of Business Enterprises," *APB Statement No. 4* (New York, October 1970), par. 199.

ciples Board (APB) and its predecessor committees. Companies that file reports with the Securities and Exchange Commission (SEC) must include disclosures required by that agency. The discussion in this chapter will be limited to disclosures ordinarily found in the notes to financial statements included in reports to shareholders. Regulations of the SEC will be dealt with only to the extent that related disclosures are frequently found in published reports. Some of the disclosures currently required and related pronouncements include:

Inventory—"Inventory Pricing," Chapter 4 of *Accounting Research Bulletin No. 43.*

Depreciable assets and depreciation—*APB Opinion No. 12.*

Income taxes—*APB Opinion No. 11.*

Income taxes, special areas—*APB Opinions Nos. 23* and *24.*

Investment credit—*APB Opinions Nos. 2* and *4.*

Earnings per share—*APB Opinion No. 15.*

Statement of accounting policies—*APB Opinion No. 22.*

Accounting changes—*APB Opinion No. 20.*

Consolidation policy—*Accounting Research Bulletin No. 51.*

Pension plans—*APB Opinion No. 8.*

Business combinations—*APB Opinion No. 16.*

Investments—*APB Opinion No. 18.*

Lease commitments by lessee—*APB Opinion No. 31.*

Research and development costs—*Statement of Financial Accounting Standards No. 2.*

FOOTNOTES

A substantial portion of the information presented in footnotes could be shown on the face of the financial statements. However, the reporting of details of accounts such as inventories, property, long-term debt, and capital stock in separate notes to the financial statements generally is considered to make for a more effective presentation of the necessary data.

The illustrative items presented in this section are examples of disclosures which are commonly found in notes to financial statements; they are not an all-inclusive listing of required disclosures. The specific circumstances of an individual entity must be considered to determine what disclosures are necessary for that entity.

Inventories

The basis of inventory pricing generally is disclosed in the statement of accounting policies. Additional footnote disclosure usually includes the nature and amount of major classes of inventory (i.e. raw materials, work in process, finished goods, and supplies). If the Lifo method of determining inventory cost is used, the excess of current or replacement cost over the Lifo cost generally is shown. The accompanying note on inventories appeared in the 1973 annual report of American Can Company (Exhibit 1).

EXHIBIT 1
Inventories (a summary of inventories follows)

	In thousands of dollars *December 31*	
	1973	*1972*
Raw materials and supplies	$117,318	$ 93,050
Work in process	90,845	90,320
Finished product	115,921	113,579
	$324,084	$296,949

For inventories stated on the last-in, first-out (LIFO) basis (approximately 25% and 26% in 1973 and 1972, respectively), the current replacement cost exceeds LIFO value by approximately $51-million at December 31, 1973 and $43-million at December 31, 1972.

Property

In most instances, disclosure of the depreciation methods used by a company is made as part of the statement of accounting policies. The composition of property usually is presented in a separate footnote, as for example, the note in the 1973 annual report of Owens-Illinois, Inc., shown in Exhibit 2.

Long-term debt

The long-term debt footnote normally includes a tabular listing showing the amount, interest rate, and due date of each issue. Segre-

EXHIBIT 2

Property, Plant, and Equipment (the major classes of property, plant and equipment are as follows)

	Thousands of dollars	
	1973	1972
Land, timberlands and mineral deposits, at cost less depletion	$ 91,843	$ 95,663
Buildings and equipment, at cost:		
Buildings and building equipment	361,964	340,787
Factory machinery and equipment	921,711	855,248
Transportation, office and miscellaneous equipment . . .	51,675	49,899
Construction in progress	44,263	32,264
	1,379,613	1,278,198
	1,471,456	1,373,861
Less accumulated depreciation	600,816	557,535
	$ 870,640	$ 816,326

At December 31, 1973, the Company owned, leased or had cutting rights to approximately 1.3 million acres of timberlands in Florida, Georgia, Louisiana, Michigan, Texas, Virginia, Wisconsin, and the Bahamas.

gation of debt according to the currency in which it is payable is becoming common with the increasing incidence of multinational financing. A requirement of the SEC that the combined aggregate amount of maturities by year be disclosed often is adopted in the annual report. Other pertinent data, such as convertibility, subordination agreements, collateral, and so on, also should be disclosed in this note. The note on long-term debt shown in Exhibit 3 appeared in the 1973 annual report of International Business Machines Corporation.

Capital stock

Details relating to capital stock often appear in the notes, such as the par value and the number of authorized shares of each class of stock outstanding, number of treasury shares, conversion features, restrictions, purposes and number of shares reserved, liquidation preference, and so on. In addition, some companies show the changes in capital stock and other stockholders' equity accounts in the notes rather than in a separate statement.

The note from the 1973 annual report of Beneficial Corporation

EXHIBIT 3
Long-term debt

	December 31, 1973	December 31, 1972
International Business Machines Corporation:		
3½% promissory note, due in annual installments,		
January 1, 1975 to 1985	$ 63,250,000	$ 69,000,000
3½% promissory note, due in annual installments,		
May 1, 1975 to 1988.	70,000,000	75,000,000
	133,250,000	144,000,000
Subsidiaries operating in foreign countries (average interest rate in parentheses) payable in:		
U.S. dollars, due 1975 to 1987 (10.5%)	364,266,640	393,595,782
French francs, due 1975 to 1991 (8.1%).	65,785,065	88,256,849
Canadian dollars, due 1975 to 1991 (8.4%)	22,504,000	24,258,351
Belgian francs, due 1975 to 1983 (7.5%)	19,001,500	1,300,000
Netherlands guilders, due 1975 to 1981 (7.8%).	17,617,174	17,771,685
Swiss francs	—	66,814,198
Other currencies, due 1975 to 1991 (9.7%)	29,811,969	36,935,909
	518,986,348	628,932,774
Consolidated long-term debt.	$652,236,348	$772,932,774

Consolidated long-term debt at December 31, 1973 was payable:	
1975	$158,125,090
1976	51,574,898
1977	221,573,099
1978	28,312,894
1979	21,517,419
1980–1984	93,645,949
1985–1991	77,486,999
	$652,236,348

shown in Exhibit 4 is illustrative of disclosures relating to capital stock.

Income tax

APB Opinion No. 11 (par. 63) prescribes disclosure requirements for income taxes as follows:

   a. Amounts of any operating loss carryforwards not recognized in the loss period, together with expiration dates (indicating separately amounts which, upon recognition, would be credited to deferred tax accounts);

   b. Significant amounts of any other unused deductions or credits, together with expiration dates; and

   c. Reasons for significant variations in the customary relationships between income tax expense and pretax accounting income, if they are not otherwise apparent from the financial statements or from the nature of the entity's business.

SEC *Accounting Series Release No. 149*, "Notice of Adoption of Amendment to Regulation S-X to Provide for Improved Disclosure

EXHIBIT 4

Capital Stock (at December 31 shares of capital stock are as follows)

	Issued and outstanding	
	1973	1972
Preferred Stock—no par value (issuable in series). Authorized, 500,000	None	None
5% Cumulative Preferred Stock—$50 par value. Authorized, 585,730	407,718(a)	407,718(a)
$5.50 Dividend Cumulative Convertible Preferred Stock—no par value—$20 stated value (each share convertible into 4.5 shares of Common; maximum liquidation value, $74,818,900 and $86,184,900). Authorized, 1,164,077	748,189	861,849
$4.50 Dividend Cumulative Preferred Stock—$100 par value. Authorized, 103,976	103,976	103,976
$4.30 Dividend Cumulative Preferred Stock—no par value—$100 stated value (each share convertible prior to November 1, 1977 into 2.1 shares of Common). Authorized, 1,069,204	949,898(b)	931,385(b)
Common Stock—$1 par value. Authorized, 60,000,000	18,896,752(c)	18,337,006(c)
After deducting treasury shares and shares held by a consolidated subsidiary:		
(a)	178,012	178,012
(b)	—	46,500
(c)	4,861,003	4,756,555

Of the authorized shares shown above as of December 31, 1973, an aggregate of 13,707 shares of $4.30 Preferred are reserved for conversion of Spiegel Subordinated Debentures and 5,417,837 shares of Common are reserved for conversion of $5.50 Preferred, $4.30 Preferred, and Spiegel Subordinated Debentures.

of Income Tax Expense," issued in November 1973, required disclosure of the separate types of timing differences and reconcilement of a company's tax or tax rate to the "normal" tax or tax rate. The required disclosure applies only to filings with the Securities and Exchange Commission; however, many companies have included these disclosures in their annual reports to shareholders.[2]

---

[2] For a discussion of the extent to which the requirements of *ASR 149* are included in annual reports, see Dean T. DuCray, "Tax Disclosure under the SEC's *ASR No. 149*," *Financial Executive*, October 1974, pp. 74–79.

Disclosures conforming to *APB Opinion No. 11* and *ASR No. 149* are included in the 1973 annual reports of Shell Oil Company and International Telephone and Telegraph Corporation, respectively. Conforming to *APB Opinion No. 11:*

Income Taxes

Items of income or income deductions are often recognized for payment of income taxes and for book purposes in different time periods; however, tax allocation accounting as prescribed by Accounting Principles Board Opinion No. 11 adjusts book income to eliminate the effect of all material book/tax timing differences.

For those differences pertaining to capital extinguishments, including intangible drilling and development costs deducted currently for tax purposes, tax deferment is computed by applying the current tax rates to the current difference in deduction. The net cumulative effect is reflected in Deferred Credits—Federal Income Taxes in the Balance Sheet.

For other timing differences tax deferment is computed by setting up initial differences at current tax rates and reversing these amounts in the appropriate subsequent period. The net cumulative effect of the latter is reflected in Receivables, Prepayments, Etc. in the Balance Sheet.

Investment tax credits are applied to reduce federal income taxes in the year realized.

For requirements conforming to *ASR No. 149* see Exhibit 5.

EXHIBIT 5

Income Taxes (an analysis of the provision for income taxes, excluding Hartford and the financial subsidiaries, is as follows)

	1973	*1972*
Current Tax Provision:		
United States Federal (including $39,036,000 and $15,600,000 relating to extraordinary items). . .	$ 47,397,000	$ 9,919,000
State and local	9,568,000	10,310,000
Foreign.	224,033,000	143,418,000
	280,998,000	163,647,000
Deferred Tax Provision:		
United States Federal (including $8,833,000 tax and $5,585,000 tax benefit relating to extraordinary items)	19,045,000	32,415,000
Foreign and other.	49,843,000	37,000,000
	68,888,000	69,415,000
	349,886,000	233,062,000
Less taxes relating to extraordinary items	47,869,000	10,015,000
Income Taxes—Consolidated Income Statement . . .	$302,017,000	$223,047,000

EXHIBIT 5 (*continued*)

Deferred income taxes arise principally from the use of accelerated depreciation for income tax purposes and straight-line depreciation for financial reporting purposes, and from the reflection of other revenues and expenses in differing periods as required by generally accepted accounting principles and by the various taxing authorities. Deferred income taxes applicable to accelerated depreciation amounted to $48,975,000 and $45,857,000 in 1973 and 1972, respectively. Other timing differences are not individually significant. Investment tax credits allowed by United States and foreign governments amounting to $16,100,000 and $19,000,000 in 1973 and 1972, respectively, are included in income on a "flow-through" basis.

A reconciliation of the effective tax rate of the Corporation to an arbitrarily selected 48% United States tax rate, after excluding the equity in earnings of Hartford and the financial subsidiaries and before extraordinary items, is as follows:

	1973	1972
Effective income tax rate	43.2%	39.7%
Lower effective foreign income tax rates.	10.6	9.5
Income taxes on dividends from foreign subsidiaries, net of foreign tax credits.	(4.0)	(2.4)
Loss of U.S. tax benefits on U.S. expenses incurred to generate foreign source income	(4.9)	(2.0)
Investment tax credits allowed by the U.S. and foreign governments.	2.3	3.4
Capital gains benefit	1.8	0.9
State and local income taxes.	(.7)	(.9)
Other, net	(.3)	(.2)
United States normal and surtax rate.	48.0%	48.0%

No added provision has been made for taxes payable upon distribution of retained earnings of subsidiaries amounting to $2,294,000,000 (including $980,000,000 of retained earnings of foreign subsidiaries), since these earnings have been permanently reinvested in the related businesses, are included in the Corporation's consolidated United States Federal Income Tax Return, or because taxes payable on foreign earnings will be substantially offset by foreign tax credits.

Earnings per share

APB Opinion No. 15, paragraph 20, reads in part ". . . a schedule or note relating to the earnings per share data should explain the bases upon which both primary and fully diluted earnings per share are calculated." For a company with a simple capital structure this requirement often can be satisfied by a simple statement such as:

> The earnings per share of common stock are based on the average shares outstanding.

However, where there is a complex capital structure a more detailed explanation is called for such as the note shown in Exhibit 6, which appeared in the 1973 annual report of Trans World Airlines, Inc.

EXHIBIT 6
Earnings per Common Share (the earnings per common share is computed as follows)

	Amounts in thousands	
	1973	*1972*
Adjustment of Net Income:		
Net income	$46,476	$43,078
Dividends on preferred stock	(2,096)	(2,096)
Reduction in interest expense, net of income tax, for the assumed tender of 6½% Subordinated Income Debentures if warrants had been exercised	2,085	2,277
Adjusted Net Earnings—Average Common and Common Equivalent Shares	46,465	43,259
Further adjustments assuming full dilution:		
Reduction in interest expense, net of income tax, for the assumed conversion of convertible debentures:		
4% debentures issued in 1967.	3,040	3,040
5% debentures issued in 1969.	5,699	5,699
Adjusted Net Earnings—Assuming Full Dilution . .	$55,204	$51,998
Adjustment of Shares Outstanding:		
Average shares of common stock outstanding.	12,379	12,260
Assumed exercise of warrants (expired December 3, 1973) and options:		
Warrants.	1,932	2,095
Employee stock options	2	34
Total Average Common and Common Equivalent Shares.	14,313	14,389
Further adjustments assuming full dilution:		
Assumed conversion of convertible debentures:		
4% debentures issued in 1967.	1,197	1,197
5% debentures issued in 1969.	2,778	2,778
Total Average Shares of Common Stock— Assuming Full Dilution.	18,288	18,364
Earnings per Common Share:		
On Average Outstanding and Equivalent Shares.	$3.25	$3.01
Assuming Full Dilution	$3.02	$2.83

EXHIBIT 6 (*continued*)

See Notes 9 and 10 for a description of rights and privileges of outstanding convertible securities, warrants, and options entering into the computation of earnings per share. Earnings per common share are computed by dividing adjusted earnings available for such shares by the weighted average number of shares assumed to be eligible for participation in such earnings. Warrants and options are considered to be common share equivalents from date of issuance except that they are excluded from the computation whenever they have the effect of increasing the earnings per share. As to warrants, net earnings were adjusted for the portion of the interest expense, net of tax effect, that would not have accrued under the assumption that the 6½% Subordinated Income Debentures were surrendered in an amount sufficient to exercise all warrants outstanding. Unexercised warrants, originally issued with the 6½% Subordinated Income Debentures, expired on December 3, 1973. As to employee stock options, the increase in the number of shares that would occur if such options were exercised was reduced by the number of shares that presumably could have been repurchased in the open market, at the average market price during the period, with the assumed proceeds from exercise of such employee stock options. As to convertible debt, net earnings were further adjusted for the interest expense, net of tax effect, that would not have accrued under the assumption that such debt was converted to common stock at the beginning of the year or date of issuance, whichever occurred later. These adjustments are excluded from the computation in any period in which they would have the effect of increasing the earnings per share.

Employee benefits

Retirement plans today are practically universal among publicly owned companies; many of these companies also have incentive plans as part of their compensation programs. Depending on the number and nature of such plans, one or more notes in the annual report may be devoted to employee benefits.

Accounting Principles Board Opinion No. 8, "Accounting for the Cost of Pension Plans," requires the following disclosures:

1. A statement that such plans exist, identifying or describing the employee groups covered.
2. A statement of the company's accounting and funding policies.
3. The provision for pension cost for the period.
4. The excess, if any, of the actuarially computed value of vested benefits over the total of the pension fund and any balance-

sheet pension accruals, less any pension prepayments or deferred charges.

5. Nature and effect of significant matters affecting comparability for all periods presented, such as changes in accounting methods (actuarial cost method, amortization of past and prior service cost, treatment of actuarial gains and losses, etc.), changes in circumstances (actuarial assumptions, etc.) or adoption or amendment of a plan.[3]

The Board also gave an example of what is considered to be appropriate disclosure:

The company and its subsidiaries have several pension plans covering substantially all of their employees, including certain employees in foreign countries. The total pension expense for the year was $. . . . . , which includes, as to certain of the plans, amortization of prior service cost over periods ranging from 25 to 40 years. The company's policy is to fund pension cost accrued. The actuarially computed value of vested benefits for all plans as of December 31, 19 . . . , exceeded the total of the pension fund and balance-sheet accruals less pension prepayments and deferred charges by approximately $. . . . .

A change during the year in the actuarial cost method used in computing pension cost had the effect of reducing net income for the year by approximately $. . . . .

A description of the provisions of incentive compensation plans often is necessary as part of a fair presentation of financial statements. The 1973 annual report of Uniroyal, Inc., included the disclosures shown in Exhibit 7.

Lease commitments

APB Opinion No. 31, "Disclosure of Lease Commitments by Lessees," requires disclosure of minimum rental commitments under

EXHIBIT 7
Employees Stock Purchase and Savings Plans

The 1971 Employees Stock Purchase Plan permitted eligible employees to purchase shares of common stock by payroll deductions which began October 15, 1971 and continued until September 30, 1973. On October 1, 1973, because of adverse market conditions, all amounts collected from employees under the Plan, together with interest thereon, were refunded.

---

[3] AICPA, "Accounting for the Cost of Pension Plans," *APB Opinion No. 8* (New York, November 1966), par. 46.

EXHIBIT 7 (*continued*)

The Uniroyal Savings Plan for Salaried Employees permits eligible employees, through payroll deductions of up to six percent of their current earnings, to invest such amounts in a combination of common stock of the Company, at the market value, and U.S. Government securities.

Under the Savings Plan, the Company contributes not less than 25%, nor more than 100% of the contributions made by each participant. Currently, the Company is making contributions of 50% of payroll deductions. The Company's contribution is invested in shares of common stock and the right to these shares vests in the employees after five years of continuing participation.

Stock Options

Options are granted to officers and other key employees at market price, are not exercisable for certain periods after grant and generally expire five years from dates of grant. At the close of fiscal 1971, options were outstanding for 249,695 shares. Based on the average option price of $21.98 per share, the aggregate value was $5,488,000. In addition, there remained 695,759 shares of common stock available for further options.

During fiscal 1973 and 1972 options:

	Were granted		Became exercisable		Were exercised	
	1973	1972	1973	1972	1973	1972
	(in thousands except per share amounts)					
Shares	48.7	39.0	39.0	9.3	3.2	–0–
Option Price:						
Per Share*	$13.00	$17.72	$17.72	$20.86	$11.27	–0–
Aggregate	$ 633	$ 691	$ 691	$ 193	$ 37	–0–
Market Value:						
Per Share*	$13.00	$17.72	$12.87	$18.05	$13.85	–0–
Aggregate	$ 633	$ 691	$ 502	$ 167	$ 45	–0–

* Average value.

During the two year period options expired or were cancelled for 124,692 shares.

At the close of fiscal 1973, options were outstanding for 209,463 shares. Based on the average option price of $19.69 per share, the aggregate value was $4,125,000. In addition, there remained 732,751 shares of common stock available for granting further options.

Class B Bonus and Management Incentive Plans

The amount charged to operations under the Company's Class B Bonus and Management Incentive Plans amounted to $2,390,000 for 1973 and $1,792,000 for 1972.

all noncancelable leases for (a) each of the five succeeding fiscal years; (b) each of the next three five-year periods; and (c) the remainder as a single amount. The Board also recognized the usefulness of disclosure of the present value of such commitments. The Securities and Exchange Commission's *Accounting Series Release No. 147* requires this present value disclosure of financing leases in reports filed with the Commission. A financing lease is defined by the SEC as:

> A lease which, during the noncancelable lease period, either (i) covers 75 percent or more of the economic life of the property or (ii) has terms which assure the lessor a full recovery of the fair market value (which would normally be represented by his investment) of the property at the inception of the lease plus a reasonable return on the use of the assets invested subject only to limited risk in the realization of the residual interest in the property and the credit risks generally associated with secured loans.

EXHIBIT 8
Lease obligations

United currently leases 92 of its aircraft, the majority of which have terms of 15 years and expiration dates ranging from 1975 through 1988. Under the terms of leases for 30 of the aircraft, United has the right of first refusal to purchase the aircraft for fair market value at the end of the lease term. One leased DC-10 aircraft is subleased to another airline and will be returned to United in 1975. Other leases include airport passenger terminal space, aircraft hangars and related maintenance facilities, cargo terminals, flight kitchens and other equipment.

Majority-owned subsidiaries of Western International hold leases on six hotels expiring from 1982 through 2003. Most of these leases grant the lessee an option to renew.

Rental expense for 1973 and 1972 was comprised of:

	1973	1972
Basic or minimum rentals—		
Non-capitalized financing leases.	$100,192,000	$ 86,958,000
Other.	13,238,000	11,760,000
	113,430,000	98,718,000
Contingent rentals—		
Non-capitalized financing leases.	1,673,000	1,203,000
Other.	277,000	605,000
	1,950,000	1,808,000
	$115,380,000	$100,526,000

EXHIBIT 8 (*continued*)

Financing leases, above, refer to leases which cover 75 percent or more of the economic life of the property, or have terms which assure the lessor full recovery of his investment plus a reasonable return. Contingent rentals relate to hotel operations and are generally based on a percentage of operating profits.

As of December 31, 1973, the companies' commitments for minimum or fixed rentals were as follows:

	Financing leases	Other leases
Payable during—		
1974	$108,293,000	$4,166,000
1975	102,715,000	3,711,000
1976	100,202,000	3,228,000
1977	98,745,000	2,802,000
1978	92,306,000	2,518,000
1979–1983	392,283,000	8,161,000
1984–1988	215,894,000	2,915,000
1989–1993	91,919,000	4,475,000
1994 and later.	96,879,000	2,704,000

The present values of minimum commitments for financing leases, based on interest rates implicit in the leases ranging from 5 to 11.25 percent for aircraft and from 1.9 to 8.5 percent for all other property (weighted average of 6.71 percent for 1973 and 6.57 percent for 1972), were:

	December 31	
	1973	*1972*
Airline—Aircraft.	$481,705,000	$400,507,000
Ground facilities	245,384,000	213,219,000
Other.	3,486,000	4,465,000
Hotels	84,639,000	63,173,000
	$815,214,000	$681,364,000

Assuming the companies were to have capitalized their financing leases, amortized the cost of the rights to the leased assets on a straight-line basis and reflected interest expense on the basis of the outstanding lease liability, net earnings would have been reduced by $7,811,000 in 1973 and $6,981,000 in 1972. This reduction in net earnings is caused by the aggregate of the assumed amortization ($63,993,000 in 1973 and $55,857,000 in 1972) and interest expense ($51,220,000 in 1973 and $44,526,000 in 1972) being greater than the actual rentals paid.

It has become general practice for companies with financing leases to include the SEC-required disclosures in their annual reports to shareholders. A footnote on leases meeting the disclosure requirements of *ASR No. 147* and *APB Opinion No. 31* is presented in the 1973 annual report of UAL, Inc. (see Exhibit 8).

Contingencies and commitments

The most commonly mentioned contingency is litigation. The note usually describes the circumstances of the litigation and indicates the opinion of management and/or counsel as to its probable impact. Other contingencies frequently described are the possible effects of environmental legislation, proposed tax adjustments, renegotiation proceedings, and guarantees of debt of an affiliate. Commitments normally require disclosure only if they are significant and are not in the normal course of business, or if they are peculiar to a particular industry. For example, a purchase commitment for reorder of inventory items normally would not be disclosed, but a commitment for substantial property additions generally would.

A comprehensive note dealing with commitments and contingencies is presented in the 1973 annual report of Liggett & Myers Incorporated:

> *Commitments and Contingent Liabilities*
>
> At December 31, 1973, commitments for the acquisition of property, plant, and equipment aggregated approximately $1,800,000.
>
> Under an agreement with the Company, Star Industries, Inc., has the right to sell to the Company, at any time prior to April 19, 1974, its remaining holdings of Carillon Importers Ltd. common stock for approximately $650,000 which would be approximately $300,000 in excess of the equity in net assets applicable to such shares as of December 31, 1973.
>
> Carillon has agreed to purchase, under certain circumstances, its common stock held by certain minority stockholders for a price per share equal to 14 times the average net earnings (as defined) per share of such common stock for the two fiscal years preceding the year in which such stock is purchased. If all such shares were purchased, the cost thereof would aggregate approximately $2,500,000 on the basis of the purchase price currently in effect;

such cost would be approximately $1,200,000 in excess of the equity in net assets applicable to such shares as of December 31, 1973.

At December 31, 1973 the Company was contingently liable as guarantor for borrowings of certain unconsolidated subsidiaries in an amount aggregating approximately $1,622,000.

On February 15, 1972, the Company filed a complaint in the U.S. District Court for the Southern District of New York alleging violations of the Securities Exchange Act of 1934 in connection with the Company's 1971 acquisition of Mercury Mills, Inc. for 163,266 shares of common stock. To the extent that such a violation may have damaged the Company, the complaint seeks, among other relief, recovery of up to 37,551 shares of the Company's common stock issued at the time of the acquisition. The defendant in this litigation has asserted claims against the Company in a 1972 Georgia State Court action (in which all proceedings have been stayed pending trial of the Company's New York Federal action) and, on September 13, 1973, in a counterclaim filed in the New York Federal action seeking, among other things, damages aggregating $9,000,000, which claims, actions, and counterclaim are, in the opinion of the Company and its counsel, without merit.

The Federal Trade Commission has filed a complaint against the Company alleging violations of Section 7 of the Clayton Antitrust Act, in which it seeks relief in the form of divestiture of the Company's subsidiary, Perk Foods Co. Incorporated. It has been the Company's belief from the outset that the acquisition of Perk Foods was lawful; and, in the opinion of the Company and its counsel, it has meritorious defenses which will prevail against the complaint. The complaint does not involve the Company's principal pet food subsidiary, Allen Products Company, Inc.

At December 31, 1973, there were several other lawsuits pending against the Company and certain of its consolidated subsidiaries. In the opinion of the Company and its counsel, none of the plaintiffs should prevail on the merits of such actions.

Borrowing arrangements

Disclosure of compensating balances and of certain short-term borrowing arrangements has been required by the SEC in *Accounting Series Release No. 148*. Many companies have incorporated some or all of these requirements in their annual reports to shareholders. The accompanying note from the 1973 annual report of Amfac is an illustration of disclosure of credit arrangements (see Exhibit 9).

EXHIBIT 9
Debt and Interest (certain information regarding borrowing arrangements follows)

	Banks	Com-mercial paper	Total (in thou-sands))	Bank revolving credit	Total
			Short-term borrowings		
Highest month-end balance of aggregate borrowings during the year:					
1973	$27,200	$25,000	$52,200	$50,000	$102,200
1972	30,050	15,000	45,050	50,000	95,050
Average borrowings outstanding during the year:					
1973	$19,500	$ 9,300	$28,800	$38,100	$ 66,900
1972	17,100	16,300	33,400	35,700	69,100
Weighted average interest rate on borrowings outstanding during the year:					
1973	8%	8½%	8¼%	8½%	8½%
1972	5¼%	4¾%	5%	5¾%	5½%
Maximum borrowings available under borrowing arrange-ments:					
12/31/73.	$40,000		$40,000	$60,000	$100,000
12/31/72.	40,000		40,000	60,000	100,000
Unused lines of bank credit:					
12/31/73.	$20,800		$20,800	$35,000	$ 55,800
12/31/72.	24,200		24,200	45,000	69,200

Amfac has informally agreed with banks to provide compensating balances which averaged about $7,900,000 during 1973 and about $7,800,000 during 1972.

Under terms of the bank revolving credit agreement, Amfac may convert any such loans outstanding prior to May 31, 1974 into a five-year term loan with interest at ½ percent above the prime rate.

Annual maturities of long-term debt (assuming bank revolving credit outstanding on December 31, 1973 is converted to a term loan on May 31, 1974) will be $10,399,000 in 1974, $11,321,000 in 1975, $10,557,000 in 1976, $10,374,000 in 1977 and $10,727,000 in 1978.

Subsequent events

Subsequent events requiring disclosure, but not requiring adjustment of the financial statements, are described by the Committee on Auditing Procedure of the AICPA as:

. . . those events that provide evidence with respect to conditions that did not exist at the date of the balance sheet being reported on but arose subsequent to that date. These events should not result in adjustment of the financial statements. Some of these events, however, may be of such a nature that disclosure of them is required to keep the financial statements from being misleading.[4]

Events which might require disclosure in the notes if they occur subsequent to the balance sheet date include agreements concerning business combinations, disposal of a significant part of the business, issuance of debt, and approval of stock distributions. Disclosures of such events were included in the 1973 annual reports of Ethyl Corporation; Castle & Cooke, Inc.; Anheuser-Busch, Incorporated; and Aetna Life and Casualty Company.

Ethyl Corporation:

Subsequent Events

On January 7, 1974, the Corporation acquired 283,050 shares (27%) of the common stock of The Elk Horn Coal Corporation at $25 per share and offered to purchase the balance of the shares outstanding for the same price. As of February 22, 1974, the Corporation had acquired approximately 95% of the outstanding shares at a total cost of about $25,000,000.

Castle & Cooke, Inc.:

Subsequent Events

Subsequent to the end of the fiscal year, the Company completed negotiations for the sale of the assets of the Royal Hawaiian Macadamia Nut Division. The net gain from the sale will be approximately $3,500,000 after deducting income taxes of $2,000,000.

Anheuser-Busch Incorporated:

Note 9: Subsequent Event

In February, 1974, the company sold $100,000,000 of 7.95% sinking fund debentures, due February 1, 1999. On February 7, 1974, $83,875,000 of these debentures were issued. The remaining $16,125,000 are subject to delayed delivery contracts providing for delivery and payment on July 15, 1974. The debentures mature annually from 1985 through 1999.

---

[4] AICPA, *Statement on Auditing Standards No. 1* (New York, November 1972), par. 560.05.

Aetna Life and Casualty Company:

Subsequent Event

On January 24, 1974, the Board of Directors approved a two-for-one stock split of Aetna's common stock, subject to shareholder approval at the 1974 Annual Meeting. Certificates for the additional shares would be distributed in May 1974 to shareholders of record at the close of business April 8, 1974. The split would increase the number of authorized common shares to 80 million and reduce the par value per share to $1.75. Such reduction in par value is subject to approval of the Connecticut Insurance Commissioner. Concurrent with the split, each share of cumulative convertible preferred stock now convertible into three-fourths of a share of common stock would become convertible into one and one-half shares of common stock.

REPORTING ACCOUNTING POLICIES

Since alternative accounting principles exist, it is essential that users of financial statements know which principles are being employed by an entity. *APB Opinion No. 22,* "Disclosure of Accounting Policies," requires reporting entities to "identify and describe the accounting principles followed by the reporting entity and the methods of applying those principles. . . ."[5]

In paragraph 15 of that *Opinion* the APB expressed its preference for a separate accounting policy statement preceding the notes to financial statements or as the initial note. Generally, this procedure is observed. Certain companies, however, present their accounting policies throughout the notes. General Electric Company uses this approach. They identify accounting policies by printing them in a distinctive ink color.

Paragraph 12 of the *Opinion* describes the disclosures to be made in the statement of accounting policies as follows:

> In general, the disclosure should encompass important judgments as to appropriateness of principles relating to recognition of revenue and allocation of asset costs to current and future periods; in particular, it should encompass those accounting principles and methods that involve any of the following:

---

[5] AICPA, "Disclosure of Accounting Policies," *APB Opinion No. 22* (New York, April 1972), par. 12.

a. A selection from existing acceptable alternatives;
b. Principles and methods peculiar to the industry in which the reporting entity operates, even if such principles and methods are predominantly followed in that industry;
c. Unusual or innovative applications of generally accepted accounting principles (and, as applicable, of principles and methods peculiar to the industry in which the reporting entity operates).

Examples of disclosures required because of existing acceptable alternatives include basis of consolidation, depreciation methods, inventory pricing, recognition of profit on long-term construction-type contracts, the successful effort or full-cost methods of accounting in the extractive industry, lease transactions by lessors, and amortization of intangibles. Often the circumstances of an entity determine what alternative is to be used but the user of financial information still must know what alternative is employed.

The following illustrations of disclosures of the type described above were presented in these 1973 annual reports:

Caterpillar Tractor Co.:

Basis of Consolidation

Caterpillar Tractor Co. has investments in subsidiaries, all of which are wholly owned, and in affiliated companies, which are 50% owned. The accompanying financial statements include the accounts of Caterpillar Tractor Co. and all of its subsidiaries except those engaged solely in financing. These financing subsidiaries, Caterpillar Credit Corporation and Caterpillar Overseas Credit Corporation S. A., are accounted for by the equity method; accordingly, their profit is included in the consolidated results of operations as a separate item and the consolidated financial position reflects the cost of the Company's investments in and advances to these subsidiaries plus the profit retained by them. The affiliated companies are also accounted for by the equity method.

Allied Chemical Corporation:

Property, plant and equipment are carried at cost. Depreciation and amortization are computed for groups of assets using lives which range from 3 to 33 years. The Company computes depreciation for financial reporting purposes principally on the sum-of-the-years-digits method for assets acquired prior to 1970 and on the straight-line method for subsequent capital additions. The accelerated method is utilized for tax purposes.

American Can Company:

Inventories

Inventories are stated at the lower of cost (principally first-in, first-out and last-in, first-out) or market.

Morrison—Knudsen Company, Inc.:

Accounting for Construction Contracts: Contracts usually cover construction and engineering work for periods in excess of one year. Profits on contracts of the Companies and their share of earnings on joint venture contracts are recorded on the percentage-of-completion method, whereby profits are recognized at the percentage of estimated total profit that costs incurred to date bear to the estimated total costs of the contract at completion. Revenue from operations and cost of revenue include the Companies' proportionate share of joint venture operations.

Provision is made for estimated future losses on the entire contract at the date it is first estimated that a loss will result from a contract in progress. Claims for additional contract compensation are not recognized in the accounts until claims have been allowed.

Since profits or losses are determined periodically during the time the contracts are in progress and, therefore, before all items of revenues and costs have been finalized, the amount of profit or loss for a particular contract during a particular period may include transactions applicable to other periods.

Mobil Oil Corporation:

Exploration and Mineral Rights (Leases)

Direct acquisition costs of unproven mineral rights (leases) are capitalized and then amortized in the manner stated below. Payments made in lieu of drilling on non-producing leaseholds are charged to expense currently.

Geological, Geophysical, and Intangible Drilling Costs

Geological and geophysical costs are expensed as incurred. Intangible drilling costs for wells that are not considered commercially successful are expensed. Intangible drilling costs attributable to wells that are determined to be commercially successful are capitalized when that determination is made and amortized in the manner stated below.

United States Leasing International, Inc.:

Basis of Accounting—Direct Finance Leases

Lease contracts under which total noncancellable rentals exceed the cost of leased equipment plus anticipated financing costs are accounted for as financing leases. At the time a direct finance lease transaction is closed, the Company records on its balance sheet the gross lease receivable, estimated residual valuation of the leased equipment, and the unearned lease income. The unearned lease income represents the excess of the gross lease receivable plus the estimated residual valuation over the cost of the equipment leased. A portion of the unearned lease income (13% in 1973 and 1972) plus an amount equal to the provision for losses is recognized as revenue at the time the lease is closed to offset expenses incurred in consummating the lease. The remainder of the unearned lease income is recorded as revenue over the term of the lease using the sum-of-the-digits method commencing with the second month of the lease.

This procedure results in recognizing the remainder of the unearned lease income as revenue approximately in proportion to the declining receivable balance.

Basis of Accounting—Operating Leases

Lease contracts under which total noncancellable rentals do not exceed the cost of lease equipment plus anticipated financing costs are accounted for as operating leases. Rental equipment is recorded at cost, and is depreciated over the useful life of the equipment on the straight line basis. Rentals are recorded as revenue when billed and are reported net of depreciation expense of $3,249,000 and $28,000 in 1973 and 1972, respectively.

Liggett & Myers Incorporated:

Franchises and Goodwill and Amortization

At December 31, 1973, the unamortized portion of the cost of an exclusive franchise held by The Paddington Corporation (a subsidiary) to import J&B Rare Scotch Whisky aggregated $56,347,447, and the unamortized excess cost applicable to the acquisition of Paddington and Carillon Importers Ltd. (a subsidiary) aggregated $13,560,263. The franchise and the unamortized excess costs are being amortized on the straight-line method over the remaining lives of the J&B franchise and a franchise held by Carillon. In 1973, such excess cost was increased by $4,216,193 resulting from the cash purchase by the Company of the remaining minority interest in Paddington at a cost of $6,042,477.

At December 31, 1973, the remaining excess of cost of investments over equity in net assets at dates of acquisition, all arising from acquisitions prior to November 1, 1970, aggregated $53,053,866. Such excess costs are not being amortized because in the Company's opinion they have not declined in value since acquisition.

Accounting principles unique to an industry should be disclosed in the accounting policies statement. Regulated industries such as utilities, transportation, insurance, and banks, and specialized industries such as finance, land development, and agribusiness characteristically have practices which are unique to their industry.

The following excerpts from 1973 annual reports represent illustrations of disclosure of industry accounting practices:

Union Pacific Corporation:

> *Depreciation*—Provisions for depreciation are computed principally on the straight-line method based on estimated service lives of depreciable properties, except for rails, ties and other track material owned by Union Pacific Railroad Company (Railroad). With respect to the latter, the generally accepted industry alternative of replacement accounting is utilized. Under this method, replacements in kind are charged to expenses and betterments (improvements) are capitalized.

Consolidated Natural Gas Company:

> *Gas Sales Revenues*
>
> In accordance with customary industry practice, revenues from residential and small commercial customers are included in income as billed on the basis of scheduled meter readings and do not include deliveries of gas from the meter reading date to the end of the month, except for estimated deliveries applicable to customers billed on a budget plan basis. Revenues from industrial, wholesale and large commercial customers are based upon deliveries to the end of the period.

Philip Morris Incorporated:

> *Inventories*
>
> Inventories are valued at the lower of cost or market. The cost of leaf tobacco is determined on an average cost basis and the cost

of other inventories is determined generally on a first-in, first-out basis. It is a generally recognized industry practice to classify the total amount of leaf tobacco inventory as a current asset although part of such inventory, because of the duration of the aging process, ordinarily would not be utilized within one year.

The third criterion cited in the *Opinion*—"unusual or innovative applications of generally accepted accounting principles. . ."— acknowledges that accounting principles are not static, and that they must evolve to meet changing conditions. Disclosure of the accounting followed for leveraged lease transactions by a lessor is an example of the application of this criterion.

Items which most companies present in separate notes to financial statements are included by some companies in the summary of accounting policies. Examples are earnings per share, income tax, and retirement plan information. The presentation may be in lieu of a separate footnote or it may set forth broad policy which is supported by greater detail in a separate footnote.

ACCOUNTING CHANGES

The accounting process requires estimates and choices among alternative accounting principles. Circumstances sometimes require a change in these estimates or choices. The term *accounting change* is defined in *APB Opinion No. 20* as ". . . a change in (a) an accounting principle, (b) an accounting estimate, or (c) the reporting entity."[6] The *Opinion* specifies the accounting for these changes and the accounting for a correction of an error in previously issued financial statements.

A change in accounting principle may be made only if the reporting entity justifies the use of the alternative acceptable accounting principle as preferable. The issuance of a statement of financial accounting standards

> . . . that creates a new accounting principle, that expresses a preference for an accounting principle, or that rejects a specific accounting principle is sufficient support for a change in accounting principle. The burden of justifying other changes rests with the entity proposing the change. . . . However, a method of accounting that

---

[6] AICPA, "Accounting Changes," *APB Opinion No. 20* (New York, July 1971), par. 6.

EXHIBIT 10
Change in accounting principle

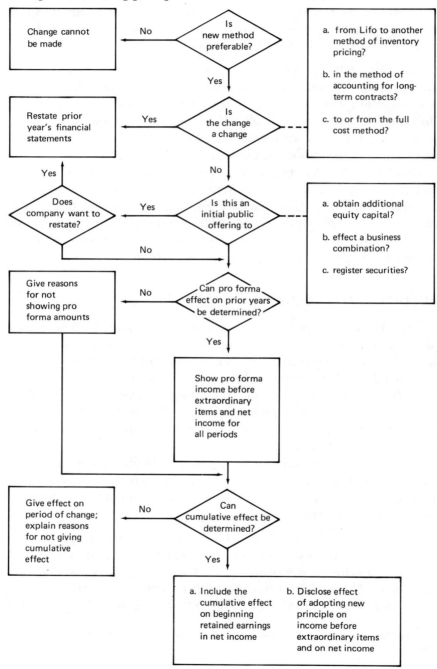

was previously adopted for a type of transaction or event which is being terminated or which was a single nonrecurring event in the past should not be changed.[7]

In addition to FASB pronouncements some other frequently cited justifications for changes in accounting principle include (*a*) conforming to a general industry practice, (*b*) improved matching of revenue and expense, and (*c*) conforming the accounting practices of the components of an enterprise.

Paragraph 8 of *Opinion No. 20* states that

neither (a) initial adoption of an accounting principle in recognition of events or transactions occurring for the first time or that previously were immaterial in their effect nor (b) adoption or modification of an accounting principle necessitated by transactions or events that are clearly different in substance from those previously occurring is a change in accounting principle.

Most changes in accounting principle should be reported as described in *APB Opinion No. 20*, paragraph 19:

a. Financial statements for prior periods included for comparative purposes should be presented as previously reported.
b. The cumulative effect of changing to a new accounting principle on the amount of retained earnings at the beginning of the period in which the change is made should be included in net income of the period of the change.
c. The effect of adopting the new accounting principle on income before extraordinary items and on net income (and on the related per share amounts) of the period of change should be disclosed.
d. Income before extraordinary items and net income computed on a pro forma basis should be shown on the face of the income statements for all periods presented as if the newly adopted accounting principle had been applied during all periods affected.

The cumulative effect of a change in accounting principle is the direct effect of the change and the related income tax effect on beginning retained earnings had the change been applied retroactively. The pro forma effect includes both direct effects and nondiscretionary adjustments, such as profit sharing expense, royalties,

---

[7] Ibid., par. 16 (par. 16 refers to an Opinion of the Accounting Principles Board; since the FASB is now the body which issues official rulings on accounting principles we have substituted the wording "Statement of Financial Accounting Standards.")

and so on, that would have been recognized if the newly adopted accounting principle had been followed in prior periods.

In its 1973 annual report Lykes-Youngstown Corporation presented the disclosures relating to an accounting change shown in Exhibit 11.

Retroactive change

A few special changes in accounting principle are applied retroactively since the advantages of retroactive treatment in prior period statements outweigh the disadvantages. Paragraph 27 of *APB Opinion No. 20* lists these changes as "(a) a change from the LIFO method of inventory pricing to another method, (b) a change in the method of accounting for long-term construction-type contracts, and (c) a change to or from the 'full cost' method of accounting which is used in the extractive industries." A special exemption described in paragraph 29 of *APB Opinion No. 20* allows companies the option to restate financial statements retroactively when such statements are first issued for: "(a) obtaining additional equity capital from investors, (b) effecting a business combination, or (c) registering securities."

When a change in accounting principle is applied retroactively, the nature of, and justification for, the change should be disclosed. In addition, unless the change is a special exemption for an initial public distribution, the effect of the change on income before extraordinary items, net income, and the related per share amounts should be disclosed in the notes or on the face of the income statement for all periods presented. Financial statements of subsequent periods need not repeat these disclosures.

The following disclosure of a change from the Lifo method appears in the 1973 annual report of Magnetic Metals Company:

Change in Accounting Method and Restatements

Effective January 1, 1973, the FIFO (first-in, first-out) method of inventory valuation was adopted for inventories previously valued on the LIFO (last-in, first-out) basis. This results in a more uniform valuation method throughout the Company and a more representative presentation of the current inventory investment.

As a result of adopting the FIFO method, the net income for 1973 is approximately $10,700 ($.01 per share) more than it would have been on the LIFO basis. The financial statements for prior

EXHIBIT 11

	1973	*1972*
Income before extraordinary item and cumulative effect of accounting change	$24,856,000	$17,580,000
Extraordinary item—gain on sale of investment, less income tax of $2,447,000 (Note 2)		8,018,000
Cumulative effect on prior years of an accounting change, less income tax effect of $4,040,000 (Note 2)	11,552,000	
Net Income for the Year	$36,408,000	$25,598,000

Per common share:
Primary:

	1973	*1972*
Income before extraordinary item and cumulative effect of accounting change	$1.24	$ .43
Extraordinary item		.90
Cumulative effect of accounting change	1.29	
Net income	$2.53	$1.33

Fully diluted:

	1973	*1972*
Income before extraordinary item and cumulative effect of accounting change	$1.26	$ .89
Extraordinary item		.41
Cumulative effect of accounting change	.59	
Net income	$1.85	$1.30

Pro forma income amounts assuming the change in accounting method had been applied retroactively (Note 2):		
Income before extraordinary item	$24,856,000	$15,442,000
Net income	$24,856,000	$23,460,000

Per common share:
Primary:

	1973	*1972*
Income before extraordinary item	$1.24	$ .20
Net income	$1.24	$1.09

Note 2—Accounting Changes. Effective January 1, 1973, expenditures for relining and rehabilitation of blast furnaces were capitalized and will be depreciated over the estimated productive life of the respective furnace linings. Prior to 1973 such expenditures were charged to cost of products sold in the year in which the expenditures were incurred. This change in accounting principle was made to recognize that blast furnace relinings last for several years and should be charged to the operating costs of the period in which the related benefits are obtained, resulting in a more appropriate matching of revenues and costs. Had this change not been made, income before extraordinary item and cumulative effect of an accounting change would have been $4,286,000 ($.48 per share) less for the year ended December 31, 1973. The cumulative effect on prior years of this change, in the amount of $11,552,000 (after reduction for federal income taxes of $4,040,000) is included in net income for the year ended December 31, 1973. The proforma amounts shown on the consolidated statement of income have been computed assuming retroactive application of the newly adopted accounting principle. Proforma fully diluted earnings per share are not presented pursuant to the limitations imposed by the concept of anti-dilution.

As a result of a study conducted during the year, the Company adopted a new method for depreciating 1973 and subsequent steel mill roll acquisitions. The new method charges cost, less scrap value, to operating expense over the estimated useful life of the roll on a straight-line basis. The majority of rolls purchased have an estimated useful life of from 18 to 48 months. Under the previous method, the cost of rolls, less scrap value, was charged to operating expense in the year of acquisition. Had the change not been made in respect of the 1973 acquisitions, income before extraordinary item and cumulative effect of an accounting change, and net income, would have been $3,034,000 ($.34 per share) less for the year ended December 31, 1973.

Refractory brick and other supplies, previously expensed upon purchase, were included in raw materials and supplies inventories at December 31, 1972, thereby increasing net income in 1972 by $1,361,000 ($.15 per share). This change was made to provide improved custodial and financial control over these items. The proforma and cumulative effects on net income of prior years are not determinable because the necessary data are unavailable.

years have been retroactively restated for this change and, as a result, retained earnings have been increased by $156,895 as of January 1, 1972. Also, the 1972 statement of income has been restated resulting in an increase in net income of $14,253 ($.02 per share). Inventories at December 31, 1973, and 1972 are $363,737 and $342,295 more than they would have been under the LIFO method.

Cumulative effect not determinable

Paragraphs 25 and 26 of *APB Opinion No. 20* deal with instances where the pro forma amounts and/or the cumulative effects of a change in accounting principle cannot be determined. The reasons for omitting these amounts and the effect on income for the period of change (including per share data) must be disclosed.

The most common example of this situation is a change to the Lifo method of pricing inventory, since determination of the cumulative effect and pro forma amounts would require reconstruction of inventory records from inception of the company. Such a change was made by Badger Paper Mills, Inc., in 1973 and the following disclosure appeared in its annual report:

Change in Accounting for Certain Items of Inventory:

During the year, the Company changed its method of determining cost for certain items of inventory from the first-in, first-out (FIFO) basis to the last-in, first-out (LIFO) basis. As a result, cost has been determined on a LIFO basis for $1,996,000 and $882,000 of the inventory value at December 31, 1973 and 1972, respectively. Current cost of these inventories was $3,230,000 and $1,689,000 at December 31, 1973 and 1972, respectively.

This change was made to recognize the inflationary effects of inventory and thereby more effectively match current costs with current revenues for both financial and income tax reporting purposes.

This change had the effect of decreasing net earnings by $162,000 ($.61 per share) for the year ended December 31, 1973. Due to its nature, it is impossible to determine the cumulative effect of this change on retained earnings at the beginning of the year and accordingly pro forma results of operations for the prior year, had this principle been followed in that period, is not determinable.

Prospective changes

Other accounting changes which do not require cumulative adjustments are those in depreciation, depletion, and amortization methods which are applied prospectively. Paragraph 24 of *APB Opinion No. 20* reads in part:

> Various factors are considered in selecting an amortization method for identifiable assets, and those factors may change, even for similar assets. For example, a company may adopt a new method of amortization for newly acquired, identifiable, long-lived assets and use that method for all additional new assets of the same class but continue to use the previous method for existing balances of previously recorded assets of that class. . . .

For prospective changes a description of the nature of the change in method and its effect on income before extraordinary items and net income of the period of the change, together with related per share amounts, should be disclosed. The following excerpt from the 1973 annual report of Bunker Ramo Corporation illustrates the manner of reporting a prospective change:

> The method of computing depreciation was changed to straight-line from accelerated with respect to 1973 additions to improve the matching of revenues and related expense. Net income in 1973 was increased $315,000 or five cents per share as a result of this change.

Changes in accounting estimates

Informed estimates concerning the collectibility of receivables, the service lives of depreciable assets, warranty costs, and so on, are a significant part of the accounting process. "Accounting estimates change as new events occur, as more experience is acquired, or as additional information is obtained."[8]

Paragraph 31 of *APB Opinion No. 20* requires that the effect of a change in an accounting estimate be accounted for in "(a) the period of change if the change affects that period only or (b) the period of change and future periods if the change affects both." If the change in estimate results from the final settlement of a claim or liability or in the realization or disposition of an asset, the change would be reported in the current period only. A change in the service life of an identifiable asset is an example of a change which affects the current and future periods.

Disclosure is required in the period of change of the effect on income before extraordinary items, net income, and related per share amounts of the current period for a change in estimate that

---

[8] Ibid., par. 10.

affects future periods. Disclosure of changes in estimates which characteristically are made each year to reflect current circumstances, such as uncollectible accounts or inventory obsolescence, is not required but is recommended if the effect of the change in the estimate is material.

A special type of change in accounting estimate is one that is recognized in whole or in part by a change in accounting principle. Paragraph 32 of *APB Opinion No. 20* requires that this kind of change be accounted for as a change in estimate since "the cumulative effect attributable to the change in accounting principle cannot be separated from the current or future effects of the change in estimate." Thus when a company's judgment that a cost should be deferred as recoverable proves subsequently to be incorrect, a change in accounting principle to expensing those and similar costs would be appropriate. The 1973 annual report of Carolina Pipeline Co. included the following disclosure:

Changes Arising from Declining Gas Supplies:

During 1972, one of the Company's gas suppliers began curtailing deliveries. Because of this and other indications of declining gas supplies, management became concerned that future gas supplies would not be adequate to permit previously anticipated sales to certain industrial customers; accordingly, unamortized gas conversion costs of $742,589 applicable to these customers were written off during 1972.

Curtailments in deliveries continued in 1973 and both of the Company's suppliers have predicted significant curtailments in future years. Because of this continued deterioration in the outlook for future gas supplies, the Company obtained approval of the South Carolina Public Service Commission to write-off, during 1973, the remaining unamortized conversion costs of $471,000 applicable to residential and commercial customers.

Also during 1973, the Company increased depreciation rates for certain transmission property utilized primarily for industrial customers and began depreciating rights-of-way to recognize the possible effect of declining gas supplies on the economic life of this property. These changes increased 1973 depreciation expense by $262,000.

The effect of these changes was to reduce net income for 1973 by $358,000 ($0.27 per share) and for 1972 by $363,000 ($0.28 per share) from amounts which would have been reported if the amortization periods and depreciation lives and practices had not been changed.

Change in the reporting entity

Paragraph 12 of *APB Opinion No. 20* describes a change in the reporting entity: "This type is limited mainly to (a) presenting consolidated or combined statements in place of statements of individual companies, (b) changing specific subsidiaries comprising the group of companies for which consolidated financial statements are presented, and (c) changing the companies included in combined financial statements." For these changes financial statements of all prior periods should be restated. "The effect of the change on income before extraordinary items, net income, and related per share amounts should be disclosed for all periods presented."[9]

The following disclosure was presented in the 1973 annual report of Reliance Electric Company:

> As of November 1, 1972, the Company adopted the policy of consolidating all subsidiaries and of accounting for investments in affiliated companies by the equity method. Prior to fiscal 1973 only North American subsidiaries were consolidated. Investments in subsidiaries outside North America and in affiliated companies were reported at the Company's original cost. The consolidated financial statements have been restated to reflect these changes in accounting policies. The changes increased net earnings for 1973 by $2,572,000 ($.29 primary and $.19 fully diluted earnings per share), and for 1972 by $289,000 ($.03 primary and $.02 fully diluted earnings per share).

Correction of an error

A correction of an error in previously issued financial statements is reported as a prior period adjustment. Paragraph 37 of *APB Opinion No. 20* states: ". . . the nature of an error in previously issued financial statements and the effect of its correction on income before extraordinary items, net income, and the related per share amounts should be disclosed in the period in which the error was discovered and corrected."

The following note describes a correction of an error resulting from misclassification of certain inventory as work in process rather than as raw material:

> At December 31, 1972 certain inventory items were classified as work in process rather than raw material, resulting in labor and

[9] Ibid., par. 35.

manufacturing expenses being included in the valuation of these items. The accompanying financial statements have been restated to reflect this change in inventory classification and valuation, resulting in a decrease in net income of $——— ($—— per share of common stock) from amounts previously reported for the year ended December 31, 1972.

SUMMARY

In this chapter we have tried to illustrate disclosures commonly made in notes to financial statements. Additional illustrations are included in two AICPA publications, *Illustrations of Reporting Accounting Changes* by Hortense Goodman and Thomas W. McRea and *Illustrations of Accounting Policy Disclosure* by Hortense Goodman. Two annual publications which illustrate current disclosures of accounting practices are *Accounting Trends and Techniques,* published by the AICPA, and *Accounting Practices,* published by Haskins & Sells.

SELECTED REFERENCES

American Institute of Certified Public Accountants *Accounting Trends and Techniques.* New York, 1973.
——— *APB Opinion No. 8.* New York, November 1966.
——— *APB Opinion No. 15.* New York, May 1969.
——— *APB Opinion No. 20.* New York, July 1971.
——— *APB Opinion No. 22.* New York, April 1972.
——— *APB Statement No. 4.* New York, October 1970.
——— *Statement on Auditing Standards, No. 1.* New York, November 1972.
DuCray, Dean T. "Tax disclosure under the SEC's ASR No. 149." *Financial Executive,* October 1974, pp. 74–79.
Goodman, Hortense *Illustrations of Accounting Policy Disclosure.* New York: AICPA, 1972.
———, **and McRae, Thomas W.** *Illustrations of Reporting Accounting Changes.* New York: AICPA, 1972.
Haskins & Sells *Accounting Practices, 1974.* New York, 1974.
Pacter, Paul "Some Comments on Applying APB Opinion No. 22," *The Journal of Accountancy,* December 1972, pp. 60, 61.
Richter, Robert F. "A Review of APB Opinion No. 22: 'Disclosure of Accounting Policies.'" *The CPA Journal,* January 1973, pp. 27–36.

Chapter 32

Reporting financial highlights, statistical summaries, and nonfinancial and external economic data

*Jack Kincannon**
Ben Hinsdale†
Carl Brauweiler‡

Every annual report should contain, in addition to an income statement, a balance sheet, and a statement of changes in financial position, a *statistical summary.* The summary usually covers five or ten years and includes important financial and nonfinancial items necessary to understand and evaluate the company. The important items in the statistical summary may be statistical computations from the financial statements, component items not specifically identified in the statements, or external data relevant to the company operations.

FINANCIAL HIGHLIGHTS

The financial highlights are key lines from the standard statements and summaries contained in the annual report. The reason

* Senior Vice President, Finance, Sears, Roebuck and Co.
† Director Shareholder Relations, Sears, Roebuck and Co.
‡ Director Accounting Research, Sears, Roebuck and Co.

for highlighting these key lines is to help the reader make a quick but accurate evaluation of the operations for the reported period.

The highlights should be presented early in the report: on the inside of the cover, on the facing page, or on the first page devoted to the report. The form of presentation is usually tabular, although the tables may be combined with a short narrative, graphs, or pictorial highlights. In some instances, the inside back cover or a centerfold is used; but the purpose is nullified if the highlights are found after all or a part of the report is read.

In order to make comparisons, it is necessary to have a minimum of two years in the highlights section. Frequently, three to five years will be presented along with a column or table showing the percent of increase or decrease for the current year. If the highlights are limited to two years, more key items should be presented for review.

The financial highlights should be presented in an appropriate form and in sufficient detail to allow not only an evaluation of past results but also an interpretation of the effect of current conditions and a forecast of the company's trend. At the same time, highlights should be limited or condensed to fulfill the main purpose of a quick overview of the company. The highlights are intended primarily for those who have some knowledge of the company or the basic industry of the company. For complete information, all of the statements, analyses, and narrative in the report must be read.

Usually, the most important financial highlight is the *net income or loss* for the period. Almost equally important is the *gross volume of business*. There are other very important items, but they do not apply to all industries or to all companies within an industry. Companies may wish to highlight specific parts of their operations, expansion for example, only when the information is necessary for an accurate evaluation of current results or trends. Other items which are important in many industries are cash flow, debt, interest expense, retained earnings, dividends, equity, book value per share, receivables, inventories, cost of sales, investments, capital expenditures, depreciation, taxes, sales by lines, and order backlogs.

Exhibit 1 is the highlights page from the 1973 Raytheon Company Annual Report. No rate of increase or decrease is given. It is necessary to read the report to find out why the stockholders' equity increased during the year while the outstanding shares de-

EXHIBIT 1

Comparative Highlights

	1973	1972
Net sales	$1,590,461,000	$1,465,031,000
Income before extraordinary item	$ 46,162,000	$ 41,174,000
Extraordinary item	—	$ 3,275,000
Net income	$ 46,162,000	$ 37,899,000
Earnings per common share:		
Income before extraordinary item	$3.03	$2.59
Extraordinary item	—	(.21)
Net income	$3.03	$2.38
Cash dividends paid:		
Common stock	$ 9,914,000	$ 9,370,000
Per share	$ .65	$ .60
Net working capital	$ 247,107,000	$ 236,051,000
Net property, plant and equipment	$ 148,580,000	$ 136,180,000
Stockholders' equity:		
Total	$ 356,138,000	$ 336,013,000
Per common share	$23.79	$21.59
Outstanding shares of common stock:		
At end of year	14,971,613	15,564,578
Average outstanding during year	15,217,912	15,898,052
Stockholders of record	22,864	24,736
Backlog:		
Total orders	$1,421,112,000	$1,008,634,000
U.S. Government funded orders included above	$ 653,256,000	$ 542,345,000

Source: 1973 Raytheon Company Annual Report.

creased. There is a large increase in order backlog, and the ratio of U.S. government orders to the total order backlog decreased.

The highlights section for Lowe's Companies, Inc., for the fiscal year ended July 31, 1973, shown in Exhibit 2, is an example of how stress can be placed on growth and performance in the data.

The increase of 39.3 percent in sales and 39.5 percent in net earnings is highlighted and then the information is repeated on a

EXHIBIT 2

Here's How We Did

Highlights *of the Year Ended July 31:*

	Change 1972-1973	1973	1972	1971
Total Dollars:				
Sales	+39.3%	$326,846,108	$234,556,133	$169,722,859
Pre-Tax Earnings	+39.9%	$ 25,393,076	$ 18,142,568	$ 13,027,470
Taxes on Earnings	+40.4%	$ 12,665,144	$ 9,021,981	$ 6,479,881
Net Earnings for Shareholders	+39.5%	$ 12,727,932	$ 9,120,587	$ 6,547,589
Cash Dividends Paid	+ 7.5%	$ 1,017,268	$ 946,119	$ 907,027
Earnings Retained and Reinvested	+43.2%	$ 11,710,664	$ 8,174,468	$ 5,640,562
Per Share:[1]				
Sales	+38.7%	$38.57	$27.81	$20.16
Earnings	+38.9%	$ 1.50	$ 1.08	$ .78
Dividends	+ 7.0%	$ .12	$ .11	$ .11
Earnings Retained and Reinvested	+42.3%	$ 1.38	$ .97	$ .67
Performance Measurements:[2]				
Asset Turnover		3.65	3.40	3.43
Return on Sales		× 3.89%	× 3.89%	× 3.86%
Return on Assets		= 14.22%	= 13.20%	= 13.25%
Leverage Factor		× 2.28	× 2.26	× 1.99
Return on Shareholders' Equity		= 32.42%	= 29.81%	= 26.31%
Five Year Earnings Per Share Growth Rate		28.39%	26.01%	18.07%

(1) To nearest whole cent. Change % computed from precise figures, page 17.
(2) See pages 14, 49 and 50 for explanatory notes.

Copyright 1973 Lowe's Companies, Inc.

LOWE'S
Companies, Inc.

1

EXHIBIT 3

Financial Highlights (in millions except per share data)	1974	1973
Revenues	$314.0	$290.6
Income Before Corporate Administrative, Interest Expense and Income Taxes	$ 33.5	$ 24.8
Corporate Administration	9.5	9.9
Corporate Other	.4	.2
Interest Expense	11.3	7.5
Income Taxes	5.4	3.2
Net Income	$ 6.9	$ 4.0
Per Share	$.74	$.21

Source: Bunker Ramo Corporation 1974 Annual Report.

per-share basis. Because of its excellent performance, the company is emphasizing the performance data in the highlights. The return on equity and growth rate lines in the highlights are indications that the company has confidence that the trend can be maintained. It should be brought out that regardless of the performance or the trend, net income is the one item which should always be included in the highlights of every company report.

The highlights page from the Bunker Ramo Corporation 1974 Annual Report, shown in Exhibit 3, is an example of less disclosure, but the facing page (Exhibit 4) had a narrative analysis of "The Year in Review" beginning with two five-year graphs for net revenues and net income. The pages which followed had detailed explanations of the corporate results including five-year graphs of interest expense, dividends paid, employees at year end, and equity per share.

STATISTICAL SUMMARY

The *quick current evaluation* of the company, which is the desired effect of reviewing the *financial highlights,* requires that this section be located in the front of the report. The *statistical summary,* on the other hand, is intended to portray the long-term operating results and is usually presented after all of the other statements, analyses, and descriptive narrative.

EXHIBIT 4

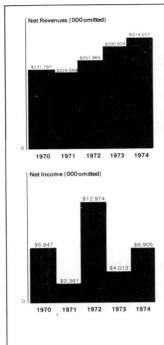

The Year in Review

Net revenues for 1974 were $314 million, an increase of $23.4 million over last year. Net income was $6.9 million or 74 cents per share, compared to $4 million or 21 cents per share last year. Net income for 1973 has been restated for the change in accounting method to expense research and development costs as incurred.

The downturn in the U.S. economy has had a negative impact on 1974 earnings. The textile, auto and brokerage industries and certain parts of the electronics industry were severely affected by the economic slowdown and consequently adversely affected our results for the year.

The 1973 electronics sales boom ended abruptly in mid-1974, leaving the Components Group with slackened orders in certain connector markets. The sales decline in the deep-pile segment of the textile industry caused Textile Group earnings to dip $2.6 million from 1973. Information Systems Group income was less than expected due to lower demand by the depressed U.S. securities market. The sales slump in the U.S. auto industry decreased 1974 car clock revenues.

Inventories increased approximately $12 million in 1974. These increases resulted from inflationary cost pressures such as higher raw materials costs and service costs, plus stockpiling of certain critical raw materials to assure a continuing supply.

One of the most significant impacts on earnings in 1974 was a $3.8 million rise in interest expense. The increased charges were due to both higher interest rates and higher borrowing levels.

To ensure continued credit availability, during 1974 the company replaced $20 million of short-term debt with a seven-year loan with our principal U.S. banks. Overseas debt has also been restructured with substantial amounts of short-term debt having been replaced with long-term. The recent downward trend of interest rates throughout the world should help to improve future earnings. The company in 1975 is also emphasizing internally generated cash-flow programs to reduce borrowing requirements.

Other factors which reduced income were certain government contracts, discussed in Notes 3 and 17 of the Notes to Consolidated Financial Statements. Income was increased by receipt of $7.5 million from IBM Corporation, as explained in Note 4.

Components Components Group sales were $174.1 million in 1974, an increase of $11.8 million over 1973. Group earnings were $23.6 million compared to $25.3 million in 1973.

European and Canadian Components Group operations achieved record sales and earnings during 1974. Good growth is expected to continue in both of these markets.

Bunker Ramo's Amphenol Industrial Division completed the acquisition of Progressive Tool Company of York, Pennsylvania, in March, 1974. Founded in 1956, Progressive Tool is a designer and supplier of tools, dies, and molds and also has a stamping facility. The acquisition has allowed the Industrial Division to increase its tool and die capacity and to expand high-speed stamping capabilities.

Source: Bunker Ramo Corporation 1974 Annual Report.

In order to show trends, most companies publish statistics for a minimum of ten years. If there is an industrial or corporate business cycle, the statistical summary should be broad enough to cover the cycle. Some companies list data from the year of inception. Exhibit 5 shows the statistical review from the Lowe's Companies, Inc., 1973 Annual Report as an example of the amount and type of information which can be presented in statistical summaries.

The annual report of most companies will not contain the

volume of information that the 1973 Lowe's Companies, Inc., report does; however, Lowe's statistical review gives an excellent quantitative history of the company. It includes the computation of the return on equity for each year, the compound growth rate in total sales by five-year periods, and the corresponding growth rate in net earnings.

Usually, the statistical summary is placed on two facing pages so that there is sufficient space for columns for ten or more years. The requirement of the Securities and Exchange Commission for a minimum of five years disclosure of operating results by line of business is frequently satisfied by the statistical summary. The primary problem is to limit the presentation to items of significant impact consistent with available space in the report after listing the data for mandatory disclosure requirements.

Although statistical summaries contain much additional information about the company operations, the summary should be limited to statistical data which show trends in company performance, or direct relationships to established criteria within the industry. The typical summary will cover ten years and will be divided into four sections: *annual operating results* from the income statement, *year-end balance sheet accounts*, *statistics on a per-share basis*, and *miscellaneous other data* and information. The statistics for prior years should be adjusted for stock splits, accounting policy changes, company acquisitions, or other significant financial events so that the amounts will be as nearly comparable as possible over the years.

The *annual operating results* section will usually be at the head of the statistical summary. Growth in absolute terms is best measured by total revenues, and this should be the top line. Net income measures the relative success of the company. If this line does not follow total revenues, ordinarily it will be set off or underlined so that the growth in net income can be followed to see how closely the trend parallels revenues. To help in comparing the trends, the statistical summary from the Inland Steel Company's 1974 annual report, Exhibit 6, also gives the net income as a percent of sales and as a percent of stockholders' equity.

If the company has more than one line of business the breakdown by line should be given in the summary so that the growth or decline in revenues and profit contribution can be evaluated. Income taxes, extraordinary items, depreciation, interest expense, cost of

EXHIBIT 5

16 Year Review of Performance

These figures reflect Lowe's internal growth since no acquisitions have been made during these years.

Year Ended July 31	15 Year Compound Growth Rates 1958-1973	10 Year Compound Growth Rates 1963-1973	5 Year Compound Growth Rates 1968-1973	1973
Stores and People				
1 Number of Stores	17.4%	16.4%	13.5%	100
2 Number of Employees	18.1%	19.5%	21.9%	3,296
3 Customers Served (Thousands)	18.0%	18.2%	18.3%	4,717
4 Average Customer Purchase				$ 69.29
Comparative Income Statement (Thousands)				
5 Total Sales	20.3%	23.7%	27.5%	$326,846
6 Pre-Tax Earnings	25.6%	26.4%	28.7%	$ 25,393
7 Taxes on Income	25.3%	26.2%	28.5%	$ 12,665
8 Net Earnings	25.9%	26.6%	28.8%	$ 12,728
9 Cash Dividends Paid	n/a	9.5%	6.1%	$ 1,017
10 Earnings Retained and Reinvested	25.2%	30.9%	32.8%	$ 11,711
Dollars Per Share (Nearest Cent) (1) (3)				
11 Sales	19.8%	22.9%	27.1%	$ 38.57
12 Earnings (2)	25.5%	25.1%	28.4%	$ 1.50
13 Cash Dividends	n/a	9.2%	5.9%	$ .12
14 Earnings Retained and Reinvested	24.8%	28.8%	32.3%	$ 1.38
15 Shareholders' Equity	23.1%	22.5%	24.6%	$ 6.10
Performance Measurements*				
16 Asset Turnover (Sales per Asset Dollar)				$ 3.65
17 Return on Sales (Earnings as % of Sales)				× 3.89%
18 Return on Assets				= 14.22%
19 Leverage Factor (Asset Dollars per Equity Dollar)				× 2.28
20 Return on Shareholders' Equity				= 32.42%
Comparative Balance Sheet (Thousands)				
21 Current Asset Totals	22.5%	21.3%	27.5%	$ 96,391
22 Cash	18.9%	11.1%	13.7%	$ 7,859
23 Accounts Receivable (Net of Reserve)	25.0%	22.4%	25.9%	$ 37,603
24 Inventories (Lower of Cost or Market)	21.7%	23.3%	32.3%	$ 50,639
25 Other Current Assets				$ 290
26 Fixed Assets	29.2%	34.3%	35.0%	$ 29,238
27 Other Assets				$ 85
28 Total Assets	23.6%	23.2%	28.9%	$125,714
29 Current Liabilities Totals	22.9%	22.8%	30.1%	$ 55,694
30 Accounts Payable	22.5%	21.8%	30.1%	$ 36,101
31 Income Tax Provisions	19.1%	16.8%	13.4%	$ 5,073
32 Other Current Liabilities	26.7%	30.5%	42.2%	$ 14,520
33 Long-Term Debt	25.7%	23.9%	39.7%	$ 18,238
34 Total Liabilities	23.6%	23.0%	32.2%	$ 73,932
35 Shareholders' Equity	23.6%	23.4%	24.9%	$ 51,782
36 Ratio: Equity ÷ Long Term Debt				2.84
37 Year End Leverage Factor: Assets ÷ Equity				2.43
Shareholders and Shares				
38 Shareholders of Record, Year End				3,704
39 Shares Outstanding, Year End (Thousands) (1) (3) (4)				8,487
40 Stock Price Range During Year (1)				$72.00-49.00

Explanatory Notes

(1) As adjusted to reflect a 100% stock dividend in May, 1966, a 2 for 1 stock split in November, 1969, a 50% stock dividend in December, 1971, and a 33⅓% stock dividend as of July 31, 1972.

(2) After deducting $2,250 dividends per year on preferred stock outstanding, for 1961 through 1972.

(3) For 1956 through 1961, per share figures are based on 8,000,000 shares, the restated shares outstanding at October 10, 1961, the original public offering date.

(4) Variation in the outstanding shares is the result of employee stock option transactions. No additional shares have been sold, or issued for acquisitions.

sales, and operating income are frequently shown in the statistical summary. The type of business, the debt-equity relationship, and the labor-materials-plant relationship are the primary factors which influence the types of statistical information which are necessary to evaluate the company properly.

The *year-end financial position* items listed in the statistical summary will generally include the accounts shown in the Inland Steel statistical summary above: working capital, property, long-term

1972	1971	1970	1969	10 Year Compound Growth Rates	5 Year Compound Growth Rates	Base Year 1968	1967	1966
86	75	64	58	19.2%	19.2%	53	44	39
2,630	2,071	1,670	1,450	16.2%	17.1%	1,223	1,017	891
3,820	3,194	2,729	2,290	17.9%	18.2%	2,034	1,755	1,636
$ 61.40	$ 53.13	$ 47.09	$ 51.98			$ 47.70	$ 43.14	$ 47.10
$234,556	$169,723	$128,491	$119,053	16.9%	20.0%	$ 97,031	$ 75,695	$ 77,043
$ 18,143	$ 13,027	$ 9,938	$ 9,514	24.1%	24.2%	$ 7,202	$ 5,151	$ 5,286
$ 9,022	$ 6,479	$ 5,068	$ 4,906	23.7%	24.0%	$ 3,609	$ 2,381	$ 2,496
$ 9,121	$ 6,548	$ 4,870	$ 4,608	24.4%	24.4%	$ 3,593	$ 2,770	$ 2,790
$ 946	$ 907	$ 844	$ 780	n/a	13.0%	$ 756	$ 661	$ 616
$ 8,174	$ 5,641	$ 4,026	$ 3,828	21.5%	29.0%	$ 2,837	$ 2,109	$ 2,174
$ 27.81	$ 20.16	$ 15.27	$ 14.15	16.4%	18.9%	$ 11.65	$ 9.20	$ 9.44
$ 1.08	$ .78	$ .58	$ .55	24.0%	21.9%	$ .43	$ .34	$ .34
$ .11	$ .11	$ .10	$ .09	n/a	12.5%	$ .09	$ .08	$ .08
$ .97	$ .67	$ .48	$ .46	21.1%	25.3%	$ .34	$ .26	$ .26
$ 4.64	$ 3.64	$ 2.96	$ 2.48	22.4%	20.5%	$ 2.03	$ 1.69	$ 1.43
$ 3.40	$ 3.43	$ 3.09	$ 3.37			$ 3.24	$ 2.65	$ 3.34
× 3.89%	× 3.86%	× 3.79%	× 3.87%			× 3.70%	× 3.66%	× 3.62%
= 13.20%	= 13.25%	= 11.72%	= 13.03%			= 11.98%	= 9.70%	= 12.09%
× 2.26	× 1.99	× 1.99	× 2.08			× 2.15	× 2.42	× 2.43
= 29.81%	= 26.31%	= 23.34%	= 27.07%			= 25.76%	= 23.49%	= 29.40%
$ 70,110	$ 54,911	$ 38,878	$ 33,433	20.0%	15.4%	$ 28,617	$ 24,164	$ 23,396
$ 7,802	$ 6,304	$ 4,658	$ 4,640	21.6%	8.6%	$ 4,129	$ 4,814	$ 3,024
$ 27,440	$ 20,944	$ 14,887	$ 14,559	24.5%	19.0%	$ 11,880	$ 9,675	$ 9,310
$ 34,475	$ 27,332	$ 19,040	$ 14,183	16.7%	15.0%	$ 12,475	$ 9,532	$ 10,931
$ 393	$ 331	$ 293	$ 51			$ 133	$ 143	$ 131
$ 19,330	$ 14,087	$ 10,390	$ 7,918	26.4%	33.7%	$ 6,546	$ 5,729	$ 5,058
$ 45	$ 88	$ 148	$ 209			$ 205	$ 99	$ 105
$ 89,485	$ 69,086	$ 49,416	$ 41,560	21.0%	17.7%	$ 35,368	$ 29,992	$ 28,559
$ 40,217	$ 31,198	$ 21,212	$ 18,505	19.5%	15.9%	$ 14,911	$ 12,503	$ 13,630
$ 27,684	$ 21,999	$ 15,178	$ 10,997	18.9%	14.0%	$ 9,703	$ 8,425	$ 9,496
$ 5,086	$ 4,293	$ 2,833	$ 3,380	22.0%	20.3%	$ 2,706	$ 2,177	$ 2,182
$ 7,447	$ 4,906	$ 3,201	$ 4,128	19.6%	19.8%	$ 2,502	$ 1,901	$ 1,952
$ 10,014	$ 7,296	$ 3,315	$ 2,192	19.3%	10.0%	$ 3,434	$ 3,527	$ 3,127
$ 50,231	$ 38,494	$ 24,527	$ 20,697	19.5%	14.5%	$ 18,346	$ 16,033	$ 16,765
$ 39,254	$ 30,592	$ 24,889	$ 20,863	22.9%	21.9%	$ 17,022	$ 13,959	$ 11,794
3.92	4.19	7.51	9.52			4.95	3.95	3.77
2.28	2.26	1.99	1.99			2.08	2.15	2.42
3,038	2,463	2,117	1,916			1,976	2,154	1,985
8,455	8,419	8,415	8,415			8,406	8,250	8,211
$66.50-30.00	$34.50-14.50	$18.00-9.50	$18.00-11.50			$12.00-6.00	$6.00-3.00	$5.00-3.50

Performance Measurements*

Line 20, Return on Shareholder Equity, may be derived by dividing Net Earnings by Shareholder Equity. But this approach provides no understanding of why and how this return was attained. It is better to "take it from the top" and think through each major variable, to facilitate understanding of their interrelationships.

Asset Turnover is affected by sales volume, by the cash-credit marketing mix and by the composition and performance of left-side balance sheet factors. The amounts of assets allocated to inventory, accounts receivable, and fixed assets, and the turnover rate of inventory and receivables, all affect Asset Turnover. For every $1.00 in Assets at the beginning of fiscal 1973, Lowe's achieved $3.65 in sales.

debt, and stockholders' equity. If important for a company, some of the components of working capital also may be listed. These would generally be inventories and receivables. If there is a major difference among components of the property account, timberlands and pulp factories as an example, these should be listed separately.

The statistics which should be listed on a *per-share basis* are income before extraordinary items, net income, net income on a fully diluted basis, dividends, and stockholders' equity (book value per share). Some companies also list cash provided by operations and the tax burden on a per share basis. Because of Securities and Exchange Commission requirements to show elsewhere in the annual report

EXHIBIT 5 (*continued*)

	1965	1964	5 Year Compound Growth Rates	Base Year 1963	1962	1961	1960	1959	Base Year 1958
1	35	28	19.6%	22	18	15	15	13	9
2	762	636	15.3%	555	491	399	360	334	273
3	1,284	1,141	17.6%	883	703	651	581	514	393
4	$ 44.44	$ 42.66		$ 44.?0	$ 46.52	$ 47.85	$ 52.80	$ 52.00	$ 52.00
5	$ 57,044	$ 48,680	13.8%	$ 39,012	$ 32,716	$ 31,128	$ 30,679	$ 27,005	$ 20,444
6	$ 3,942	$ 3,086	24.0%	$ 2,438	$ 2,054	$ 1,890	$ 1,359	$ 1,516	$ 833
7	$ 1,896	$ 1,518	23.5%	$ 1,233	$ 1,034	$ 956	$ 641	$ 760	$ 429
8	$ 2,046	$ 1,568	24.4%	$ 1,205	$ 1,020	$ 934	$ 718	$ 756	$ 404
9	$ 519	$ 460	n/a	$ 411	$ 402	$ 102	—	—	—
10	$ 1,527	$ 1,108	14.5%	$ 794	$ 618	$ 832	$ 718	$ 756	$ 404
11	$ 7.10	$ 6.14	13.9%	$ 4.91	$ 4.09	$ 3.89	$ 3.83	$ 3.38	$ 2.56
12	$ .25	$ .20	26.2%	$ .16	$ .13	$ .12	$ .09	$ .10	$ .05
13	$ .06	$ .06	n/a	$ .05	$ .05	$ .01	—	—	
14	$ .19	$ .14	17.1%	$ .11	$ .08	$ .11	$ .09	$ .10	05
15	$ 1.17	$ .97	24.3%	$ .80	$ .71	$ .63	$ .46	$ .37	$ .27
16	$ 3.20	$ 3.11		$ 2.98	$ 2.76	$ 3.32	$ 4.35	$ 5.13	$ 5.38
17	× 3.59%	× 3.22%		× 3.09%	× 3.12%	× 3.00%	× 2.34%	× 2.80%	× 1.98%
18	= 11.49%	= 10.03%		= 9.20%	= 8.62%	= 9.96%	= 10.18%	= 14.36%	= 10.65%
19	× 2.31	× 2.47		× 2.31	× 2.34	× 2.57	× 2.40	× 2.43	× 2.20
20	= 26.55%	= 24.78%		= 21.28%	= 20.23%	= 25.60%	= 24.43%	= 34.89%	= 23.40%
21	$ 19,187	$ 15,350	24.8%	$ 13,976	$ 11,702	$ 9,305	$ 8,071	$ 5,737	$ 4,618
22	$ 3,801	$ 3,374	36.2%	$ 2,735	$ 1,956	$ 1,299	$ 442	$ 365	$ 583
23	$ 7,165	$ 5,586	30.3%	$ 4,968	$ 3,769	$ 3,108	$ 2,858	$ 2,112	$ 1,324
24	$ 8,156	$ 6,337	18.5%	$ 6,214	$ 5,868	$ 4,801	$ 4,755	$ 3,164	$ 2,655
25	$ 65	$ 53		$ 59	$ 109	$ 97	$ 16	$ 96	$ 56
26	$ 3,832	$ 2,381	19.4%	$ 1,531	$ 1,261	$ 1,229	$ 1,253	$ 1,281	$ 630
27	$ 77	$ 73		$ 123	$ 134	$ 1,301	$ 58	$ 30	$ 19
28	$ 23,096	$ 17,804	24.3%	$ 15,630	$ 13,097	$ 11,835	$ 9,382	$ 7,048	$ 5,267
29	$ 11,213	$ 7,454	23.2%	$ 7,123	$ 5,696	$ 4,922	$ 4,874	$ 3,130	$ 2,513
30	$ 7,913	$ 5,149	23.9%	$ 5,036	$ 4,255	$ 3,187	$ 2,827	$ 1,562	$ 1,724
31	$ 1,671	$ 1,142	23.7%	$ 1,073	$ 855	$ 716	$ 521	$ 642	$ 371
32	$ 1,629	$ 1,163	19.4%	$ 1,014	$ 586	$ 1,019	$ 1,526	$ 926	$ 418
33	$ 2,377	$ 2,615	29.4%	$ 2,139	$ 1,680	$ 1,791	$ 862	$ 986	$ 589
34	$ 13,606	$ 10,097	24.6%	$ 9,304	$ 7,435	$ 6,792	$ 5,736	$ 4,116	$ 3,102
35	$ 9,490	$ 7,707	23.9%	$ 6,326	$ 5,662	$ 5,043	$ 3,646	$ 2,932	$ 2,165
36	3.99	2.95		2.95	3.37	2.81	4.23	2.97	5.26
37	2.43	2.31		2.47	2.31	2.35	2.57	2.40	2.43
38	1,871	1,967		2,034	2,047				
39	8,122	7,946		7,904	8,000	P,000	8,000	8,000	8,000
40	¼4.00-2.50	$3.00-1.50		$1.50-1.00	$2.50-1.50				

Return on Sales is the measurement of the efficiency of the sales organization. It is affected by sales volume, customer and product mix, and income statement factors — margin rates, fixed and variable expenses, and tax rates. 1973's 3.89% was our highest return on sales to date. This, multiplied by Asset Turnover, gives Return on Assets of 14.22%. This is the same as dividing Net Earnings by Beginning Assets.

Leverage gets us into right-side balance sheet factors, and measures equity dollars versus total asset dollars. For every $1.00 of shareholders' equity at the beginning of 1973, Lowe's had $1.28 in other liabilities, thus financing $2.28 in assets. This 2.28 leverage factor times the 14.22% Return on Assets gives Return on Beginning Shareholder Equity of 32.42%. See page 14 for further discussion.

Source: Lowe's Companies, Inc., 1973 Annual Report.

market price information if the common stock is traded on an exchange, more companies are now listing market price information in the statistical summary. This will usually consist of the range (the highest and lowest prices during the year), the year-end closing price and the price/earnings ratio based on the year-end price, and the earnings per share.

In order to tell the full story, *miscellaneous other data* are listed in the statistical summary. This information may require an additional computation using statement data, or it may not come from the

EXHIBIT 6

Ten-Year Summary of Financial and Operating Results

Inland Steel Company and Subsidiary Companies

	1974	1973	1972	1971	1970	1969	1968(1)	1967	1966	1965
Results of Operations dollars in millions										
Net sales	$2,450.3	$1,829.0	$1,469.8	$1,253.6	$1,195.1	$1,216.4	$1,129.8	$1,022.5	$1,082.6	$990.9
Taxes on income	125.0	73.6	49.5	40.2	30.5	45.3	58.8	37.1	49.7	56.4
Income before extraordinary items	148.0	83.1	65.9	47.8	52.3	58.7	77.6	53.6	66.1	68.8
Extraordinary gains or (losses)	—	—	—	—	(5.6)	2.2	4.1	1.2	2.3	—
Net income for the year	148.0	83.1	65.9	47.8	46.7	60.9	81.7	54.8	68.4	68.8
As a % of sales	6.0%	4.5%	4.5%	3.8%	3.9%	5.0%	7.2%	5.4%	6.3%	6.9%
As a % of stockholders' equity	16.5%	10.0%	8.2%	6.1%	6.0%	8.0%	11.2%	7.8%	10.1%	10.7%
Dividends paid—common and preferred	$ 52.2	$ 42.5	$ 39.6	$ 39.7	$ 39.7	$ 36.5	$ 36.5	$ 36.7	$ 36.6	$ 36.5
Capital expenditures	101.4	100.0	91.6	66.8	89.0	147.8	139.2	126.4	123.4	131.0
Depreciation, amortization, and depletion	74.0	71.2	69.6	61.4	62.5	52.7	42.4	80.8	76.9	72.3
Financial Position At Year End dollars in millions										
Working capital	$ 362.7	$ 272.9	$ 247.8	$ 228.9	$ 217.4	$ 137.5	$ 162.1	$ 194.0	$ 169.4	$175.7
Property (net)	934.1	908.6	870.6	851.6	852.4	841.0	773.1	685.2	644.1	625.7
Long-term debt	389.5	346.8	330.1	326.8	335.2	240.5	199.0	203.2	163.6	170.4
Stockholders' equity	939.3	849.3	811.5	786.9	782.1	774.7	750.1	708.5	691.1	658.8
Stockholder Data Applicable To Common Stock										
Approximate number of stockholders	72,000	71,000	71,000	75,000	79,000	69,000	59,000	52,000	49,000	41,000
Average number of shares (in thousands)	18,219	18,258	18,345	18,346	18,390	18,235	18,239	18,326	18,292	18,251
Primary earnings per share before extraordinary items	$ 7.96	$ 4.39	$ 3.43	$ 2.44	$ 2.68	$ 3.05	$ 4.11	$ 2.77	$ 3.48	$ 3.64
Extraordinary gains or (losses) per share	—	—	—	—	(.30)	.12	.22	.07	.13	—
Net earnings per share	7.96	4.39	3.43	2.44	2.38	3.17	4.33	2.84	3.61	3.64
Dividends per share	2.70	2.16	2.00	2.00	2.00	2.00	2.00	2.00	2.00	2.00
Stockholders' equity per share	49.10	43.75	41.51	40.10	39.64	39.40	38.43	36.02	35.46	33.73
Production and Employment Statistics dollars and tons in millions										
Tons of raw steel produced	8.0	8.2	7.8	6.5	7.1	7.5	7.0	6.8	6.9	6.5
Tons of steel shipped	6.1	5.9	5.2	4.7	4.7	4.7	4.8	4.5	4.7	4.5
Average number of employees	34,928	34,604	33,364	31,816	32,159	32,143	31,628	31,272	31,554	31,682
Total employment costs (2)	$ 612.3	$ 527.1	$ 457.9	$ 388.6	$ 364.4	$ 361.3	$ 329.5	$ 302.4	$ 306.5	$290.1

(1) As of January 1, 1968, the Company changed from the accelerated method of computing depreciation to the straight-line method for all assets, and changed from the "deferred method" to the "flow-through" method of accounting for investment tax credits. These two changes increased 1968 income $22,828,000.

(2) 1965-1973 were restated for comparative purposes.

Source: Inland Steel Company 1974 Annual Report.

regular statements. The Lowe's Companies statistical review shown earlier begins with items not available from statements: the number of stores, the number of employees, the number of customers, and the average purchase amount. The computations of various ratios also are presented: asset turnover, return on sales, return on assets,

EXHIBIT 7

Ten Year Summary

(Dollar amounts in thousands, except per share figures)

See Analysis of Summary on pages 12-15.

	1974	1973	1972
Summary of Operations:			
Net sales	$4,471,427	$3,601,535	$3,196,789
Costs and expenses	4,294,578	3,403,664	3,000,746
Income before taxes and extraordinary charge	176,849	197,871	196,043
Provision for taxes on income	82,222	94,443	95,408
Income before extraordinary charge	94,627	103,428	100,635
Extraordinary charge (net of taxes)	—	—	12,300*
Net income	$ 94,627	$ 103,428	$ 88,335
Dividends	$ 52,161	$ 49,331	$ 49,741
Per share of common stock:			
Net income	$3.41	$3.70	$3.13**
Net income—fully diluted	$3.38	$3.66	$3.10
Dividends	$1.882	$1.768	$1.768
Average number of common and common equivalent shares (in thousands)	27,741	27,945	28,190
Financial Position:			
Cash and temporary investments	$ 36,240	$ 33,987	$ 68,012
Notes and accounts receivable (net)	300,666	260,978	207,592
Inventories	793,045	558,611	464,269
Total current assets	$1,129,951	$ 853,576	$ 739,873
Total current liabilities	582,443	410,859	313,974
Working capital	$ 547,508	$ 442,717	$ 425,899
Property, plant and equipment (net)	524,393	479,612	459,475
Total assets	1,710,438	1,390,897	1,245,193
Long-term debt	237,473	143,019	135,466
Stockholders' equity	850,011	807,664	768,744
Per share of common stock	$30.67	$29.14	$27.41
Statistical Information:			
Capital expenditures	$ 94,164	$ 70,374	$ 87,139
Depreciation charged during the year	49,150	46,690	43,727
Total taxes—income, property, payroll and other	130,850	138,491	133,025***
Per share of common stock	$4.72	$4.96	$4.72***
Interest expense	39,281	16,957	11,829
Payroll	498,153	452,643	431,349
Average number of employees	50,410	48,909	48,948
Number of stockholders at year end	66,320	67,556	69,999
Number of shares of common stock outstanding at year end (in thousands)	27,718	27,720	28,046

*Extraordinary charge before tax benefit was $22,500,000.

**Income before extraordinary charge was $3.57 per share for 1972.

***Before tax benefits on extraordinary charge.

Income before taxes for all years has been restated to reflect state and local income taxes as part of the provision for taxes on income. Per share figures for 1965 have been adjusted to reflect the two-for-one stock split in 1966.

Source: Kraftco Corporation 1974 Annual Report.

return on equity, leverage factor, debt/equity ratio, and compound growth rates for all items. An explanation of the computation is given.

The statistical summary should also list the number of shares outstanding, and most companies will also list the number of shareholders. In order to make comparisons, some operating results or

Kraftco Corporation . . . and Subsidiaries

1971	1970	1969	1968	1967	1966	1965
$2,959,636	$2,751,129	$2,580,905	$2,428,106	$2,318,587	$2,251,725	$2,017,280
2,772,838	2,581,104	2,419,206	2,271,646	2,174,619	2,112,694	1,884,844
186,798	170,025	161,699	156,460	143,968	139,031	132,436
95,451	88,019	86,074	80,298	67,848	65,570	62,534
91,347	82,006	75,625	76,162	76,120	73,461	69,902
—	—	—	—	—	—	—
$ 91,347	$ 82,006	$ 75,625	$ 76,162	$ 76,120	$ 73,461	$ 69,902
$ 47,642	$ 47,507	$ 47,077	$ 44,886	$ 41,641	$ 40,413	$ 37,664
$3.25	$2.93	$2.69	$2.67	$2.65	$2.55	$2.41
$3.21	$2.92	$2.69	$2.67	$2.65	$2.55	$2.41
$1.70	$1.70	$1.675	$1.575	$1.45	$1.40	$1.30
28,094	27,978	28,111	28,497	28,718	28,861	28,936
$ 84,990	$ 51,653	$ 55,511	$ 92,913	$ 84,701	$ 69,466	$ 117,082
192,727	184,773	178,573	159,044	140,469	134,830	121,815
410,872	363,030	341,083	310,453	310,831	310,832	250,928
$ 688,589	$ 599,456	$ 575,167	$ 562,410	$ 536,001	$ 515,128	$ 489,825
267,270	241,027	249,308	202,750	190,449	189,524	180,824
$ 421,319	$ 358,429	$ 325,859	$ 359,660	$ 345,552	$ 325,604	$ 309,001
430,326	389,037	359,899	346,691	343,650	334,347	330,866
1,163,791	1,031,365	977,684	948,145	915,344	884,518	852,652
140,325	82,875	57,377	87,728	85,145	87,732	89,322
732,391	685,055	649,119	638,697	622,280	592,680	566,239
$26.10	$24.50	$23.25	$22.41	$21.66	$20.58	$19.56
$ 87,356	$ 75,526	$ 56,511	$ 45,799	$ 51,600	$ 42,481	$ 37,767
40,733	42,029	42,305	41,206	39,980	38,481	38,222
129,009	118,438	114,096	105,876	92,425	89,072	82,636
$4.59	$4.23	$4.06	$3.71	$3.21	$3.09	$2.85
9,777	7,589	5,436	4,865	4,397	4,471	4,157
392,997	368,038	346,973	323,257	309,905	301,407	280,983
48,091	48,179	48,160	47,007	47,060	46,525	45,157
71,461	71,538	71,584	71,702	72,352	71,240	68,762
28,064	27,965	27,921	28,339	28,672	28,801	28,936

balance sheet information may be listed under a miscellaneous statistical information caption as in Exhibit 7, the summary from the Kraftco Corporation's 1974 annual report.

Kraftco lists the capital expenditures for the year and then the depreciation expense. This shows the relationship between the funds generated from depreciation and the amount spent for replacement of facilities or expansion. The number of employees is listed with the total payroll expense. The Inland Steel Company statistical summary shown earlier also lists the average number of employees and total payroll together, and in addition, lists the tons of steel produced and steel shipped. Generally a company should list any item which would help to explain variations in its annual operating results, or which might be an important factor in estimating future operations.

NONFINANCIAL AND EXTERNAL ECONOMIC DATA

Corporate quarterly and annual communications to shareholders and other financial statement users are increasing editorial comment and graphics beyond the traditional financial contents. Although stockholders are most interested in comments directly relating to the company, pressures on large corporations from public advocates and government agencies have recently intensified.

Evidence of these pressures is the 66 shareholder resolutions brought to votes in the 1975 corporate annual meeting season. Exhibit 8 is a summary of shareholder annual meeting resolutions receiving significant shareholder support.

EXHIBIT 8

The 3-percent mystique: The Securities and Exchange Commission established 3 percent as the magic number that would ensure the survival of a resolution, taking the view that a corporation should not be required to go to the expense of circulating a shareholder proposal year after year unless the proposal obtained significant, and somewhat expanding, shareholder support. Thus, in Rule 14a-8, the commission provided that a corporation could omit a proposal from its proxy materials if "substantially the same" proposal has been included in the proxy materials and voted upon in any of the last five years, and the proposal either (a) did not get 3 percent of the votes the first time it was voted upon, or (b) did not get 6 percent of the votes the second time it was voted upon, or (c) did not get 10 percent of the votes any subsequent time it was voted upon.

At least until this year, the principal problem for shareholder proponents has been to obtain 3 percent of the votes, so that their resolutions will stay alive for a second year. On the basis of IRRC's preliminary figures from the 1975 annual meetings, it appears that

EXHIBIT 8 (*continued*)

proponents might expect in future years to receive at least 3 percent of the votes more often than not, and that their main problem will be to obtain the levels of support necessary to keep their resolutions alive for a second or third year, and then permanently. This year, five resolutions received more than the 10-percent level of shareholder support which, if maintained, would allow the sponsors to reintroduce those resolutions indefinitely.

The steady increase in 3-percent-support levels over the last three years is shown in this chart:

		Resolutions receiving more than 3%	
Year	*Total resolutions*	*Number*	*Percentage of total*
1973.	40	7	17.5
1974.	72	29	40.3
1975.	66	46	69.7

(It should be noted that not all the resolutions that received 3 percent or more were guaranteed survival. One of those resolutions in 1973, four in 1974 and 12 in 1975 needed either 6 percent or 10 percent to survive, but received less than 6-percent support, so for five years they cannot be proposed again.)

The 1975 survivors: Here is the breakdown of surviving and non-surviving resolutions, by issue:

		Total survivors		Total nonsurvivors	
Issue	*Total resolutions*	*Needing 3%*	*Needing 6%*	*Receiving over 3%*	*Receiving under 3%*
Political activity.	31	16	2	7	6
Strip mining	10	3	1	2	4
Equal employment	4	0	1	1	2
South Africa.	3	1	0	0	2
Media accuracy	2	1	0	0	1
B-1 bomber	2	1	0	0	1
Infant formula	1	1	0	0	0
South Korea.	1	1	0	0	0
Corporate governance	12	5	1	2	4
Totals	66	29	5	12	20

Source: Investor Responsibility Research Center, *News for Investors,* vol. 11, no. 6 (June 1975), p. 108.

An example of disclosure in the social responsibility area is shown in Exhibit 9 from Sears 1974 annual report to shareholders (table also disclosed in Sears 1973 annual report).

Since 1957 Sears Roebuck Acceptance Corporation, the wholly

EXHIBIT 9

Progress in Equal Employment Opportunity

Sears continued to make progress in its commitment to Equal Employment Opportunity last year. Our formal Affirmative Action Program establishes goals designed to balance our work force in all job categories, reasonably reflecting the labor force availability of the area surrounding each Sears employment unit. And as the figures below indicate, we have been making a successful effort to hire and promote minorities and women into jobs where they have previously been underrepresented.

Administering an effective Affirmative Action Program is a most difficult task. Management's challenge has been to increase the representation of minorities and women at all levels of our work force and to continue identifying and advancing qualified white male employes. In administering the Program, we are bound to disappoint some elements of our work force and of our concerned society. With both groups, our approach has been to seek a broader understanding of the requirements of the law and company policy as we hire and promote qualified and quali-fiable minorities and women at a rate which will achieve our long-term goals.

A graphic example of our achievements is in the important area of Officials and Managers. While the total number of Officials and Managers has risen by 7,481 (19 per cent) since 1969, the number of female Officials and Managers has increased 5,926 (78 per cent) and the number of male minority Officials and Managers has increased 1,333 (171 per cent). We have achieved this success both by promoting minorities and women into the category of Officials and Managers and through our College Recruiting Program. As of January 1975, 55 per cent of those college recruits in our Management Training Program were minorities or women.

Sears will continue to demonstrate good faith efforts to provide equal employment opportunity, and we will place great emphasis on full compliance by all company units with our policy of equal opportunity and non-discrimination in hiring, training, advance-ment, compensation and all other conditions of employment.

The table below shows the percentages and total number of Sears employes in each EEOC job category as of February 1969 and January 1975.

**Percentage of Male, Female and Minority Employes
In Each EEOC Job Category***

Job Categories	Male %		Female %		Black %		Asian American %		Native American %		Spanish-Surnamed American %		Employes in each job category (in thousands)	
Date	Feb. '69	Jan. '75	Feb. '69	Jan. '75	Feb. '69	Jan. '75	Feb. '69	Jan. '75	Feb. '69	Jan. '75	Feb. '69	Jan. '75	Feb. '69	Jan. '75
Officials and Managers	80.3	70.6	19.7	29.4	1.2	4.7	.2	.2	.1	.2	1.0	1.8	38.6	46.1
Professionals	85.3	52.4	14.7	47.6	.7	4.6	.2	.8	.0	.1	.3	1.7	1.6	3.3
Technicians	86.6	59.8	13.4	40.2	3.7	9.6	.6	1.5	.3	.1	2.6	3.4	3.4	2.1
Sales Workers	41.3	37.8	58.7	62.2	4.4	10.4	.6	.5	.1	.2	1.9	3.1	120.7	132.0
Office and Clerical	13.1	12.8	86.9	87.2	5.4	11.5	.7	.7	.1	.2	2.6	4.3	93.2	104.7
Craft Workers	94.6	94.4	5.4	5.6	4.0	6.2	.8	.7	.2	.3	3.4	4.8	24.7	26.6
Operatives	87.1	76.7	12.9	23.3	16.7	17.9	.7	.7	.1	.2	4.7	6.4	30.1	12.2
Laborers	59.6	73.2	40.4	26.8	24.7	21.9	.2	.6	.2	.3	9.1	6.1	14.1	41.4
Service Workers	64.4	60.6	35.6	39.4	39.0	31.6	.7	.7	.1	.2	2.5	5.6	13.3	15.3
All Categories	48.3	45.1	51.7	54.9	7.6	12.0	.6	.6	.1	.2	2.7	3.9	339.8	383.6

*Job Categories as defined by U.S. Equal Employment Opportunity Commission

Source: Sears, Roebuck and Co. 1974 Annual Report, "Progress in Equal Opportunity," p. 4.

owned consolidated finance subsidiary of Sears, has released a quarterly brochure entitled "Interpretation of Consumer Credit." This brochure is made available to corporate, institutional, and educational readers. The May 1975 report that follows is an example of external economic data which has received widespread interest.

Explanation of Exhibit 10 from the Sears Acceptance Brochure:

The Federal Reserve Board publishes seasonally adjusted monthly figures on the amount of instalment credit extended and the amount repaid. Disposable personal income estimates by the Department of Commerce are in terms of annual rates for each calendar quarter. To put the three series of figures on a comparable chronological basis, the monthly credit-extended and credit-repaid series are converted to annual rates for each calendar quarter (sum of the three months multiplied by four).

The excess of instalment credit extended over instalment credit repaid represents the extent of growth in the instalment debt outstanding, and since the first two are in terms of annual rates by calendar quarter, the same will be true of the latter.

The annual rate of growth in instalment debt has more meaning when it is related to the current level of disposable income than when it is expressed only in terms of dollars. Thus, for example, instalment debt was growing at the annual rate of $7.6 billion in the third quarter of 1965, and at the rate of $11.8 billion in the fourth quarter of 1971, but because of the higher level of disposable personal income at the later date, both rates of growth were equivalent in relation to the respective levels of income.

By expressing the dollar rate of growth in instalment debt as a percentage of the current disposable income, quarter to quarter, we find that the graph of these percentage ratios is a wave-shaped curve. Until the most recent expansion in the credit cycle, the wave usually crested around 2%–2.2%. 1.9% in III-1959, 2.1% in II-1965, and 1.9% in II-1969. (The relatively high 2.8% peak recorded in I-1973 was probably the result of some anticipatory buying of big ticket goods, particularly autos, plus a sharp growth in mobile home credit in recent years.)

In IV-1974 the ratio fell below the zero line; the last time this had occurred was II-1961. This means that instalment debt repayment exceeded extensions, thus reducing total outstanding instalment debt.

Approximately 30 million shareholders have no organized voice to combat the misinformation prevalent in our economic system

EXHIBIT 10

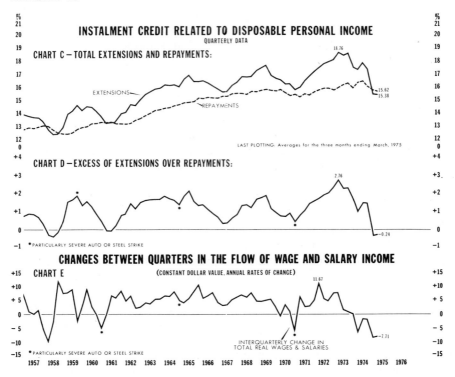

Source: Economic Research and Business Analysis Division Sears, Roebuck and Co.

CHART C. Extensions and repayments both rose less than Disposable Personal Income, as noted by the slight declines in the two ratios. In the current quarter, the extensions at 15.38% was below that of the trough in the 1969-70 recession, and the 1966-67 mini-recession, but much higher than the troughs of the 1960-61 or 1957-58 recessions.

CHART D. Net extensions of total credit stayed below zero for the second consecutive quarter. The ratio does show a slight uptick from the previous period due to a smaller rate of decline in extensions than in the repayments ratio. Net extensions for all components of credit were weak in the first quarter, but the monthly trends of each were unique and worth noting: Net Auto extensions were negative in January and March, but extensions exceeded repayments in the February rebate promotion. The Other Consumer Goods net remained steadily negative throughout the quarter. And Personal Loans began the quarter with repayments exceeding extensions, but in February and March repayments dropped below extensions so that the net ratio turned positive.

CHART E. Due to the large first quarter cutbacks in employment and hours, current-dollar wages and salaries declined at a 2.2% annual rate compared to the fourth quarter's 3.3% increase. This was the first decline in nominal terms since the 1969-70 recession. However, the rate of increase in the Personal Consumption Expenditures deflator slowed to a 6% annual rate, half of the previous quarter's increase. Consequently, real wage

and salary income eased to a 7.7% rate of decrease from the fourth quarter's 8.2% drop.

OUTLOOK. Price behavior, particularly in regard to food, as well as the tax rebates are helping to restore both real buying power and consumer confidence. Durable goods spending has already bottomed out, and should begin a very gradual uptrend from the second quarter on, but initially will lag behind the growth rate of real disposable income. Consequently, the net extensions ratio should remain below zero in the second quarter, but will move into positive territory in the second half of 1975.

today. Recent surveys of student attitudes indicate that students, both liberal and conservative, are misinformed about the level of corporate profits in our incentive economic system—the most productive ever devised.[1] Business has started to "speak out" and must

[1] James J. Kilpatrick, "Why Students are Hostile to Free Enterprise," *Nations Business*, July 1975.

adopt an internal and external approach to make its voice heard. An example of a meaningful internal approach is found in an eight-page section with specific graphic illustrations covering Consumer Information and Education in Sears 1973 annual report. This article outlined Sears policy, "Satisfaction Guaranteed or Your Money Back," and backed this up with the necessary criteria such as: (1) specific product guarantees, (2) information on product performance and serviceability, (3) point-of-sale literature, and (4) consumer education booklets covering a broad range of products.

In its 1974 annual report Sears eliminated the internal theme; however, Arthur M. Wood, chairman of the board and chief executive officer, sent each shareholder a special letter, Exhibit 11, which

EXHIBIT 11

Sears

Dear Shareholder:

Sears, Roebuck and Co. is a member of The Business Roundtable, an organization of 150 leading U.S. companies which concerns itself with national problems facing business. The following article is the third of a 12-part series of advertisements dealing with "Our Economic System", prepared and being published by the Reader's Digest under the sponsorship of The Roundtable.

This article, which appears in the April, 1975, issue of Reader's Digest, concerns itself with the subject of business profits. We hope that you will find it informative and that it will stimulate your interest in reading the full series.

In order for our system to survive there must be a broader understanding of how it works and the importance of supporting it. The Business Roundtable believes that the Reader's Digest series will help explain some of the fundamental precepts of our free enterprise system.

Arthur M. Wood
*Chairman of the Board and
Chief Executive Officer*

---

is an example of external disclosure dealing with "our economic system."

The article "THEM" explains the role of American business in our society. The article explains that income is the basis of creating a million new jobs in the United States each year, that business paid federal, state, and local governments more than $41 billion in annual tax revenues, and that the average U.S. company now makes a little less than a nickel profit on each sales dollar (not 28 cents profit on every dollar as polls indicate that the majority of Americans believe). Finally the article illustrates, as shown in Exhibit 12, that on a dress selling to a customer at $50, the manufacturer's profit was 92 cents and the retailer's profit was $1.30!

EXHIBIT 12

MANUFACTURER'S
COST AND PROFIT

Fabrics and accessories	$ 8.11
Design and factory operations.	4.91
Production wages and benefits	6.86
Administrative and sales salaries	3.97
Taxes.	.98
Profit from sales to retailer	.92
Wholesale price to retailer.	$25.75

RETAILER'S COST
AND PROFIT

Dress from manufacturer	$25.75
Advertising, sale markdowns, freight	5.55
Store operations	6.20
Payroll.	9.10
Taxes.	2.10
Profit from sales to customer	1.30
Selling price to customer	$50.00

The amount and type of nonfinancial data which a company includes in its shareholder reports depends on the company, the industry, and the competitive situation. The information can be included in the annual report within the statements, the statistical summary, and the narrative explanation—or it can be sent as a separate report to the investor. Almost all companies will show the number of employees in their statistical summary. The Inland Steel statistical summary, Exhibit 6 shown earlier, shows the following nonfinancial data: number of employees, tons of steel produced, tons of steel shipped, average number of shares outstanding, and the approximate number of shareholders.

In addition to the number of employees, many companies will have an organization chart; an outline of corporate objectives; the number and location of stores, factories, warehouses, and distribution centers; and other internal organization information. The merit of disclosing internal information must be balanced with the competitive situation and potential use by other companies in the same industry. It is becoming more common now to distribute a synopsis of the annual shareholders' meeting to all shareholders. These reports usually contain answers to questions relative to corporate operations which may not be clear in other corporate reports.

External data is used to show the position of a company in an industry, the effect of outside events or trends, and the relationship of the company performance to the economy as a whole. The external data is usually in tabular form, and the relationship of the data to the company should be explained. Exhibit 13 consists of

EXHIBIT 13

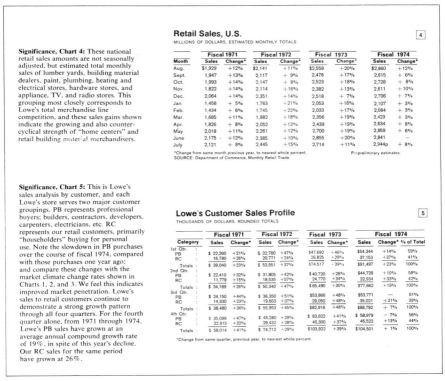

Retail Sales, U.S.
MILLIONS OF DOLLARS, ESTIMATED MONTHLY TOTALS [4]

Significance, Chart 4: These national retail sales amounts are not seasonally adjusted, but estimated total monthly sales of lumber yards, building material dealers, paint, plumbing, heating and electrical stores, hardware stores, and appliance, TV, and radio stores. This grouping most closely corresponds to Lowe's total merchandise line competition, and these sales gains shown indicate the growing and also counter-cyclical strength of "home centers" and retail building material merchandisers.

Month	Fiscal 1971 Sales	Fiscal 1971 Change*	Fiscal 1972 Sales	Fiscal 1972 Change*	Fiscal 1973 Sales	Fiscal 1973 Change*	Fiscal 1974 Sales	Fiscal 1974 Change*
Aug.	$1,929	+12%	$2,141	+11%	$2,559	+20%	$2,860	+12%
Sept.	1,947	+13%	2,117	+ 9%	2,478	+17%	2,615	+ 6%
Oct.	1,993	+14%	2,147	+ 8%	2,523	+18%	2,728	+ 8%
Nov.	1,822	+14%	2,114	+16%	2,382	+13%	2,611	+10%
Dec.	2,064	+14%	2,351	+14%	2,518	+ 7%	2,706	+ 7%
Jan.	1,458	+ 5%	1,763	+21%	2,053	+16%	2,107	+ 3%
Feb.	1,434	+ 6%	1,745	+22%	2,033	+17%	2,084	+ 3%
Mar.	1,685	+11%	1,982	+18%	2,356	+19%	2,423	+ 3%
Apr.	1,826	+ 8%	2,052	+12%	2,439	+19%	2,634	+ 8%
May	2,018	+11%	2,261	+12%	2,700	+19%	2,859	+ 6%
June	2,175	+12%	2,385	+10%	2,855	+20%	2,841	—
July	2,121	+ 8%	2,445	+15%	2,714	+11%	2,944p	+ 8%

*Change from same month previous year, to nearest whole percent.   P=preliminary estimates.
SOURCE: Department of Commerce, Monthly Retail Trade

Significance, Chart 5: This is Lowe's sales analysis by customer, and each Lowe's store serves two major customer groupings. PB represents professional buyers; builders, contractors, developers, carpenters, electricians, etc. RC represents our retail customers, primarily "householders" buying for personal use. Note the slowdown in PB purchases over the course of fiscal 1974, compared with those purchases one year ago; and compare these changes with the market climate change rates shown in Charts 1, 2, and 3. We feel this indicates improved market penetration. Lowe's sales to retail customers continue to demonstrate a strong growth pattern through all four quarters. For the fourth quarter alone, from 1971 through 1974, Lowe's PB sales have grown at an average annual compound growth rate of 19%, in spite of this year's decline. Our RC sales for the same period have grown at 26%.

Lowe's Customer Sales Profile
THOUSANDS OF DOLLARS, ROUNDED TOTALS [5]

Category	Fiscal 1971 Sales	Fiscal 1971 Change*	Fiscal 1972 Sales	Fiscal 1972 Change*	Fiscal 1973 Sales	Fiscal 1973 Change*	Fiscal 1974 Sales	Fiscal 1974 Change*	Fiscal 1974 % of Total
1st Qtr.									
PB	$ 22,260	+21%	$ 32,780	+47%	$47,692	+46%	$54,344	+14%	59%
RC	16,780	+26%	20,771	+24%	26,825	+29%	37,153	+37%	41%
Totals	$ 39,040	+23%	$ 53,551	+37%	$74,517	+39%	$91,497	+23%	100%
2nd Qtr.									
PB	$ 22,410	+32%	$ 31,805	+42%	$40,720	+28%	$44,728	+10%	58%
RC	11,779	+15%	18,535	+57%	24,770	+34%	32,934	+33%	42%
Totals	$ 34,189	+26%	$ 50,340	+47%	$65,490	+30%	$77,662	+19%	100%
3rd Qtr.									
PB	$ 24,150	+44%	$ 36,350	+51%	$53,866	+48%	$53,771	—	61%
RC	14,330	+23%	19,603	+37%	29,050	+48%	35,021	+21%	39%
Totals	$ 38,480	+36%	$ 55,953	+45%	$82,916	+48%	$88,792	+ 7%	100%
4th Qtr.									
PB	$ 35,099	+47%	$ 45,280	+29%	$ 63,622	+41%	$ 58,979	− 7%	56%
RC	22,915	+32%	29,432	+28%	40,300	+37%	45,522	+13%	44%
Totals	$ 58,014	+41%	$ 74,712	+29%	$103,922	+39%	$104,501	+ 1%	100%

*Change from same quarter, previous year, to nearest whole percent.

Source: Lowe's Companies 1974 Annual Report.

"Chart 4, Retail Sales, U.S." and "Chart 5, Lowe's Customer Sales Profile" from the Lowe's Companies' 1974 annual report. The significance of the Department of Commerce statistics, the company statistics, and the relationship of the increases for both are explained in adjoining columns.

In addition to trade association statistics, the primary sources of external data are state and federal reports. Government reports are usually available for many years for comparative purposes. The Jos. Schlitz Brewing Company, in a preliminary prospectus dated November 18, 1974, for a debenture issue (Exhibit 14), is able to esti-

EXHIBIT 14

Competition

The United States beer industry is highly competitive and the Company competes with national, regional and local brewers, and with imported beers. The Company's brands compete in different price markets, although all brands compete against the total market. *Schlitz* is sold in the premium beer market; *Old Milwaukee* and *Primo* are sold in the popularly priced beer market; and *Schlitz Malt Liquor* is sold as a premium specialty product.

The Company is the second largest brewer in the United States. In 1973 the Company accounted for 15.24 percent of the total industry tax paid sales in the United States (substantially equivalent to domestic sales). Expansion of brewing industry sales in the United States and those of the Company in the last ten years are shown in the following table:

COMPANY AND INDUSTRY SALES IN THE UNITED STATES

	In Barrels			Tax Paid Company Sales as
	Brewing Industry Tax Paid Only(1)	Company Tax Paid Only	Total Company Including Tax Free Export(2)	% of Tax Paid Industry Sales
1964	98,643,644	8,080,607	8,257,477	8.19
1965	100,411,085	8,371,243	8,607,104	8.34
1966	104,262,499	9,182,272	9,466,851	8.81
1967	106,974,363	9,794,311	10,099,598	9.16
1968	111,415,455	11,119,735	11,576,374	9.98
1969	116,271,320	13,175,459	13,709,359	11.33
1970	121,860,006	14,722,738	15,129,396	12.08
1971	127,374,997	16,367,166	16,707,934	12.85
1972	131,811,756	18,571,749	18,905,867	14.09
1973	138,449,266	21,096,280	21,343,071	15.24
1974 through August	100,633,314	15,906,570	16,102,175	15.81

(1) The data given with respect to the brewing industry represent tax paid withdrawals of malt beverages manufactured in the United States, as reported by the Internal Revenue Service of the U. S. Treasury Department.

(2) Export sales consist principally of sales to the United States Armed Forces.

Source: Jos. Schlitz Brewing Company, Preliminary Prospectus, November 18, 1974.

mate its share of the beer industry based on taxes paid for a ten-year period.

Data relative to market prices and price/earnings multiples are available from *The Wall Street Journal* and other publications. Although the tabular form is appropriate for most data, the effect of such items as the following may be difficult to quantify specifically: wage and price controls, bad weather, credit availability, strikes, and material shortages.

The company should determine the method—narrative, tabular, graphic, or a combination—for the clearest presentation of the point to be made. The information should be listed in the part of the report in which the relationship can be best established. If a long-term trend is depicted, the statistical summary is frequently used. The source of the external comparative data should be given. The greater use of internal nonfinancial data and external economic data to explain or clarify changes, trends, ratios, and balances has increased the understanding of financial reporting.

Chapter 33

Scope of the audit report: Coverage of the accountant's opinion

*Robert J. Sack**

AN OVERVIEW

The preparation of the annual report to stockholders is the responsibility of company management. Generally, the only item in the annual report which is not prepared by management is the report of the independent auditor. In the auditor's report, the auditor expresses an opinion on the presentation of the company's basic financial statements including the referenced footnotes. In the great majority of cases, the auditor's opinion is specifically limited to those basic statements, and it is not intended to cover any other part of the annual report. Occasionally, the company and the auditor will agree that the scope of the auditor's work and the auditor's opinion should be explicitly expanded to cover statistics, schedules, or other financial information presented. However, most of the text presentations in the annual report—the traditional president's letter, the newer management analysis of operations, and the organizational or component reports—are typically very qualitative and subjective, and given today's auditing standards, the auditor is precluded from providing any assurance on those commentaries.

* Partner, Touche Ross & Co.

Many auditors read the draft of their client's annual report before it is published, looking simply for inconsistencies between the basic financial statements and any of the other presentations in the annual report. And of course, the auditor may be one of a number of people to advise management and the board of directors as to the appropriateness of presentations in the annual report, the interim reports, and the other financial disclosures the company makes during the year. However, the purpose and scope of these reviews is, by definition, limited, and the auditor will not be able to express an opinion on the totality of the client's financial presentations to the public. The auditor's responsibility must be understood to be limited to those financial presentations which are explicitly identified in the scope paragraph of the auditor's report.

THE BASIC FINANCIAL STATEMENTS

A combination of common practice and regulatory and professional action has established a set of basic financial statements—the balance sheet, the statement of income, and the statement of changes in financial position. These basic statements are the standards by which a company's financial disclosures are measured. It is not clear why these statements were selected, and why some other presentations have been excluded. The selective process has simply been evolutionary.

The SEC's proxy rules specify only that an annual report must include such financial statements as management believes necessary to reflect adequately the financial position of the company at the end of each of the two most recent years, and the results of its operations for those two years. Kohler's *Dictionary for Accountants* defines financial position as "the assets and liabilities of an organization as displayed on a balance sheet. . . ." Kohler does not define results of operations, but *Accounting Principles Board Opinion No. 9* states, "The statement of income and the statement of retained earnings (separately or combined) are designed to reflect, in a broad sense, results of operations." For many years, the balance sheet and the statement of income were the traditional vehicles used by commercial entities to describe their financial affairs.

In 1967 the Accounting Principles Board issued *Opinion No. 12*, requiring disclosure of all material changes in the capital accounts. The *Opinion* provides that disclosure of those changes may take the form of separate statements, may be made within the "basic" financial statements, or may be shown as part of the footnotes. In *Opinion No. 19* (1971) the Board upgraded the flow of funds statement, taking the position that it was "essential for financial statement users, particularly owners and creditors, in making economic decisions." In that *Opinion*, the Board identified the "basic financial statements" as the balance sheet, the statement of income and retained earnings, and the statement of changes in financial position, as the funds flow statement was then renamed.

By definition, an evolutionary process responds to outside pressures. It may be that in future years the definition of basic statements—the basic statements which are essential to financial statement users—will again be expanded, perhaps to include some of that data which is now considered supplemental, such as a line-of-business statement or an analysis of historical trends. User needs will dictate any required expansion, and ultimately the accounting profession will acknowledge and codify those needs.

At this time, however, the three basic financial statements have become the standard vehicle for financial disclosures in the annual report. A company may present other financial and statistical information, but those presentations will be considered supplemental to the basic statements. Auditors may consult with their client regarding many different kinds of supplemental presentations in the annual report, though they do not commonly express a public opinion on those presentations. Auditors express their opinion on their clients' financial disclosures in the context of the basic statements, saying that they ". . . present fairly in accordance with generally accepted accounting principles the company's financial position, results of operations, and changes in financial position. . . ."

DISTINGUISHING RESPONSIBILITIES

Traditional accounting literature emphasizes management's responsibility for the preparation of the financial statements and, of course, for the annual report to stockholders. The SEC's *Accounting Series Release No. 62* (1947) discusses the possibility of extending the auditor's opinion to cover other data in a filing with the Commission, a subject of some controversy at that time. The ASR quotes the Commission in the Interstate Hosiery Mills matter as follows:

The fundamental and primary responsibility for the accuracy of information filed with the Commission and disseminated among the investors rests upon management. Management does not discharge its obligations in this respect by the employment of independent public accountants, however reputable.

That position had originally been stated by the accounting profession in a 1936 publication, *Examinations of Financial Statements by Independent Public Accounts*. The profession's current position is stated in *Statement on Auditing Standards No. 1* (the 1973 codification) in Section 110.02, as follows: ". . . the fairness of the representations made through the financial statements is an implicit and integral part of management's responsibility." That responsibility obviously holds for all of the company's communications with the public, not just for the financial statements.

Section 110 from *SAS No. 1* goes on to say that the auditor's "responsibility for the statements he has examined is confined to the expression of his opinion on them." In the context of that section of *SAS No. 1*, the purpose of that statement is to emphasize that auditors are responsible for their reports and that management is responsible for the statements. However, in the context of this discussion, emphasis should be placed on the fact that the auditor can only be responsible "for the statements *he* [or she] *has examined.*"

This identification of responsibility has legal ramifications, of course. But perhaps even more important, the reader of the annual report needs to understand the scope of the auditor's report in order to be able to differentiate between those presentations which have been examined by an independent auditor and those presentations which are solely the responsibility of management.

IDENTIFYING THE AUDITOR'S RESPONSIBILITY

The auditor's responsibility for the enumerated financial statements

In simpler days, it was easier for the reader of the annual report to understand the relationship between the basic financial statements and the supplemental data, between the data attested to by the auditor and the material which was management's responsibility only. In the past, the annual report was often little more than a president's letter, the basic financials, the related footnotes, and the auditor's report. Today, however, many companies provide the annual report reader with considerable additional information. A large part of this increase can be traced to the SEC's *Release No. 11-079* which required a number of new substantive presentations in the published annual report:

1. A five-year earnings summary and a qualitative management analysis of the significant changes.
2. A line-of-business analysis for the same period.
3. The market price performance of the company's stock during the latest year.

Also, the Accounting Principles Board in *Opinion No. 28* and the Financial Accounting Standards Board in *Statement No. 3* focused new attention on events (or year-end adjustments) in the fourth quarter. As a result, a number of companies have included a separate fourth quarter report as a part of the annual report. Finally, many companies, apparently responding to requests from the financial community, have been providing ten-year summaries, showing sales, net earnings, equity, number of locations, number of employees, and other significant statistics over the preceding decade.

This expansion of financial data in the annual report has blurred the distinction between the basic financial statements, audited and reported on by the independent accountant, and the remainder of the annual report which, as has been noted, is the sole responsibility of management. In an effort to avoid any confusion as to the items covered by the auditor's opinion—and the responsibility the auditor is taking—the auditor's report will usually refer precisely to the statements the auditor has examined, referring to the exact titles used by the company. For example, some scope paragraphs from 1974 audit reports read as follows:

> We have examined the consolidated balance sheets of Republic Steel Corporation and consolidated subsidiaries as of December 31, 1974 and December 31, 1973, and the related consolidated statements of income, income retained and invested in the business and changes in financial position for the years then ended.

> We have examined the accompanying consolidated balance sheet of Chrysler Corporation and consolidated subsidiaries as of December 31, 1974 and 1973, and the related statements of net earnings and changes in financial position for the years then ended.

> We have examined the balance sheets of Virginia International Company as of December 31, 1974 and 1973, and the related statements of income (loss) and deficit, changes in financial position, and capital in excess of par value for the years then ended.
>
> We have examined the consolidated balance sheet of Russ Togs, Inc., and Subsidiaries as of February 1, 1975 and February 2, 1974, and the related consolidated statements of operations, stockholders' equity and changes in financial position for the fiscal years (fifty-two weeks) then ended.
>
> We have examined the consolidated statements of financial condition of Richard D. Irwin, Inc., and consolidated subsidiaries as of February 28, 1975 and February 28, 1974, and the related consolidated statements of income, changes in shareholders' equity, and changes in financial position for the years then ended.

Still, that specific referencing may leave some confusion. The auditor's report in one 1974 annual report refers to the client's "Balance Sheets as of October 31, 1974, and 1973 and the related Summary of Operating Results and Statement of Changes in Financial Position for the years then ended." By coincidence, that company's annual report also includes a statement captioned "Ten-Year Summary of Operations," which presents earnings and balance sheet information for the most recent ten years. The ten-year summary is contiguous to the financial statements; in fact, it separates the basic financial statements from the auditor's report. Given this location and the similarity of titles between the ten-year summary and the earnings statement, a reader of the annual report, reading quickly, could be confused as to whether the auditor intended to cover the ten-year summary or not.

Some auditors have dealt with a potential ambiguity in responsibility by asking their client to mark certain data "unaudited." In the 1974 annual report from Evans' Products Company, the fourth quarter financial statements follow immediately after the auditor's report on the basic financials for the year. The company labeled that fourth quarter statement "unaudited." In the 1974 Avco Corporation report, the management discussion and analysis section is specifically captioned "not reported on by certified public accountants." In a number of situations, the auditor dealt with this question of coverage by specifically referring in the scope paragraph of the audit report to the page numbers of the statements examined. For instance, the auditor's report on the Westinghouse Electric Corporation 1974 financial statements does not refer to the individual financial statements examined but simply says:

> In our opinion . . . the consolidated financial statements appearing on pages 24 through 35 present fairly. . . .

The auditor's responsibility for footnote data

Interestingly, under traditional referencing practices, auditors very carefully identify the financial statements they are reporting on, but say nothing in their report about the supporting footnotes. However, it is clearly understood by all that the auditor accepts responsibility for the notes equal to that for the financial statements themselves. In fact, auditors understand that they are reporting not just on the fairness of the statements themselves but on the adequacy of the disclosures in the statements—which of necessity includes certain footnote data. Some would argue that the footnotes are simply one part of the related statement, and therefore the notes are covered automatically by reference to the specific statements. Technically, it can be said that the footnotes are covered by the auditor's opinion because each of the basic financial statements (which auditors itemize specifically in their report) includes a legend similar to "see notes to financial statements." Still, given the complexity of some of today's annual reports, a more explicit referencing scheme is occasionally necessary.

For example, the presentation of accounting policies may present unusual referencing problems. The Accounting Principles Board in *Opinion No. 22* required a statement of accounting policies with all financial statements. The method of presentation was optional, however: a company could present the statement of accounting policies as a separate stand-alone schedule or it could be included as an integral part of the footnotes to the statements. Practice appears to be mixed. Where a company presents a separate schedule of accounting policies, it would seem appropriate to have the financial statement legend read, "see summary of accounting policies and notes to financial statements," as for example in the Universal Foods Corporation annual report for 1974. The W. R. Grace & Company annual report for 1973 includes the following legend on all the basic financials:

The Statement of Accounting Policies, page 29, and the Notes to Financial Statements, pages 34 to 38, are an integral part of this Statement.

Some companies integrate the otherwise dry footnote data into the text of the annual report, and that practice also requires careful referencing. Associated Dry Goods Corporation in its 1973 annual report worked its footnote data into a section of its annual report captioned "Year in Review." The auditor, of course, was not in a position to assume responsibility for all of the management discussion in that section, but it was necessary that the auditor's report cover the footnote data contained therein. The company and the auditor resolved that problem by referencing the appropriate pages from the "Year in Review" within the legend on the basic financial statements. The legend reads:

See pages 9 to 14 of the Year in Review [which contained the footnote data] and pages 24 and 25 [which contained the Summary of Significant Accounting Policies].

The accountant's report simply refers to the traditional basic financial statements.

Ferro Corporation dealt with a similar concern by including the following statement as the last item in the Notes to the 1974 Consolidated Financial Statements:

Other Comments in Financial Review Section:
Refer to the Financial Review section of this report for comments under "Income Tax Expense," "Financing" and "Translation of Foreign Currencies."

Reporting on subsidiary statements

Often when a company carries a subsidiary (or an affiliate) on the equity basis, it is appropriate to present summarized financial statement information for the subsidiary in the footnotes to the basic financial statements. Typically, this presentation is appropriate when the subsidiary is "significant" as defined by the SEC and separate subsidiary financials are required for filings with the Commission. For example:

1. The Mead Corporation, in the footnotes to its 1974 financials, presents selected combined financial data for a group of jointly owned companies. Several of the jointly owned companies sup-

ply some of Mead's raw materials; the others are engaged in independent but related ventures.

2. Rockwell International Corporation, in the footnotes to its 1974 financial statements, presents combined summarized financial information for affiliates (apparently less than majority owned) and a somewhat more expansive presentation of summarized financial information for its wholly owned finance subsidiaries.

3. Hardee's Food Systems, Inc., in its footnotes for 1974, presents combined, condensed financial data for a group of partnerships with certain of its licensees.

Because these condensed presentations are included as part of the footnotes to the basic financial statements, they must be considered to be covered by the auditor's opinion on the financial statements. As noted earlier, the Westinghouse auditor explained his scope by saying, "The consolidated financial statements, appearing on pages 24 through 35, present fairly the financial position of Westinghouse Electric Corporation and its subsidiaries. . . ." The condensed financial statements of Westinghouse Credit Corporation are presented on page 35.

Occasionally, a company may decide to present more comprehensive financial statements of a nonconsolidated subsidiary, and will ask the auditor to specifically cover those statements in the auditor's opinion. For example,

1. Fruehauf Corporation, in its 1974 annual report, presents a full set of financial statements for Fruehauf Finance Company. The auditor's report on the parent specifically mentions the finance company statements in the scope paragraph and in the opinion paragraph. The scope paragraph includes these phrases, "We have examined the accompanying consolidated balance sheet of Fruehauf Corporation and consolidated subsidiaries . . . ," "We have also examined the accompanying consolidated balance sheet of Fruehauf Finance Company and consolidated subsidiary . . . ," and finally, "Our examinations were made in accordance with. . . ."

2. Anderson, Clayton & Company presents combined financial statements of its unconsolidated international subsidiaries in its 1974 annual report. Again, the auditor's report on the parent specifically covers these subsidiary statements: The opinion paragraph begins, "In our opinion, the aforementioned financial statements present fairly the respective financial positions of

Anderson, Clayton & Co., and Consolidated Subsidiaries and of the Combined Nonconsolidated International Subsidiaries of Anderson, Clayton & Co., at June 30, 1974. . . ."

3. Allis-Chalmers Corporation presented separate combined financial statements for its Credit, Financial, and Leasing Services subsidiaries. The auditor issued a completely separate stand-alone report, covering those specific statements as well as the traditional report on the consolidated statements.

In all of these cases the auditor expresses an opinion on the consolidated financial statements, and that opinion is intended to cover the company's investment in the unconsolidated subsidiary and the subsidiary's net earnings or loss included as a part of the consolidated statements. By extending his or her opinion to the full financial statements of the subsidiary, the auditor is acknowledging a normal examination of the subsidiary just as though it had been a stand-alone entity. And the auditor is accepting greater responsibility than if an opinion was only expressed on the consolidated statements, which included the subsidiary's numbers as a single item. From a practical standpoint that extended responsibility means that the auditor will have to make a much more intensive examination of the subsidiary's accounts and records than if he or she were simply reporting on the consolidated financial statements. It also means that the materiality standard is different: for purposes of reporting on the subsidiary, questions of materiality must be decided by using the subsidiary's assets (or revenues or net worth, as appropriate) as the basis, not the assets in the consolidated financial statements.

OTHER PROBLEMS IN IDENTIFYING RESPONSIBILITIES

Engagements with more than one auditor

Some companies have found it necessary to use more than one auditor to cover the entire entity. After the unfortunate Atlantic Acceptance case, the accounting profession developed strong guidelines for the conduct of such engagements. The requirements established by the profession in the United States are included in *SAS No. 1*, Section 543. These professional requirements permit a principal auditor to express an opinion on the financial statements taken as a whole without making reference to the participation of another auditor. However, many auditors prefer to mention in their report the "other auditor's" involvement because of a concern that by remaining silent they could be construed as accepting responsibility for the other auditor's work. Typically, a principal auditor will only accept another auditor's examination of the financial statements of a component where the component is relatively immaterial to the total entity.

Where the principal auditor decides to refer to the participation of another auditor, standard words will be used which the profession has agreed on for the scope and the opinion paragraphs of the audit report. It is understood that these "reference comments" are not intended to be qualifications in the principal auditor's report but are intended simply to indicate a sharing of the responsibility. For example, the audit report on the financial statements of The Upjohn Company for 1973 includes the following sentence in the scope paragraph:

> We did not examine the financial statements of certain consolidated foreign subsidiaries which statements reflect total assets and revenues constituting 17% and 18% respectively of the related consolidated totals. These statements were examined by other auditors whose reports thereon have been furnished to us and our opinion expressed herein insofar as it relates to the amounts included for such foreign subsidiaries, is based solely upon such reports.

The opinion paragraph begins with this sentence:

> In our opinion, based upon our examination and the reports of other auditors, the aforementioned financial statements present fairly the consolidated financial position of The Upjohn Company and Subsidiaries. . . .

SAS No. 1 requires the principal auditor to cite the magnitude of the components examined by the other auditor. It permits, but does not require, the identification of the other auditor. In practice, the other auditor is rarely identified in the published annual report. In filings with the SEC, however, if the principal auditor refers to the participation of another auditor, the other auditor's report must be provided in the filing.

Reporting on two years

Most companies present comparative financial statements for the current year and the prior year in their annual reports. If the auditor has examined both years' financial statements, the report can easily be written to express an opinion on both years. If another auditor examined the prior year, however, the presentation is a little more complicated. The auditor for Coquina Oil Corporation solved the problem by covering the current year (1973) in the scope and opinion paragraphs of the current report and adding the following paragraph immediately after the opinion:

> The financial statements of Coquina Oil Corporation and its subsidiaries for the year 1972 were examined by other independent accountants.

The other accountants were not named nor was their report presented. Mountain Banks, Ltd. solved the problem in a different way in their 1974 annual report: The current auditor's report on the 1974 financials and the prior auditor's report on the 1973 financials were both presented, side by side, on the same page.

Subsequent events

The financial statements reflect the company's status as of the fiscal year-end, the balance sheet date. The auditor and client monitor events which occur subsequent to the balance sheet date to see whether those events should be reflected in the financial statements under examination, or whether they are more appropriately reflected in the results of the next year. That discovery and allocation process continues throughout the post-balance sheet period, from the balance sheet date to the date the auditor completes the audit. It is understood that the auditor dates his or her report on the date the audit was completed. It is also understood that the auditor has considered any important transactions which occur during this specifically identified post-balance sheet period.

Occasionally something happens during that hiatus between the time the auditor finishes the examination and the time that the annual report can be assembled and published. Typically, a company will want to recognize any such event in a "subsequent events" footnote, even though the auditor has already signed off on the financial statement presentation. In this situation, there are three ways to proceed: First, the auditor can bring the subsequent event footnote within the scope of his or her opinion simply by dating the report as of the current date. To do so, however, the auditor will be required to extend the review of all post-balance sheet events up to the current date. Because of the additional cost and time involved in that review, some clients prefer to keep the subsequent event footnote outside the scope of the auditor's opinion. The Damon Corporation included a footnote in its 1973 annual report describing a post-balance sheet agreement to acquire two businesses. The caption to the footnote read:

> Event (unaudited) subsequent to the date of the report of certified public accountants.

In some cases, the subsequent event is important to the auditor's evaluation of the financial statements and the event must be covered in the auditor's opinion. If the auditor cannot extend his or her review of subsequent events beyond the date the audit was originally completed, the auditor may simply double-date the audit report, to indicate the recognition of the one isolated event. The auditor reporting on the 1974 financial statements of Nease Chemical Company, Inc., dated the audit report:

> February 21, 1975 (March 27, 1975 as to note five).

Note five described an important amendment to the company's term loan agreement which was consummated in March 1975.

Expanding the auditor's traditional coverage

So far this chapter has dealt only with the auditor's responsibility for the financial statements and the related footnotes. As noted earlier, there is considerable additional financial information now being included in annual reports to stockholders. And a logical question to ask is, Why shouldn't the auditor extend his or her opinion to this additional financial data, beyond the basic financial statements? It would appear that there is a small trend in the direction of expanding the coverage of the auditor's report, and it will be useful to explore some specific examples from recent annual reports. First, however, it would be well to review some of the criteria which can be used to decide what information can be and what information should not be attested to by the auditor. There are several places to look for guidance.

1. A committee of the American Accounting Association issued *Studies in Accounting Research No. 6*, "A Statement of Basic Auditing Concepts" (1973), which suggests the following conditions to the coverage of any information by the auditor.

    a. The information must be supported by evidence; it must be quantifiable and verifiable.

    b. The information to be reported on must be the result of an information system.

    c. There must be accepted criteria for evaluating the presentation.

2. D. R. Carmichael, the director of the AICPA's Auditing Standards Division, reviewed this question in an article in the September 1974 issue of the *Journal of Accountancy.* He suggests that the conditions outlined in the AAA report are satisfactory precedents for a traditional auditor's report, equivalent to that customarily given on the basic financial statements. However, he argues that for some "other information" it may be appropriate for the auditor to offer (and the public to accept) a different level of assurance than might be expected for the basic financial statements. He concludes that the auditor's examination can be extended beyond traditional, quantifiable financial data, but that it is probably not possible to give the same level of assurance as had been traditionally expected.

3. The AICPA's *Statement on Auditing Standards No. 1* describes "long form reports" and "special reports" and suggests that an auditor may report on various financial and nonfinancial presentations. These reporting sections of *SAS No. 1* do not specifically deal with the auditability of presentations other than the traditional financial statements, but there is a useful analogy in the section on *comfort letters. SAS No. 1* Section 630, suggests that an auditor should only comment on items in a comfort letter which:

    a. Is information expressed in dollars (or percentages) and which has been obtained from records subject to the company's system of internal control, or

    b. Which has been derived directly from such records by analysis or computation, or

    c. Which is quantitative information that is subject to the same controls as the dollar data.

That section of the SAS specifically cautions the auditor not to comment on "matters involving primarily the exercise of business judgment of management." It appears to be saying that in these areas of "business judgment" there are no objective standards for an auditor to use in measuring and reporting.

The auditors are adhering to these guidelines and constraints. A number of 1974 annual reports show some expansion of the auditor's traditional opinion, but generally not beyond quantitative, systems based, evidence supported, financially oriented information. For example:

1. The auditor's report on the Polychrome Corporation's financial statements says, "We have also examined the summary of operations (included on page 3) for the five years ended December 31, 1974." The auditor's opinion concludes, ". . . and the summary of operations summarizes fairly the results for the five years ended December 31, 1974. . . ."

2. The auditors for Puget Sound Power & Light Company included the following third paragraph in their report on the 1974 financials:

   "In addition, we have read certain historical accounting information included in the nonfinancial statement sections of this annual report as identified therein; have compared it to data taken from the audited financial statements; have subjected it to audit procedures; have verified its mathematical accuracy. In our opinion, such data is fairly stated in relation to the audited financial statements taken as a whole."

3. The chartered accountants reporting to Westinghouse Canada Limited included this final paragraph in their accountant's report:

   "We have also examined the statement of ten-year highlights for the years 1965 to 1974 inclusive, presented as supplementary information. In our opinion, this statement presents fairly the information shown therein."

4. In the Avco annual report, the audit opinion concludes with this final sentence:

   "Further, in our opinion, the business line analysis for the 1974 and 1973 years in the Financial Review, when read in conjunction with the consolidated financial statements, is fairly stated in all respects material to the consolidated and combined results of operations."

5. In the J. C. Penney Company, Inc., annual report for 1974, the auditor concludes:

> "Also, in our opinion, the accompanying statistical data on pages 30, 31 and 33 present fairly the information shown therein."

> Page 30 includes the traditional ten-year financial summary. Page 31 is a ten-year operations summary detailing statistics about numbers of stores, store sizes, and store characteristics. Page 33 is an analysis of store space opened during the fiscal year.

A number of companies bind their annual report to the SEC, the Form 10-K, into their published stockholder annual report. The SEC has always insisted that the auditor's report cover specifically the schedules which are required to be furnished with the Form 10-K. And in each case where the Form 10-K was included in the annual report to the stockholders, the auditor's opinion was extended to cover the schedules which were included. See for example the auditor's reports in the 1974 annual reports of:

> Kewanee Oil Company—"Our examination, referred to above, also included the financial schedules listed in answer to Item 10. In our opinion, such financial schedules present fairly the information required to be set forth therein."

> NVF Company—"and the supporting schedules, in our opinion, present fairly the information set forth therein."

Note that in each of the above cases, the auditor introduces his or her comments on this other information by using the words "also" or "in addition." The auditor's primary obligation is to see that the disclosure requirements of the basic statements are met. If the basic statements are complete in and of themselves, then by definition any other presentations must be considered supplemental. Where the auditor reports on data outside the basic statements, the auditor will be careful to designate that information as simply additional information—and therefore not necessary for a fair presentation of financial position or results of operations.

The concern about inflation has prompted several interesting extensions of the audit report. For a number of years Indiana Telephone Corporation has presented financial statements with two columns, one on the historical cost basis and one on a price-level adjusted basis. ITC's auditor has covered the historical cost financial statements with the traditional two-paragraph report and has also included a third paragraph which covers the restatement to reflect price-level adjustments. That third paragraph reads:

> In our opinion, however, the accompanying financial statements shown under Column B more fairly present the financial position of the Corporation as of December 31, 1973, and the results of its operations for the year then ended, as recognition has been given to changes in the purchasing power of the dollar as explained in Note 1(a).

Barber-Ellis of Canada, Limited, took a different approach. In their annual report for 1974 they presented the normal historical financial statements with the traditional chartered accountant's report. But the company also presented, as supplementary information, a full set of financial statements restated on a current replacement cost basis. The chartered accountants reported on the supplementary financial information as follows:

> In conjunction with our examination of and report on the financial statements of Barber-Ellis of Canada, Limited for 1974 we have also examined the accompanying supplementary financial statements which have been prepared on a current replacement cost basis.

> Uniform criteria for the preparation and presentation of such supplementary financial information have not yet been established and accordingly, acceptable alternatives are available as to their nature and content. In our opinion, however, the accounting basis described in the notes to the supplementary financial statements has been applied as stated and is appropriate in these circumstances.

The auditor's responsibility for the remainder of the annual report

The auditors have tried to be very precise in explaining the degree to which they have been involved in their client's annual report, by defining as precisely as possible the statements and schedules covered by their opinion. The annual report reader must assume that the auditor has not examined any other part of the annual report, and that any presentation not specifically referred to in the auditor's report is solely the responsibility of company management. This division of responsibilities is a given assumption for both the auditor and the client. The audit staff and the client's financial people plan the scope of their work based on this understanding.

Even with understanding of the formal division of responsibilities, many auditors make it a practice to read carefully the draft of their client's published annual report in its entirety. There are two reasons for such a review: First, because of broad experience in evaluating financial presentations and familiarity with the requirements of the SEC and other regulatory bodies, the auditor is often able to make independent recommendations to a client about presentations in the annual report, particularly where there have been unusually complicated accounting transactions during the year. Second, and perhaps more compelling, the auditor feels that a reading of the complete draft of the published report is an important audit step, a challenge for possible inconsistencies between the representations in the basic financial statements and the other financial and statistical representations made in the highlights, the President's letter, the five-year summary, or in any of the other sections of the annual report. For example, the division managers, in their text report to the shareholders, may provide a new perspective on a transaction, and the auditor may conclude that the financial statements should be revised to reflect the substance of the transaction as it is now understood. Or, there may be a situation where the auditor concludes that the presentation in the text is inconsistent with the presentation in the basic financial statements, but the financials appear to be correct.

Most often the auditor and the client will agree as to the change required. Unfortunately, however, a disagreement will sometimes develop, and the auditor will then be faced with a difficult decision. If, after studying the matter, the auditor concludes that the financial statements are in error and the text presentation is correct, the auditor may decide that his or her report on the financials should be qualified. Or the inconsistent presentations may simply raise questions about the financial statements which cannot be resolved—and that uncertainty may also have to be expressed as a qualification in the auditor's report. It is possible that the auditor will conclude that the financial statements are correctly stated but the other presentation is in error. It is not clear what the auditor should do in that situation. Auditors have no stated responsibility for the non-financial statement presentation, but most auditors would acknowledge an implied responsibility for an apparent misstatement which had come to their attention. The auditor for Kingstip, Inc., was confronted with this very difficult problem and dealt with it by including the following final paragraph in his report:

> Attention is drawn to the fact that the presentation with regard to the loss from disposition of discontinued plant operations in 1974 as displayed in the President's Letter on page 3 and in the Eight-Year Summary on page 8 is presented in a manner different from the above-mentioned Consolidated Statement of Earnings, which is presented in accordance with generally accepted accounting principles.

The auditing profession has been concerned about the conflict between good business practice, which seems to require at least a reading of the client's annual report, and the exposure to greater responsibility which is certain to come if the auditor becomes "associated with" nonfinancial statement presentations. The Auditing Standards Executive Committee of the AICPA has been working on a project to define specifically the auditor's responsibility for information in the annual report, apart from the basic financial statements, and to describe the procedures an auditor should follow when the auditor's report is incorporated in documents published by a client. The Committee issued an exposure draft of a position paper on March 15, 1975, entitled, "Other Information in Documents Containing Audited Financial Statements." The exposure draft restates the classic position that the auditor's responsibility does not extend beyond the specific presentation identified in the auditor's report. It goes on to say, however, that while the auditor need not corroborate any of the other information included in a client's annual report, the entire report should be read, looking for conflicts or inconsistencies. The exposure draft does not tell the auditor what to do if the auditor concludes that there is a conflict which he (or she) is not able to resolve, except to say that "the action to be taken will depend on his [or her] judgment in the particular circumstances."[1]

The comments on the exposure draft have been mixed. Some have said that it is too general, and that the auditor should be given specific guidance as to the scope of the review of such "other

---

[1] In December 1975, the Auditing Standards Executive Committee of the AICPA approved *Statement on Auditing Standards No. 8*, "Other Information in Documents Containing Audited Financial Statements." The substance of the final statement is as described here.

information" and the procedures to be followed in resolving problems. Some have argued that the draft statement should not be issued because it might extend the auditor's responsibility in an undefined, unmanageable way. Some have said that the draft does not go far enough and that the auditor should assume greater responsibility for a client's annual report presentations.

No matter how this exposure draft is dealt with finally, it seems quite clear to the author that the auditor's reading of a client's draft annual report is a worthwhile audit procedure. Normally, this reading by the auditor can be accomplished with a minimum of cost and disruption. It requires only reasonable coordination and some specific timing commitments between all parties.

Typically, one of the senior people on the audit engagement will read the entire report. The reading is more productive if it is performed by someone with a long-time association with the client and a broad business background. The less experienced people on the audit staff will be responsible for cross-referencing the numbers and the statistics in the body of the annual report and in the basic financial statements with the audit workpapers.

Incidentally, someone on the audit team should be responsible for proofreading the auditor's report which has been reproduced in the draft annual report. Frequently, auditors deliver a series of audit reports to their clients: at the same time, they will deliver their opinion on the basic financial statements to be included in the annual report, the audit report to accompany the financial statements and schedules to be filed with the 10-K, and perhaps even an audit report to be furnished to a bond trustee describing the company's compliance with the terms of the indenture. All too often, in the last-minute rush of assembling the material for the printing of the annual report, the wrong audit opinion is published. And in one situation, the printer's composing room found that they really did not have space for the full, two-paragraph auditor's report. They rewrote the audit report, squeezing into one line at the bottom of the page the following shortcut, "In our opinion, the financial statements above present fairly the financial position of. . . ." It's hard to argue with the clarity of that phrase, but unfortunately, it does not meet the auditing profession's technical standards. The client and the auditor both put considerable effort into the financial statements and the annual report presentations; a last-minute touching of all the bases would seem to be well justified.

PROSPECTS FOR THE FUTURE

While it is true that there are some interesting examples of expanded auditor reports, nothing in 1974 practice indicates a dramatic extension of the auditor's attest function to other areas of the annual report, beyond the basic financial statements. However, there are some new developments in financial reporting which could require (or give an opportunity to) the auditor to accept a broader responsibility.

1. Some of the more actively traded companies will be required to present a footnote with their 1976 financial statements, summarizing quarterly operating and earnings information as previously reported in their 1976 interim reports. (*ASR 177;* September, 1975.) The accounting profession objected originally to this proposal because it would apparently have brought the interim data under the auditor's opinion. The SEC has agreed that the interim data footnote could be labeled "unaudited," but it has insisted that the auditor review the data and report any unadjusted differences. The profession accepted that compromise and, in fact, the AICPA's Auditing Standards Executive Committee has suggested some minimum review procedures.[2] Most companies will ask their auditors to perform that review before the quarterly financials are released, to avoid the possibility of making a significant adjustment at year-end.

    It is not clear, however, whether the auditor's reports on the 1976 annual financial statements explain the scope of work done on the interim data footnote, or whether the auditors will remain silent about the review procedures performed. It may be that because of the limited scope of the review procedures, the auditors will be reluctant to explicitly extend their responsibility to the interim data. That decision will be understandable, but in the author's opinion it will be regrettable. The financial community will be aware of the auditor's involvement, particularly if they believe that there is a need for an independent review of the interim statements. If the auditor has performed such a review, he (she) has an obligation to remove any ambiguity about his (her) responsibility. The profession must find a way to communicate the results of a review of less than full scope.

---

[2] *Statement on Auditing Standards No. 10,* "Limited Review of Interim Financial Information," was formally adopted in December 1975.

2. It seems likely that companies will eventually provide some
    forecast data regarding next year's operating results in their
    annual reports. The SEC recognized that many companies pro-
    vide informal forecasts to financial analysts and some special
    investor groups. The Commission suggested that forecasting be
    formalized and included as part of the regular corporate dis-
    closure system. That proposal ran into unexpectedly strong
    criticism, however, and it may be put on the backburner for the
    time being.

    Nonetheless, it seems inevitable that a few companies will
    capitalize on their strong forecasting systems and include an
    estimate of next year's results in a current year's annual report.
    Competitive pressures might move more companies to follow
    suit—and to ask for an auditor's attestation. An auditor ought
    to be able to report on a forecast. The forecast financial data
    would appear to meet the three criteria suggested by the Amer-
    ican Accounting Association, which were described earlier.

    a. The forecast presentation would certainly be quantitative.
        Presumably, the presentation would follow a normal financial
        statement format, and would also compare this year's actual
        against last year's forecast.

    b. A company is not likely to step into the forecasting area
        unless it has a substantial system for developing the data.
        An auditor ought not to be associated with a forecast un-
        less the client's forecasting system has demonstrated its
        effectiveness.

    c. Several committees of the AICPA have established stan-
        dards for the preparation and presentation of forecast data.
        The MAS Division published the third in its Guideline
        Series, "Guidelines for Systems for the Preparation of Finan-
        cial Forecasts." The Accounting Standards Executive Com-
        mittee has issued a Statement of Position, "Presentation and
        Disclosure of Financial Forecasts."

    An auditor's report on a forecast should specifically comment
on the conformity of the underlying system and the actual presentation with the established standards; and it should also comment on the reasonableness of the assumptions, because it is the
assumptions that give life to the numbers.

    The SEC's Chief Accountant has recently been suggesting an
even greater level of auditor involvement in financial reporting.

He has suggested that an auditor be appointed as an *"independent accountant of record."* He has suggested that the auditor and the client assume a kind of partnership in the preparation and presentation of financial data and that the auditor carry a certain level of responsibility for all of a client's financial disclosures.

The phrase, "independent accountant of record," has not been defined, but from speeches and presentations by SEC people, it is possible to develop an idea of what is implied. One aspect of this proposal might require the auditor to express an opinion, not just that the client's statements were "fairly presented in accordance with generally accepted accounting principles," but also that the accounting principles which the client selected from various acceptable alternatives available were the most preferable in the circumstances. Also, the proposal implies that the auditor would be much more involved in the client's detailed financial reporting and decision making regarding the extent and timing of disclosures. The auditing profession is likely to object to this evolving idea because it conflicts with the traditional concept of independence. The profession (and for that matter, the SEC) has insisted that an auditor be removed from the client's decision making so that the auditor is in a position to report objectively and independently on the financial statements which have been prepared by responsible management.

Of more concern, however, is the uncertain level of responsibility which is implied by the "independent accountant of record" concept. The auditor would apparently have responsibility, to a greater or lesser degree, for all of the items in the annual report, for the interim financials, and perhaps even for the speeches which management makes before financial analysts. Auditors will be concerned about an imprecise boundary of responsibility because of the legal liability implications. But the financial community will also be concerned: it is not enough to know that an auditor has simply been "involved." In evaluating a company's financial presentations, it is important for the reader to know where the independent auditor's examination begins and ends.

Chapter 34

Developing effective relations with the independent auditor

Robert A. Morgan*   *Donald G. Disney‡*
Glenn V. Schultz†   *Dean H. Secord§*

The development of effective relationships between a company and the independent auditor is a process as challenging as it is essential. The primary challenge is the development of a communication network between people who may be separated by miles, borders, responsibility levels, language—to list only a few communication barriers. A skeptic might view this process and observe that truly effective relationships are never fully achieved; however, some techniques are available which, together with continual effort and hard work, can improve the potential for achieving more effective relationships. This chapter identifies and discusses those techniques as they affect both the company and the independent auditor. It focuses on those matters considered important, first, from the company's point of view and, second, from the independent auditor's point of view. This somewhat artificial separation should not obscure

* Controller, Caterpillar Tractor Co.
† Manager, Office Systems & Procedures, Caterpillar Tractor Co.
‡ Manager, Office Methods & Procedures, Caterpillar Tractor Co.
§ Partner, Price Waterhouse & Co.

the obvious mutuality of interest that both company and auditor have in the activities of the other. Nor should it be assumed that the results of their combined efforts affect only the two parties. Exhibit 1 depicts the scope and far-ranging effect of the company/independent

EXHIBIT 1
The independent but overlapping relationships of the company,
independent auditor, and third parties

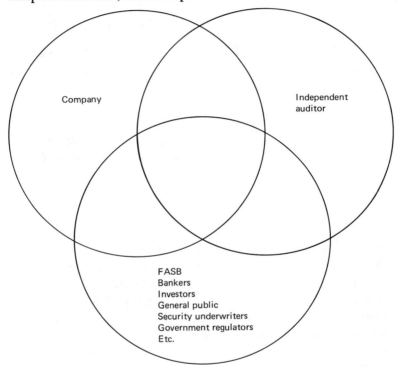

auditor relationship as it impacts on and, in turn, is influenced by, third parties. The illustration points out the independence maintained by all but recognizes a certain overlapping of interests and activity.

It may be helpful if the reader recognizes the perspective from which this chapter was prepared. It was developed and written from the point of view of a large, multinational company and its independent auditor; however, the issues proposed for consideration should prove appropriate and useful to companies of any size.

THE COMPANY'S VIEW

The foundation upon which a lasting and effective relationship between the independent auditor and the company is built consists of understanding and respect. Although these principles are conceptual and may be subject to different interpretations, they are essential ingredients in any arrangement where two parties work together in an independent but complementary fashion. How to translate these principles into everyday working tools that can build and enhance the company/independent auditor relationship is the objective of this section.

If the relationship is to develop, each must recognize the issues that are considered important to the other party. In any listing of significant matters between auditor and company, the following may be considered basic and elemental:

1. An open and frank relationship.
2. Financial statement preparation—company and independent auditor's responsibilities.
3. Mutual respect for the other's professional competence.
4. Auditor's knowledge and understanding of company operations.
5. Independence.
6. Accessibility.

Each of these in turn is explained below.

Open and frank relationship

A relationship founded upon open conduct and a frank expression of views creates the climate in which both the independent auditor and the company can develop optimum effectiveness. The problems that might plague any relationship between two parties working together are minimized as openness is expanded. Communication breakdowns are reduced, and misunderstandings occur with less frequency. Of the various methods that exist to develop this free and open climate for improved relations, the following seem sufficiently important to deserve special attention.

Contact throughout the year. A fundamental principle underlying the auditor/company relationship is "no accounting surprises." The auditor can contribute immeasurably here by maintaining contact throughout the year and not just at year-end. The means at hand are many. Letters, memoranda, reports, meetings, visits, and telephone calls are typical examples.

The requirements set forth in *APB Opinion No. 28,* "Interim Financial Reporting," encourage a more formalized structure for increasing contact during the year; however, SEC *Accounting Series Release* No. 177 (Sept. 16, 1975) virtually requires more frequent, in-depth contact by providing for inclusion of summarized quarterly results in the notes to the annual financial statements filed with the Commission (on Form 10-K). To improve the effectiveness of this contact, auditors must be guided by their experience and judgment to determine the optimum number and type for each company. Management must be guided by an appreciation for the limited time available to auditors weighed against the benefits to be gained by both parties.

Working and communicating with management. Most financial executives prefer that auditors share their thoughts before comments are incorporated into audit reports or other reports to management.

One good practice which some independent auditors follow is to review drafts of proposed reports with the company to make certain that facts and assumptions are correct. Such review ensures that the resulting final reports are factually correct and the recommendations are clearly understood.

Another important procedure to follow is to use the chain of command. During the course of the audit, the effective auditor deals directly with functionally responsible managers. Auditors who go around these managers to top officials do so at the risk of destroying future relationships. An appropriate reconciliation of different viewpoints can in almost every case be worked out between the auditor and management below the top level. In the event of an unusual situation where differences persist, both should jointly address the problem to top officials. Of course, the auditors must not be denied access to top management and the board of directors.

Scheduling the audit work at times mutually convenient to both management and the auditor provides assurance that the auditor will have reasonable access to management's time during the least busy periods of the quarterly and yearly closing cycles. A related suggestion for auditors is to coordinate their audit program with that of the company's internal audit staff to reduce duplication and redundancy of effort. Working together harmoniously and effectively produces the greatest coverage for the amount of the audit fee, an obvious advantage.

Correcting internal control weaknesses. Detection of internal control weaknesses, by either the independent auditor or the company's internal audit staff, is vital. Significant weaknesses must be brought to the attention of management immediately upon detection. A written report with recommendations for corrective action should be provided management to establish understanding and to serve as a basis for assuring that appropriate corrective action is taken.

As a follow-up to insure understanding and compliance with the auditor's recommendations, the company should install a formal response system. This requires that a written reply be prepared and submitted within a specified time frame, setting forth the action to be taken. If the auditor's suggestions can be drafted and discussed with management before the final report is prepared, the auditor can include management's response following each comment. This can reduce or eliminate the need for a separate management report that comments on each recommendation. Subsequent programs should include a reaudit of previously detected areas of weaknesses.

Fee charged by independent auditor. There must be agreement that audit fees are reasonable and fair. What is not so evident, perhaps, is that management wishes to be better informed of the nature and substance of services provided by the auditor. Some portion of the auditor/company communications recommended above should be devoted to increasing management's understanding and acceptance of the various aspects of audit work performed and other services provided, and the corresponding fees charged. The reason for this should be apparent. A practice engaged in by many companies and their auditors is to schedule a meeting which precedes the company's budget process to discuss prospective audit fees.

Financial statement preparation—company and independent auditor's responsibilities

The management of a company is fully responsible for the preparation and distribution of financial statements, whereas the basic function of the independent auditor is the attestation to the fairness of these financial statements.

It should always be this way if we are to continue prudent business practices—each has unique responsibility and should accept it and carry it out completely. While auditor and management have separate and distinct responsibilities in the preparation and issuance of financial statements, a close working relationship throughout this process is imperative if each is to perform the respective functions effectively. The following three subsections highlight auditor and company responsibilities and interrelationships regarding financial statements for internal and external reporting purposes.

Report on fairness and consistency of statements. The report of the independent auditor on published financial statements usually contains wording such as "In our opinion, the accompanying statements present fairly . . . in conformity with generally accepted accounting principles consistently applied." This is well known as a "clean opinion" and is what executives always wish to see on their published financial statements. There are occasions when the auditor's opinion recognizes changes in the company's accounting principles which produce a material effect. How changes in accounting principles should be reported in financial statements and what is required to justify these changes are covered in Accounting Principles Board (APB) *Opinion No. 20.* In that *Opinion,* the definition of the term *accounting principle* includes "not only accounting principles and practices but also the methods of applying them."

The auditor's opinion will indicate whether the accounting change is approved by them and also whether or not the statements have been prepared in compliance with generally accepted accounting principles. When there is a material difference of opinion between the auditor and management which cannot be resolved before issuing statements, the auditor may issue a qualified opinion setting forth the qualification.

In the event any significant change in accounting principle takes place between years, the auditor and management should always discuss the change and its effect sufficiently in advance to obviate disagreement at the time of issuing statements. If management has approached the change rationally, included justification for the change, explained the change adequately, and not violated generally accepted accounting principles, the auditor will generally be receptive to the change. If, on the other hand, the auditor believes the change will distort the fairness and consistency of statements, the auditor is required to bring this concern to the attention of management. Generally, differences of opinion on the reasonableness and materiality of changes can be resolved if there is a good working relationship between the parties.

Application of generally accepted accounting principles. The management accountant, in the ever-increasing desire for "professional" acceptance within accounting circles, increases acceptance through the use of good judgment in the development and application of accounting procedures and practices by following generally accepted accounting principles. Management should be totally knowledgeable of these principles and develop supporting internal operating procedures which assure the appropriate financial statement results. For example, when a specific inventory valuation system (Lifo, Fifo, average) is implemented, all necessary record-keeping and control functions must be diligently adhered to so that year-end values are properly stated. Complex systems should always be documented adequately for internal use and for review, acceptance, and utilization by the independent auditor, in following the transactions from step to step.

The alert and knowledgeable company accountant will apply procedures that are based on acceptable accounting concepts. Among other matters, consideration should be given to the correct asset lives, appropriate depreciation rates, and accounting for the investment tax credit, as well as an inventory valuation basis which recognizes the relationship between costs and revenues. The accounting concepts selected should be those that are deemed appropriate for the particular circumstances of the company and which are acceptable to the independent auditor. An early discussion with the auditor before adoption is a good practice. Once this is done, procedures which will achieve the results expected by using the concept should be developed and applied.

Quality of statements. William Blackie, retired chairman of Caterpillar Tractor Co., has made this most appropriate comment: "Not only tell the accounting truth, *but tell it well.*" The test of how well accountants fulfill their responsibility of effective reporting is the understanding level achieved. The intelligence and business acumen exhibited by accountants in performing their functions will be fully visible in the statements produced. Readers of financial statements should be provided with the opportunity to obtain a fair picture of the condition of a business. Statements should be designed to help, rather than hinder, their readability. Significant accounting practices are required to be highlighted in footnotes to the statements. The use of terms which are meaningful to the general public, and not only to other accountants, should always be encouraged. A one-page, or shorter, story of the financial history of the business should be presented. Achieving brevity with a completeness of content is a challenge for accounting management in published financial statements.

Professional competence of independent auditor and manager

An important aspect of the auditor/management relationship is mutual respect. When each party respects the other's professional competence, the relationship will flourish and develop fully. A genuine, honest appreciation for the other can be the very essence of a sound and lasting relationship.

Confidence in each other's abilities. Although a sense of mutual confidence in the other's role must exist for an effective relationship, this section deals primarily with the relationship as viewed by management. In addition to the normal audit services, management expects the independent auditor to be competent in many areas. As tax laws change, the company frequently needs counsel to determine the record keeping necessary to comply. Preparing various mandatory governmental reports, such as the Securities and Exchange Commission 10-K, requires special understanding and expertise that the independent auditor is frequently expected to provide. Advice on new techniques for profit planning, data processing, and management reporting are other potential service areas for the auditor. In short, the auditor should offer a full range of professional services.

Continuity of independent auditor's audit team. A good portion of a new independent auditor's early training comes from contact with the company. Therefore, management rightly expects a nominal return on the time and effort expended. This usually takes the form of an expectation that the auditor will be reasonable and fair in rotating new personnel into the company's account. Following this simple guideline can go far toward building successful relations. The reader will note that in the section *Audit Responsibility Structure* (below), this matter is also referred to as one important to the independent auditor.

Keeping abreast of "generally accepted accounting principles." For many years the establishment of accounting principles was carried on by the independent auditing profession through the Accounting Principles Board. Today, this responsibility is being performed by the Financial Accounting Standards Board. Several thorny accounting problems such as product-line reporting, translation of foreign accounting transactions, leases, and mergers have created controversy throughout the accounting profession and the business world. How to account for these has never been a simple or easy matter to resolve. With increased attention being given these issues, the company looks to and expects advice from its independent auditor.

Independent auditor's knowledge of management's internal operations

The independent auditor's value to a company has a direct correlation to the level of understanding of the company's business operations. It is the responsibility of the auditor to work out a plan, acceptable to management, which assures continuing understanding of the business. A series of meetings with key management personnel to discuss various aspects of the company's business operations is probably the best means to achieve the desired level of understanding.

Complementary program between the company's internal audit staff and the independent auditor to review internal control. Generally, the independent auditor will concentrate on items important to the financial statements while the company's internal audit staff will emphasize operations reviews. A synergistic result will be realized when management's internal audit program is used to complement the auditor's efforts. There would seem to be no purpose served by having the independent auditor perform the same activities which are included in the company's internal audit program. An exchange of reports identifying the extent of the audit and areas covered can be invaluable to both parties. A broader base of activities can be covered at the lowest cost. The independent auditor should become fully involved with the company's internal audit, which detects serious control defects. A coordinated program whereby the two groups rotate areas of audit over a reasonable period of time should be worked out in advance.

Although the auditing thrust may be slightly different between the auditor and the company, all efforts should be coordinated to produce the greatest benefit to both. The adoption of fundamental principles of internal check can be useful to both the independent auditor and the internal auditor in planning the scope of their audit programs. Examples of internal check principles that cover sensitive areas can be found in available books and texts on the controllership function. For illustration purposes, some typical examples are listed below. Each company should develop principles appropriate to its needs.

1. The bookkeeping function should be separated from the custodianship function. For example, whoever keeps the asset record should not have access to the asset.
2. An effective perpetual inventory control should be maintained over all merchandise, supplies, and fixed assets.
3. Checks, blank as well as signed, should be as carefully guarded as cash. (Many forgeries by professional forgers are committed through the use of stolen blank company checks.)
4. Signed checks should not be mailed either by the person who signed the checks or by the person who prepared or approved the supporting documents on the basis of which the checks were issued. All invoices, petty cash vouchers, notes, and other documents that have been paid should be immediately perforated or indelibly stamped "PAID," with the date. This should be done preferably by or under the direction of the individual signing the payment check.
5. Authority for the approval of disbursements should be segregated from the authority for making payment. For example, payrolls should be approved by one person, but payroll checks should be prepared, signed, and issued by others.
6. Prenumbering should be used in connection with all original memoranda prepared in the support of the receipt or disbursement of cash, inventories, or other assets.
7. Credits, allowances, contributions of merchandise, and other such transactions should be carefully supervised and approved by proper authority.
8. Departure from established routines or systems and procedures should not be permitted until the internal check aspects have been considered and approved by proper authority. The development of new EDP systems must follow the same constraints of internal check review.

Multinational and joint venture operations. The company's business operations are more complex today than ever before as they expand internationally through wholly owned subsidiaries and joint ventures. This places an added burden on the independent auditor. To help assure consistency in consolidated statements, common accounting practices must be followed throughout the company's organization. The auditor must extend the audit program to include necessary checks of the records of subsidiary companies. This effort is made easier if the independent auditor is represented in foreign countries and can coordinate audit activities on a worldwide basis for the company. Occasional visits to overseas locations by parent company management and auditor can assist in developing a closer relationship with the auditor's foreign representative, the company's subsidiary accounting management, and the corporate coordinators. Exhibit 2 illustrates the communication lines that should be fol-

EXHIBIT 2
Communication lines for multinational operations

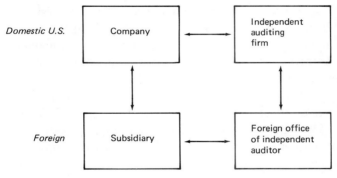

lowed when questions are raised on policy issues. Questions that concern purely informational matters could be directed to anyone.

The independent auditor can be very useful to multinational companies where the subsidiary's internal audit staff is either understaffed or inexperienced. Some countries have not adopted modern auditing requirements, and therefore have not encouraged the development of auditing programs in schools. Internal auditors with knowledge and experience are often difficult to find. They have to be supplemented, or even replaced completely in some cases, by the independent auditor. In situations where it may not be diplomatic to use the internal audit staff to review operations of a joint venture, the independent auditor can fill this void.

Independence

The financial statements issued by a company are just that: the company's—not the auditor's. The auditor renders an opinion about the fairness and consistency of the statements, and whether the transactions have been reported in accordance with generally accepted accounting principles. But the company is responsible for adoption of appropriate accounting practices and for issuing proper financial statements to the public. The independence exercised by both management and the independent auditor in the preparation of the financial statements is essential to the continued acceptance of the statements by the public, bankers, investors, and so on. A fairly recent development that has resulted in strengthening this independent relationship has been the increased involvement by the audit committee of the board of directors.

Board of directors audit committee. The establishment of corporate board of directors audit committees has been adopted by most large companies and many smaller ones as a means to enhance internal controls by making direct communication between the independent auditor and the outside directors very convenient. The corporate audit committee can be an active force in the efforts to improve financial reporting to stockholders and prospective investors. How this is accomplished can vary in significant degree from one company to another. This is due to the different ways individual directors function in performing their work. But the end result is the same—more independence by auditors and improved financial statements for users.

Accessibility

As stated in the introduction of this chapter, the foundation upon which a lasting and effective relationship between the independent auditor and management is built consists of understanding and respect. In addition to these attitudinal considerations, physical considerations play an important part in a good relationship between auditor and management. Physical space requirements for the auditor to work, accessibility to operating personnel and source transactions (to reduce the time and effort required to perform an audit), and appropriate size of the auditor's staff are discussed in this section.

Adequate accommodations for independent auditor. In all due respect to the independent auditor's efforts to complete an effective audit at the least cost to the company, the auditor should expect adequate physical accommodations to be provided at the company's places of business. This should include desk and file space close to the company's accounting personnel or other operating areas where the majority of the audit is to take place. Telephones are also necessary to speed up communications with the auditor's head office, with other members of the auditor's staff located throughout the company's business, and with members of management's staff. If mechanized auditing techniques are utilized as part of the audit, provisions for computer time and input-output devices should be made at mutually convenient times. In summary, the auditor should be treated in a similar fashion to management's staff in respect to physical accommodations.

Cooperation by management. Management's staff should be fully aware that the auditor is on the premises at the request and for the benefit of the company. Therefore, they are to cooperate completely at all times. This can best be accomplished if the audit schedule is known in advance and has been developed with an understanding of the limited time available to the auditor and company personnel. Data required to complete the audit must be readily available upon request—nothing should be withheld. If it is felt that some data is highly proprietary, the auditor should designate a key member of the audit staff to be given access to this data. For example, not every member of the auditor's staff needs to have access to the salaries of management personnel. It should be understood, however, that withholding significant amounts of data from the auditor could be interpreted as attempting to cover up irregularities. Remember that the auditor's opinion is based on being satisfied that the statements of the company fairly present the financial position at a specific point in time. Auditors can only express this opinion if they have had an opportunity to conduct their audit in accordance with generally accepted auditing standards. This means expecting the complete cooperation of and communication with management.

Size of independent auditor's firm and size of the company's firm. Today, independent auditing firms exist in varying sizes and in varying locations. A small or medium-sized company with operations at one location may select a local independent auditor who will adequately meet its requirements. Smaller auditing firms generally may not be able to afford the specialized expertise of systems analysts or computer specialists. However, auditors can usually assist management in acquiring the services of specialized experts through their association with larger auditing firms or management consultants.

The large multilocation company should solicit the services of an auditor who has offices or affiliations throughout the United States and in foreign countries. Auditors should also have access within their organization to specialized talents. The multinational company will find that it is more efficient, and in most cases more economical, to use the same auditing firm for all of its domestic and foreign locations.

Regardless of size or location, management should be convinced that it is associated with an auditor of high standards, who is deeply interested in the affairs of the company, and who will provide adequate service at a fair price.

THE INDEPENDENT AUDITOR'S VIEW

The second part of this chapter focuses on the development of effective company/auditor relationships from the independent auditor's view. As indicated earlier, the approach is oriented to the audit of a large multinational company with the hope that there are some aspects which have application to the audits of varying sizes of companies. The broad topics which will be covered are the following:

1. Audit responsibility structure.
2. Audit planning process.
3. Coordination with key financial groups.
4. Foreign field visits.
5. Reporting.
6. Expediting audit work.
7. Accounting, auditing, and communication problems.

Audit responsibility structure

A corporation's organizational structure is usually well understood by the independent auditor, since it is studied carefully. However, the company's management may not be so well informed about the auditor's organizational structure. A clearer understanding of the independent auditor's responsibility structure should be a helpful starting point to engender more effective relationships.

The audit is a team effort. The team comprises the partner, manager, senior, and staff accountant. The various members of this team carry out assignments that support and assist each other in much the same fashion as that of the coach and members of a football team. The audit partner's function can be likened to that of the coach, while the audit manager plays the captain's role. The audit senior quarterbacks the day-to-day audit effort which is carried out by staff accountants.

Roles of partner, manager, senior, staff accountant. The audit partner is the person ultimately responsible for the audit. The partner signs the auditing firm's signature on the independent auditor's report to the board of directors and shareholders. This report indicates the independent auditor's opinion on the fairness of the company's annual financial statements. The audit partner is in frequent contact with the entire audit team as well as with key company officials.

There are several assistant coaches involved with the audit. One is the alternate audit partner, whose function is to be sufficiently abreast of the company's affairs to provide an intelligent sounding board for consultation on accounting, reporting, and auditing problems. The alternate audit partner also substitutes for the regular audit partner in unavoidable emergency situations.

Other assistant coaches are tax and management advisory service (MAS) partners. Because of the importance and complexity of the tax area, tax specialists are essential not only to determine the propriety of the tax expense and liability accounts but also to provide consultation on major business transactions with tax consequences, revenue agents' examinations, and so on. The tax partner coordinates these services and is assisted by a tax manager.

The technical nature of the company's EDP function has required increasing audit support from EDP specialists on the MAS staff. The MAS partner and consultants, on an as needed basis, become intimately involved in the EDP audit effort and in many other areas of assistance in design or critique of information structures and systems to facilitate management's tasks.

The audit manager is the captain of the audit team and is the leader directly responsible for the conduct and completion of the audit. Audit managers control the approach to each phase of the work (including tax and MAS efforts) and must bring each matter of significance to the attention of the audit partner.

The audit senior directs the day-to-day audit work and calls the plays pursuant to the overall game plan approved by the partner and manager. The senior is intimately involved in the details of planning the audit, supervises its execution, and reviews the working papers which form the record of the audit. One of the audit senior's most challenging roles involves the development of the capabilities of the audit staff accountants who are team members.

Continuity. An effective audit requires the auditor to go beyond the financial books and records. It requires a broad understanding of the company's business. To develop and carry out a well-conceived audit, the auditor needs to give consideration to the company's organization, operating and information control systems, and its business environment. Continuity of the audit team is important because an appreciation of the company's business and an acquaintance with management's financial personnel can be fully developed only over a period of time.

Continuity does not mean that the auditor performs the same audit work twice. Typically, just the opposite is the case. The staff accountant may work on cash and payrolls during the first year and then progress to the more complex areas of receivables and inventories in successive years. The reason for this nonrepetitive approach is not only to provide a challenge for the auditor but also to provide a fresh audit approach each year. Of course, this does not involve starting from scratch each year. Rather, there is cumulative knowledge carried forward in the working papers, and the prior staff accountant and the audit senior are available for consultation.

At the core of continuity is the advancement of the auditor. An ideal career plan might result in a staff accountant's performing successively more difficult audit assignments at the corporate office and at manufacturing plants and then being promoted to senior accountant. A three-year period is usually required for this process to be completed. Generally, after three more years of directing the audit at plants and corporate headquarters, the senior would be promoted to audit manager. After six years in that capacity, the audit manager would become the audit partner.

The continuity resulting from this extensive development and exposure is invaluable to the auditor and the company.

Rotation of people. The positive effects of continuity should be balanced with the equally positive effects of a fresh perspective as a result of a change in audit management personnel every few years. There are solid advantages to long-term rotation of partners and managers. The effective auditor does not take anything for granted. Facts, systems, and controls once clearly understood may change, yet the changes may not be obvious. If there are systems changes, appropriate changes must be made in the audit approach.

Thus, after several years of involvement, the partner and manager are often relieved of responsibility for the engagement, but not in the same year. The not surprising result is that a matter seen in one light by one person is seen in a different light by a different person. The result of this process is that the needed continuity at the management level is retained and, at the same time, fresh and penetrating thinking applied to the company's operations is assured.

Audit planning process

A basic understanding of how the independent auditor plans the audit should be useful in promoting a more effective relationship between management and auditors. In the auditor's report on the company's financial statements, the independent auditor states that the audit was made in accordance with generally accepted auditing standards. One of these auditing standards requires the audit to be "adequately planned."

It is important to begin the audit with a formal plan. In practice, at the conclusion of the current year's audit a beginning is made on the formal plan for the next year's audit. One approach would be for the output of the planning process to encompass two documents, viz., the audit plan control and the planning memorandum.

Audit plan control. The audit plan control is a document which is designed to record formally in one place the logic of the independent auditor's overall audit approach. It deals with the "why" of audit tests. It replaces the decentralized situation where, for many audits, the audit logic would be contained in written audit programs, in memoranda that are carried forward from year to year, in the annual planning memorandum and, to a great extent, in the minds of the audit staff involved.

Included in Exhibit 3 is the broad outline of such an audit plan control. Once the audit plan control is developed, only minor revi-

EXHIBIT 3
Audit plan control contents (selected items)

Company Background Data:
  Principal products and facilities
  Subsidiary companies
    United States
    Outside United States
  Organization
    Overall management chart
    Financial function chart
  Competitive environment
  Information system
  Control systems
    Accounting
    Organization
    Operating
    Information

Company Accounting Data:
  Significant accounting principles
  Accounting manuals

Reports Required:
  External
  Internal

Timing Requirements:
  United States
  Outside United States

Coordination—Key Financial Groups:
  Accounting
  Treasury
  Tax
  EDP
  Internal audit

Coordination with Specialists:
  Tax
  International tax
  MAS
  SEC
  Accounting research
  Government contracts

Audit Approach (by Functional Audit Area):
  Sales and receivables
  Production costs and inventories
  Purchases and accounts payable
  Labor costs and employee benefits
  Property, plant, and equipment
  Cash
  Investments and other assets
  Liabilities, deferred credits, and contingencies
  Capital stock and other equity accounts
  Consolidation

Audit Administrative Guide:
  Communications
    Inquiry form
    Information form
  Information retrieval
    Working papers
    Correspondence control

sions are required to recognize changes in the organization, its accounting and control systems, and the environment in which it operates. The existence of this control document allows the auditor to spend considerably more time in areas of change and exception. Without such documentation, it is likely that considerable effort may be invested relocating and restudying facts that were previously well understood, but have faded from memory or easy accessibility.

Planning memorandum. The audit planning memorandum is rewritten every year. This memorandum describes when and how the audit approach will be specifically applied to the current year. The audit senior and manager formalize the plan, subject to the overall guidelines and approval of the audit partner. The annual audit plan gives consideration to the possibilities of rotation of audit emphasis. This concept attempts to focus on areas and company locations where the auditor can vary the extent of the work performed from year to year.

In formulating the audit plan, the auditor studies what significant changes have occurred in a number of areas, for example:

1. The economic environment.
2. The company's operations.
3. Key financial and operating personnel.
4. Control systems—accounting, organization, operating, information.
5. Interim results of operations and changes in financial position.

Once the audit impact of change is thoughtfully considered, the audit planning memorandum is written. It sets out major audit problems and how they will be dealt with. The planning memorandum also deals with the timing of critical phases of the examination and reporting requirements. Finally, the plan must be flexible enough to provide for changes in audit work occasioned by changes in circumstances.

Coordination with management. The auditor works closely with management in learning the significant changes that will have an impact on the annual audit plan. Schedules must be established with common completion dates in mind: for example, annual report and 10-K printing dates. Timing of visits to plants and branches is shared with management to provide opportunities for resolution of schedule conflicts. Further, significant changes in audit emphasis from year to year which may have a significant impact on fees should be discussed in advance with management. For example, the typical audit approach should not require an in-depth review of controls in the data processing department at every location each year. In the year a special in-depth review is expected, the company should be alerted in advance to the possibility of increased costs.

Coordination with key financial groups

The independent auditor must have a clear line of communication to top management. This direct contact is important to insure cooperation at all levels and to provide an essential broad perspective of the philosophy and operations of the company.

Close coordination with key financial groups also is essential to performing an effective audit. The auditor's interaction with the following financial groups is discussed in this section:

1. Accounting.
2. Treasury.
3. EDP.
4. Tax.
5. Internal audit.

Accounting.   The independent auditor should meet with the controller and chief assistants on a regular basis. Once a month would seem to be the minimum in most circumstances. Subjects discussed at these sessions include accounting and auditing matters which have arisen during the course of the audit. The impact on financial reporting of proposed pronouncements of the FASB and SEC also should be covered. These meetings provide the company with opportunities to alert the auditor to matters that are under consideration so that advance background study can begin.

The most effective approach to discussions of technical matters requires the company's accounting group to research the relevant facts and to develop a well-reasoned position. The auditor can then study the company's position and express agreement, disagreement, and alternative approaches.

Treasury.   The independent auditor requires close cooperation with the treasury function to perform an effective audit of the company's finances—for example, cash and investments. In addition, in a multinational company it is essential for the auditor to inquire into the management of foreign exchange, which is normally overseen by the treasury function.

The treasury function also serves as liaison between the independent auditors and the company's bankers and actuaries. The disclosure of informal compensating balance arrangements has resulted in expanded communication between bankers and auditors. The significance of pension costs has led to greater need for contact between the auditor and actuaries. Generally, the auditor corresponds with and contacts such outsiders as arranged through appropriate company representatives.

EDP.   Auditors should not simply be concerned with auditing the computer systems that are critical to the reliability of the current year's financial statements. They also must have a clear understanding of management's plans for developing new systems and facilities so that they can raise internal control considerations in the development stage and can be prepared to audit the new systems effectively when they become operational.

An approach to the auditor's gaining such understanding is to hold an annual review with the top-level EDP managers. Such a review would be a status report and would cover for the next three years: status of major systems, modifications, and changes previously discussed; major systems scheduled for revision; and major facilities and equipment changes. Attendance at this meeting would include the audit team (audit partner, manager, senior, and the MAS consultants who will assist them). Representatives from the controller's and internal auditor's groups would also be invited. One ancillary advantage is having all audit team members hear the EDP plans at the same meeting.

Tax. The reporting of the company's taxes currently payable is an important matter. It is rendered exceedingly complex by the existence of foreign operations. A further complexity in the tax picture is the requirement for recording deferred taxes. Both management and independent auditor have resolved part of the difficulties of dealing with taxes by relying on tax specialists.

An approach to coordinating the audit of the company's tax position is to separate the audit effort into two phases. The more difficult first phase is the redetermination of the company's tax liability position at the beginning of the year after the U.S. tax return has been filed. The second phase is the review of the tax provision for the year. Both of these phases are covered in a memorandum which documents major aspects of the company's tax position.

The theory of this approach is that if the auditor is satisfied with the company's beginning tax liability, after considering pending issues arising from the examination of prior returns, and with the provision for the year, the auditor will be satisfied with the year-end liability. The approach allows the first phase to be completed prior to December and greatly expedites the year-end tax review. Usually, the company's tax department develops the initial analytical data and it is reviewed by the auditor's tax representatives.

Internal audit. The independent auditors have the responsibility to carry out their examinations in sufficient scope to enable them to express an unqualified opinion on the consolidated financial statements. The responsibility is fulfilled in an efficient manner when their work is coordinated to the fullest extent possible, both in the

United States and abroad, with the company's internal audit department. The internal audit effort usually emphasizes functional audits, involving the review and checking of physical, managerial, and accounting controls, adherence to company policies and procedures, and the operational efficiency within the organization. Often the internal audit view is focused on evaluating the effectiveness of the particular activity from a profit improvement standpoint. It places emphasis on how well a particular function has been carried out rather than on substantiating the recorded results of the activity.

An effective internal audit function is an important part of the company's system of internal accounting control. The internal auditor's work cannot be substituted for the work of an independent auditor, but it is considered in determining the extent of audit tests in particular areas and in visits to domestic and foreign locations. Early each year the independent auditors meet with the chief internal audit manager to coordinate their respective examination plans for that year.

Copies of reports prepared by the internal auditors following the conclusion of each audit should be furnished to the office of the independent auditor responsible for the audit and to the other office that performs audit work for the location involved. These reports can be reviewed to help establish the scope of work and to determine the status of recommendations made. Copies of reports to management by the independent auditor similarly should be furnished to the internal auditor. In addition, the internal audit staff, in connection with its examinations of foreign subsidiaries, should meet with the independent auditor's representatives to assure coordination of effort and to exchange ideas.

Foreign field visits

Written correspondence and telephone conversations alone are usually not adequate for the independent auditor to serve adequately a multilocation and multinational company.

The audit partner and/or audit manager responsible for the examination should make it a practice to visit major company locations which are audited by the independent auditor's overseas offices. Normally it is not practical or particularly useful to make a complete circuit every year, but a scheme of coverage over a three- or four-year period is a reasonable goal. These visits also afford an opportunity for discussions at the auditor's overseas office with the audit team responsible for the audit.

The basic objectives of foreign field visits are as follows:

1. Coordinate overall audit objectives.
2. Assess auditing and accounting needs from the local perspective.
3. Exchange viewpoints on the conduct of examination.

One particularly useful approach for these field visits is a joint visit with management officials, principally the controller. (At times, however, treasury, tax, internal audit, or other corporate officials may also make such joint visits.) The joint visit provides the opportunity for complete and frank discussions with all interested parties. Further, an important common denominator is achieved in that opportunities are provided for the various parties to focus on a particular matter at the same time.

To be most effective, considerable effort must be expended prior to the visit in studying the relevant reports, memoranda, letters, and so on. The result of this study is a listing of points for discussion. The listing should be distilled and amended by both management and the independent auditor.

The visit schedule should provide for a number of joint and separate meetings, for example:

1. Initial separate meetings:
    Corporate officials and local management personnel at the company's facilities.
    Independent auditor and local audit personnel at the auditor's offices.
2. Joint meetings:
    All parties at the company's facilities.
    All parties at the auditor's offices.
3. Separate wind-up meetings.

The length of the visit will depend upon the complexities of the points to be discussed and the logistics of visiting the company's facilities and the auditor's offices. An essential part of each visit is the opportunity for contacts outside of normal office hours. A joint dinner is often a useful way of improving mutual understanding. The dividends from these field visits continue long after the visits are made. Experience has shown that subsequent written and oral consultations on accounting, auditing, and tax problems are greatly facilitated by having met on an "eyeball-to-eyeball basis" the individuals with whom one is dealing.

Reporting

The independent auditor's basic concern is the expression of an opinion on the fairness of the company's financial statements. How this is done by using company reports is the subject of this section.

Audit report. Coordination with management on the audit report is primarily focused on the timing of its issuance. The report date represents the day the audit process is completed with respect to the annual financial statements that will be issued to stockholders. All significant audit work supporting the auditor's opinion is expected to be finished by that date. Accordingly, both management and the auditor devote considerable attention to setting a realistic completion date based upon a carefully developed timetable. Such a timetable might be as follows (for a December 31 year-end):

November 15	Completion of interim audit work
December 1	Resolution of all known year-end accounting problems
December 15	Complete review of draft of annual report
December 26	Year-end audit begins
January 10	Subsidiaries' closing date
January 20	Consolidation completed by company
January 22	Audit clearance for subsidiaries
January 31	Report on consolidated financial statements

Both management and the auditor must monitor the process of the closing and the audit to ascertain that unforeseen circumstances are appropriately handled. If they are not, the report date may have to be delayed.

A smooth year-end closing can be greatly facilitated by careful attention to two items on the above timetable: early resolution of possible year-end accounting problems and early attention to drafting the annual report to stockholders. By setting a date early in December to discuss with management all important accounting problems or potential problems known at that time, the process of resolving these matters can be concluded on a timely basis rather than at the last minute. If such matters are unduly delayed, there is a risk of hasty action based on inadequate study. Both of these risks can be avoided if all parties work toward the early resolution deadline.

The auditor has an interest not only in the financial statements on which the auditor's report is rendered but also in the remainder of the textual and statistical data that appear in the annual report to stockholders. The auditor's interest includes determining that there are no inconsistencies between the financial statements and the remaining portions of the report.

For a company with a December fiscal year-end, October is not too early to begin the process of drafting the annual report. By then the results of the first three calendar quarters have been released. The responsibility for preparing the financial data for the annual report usually falls on the controller's group. By setting a date in mid-December for completion of the drafting process, attention can be devoted after year-end to the inevitable unexpected problems which arise.

Reports to management. During the examination, the auditor is primarily concerned with those accounting controls which are directly related to the fairness of the financial statements. The extent of audit tests is based upon the effectiveness of the company's system of controls. Control deficiencies may require additional audit work.

From time to time, the auditor points out to management the potential improvements that might be made in internal accounting controls and in other aspects of the company's operations. At the completion of each phase of the examination, the auditor discusses findings with appropriate company officials and offers the recommendations developed during the work. It is customary to incorporate the recommendations considered important into a "report to management." Such a report is usually issued on each entity subjected to audit for which recommendations are developed. Those recommendations thought to have minor impact are usually discussed orally.

The timing of issuance of the report and the comments of company officials are areas where coordination between the auditor and management is vital. The most effective timing is to issue the report after the completion of the interim work. This approach gives corporate management the opportunity to review both the auditor's recommendations and the reactions of local officials in advance of completion of the year-end audit. Management is then able to take whatever corrective action is deemed appropriate on a timely basis. If the report to management is to be issued after the year-end audit, it should be issued as expeditiously as possible. Both parties should take appropriate action to insure an early report.

A particularly useful format for comments by local management is to reflect on them following the auditor's recommendation. This juxtaposition may eliminate the need for a separate report from management covering these comments. By using this report format, corporate management can review both the recommendations and responses to determine areas of agreement and disagreement. Where the latter situation arises, corporate management must take steps to deal with the disagreement.

Reporting to the board of directors audit committee. The audit committee is the usual vehicle through which the independent auditor communicates with the board of directors. The independent auditor meets with the board's audit committee at least once a year and in some cases two or more times. Normally, a written report from the auditor serves as the agenda for the oral discussion at the meeting. The audit committee members explore areas of concern that they deem appropriate. Matters covered in such a report to be reviewed at the conclusion of the year-end audit are described in Exhibit 4. In this report the auditor goes on record with specific

EXHIBIT 4
Report to the audit committee of the board of directors

CONTENTS

19x1 examination:
  Organization and staff
  Planning and scope
  Internal accounting controls, including data processing controls
  Coordination with internal auditors
  Visits to major locations

Current financial and accounting matters

Status of matters previously discussed with the audit committee:
  Federal income taxes
  Translation of foreign currencies

Matters likely to affect future accounting and reporting:
  Pension disclosure
  Pronouncements of the Financial Accounting Standards Board
  SEC developments

comments about the audit and about the company's compliance with accepted accounting practices, internal controls, and with current authoritative pronouncements.

Coordination between the auditor and management on the audit committee report attempts to achieve the goal of providing for thorough discussion of the agenda in advance of the meeting. In practice, a final draft is provided to the company a few days before the meeting. Study of this draft presents management with an opportunity for final study and resolution of any matters of disagreement with the auditors. Such final study is important because the audit committee is vitally interested in any such disagreements.

Foreign subsidiary reports.   It is common practice for companies with foreign subsidiaries to require a full audit in conformity with generally accepted auditing standards in the United States. In many countries there is also a requirement for a statutory audit. The reporting requirements are most effectively monitored by the auditor's office that is responsible for the corporate audit.

Instructions issued by the auditor to the office which is conducting the foreign subsidiary audit are primarily focused on the timing of various reports that must be submitted. An example of such reporting requirements and deadlines is outlined in Exhibit 5. The timing and nature of the reporting requirements are closely coordinated with the company.

EXHIBIT 5

ABC, INCORPORATED
Reporting Requirements and Deadlines Relating to Examination
For Year Ending December 31, 19x1

	Instructions page	*Due on or before*
Fee estimate	10	September 30, 19x1
Memorandum of significant accounting and auditing points resulting from interim examination	3	November 15, 19x1
Memorandum on income tax position	7	December 10, 19x1
Internal control memorandum based on interim examination	4	December 15, 19x1
Copy of company-prepared balance sheet and statement of income	6	January 13, 19x2
Cable (Telex or telephone) clearance for consolidation	6	January 22, 19x2
Memorandum on examination	6	January 25, 19x2
Report and year-end financial statements (U.S. dollar statements)	8	February 25, 19x2
SEC schedules	9	March 1, 19x2
Internal control memorandum	4	March 15, 19x2
Statutory audit reports	2	As issued
Copy of bill	10	April 15, 19x2

U.S. personnel responsible for examination:

Partner: James Able
Manager: Joseph Baker

Clearance of subsidiaries' financial statements. The audit of the financial statements of subsidiary companies is normally conducted for two purposes:

1. To determine their fairness for inclusion in the consolidated financial statements.
2. To comply with local requirements for statutory report.

Frequently the subsidiary is consolidated as of its fiscal year which may end from one to three months earlier than the parent's year-end. While it is customary to receive an auditor's report and related financial statements in due course, the subsidiary's financial statements are usually consolidated based upon telex clearance from the auditor's local representatives.

The coordination between the company and auditor requires close communication to deal with and resolve the accounting and auditing problems which seem to arise inevitably. While audit exceptions discovered at the subsidiary level, in and of themselves, may not result in a material problem at the consolidated level, each matter must be carefully evaluated, especially in light of its impact on other subsidiaries.

Expediting audit work

The company and auditor share the common goals of the best possible audit at the least possible cost. Since audit fees are primarily a function of time spent, the continuing challenge is to reduce, or at least hold constant, the audit time charges. Continuing review of the audit logic and programs and coordination with company personnel are two areas that require attention in fulfilling this goal.

The auditor must subject the audit process to continual review. Elementary questions that must be applied to major audit areas are: (1) Have circumstances changed which affect our tests? (2) Do the tests fulfill their purpose? (3) Are the most important tests emphasized?

Audit staff members are expected to understand the specific objective that each test is intended to accomplish and to be imaginative in carrying out audit tests. At the completion of the audit program, they are asked to crystallize their thoughts by annotating a draft of the audit program for next year.

Coordination with management personnel often involves using them to prepare schedules and retrieve documentation. Many useful analytical schedules can be prepared by management if the auditor provides advance direction. Development of pro forma schedules by the auditor can be a considerable help.

A number of specific matters that require careful consideration in executing a more efficient audit are set forth below:

1. Take full advantage of management's computer and other EDP equipment to reduce manual audit time.
2. Plan to reduce unnecessary scheduling and, where appropriate, work directly to company records.
3. Use management's personnel to:
   a. Prepare schedules for SEC reports, tax returns, or supporting account balances, such as reconciliations of cash, summaries of properties, and analyses of selected profit and loss accounts.
   b. Prepare trial balances of detailed accounts supporting selected general ledger controls.
   c. Prepare confirmation requests.
   d. Procure and refile vouchers, invoices, and other documents.
   e. Type confirmation letters, report drafts, and so on.
4. Where adequate direct supervision and control can be exercised, also consider using company personnel to:
   a. Sort checks.
   b. Assist in readying confirmation requests for mailing.
   c. Reconcile amounts reported by customers, vendors, and others to books.
   d. List and accumulate shipping papers, subsequent remittance advices, and other data to facilitate follow-up of confirmation "no replies."

Accounting, auditing, and communication problems

Probably the most important area of effective coordination between the independent auditor and the company is in dealing with accounting, auditing, and communication problems.

Accounting and auditing problems. The company wants no surprises that relate to the technical areas of accounting and auditing. Both management and auditor wish to avoid last-minute major surprises; however, if there is to be a surprise, both want it to be minor in nature.

The auditor's task is to set up a timely review system to assure that problems are brought up for attention in an orderly and timely manner. Thus, the company should be alerted to the facts soon after the auditor has discovered the problem. It is not essential that all research avenues be completely exhausted prior to informing the company about a potential problem.

Communication. Free and open communication between the independent auditor and management is essential. The independent auditor must communicate with management and with other offices involved in the audit. The management at corporate headquarters usually communicates just with the headquarters' audit team, which in turn controls contact with other offices.

Effective communication often represents the key ingredient to avoiding misunderstandings. One way this is accomplished for a multilocation company is for the local auditor at each subsidiary location to maintain continuing contact throughout the year. The independent auditor at corporate headquarters must adopt and adhere to the policy of sharing with management any matter that comes up for attention. Such a policy should be clearly understood.

In short, without effective communication, there is no possibility of developing effective relations between management and the auditor.

Chapter 35

Scope and objectives of the interim financial report

John V. van Pelt, III [*]

Interim financial reporting to the public has, until relatively recently, been on a *laissez-faire* basis. Accounting opinions of the American Institute of Certified Public Accountants were practically silent on matters relating to financial statements that did not conform to the corporate fiscal year. As a result, corporations had no formal guidance in establishing the accounting principles which allocated revenues and costs among the various interim periods of a fiscal year. There was no specified form or content for interim reports required to be issued by listed corporations to their stockholders under provisions of listing agreements entered into with the New York Stock Exchange, and in more recent years with the American Stock Exchange. The Securities and Exchange Commission has required a reporting of certain significant events ever since the adoption of the Securities Exchange Act of 1934, but interim financial data was called for only in connection with stub filings related to registration statements, certain economic reports and, for most recent years since 1946, either quarterly or semiannual data setting forth key operating figures.[1]

---

[*] Vice President–Finance (Retired), Vulcan Materials Company.

[1] For a more complete discussion of the evolution of interim reporting matters, see Robert G. Taylor, "A Look at Published Interim Reports," *The Accounting Review*, January 1965, pp. 89–96; and "The Published Interim Report and the CPA," *The Journal of Accountancy*, September 1965, pp. 55–58.

In 1970 the Securities and Exchange Commission adopted Form 10-Q, concurrently rescinding Form 9-K. In 1971 the Management Accounting Practices Committee of the National Association of Accountants issued a statement entitled "Guidelines for Interim Financial Reporting." In 1973 the Accounting Principles Board of the American Institute issued *Opinion No. 28*, "Interim Financial Reporting." Additionally, Rule 10b-5 has become increasingly important in connection with issuance of material information relating to a company's operations, as its scope has been extended following the Texas Gulf Sulphur case which was adjudicated in the Southern District Court of New York in 1966.

(*Note:* The reader should consult Chapter 37, particularly the section "Quarterly Reporting—Form 10-6" beginning on page 863. This section summarizes the expanded SEC requirements for interim reporting contained in *ASR No. 177*, issued in September, 1975.)

THE PURPOSE OF THE INTERIM FINANCIAL REPORT

The changed atmosphere surrounding the interim report relates in a large measure to the reason for its issuance. Years ago when the New York Stock Exchange was the primary force pushing for the issuance of these reports, the general corporate attitude was one of condescension.

Today the interim report is an element in a required pattern of maintaining publicly issued information on a current basis. By failing to keep up a constant flow of information regarding material events which might affect the market value of a company's stock, the company creates problems for its executives and employees who might wish to enter into transactions in the company's stock.

A corporation which is publicly owned avails itself of many avenues for the dispersion of information. There is a question as to the extent to which all information releases must be fully consistent. This will be touched upon subsequently. However, there is no question that information which is material in its impact on the market value of the company's stock must be made available to all who are potential traders. On this basis, information which the management deems to be material should probably be included in all releases, whether they are in the form of required filings with the SEC or interim statements mailed to the company stockholders.

Additionally, at the time the events first occur or where probability of occurrence is first disclosed to anyone, they should be made the subject of press releases.

Obviously, there are situations in which, for competitive reasons, disclosure of impending developments would hurt the company. Under such situations, so long as no outsider has knowledge of the event and no insider avails himself or herself of this knowledge for personal gain, failure to disclose would be acceptable.

Primarily, the interim financial report is a mechanism for indicating earnings progress within the fiscal year, but modern concepts make it imperative that the report contain far more than the bare figures of net income and earnings per share.

THE INDEPENDENT AUDITOR

In few instances do independent public accountants render an opinion with respect to interim financial information. Dr. L. Todd Johnson explores three avenues of approach that could lead to ultimate acceptance by independent accountants of responsibility for data contained in interim reports.[2] First, it would be possible to adopt now the requirement that auditors disclose known misrepresentation in interim financial statements issued by the client during the year under examination. Second, an extension of the auditor's area of responsibility would call for a mandatory year-end review of interim reports issued with respect to the fiscal year and correction in the annual report of any discrepancies, or a "negative assurance" that no discrepancies were discovered during the course of the examination. The third avenue would call for a program of "continuous auditing" to permit rendering of an opinion on the interim statements at the time of issuance. Dr. Johnson recognizes that such factors as higher cost and a delay in the issuance of data may create problems, but he contends that ultimately the benefits of full attestation would justify the added costs or inconveniences.

For many years, independent accountants have given "negative assurance" with respect to stub statements filed in connection with securities registrations. In the early days of Securities Act registrations they gave opinions related to stub periods, but such situations are rare today. However, agreements between issuers of securities

---

[2] L. Todd Johnson, "Extending the Attest Function to Interim Reports," *The CPA Journal*, June 1974, pp. 43–46, 50.

(or selling stockholders) and investment bankers providing for the offering and sale of securities to the public usually are conditioned upon the receipt by the investment bankers of a letter from the issuer's independent public accountants. Among other matters, the accountants will be asked to comment on unaudited financial statements included in the registration statement. The resultant letter is usually termed a "comfort letter." With respect to the unaudited financial statements the accountants can only furnish "negative assurance."

In October 1971 the AICPA Committee on Auditing Procedure issued *SAP No. 48*, "Letters for Underwriters." This *SAP* made a primary change from earlier procedures by making it clear that the underwriters are responsible for the sufficiency of the procedures employed by the independent auditors in furnishing negative assurance with respect to unaudited interim financial statements and other matters included in the comfort letters.

SAP No. 48 includes an example of a typical comfort letter. Additionally, the procedure indicates that the comfort letter should set forth the work to be performed by the accountants. Other than reading minutes of corporate meetings and reviewing the unaudited statements the principal work done by the accountants is described in the words "made inquiries of certain officials of the company, . . ." in the example referred to above.

Obviously, the scope of the "inquiries" is the real meaning of the extent of the examination made by the independent accountants. Louis H. Rappaport, a former partner of Coopers & Lybrand, includes in his book copies of programs used by his firm covering three types of industries.[3]

The extent of the inquiries covered by the foregoing examples is quite detailed, and includes examination of the client's ledgers to insure that the financial statements conform to those records, comparisons with prior periods, and reviews of the client's underlying working papers supporting any of the interim financial statements. Additionally, tax returns and internal audit reports are examined and tax provisions checked. Letters are obtained from company's counsel. These steps are supplemented by questions addressed to company personnel.

The above procedures presently permit a negative assurance, and

[3] Louis H. Rappaport, SEC *Accounting Practice and Procedure*, 3d ed. (New York: Ronald Press Co., 1972) pp. 12–57.

possibly this might be considered sufficient to cover any interim statement. It is not beyond the imagination that the profession could apply such procedures to interim statements on a widespread basis without unduly burdening industry with additional cost. Time delays would probably be minimal, though such examinations would hardly be possible in situations where companies follow the practice of issuing interim figures only a few days after the end of a quarter.

SEC FILING REQUIREMENTS

Form 8-K

This is a report that must be filed upon the occurrence of significant events. It must be filed by companies having securities listed on a national securities exchange and also by publicly owned, unlisted companies registered pursuant to Section 12(g) of the 1934 Act. Exemption from reporting is granted to foreign governments, certain foreign private issuers, issuers of American Depository Receipts for securities of any foreign issuer, or investment companies reporting quarterly under Rule 13a-12. The form must be filed within ten days after the end of the month in which any of the following events occur, unless the same information as that required by Form 8-K has been previously reported by the company to the SEC:

Item 1. Changes in control of registrant.
Item 2. Acquisition or disposition of a significant amount of assets otherwise than in the ordinary course of business.
Item 3. Material legal proceedings.
Item 4. Changes in registered securities.
Item 5. Changes in collateral for registered securities.
Item 6. Material defaults upon senior securities.
Item 7. Material increases in amounts of outstanding securities.
Item 8. Material decreases in amounts of outstanding securities.
Item 9. Granting or extension of options to purchase securities of the registrant or its subsidiaries.
Item 10. Material charges or credits of an unusual nature (such as write-downs, write-offs, or abandonments of assets or obsolescence of inventory), material credits to income

from disposition of assets, or material restatements of capital share accounts.

Item 11.   Matter submitted to vote of security holders.

Item 12.   Changes in registrant's certifying accountant.

Item 13.   The registrant may, at its option, report under this item any events, with respect to which information is not otherwise called for by the form, that the registrant deems of material importance to security holders.

Item 14.   Financial statements and exhibits.

Form 8-K was amended in 1971 by the addition of Item 12 noted above. This item provides that if a registrant engages as its principal accountant to audit the registrant's financial statements an independent accountant, who was not the principal accountant for the registrant's most recently filed certified financial statements, the date when such independent accountant is employed must be stated. Additionally, a statement is required from the registrant outlining any disagreements with the former independent accountant which, if not resolved to the former accountant's satisfaction, would have caused the former accountant to refer in his or her opinion to the subject matter of such disagreement. Furthermore, the registrant is required to request the former accountant to write a letter to the Commission indicating the extent of his or her agreement or disagreement with the statement.

Item 14 of Form 8-K relates primarily to acquisitions described in Item 2. The test of significance to determine the necessity for inclusion in Item 2 is (1) if the net book value of such assets or the amount paid or received therefor upon such acquisition or disposition exceeded 15 percent of the total assets of the registrant and its consolidated subsidiaries, or (2) if it involved the acquisition or disposition of a business whose gross revenues for its last fiscal year exceeded 15 percent of the aggregate gross revenues of the registrant and its consolidated subsidiaries for the registrant's last fiscal year.

A balance sheet of an acquired business must be filed as of a date reasonably close to the date of acquisition. This balance sheet need not be certified, but if it is not certified, there shall also be filed a certified balance sheet as of the close of the preceding fiscal year. Income and retained earnings statements of the business must be filed for each of the last three full fiscal years and for the period, if any, between the close of this latest of such fiscal years and the date of the latest balance sheet filed. The income and retained earnings statements must be certified up to the date of the certified balance sheet.

If the business was in insolvency proceedings immediately prior to its acquisition, the balance sheets referred to above need not be certified. In such case, the income and retained earnings statements required must be certified to the close of the latest full fiscal year. In general, principles applicable to a registrant and its subsidiaries with respect to the filing of individual, consolidated, and group statements are the same as those relating to original registration statements of annual reports. Regulation S-X contains requirements as to certification and form and content of financial statements, except that no supporting schedules need to be filed. Instructions for Form 8-K also contain provisions relating to the filing of other statements or the omission of statements.

Form 10-Q

Every issuer of a security registered under Section 12 of the Securities Exchange Act of 1934 which is required to file annual reports with the SEC on Forms 10-K, 12-K, or U-5-S, has to file a quarterly report on Form 10-Q. The report must be filed for each of the first three quarters of the fiscal year, beginning with the first of such quarters that ends after securities of the issuer become registered.

Certain classes of issuers are exempt from the requirement to file these reports:

1. Investment companies required to file quarterly reports under Rule 12a-12;
2. Real estate companies filing on Form 7-Q;
3. Foreign private issuers filing on Form 6-K;
4. Life insurance companies and holding companies having only life insurance subsidiaries; or
5. Companies in the promotional or development stage to which paragraph (b) or (c) of Rule 5A-01 of Article 5A of Regulation S-X is applicable.

Certain public utilities may, at their option, file as exhibits to Form 10-Q copies of their reports to regulatory authorities for the preceding fiscal quarter or for each month of such quarter as the case may be, together with copies of their quarterly reports, if any, for such periods sent to their stockholders.

Subject to the above-noted exemptions, the requirement to file quarterly reports on Form 10-Q is also applicable to every issuer that registered securities pursuant to the Securities Act of 1934 and is required to file annual reports pursuant to Section 15(d) of the 1934 Act on Form 10-K, 12-K, or U-5-S.

Form 10-Q calls for three kinds of financial information:

A. Summarized profit and loss information.
B. Summarized capitalization and stockholders' equity information.
C. Information concerning sales of unregistered securities.

The information submitted need not be certified. Information is to be given as to the registrant or, if the registrant includes consolidated financial statements in its annual reports filed with the Commission, it shall be given for the registrant and its consolidated subsidiaries. If information is given for a consolidated group, it need not be given separately for the registrant. The same requirements of presentation apply to Form 10-Q with respect to unconsolidated subsidiaries, 50 percent owned companies, or similar companies or groups as apply to reports filed with the Commission, except that no information need be furnished for any unconsolidated subsidiary or company which would not be required to file quarterly financial information if it were a registrant pursuant to Rule 12a-13 or 15d-13. Some delay is permitted with respect to information applicable to unconsolidated foreign companies, but the delayed information must be filed by amendment when available.

The summarized financial information called for by Part A has to be furnished in comparative columnar form for (1) the interim period between the end of the last fiscal year and the end of the latest fiscal quarter, and (2) the corresponding period of the preceding fiscal year. In cases of reports for the second and third fiscal quarters the summarized financial information may also be furnished, at the registrant's option, for the most recent fiscal quarter and the corresponding period of the preceding fiscal year.

In situations involving material seasonal cycles, or material variations in operating results from other causes, the required information may be supplemented with comparative figures for the 12 months to the end of the period for which the report is filed, and the corresponding 12 months in the preceding year. For registrants engaged in seasonal production and seasonal sale of a single-crop agricultural commodity, the summarized financial information may include information for the 12 months ended with the current interim quarter, with comparative data for the corresponding period in the preceding year, in place of year-to-date information specified in the preceding paragraph.

The financial information to be included must be prepared in conformity with the accounting principles or practices (including consolidated practices) reflected in the financial statements included in the annual report filed with the Commission for the preceding fiscal year, unless a change in accounting principle or practice which would materially affect the financial statements filed or to be filed for the current year with the Commission, and not previously reported, is described. The description must state the date of change and the reasons therefor, and be accompanied by a letter from the registrant's independent accountants (filed as an exhibit) approving or otherwise commenting on the change.

While Form 10-Q specifies certain captions for both Parts A and B, captions may be varied or added to where appropriate to conform to the nature of the business of the registrant and its subsidiaries. Furthermore, any material information necessary to make the material called for not misleading must be furnished, including statements that results for interim periods may not be indicative of results for the full year, due to seasonal or other specified factors, or explanations of unusual increases or decreases in net sales or income.

The information furnished has to reflect all adjustments which are, in the opinion of management, necessary to a fair statement of the results for the interim periods. A statement to that effect must be included. Such adjustments have to include, for example, appropriate estimated provisions for bonus and profit sharing arrangements normally determined or settled at year-end.

Any material retroactive prior period adjustment made during any period in the report needs to be disclosed, together with the effect thereof upon net income—total and per share—of any period included in the report and upon the balance of retained earnings. If results of operations for any period reported on have been ad-

justed retroactively by such an item subsequent to the initial reporting of such period, similar disclosure of the effect of the change
has to be made.

The registrant may furnish any additional information related
to the periods being reported on which, in the opinion of management, is of significance to investors, such as a statement of changes
in financial position, the dollar amount of backlog of firm orders,
and an explanation of commitments and contingent liabilities.

If appropriate, the summary of income information must be
prepared to show earnings applicable to common stock. Per-share
earnings and dividends declared for each period of the summary
must be included and the basis of the computation stated, together
with the number of shares used in the computation. Unless set
forth in some other part of Form 10-Q, the computation of per-share
earnings in detail must be filed as an exhibit.

If a registrant has both gross sales and operating revenues they
must be separately shown, unless one of them is not more than 10
percent of the sum of the two. If gross sales and operating revenues
include excise taxes in an amount equal to 10 percent or more of
the total of such items, the amount of excise taxes shall be stated
separately. If the provision for income taxes includes any material
provisions for deferred income taxes, they shall be disclosed and
explained. The methods used (e.g., proportion of year expired or
estimated annual effective tax rate) in the allocation to the interim
periods of the income tax effects of operating loss carrybacks, carryforwards, or other tax credits shall be described.

Additional instructions apply if there have been acquisitions of
other businesses or dispositions of significant portions of the registrant's business. If an acquisition was treated as a pooling of interests, the results of operations for both the current and the prior
year must reflect the combined results including the pooled business.
Supplemental disclosure of the separate results of the combined
entities for periods prior to the combination must be given, with
appropriate explanations. In case the registrant has disposed of any
significant portion of its business or has acquired a significant
amount of assets in a transaction treated for accounting purposes
as a purchase during any of the periods covered by the report,
the effect on revenues and net income—total and per share—for
all periods has to be disclosed.

As an addendum to Part C, under most situations in which

new debt is incurred (but not when leases are capitalized for accounting purposes) an EDP attachment is required, which is used by the Commission for statistical purposes. The attachment is a punch card upon which the registrant records certain data relating to the newly incurred debt.

The 10-Q report is due to be filed within 45 days after the end of each of the first three fiscal quarters of each fiscal year. If an interim report to stockholders contains all of the required information, it may be filed as an exhibit and the information incorporated by reference.

Form 7-Q

Quarterly reports on Form 7-Q have to be filed by issuers of securities registered under Section 12 of the 1934 Act, a substantial portion of whose business is that of acquiring and holding for investment: (1) real estate or interests in real estate, or (2) interests in other issuers, a substantial portion of whose business is that of acquiring and holding for investment real estate or interests in real estate, and which as a matter of policy or practice make cash distributions from any source other than current or retained earnings. The report must also be filed by real estate companies which register securities under the 1933 Act and are obligated to file reports pursuant to Section 15(d) of the 1934 Act.

The 7-Q report has to be filed for each of the first three fiscal quarters of each fiscal year, commencing with the first such quarter that ends after securities of the issuer become registered.

The form need not be filed with respect to (1) any investment company that has an obligation to report quarterly pursuant to Rule 13a-12, (2) foreign private issuers required to file Form 6-K, or (3) any partnership all of whose properties are under long-term net leases to other persons.

Form 7-Q consists of four parts:

A. Profit and loss information prepared on an accrual basis.
B. Funds generated and funds disbursed.
C. Cumulative amounts of excess (deficiency) of funds generated over distributions, after realized gains (losses) on investments (exclusive of minority interests).
D. Summary of capitalization and stockholders' equity.

The instructions for Form 7-Q are substantially the same as those for Form 10-Q, except that the summarized financial information is set forth in a format designed solely for a registrant involved in real estate operations. In Part B material minority interests must be separately columnarized.

RULE 13a-10 INTERIM REPORTS

Rule 13a-10 relates to issuers registered under Section 12 of the 1934 Act which change fiscal closing dates. If such companies change their fiscal years after the end of the last fiscal year shown in financial statements included in a filing pursuant to Section 12 of the Act, they shall file a report covering the resulting interim period. This report is ordinarily due within 120 days of the close of the interim period or after the date of determination to change the closing fiscal date, whichever is later. There is an exception to the requirement if the interim period is less than three months, or if the interim period for the preceding fiscal year or the annual report for the succeeding fiscal year covers the interim period as well as the fiscal year.

The rule also requires interim reports in connection with applications for registration on Form 8-B which relates to the succession by a registrant to the business of a predecessor or predecessors having outstanding registered securities.

The rule requires certification of the financial statements included in the interim reports, either at the time of filing the interim report if the statements are for a period of more than six months, or in conjunction with the filing of the next annual report of the registrant.

SEC RULE 10b-5

Rule 10b-5 deals with a wide variety of transactions. Much of the extent of the rule's application has been developed by the SEC. The development of judicial decisions has been spotty, mostly occurring at the district court level. Professor Alan R. Bromberg of Southern Methodist University has explored the rule in detail.[4] Business executives should read this study in order to understand

---

[4] Alan R. Bromberg, *Securities Law Fraud-Rule 106 S*, Revised to 1973 (New York: McGraw-Hill Book Company).

the potential ramifications of the rule. The following comments are merely indicative of some of the areas that can be covered.

The *Texas Gulf Sulphur* case[5] went a long way in making people realize how far-reaching the rule was in regard to the issuance of interim information. In this case there were widespread and highly exaggerated rumors regarding a raw material strike. The extent of the find had not been determined by the company, so it put out a very lukewarm report on the matter. Shortly thereafter, the find was proved to be valuable. Before the second public announcement two employees had purchased stock, not knowing that this was an improper act. They were guilty of fraud. Two directors who placed orders for the stock 20 minutes after the announcement were not guilty. It is quite clear from this case that any insider who possesses information which has not been made public, that may affect the market value of a company's securities, engages in transactions involving company securities at his or her peril.

In the case of *Cady, Roberts & Co.*, 40 SEC pp. 912–1961, it was held that a broker who received information from a company director that the company was about to cut its dividend sharply was an insider. The extension of the rule is such that failure to release information while others are involved in trading may create liability.

No final determination has been made in the case of the analyst who determined from his analysis that there were problems at Equity Funding which could result in bankruptcy. The analyst used the findings to benefit his customers, rather than making the information public. There have been allegations that the analyst operated improperly, and these actions could be susceptible to a claim of fraud under the rule, but no formal action has been brought. An interesting feature of 10b-5 is that there is no statute of limitations under its provisions. Obviously there are situations in which, to protect the company's position during development of a competitive situation, release of information may not be possible. Insiders in such situations must not indulge in security transactions if values might be affected by the outcome of the development, nor disclose information which they possess to others.

Clearly, Rule 10b-5 must be considered when preparing financial statements as part of an interim report. The rules set forth under

---

[5] *S.E.C.* v. *Texas Gulf Sulphur Co.*, 258 F. Supp. 262, S.D., N.Y. 1966.

Form 10-Q, which are also common to Form 7-Q, require the management to furnish any material information to make the material called for not misleading, as well as explanations as to why the results of the interim period may not be indicative of the results for the full fiscal year. A management which ignored an action or event that could have a significant impact upon results beyond the end of the fiscal year would do so at its peril.

Of course, Rule 10b-5 is not specifically aimed at interim financial statements, but it calls for immediate announcement of the event in question as soon as it becomes known. However, since such information would be announced only if material in its impact on the company's present or future results, it must become a part of future financial statement presentations until its impact is reflected in the results shown, or until there is a change in the conditions.

GUIDELINES FOR INTERIM FINANCIAL REPORTING

In the late 1960s discussions between the National Association of Accountants, The Financial Executives Institute, and The American Institute of Certified Public Accountants, resulted in agreement that the NAA would undertake an initial research project to determine the basic principles that should be applied to interim reports. The results of this study were finally published by the NAA in 1972.[6]

In 1971 the Committee on Management Accounting Practices of the NAA issued a statement based in part on early drafts of the research study, but more importantly on the findings of a subcommittee to which the work was delegated, which set forth "Guidelines for Interim Financial Reporting." In general, the statement was designed to provide guidance for current practice and to suggest a basis for further development of the subject.

The guidelines are presented herewith:

1.   *Preamble*
1.1   Interim statements are designed to provide a timely reporting

---

[6] James W. Edwards, Geraldine F. Dominiak, and Thomas V. Hedges, *Internal Financial Reporting* (New York: The National Association of Accountants, May 1972).

of pertinent financial information with highlights of significant happenings. The report is intended to assist the investor and other users in following the trends of the business.

1.2 The purpose of these guidelines is to set standards for the reporting of interim financial information.

2. *Guidelines*

2.1 Those companies that currently report publicly should supplement their annual financial information with interim financial information. As a minimum, interim financial reports should be published on a quarterly basis for the first three quarters of the fiscal period. The practice followed by a number of companies of publishing an interim report for the fourth quarter is encouraged.

2.2 The interim reporting period should be regarded as a portion of the annual fiscal period rather than a fiscal period in itself.

2.3 The preparation of the interim financial reports and the recognition of revenues and expenses should be based on accounting principles and practices which are consistently applied and conform with those used in the preparation of annual financial statements. Revenues should be reported in the period in which earned. While arbitrary adjustments to net income should be avoided, meaningful interim reporting recognizes that costs and expenses incurred, or to be incurred, in one interim period for the benefit of the fiscal year may be prorated over that year. Thus, a company which accounts for particular transactions as incurred on an annual basis might accrue or defer such transactions for interim reporting periods.

2.4 The interim statement, as a minimum, should include sales and revenue, income taxes, income before extraordinary items, and net income for the interim period and year-to-date, together with comparative data for the same period of the prior year. Income before extraordinary items per share and net income per share should be shown for the current interim period and year-to-date with comparative data for the prior year. In addition, a condensed balance sheet or statement of changes in financial position should be included when a material financial transaction has taken place which would lead the company to believe that these reports are significant.

2.5 A change in interim or general accounting practice or policy should be disclosed in the report for the period in which the change is made. The dollar impact of the change applicable to the interim period and the effect on year-to-date amounts should be reported. Whenever possible, accounting changes should be made effective at the beginning of a fiscal year.

2.6 No restatement of prior interim periods should be made for changes in estimates or assumptions used as a basis for prior period reporting.

2.7 Interim reports should comment on important developments, extraordinary items, and unusual transactions and disclose them in the period in which they occur.

2.8 Extraordinary items for purposes of interim financial reporting should consist of those that will be expected to be set forth in the fiscal year financial statements as extraordinary items. Unusual transactions, the amounts of which are material with respect to the operating results of the interim period but which are not expected to be shown as extraordinary items in the fiscal year statements, should be explained along with the impact on earnings per share.

2.9 Interim financial statements should be presented on a consolidated basis by companies which present their annual financial statements on a consolidated basis.

2.10 Interim financial statements should recognize the combined results of pooled businesses for the current period and all prior periods included in the report. The effect of any material divestiture should be reported in the period in which it occurs.

2.11 Attestation by independent public accountants of interim financial reports is not required. However, to provide for consistency with the annual report, companies should counsel with their public accountants relative to any change in accounting methods, extraordinary items, or other significant transactions which might arise within an interim period.

2.12 These guidelines are intended to require that to the extent financial data included within the interim report is also furnished to the SEC, such data should be consistent.

In reviewing the guidelines, it should be recognized that they were issued before *Opinion No. 30* of the Accounting Principles Board, which was released in June 1973. At the time the guidelines were first published there were many more extraordinary items that appeared in financial statements when compared to the specification of such items under *Opinion No. 30*. It is quite possible that the statement would have been worded differently in this area if corporate practices had conformed to present-day rules.

Except that the SEC expects information regarding pooled businesses on a separate basis for prior periods as well as the reflecttion of the prior periods on a pooled basis, the guidelines conform to SEC requirements. The guidelines go considerably further than the SEC requirements in laying down accounting rules that should apply to interim statements. Paragraphs 2.2 and 2.3 were possibly the first clarification of grey areas that had existed in connection with the preparation of interim statements.

OPINION NO. 28

The Accounting Principles Board, as one of its last acts, issued *Opinion No. 28* dealing with interim reporting in May 1973.[7] A summary of the provisions of the *Opinion* follows:

1. The interim period should be viewed primarily as an integral part of an annual period.
2. Revenues should be recognized as earned during an interim period on the same basis as followed for the full year.
3. Costs may be classified as:
   a. Costs associated with revenue which are charged to income in periods in which the revenue is recognized.
   b. All other costs that are not allocable to products sold or services rendered may be charged to income as incurred or allocated among periods on the basis of an estimate of time expired, benefit received, or other activity associated with the periods.
4. Companies should generally use the same inventory pricing methods and use the same basis for write-down to market at interim dates as at annual inventory dates. However, the following exceptions are appropriate at interim reporting dates:
   a. Some companies use estimated gross profit rates to determine cost of goods sold during interim periods, or some other method different from that used at annual inventory dates. These companies should disclose the method used at interim dates, and any significant adjustments should such arise in reconciling with the annual physical inventory.
   b. Companies using the Lifo method should provide reserves

---

[7] AICPA, "Interim Financial Reporting," *Accounting Principles Board Opinion 28* (New York, May 1973).

for replacement for interim period declines in base levels that are expected to be replaced by year-end.

c.   Inventory losses from market declines should be recognized in the period the decline occurs and future recoveries in the same fiscal year should be treated as gains, but only to the extent of previously reflected losses. This proviso would not apply if management deemed a decline to be a temporary situation within the fiscal year.

d.   Standard cost variances that are planned (for example, volume variances) should be deferred at interim reporting dates. Unplanned or unanticipated variances should be absorbed on an interim basis.

5.   When a cost or expense item which is charged to expense for annual reporting purposes benefits more than one interim period, the cost or expense should be allocated to those periods.

6.   Some costs and expenses incurred in an interim period cannot be readily identified with activities or benefits of other periods and should be charged to the interim period in which incurred. Disclosure should be made as to the nature and amount of such costs, unless items of a comparable nature are included in both the current interim period and the interim period of the preceding year. Arbitrary assignment of such costs to an interim period should not be made. Gains and losses that arise in any interim period similar to those that would not be deferred at year-end should not be deferred to later interim periods within the same fiscal year.

7.   The amounts of certain costs and expenses are frequently subjected to year-end adjustments even though they can be reasonably approximated at interim dates. To the extent possible, such adjustments should be estimated and the resultant costs and expenses assigned to interim periods on a reasonable basis.

8.   Significant seasonal variations should be disclosed.

9.   Income taxes should be accrued on the basis of effective tax rates estimated for the fiscal year, excluding the tax related to unusual or extraordinary items.

10.   Effects of tax losses arising in early portions of a fiscal year (assuming carry-back of such losses is not possible) should be recognized only when realization is assured beyond a reasonable doubt. A pattern of early year losses offset by income

in later periods of the year should negate such doubt under normal situations. Tax effects of losses in an early interim period may be recognized in a later interim period of the year if realization, though initially uncertain, becomes reasonably assured. When tax effects of losses in early periods are not recognized, no tax provision on later income of the year should be made until all interim losses are utilized. Changes resulting from new tax legislation should be reflected after the effective dates prescribed in the statutes.

11. Extraordinary items included in an interim period should be disclosed separately. Effects of disposals and other unusual items not classified as extraordinary should be separately disclosed in interim statements of affected periods. Disclosure should be made of unusual seasonal results, poolings of interest, and significant purchases. Extraordinary items, gains and losses from disposition of a business, and unusual or infrequent items should not be prorated over the balance of the year.

12. Disclosures of contingencies, changes in accounting principles or practices, and changes in estimates are required. The *Opinion* covers those changes of principle which require retroactive restatement. The effect of a change in estimate should be accounted for in the period in which the change is made, but the effect on earnings of a change made in a current interim period should be reported in the current and subsequent periods, if material to the period presented. It should continue to be reported for as long as necessary to avoid misleading comparisons.

13. In determining materiality, except as mentioned in the note above, the effect of the change or extraordinary item should be related to the estimated income for the full fiscal year and also to the effect on the trend of earnings.

14. The *Opinion* offers the following guides to minimum disclosure for publicly traded companies, recognizing that early issuance of data may be more desirable than complete financial statements.

  a. Sales or gross revenues, provision for income taxes, extraordinary items (including related income tax effects), cumulative effect of a change in accounting principles or practices, and net income.

    b.   Primary and fully diluted earnings per share data for each period presented.

    c.   Seasonal revenues, costs, or expenses.

    d.   Significant changes in estimates or provisions for income taxes.

    e.   Disposal of a segment of a business and extraordinary, unusual, or infrequently occurring items.

    f.   Contingent items.

    g.   Changes in accounting principles or estimates.

    h.   Significant changes in financial position.

    When financial data are furnished it should be done on a comparative basis with the prior year and should also include year to date or the last 12 months to date.

15.   If a fourth quarter report is not separately issued, the annual report should include fourth quarter information.

16.   The *Opinion* indicates that publishing of balance sheets and funds flow data should be encouraged for publicly traded companies and the inclusion of the item indicated as 14(h) above is applicable only in situations where this cannot be accomplished.

17.   The *Opinion* is effective for interim information issued for all periods relating to fiscal years beginning after December 31, 1973.

UNSETTLED AREAS

Though an APB *Opinion* has been issued, it is possible that the last word has not been said in establishing the accounting principles to be applied in preparing interim statements. Five of the 18 members of the APB disagreed on one major point. The *Opinion* favored the treatment of the interim period as a part of an annual period, as did the NAA statement. The five dissenters contended that the interim period should be a discrete accounting period.

The NAA did not disclose any dissent in the subcommittee that drafted its statement, but in that instance there was also opposition on this same point. It is possible that further examination of this particular area should be made before the issuance of authoritative statements results in the establishment of an inflexible and possibly misleading application. Those who oppose the theory of the interim period being considered part of a fiscal year point to two difficulties. First, the fiscal year, just like a shorter span of time, is also an interim period in the life of a business, and in a multiproduct line corporation will probably involve several differing natural business years. Second, the opposition group feels that treating any period as part of a longer period tends to obscure the events that arise in that period.

The only enforcement authority wielded by the American Institute is under Rule 203 of the Institute's Rules of Conduct. Since few independent accountants' opinions are issued to cover interim statements, the Institute has little enforcement authority in this instance. Many principal financial officers of corporations are members of the Institute, so conceivably the Institute could move against them if they did not comply with the provisions of the opinion. In that portion of the *Opinion* that deals with accounting principles, as opposed to statement presentation and disclosure, the SEC is in a position to provide some measure of enforcement since the SEC has indicated that it will generally require adherence to the opinions of the APB in financial statements filed with the Commission. Corporations filing Forms 10-Q or 7-Q would thus have to follow such principles.

The authority with the greatest enforcement power in regard to interim financial statements prepared for stockholders would be either the New York Stock Exchange or the American Stock Exchange, both of which provide in listing agreements signed in recent years for quarterly issuance of such statements. Under threat of delisting, the Exchanges could go a long way toward forcing adherence to the *Opinion* in all of its provisions.

While it would seem axiomatic that the same principles would have to be applied in constructing the accounting results for a given period no matter who the ultimate user of the information might be, it is so clear that the content of the statements issued should always be the same. A. A. Sommer, Jr., a commissioner of the SEC, pointed out in an address in March, 1974,[8] that Securities Act *Release No. 5427* contains a section that indicates that the Commission may feel that financial statements might be something other than unitary—that is, there might be financial statements for

---

[8] A summarization of the address by A. A. Sommer, Jr., given as the Second Emanuel Saxe Distinguished Accounting Lecture at Baruch College, New York, on March 19, 1974, is contained in *The Journal of Accountancy*, August 1974, pp. 55–58.

the sophisticated investor and professional analyst, and financial statements for the average investor.

The paragraph that raises this point states:

> The proposals set forth in this release are primarily designed to assist professional analysts who have the responsibility of developing an understanding in depth of corporate activity. They are not primarily intended to serve the direct needs of the "average investor." Such an investor does not usually have the time to study or the training necessary to fully understand the data which are called for herein. It is not appropriate, however, for such data to be unavailable to the average investor who does wish to devote the time necessary to consider it. By being included in financial statements filed with the Commission, therefore, data will become "data of public record" and, hence, available to all. Disclosure will not be discriminatory even though usage will mostly be by professionals. Data of this kind would not be expected to be sent routinely to all shareholders, although it would be useful if its availability was mentioned in communications with shareholders and if management took steps to make it available on request.

Securities Act *Release No. 5427* related primarily to annual filings and Registration Statements, but since it proposed amendments to Regulation S-X, the same principles of inclusion of data submitted to the Commission in Form 8-K, Form 10-Q, or Form 7-Q would apply in determining the content of an interim report to stockholders.

It would seem to be clear that questions as to the need for furnishing the same information to all parties would be affected by the materiality of the information in its potential impact on the market price of a company's securities. SEC Commissioner Phillip Loomis made these cogent comments regarding materiality in a group discussion which was reported in the *Financial Analysts Journal:*

> . . . materiality has to be judged in the total context of the corporation.—I don't think it (materiality) should be judged purely on the basis of the magnitude of a market movement,—but if you have an event that could reasonably be expected to have a market impact, and it does, then maybe you've got a material event.—it is a good thing for a company to disclose material events in its life promptly. By prompt disclosure, the company complies with its obligations under the Exchange rules if it is a listed company and avoids a problem for its executives and employees. Once information is public, insiders can trade; before that they can't.—highly

specific information is a simple, concrete event or determination or fact, as opposed to a mosaic of general information, some of which is public and some of which isn't. We are not trying to inhibit securities research. That's one of the reasons why we refer to a specific event rather than the result of research.[9]

WHAT SHOULD INTERIM REPORTS INCLUDE?

With the foregoing background, it is obviously impossible to lay down any single set of rules for inclusion or exclusion that would satisfy all parties. However, there seem to be enough guidelines, opinions, required data, and statements available to establish the following as relatively defensible standards for interim reporting.

1. No information should be given to security analysts that has not been publicly released, unless it is to be released concurrently, except for general economic data which could be attained by anyone performing research outside the company.
2. So long as *Opinion No. 28* is in force, its provisions should govern the allocation of revenues and expenses within the fiscal year.
3. Information required to be submitted to the SEC is clearly spelled out, except that a determination as to materiality of significant events is a matter of judgment. As suggested in the guidelines submitted by NAA, the company should consult with its independent accountants in connection with the compilation of interim reports. The judgment as to materiality should be joint between management and the accountants, with the understanding that information considered material on an annual basis for purposes of the interim report will be included in the annual report.
4. Reports to stockholders should be issued at the end of each of the first three quarters of the year, and if no separate fourth quarter report is issued, the operating results for that quarter should be summarized in the annual report.
5. Reports to stockholders should include, on a comparative basis with the preceding year:
   a. Results for the current quarter.
   b. Results for the fiscal year to date.

---

[9] "Loomis on Inside Information" (an edited transcript), *Financial Analysts Journal*, May–June 1972, pp. 20–25, 82–88.

c. For companies with significant seasonal variations, or for companies with varied product lines that create natural business years that do not conform in all instances to the fiscal year, results for the 12 months ending at the end of the current quarter. (Form 10-Q suggested that "companies" engaged in the seasonal production and seasonal sale of a single-crop agricultural commodity might limit operating results to those of the current quarter and of the 12 months ending at the end of the current quarter.)

d. Operating results should be furnished at least in the detail called for by *Opinion No. 28.*

e. While neither the guidelines issued by NAA nor *Opinion No. 28* covered the point, it would seem to be essential that those companies which furnish a breakdown of revenues and earnings (generally before certain unallocated items such as income taxes, interest, or administrative expenses) by product lines in their annual reports should also furnish such information in interim reports. One important reason for this position is that such companies are almost surely going to be furnishing such data to security analysts, and the flow of business in differing product lines can have highly significant impacts on the overall direction of company earnings.

f. Interim reports to stockholders should include, at the least, summarized balance sheet data for the end of the current quarter and for the comparable date in the previous year. Additionally, the reports should include funds flow data for the current fiscal year to date.

g. Notes or other comments should explain (to the extent the financial information does not clearly describe the transaction) effects of disposals of a segment of the business, extraordinary items, and unusual and infrequently occurring transactions and events that are material with respect to the operating results of the interim period.

h. Notes or other comments should also explain matters such as unusual seasonal results, pooling of interests, and acquisitions of significant business interests in a purchase.

i. Notes or other comments should cover contingencies and other uncertainties that could be expected to affect the fairness of presentation of financial data.

j. Changes in accounting practices and changes in accounting estimates should be described.

k. Comments accompanying the interim financial statements should cover significant events that may change the course of future earnings. Whether or not estimates of earnings for the full fiscal year are mentioned should be determined entirely on the basis of the company's practice in its use of such information in annual reports, and in discussions with security analysts or major investors.

l. Comments should cover any other items mentioned in 8-K reports for the current quarter.

m. Summarization of any data furnished to the SEC for interim purposes under *ASR Nos. 148* and *149* related to bank deposits covering short-term credit and components of income tax expenses, respectively.

n. Attestation by an independent public accountant should not be required.

THE FUTURE

The entire scope of interim reporting is undergoing change. There is a somewhat nebulous policing possible under existing conditions. Most companies tend to change their practices slowly unless pressure is applied. This is not to say that in isolated cases companies do not face up to the changing scene without hesitation. As an example, the Midland Company, in its report for the quarter ended June 30, 1973, revised its presentation of financial information and included in its president's letter the following statement:

> You will note that the financial information herein is presented in greater detail than has been our practice, as well as that of most other publicly owned companies in the past. The expanded presentation, which includes certain balance sheet and other statistical data (see facing page) in addition to the traditional earnings highlights, conforms to the disclosure of interim financial information suggested by the Accounting Principles Board of the American Institute of Certified Public Accountants in its recent Opinion 28. While the requirements of the opinion are not effective until 1974, we believe that compliance at this early date is in keeping with the best interest of you, our shareholders. We think it is also responsive to the many favorable comments received regarding the comprehensive data in our 1972 annual report which was similar in style and

presentation to the Annual Report on Form 10-K filed with the Securities and Exchange Commission. We hope you find this additional data informative as we continually endeavor to keep you currently appraised of the progress of our company.

It is possible that a coercive force may be injected into the picture. Ray Garrett, Jr., chairman, Securities and Exchange Commission, made the following comments before the Financial Analysts Federation Annual Conference in 1974:

> Another area which will be receiving attention is that of interim reporting. Historically, interim reporting has been on a highly summarized basis—somewhat of a stepchild to accountants and registrants alike. However, there is plenty of reason to believe that interim reports have a very substantial effect upon market behavior, and we believe that it is desirable to give this matter a new look. We certainly do not contemplate a requirement for the publication of full audited financial statements for interim periods, but we think that summary figures now made available may be too summary and may not be the most useful figures to most investors. We would welcome your thoughts on this subject. We will also be working with the AICPA in determining the responsibility of independent public accountants in the interim reporting field.[10]

If the SEC injects itself into the picture with regard to interim reports to stockholders, it is probable that conformity with *Opinion No. 28* will at least be assured. Possibly, there may be changes in that *Opinion* issued by the Financial Accounting Standards Board. It is not possible to contemplate regulations by the SEC expanding the form and content of the interim financial statements issued to stockholders.

While this discussion is centered on the publicly held company, some comment should be directed toward the privately held company. To the extent that creditors require interim statements they should be able to dictate the form and content, so that it would seem to be unnecessary to establish elaborate requirements for repetitive issuance of reports that have no real use or need. Where interim statements are required because of purchase investigations and comparable one-shot situations, the outside negotiator may well have to be satisfied that accounting procedures conform to

---

[10] "The S.E.C. Chairman Looks Ahead," an excerpt from Mr. Garrett's talk entitled "Improved Disclosure—Opportunity and Responsibility for Financial Analysts," *The C.P.A. Journal*, August 1974, pp. 12–13.

accepted practices for all purposes, not solely for interim statements. The privately owned company may well be keeping a set of books designed for a special purpose, such as minimization of income taxes, and all too often its public accountant is a party to, or instigator of, the practices followed.

Duality of reporting for different classes of investors or analysts for publicly owned companies is a dangerous practice. An investor should not have to halt his or her study of a company in order to ask the company to furnish information that might alter expectations as to the future trend of its earnings, while such data would be routinely sent to a professional analyst. If such data were not distributed to all interested persons alike, it would seem that anyone who might have spotted disadvantageous trends had the information been supplied routinely, would have an excellent cause of action. Who is to decide which investor is intelligent enough to use the information and which investor is not? Granted that a majority of investors would not be competent to analyze much of the submitted data, by making it available to everyone on an equal basis the company shifts any blame for not having sought out professional advice to the shoulders of the majority who are not competent.

PART 6

Accounting policy and corporate liability

Chapter 36

Pervasive role of accounting
(in harmonizing adverse economic interests, allocating economic resources, and resolving social conflicts)

*LeRoy Layton**

Is accounting, as many outsiders believe, just a clerical function, performed so that financial statements and tax returns can be prepared accurately? Is it the realm of limited imagination and exacting mathematical computations aimed simply at bringing financial statements in balance "to the penny"?

Bookkeeping is a clerical function and accounts do balance. But to view the accounting discipline in that narrow a perspective is to wholly ignore its intricacy, its recognized contributions to our social well-being, its role as mediator to a myriad of economic needs, and the internal efforts that continually extend and improve it.

Accounting has manifold uses in adjusting the values of many adverse economic interests; in helping to allocate financial, material, and human resources; and in resolving social conflicts. Accounting has served these purposes in the United States and other developed nations during a period of great change; and accounting has had to develop and improve considerably to be able to cope with change and to provide meaningful answers to questions of critical impor-

* Senior Partner, Main Lafrentz & Co., retired. Chairman of Board, McLintock Main Lafrentz—International.

tance to society. The pace of change in the past century, swift as it may have been, very likely will be exceeded by that of the next century. Accounting as we know it today may have to be drastically modified to continually stay abreast of future conditions. How well it succeeds will have significant bearing on the quality of life in the years ahead.

GENERAL

Accounting is an indispensable management tool in planning, programming, and controlling the continued financial vigor and health of individual enterprises and institutions, whether they be private or public, profit making or otherwise. All of these enterprises and institutions exist to serve society in a multitude of different ways. The efforts of many are supportively intertwined with others, but some act as agents of limit or control. The relative value of each institution to society is very difficult to determine. Yet each lays claim to financial, material, and human resources that are in limited supply.

Accounting has developed over the years to serve an economic system that has become increasingly complex and that is based on varied inputs and other factors that have become, to a considerable degree, interdependent. It has served an economy in which the private, free market system, in retrospect, may have been excessively effective and, in some measure, counterproductive, during an extended period of spectacular growth.[1] Whether this is or is not true, the government (mainly federal but also state and local) has stepped in as regulator, referee, or mediator whenever it has perceived a significant segment of the public interest to be in jeopardy. This integration of the traditional free market system with government planning and regulation has produced what some call a "mixed economy."[2]

---

[1] For some extraordinary insight and outlook on this matter, see D. H. Meadows, D. L. Meadows, Jorgen Randers, and W. W. Behrens III, *The Limits to Growth—A Report for the Club of Rome's Project on the Predicament of Mankind,* (A Potomac Associates book published by Universe Books, New York, 1972), 205 pp. *See also* a companion work by M.I.T. Professor J. W. Forrester, *World Dynamics* (Cambridge, Mass.: Wright-Allen Press, 1971).

[2] See Albert T. Sommers, ed., *The Free Society and Planning—A Conversation on the Future of the Mixed Economy* (New York: The Conference Board, Inc., 1975), 36 pp.

In this mixed economy, accounting provides the basic information for use in financial statements and an endless number of other documents and communications that are necessary in harmonizing the monetary claims and demands of all segments and constituents of our society. Accordingly, let's look at the role of accounting, first as it serves the diverse interests of the *private sector,* and second, for its many uses in the *public sector.*

PRIVATE SECTOR

Following are some of the roles played by accounting to assist and inform diverse parties at interest in the private sector, whether management, stockholders, potential stockholders, financial analysts, credit grantors, employees, suppliers and contractors, customers, or others, such as lessors, licensors, franchisors, or private nonprofit organizations.

Management

At the present time in the United States, the private business sector plays the central role in our economy. Managements set their individual corporate goals for producing and distributing the great majority of goods and services required to meet not only the needs of our domestic society but also (via exports) to satisfy in part the wants of other economies. They cope with the vagaries of the public's wants and needs, constrained by limited resources and public regulation—an effort that needs varying degrees of energy, ingenuity, technical knowledge, and risk taking. Managements provide employment for a large majority of the country's productive work force, and the taxes that they and their employees pay enable governmental bodies to function. Their contributions and those of their employees support most not-for-profit organizations. They also play a major part in implementing an all-important, and continuing, research and development effort.

Business managements have the prime responsibility for the vigor and health of the corporations under their care, and are completely dependent in this respect on managerial and financial accounting systems. *Managerial accounting* is used almost exclusively internally, while *financial accounting* produces data for both internal and external use.

Managerial accounting. Managerial accounting, although generally anchored to the financial accounting framework, involves a broader information-processing system. It deals in many units of measure and produces a variety of reports designed for specific purposes. Its scope encompasses the past, the present, and the future. Its purposes include short- and long-range planning, cost determination, control of activities, assessment of objectives and program performance, and provision of basic information for decision making. The following are a few of the many areas where managerial accounting can play a key role:

1. All facets of the budgetary process—financial, operating, capital, and so on.
2. Product costing by job order or process cost systems.
3. Establishment of standard costs and analyses of the amounts and meaning of variances.
4. Assistance with product pricing.
5. The setting of production schedules, control of production, and the maintenance of balance between purchases, inventory levels, marketing prospects, and so on.
6. Analytical support for decision making; for example:
    a. On feasibility of new products.
    b. On continuance or discontinuance of old products.
    c. On determinations of whether to buy or lease plant and heavy equipment.
    d. On questions of whether to manufacture or purchase product components.

Financial accounting. Financial accounting data, among many other uses, permits management:

1. To monitor the volume of sales and purchases.
2. To keep the value of inventory aligned with the rate of sales and purchases.
3. To know who owes them, how much, and when it is due, and to whom they owe money and when it is due.
4. To know and predict cash balances and cash flows.
5. To forecast and satisfy working capital needs.
6. To meet financing requirements of expansion or modernization programs.
7. To have funds available for the payments of taxes, and so forth.

In other words, financial accounting offers the information that management needs to keep the "cash to cash" cycle moving at an adequate pace. Corporate fiscal constipation can be more damaging and more difficult to cure than its human counterpart. An ill corporation will not adequately serve its customers nor offer sufficient opportunity to its employees. It probably will not be able to deal equitably with its creditors, and its stockholders will have their capital placed in jeopardy. It is likely to waste limited financial, material, and human resources, with a resultant loss to all of society. This leads to consideration of those outside the corporation who have an interest in its success or failure.

Financial statements

Financial statements provide the major source of economic information for stockholders, potential stockholders, financial analysts, credit grantors, employees, suppliers, and all other interested parties. These statements are contained in stockholders' annual and quarterly reports, filings with the Securities and Exchange Commission (SEC), direct submissions to interested parties in private financing arrangements, and sometimes in submissions to credit information services.

Management has the responsibility to prepare financial statements that present fairly the financial position of the corporation, the results of its operations, and the changes in its financial position. Generally, a comparison of the two latest years is reflected. The statements contain supplemental footnote information considered necessary to make them meaningful and not misleading to the reader. Guidelines in the preparation of financial statements come from a set of accounting conventions called *generally accepted accounting principles* (GAAP), some of which have been precisely articulated by: (*a*) the Accounting Principles Board (APB); (*b*) its successor, the Financial Accounting Standards Board (FASB); (*c*) the SEC; and (*d*) to a lesser extent, other regulatory agencies. The remainder of GAAP, however, has only the authority of acceptance through general usage.

The independent audit function

The interests of the corporation and its management generally are considered to be identical. The success of one brings rewards to the other. These rewards—whether they be power, prestige, high income, or wealth—are intended to attract, hold, and motivate key executives in the interests of their corporations. They also leave key executives open to the temptation of "putting the corporation's best foot forward" in the preparation of financial statements. No matter how scrupulously objective key executives may be, they remain suspect by most of the investing public. It is considered imperative that this doubt be dispelled so that financial statements can fulfill their essential role in communicating economic data to the rest of society.

This assurance is supplied by the *independent audit* function. Audits are performed in accordance with generally accepted auditing standards which have been promulgated by the AICPA, and result in the auditor's expression of an opinion on the fairness of the financial statements in accordance with GAAP, applied on a basis consistent with the prior year.

Diverse interests in the private sector

Private sector users of financial statements have differing needs for economic information to determine that their interests are, or are not, being satisfied or preserved. The following briefly analyzes those interests and the extent to which financial statements can provide adequate information.

Stockholders and potential stockholders are interested in a clear portrayal of a corporation's financial condition and results of its operations. They seem less interested in the former, which possibly reduces the potential detrimental impact of carrying most assets at historical costs regardless of their current values. While earnings are of greater interest, even their value to many shareholders seems to rest on the extent to which past earnings are considered predictive of future earnings. For example, the market places considerable value on upward trends in earnings, which can be quickly lost when the trend line flattens out or starts down.

While forecasts of future earnings, though being urged by the SEC, are in little use today, there is an increasing tendency to require disclosure of events and transactions in the current year that will have a material impact on future years' operations.

Many stockholders do not use, and probably do not fully understand, much of the information included in financial statements, particularly the detailed footnotes. Yet the more sophisticated investors and the *financial analysts* who serve investors need the more detailed information. Their needs are met even though clarity for some of the less sophisticated may be diminished somewhat. Other focal points of interest, where financial statements play a prominent role for investors, include:

1. Earnings per share calculations.
2. Price/earnings ratio of the shares.
3. Dividend policy and assurance of its continuation, ratio of dividends to earnings, earnings trend, and so on.
4. Factors dilutive of stockholders' equity.
5. Timely and full disclosure of uncertainties and contingencies, and their possible impact on the corporation.

An area where financial statements are not sufficiently effective is in providing comparability between different corporations. Many believe that with adequate disclosure in financial statements, the market will accurately judge the quality of earnings and will price securities accordingly.

Credit grantors. Some credit grantors have made the point that they are entitled to more financial information than stockholders (and indeed many of them get it) because they have their entire "investment" to lose and only interest income to gain. Common shareholders, they point out, have the possibility of unlimited gain as the reward for risking their investment. While credit grantors have a strong interest in earnings and their continuation, they have an equally keen interest in the debtors' financial condition and probable future changes therein. For example, they are interested in:

1. Current corporate liquidity.
2. Future liquidity and cash flows.
3. Assets available for collateral and their current values. These values are readily available from financial statements for marketable securities, receivables, and most inventories; they can be obtained outside the financial statements for assets such as plant, equipment, and Lifo inventories.
4. Earnings coverage of interest charges.
5. Determination of adherence to restrictive covenants in bond indentures. These can range from simple ratios obtainable from financial statements, to more complicated restrictions determin-

able only after special analyses of information not generally carried in financial statements.

Suppliers and contractors. As credit grantors, vendors' interests are somewhat similar to those covered above. Vendors rarely can arrange for the protection afforded by collateral or indenture instruments. Generally, they have traded goods or services on credit extended for a relatively short period of time. Financial statements do reveal sufficient information to judge ability to pay, but do not satisfactorily indicate payment patterns (discount, slow, delinquent). However, this information is available from other sources. Vendors, except where financial information is fraudulent, can knowledgeably determine whether to extend normal credit, to alter the terms of credit, to require COD basis for their shipments, or to refuse to sell at all.

Employees. Despite the history of labor-management strife, the interests of a corporation and its employees are more closely aligned than they may appear to be. It is true that most of labor's wants are directly related to costs which the corporation, and ultimately the consumer, must bear. Examples of their wants are:

1. Assurance of continued employment.
2. Adequate compensation, including protection from inflation.
3. Opportunity for advancement.
4. Reasonable hours of work with sufficient allowance for illness, vacation, leisure time, and so on.
5. Benefit plans for meeting health-care costs, for income continuation during sickness and disability, for life insurance protection, retirement pensions, and so on.
6. Safe working conditions.

The chances of securing the above and retaining them over an extended period of time are enhanced by the sound financial health and success of the employer. Financial statements reflect this information, although the degree to which it has influenced the results of collective bargaining is difficult to determine. Undoubtedly it has whetted appetites when profitability was up and brought a degree of sobering reality when financial viability was threatened.

Other focal points of interest where accounting or financial statements play an important role include:

1. Computation of profit sharing bonuses.
2. Computation of contributions to trusteed profit sharing plans.
3. Compliance with funding requirements and vesting provisions of pension plans.

Customers. Customers generally are interested in the price and adequacy of the product or service they are purchasing. Beyond this, their concerns run to such matters as: prompt service or repairs when needed, availability of replacement parts, product guarantees, and product safety. The ability of the seller to provide the above will be judged in most instances on his or her reputation, with financial statements playing a lesser role. However, there are situations where financial statements are important. For example, adequate financial strength is a prime concern where long-term contracts (generally construction) are being negotiated. Financial statements are submitted to bonding companies where completion or performance bonds are required, and, in most cases, are submitted directly to the owners (purchasers) where bonds are not required.

Other areas of accounting influence—private sector

There are many other situations where accounting or financial statements play an influential role in harmonizing economic interests, allocating economic resources, and resolving conflicts. A few examples are described briefly below.

1. Landlords' rentals and licensors' royalties are often dependent partially or wholly on sales volume (dollars or units), or profits. These may be based on an entire corporate operation, but generally they are based on those sales or profits of a particular location or a particular product, and are produced by analyses of the accounting records.
2. Both franchisors and franchisees need knowledge of the financial responsibility of the other, and franchise fees are often dependent on operating factors.
3. One of the key factors in contemplating corporate acquisitions is an appraisal of the operating performance, the quality of earnings, and the future prospects of the acquiree. Such ap-

praisals are, in fact, made by both parties to a business combination.

4. Competing firms use every source available to obtain operating information about each other. Not the least interesting to them in this respect are financial statements presenting product-line and regional operating results.

5. Many types of disputes (contract interpretations and breaches, acts of negligence, etc.) directly involve accounting matters. Others, not directly involved with accounting, often need accounting for measuring resultant damages: for example, lost profits due to patent infringements. The testimony of expert witnesses concerning accounting matters is often necessary in courts of law and arbitration proceedings.

6. Estimation of losses in connection with business interruption (use-and-occupancy) and casualty insurance claims depends heavily on the interpretation of, and in some cases, the reconstruction of, accounting records.

7. Loss of property in eminent domain proceedings, where "going-concern" values in excess of pure property values are involved, requires the use of accounting information. Closely allied to this are claims for property expropriated by foreign governments.

8. The relative interests of partners and co-venturers in the assets and operations of partnerships and joint ventures are maintained by accounts and reported in financial statements.

Private not-for-profit organizations

Most of the foregoing applies equally to not-for-profit organizations in the private sector. For years, however, many of these organizations did not receive equal attention in the areas of efficient administration and management and effective accounting systems. Efforts are now being made to eliminate this inequality, as it is realized that these organizations are competing with private enterprise and governments for the same material, financial, and human resources. Their efficiency and effectiveness, their costs, and their contributions to society need to be measured and compared to those of private enterprise and governments. An informative publication along this line is *Accounting and Financial Reporting—A Guide for United Ways and Not for Profit Human Service Organizations*, prepared by the Systems, Planning, and Allocations Division of United Way of America (December 1974).

THE PUBLIC SECTOR

Consideration of the role of accounting to this point has been isolated almost entirely within the private sector. The public sector deserves equal attention. The past four decades have been marked by phenomenal growth in population, production, consumption, technological advancement, and size and power (and multinational proliferation) of corporations. The years have also witnessed a drain on natural resources, social unrest, wars, inflation, and a host of other persistent problems. The greatest incidence of growth, however, is in the size, cost, and influence of our governments (federal, state, and local). This growth has led to multifold and multiform extension of the requirements for accountability, which will be explored under the categories of—

1. Government as tax collector.
2. Government as customer.
3. Government as protector.
4. Administration of government.

Almost all matters considered will involve the federal government, although in varying degrees some of them apply to state and local governments as well.

Government as tax collector

Income taxes are the main source of revenue for the federal government, a major source for many states, and have been a key enabling factor in the federal government's phenomenal growth over the last several decades. In the early years of the income tax, the need to determine taxable net income for filing returns did much to improve the accounting systems of many businesses, particularly smaller ones. Accounting has returned the favor since. With few exceptions, generally accepted accounting principles (GAAP) are acceptable for determining taxable net income. In a number of instances, one GAAP alternative is used for tax purposes while a different acceptable principle is used in preparing financial statements. The government to this point has been loath to require for tax purposes only those accounting principles used in financial statements (with the Lifo inventory basis being the notable exception), to avoid undue governmental influence in the development of accounting principles; but this attitude may be changing.

Government as customer

Governments, particularly the federal agencies and departments, have become major purchasers of highly technical services, supplies, and property. Because of the sophisticated nature of these purchases, considerable outlay of public funds is being made under negotiated contracts. This form of procurement is dependent on accurate accounting information for protection of the interests of both the contractor and the public.

Procurement policies are set by the—

1. Department of Defense for purchases of the Air Force, Army, Navy, and Defense Supply Agency.
2. National Aeronautics and Space Administration for purchases relating to the National Space Act.
3. Nuclear Regulatory Commission and the Energy Research and Development Administration (successors to the Atomic Energy Commission) for purchases relating to the Energy Reorganization Act of 1974.
4. General Services Administration for purchases by federal agencies other than the aforementioned.

While not all procurement policies are identical, almost all purchases over $100,000 are subject to cost accounting standards promulgated by the Cost Accounting Standards Board (CASB). Larger contractors (based on the level of their annual sales to the government) are required to file disclosure statements for each of their profit centers. These statements, developed by the CASB, contain a description of the cost accounting procedures which the contractor will use in estimating, accumulating, and reporting costs.

A contractor's accounting records, cost estimates in support of bid proposals, and cost accumulations and allocations during contract performance are subject to examination by several governmental agencies. Similar information is also necessary in other situations, such as:

1. Cost data submission for the purpose of escalation and price redeterminations.
2. Cost and fee settlements upon contract terminations for convenience of the government.
3. Submission of reports to the Renegotiation Board for determination of the reasonableness (or excessiveness) of profits on contracts directly related to the national defense effort.

Inadequate accounting records can mean rejection of bid proposals or failure on the contractor's part to recover funds otherwise equitably due. Procurement agencies recognize the necessity of allowing the contractor a fair profit, but they are trying to eliminate profiteering. The private sector, including the contractors, should recognize the long-range benefits of this effort.

Government as protector

Local and state governments perform those services that they perceive cannot be effectively performed by individuals (police and fire protection, road maintenance, public schooling, etc.). Similarly, the federal government has enacted numerous laws designed to protect or improve society, or segments of it. Various departments and agencies have been created to administer and enforce these laws, and the majority of their regulatory processes could not exist without accurate, timely information derived from accounting systems and transmitted through a welter of reports. In several areas, the information is considered of such importance that agencies have prescribed uniform accounting systems. In most instances the financial reports are required to be audited, generally by independent auditors, but in some cases by government auditors.

An attempt will be made to describe briefly the purposes of some of the major federal agencies and the degree of their dependency on accounting. The agencies are categorized roughly by major goal or objective, although the efforts of some fall into several categories. The first, national defense, was covered earlier and is excluded here. The other broad objectives might be classified as follows:

1. Preservation of the economy and the free enterprise and free market systems—by the Securities and Exchange Commission, Antitrust Division of the Justice Department, Small Business Administration, Federal Reserve System, Comptroller of the

Currency, Federal Deposit Insurance Corporation, and the Federal Home Loan Bank Board.

2. Regulation of those industries where monopolistic powers have been granted—by the Federal Communications Commission, Federal Power Commission, Interstate Commerce Commission, Federal Maritime Commission, Civil Aeronautics Board, and numerous similar state commissions.

3. Improvement in the quality of life and the safety of individuals—by the Department of Health, Education and Welfare, Department of Housing and Urban Development, Office of Economic Opportunity, Rural Electrification Administration, Civil Aeronautics Board, and the Environmental Protection Agency. Also within this category are a number of recent acts concerning pollution, occupational safety and health, pension reform, and product safety.

4. Aid to scientific development—by the National Aeronautics and Space Administration, Nuclear Regulatory Commission, and Energy Research and Development Administration. Procurement procedures of these agencies were covered previously in this chapter.

5. Administration of government—by the Bureau of the Budget, General Accounting Office, Internal Revenue Service, General Services Administration, Renegotiation Board, and many others.

Securities and Exchange Commission (SEC). The SEC regulates the securities markets and protects the interests of investors and potential investors in the offering and sale of securities. The SEC administers the Securities Act of 1933, the Securities Exchange Act of 1934, the Public Utility Holding Act of 1935, the Trust Indenture Act of 1939, the Investment Company Act of 1940, and the Investment Advisers Act of 1940. It also has an advisory role (to Federal District Courts) under Chapter X of the National Bankruptcy Act.

The SEC has contributed more to the improvement of the private sector's financial reporting than any other federal agency. This is due probably to the nature of its function, which results in a greater need for timely, fair audited financial statements than that of any other federal agency.

The SEC has the power to prescribe the form of financial statements and the accounting principles to be used in their preparation for registrations of securities and other filings with the Commission. However, it has refrained from doing so on the basis that imposing a set of rigid, uniform accounting practices would not adequately protect the public. Instead, it has permitted the accounting profession to develop generally accepted accounting principles, a task now in the hands of the Financial Accounting Standards Board (FASB). Many others are contributing to this development process besides the SEC and the accounting profession—stock exchanges, corporate financial executives and other preparers of financial statements, financial analysts, academia, and others.

Guardians of the free enterprise system. The actions of the Justice Department's Antitrust Division in maintaining the validity of the free enterprise system are too varied and intricate to be covered here. However, accounting often plays an important role for both plaintiffs and defendants, not only in establishing guilt or innocence but in measuring the extent of damages.

The Small Business Administration (SBA). The SBA exists to help small business executives survive in an economic climate that continues to grow more turbulent. Small businesses are adversely affected not only by strong competition from large competitors but also by greater difficulty in dealing with the energy shortage and complying with governmental standards in areas such as health, safety, and antipollution.

Basically the SBA provides financial counseling and loans under four programs: the regular business loan program, the minority enterprise loan program, the regulatory compliance assistance program, and the emergency energy shortage assistance authority. Also, the SBA licenses, regulates, and helps finance Small Business Investment Companies (SBICs), which make venture capital available to small business concerns. SBICs are required to submit financial reports to their stockholders and to the SBA (audited statements annually and unaudited statements semiannually).

Those who borrow from SBICs and from the SBA must qualify under the terms of the programs and prove their creditworthiness, which, though less stringent than regular credit channels, requires adequate accounting records and financial reports.

Regulation of banks and currency. The banking system and the control of currency and credit are supervised in the United States by several bodies: the Board of Governors of the Federal Reserve

System, the Comptroller of the Currency, the Federal Deposit Insurance Corporation, and the Federal Home Loan Bank Board, which covers federal savings and loan associations. Their collective supervision is intended to afford financial soundness, depositors' insurance, regulation of the issuance of banks' own securities, adequate accounting and reporting, audits, and the control of credit. The last-named includes regulation of bank reserves; credit granted by brokers, dealers, and members of national security exchanges; credit granted by anyone for the purpose of purchasing or carrying registered securities; and payment and rate of interest on deposits.

This entire area is a sensitive and vital one for the U.S. economy. A decline or breakdown of depositor confidence could be catastrophic. Prompt, accurate reporting of financial and statistical information is necessary to support the decision-making processes involved.

Regulation of monopolies. The nature of some industries, the type of services they render, and the enormous capital outlay needed to render these services are such that it is not considered possible for them to operate in a completely free market. Therefore, they are granted certain monopolistic rights. In return, these industries are subject to close regulation, particularly as to the rates they can charge for their services. This regulation is handled by five federal agencies and numerous state commissions. The former are the Federal Communications Commission, Federal Power Commission, Interstate Commerce Commission, Federal Maritime Commission, and Civil Aeronautics Board. The CAB has additional responsibilities of encouraging and developing civil aviation in the United States and establishing safety rules. These agencies must arbitrate between a fair rate of return for the company and a fair price to the consumer for services rendered.

Accounting and reporting are considered so important to the regulation and rate-setting process that each of the five federal agencies has prescribed uniform systems of accounts that must be followed in preparing financial reports and statistics for submission to the agencies. The agency statements differ in several respects from generally accepted accounting principles, and are not considered adequate by the accounting profession for reporting to stockholders.

Department of Health, Education, and Welfare (HEW). This department has the responsibility of improving the administration of government agencies which promote the general welfare in the fields of health, education, and social security. It issues accounting regulations governing payments to providers of services to enrollees under the Medicare program (health insurance for the aged) and has also issued several manuals thereon.

A regulation[3] effective August 8, 1974, but not finalized until July 1975, establishes rules for qualifications of Health Maintenance Organizations. It is interesting to note that submission of financial documents is required, including:

1. Complete financial statements for each of the three preceding, fiscal years.
2. A complete current financial statement audited by a certified public accountant.
3. Projected financial statements for the next three years, including projected capital expenditures, expected loans, and cash flow schedules.

Obviously, sound financial planning and adequate financial and cost accounting procedures are an integral part of this program.

Not particularly complicated, but absolutely necessary, is the extensive accounting required by both employers and the government to collect, compute, and transfer social security taxes and to pay social security benefits.

Department of Housing and Urban Development. This department attempts to achieve coordination among those federal agencies whose activities bear upon urban, suburban, or metropolitan development. The Federal Housing Authority (FHA), in carrying out its program of loan and mortgage insurance, has issued a handbook of FHA requirements, which include the maintenance of accounting records and submission of financial reports.

Office of Economic Opportunity. The purpose of this office, established by the Economic Opportunity Act of 1964, is to "eliminate the paradox of poverty in the midst of plenty in this Nation by opening to everyone the opportunity for education and training, the opportunity to work and the opportunity to live in decency and dignity." The office is encouraging local Community Action Programs to fight poverty and makes grants of funds therefor. Require-

---

[3] See Public Health Service, Department of Health, Education, and Welfare, *Qualification of Health Maintenance Organizations,* (42 CFR, Part 110, Subpart F), published as Part II in *Federal Register* for August 8, 1975, pp. 33, 519–33,524.

ments for operating these programs include audits and accounting system surveys by independent auditors, and instructions have been issued pertaining to them.

Rural Electrification Administration (REA). This agency administers loan programs for rural electrification and rural telephone services. It has issued instructions concerning a uniform system of accounts for borrowers, monthly financial and statistical reports for filing with the REA, and auditing requirements. Borrowers are required to have their accounts audited annually by certified public accountants.

Recent acts concerning the quality of life. There have been a series of recent congressional acts which will have a tremendous impact on the operations and costs of both private enterprises and governments. This impact must be considered in all future financial planning, particularly long range, as costs of achieving program goals have been estimated to run into the hundreds of billions of dollars. Yet accounting in most instances has not developed sufficiently to provide the knowledge necessary to measure the resultant benefits to be derived from these expenditures, or to determine that the goals are or are not achievable. These acts include the National Environmental Policy Act of 1969 (NEPA), Clean Air Act (1970), Water Pollution Act (amendment of 1972), Noise Control Act of 1972, Federal Environmental Pesticide Control Act of 1972, Fish and Wildlife Coordination Act of 1970, Occupational Safety and Health Act of 1970, Consumers Product Safety Act of 1972, Employee Retirement Income Security Act of 1974, and a number of others. Most antipollution acts are administered by the Environmental Protection Agency (EPA). The National Environmental Policy Act requires all federal agencies to consider environmental effects and values in all their major decisions or actions, and to support them with "impact statements." Preparation of these statements involves consultation with all other federal agencies involved, including EPA, and with appropriate state or local agencies, if any. The statements are exposed for public comment for at least 90 days prior to final action. Accounting, which is largely ignored in this process now, should be one of the many skills involved in producing, reviewing, and commenting upon these environmental impact statements.

The income tax statutes are being changed to help "finance" some of these programs. For example, special short-term amortization charges, rather than lesser depreciation deductions, are allowed for pollution control facilities, coal mine safety equipment, on-the-job training or child care facilities, and employment of welfare people. Others include an additional investment credit where employee stock ownership plans are instituted to achieve wider spread of ownership of American business, amortization of rehabilitation expenditures of the Federal Housing Act, and special treatment for soil and water conservation expenditures by farmers.

Administration of government

Few can quarrel with the objectives or goals of most of the programs of federal, state, and local governments. In fact, some of the most expensive (pollution control) and some not yet dealt with (population growth control and diminishing natural resources) are probably far more critical than most realize. Yet there are limits to what the country can afford without seriously damaging its economy. The harsh realism of the private sector's marketplace, where the "bottom line" is relatively easy to determine and must be faced constantly, is missing from the operation of governments.

Two goals, easily stated but difficult to implement, must be attained:

1. All governmental waste needs to be attacked at every level until it reaches an irreducible minimum.
2. Priorities must be set on a benefit-cost basis, and difficult choices must be made.

The General Accounting Office (GAO), in monitoring numerous grants-in-aid and revenue sharing programs, has expanded its scope of auditing to include not only the traditional financial examinations but also—

1. A review of compliance with applicable laws and regulations.
2. An evaluation of efficiency of operations.
3. An evaluation of program effectiveness.

Such an audit of all grantees is required, either by GAO auditors or independent auditors from the private sector. In this writer's opinion, the accounting profession, and probably the GAO also, has not developed sufficiently sound standards for effectively fulfilling the GAO's requirements. This effort should be made. The accounting profession possesses the requisite interdisciplinary skills necessary to develop adequate standards, and a number of independent audit firms are equipped to make compliance, efficiency, and effectiveness audits thereunder.

Similar examinations, whether they be made by auditors from the private sector, by government examiners, or by a combination thereof, should be made of all governmental operations, not just of grantees. Waste and ineffectiveness must be reduced to a minimum or some worthy programs will suffer from lack of funds.

More difficult, but even more pressing, is the development of methods for determining the cost to society of not accomplishing goals such as pollution control, poverty reduction, population growth control, and depletion of natural resources. This is truly a multidisciplinary effort, but one where the independent accountant's objectivity and analytical skills should be helpful.

EFFECTIVENESS OF ACCOUNTING

Many have criticized accounting principles and financial reporting in the United States. Spectacular frauds and bankruptcies have fanned this criticism, although they represent a minute percentage of the profession's total endeavor. Use of current or fair values of assets rather than historical costs is being widely suggested, but inclusion of value increases in income would seem contrary to the stress on "cash return" contained in the Special Study Group's report on the Objectives of Financial Statements. Further, in those relatively few instances where fair current values of assets are considered critical, they should be disclosed in the statements or be reflected in special-purpose statements. All agree that current inflation rates reduce the effectiveness of financial statements, but there is strong disagreement on how to correct the situation. This issue probably will be resolved within the next year. Accounting alternatives still exist but are being refined gradually by studies of conditions under which each is likely to afford the fairest presentation.

Improvements will never seem to come soon enough, but progress has been made and seems to be continuing at a satisfactory pace under the FASB/SEC effort. If the pace of change were to become too swift, particularly if hasty steps had to be retraced, the results could be disruptive. Accounting principles are not an academic plaything to be flipped or flopped everytime they fail to prevent a misleading presentation. They are measuring tools; and no amount of rigid articulation on the one hand, or broadly stated principles on the other, will eliminate occasional misuse of the measuring tools. Improvement here lies with the preparers and auditors of financial statements.

SUMMARY OF ACCOUNTING'S ROLE

Described in this chapter are some, but not all, of the situations and conditions where accounting plays a vital role in harmonizing adverse economic interests, allocating economic resources, and resolving conflicts. Financial statements serve as summary indicators of an accounting entity's resources; claims against these resources; its liquidity and solvency; its major sources of capital; the use of its funds; the scope, magnitude, and trend of its operations; relative profitability; contingencies affecting the enterprise; and other favorable or unfavorable circumstances that could affect the enterprise. Much supplemental financial and statistical information can be obtained from underlying accounting records when needed. Management and cost accounting produces information for controlling costs and insuring efficient operations, for budgeting and planning, for supporting contract reimbursements, and for making decisions in many areas at numerous levels.

Accounting is an indispensable aid to governments in raising tax revenues, enforcing effective procurement policies, and in pursuing or regulating almost all of its many programs designed to aid or protect the public and the country's economy.

The auditing function assures the objectivity of, and adds credibility to, the financial statements; it is the bulwark of fair presentation and full disclosure. Fraud in the presentation of accounts (false financial statements) does exist and sometimes goes undetected by the auditor. However, the manifold positive uses of accounting strongly suggest that for each misuse of accounts, there are hundreds of daily instances where accounting faithfully serves its intended purpose.

Only in the area of "social measurement" does accounting fall materially short. This was touched upon briefly in several previous paragraphs, particularly in measuring the cost to society of failure to accomplish the goals of some of the more urgent governmental programs. Another dimension of this problem is the need to consider the net costs to society of corporate operations in terms of pollution damage, use of irreplaceable natural resources, beneficial use or misuse of human resources, production of safe or unsafe goods, and so on. A number of studies by the AICPA and others both in and outside the accounting profession are underway. It is a multidisciplinary problem and will not easily be solved. This does not lessen its importance, though, as life on our finite planet (not just its quality) will someday depend upon a complete balancing of many opposing forces.

Chapter 37

Annual and interim reporting under the Securities Exchange Act of 1934

*John W. Nicholson**

The Securities Act of 1933 (1933 Act) was enacted by Congress with the objective of providing investors with material information for offerings of securities to the public, whether the offering is to be by the issuer of securities (i.e., the company) or by major shareholders. The Securities Exchange Act of 1934 (1934 Act), together with its subsequent amendments, has extended the disclosure doctrine for investor protection that had been established in the 1933 Act to cover public trading in securities on national securities exchanges and in the over-the-counter markets.

Companies which have their securities listed on a national securities exchange and over-the-counter companies which have assets in excess of $1 million and 500 or more shareholders for any one class of equity securities must file a registration statement with the Securities and Exchange Commission (the "SEC" or the "Commission") under the 1934 Act. The principal form for such a registration is the Form 10, though other forms may be authorized or prescribed under certain circumstances. Following registration of its securities under

* Director of SEC Practice & Research, Arthur Young & Company.

the 1934 Act, a company must file annual and other periodic reports to keep current the information available to the public. Under Section 15(d) of the 1934 Act, similar periodic reporting requirements exist for over-the-counter companies that have registered with the SEC only under the 1933 Act.

The primary periodic reporting forms that are to be filed with the SEC under the 1934 Act are as follows:

Form 10-K—An annual report which is due within 90 days after the end of each fiscal year.

Form 10-Q—A quarterly report which is due within 45 days after the end of each of the first three fiscal quarters of each fiscal year; a Form 10-Q need not be filed for the fourth quarter.

Form 8-K—A report which must be filed within ten days after the close of any month during which any of certain specified events occur.

Other periodic reporting forms may be authorized or prescribed for companies in certain industries, for foreign issuers of securities, and for other special situations. This chapter concentrates on the Forms 10-K, 10-Q, and 8-K, the primary periodic reporting forms under the 1934 Act, and does not deal with special situations.

FORM 10-K

The *Form 10-K* is the general form that is used for annual reports that must be filed with the SEC when no other report form is authorized or prescribed. Reports on this form are to be filed within 90 days after the end of the fiscal year covered by the report; however, supplemental financial schedules may, at the option of the company, be filed as an amendment to the report not later than 120 days after the end of the fiscal year. Any such amendment is to be filed on a Form 8.

Form 10-K consists of two parts, the contents of which are summarized below.

Part I

Item 1. Business (description of the business, including line-of-business or class-of-product-or-service data)
Item 2. Summary of Operations
Item 3. Properties
Item 4. Parents and Subsidiaries
Item 5. Legal Proceedings

Item 6. Increases and Decreases in Outstanding Securities
Item 7. Approximate Number of Equity Security Holders
Item 8. Executive Officers of the Registrant
Item 9. Indemnification of Directors and Officers
Item 10. Financial Statements and Exhibits Filed

Part II

Item 11. Principal Security Holders and Security Holdings of Management
Item 12. Directors of the Registrant
Item 13. Remuneration of Directors and Officers
Item 14. Options Granted to Management to Purchase Securities
Item 15. Interest of Management and Others in Certain Transactions

The information called for by Part I of Form 10-K is to be furnished by all registrants required to file a report on this form. Part II may be omitted from the report by any company which, since the close of the fiscal year being reported on, has filed with the SEC (or will file within 120 days after the close of the fiscal year) a definitive *proxy statement* pursuant to Regulation 14A of the SEC or a definitive *information statement* pursuant to Regulation 14C, which involves the election of directors.

All sections of the annual report to the SEC on Form 10-K are important to company executives and should be critically reviewed (generally by a high-level financial officer) prior to any filing. A review should also be made by the company's independent accountants to make certain that legal or narrative disclosures are not in conflict with, or do not include data that should be, but are not, in the financial statements. In some cases, the independent accountants may assist in preparing data for the sections of the Form 10-K other than those directly involved with financial statements. However, the auditors' chief concern is generally with the "Summary of Operations" (Item 2) and audited financial statements (Item 10).

Basic financial statements

The "Instructions as to Financial Statements" for Form 10-K set forth the requirements as to the basic financial statements that must be filed as part of the annual report to the SEC. These are summarized below.

1. Balance sheets as of the end of the last two fiscal years.
2. Statements of income for the last two fiscal years.
3. Statements of changes in financial position for the last two fiscal years.

4. Statements of retained earnings and paid-in capital for the last
    two fiscal years.

Note. If there has been a change in the fiscal year end, Rule
13a-10 under the 1934 Act should be referred to for guidance.

The foregoing statements are to be in comparative columnar form
and accompanied by notes required by generally accepted accounting principles and the SEC's Regulation S-X. In addition, the financial statements must be examined and reported on by independent
accountants.

Both parent-company-only and consolidated financial statements
must be filed in a Form 10-K, except that the individual financial
statements of the company may be omitted if consolidated statements are filed, if the basis for the omission is set forth in the index
to financial statements in the Form 10-K, and if certain conditions
specified in the "Instructions as to Financial Statements" in Form
10-K are met (see note).

Note. SEC Form 10-K, Instruction 1(b) as to Financial Statements, states:

> . . . the individual financial statements of the registrant may be
> omitted if (1) consolidated financial statements of the registrant
> and one or more of its subsidiaries are being filed, (2) the condi-
> tions specified in either of the following paragraphs are met, and
> (3) the basis for the omission is stated in the list of financial state-
> ments filed under Item 10.
>
> (i) The registrant is primarily an operating company and all
> subsidiaries included in the consolidated financial statements being
> filed, in the aggregate, do not have minority equity interests and/or
> indebtedness to any person other than the registrant or its consoli-
> dated subsidiaries in amounts which together exceed 5 percent of
> the total assets as shown by the most recent year-end consolidated
> balance sheet. Indebtedness incurred in the ordinary course of busi-
> ness which is not overdue and which matures within one year from
> the date of its creation, whether evidenced by securities or not, and
> indebtedness of subsidiaries which is collateralized by the registrant
> by guarantee, pledge, assignment or otherwise are to be excluded
> for the purpose of this determination.
>
> (ii) The registrant's total assets, exclusive of investments in and
> advances to its consolidated subsidiaries, as would be shown by its
> most recent year-end balance sheet if it were filed, constitute 75
> percent or more of the total assets as shown by the most recent
> year-end consolidated balance sheet; and the registrant's total sales

and revenues, exclusive of interest and dividends received from or its equity in the income of the consolidated subsidiaries, as would be shown by its income statement, for the most recent fiscal year if it were filed, constitute 75 percent or more of the total sales and revenues shown by the most recent annual consolidated income statements.

While the "Instructions as to Financial Statements" for the Form 10-K delineate the financial statements that are to be included in the annual report to the SEC, the form and content of those financial statements are governed by Regulation S-X and the accounting series releases of the SEC.

A company must also consider and apply generally accepted accounting principles when preparing financial statements for public reporting purposes. While the Commission has broad powers under the statutes it administers to establish accounting principles, it has rarely exercised its authority in this area and for the most part has looked to the private sector of our economy for the establishment and improvement of accounting principles. This position was reaffirmed in *Accounting Series Release No. 150* issued in 1973. The Financial Accounting Standards Board is currently the dominant body in the United States of America for establishing and improving accounting principles. Over the years, accounting principles have also been developed by the predecessor Accounting Principles Board and the Committee on Accounting Procedure, both of which were, during the periods of their existence, part of the organizational structure of the American Institute of Certified Public Accountants. Accounting principles have also been influenced to a significant extent by customs and precedents, recommendations of industry groups, and accounting rules of regulatory authorities.

If a company's financial statements are not prepared in conformity with generally accepted accounting principles, it can expect to be confronted with a qualified or adverse opinion on its financial statements by its independent accountants. The absence of an unqualified (or clean) auditor's opinion could in turn lead to a questioning by the SEC and possible problems for the company. In an early accounting series release, the SEC set forth the following administrative policy which bears on this matter:

> In cases where financial statements filed with this Commission pursuant to its rules and regulations under the Securities Act of 1933 or the Securities Exchange Act of 1934 are prepared in accord-

ance with accounting principles for which there is no substantial authoritative support, such financial statements will be presumed to be misleading or inaccurate despite disclosures contained in the certificate of the accountant or in footnotes to the statements provided the matters involved are material. In cases where there is a difference of opinion between the Commission and the registrant as to the proper principles of accounting to be followed, disclosure will be accepted in lieu of correction of the financial statements themselves only if the points involved are such that there is substantial authoritative support for the practices followed by the registrant and the position of the Commission has not previously been expressed in rules, regulations, or other official releases of the Commission, including the published opinions of its chief accountant.[1]

Publicly held companies rarely follow accounting principles that will result in anything other than an unqualified opinion.

Exceptions in auditors' opinions

Qualifications, or *adverse* or *disclaimed opinions* based on departures from generally accepted accounting principles or limitations on the scope of an auditor's examination are not acceptable to the SEC. Their issuance by the auditors can result in questions being raised by the Commission and possible significant problems for a company.

A qualification relating to a major uncertainty or contingency which cannot be resolved as of the statement or filing dates (and which does not also involve a departure from generally accepted accounting principles or an audit scope limitation) are generally accepted by the SEC. Also, a consistency exception in the independent accountants' opinion because of a change in an accounting principle or procedure will generally not result in questions being raised by the SEC (unless, for example, the company has changed to an accounting principle or procedure which either the auditors or the SEC staff members view as not preferable).

If the independent accountants have a serious qualification in their opinion, if they disclaim an opinion, or if they issue an adverse opinion, consideration should be given to discussing their report with the Division of Corporation Finance of the SEC prior to the filing of a Form 10-K. Similar discussions with stock exchanges should also be considered by listed companies in these situations.

---

[1] *SEC Accounting Series Release No. 4,* 1938.

Both executives from the registrant and representatives of the auditors should participate in such discussions; at times it may also be desirable to have legal counsel attend.

Reports of predecessor and successor auditors

If there has been a change in the principal auditors, and different accounting firms have reported on the two sets of annual financial statements in the Form 10-K, the opinions of both the successor and predecessor independent accountants must be included in the Form 10-K. Both opinions are also required for the annual report to shareholders under the SEC's 1934 Act proxy rules. If there is a significant problem in obtaining the predecessor auditor's opinion, the matter should be discussed with the staff of the Division of Corporation Finance of the SEC.

Summary of operations

The *summary of operations* in a Form 10-K is not a financial statement (as that term is used in customary SEC parlance); however, a company may elect to present its summary of operations in the form of a full income statement and to have it covered by the opinion of the independent accountants. This enables the company to omit the separate two-year income statement (if it so desires) required by the instructions to the basic financial statements. The summary of operations is viewed by many users of financial statements as the most important of the various sets of financial data presented. This, plus the advantages of not repeating essentially the same information in two places within a report, to a large extent explains the popularity of the practice of presenting the summary in the form of a full statement of income.

The instructions for the summary of operations in Form 10-K require a summary for five years or for the life of the company, if shorter; information for additional years may also be necessary to keep the summary from being misleading. This latter requirement has in general been interpreted as applying if trends shown by a five-year summary are not indicative of trends over a longer period. For example, a five-year summary may show a strong growth trend whereas additional years' data might show sharp declines in sales and profits immediately prior to the most recent five-year period, or might provide other evidence of fluctuations in operations.

The instructions call for a summary on both a parent company and a consolidated basis, "as appropriate;" there are similar instructions as to summaries in other SEC forms. The Commission has not defined what "as appropriate" means in this context. In filings under both the 1933 and 1934 Acts, the summary has almost universally been presented only on a consolidated basis, even when both parent company and consolidated financial statements are required by instructions as to financial statements.

A reconciliation with amounts of sales and net income reported in prior periods must be given with the summary when changes have been made because of acquisitions accounted for as poolings of interests or because of other reasons, except that such reconciliations need not be made (1) if they have been made in filings with the SEC in prior years or (2) the financial statements which are being retroactively adjusted have not previously been filed with the SEC or otherwise made public.

Earnings per share in summary of operations

An instruction to the "Summary of Operations" of Form 10-K requires the company to set forth clearly the computation of per-share earnings, together with the number of shares used in the computation. If this data can be presented understandably on the face of the summary, in a note to the summary of operations, or in a note to the basic financial statements, such a presentation is preferred. If the computation is complex and requires a lengthy detailed presentation, the computation should be set forth in a separate exhibit to the Form 10-K.

The company must also furnish by exhibit earnings per share on a fully diluted basis, even if such computations result in improved earnings per share or the dilution is less than 3 percent and such per-share data are not required to be shown on the statement of income under *APB Opinion No. 15.*

Management's analysis of the summary of operations

In August 1974, the Commission issued *Accounting Series Release No. 159.* This release adopted Guide 1 of *Guides for Preparation and*

Filing of Reports and Registration Statements under the Securities Exchange Act of 1934. Guide 1 effectively mandates that a separately captioned section entitled "Management's Discussion and Analysis of the Summary of Operations" be included immediately following the summary of operations to explain (*a*) material changes from period to period and (*b*) changes in accounting principles or practices. The section should include a discussion of changes in revenue and expense for each item required to be set forth in the summary (or statement of income) or disclosed pursuant to S-X Rule 12-16 on "Supplementary Income Statement Information," if such changes meet specified materiality criteria. Management's analysis should be considered at an early stage in the annual report preparation process so that management can be well prepared to provide interpretive comments that are called for. Management—not the independent auditor—should prepare the discussion and analysis prepared under Guide 1.

Periods covered by the analysis are limited in Form 10-K to the most recent fiscal year compared to the immediately preceding fiscal year, and the second most recent fiscal year compared to its immediately preceding year. There may also be circumstances under which explanation of changes between earlier periods may be necessary to an understanding of the summary.

The summary of operations and management's analysis must also be included in the annual report to shareholders. The five-year summary of earnings and the analysis from the annual report to shareholders can be incorporated by reference in a Form 10-K. The summary of operations and analysis of the summary by management in the annual report to shareholders should satisfy the requirements for such information in the Form 10-K in the normal case. This is true even though the analysis in the annual report to shareholders is set forth in separate sections of the report and not located in one place, provided there appears to be good faith in complying with the Commission's rules and regulations.

Companies should not request nor expect the independent accountants to express an opinion on the "Management's Discussion and Analysis of the Summary of Operations," as such a discussion and analysis would normally be based in part on nonfinancial information and include judgmental comments that the independent accountant could not attest to. However, the auditors should read the discussion and analysis to determine that management's explanations are consistent with the audited financial statements included in Form 10-K.

Other financial statements

In addition to the basic financial statements of the company and the summary of operations, it is also necessary to file supplemental financial schedules in a Form 10-K if materiality criteria for the individual schedules are met. For commercial and industrial companies, the requirements as to the schedules to be filed are set forth in Regulation S-X, Article 5-04. These schedules require additional detailed financial information on such matters as:

1. Marketable securities.
2. Long-term investments.
3. Receivables from officers, directors, and affiliates.
4. Property, plant, and equipment.
5. Intangible assets.
6. Long-term debt.
7. Capital shares.
8. Supplementary income statement information (i.e., maintenance and repairs, depreciation and amortization, taxes other than income taxes, rents, royalties, advertising costs, and research and development costs).

Furthermore, complete financial statements may be needed for subsidiaries not consolidated, consolidated subsidiaries that are financial institutions, and 50 percent or less owned persons if they meet certain materiality criteria. These additional statements may at times be filed on a group or summarized basis.

An instruction in Form 10-K states that financial statements other than those specified in the instructions may be filed upon the written request of the company and with the approval of the Commission. In addition, the Commission may require the filing of other financial statements which are considered necessary or appropriate for the protection of investors. Cases are rare where the Commission has permitted or requested financial statements other than those specified in its basic instructions under the provisions of this rule. However, this rule has at times been useful to companies that were encountering problems in technical compliance with basic rules and regulations. If it is to be availed of by a company, that company and its independent accountants should agree on the alternative financial statement presentations which provide significant data for investors. They should then submit the proposed alternative statements for review by the SEC staff and also discuss them at a prefiling conference.

Quarterly financial data in notes to annual financial statements

In September 1975, the SEC issued a rule that for the first time required companies to disclose selected quarterly information in notes to annual financial statements. This new requirement was promulgated in *Accounting Series Release No. 177* and is set forth in Regulation S-X Rule 3-16(t). Under the new rule, companies must disclose selected quarterly information for the two most recent fiscal years and any subsequent interim period for which an income statement is presented. The Commission is, however, permitting a transitional period and is not requiring the inclusion of such data in financial statements for fiscal periods beginning prior to December 26, 1975. The disclosure requirements of S-X Rule 3-16(t) are not applicable to "parent company only" financial statements presented in addition to consolidated financial statements or to supplemental financial statements required to be filed for unconsolidated subsidiaries, 50 percent or less owned persons, or consolidated subsidiaries engaged in financial activities. If the note is part of audited financial statements, it may be marked as "unaudited"; the manner in which the independent auditor handles his association with such published unaudited quarterly information should follow pronouncements by the Auditing Standards Executive Committee of the American Institute of Certified Public Accountants.

The minimum information needed to meet the SEC disclosure rule is the following:

Net sales.

Gross profit.

Income before extraordinary items and cumulative effect of a change in accounting.

Per share data based upon such income.

Net income.

Data such as net income per share may also be needed to meet the requirements of generally accepted accounting principles. In addition, the note should describe the effects of the disposal of segments of a business and extraordinary, unusual, or infrequently occurring items recognized in each quarter presented, as well as the effect of year-end or other adjustments that are material to the results of any such quarter. Furthermore, if quarterly data presented pursuant to S-X Rule 3-16(t) varies from information presented in a quarterly report on Form 10-Q, a reconciliation of any difference together with the reason therefor must be presented.

Regulation S-X Rule 3-16(t) also provides that it shall not apply to any registrant that does not meet the following conditions:

> (a) The registrant (1) has securities registered pursuant to Section 12(b) of the Securities Exchange Act of 1934 or (2) has securities registered pursuant to Section 12(g) of that Act which also (i) are quoted on the National Association of Securities Dealers Automated Quotation System and (ii) meet the requirements for continued inclusion on the list of OTC margin stocks set forth in Section 220.8(i) of Regulation T of the Board of Governors of the Federal Reserve System; and
>
> (b) The registrant and its consolidated subsidiaries (1) have had a net income after taxes but before extraordinary items and the cumulative effect of a change in accounting, of at least $250,000 for each of the last three fiscal years; or (2) had total assets of at least $200,000,000 for the last fiscal year end.

In *Accounting Series Release No. 177*, the SEC also expressed the view that companies should include the disclosures required by S-X Rule 3-16(t) in the financial statements furnished to stockholders as well as in filings with the Commission. Under an administrative interpretation by the Chief Accountant of the SEC and the Division of Corporation Finance, the absence of such disclosures from the annual report to stockholders will preclude its incorporation by reference in a Form S-8 or Form 10-K filing.

Changes in SEC rules—guidance as to retroactive application

Where there have been major changes in Regulation S-X or other SEC rules and regulations, the basic financial statements for the prior year as well as the current should be conformed to the currently effective rules and regulations. It is also recommended that supplemental financial schedules be conformed. However, to date the Commission has accepted prior period schedules which followed instructions in effect for the period for which they were prepared.

Incorporation by reference

It is becoming an increasingly prevalent practice to incorporate the financial statements from the published annual report to shareholders to meet the financial statement requirements of the annual report on Form 10-K. This may, however, necessitate some expansion of data in the financial statements or notes to the annual report to shareholders so that they substantially comply with the rules and regulations of the SEC. If data in the shareholder report does not comply in certain areas (e.g., depreciation and amortization policies or stock option disclosures), it is often practicable to provide the additional data through the inclusion of so-called "SEC compliance financial information" in the body of the Form 10-K while incorporating the basic financial statements from the annual report to shareholders. In addition, separate complete financial statements may be required by SEC rules for certain unconsolidated and consolidated subsidiaries or for certain investees, though such financial statements may not be included in the printed annual reports to stockholders. Again in such cases, a company can incorporate basic consolidated financial statements from the annual report to shareholders, while including the separate financial statements of subsidiaries or investees in the Form 10-K.

The procedure of incorporation by reference is not practicable for all entities. In general, it is most practical for those companies which need report to the SEC only on the basis of the consolidated financial statements of the company, or which can supply supplemental financial data on a relatively facile basis. It must also be noted that data to be incorporated by reference must be physically filed with the Form 10-K. Furthermore, "piecemeal" incorporation of data by reference (i.e., one financial statement from one document, a second from another, etc.) is not acceptable to the SEC, since it could seriously reduce the effectiveness of the Commission's service for making financial data available to the public.

It is also possible to incorporate financial statements or financial data by reference from other SEC filings. One such example is a registration statement under the 1933 Act. This may, however, necessitate the inclusion of a comparative balance sheet in the 1933

Act filing. Data may be incorporated from a 1933 Act document based on a registration that is filed but not yet effective. If a material amendment must be filed to make the 1933 Act registration statement effective, a corresponding amendment to the Form 10-K must also be filed.

The practice of incorporation by reference must meet technical requirements of the Commission; these are set forth in General Instruction F to Form 10-K and in Rule 12b-23 under the 1934 Act.

Combining the annual report and Form 10-K

There has also been a growing practice in recent years whereby some companies, in effect, use the Form 10-K as the annual report to shareholders. In such cases there may be a cover for the annual report "wrapped around" the Form 10-K, or there may be a letter from the president of the company which also serves as a transmittal letter for the Form 10-K being sent to the company stockholders.

If the Form 10-K and the annual report are to be combined into one document, the following guidelines, which have been summarized from an interpretive letter of the Commission, should be followed:

> The combined report shall contain full and complete answers to all items required by Form 10-K. If the responses to a certain topic of disclosure required by Form 10-K are separated within the report, appropriate cross-references must be included.

> If Part II information, which is generally textual data of a legal nature, is omitted from the report in reliance upon General Instruction H to Form 10-K, "Omission of Information Previously Filed," a definitive proxy or information statement must be filed in accordance with the provisions of Instruction H.

> Any additional information or exhibits contained in the report (i.e., message to stockholders, financial highlights, pictures, graphics, etc.) must meet the requirements of the 1934 Act rules which require that there be added to the report such further material information as may be necessary to make the statements not misleading, and permit the inclusion of such exhibits as the registrant may desire so long as the exhibits are marked to indicate the subject matter to which they refer. Furthermore, the provision of Guide 8 of *SEC Release No. 33-4936* which relates to photographic repro-

ductions, should be complied with, though it is technically a 1933 Act rule. The report must include the Form 10-K cover page, the answer to Item 10 of Form 10-K, and manual signatures on at least one complete copy filed with the Commission and each securities exchange on which the registrant has a listing.

Schedules need not be included in the report but may be filed by amendment on Form 8.

The report must include the following disclaimer of any action on the part of the SEC: "This Form 10-K has not been approved or disapproved by the Securities and Exchange Commission nor has the Commission passed upon the accuracy or adequacy of the data included herein."

When a company elects to combine its annual report to shareholders with its Form 10-K, the annual report will be deemed to have been "filed" and will become subject to the liabilities of Section 18 of the 1934 Act.

A combined report is not practicable for all corporations filing with the Commission and should only be adopted after due consideration of all accounting, legal, stockholder communication, printing, and distribution problems.

QUARTERLY REPORTING—FORM 10-Q[2]

In September 1975, the SEC issued *Accounting Series Release No. 177*. This release, which amends Form 10-Q, requires an expanded reporting of interim financial information. The requirements of the form, as amended, are summarized in succeeding sections.

Every issuer of a security (unless covered by an exemption) which is required to file annual reports with the SEC under the 1934 Act must also file quarterly reports on Form 10-Q. This form is filed for each of the first three quarters (but not the fourth quarter) of each fiscal year of the issuer, beginning with the first of such quarters that ends after securities of the issuer become registered. The report is due to be filed within 45 days after the end of each quarter. The instructions for Form 10-Q provide for inclusion of the information in the following categories:

1. Condensed financial statements (based on Regulation S-X except as to notes).

---

[2] For additional information see Chapter 35, "Scope and Objectives of the Interim Financial Report."

2. An analysis by management of the results of operations.

3. Additional financial disclosures of significance to investors.

This information is to be presented on a consolidated basis and need not include "parent company only" information, though the latter may be required in other SEC filings.

Instruction D(b) to Form 10-Q remains unchanged by *Accounting Series Release No. 177* and continues to provide that quarterly information be given for unconsolidated subsidiaries and investee companies for which separate or group financial statements are required in a company's annual report filed with the SEC. However, SEC *Staff Accounting Bulletin No. 6* provides that, in lieu of the financial information required by this instruction, summarized income statement information of unconsolidated subsidiaries and investee companies will be accepted in a note to the registrant's quarterly financial statements in Form 10-Q. In addition, *Staff Accounting Bulletin No. 2* indicates that separate condensed financial statements of financial-type consolidated subsidiaries are not required in Form 10-Q filings, though separate data on such subsidiaries may be required in other SEC filings pursuant to S-X Rule 4-02(e).

**Presentation of condensed S-X financial
statements**

Form 10-Q requires that the condensed financial statements shall be provided for periods set forth below:

(1) The condensed income statement shall be presented for the most recent fiscal quarter, for the period between the end of the last fiscal year and the end of the most recent fiscal quarter, and for corresponding periods of the preceding fiscal year. It also may be presented for the cumulative 12-month period ended during the most recent fiscal quarter and for the corresponding period of the preceding fiscal year.

(2) The balance sheet shall be presented as of the end of the most recent fiscal quarter and for the end of the corresponding period of the preceding fiscal year. However, balance sheets for dates prior to December 26, 1975, are not required.

(3) The statement of source and application of funds shall be presented for the period between the end of the last fiscal year and the end of the most recent fiscal quarter, and for the corresponding period of the preceding fiscal year. It also may

be presented for the cumulative 12-month period ended during the most recent fiscal quarter and for the corresponding period of the preceding fiscal year.

The presentation of condensed balance sheet and statement of source and application of funds data is a new requirement; a transition rule provides that disclosure of comparable data for prior years shall not be required for interim periods beginning prior to December 26, 1975. No similar exception is provided for comparative prior-period condensed income statements.

The condensed financial statements required to be furnished in Form 10-Q are to follow the general form of presentation set forth in Regulation S-X and must conform with standards of accounting measurement set forth in *APB Opinion No. 28*. The following guidance summarized from instruction "H" of Form 10-Q and the SEC's *Staff Accounting Bulletin No. 6* should be followed:

Condensed balance sheets need only present major captions set forth in Regulation S-X. Subordinate captions may be omitted with the exception of inventories, where data as to raw materials, work-in-process, and finished goods shall be included (if applicable). Major captions may be combined with others if the amount of any such caption represented is less than 10 percent of total assets and the amount in the caption has not increased or decreased by more than 25 percent since the balance sheet at the end of the preceding quarter.

Condensed income statements need only present major captions set forth in Regulation S-X; captions may, however, be combined if the caption is less than 15 percent of average net income for the most recent three years and the amount in the caption has not increased or decreased by more than 20 percent as compared to the next preceding comparable income statement. When calculating average net income, registrants should exclude loss years unless all years had losses. In the latter case, the average net loss shall be used. Earnings per share and dividends per share data are to be presented, together with the basis of the computation and a schedule setting forth the computation (unless such computation is otherwise clearly set forth in the Form 10-Q).

Statements of source and application of funds can be abbreviated, starting with the amount of funds provided by operations and showing other sources and applications of funds individually only when they exceed 10 percent of the average funds provided by operations for the most recent three years. When calculating average funds provided by operations, registrants should exclude years where there was a net outflow of funds from operations unless all three years had such a net outflow of funds. In the latter case, the average net outflow of funds should be used for the 10 percent test. An analysis of each element of working capital need not be included. If a registrant previously combined captions in a Form 10-Q but is required to present such captions separately for the current quarter based on the above-noted tests, the prior period comparative financial statements must be reclassified to conform with the captions presented for the current period.

Notes to financial statements and schedules as required by S-X Rules are not required in a Form 10-Q. The instructions, however, carry an admonition that "As with all information filed with the Commission . . . disclosures must be adequate to make the information presented not misleading." This instruction effectively retains for the Commission broad discretionary powers to determine the footnote disclosures to be provided in Form 10-Q filings. The Commission's staff has indicated that footnote disclosures should include such data as are needed to keep other published information about a company up to date.

Management's narrative analysis

Form 10-Q requires a narrative analysis by management of the results of operations. Such analysis provides explanations of the reasons for material changes in revenues and expenses between the current quarter and the immediately preceding quarter and the same quarter of the preceding year. If applicable, explanations are also required of changes of the current-year-to-date amounts from the preceding year-to-date amounts. The analysis should also include an explanation of the effect of any changes in accounting principles or practices.

Additional financial disclosures of significance
to investors

The instructions to Form 10-Q should be referred to for specific disclosure requirements related to the following:

1. *Management representation.* A representation to the effect that all adjustments which are, in the opinion of management, nec-

essary to a fair statement of the results for the interim periods is to be included in the Form 10-Q.

2. *Changes in accounting.* In addition to meeting the reporting requirements for accounting changes under generally accepted accounting principles, a registrant should state the date of any change in accounting during the quarter being reported on and the reasons for making the change. In the first Form 10-Q filed subsequent to the date of an accounting change, a letter from the registrant's independent accountant must be filed as an exhibit indicating whether or not the change is to an alternative principle which in his judgment is "preferable" under the circumstances. No letter is needed, however, when a change is made in response to a standard adopted by the Financial Accounting Standards Board which requires such a change. When there has been an accounting change in other than the first interim period of a fiscal year, *FASB Statement No. 3* requires that financial statements for prechange interim periods be restated. In an interpretive letter addressed to the then chairman of the Committee on SEC Regulations of the American Institute of Certified Public Accountants, the Chief Accountant of the SEC indicated that such restatements would not necessitate amending previously filed Form 10-Qs for the prechange interim periods; however, comparative data in subsequent Form 10-Qs should be restated. A company could, of course, voluntarily amend previous Form 10-Qs. Furthermore, if a company publishes prechange interim data in a report to shareholders, a prospectus, a merger proxy, or otherwise, the prechange data should be restated.

3. *Prior period adjustments.* Any material prior period adjustment made during any period included in a Form 10-Q shall be disclosed, together with the effect thereof upon net income (total and per share) of any period reported in the form and upon the balance of retained earnings.

4. *Business combinations and dispositions.* Form 10-Q requires certain disclosures when a business combination or a disposition of any significant portion of the business occurs in a quarter. The business combination disclosures vary, depending on whether the nature of the transaction is a purchase or a pooling of interests.

5. *Issuances of unregistered securities.* Form 10-Q requires a reporting of the sales, exchanges, or guarantees of unregistered securities.

6. *Form 8-Ks filed in quarters.* The registrant should indicate

whether any Form 8-K applicable to the most recently completed fiscal quarter was filed, reporting (*a*) any material unusual charges or credits to income or (*b*) a change in independent accountants.

7. *Other financial information.* Other financial information related to the periods being reported on, that management may consider significant to investors, may also be disclosed in the Form 10-Q. This includes the seasonality of the company's business, major uncertainties currently facing the company, significant accounting changes under consideration, and the dollar amount of backlog orders.

Incorporation by reference

The Form 10-Q instructions provide that if the registrant makes available to its shareholders or otherwise publishes an interim financial statement containing the information required by Form 10-Q, the information called for may be incorporated by reference from the published statement, provided copies thereof are filed as an exhibit.

Review by independent auditors

The instructions to Form 10-Q indicate that the financial information included in such form need not be reviewed by an independent accountant prior to filing. The instructions further provide that if a review of the financial information in the Form 10-Q is made in accordance with established professional standards and procedures for such a review, the registrant may state that the independent accountant has performed such a review. If such a statement is made, the registrant is required to indicate whether all adjustments or additional disclosures proposed by the independent accountant have been reflected in the data presented, and if not, why not. In addition, a letter from the registrant's independent accountant confirming or otherwise commenting upon the registrant's representations and making such other comments as the independent auditor deems appropriate may be included as an exhibit to the form.

FORM 8-K

Form 8-K is a report that is to be filed with the SEC when any one or more of certain specified events occur. The form is due within ten days after the close of each month; if none of the specified events occurs, the form need not be filed. In addition, if substantially the same information as that required by the Form 8-K has been previously reported to the SEC by the company, an additional report on Form 8-K is not required. Incorporation of data by reference from other filings with the SEC is permitted in answering items on Form 8-K, provided Rule 12b-23 under the 1934 Act is complied with. Also, any item in the Form 8-K which is not required to be reported may be omitted.

Events to be reported in Form 8-K

The Form 8-K lists the 13 following categories of events that must be included in a monthly report to the SEC if they have occurred:

Item
1. Changes in Control of Registrant
2. Acquisition or Disposition of Assets
3. Legal Proceedings
4. Changes in Securities
5. Changes in Security for Registered Securities
6. Defaults Upon Senior Securities
7. Increase in Amount of Securities Outstanding
8. Decrease in Amount of Securities Outstanding
9. Options to Purchase Securities
10. Extraordinary Item Charges and Credits, Other Material Charges and Credits to Income of an Unusual Nature, Material Provisions for Loss, and Restatements of Capital Share Account
11. Submission of Matters to a Vote of Security Holders
12. Changes in Registrant's Certifying Accountant
13. Other Materially Important Events

Many of the foregoing items are predominantly legal in nature in terms of reporting; however, both the company financial officers and the independent auditors should be alert to what has been reported on each Form 8-K, since this data often has significance to financial accounting and reporting. The items in which the accountants are most likely to be directly involved are Item 2, "Acquisition or Disposition of Assets" (where the acquisition of another business is involved); Item 10, "Extraordinary Item Charges and Credits,

Other Material Charges and Credits to Income of an Unusual Nature, Material Provisions for Loss, and Restatements of Capital Share Account"; and Item 12, "Changes in Registrant's Certifying Accountants."

Financial statements of businesses acquired (Item 2). If a registrant has purchased another business or succeeded to it through a pooling of interests and certain materiality tests are met, financial statements of the acquired company must be filed in the Form 8-K. These financial statements would include balance sheets as of the end of the latest fiscal year on an audited basis and as of a subsequent date reasonably close to the date of acquisition on an unaudited basis. In addition, statements of income, changes in financial position, retained earnings, and paid-in capital accounts are to be presented for the last three fiscal years (audited) and for the unaudited period between the end of the latest fiscal year and the date of the subsequent interim balance sheet. Regulation S-X governs the form and content of the statements to be filed for companies acquired, including the basis of consolidation. If the acquisition involves two or more related companies, combined statements may also be filed if appropriate. No supporting schedules need be filed.

The Commission can permit the omission or the substitution of other statements. The most common situation that creates problems is the one where it is impossible or impractical to obtain audited financial statements of the acquired entity for all periods specified in Form 8-K. In this connection attention is directed to *Release 4950* under the 1933 Act, which sets forth criteria as to when audited financial statements can be waived in 1933 Act filings which require disclosures of financial statements of companies acquired or to be acquired. While *Release 4950* does not technically apply to a Form 8-K which is under the 1934 Act, the SEC staff as a practical matter has utilized the 1933 Act criteria in granting relief from audited financial statement requirements under the Form 8-K.

Significant charges and credits to income (Item 10). In January 1973, the SEC issued *Accounting Series Release No. 138*, which increased disclosure requirements with respect to unusual charges and credits to income. The objective of this release was to obtain prompter and more complete public disclosure of unusual transactions, losses on write-downs of assets, provisions for losses on major contracts or purchase commitments, and similar items. The new rules applied not only to those items that meet the criteria for "extraordinary items" under generally accepted accounting principles, but also applied to material unusual charges and credits reported in the income statement as components of revenues, costs, or expenses and not as extraordinary items. The decision as to what constitutes a material unusual charge or credit to income may involve a subjective decision by a company where the charge or credit is not classified as extraordinary. In such cases, the company should consult with its independent accountants and possibly also its legal counsel.

The charges or credits reported in a Form 8-K will at times be based on estimates and will be subject to modification when the actual amounts are ascertained. In such cases, an amended Form 8-K may have to be filed or a summary of differences between estimated and actual amounts may have to be included in the annual report on Form 10-K and/or in 1933 Act registration statements forms that may be filed.

Accounting Series Release No. 138 also provided for the timely review by independent accountants of extraordinary or material unusual charges and credits to income or material provisions for losses effected by companies. Form 8-K now requires a "report" from the registrant's independent accountants with respect to the accounting principles applied. There is no requirement for auditor verification with respect to the facts or the amounts reported in Item 10; the report is to be based on the accountant's reading of the description by the registrant of the facts set forth in the Form 8-K and the accounting principles applied. Accordingly, a disclaimer of opinion on the factual data is usually included in the report because the independent accountant has done limited work.

Changes in registrant's certifying accountants (*Item 12*). Objective reporting by independent accountants is one of the basic supports to the SEC in its administration of the federal securities laws. Independent accountants' reports provide the assurance of an outside expert's examination and opinion, thereby substantially increasing the reliability of financial statements. The independence of auditors is essential to the system for investor protection, and the SEC has from time to time taken steps to strengthen that independence.

One such step was the inclusion of Item 12 in Form 8-K. This item was initiated in 1971 and amended in 1974. It currently provides as follows:

Item 12. Changes in Registrant's Certifying Accountant

If an independent accountant who was previously engaged as the principal accountant to audit the registrant's financial statements resigns (or indicates he declines to stand for re-election after the completion of the current audit) or is dismissed as the registrant's principal accountant, or another independent accountant is engaged as principal accountant, or if an independent accountant on whom the principal accountant expressed reliance in his report regarding a significant subsidiary resigns (or formally indicates he declines to stand for re-election after the completion of the current audit) or is dismissed or another independent accountant is engaged to audit that subsidiary:

(a) State the date of such resignation (or declination to stand for re-election) dismissal or engagement.

(b) State whether in connection with the audits of the two most recent fiscal years and any subsequent interim period preceding such resignation, dismissal or engagement there were any disagreements with the former accountant on any matter of accounting principles or practices, financial statement disclosure, or auditing scope or procedure, which disagreements if not resolved to the satisfaction of the former accountant would have caused him to make reference in connection with his report to the subject matter of the disagreement(s); also, describe each such disagreement. The disagreements required to be reported in response to the preceding sentence include both those resolved to the former accountant's satisfaction and those not resolved to the former accountant's satisfaction. Disagreements contemplated by this rule are those which occur at the decision-making level; i.e., between personnel of the registrant responsible for presentation of its financial statements and personnel of the accounting firm responsible for rendering its report.

(c) State whether the principal accountant's report on the financial statements for any of the past two years contained an adverse opinion or a disclaimer of opinion or was qualified as to uncertainty, audit scope, or accounting principles; also describe the nature of each such adverse opinion, disclaimer of opinion, or qualification.

(d) The registrant shall request the former accountant to furnish the registrant with a letter addressed to the Commission stating whether he agrees with the statements made by the registrant in response to this item and, if not, stating the respects in which he does not agree. The registrant shall file a copy of the former accountant's letter as an exhibit with all copies of the Form 8-K required to be filed pursuant to General Instructions F.

A significant problem that has arisen with respect to Item 12 insofar as the independent auditors are concerned is the interpretation of the term "disagreement." Explanatory material in *Accounting Series Release No. 165* indicated that this should be interpreted as follows:

> 5. The term "disagreements" should be interpreted broadly in responding to this item. For example, if an accountant resigned or was dismissed after advising the registrant that he had concluded that internal controls necessary to develop reliable statements did not exist, this would constitute a reportable disagreement in the event of a change of accountants. Similarly, if an accountant were to resign or be dismissed after informing the registrant that he had discovered facts which led him no longer to be able to rely on management representations or which made him unwilling to be associated with statements prepared by management, such situations would constitute reportable disagreements.

This has not resolved issues in all practical cases. However, a precise objective definition of "disagreements" is probably not possible for this purpose, and it might even be inadvisable to attempt to have such a definition. There are many concepts in accounting and financial reporting that cannot be objectively or precisely defined.

If there are disagreements, it is preferable that the registrant and the former auditors meet and agree on the description of the disagreement that is to be reported under Item 12 of Form 8-K. In many cases the company explains the disagreement in its letter, with the auditor stating that he or she concurs in the explanation of the company. Cases where there is a lack of concurrence as to whether a disagreement existed or as to the explanation that should be given of the disagreement are rare. These have to be handled on a case-by-case basis. Under these situations, the independent auditor should be particularly careful that his or her position is well documented.

For further background information on reporting changes in auditors and for related provisions in Regulation S-X and the proxy rules, the SEC's *Accounting Series Release No. 165* (1974) should be reviewed.

TIMELY FILINGS AND EXTENSIONS

It is important that a Form 10-K and other periodic reports be filed within the period specified, not only from the standpoint of getting data out promptly to the investing public but also because the eligibility to use certain streamlined registration procedures under the 1933 Act (e.g., a Form S-7 or Form S-16) depends in part on compliance with the filing requirements, including timeliness, of the 1934 Act reports such as Form 10-K, 8-K, and 10-Q. In recent years, the Commission has been placing an emphasis on the timely filing of periodic reports.

If a filing date cannot be met for a valid reason, Rule 12b-25 under the 1934 Act governs the granting of extensions of filing dates. This rule provides for an extension, in appropriate cases, of 30 days which can be renewed for an additional 30 days. Applications, which must be filed on Form 12b-25 as soon as possible but not later than the last day of the specified period, are deemed to be granted unless denied within 15 days after receipt. Thereafter, any request for further extension shall be deemed to have been denied unless the Commission enters an order granting it within 15 days after receipt. The rule spells out the procedures to be followed in applying for extensions.

Rule 12b-25 also provides that if the requested extension is necessitated by the inability of any person other than the company to furnish any required opinion, information, report, or certification, the application on Form 12b-25 shall have attached as an exhibit, a statement signed by such person stating the specific reasons why he or she is unable to furnish the required opinion, information, report, or certification.

A company must have a good reason to obtain an extension. A note to Rule 12b-25 states, in part: "Only the most compelling and unexpected circumstances justify a delay in the filing of a report and the dissemination to the public of the factual information called for therein."

Chapter 38

Corporate accounting policy under uniform cost accounting standards

*Robert K. Mautz**

A number of factors may have contributed to the movement leading to establishment of the CASB. To some people, Admiral Hyman G. Rickover's testimony before congressional committees stands as the original impetus. He contended that his own work as an engineer in charge of the U.S. Navy nuclear propulsion program suffered because the lack of uniform cost accounting standards made government contract administration difficult, time-consuming, and unsatisfactory. Although the accounting profession had long given attention to financial accounting standards, no authoritative organization had attempted to formulate cost accounting standards. The Armed Services Procurement Regulations, Section XV, provided some guidance for contract accounting, but Admiral Rickover and others found the ASPR provisions inadequate for their purpose.

Influential members of Congress were won over to the Admiral's view, extensive hearings were held, the conclusions and recommendations of the GAO feasibility study were considered, and finally the CASB was established by amendment to the Defense Production Act. In the public hearings, industry vigorously opposed creation of the CASB, arguing that uniform cost accounting stan-

* Partner, Ernst & Ernst.

dards were neither necessary nor desirable. Professional accountants, including the official representatives of the AICPA, supported establishment of the CASB.

AUTHORIZING LEGISLATION

The Cost Accounting Standards Board was established by Public Law 91–379 signed by the President August 15, 1970. The General Accounting Office had previously completed a feasibility study, at the request of Congress, on the basis of which it concluded that cost accounting standards for negotiated defense contracts were feasible and that a means for promulgating them should be established. The Board was formally organized in January 1971 following the initial appropriation of funds for its operations.

PURPOSE

The CASB is an agent of the Congress established independent of the executive departments. Its purpose is stated to be:

> The Board shall from time to time promulgate cost-accounting standards designed to achieve uniformity and consistency in the cost-accounting principles followed by defense contractors and subcontractors under Federal contracts. Such promulgated standards shall be used by all relevant Federal agencies and by defense contractors and subcontractors in estimating, accumulating, and reporting costs in connection with the pricing, administration and settlement of all negotiated prime contract and subcontract national defense procurements with the United States in excess of $100,000, other than contracts or subcontracts where the price negotiated is based on (1) established catalog or market prices of commercial items sold in substantial quantities to the general public, or (2) prices set by law or regulation.

ORGANIZATION

The Comptroller General of the United States serves as chairman of the five-man CASB and appoints the other members who serve four-year terms. The enabling legislation requires that two members be appointed from the accounting profession, one from industry, and one from a department or agency of the federal government. Board members serve on a part-time basis.

The staff of the CASB includes 22 full-time professionals in addition to secretarial and clerical personnel. It is headed by an executive secretary assisted by a general counsel and four project directors.

PROCEDURES IN DEVELOPING STANDARDS

Other than the requirement for exposure of proposed standards through the *Federal Register,* the Board is not bound by any formalized procedures. At least the following steps are included in the development of most standards:

1. In response to a request from the staff, the Board authorizes research aimed at developing a cost accounting standard on a specific topic.
2. A library study is undertaken to acquaint the project team with available materials, data, and views.
3. Staff members visit contractors' plants to discuss possibilities, problems, and usefulness of the proposed standard.
4. Questionnaires, discussion outlines, interview guides, and illustrative cases are used to elicit views from contractors, agency representatives, professional organizations, consultants, and others.
5. A draft standard is developed by the staff and circulated to interested parties for comment.
6. Intensive staff discussion of the draft standard and comments from interested parties lead to a revised draft.
7. The revised draft standard is presented to the Board with a request for review and initial publication in the *Federal Register.*
8. Intensive Board discussion may lead to further revision of the revised draft standard and ultimately to publication of a proposed standard in the *Federal Register* with a request for comments. Typically, 60 days or more are allowed for comment.
9. Comments on the published proposal are reviewed and evaluated independently by staff and Board members.
10. Revised wording is considered, final promulgation of the standard in the *Federal Register* is provided, and a copy of the standard is sent to Congress.
11. After 60 days of continuous session of Congress, the standard

becomes effective unless the two Houses of Congress pass a concurrent resolution stating in substance that the Congress does not favor the proposed standard. Promulgated standards have the full force and effect of law.

IMPLEMENTATION AND ENFORCEMENT

Other than an obvious interest in the effectiveness of its standards, the CASB is not involved in their implementation. The responsibility for securing compliance with cost accounting standards for affected contracts falls upon the executive agencies.

Both before and after promulgation, the CASB and its staff seek any and all information from the agencies, from contractors, and from others that bears on the usefulness, effectiveness, and cost of applying standards.

EXEMPTIONS AND WAIVERS

The Board has the authority to grant exemptions and waivers when conditions or circumstances so require. It has generally rejected blanket requests to exempt any entire industry, class or group of contractors, or type of contract, from its requirements. Exemptions or waivers have been granted only in individual cases in which the interests of the government were best served by such action.

OPERATING POLICIES

In March of 1973, the CASB published a small booklet entitled *Statement of Operating Policies, Procedures and Objectives.* The following excerpts from that document assist in explaining the attitude and approach of the Board.

Objectives

A Cost Accounting Standard is a statement formally issued by the Cost Accounting Standards Board that (1) enunciates a principle or principles to be followed, (2) establishes practices to be applied, or (3) specifies criteria to be employed in selecting from alternative principles and practices in estimating, accumulating, and reporting costs of contracts subject to the rules of the Board.

A Cost Accounting Standard may be stated in terms as general or as specific as the Cost Accounting Standards Board considers necessary to accomplish its purpose.

Increased uniformity and consistency in accounting are desirable to the extent that they improve understanding and communication, reduce the incidence of disputes and disagreements, and facilitate equitable contract settlements.

Uniformity

Uniformity relates to comparison of two or more accounting entities, and the Board's objective in this respect is to achieve like treatment under like circumstances. The Board recognizes the impossibility of defining or attaining absolute uniformity, largely because of the problems related to defining like circumstances. The Board will, nonetheless, seek ways to attain a practical degree of uniformity in cost accounting.

Uniformity is achieved when contractors with the same circumstances (with respect to a given subject) follow the practice appropriate for those circumstances. Any increase in uniformity will provide more comparability among contractors whose circumstances are similar.

The Board does not seek to establish a single uniform accounting system or chart of accounts for all the complex and diverse businesses engaged in defense contract work. On the other hand, if the Board were to be satisfied that circumstances among all concerned contractors are substantially the same, the Board would not be precluded from establishing a single accounting treatment for use in such circumstances.

Consistency

Consistency pertains primarily to one accounting entity over periods of time. Like uniformity, the attainment of absolute consistency can only be measured when like circumstances can be defined. The Board believes that consistency within an entity, from one time period to another, can be improved, thereby enhancing the usefulness of comparisons between estimates and actuals. It will also improve the comparability of cost reports from one time period to another where there are like circumstances.

Allocability and allowability

Allocability is an accounting concept affecting the ascertainment of contract cost; it results from a relationship between a cost and a cost objective such that the cost objective appropriately bears all or a portion of the cost. To be charged with all or part of a cost, a cost objective should cause or be an intended beneficiary of the cost.

Allowability is a procurement concept affecting contract price, and in most cases is expressly provided in regulatory or contractual provisions. An agency's policies on allowability of costs may be derived from law and are generally embodied in its procurement regulations. A contracting agency may include in contract terms or in its procurement regulations a provision that it will refuse to allow certain costs, incurred by contractors, that are unreasonable in amount or contrary to public policy. In accounting terms, those same costs may be allocable to the contract in question.

Cost Accounting Standards should result in the determination of costs which are allocable to contracts and other cost objectives. The use of Cost Accounting Standards has no direct bearing on the allowability of individual items of cost which are subject to limitations or exclusions set forth in the contract or are otherwise specified by the government or its procuring agency.

It should be emphasized that contract costs, with which Cost Accounting Standards are involved, are only one of several important factors which should be involved in negotiating contracts. Therefore, the promulgation of Cost Accounting Standards, and the determination of contract costs thereunder, cannot be considered a substitute for effective contract negotiation. At the same time, it should be emphasized that where contract costs are required to be determined and Cost Accounting Standards are applicable, the latter are determinative as to the costs allocable to contracts. It is a contracting agency's prerogative to negotiate the *allowability* of allocated costs, but not the allocation itself.

The Cost Accounting Standards Board will establish standards to:

1. Measure the amount of costs which may be allocated to covered contracts,
2. Determine the accounting period to which costs are allocable, and

3. Determine the manner in which allocable costs can be allocated to covered contracts. The resulting cost measurements and allocation determinations are binding on both the contractor and the contracting agency, as indicated above.

Fairness

The Board considers a Cost Accounting Standard to be fair when, in the Board's best judgment, the standard provides for allocating costs to affected contracts without bias or prejudice to either party.

The results of contract pricing may ultimately be regarded as fair or unfair by either or both parties to that contract. But if the Cost Accounting Standards utilized in the negotiation, administration, and settlement of the contract provide the contracting parties with accounting data which are representative of the facts, the standards themselves are "fair" regardless of the outcome of the contract.

Materiality

The Board believes that the administration of its rules, regulations, and Cost Accounting Standards should be reasonable and not seek to deal with insignificant amounts of cost. Although this rule of common sense is already practiced by the government, the Board recognizes that in particular standards, a specific "materiality" statement may be useful; and in such cases it will include one.

Verifiability

Verifiability is generally accepted as a goal for information used in cost accounting. Contract cost accounting systems should provide for verifiability. Contract costs should be auditable by examination of appropriate data and documents supporting such costs or by reference to the facts and assumptions used to assign the costs to the contract. Contractor records of contract costs should be reconcilable with the general books of account.

Relationship to other authoritative bodies

Promulgations by the Cost Accounting Standards Board may involve the areas of interest of other authoritative bodies. Contract cost accounting often deals with the same expenditures and the same problems of allocation to time periods as are of interest in financial and income tax accounting.

The Cost Accounting Standards Board seeks to avoid conflict or disagreement with other bodies having similar responsibilities and will through continuous liaison make every reasonable effort to do so. The Board will give careful consideration to the pronouncements affecting financial and tax reporting, and in the formulation of Cost Accounting Standards it will take those pronouncements into account to the extent it can do so in accomplishing its objectives. The nature of the Board's authority and its mission, however, is such that it must retain and exercise full responsibility for meeting its objectives.

Nondefense applications

The Board is of the opinion that uniformity among all government agencies in contracting costing is a highly desirable objective. It is, therefore, the Board's view that extension of Board pronouncements to nondefense agencies would be markedly beneficial both to the agencies concerned and to their contractors. Companies with a mixture of defense and nondefense contracts will be benefited substantially by having a single set of cost accounting principles applicable to all their government contracts.

Single government representative

To assure maximum uniformity of interpretation of its promulgations, the Board believes that it is highly desirable to have federal agencies agree upon a single representative to deal with a given contractor regarding application of the requirements of the Board. Because of its conviction of the merit of such a procedure, the Board recommended that the agencies arrange for a single contracting officer for each contractor, or major component thereof, to be designated to negotiate as needed to achieve consistent practices relating to the standards issued by the Board.

Interpretations

The Board notes the existence of contractual and administrative provisions for the resolution or settlement of disputes arising under a contract, and the Board will not intervene in or seek to supersede such provisions. When there are widespread and serious questions of the Board's intention or meaning in its promulgations, the Board may at its discretion respond to requests for authoritative interpretations of its rules, regulations, and Cost Accounting Standards. Such interpretations will be published in the *Federal Register* and will be considered by the Board as an integral part of the rules, regulations, and standards to which the interpretations relate. This formalized procedure does not preclude unofficial consultation between inquirers and the executive secretary and members of the Board's staff.

Exemptions

The Board anticipates that it will grant exemptions only in rare and unusual cases. In reviewing a request for an exemption, the Board would be persuaded that an exemption is justified only if—

1. The administrative burden is grossly disproportionate to the benefits which could be expected, or
2. Failure to grant an exemption will prevent the orderly and economical acquisition on a timely basis of supplies and services essential to the needs of the government.

The Board notes that the granting of an exemption would reduce the extent to which the primary goals of increased uniformity and consistency are achieved.

Consideration of existing practices

To be effective, Cost Accounting Standards must have both theoretical validity and practical applicability. So that practical considerations wll not be overlooked, the Board seeks reliable information about current practices in a variety of ways. Disclosure Statements, questionnaires, intensive discussions with contractors, responses to *Federal Register* publication of proposed standards, and study of published research results all supply useful information about current practice.

The Board's purpose in this is, first, to establish what practice is; second, to discover the reasons supporting different practices in apparently similar circumstances; and, third, to determine the appropriate criteria for the selection of practices in given circumstances. There is no presumption that the most common practice is or is not the most desirable practice.

Comparing costs and benefits

The Board views costs and benefits in a broad sense. All disruptions of contractors' and agencies' practices and procedures are viewed as costs. Diligent research into current practice is helpful in appraising the probable cost impact of proposed standards. Benefits include anticipated reductions in the number of time-consuming controversies stemming from unresolved aspects of cost allocability. The Board also expects that benefits will be achieved through simplified negotiation, administration, audit, and settlement procedures. Finally, and most importantly, the availability of better cost data stemming from the use of Cost Accounting Standards will permit improved comparability of offers and facilitate better negotiation of resulting contracts.

The Board is interested in data which will enable it to gauge the impact of a proposed standard on the amount of costs that will shift to or from government contracts as a result of one or more standards. The Board recognizes that a fair Cost Accounting Standard may result in a shift of cost from the government to contractors or from contractors to the government. In formulating standards, the Board will not regard such shifts of costs as determinative.

Cost allocation concepts

Cost accounting for negotiated government contracts has long been on the basis of full allocation of costs, including general and administrative expenses and all other indirect costs. The allocation of all period costs to the products and services of the period is not a common practice either for public reporting or for internal management purposes; yet this has long been the established cost principle for costing defense procurement. The Board will adhere to the concept of full costing wherever appropriate.

Direct identification of costs

As an ideal, each item of cost should be assigned to the cost objectives to the extent practical. The Board recognizes the need for care in application of the concept of direct identification of costs with final cost objectives. Therefore, Cost Accounting Standards developed by the Board will reflect the desire for direct identification of cost and at the same time provide safeguards to assure consistency and objectivity in allocating costs incurred for the same purpose.

Hierarchy for allocating cost pools

Costs not directly identified with final cost objectives should be grouped into logical and homogeneous expense pools and should be allocated in accordance with a hierarchy of preferable techniques. The costs of like functions have a direct and definitive relationship to the cost objectives for which the functions are performed, and the grouping of such costs in homogeneous pools for allocation to benefiting cost objectives results in better identification of cost with cost objectives.

The Board believes there is a hierarchy of preferable allocation techniques for distributing homogeneous pools of cost. The preferred representation of the relationship between the pooled cost and the benefiting cost objectives is a measure of the activity of the function represented by the pool of cost. Measures of the activities of such functions ordinarily can be expressed in such terms as labor hours, machine hours, or square footage. Accordingly, cost of these functions can be allocated by use of a rate, such as a rate per labor hour, rate per machine hour, or cost per square foot, unless such measures are unavailable or impractical to ascertain. In these latter cases, the basis for allocation can be a measurement of the output of the supporting function. Output is measured in terms of units of end product produced by the supporting functions, as for example, number of printed pages for a print shop, number of purchase orders processed by a purchasing department, number of hires by an employment office.

Where neither activity nor output of the supporting function can be measured practically, a surrogate for the beneficial or causal relationship should be selected. Surrogates used to represent the relationship are generally measures of the activity of the cost objectives receiving the service. Any surrogate used should be a reasonable measure of the services received and should vary in proportion to the services received.

Pooled costs which cannot readily be allocated on measures of specific beneficial or causal relationship generally represent the cost of overall management activities. These costs should be grouped in relation to the activities managed, and the base selected to measure the allocation of these indirect costs to cost ʼobjectives should be a base representative of the entire activity being managed. For example, the total cost of plant activities managed might be a reasonable base for allocation of general plant indirect costs. The use of a portion of a total activity, such as direct labor costs or direct material costs only, as a substitute for a total activity base, is acceptable only if the base is a good representative of the total activity being managed.

PROMULGATIONS TO DATE

The following paragraphs in this section provide brief descriptions of the Contract Clause, Cost Accounting Standards, and other promulgations of the Board. As summaries, they should not be relied on as guides to implementation of the stated requirements.

Contract clause

A clause to be included in all contracts subject to CASB requirements has been developed. It commits the contractor to file a Disclosure Statement to the extent required by other regulations of the Board, and to follow disclosed practices consistently. It further commits all covered contractors to comply with all Cost Accounting Standards in effect during the performance of the contract; to agree to a contract price adjustment if contract cost is affected by additional Cost Accounting Standards, changes in the Disclosure Statement, or failure to comply with an applicable Cost Accounting Standard; to follow prescribed procedures should a dispute arise; and to include the substance of the clause in all negotiated subcontracts not exempted by law.

Disclosure statement

Public Law 91-379 directed the CASB to establish regulations that would ". . . require defense contractors and subcontractors as a condition of contracting to disclose in writing their cost-accounting principles, including methods of distinguishing direct costs from indirect costs and the basis for allocating indirect costs. . . ." The Disclosure Statement, a 32-page document, including instructions plus continuation sheets provided for explanatory purposes, is the device used by the CASB to obtain a description of the contractors' or subcontractors' cost accounting practices. Blank copies of the Disclosure Statement may be obtained from the contracting agency.

A Disclosure Statement is required for every covered organization unit within a corporate organization. Some companies must therefore file more than one statement.

When first imposed, the Disclosure Statement requirement was restricted to companies which together with subsidiaries received net awards of negotiated national defense prime contracts during federal fiscal year 1971 (July 1, 1970, through June 30, 1971) totaling more than $30 million. Effective April 1, 1974, companies having prime contracts of $10 million or more in either fiscal 1972 or 1973 of the type that are subject to Cost Accounting Standards are required to file a Disclosure Statement. The Board has authorized research by the staff to determine when to bring subcontractors under the Disclosure Statement requirement and to recommend a minimum activity in government contracting below which the requirement will not be applied.

Cost accounting standards

The official statement of a Cost Accounting Standard includes the following sections:

1. General applicability.
2. Purpose.
3. Definitions.
4. Fundamental requirement.
5. Techniques for application.
6. Illustrations.
7. Exemptions.
8. Effective date.

Standard No. 401—Consistency in Estimating, Accumulating, and Reporting Costs

This standard requires that practices followed in estimating costs to price a proposal and practices followed in accumulating and reporting costs must be mutually consistent, especially the classification of elements or functions of cost as direct or indirect, the indirect cost pools to which each element or function of cost is charged or proposed to be charged, and the methods of allocating indirect costs to the contract. Costs estimated for proposal purposes shall be presented in such a manner and in such detail that any significant cost can be compared with the actual cost accumulated and reported for the contract.

Standard No. 402—Consistency in Allocating Costs Incurred for the Same Purpose

This standard is intended to prohibit so-called "double counting" of costs. Double counting occurs most commonly when cost items are allocated directly to a cost objective without eliminating like cost items from indirect cost pools which are also allocated in some part to that cost objective. Thus a contract might be charged directly with all of the specific cost which it caused but get an additional share of the same kind of cost incurred for other purposes through an indirect cost allocation.

The standard requires that all costs incurred for the same purposes in like circumstances be treated either as direct costs only or as indirect costs only in making allocations to final cost objectives. Then, no final cost objective shall have charged to it directly any cost if other costs incurred for the same purpose in like circumstances have been charged to it, or to any other final cost objective, indirectly through allocation of an indirect cost pool. And no cost should be charged to it indirectly if other costs incurred for the same purpose in like circumstances have been charged directly to it.

Standard No. 403—Allocation of Home Office Expenses to Segments

Appropriate allocation of indirect costs to final cost objectives is a major problem in cost accounting. For contract accounting purposes, home office costs must be allocated to contracts and other final cost objectives. This standard is concerned only with the first of these steps, allocation of home office costs to segments.

The standard divides home office expenses into three categories:

1. Expenses incurred for a specific segment. Such costs should be allocated directly to the segment.
2. Expenses incurred for more than one segment and whose relationship to the segments for which incurred can be measured at least approximately on some objective basis. Such expenses should be grouped on the basis of their relationship to the segments and allocated on the most objective basis available.
3. Expenses incurred to manage the enterprise as a whole which have no identifiable relationship to any specific segment or segments. The total of such residual expenses is to be allocated to segments either (*a*) on the basis of a three-factor formula (payroll dollars, operating revenue, and net book value of tangible capital assets), or (*b*) on any basis representative of the total activity of the segments. The three-factor formula is required when the residual expenses exceed a stated proportion of the aggregate operating revenue of all segments for the previous fiscal year.

The standard provides for allocation of all home office expenses to segments on the basis of the beneficial or causal relationship between supporting and receiving activities. To accomplish this, the standard suggests the following classes and allocation bases of home office expenses in the second category:

1. Centralized service functions such as personnel administration and data processing—allocated on the basis of the service furnished to or received by each segment.
2. Staff management of certain specific activities of segments such as manufacturing, accounting, and engineering—allocated over a base or bases representative of the total specific activity being managed.
3. Line management of particular segments or groups of segments—allocated over a base or bases representative of the total activity of the segments involved.
4. Central payments or accruals such as pension costs, group insurance, state and local taxes—allocated directly to segments concerned if so identifiable; otherwise, on a basis representative of the factors on which the total payment is based.
5. Independent research and development and bidding and proposal costs—allocated pursuant to provisions of existing laws, regulations, and other controlling factors.

6. Staff management not identifiable with any certain specific activities of segments—allocated as residual expenses.

To assist in identifying appropriate allocation bases, the standard sets forth a "hierarchy" of preferable allocation techniques which represent beneficial or causal relationships:

Preferred. A measure of the activity of the organization performing the supporting function, usually a measure of labor effort, machine time, or space.

Second. A measure of the output of the supporting function in terms of units of end product.

Third. A measure of the activity of the segments receiving the service provided that the cost varies in proportion to the services received.

Where a particular segment receives significantly more or significantly less benefit from residual expenses than would result from the required allocation, the government and the contractor may agree to a special allocation of residual expense to such segment commensurate with the benefits received.

Standard No. 404—Capitalization of Tangible Assets

A number of cost accounting standards may be necessary to provide guidance for fixed asset accounting. This standard constitutes a first step. It requires the contractor to have and apply a written policy on tangible asset capitalization that designates the economic and physical characteristics on which the policy is based and identifies asset accountability units to the maximum extent practical. Any tangible asset with a minimum service life of two years or more and a cost of $500 must be capitalized. Lower, but not higher, limits may be set in the contractor's policy.

Tangible capital assets constructed for a company's own use shall be capitalized at amounts which include general and administrative expenses when such expenses are identifiable with the constructed asset and are material in amount. When the constructed assets are identical with or similar to the contractor's regular product, such assets shall be capitalized at amounts which include a full share of indirect costs.

Donated assets which, at the time of receipt, meet the contractor's criteria for capitalization shall be capitalized at their fair value at that time.

Provisions for determining cost, accounting for assets acquired at less than arm's length, accounting for assets acquired through a business acquisition, and accounting for assets retired call for no unusual practices.

Standard No. 405—Accounting for Unallowable Costs

This standard does not govern the allowability of costs, which is a function of the appropriate procurement or reviewing authority. It does require:

1. The identification in the accounting records, and exclusion from claim, of costs specifically described as unallowable either by the express wording of laws or regulations or by mutual agreement of the contracting parties.
2. The identification of costs specifically designated as unallowable by a written decision of a contracting officer pursuant to contract disputes procedures.
3. The identification of mutually agreed or contracting-officer designated "directly associated costs," defined for this purpose as any cost which is generated solely as the result of the incurrence of an unallowable cost and which would not have been incurred had the unallowable cost not been incurred.
4. Inclusion of identified unallowable costs and directly associated costs in any indirect cost allocation base or bases in which they normally would be included. This has the effect under existing procurement regulations of including in the amount disallowed (*a*) the specific unallowable cost, (*b*) any directly associated costs, and (*c*) the share of indirect costs that normally would have been charged to a contract as the result of inclusion in the allocation base of the unallowable costs and costs directly associated therewith.

No special type of detailed records or reports are required to be used for identification purposes as long as the means selected permit ready identification of amounts and descriptions.

Standard No. 406—Cost Accounting Period

This standard requires that, with four possible exceptions, a contractor shall use the fiscal period as the cost accounting period in accumulating and allocating costs. The exceptions are:

1. If an indirect function exists for only a part of a cost accounting period, its costs may be allocated to cost objectives of that same part of the period if the cost (*a*) is material, (*b*) is accumulated in a separate cost pool, and (*c*) is allocated on the basis of an appropriate direct measure of the activity or output of the function during that part of the period.
2. If use of a fixed annual period other than the fiscal year is an established practice of the contractor and it is consistently used for managing and controlling the business, and if appropriate accruals, deferrals, or other adjustments are made with respect to such annual period, that period may be used as the contractor's cost accounting period upon mutual agreement with the government.
3. If a change of fiscal year occurs, for the transitional period the contractor may select any one of (*a*) the period, less than a year in length, extending from the end of the contractor's previous cost accounting period to the beginning of the next regular cost accounting period; (*b*) a period in excess of a year, but not longer than 15 months, obtained by combining the period described in (*a*) above with the previous cost accounting period; or (*c*) a period in excess of a year, but not longer than 15 months, obtained by combining the period described in (*a*) above with the next regular cost accounting period.
4. If the contractor's cost accounting period is different from the reporting period required by Renegotiation Board regulations, the latter may be used for such reporting.

Standard No. 407—Use of Standard Costs for Direct Material and Direct Labor

A significant number of defense contractors use standard costs in their books of account. The CASB recognizes the usefulness of standard costs for management control purposes and seeks to facilitate their use as long as they do not conflict with the stated purpose of cost accounting standards. In time, additional cost accounting standards are expected to cover other aspects of standard costs. This standard states that standard costs may be used for estimating, accumulating, and reporting costs of direct material and direct labor if—

1. Standard costs are entered in the books of account;
2. Standard costs and related variances are appropriately accounted for at the level of the production unit; and
3. Practices with respect to the setting and revising of standards, use of standard costs, and disposition of variances are stated in writing and are consistently followed.

The standard requires that material price variances be accumulated either at the time purchases of direct material are entered in the books of account or at the time direct material cost is allocated to production units. Material price variances should be allocated at least annually to cost objectives in a way that adjusts the cost objectives to actual costs of direct materials used.

Direct labor cost variances likewise should be allocated at least annually to cost objectives in a way that adjusts the cost objectives to actual cost of direct labor used. Bases for such allocation are specified. Allocations of variances may be made in memorandum worksheet adjustments rather than in the books of account.

The standard seeks to put the accounting for such costs as paid time off for illness, vacations, holidays, jury duty or military training, or other personal activities on an accrual basis. The basis for recognition is the concept of "entitlement" which is an employee's right, whether conditional or unconditional, to receive a determinable amount of compensated personal absence, or pay in lieu thereof.

The fundamental requirement for this standard states:

1. The costs of compensated personal absence shall be assigned to the cost accounting period or periods in which the entitlement was earned.
2. The costs of compensated personal absence for an entire cost accounting period shall be allocated pro rata on an annual basis among the final cost objectives of that period.

Standard No. 409—Depreciation of Tangible Capital Assets

This standard provides that the cost of a tangible capital asset, less its estimated residual value, shall be assigned to the cost accounting periods representing its estimated life in a manner that reflects the pattern of consumption of service over the life of the asset.

The estimated service lives initially established for tangible capital assets shall be reasonable approximations of their expected actual periods of usefulness considering (*a*) quantity and quality of expected output and the timing thereof, (*b*) costs of repair and maintenance and the timing thereof, and (*c*) technical or economic obsolescence of the asset or of the product or service it is involved in making. The expected actual periods of usefulness shall be those periods which are supported by records of either past retirement or withdrawal from active use for like assets used in similar circumstances, appropriately modified for specifically identified factors expected to influence future lives. The burden shall be on the contractor to justify estimated service lives which are shorter than experienced lives.

If not available when the requirements of this standard must first be followed by a contractor, the records required shall be developed from current and historical fixed asset records and be available following the second fiscal year after the date the contractor becomes subject to the standard. Estimated service lives used for financial accounting purposes, if not unreasonable, shall be used until adequate supporting records are available. Estimated service lives for tangible capital assets for which the contractor has no data available, or no prior experience for similar assets, shall be established based on a projection of the expected actual period of usefulness until the contractor is able to develop estimates supported by personal experience. Lives so established shall not be less than asset guideline periods (mid-range) published by the Internal Revenue Service. The contracting parties may agree on estimated service lives of assets acquired for unique purposes or in special circumstances.

The method of depreciation used for financial accounting purposes shall be used for contract costing unless such method does not reasonably reflect the expected consumption of services or is unacceptable for federal income tax purposes. An accelerated method is appropriate where the expected consumption of asset services is significantly greater in early years of asset life. The straight-line method is appropriate where the expected consumption of asset services is reasonably level over the service life of the asset or group of assets.

Gains and losses on disposition of tangible capital assets shall generally be considered as adjustments of depreciation costs previously recognized and shall be assigned to the cost accounting periods in which disposition occurs. Any gains on disposition to be recognized for contract costing purposes shall be limited to the difference between the original acquisition cost of the asset and its undepreciated balance.

Standard No. 411—Accounting for Acquisition Cost of Material

Most material used on government contracts subject to Cost Accounting Standards is purchased specifically for and charged directly to the appropriate contract. This standard permits direct charging of such costs provided the contract was specified at the time of purchase or production of the units.

Some materials, of course, are drawn from existing inventories. Such material may be priced into contracts using one of the following costing methods consistently applied:

1. The first-in, first-out (Fifo) method.
2. The moving average cost method.
3. The weighted average cost method.
4. The standard cost method.
5. The last-in, first-out (Lifo) method.

Contractors are required to have and consistently apply written statements of accounting policies and practices for accumulating material costs and allocating them to cost objectives. The cost of materials which are used solely in performing indirect functions or which are not a significant element of producton cost may be charged to an indirect cost pool and allocated as part of the pool.

EVALUATION OF CASB ACTIVITIES TO DATE

Although opposed in principle to the establishment of the CASB, once the Board was in operation, industry has cooperated generously in responding to questionnaires, granting interviews to CASB staff members, and commenting on issues, papers, and exposure drafts. The Board on its part has attempted to maintain open relations with all interested industry representatives, welcoming comments of all kinds.

To this end, the Board has held an all-day Evaluation Conference at which all interested parties were invited to express both orally and in writing their views on those cost accounting standards now in effect.

Three major criticisms were voiced by those commenting in connection with the Evaluation Conference. First, although the Board strives to develop standards which are fair and reasonable, problems arise in the implementation of those standards; and although the Board has neither responsibility nor authority for implementation, failure to consider the problems involved therein may nullify the Board's best efforts. Second, the definition of an "accounting change" in connection with revision of required Disclosure Statements has not yet been established on any consistent or satisfactory basis. Third, the subject of materiality, although treated by the Board in its Statement of Operating Policies, Procedures, and Objectives, needs additional attention if continuing problems of implementation are to be avoided.

With respect to specific standards, No. 403 and No. 409 have aroused the greatest opposition. In practice, No. 403 appears to have worked out well except for its recommended treatment of state and local income taxes and franchise taxes, which receives continuing criticism. No. 409 was strongly criticized as likely to reduce cash flow to contractors during a period of inflation and recession; to make more difficult, if not impossible, the recovery of real cost of facilities used in defense production; and thereby to discourage investment in defense facilities. The Board's response was that built into the standard is sufficient delay in its application that the Board will have time to complete its consideration of the impact of inflation on defense contract accounting as well as its study of the cost of capital. Both of these subjects have been placed on the Board's top priority list.

A number of people have expressed concern that the work of the CASB is likely to overlap that of the Financial Accounting Standards Board. Some contend that certain standards, such as No. 403, No. 404, No. 409, and proposed No. 412—Composition and Measurement of Pension Cost—have already invaded topics that belong to the assignment given to the FASB. The CASB's unofficial response has been to the effect that any cost of importance in negotiated defense contracts falls within its realm of cognizance established by Congress and that it has not yet imposed, and does not now intend to impose, any requirements directed at external financial reporting. To the extent that cost accounting standards offer useful solutions to important accounting problems and therefore are adopted for financial as well as cost accounting purposes, such a result is gratifying but not a primary consideration in the CASB's work.

INDUSTRY OPPORTUNITY

The openness with which the CASB conducts its deliberations, its willingness to hear all views, and its responsiveness to criticism of proposed standards provide industry representatives with an exceptional opportunity to participate effectively in the standard setting process. Companies engaged in government contracting already find the CASB's work a matter of vital interest. Other companies should become more involved in CASB activities. Accounting is a unitary subject, and the fact that the standard-setting process has been fragmentized through the establishment of a number of authoritative bodies quite independent of one another requires that all concerned with accounting exert sincere efforts to keep the work of those bodies reasonably harmonious.

Chapter 39

Corporate tax management

*Paul L. Dillingham**

In today's complex business society where government tax agencies are more than a 50 percent partner in the earnings of the business, it is natural that top executives are taking a harder look at the management of the company's tax responsibilities. The tax executive belongs to a new profession—not legal, not financial, not engineering—but oftentimes a blend in education and/or experience of two or more of these seemingly unrelated areas of expertise. Having grown like Topsy, the tax executive is ever-increasingly finding his or her place in the corporate scene. This chapter is designed to discuss the evolution of the corporate tax function and to explain ways of maximizing its effectiveness, whether improving an existing department or forming a new one. Nobody likes paying taxes, but it is the price of a free civilization. Given this necessary part of doing business, does not it behoove us to so arrange our affairs so that we pay our fair share but no more or no less than required by law?

WHY A CORPORATE TAX DEPARTMENT?

Prior to World War II very few companies, even the largest in size, had separate tax departments. Instead, it was common practice

* Vice President–Director of Taxes, The Coca-Cola Company.

for a member of the accounting department staff to merely transcribe data from the financial records to appropriate tax return forms and mail the tax returns. Tax return preparation was considered a routine chore, followed without imagination. Generally, there was little effort made to look for possible tax savings or to question the rulings of government tax officials. State and local tax rates were relatively low and little attention was given to these requirements.

By the late 1940s, as demands grew for more government services, new taxes became prevalent and tax rates moved upward. In this period of prosperity business expanded and became more complex. The combination of these factors brought into focus the need for more sophisticated handling of tax matters and recognition by management that more attention to this area of the business was essential. Public accounting or law firms were perhaps in the best position initially to provide tax counsel and to assist in tax planning as well as to prepare tax returns, mainly because this service was closely related to other financial and legal matters handled for a client. Additionally, these firms were in a better position to employ specialists whose services could be utilized by a number of clients. Reliance on such outside specialists was subject to time limitations and availability, which oftentimes presented problems when management decisions needed to be made quickly.

The importance of having tax specialists available on a full-time basis and the advantage of dealing with people who had an intimate knowledge of the company's business led management to the inescapable conclusion that it must develop its own in-house tax staff. Many companies looked to their outside legal counsel or public accounting firm for an individual to organize and manage the tax function in the company. Companies continue to hire experienced tax specialists from accounting and legal firms as their tax staffs are enlarged, but there has been a growing trend in recent years to look for people with experience in the government sector. The U.S. Treasury Department and Internal Revenue Service, as well as many state tax departments, have produced many excellent tax specialists, and it is sometimes refreshing as well as enlightening to have on one's tax staff an individual who has worked the other side of the street. This varied experience not only broadens the individual's perspective but also serves well to help understand administrative and procedural problems encountered by government tax agencies.

TAX COMPLIANCE

The major responsibilities of a corporate tax department logically fall into two areas—tax compliance and tax planning.

By *tax compliance* is meant the routine task of collecting, scheduling, adjusting, and transcribing financial data to various government tax forms, affixing signatures of appropriate company officers, and transmitting the return with payment to the specified government tax agency. This function is not simple or unimportant. To the contrary, a larger tax department will have a number of people assigned to monitoring the flow of information from various segments of the business, maintaining a tax calendar to see that required forms are available and deadlines for filing are met (or extensions of time for filing requested and approved), tracking down officers of the company or subsidiaries to sign returns, requesting checks for payment of taxes, preparing tax accruals or budgets for the financial staff, and a myriad of other details.

Compliance is an absolutely essential part of the tax business to avoid penalties for late payment or failure to file returns. Constantly changing business operations, formation of new subsidiaries or branch offices, new laws, or changes in old ones by court decisions may require tax returns in new jurisdictions or eliminate the need for returns in others. In the case of property taxes, the general practice is to prepare and file a tax return reporting the company's assets located in a specified jurisdiction. After receipt of this report, the government agency advises the taxpayer of the value assigned to his or her property and the amount of tax due. Good tax administration requires comparing these invoices with the values reported by the company to decide whether objection should be taken or whether the government's valuation is to be accepted and tax paid as assessed. In larger companies where business operations extend to many states or to foreign countries, the number of tax returns required to be filed annually may well run into the hundreds or thousands. Given such a volume of returns to be handled, it is not surprising that there will be many occasions where disagreements arise between taxpayer and tax official. Settlement of such controversies may be accomplished in many cases simply by correspondence or a telephone call. More complex issues may require preparation of more formal and detailed briefs or protests, followed by one or more personal conferences to air more fully the facts and circumstances pertinent to the issue.

A company which does business in a number of states will find it necessary to develop procedures which will provide certain financial data identified by states, counties, cities, and in some cases even smaller political subdivisions such as townships or school districts. This information may be required to compute accurately state or local income taxes or sales and use taxes. Practically all states in the United States now have sales taxes, and many counties and cities have them as well. For the corporate tax department, a sales tax presents problems in two areas—as a *vendor* and as a *purchaser*.

Sales tax of vendors

Companies engaged in retail merchandising must collect sales taxes from purchasers and remit the tax to the appropriate government agency on a monthly or quarterly basis. An organization with a number of retail stores located in several states will find that considerable time is required to keep abreast of changes in tax laws and regulations, to advise store managers of such changes, to arrange for reporting of necessary data by stores to the tax department for completion of tax returns, and to file returns with payment of tax.

Subsequently, when tax returns are audited by government agents, tax department personnel will be required to work with the auditor to convince the auditor that company procedures are adequate to assure full compliance with the law. This may require having a member of the tax department staff accompany the auditor if the auditor wishes to visit a store to observe how a salesclerk actually follows established procedures. A company selling its products at other than retail generally will not collect sales taxes from customers, provided it obtains from the customer some evidence that the goods will be resold; or if the customer does not resell the goods, evidence will be necessary to show that the tax will be paid directly to the state involved. Normal practice with respect to sales at other than retail is for the vendor to request from each customer a "resale certificate," which is a simple document relieving the vendor of liability for collecting the tax and transferring responsibility to the purchaser to either collect sales tax when the goods are resold or to pay the tax directly if the goods are used in the purchaser's own business.

Sales tax of purchaser

The second part of the problem for the corporate tax staff relates to the company's role as a purchaser. If it has not furnished a resale certificate to the vendor, it should expect the vendor to include sales tax on the invoice for the goods. But what if the vendor ships the goods from another state and, because of limited activities in the purchaser's state, is not required to collect sales tax in the destination state? In that event, the burden shifts to the purchaser to pay the tax directly to the state.

These examples point up some of the problems of properly accounting for sales and use taxes and emphasize the need for close attention by the tax department to this area.

Information for income tax returns

Gathering information from various sources for completion of income tax returns—state, federal and foreign—likewise requires adequate advance planning and communication with the accounting department or other departments to specify precisely what is required and when it is needed. It is essential in a sizable company that such requests be in writing. Attaching to the request a blank form suggesting the format for providing the information is generally helpful. Requests should be as complete as possible to avoid the necessity of a follow-up, which is not only time-consuming but can be irritating, as well, to the person supplying the data.

TAX PLANNING

Tax planning, on the other hand, should involve a very imaginative and creative approach to tax management. Management decisions as to acquisitions of new businesses, plant location, compensation programs, type of business entity (subsidiary or branch), abandonment of products or facilities, and many other day-to-day decisions generally have tax implications. To ignore these implications may be costly either from the standpoint of attracting unnecessary additional taxes, or of losing tax incentives or other reductions which otherwise might be used to advantage. Countless added tax costs result from poor tax planning or lack of planning. So often there are several alternative means of accomplishing a desired business objective but one may be much better from a tax standpoint. Tax planning, then, is where real savings may be enjoyed, and for this reason this part of the tax department's responsibilities is of extreme importance.

Sound tax planning requires, of course, competent tax specialists with a thorough knowledge of tax laws, rulings, regulations, and court decisions, as well as ability to think creatively. Essential to this part of tax management is an intimate knowledge of the company's business operations and an extremely reliable communications network within the company and to top management. The tax department must alert top management to situations that may have tax implications. The tax executive who learns of tax problems *after* they exist can be expected to do no more than a salvage operation, which is likely to produce limited savings. However, if the tax executive is made aware of and participates in matters at the planning stage, it is likely that alternatives will be suggested which will produce maximum tax savings. Obviously, taxes are not the most important factor in many management decisions, but is not management entitled to have the benefit of this input when making its judgments?

Use of computers in tax compliance and planning

In this age of computers and sophisticated electronic processing equipment many companies are beginning to consider use of such equipment for tax compliance as well as tax planning. Companies who utilize computers for processing financial data find it relatively simple to adapt the system to tax needs for actual preparation of property tax returns and state and federal income tax returns. For multinational companies, this can be a valuable tax planning tool in meeting tax requirements for distribution of earnings of foreign subsidiaries, as well as for utilizing fully the available foreign tax credits. Companies limited to U.S. operations in a number of states will also find significant benefit in using the computer for projections of costs of plant locations, inventory storage, alternative methods of computing state income tax liabilities, and other matters.

When should a tax department be formed?

There is no hard and fast rule as to the point at which a successful corporation should form its own tax department. That is to say, there is no dollar and cents rule that states, for example, that if a corporation's sales are at least $40 million or its profits exceed $5 million it should have a tax department. The decision of when and if a tax department should be formed, taking all things into consideration, has to be made on an individual corporation-by-corporation basis. Keeping this in mind, there are certain criteria that can be helpful as a guide to determine the point at which a corporation should form its own tax department. The criteria to be used in arriving at this decision include, but are not limited to, the following:

1. Management believes that the corporation is overpaying its taxes and that if someone had daily control of the tax burden then the overall tax outlay could be reduced.
2. Management is getting involved with increasingly complex and time-consuming tax-oriented business transactions requiring extensive use of outside tax assistance, with resulting higher and higher billings for such tax advice.
3. Management is becoming increasingly aware of the tax implications of decisions they make as well as of transactions they enter into.
4. The need has developed for an individual located within the organization who is well versed in taxes as well as the company's operations and policy, and who would be available to render valuable assistance in management's decision-making process.
5. The corporation's operations have expanded into several states and/or foreign countries, becoming subject to taxation in those jurisdictions.
6. Accounting personnel are spending an excessive amount of their time in the handling of tax audits and other tax procedures.

If three or more of these conditions exist, then the point has been reached when a tax department should be formed. On the other hand, if only one or two of these conditions exist, then the time has been reached when a detailed study should be made to determine whether or not a tax department should be formed. The major part of such a study should be a cost analysis comparing the current and projected costs of outside tax assistance with the costs of an in-house tax department. If the results of the cost analysis indicate that the annual costs of outside tax assistance will equal or exceed the costs of having an in-house tax department, then the decision should be in favor of forming a tax department. Furthermore, even if the results of the cost analysis indicate that the annual costs of outside tax assistance will be somewhat less than the costs of an in-house tax department, the factors of availability and service should be weighed in reaching a final conclusion.

How should a tax department be structured?

Various organizational structures are prevalent today in corporate tax departments. Some are arranged with subdepartments or sections, each of which has total responsibility for compliance and planning with respect to a certain type of taxes. For example, one section may handle state income and franchise taxes, another property taxes, another federal income taxes, another sales and use and payroll taxes, and so on. Other tax departments are divided so that one subdepartment does all tax compliance for all taxes, another subdepartment does tax planning and research, and another deals with tax litigation and/or tax legislation. Which structure is chosen will likely be dictated to a large degree by the type of business and its specific set of tax problems. In any event, it is the view of most tax executives that a single, integrated tax department is most effective and efficient, as opposed to divided responsibilities between fiscal and legal or other areas of the business.

Should the tax department be centralized or decentralized? By this is not meant physical location of tax personnel but rather the line of reporting and supervision in the corporate organization. It may be desirable, for example, to station tax personnel at foreign locations or at division or subsidiary offices which may be located away from corporate headquarters. In such a situation most tax executives prefer to have these personnel report to corporate headquarters rather than to local branch or division or subsidiary management. The reason for this is the importance of managing the tax function on a companywide basis to avoid tax decisions on a localized basis which may have an adverse effect on the companywide tax picture. A tax specialist who is responsible only to a local manager may be persuaded to give tax advice or make tax decisions which are not always in the best interests of the overall company business. This is not to say that a local tax specialist should operate in a vacuum—he or she must be responsive to the problems of the local manager and provide tax counsel on a day-to-day basis. But what should be avoided is any undue pressure on the tax counsel to tailor advice solely to the local problem while disregarding the overall picture. Perhaps the most workable solution is a mixed reporting relationship where the tax executive at corporate headquarters has primary responsibility for supervising the technical aspects and for granting salary increases and promotions to the staff in the field, but where the local manager administratively supervises the individuals involved.

While it is highly desirable to control the tax function from a centralized location at corporate headquarters, a certain amount of day-to-day tax management of subsidiaries or divisions is necessary at headquarters. The degree of such local decision making on tax matters will vary depending on the complexity of the business, the uniqueness of its tax problems, the attitude of local management, and other factors. Perhaps the most workable arrangement results when certain routine tax returns such as payroll reports, information returns on wages or other payments, sales and use tax returns, and certain local property tax returns are prepared by subsidiary or division offices under instructions and supervision of the corporate tax department. In most cases, it is perhaps not economical to maintain a sizable tax library at a number of locations. Thus, it normally is prudent for the corporate tax department located at corporate headquarters to assume responsibility for maintaining a tax library and to keep abreast of changes in tax laws, regulations, court decisions, and other developments and to pass along pertinent advice and instructions to other offices.

Acquiring and training professional tax staff

Once the decision has been made to go ahead with the formation of a tax department, the next step is deciding what is needed to make that department operational. The basic need, besides adequate available space and the supporting furniture and fixtures will be, of course, personnel.

An individual will have to be hired to supervise or manage the tax department. This individual should be well experienced in dealing with compliance problems as well as being a good tax planner. The most likely places to obtain such an individual are from the tax department of the certified public accounting firm currently servicing the company, the tax department of a law firm or another certified public accounting firm, or the tax department of another corporation.

The manager's job will likely be a shirt-sleeve one at first, with actual preparation of tax returns and other details taking up a considerable amount of the manager's time. This fact should be communicated to prospective applicants for the position. These details should become divorced from the manager's duties as the department matures, enabling the manager to concentrate on problems involving policy, planning, and research. The compliance function would then be delegated to subordinates with the manager reserving and exercising the right to review all tax returns.

In addition to secretarial help, at least one assistant should be provided the tax manager. It would be best if someone from the accounting department who is familiar with the accounting and reporting systems of the company is transferred to fill the assistant's position. The tax manager will then have someone to rely on who will know where and how to obtain the data necessary to carry out the compliance function properly.

Tax library

Besides personnel, the tax manager will need an adequate tax library to assist in the solution of day-to-day tax problems as well as complicated tax research problems. The basic tax library should consist of the following:

1. A current copy of the Internal Revenue Code and the Regulations thereunder.
2. A complete federal tax service—income tax, excise tax, payroll tax, and so on, as required.
3. Complete state tax services for those states in which franchise, income, and similar tax returns are required to be filed.

4. Tax reference books—leading works in each area of specialization.
5. Tax periodicals—monthly publications of tax and accounting organizations.

Sources of tax department personnel

As the tax department matures and finds its place in the corporate scheme, it will likely be forced to expand in order to be more responsive to the needs of management. The tax executive will need to recruit additional specialists to fit the needs of the particular business.

For years there have been conflicting opinions as to whether accountants or attorneys are better equipped to deal with tax matters. Attorneys argue that interpretation of tax laws requires a legal background, while accountants argue that financial data must be analyzed to calculate tax liability and this requires expertise in accounting. Obviously both arguments have validity, and this leads one to the conclusion that the person best equipped to handle a company's tax matters is one who is trained in both fields. In a broader sense, then, the ideal corporate tax department should have some accountants, some lawyers, perhaps one or more engineers if the company has substantial physical property holdings, and even someone trained in computer programming if computers are utilized in tax planning and compliance.

A tax executive seeking to employ tax specialists with previous experience will naturally look to public accounting firms, law firms, government tax agencies, or other company tax departments. For junior tax people, recent graduates of law schools or accounting graduates provide the best source. However, transfers from other departments within the company, particularly in the financial area, should not be overlooked. Training in internal auditing, for example, appears to provide ideal background in many cases.

Continuing education

A tax professional, like other professionals, requires a heavy program of continuing education. Tax laws are constantly being changed, and interpretations by government agencies as well as the courts are often reversed or modified. Thus, a training program for tax professionals, whether fresh out of college or senior employees with many years of experience, is absolutely essential. In-house and on-the-job training is perhaps most appropriate for junior employees, while experienced staff members will be well advised to continue their education by attendance at symposiums and seminars sponsored by various universities as well as professional organizations.

In this connection it should be noted that one professional organization in particular, Tax Executives Institute, Inc., has recently embarked on an ambitious program of expanding its professional development program and provides one- and two-week programs annually on several areas of tax practice, such as U.S. income tax, state and local taxes, and international taxes. This program by TEI, an international organization of some 2,800 corporate tax executives representing most of the major corporations in the United States and Canada, was begun a few years ago to fill a need for development of corporate tax specialists.

Many fine universities throughout the United States annually sponsor tax institutes lasting from three days to two weeks, but most of these programs are designed for public tax practitioners and devote a large portion of their programs to matters of less interest to tax people in the private sector. Other professional organizations, such as the American Institute of Certified Public Acountants, also offer tax courses in their professional development program, but these also generally have more appeal to public practitioners.

Some operating guidelines

Having decided where in the corporate structure the tax department will fit, the next order of business is to institute operating procedures coordinating the day-to-day operations between the tax department and the other departments of the company. Ideally, all tax functions and responsibilities should be transferred to, and placed under the direct control of, the tax department in order that no tax-related decision is made unless directed or approved by the tax department. In some instances, especially in the early stages of development of the tax department, this is not practical. Therefore, in those situations the tax department should service the other departments by acting in an advise and consent capacity.

Tax procedures guidelines. In either instance, the tax department should immediately set up procedures for handling tax inquiries from other departments involving both routine and special tax inquiries. All inquiries should be answered as soon as possible, preferably in writing. Tax department files should contain a copy of the inquiry and the response given for future reference purposes.

Consideration should also be given to the production by the tax department, as soon as time permits, of a Tax Procedure Guide (in loose leaf format) to be distributed to all other departments. This guide should contain the procedures to be followed in all routine tax matters that other departments would be involved with. For example, such items as the following should be included:

1. Accounting department
   a. Guidelines for choosing life and class of capital asset acquisitions for depreciation purposes.
   b. Investment credit guidelines—life categories, percentage credit available, new versus used property, recapture.
   c. Guidelines for collecting sales tax, obtaining resale certificates, accruing use tax.
   d. Guidelines for reimbursed expenses—substantiation, reports.
   e. Guidelines for filing information reports to various taxing authorities.
   f. Guidelines for destruction of records.
2. Payroll department
   a. Instructions relative to withholding of federal, state, and local income taxes; social security tax; and other payroll taxes.
   b. Guidelines for preparation of quarterly wage reports, W-2s, and annual payroll tax returns.
3. Personnel department
   a. Guidelines for checking out unemployment insurance claims.
   b. Guidelines for tax responsibilities relative to employee benefit programs; for example, reimbursed moving and tuition expenses, stock option programs, and prizes and awards.
4. Internal auditing department
   a. Guidelines for checking customer resale certificates.
5. Public relations department
   a. Guidelines for tax implications relative to issued public statements.
6. All operating departments, divisions, and subsidiaries
   a. Guidelines to be followed upon notification of any tax audits.
   b. Guidelines to be followed upon receipt of any tax-oriented inquiries from outside sources.

Of course, the guide should be updated as necessary to reflect any applicable changes that may occur.

This communication process should be extended one step farther, by the tax department's initiating a flow of memorandums to keep management informed of current changes as well as impending changes in both corporate and personal taxes.

Tax calendar. Internally, one of the first priorities of the tax department should be to develop a tax calendar. The tax calendar is a must for compliance purposes in order to assure that all returns are prepared and filed on time. To attain this objective, entries must be religiously made on the tax calendar to reflect the filing of returns, extension of returns, and the payment of taxes due. Additionally, the setting of compliance priorities is automatically dictated by use of the tax calendar.

A tax calendar is a listing of all tax returns and their due dates, including tax payment dates. The format, in monthly due date order, can be either on a strict chronological basis, or by jurisdiction, or by type of tax. From a control point of view, it would be best to have at least one set of calendars containing all three formats for the manager's use. The tax calendar can be prepared either manually, by hand or typewriter, or mechanically by making use of a computer to print out the calendar at the beginning of each taxable year.

Tax workpapers. One additional matter of importance that the tax department should be concerned with involves the development of tax workpapers. Tax workpapers should be designed with one object in mind, the aiding in the preparation of federal income tax and state income/franchise tax returns. In this context, workpapers should be developed for submission to the accounting department for a restatement of financial data in a more appropriate format that will aid in the preparation of the federal income tax return. Workpapers should also be developed for submission to operating divisions and subsidiaries so that data necessary to make any applicable tax adjustments can be furnished in a standardized format. Additionally, workpapers should be developed whereby state allocation factors can be summarized and listed on a master schedule to aid in the preparation of state income/franchise tax returns. It should be borne in mind that the preceding examples represent only a small number of the possibilities for the development of tax workpapers. There are many other areas where specially developed workpapers would be a definite aid in carrying out the tax function.

Relationships within and outside the company

The corporate tax executive must first of all be technically competent in the field of taxes, but also must be a salesperson with some ability in public relations as well. The everyday work of the corporate tax executive is on matters which are not necessarily pleasant to associates in the company. The corporate tax executive must avoid the reputation of being a negative thinker who frequently responds to requests for advice with the answer "it can't be done that way." Instead, the executive should look for alternatives which will meet the business objective but minimize the tax impact. The corporate tax executive who is a roadblock to many projects will probably be avoided by associates and the most valuable tool—communication—will be lost.

The corporate tax executive for the most part is a staff person who is relied on for advice and counsel in the executive's specialized area of expertise. Seldom does the corporate tax executive have the authority to force managers to follow his or her recommendations, so this must be done in more subtle ways by selling ideas.

The relationships of the corporate tax executive outside the company are equally important in dealing with government tax representatives, who are generally in an adversary position. The respect of adversaries for integrity and technical competence must be developed and maintained. The corporate tax executive must be skillful in the art of compromise, as most tax controversies are settled short of the courthouse. Many companies recognize the desirability—indeed the responsibility—for their executives to participate in outside professional organizations. As Theodore Roosevelt said, "Every man owes some of his time to the upbuilding of the profession to which he belongs." Such participation not only satisfies a personal need but more often than not redounds to the benefit of the company. There are numerous organizations whose membership is open to corporate tax administrators and public practitioners in addition to government officials. Even those groups who do not admit nongovernment people to membership normally welcome them to their public conferences. These conferences provide excellent opportunities to keep abreast of the latest developments and to gain insight into the development of new or changing policies on the part of government officials. Equally important is the availability of these people for informal discussions of specific problems of concern to the corporate tax executive. The tax executive will no doubt find it extremely useful to develop and maintain a personal acquaintanceship with various government tax officials by attending such conferences.

SUMMARY

This chapter is intended to give a broad overview of the growing need for more attention by top management to corporate tax matters and their effect on day-to-day business operations. Once the need is recognized, it is important to assign responsibility for the tax function to able people who are appropriately positioned within the corporate organization so as to be more effective in dealing with and counseling top executives and other managers in the company. Absent this relationship with top management, the tax executive will be unable to become involved in important matters early enough to be able to provide meaningful tax counsel and alternative possibilities for solving problems and making decisions. This is extremely important in the tax planning area. If there are several layers of supervision between the chief tax executive and top management, there is always the danger that information coming down to the tax executive or recommendations going up will be garbled and may be misinterpreted. Recognizing the need to enhance the stature of the corporate tax department, a number of companies have elevated the chief tax executive to a position of senior vice president, vice president, or other comparable level of management. The tax executive is an essential part of the management team and must have the stature and respect of colleagues to do the best job. Communication and flow of information between the tax executive and others in the company is the key to success in handling this responsibility.

PART 7

Accounting standards for special profit and nonprofit enterprises

Chapter 40

Current problems and practical solutions of accounting and reporting for regulated electric and gas utilities

*Robert O. Whitman**

CHANGED ECONOMIC AND SOCIOLOGICAL ENVIRONMENTS

The accounting process is a practical "art" rather than a mechanical application of rigid and inflexible rules. The goals of accounting as an "art" are to serve useful purposes and possess the capability to deal with problems of recording costs and revenues. For regulated public utilities accounting must meet the needs of investors, rate regulatory authorities, and consumers.

The practical art aspects of accounting have become increasingly important to utility accountants as a result of the changed economic and sociological environments in which utility companies have been operating. To meet successfully the forces of changing environments, accounting cannot be rigid and must be sufficiently flexible to fulfill its purpose.

For many years prior to the mid-60s, the operations of public utility companies were characterized by moderate inflation, rela-

---

* Senior Executive Vice President, Treasurer, and Chief Accounting Officer, American Electric Power Service Corporation (Management Arm of AEP System).

tively low capital costs, the ability to obtain funds when needed at moderate costs, a bullish common stock market, relatively stable fuel costs, less stringent environmental quality regulations, a steadily increasing demand for service, and electric rate decreases by some companies made possible largely by economies of scale and operating efficiencies.

That era, however, gave way to much more difficult times. The explosive inflationary trends of the late 60s and early 70s raised numerous challenges and issues in public utility accounting, financial reporting, and rate regulation. The cost of money increased significantly, as did the cost of fuel and other resources. A depressed stock market for utility equities, reductions in interest and preferred dividend coverages, greatly extended construction periods, user conservation and less than adequate rate increases, exacerbated by regulatory lag in the granting of such increases, have resulted in many new problems for regulated public utility companies.

Inflation, of course, causes accounting and financing problems for all industries; utilities are not unique in this respect. However, the special characteristics of the utility industry—a high degree of regulation, debt-heavy capital structures, and the requirement for continuing investment in capital equipment for replacements and for increased needs of customers—intensify the impact of inflation on the financial integrity of all regulated utilities.

Also, beginning about the mid-60s, air and water quality standards became much more stringent and have resulted in significant increases in plant investment that produce no additional revenues but at the same time produce increases in operating costs.

The drastically changed economic and sociological environments in the last decade have raised many of the accounting, financial reporting, and regulatory issues and problems to be discussed in this chapter. The companies, their customers, and rate regulatory authorities have been striving to adapt to these changed environments; however, much remains to be done by all involved.

The topics to be discussed herein include:

1. Public utility accounting—special considerations.
2. The problem of eroding interest coverage.
3. Accounting for cost of funds during construction (AFDC).
4. Deferred fuel cost accounting.
5. Flow-through versus normalization accounting.

6. The costs of more stringent environmental regulation.
7. Financial implications of lease capitalization.
8. Some new and some not-so-new rate-making concepts which can help alleviate many of the financial problems of utilities.[1]

PUBLIC UTILITY ACCOUNTING: SPECIAL CONSIDERATIONS

Before specific issues and problems facing regulated public utilities are taken up, attention should be directed to the fundamental consideration that the accounting and financial reporting for these companies must reflect the impact of the rate-making process, and to the accounting requirements of the regulatory authorities as set forth in the promulgated uniform systems of accounts, which conform to the principle of matching costs and revenues.

Impact of rate making on application of generally accepted accounting principles to utility accounting

The basic postulates and broad principles of accounting, usually referred to as "generally accepted accounting principles," generally apply to all business enterprises, including public utility companies. However, the application of "generally accepted accounting principles" to public utilities must reflect the impact of the rate-making process in order to achieve the proper matching of costs and revenues. Thus, the application of generally accepted accounting principles to regulated public utilities may be different from the application thereof to nonregulated businesses. Recognition of this is set forth in the following statements contained in the *Addendum* to *Accounting Principles Board (APB) Opinion No. 2,* "Accounting for the Investment Credit":

> . . . Differences may arise in the application of generally accepted accounting principles as between regulated and non-regulated businesses, because of the effect in regulated businesses of the rate-

---

[1] Readers desirous of obtaining a detailed background in public utility accounting may refer to J. Rhoads Foster and Bernard S. Rodey Jr.'s *Public Utility Accounting* (Englewood Cliffs, N.J.: Prentice-Hall, Inc., 1951); and James E. Suelflow, *Public Utility Accounting: Theory and Application* (East Lansing, Mich., Institute of Public Utilities, Michigan State University, 1973).

Readers whose interests include further inquiry into the economics of regulated utilities are directed to Paul J. Garfield and Wallace F. Lovejoy, *Public Utility Economics* (Englewood Cliffs, N.J.: Prentice-Hall, Inc., 1964).

making process, a phenomenon not present in non-regulated businesses.

and:

> Such differences usually concern mainly the time at which various items enter into the determination of net income in accordance with the principle of matching costs and revenues.

Other *Opinions* of the Accounting Principles Board suggesting possible conflict with the recognition of the impact of the rate-making process have included the same provision, as, for example, paragraph 6 of *APB Opinion No. 11*, "Accounting for Income Taxes":

> It [*APB Opinion No. 11*] does not apply (a) to regulated industries in those circumstances where the standards described in the *Addendum* (which remains in effect) to *APB Opinion No. 2* are met. . . .

More recently, in *Statement of Financial Accounting Standards No. 2*, "Accounting for Research and Development Costs," the Financial Accounting Standards Board (FASB) explicitly recognized the concept that accounting principles may in certain cases be applied differently in regulated enterprises in order to effect an appropriate matching of costs and revenues and that these incurred costs may be deferred in the accounts rather than be charged to current expenses as is required for all other businesses.

Another example of this cost and revenue matching principle is normalization of certain allowable income tax reductions by some utilities, while other utilities account for these tax reductions on an actual taxes paid basis because these tax benefits "flow through" directly to customers.

Both methods are acceptable, but the method prescribed by the regulatory authority having primary rate jurisdiction must be used for financial reporting purposes if reporting is to be meaningful. Increasingly, normalization of specific tax reductions is being considered by regulatory commissions in the establishment of rates. When this occurs, normalization accounting is prescribed in the uniform systems of accounts, and utilities are required to switch to normalization accounting for financial reporting purposes.

Public utility accounting regulation

As previously stated, public utilities are regulated by a number of authorities which prescribe the accounting to be followed. For electric public utilities, accounting and financial reporting are regulated by three authorities:

1. State public utility commissions,
2. The Federal Power Commission (FPC), and
3. The Securities and Exchange Commission (SEC).

Regulation by state commissions. There are state government agencies in nearly all of the 50 states with authority to regulate the intrastate operations of public utilities. Such regulation includes the authority to establish reasonable rates and to prescribe uniform accounting and periodic and special reporting. As stated previously, the accounting prescribed for regulated public utilities generally conforms to the rate-making treatment of the regulatory authority having primary rate jurisdiction.

Regulation by the Federal Power Commission. The Federal Power Commission was created in 1920 to administer the Federal Water Power Act of 1920, and was given jurisdiction over electric power and natural gas companies engaged in interstate commerce by the Federal Power Act of 1935. The FPC has control over the accounting and depreciation practices of licensees, electric public utilities, and natural gas companies over which it has jurisdiction. Also, the Commission has other powers which give it the ". . . comprehensive authority to regulate the rates and services of the electric utility industry with respect to both wholesale sales and interstate commerce for resale to the public and interstate transmission of electricity."[2] In addition, the FPC has assumed jurisdiction over financial reporting to the public by requiring that these reports conform to the accounting requirements prescribed in the FPC Uniform Systems of Accounts. This power was affirmed in the case of *Appalachian Power Company* v. *Federal Power Commission* in which the U.S. Court of Appeals held:

> We agree with the Commission's determination that it [the FPC], rather than state agencies, has the power to regulate the basic accounts which a company subject to its jurisdiction must use for financial reporting purposes.[3]

Although the FPC has primary jurisdiction over accounting and reporting, it has generally recognized the impacts of the rate-making process which are reflected in the accounting prescribed by state

---

[2] Garfield and Lovejoy, *Public Utility Economics,* p. 269.
[3] 328 F. 2d 237 (1964) 479.

regulatory commissions. Thus FPC *Order No. 505*, issued February 11, 1974, in part provides that any gain or loss on reacquisition of debt shall be amortized over the remaining life of the respective security issues; however, this Order also provides that such amounts may be recognized currently in income when that practice is allowed by the regulatory authority having primary jurisdiction over the utility company's rates. The Commission's specific recognition is stated as follows:

> . . . We believe that the accounting and financial statements of a regulated utility should reflect the economic effects of rates, as provided for by the *Addendum* to the Accounting Principles Board's *Opinion No. 2.*

Regulation by the Securities and Exchange Commission. The Public Utility Holding Company Act (a part of the Public Utility Act of 1935) gives the Securities and Exchange Commission jurisdiction over the issuance of securities of public utility holding companies and power to simplify and integrate public utility holding companies. The Act applies to holding companies, their subsidiaries, affiliates, and mutual service companies (and to those whose main business is the performance of service, sales, or construction work for them).

Section 15 of the Act is especially noteworthy in that the SEC is given the authority to establish uniform accounting procedures for registered holding companies, subsidiaries, and service companies.

As with all corporations, security issues by public utility companies come under the rules and regulations of the Securities Act of 1933. Financial statements included in filings with the SEC are generally prepared on the basis of accounting as prescribed by the FPC.

ERODING INTEREST COVERAGE: A CRITICAL SITUATION FOR UTILITIES AND THEIR CUSTOMERS

What is coverage?

Coverage refers basically to the number of times a company's current earnings (increased by adding back interest charges, income taxes, and certain rentals) are able to meet fixed charges. Traditionally, earnings coverage is a primary financial indicator used by the investor in fixed income debt and preferred stock securities to evaluate the security and safety of the investment. All other things being equal, debt issued by a company with a coverage ratio of 3, for example, is more secure than debt issued by a company with a coverage ratio of 2½ or lower.

Registration statements submitted pursuant to the Securities Act of 1933 when debt securities are to be registered require a statement of the ratio of earnings to fixed interest charges.

The SEC defines "fixed charges" as:

1. Interest and amortization of debt discount and expense and premium on all indebtedness;
2. Such portion of rentals as can be demonstrated to be representative of the interest factor in the particular case; and
3. In case consolidated figures are used, preferred stock dividend requirements of consolidated subsidiaries, excluding in all cases items eliminated in consolidation.

Most mortgage indentures and debenture agreements provide for a coverage test which must be met if additional debt securities are to be issued. In such cases, the provisions of each individual instrument must be considered to determine the definitions of "earnings" and "fixed charges." For example, the amount of nonoperating income includible in earnings may be restricted to either a sum certain or a percentage of operating income before income taxes.

The problem

Generally, the amount of debt and preferred stock a utility may issue is governed by three key factors: (1) capitalization ratios established by state regulatory authorities, or by the SEC in the cases of members of holding company systems; (2) coverage ratios established by mortgage indentures, debenture and preferred stock agreements, or corporate charters; and (3) amounts of bondable property.

Aside from the fact that coverage requirements may restrict the issuance of additional debt, coverage for the most part determines the bond ratings as established by bond rating agencies; the continued deterioration of interest coverage will often prompt rating services to downgrade a utility's bond ratings.

During the ten years ended in 1973 significant changes have taken place in interest costs and interest coverage of privately owned Class A and B electric utilities, as Table 1 shows.

TABLE 1

	Class A and B electric utilities		
	1973	*1964*	*Increase*
Total debt	$60.5 billion	$24.1 billion	151%
Total interest charges.	$ 3.5 billion	$ 0.9 billion	289%
Interest charges as a percentage of revenues	10.6%	5.7%	—
Average cost of embedded debt*	5.8%	3.7%	—
Times interest earned†	2.7	4.9	—

* If current costs are considered, the comparison is even more significant: approximately 9 percent in 1973 versus 4 percent in 1964.

† Number of times operating income (before income taxes) is able to meet interest on long-term debt.

As a result of the spiraling costs of debt capital, at the same time that earnings have failed to keep pace because of increased operating costs, lesser growth resulting from conservation by users, and lagging rate increases, the coverage ratios of many utilities have dropped well below the two and one-half to three times multiple that many investors consider necessary for security of investment.

The result

Eroding interest coverages have resulted in increased difficulties for utilities in obtaining funds for required replacement and expansion of utility plant by the sale of debt and preferred stock securities. The cancellation or postponement of acquisition of new plant facilities or curtailment of critically needed replacement eventually must result in deterioration of service and reliability.

Failure or delay by regulatory authorities in setting rates which will permit utility companies actually to earn reasonable and adequate rates of return and thus boost sagging coverage ratios will adversely affect the ability of utility companies to meet present and future needs for service to their customers.

Possible solutions

Essentially, the basic remedy to eroding interest coverage lies in increasing the earnings available for coverage. With increasing costs and limited growth this calls for increases in established rates for service. Regulated electric utility companies have been urging the regulatory authorities to make the following changes in the rate-making process:

1. Establishing rates which will provide the allowable rate of return in the period covered by the increased rates. This can be achieved by the use of projected test periods as opposed to a past historical test year.
2. Adopting normalization accounting for certain income tax benefits. Normalization of such tax benefits results in requirements for higher rates initially than are derived from flow through of tax benefits, although over the life of the related property, the total amounts charged to the rate payers are substantially the same under both conditions.
3. Including in rate base for establishing rates specific amounts of interest-bearing construction work in progress (with corresponding reduction in the credits for allowance for funds during construction), especially when all or part of the allowance cannot be included in earnings for interest coverage.

Increases in earnings for interest coverage can also be achieved by the issuance of additional preferred stock or additional common stock. If earnings for interest coverage are not adequate, earnings for preferred dividends would probably also not be adequate, so that the remaining alternative to the sale of bonds or preferred stock is the issuance of additional common stock. However, deteriorating earnings, combined with a poor stock market for utility equities, makes it difficult to sell substantial amounts of common stock on a reasonable basis. Most utility common stocks have been selling below book value. The sale of additional stock at depressed market prices results in dilution that penalizes the position of current stockholders. If continued long enough, such dilution would make it impossible to obtain funds by issuance of common stock.

As previously indicated, the basic solution to the coverage problem is for the regulatory authorities to allow adequate returns on common equity. While proposals for rate increases must be initiated by utilities, approvals therefor rest squarely on the shoulders of rate regulatory commissions. Such commissions should grant utilities rate increases sufficient to enable the companies to earn the allowable return on common equity in the period in which the rate increases are made effective. The alternatives to higher rates— curtailments of service or the furnishing of inadequate service—are unacceptable.

ALLOWANCE FOR FUNDS USED DURING CONSTRUCTION (AFDC)

The income statements of regulated public utilities frequently include amounts under the caption "Allowance for Funds Used during Construction" (AFDC), formerly characterized as "Interest during Construction-Credit." AFDC is defined in the uniform systems of accounts prescribed by the FPC and state regulatory authorities as consisting of "the net cost of borrowed funds used for construction purposes and a reasonable rate on other funds when so used." Capitalizing the cost of funds during the period of construction has been a long-standing practice of regulated public utilities. It is the means by which the companies recover such costs by charges to customers in the form of depreciation over the life of the plant assets.

It should be pointed out that regulated public utilities are capital intensive. In the electric utility industry, about $4.50 to $5 of capital is required to produce $1 of revenue. The construction period for electric utility property may run upwards of four years for a fossil-fueled generating plant, and generally much longer for a nuclear generating plant. A decade ago, these construction periods were generally shorter. Also, the costs of construction are now higher, resulting in much larger amounts of capitalization of the costs of funds during the construction period.

When plant under construction is not included in the rate base, the investment therein is not contributing to the production of operating revenue. Nevertheless, extensive capital costs are being incurred for interest on debt, dividends on preferred stock, and cost of common shareholders' equity.

It is generally agreed that the cost of funds during construction represents a cost of plant, and that to require a utility to incur very large costs in connection with such investment, without corresponding recovery of such costs, would be confiscatory. By its franchise, a regulated electric utility is required to provide plant facilities sufficient to meet the service needs of all customers. In return, it is granted the right to earn ". . . a fair return upon the value of that which it employs for the public convenience."[4]

Regulatory authorities have therefore provided in the uniform systems of accounts for a credit to "Other Income," representing an allowance for the economic cost of construction, funds during the construction period. The charge corresponding to the AFDC credit in the income statement is to the Construction Work in Progress account. The latter account is subsequently included in Electric Plant in Service as part of the overall cost of the completed facility and thus becomes a part of the utility's rate base, to be recovered in charges to customers over the life of the plant.[5] The interest portion of AFDC, as shown in the income statement, represents the transfer of interest costs applicable to construction. The remainder of AFDC represents the cost of preferred stock and return on common stock equity funds used for construction.

Although AFDC is an accepted accounting concept, there has been considerable discussion of AFDC accounting, principally because the amounts have become considerably larger as a result of the higher plant costs, increased costs of capital funds, and longer periods of construction.

In 1973, total AFDC represented 29 percent of net income for common stock of privately owned Class A and B electric utilities.[6] This is in sharp contrast to 1964 when Interest during Construction-Credit (as it was termed then) represented less than 4 percent of net income for common stock.

The other concerns expressed relative to AFDC are that it does not represent cash income and that the rates for calculating AFDC may differ among companies.

The fact that there is no single method of calculating AFDC has caused some confusion; however, if one considers the many factors

---

[4] *Smyth* v. *Ames,* 169 U.S. 466, 547 (1898).

[5] Rate base is defined by Garfield and Lovejoy as ". . . the net (or depreciated) valuation of the public utility's tangible property, comprising the plant and equipment used and useful in serving the public. (Such tangible property is called 'plant in service' in the Uniform System of Accounts prescribed for the public utilities.) In addition, the rate base includes an allowance for working capital. . . ."

[6] The percentage for the year 1974 is expected to be much greater, although this percentage is not yet available.

that enter into the calculation of the AFDC rate, it is understandable that there may be several acceptable ways for calculating and applying the allowance. Additional guidelines to the computation of the allowance would probably aid analysts and investors in better understanding AFDC accounting, but the mechanics of the calculation should not overshadow the substance of the objective of recording this type of cost.

Because AFDC is a noncash credit it has been regarded as a lower quality of earnings, particularly when portions of the amounts cannot, because of indenture or other restrictions, be included in earnings for coverage of bond interest or preferred stock dividends. However, analysts must consider that earnings would not be reported properly if costs of financing construction work were not recognized in the accounts. AFDC, to the extent that it relates to interest, is a proper offset to current costs which are not contributing to the production of current operating revenues. Similarly, the portion of AFDC which relates to the cost of preferred stock attributable to funds devoted to construction should offset the amount of preferred stock dividends deducted in the computation of net income applicable to common stock. Finally, it should be recognized that the inclusion in current income of AFDC attributable to common stock funds devoted to construction represents return on investment which will be recovered through depreciation charges.

Factors to be considered in computing the allowance for funds used during construction

If one were able to trace each dollar of construction capital to its original source, the computation of AFDC would be fairly straightforward. However, for most utility plant construction this is not feasible, and a composite AFDC rate, which takes into account all sources of funds and their related costs, must be derived.

Before looking at a simplified example of one of the ways the AFDC rate may be determined, let us consider some problems encountered in determining that rate.

Current cost of capital versus embedded cost.   One problem is the determination of costs of debt and preferred stock financing representing costs of current construction. Overall *embedded cost* (that is, the cost of all debt and all preferred stock outstanding at a particular date) cannot be considered appropriate for determining the AFDC rate because embedded cost does not reflect current costs of funds relative to the period of construction.

Capitalization ratio. Use of a composite AFDC rate requires appropriate weighting of the actual costs of debt and preferred stock, and a reasonable allowance on common equity capital funds obtained and invested in the specific construction projects.

Consideration of the federal income tax effect of debt. Another consideration relates to the federal income tax effect of the debt component of AFDC. Undoubtedly this should be recognized—not by reduction in the rate for AFDC but by removing the tax benefit of the interest costs included in federal income tax charged to operations and recording this as an "Other Income" credit. In this manner federal income tax chargeable to operating costs is not reduced because of nonoperating construction activities. The accounting mechanics for this calls for a charge to the federal income tax account "above the line"[7] and a credit to the federal income tax account "below the line"[8] for the tax effect of the debt component of the AFDC rate.

Propriety of including the cost of common equity in the AFDC rate. "The cost of capital is not measured by interest payments alone, but rather by all the economic costs of the entire financing arrangement."[9] This includes the cost of common stock capital—the return required to attract investment by common stockholders— which must be considered in arriving at the total cost of capital.

During the construction period, the investment represented by equity funds is not producing revenues when construction work in progress is not included in the rate base upon which rates are established. The cost of such equity capital for extended periods of time is an appropriate cost of utility plant and, therefore, should be considered in arriving at the AFDC rate.

Other considerations. Other items to be considered in determining the cost of capital and, therefore, the AFDC rate are:

Compensating balance requirements. The requirement by many lending institutions that compensating balances be maintained by

---

[7] "Above the line": operating expenses, including provisions for depreciation, income and other taxes, are described as "above the line" items which are properly includible in rates charged to customers.

[8] "Below the line": expenses and credits such as interest expense and AFDC which are not included in cost of service for establishment of utility rates charged to customers.

[9] Arthur L. Litke, "Allowance for Funds used during Construction," *Public Utilities Fortnightly*, vol. 90, No. 7 (September 28, 1972), p. 20.

borrowers increases the effective cost of debt. For example, on a term loan of $100 million with a fixed interest rate of 10 percent per annum, a 20 percent compensating balance requirement increases the effective cost of funds actually available to 12.5 percent:

$$\frac{\text{Yearly Interest Cost}}{\text{Usable Funds}} = \frac{\$10 \text{ Million}}{\$80 \text{ Million}} = 12.5 \text{ Percent Effective Cost}$$

It is this effective cost which must be considered in determining the weighted AFDC rate, since it represents the full cost of the borrowing to the company.

Commitment fees. On certain long-term bank loan agreements, the borrower is required to pay a commitment fee on committed but unborrowed funds. The cost of commitment fees must also be included in calculations to arrive at the effective cost of borrowed funds.

SEC disclosure requirements

The SEC has been requiring more extensive disclosure in registration statements for the allowance for funds used during construction. When the AFDC credit has been significant, the SEC has generally required:

1. Disclosure of the rate for AFDC and the portions of AFDC attributable to funds provided by common stock equity of net income for common stock.
2. An exhibit supporting the calculation of the portion of net income attributable to the common equity component of AFDC.
3. The deduction of AFDC (or a portion thereof) from "sources of funds from operations" in the statement of changes in financial position.

Example of AFDC calculation

The following is an illustrative example of how the AFDC rate may be determined. It is by no means all inclusive since numerous other considerations may affect the AFDC rate.

Assume the following factors:

1. *Recently issued debt.* Consists of a $200 million long-term bank commitment, $150 million borrowed and outstanding; regular

interest (on borrowed funds) at 10 percent per annum, no commitment fee on funds not borrowed, and a requirement for the company to maintain a 20 percent compensating balance on borrowed funds.

2. *Recently issued preferred stock.* Consists of a 8½ percent, $40 million issue; effective cost to the company is 8.43 percent after considering premium on issuance.

3. *Common equity.* The cost of common equity has been estimated to be 15 percent.

4. The average capital ratios for the last two years (which the company calculated is the average period for investment in projects under construction for this computation) are:

Debt	57%
Preferred stock	12
Common equity.	31
	100%

Calculation

a. *Cost of debt:*
   Annual interest cost:
   $150 Million @ 10% = $15,000,000
   Usable borrowed funds:
   $150 Million @ 80% = $120,000,000
   Effective annual cost:

   $$\frac{\$15,000,000}{\$120,000,000} = 12.50\%$$

b. *Weighting process:*

	Average capital ratios	Effective cost	Weighted cost
Debt	57%	12.50%	7.13%
Preferred stock	12	8.43	1.01
Common equity.	31	15.00	4.65
Indicated AFDC rate			12.79%

An accounting mechanism to meet changed conditions

Fuel costs represent the largest component of the operating costs of electric utilities, as do purchased gas costs for gas utilities. If the prices of fuel did not change or if such changes were immediately reflected in rates approved by regulatory authorities, there would be no necessity for fuel adjustment clauses.[10]

Fuel costs can increase very significantly in a relatively short period of time. In addition to the quadrupling of oil prices in 1973 and 1974, coal prices increased nearly 75 percent between June 1973 and June 1974, and natural gas prices also significantly increased.[11]

Fuel costs have in many cases been further increased because of environmental considerations to eliminate sulphur oxide emissions into the atmosphere by increased use of costlier low-sulphur fuels.

Fuel adjustment clauses included in rate schedules give recognition to the extended time lag between changes in the prices of fuels and changes in approved rate schedules. In fairness to the utility companies and to their customers, regulatory commissions have authorized that these charges be passed through to customers on a more current time basis than is possible in the time required for overall changes in rate schedules.

However, in the operation of the fuel adjustment clauses, there is usually a lag of one to two months between the time increased fuel costs are incurred and the time customers are billed, principally because regulatory authorities generally require that fuel adjustment charges be based on experienced actual costs rather than on projected estimated costs. This time period lag has a minor impact on the statement of earnings, interest coverage, and cash flow during periods of stable prices. But when very sharp changes take place in fuel prices, such as those experienced in 1973 and 1974, failure to recognize the significant increased amounts to be recovered from customers results in a mismatching of costs and revenues and in resulting distorted statements of results of operations and interest coverage.

In order to overcome this mismatching and to reflect appropriately the changed conditions, many utility companies have adopted so-called *deferred fuel cost accounting*. Recoverable fuel costs at the end of each month are set up in a deferred debit

---

[10] A fuel adjustment clause in a rate schedule provides for adjustment in the billings to customers for the price variation in fuel from the base price of fuel included in the calculation of established rates.

[11] Federal Power Commission, "Monthly Fuel Costs and Quality Information," Press Release No. 20707, September 27, 1974.

account with a contra credit to the fuel expense account. In each succeeding month, the previous month's amounts for deferred fuel recoveries are reversed. The net result is that each month's fuel expense costs include only amounts representing the quantities of fuel consumed, priced at the base cost of fuels upon which scheduled rates were established.

Compensating for the recovery lag

The adverse cash flow effects of delayed billing for increases in fuel costs are lessened by reducing the "lag" between the time when the recoverable fuel costs are incurred and the time when they are billed to customers. This lag was originally built into fuel clause tariffs because of the time required to determine actual costs for billing application. As the impact on cash flow resulting from these time lags has become greater, utilities have been attempting to shorten the time lag by use of electronic data processing equipment to determine fuel costs more quickly, and to file updated fuel adjustment clauses in which the lag has been reduced to one month.

Shortening the period between the incurring of fuel costs and billing the fuel adjustment charges to customers, or changing the base cost of fuel included in establishment of new rates, produces the problem of how to dispose of the fuel costs that have not been recovered. Rather than include more than one month's fuel adjustment charges in monthly bills to customers, regulatory commissions have permitted the recovery of these amounts over a reasonable number of months.[12]

FLOW THROUGH VERSUS NORMALIZATION ACCOUNTING: TWO ACCEPTABLE METHODS FOR ACCOUNTING FOR FEDERAL INCOME TAX REDUCTIONS DEPENDING UPON METHOD ADOPTED IN ESTABLISHING RATES

Depending upon the method adopted by regulatory authorities in establishing prescribed rates, there are currently two accounting

---

[12] Case 26446, Orange and Rockland Utilities, Inc.—Electric Rates, New York State Public Service Commission, July 16, 1974, where the company was permitted to spread the unrecovered fuel charges over a 12-month period, is an example of this approach which has been prescribed by several commissions.

treatments for accounting for federal income tax benefits resulting from liberalized tax depreciation and from investment tax credits:

1. Deferred method (commonly referred to as "normalization").
2. Actual tax method (commonly referred to as "flow-through").

Normalization accounting

Normalization accounting for liberalized depreciation is the method under which the tax reduction effects of timing differences between taxable income and accounting income are deferred currently, and applied as reductions of income tax expenses in future periods when the timing differences are reversed. Normalization accounting for investment tax credits is the accounting method whereby current investment tax credit tax reductions are credited to income over the productive lives of the acquired assets, or other extended time periods. Under normalization accounting the charges to the income account for income tax expense in the year in which the tax benefits are realized are stated at amounts exclusive of such tax benefits. The tax benefits are credited to income over future accounting periods.

Flow-through accounting

Flow-through accounting for liberalized depreciation and investment tax credits is the method under which these benefits are included as reductions of income tax expense in the year realized.

In accordance with the *Addendum to APB Opinion No. 2* (as discussed earlier), regulated companies are required to account for the aforementioned federal income tax benefits using normalization or flow through consistent with the method adopted by the regulatory authority in establishing rates.

Flow through: A sound concept—under conditions that have ceased to exist. The flow-through method for accounting and rate making was prescribed by a large number of regulatory commissions during the 1950s and 1960s. The requirement for passing on the tax benefits of liberalized depreciation and investment tax benefits to current customers was predicated upon the assumptions that plant additions would increase or at the very least would not be less than plant retirements; that IRS regulations would remain unchanged; and thus, that future customers would receive similar benefits.

Flow-through accounting could be justified during a period in which capital funds were readily available at reasonable costs, and interest and preferred dividend coverages were adequate or more than adequate. Some utility companies by flowing through income tax reductions to customers were able to institute rate reductions which in turn encouraged consumer usage and resulted in growth of new and profitable business.

A need to reexamine the alternative to flow-through accounting. In recent years economic conditions are forcing regulatory commissions to reconsider the rate and accounting consequences of flow-through of certain income tax benefits. Inflation, user conservation, and environmental regulations have placed burdens upon utility companies which require such reconsideration.

Flowing through currently the tax benefits of liberalized depreciation and investment tax credits deprives the utility companies of cash flow and thus increases outside fund requirements for plant replacements and plant extensions. This becomes particularly acute under conditions like those experienced in the 1970s when plant replacements require three or four times the original cost of plant replaced. In addition, normalization of tax benefits, assuming commensurate rate relief, results in improved earnings coverages for interest and preferred dividends at about twice (based upon a tax rate of 48 percent) the amount of tax reductions normalized.

Congress has recognized that the flow-through method results in reductions of tax revenues. The Tax Reform Act of 1969 and the Revenue Act of 1971 require public utility companies to normalize the tax benefits of liberalized depreciation, asset depreciation range, and investment tax credits, but make an exception for utility companies which, as of the effective date of the amendments to the Internal Revenue Code and under commission order, were using the flow-through method by permitting these companies to continue this method. By these provisions Congress conveyed to regulatory commissions that the intent of the tax benefit provisions of the Internal Revenue Code was to make funds for construction available to the utility companies and not for the immediate benefit of current customers.

While both flow-through and normalization are acceptable accounting methods, depending upon the rate-making treatment, economic conditions may require the adoption of the normalization method for establishing rates and for accounting when increased funds for capital improvements must be made available to the companies and earnings coverages must be improved, as is increasingly becoming the case.

THE COST OF IMPROVING THE ENVIRONMENT: ADDING TO THE FINANCIAL BURDEN

Prior to the mid-1960s pollution control regulations had a relatively minor financial impact on electric utilities and other industries. However, toward the latter part of the 1960s numerous federal and local regulations were imposed which have made compliance much more costly.

The increases in operating and capital costs associated with these more stringent environmental regulations represent major challenges to public utilities. The increases in costs of constructing and operating air and water pollution control facilities have added further to the already heavy financial burdens that utilities and their customers must bear.

Table 2 indicates the magnitude of the financial burden for capital expenditures placed on electric utilities and other business as a consequence of the current stringent environmental regulations.

TABLE 2
The cost of a cleaner environment (millions of dollars)

	Electric utilities	All businesses	Percent relationship
How much must be spent*.	$5,270	$24,670	21.4
Investment in air and water pollution controls:			
1973†	$1,212	$ 5,687	21.3
1974‡	1,549	7,403	20.9
1977‡	3,841	9,319	41.2
Pollution control expenditures as a % of total capital spending:			
1973†	7.6%	5.7%	—
1974‡	8.3	6.2	—
1977‡	13.2	7.0	—

* The total cost of bringing industries' existing facilities up to present pollution control standards as of January 1, 1974.
† Actual expenditures.
‡ Planned expenditures.
Source: Data abstracted from McGraw-Hill, "7th Annual Survey of Pollution Control Expenditures," May 17, 1974.

It should be noted that the numerous "clean-up" technologies and devices have added significantly to the cost of service, without contributing any efficiency savings. To the contrary, many of the technologies and devices now in use and proposed tend to decrease efficiency and revenues and increase costs.

Industrial development bonds and tax incentives: Helping to lighten the burden

In order to lighten the financial burden of meeting the costly environmental regulations of the 1970s, utilities have turned to financing pollution control facilities with tax-exempt industrial development bonds.

The Revenue and Expenditure Control Act passed by Congress in 1968 limited the issuance of industrial revenue bonds to a maximum of $5 million per issue. However, the act permits, under certain conditions, unlimited use of tax-exempt industrial revenue bond financing provided that the security issues are used to finance air or water pollution control facilities.

In industrial revenue bond financing, the instrument is issued by a local political subdivision (state, county, city), which uses the proceeds to build pollution control facilities. In turn, the political subdivision leases or sells such facilities to the utility at a rental or installment sales price sufficient to compensate the issuer for the interest and principal of the borrowing.

The financial advantages to the utility company of industrial revenue bond financing are that interest rates on revenue bonds are lower by reason of their tax-exempt status, and that all federal income tax benefits for liberalized depreciation, investment tax credit, and interest deductions are retained by the utility company.

The need for environmental quality protection (EQP) clauses in electric utility rate schedules

A proposal still in the discussion stage by utilities and regulatory bodies is the inclusion of an environmental quality protection clause in electric utility rate schedules. Such a clause would be similar to the automatic fuel adjustment clauses in that added service costs attributable to environmental quality protection would be passed on to current customers without awaiting a formal rate proceeding.

Federal, state, and other authorities realize that industry must recover the costs of providing a cleaner environment, but for the most part they have not recognized that these costs cannot be fully recovered unless customers are currently charged therefor by use of automatic rate clauses.

LEASE CAPITALIZATION: WHAT WILL BE THE IMPLICATIONS?

Leasing of plant and equipment has become a major vehicle for financing capital expenditures in our nation's economy. A large segment of the national economy, including electric utilities and other capital-intensive industries, depends upon leasing as a means of financing advantageously the requirement for modernized or expanded plant and equipment.

Why public utilities lease

Regulated electric public utilities are required by franchise to furnish adequate service to customers to meet present and future needs. To accomplish this they must, of necessity, continuously replace and expand plant facilities. The use of long-term leases, in addition to conventional financing through issuance of bonds and preferred and common stock securities, has become necessary to relieve utility companies of overburdened debt and dilution of common stock earnings.

In a typical lease, the interest costs are frequently lower than can be obtained by the electric utility on its own long-term debt financing. Moreover, the leasing costs can still reflect the depreciation and investment tax credits that are available to the lessor.

Leasing is advantageous to the utility investor. By lowering the cost of service, leasing can be equally advantageous to the consumers of utility services.

The capitalization controversy

For several years now, accountants have wrestled with the problem of what circumstances require lessees to capitalize lease agreements.

Restating the issues involved in the controversy as to whether or not to capitalize leases may be academic, since the controversy may have been resolved by the time this book is published. It would be more useful, therefore, to examine the consequences of lease capitalization for regulated utility companies.

Lease capitalization and its effect on capital structure. The effect of lease capitalization on the ratio of debt to preferred and common stock equity has long been considered the major impact of lease capitalization by utilities. Consider the case of a utility company which is required by the SEC to maintain a capital structure not to exceed 60 percent debt and 10 percent preferred stock, and which has the following capital structure:

Actual capital structure

Component	Amount (in millions)	Percentage
Debt	$ 600	60%
Preferred stock	100	10
Common equity.	300	30
Total.	$1,000	100%

Now consider the effect on the utility's capital structure if it were required to capitalize its so-called financing-type leases totaling $40 million present value.

Pro forma capital structure giving effect to capitalization of financing-type lease commitments

Component	Amount (in millions)	Percentage
Debt	$ 640	61.5%
Preferred stock	100	9.6
Common equity.	300	28.9
Total.	$1,040	100.0%

The end result is that this utility would have to increase its common stock equity by approximately $18 million in order to conform its capital structure to the requirements of regulatory authorities.

The author's views. Changes in accounting principles and in financial accounting and reporting requirements should be made only to the extent that these changes serve useful purposes. When accounting principles are established, or changes are made in previously established generally accepted accounting principles, due consideration must be given to the resulting financial effects. In the author's opinion, capitalization of leases by public utility lessees can result in serious damage to the investor, the consumer, and the national economy that far outweighs any theoretical advantages that may be derived from this change in accounting policy.

We should not lose sight of the implications of opening the Pandora's box of *"as if"* accounting which would be a logical consequence of some of the arguments of the proponents of lease capitalization.

RATE MAKING: THE KEY TO PROBLEMS

Many of the accounting and financial problems of public utilities are directly related to the impacts of the rate-making process which must be reflected in the accounting and financial reporting. As a result of price inflation, increases in financing costs, increased emphasis on environmental protection, and other factors, frequent rate increases have become necessary.

An era gone by

Public utilities can, for the most part, point with pride to rate levels charged for utility service during the 20 or 30 years preceding the 1970s. During that period rate decreases were made possible by economies of scale, operating efficiencies, flow-through accounting, increased usage, and relatively mild inflation; however, it appears that that is an era gone by—not soon, if ever, to return.

A changed climate

There are a number of factors which have turned the climate for establishing rates from one of rate decreases to one which calls for badly needed rate increases. The most important change in the economic climate is inflation.

As stated previously, the effects of inflation are much more acute on regulated companies than on nonregulated industry. Nonregulated industry can for the most part meet inflation head-on by immediately passing on increased costs to the consumer. However, regulated utility companies cannot recover increased costs by arbitrarily increasing rates. Rate adjustments are subject to regulatory approval, which involves considerable lag between the time the increased costs are incurred and the time that these costs are reflected in increased rates.

Rate regulation responsibility: Fair treatment for both consumer and investor

Rate-making authorities are charged with a weighty responsibility which has taken on new and more important significance during the last several years. Rate-making bodies must establish rates which are just and equitable for both the consumer and the investor.

The basic rule is that utility rates must be sufficient to allow the utility to earn a "fair rate of return" on its capital investment. What constitutes a "fair return" has been the subject of much controversy, but long experience has shown that the variations in rate of return allowed have been considerably narrowed.

The landmark court cases which established the criteria for a "fair rate of return" were *Bluefield Water Works & Improvement Co.* v. *Public Service Commission of West Virginia* (1923)[13] and *Federal Power Commission* v. *Hope Natural Gas Co.* (1944).[14]

The considerations for determining "fair return" as established by these cases are summarized as follows:

1. Rate of return for a public utility should be commensurate with that of businesses having corresponding risks and uncertainties.
2. Return must be sufficient to assure confidence in the financial soundness of the utility.
3. The return allowed a utility should be adequate to allow it to maintain its credit and enable it to attract capital in amounts sufficient to meet its legal and moral responsibilities to the public.
4. Return should provide for both operating expenses and capital costs of the business, including dividends to common stockholders.

While the legal principles established by the *Bluefield* and *Hope* cases have been followed by regulatory authorities, risks of the

---

[13] *Bluefield Water Works and Improvement Co.* v. *Public Service Commission of West Virginia*, 262 U.S. 679 (1923).

[14] *FPC* v. *Hope Natural Gas Co.*, 320 U.S. 591 (1944).

"utility business" have increased significantly in the past decade because rate increases as allowed by the authorities have not kept pace with increases in operating, tax, and capital costs. One need only compare utility bond ratings in the 1970s with the previous decade to see how rapidly earnings coverages for interest and preferred dividends have been dwindling. The consequences have been higher capital costs and increasing difficulties in attracting capital. The results of rate making cannot be considered "fair" when the financial integrity of the utility is threatened.

The necessity for changes in rate making

Both utility companies and rate regulatory authorities understand that ways must be found to assure that the companies actually realize a fair rate of return. Some of the suggested changes in rate-making procedures will now be considered.

Compensate for regulatory lag

One step toward realizing the fair rate of return is reducing the time period required for establishing new rates.

Delay of months and sometimes years in allowing justifiable rate increases has greatly added to the financial deterioration of utility companies. Regulators must do everything possible to shorten the processing time of rate cases. Much can be accomplished in this respect by increasing commission staffs and consultants.

Regulatory authorities should also adopt procedures which permit immediate rate relief in emergencies by granting temporary rates, with provisions for refunds with interest to the extent that rate increases are found not justified after completion of formal rate proceedings.

Additionally, regulatory authorities and public utility statutes should permit utilities to recover losses in revenues to the extent that the allowable rate of return was not realized during the regulatory lag period. Such a procedure was developed in 1949 by the Board of Public Utility Commissioners of the Province of Alberta, Canada. The Alberta method, as it is known, compensates the utility for the revenues lost as a result of regulatory lag by (*a*) adding to the rate base the amount of revenue "loss"; and (*b*) amortizing that amount over a relatively short period of time.[15] Although this method is a fair method for rate making and has been used in Canada for approximately 25 years, it has not gained acceptance by commissions in the United States.

Increase the use of automatic escalation clauses

As discussed earlier, most utility tariffs provide for recoveries of changes in the price of fuels by means of fuel adjustment clauses, and some commissions permit immediate pass through of certain taxes. A logical extension for immediate recoveries of increased costs is to apply automatic adjustment clauses to costs of purchased power and increases in costs due to environmental requirements.

Use projected test years

A number of regulatory authorities have adopted future projected test periods for measuring the amounts of rate increases that should be allowed, and have abandoned the purely historical test year for rate increase determinations. Adoption of projected test periods in rate proceedings provide the utility company with rates sufficient to realize a fair rate of return on investment in the time periods in which such rate increases are made effective.

Include construction work in progress in rate base

As a result of increased costs and the lengthening of time for the construction of plant facilities, construction work in progress (CWIP) upon which interest is capitalized has increased significantly.

CWIP has been included in the rate base by regulatory authorities to a limited extent in some jurisdictions, but for the most part utility companies have been compensated for CWIP by the Allowance for Funds Used during Construction credited to Other Income. The inclusion of all or a portion of CWIP in the rate base permits immediate return on investment, and although the plant is not in service, this procedure recognizes that most plant investment is

---

[15] Garfield and Lovejoy, *Public Utility Economics*, p. 268.

being made for the future needs of current customers. The inclusion of CWIP in the rate base, and the concomitant termination of accrual of AFDC on that portion of CWIP included therein, produces the following benefits to the utility:

1. A reduction in the need for outside financing, since the investment in CWIP is producing cash revenues.
2. An improvement in interest coverage ratios. For every dollar of AFDC realized from increased revenues, earnings coverage before federal income taxes at the current income tax rate is increased by approximately two dollars. In addition, where bond indenture agreements limit Other Income to a specified percentage of Operating Income for the calculation of earnings coverage, increases in Operating Income allow for larger amounts of Other Income to be included in earnings coverage.
3. An improvement in the quality of earnings in the eyes of analysts by lowering the amounts of AFDC and the proportions of AFDC included in common stock earnings.

An essential consideration in the inclusion of CWIP in the rate base is that the effective date of ending the accrual of AFDC must coincide with the time that the increased rates are made effective, so that reported common stock earnings are not decreased.

A related problem is the determination of the specific amounts of CWIP to be included in the rate base and to be excluded from computation of AFDC. This is especially important where the FPC has jurisdiction over certain rates, and state or other regulatory commissions over other rates. Because the same physical plant may be involved in providing service to customers located in more than one jurisdiction, there must be agreement as to the number of dollars of CWIP that are allocated to each jurisdiction and considered by each authority in establishing rates.

The increasing trend toward inclusion of CWIP in the rate base reflects the recognition of the need of utilities for immediate return on capital invested in projects under construction. If complete recognition of such investment at one time is not practical because such change might produce an unusually large rate increase, an orderly transition might be accomplished by progressive increases in percentages of CWIP to be included in the rate base over a reasonable period of time.

Increase the usage of normalization accounting

As discussed previously, a change from flow-through accounting to normalization accounting, with corresponding increase in rates, increases internal cash generation and improves earnings coverages. However, because of inadequate earnings, actual federal income taxes have fallen in many cases to very low levels so that the amounts of increases in cash earnings and improvements of earnings coverage resulting from normalization of income tax reductions have become limited. Rate increases are now needed to achieve the full benefits of normalization.

Provide for a return on efficiency

Commissions should reward efficiency of management by providing for an added return to utilities which can demonstrate operating efficiency above average levels. Basing return solely on amounts invested fails to place a value on superior management. Although some commissions have recognized that a reasonable share of the savings resulting from superior efficiency should accrue to the utility, there is urgent need to extend such rewards.[16]

Recognize appropriate differentials between rate of return for equity capital and interest costs for long-term debt

The record amply demonstrates the need to allow for higher returns for common equity capital than in the past. In just a few years long-term debt interest and preferred stock dividend rates have more than doubled, leading to drastic declines in interest coverage and a sharp reduction in the differential between cost of capital for long-term debt and preferred stock and the return on common equity. This has led to lessening investor interest in utility common equity securities, which in turn has increased the costs and the difficulties of obtaining funds through the issuance of long-term debt and preferred stock securities.

To restore investor confidence and interest in utility securities, there is a need to provide for improvement in the return on com-

---

[16] Public Service Commission of Wisconsin, 74 *PUR* NS5.

mon stock equity proportionate to the increases that are being realized currently by investors in the long-term debt and preferred stock securities of these companies.

THE MANAGEMENT ACCOUNTING
APPROACH AND UTILITY ACCOUNTING

As the reader can appreciate, there are many problems facing public utilities, and only a concerted effort and coordination by all the organizational functions—accounting, finance, rates, legal, engineering, and others—will enable regulated public utilities to overcome the current problems of the industry.

In this respect, accounting, as a service function, should interrelate, and where necessary interact, with all other functions in the corporate organization. Interrelation and interaction enable the accounting function to perform creatively and dynamically in recognizing, evaluating, and solving the many problems facing the industry today.

This management accounting approach can be applied to companies in all industries; however, it is especially important to regulated public utilities in light of the many and varied challenges that have been brought about by the changed economic and sociological environments.

Chapter 41

Financial accounting and reporting for real estate developments

Edward C. Harris*
James J. Klink*

This chapter includes the accounting for real estate development and accounting for the sale of all types of real estate. This chapter does not include accounting for the ownership and operation of long-term real estate investments, and it does not include accounting for depreciation or real estate leases. The following are the major topics considered in this chapter:

Recent changes in the real estate industry
Sales of real estate (except retail land)
Sales of retail land
Condominiums
Investor accounting for joint ventures
Allocation of costs
Financial statement presentation

RECENT CHANGES IN THE REAL ESTATE INDUSTRY

During the last two decades, the real estate industry has undergone substantial growth and change. Real estate, in 1973, was the

---

* Partner, Price Waterhouse & Co.

third largest industry in the United States. The industry comprised approximately 350,000 construction firms and 150,000 real estate service and financing establishments. These 500,000 establishments employed approximately 4.6 million workers[1] and accounted for $194 billion (approximately 15 percent) of the gross national product.[2] Traditionally, this industry has been dominated by the small private builder. However, some 300 of Fortune's "500" companies have been involved in real estate investment or development.[3]

Certain of the principal factors which contributed to this growth are listed below:

1. Demographic factor. Significant increases in the 25- to 34-year-old age group account for most new household formations.
2. Increases in disposable income and the emergence of shorter workweeks caused increased demand for second homes, recreation facilities, and retail land lots.
3. Deterioration of the inner cities caused substantial movement to suburban localities.
4. Private investors have heavily invested in real estate as an alternative to the stock market. Such investments have been placed principally in tax shelter type investments, including syndications, or real estate investment trusts.

The significant growth of real estate investment trusts, along with the significant expansion of the economy in the late 1960s and early 1970s, resulted in excessive funds available for development and construction. The pressure to invest these funds aided in the rapid expansion of the real estate industry. Large-scale developments, including new towns, planned unit developments, resorts, and the like, which were previously considered to carry too high an investment risk by many developers, were undertaken in a lemming-like manner. Overbuilding occurred in a number of geographic areas. Management of this expansion demanded a much higher level of management skills than was available in the industry.

During the early 1970s, inflation was occurring at a level unprecedented during peacetime in the United States. Significant shortages of construction materials (e.g., lumber, concrete, steel,

---

[1] *County Business Patterns 1973,* December 1973, pp. 15 and 25.

[2] *Survey of Current Business,* July 1974, p. 21.

[3] Maklon Apgar, IV, "Do Big Corporations Belong in Real Estate?" *Corporate Financing,* May/June 1972, p. 45.

etc.) developed, and the money supply became critically short, causing interest rates to soar to unprecedented high levels. Furthermore, the federal government suspended various housing programs, causing a further reduction in available construction and development funds. Gasoline and other energy sources became critically short and more expensive. During the same period, the activities of the ecological interest groups, both public and governmental, resulted in substantial delays for many developments. Sales of new homes decreased significantly as buyers were unable to get financing. Overbuilding occurred in a number of geographic areas. Contractors found that they were no longer able to fulfill economically their long-term contracts or commitments. Administration of The Interstate Land Sales Full Disclosure Act, passed in 1968, required significantly greater disclosure for the benefit of the buyer; the administrative cost of compliance also caused many developers to discontinue or not pursue sales to the public. By 1974 the culmination of these factors brought the real estate industry almost to a stop. The number of foreclosures and bankruptcy filings was on the rise.

The rapid growth and changing environment of the real estate industry has caused the developer and his or her accountant significant problems.

Early accounting problems

Until 1973, even though the real estate industry had been growing rapidly in the late 1960s and early 1970s, there was almost no authoritative literature specifically dealing with the accounting for real estate transactions. The only literature at that time was the Securities and Exchange Commission's *Accounting Series Release No. 95* issued in 1962, listing a number of conditions which would raise a question as to the propriety of current recognition of profit. *Accounting Principles Board Statement No. 4* issued in October 1970 described the existing accounting principles, but application of these principles to real estate transactions was frequently difficult.

The real estate industry differs from most industrial and commercial companies, primarily because of the relative size of individual transactions, the length of the business cycle, the use of leverage, tax considerations, and because most real estate transactions are more often based upon the value of property as opposed to the quality of credit. Most sales prices of income properties are based upon cash flow rather than income reported under generally accepted accounting principles.

Other factors which caused a need for development of accounting methods specifically suitable for the real estate industry were:

1. Multiple roles of a seller including developer, financier, manager, and guarantor.
2. Lack of enforcement of contract obligations prior to closing.
3. New areas of implied warranty.
4. Buyer's refusal to perform.
5. Uncertainties as to future costs.

These difficulties led to various accounting practices which received considerable adverse publicity in the late 1960s and the early 1970s, leading ultimately to the development of two accounting guides by committees of the American Institute of CPAs. Both of these guides were issued just before the Financial Accounting Standards Board assumed responsibility for the development of accounting principles in early 1973. These two guides do not provide answers for all the accounting problems in the real estate industry. One of the guides, "Accounting for Profit Recognition on Sales of Real Estate," deals with the recognition of revenue but does not deal with cost accounting or disclosure. The other accounting guide, "Accounting for Retail Land Sales," although including consideration of revenue, cost accounting, and disclosure, deals with a relatively small segment of the real estate industry. There is still a need for literature and research in a number of areas including cost accounting, financial presentation, and accounting for real estate joint ventures.

Government regulation

Interstate Land Sales Full Disclosure Act.   The act, enacted in 1968, requires a land developer who sells or leases through the instrumentalities of interstate commerce 50 or more lots of undeveloped land pursuant to a "common promotional plan," to register the land with the Secretary of Housing and Urban Development and to make full disclosure concerning the lots to purchasers or lessees. Registration is effected through the filing by the developer of a statement of record with the Office of Interstate Land Sales Registration (OILSR), a unit of the U.S. Department of Housing and Urban Development. The required disclosure is made by delivery to the purchaser or lessee, prior to the signing of an agreement, of a property report containing certain prescribed items of information. Certain transactions are exempted by the act from the registration and disclosure requirements. Contracts for the purchase or lease of lots are voidable at the option of the purchaser or lessee if the lots are not registered or if the purchaser or lessee has not been furnished with the required property report. Various financial statements are required to be filed with HUD as well as included in the property report furnished to the buyer.

Securities and Exchange Commission. Various types of real estate transactions are the equivalent of an offering of securities in a form of an investment contract or a participation in a profit sharing arrangement within the meaning of the Securities Act of 1933 and the Securities Exchange Act of 1934. The more common types of real estate transactions that may require registration under the Securities Act are sales of interests in limited partnerships and resort condominiums. The condition under which an offering of condominium units is construed to be an offering of securities is covered in SEC *Securities Act Release No. 5347.*

SALES OF REAL ESTATE (EXCEPT RETAIL LAND)

The AICPA Accounting Guide, *Accounting for Profit Recognition on Sales of Real Estate,* was effective for transactions after July 1, 1973.

Scope of guide

The Guide applies to:

1. All sales of real estate, regardless of the nature of the seller's business, except for retail lot sales, the accounting for which is described under a separate heading, "Sales of Retail Land."
2. The seller's accounting only—not to the buyer's accounting.

3. A sale of a business, including the sale of corporate stock, if the sale is in economic substance a sale of real estate.
4. Sales of options to purchase real estate.

The Guide does not cover:

1. Cost capitalization or allocation.
2. Accounting for lease transactions (including sale-leasebacks), except in paragraphs 30–33 which relate to a sale of improvements and a lease of land.
3. The appropriate accounting for nonmonetary transactions, which are covered by *APB Opinion No. 29.*
4. Rules for imputation of interest, which is covered by *APB Opinion No. 21.*
5. Accounting for assets and liabilities, except by inference.
6. Rules for disclosure.

General principles

In the development of the Profit Recognition Guide, the AICPA drew upon principles in *Accounting Principles Board Statement No. 4*, specifically principles of realization and substance over form. The key statements in introductory paragraphs 6–13 are based upon these principles and include:

1. "Revenue (and profit) is conventionally recognized at the time an asset is sold, provided (a) the amount of the revenue is measurable—that is, the collectibility of the sales price is reasonably assured or the amount uncollectible can be estimated—and (b) the earnings process is complete or virtually complete—that is, the seller is not obligated to perform significant activities after the sale in order to earn the revenue."
2. "Economic substance should determine the timing of recognition, amount, and designation of revenue if the economic substance of a transaction differs from its legal form."
3. In order to justify profit recognition ". . . a transaction should transfer from the seller to the buyer (a) the usual risks of ownership . . . and (b) all or most of the rewards of ownership. . . . Any risk that is retained by the seller in the asset sold should be limited essentially to that of a secured creditor."
4. "If, at the time of sale, the terms of the transaction are such

that the buyer may expect to recover his investment plus a return through assured cash returns, subsidies, and net tax benefits, even if he were to default on his debt to the seller, the transaction is probably not in substance a sale. . . ."

The Guide prescribes specific rules which usually must be followed in order to satisfy the objectives of the general principles. The three main subdivisions of the Guide described in the following sections are:

1. Time of sale.
2. Buyer's investment in purchased property.
3. Seller's continued involvement with property sold.

Time of sale

Profit on most real estate sales should not be recorded prior to the time of closing. According to the Guide, "A sale is consummated when the parties are bound by the terms of a contract, all consideration has been exchanged, and all conditions precedent to closing have been performed. Usually all of those conditions are met at the time of closing, not at the time of a contract to sell or a preclosing."

Exceptions to the portion of the above related to "conditions precedent to closing" are described in the section of the Guide dealing with seller's involvement. The exceptions are permitted because of the length of the construction period and provide that under certain conditions, partial income recognition is acceptable as construction or similar seller performance progresses. Typical transactions include profit recognition on condominiums (especially highrise) during construction, sales of land which include requirements for the seller to perform certain development or construction work, and certain sales of income-producing properties requiring construction and/or initiation and support of operations. The exceptions are not considered to include single family housing.

Buyer's investment in purchased property

The Guide concludes that since uncertainty about collectibility of a receivable in a real estate sale may be greater than in other commercial transactions, the buyer's initial investment must be large enough to give a buyer an equity in the property sufficient that the risk of loss through default motivates him to honor his obligation to the seller. As a consequence of this position and the need to establish a general standard for buyer's commitment, the Guide provides specific requirements for down payment and payment of the remaining balance of the purchase price. Although specific requirements for buyer's investment may have been met, the requirement for a continuing evaluation of collectibility of receivables remains.

Size of down payment. General rule: The Guide sets forth in Exhibit A minimum down payments based upon usual loan limits for various types of properties. In addition, the Guide states that ". . . if a newly placed permanent loan or firm permanent loan commitment for maximum financing of the property exists with an independent established lending institution, the minimum down payment needed to recognize profit on a sale of real estate should be the greater of (a) the amount derived from Exhibit A (page 955) or (b) the amount by which the sales value of the property exceeds 115% of the amount of loan or commitment by the primary lender." (The 115 percent test for down payment does not apply unless a newly placed permanent loan or firm loan commitment from an independent lender is involved in the transaction.) The Guide provides a modification of the general rule with the statement ". . . in most instances a down payment of 25% of the sales value of the property is an initial financial investment by a buyer adequate to support recognizing profit at the time of sale."

Even if the down payment required under Exhibit A is only 10 percent, the transaction must be accorded instalment or deposit accounting as the down payment is inadequate because of the newly placed first mortgage.

Sales value. Buyer's investment must be related to sales value which is described as ". . . stated sales price increased or decreased for other considerations that clearly constitutes additional proceeds on the sale, services without compensation, imputed interest, and so forth." An illustration of sales value versus sales price is:

Down payment paid to seller	$ 100,000
First mortgage (newly placed with outside lender)	700,000
Second mortgage given to seller at market rate of interest	200,000
Sales value	$1,000,000
115 percent of first mortgage 1.15 × $700,000	805,000
Down payment required	$ 195,000

EXHIBIT A
Minimum down payment requirements

This schedule of minimum down payments of various types of real estate property has been developed by the Committee to help determine whether a buyer's initial investment in the property is adequate to recognize profit at time of sale. Use of the schedule is described in paragraphs 18 to 24 and illustrated in Exhibit B.

	Minimum down payment expressed as a percentage of sales value
Land:	
Held for commercial, industrial, or residential development to commence within two years after sale	20%*
Held for commercial, industrial, or residential development after two years	25%*
Commercial and industrial property:	
Office and industrial buildings, shopping centers, etc.:	
Properties subject to lease on a long-term lease basis to parties having satisfactory credit rating, cash flow currently sufficient to service all indebtedness	10%
Single tenancy properties sold to a user having a satisfactory credit rating	15%
All other.	20%
Other income-producing properties (hotels, motels, marinas, mobile home parks, etc.):	
Cash flow currently sufficient to service all indebtedness	15%
Start-up situations or current deficiencies in cash flow.	25%
Multi-family residential property:	
Primary residence:	
Cash flow currently sufficient to service all indebtedness	10%
Start-up situations or current deficiencies in cash flow	15%
Secondary or recreational residence:	
Cash flow currently sufficient to service all indebtedness	15%
Start-up situations or current deficiencies in cash flow	25%
Single family residential property (including condominium or cooperative housing):	
Primary residence of the buyer	5%†
Secondary or recreational residence	10%†

* Not intended to apply to volume retail lot sales by land development companies.
† If collectibility of the remaining portion of the sales price cannot be supported by reliable evidence of collection experience, a higher down payment is indicated and should not be less than 60% of the difference between the sales value and the financing available from loans guaranteed by regulatory bodies, such as FHA or VA, or from independent financial institutions.

* * * * *

This schedule cannot cover every type of real estate property. To evaluate down payments on other types of property, analogies can be made to the types of properties specified, or the risks of a particular property can be related to the risks of the properties specified.

Example of down payment test—Exhibit A versus new loan

Down payment	$ 150,000
Balance of existing first mortgage payable by seller but assumed by buyer.	500,000
Second mortgage payable to seller, noninterest bearing	400,000
"Sales price"	$1,050,000
Amount required to discount second mortgage to fair market value.	75,000
"Sales value"	$ 975,000

Composition of down payment.   Acceptable forms of down payment are:

1. Cash.
2. Buyer notes supported by irrevocable letters of credit covering the period of the notes from an established lending institution which issues such letters in the normal course of business.
3. Cash payments by buyer to third parties to reduce existing indebtedness.
4. Cash payments which are in substance additional sales proceeds such as prepaid ". . . interest or fees that by the terms of the contract are maintained in an advance status and are applied against principal at a later date."

Some unacceptable forms of down payment are:

1. Payments to third parties for improvements to the property.
2. Prepaid interest not meeting the test described above.
3. Marketable securities or other assets (acceptable when converted to cash).

Funds that have been or will be loaned to the buyer or otherwise provided directly or indirectly by the seller must be deducted from the down payment.

Buyer's continuing investment.   The Guide concludes that ". . . a seller should recognize the profit on a sale of real estate at time of sale only if the buyer is required to continue to increase his investment in the property each year after he pays an adequate down payment."

The specific requirements may be summarized to the effect that, as a minimum, the buyer must reduce his or her total indebtedness—

a. Annually (beginning no more than one year after recording the sale),
b. In level payments, including principal and interest,
c. Based upon a maximum term—

> For land . . . .   20 years
> For other property . . . .   over customary term of first
> mortgage by independent lender

The composition of annual payments must be the same as the down payment.

Exception.   If the preceding requirements for continuing investment are not met, a reduced profit may be recognized if the annual payments are at least equal to the sum of—

a.　Level payment of principal and interest payment on a maximum available first mortgage, *and*
b.　Interest at an appropriate rate on the remaining indebtedness.

The reduced profit is calculated by valuing the receivable from the buyer at the present value of the lowest level of annual payments due over customary term of first mortgage.

Example

Down payment (meets applicable tests)		$ 150,000
First mortgage at market rate of interest (new, 20 years—meets required amortization)		750,000
Second mortgage, interest at a market rate is due annually, with principal due at end of 25th year (the term exceeds the maximum permitted)		100,000
Stated selling price		$1,000,000
Second mortgage	$100,000	
Less present value of 20 annual interest payments on second mortgage (see Note below)	70,000	30,000
Adjusted sales value for profit recognition.		$ 970,000

Note: Lowest level of annual payments over *customary term* of first mortgage—thus, 20 years, not 25.

The test could also be applied if the seller held one first mortgage of $850,000 with terms similar to those of the second mortgage.

Cumulative application of buyer investment requirements.　The requirements for down payment and continuing investment previously described—

a.　Are cumulative, and
b.　Must be applied at the closing date and annually thereafter (excess payments may be applied as needed).

The closing date for this purpose may be interpreted as being the date of recording when the sale (or income therefrom) is required to be recorded subsequent to the closing date for accounting purposes.

Receivables subject to subordination.　Profit recognition is limited to an amount determined under the cost recovery method if the seller's receivable is subject to later subordination, unless proceeds of the loan to which the receivable is subordinated are applied in reduction of the receivable. However, the receivable may be subordinate to a mortgage on the property existing at the time of sale.

Release provisions.　If the sale transaction provides for releases from lien, the buyer must be required to have made adequate cumulative payments at the time of each release with respect to the sales value of the unreleased property in order for full profit recognition to be acceptable. The seller must look forward to each release date to determine if the investment test will be met at each date.

Example—Sale of land

1. Property sold—200 acres.
2. Value per acre—$5,000.
3. All acres of equal value.
4. Release requirements are:
   a. 125 percent of selling price per acre
   b. *All* payments applied to release

Composition of sales price

Down payment (25%)	$ 250,000
Ten-year mortgage to seller at 11%	750,000
Sales price	$1,000,000

First release—55 acres at end of year 1

Sales price $275,000 × 125% equals $343,750 required for release, paid as follows:

Down payment		$250,000
First instalment		44,850
Additional release payment (minimum necessary under agreement)		48,900
		$343,750
Remaining unpaid balance ($1,000,000 less $343,750)		$656,250
Remaining unreleased acres:		
145 acres × $5,000 each (sales value)		$725,000
Down payment test (25%).	$181,250	
Amount required for amortization of principal from date of sale to date of release equals $725,000 – $181,250 × 1.56% (1.56% is first year amortization of principal based upon a maximum allowed 20-year amortization)	8,483	189,733
Maximum allowed unpaid		$535,267

As the unpaid debt after the first release ($656,250) exceeds the maximum allowed to be unpaid ($535,267), the acreage released must be accounted for as a separate sale and the profit on the unreleased acreage must be deferred.

Sale of improvements and concurrent lease of land. According to the Guide,

> If property improvements are sold subject to a lease of the underlying land to the buyer of the improvements, the computation of the relative size of a down payment in relation to the sales value of the property to determine the adequacy of the buyer's initial investment . . . should include the effect of the lease. . . . The lease

affects only the tests of buyer's initial investment if the lease is between the buyer and a third party lessor. . . . If the seller of the improvements is also the lessor of the land, however, the lease also affects the calculation of profit on the sale of the improvements.

Examples of the above are included in Exhibit B to the Guide.

Inadequate buyer investment. "If the buyer's initial and continuing investment in the property in a real estate transaction fails to conform to the requirements specified in this guide, a method of recognizing revenue that is appropriate to the circumstances of the transaction should be selected." The methods, which are described in the Guide are the deposit, instalment, and cost recovery methods. Simple illustrations of when these methods are to be applied are given below.

Deposit method

Down payment	$ 10,000
Mortgage to seller (interest only for 10 years, with balloon)	990,000
Sales price	$1,000,000

Down payment insignificant—substance appears to be an option. The $10,000 would be recorded as a liability, no income recognized.

Cost recovery method

Cost of property sold.	$ 250,000
Down payment	$ 400,000
Mortgage payable to seller with interest only for 5 years, with balloon payment, subordinated to development loan and payable only out of development profits (collection uncertain)	600,000
	$1,000,000
Profit at closing ($400,000 cash received less total cost of $250,000).	$ 150,000

The $600,000 is obviously a contingency (a participation in future profits, if any) and should be considered to have no value for accounting purposes.

Instalment method

Cost of property sold.	$ 650,000
Down payment 15% (assume 25% required under Exhibit A). . .	$ 150,000
Mortgage to seller due over 10 years (level payments)	850,000
Sales price	$1,000,000
Profit at closing—$150,000 (cash received at closing) divided by $1,000,000 (total principal to be received) × $350,000 profit.	$ 52,500

The down payment is inadequate for full profit recognition but is significant; thus, partial recognition appears appropriate.

In the application of any of these alternative methods of accounting, it is important to note the stipulation in the Guide that "under any of these methods of accounting for sales using deferred recognition, caution should be exercised that the recorded asset amounts less deferred profit, if any, do not exceed the depreciated values had the property not been sold. It would be inappropriate to avoid charging losses in value to income by accomplishing a thinly financed 'sale' under which the risk of losses in value continue to rest with the seller."

Seller's continued involvement with property sold

A seller frequently continues to be involved over extended periods with property that he or she has legally sold; this involvement can be in the form of:

Financing	Repurchasing
Management	Guarantees
Development	Equity participation
Construction	Leasebacks

The Guide describes the effect on accounting of these involvements in two ways:

> . . . recognition of all or part of the profit from a sales contract should be postponed to await performance by the seller if continued involvement by the seller includes obligations to perform specific significant parts of the contract after the time of sale.

> . . . a sales contract should not be accounted for as a sale if the "seller's" continued involvement with the property carries in essence the same kinds of risks as does ownership of property. For example, an obligation by the "seller" to repurchase the property or to guarantee cash flow from the property or returns to investors ("buyers") for an extended period, or an arrangement by which the "seller" continues or is obligated for extended periods to continue to operate the property and may suffer directly or indirectly, most of the consequences of unprofitable operations usually prevent the transaction from being accounted for as a sale.

The following sections describe the application of these principles to several common types of continuing involvement by sellers.

Participation solely in future profits. "A contract for sale of real estate may include or be accompanied by an agreement that provides for the seller to participate in future profit from the property without risk of loss." Under these circumstances, profit recognition on the sale need not be deferred; however, no costs may be deferred.

Permanent financing. If the seller is responsible for obtaining or providing permanent financing for the buyer, obtaining the financing is prerequisite to a sale for accounting purposes.

It should be noted, however, that even if obtaining financing is not the obligation of the seller, collectibility of the receivable may be questionable if the buyer does not have financing.

Services without compensation. When a sales contract is accompanied by an agreement to provide management services without adequate compensation, the value of the services should be imputed, deducted from the sales price and recognized over the term of the management contract. Taken out of context, the above could be read to imply that profit recognition at time of any sale is appropriate as long as the future costs are estimable and provided for. Such is not always the case, as will be noted in the subsequent discussion of initiating and supporting operations.

Seller's involvement with development, construction, and operations. Paragraphs 47 through 55 and paragraph 60 of the Guide relate specifically to the seller's involvement in the development, construction, and operation of a property after the sale. The seller's involvement may be stated or implied, and the Guide describes conditions under which a sale or profit may be recognized.

Paragraphs 47–50 involve primarily a sale of land with a related development or construction obligation. If the property sold or being constructed is an operating property (e.g., apartment, shopping center, office building, warehouse, etc.) as opposed to a nonoperating property (e.g., land lot, condominium unit, single family detached housing), then paragraphs 51–55, "Initiating and Supporting Operations" may also apply.

The sale of condominium units is covered by paragraph 60.

Development and construction (paragraphs 47–50). "A contract for sale of undeveloped or partially developed land or other property may include or be accompanied by an agreement requiring the seller to develop the property in the future, to construct facilities on the land, or to provide offsite improvements." Under these circumstances, ". . . recognizing profit on the basis of costs incurred or to be incurred in development or construction is appropriate, provided that uncertainties can be reliably quantified. A completed contract method should be used if total cost and total profit cannot be reasonably estimated from the seller's previous experience."

If the cost incurred method is used, profit should be allocated to the sale and later development on the basis of estimated *costs* of each activity. Thus, if the land was a principal part of the sale and its market value greatly exceeded cost, part of the profit which could be said to be related to the land sale would be deferred and recognized during the development or construction period.

Initiating and supporting operations (**paragraphs 51–55**). The following is a condensed description of the requirements for sale and profit recognition as described in this section of the Guide. A specific example of profit recognition is given as Exhibit C to the Profit Recognition Guide.

The Guide first requires a determination (paragraph 53) of whether or not the transaction is in economic substance a sale. If the transaction is considered a sale, the Guide gives circumstances considered to be either stated support or implied support and generally describes the accounting under each set of circumstances.

Stated support. ". . . if the seller is contractually obligated under short-term sale and leaseback agreements or otherwise, to guarantee returns on investment to the buyer for limited periods, the Committee believes that a sale should not be recognized and therefore Exhibit C should not be applied until such time as actual rental operations are at a level sufficient to cover all obligations, such as operating expenses, debt service, and other contractual payments, including payments to the seller." However, the Guide treats returns on investment differently from other cash flow guarantees. If, for example, the seller guaranteed the buyer that there would be no negative cash flow from the project, but did not guarantee a positive return on investment, then ". . . if the seller has contractual obligations which do not include returns on investment, profit recognition under Exhibit C should commence (see paragraph 55) when rentals on underlying leases attain levels that assure coverage of operating expenses and debt service (including payments due the seller under the terms of the transaction) unless objective information regarding occupancy levels and rental rates in the immediate area provides reasonable assurance that rental income will be sufficient to meet those expenses and cash flow requirements." If the "objective information" described above is available, the profit recognition method described in paragraph 55 and Exhibit C of the Guide may then be used.

Implied support. The conditions under which support is implied (i.e., the seller is "presumed to be obligated to initiate and support operations of property he has sold, even in the absence of specified requirements in the sale contract or related document. . .") are described in paragraph 52. They are:

> A seller obtains an interest as general partner in a limited partnership that acquires an interest in the property sold.

> A seller retains an equity interest in the property, such as an undivided interest or an equity interest in a joint venture that holds an interest in the property.

> A seller holds a receivable from a buyer for a significant part of the sales price and collection of the receivable is dependent upon the operation of the property.

> A seller enters into a management contract with the buyer that provides for compensation on terms not unusual for the services to be rendered and that is not terminable by either seller or buyer.

It should be noted that when the seller is a general partner in a limited partnership and has a significant receivable related to the property, the transaction should be accounted for as described under the section "Financing, Leasing, and Profit-Sharing Arrangements."

Profit recognition under Exhibit C (paragraph 55). When commencement of profit recognition is appropriate under the circumstances described under *Stated support* or *Implied support,* the following conditions apply:

1. Profit is recognized on the basis of costs incurred as compared to total costs to be incurred during this support period. It should be noted that costs include land and operating expenses as well as other costs.

2. Estimated profit should be adjusted by reducing estimated future rent receipts by a safety factor of 33⅓ percent unless signed lease agreements have been obtained to support a projection higher than the rental level thus computed (when signed leases amount to more than 66⅔ percent of estimated rents, no additional safety factor is required but only amounts under signed lease agreements can be included).

3. ". . . support should be presumed for at least two years from the time of initial rental unless actual rental operations are able earlier to cover all obligations, such as operating expenses, debt

service, and other contractual commitments including payments to the seller. Where the seller is contractually obligated for a longer period of time, profit recognition under Exhibit C should continue until the expiration of the contractual period."

Financing, leasing, and profit sharing arrangements ("no sale" conditions). "No sale is recognized if the transaction is in substance a financing, leasing, or profit-sharing arrangement. Payments from 'buyer' to 'seller' are accounted for as funds loaned, rental payments, or transfers needed to effect division of profits as the substance of the transaction indicates the parties have agreed."

Under the following conditions, the transaction is required to be accounted for as a financing, leasing, or profit sharing arrangement:

1. The seller is directly or indirectly a general partner in a limited partnership holding the property and holds a "significant receivable" which is defined as a receivable in excess of 15 percent of the maximum available first lien financing. This condition is described in greater detail in paragraph 53 of the Guide.
2. "A seller has an obligation or an option to repurchase the property. (A right of first refusal based on a bona fide offer by a third party is ordinarily not an obligation or an option to repurchase.)"
3. "A buyer has an option to compel the seller to repurchase the property."
4. "A seller guarantees the return of the buyer's investment (see paragraph 13)."

Partial sales. The Guide accepts income recognition in a sale of a partial interest in an asset if the following conditions exist:

1. Sale is to an independent buyer.
2. Collection of sale price is reasonably assured.
3. Seller is not required to support property, its operations, or related obligations to an extent greater than the seller's proportionate interest.

If the transaction is in substance a sale, but the seller retains an interest and the buyer receives preferences, the seller may use a cost recovery method for profit recognition. The preference might include profits, cash flow, return on investments, and so on.

"A sale of property in which the seller holds or acquires an equity interest in the buyer should result in recognizing only the part of the profit proportionate to the outside interest in the buyer. No profit should be recognized if the seller controls the buyer. . . ."

Sales of condominium units (paragraph 60 of the Guide) are covered in a separate section of this chapter.

SALES OF RETAIL LAND

The AICPA Accounting Guide, *Accounting for Retail Land Sales,* was effective on a retroactive basis for all financial statements for periods ending on and after December 31, 1972. The following is a condensed summary of the accounting principles set forth in the Guide.

Scope of guide

The dominant activity of the retail land sales industry is retail marketing of numerous lots, subdivided from a larger parcel of land, for use by the original or a subsequent purchaser as a primary or secondary homesite or as recreational property for placement of motor homes or other recreational vehicles. The Guide applies to "retail lot sales on a volume basis with down payments that are less than those required to evaluate collectibility of casual sales of real estate. Wholesale or bulk sales of land and retail sales from projects comprising a small number of lots are subject to the general principles for profit recognition on real estate sales." Where retail land is sold in an improved state with a down payment of 10 percent or more accompanied by a general obligation note receivable, secured by a first mortgage and marketable at banks without substantial discount and without recourse to the seller, many provisions of the Guide do not apply because the earnings process is complete.

Standards for selection of accounting method

Conditions for recording a sale. Sales should not be recorded until:

1. The period of cancellation with refund has expired and the customer has made all required payments.
2. Aggregate payments (including interest) equal or exceed 10 percent of contract sales price.
3. The selling company is clearly capable of providing all improvements and offsite facilities promised.

If these conditions are met, either the accrual or the instalment method must be selected; if the conditions are not met, the deposit method of accounting should be used.

Requirements for accrual method

1. Properties clearly will be useful for residential or recreational purposes at the end of the normal payment period.
2. Project's improvements have progressed beyond preliminary stages, and there is evidence that the work will be completed according to plan.
3. Receivable is not subject to subordination to new loans on the property, except subordination for home construction purposes under certain conditions.
4. Collection experience for the project indicates that collectibility of receivable balances is reasonably predictable and that 90 percent of the contracts in force, six months after sales are recorded, will be collected in full or alternatively, down payments are 20–25 percent of sales price.

These tests should be applied on a project-by-project basis. Unless all conditions for use of the accrual method are met for the entire project, the instalment method of accounting should be applied to all recorded sales. The Guide permits prior experience to be applied with limitations.

According to a "1975 Survey of Accounting and Reporting Practices of Real Estate Developers," annual reports of 20 publicly held retail land sellers (fiscal years ended in 1974 and early 1975) disclosed that:

    10 used instalment method
     6 used accrual method
     4 used a combination of the above methods
    ———
    20
    ===

General procedures

Accrual method. The following general procedures should be used to account for revenues and costs under the accrual method of accounting:

1. Record sales contracts gross.
2. Discount receivables to reflect an appropriate interest rate.
3. Establish an allowance for contract cancellation.
4. Defer revenues based on ratio of future costs to be incurred to

total costs—deferred revenue to be recognized as development is performed.

5. Calculate cost of sales only on net sales recorded after eliminating sales expected to be cancelled before maturity.

Financial statement presentation is illustrated in exhibits to the Guide.

Interest rate. Regardless of the stated rate of interest, ". . . the effective annual yield on the receivable . . . should not be less than the minimum annual rate charged locally by commercial banks and established retail organizations to borrowers financing purchases of consumer personal property with instalment credit. In the absence of more definitive criteria, the objective of evaluating the gross receivable less contract cancellation allowance should be to record the net receivable at the value at which it could be sold on a volume basis at the time of the initial transaction without recourse to the seller." According to the Guide "for 1972 and recent prior years, a rate of not less than 12 percent is appropriate." A 1975 survey of reports of major retail land developers for 1974-75 indicated discounting of receivables to yield an effective interest rate of 12 percent.

Delinquency and cancellation

Evaluating historical data to establish the ability to predict the collection of receivables from current sales requires experience with a representative sample of receivables over an adequate period of time . . . the Committee concludes that the receivables should be considered uncollectible and the contracts presumed to be cancelled (for this purpose) if regular payments due are unpaid for the following delinquency periods:

Percent of contract price paid	*Delinquency period*
Less than 25%	90 days
25% but less than 50%	120 days
50% and over	150 days

The historical data should be continually updated, and the allowance for contract cancellations should be adjusted accordingly to reflect any changes therein.

Deferral of revenues related to future performance. Unless all improvements and amenities for which the seller is obligated are complete, a portion of the revenues must be deferred until completion. The deferral should be based on the ratio of costs yet to be incurred to total costs. Total cost in the denominator should also include costs previously expensed, such as costs for interest and marketing.

Exhibits to the Guide give several examples of financial statement presentation; the illustration of measuring initial consideration (Exhibit 1) follows.

Instalment method. If the instalment method is required, the following general procedures should be used to account for revenues and costs:

1. The entire contract price, net of stated interest (a market rate of interest need not be imputed), should be reported as revenue in year of sale.
2. Cost of sales (including a provision for future improvement costs to be incurred) and selling costs should be charged to income in the current period.
3. Gross profit less selling costs directly associated with the project should be deferred and recognized in income as payments of principal are received on the sales contract receivable.
4. Selling costs to be deducted in determining the gross profit to be deferred above should be limited to amounts expected to be recovered from collectible contracts.

Change to accrual method from instalment method. The Guide states that "at the time that all four conditions (required for use of the accrual method) are satisfied on a project originally recorded under the instalment method, the accrual method of accounting should be adopted for the entire project (current and prior sales) and the effect accounted for as a change in accounting estimate due to changed circumstances in accordance with the provisions of *APB Opinion No. 20,* 'Accounting Changes,' Paragraphs 31–33." The problems involved in evaluating the last requirement (adequacy of collection experience) make it very difficult to determine a precise time at which the change is appropriate.

Deposit method. All cash received is credited to a liability account. No revenue is recorded; direct selling costs may be deferred but not in excess of amounts expected to be recovered.

Costs

Future performance costs. Estimates of costs to complete a project, when required under either of the accrual or instalment

EXHIBIT 1
Initial measure of consideration (accrual method) (amounts in thousands)

Assumptions:

Gross sales contracts recorded at Point 0 (stated interest of 6%) $1,000
Estimated uncollectible principal amount (sales contracts of $200* less
estimated down payments to be forfeited of $20) . . . . (180)

Net sales contracts receivable . . . . $ 820
Down payments and collections at Point 0 relative to above sales contracts
($80 + $20) 100

Collections projected (principal amounts) for years 1 through 9 . . . . $ 720

Land cost (applicable to sales contracts of $800). . . . . $ 60
Selling expenses at Point 0 . . . . $ 300
Future improvement costs (applicable to sales contracts of $800) . . . . $ 120
Minimum annual yield required on contracts receivable 12%
Discount required:
Sales contracts receivable at Point 0 (see above) . . . . $ 720
Present value of 108 level monthly payments of $8.65 on sales contracts
receivable (discounted at 12%) (Schedule A) 570

Discount required . . . . $ 150

Computation of deferred revenue applicable to future improvements:

$$\frac{\$120}{\$60 + \$300 + \$120} = 25\%$$

$$25\% \times \$650 \ (\$1{,}000 - \$200 - \$150) = \$163$$

Profit recognition at Point 0:

Revenue recognized: Cash received at Point 0. $ 100
Present value of balance of sales contracts receivable 570

(Net sales $820, less discount $150) . . . . $ 670
Less: Deferred revenue applicable to future improvements 163

Net revenue. . . . . $ 507
Less: Costs and expenses ($60 + $300) 360

Pretax income. . . . . $ 147

* It is assumed that experience shows that 90 percent of contracts in force six months after sales are recorded will ultimately be collected in full.

EXHIBIT 1—Schedule A
Present value of sales contracts receivable (amounts in thousands)

Year	Receivable collections		Annual collections	Present value @ 12%
	Principal	Interest*		
1	$ 62	$ 42	$104	$ 97
2	66	38	104	87
3	70	34	104	77
4	75	29	104	68
5	79	25	104	60
6	84	20	104	53
7	89	15	104	47
8	95	9	104	43
9	100	4	104	38
	$720	$216	$936	$570

* Assumes no interest for year 0.

methods, should be based on adequate engineering studies. Such estimates should contain reasonable provisions for (1) unforeseen costs; (2) anticipated cost inflation generally experienced in the construction industry locally; and (3) unrecoverable costs of offsite improvements, utility and recreation facilities, and any related anticipated operating losses of the facilities. Estimates of anticipated proceeds from future sale of facilities should be discounted to present value as of the date the net unrecoverable costs are recognized.

Costs to be capitalized. "Costs directly related to inventories of unimproved land or to construction required to bring land and improvements to a saleable condition are properly capitalizable. . . ." Costs would include certain interest and property taxes. "Interest is properly capitalizable if it results from (a) loans for which unimproved land or construction in progress is pledged as collateral or (b) other loans if the proceeds are used for improvements or for acquiring unimproved land." Capitalization of carrying costs should be discontinued when a saleable condition is reached. In addition, "the carrying amount of capitalized costs should not exceed net realizable value."

Methods of allocating costs to parcels sold. Cost allocation methods are not peculiar to this segment of the industry; therefore, a more complete discussion of this subject appears beginning on page 999.

Disclosure in financial statements

The Guide outlines various disclosures which should be made by companies engaged in retail land sales operations. In addition, numerous exhibits are presented which illustrate financial statement presentation.

ACCOUNTING FOR NONMONETARY TRANSACTIONS

Accounting Principles Board Opinion No. 29 sets forth the principles of accounting for nonmonetary transactions. In general terms, the *Opinion* limits the occasions where noncash real estate exchanges result in recognition of profit.

The basic principle stated in the *Opinion* is that ". . . accounting for nonmonetary transactions should be based on the fair values of the assets (or services) involved which is the same basis as that used in monetary transactions. Thus, the cost of a nonmonetary asset acquired in exchange for another nonmonetary asset is the fair value of the asset surrendered to obtain it, and a gain or loss should be recognized on the exchange." However, the *Opinion* modified the basic principle for situations where (1) fair value is not determinable within reasonable limits and (2) where the earnings process is not culminated. Such circumstances are often typical in nonmonetary real estate transactions.

The second modification stated that

> If the exchange is not essentially the culmination of an earning process, accounting for an exchange of a nonmonetary asset between an enterprise and another entity should be based on the recorded amount (after reduction, if appropriate, for an indicated impairment of value) of the nonmonetary asset relinquished . . . the following two types of nonmonetary exchange transactions do not culminate an earning process:
>
> a. An exchange of . . . property held for sale in the ordinary course of business for . . . property to be sold in the same line of business to facilitate sales to customers other than the parties to the exchange, and
> b. An exchange of a productive asset not held for sale in the ordinary course of business for a similar productive asset or an equivalent interest in the same or similar productive asset. . . .

The above would seem to eliminate profit recognition on most nonmonetary real estate exchanges; however, under circumstances where one party purchases a property for monetary consideration and simultaneously exchanges that property for another, profit recognition would seem to be appropriate as the transaction is essentially monetary.

Although practice is not settled, transactions involving exchanges of properties such as manufacturing plants and headquarters buildings for certain other real estate investments such as raw land, apartments, and so on, may qualify for income recognition.

CONDOMINIUMS

A condominium is normally defined as a multiunit structure in which persons hold fee simple title to individual units (apartments) together with an undivided interest in the common elements associated with the structure. The common elements comprise all portions of the property other than the individual units and may include such items as the hallways and elevators contained in the building, the underlying land, private roads, parking areas, and recreation facilities.

The actual definition of a condominium varies by state. In certain states, the units need not be part of a multiunit structure, thereby making possible a condominium subdivision of single-family detached homes. As a result, there is a wide variety of condominiums which vary in use such as (*a*) a primary residence; (*b*) a secondary residence, often oriented towards recreation facilities; or (*c*) commercial property. In many instances, uses can be commingled as in a highrise condominium where the main floor may contain commercial units while the upper floors contain single family residences. In addition, the rights of ownership with respect to the condominium units may vary substantially as follows:

1. Standard—owner has fee simple title to the unit with no substantial restrictions as to its use.
2. Restricted—owner has fee simple title; however, he or she may only occupy the unit for a stated period of time each year. During the remaining period, the unit is held for rent to the public.
3. Timesharing—two or more owners hold individually undivided interests in a given unit. Through a separate agreement, each owner may only occupy the unit during stated period(s) each year.

It is evident from the above that there is a wide variety in the form and use of condominiums and, since its introduction, the condominium form of ownership has created unique accounting problems.

Accounting principles

Prior to the issuance of the Profit Recognition Accounting Guide, there was no authoritative literature on accounting for sales of condominiums, as the condominium was still a relatively new form of ownership. The Accounting Guide discussed in broad terms the timing of profit recognition on real estate sales, covering condominium sales specifically in paragraph 60. The Guide stated a number of conditions which must be met before profit recognition would be appropriate on condominium sales. As stated earlier in this chapter, the Accounting Guide is broken down into three major sections (i.e., time of sale, buyer's investment in purchased property, and seller's continued involvement with property sold). The following is a discussion of the special problems for condominiums arising under all the general areas of the Guide as well as under paragraph 60.

Time of sale

According to the Guide, "All parties must be bound by the terms of the contract." In order for the buyer to be bound, he or she must be unable to require a refund. Certain states require that a "Declaration of Condominium" be filed with appropriate authorities before the sales contract is binding and not voidable at the option of the buyer.

All conditions precedent to closing, except completion of the project, must be performed. Although paragraph 14 of the Guide includes a requirement that *all* conditions precedent to closing must be performed, paragraph 60 clearly permits an exception to the completion requirement for condominium projects, as it permits profit to be recognized on the sale of a condominium unit in accordance with the percentage of completion method.

In light of paragraph 14 of the Profit Recognition Accounting Guide, a question arises when using the percentage of completion method of accounting as to whether the seller must file the Declaration before profit recognition is appropriate. While there are differences of opinion within the accounting profession, the following guidelines seem to be acceptable in light of current practice:

1. If state laws require that the Declaration must be filed before a sales contract is binding and not voidable, then the Declaration must be filed before profit recognition is appropriate.
2. If the filing of the Declaration is not a prerequisite to a binding sales contract, then profit may be recognized in accordance with the percentage of completion method provided that all other criteria for sale and profit recognition are met.

In addition, certain types of condominium units are required to be registered with either the Office of Interstate Land Sales Registration of the United States Department of Housing and Urban

Development or the Securities and Exchange Commission before any sales documents may be considered to be valid and binding.

Buyer's investment in purchased property

Buyer's investment requirements are generally covered in the previous discussion on pages 953–60. However, when the seller uses the percentage of completion method of accounting and where there is more than a one-year delay between sale and closing, the cumulative test of buyer investment will not be met unless down payments in excess of the minimum prescribed have been made and can be applied toward meeting the required annual payments. Alternatively, the deposit method can be used until the closing is one year or less from the date of sale.

When the percentage of completion method of accounting is used, either (1) the buyer must have a permanent loan commitment, or (2) the seller must be financially able and willing to provide financing at an acceptable cost to the buyer before profit recognition would be appropriate.

Seller's continued involvement with property sold

Permanent financing. Often sales contracts are subject to the buyer obtaining permanent financing at an acceptable cost, the arrangement of which is often the responsibility of the seller. In such cases, providing or obtaining financing is a prerequisite to a sale for accounting purposes.

Option or obligation to repurchase the property. Where the seller has the option or obligation to repurchase property, no sale can be recognized. However, a commitment by the seller to assist or use his or her best efforts (with appropriate compensation) on a resale would not preclude profit recognition.

Additional criteria for profit recognition

Whether the percentage of completion or the closing methods (described on pages 976–77) are used to report profits, certain additional criteria must be met.

The developer must have the ability to estimate costs not yet incurred. Consideration must be given to the prior experience of the developer, the type of construction contract, and the current economic conditions affecting the cost of construction and money. See the section entitled "Cost Capitalization and Allocation" in this chapter for a discussion of estimating future costs and accounting for changes thereof.

A problem unique to condominium developers is support of the condominium association. As a sales inducement, the seller may at times guarantee that the monthly assessments to be charged the buyers by the condominium association will not exceed a certain amount for a stated period of time or until a certain percentage of occupancy is obtained. In some circumstances, the costs of such support could be significant. In such instances, full deferral of profit until the guarantee lapses is appropriate when there is uncertainty as to the cost of the guarantee.

Construction must be beyond a preliminary stage. This requirement generally means that construction has started and, as a minimum, the building foundation is completed. Some developers use a general rule of thumb for the preliminary stage test to the effect that 25 percent to as much as 50 percent of total direct construction costs must be incurred and in place (not just onsite), depending on the nature of the project.

Sufficient units must be sold to assure that the property will not revert to rental property. In determining whether this requirement has been met, the following factors should be considered:

1. Economic conditions.
2. Developer's history.
3. State laws requiring a specified percent of units to be sold before the Declaration of Condominium may be filed.
4. Sale contracts giving buyer a right of rescission until a specified percent of units are sold.
5. Seller's right to convert to rental basis.
6. Construction loans requiring a specified percent of units to be sold before the lender will release any unit.
7. End loan financing commitments providing for a specified percent of units to be sold before closing of any sale.

All of the above factors should be considered before profit recognition is determined to be appropriate. In the absence of other specific requirements, such as those imposed by state laws or financing agreements, many accountants and developers have used a rule of thumb that 50 percent of the units in the project must be sold.

The developer must be able to reasonably estimate aggregate sales proceeds. Consideration should be given to sales volume, trends of unit prices, developer experience, geographical location, environmental factors, and so forth.

Methods of accounting for profit recognition

General. There are two alternative methods of accounting for profit recognition on condominium sales:

1. Closing method—sales and the related profit are generally recorded at the time of closing of each unit. This method is often referred to as the completed contract method.
2. Percentage of completion method—unit sales are generally recorded on the date of sale. However, profit is recognized as construction progresses on the project.

For profit recognition purposes under either method, the project may be defined as a building, group of buildings (phase), a single structure, or a complete project, depending on the circumstances. The principal consideration in defining the project is cost accounting; that is, the developer's ability to identify direct construction costs with individual segments of a development.

Under either method of accounting, if the total estimated costs exceed the estimated aggregate proceeds, the total anticipated loss should be charged to income in the period in which the loss becomes evident so that no anticipated losses are deferred to future periods.

A 1975 survey of 100 annual reports for 1974 indicated 52 disclosures of accounting policies with respect to sales of 38 condominiums of which 38 recorded sales at time of closing or passage of title. The percentage of completion method reported by 12 companies was applied to midrise or highrise projects.

Closing method. This method of accounting is widely used by developers who construct and sell townhouse or garden apartment condominiums since the construction period is relatively short. The principal advantage of the closing method is that profit recognition is based on actual costs and eliminates the need for reliance on estimates.

Percentage of completion method. This method of accounting has been adopted principally by developers constructing midrise or highrise condominiums where the period of the construction cycle may extend up to two to three years. The principal advantage of this method is that it allows recognition of some profit as construction progresses on units sold. However, this method requires heavy reliance on estimates or aggregate project costs and revenues which are, of course, subject to uncertainties.

Under the percentage of completion method, "profit to be recognized should be calculated on the basis of the percentage of completion of the project times the gross profit on the units sold." Since the Guide does not define how percentage of completion is to be determined, either of the following alternatives may be used:

1. Actual stage of direct construction as determined through architectural or engineering studies, or
2. The relationship of costs already incurred to total estimated costs to be incurred. Total costs would properly include direct construction costs and the allocated share of common costs such as site improvements and amenities. Practice is divided, however, with regard to the inclusion of other common costs such as land, predevelopment costs, and construction interest if capitalized. The costs selected for inclusion should be those which most clearly reflect the earnings process.

Condominiums sold under time-sharing concept. Some developers sell undivided interests in each of the individual units to two or more buyers with restrictions as to the periods of time in which each buyer may occupy the unit. The closing method of accounting is probably warranted in such situations. Profit on the accrual or instalment method should not be recognized until all undivided interests for a given unit are sold and closed; however, the cost recovery method of accounting might be utilized in appropriate circumstances.

Condominium conversion. In the past few years, conversion of apartments to condominiums has become common because of reduced returns on investment, or in many instances operating losses, which have resulted principally from rent controls, rising real estate taxes, and increased operating and maintenance costs.

Conversion costs. Conversion costs include the direct cost of conversion, interest during the conversion period, assessments on unsold units and, of course, the original cost of the units. Revenue and expenses related to rental operations during the conversion period should normally be included in results of operations. However, there may be justification for capitalizing losses created solely by increased vacancies directly attributable to the conversion of the property. Any prepaid penalty associated with required refinancing should generally be expensed as incurred in accordance with *APB Opinion No. 26,* "Early Extinguishment of Debt."

The accounting for the results of rental operations and for prepayment penalties, as described above, is generally appropriate for the typical conversion, that is where the conversion is made by the owner who operated the property as a rental operation. However, where the conversion is made by a converter who acquired the property for immediate conversion rather than for operation, such costs are typically taken into consideration in determining the purchase price of the property and are, therefore, clearly costs of conversion which are capitalizable.

Methods of accounting. Either the closing method or percentage of completion method is appropriate for accounting for condominium conversions. Most converters are using the closing method of accounting with deferrals as appropriate or necessary.

The percentage of completion method is seldom used for condominium conversions. If used, however, the stage of completion should be determined on the basis of costs incurred to total estimated costs to be incurred. In any calculation of the percentage of completion or other deferral of income, there is a problem in determining which costs should be included. In this type of development, the selling and interest costs could exceed the direct conversion cost. Logically, all selling, interest, and direct conversion costs, including any capitalized losses of rental operations as discussed above, would be factored into the determination of percentage of completion for income recognition.

INVESTOR ACCOUNTING FOR JOINT VENTURES

General

In recent years, joint ventures have been widely used for real estate development. Generally, real estate joint ventures are entered into by two or more venturers for the purpose of pooling knowledge and resources.

The four types of parties normally found in a joint venture are land owner, investor, developer, and lender (typically, more than one of these interests are combined in one venture). Some types of interests obtained by a venturer are:

1. *Land owner* (usually relatively inactive unless filling two roles)
   a. Contributes land for joint venture interest.
   b. Contributes land for joint venture interest and preferred cash flow.
   c. Sells land for note subordinated to other lenders and for joint venture interest.
2. *Investor* (other than land owners—usually relatively inactive)
   a. Invests cash for joint venture interest:
      (1) May or may not get preferred return.
      (2) May get preference on tax attributes.
3. *Developer* (usually has operational control within predetermined constraints)
   a. Contributes services for joint venture interest.
   b. Sells services *and* gets joint venture interest for management without cash involvement.
   c. Acts as general partner in limited partnership.
   d. May guarantee cash flow.
4. *Lender* (usually relatively inactive)
   a. Lends development funds and receives joint venture interest.
   b. Lends funds and makes equity investment in joint venture.

A party upon entering a real estate joint venture may have an interest in (1) the joint venture equity in net assets and future profits and losses; (2) only future profits and losses; or (3) only future profits. Real estate joint ventures are organized as corporate entities or, more frequently, as partnerships. Limited partnerships are often used because of the advantages of limited liability and the maximization of tax advantages. In a limited partnership, the general partner is normally in control of day-to-day operations, while the limited partners remain relatively inactive.

Definition. A joint venture for accounting purposes has the following characteristics:

1. The entity is owned and operated by a small group of venturers as a separate business or project for the mutual benefit of the members of the group.
2. Each venturer participates, directly or indirectly, in overall man-

agement. These arrangements are usually made through a joint venture or partnership agreement entered into at formation.

3. Significant influence of each of the investors is presumed to be present.

4. One investor does not have control by direct or indirect ownership of a majority voting interest (otherwise, the venture is likely to be a subsidiary of the controlling investor).

Legal entities within the accounting definition of a joint venture are as follows:

1. Corporations.
2. Partnerships.
3. Undivided interests.

Regardless of the legal form of a joint venture, the accounting principles should be the same for recognizing profits and losses.

There is little authoritative literature on investor accounting for real estate joint ventures.

Because of the variation in accounting for investments generally, the Accounting Principles Board (APB) issued *Opinion No. 18* on the equity method of accounting for investments in common stock in March 1971, which (by an AICPA accounting interpretation in November 1971) may be considered applicable to unincorporated joint venture investments. However, this *Opinion* does not cover many areas of real estate joint venture transactions. The following discussion is, unless stated otherwise, based on a combination of practice in light of the accounting principles as set forth in *Opinion No. 18* and the Profit Recognition Guide.

Investor accounting for joint venture income

APB Opinion No. 18 concluded in paragraph 16 that "investors should account for investments in common stock of corporate joint ventures by the equity method regardless of the percentage interest held." The general investment requirement of 20 percent before applying the equity method of accounting as set forth in *APB Opinion No. 18* is not applicable to joint ventures. An interpretation issued by the AICPA in November 1971 stated that "many of the provisions of the Opinion would be appropriate in accounting for investments in . . . unincorporated entities." Therefore, as a general rule, investors should account for all unincorporated joint venture interests (including limited partnership interests) on the equity method. The two principal exceptions to the general rule relate to (a) ventures operating in a foreign country where realization is subject to major uncertainties (cost method is appropriate), and (b) ventures in which one venturer has control through a voting interest in excess of 50 percent (consolidation is appropriate unless such control is temporary).

In a 1975 survey of annual reports of 100 selected real estate developers or companies with development activities, 61 companies disclosed the following accounting for investments in joint ventures and partnerships:

Investment interest	Number of instances			
	Consolidated	Equity	Cost	Total
Over 50%	12	11		23
50%.	2	23	1	26
Under 50%.		25	3	28
Not specified		11	1	12

Elimination of inter-entity profits and losses

APB Opinion No. 18 provides that in applying the equity method, intercompany profits should be eliminated by the investor until realized by the investee as if the investee company were consolidated. An AICPA Accounting Interpretation issued in November 1971 clarified this by stating that intercompany profit should be eliminated by the investor only to the extent of his or her ownership interest in the investee. Complete elimination of the intercompany profit is required by the investor, however, where the investor controls the investee (through majority voting interest or when control is exercised through guarantees of indebtedness, extension of credit and the like) or enters into a transaction with the investee which is not at "arm's length." The elimination process would not apply to losses to the extent they represent permanent loss of value.

Generally, when accounting for investor profit on contribution or sale of goods or services to a joint venture, there are two separate elements of profit which must be accounted for:

1. The portion applicable to the equity interest of the investor.
2. The portion applicable to the equity interest of the outside investors.

With respect to the accounting for the investor's own portion, such profit should be deferred until the cost to the venture is charged to expense in the venture financial statements and thus is recognized by the investor in recording his share of earnings or losses of the venture. At such time, this portion of the profit to the investor and the expense of the venture would be eliminated. This approach would also be applicable for interest income on investor loans to the joint venture.

The next seven sections will discuss in detail the accounting for the portion of profit applicable to the equity interest of the outside investors for the following types of transactions:

1. Cash contributions.
2. Contribution of real estate by one venturer.
3. Contribution of real estate by more than one venturer.
4. Contribution of services by one venturer.
5. Interest income on loans and advances to joint ventures.
6. Investor sales of real estate to the joint venture.
7. Investor sales of services to the joint venture.

If an investor reports profit on a transaction with a venture in a period different from that in which a gain is reported for tax purposes, deferred income taxes should be provided on the timing difference in accordance with *APB Opinion No. 11,* "Accounting for Income Taxes."

Cash contributions. No accounting problems result when all venturers contribute cash at formation of the joint venture in proportion to their respective interests. The investor should record an investment in the venture in the amount of cash contributed.

Contribution of real estate by one venturer (contributor's accounting for profit applicable to outside venturers). No existing authoritative literature deals specifically with the accounting to be followed when an investor contributes real estate in exchange for an investment in a joint venture. Frequently, the fair market value of the contributed real estate exceeds cost by a substantial amount. In most cases, the investor should record his or her investment in the joint venture at the same cost as the real estate contributed. However, in circumstances where the contribution of real estate by *one investor* is virtually the same as a sale to a willing buyer, income recognition may be appropriate. Thus, if fair market value of the real estate contributed can be objectively determined by an unrestricted contribution of cash to the venture by another informed investor, the transaction, to the extent of the other investor's interest, may be the same as a sale to a willing buyer; that is, the contributor of the real estate may have effectively sold a partial interest in the property to the outside venturer in exchange for an interest in the venture cash. Thus, the following general rule appears appropriate: when real estate is contributed by an investor to the joint venture, profit recognition to the extent of the other investors' proportionate interest only may be appropriate by the investor when the other investors contribute cash for their proportionate interest, provided that the contributor of the real estate has no continuing involvement with the venture, such as that requiring deferral of profit under the Profit Recognition Accounting Guide. In addition, depending upon the circumstances, the existence of other significant transactions directly with the other investors or with the venture may require deferral of profit.

The application of the general rule relating to profit recognition is illustrated by the following example:

Assumptions:

1. Venturer A contributes a parcel of land for a 50 percent interest in an unincorporated joint venture.
2. Venturer B contributes $200,000 in cash for its 50 percent interest.
3. Venturer A had originally purchased the land for $120,000.
4. There is no continuing involvement of Venturer A requiring deferral of profit.

Result:

1. An objective basis exists for valuing the noncash asset at $200,000.
2. Venturer A now effectively owns a 50 percent interest in the land and a 50 percent interest in the venture cash.

Value of venture assets	$400,000
Venturer A 50% interest	$200,000
Cost of land	120,000
Indicated gain	$ 80,000
Less Venturer A share of gain to be deferred until venture sells land to third parties	40,000
Venturer A recognizes gain on "sale" of 50% in land for cash	$ 40,000

Contribution of real estate by more than one venturer (contributor's accounting for profit applicable to outside venturers).

Gain from an excess of value assigned to capital contributions by the venture over investors' cost should ordinarily be deferred in its entirety by the investors until confirmed by transactions between the venture and third parties in any of the following circumstances:

1. The venturers contribute real estate.
2. The venturers contribute cash in proportion to their ownership interests and also real estate.
3. The portion of total capital contributed in cash is not significant.

In such cases, the absolute value of the assets contributed is not measurable and the gain to the venturers should be deferred regardless of what amount is recorded on the books of the venture.

Contribution of services by one venturer (contributor's accounting for profit applicable to outside venturers). Contribution of "know how" would not generally result in profit until realized by venture transactions with third parties.

Normally, the investor contributing services should record as its investment the cost of the services contributed plus income to the extent of the portion of the profit on the services applicable to the other investors' ownership interests. The value of the services should be the lesser of: the value assignable to such services based on cash contributions by other investors, or the fair value of such services not exceeding the price of comparable services to independent third parties. The portion of the income recorded should be recognized on the basis of actual costs incurred. Costs related to prior services must be clearly identifiable as a direct cost of the project.

With respect to the recognition of profit on such services, however, the following conditions must be met:

1. There should be no substantial uncertainties as to the ability of the investor to perform (such as when the investor lacks experience in the business of the venture) or as to the cost of any future services to be rendered.
2. The investor contributing the service has no other continuing involvement with the venture such as that requiring deferral of profit under the Profit Recognition Accounting Guide.

Interest income on loans and advances to joint ventures (investor-lender's accounting for interest income applicable to outside investors). Interest income applicable to the equity interest of the outside investors only may be recognized under the condition that the loan is on the same basis and terms as that of an independent lender. The investor/lender's risks may be substantially different from those of an independent lender, requiring full deferral of the portion of interest income applicable to the other investors until confirmed by venture transactions with third parties, when conditions such as the following are present:

1. Lack of adequate collateral and other conditions normally required by an independent lender.
2. Situations where all venturers make loans and equity investments in proportion to their equity interests (causing a lack of objective evidence to differentiate between the role of the independent lender and investor).
3. Circumstances where the investor's risks exceed his or her investment, loans, and advances (unless the other venturers have a sufficient capital investment in the venture so that they may reasonably be expected to bear their share of the risks of ownership).
4. Additional continuing involvement as outlined in the Profit Recognition Accounting Guide.

Example. Investors A, B, and C are all investors in a corporate joint venture; each invests $1 million for a one-third interest and, in addition, each lends $2 million to the venture. In this case, none of the venturers may record interest income. If, however, A had loaned $5 million instead of $2 million, interest income to the extent of two thirds of the income on the additional $3 million would be eligible for income recognition if the other requirements were met.

Investor sales of real estate to the joint venture (investor-seller's accounting for profit applicable to outside investors). With respect to a sale of real estate by the investor to the joint venture (distinguished from a capital contribution), profit recognition to the extent of other investors' proportionate interests in the joint venture only is appropriate if all necessary requirements for profit recognition set forth in the AICPA Accounting Guide entitled *Accounting for Profit Recognition on Sales of Real Estate* are satisfied.

Investor sales of services to the joint venture (accounting for profit applicable to outside investors). When services are performed by an investor for the joint venture, profit recognition to the extent of outside interests in the joint venture only is appropriate if—

1. The transaction was entered into at a price determinable as being on an arm's-length basis; that is, the fair value of such services as measured by comparable services to independent third parties and on the same terms.
2. There are no substantial uncertainties as to the ability of the investor to perform (such as when the investor lacks experience in the business of the venture) or as to the cost of any future services to be rendered.
3. The investor performing the services has no other continuing involvement with the venture such as those requiring deferral of profit under the Profit Recognition Accounting Guide.

The portion of income recorded should be recognized on the basis of performance.

Venture sales of real estate or services to an investor

Since an investor cannot recognize profit on a sale to itself, it must defer its interest (proportionate share) in such joint venture profit; the investor's share of such income should be recognized as the asset is depreciated or sold to a third party.

If services for an investor are performed by the joint venture and the costs are capitalized by the investor, the general rule as stated above for a sale of assets would be applicable, but the costs capitalized should be reduced by the investor's interest in the joint venture profit on the services performed. However, when a joint venture renders services to an investor and the investor expenses the cost of such services, deferral of profit is not appropriate.

Accounting principles for the separate financial statements of a joint venture

Generally, the financial statements of a joint venture should be prepared in accordance with generally accepted accounting principles. When there is a variance, the investor, in applying the equity method, should adjust the financial statements of the venture to conform with generally accepted accounting principles. In addition, it is appropriate to adjust the venture financial statements to conform to accounting policies followed by the investor.

Lag in venture reporting

In accordance with *APB Opinion No. 18,* the most recent financial statements of the joint venture should generally be used by an investor to apply the equity method. A lag in reporting should be consistent from period to period. When a lag does exist, intervening events materially affecting the financial position or results of operations of the joint venture should be analyzed to determine whether or not the financial statements of the investor should be adjusted or whether disclosure of such events is necessary.

Varying profit participations for accounting purposes

In some instances, joint venture agreements for other than corporate joint ventures may designate different allocations among the venturers of profits and losses, distributions of cash from operations and distributions of cash proceeds on liquidation; and one or more of the allocations may change with the lapse of time or the occurrence of specified events. In such circumstances, accounting for an investor's equity in venture earnings must be carefully considered, as the allocation of profits and losses specified in the venture agreement may not be in agreement with the economic substance of the transaction.

Equity in investee earnings must be determined on a realistic pretax income basis. A good approach to determine the share of the investee's pretax income (loss) is to consider how any reported increase (decrease) in net assets will ultimately affect cash payments to the investor, whether over the life of the venture or in liquidation.

Loss in value of joint venture investment (including loans and advances)

If a permanent decrease in value of a joint venture investment has occurred, a write-down to realizable value should be recognized in excess of what would otherwise be recorded by applying the equity method. Such write-downs would rarely be encountered since the financial statements of the venture, which must be stated in accordance with, or adjusted to, generally accepted accounting principles, are presumed to present fairly financial position and results of operations of the venture.

Recognition of losses in excess of an investor's investment (including loans and advances)

Accounting for losses in excess of investment. Recognition of venture losses in excess of an investor's investment (including loans and advances) by continuing to apply the equity method may be appropriate in circumstances where the investor is committed to absorb such losses because of its stated or implied guarantee of investee obligations and support of operations. The resulting negative balance in the investment account should be reflected as a liability in the financial statements. Examples of such circumstances may be as follows:

1. Legal obligations.
2. Quasi-legal obligations based on business reputation, intercompany relationships, credit standing.
3. A presumption supported by past performance that the investor would make good venture obligations.
4. Operating considerations, such as losses resulting from a material nonrecurring investee loss or from expected start-up costs.
5. Publicly stated investor intentions to support.

When venture losses in excess of investment are not recognized and the venture subsequently reports income, the investor should resume recognition of venture earnings only after his or her share of subsequent net income equals the share of net losses not recognized during the period the equity method was suspended.

Accounting required for other investors. In situations where an investor has no legal obligation to contribute his or her share of losses in excess of the investment (or where the investor is not financially capable of fulfilling such a legal obligation), the other investors will have to absorb such excess losses by recording their allocable share thereof until the aggregate operating losses recognized by such other investors equal their investment (including loans and advances), unless the imminent return to profitable operations by the venture appears to be assured.

If future earnings materialize, the other investors should record all such earnings until the excess losses recorded by them have been recovered.

Accounting for the difference between investor cost and underlying equity in net assets of venture at date of investment

Normally, there will not be a difference between an investor's cost and underlying equity in venture net assets at formation. Such a difference may frequently exist, however, upon acquisition of a venture interest subsequent to formation. Paragraph 19n of *APB Opinion No. 18* requires that the difference between the cost of an investment and the amount of underlying equity in net assets of an investee should be accounted for in the same way as if the investee were a consolidated subsidiary. Therefore, the difference at the date of investment should be dealt with according to its nature. Any unidentified difference, sometimes designated as goodwill, will normally apply entirely to the real estate assets.

COST ACCOUNTING FOR REAL ESTATE DEVELOPMENTS

Introduction

Little authoritative literature exists regarding the principles of accounting for costs of real estate developments, except for retail land operations. The AICPA Industry Accounting Guide, *Accounting for Retail Land Sales,* sets forth certain broad guidelines concerning cost capitalization and allocation methods. This section will summarize and discuss certain of the more significant alternative cost capitalization and allocation methods which are currently being utilized in this industry.

Industry characteristics. The cost accounting problems which the real estate developer and his or her accountant encounter can be best illustrated by considering the peculiar characteristics of this industry. Certain of these peculiar characteristics are (*a*) the extended business cycle, (*b*) the nature of the common costs, and (*c*) the materiality of transactions.

Business cycle. It is not uncommon for a large real estate development to have a business operating cycle (i.e., the average time intervening between the acquisition of materials or real estate and the final cash realization) which spans a number of years and may include several economic cycles. It is difficult to develop a complete master plan with a high degree of certainty for a real estate development which requires a development period of five years or more. Master plans for such developments are often revised numerous times before the project is completed.

Common costs. Costs incurred are frequently large in dollar amount and may benefit more than one project within a development. For example, sewage treatment facilities and amenities may benefit all or a major portion of the total development. This communal benefit coupled with the heterogeneity of development projects must be weighed in the selection of capitalization and allocation methods.

Size of transaction. Individual real estate transactions are relatively large, ranging from thousands to millions of dollars.

Pervasive measurement principles. Cost incurred in real estate operations range from "brick and mortar" costs which are clearly capitalizable to general administrative costs which are not capitalizable. There is a broad range of costs between these two extremes which sometimes are difficult to identify and subject to interpretative classifications. Judgmental decisions must be made as to whether such costs should be capitalized. *Accounting Principles Board Statement No. 4*, "Basic Concepts and Accounting Principles," sets forth certain pervasive measurement principles concerning the accounting for costs. The *Statement* states that

> Income determination in accounting is the process of identifying, measuring, and relating revenue and expenses of an enterprise for an accounting period. . . . Expenses are determined by applying the expense recognition principles on the basis of relationships between acquisition costs and either the independently determined revenue or accounting periods. To apply expense recognition principles, costs are analyzed to see whether they can be associated with revenue on the basis of cause and effect. If not, systematic and rational allocation is attempted. If neither cause and effect associations nor systematic and rational allocations can be

made, costs are recognized as expenses in the period incurred or in which a loss is discerned.

Modifying convention—conservatism. Historically, managers, investors, and accountants have generally preferred that possible errors in measurement be in the direction of understatement rather than overstatement of net income and net assets. This has led to the convention of conservatism, "including . . . the rules that inventory should be measured at the lower of cost and market. . . ."

Lower of cost or net realizable value

The accounting for decreases in market value or utility of real estate varies depending upon the nature and type of real estate.

The carrying value of real estate inventories is subject to the same general tests required for inventories of a manufacturing concern; that is, inventories must be stated at the lower of cost or market. *Accounting Research Bulletin No. 43,* Chapter 4, "Inventory Pricing," states that "the term market means current replacement cost (by purchase or by production . . .) except that:

1. Market should not exceed the net realizable value (i.e., estimated selling price in the ordinary course of business less reasonably predictable costs of completion and disposal), and
2. Market should not be less than net realizable value reduced by an allowance for an approximately normal profit margin."

Major questions about the applicability and the application of the above principles are:

1. What types of real estate should be regarded as inventory and what should be regarded as a long-term investment?
2. Should cost of completion and disposal include the cost (especially interest cost) to carry the inventory to date of sale?
3. Should the above principles be applied to individual items or groups of items?

Once these questions are answered, net realizable value of real estate inventory can be calculated with only minor complications.

Inventory versus long-term investment. It is generally agreed that real estate held for sale falls in the category of inventory. The greatest difficulties arise in the classification of raw undeveloped land as between inventory and long-term investment. One view, which seems most appropriate, is that developers hold most raw land for future development and sale; since the land will in time become inventory, it should be classified as inventory. Another view is that the anticipated holding period should determine the classification (i.e., an anticipated long or indefinite holding period is evidence of a long-term investment).

On the other end of the spectrum, it is generally agreed that long-term investments should include (*a*) income producing properties held for long-term investment; (*b*) real estate used in the business; and (*c*) land held for use in development of (*a*) or (*b*).

Inclusion of interest in cost of completion and disposal. In manufacturing and commercial enterprises, interest is generally regarded as a period cost and excluded from inventory and from any calculation of net realizable value. However, most real estate development companies capitalize, as a cost, the interest incurred (*a*) during the holding period of land and (*b*) to completion of inventory or to the point inventory is ready for sale (see "Costs to Be Capitalized"). Interest incurred subsequently is usually treated as a period cost. Because market values prior to the mid-70s had been stable and generally increasing with the result that write-downs had not been common, the methods of calculating net realizable value were not reviewed thoroughly. The recession of the mid-70s brought this question sharply into focus, and the AICPA Real Estate Accounting Committee is currently studying this question. Practices with respect to the treatment of interest may be described very briefly as:

Calculate a net realizable value (as described earlier) excluding interest and—

1. Compare to net book value at the valuation date and reserve any excess over net realizable value (excluding interest to carry),
2. Add, to net book value, the cost of interest to carry the inventory to date of sale and reserve any excess over net realizable value,
3. Add, to the net book value, the cost of interest to carry the inventory to the point at which capitalization of interest is usually discontinued (completion, ready for sale, etc.) under the developer's accounting policy and reserve any excess over net

realizable value. If interest is not capitalized at all then future interest cost is not included in the calculation.

Current practice at December 31, 1975, varies, and all of the above may be in use to some extent. However, where interest has been considered to be a cost of the property for accounting purposes, it seems logical and consistent that future interest is also a cost of the property, with the result that the first method described above would not be appropriate. It appears from annual reports that the majority capitalize interest not *beyond* net realizable value but without describing the basis for calculation of net realizable value. It appears common, however, to consider future interest in the calculation in respect of obvious inventory items such as houses, condominiums, lots, and the like, but less common in respect of raw land.

The calculation of interest cost to be used in the calculation of net realizable value also varies from specific identification of debt with property to a calculation of average interest cost including equity. It seems appropriate to calculate future interest cost on a basis consistent with the developer's capitalization policy.

Valuation of inventories—group convention. ARB No. 43, Chapter 4, further states that "depending upon the character and composition of the inventory, the rule of cost or market, whichever is lower may properly be applied either directly to each item or to the total of the inventory (or, in some cases, to the total of the components of each major category). The method should be that which most clearly reflects periodic income. . . . The most common practice is to apply the lower of cost or market rule separately to each item of the inventory." The group convention was principally established for a manufacturing concern. For the group convention to be appropriate, there must be a high volume of transactions with each individual component of the group having approximately the same rate of turnover. Since this condition is not usually present in the real estate industry, the group convention is not normally used.

As a general rule, because of the relatively low volume and the significance of individual sales transactions in the real estate industry, the lower of cost or market test should be applied to each individual sales unit, except where the units are homogeneous such as units in a condominium project. In situations where the developer uses current market values to allocate costs to individual units, net realizable value as determined either on a project-by-project basis or on an individul unit basis should be the same.

Costs to be capitalized

A research study by the Canadian Institute of Chartered Accountants entitled *Accounting for Real Estate Development Operations,* sets forth the general premise, "land development costs are those costs that are directly attributable to the development of land and to its ownership during the period of the development." Additionally, the AICPA Industry Accounting Guide, *Accounting for Retail Land Sales,* states:

> Costs directly related to inventories of unimproved land or to construction required to bring land and improvements to a saleable condition are properly capitalizable until a saleable condition is reached. Those costs would include interest, real estate taxes and other direct costs incurred during the inventory and improvement periods.

While the propriety of capitalizing certain costs is obvious and does not warrant comment in this chapter, other costs are treated inconsistently in practice within the real estate industry and will be discussed below. They are the costs of interest, incremental (direct) overhead and selling, startup and preoperating, and amenities.

Interest and other carrying costs. A disagreement exists as to the proper accounting treatment of interest costs incurred in connection with development and construction of real estate properties held for either sale or investment. Proponents of capitalization argue that such interest costs are a necessary cost of the asset the same as "brick and mortar" costs. Proponents of charging off interest costs as a period cost argue that interest is solely a financing cost, a cost which varies directly with the capability of a company to finance the development and construction through equity funds. A similar disagreement can be cited concerning the accounting for other carrying costs such as real estate taxes and insurance.

These alternative approaches are recognized in the AICPA Industry Accounting Guide, *Accounting for Retail Land Sales.* The Guide states in paragraph 51 that "costs which may be capitalized" . . . include interest, real estate taxes, and other direct costs incurred during the inventory and improvement periods." However, paragraph 40 of the Guide recognized that certain companies expense interest and other carrying costs as period costs. It states, "Interest and project carrying costs incurred prior to sale on some projects may have already been charged to expense and would therefore not be included in cost of sales at the time the sale is recorded."

In November 1974, the SEC issued *Accounting Series Release No. 163,* "Capitalization of Interest by Companies Other Than Public Utilities." The release prohibits SEC reporting companies from adopting a policy of capitalizing interest in financial statements filed with the SEC for periods ending after June 21, 1974, unless the company had previously publicly disclosed an accounting policy of capitalizing interest costs (except for transactions covered by the AICPA Industry Accounting Guide, *Accounting for Retail Land Sales*). In addition, companies which previously disclosed an interest capitalization policy may not extend such policy to new types of assets.

The question of capitalization of interest is currently on the agenda of the Financial Accounting Standards Board.

A 1975 survey of accounting and reporting practices of real estate developers reported the following results regarding policies of capitalizing interest for 93 of 100 companies surveyed:

Interest capitalized:	
On all real estate	76
On properties under development and construction,	
but not undeveloped land	14
	90
Interest not capitalized.	3
	93

It was not determinable whether the other seven companies not disclosing capitalization policies capitalized or expensed interest.

Methods of interest capitalization. There are three primary methods of capitalizing interest used in practice by the real estate industry. The most predominant method used is the specific identification method. In accordance with the specific identification method, interest on all debt directly related to the properties would be capitalized.

The other two methods of capitalizing interest as used in the real estate industry, but to a far lesser degree, involve an allocation of all interest expense to all assets as follows:

1. Interest cost of specific identified debt is capitalized to the specific asset, and the remaining general interest cost for the period is allocated to all assets based upon the weighted average of the asset carrying values net of specific identified debt.
2. Total interest costs for the period are allocated to all assets based upon the weighted average of the gross asset carrying values during the period. The portion of interest allocated to real estate assets under development and construction is capitalized.

With respect to the 93 companies referred to above which did capitalize interest, 68 companies disclosed what type interest was being capitalized as follows:

Interest on debt directly related to the properties 59
Interest on directly related debt, plus an allocation of
   interest on general debt 8
Allocation of interest on all debt 1
                                                       68

When to stop capitalization. The point at which capitalization of interest and other carrying costs should stop is not clearly defined in authoritative literature, with the exception that capitalization of carrying costs should not result in a carrying value greater than net realizable value. The 1975 survey, cited previously, indicated that of 100 companies surveyed 57 companies disclosed the point to which interest costs were capitalized as follows:

Completion of construction 38
Date rental or sales operations begin 8
Certain percentage of occupancy or period of
   time after occupancy begins. 7
Date of sale 4
                                              57

In addition, 44 companies disclosed that capitalization was discontinued when the capitalization of such costs would result in a carrying cost in excess of net realizable value.

Overhead costs. It is generally accepted in practice to capitalize certain overhead costs which are directly related to the development and construction of real estate projects. The principal problem is in defining and identifying overhead costs to be capitalized. It would be appropriate to consider several questions prior to capitalization of overhead costs:

1. Is specific information available (such as timecards) to support the allocation of overhead costs?
2. Is the overhead cost incurred an incremental cost; that is, in absence of the project or projects under development or construction, would these costs have been incurred anyway?
3. Is the impact of capitalization of such overhead cost on the results of operations consistent with the pervasive principles of matching costs with related revenues?
4. Has the principle of conservatism been considered?

Selling costs. As a general rule, selling and advertising costs should be expensed as incurred. However, deferral of direct selling costs (e.g., salesperson's commission, title fees, and revenue stamps) is, at times, appropriate depending upon the accounting method utilized for profit recognition. For example, it would be appropriate to defer direct selling costs when using the deposit method of accounting. In addition, *APB Statement No. 4,* "Basic Concepts and Accounting Principles," provides that when using either the instalment or cost recovery method of accounting, costs directly associated with the revenue (which would include direct selling costs), should be recognized as expenses as the related revenue is recognized. These principles were also recognized in the AICPA Accounting Guide, *Accounting for Retail Land Sales.* Obviously, tests for net realizable value must also be considered when deferring selling costs.

Start-up and preoperating costs. Generally, established industrial and commercial companies have expensed start-up and preoperating costs in the period incurred. However, in an attempt to achieve a better matching of costs and revenues, certain real estate companies have deferred these expenses. Such costs might include project overhead, advertising and promotion costs, initial rent-up costs, and so on. Typically, the deferral of such costs is stopped when a specific event takes place (e.g., the initiation of an active sales program or when a certain level of occupancy is attained or when a predetermined period of time expires).

A 1975 survey of accounting and reporting practices of real estate developers reported that 14 of the 100 companies disclosed accounting policies of 15 instances of deferring start-up and preoperating costs applicable to a variety of operations. This represents a decrease from 17 companies of 100 for the previous year.

	Number of deferrals	*Amortization period*
Preoperating expenses of hotels, motor inns, and resort facilities	5	3–10 years
Start-up costs of rental properties until properties become operational	5	5–10 years or over period approximating term of major leases
Start-up costs of new housing or condominium projects until the projects open or deliveries have begun	2	1–5 years
Start-up costs relating to new region, branch, or division	2	2–3 years
Preopening costs relating to development of model home areas	1	Estimated sales period
	15	

Amenities. Real estate developments often include amenities such as golf courses, utilities, clubhouses, swimming pools, and tennis courts. The accounting for the costs of these amenities should be based upon management's intended disposition:

1. Amenities sold with sales units—costs should be allocated to cost of sales upon the sale of the related units.
2. Amenities to be sold separately—costs should be capitalized to the extent of the present value of anticipated proceeds on the sale. Costs, including expected operating losses prior to sale, in excess of anticipated proceeds should be allocated to cost of sales upon the sale of the related units.
3. Amenities to be retained by developer—unrecoverable costs incurred in developing amenities that are not expected to provide a return sufficient to recover costs of both operation and construction should be allocated to cost of sales upon the sale of the related units (after giving effect to the present value of amounts obtainable from operations, future sales, recovery, or salvage).

ALLOCATION OF COSTS

Costs to be allocated

Regardless of the size of a real estate development, the capitalizable costs can be summarized as follows:

1. Common to the entire development.
2. Common to only certain segments or projects within the development.
3. Related directly to the individual sales transaction.

The first two types of costs must be allocated in an appropriate manner to individual sales transactions.

Methods of cost allocation

The method used to allocate costs should accomplish the objective of matching costs with related revenues. A 1975 survey of accounting and reporting practices of real estate developers reported that 45 of 100 companies surveyed disclosed their cost allocation accounting policies. The following is a summary of the policies disclosed:

Method	*Number of companies*
Value	26
Area	18
Specific identification	2
Hybrid	7
	53

Note: Eight of the 45 companies indicated that they used different cost allocation methods depending upon the nature or size of the project.

Value method. As indicated in the survey results above, the value method is predominantly used in practice. Under this method, the allocation of costs is based on relative values such as estimated selling prices or appraised values. Although the Retail Land Sales Guide states that the value method may be applied using values either "gross or net after estimated future improvement costs," in developments which contain multiple forms of development, common costs are normally allocated based on estimated selling prices net of direct or indirect development and construction costs. This approach is preferred in practice as it is less likely to result in deferral of losses.

Example of value method. The following is an illustration of the use of the value method to allocate common costs for a condominium project which consists of three buildings, each being defined as an individual "project" for accounting purposes.

	Project		
	A	*B*	*C*
Number of units	75	75	100
Estimated sales value	$2,600,000	$3,000,000	$3,200,000
Less: Direct construction costs	1,800,000	2,100,000	2,500,000
Sales value net of direct costs (aggregate of $2,400,000)	$ 800,000	$ 900,000	$ 700,000
Allocation of common costs aggregating $1,500,000			
1,500,000 × 800,000/2,400,000	500,000		
1,500,000 × 900,000/2,400,000		562,500	
1,500,000 × 700,000/2,400,000			437,500
Gross Profit	$ 300,000	$ 337,500	$ 262,500
Percent of Sales	11.5%	11.3%	8.2%
Had the value method been applied based on gross sales value, the results would have been—			
Allocation of common costs	$ 443,200	$ 511,400	$ 545,400
Gross profit	356,800	388,600	154,600
Percent of sales	13.7%	13.0%	4.8%

Area method. This method of cost allocation is based upon square footage, acres, frontage, and so on. Often, the use of this method will not result in a logical allocation of costs. When negotiating the purchase price for a large tract of land, the purchaser considers the overall utility of the tract, recognizing that various parcels contained in the tract are more valuable than others. For example, parcels which are on a lake front are usually more valuable than those further back from the lake. In such a situation, if a simple average based on square footage or acreage was used to allocate costs to individual parcels, certain parcels could be assigned costs in excess of their net realizable value. Generally, the use of the area method should be limited to those situations where each individual parcel is estimated to have approximately the same relative value. Under such circumstances, the cost allocations as determined by either the area or value methods would be approximately the same.

FINANCIAL STATEMENT PRESENTATION

Balance sheet

Presentation of current assets and liabilities. Typically, the balance sheets of real estate companies are not classified so as to distinguish between current and noncurrent assets and liabilities. *Accounting Research Bulletin No. 43*, Chapter 3A, entitled "Current Assets and Current Liabilities," emphasizes that in determining current assets and liabilities, criteria developed must relate to the operating cycle of the business. The operating cycle is defined as the average time intervening between the acquisition of materials or services entering the business process and the final cash realization. The bulletin further states that:

> A one-year time period is to be used as a basis for the segregation of current assets in cases where there are several operating cycles occurring within a year. However, where the period of the operating cycle is more than twelve months, as in, for instance, the tobacco, distillery, and lumber businesses, the longer period should be used. Where a particular business has no clearly defined operating cycle, the one-year rule should govern.

While the operating cycle of a real estate company ordinarily exceeds one year, it is not possible in most instances to clearly define it precisely. Therefore, the classification of current assets and liabilities on the basis of the one-year rule would not be meaningful for most real estate companies. Both the *Accounting Research Bulletin* and the SEC Regulation S-X recognized that there may be exceptions to the general rule. SEC Regulation S-X provides some guidelines for disclosure in those circumstances whereby a company elects to present a classified balance sheet based on an operating cycle which exceeds more than one year.

A 1975 survey of accounting and reporting practices of real estate developers reported the following results with respect to the classification of balance sheets:

	1973 reports	1974 reports
Classified	22	10
Unclassified	64	74
	86	84

Arrangement of assets. The predominant method for real estate companies is to arrange assets in the order of liquidity (i.e., the order of expected conversion to cash). A second method is to arrange the assets in the order of significance to the operations of the company. In this case, the first assets listed might be "real estate" or "properties."

Grouping of real estate assets. Real estate assets should be grouped and presented in a manner which assists the reader of the financial statements to better understand the operations and financial position of the business. Real estate assets are usually grouped according to general classifications such as the following:

1. Unimproved land.
2. Land under development.
3. Residential lots.
4. Condominium and single-family dwellings.
5. Rental properties.

Offsetting nonrecourse debt against real estate properties. In the real estate industry, debt agreements secured by real property often provide that the lender has no recourse against the debtor in the event of default. When an event of default occurs, the lender can only seek to take possession and title to the related real property in settlement of the debt. Some accountants believe that the property should be net of the nonrecourse debt in the financial statements. However, *Accounting Principles Board Opinion No. 10* states that "It is a general principle of accounting that the offsetting of assets and liabilities in the balance sheet is improper except where a right of offset exists." Under the going concern concept of accounting, the real property theoretically will not be utilized in payment of the nonrecourse debt and thus, the nonrecourse debt would not be offset against the real property in the balance sheet. The Securities and Exchange Commission, *Staff Accounting Bulletin No. 1*, indicates that offsetting is not appropriate. However, some developers do disclose in a note to the financial statements the amount of and the interrelationship of the nonrecourse debt with the cost of the related properties. A 1975 survey of annual reports of real estate developers did not disclose any examples of offsetting mortgage debt against the related property in the balance sheet.

Income statement

As a general rule, it is desirable to classify revenues and cost of sales or operations by principal sources or type of activity. Typically, these classifications will be similar to those used for inventories. Such disclosure assists the reader of the financial statements to understand better the results of operations of the business.

To further assist the readers of financial statements, the Securities and Exchange Commission issued SEC *Release 11079* which requires that annual reports to shareholders of SEC reporting companies must contain disclosure of various data previously required for inclusion only in filings with the SEC. One of the significant requirements of the release was disclosure by lines of business. The impact of this requirement is unclear, as many developers consider themselves to be only in one line of business.

Statement of changes in financial position

Accounting Principles Board Opinion No. 19, "Reporting Changes in Financial Position," requires that a statement summarizing the changes in financial position be presented as a basic financial statement for each period for which an income statement is presented. Statements of changes in financial position of real estate companies usually comprise changes in cash rather than changes in working capital, as they usually do not distinguish between current and noncurrent assets and liabilities. The 1975 survey of accounting and reporting practices of real estate developers reported the following results with respect to presentation of changes in financial position by 84 real estate companies:

Cash	62
Cash and marketable securities	11
Working capital	10
Other	1
Total Companies	84

Other disclosures

The following is a discussion of certain financial statement disclosures which are appropriate in the financial statements of a real estate developer as opposed to a manufacturing or service enterprise. This discussion is not intended to cover disclosure requirements for retail lot sales, which are set forth in the *Retail Land Sales Guide.*

Principles of income recognition.   The methods of income recognition (e.g., completed contract, closing method, percentage of completion method, instalment method, etc.) should be disclosed. When more than one method is utilized for similar projects, a company should disclose the circumstances under which each method is used. When the percentage of completion method is utilized to account for condominium sales, disclosure is sometimes made of the minimum percentage of units which must be sold and the minimum percentage of construction which must be completed before the entity begins profit recognition.

Because of the complexity of real estate transactions, it is appropriate to disclose also the time of recording the sale and related income (i.e., at closing, at time of sale, etc.). Where the initial valuation of the consideration includes imputation of interest (in accordance with *APB Opinion No. 21*), the interest rates used should be disclosed.

The method of allocating cost to unit sales should be disclosed (i.e., relative market values, area, unit, specific identification, etc.). Disclosure should include how market is determined when inventory is carried at an amount lower than cost.

Capitalization policies.   Generally, financial statement disclosure should include, where applicable, the following:

1. Capitalization policies for interest, property taxes, and other carrying costs including point to which such costs are capitalized.
2. Policies for deferral of start-up or preoperating expenses, including the method and period of amortization.

In November 1974, the SEC issued *Accounting Series Release No. 163,* "Capitalization of Interest by Companies Other Than Public Utilities." The release requires the following disclosure for companies reporting to the SEC which follow a policy of capitalizing interest:

1. Interest capitalized must be shown in the income statement.
2. The reason for the policy of interest capitalization and the way in which the amount of interest capitalized is determined.
3. The effect on net income for each period for which an income

statement is presented of following a policy of capitalizing interest as compared to a policy of charging interest to expense as incurred.

Commitments and contingencies. Exceptionally large commitments, particularly those arising other than in the ordinary course of business, should be disclosed. Such commitments might include, among other items, commitments to purchase (or construct) real estate; to purchase long-term investments; to provide financing to affiliates, including joint ventures; and to guarantee debt of others. In addition, real estate companies often sell properties subject to permanent mortgages. When a company remains contingently liable for such mortgages assumed by others, the amounts of the mortgages should be disclosed.

Uncertainties. In 1974 the SEC issued *Accounting Series Release No. 166*, "Disclosure of Unusual Risks and Uncertainties in Financial Reporting," which requires that any SEC reporting company disclose in its financial statements significant changes in the degree of business uncertainty of the company.

Cash flow versus earnings per share. SEC *Accounting Series Release No. 142* states that "per share data other than that relating to net income, net assets and dividends should be avoided in reporting financial results." The release was issued to limit certain presentations of per share data relating to cash flow.

Joint ventures. Most of the disclosures required for joint ventures are included in paragraph 20 of *APB Opinion No. 18* for investments which are significant, either individually or in the aggregate, to an investor's financial statements.

SELECTED REFERENCES

"Accounting for Condominium Sales." Price Waterhouse & Co., July 1975.

AICPA "Accounting for Nonmonetary Transactions," *Accounting Principles Board Opinion No. 29*. New York, May 1973.

———— "Interest on Receivables and Payables," *Accounting Principles Board Opinion No. 21*. New York, August 1971.

———— "The Equity Method of Accounting for Investments in Common Stock," *Accounting Principles Board Opinion No. 18*. New York, March 1971, and an Interpretation issued in November 1971.

Canadian Institute of Chartered Accountants "Accounting for Real Estate Development Operations," *A Research Study*. Toronto, 1971.

Colemon, H. A., ed. "Financing Real Estate Development." Englewood: The American Institute of Architects, 1974.

"Investor Accounting for Real Estate Joint Ventures." Price Waterhouse & Co., February 1975.

Office of Interstate Land Sales Registration, U.S. Department of Housing and Urban Development "Condominium and Other Construction Contracts." *Federal Register,* vol. 39, No. 41 (February 28, 1974).

"Q&A: Real Estate Transactions." Marvin L. Baris, Coopers & Lybrand, 1973.

Real Estate Developers *1975 Survey of Accounting and Reporting Practices,* Price Waterhouse & Co.

Securities and Exchange Commission "Accounting for Real Estate Transactions Where Circumstances Indicate the Profits Were Not Earned at the Time the Transactions Were Recorded," December 28, 1962.

—— "Advertising and Sales Practices in Connection with Offers and Sales of Securities Involving Condominium Units and Other Units in Real Estate Developments," *Release No. 5382.* April 1973.

—— "Capitalization of Interest by Companies Other than Public Utilities," *Accounting Series Release No. 163.* November 14, 1974.

—— "Disclosure of Unusual Risks and Uncertainties in Financial Reporting," *Accounting Series Release No. 166.* December 23, 1974.

—— "Guidelines as to the Applicability of the Federal Securities Laws to Offers and Sales of Condominiums or Units in a Real Estate Development," *Release No. 5347.* January 4, 1973.

—— "Reporting Cash Flow and Other Related Data," *Accounting Series Release No. 142.* March 15, 1973.

—— *Staff Accounting Bulletin No. 1.*

Chapter 42

Earnings measurement and return on investment of franchise sales companies

Charles Evans *
Charles Calhoun †

Definition of franchising

Any discussion of a franchise sales company or the measurement of its earnings must begin with a rather comprehensive definition of franchising itself. *Franchising* has been described as simply a method of distribution and a technique for financing growth. However, a study by The Conference Board entitled "Some Guideposts to Definition" elaborates further on a set of general criteria to be met if an arrangement is to be considered a franchise.[1] These criteria are:

1. The relationship between the parties is contractual and for a specified period of time.
2. The purpose of the relationship is the efficient distribution of a product, service, or business concept.

---

* Treasurer, ServAmerica, Inc.

† Department of Accounting, University of South Carolina.

[1] E. Patrick McGuire, *Franchised Distribution*, Report No. 253 (New York: The Conference Board, Inc., 1971), p. 3.

3. Both parties contribute resources toward the establishment and maintenance of the franchise.
4. The contract outlines certain standards and practices of operating procedure to which both parties agree to conform.
5. The relationship creates a business entity which will, in most cases, require and support the full-time business activity of the franchisee.
6. Both the franchisee and franchisor participate in a common public identity.

Consequently, the *franchise sales company* is probably best defined as a company engaged in the sale of rights to others. These rights might include the use or sale of a product, service, process, brand name, trademark, or business method which has been developed by or is the property of the franchise sales company.

Distinction between franchise and license

It seems appropriate to discuss briefly the similarities and contrasts between the terms *franchise* and *license*. These terms are used almost interchangeably in the literature, as well as in actual contracts. Many contracts include both terms, and it is generally unclear whether the contract intends to make any distinction. In many contracts compensation is discussed in terms of a royalty fee, which appears to be a payment for the use of the trademarks and seems therefore to be tied to a license; however, several of these same contracts also include a franchise fee which is attached to the franchise itself.[2]

As a practical matter there are at least two reasons for making the distinction between franchise and license:

1. The federal taxation of receipts to the franchisor may be different.
2. Franchise fees are commonly associated with the initial fee, and license fees are generally associated with continuing fee receipts. The financial reporting of these receipts may differ if, in fact, this distinction is appropriate.

---

[2] See Charles H. Calhoun, III, "Accounting by Franchising Corporations for Franchise Sales: Revenue Recognition and Receivable Valuation" (D.B.A. dissertation, Florida State University, 1973), pp. 23–24, for several examples of actual contracts.

Let us now examine the various types of consideration that may be received by the franchise company.

Consideration given for the franchise

The sale of a franchise usually calls for consideration to be paid to the franchise sales company (the *franchisor*) by the buyer (the *franchisee*). This consideration normally takes the form of an *initial fee* which represents compensation for establishing the relationship, some form of *continuing fees* which are paid for the continuing rights granted under the agreement, and possibly *other forms of continuing revenue* generally associated with the sale of products or for providing services such as advertising and record keeping.

Hagler describes the relationship between the franchisor and the franchisee as follows:

1. The franchisee invests money (the franchise fee), and the franchisor contributes "know-how." The franchisor uses the fee to cover costs of setting up the franchise unit and making it operational.
2. When the unit is operational, the franchisor receives a royalty. The franchisee receives the remaining net profits.
3. The franchisee operates the franchise outlet on a day-to-day basis, making routine decisions, but many of the major decisions are made by the franchisor.[3]

Earnings measurement of franchise sales companies poses two major problems: the *recognition of revenue* in the proper period and the proper *matching of costs* with that revenue, which may entail deferral of certain related costs and expenses. While these problems are not unique to franchise sales companies, certain aspects of the problems are not generally faced by other industries.

During the franchise decade, that is, 1960–69, numerous new franchise sales companies were organized and financed by the public through the issuance of a variety of securities. Earnings which many accountants felt should have accrued to future accounting periods were being run through the current income statement in accordance with a revenue procedure known as "immediate recognition." Other diverse accounting practices of franchise companies, relating mainly to recognition of revenue from initial franchise fees, caused the

---

[3] J. L. Hagler, "The Franchise Fee," *Management Accounting*, July 1974, p. 50.

investment community to show an increasing lack of confidence in the financial statements of many franchise sales companies.[4] A January 1970 article by Archibald MacKay in the *Journal of Accountancy* soon became accepted as the AICPA's unofficial position on the recognition of franchise fee revenue.[5] The February 1973 publication of an Industry Guide entitled *Accounting for Franchise Fee Revenue* essentially incorporated MacKay's article into an "official" AICPA position.[6] Without debating the merits of the AICPA's position at this point, suffice it to note that there are those who disagree with the treatment "encouraged" by the Accounting Guide.[7]

RECOGNITION OF REVENUE

Initial fees

The single most difficult problem in measuring earnings of the franchise sales company is the recognition of revenue from initial franchise sales or fees in the proper accounting period. These initial fees are generally paid to the franchisor by the franchisee as consideration for *establishing the franchise relationship.* This includes certain *key initial services,* such as: (1) adequate training programs for the franchisee and/or key employees, (2) assistance to the franchisee in selecting the location of the franchise operating unit, (3) initial advertising and promotion assistance, (4) installation of accounting and information systems, (5) protection of territorial rights, (6) operating manuals and procedural guides, and (7) providing franchisor personnel to assist in opening the franchise unit.

Because this initial fee may be, in part at least, consideration for intangible rights, revenue recognition in the proper accounting period may become complicated.

The American Institute of Certified Public Accountants' Industry Accounting Guide, *Accounting for Franchise Fee Revenue,* discusses several bases of recognizing revenue from these sources which have

---

[4] J. Richard Elliott, "Speculative Bellyache?" *Barron's,* August 25, 1969, pp. 3, 17–19; "Sticky Fingers?" *Barron's,* September 15, 1969, pp. 3, 14, 18, 22; "Home to Roost," *Barron's,* September 22, 1969, p. 5; and "Chicken Delight?" *Barron's* September 29, 1969, p. 5.

[5] Archibald E. MacKay, "Accounting for Initial Franchise Fee Revenue," *Journal of Accountancy,* January, 1970, pp. 66–72.

[6] AICPA, *Accounting for Franchise Fee Revenue* (New York, 1973).

[7] Charles H. Calhoun III, "Accounting for Franchise Fee Revenue: Is It a Dead Issue," *Journal of Accountancy,* February 1975.

been previously used and/or advocated. These various bases are: (1) the cash basis, (2) spreading revenue over the life of the agreement, (3) recognizing revenue at the date of execution of the franchise contract, and (4) recognizing revenue on substantial performance by the franchisor of its contractual obligations.[8] All of the methods, other than the substantial performance method, have been deemed by the Committee on Franchise Accounting and Auditing to be deficient for the reasons discussed below.

Cash basis. The receipt of cash does not, in and of itself, generate revenue and is not a reliable method of recognizing revenue. The recognition of revenue in accordance with the rules of accrual accounting is based on the concept of *earning*. Until goods have been delivered or services rendered, revenue has not been earned. The receipt of cash is often unrelated to the earning process.[9]

Example 1:

Worldwide Foods, Inc., sells five franchises in December 1975. Initial fees per unit are $10,000; 50 percent is received at signing, and the remainder is due upon the determination of a mutually agreeable location. The $5,000 down payment is to cover costs associated with the location efforts. The 1975 financial statement of Worldwide should not include the $25,000 as income; it has not been "earned."

The cash basis illustrated above is the *cash receipts* basis. Other cash bases include the *cost recovery* method and the *installment sales* method. These will be discussed briefly in the section dealing with collectibility considerations.

Spread revenue over life of agreement. Most franchise contracts cover a specific period of time (usually a relatively long period); however, recognition of revenue over this period does not give adequate consideration to the substantial, and sometimes costly, initial services provided by the franchisor. Once these obligations and services are performed by the franchisor, the initial fee is usually nonrefundable.

The decision as to whether or not the franchise fee revenue should be spread over the life of the contract should be based on a comparison of the amount of the initial fee with the cost of services

---

[8] AICPA, *Accounting for Franchise Fee Revenue.*

[9] E. H. Kohler, *A Dictionary for Accountants*, 4th ed. (New York: Prentice-Hall, Inc., 1970), p. 78.

provided for that fee. No one is in a better position to make that judgment than the accounting management of the franchise firm. On what basis was the franchise fee established? Does the fee cover only the cost of initial services and some reasonable rate of return, or is the fee totally unrelated to initial services?

Example 2:

Straight-Arrow Business Methods, Inc., has established an initial franchise fee of $12,500 determined as follows:

Cost of site selection	$ 2,000
Initial advertising and promotion	1,000
Home office training of franchisee	4,000
Overhead allocation—operating manuals, etc.	1,000
Personnel assistance for opening week	2,000
	$10,000
Add-on for profit and other overhead	2,500
Total	$12,500

The term of the franchise agreement is ten years.

Assuming the validity of these costs, it appears highly unlikely that the $10,000 (not to mention the $2,500) could be considered to be earned over the life of the contract. Therefore, spreading revenue recognition over the life of the contract is inappropriate unless management has established a significant initial fee intended to compensate the franchisor for granting the franchisee the use of intangible rights over the contract's term.

Recognize revenue at date of execution of franchise contract. The execution of a contract does not imply a consummated transaction. The franchise contract usually calls for the performance of services by the franchisor, and indeed the initial franchise fee is, in part, consideration for those services. Revenue should not be recognized before services are rendered by the franchisor.

Example 3:

Bump-Hustle Dance Schools, Inc., has just completed the signing of an agreement with a franchisee for an initial fee of $7,500 and a term of five years. The franchisee has paid $1,500 down and will pay the remainder based on various measures of success for the franchise.

Clearly the fact that the contract has been negotiated does not mean that the franchisor has "earned" the initial fee. This type of "immediate recognition" was one of the questionable reporting practices employed by some franchise firms in the 1960s.

Recognize revenue on substantial performance. Substantial performance is said to have occurred when a seller has performed all, or essentially all, of the services required of him or her. At the same time the seller has a valid claim against the purchaser to be compensated for the services performed. In accordance with this theory, initial franchise fee revenue should be recognized in the accounting period in which the initial franchise transaction has been consummated; that is, when substantially all of the services contracted for by the franchisee to be performed by the franchisor have been performed.[10]

Due to the practical difficulty in determining the adequate performance of certain of these services, such as consultation, advice, and so on, MacKay proposed—and the AICPA adopted—the requirement that substantial performance be signaled upon the opening of the franchisee operation for business. This method has met with considerable acceptance because of the ease in determining when it occurs and the fact that most of the required franchisor services have been performed at opening date.[11] The method is based on the concept that the function of the franchisor is to put the franchisee into business, not just to grant franchises. Obviously, good judgment must prevail in applying this general rule. If the franchisor performs all of its obligations under the contract and the franchisee never opens for business, strict adherence to the rule would improperly defer revenue beyond when it is actually earned. However, if receivables are involved, proper valuation becomes an additional concern.

Example 4:

On September 5, 1975, John Smythe enters into a franchise contract with Franchisor International, Inc., to open and operate a specialty clothing outlet under the Franchisor International, Inc., franchisor system. Mr. Smythe pays $10,000 upon execution of the contract as an initial franchise fee and agrees to pay 2 percent of gross revenue as a continuing fee, or royalty. Franchisor International agrees to assist Mr. Smythe in selecting an operating site, to train Mr. Smythe in the Franchisor

---

[10] AICPA, *Accounting for Franchise Fee Revenue.*

[11] MacKay, "Accounting for Initial Franchise Fee Revenue."

International, Inc., method, and to assist Mr. Smythe with a preopening advertising campaign. Mr. Smythe opens for business on January 10, 1976. Franchisor International, Inc., reports on a calendar year basis.

Under the *substantial performance* method of recognizing revenue from initial franchise fees, the entries relating to revenue recognition only would be as follows:

September 5, 1975	Dr.	Cr.
Cash	10,000	
Deferred Franchise Revenue		10,000
January 10, 1976		
Deferred Franchise Revenue	10,000	
Franchise Fee Revenue		10,000

Obviously, this method might defer recognition of revenue from one accounting period to another, as exhibited by Example 4. This revenue basis recognizes, however, that Franchisor International, Inc., has significant obligations to perform under the franchise contract before the $10,000 initial franchise fee is earned. The costs incurred in performing the obligations and the related accounting treatment of those costs are discussed below.

Royalties (continuing fees)

Royalties, or continuing fees, are paid by the franchisee to the franchisor over the life of the contract as consideration for the continuing franchise relationship (the use of the intangible rights owned by the franchisor) and for continuing services which are rendered by the franchisor to the franchisee. These services might include field supervision, quality inspections, new product innovations, centralized purchasing, and record-keeping assistance. The amount of the royalty fee is determined by one of two systems. Most common is a fee that is stated as a *percentage of gross sales* of the franchisee. Other franchisors use a *flat rate charge* that is *based on units sold.*

The amount the franchisor will receive is therefore based to some degree on the success of the franchisee. If the intangible assets of the franchisor are valuable from the standpoint of attracting customers to the franchisee's place of business, this may be important evidence that the fee is the primary source of revenue that compensates the franchise company for the transfer of the intangible rights.

It is possible that intangible rights may serve as a basis for the royalty fee. A former treasurer of the International Franchise Association, Ray Burch, related his opinion of the relationship between the intangible rights conferred and royalty fee in the following statement:

> It is the use of a trademark which almost invariably distinguishes true franchising from spurious "franchising." . . . Granting the use of a trademark or service mark for a fee or royalty is indeed the essence of the franchise relationship. This is recognized by the definition of 'franchise' in the California Investment Law, the International Franchise Association's "Model Bill," and by most other state laws to regulate franchising. . . .[12]

The collection of royalty fees appears to be the primary method that companies engaged in franchising services have adopted to compensate them for the use of their trademark or trade name. The franchisor uses the royalty fee to compensate it for allowing the franchisee to be a part of the system developed by the franchisor. When little or no cost is incurred for the continuing services that are provided to the member units of the franchise system, the willingness of members of the system to pay a continuing royalty fee would appear to confirm that the royalty fee is in payment of the intangible rights conferred. When this situation exists and a franchisor also charges an initial fee, but provides several initial services, it is likely that the initial fee includes no charge for the intangible rights conferred. These royalties should be recognized as revenue on the accrual basis when the fees are earned and become due from the franchisee. Related expenses should be matched as closely as possible with that revenue.

Other sources of revenue

Other common sources of revenue of the franchise sales company include product sales to the franchisee, area franchise sales, and management fees.

Under certain agreements, some or all of the *products marketed* by the franchisee are sold to the franchisee by the franchisor. When

---

[12] "Dear F.T.C. . . . ," *Franchise Journal*, July, 1972, p. 12.

the franchisor has no equity interest in the franchisee, no particular accounting problems arise. Revenue should be recognized on the conventional basis of when the sale transaction is consummated.

Area franchise sales generally arise by the sale of geographical territorial rights to a middle person franchisee, who in turn sells individual franchise outlet rights to others. These arrangements are generally quite complex; however, the same criteria used for initial franchise fees should be used to recognize revenue from area franchise sales. It should be noted that under many area sales arrangements the franchisor has no further substantial obligation to the franchisee after the sale. Under these conditions, the substantial performance criteria should have been met at contract date and revenue would be recognized at that time.

While the sale of territorial franchises can be an important source of revenue to corporations which sell them, a note of caution must be issued. Territorial sales should not be considered a continuing source of revenue, because as more franchises are sold, the remaining area diminishes and eventually sources of revenue from territorial franchises will disappear. Disclosure of this situation should be made in published financial reports.

Management fees are charged by the franchisor when it operates the franchised unit for the franchisee owner. These arrangements are made generally when absentee-owner franchisees are involved and are not available to manage the franchise outlet. No special problems are encountered when recognizing revenue from management fees. Revenue should be recognized on the accrual basis at the time when the fees are due from the franchisee.

Collectibility considerations

Collectibility considerations usually present no unusual problems with regard to revenue recognition of initial franchise fees. The essential key to recognition is still the "earning process." When the consideration paid to the franchisor for initial franchise fees is in a form other than cash (usually receivables of some nature), an investigation must be made to determine the collectibility of those receivables. Appropriate reserves should be established if possible. However, there may be some limited situations in which the adoption of a cash basis is acceptable. The cost recovery method or the installment sales method may be used in unusual circumstances.

The *cost recovery method* is one of the AICPA's exceptions to the general rule disallowing the use of a cash basis in recognizing revenue. Periodic cash receipts are first applied to the recovery of any expenses incurred in making the sale, and after all expenses are covered, additional receipts are recognized as income. This procedure is considered to be applicable only for long-term contracts where there is extreme uncertainty as to the ultimate receipt of payment. As receipt takes place revenue is recognized, but equal amounts of expense are matched to this revenue so that no profit is recognized until all costs have been covered.[13]

Installment sales are sales made on terms whereby the purchaser agrees to pay for the purchase over a specific period of time by a series of periodic payments. Usually, but not always, a cash down payment precedes the periodic payments.[14] The installment sales method recognizes revenue in conjunction with the receipt of the periodic payments. The amount of revenue so recognized is a portion of the gross margin (total contract price less total estimated contract costs) that will be received over the term of the contract. The same circumstances necessitating the cost recovery method exist for the application of the installment sales method except that the ability is present to make a reasonable estimate of the total cost to be incurred in performing the contract. When these costs can be reasonably estimated, the ratio of gross profit to total contract price can be determined and multiplied by the payments received in a period to compute the amount to be taken into income during that period. The use of the installment basis receives its authoritative support from certain pronouncements of the AICPA.[15]

Most franchisors do not accept notes in payment of the initial franchise fee, so the potential application of these methods is limited. It is also unlikely that a franchisor would willingly accept notes that are highly likely to prove uncollectible. However, it is possible that some franchisees will default on their obligations. The credit policy of the franchise firm may require modification if the facts indicate a high rate of uncollectibility. Even in the few cases where franchisors do accept notes for a portion of the franchise fee, reasonable estimates of uncollectibles can usually be made by using

---

[13] AICPA, *Accounting Research Bulletin No. 43* (New York, 1953), chap. 1, sec. A, par. 1.

[14] Kohler, *A Dictionary for Accountants*, p. 234.

[15] AICPA, Accounting Principles Board, "Omnibus Opinion—1966," *Opinion No. 10* (New York, 1966), par. 12.

historical results, industry averages, aging, or some other method. The Industry Accounting Guide mentions the installment sales basis of revenue recognition but clearly discloses the exceptional circumstances that must exist before it is acceptable.

DEFERRAL OF COSTS AND EXPENSES

The discussion of revenues has touched on several inherent problems, but has centered finally on the *timing* of revenue as the most critical problem in accounting for franchise fee revenue. Almost the same questions arise when seeking the appropriate method of accounting for the related expenses. Again, the critical problem is timing.

The concept of *matching costs and revenues* applicable to commercial companies presents certain unique problems to the franchise sales company, mainly as it relates to initial franchise fees.[16] The substantial performance doctrine which should be applied to the recognition of revenue, according to the AICPA, is the key to proper cost deferral. The cost of services and expenses which are directly associated with a specific franchise sale and are expended in connection with the franchisor's performance of contractual obligations under the franchise contract should be deferred until the revenue from that sale is recognized. These costs and expenses are usually incurred by the franchisor in performing the key initial services called for by the franchise contract and have been discussed above.

The difficulty in determining which costs to defer is due to the fact that the initial franchise fee of some franchise companies is for both services and *intangible rights*, and the costs incurred related to that revenue may be irregular, nonrecurring, or related to a specific franchise contract under which revenue has been deferred. An analysis of all franchisor incremental expenses must be made to determine whether or not they qualify for deferral and subsequent matching with deferred revenue. Obviously, deferred costs should not be allowed to exceed expected revenues, in that the application of the doctrine of conservatism would require recognition of the loss in the accounting period in which the loss is determined.

---

[16] For a theoretical discussion of "The Matching Concept," see American Accounting Association, 1964 Concepts and Standards Research Study Committee, "The Matching Concept," *The Accounting Review*, April 1965, p. 369; and Delmer P. Hylton, "On Matching Revenue with Expense," *The Accounting Review*, October 1965, p. 826.

Deferral of expense recognition is necessary for those costs which are directly related to the sale of a franchise but for which the revenue from the sale has not been recognized. Examples of types of costs which may properly require deferral are:

1. Sales commissions.
2. Specific site selection expenses, such as travel and real estate commissions.
3. The cost of training the franchisee and/or his or her designates.
4. Direct local initial advertising costs.
5. Trademark registration costs for specific countries or areas.

Example 5:

Assume the same facts as in Example 4 above. Franchisor International, Inc., incurred costs relating to Mr. Smythe's franchise of $6,000. These represented a sales commission to the marketing organization which sold Mr. Smythe the franchise and other direct costs related to setting up the franchise unit and making it operational. The entries are:

September 5, 1975	*Dr.*	*Cr.*
Deferred Franchise Costs	6,000	
Accounts Payable		6,000

January 10, 1976		
Franchise Costs and Expenses	6,000	
Deferred Franchise Costs		6,000

Reviewing the entries of Examples 4 and 5 shows the effects of the sale of the franchise to Mr. Smythe on 1975 financial statements. There is no revenue recognized in connection with the Smythe franchise sale. The balance sheet shows $10,000 deferred franchise revenue in the liability section and $6,000 of deferred franchise costs in the asset section. Financial statements for 1976 would reflect franchise revenue of $10,000, together with direct costs of $6,000, or a contribution to fixed costs of $4,000.

Other franchise company costs and expenses which are fixed and are related to the general sales and administrative functions should be expensed when incurred.

Alternatives to substantial performance

The accounting management of franchising corporations is not totally locked in by the recommendation of the AICPA to use the *substantial performance* basis of revenue recognition. Recommenda-

tions of an industry audit guide are not binding on members of the
accounting profession to the extent that *APB Opinions* are binding.
If in the opinion of the accountant the application of another
method provides more meaningful financial reporting, some other
method may be used. In addition, the use of another method which
is at variance with the industry accounting guide need not be disclosed in the financial statements, nor does it require the auditor
to qualify his or her opinion.[17]

Several articles have suggested that the *percentage-of-completion*
method of accounting should be applied to the initial franchise fee
if the fee includes little or no compensation for the transfer of intangible rights granted the franchisee. Corporate accountants know
how the fee was developed, what initial services are to be provided
for the fee, and the costs that are associated with those services. The
completion of a particular service should trigger the recognition of
revenue; the recognition of cost expiration can be needlessly postponed by using the substantial performance method.

USE OF CAPITAL

There are many reasons that franchising came into existence and
has grown to the point that it is now a significant sector of the
economy. One reason franchising has evolved to its present size is
that franchising corporations may expand their market influence
without the use of large amounts of capital. *Franchised Distribution*
stated that:

> Often, the single most important reason for adopting franchised
> distribution would be to conserve or acquire capital, while at the
> same time attempting to establish an effective distribution network
> as quickly as possible. . . .
>
> John Y. Brown, President of Kentucky Fried Chicken Corporation,
> has stated that it would have required $450 million for his company
> to have established its first 2,700 stores. This sum was simply not
> available to his corporation during the initial stages of its hoped-for
> expansion. . . .
>
> The franchise company that sells franchises to its distributors not
> only accumulates interest-free capital but also enjoys a good deal

[17] Charles H. Calhoun, III, "Accounting for Franchise Sales: Is Substantial Performance the Answer?" *The National Public Accountant* (March 1975), p. 13.

of discretion on how the funds are to be employed. This is not the case with many other types of funding arrangements, some of which restrict the loan funds to specific areas of corporate activity.[18]

This view of franchising as a method of raising capital to expand an organization is one which must be examined closely when attempting to determine the return on investment of a franchise sales company. The funds which are raised in this manner do not appear as paid-in capital on the balance sheet, and the cost of this capital does not appear on the income statement. The net effect shows up as "earnings" in the form of continuing royalty fees and initial fees less related costs.

Hagler views the initial franchise fee as an investment transaction rather than a revenue transaction, stating:

> In reporting . . . to stockholders, the franchise fee would be reported as "contributed capital from franchisees." Those expenses related to the sale . . . would be estimated and accrued at the same time. These costs would be charged against the capital in the same manner as costs related to the issuance of securities.[19]

Example 6:

Assume the same facts as in Examples 4 and 5. The entries under the *investment concept* would be:

	Dr.	Cr.
Cash	10,000	
Capital Contributed from Franchises		4,000
Estimated Franchise Cost Payable		6,000

This method of accounting for initial franchise fees, while not generally accepted, would provide a much different picture of invested capital in the equity section of a franchise sales company. This new invested capital base would include the contributions of shareholders plus those of the franchisees. Earnings from franchising (royalties) and related activities (equipment, sales, etc.) could then be related to this expanded invested capital to arrive at return on investment. In order to arrive at realistic return on investment results under this view, recognition of the significant capital contribution from the franchisees is necessary.

A study by Bernstein also suggested somewhat similar alternative

---

[18] McGuire, *Franchised Distribution*, pp. 6–7.
[19] Hagler, "The Franchise Fee."

reporting procedures. In his discussion of various alternatives he made the following comments:

> The franchisor exerts substantial control over the operations of his franchisees. The extent of this control is similar to that exercised by a parent corporation over its subsidiaries. In addition, the franchisor often invests heavily in franchise units, and assumes substantial financial risk. He also receives a royalty or share of the profits from his franchisees, which tend to make the franchisor somewhat of a partner. Consequently, the continued profitability of the franchisor is dependent upon the success of his franchisees.
>
> . . . A franchisor may, in substance, control the operations of hundreds of individual franchise units. Nevertheless, under current reporting procedures, *the franchisor is never held accountable for this vast area of control.* In addition, *the financial interdependencies between the franchisor and his franchisees are not disclosed.* . . .
>
> . . . The continued profitability and stability of the franchisor are a function of the success of the individual franchise units. . . .
>
> . . . Current reporting procedures do not provide financial statements for franchisees. As a result, investors, creditors, and potential franchisees are unable to estimate the future stability and profitability of the franchisor. . . .[20]

The appropriate numbers to use in making return on investment calculations would seem to depend in part on the relative position and viewpoint of the person making the calculation.

Example 7:

The controller of Pieright Franchise, Inc., is preparing to determine the rate of return on capital invested by the corporate shareholders. In making this calculation the controller considers corporate philosophy to include the following:

1. Franchising was especially selected as a means of expansion so that no additional stockholder capital would be required.
2. The company has absolutely no plans to acquire any franchise units from franchisees.

---

[20] Michael M. Bernstein, "Accounting and Reporting for Business Franchises" (unpublished doctoral dissertation, University of California, Los Angeles, 1970), pp. 155–57.

In light of this, the controller would not treat the franchise fee as part of equity capital in measuring return on investment.

TAXATION OF FRANCHISE SALES

The tax concerns of the franchisor company are very similar in many respects to those of any other business. This section of the chapter is intended to provide only a brief discussion of the tax consequences that attach to the transfer of a franchise and to the payments received by the franchisor from franchisees.

Amounts received other than initial fees

Amounts received by the franchisor for management services, sales of product, or in connection with contingent fees (usually based on a percentage of gross franchisee sales) are taxed in the period in which the receipts are earned. These receipts are taxed as ordinary income.[21]

Example 8:

Freezee Corporation requires its franchisees to pay 4 percent of their monthly gross sales as a continuing royalty. During August the gross sales of franchisees totaled $800,000. Freezee Corporation would report $32,000 of ordinary income related to those sales.

Initial fees

The tax treatment accorded the receipt of initial fees by franchisors was an area of much controversy, so in 1969 Congress enacted Section 1253 with a view toward ending the confusion. Section 1253 provides a set of basic guidelines to be used in determining the proper tax treatment. These guidelines are summarized as follows:

The effect of Section 1253 is essentially to disallow capital gains treatment on receipts because franchisors usually retain a "significant power, right, or continuing interest" because of contractual and operating relationships they establish with their franchisees.[22]

---

[21] IRC, Sec. 1253 (c); Prop. Reg. Sec. 1.1253-1 (b).

[22] Charles H. Calhoun, III and Dale L. Davison, "Tax Aspects of Franchising," *Tax Ideas* (Englewood Cliffs, N.J.: Prentice-Hall, Inc., 1975), par. 25,038.3.

It is possible that the initial fee might be accorded capital gains treatment in certain circumstances, but in most cases it will likely be taxed as ordinary income. Even if the franchisor company does not retain a "proprietary interest" in its franchisees, the IRS may adopt the position that the individual franchises constitute property held primarily for sale in the ordinary course of business.[23]

If corporate management is uncertain as to the tax status of initial franchise fees, the matter may be researched in the sources cited.

SUMMARY

The solutions to problems relating to earnings measurement and return on investment computations of franchise sales companies lie in a careful analysis of the initial franchise fee. Does this fee call for the performance of services by the franchisor? Over what period will these services be performed? How much will these services cost? Once these and other questions are answered, the accountant can then choose the proper method of revenue recognition. Cost deferral problems should be solved by the same process.

Return on investment computations have haunted accountants for decades. In attempting to make these computations for franchise sales companies, it is again the initial fee which must be analyzed. Should the fee be included in the stockholders' equity section of the franchisor, or does the philosophy of a corporation concerning its future growth preclude this approach? ROI computations do, indeed, depend on the viewpoint and philosophy of those making the calculations.

---

[23] IRC, Sec. 1221 (1).

Chapter 43

Accounting standards for not-for-profit organizations

*Charles W. Lamden**

Not-for-profit organizations include a wide variety of organizations in the present social and economic milieu. They include governmental units—federal, state, and local—colleges and universities and other educational institutions, hospitals and other health-care organizations, voluntary health and welfare organizations, clubs and professional associations, churches and related religious organizations, research organizations, foundations, and other social and cultural organizations such as museums, symphony associations, and ballet and theater companies. The receipts and disbursements of these organizations account for a material segment of the gross national product in the United States, and the property and resources which they own or control reflect a very substantial portion of the nation's total resources. It is conservatively estimated that there are over one-half million not-for-profit organizations for which American accountants and auditors must keep records, maintain accountability for the resources, and attest to such accountability.

PURPOSES AND DEFINITIONS

The objective of record keeping and the presentation of financial data is to make available meaningful financial information. This re-

* Partner, Peat, Marwick, Mitchell & Co.

quires appropriate and adequate disclosure of the information required by the users of the financial data.

The purposes of preparing and presenting such data are comparable to the purposes of presenting financial statements for commercial profit-seeking corporations. There are similarities with respect
to the users of such data also. Each of the organizations has a management for whom reports must be prepared. And depending upon
the nature of the not-for-profit organizations, various public groups
—or the general public—require financial information. There are
similarities, also, as to other users such as credit grantors and regulatory agencies.

Because of both the special nature of the data required and historical developments, specialized accounting principles and reporting
practices can and, in a number of instances, do differ materially
from the principles and reporting practices of commercial organizations. To understand the reasons for these differences it is necessary
to examine the different perspectives or approaches taken in the
two areas—profit and not-for-profit organizations.

It may be wise to begin the analyses with the basic definition of
accounting, which has generally been accepted as follows: "Accounting is the art of recording, classifying and summarizing in a significant manner and in terms of money, transactions and events which
are, in part at least, of a financial character, and interpreting the
results thereof."[1]

This definition is applicable to not-for-profit organizations as well
as to commercial profit-oriented organizations. Fundamentally then,
the reasons for the differences are not found in the purpose, function, and definition of accounting nor in the general character of
the users. The differences arise when the proper perspective is
placed on profit-oriented organizations (business enterprises) and
not-for-profit organizations. This becomes evident in the definition
of accounting given in *Accounting Principles Board Statement No. 4*
(October 1970), which is concerned basically with accounting for
business enterprises. That definition states that accounting is a "service activity" which "is to provide quantitative information primarily
financial in nature, about economic entities that is intended to be
useful in making economic decisions—in making reasoned choices

---

[1] AICPA *Accounting Terminology Bulletin No. 1.*

among alternative courses of action" (paragraph 40). This reflects the change of emphasis to a measurement of profit which requires the matching of costs and revenues in order to make choices among alternative courses of action.

The emphasis in not-for-profit accounting is on "stewardship" rather than on matching costs with revenues. This emphasis arises from the fact that not-for-profit organizations receive funds for which they must maintain accountability. This takes the form of general accountability and specific accountability. The not-for-profit organization (school or college, church, hospital, community fund, etc.) is established to carry out special functions and to meet the designated objectives of the organization. The organization has the general accountability to use the funds and resources it receives for its established objectives. In some cases, funds are contributed for use in a specific project. In those cases the organization has a specific accountability to be certain that the specific requirements of the donor are carried out. These underlying concepts, (1) stewardship and (2) accounting for funds for restricted purposes, are the basic reasons for the system of accounting used by not-for-profit organizations which has generally been identified as "fund accounting." In fund accounting the records for funds for restricted purposes are kept in self-balancing *funds* and separate reporting is maintained for each fund group. The emphasis is on the receipt of resources and the utilization of those resources for the designated objectives.

While the general characteristics of recording and reporting data for the various types of not-for-profit organizations are similar, the historical development of accounting principles and procedures has resulted in a variety of record-keeping procedures and forms of presentation of the financial data. Some of these differences resulted from differing objectives of the organizations; in some cases, however, there is no apparent justification for the differences.

Recognizing the need for uniformity in reporting, some of the organization groups (e.g., colleges and universities, hospitals, state and local governments, voluntary health and welfare organizations) developed manuals for use by their group. Some illustrations of these basic "authoritative" documents are described in the following pages.

In some instances, however, subgroups of the larger organization groups issued manuals or procedural instructions which differed from the major groups. Also, some organizations such as museums, art galleries, zoological societies, foundations, fraternal organizations, and so on, do not fall directly within the categories for which manuals have been issued, and their reporting practices vary. For various reasons, also, some logical and some not so logical, individual organizations have not followed the standards established by their group. The result is that there is a variety of practices among the groups, and in some cases within the groups.

Historically, the public accounting profession did not concern itself with the establishment of accounting principles for not-for-profit organizations. The American Institute of Certified Public Accountants (AICPA) *Accounting Research Bulletins* and *Accounting Principles Board Opinions* were designed primarily for profit-oriented organizations, and in some instances specifically excluded not-for-profit organizations.

While little attention was paid to the development of accounting standards for not-for-profit organizations by the accounting profession, the AICPA Committee on Auditing Procedure issued *Statement No. 28* in 1957, which recognized that "special" reporting was required for not-for-profit organizations which followed "special" accounting practices and procedures.

Paragraph 11 of *Statement on Auditing Procedure No. 28* (*SAP No. 28*) reads as follows:

> If the statements are those of a nonprofit organization they may reflect accounting practices differing in some respects from those followed by business enterprises organized for profit. It is recognized that in many cases generally accepted accounting principles applicable to nonprofit organizations have not been as clearly defined as have those applicable to business enterprises organized for profit. In those areas where the auditor believes generally accepted accounting principles have been clearly defined (as indicated by authoritative literature and accepted practice, etc.) he may state his opinion as to the conformity of the financial statements either with generally accepted accounting principles, or (alternatively, but less desirably) with accounting practices for nonprofit organizations in the particular field (e.g., hospitals, educational institutions, etc.), and in such circumstances he may refer to financial position and results of operations; in either event, it is assumed that the auditor is satisfied that the application of such accounting principles and practices results in a fair presentation of

financial position and results of operations or that he will state his exceptions thereto. In those areas where the auditor believes generally accepted accounting principles have not been clearly defined, the other provisions of this statement apply.[2]

Thus, even though the responsibility for determining whether accounting principles have been defined for a particular not-for-profit entity rested with the independent auditor, the accounting profession did recognize that such principles existed.

Over the years, however, accountants in public practice have participated as individuals in the various committees of educational, governmental, and philanthropic groups which were charged with the responsibility for developing charts of accounts and accounting procedures and standards. AICPA and state CPA society committees, which included both public accountants and internal accountants in not-for-profit organizations, were also formed.

The most important accomplishment of the accounting profession committees was the issuance of four AICPA Industry Audit Guides. These guides are important because they confirmed the existence of generally accepted accounting principles and identified, more specifically, appropriate reporting procedures for hospitals, colleges and universities, voluntary health and welfare organizations, and state and local governmental units. It is interesting to note that even though these publications are called "audit guides," they have the effect of establishing accounting standards for the accounting profession in the not-for-profit areas that are covered.

Since each of the audit guides was based on the principles and procedures already established by the organization group, and in general incorporates the existing manuals of the group as part of the audit guide, the principles and reporting procedures differ as between the audit guides. Nonetheless, the development of the audit guides is a major step forward since major variations in the reporting procedures within the organization groups should be substantially reduced or eliminated if the established procedures have the weight of "generally accepted accounting principles."

The next efforts undoubtedly will be to develop audit guides for

---

[2] The substance of paragraph 11 of *SAP No. 28* was also included in *SAP No. 33*, chap. 13, par. 8, and is now incorporated as Section 620.08 of *Statement on Auditing Standards No. 1* (*SAS No. 1*).

those areas that are not now specifically covered, such as foundations, churches, research organizations, trade associations, labor
unions, civic and fraternal organizations, and various cultural organizations. After uniform reporting procedures are established for
each of the groups, the next logical step would be an overall audit
guide for not-for-profit organizations that would eliminate unnecessary differences between the groups.[3]

AUTHORITATIVE SOURCES

Until a uniform set of accounting standards is established for all
not-for-profit organizations it will be necessary to follow the standards established for the specific areas (e.g., state and local governments, hospitals, colleges and universities). The authoritative manuals and guides in these areas often supply statements of accounting
principles, charts of accounts, and illustrative formats for financial
statements.

The use of the authoritative manuals and guides is necessary if
uniformity of principles and presentation is to be achieved within
the discrete groups of not-for-profit organizations. It is also necessary to utilize these authoritative sources if the organization plans
to have the outside auditor issue his or her report "in accordance
with generally accepted accounting principles." This is particularly
true if the AICPA has issued an "Industry Audit Guide" for the
area.

To accomplish these objectives it is necessary to be able to identify the appropriate "authoritative sources" for each area. It will,
of course, be necessary to obtain the most current revisions of the
manuals and guides, and to determine if new authoritative manuals
or guides have been issued for areas not specifically covered in the
listing set forth below.

---

[3] Efforts in this direction have already begun. The AICPA Subcommittee on Non-
Profit Organizations of the Accounting Standards Executive Committee has been
organized to provide guidance for not-for-profit organizations not currently covered
by audit guides and to explore ways of eliminating unnecessary differences between
the current audit guides. Also, the October 1974 report of the Accounting Advisory
Committee of the *Commission on Private Philanthropy and Public Needs* (the Filer
Commission) has recommended a uniform "Standard Accounting Report" (SAR) for
use in the preparation of the annual financial reports of all philanthropic organizations.

The areas which are specifically covered and the authoritative sources for those areas are as follows:

I. *State and Local Governmental Units*
   A. AICPA Industry Audit Guide—*Audits of State and Local Governmental Units.*
   B. Industry Manual—*Governmental Accounting, Auditing and Financial Reporting* (GAAFR), published by the National Committee on Governmental Accounting of the Municipal Finance Officers Association.
   C. While GAAFR is incorporated by reference in the Audit Guide, it should be noted that there are certain variations in the Audit Guide from GAAFR. The Audit Guide takes precedence as an authoritative source when the report is prepared "in accordance with generally accepted accounting principles."

II. *Colleges and Universities*
   A. AICPA Industry Audit Guide—*Audits of Colleges and Universities.*
   B. Industry Manual—*College and University Business Administration* (CUBA), published by the National Association of College and University Business Officers (Third Edition).
   C. The Audit Guide includes material that was in the earlier edition of the Manual and incorporates some data by reference. The guide explains the relationship as follows: "Much of the material in this guide is presented as it appears in the Manual. In some instances, however, the guide recommends practices, both accounting and reporting, which differ from the Manual or which clarify or expand practices recommended by it. Also, some disclosure requirements recommended by the Accounting Principles Board are not mentioned in the Manual. Significant items added to the guide or requiring accounting or reporting practices which are different from those recommended in the Manual. . . ." are then listed in the balance of Chapter I of the Guide. The third edition (1974) of CUBA states that ". . . the effort that produced the AICPA guide was a significant part of the total effort that went into the

present revision." Accordingly, the third edition of the manual is substantially in agreement with the guide.[4]

III. *Hospitals*
   A. AICPA Industry Audit Guide—*Hospital Audit Guide.*
   B. Industry Manual—*Chart of Accounts for Hospitals* published by the American Hospital Association.
   C. The Audit Guide states that "Recommendations in the revised American Hospital Association's *Chart of Accounts for Hospitals* (1966) are generally compatible with generally accepted accounting principles and this guide. However, two recommendations in that publication presently are not in accordance with generally accepted accounting principles:
      1. Carrying property, plant, and equipment at current replacement cost and basing depreciation on these values.
      2. Carrying long-term security investments at current market value."

In addition to the *Chart of Accounts for Hospitals* other American Hospital Association publications are incorporated by reference for purposes of understanding terminology, accounting and auditing procedures, and cost determinations. These include:
   Uniform Hospital Definitions.
   Cost Finding and Rate Setting for Hospitals.
   Internal Control and Internal Auditing for Hospitals.

IV. *Voluntary Health and Welfare Associations*
   A. AICPA Industry Audit Guide—*Audits of Voluntary Health and Welfare Organizations* (1974).

---

[4] The Accounting Standards Division of the AICPA has addressed to the Financial Accounting Standards Board (FASB) a Statement of Position, "Financial Accounting and Reporting by Colleges and Universities." It proposes that the AICPA Industry Audit Guide, *Audits of Colleges and Universities,* be amended. The Task Force on Colleges and Universities, which prepared the paper, had previously participated in a consultative capacity in the development of two recent publications that recommended expansion, clarification, and revision of the Audit Guide. The two publications are: *College and University Business Administration* (*Manual*—Third Edition), published by the National Association of College and University Business Officers and *Report of the Joint Accounting Group* published by the Western Interstate Commission for Higher Education. The purpose of the position paper is not only to bring to the attention of the FASB the amendments to the Audit Guide that were recommended by the Task Force but also to conform the guide to the third edition of the manual.

B. Industry Manual—*Standards of Accounting and Financial Reporting for Voluntary Health and Welfare Organizations* (Revised 1974) published by the National Health Council, Inc.; National Assembly of National Voluntary Health and Social Welfare Organizations, Inc.; and United Way of America.

C. It should be noted that the AICPA published its first audit guide in 1966. The current Industry Audit Guide (1973) supersedes the previously issued audit guide. The status of the revised audit guide and its relationship to the industry manual (1964 edition) is set forth in the preface of the Audit Guide as follows:

> This revised audit guide has been prepared by the Committee on Voluntary Health and Welfare Organizations of the American Institute of Certified Public Accountants, in consultation with the Joint Liaison Committee formed by the National Health Council, the National Assembly for Social Policy and Development, and the United Way of America, and supersedes the audit guide previously issued in 1966.

> This revised audit guide describes generally accepted accounting principles applicable to financial reporting by health and welfare organizations. In most instances, these principles are compatible with those set forth in the *Standards of Accounting and Financial Reporting for Voluntary Health and Welfare Organizations.* The National Health Council and the National Assembly have advised the Committee that it is their intent to revise the *Standards,* as necessary, to achieve maximum possible uniformity with this guide.

Another industry manual, while specifically applicable to "human service" organizations, has been issued to comply with the AICPA Audit Guide, and should be useful for all voluntary health and welfare organizations. It is *Accounting and Financial Reporting—A Guide for United Way and Not-for-Profit Human Service Organizations,* published by the United Community Funds and Councils of America.

V. *Other Not-for-Profit Organizations*

The AICPA has not issued an audit guide for a large variety of organizations which are not specifically covered by the four audit guides referred to above. Examples of such organizations are:

Churches.
Foundations.
Research and scientific organizations.
Business and professional trade associations.
Labor unions.
Community, civic, social, and fraternal organizations.
Cultural organizations, including libraries, museums, zoos, symphony associations, and ballet and theater companies.

Some of these groups have issued manuals which are helpful in establishing charts of accounts and preparing financial reports for these organizations. To the extent that they follow general principles of fund accounting and appropriate disclosure of restricted funds, it may be possible for outside auditors to report that the financial statements of these organizations are "in accordance with generally accepted accounting principles." To the extent that these Manuals recommend cash basis accounting or other procedures not "generally accepted" (e.g., use of current market values for land and building, etc.), reports presented in accordance with the manuals should be presented as "special reports," following the requirements set forth in AICPA *Statement on Auditing Standards No. 1*, Section 620.

Illustrations of manuals which may be helpful for some of these areas are:

Diocesan Accounting and Financial Reporting, issued by the National Conference of Catholic Bishops.
Handbook for the Finance Officers of a Local Church, issued by Evangelical and Reformed Church.
Uniform System of Accounts for Clubs, issued by the Club Managers Association of America.

BASIC ACCOUNTING STANDARDS FOR THE NOT-FOR-PROFIT GROUPS

To understand the nature of accounting standards for not-for-profit organizations, it is necessary to understand the objective of recording financial data and presenting financial statements. A fundamental objective in these organizations is to record the receipt of gifts, grants, and taxes and to record the expenditures in accordance with the instructions of the donors or those who provided the funds. Funds received but not yet expended for the designated purposes must be accounted for in a manner which will clearly identify the purposes for which they will be expended. The emphasis is on accountability or stewardship for the resources received. (There is also a legal responsibility of the organization to the donor in that, having accepted his gift with restrictions, the organization has contracted to meet that restriction in the use of the donated funds.)

This objective differs from the objective of financial statements for commercial organizations which is the recording and presentation of information useful for making profit oriented economic decisions. To make such decisions, it is necessary to compare what must be given up with what is expected to be received. To determine the results from this process, the accounting procedure is to match costs with revenues.[5] This difference, however, is one of degree (or emphasis) since decision makers (e.g., tax levying agencies or donors) in not-for-profit organizations allocate funds to government agencies, approve or reject tax referendums, or donate to hospitals, universities, or churches to achieve their goals just as investors buy securities or consumers buy goods to achieve their goals. In commercial enterprises the benefits resulting from the sacrifices can be measured as net income. In not-for-profit organizations, the measurement is much more difficult since attainment of the goals can be measured only in terms of "performance." This requires a different kind of reporting.

While commercial organizations do have the responsibility to report on the stewardship of their resources, the emphasis of their accountability is on the utilization of the resources to earn a profit. In not-for-profit organizations the emphasis is placed on accountability and stewardship.

It is important to understand that the standards of reporting for not-for-profit organizations have developed differently from commercial accounting standards because there is a difference in emphasis in the objectives for recording and reporting the data and

---

[5] See the Report of the AICPA Study Group on the Objectives of Financial Statements, p. 13. It should be noted that the "matching process" is required in several aspects of not-for-profit accounting. For example, this matching is required for hospitals in addition to the stewardship and contractual responsibilities. It is also required in "enterprise-type" funds of governmental units.

because of legally binding restrictions in not-for-profit organizations which have no real counterpart in business enterprises. It also must be kept in mind that there are some differences among governments, hospitals, educational institutions, and health and welfare organizations which result in different reporting standards, which are merely "historical." It is also important to recognize that some activities of not-for-profit organizations carry on enterprise activities where costs are matched against revenues (enterprise funds and intragovernmental service funds of governments and the unrestricted funds of hospitals). Finally, as desirable as it may be to quantify performance measures, generally accepted standards have not yet been established for "performance reporting."[6]

Based on the objectives, historical background, and constraints that have been set forth above, the balance of the chapter will list briefly some of the more significant accounting standards in each of the not-for-profit groups.[7]

I. *State and Local Governmental Units*
    A. Fund accounting is required. Each fund of a governmental unit will fall into one of eight types: (1) the general fund, (2) special revenue funds, (3) debt service funds, (4) capital project funds, (5) enterprise funds, (6) intragovernmental service funds, (7) trust and agency funds, and (8) special assessment funds. (In addition fixed assets generally will be carried in a general fixed asset group of accounts and long-term liabilities generally will be carried in a general long-term debt group of accounts. See standards E and F below.)

---

[6] Considerable efforts are being made to develop standards for "performance" reporting in government. A major step was taken by the General Accounting Office with the issuance of *Standards for Audit of Governmental Organizations, Programs, Activities and Functions,* and various accounting firms and professional organizations are continuing to study and experiment with such standards.

[7] The accounting standards set forth in this section are taken from, or based upon, the AICPA Industry Audit Guides for (1) *State and Local Governmental Units,* (2) *Colleges and Universities,* (3) *Hospitals,* and (4) *Voluntary Health and Welfare Organizations.* To date, these are the basic authoritative standards which are required to present financial statements in these not-for-profit areas in accordance with "generally accepted accounting principles." While the statements of the standards have been summarized, reorganized, or adapted in some instances for the purposes of presentation in this chapter, the intent is to present the standards which have been included in the audit guides and authorized and approved by the Accounting Principles Board. (At this writing the Financial Accounting Standards Board has not acted to modify these standards.)

B. Budgets and budgetary accounting are required for general funds and significant special revenue funds.

C. A governmental accounting system should incorporate the accounting records necessary to show compliance with applicable legal provisions.

D. Accrual accounting (or a modified accrual basis) is generally recommended. (Special and rather restricted rules are set forth in those cases where variations from the accrual method are made because of the purpose for which a fund has been established.)

E. Accounting for fixed assets and depreciation thereon depends upon the nature and purpose of the fund. Thus, fixed assets should be recorded in enterprise, intragovernmental service, and certain trust funds. All general fixed assets (those not accounted for in the above-mentioned funds) should be recorded in the general fixed asset group of accounts.

In general, fixed assets should be capitalized and recorded at historical cost (or appraisal value, if contributed), and depreciation should be recorded only where the function of the fund is to match costs with revenues. Exceptions to these rules, designated as "acceptable alternatives," are specifically stated as follows:

1. In the general fixed asset group, certain "improvements other than buildings" are not required to be capitalized.

2. An allowance for depreciation may be deducted from related assets in the general fixed assets group of accounts, with a corresponding reduction in the investment in the general fixed assets account.

F. Except for enterprise and special assessment funds (and certain trust funds), long-term liabilities should not be carried as liabilities of any fund but should be set up in a separate, self-balancing group of accounts known as the General Long-Term Debt Group of Accounts. In addition to general obligation bonds (obligations of a governmental unit as a whole which are supported by general revenues) this debt group may include time warrants and notes which have a maturity of more than one year from date of issuance.

Long-term liabilities (including bonds) of enterprise, special assessment, and certain trust funds should be carried as obligations of those funds. Also, general obligation bonds (backed by the full faith and credit of the governmental unit) being repaid by enterprise, special assessment, or certain trust funds should be carried as liabilities of those funds to reflect the intention to retire such liabilities out of the resources of those funds.

Under no circumstances should debt of any type be recorded in more than one fund or group of accounts. When general obligation bonds are carried in other funds, their existence should be reported in a note to the statement of general long-term debt to reflect the contingent liability for payment.

G. Financial statements should be presented utilizing a common terminology and classification of accounts. The terminology and classification should reflect the requirements of the various funds or account groups. Each fund of a governmental unit constitutes a separate entity. Homogeneous funds may be consolidated in a single balance sheet, but funds or account groups of different types may not be consolidated. Separate financial statements are required, since a single set of consolidated financial statements for all funds and account groups will not fairly present financial position and results of operations of the individual funds in accordance with generally accepted accounting principles. The individual balance sheets of the respective funds may be presented in a *combined balance sheet*.

A proper balance must be achieved between the full disclosure of necessary data in a limited number of financial statement captions and notes and the presentation of voluminous detail. Unless there is a specific reason that professional pronouncements of accounting standards would not be applicable (e.g., pronouncements on earnings per share or income tax allocation) or there is a specific authoritative preference for a procedure that must be followed by state and local governmental units, authoritative pronouncements of professional bodies (APB and FASB) on accounting standards are applicable in the financial statements of state and local governmental units.

II. *Colleges and Universities*

    A. Fund accounting is required. The fund groups usually encountered in educational institutions are: (1) current funds, (2) loan funds, (3) endowment and similar funds, (4) annuity and life income funds, (5) plant funds, and (6) agency funds.

    B. Financial reporting utilizes the three following basic types of statements: (1) balance sheet, (2) statement of changes in fund balances, and (3) statement of current funds revenues, expenditures, and other changes.

    C. A clear distinction between the balances of funds which are externally restricted and those which are internally designated within each fund group should be maintained in the accounts and disclosed in the financial reports.

    D. Accrual basis accounting is required. (In practice, minor variations are accepted for accruals and deferrals such as investment income and interest on student loans when the amounts are not material. Also a special rule is recognized for revenues and expenditures of an academic term, such as a summer session which is conducted over a fiscal year-end. In the latter case, all revenues and expenditures of such summer session should be reported totally within the fiscal year in which the program is predominantly conducted.)

    E. Gifts, bequests, grants, and other receipts restricted as to use by outside grantors or agencies should be recorded as additions directly in the fund group appropriate to the restricted nature of the receipt. Unrestricted gifts, bequests, and grants should be recorded as unrestricted current funds revenues. Special note disclosure is required for pledges of gifts, including uncollected subscriptions, subscription notes and estate notes, and for uncollected grant awards. (Pledges may be recorded as receivables at their estimated net realizable values; however, grant awards not yet funded and for which the institution has not yet performed services should not be considered as assets to be accounted for in the financial statements.)

F.   Investments purchased generally should be reported in the financial statements at cost, and investments received as gifts at the fair market value at the date of gift. Investments in wasting assets, other than institutional plant, should be reported net of allowance for depreciation or depletion.

The use of current market value for investments (excluding physical plant) is an acceptable alternative, provided this basis is used for all investments of all funds. (When current market value is used unrealized gains and losses should be recognized in the financial statements in the same manner as realized gains and losses.)

Special rules are also established for interfund sales of investments, the pooling of investments, premiums and discounts on long-term interest-bearing obligations, and investments in wasting assets in endowment and similar funds. (In the latter case depreciation or depletion should be provided in order to maintain the distinction between income and principal of the endowment funds.)

G.   Depreciation of physical plant should not be recorded either in the statement of current funds revenues, expenditures, and other changes or in the statement of changes in unrestricted current funds balance. However, depreciation allowances may be reported in the balance sheet and the provision for depreciation reported in the statement of changes in the balance of the investment-in-plant fund subsection of the plant funds group.

H.   Interfund borrowings of a temporary nature should be reported as assets of the fund group making the advances as well as liabilities of the fund group receiving the advances.

Disclosure is required of (1) terms and due dates for long-term interfund borrowings and (2) interfund borrowing where funds share a joint bank account and one of the funds has, in effect, an overdraft. (Caution is also advised in the handling of advances from unrestricted current funds or quasi-endowment funds, which may be permanent transfers, and advances from donor restricted plant funds and endowment funds to other funds, which may be improper.)

I. Funds held in trust by others preferably should not be included in the balance sheet with other funds administered by the institution. Adequate disclosure of such amounts (either parenthetically in the endowment and similar funds group in the balance sheet or in the notes to the financial statements) is required. Only if the institution has legally enforceable rights or claims, including those as to income, may such funds be reported as assets, properly described, in the financial statements. The value of such funds should be supported by annual trust reports available to the institution.

The reporting of income from funds held in trust by others depends upon the terms of the trust instrument. Income from irrevocable trusts, with no discretionary power resting with the trustees as to the distribution of income, should be included either as endowment income with a notation of the amount, or should be separately stated. Income from revocable trusts, or where the trustees have discretion as to the amounts to be distributed to the beneficiaries, is tantamount to gifts and should be so reported with disclosure of the amounts.

J. Where institutions are operated by religious groups, facilities made available to the educational entity by the religious group should be disclosed in the financial report together with any related indebtedness.

In order to account for the proper revenues and expenditures as a separate educational entity, the monetary value of services contributed by members of the religious group should be recorded in the accounts and reported in the financial statements. (Such amounts may be determined by reference to lay-equivalent salaries.) The value of such services less any maintenance, living costs, or personal expenses which may be incurred for the contributing personnel should be recorded as gift revenue.

III. *Hospitals*

A. The basic standards of fund accounting are applicable. The funds should be presented in two major categories: unrestricted funds and restricted funds.

1. All unrestricted resources should be shown in the balance sheet under the "unrestricted" caption or

otherwise disclosed in order to indicate the resources available at the discretion of the governing board. The total of all unrestricted funds should be presented.

2. Restricted funds generally fall into the following categories: (*a*) funds for specific operating purposes, (*b*) funds for additions to property, plant, and equipment, and (*c*) endowment funds.

When appropriate, other categories of restricted resources may be presented in restricted funds such as student loan, annuity, life income, agency, or retirement of indebtedness funds.

Donor restricted resources for specific operating purposes should be accounted for in a restricted fund or may be shown as deferred revenue in the unrestricted fund. These resources should be reported as "other operating" revenue in the financial statements of the period in which expenditures are made for the purpose intended by the donor.

Resources restricted by donors for additions to property, plant, and equipment should be included in the restricted fund balance until such time as the expenditures are made for the purpose intended by the donor, at which time a transfer of resources from restricted fund balance to unrestricted fund balance should be shown in the financial statements.

Endowment resources (including term endowments) should be accounted for as restricted funds. When term endowment funds become available to the governing board for unrestricted purposes, they should be reported as "nonoperating revenue." If these funds are restricted, they should be shown as a transfer to specific purpose or other restricted funds.

3. Board-designated funds should be accounted for as part of unrestricted funds. Disclosure of board designations should be made in the financial statements. The term "restricted" should not be used in connection with board designations (or other internal hospital appropriations) of funds.

B. Property, plant, and equipment (at cost) and related liabilities should be accounted for as part of unrestricted funds. If limitations exist on the use of proceeds from a disposition of property, plant, and equipment, such limitations should be disclosed.

C. Depreciation should be recognized in hospital financial statements. If third parties reimburse hospitals for depreciation and restrict all or part of the reimbursement payment to replacements of, or additions to, property, plant, and equipment, such payment should be included in revenue in order to match this revenue with depreciation expense. In the statement of changes in fund balances, the amount of the payment should be shown as a transfer from unrestricted to restricted funds and returned to unrestricted funds when expended.

D. Accrual basis accounting is required. Patient revenue should be accrued at established rates during the period the services are being provided. Charity allowances, other arrangements for providing service at less than established rates, and the provision for uncollectible accounts should be reported either separately from gross revenues under "deductions from gross revenues" or by some other disclosure. Such allowances should also be accounted for on the accrual basis.

E. Gifts, grants, and bequests that are not restricted by donors should be reported as nonoperating revenue, and *not* credited directly to fund balances. Appropriation of these contributions by the governing board does not alter this treatment; rather such action is a designation of the unrestricted fund balance. Grants and subsidies given by a governmental or community agency for general support of the hospital ordinarily should be shown as nonoperating revenue. However, where the grantor specifies that this revenue is to be used for indigent care, it should be accounted for as a specific purpose (restricted) gift and offset against allowances and uncollectible accounts when used.

F. Long-term security investments generally should be recorded in the financial statements at cost. (The accounting profession is currently studying the feasibility of carrying marketable securities at market value, as an acceptable alternative.) Income from investment of board-designated and other unrestricted funds, unrestricted income from endowment funds, and realized gains (or losses) on sale of investments of board-designated or other unrestricted funds should be included in the statement of revenue and expenses. Realized gains (or losses) on sale of investments of endowment funds should be added to (deducted from) endowment fund principal unless such items are legally available for other use or chargeable against other funds. In the latter case, the gain or loss from these endowment funds should be accounted for as resources for specific operating purposes, if restricted, or nonoperating revenue, if not restricted, and must be accounted for as a fund balance transfer.

Investment income and net realized gains or losses from investments of restricted funds, other than endowment funds, should be added to the respective fund balances, unless legally available for unrestricted purposes. In the latter case these items should be included in nonoperating revenue.

Gains or losses on investment trading between unrestricted and restricted funds should be recognized in the originating fund and separately disclosed; however, such gains or losses resulting from transactions between designated portions of the unrestricted fund should not be recognized.

G. Financial reporting should utilize the following basic types of statements: (1) balance sheet, (2) statement of revenues and expenses, (3) statement of changes in fund balances, and (4) statement of changes in financial position of the unrestricted fund. When a hospital is a part of a larger organization such as a medical school, a university, a governmental unit, or a corporate conglomerate, the reporting may be conformed to that of the larger unit as a whole. However, accounting practices and reports of the hospital entity alone should conform to the basic standards for hospitals.

When auxiliaries, guilds, fund raising groups, or other organizations that assist hospitals are independent (as characterized by their own charter, bylaws, tax-exempt status, and governing board) the financial reporting of these organizations should be separate from reports of the hospital. If significant resources or operations of a hospital are handled by such organizations, full disclosure should be made of the related facts and circumstances. If such organizations are under control of (or common control with) hospitals and handle hospital resources, their financial statements should be combined with those of the hospital.

Unless there is a specific reason that professional pronouncements of accounting standards would not be applicable, or there is specific authoritative reference for a procedure that must be followed by a hospital, authoritative pronouncements of professional bodies (APB and FASB) on accounting standards are applicable to the financial statements of hospitals.

H. All pledges, less a provision for amounts uncollectible, should be accounted for in the financial statements and appropriately classified as unrestricted or restricted. Revenue from unrestricted pledges (net of provision for uncollectibles) should be recorded as nonoperating revenue in the period in which the pledge is made. That part of a pledge that is to be applied during some future period should be reported in the period in which it is received as deferred revenue, or added to a restricted fund balance. Pledges restricted in any other way should be reported as restricted funds.

I. When endowment-type funds are held in trust by outside parties, and not directly or indirectly controlled by the hospital, they should be disclosed, but they should not be included in the financial statements of the hospital. Where the trustee is required to make distributions to the hospital, such distributions should be recorded on the accrual basis as endowment income. Appropriate disclosure in a footnote of the right to future income is also recommended. If the distribution the trustee makes to the hospital is discretionary, the hospital should report such a distribution as a gift (or in any manner specified by the terms of the trust or directions of the trustee).

J.   Fair value of donated services should be recorded when there is the equivalent of an employer-employee relationship and there is an objective basis for valuing such services. In hospitals operated by religious groups, the monetary value of services contributed by members of the religious group (determined by reference to lay-equivalent salaries) should be reported as expense with a corresponding credit to nonoperating revenue.

Donated medicines, linen, office supplies, and other materials which normally would be purchased by a hospital should be recorded at fair market value and reported as other operating revenue.

Donations of property and equipment should be recorded at fair market value at the date of contribution in the unrestricted fund balance, unless designated for endowment or other restricted purposes.

IV.   *Voluntary Health and Welfare Organizations*

A.   The basic standards of fund accounting are applicable. The most commonly used funds are: (1) current unrestricted fund, (2) current restricted funds, (3) land, building, and equipment fund (often referred to as plant fund), (4) endowment funds, (5) custodian funds, and (6) loan and annuity funds.

Appropriate segregation should be made between those resources available for use at the discretion of the governing board (unrestricted funds) and those resources over which the board has little, if any, discretion as to use because of externally imposed restrictions (restricted funds).

Board-designated funds should be accounted for within the current unrestricted fund. Separate accounts may be maintained for such designated funds, and the designated and undesignated portions of the fund segregated in the fund balance section of the unrestricted fund balance sheet. Board-designated funds should not be included with donor restricted funds, and the term "restricted" should not be used in connection therewith.

B.   Fixed assets should be carried at cost (and donated assets at their fair value at the date of the gift) in the land, building, and equipment fund (plant fund). This fund should include the total investment in fixed assets, which reflects both unrestricted and restricted amounts invested in land, buildings, and equipment. In addition this fund should include (1) unexpended resources contributed specifically for the purpose of acquiring or replacing land, buildings, and equipment for use in the operations of the organization; and (2) mortgages or other liabilities relating to these assets.

When additions to land, buildings, or equipment used in carrying out the organization's program and supporting services are acquired with unrestricted fund resources, the amount expended for such assets should be transferred from the unrestricted fund to the plant fund and should be accounted for as a direct addition to the plant fund balance.

Donated fixed assets that are to be used by the organization should be recorded as a contribution in the land, building, and equipment fund. If donor imposed restrictions prevent such fixed assets from being immediately disposed of, or currently used in the organization's normal program, they should then be recorded as contributions in a donor restricted fund. When the restrictions lapse, the assets should be transferred to the land, building, and equipment fund if the assets are to be used in the organization's normal operations, or to the unrestricted fund if they are to be held for resale or other use. Receipt of donated fixed assets with no restrictions as to use or disposition, and which will be held for conversion to cash or for production of income, should be recorded as support within the unrestricted fund and as an asset on its balance sheet.

Gains or losses on the sale of fixed assets should be reflected as income items in the plant fund accounts. Proceeds from the sale of fixed assets should be transferred to the unrestricted fund and reflected as direct reductions of or additions to the respective fund balances.

C. Depreciation expense should be recognized as a cost of rendering current services and should be included as an element of expense in the statement of support, revenue, and expenses and changes in fund balances of the fund in which the assets are recorded and in the satement of functional expenditures.

D. Accrual basis accounting is required. Financial statements prepared on a cash basis, or a modified accrual basis, may be acceptable only if they do not differ materially from financial statements prepared on an accrual basis.

E. Gifts, grants, and bequests that are not restricted by donors should be reported in the current unrestricted fund. Appropriation of these contributions by the governing board does not alter this treatment; rather, such action is a designation of the current unrestricted fund balance.

    Gifts, grants, bequests, and income from endowment funds or other similar sources, where the donor has specified the operating purpose for which the funds are to be used, should be accounted for in current restricted funds.

    Gifts, grants, and bequests accepted with the donor stipulation that the principal be maintained intact in perpetuity or until the occurrence of a specified event, or for a specified period, should be accounted for in endowment funds.

    If endowment fund income is not subject to donor-imposed restrictions, it should be credited as earned to the appropriate revenue account of the unrestricted fund. If endowment income is subject to donor restriction, it should be credited as earned to the appropriate restricted fund.

    When restrictions on endowment fund principal lapse, the resources released should be transferred to the unrestricted fund or to a specific restricted fund, according to the terms of the original gift, grant, or bequest.

F. Investments purchased by voluntary health and welfare organizations should be recorded at cost. Securities donated to the organization should be recorded at their fair market value at the date of gift. The carrying of investments at market value is also deemed acceptable. However, the basis of carrying investments should be the same in all funds and should be clearly disclosed in the financial statements. Also, market value (if the investments are carried at cost), or cost (if investments are carried at market), should be disclosed parenthetically in each fund, or set forth in the footnotes.

If investments are carried at market, the unrealized appreciation (or depreciation) should be separately identified and included in revenues (or other expenses) of the appropriate fund in the statement of support, revenue, and expenses and changes in fund balance.

Assets transferred to other funds because of the lapse of restrictions should be transferred at market value. Gains or losses on such assets should be recorded by the fund making the transfer.

Investment income and realized gains and losses (and unrealized gains and losses, where investments are carried at market value) on investments of unrestricted funds should be reported in unrestricted revenue. Investment income and gains of restricted funds, other than endowment funds, should be included in the revenue of restricted funds unless legally available for unrestricted purposes.

Unrestricted investment income of endowment funds should be included in the revenues of the current unrestricted fund. Donor restricted income of an endowment fund should be included in the revenue of the appropriate restricted fund.

Generally, realized gains and losses on investments of endowment funds should be recorded as principal transactions. However, when the endowment instrument specifically states that such gains and losses are not restricted, they should be recorded as income. Also, where the statutes of the state so provide, net realized (and in some cases, unrealized) gains on investments of endowment funds may be available for unrestricted use. Where permitted by law, the designated amount of appreciation to be transferred to the unrestricted fund should be reflected as a transfer of fund balances. Further, disclosure should be made of realized (or where applicable unrealized) investment gains in endowment funds that are available for transfer to the unrestricted fund at the discretion of the governing board. The statutory authority for such transfers should also be disclosed.

G. Financial reporting should utilize the following basic types of statements: (1) statement of support, revenue, and expenses and changes in fund balances, (2) statement of functional expenses, and (3) balance sheets.

The functional classification of expenses should include two categories: (1) specific "program services" which describe the organization's social service activities and (2) "supporting services" under which management (or administrative) and general expenses and fund raising costs are shown as separate items. The various functions should be adequately described to portray their purpose, and each functional classification should include all of the costs that are applicable to the service described. The financial statements should clearly disclose the total support received and the related fund-raising costs incurred for the period. Overall, the financial statements should contain sufficient information to enable the reader to obtain a general understanding of the nature of the costs of carrying out the organization's activities.

H. Donations and pledges should be recorded as support when received, unless the donor specifies use in future periods. In the latter case, donations (including pledges) should be recorded as a deferred credit in the balance sheet of the appropriate fund and recorded as support in the year they may be used.

Provision should be made for uncollectible pledges. The allowance for uncollectible pledges and the net amount of pledges receivable should be disclosed in the financial statements.

Amounts allocated, but not received at the balance sheet date, from donations arising from United Way campaigns or collected by other agencies should be recorded in the same way as pledges receivable.

I. Funds held as custodian, which are held or disbursed only on instructions from the person or organization from whom they were received, should not be considered as a part of the organization's revenue or support.

J.   Donated materials of significant amounts should be recorded at their fair value when received and valued on a clearly measurable objective basis. (Care should be taken in recording such contributions as gifts when the nature of the materials is such that valuation cannot be substantiated.)

Donated materials used in providing the service rendered by the organization should be reflected in the cost of that service at the value previously recorded for the contribution.

If significant amounts are involved, the value of the materials recorded as contributions and expenditures should be clearly disclosed in the financial statements. Free use of facilities and other assets useful in fulfilling the organization's purposes should also be recorded as contributions, and the basis of valuation fully disclosed.

Donated services should be recorded when: (1) the services performed are a normal part of the program or supporting services and would otherwise be performed by salaried personnel, (2) the organization exercises control over the employment and duties of the donors of the services, and (3) the organization has a clearly measurable basis for the amount. Supplementary efforts and periodic services of volunteers, and research and training activities of personnel without pay (or with a nominal allowance), which are not under the direct control of the organization, and which cannot be readily valued, should not be recorded as contributions (even though such services constitute a significant factor in the operation of the organization).

The financial statements should disclose the methods followed by the organization in evaluating, recording, and reporting donated services and should clearly distinguish between those donated services for which values have been recorded and those for which they have not been recorded.

V.   *Other Not-for-Profit Organizations*

Since authoritative industry audit guides or similar professional pronouncements have not been issued for other not-for-profit organizations (churches; foundations; research and scientific organizations; trade associations; labor unions; community, civic, social, and fraternal organizations and clubs; cultural organizations such as libraries, museums, zoos, symphony associations, ballet and theater companies; etc.), authoritative accounting standards cannot be listed for these organizations. As indicated in the earlier part of this chapter in the discussion of authoritative sources for these areas, reference should be made to the AICPA *Statement on Auditing Standards No. 1,* Section 620.

In those areas where the literature clearly defines acceptable acounting principles, the industry manuals may be utilized. If the auditor feels that the principles are adequately defined, the auditor may state the opinion that the financial statements are presented in accordance with generally accepted accounting principles or (less desirably) with accounting practices for not-for-profit organizations in the particular field. In those areas where the auditor believes generally accepted accounting principles have not been clearly defined, or where cash basis or other "nonaccepted" procedures have been used, the data must be presented and reported on as a "special report."

For practical purposes, another approach is to utilize the applicable provisions of the four audit guides that have been issued. A careful review of the standards that have been outlined in this chapter will indicate that the basic concepts of (1) fund accounting; (2) the segregation of restricted and unrestricted assets; (3) the recording of fixed assets (except for depreciation in some instances); (4) the use of the accrual basis; (5) the handling of gifts, grants, and bequests; (6) the handling of investments (except for the alternative use of market value in some instances); (7) and the handling of other items such as pledges, funds in trust, custodial funds, and donated services, do not differ materially. There are major differences in reporting format and a variety of other procedures depending on the nature of the organization.

In deciding which format to use for one of these other not-for-profit areas, an analysis should be made of the functions of the organization covered in one of the four audit guides.

Other health-care institutions could use the Hospital Audit Guide reporting format to the extent applicable.

Libraries, museums, zoos, and local school districts that are directly under the jurisdiction of cities, counties, or states probably should utilize the reporting format in the *audit guide for state and local governmental units.*

To the extent that they conduct educational activities of various types; receive gifts, grants, bequests, and contributions which are both restricted and unrestricted; and receive tuition, fees, memberships or dues from participants and have other accountability characteristics of educational institutions, the following organizations can satisfactorily adapt the *college and university reporting format* to their needs: churches, research and scientific organizations, professional organizations, and autonomous associations for libraries, museums, zoos, symphony associations, and ballet and theater companies.

Foundations and civic, social, and community organizations generally will find that the *voluntary health and welfare organization format* can be adapted to meet their needs.

CONCLUSION

While there is a great deal that can and should be done in the continued development of accounting standards in the not-for-profit areas, much progress has been made. Recognized authoritative accounting standards and standardized reporting formats have been established in four major areas—state and local governmental units, colleges and universities, hospitals, and voluntary health and welfare organizations. Authoritative literature is available in each of the areas based on AICPA audit guides and industry manuals. Moreover, professional committees are at work in all of the areas, sponsored both by the AICPA and the not-for-profit organizations. Regardless of the sponsorship, most of these committees have both professional accounting and not-for-profit organization representatives as committee members. Their objectives in each of the areas are to improve, and make more uniform, accounting standards for not-for-profit organizations.

PART 8

Planning and control

Chapter 44

Costing systems for control—Job order and process

*J. B. Campbell**
H. R. Anderson†

A costing system is an integral part of a company's total information system. Fundamental to a costing system is its role in controlling resource inputs. In analyzing costing systems for control, emphasis will be directed toward a review of the traditional costing systems, the fundamental purposes of a cost system, operational aspects of a costing system, the influence of federal cost accounting standards on costing systems, and a summary of controllership responsibilities.

THE TRADITIONAL COSTING SYSTEMS[1]

In many areas of accounting, a single term may have more than one common usage. It is appropriate to recognize this condition when discussing costing systems. To illustrate, are all of the following considered traditional costing systems?

---

* Vice President and Controller, Northrop Corporation.

† Professor of Accounting, California University, Fullerton.

[1] Information in this section condensed from H. R. Anderson and M. H. Raiborn, *Basic Cost Accounting Concepts* (Boston, Mass.: Houghton Mifflin Company, 1977).

Absorption costing	Direct costing
Standard costing	Process costing
Normal costing	Joint costing
Job order costing	Historical costing

All of these methods, systems, or techniques involve product costing but they can be separated into three distinct groups:

1. *Absorption costing* and *direct costing* have a similar characteristic in that they determine the elements of cost included for product costing purposes.
2. *Standard costing, normal costing,* and *historical costing* also have a similar feature. Each represents a different type of cost to be used for product costing purposes—either estimated (standard), part estimated and part actual (normal), or actual (historical) costs.
3. Only *job order costing* and *process costing* are product cost accumulation systems. The remaining costing techniques or methods become a part of a job order or process cost accumulation system. For instance, a standard, direct job cost system would use predetermined costs, and only predetermined variable production costs would be used for product cost determination and inventory valuation purposes. Actual costs would be used in an historical, absorption process cost system, and all elements of manufacturing costs (variable and fixed costs) would be used to compute product costs.

Job order costing system

One traditional costing system is known as a job order system. By definition, a *job order cost system* is a product costing system applicable to unique products or specific customer orders in which raw materials (purchased parts, assemblies, and other direct material costs), labor, and manufacturing overhead costs are assigned to specific job orders or batches of products. Unit costs are computed by dividing total manufacturing costs accumulated for each job order by the number of good units produced.

Characteristics of a job order cost system are identified below.

1. Manufacturing costs are accumulated for specific contracts, jobs, or batches of products.
2. Costs are accumulated for particular quantities (or orders) of

goods without primary regard given to the period of time it takes to produce them.

3. A single work in process inventory control account is maintained and is supported by a subsidiary ledger comprised of job order cost sheets, each containing a cost summary for one job order.

A job order costing system is used in situations where identification of specific units and orders is possible. Production processes which use a job order costing system include large milling machine manufacturing, jet aircraft assembly, and any job shop where special orders are their primary business. In addition, government contract costing is a type of job order costing.

Process costing system

Process costing is the second traditional costing system. A *process cost system* assigns costs to *cost centers* rather than specific job orders. Raw materials, labor, and manufacturing overhead costs are assigned to processes or cost centers. An average unit cost is computed by dividing total manufacturing costs in each department or process by the equivalent whole units produced during the period.

A process costing system has the following characteristics:

1. Manufacturing costs are accumulated for entire departments or processes, and no effort is made to determine the cost of particular jobs or batches of product.
2. Costs are accumulated for specific departments, and production is measured for specific time periods.
3. Individual work in process inventory accounts are established for *each* production department or process to accumulate manufacturing costs. The number of work in process accounts will vary depending on the number of production processes required.

Process costing systems are used for production operations employing sequential processes in which materials move continuously from one department to the next. Examples include food processing, oil refining, paint manufacturing, and any other process producing similar products in long, "standard" runs.

Hybrid costing systems

No two cost accounting systems are exactly alike. Industry traits and characteristics, company size, product mix, product diversity, seasonal factors, labor unions, plant location, and many other factors affect the existing costing system. Although job order costing is the more widely used system, many firms use a mixture of the two. Process costing is used for long production runs while job order costing is applied to special order business.

Many costing systems contain selected characteristics from the two traditional costing systems. There is nothing sacred about adhering to one system or the other. The important thing is to assemble a costing system that fits a particular production operation and that provides information to management on a timely basis.

FUNDAMENTAL PURPOSES OF A COST SYSTEM

Cost control for financial target realization

In a single plant as well as in the more complex business environments, the financial plan usually includes regular or firm jobs, jobs that are continuations of work presently under contract, and a projection of new business. Considerable risk is attached to this forecast of business volume because such forecasts affect product mix and resource requirements. To effectively control the incurrence of direct and indirect production costs, a company must be certain of its product mix and should exercise strict control over all resource inputs. The costing system employed must be capable of continuously monitoring the validity of a forecast and must recognize the probability of significant variances occurring in plant sales and direct and indirect costs. The impact of changes must be assessed and corrective measures taken immediately to help assure the attainment of sales and profit targets.

Single-plant, single-product companies. There are many small job order or process type companies that perform essentially the same operation for a variety of customers. This type of company will usually employ a costing system that is based on machine-hours or labor cost and/or hours. Material is either furnished by the customer or treated as a separate direct charge to the customer's job order. Normally, one overhead (or burden) rate is used to assign indirect manufacturing costs to each job. Direct labor costs are traceable to each order processed. Selling and general and administrative costs (operating costs) are recovered by inclusion in an add-on type of G&A overhead for each job, based on a percentage of assigned production costs.

Typically, this type of operation uses a *time and material job cost system.* The "financial plan" is comparatively uncomplicated and is often in schedule form, especially if the company uses bank financing or is dealing directly or indirectly (as a contractor or subcontractor) with the government. Work volume forcasts are important for establishing overhead rates, labor rates for the period, total material costs, and material allowances for scrap if material is furnished. Often the owner is a member of the labor force and his/her salary must be determined for job costing purposes.

Single-plant, multiproduct companies. When a single-plant company produces several products, a more formal costing system is necessary. Raw material and labor costs are still traceable directly to specific jobs, but overhead costs are more of a problem. If different classes of labor are involved or if radically different processes and equipment are used on the various products, the costing system must include several overhead pools. Each pool is comprised of homogeneous overhead costs having a similar causal or beneficial relationship with the allocation base used for cost assignment purposes. Applied overhead will differ among the various products. General and administrative overhead, however, is applicable to all products produced during the period.

The complexity of financial planning increases as the number of products increases. Product mix determines material, labor, and overhead resource usage. Volume changes in product sales will affect overhead cost assignment and financial performance. Such changes are more common in new product lines, but unforeseen market changes in mature product lines should also be anticipated. A comprehensive costing system should produce information to help minimize the financial impact of product demand changes.

Multiplant, multiproduct companies. The cost control problems described for single-plant companies increase in direct proportion to the number of plants owned and operated by the company. The biggest danger is loss of cost control as a result of divisional communication breakdown. (Another cause of poor divisional performance is the lack of total corporate objectives and/or the failure of all segments to adhere to them.) Multiplant job cost systems usually depend on thousands of documents. Effective cost control can result only from companywide organization, cooperation, and communication.

Old product obsolescence and the creation of new product lines requiring research and development costs augment the problems of all companies. Such changes do not affect the type of costing system used but do require additional reports to determine the differences between actual direct labor learning curves and planned curves. In addition, actual raw material usage must be compared to the estimated allowances for such costs. A change order system should be established that will identify customer-authorized product changes and provide billing methods which will charge such costs directly to the customer. New overhead pools must be established to identify the costs which are applicable to product design and development and which are allocable on the basis of direct engineering labor. If the contracts (jobs) require work over more than one year, problems also arise in inventory pricing.

In summary, the complexity of financial planning is increased by the risk of new products which may or may not be successful and by the possible differences between estimated and actual delivery schedules, quality experience, and labor and material costs.

Cost analysis for pricing and contract negotiation

Costing systems with historical data from predecessor contracts play a very important role in product price determination and contract negotiation. Price quotes and contract bids require detailed information concerning raw material costs, labor rates, manufacturing and general and administrative overhead rates, and allocation bases. Interest costs, cost of capital, and profit are added using a predetermined percentage (or factor) of total costs.

A detailed listing of source data for price determination purposes is shown in Exhibit 1. Raw materials, if not furnished by the customer, can be traced to invoices or requisitions supported by invoices. Quantities of raw material are estimated on the basis of past experience, including supported material allowances for scrap. Prices actually used in bidding are derived from purchase orders or firm quotations. Material is purchased and recorded in job or contract inventory by various categories. Material for the job or contract could be under firm purchase orders with delivery dates spread over

EXHIBIT 1
Costing records for price determination

For price determination purposes, the following records may be useful:

Materials
  1. Raw materials, with scarce or exotic materials identified.
  2. Customer furnished materials.
  3. Purchased parts.
  4. Equipment to be included as customer property.
  5. Customer furnished equipment.

Direct Labor
  1. Assembly.
  2. Fabrication.
  3. Tooling.
  4. Engineering.
  5. Quality control.

Subcontract
  1. Parts.
  2. Sections of completed product.

Make or Buy Information
  To support in-house fabrication versus subcontract work.

Services Direct to the Job

Other Costs Direct to the Job

Overhead
  1. Factory.
  2. Administrative.
  3. Quality control.
  4. Engineering.
  5. Corporate.

the life of the contract. Excess material is transferred at cost, or sold and credited to the job or contract. For internal control purposes, the auditors check invoices as well as purchase orders.

Payroll records for work performed provide labor rate and hour information. Previous job cost reports for the same or a similar product are useful for projecting labor rate trends, as well as support for the bid. The various classes of labor costs increase and decrease at various rates during the life of the contract. For example, tooling and engineering are heaviest at the beginning of the contract, then fabrication, and final assembly, with quality control comparatively static. In the preparation of labor estimates, it is prudent to assume that negotiators or contract officers will expect labor unit costs to decrease based on learning curve theory, and wage rates to increase by a reasonable inflation factor.

Specific records should be maintained for purchased parts and services and for all subcontract items. In many cases, purchase orders are written for the entire contract amount to get the best price. Procurement of parts, service, or subcontract work should be finalized only after three or more bids have been received and justification made for the bid finally accepted. Overhead in all categories is generally bid on the basis of experienced cost, factored for planned increases and inflation. Estimates of future overhead cost will vary from experienced costs because of expected volume changes in each category and expected changes in rate ranges and inflationary expectations in supply costs. Historical records of cost experienced in each overhead pool should be reviewed in detail for expected changes. Care should be taken to trace labor costs to payroll records and supply costs to invoices. Problems in overhead do not generally arise from the question of whether the cost was actually incurred but focus on whether a cost was correctly allocated to the contract. Documentation of all costs should include justification in all questionable areas.

General and administrative expenses are applicable for government contract pricing purposes. Section XV of ASPR (Armed Services Procurement Regulations) contains abbreviated costing guidelines in this area. More specific costing rules are described in Cost Accounting Standards (CASs) Nos. 403 and 410.

Records supporting inventory valuation

One of the objectives of a costing system is the determination of product unit cost. The focal point of any costing system is the *work in process inventory* account. All material, labor, subcontract, and factory costs flow into this account. There is little difficulty in costing resource inputs. Costing product output is not as easy. Once resource inputs have entered the production process and their costs have been charged to work in process, their identity is lost. All resource input costs are channeled or reassigned to units of output. This cost reassignment process (product costing) is one of the functions of a costing system. As described in the chapter section "Traditional Costing Systems," once product unit cost has been determined, total cost of units completed can be computed. This amount is transferred to finished goods inventory or cost of goods sold. Any amount remaining in work in process inventory represents the costs attached to partially completed units.

Special problems arise when customers require product changes or when an order or a contract is terminated. These situations require specific accounting approaches and are not normal product costing influences.

Performance measurement

Cost estimates generated through a costing system are subject to rigorous scrutiny during the period of implementation. Cost control is maintained if estimated costs are realistic and if differences between estimated and experienced costs are minimized. The main reason for such close attention is the possible effect on planned profits and distribution of overhead costs to contracts caused by changes in costs and product mix.

As a company increases in complexity, it is not unusual for total costs to be 50 percent overhead. Volume changes in sales or sales mix could have a significant financial effect. If sales volumes are in accordance with the financial plan, the overhead should be relatively easy to control. Problems arise when there are strikes or fires or changes in volume. Generally, overhead costs are included in well-defined pools of cost categories by organization responsibility, and assignment for cost control is separate from direct cost controls. Reports by overhead pool by organizational segment should show forecasted versus actual costs, with significant variances explained.

For control and performance measurement purposes, detailed records are maintained on direct material and direct labor. Material prices and quantities used should be reviewed often and compared to projected data to determine if variances exist. Any major differences should be analyzed and explained.

Direct labor control includes hours and rate ranges. Variances from plan should include explanations as to overtime usage and rate changes. Learning curve analysis is applicable for assembly and certain fabrication labor. Actual results are compared closely to original projections, and variances are noted. Tooling and Design Engineering normally control their own costs to budget and can determine progress by tools made compared to tools required, and design prints compared to total required.

Effective performance measurement requires lower level detail job reports of actual versus planned costs. All major jobs are reported in such detail. Minor jobs are reported in less detail, but even minor jobs can be reported in a schedule estimating progress cost versus plan. At least monthly, each individual plant should make a summary report of all jobs in process, showing estimated progress on cost compared to plan and reasons for significant variances.

Accurate and timely reports

Reports to management.   Management reporting starts with the lowest tier of detailed records on individual jobs and continues through major cost categories, summarized by category, to an individual job summary; then to a plant summary by jobs; and finally to a corporate report summarized by plant and contract. The controller should be able to trace any significant variance by job or contract through the reporting system to the job or contract material, labor, subcontract, or overhead cost category which has problems. The lower tier cost controllers should provide explanations by the time the summary is received in the corporate office and be able to discuss corrective measures needed.

Reports to government and higher tier contractors.   Good business practice dictates that the essential requirements of the customer must be recognized, especially when supported by contract clauses. The customer must have factual support for progress payments and billings and enough detail to support contract costs.

An existing costing system which has been satisfactory to the company for many years cannot always be easily adapted to customers' report forms. Therefore, the controller must make certain that the company's and customer's systems are reconcilable by date, amount and units of product, and man-hours. Failure to take care of this reconciliation or failure to educate the customer's auditors and company personnel in the need for system reconciliation may lead to endless questions, disputes, and litigation.

Historical records and documentation

Historical documentation of past performance provides initial input to the forecasting function. Care should be taken to preserve historical data, and such information should be easy to retrieve when needed. Other reasons for maintaining historical records are included in the following situations:

1.   Detailed job records must be kept on file for historical purposes for the duration of the job at a minimum, or for whatever period is required in the contract.

2. As overhead is a large portion of job cost and applies to periods rather than jobs, records must be kept for whatever period of years is necessary to satisfy all claims.
3. Supporting detail such as timecards, payroll rates, and materials, supplies, and subcontract invoices must be filed as long as support for the contract is necessary.

Accumulation of data for special studies

Overhead cost studies. Fixed and variable overhead studies lead to endless arguments. Obviously, some overhead costs are more variable than others. Some are easier to discontinue during periods of cost reduction. Data for these studies may come from historical cost information and/or from planned increases in overhead costs.

Alternative investment of resources studies. A company may own fully depreciated assets with high maintenance costs and low productivity. A study may be needed to compare cost advantages and disadvantages of new asset investment, and relative cost savings in labor and unit costs. Buy versus rent studies are also based on historical records.

Corrective measure studies. A costing system yields reports and variance analysis studies centering on specific problem areas. The next step is to conduct a study to determine the corrective measures available to management.

Audit support detail

Government audit. Contract review is one objective of a government audit. Armed Services Procurement Regulations Section XV contains abbreviated and sometimes ambiguous statements of allowable and unallowable costs. Other regulations affect material purchases, subcontractor relationships, purchases of foreign goods, make or buy lists, obligatory records, use of government owned material and equipment, and government inspection. Support detail may include not only purchase orders, requisitions, invoices, and ledgers, but also memoranda and reports concerning overhead allocated to the contract. In addition, when the government is a major customer, the audit may include the entire accounting system and management policies and procedures.

Commercial audit. A well-defined costing system provides for internal audit reviews and methods for implementing improvements within the system. Independent auditors are expected to check out the costing system to determine its effect on the valuation of work in process and finished goods inventories and the amount shown in the Cost of Goods Sold account. Certification of financial position and operating results is not possible without a thorough examination of a company's costing system.

OPERATIONAL ASPECTS OF A COSTING SYSTEM

Support records, documents, and files

Data retention varies in size and sophistication among companies. Detail of documentation is a function of the cost to install and maintain the system and the benefits derived from the system by management. As a general rule, the larger and more decentralized the company, the more detailed is the record system.

Master job file. Maintenance of a master job order (or processing order) file is essential to control of the production operation. All resource utilization is dependent upon the contents of the master job file. Production scheduling, raw material purchasing, labor scheduling, and subcontract needs are all determined from job orders on hand.

A contract is a living document until completed or terminated. Changes to the contract are negotiated and included in the contract file. The master job order translates the contract into terms of requirements of labor and material, subcontracts, purchased parts, and other direct costs. Performance and schedule requirements and budgets are assigned by suborders (related by code to the master job order) to various managers responsible to the plant manager.

Direct cost records. Control of operating costs and preparation of contract bids and sales proposals are facilitated by a complete set of direct cost records. Direct labor is supported by a set of payroll records and related job timecards. Payrolls are on file which identify employee names, numbers, and rates. Job cards indicate employee name, number, and rate, and hours and rates charged to jobs, and are auditable to the payroll and balanced against total hours paid.

Invoice, purchase order, material requisition, and receiving report forms provide adequate support for cost verification of raw material and supplies. Specific records should be maintained for all costs classified as "other direct costs." Other direct costs, either equipment or services, are supported by invoices, requisitions, purchase orders, and receiving reports and all are charged to the appropriate job code. Some items are charged to the job through the supplies inventory. The auditable file in this case includes the purchase order and invoice charge to inventory, the requisition to the job from inventory, and the inventory pricing system. All of these documents help to measure the costs charged to work in process inventory. The existing inventory records and valuation methods should provide proof of cost transfers from work in process inventory to finished goods inventory and from finished goods inventory to cost of goods sold.

Indirect (overhead) cost support. Documentation of indirect costs is more difficult because of numerous minor cost items and because methods of assignment of these costs to cost objectives (products or contracts) prevent specific unit cost verification. Indirect cost incurrence should, to the extent practicable, be supported by invoices, purchase requests, purchase orders, and other forms of cost authorization. Once incurred, indirect costs are charged to various overhead pools. Each overhead pool maintained should be described in detail, including purpose of the pool, types of costs to be charged to the pool, and reasons supporting the allocation base used to apply overhead costs to cost objectives. Support for an allocation base should stem from the causal or beneficial relationship between the costs contained in the respective pool and the final cost objective.

Financial plan. In order to control costs, actual costs incurred must be compared with some cost target to determine if excessive spending has occurred. The company's financial plan provides a detailed set of cost targets for the review process. Therefore, establishment and maintenance of an annual profit plan, master budget, or financial plan is an integral part of a total company cost control program. An updated financial plan file for each major job or contract can serve a variety of useful purposes, including:

1. Reconciliation of original detailed bid with the bid accepted by the customer;
2. Reconciliation of the bid in detail with the master job order;

3. Basis for changes in schedule, design, and production requirements and the changes in budgets; and
4. Basis for report of estimated versus actual cost and progress to date.

Management reports. Cost control is fostered by various forms of reports to management. Routine analysis reports prepared by people in the controller's area and the internal audit staff may provide information to facilitate cost control. Variance reports prepared from comparisons of actual versus planned or budgeted costs often pinpoint areas of costs requiring corrective action. In addition, management may request special reports to be prepared to analyze performance in specific areas of operations. These reports together provide most of the information needed to control operating costs adequately.

The following contract job analysis reports are usually made, and all should be included in the permanent contract or job files:

1. Reconciliation of detailed bid to the signed proposal.
2. Reconciliation of the signed proposal to the master job order.
3. Reconciliation of the master job order to the budget releases.
4. Engineering change analyses.
5. Changes in schedule analyses.
6. Production line stations and schedule of parts and sections to the production line.

In addition to regular reports filed as permanent records, a provision should be made to expand the system when necessary with special reports to meet special situations. For example, reports should be made for (1) significant changes in engineering design or quantity increases or decreases with possible effects on costs and profits, (2) material shortages or subcontract failures, and (3) any other situation where early warning is necessary to produce corrective action.

Internal analysis and reporting

Successful cost control depends on a strong costing system, defined methods of classifying and accounting for costs, and full cooperation from all levels of management. Production scheduling must have adequate information concerning open orders and resource availability. Every link of the company's information system must be operational, supplying data on a timely basis. Top management should encourage full company support and should specify the types of information and reports needed to guide company operations.

The costing system, just like other parts of the accounting system, should contain internal control devices. A system of checks and balances should be established to verify resource input data, and trained internal auditors should conduct a continuous surveillance of operations. In addition, each costing system should contain provisions for special studies to identify approaches to corrective action or cost improvement, i.e., cost versus plan variance analysis, value analysis, and asset utilization studies.

Controlling change orders

Change orders are negotiated for any changes in product design and schedule or any changes in unit quantities and result in adjustments in direct costs and possible changes in overhead application rates, and different labor skills. Such changes can originate from either customer authorized changes or internal changes authorized by management.

Customer authorized changes. Change orders initiated by the customer require a special information gathering system. Costs of such changes are usually chargeable directly to the customer. Therefore, some means should be provided for assembling increased costs resulting from product changes. Product volume changes could result in increases or decreases in unit costs and overhead application rates. If a contract or job termination is involved, a special analysis should be conducted before a proper settlement can be negotiated.

Often change orders result in production delays. Price escalation usually accompanies production delays and a means of identifying these cost increases should be available. Engineering design changes often result in partial terminations and obsolete units. These costs must also be charged to the customer.

Internal changes authorized by management. Internal change orders can result from mistakes being corrected, engineering design improvements, or production improvements in tooling and/or processing. These changes may result in significant cost increases or decreases. Costs associated with general betterments in product design or manufacturing processes should be charged against overhead for the period, while the cost of improvements in a specific contract should be treated as a direct cost to the job which receives the benefit of the improvement. Costs resulting from correction of mistakes should be accounted for by job order or overhead account and explained in variance analysis reports.

Cost control through systems management

Cost control can be accomplished in many ways. The most cumbersome, unorganized approach is to analyze operating segments selected on an arbitrary basis. "Small fires" or operational trouble spots are analyzed after the fact with little or no effect on cost control. Cost control through *systems management* is at the opposite end of the spectrum. Under this concept, cost control is a by-product of an effective, coordinated information system. Control mechanisms are woven into the costing system.

Exhibit 2 identifies the segments of a costing system utilized for effective cost control. Each of the segments listed has primary functions other than cost control. However, integrated into a system of complementary functions, costs are controlled through efficient resource management.

EXHIBIT 2
Segments of a costing system for control

Bid and Proposal Preparation
1. Direct labor.
2. Direct material.
3. Purchased parts.
4. Subcontract items.
5. Special equipment (customer ownership).
6. Factory overhead.
7. Administrative overhead.
8. Special costs (marketing and research and development).

Master Job Control
1. Analysis of total job requirements.
2. Production orders.
3. Material control.
4. Direct labor control.
5. Control of overhead costs.
6. Quality control.
7. Management reporting.
8. Internal audit controls.

   Note: A sample set of source and transmittal forms used in a costing system is illustrated in the Appendix to this chapter.

Bid and proposal preparation.   Preparing contract bids and job proposals are critical factors in the financial success of a company. If care is not taken, overpricing or underpricing occurs, resulting in lost business or monetary losses in income. In addition, bids and proposals constitute target costs for cost control and performance evaluation purposes.

When preparing bids for defense contracts, the contractor must now categorize costs in a manner similar to the way costs will be accounted for (see Cost Accounting Standard No. 401). In the past, engineering or some other organizational segment other than accounting would prepare bids and proposals. Under those conditions, job performance was difficult to evaluate because of the absence of cost comparability.

A detailed bid or job proposal should include itemized projections for direct labor, raw material needs, purchased parts, areas requiring subcontract work, special equipment needs, estimates of factory overhead costs, general and administrative expense allotments, and special analyses including marketing studies and research and development cost projections. Records of each segment of the proposal should be maintained for performance evaluation and control purposes.

Master job control.   All parts of the costing system used to accumulate and account for actual costs incurred are referred to collectively as the "Master Job Control." A listing of these segments is shown in Exhibit 2. First, job requirements are summarized from information included in the bid or job proposal (adjusted to agree with the contract as finally negotiated). Initial analyses should identify organizational segments responsible for specific job requirements.

Issuance of production orders to work centers is the second step. This part of the master job control contains the responsibilities of scheduling production, identifying quality and performance requirements, and communicating targets for costs and hours to responsible managers. Control of raw material, labor, and factory overhead costs is an extension of a costing system's cost accumulation process. Material control results from (1) adequate procurement scheduling of raw materials, purchased parts, and subcontract items; (2) comparisons of price and quantity allowances with actual cost and usage information; and (3) a functioning inventory control system. Labor costs are controlled by rate and efficiency variance analyses and a fully operational payroll and labor time system. Spending and efficiency differences are analyzed for control purposes in the areas of factory, engineering, and general and administrative overhead. Other control functions in the factory include surveillance of labor learning curves, quality control reports, comparisons of progress cost reports with target costs, and actual versus planned production scheduling analyses.

All of this information enters the flow of a company's information system. Each company's information system will be unique, designed specifically for a particular industry and operating environment. An illustrative outline of one management reporting system is shown below.

1. Corporate level—special analyses of major jobs by division.
2. Divisional level—analyses of actual versus planned costs for all jobs.
    a. Schedule reports.
    b. Quality reports.
    c. Target realization reports.
    d. Changes reports.
        (1) Make or buy decisions.
        (2) Customer-authorized changes.
        (3) Scrap and error reports.
        (4) Improvements in operating processes.
    e. Comparison of improvement curves with planned improvement curves.
    f. Planned versus actual overhead reports.
        (1) Numerical controls.
        (2) Hourly usage controls.
    g. Risk reports.
    h. Corrective action reports.

Internal audit controls tie together the various elements of a control system. An internal audit involves a critical review of the entire management reporting system. Subcontractor prices must be verified. Elements of the inventory control system must be checked to determine if the system is functioning properly. Cost classification must be verified through analyses of direct and indirect costing techniques and guidelines. In summary, the internal audit function polices the entire management information system, providing the catalyst for a coordinated reporting network. An illustrative set of information forms to support this cost control system is shown in the appendix.

FEDERAL COST ACCOUNTING STANDARDS[2]

The creation and background of the Cost Accounting Standards Board was described in Chapter 38. Concern here is the effect that Cost Accounting Standards (CASs) have on costing systems. CASs are applicable to defense contracts in excess of $100,000. Certain companies and industries are exempt from a few of the standards. For the most part, however, CASs apply to most government defense contracts, and contractors must comply with the rules of each standard if they have a covered contract. Although CASs are not designed for cost control purposes on the side of the contractor (they may limit revenue more than control costs), failure to comply will subject the contractor to stiff penalties, thereby increasing the cost of the contract.

This section is intended to review existing topics covered by CASs and to discuss their effect on costing systems. For more specific information about each standard, consult Commerce Clearing House's "Cost Accounting Standards Guide."

CAS No. 401—Consistency in Estimating, Accumulating, and Reporting Costs

The purpose of this standard is to insure that each contractor's practices used in estimating costs for a proposal are consistent with cost accounting practices used by the contractor in accumulating and reporting costs.

CAS No. 402—Consistency in Allocating Costs Incurred for the Same Purpose

The purpose of this standard is to require that each type of cost is allocated only once and on only one basis to any contract or other cost objective.

CAS No. 403—Allocation of Home Office Expenses to Segments

The purpose of this standard is to establish criteria for allocation of the expenses of a home office to the segments of the organization

---

[2] Only companies contracting with the federal government need to be interested in this section of the chapter.

based on the beneficial or causal relationships between such expenses and the receiving segments.

CAS No. 404—Capitalization of Tangible Assets

This standard requires that for purposes of cost measurement, contractors establish and adhere to policies with respect to capitalization of tangible assets which satisfy criteria set forth in the standard.

CAS No. 405—Accounting for Unallowable Costs

The purpose of this standard is to facilitate the negotiation, audit, administration, and settlement of contracts by establishing guidelines covering (1) identification of costs specifically described as unallowable, at the time such costs first become defined or authoritatively designated as unallowable; and (2) the cost accounting treatment to be accorded such identified unallowable costs in order to promote the consistent application of sound cost accounting principles covering all incurred costs.

CAS No. 406—Cost Accounting Period

The purpose of this standard is to provide criteria for the selection of time periods to be used as cost accounting periods for contract cost estimating, accumulating, and reporting.

CAS No. 407—Use of Standard Costs for Direct Material and Direct Labor

The purpose of this standard is to provide criteria under which standard costs may be used for estimating, accumulating, and reporting costs of direct material and direct labor; and to provide criteria relating to the establishment of standards, accumulation of standard costs, and accumulation and disposition of variances from standard costs.

CAS No. 408—Accounting for Costs of Compensated Personal Absence

The purpose of this standard is to improve, and provide uniformity in, the measurement of costs of vacation, sick leave, holiday, and other compensated personal absence for a cost accounting period, and thereby increase the probability that the measured costs are allocated to the proper cost objectives.

CAS No. 409—Depreciation of Tangible Capital Assets

The purpose of this standard is to provide criteria and guidance for assigning costs of tangible capital assets to cost accounting periods and for allocating such costs to cost objectives within such periods in an objective and consistent manner.

CAS No. 410—Allocation of Business Unit General and Administrative Expense to Final Cost Objectives

This standard provides criteria for the allocation of business unit general and administrative (G&A) expenses to business unit final cost objectives based on their beneficial or causal relationships. (This is a proposed standard at time of writing.)

CAS No. 411—Accounting for the Acquisition Costs of Material

This standard provides criteria for the accounting for acquisition costs of material and includes provisions relating to the use of inventory costing methods.

CAS No. 412—Composition and Measurement of Pension Cost

This standard provides guidance for determining and measuring the components of pension cost and establishes the basis on which pension costs shall be assigned to cost accounting periods.

Note: There are other Cost Accounting Standards proposed or in process that will have significant impacts on the cost accounting and control system. It is imperative that controllers keep current on these Standards and make sure that appropriate changes are made. Areas of current research include termination accounting, accounting for scrap, accounting for manufacturing overhead, direct versus indirect costs, cost of capital, and accounting for independent research and development costs. In addition to the various regulations mentioned above, it is now necessary to make a formal disclosure of cost accounting practices followed in each segment of the business. Once formalized, the disclosure may be changed only after formal notice has been given to the government.

The work of the Cost Accounting Standards Board places constraints on the flexibility of the costing system. The controller should be fully aware of these constraints and know how they may or may not restrict the flexibility of his system. A costing system, as described in the company's Disclosure Statement, may not be changed except through a prescribed channel. Delays will arise from necessary changes unless a workable liaison can be established.

Assuming that Cost Accounting Standards are concerned only with generally accepted accounting principles, delays in changes need not impede progress substantially if they are kept to reasonable time limits. A flexible costing system should not be hampered by the work of the Cost Accounting Standards Board. Cost Accounting Standards should be treated simply as an expansion of the "advance agreements" or "special accounting agreements" normally found in the contracting business, especially with the federal government.

THE CONTROLLER'S FUNCTION

Organization

The corporate controller is normally remote from the plant's detailed cost system and usually relies on summary type reports for information. Action is required when there are significant variances between the plan and actual performance. The fundamental causes for variances are usually found in the operating organizations—factory, engineering, tooling, material, and subcontract—and it is inadvisable and impractical for the controller to intervene directly where the lower tier organizations are concerned. He or she should, however, require as a part of the cost system that the plant-level controller have on file functional outlines and job descriptions for the personnel directly concerned in the operation of the cost-bid system from original proposal to the cost ledger. The plant controller must be able to trace the variance to the source expeditiously, obtain information from the executives concerned, and report back through the plant manager when circumstances warrant.

In large, decentralized companies, an organization chart of the controller's function should be prepared. In addition to normal organization charts, the plant controller should have a chart for each major contract or job disclosing who is responsible for the bid and for performance reports or realization against contract budget in all organizational units outside those reporting to the plant controller. The plant controller also should have a time-phased report chart showing how the contract or job budget versus actual cost summary is built up from all plant organizations.

The functional outline of job descriptions and organization charts described above will disclose some employees responsible for cost reports who are not members of the accounting organization. It must be understood by all concerned that the controller has a legitimate interest in the quality of the cost reports and is, in fact, responsible to management for the financial statements. However, the controller has no need to disrupt the budget system established by the other organizations. The controller's main objective is training and integrating the personnel and reports into the cost system to facilitate performance reporting and cost control.

Responsibilities

1. A fundamental responsibility of a controller is to ensure that appropriate costing systems have been established to serve the needs and requirements of all levels of management. It is not sufficient to develop systems simply for the accumulation of historical costs, but rather to make effective utilization of the cost data. This requires that the cost systems be designed to provide for expeditious or even automatic analysis, comparisons to measurement norms, and summarizations. In addition, the system should be flexible in its ability to change with changing conditions in the business cycle, in sales volume, and in product mix. The system should provide for changes in level of detail for the various levels of management and should be capable of changing to focus attention on currently significant cost problems.

2. The controller should take the lead role in developing a sound cost control philosophy. He or she must understand the business thoroughly, create a costing system responsive to the needs of the company, and establish proper communication channels with the executives concerned. Basic and detailed knowledge of all facets of the manufacturing and productive processes, design

engineering, sales, distribution, and warehousing are required to develop effectively the type of cost system that will provide the necessary cost data to make intelligent decisions.

3. Maintenance of the cost system is necessary because it must be responsive to the needs of the business, whether they concern planning, control, pricing, or valuation. The mere collection of costs without an objective or clear understanding of the reason for the data is of little value. The system must respond to the changing environment and provide management with all necessary cost information.

4. Presenting the data in tabular form is not sufficient; the data must be communicated. It is a prime responsibility of the controller to interpret and convey the cost information in proper terms to affected management personnel. The right cost information must be delivered in a timely manner to the personnel who have the opportunity and responsibility to take corrective action. This may require an education process for the users of the cost information so that they may utilize effectively the data provided. The report recipients are often not accountants and should have a clear, concise understanding of the cost system. The presentation of the cost reports should be made in such a manner as to motivate the decision makers to take timely and effective action.

5. Reports are good only if acted upon or if the information is useful. Quick formulation of reports is the controller's responsibility. They must be accurate and timely if corrective action is possible, especially if they form the basis of other reports. An integrated cost information system is built upon a low level of detailed reports, with essential information summarized for top management. When some of the bricks are missing or weak at low levels, the whole edifice is weak.

6. In many companies pricing is based on cost, using a job cost system. The estimated rate of profit will probably be low under competitive circumstances, especially with a mature production process. When a new product which involves a high degree of research and development is proposed, there may be a high degree of risk in the estimated profit. The controller should require risk analysis in written form from the cost estimator. Risks are of various types: contract termination risk, production and engineering risk, risk of strike, and risk of material shortages.

Known risks must be reviewed constantly. Whenever an analysis discloses a substantial variance between the financial plan and contract or job performance, explanations and corrective reports should be required.

7. New products and processes require heavy asset and plant re-arrangement expenditures. The controller is part of the check and balance decision system. Marketing and manufacturing executives understandably want increased sales. The controller must determine if the investment is justified, either for new business or for cost improvement purposes.

8. In the paragraphs above, the controller was shown to be responsible for the orderly operation of the cost system, including books, records, reports, and all other necessary documentation. These are all duties for which he or she has been trained as an executive accountant. A successful controller has to go beyond technical performance and become a representative of the company's financial structure when working with people outside the company.

Dealing with government auditors, regulators, and contracting representatives is especially important to a company contracting with the government. In addition, all companies have to work with federal, state, and local taxing authorities, the SEC, and other trade regulators. Cooperating with internal and independent auditors is another challenge to a controller who has usually been an auditor and knows the strengths and weaknesses of auditors and audit programs. When a controller has confidence in existing records and the reporting system, working with outsiders can be very frustrating and time-consuming unless there exists a preconceived procedure for handling questions and required reports. The following are suggested guidelines to cope with such situations:

a. All policies and procedures should be in writing.

b. All regular internal reports and reports to outsiders should be described and time-phased and responsibly assigned for accuracy and scheduling purposes.

c. All special reports should be closely controlled for impact on schedule and for value to the company.

d. Agreement should be negotiated in advance with concerned auditors and contracting representatives for changes in the system which affect contract costs.

e. Authority of auditors to review cost documentation affecting the contracts with which they are concerned should be recognized and made known to all employees.

f. Authority to give access to records to auditors and responsibilities for answering accounting questions should be specifically assigned at low enough levels to speed the audit process, while still providing informative answers.

9. Finally, the controller should be engaged more with future operations than with those in the past. If the system functions properly, sufficient time will be allowed to conduct top-level analyses leading to formulation of future plans and policies.

APPENDIX: SAMPLE SET OF SOURCE AND TRANSMITTAL FORMS USED IN A COSTING SYSTEM

AUTHORIZED TIME-REPORTING DOCUMENTS	
	PAGE
	EFFECTIVE
	SUPERSEDES

I. Purpose
   To establish responsibilities and the procedure for the use and control of authorized time-reporting documents.

II. General
   A. Work Authorization Document: A document which authorizes the department to which it is issued to expend labor and procure material as required to accomplish the task described therein.
      1. The work authorization document is authority for the affected department to issue appropriate internal work order documentation defining the tasks. Examples are sales order, work package authority, interdivision work order, etc.
      2. Direct labor hour expenditure shall not be reported directly against the work authorization document, except in special cases where the scope of the project is such as to make a further functional or task separa-

tion organizationally impractical and economically not justifiable.

B. Authorized Time-Reporting Document: A document issued, except in special instances cited herein, on the operational department level, which describes and authorizes a task to be accomplished, and to which direct labor hours expended shall be charged. Examples are production order, tool order, planning order, etc.

    1. An authorized time-reporting document will have a Division form number and will be issued through Forms Management, with the concurrence of Timekeeping and Management Services. If the document is serialized, the serial range must be obtained from Cost Accounting.

    2. All approved authorized time-reporting documents, including those documents having the dual function of work authorization and direct labor reporting, are listed as Attachments to this procedure.

C. Time-Reporting Department: A department which reports the expenditure of labor hours to Finance.

D. Each department using Authorized Time-Reporting Documents under this procedure shall maintain instructional material for its use and control as required.

III. Procedure

A. Direct Labor Reporting Organizations

    1. The manager of each department reporting direct labor hours will ensure that all hours expended have been authorized by, and charged to, a time reporting document cited in the Attachments to this procedure.

    2. Every direct-labor-reporting employee will have the appropriate authorizing document available at his work station to verify the effort being performed. All work efforts are subject to Finance and customer audit to determine compliance with standard time charge practices and time charging authority.

    3. In any department where time-reporting documents are not available the Work Authorization Document will be available in the immediate work area, at the work station of the employee or his immediate

manager. In cases where it would be impractical to furnish employees with Work Authorization Documents, the department will publish a list of active time charges and work effort description to enable the employee to accurately select applicable time charges.

    4. Request for new documents or revised applications for existing documents will be approved by a manager reporting to a vice president and forwarded to Timekeeping.

B. Timekeeping

    1. Timekeeping will accept direct labor hours reported only when supported by an approved time-reporting document applicable to that particular department. Timekeeping will report to the management of departments concerned any instance where direct labor hours are being reported without approved time-reporting documentation.

    2. In the case of requests for new documents or revised functions for existing documents Timekeeping will perform the following functions:

       a. Review each request for conformance with Timekeeping procedures.

       b. Coordinate with Accounting in cases where a work authorization document is to be used also as a time-reporting document, and in other cases as required.

       c. Return disapproved requests to the requesting department with reasons noted.

       d. Refer approved requests to Management Services.

       e. Instruct affected department and supporting Timekeeping activity to accept direct labor hours reported on the newly approved or revised document.

TIME REPORTING AND WORK AUTHORIZATION DOCUMENTS — MANUFACTURING

	Facilities	Manufacturing Research and Development	Manufacturing Engineering	Tool Design Numeric Design	Tool Fabrication	Production Fabrication	Prototype Fabrication and Assembly	Military Subassembly and Assembly	Commercial Subassembly and Assembly	Overdale Military Assembly	Overdale Manufacturing Engineering and Maintenance
	51XX	5205	52XX	5254 5261	54XX	55XX	553X 556X	57XX	59XX	R58XX	R5880
TIME REPORTING DOCUMENTS											
20-779A Engineering Fabrication Order (EFO)							•	•	•	•	•
29-18A Plant Engineering Work Order (PEWO)	•										•
60-282A Numeric Design Request				•							
60-443A Assembly Line Operation Order (ALOO)							•	•	•	•	
76-42 Planning Order			•								
76-68 Parent Tool Order				•	•				•		•
76-69 Split Tool Order				•	•				•		•
76-72 Production Order						•	•	•	•	•	
76-78A Customer Repair Order (CRO)							•	•	•	•	
76-86B Limited Production/Rework Order (LPRO)		•			•		•	•	•	•	
76-94B Limited Work Order		•									
WORK AUTHORIZATION DOCUMENTS											
25-105 Travel Authority	•	•	•	•	•	•	•	•	•	•	•
40-2A Sales Order (90,000 Series only)	•	•	•	•	•	•	•	•	•	•	•
C-34 Interdivisional Work Order (IWO)	•	•	•	•	•	•	•	•	•	•	•

TIME REPORTING AND WORK AUTHORIZATION DOCUMENTS — ENGINEERING PRODUCT SUPPORT

	Engineering	Flight Test	Manufacturing Engineering	Assembly	Project	Test and Evaluation	System Engineering	Engineering Data Standards and Check	Design Engineering	Advanced Systems	Research and Technology Development Programs	Product Support
	26XX	27XX	281X	2830	3030	31XX	32XX	3340	34XX	36XX	37XX	88XX
TIME REPORTING DOCUMENTS												
11-7 Machine Sketch		•				•						
20-231A Test Work Order	•	•				•			•		•	
20-235 Test Shop Order		•				•					•	
20-421 Research Laboratory Release						•					•	
20-779A Engineering Fabrication Order (EFO)				•		•					•	
20-827 Materiel Research Lab Work Order						•					•	
29-18A Plant Engineering Work Order (PEWO)			•			•			•		•	
60-443A Assembly Line Operation Order (ALOO)			•			•					•	
76-42 Planning Order			•									
76-68 Parent Tool Order			•									
76-69 Split Tool Order			•									
76-72 Production Order												
76-78A Customer Repair Order (CRO)				•		•						
76-86B Limited Production/Rework Order (LPRO)				•		•						
WORK AUTHORIZATION DOCUMENTS												
25-105 Travel Authority	•	•	•	•	•	•	•	•	•	•	•	•
39-669 Work Package Authority (WPA)	•	•	•	•	•	•	•	•	•	•	•	•
40-2A Sales Order	•	•	•	•	•	•	•	•	•	•	•	•
C-34 Interdivisional Work Order (IWO)	•	•	•	•	•	•	•	•	•	•	•	•

TIME REPORTING AND WORK AUTHORIZATION DOCUMENTS

GRAPHICS, INDUSTRIAL ENGINEERING, OPERATIONS CONTROL, QUALITY CONTROL, SPARES

		Graphic Operations	Industrial Engineering	Production Control & Storerooms & Stockrooms	Shipping	Transportation Services	Production Programs QC	Functional Test	Quality Engineering	Military Spares	Commercial Spares
		115X	5041	53XX 65XX	6841	685X	75XX 77XX	N7300	76XX	8321	8331
TIME REPORTING DOCUMENTS											
20-231A	Test Work Order				●						
20-779A	Engineering Fabrication Order				●			●			
26-2A	Invoice and Packing Sheet				●	●					
26-2F	Packing Sheets/Debit Memo				●						
26-9	Shipping Container Request				●						
28-7A	Purchased Part Requisition				●						
28-8	Material Requisition				●						
28-8A	Raw Material Request – Limited Use				●						
31-47	Shipping Authority				●						
31-146A	Receiving Report				●						
48-16	Graphics Work Order	●									
52-23	Reproduction Order	●									
52-24	Drawing or Associated Document Microdata Worksheet	●									
55-7	Subcontract Supply Requisition				●						
55-11	Shipping Advice				●						
60-819	Export Control Disbursement & Shipping Action Req.			●	●						
60-819A	Export Control Disbursement & Shipping Action Req.			●	●						
60-836	Export Control Disbursement & Shipping Action Req.			●	●						
76-68A	Tool Order Change Notice				●	●					
76-69	Split Tool Order				●	●					
76-72	Production Order				●	●		●			
76-73	Production Order (Mfg. Gross Req. System)				●	●		●			
76-78A	Customer Repair Order (CRO)				●			●			
76-86B	Limited Production/Rework Order (LPRO)				●			●			
DD-250	Material Inspection and Receiving Report				●						
DD-1149	Requisition and Shipping Document				●						
DD-1348-1	DOD Single Line Item Release/Receipt				●						
WORK AUTHORIZATION DOCUMENTS											
25-105	Travel Authority	●	●		●	●	●	●	●	●	●
39-669	Work Package Authority (WPA)	●	●		●	●	●		●	●	●
40-2A	Sales Order (90,000 Series only)	●				●					
40-2A	Sales Order		●		●	●	●		●		●
C-34	Interdivisional Work Order (IWO)	●	●			●	●	●	●	●	●

WORK PACKAGE AUTHORITY
FORM 39-669 (R.6-70)

				PAGE (1) 1 OF
RESPONSIBLE DEPT. (2)	SALES ORDER NO. (3)	BGT. ADVICE (4)	WPA NO. (5)	REV. (6)

PROGRAM (7)	SCHEDULED START DATE (8)	SCHEDULED COMP. DATE (9)	SUM. COST ELEMENT NO. (10)

CONTRACT (11)	WPPA REFERENCE REV. PAGE (12) LINE	SUMMARY ACCOUNT FUNCTION (13)

WBS ELEMENT NO. (14)	DEPARTMENT NAME (15)	(16) DETAIL ACCT. NO. MAT'L. USE ONLY

WBS ELEMENT NAME (17)	PREPARED BY (18)	DEPT. (18)	DATE (18)

CHANGE AUTHORITY/REFERENCES/REMARKS

(19)

END PRODUCT (20)	QUANTITY (21)	DIRECT PVW ASSIGNED
		HOURS (22)	DOLLARS

TYPE OF WPA (23)		PLANNED VALUE OF WORK ACCOMPLISHED (PVWA) CRITERIA AND METHOD OF DETERMINATION
☐ DISCRETE EFFORT	☐ RECURRING	(24)
☐ LEVEL OF EFFORT		
☐ APPORTIONED EFFORT	☐ NONRECURRING	

STATEMENT OF WORK

(25)

(26) MONTH/YEAR								
PVWS (27) MONTHLY								
CUMULATIVE								
PVWA (28) MONTHLY								
CUMULATIVE								

APPROVALS

ISSUE	RESPONSIBLE DEPT.	DATE	PROGRAM BUDGET	DATE	PROGRAM PLANNING	DATE
ORIGINAL						
REV. (29)	(30)	(30)	(31)	(31)	(32)	(32)
REV.						
REV.						

FORM FACSIMILE AND INSTRUCTIONS
"WORK PACKAGE AUTHORITY"

A. Purpose

The Work Package Authority (WPA) describes a Statement of
Work (SOW) that is to be performed by a department, for an

assigned dollar or hour value, within a specified schedule; the WPA also identifies the Cost/Schedule System (C/SS) number that is used to release budget and accumulate actual costs for measuring work performance. WPAs will not normally be prepared for burden, miscellaneous ODC, and other cost elements retained at the Program Controller level; if such WPAs are required, they will be prepared by the Program Controller.

B. Responsibility for Entries

WPAs are prepared by Functional Planners (FPs) in designated areas, or by the responsible department. They are scheduled by a Functional Scheduler (FS) and budgeted by a Functional Controller (FC). Responsibilities for data entries are normally as follows, but may vary for different departments.

C. Form Instructions

Entered by	Item	Instructions
FP	1	*Page 1 of*–Page number and quantity of pages making up complete WPA. Page 1 preprinted.
FP	2	*Responsible Department*–Designates the department number for department responsible to perform the work defined on the WPA.
FP	3	*Sales Order (SO) Number*–Designates the number assigned to the Sales Order, representative of the WBS element, identified in Items 14 and 17.
FC	4	*Budget Advice*–Identifies the Budget Authorization Number, as displayed on the applicable Bid-Budget Advice form.
FC	5	*Work Package Authority (WPA) Number*–The unique number (within sales order) or identification assigned to the WPA for its individual control purposes.
FP	6	*Revision*–The number sequentially assigned to identify, for control purposes, each authorized changed or revised issue of the WPA.
FP	7	*Program*–Designates title, acronym, etc., by which program/project is recognized.
FS	8	*Scheduled Start Date*–Date on which performance of the work defined on WPA is scheduled to start. May be expressed as calendar or "M" date.
FS	9	*Scheduled Completion Date*–Date by which work defined on WPA is scheduled to be completed. May be expressed as calendar or "M" date.

FP	10	*Summary Cost Element (SCE) Number*—The summary cost element (account) number, as identified in the Chart of Accounts and stipulated by Sales Order and described in Item 13.
FC	11	*Contract*—Assigned number or code by which the contract is identified.
FC	12	*WPPA Reference*—Indicates the WPPA revision number, page, and line number of planned WPA to assist in associating WPA to its parent WPPA.
FP	13	*Summary Account Function*—The applicable SCE function as indicated by the sales order and descriptive of the summary cost element number, Item 10.
FP	14	*WBS Element Number*—The unique number or coding identity assigned to the WBS element, named in Item 17, for WBS element identification purposes.
FP	15	*Department Name*—Title of the designated responsible department, Item 2.
FP	16	*Detail Account Number*—This block is for use of Material only and is used to indicate a Material Account number that converts to a WPA number.
FP	17	*WBS Element Name*—Denotes name/title/description of the WBS element represented by the WBS number identified in Item 14.
FP	18	*Prepared by/Department/Date*—Name of person who prepared the WPA, the department number, and the date the WPA was prepared.
FP	19	*Change Authority/References/Remarks*—Identifies Change Authority authorizing change to WPA, lists references and/or remarks applicable to Item 25, Statement of Work, etc.
FP	20	*End Product*—Designates the hardware, data, service, or facility to be produced or accomplished under the WPA.
FP	21	*Quantity*—Designates quantity of end product required on the WPA.
FC	22	*Direct PVW Assigned*—The Planned Value of Work in budgetary direct hour or dollar value planned to accomplish the WPA as defined.
FC	23	*Type of WPA*—Designates the type of WPA effort involved to accomplish the statement of work, and whether it is recurring or nonrecurring effort.
FC	24	*Planned Value of Work Accomplished (PVWA) Criteria and Method of Determination*—Defines the

criteria and method for determining Planned Value of Work Accomplished (PVWA) for the WPA. PVWA is synonomous with "Earned Value," "Earned Hours," "Earned Dollars," etc., terms.

FP	25	*Statement of Work*—Qualitatively and quantitatively defines in detail the work requirements necessary to accomplish the end product and other objectives covered by the WPA budget and schedule. Includes schedule network interfaces and constraints, pertinent Statement of Work and specification references that apply, as well as any other applicable factors.
FC	26	*Month/Year*—Designates the month and year applicable to each of the columns or fields on the PVWS and PVWA time-phasing grid, Items 27 and 28.
FC	27	*PVWS, Monthly Cumulative*—"Monthly" line portrays the planned estimate/budget value, Item 22, of work incrementally time phased or loaded over the monthly periods within the schedule, Items 8 and 9. Its use is optional on this form.
		"Cumulative" line portrays the running total-to-date or cumulative PVWS as of each completed period time phased. Its use is optional on this form.
FC	28	*PVWA, Monthly/Cumulative*—"Monthly" line reflects the monthly PVWA increase or decrease from the previous reported "cumulative" PVWA. Its use is optional on this form.
		"Cumulative" line states as of each completed period the value of the planned work actually earned to date in accordance with the PVWA criteria and method, Item 24. Its use is optional on this form.
FC	29	*Issue Change Number*—Identifies for approval, control, and historical information purposes the issue of the WPA released. Enter the authority for each change in Item 19.
FP	30	*Approval/Responsible Department and Date*—Signature of responsible manager or supervisor assigned direct responsibility for performance and control of the WPA and date of signing.
FC	31	*Approval/Program Budget and Date*—Signature of program controller designated to control budgetary (PVW) assignment to the WPA and date of signing.
FS	32	*Approval/Program Planning and Date*—Signature of individual assigned to approve the schedule, work loading, and release to work of the WPA.

BID – BUDGET ADVICE
FORM 39-668 (R. 2-71)   □ COST ESTIMATE   (1) □ CONTRACT VALUE   □ BUDGET ADVICE   (2)

TITLE/SUBJECT (3)		CHANGE NO. (4)	CODE (5) SALES ORDER NO (6)	SO DASH (7) BUD ADV NO. (8)

(9) □ REC □ N/R | WBS ELEMENT NO. (10) | PROGRAM (11) | CON CODE (12) CONTRACT NO. (13) | C/I (14) | ISSUE DATE (15)

FCC (16)	LINE (17)	SUM COST ELEM (18)	DESCRIPTION (19)	HOURS (20)	RATE (21)	DOLLARS (22)	OVERTIME PREMIUM DOLLARS (23)	BURDEN RATES % (24)	C.E. USE ONLY (25)
	1	423-00	ENGINEERING						
21	2	424-10	GRAPHICS						
22	3	425-10	PRODUCT SUPPORT						
	4								
	5		SUBTOTAL ENGRG						
	6	472-01	ENGINEERING BURDEN	%					
	7								
51	8	401-10	FACTORY FAB						
52	9	401-20	FACTORY ASSEMBLY						
61	10	402-10	PREP AND DEL						
31	11	403-10	TOOL DESIGN AND FAB						
32	12	404-10	TOOL ENGRG & PLNG						
41	13	405-10	QUALITY CONTROL						
	14								
	15		SUBTOTAL MFG						
	16	471-01	MANUFACTURING BURDEN	%					
	17								
13	18	431-00	ENGINEERING MATERIAL						
14	19	445-01	SUBCONTRACT ENGINEERING						
63	20	430-00	PRODUCTION MATERIAL						
64	21	441-00	SUBCONTRACT PRODUCTION						
33	22	436-00	TOOLING MATERIAL						
65	23	442-00	SUBCONTRACT TOOLING						
23	24	438-11	MYLAR SUPPLIES						
24	25	447-04	SUBCONTRACT PROD SUPPORT						
25	26	448-03	SUBCONTRACT GRAPHICS						
	27								
	28		SUBTOTAL MAT'L & SUBCONTRACT						
	29	473-01	MAT'L & SUBCONTRACT BURDEN	%					
	30						WRITE-IN		
176	31	450-00	MISCELLANEOUS O.D.C				(26)		
	32								
115	33	450-01	ENGINEERING O.D.C						
156	34	452-00	FACILITIES COST						
175	35	458-02	TRAVEL						
116	36	458-83	DATA PROCESSING – ENGINEERING						
126	37	458-84	DATA PROCESSING – PROD SUPPORT						
136	38	458-86	DATA PROCESSING – MFG ENGR						
	39	4xx-x7	OVERTIME PREMIUM						
	40		SUBTOTAL COST						
	41	474-01	ADMINISTRATIVE BURDEN	%					
	42								
266	43	460-00	INTERDIVISIONAL WORK						
286	44	499-90	UNRELEASED BUDGET			(27)			
	45								
273	46	458-37	F.S.						
	47		TOTAL BUDGETED COST	$	(28)				
	48								
271	49	459-99	RESV.	$					
	50		TOTAL BUDGETED VALUE	$	(29)				
284	51	499-97	FEE/PROFIT	% (30)	$	(31)			
	52		INTERIM BUDGET SUBTOTAL	$					
283	53	499-98	INTERIM BUDGET BALANCE	% (33)	$ (32)				
281	54	499-99	TOTAL PRICE	$ (34)	QTY (35)	UNIT PRICE (36)			

APPROVAL (37) | PREPARED BY (38) | DEPT NO. | DATE

TOOLING MATERIAL REQUISITION

Form 60-706 (2-71)

(1) N° 29002

| P.O. NUMBER (22) | ITEM (23) | COM. GRP. (24) | DIM. (25) | SPECON (2) 1500 | INV. (3) E | REQ'D DELIVERY DATE (26) | | PAGE (7) OF (8) |

INSP (4) N

| PROJ I.D. (27) | TYPE (28) / CONTRACT NO. (29) | ACCT. NO. (30) | REQUESTER (9) | DEPT (10) | EXT. (11) |

WPA/S.O. NO. (5)

(6) INTERNAL DEST./ZONE (31)

FACILITY-PLANT (12)

DATE (13)

DWG & DASH NO. (14) | SYMBOL (15) | NUM. CODE (16) | T.O. SERIAL (17)

SUPPLIER NAME (33)

REMARKS (34)

TOTAL COST (35)

QTY ORDERED (18)	UNIT (19)	SIZE (20)	MATERIAL DESCRIPTION (21)	UNIT PRICE (36)	PRICE EXT. (37)	QTY REC'D (38)

MAT'L REP. SIGNATURE (39) | EMP. NO. (40) | EXT. (41) | DATE (42) | APPROVED FOR ORDERING (43) | DATE (44)

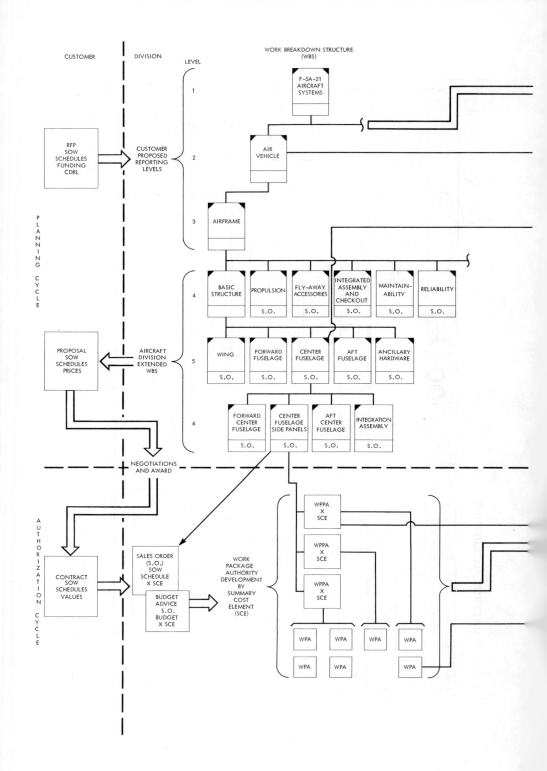

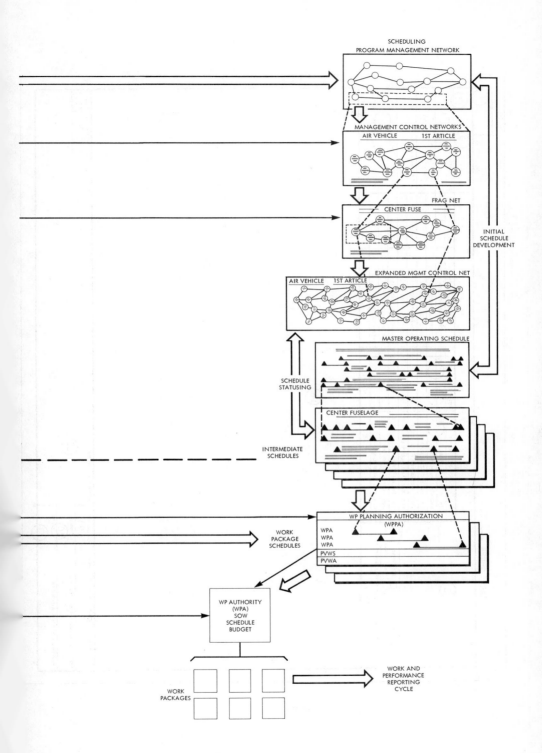

SCHEDULING
PROGRAM MANAGEMENT NETWORK

MANAGEMENT CONTROL NETWORKS
AIR VEHICLE   1ST ARTICLE

FRAG NET
CENTER FUSE

INITIAL
SCHEDULE
DEVELOPMENT

EXPANDED MGMT CONTROL NET
AIR VEHICLE   1ST ARTICLE

MASTER OPERATING SCHEDULE

SCHEDULE
STATUSING

CENTER FUSELAGE

INTERMEDIATE
SCHEDULES

WP PLANNING AUTHORIZATION
(WPPA)
WPA
WPA
WPA
PVWS
PVWA

WORK
PACKAGE
SCHEDULES

WP AUTHORITY
(WPA)
SOW
SCHEDULE
BUDGET

WORK
PACKAGES

WORK AND
PERFORMANCE
REPORTING
CYCLE

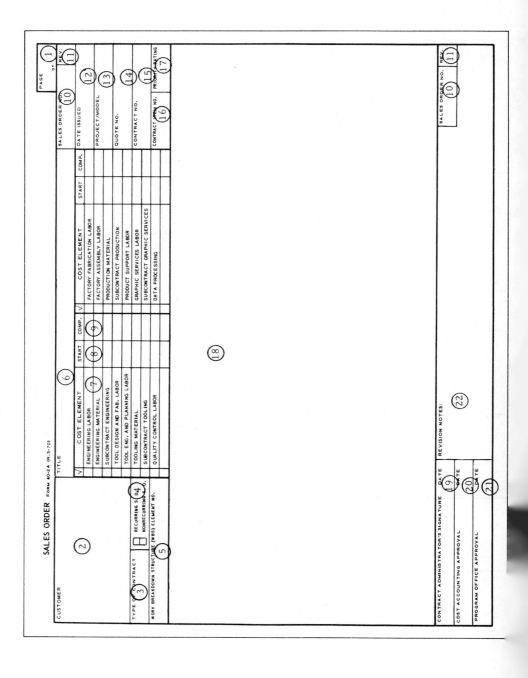

SALES ORDER FORM 40-2A (R.5-70)

PAGE (1) of REV. (11)

SALES ORDER NO. (10)

CUSTOMER (2)

TITLE (6)

DATE ISSUED (12)

PROJECT/MODEL (13)

QUOTE NO. (14)

CONTRACT NO. (15)

CONTRACT PLAN NO. (16)

PRIORITY RATING (17)

TYPE OF CONTRACT (3)

RECURRING $ (04)
NONRECURRING $

WORK BREAKDOWN STRUCTURE (WBS) ELEMENT NO. (5)

√	COST ELEMENT (7)	START (8)	COMP. (9)	√	COST ELEMENT	START	COMP.
	ENGINEERING LABOR				FACTORY FABRICATION LABOR		
	ENGINEERING MATERIAL				FACTORY ASSEMBLY LABOR		
	SUBCONTRACT ENGINEERING				PRODUCTION MATERIAL		
	TOOL DESIGN AND FAB. LABOR				SUBCONTRACT PRODUCTION		
	TOOL ENG. AND PLANNING LABOR				PRODUCT SUPPORT LABOR		
	TOOLING MATERIAL				GRAPHIC SERVICES LABOR		
	SUBCONTRACT TOOLING				SUBCONTRACT GRAPHIC SERVICES		
	QUALITY CONTROL LABOR				DATA PROCESSING		

(18)

REVISION NOTES: (22)

CONTRACT ADMINISTRATOR'S SIGNATURE (19) DATE

COST ACCOUNTING APPROVAL (20) DATE

PROGRAM OFFICE APPROVAL (21) DATE

SALES ORDER NO. (10) REV. (11)

BURDEN ACCUMULATION, ALLOCATION AND APPLICATION

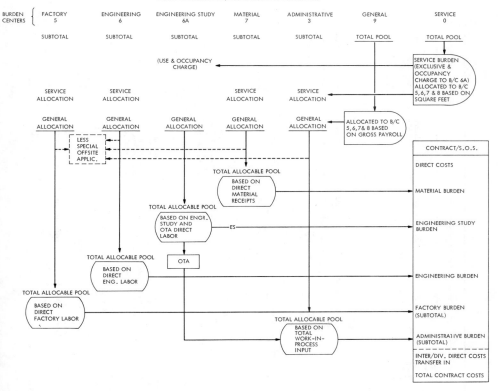

Burden centers

	(5) Factory	(6) Engineering	(6A) Engineering study	(7) Material	(8) Administrative	(9) General	(0) Service
Functions	Production operations Manufacturing engineering Production control Production flight facility Preparation and delivery Terminal services Quality control	Production system engineering Test and evaluation Product support Program management Graphics Proposal operations	Advanced systems dept Research and technical dev programs dept (excl aerosciences lab operations) Special programs	Procurement Material control Warehousing, traffic and transportation Subcontracts	General manager Customer requirements and relations Finance Contracts and pricing	Administration Industrial relations Business systems mgt Master parts listing Payroll and time-keeping Security Communications Master planning	Plant protection Facilities and plant engineering Plant and equipment maintenance Safety and parking Calibration services
Cost elements Labor and fringe payments	Indirect salaries and wages Production engineering Payments to indirect employees—fringe Payments for indirect employees—fringe	Indirect salaries and wages Payments to indirect employees—fringe Payments for indirect employees—fringe	Indirect salaries and wages Payments to indirect employees—fringe Payments for indirect employees—fringe	Indirect salaries and wages Payments to indirect employees—fringe Payments for indirect employees—fringe	Indirect salaries and wages Overhead technical activity Payments to indirect employees—fringe Payments for indirect employees—fringe	Indirect salaries and wages Payments to indirect employees—fringe Payments for indirect employees—fringe	Indirect salaries and wages Payments to indirect employees—fringe Payments for indirect employees—fringe
Other—Peculiar to one burden center	Technical activities Scrap sales Services purchased for Palmdale			Purchase discounts Transportation	Technical activities Advertising—general Bad debts Contributions Entertainment Patent expense Legal and audit Taxes franchise Insurance—general	Employee relations Training expense Medical expense Advertising—personnel Postage Repairs and maintenance—cafe Insurance—public liability Graphic services purchases Laundry and cleaning Telephone and telegraph	Communication system Depreciation and amortization Insurance—fire and aircraft Returnable container expense Rental of equipment and facilities Repairs and maintenance Services purchased Property taxes Licenses and permits Utilities
Other—Common to more than one burden center	Auto allowance Business conferences Dues and memberships Miscellaneous Professional consultants Services purchased Subscriptions and technical books Supplies Sales and use tax Travel Burden transfer between divisions	Auto allowance Business conferences Dues and memberships Miscellaneous Professional consultants Services purchased Subscriptions and technical books Supplies Sales and use tax Travel Burden transfer between divisions	Auto allowance Business conferences Dues and memberships Miscellaneous Professional consultants Services purchased Subscriptions and technical books Supplies Sales and use tax Travel Burden transfer between divisions	Auto allowance Business conferences Dues and memberships Miscellaneous Professional consultants Services purchased Subscriptions and technical books Supplies Sales and use tax Travel Burden transfer between divisions	Auto allowance Business conferences Dues and memberships Miscellaneous Professional consultants Services purchased Subscriptions and technical books Supplies Sales and use tax Travel Burden transfer between divisions (incl transfers from corporate)	Auto allowance Business conferences Dues and memberships Miscellaneous Professional consultants Services purchased Subscriptions and technical books Supplies Travel Burden transfer between divisions (incl data processing)	Auto allowance Business conferences Dues and memberships Miscellaneous Professional consultants Services purchased Subscriptions and technical books Supplies Travel Burden transfer between divisions → Other divisions
	Subtotal	Subtotal	Subtotal	Subtotal	Subtotal	Total pool	Total pool

WORK PACKAGE PLANNING AUTHORIZATION FORM 39-470A (R3-72)

PROGRAM (1)		REV (3)	SALES ORDER NO. (4) □	SALES ORDER TITLE (6)		PREPARED BY (8)		DATE (9)	PAGE (10) OF
SCHEDULE REFERENCE (2)			DEPT NO. □	FUNCTION (7)		APPROVED BY (9)		DATE	DATA, AS OF (11)

SUMMARY COST ELEMENT NO. (5)

DIRECT PVW ASSIGNED: HOURS □ DOLLARS □ (17)

MONTHLY TIME PHASED BUDGETS (HOURS OR DOLLARS) (19)

DESCRIPTION (12)	LINE (13)	WPA NO. (14)	TYPE (15)	RESP. DEPT. NO. (16)	P/V/W (18)	JUNE (20A)	JULY (20B)	AUG.	...	JULY	AUG.	SEPT.	OCT.	NOV.	DEC.	JAN.	FEB.	MAR.	APR.	MAY
					S															
					A															

BUDGET RELEASE NO. (21)	DIRECT VALUE H (22) $ (22)	WAGE RATE (23)	BUDGET $ VALUE (24)	CONV. RATE (25)	TOTAL WPA'S PVWS (26)	PVWA (27)
					CUM. VALUE PVWS (28)	(29)
					CUM. VALUE PVWA (30)	

REMARKS (31) (32)

Chapter 45

Standard costs—Uses as a management tool

*Robert M. Rice**

This chapter is concerned with the use by management of standard cost data. The discussion refers not only to standard product costs per se but also to basic quantitative standards used in computing standard costs, the variances generated by a standard cost system, and various analytical reports.

Standard costs are defined as costs which have been computed using standard quantitative data and predetermined economic factors. The data used in the computations provides for the processing of the products in the optimum practical manner at efficiency levels which are attainable with *good performance*. These standard costs typically are established for material, labor, and overhead elements and may be used in connection with systems oriented toward either a job lot or a process method of cost accumulation.

The commentary assumes the existence of an integrated standard cost financial control system which utilizes standard costs for both internal and external financial reporting, isolates differences or variances between actual results and the predetermined standard costs, and makes available to management quantitative as well as financial data.

---

* Vice President–Finance and Chief Financial Officer, Rockwell International.

Fundamentally, standard product costs and the quantitative data supporting the computation of standard product costs constitute measurement tools. Standard costs are used both as an absolute unit of measure and as a device for measuring the difference between actual results and standard performance. While there are practical limitations upon the amount of detail which should be incorporated in standard costs, their usefulness for control purposes is directly related to the amount of detail built into the standards.

The uses discussed are intended to illustrate the *potential* that exists in a standard cost system. In any particular operating situation, certain of these uses may not be feasible. Furthermore, the operating environment will determine the extent to which data is generated routinely or, alternatively, is made available through special analysis.

CONTROL OF OPERATIONS

The major reason for the introduction of standard costs is to provide better control over operations. *Control* implies the existence of a *plan* for the operations plus the exercise of a *directing* influence to achieve that plan. It involves a method for advising management when operations are not going according to plan, together with the reasons for the deviation.

Standard cost data is used extensively in the *planning process.* Standard costs are used to compute the values of projected cost of sales and planned inventory quantities. Standard quantitative data is used to estimate machine loadings, personnel and raw materials requirements, and so on. The major advantage of standard data over historical actual data for planning purposes is that historical data must be adjusted to eliminate nonrepetitive events, past inefficiencies, and off-standard operations which are not expected to recur. Furthermore, since standard costs are constructed by detailed cost elements, it is relatively easy to adjust standard costs to accommodate anticipated changes in any one element. Similar adjustments to historical actual costs are more difficult to make since the content of historical actual costs will vary with each reporting period.

Although standard cost data is used extensively in developing operating plans, it is the *analysis and use of cost variances* from standard in the exercise of the *directing* influence which have received most attention and are most frequently associated with the use of standard cost systems. Undoubtedly this results from the fact that the planning cycle tends to recur annually or at infrequent intervals, whereas variances from standard are being constantly generated, analyzed, and explained.

MOTIVATION OF PEOPLE

Another reason often advanced for the introduction of standards and standard costs is to motivate people to perform more effectively. The theory is that people will improve their performance just because they are being measured accurately and fairly. While this theory may be valid in certain situations, the successful use of standards as a motivating tool is believed to be dependent upon a number of factors including the employees' attitude toward the company and the work environment, the efforts made by management to win acceptance of the program, and employee understanding of and belief in the fairness of the standards. However, given the introduction of standards into a properly prepared environment, it appears that standards and standard costs can be used to motivate employees in all functional areas.

In subsequent sections of this chapter, the various uses of standard cost data are set out in relation to a typical manufacturing organization.

USE OF STANDARD COST DATA BY THE
GENERAL MANAGER

The general manager is responsible for the overall operation of the business; however, the functions he or she *personally* performs may be grouped as follows:

1. Formulating and approving a plan for the business.
2. Structuring the organization so that all functional elements essential to the accomplishment of the plan are assigned to specific individuals.
3. Motivating subordinates.
4. Setting goals and objectives for subordinates and evaluating their performance.
5. Making major decisions regarding alternative courses of action.

Business plans

Business plans are composed of many elements, both monetary and nonmonetary; however, they generally are summarized in financial terms. Standard costs and the standard quantitative data supporting standard costs are used extensively in the planning process. For example, standard costs are applied to the *unit sales plan* to arrive at the optimum product mix. Standard quantitative data is applied to the unit sales plan (plus or minus change in inventories) to determine the necessity for additional plant capacity or other production requirements. (See also comments by functional area in subsequent sections of this chapter.)

Organizational structure

The general manager, based upon personal knowledge and experience, has a general indication of the type of organization desired. Before that organization is finalized, however, the general manager will want to compare the cost of each organizational segment with the benefits to be derived therefrom. Standard costs, particularly the overhead element, would be used in such an evaluation.

Motivating subordinates

It was mentioned previously that one of the reasons for installing standard costs was to motivate people. This rationale applies to all levels of the organization, including the general manager's direct subordinates. At this level the motivational impact is particularly strong since these employees are capable of understanding a standards program and their compensation is frequently tied to results achieved as measured by the balances in various standard cost accounts (i.e., production manager's compensation related to labor performance and material usage variances).

Goals and objectives

To be meaningful, goals and objectives for all employees must be quantified. It must be possible to measure actual performance in relation to such goals. Specific goals for key managers are often defined in terms of standard cost data as reflected in the books of account. The purchasing manager, for example, may be committed to a negotiated purchase price variance of a certain amount per month. Many general managers assign responsibility for each standard cost variance to a subordinate, who is then motivated or caused to take corrective action.

Decisions regarding alternative actions

Perhaps the general manager's most important function is to make decisions regarding alternative courses of action. In a business situation, the alternatives are quantified and a financial evaluation is made. The information required for making such decisions is often based upon standard costs. Future projections of costs are frequently involved, and standard costs adjusted for anticipated changes in economic and other operating conditions are an appropriate tool for use in the analysis.

USE OF STANDARD COST DATA BY THE FINANCE FUNCTION

In a typical manufacturing organization, the finance function maintains the financial records and reports the operating results, both externally and internally, on a timely basis. This function also analyzes the results of current operations and issues appropriate recommendations. It provides information for estimating costs of new products and for pricing decisions. It also evaluates alternative courses of action and compiles various long- and short-term plans and forecasts. Standard costs are one of the tools used in accomplishing these various tasks.

Reporting and analyzing operating results

The most basic uses of standard costs by the finance function are to *value inventories* and to *compute cost of sales*. If the standards are established as defined at the beginning of this chapter and the predetermined economic levels approximate actual on the closing date, full absorption standard costs comply with the accounting requirements for external financial reporting and federal income taxation. Many companies annually revise their standard costs just

EXHIBIT 1
Bill of material

```
A952-615A                                          INDENTED EXPLOSION            12/19/75
                                                                                 PAGE    1

 PATTERN        PART NUMBER        DESCRIPTION    QTY PER   TOT QTY   LC     TP  A/C
0---------- 202269              AIR FIL DRY TYPE  1.0000    1.0000 01  PC  3  A
1--------- A19868               NAME PLATE        1.0000    1.0000 05  PC  1  C
1--------- 201958-155           BODY ASSY         1.0000    1.0000 02  PC  3  A
2-------- 201958-100            COVER             1.0000    1.0000 03  PC  3  C
3------- 201958-100RGH          COVER             1.0000    1.0000 04  PC  1  C
2-------- 201958-134            STUD              1.0000    1.0000 03  PC  3  C
3------- RM340080100            RAW MATERIAL      0.9430    0.9430 06  LB  2
2-------- 201958-201            SHROUD            1.0000    1.0000 03  PC  3  C
3------- RM370200030            RAW MATERIAL      8.3930    8.3930 09  LB  2
1--------- 202269-160           RETAINER          1.0000    1.0000 02  PC  3  C
2-------- 202269-159            RETAINER          1.0000    1.0000 03  PC  3  C
3------- RM440200035            RAW MATERIAL      1.9600    1.9600 06  LB  2
2-------- 202269-37             TUBE              1.0000    1.0000 03  PC  3  C
3------- RM340240065            RAW MATERIAL      0.4330    0.4330 06  FT  2
1--------- 202269-826           ELEMENT S/A       1.0000    1.0000 03  PC  3  A
2-------- 202269-06             GASKET            2.0000    2.0000 04  PC  1  C
2-------- 202269-178            CYLINDER          1.0000    1.0000 04  PC  3  C
3------- RM430340045            RAW MATERIAL      2.1565    2.1565 05  FT  2
2-------- 202269-179            INNER PERF        1.0000    1.0000 04  PC  3  C
3------- RM430340234            RAW MATERIAL      1.6473    1.6473 05  FT  2
2-------- 202269-294            DY MEDIA          1.0000    1.0000 04  PC  1  C
2-------- 202269-295            "DG" MEDIA        1.0000    1.0000 04  PC  3  C
3------- RM220499005            RAW MATERIAL      4.5400    4.5400 06  FS  2
1--------- 27706                NUT               1.0000    1.0000 02  PC  1  C
```

Explanatory Notes:
Qty Per—Quantity per assembly.
Tot Qty—Column provided to show requirements for a specified number of assemblies.
LC—Level code in the assembly sequence.
TP—Type of material—purchased part, raw material, manufactured part.
A/C—Assembly or component.

prior to the close of their fiscal year so that standards do approximate actual costs at the balance sheet date. In the event that standard costs are not current and therefore do not approximate actual costs at the balance sheet date, external reporting requirements can be met relatively easily by the association of variances based upon the proportion of total production remaining in inventory to that transferred to cost of sales.[1]

Because of the use of predetermined elements in a standard cost system, inventory and cost of sales valuations usually can be computed faster than such computations can be completed under alternative systems. The use of standard factors permits many computations to be made simultaneously rather than sequentially. Since

---

[1] For illustration of this method of inventory valuation, see Honeywell Annual Report 1975, footnote on inventories as follows: "Inventories are valued at the lower of cost or market. Cost is generally determined on a first-in first-out basis, and market is based upon estimated realizable value. The cost of manufactured products is based on standards developed for individual items from current material, labor and overhead costs at normal activity levels. Standard costs are adjusted to actual by application of manufacturing variances."

management takes corrective action based upon the cost information, speed is essential if profits are to be maximized.

In addition to the element of speed, standard cost systems generally provide *more usable information* in that costs are determinable by individual product and by element of cost within each product. For example, the *bill of materials* (see Exhibit 1) provides a detailed listing of the quantities and types of materials required to make one unit of a particular finished product. The *route sheet* (see Exhibit 2) lists every operation required to make a finished product and the elapsed time required per operation. In addition to standard quantities of materials and standard operating times, standard cost systems usually provide a comparison of standard quantitative data to actual performance. Variances between standard and actual data

EXHIBIT 2
Operations routing sheet

OPERATIONS ROUTING SHEET

PAGE 1 OF   DATE 1/23/74

Part Number 202269	(18) Material Specifications	(12) Shop Order	
Part Name FILTER ELEMENT	(16) Description REF B/M & B/P	(22) Due Date	Quantity
R/M Part Size	(19) Raw Material Size	(21)	☐ Add
DWG Number 202269	(18) Unit of Measure 1.000 PC	(8) Quantity Per Piece (12)	☐ Change
Written By (2) Date 9/27/73	(8) Revision No. (6) F	Approved (2) R/M Number (11)	☐ Delete

DEPT. NO.	OPER. SEQ.	MACH. CODE	OPERATION DESCRIPTION	TOOLING AND GAGES	STANDARD HOURS SET-UP	PER PIECE
60	10	745	ROLL "DG" AROUND "DY" MEDIA		.0	.0150
60	20	743	ASM OUTER PERF TO DG & DY MEDIA		.0	.0210
60	30	749	TRIM EXCESS DG MEDIA		.0	.0075
60	40	749	ASM INNER PERF TO DG & DY MEDIA		.0	.0125
60	50	749	PRE-GLUE ELEMENT		.0	.0133
60	60	749	PRE-GLUE GASKETS & STAMP		.0	.0167
60	70	749	ASM GASKETS TO ELEM & SEAL		.0	.0181
12	80		INSPECT		.0	.0000
13	90		STOCK		.0	.0000
					.0*	.1041*

EDP-20

may be analyzed by individual product, by cost center, or by both product and cost center, depending upon the design of the standard cost system.

Estimating costs of new products

Standard costs provide a practical basis for estimating costs of new products. Standard cost systems usually incorporate a large data bank which includes standard processing times per operation or per machine, standard labor and overhead rates for each operation, plus standard material prices and quantities per unit of finished product. Under a standard system, estimating the cost of a new product involves determining which operations are required, making adjustments to specific elements to compensate for anticipated changes in operating conditions, applying standard rates to the quantitative components, and accumulating the cost.

Pricing decisions

The finance function provides the cost information which is essential for making informed pricing decisions. Since standard costs are built up from many detailed cost elements, it is easy to react to changes in specific cost factors, such as a labor rate change or a change in the cost of a basic raw material. In evaluating sales promotion and quantity discount proposals, it is essential that the effect of a change in unit volume on average unit costs be known. A standard cost system is designed to provide both fixed and variable costs per unit of product. Thus, the incremental costs associated with an increase in volume of a particular product can be readily computed.

Plans and forecasts

Standard cost data, both quantitative and financial, is used in compiling both long- and short-range plans and forecasts. Depending upon the degree of accuracy required, these projections can be built up from detailed material explosions of finished product sales or based upon an expected average percentage relationship of cost to sales.

Alternative courses of action

The finance staff, as the custodian of financial data, evaluates various alternative courses of action under consideration by management. Such proposals may include make-or-buy decisions, product substitutions, use of alternative raw materials, capital expenditures, and so on. In all such analyses, standard product costs are advantageous to use because the data has been compiled by detailed operation and cost elements, it excludes abnormal inefficiencies and nonrecurring factors, and changes or substitutions in one or more cost elements may be effected with a minimum of clerical effort.

USE OF STANDARD COST DATA BY THE PRODUCTION FUNCTION

The production function has overall responsibility for manufacturing and is especially concerned with the efficient use of people, materials, and equipment in meeting production requirements. Variances generated by the standard cost system are used both to measure efficiency and to isolate and identify problems so that corrective action can be taken.

Direct labor performance variance

The standard cost variance of primary importance to the production function is perhaps the *direct labor performance variance*. An unfavorable labor performance variance indicates that labor in a particular area or department is performing below standard. Through recurring reports or special analyses the production manager can determine whether the variance was caused by:

1. Machine problems—lack of preventive maintenance, inadequate capacity.
2. Inefficient manning.
3. Improper materials—wrong specifications, poor quality.
4. Failure of support services—lack of materials, poor lighting, improper working conditions.
5. Supervision—improper instructions, lack of supervision.
6. Off-standard operation—wrong process, use of alternative equipment.
7. Training inadequacies.

Direct labor rate variance

The direct labor rate variance generated by a standard cost system is of major interest to the *personnel function*. However, the *production manager* may take corrective action if excess cost is attributable to:

1. Manning—excessive use of highly skilled job classifications, failure to use apprentices.
2. Abuse of incentive programs.

Direct material usage variance

The direct material usage variance is primarily the responsibility of the production function, although the production scheduling, materials control, purchasing, and plant engineering functions also may share responsibility. An analysis of the variance may indicate areas requiring corrective action by the production manager as follows:

1. Operator performance—lack of training, improper instructions, capability.
2. Machine related—failure to hold tolerances, improper tooling, worn or broken tooling or fixtures.
3. Off-standard operation—substitute operation with less favorable yield.
4. Incorrect material specifications.
5. Poor quality of materials.
6. Incorrect inspection standard.

Overhead variances

Overhead variances generated by a standard cost system are analyzed under a typical two-step approach into *spending* and *volume* elements. If an *unfavorable overhead spending variance* is reported, the production manager should review indirect labor and indirect materials purchases and usage of services, following procedures similar to those used in the analysis of direct labor and direct material.

An *unfavorable overhead volume variance* may be attributable to production limitations, to decreased sales, or to other problems. If it is found to be production related, the production manager should determine which are the bottleneck operations and then systematically review:

1. Machine capacities and performance—downtime analysis.
2. Labor productivity and manning.
3. Availability of materials.
4. Adequacy of support services.
5. Production scheduling routines.
6. Plant layout.

This type of review may reveal that purchasing, materials control, production scheduling, industrial engineering, or plant engineering also must take corrective action.

USE OF STANDARD COST DATA BY THE PURCHASING FUNCTION

The purchasing function is assigned the task of obtaining purchased materials and services in accordance with standard specifications as scheduled, in the correct quantities, at the best price, from acceptable suppliers. Standard cost data is used extensively to measure its effectiveness in carrying out this task.

Purchase price variance

Companies which use standard cost systems generally hold the *purchasing function* primarily responsible for the purchase price variance on materials and consider that account to be the principal measure of purchasing performance. The usefulness of the account will depend upon the details which were utilized to construct the standard costs; however, a standard cost system has the capability to isolate the following:

1. General price increases.
2. Price differences due to mix of suppliers.
3. Price differences resulting from purchasing negotiations.
4. Off-standard material specification.
5. Differences in price attributable to freight rates or location of suppliers.

6. Purchase orders issued for other than standard quantities.

Having thus identified the factors which contribute to purchase price variances, the purchasing function can take corrective action if appropriate.

Direct material usage variance

The direct material usage variance is often considered the responsibility of the *production function*. However, analysis of the usage variance may indicate purchasing responsibility due to:

1. Substandard quality.
2. Incorrect specifications.
3. Inadequate deliveries, necessitating material substitutions.

In all of these cases corrective action may be required by the *purchasing function*.

Direct labor performance variance

The *purchasing function* may also be held responsible for an unfavorable labor performance variance when the poor labor performance is attributable to substandard quality or otherwise off-standard materials.

USE OF STANDARD COST DATA BY THE MATERIALS CONTROL FUNCTION

The *materials control* function is responsible for control of inventories and scheduling materials to meet production requirements.

Material scheduling

Locations using standard cost systems commonly determine their material requirements by multiplying the units in the *production forecast* (adjusted for changes in inventory) by the standard quantities per unit set out in the standard bill of materials for each product (see Exhibit 3). The resulting quantities, adjusted for material usage variances if significant and repetitive, constitute the total materials required to meet the forecast.

EXHIBIT 3 — Material requirements report

```
T534-085   TIME: 11:48 P.M.        S E L E C T I V E   M R P   D E T A I L   R E P O R T
```

RUN #: 5   DATE: 08-01-75   NOUN: U-RING   DESC: LILCS AKDQ   W.S. #: 0   RECORD #: 1

PART #: 201951-08   LEAD: 14 PLAN: RR BUY: ABC: C

-TRANSACTION- DEMAND REPLEN	QUANTITY	DUE DATE	PROJECTED ON-HAND	COMMENTS	ORDER #/ REFERENCE	EXTENDED VALUE	ACTION DATE	---MAXIMUM--- ORDER QUANTITY
				UOFM: PC LOW LEVEL: 2				
600	231.00	08-01-75	231.00		ON-HAND	145.99		
640	26.00	08-08-75	205.00	007-04/ 030-99/ 000-00	ACCUM 2	129.56		
640	8.00	08-08-75	197.00	007-04/ 030-99/ 000-00	ACCUM 2	124.50		
640	6.00	08-15-75	191.00	007-04/ 030-99/ 000-00	ACCUM 2	120.71		
640	5.00	09-10-75	186.00	007-04/ 030-99/ 000-00	ACCUM 2	117.55		
640	4.00	10-08-75	182.00	007-04/ 030-99/ 000-00	ACCUM 2	115.02		
640	3.00	11-13-75	179.00	007-04/ 030-99/ 000-00	ACCUM 2	113.13		

PART #: 201957-07   NOUN: ELEMENT S/A   DESC: LEAD: 28 PLAN: RR BUY: ABC: C

-TRANSACTION- DEMAND REPLEN	QUANTITY	DUE DATE	PROJECTED ON-HAND	COMMENTS	ORDER #/ REFERENCE	EXTENDED VALUE	ACTION DATE	---MAXIMUM--- ORDER QUANTITY
				UOFM: PC LOW LEVEL: 2				
	.00		172.00		ON-HAND	.00		
620	172.00	05-09-75	142.00		01367	214.83		
620	30.00	07-11-75			41827AA	177.36		
640	80.00	08-01-75	62.00	202067	/W0000902	77.44		
640	32.00	09-05-75	30.00	202067	/W0000903	37.47		
640	10.00	09-05-75	40.00		/W0003085	49.96		
640	40.00	09-05-75	.00		/W0000904	.00		
640	45.00	02-20-76	45.00	202067	/W00030R6	56.21	08-08-75	
640	45.00	02-20-76	.00	202067	/W0000905	.00	01-23-76	

PART #: 201958-100   NOUN: COVER   DESC: LEAD: 14 PLAN: RR BUY: 1   ABC: C

-TRANSACTION- DEMAND REPLEN	QUANTITY	DUE DATE	PROJECTED ON-HAND	COMMENTS	ORDER #/ REFERENCE	EXTENDED VALUE	ACTION DATE	---MAXIMUM--- ORDER QUANTITY
				UOFM: PC LOW LEVEL: 1				
	.00		.00		ON-HAND	.00		
600	30.00	08-01-75	30.00		/W0003266	785.01	07-18-75	
640	30.00	08-15-75	.00	007-04/ 030-99/ 000-00	ACCUM 2	.00		
640	215.00	08-15-75	215.00		02734	5625.91		

PART #: 201958-100RGH   NOUN: COVER   DESC: LEAD: 98 PLAN: RR BUY: RA   ABC: C

-TRANSACTION- DEMAND REPLEN	QUANTITY	DUE DATE	PROJECTED ON-HAND	COMMENTS	ORDER #/ REFERENCE	EXTENDED VALUE	ACTION DATE	---MAXIMUM--- ORDER QUANTITY
				UOFM: PC LOW LEVEL: 2				
600	215.00		215.00		ON-HAND	3758.20		
640	215.00	08-01-75	185.00	030-99/ 000-00/ 000-00	ACCUM 4	3233.80		
	710	1000.00	10-10-75	1185.00	28352	20713.80		

Explanatory Notes: Noun—Short description.   DESC—Description.   ABC—Classification based upon total inventory value.

Inventory level

The *materials control* function usually establishes the inventory level by item on a unit or quantitative basis. On the other hand, total inventory targets or budgets for a location are commonly expressed in monetary value and, assuming a standard cost system is in use, the value assigned will represent standard cost.

Direct labor performance and direct material usage variances

Since both unfavorable labor performance and material usage variances may in some instances be attributable to the unavailability of specified materials at work stations, unfavorable balances in these accounts may result in corrective action being taken by *materials control* as follows:

1. Review of lead-time analysis.
2. Revision of safety stock levels.

USE OF STANDARD COST DATA BY THE PRODUCTION SCHEDULING FUNCTION

The production scheduling function is responsible for scheduling the personnel and equipment required to meet the production forecast. To accomplish this detailed scheduling assignment, quantitative data contained in the standard product cost route or processing sheets is used. The route sheets (see Exhibit 2) show both the specific operations required to produce a product and the processing times per operation. This data, when applied to quantities in the production forecast and related to manufacturing capacities by specific operation, results in a production schedule (see Exhibit 4). If the location has been generating significant and consistent performance variances, the production schedulers probably would adjust the standard data to effect a more realistic production schedule.

USE OF STANDARD COST DATA BY THE PERSONNEL FUNCTION

The *personnel function* is defined to include the full range of employee relations activities including setting or negotiating wages and salaries, hiring, training, and so on. The personnel function is

EXHIBIT 4
Production schedule

PRODUCTION SCHEDULE

PERIOD	PART NO.	EXPEDITER	HOURS TO COMPLETION	MATERIAL CODE	QUANTITY	DEPT	OPERATION	WORK CENTER	STANDARD RATE (1)	START DATE	DUE DATE	HOURS FOR OPERATION (2)
12	414030925001	2	74.9	2	70	08	006	7055	.0000	18	53	0.5 (M)
16	414030065002	2	325.2	4	40	08	005	7055	.0242	10	72	1.0
16	414030065002	2	324.2	4	40	08	008	7055	.0244	11	72	1.0
										PERIOD TOTAL		27.4 *
32	408010845002	2	175.7	2	70	08	010	7055	.0185	29	140	1.3
12	412030915002	1	69.4	2	280	08	015	7055	.0035	24	53	4.2 (M)
13	414010065006	2	139.9	4	50	08	057	7055	.0245	25	58	1.2
12	412030915002	1	65.2	2	280	08	018	7055	.0029	25	53	4.2 (M)
13	414010065006	2	141.1	4	50	08	056	7055	.0245	24	58	1.2
16	428030910001	4	99.9	2	140	08	005	7055	.0000	29	72	1.5 (M)
41	450010915001	2	425.6	2	70	08	006	7055	.0162	28	184	1.1
41	450010915001	2	424.5	2	70	08	005	7055	.0162	29	184	1.1
15	422061095001	1	169.9	2	170	08	005	7055	.0073	29	67	1.2
23	422060915001	1	437.5	2	90	08	005	7055	.0320	25	106	2.9
23	422060915001	1	434.6	2	90	08	006	7055	.0258	26	106	2.3
										PERIOD TOTAL		22.2 *
32	408010845002	2	174.4	2	70	08	015	7055	.0185	30	140	1.3
25	414010845001	2	74.0	2	95	08	003	7055	.0032	39	116	0.3
25	414010845001	2	74.4	2	95	08	002	7055	.0038	38	116	0.4
16	428030910001	4	98.4	2	140	08	006	7055	.0000	30	72	1.3 (M)
23	426050915002	1	248.0	2	127	08	006	7055	.0211	39	106	2.7
23	426050915002	1	250.7	2	127	08	005	7055	.0213	38	106	2.7

CONTINUING

Explanatory Notes:
(M)—Established minimum.
Period—numbered week starting from first week in January.
(1)—Standard rate from standard cost files.
Start Date } Numbered day starting from January 1.
Due Date }
(2)—Hours for operation are computed by multiplying quantity times standard rate.

primarily concerned with the standard cost variances, both rate and performance, relating to *labor*.

Direct labor rate variance

An unfavorable direct labor rate variance may point up the need for action by the personnel manager to correct situations such as the following:

1. Failure to use apprentices or other employees in the lower pay grades.
2. Excessive incentive payments as a result of administrative deficiencies.
3. Looseness in the administration of merit increase programs.
4. General wage increases in excess of planned levels.
5. Failure to hire the required number of employees, resulting in temporary transfer at higher rates of pay.

Direct labor performance variance

Along with production management, the personnel function utilizes the labor performance variance to highlight:

1. Training deficiencies.
2. Improper manning.
3. Poor employee morale as evidenced by slowdowns.
4. Lack of competent supervision.
5. Deficiencies in handling grievances.

USE OF STANDARD COST DATA BY THE INDUSTRIAL ENGINEERING FUNCTION

It is the function of the *industrial engineers* to determine how a product should be manufactured: the operations required, the time per operation, and the material requirements. The industrial engineers supply much of the quantitative data used to compute standard product costs.

Checking validity of engineered standards

Having supplied basic engineered data, the industrial engineers use data produced by the standard cost system as a check on the validity of their data. In this regard the engineers are particularly interested in the ratio of standard labor hours to actual labor hours by operation or department. A relatively large variance, either favorable or unfavorable, is cause for concern. A substantial variance indicates the possibility of an operating or production problem or an error in the basic engineering data. In either case corrective action may be required.

BWS/CWS variance

The industrial engineers are charged with improving production methods. A measure of their success in initiating improved methods is the difference between the *budgeted* or *basic work standards* (*BWS*) built into standard product cost and the *current* or *revised work standards* (*CWS*) used currently as a measure of labor performance. The BWS/CWS variance, which is computed by multiplying the difference in hours (BWS − CWS) times the standard direct labor rate, measures the direct labor cost reduction achieved by the industrial engineers through the introduction of new methods.

Selection of production method

While the engineers have knowledge of machine capacities and processing times upon which to base the selection of the optimum production method for a given product, they must rely upon standard cost financial data to select that production method which is most *cost effective*. The standard cost data which is essential for such a decision will include burden rates per machine-hour, labor rates, and material prices.

USE OF STANDARD COST DATA BY THE PLANT ENGINEERING FUNCTION

The plant engineering function is responsible for plant maintenance and construction.

Plant maintenance

Plant engineers are especially concerned with machine downtime and reduced operating speeds caused by mechanical problems, excess material usage caused by the failure of machines to hold tolerances, and parts replacement costs. Standard cost data pertaining to these areas includes analyses of labor performance, material usage variances by department, manufacturing overhead variances by department and detail account, and the machine downtime report.

Capital expenditures

To carry out its responsibilities for construction and major capital expenditures, the *plant engineering function* should have access to a long-range production forecast which is quantified in terms of machine-hours by operation to determine machine requirements. This type of information can be computed by applying the long-range production forecast, expressed in units of finished product, against the standard product cost route or process sheets.

USE OF STANDARD COST DATA BY THE MARKETING FUNCTION

The *marketing function* is responsible for the complete product distribution and sales effort and is jointly responsible with other staffs for sales price determination and product selection. Critical information needs of marketing include:

1. Profitability by product and product line.
2. The effect of additional volume upon profitability—the fixed versus variable cost relationship.
3. The profit effect of sales promotions and sales incentives.
4. The estimated cost of new modified products.

Fundamentally, marketing needs accurate current and projected cost information by individual product. This is the information that a standard cost system is designed to supply.

ADDITIONAL USES OF STANDARD COST DATA COMMON TO ALL STAFFS

All functional areas have in common the need to plan a level for their own activities which is commensurate with the operating level of the business as a whole, and to be apprised of their own performance in relation to planned levels.

Planning staff requirements

To satisfy the planning requirement, both quantitative and monetary data from the standard cost files is applied against the production and sales forecasts. The resulting data includes a great variety of information, such as amount of purchases, personnel levels, hiring requirements, and machine-hours by department. This data, in turn, is used to calculate staff requirements, such as the number of purchasing agents needed or the number of personnel recruiters required.

Performance measurement

For performance measurement, the standard cost system generates overhead variances by specific department and detailed expense account. From this data the functional head can determine whether his or her spending is in accordance with previously established targets and, if not, what specific categories of expense account for the variance.

SUMMARY

Standard cost systems are based upon, and in turn provide, a great amount of both quantitative and financial data which is correlated both to specific products and to operating areas or departments. Standard cost financial data includes all elements of cost incurred in manufacturing a product. The quantitative data pertains to all cost elements which are susceptible to practical measurement.

Standard cost data is used by every functional area of management involved with a manufacturing enterprise. The data is used both to *control* (which necessitates planning) operations and to *motivate people.* Typical uses of the data by the various functional areas of management have been presented; however, standard cost systems can be structured in different ways to satisfy the varying requirements of management. Thus, many additional or altered uses can be conceived.

Chapter 46

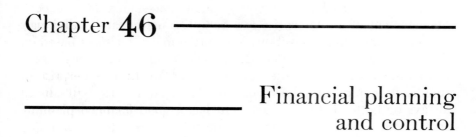

Financial planning
and control

*George E. Williams**

PURPOSE

Financial planning and control is one of the most important keys to successful management. In particular, its purpose is to aid managers in achieving their goals. Generally, the goals most affected by the financial planning and control system are those which can be expressed in terms of dollars, such as profits, sales, and assets. There are other important goals which are not as directly susceptible to financial quantification, such as improvements in product quality, personnel development, stockholder relations, and so on. However, many management goals which at first glance would not appear appropriate for inclusion in the financial plan can fruitfully be included when thought and analysis are applied. For instance, a growth in market share can be quantified, and the cost of achieving it can be planned; a new computer-based operating system in a department may be desirable, and the cost of implementation can be planned and often the benefits can be quantified.

Usually the overriding objective of the financial planning and control system is focused on sales, profits, and balance sheet figures. As noted above, many subsidiary plans and actions which will contribute over the short or long term to the financial goals can be in-

* Senior Vice President, Finance, Otis Elevator Company.

cluded in the scope of the financial planning and control system. The contribution of the financial planning and control function is to *improve the odds of success* in achieving the company's goals. The existence of such a system does not, of course, guarantee success. Management of an enterprise is a complex matter, and individuals in senior management positions must often make decisions based on their best judgment, without the benefit of quantifications which of themselves determine the best route to take. In an enterprise of significant complexity, however, the financial results will almost always be better if the management has a good financial planning and control system than they will be without this tool—assuming the same level of management skills in both cases. It can be said that financial planning and control influences results and, properly used, can make things happen.

Definition of goals

Implicit in the purpose of financial planning and control is the *definition of goals.* These may range from simple statements of desired dollar profit to very complex objectives involving rate of profit growth and market penetration, while achieving predetermined figures for key ratios such as asset turnover, current ratio, and so on. The more complex goals may involve a dozen or more ratios and a number of operating objectives such as new product development, increased geographical scope, expansion of services, decreased emphasis in certain market areas, and so on. In any event, if there are no well-understood objectives, it is not possible for managers to determine whether or not their plan is acceptable or whether or not the plans of their subordinates are acceptable. Consequently, one of the main benefits of the plan is lost. It is true that the senior manager may have an intuitive feel for what he wants the organization to accomplish and can, therefore, say whether a plan is acceptable or not. However, most people would probably agree that communication of the goals to the subordinate managers will tend to improve the chances of achieving them.

One obvious purpose in having a plan is to see that everybody is working toward the same end. If the emphasis in a given period needs to be placed on conservation of cash, it is important that decisions concerning inventory, for example, be made in the light of this overall company requirement. Another purpose in develop-

ing a plan is to require people to think ahead. Without this requirement it is very easy for a group to concentrate its efforts on one
aspect of the operation without giving sufficient consideration to
other aspects which are affected. For instance, a retail organization
pressing for growth and establishment of new outlets could, without an integrated plan, overlook the need for a significant increase
in the number of competent people to manage the stores, or the
cash resources needed for differing assumptions as to profitability,
and perhaps the need for new inventory control systems as the
company becomes more dispersed and complex. The very existence
of the plan influences success by having management think through
the required steps in achieving the goals.

The plan as a basis for measurement

The plan also provides the basis for measurement. In the sense
meant here, there is *no measurement* without a plan. The financial
statement is, of course, an important and, indeed, an essential
means of communication between the management, the board of
directors, the stockholders, potential stockholders, regulating agencies, financial analysts, and so on. It does tell those outside the company whether the results are up to their expectations and whether
they are better or worse than other companies, but it is not a very
useful package of information in helping management guide the
affairs of the company. By itself it is almost useless as a management
tool. Something more is needed. In common with most control systems, whether physical or financial, the actual results serve only as
part of the feedback loop for comparison with the desired results
in sufficient detail, at the proper level, to signal the need for meaningful corrective action. Measurement, then, implies *comparison
of actual results with planned results.* In the more sophisticated
systems it also includes *leading indicators* so as to afford the possibility of action to prevent undesirable events from occurring.

Measurement can also help influence results by providing a basis
for individual personal *incentives* for achievement of planned results. Often these are monetary incentives in the form of bonuses
for achieving or bettering the plan. During difficult times the negative incentives may be direct and firm. For example, one major
corporation advised its managers throughout the country that a
failure to reduce inventory by a certain percentage within a pre-

scribed time would be cause for dismissal. Usually, of course, such broadly disseminated bases for termination of employment are not warranted. Nevertheless, objectively one would have to say that financial plans do aid in communicating from one level of management to another what is expected of them.

Another purpose of the financial planning and control system is to provide a *baseline* upon which modifications can efficiently be introduced if circumstances change. Some companies have found their business to be sufficiently volatile to warrant preparation of *action plans* in case the business level goes up or down by predetermined steps. Even when the business is not regularly so volatile, the existence of the plan is helpful in discerning quickly where changes must be made in the event their need is indicated. Furthermore, a good measurement system probably will provide for earlier warning that circumstances are changing than would be the case without the financial planning and control system.

In summary, the financial planning and control system is a tool used by management to increase the chances of success in attaining its goals by planning the actions needed and measuring results against these plans in a way calculated to influence corrective action as early as possible.

ORGANIZATION

Operational orientation and accounting competence

The persons responsible for financial planning and control need an *operational orientation* but they must also be *competent in the field of accounting*, even though accounting per se is not their responsibility. Accounting must serve several purposes, such as those related to taxation and financial reporting to stockholders. There can be conflicts between these purposes and the requirements for management information and control. For instance, the determination of the manufacturing cost of an item might differ in amount if the purpose of the derivation were proper inventory valuation on the one hand and measurement of the manufacturing manager's performance on the other hand. The cost needed for pricing analysis might be a third figure. These complications make it essential that the financial planning and control staff be well versed in accounting matters. They are not responsible ordinarily for the books of account but are *responsible for the measurement of performance.* The accounting structure must be so arranged as to provide a rational basis for measurement so that the managers being measured both *understand and accept* the logic of the measurements. If the accounting system does not meet this requirement it should be changed, or a parallel system established. The financial planning and control staff should be well enough aware of the purposes of accounting other than performance measurement so that the final accounting system is the simplest one that fulfills all purposes.

As noted, the personnel in the financial planning and control function need to be operationally oriented. That is to say, they should have a good feel for personnel relations and for the cause and effect of various operating decisions and actions. The latter requires a very good understanding of the nature of the particular business and the interrelationship of the various functional organizations. If it is a manufacturing establishment, for example, there should be an understanding of the production process, the production control techniques being used, the influence of marketing on inventories, and so on. The staff should understand what can reasonably be expected. It should be able to communicate in a way that demonstrates this understanding.

Scope of financial planning and control activity

The scope of the activity will depend on the individual company philosophy. Some major companies have several hundred people on the corporate staff performing this function, whereas a several billion dollar, multidivision manufacturing firm may have no more than a dozen people on the corporate staff for this purpose. When the latter condition exists, its success depends on the high competence of the individuals involved, their energy and breadth of background and careful attention to the design of the system throughout the corporation. The system design in this latter case would tend to a high degree of delegation of authority to the divisions and a careful choice of the information which flows from the divisions to the corporate office. The information flow has to be extremely selective so that it can be absorbed by a small group, and yet its content has to be chosen so as to have high odds that early knowledge of significant problems is surfaced.

Size and responsibility of staff

At the division or subsidiary level, the size of the staff, of course, depends on the complexity and the size of the enterprise. Most of the detailed work of planning and measurement is done here, and in comparing a division or subsidiary of, say, $100 million volume with a multidivision corporation having sales of $100 million, one would expect the division or subsidiary staff to be larger than the corporate staff even though the two businesses are equal in dollar volume.

The corporate level staff would ordinarily be responsible for establishing the content of the plans, the definitions to be used in the preparation of the plans, and the follow-on measurement. They would also be responsible for an *appraisal overview,* including an analysis of proposed plans. To the extent possible, the content and form of the plans should be such as to maximize the requirement for self-analysis by the divisions. Thus, the divisions' plans are likely to be in better shape when presented, because major flaws would have been detected by the requirement of self-analysis. The corporate staff also has a role in motivation of division performance.

PLANNING SYSTEM

Fitting procedures to nature of business

The specific techniques and procedures must fit the nature of the business, its personality, and its business cycle. If it is a manufacturing firm with very long lead times or individual programs which require a number of years between initiation and success or failure, then obviously the plans must extend far into the future. Of course, no one is able to foretell exact results five or ten years in the future, but if business decisions are based on five- or ten-year assumptions it is logical that, to the extent useful, certain aspects of the plan extend that far out. Ordinarily the plan for the first one or two years would be in far more detail than for the succeeding years. For the immediate future year and possibly the second year, the purpose is to establish agreed-upon plans for key financial elements and then measure performance against these agreed-upon goals.

The emphasis in establishing the goals will depend on the type

of business. The key parameters would differ between a manufacturing company, a marketing company, and a financial institution. In the latter case, for instance, in addition to operating expenses, a bank would be interested in growth of deposits, loss ratios
on loans, and so on, and an insurance company would have an
abiding interest in the performance of its investment portfolio as
well as premium income, maximum unit exposure, and so on. None
of these are ordinarily significant matters in the manufacturing
firm, while inventory turnover and fixed asset turnover might be
significant but of little interest to a financial institution. Most business enterprises will find profit dollars and return on assets to be
items of high significance. The return on sales or return on through-
put, as well as asset turnover, will likewise be of general
significance.

Measurability of parameters

In establishing a planning and control system it is important
that those being measured agree that the parameters being planned
can in fact be measured within a reasonable degree of accuracy.
If experience shows an inadequacy in the measurement system
it should be corrected promptly. It must again be emphasized that
the whole procedure starts with a plan. There is no such thing as
control without a plan. This point is so important that it merits emphasizing through an illustration of an analogy in the physical
world.

Visualize a tank of water which is to be kept filled to a certain
level. If done manually, the operator is shown the valve to control
the rate of flow into the tank and is shown by a mark, or otherwise,
the desired level of liquid in the tank. The operator watches this
point (the planned level) and opens or closes the valve to maintain that level depending on the rate of flow out of the tank. This
can be done with an automatic valve providing there is a measurement of level in the tank and a predetermined or planned level
set into the measuring device which feeds back the message to
the valve and opens or closes it. This illustration shows that even
though a plan may be in someone's head rather than committed
to paper, without a plan control is not possible. Plans can be modified, of course, depending on desires, needs, or changes in circumstance. In our physical analogy this means we would simply reset

the point of control so that the water in the tank goes to a higher or lower level.

An understanding of the planning process may be helped by considering a typical sequence of events. A preliminary plan may be proposed and, depending on the timing, it may be in rather rough form. Following some analysis or interpretation, there may be some feedback to the originator as to whether the plan appears generally acceptable or whether some key elements need improvement. Typically, the next step would be the preparation and submission of a complete plan with a significant amount of detailed supporting data. This would be subjected to a very detailed analysis.

Parameters of acceptance

The analysis is best performed if there are recognized *parameters of acceptance*. A useful set of such parameters includes the following:

1. Results equal to or better than other competent companies in the same field.
2. Growth and/or improvement over time.
3. The plan represents a challenge to the manager.
4. Feasibility.

The first two parameters are fairly self-explanatory and straightforward in their determination. The last two, challenge and feasibility, ultimately represent judgments, even though such judgments may be premised on very detailed and sometimes sophisticated analyses. If there is no challenge in the plan, the management is not being stretched to do its very best. At any given point in time, some elements of the business are likely to have an opportunity to do significantly better than their competition, and other elements of the business at that point in time may be faced with exceedingly difficult situations. If those elements which have the opportunity to do extraordinarily well are not challenged to take full advantage of the opportunity, it is obvious that the overall enterprise will not be maximizing the total gains to be made. Furthermore, it is not prudent to assume that the competition is taking it easy; therefore, one should assume just the opposite. All elements of the company should be stretched to do their level best—to try a little harder and do a little better than they thought possible. However, if the challenge is too great, it is debilitating to the spirit of those being challenged and will be counter-productive; consequently, it is important to consider feasibility.

If, in a complex company having many elements, the judgments as to challenge and feasibility are made wisely, the results over time will show that not every manager achieved every element of his plan every time but that most managers achieved most elements most of the time. Some companies fail to attempt these judgments and instead rely upon more mechanistic yardsticks. By so doing they are certain to miss many good opportunities, and conversely to demand the impossible from some operations. When judgments are made, they will not be perfect but the results will be better than if judgments are not made.

Communicating during planning

During the course of the analyses of the plans there will be continuing contact between the analyst and the organization whose plan is being analyzed, because of questions that arise during the course of the analysis. Usually at the completion of the analysis there are still open questions, and there may be areas where the analyst thinks the organization being studied has either been too optimistic or too pessimistic in its proposal. There should then be an informal discussion of these matters between the corporate staff and the division management. Often this discussion will result in some questions being put to rest, and on some other items there will be developed a conviction on the part of the division management that they should modify some elements of their plan. The staff should inform the division management as to what its recommendation to corporate management will be concerning the plan. The recommendation may be to accept the plan as proposed, to accept the plan as the division has agreed to revise it, or there may be remaining areas where agreement between the staff and the division management has not been reached. Corporate management is informed of the result of this discussion meeting and receives the recommendations of the staff. Typically, the final agreement is reached at a later meeting between the chief executive officer, the division management, and the corporate staff. The chief executive officer is, of course, not bound to the staff recommendations and may agree with the division president as to the feasibility of some element or elements in dispute, or to the contrary, the chief executive officer may conclude that there are areas where the division should do better than either the division or the staff estimated. With experience in this process and an increased understanding of it, there is likely to be an improvement in the quality of the initial proposals and a decrease in the number of changes between the proposed plan and the final plan agreed upon.

MEASUREMENT SYSTEM

Frequency of measurement

The frequency of measurement of actual performance will depend on the cycle of the business. Some businesses may need input on a weekly or even daily basis. Usually a frequency of at least monthly is prudent. The monthly measurement may be augmented by a more detailed review each quarter. Good measurement requires both documents and face-to-face oral discussions.

Content of documents

The content of the documents is determined by the key factors which are planned plus the underlying elements which pertain to the key factors. For instance, if total asset turnover is one of the key factors, it is also prudent to measure performance on the major asset elements. In a manufacturing establishment the largest portions of the assets would ordinarily be receivables, inventory, and plant and equipment. Consequently, the reporting documents should include not only total assets and their turnover versus plan but also the amount and turnover, or collection period, of receivables, the amount and turnover of inventory, and the amount and turnover of fixed assets. A leading indicator of fixed assets might be included in the form of approved authorizations for fixed asset additions. Depending on the nature of the business, the turnover of various classes of inventory might be worthwhile to measure. As another example, receivables might be viewed in terms of age. Alternatively, such detail as the aging of receivables might be called for only in case the collection period was greater than planned. In any event, it is particularly important to be sure that all major elements of the plan are covered by the measurement system. The greater the degree of delegation of management authority for decision making, the greater the need for measurement of the results of the decisions. Delegation of authority without planning and measurement may be considered an abdication of top management's responsibilities to the stockholders.

Documents used in reporting may be either tabular or graphical. Each method has its place. Almost always it can be found useful to have some data in the form of the classical *budget variance report* containing, for the items to be measured, the planned and actual amounts for the month and year to date along with the variances in terms of amounts and percentages. This format illustrates an important principle of measurement: that it should be done in a way to highlight departures from plan so that attention may be focused on an *exception* basis to problem areas. An illustration of this kind of report is shown in condensed form as Exhibit 1. As illustrated here, the manager can see at a glance that the primary problem is administrative expense. These expenses will have to be studied in more detail. Secondly, there is an asset problem. Reviewing Exhibit 1 will show why the financial statement itself is

EXHIBIT 1

PROGRESSIVE GROWTH CORPORATION
Profit Plan Variance Report
As of March 31, 19—

(dollars in thousands)   Favorable/(Unfavorable)

Month					Year to date			
		Variance					*Variance*	
Actual	*Plan*	*Amount*	*%*	*Item*	*Actual*	*Plan*	*Amount*	*%*
$1,025	$1,000	$ 25	2.5	Sales	$3,060	$3,000	$ 60	2
500	500	–0–	–0–	Cost of sales	1,515	1,500	(15)	(1)
525	500	25	5.0	Operating margin	1,545	1,500	45	3
200	175	(25)	(14.3)	Administrative	605	525	(80)	(15.2)
127	125	(2)	(1.6)	Selling	373	375	2	0.5
50	50	–0–	–0–	Interest	150	150	–0–	–0–
877	850	(27)	(3.2)	Total costs	2,643	2,550	(93)	(3.6)
148	150	(2)	(1.3)	Pretax income	417	450	(33)	(7.3)
74	75	1	1.3	Income tax	209	225	16	7.1
74	75	(1)	(1.3)	Net income	208	225	(17)	(7.6)
6,100	5,900	(200)	(3.4)	Average assets	6,000	5,800	(200)	(3.4)
7.2%	7.5%	(.3) points		Return on sales	6.8%	7.5%	(.7) points	
2.0	2.0	—		Annualized asset turnover	2.0	2.1	(.1)	
14.6%	15.3%	(.7) points		Annualized return on assets	13.9%	15.5%	(1.6) points	

almost useless for purposes of measurement and control. It is only from comparing amounts and ratios with some predetermined goal, ordinarily the plan, that the manager is able to discern where action might be needed. The financial statement itself would include very little of the data shown on this budget variance report.

Face-to-face discussions

Even when the measurement and reporting documents are well conceived, it is important that there be periodic *face-to-face discussions* between the chief executive, his or her staff, and operating management. For efficiency, these discussion meetings should be structured to be sure that major topics are not overlooked, but there should be sufficient flexibility so that unanticipated items of significance can be brought forward. There will, of course, be many unplanned conversations between these individuals, but regular scheduled meetings as prescribed here are essential in minimizing the possibility of poor communication in both directions.

Graphic presentation

Mention was made earlier of using *graphics* in the measurement and reporting procedure. Such methods of presentation lack the precision of tabular figures but have the advantage of communicating quickly the direction of trends and the approximate value of any variances from plan. The two modes, graphics and tables, are complementary, and neither should be used to the exclusion of the other. One often needs to know the size of a figure within a few percentage points of accuracy, and for this the tables are necessary. On the other hand, it is nearly impossible and certainly very time-consuming to discern a *trend* from a table of numbers. Graphical means are exceptionally useful for this purpose.

Examples of graphical techniques are shown in Exhibits 2 through 8. Exhibit 2 shows *sales dollars.* In the example portrayed, we see lines for the prior year's actual experience, the plan for the current year, and the actual results for the current year. The bars give at a glance a picture of the backlog available for shipment in the current year and the following year. These would be appropriate only for companies having long lead time items. The arrow provides a means for the operation being measured to show any changes in outlook since the last reporting time.

EXHIBIT 2

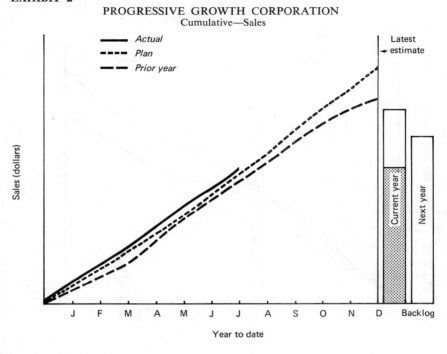

PROGRESSIVE GROWTH CORPORATION
Cumulative—Sales

The *profit curves* shown in Exhibit 3 are similar in concept to the sales data portrayed in Exhibit 2. In both cases cumulative plotting is shown. Some people may prefer month-by-month plotting rather than cumulative. In fact, both could be shown on the same chart. However, if the objective is to attain certain sales and profits by the end of the year, the cumulative results are more significant than the month-by-month amounts. Furthermore, one can get a rough idea of the monthly results versus plan by comparing the slopes of the lines.

The portrayal of *assets employed* in Exhibit 4 is also shown on a cumulative basis—in this case the cumulative average. The lines here, of course, do not start at zero since the assets at the beginning of the year equal those at the end of the prior period. One limitation of this portrayal is that one cannot easily see what the asset level is expected to be at the end of the year. However, since the cost of investments is a function of size and time, the average assets employed does represent the primary measure. The amounts at a point in time can be added if desired.

EXHIBIT 3

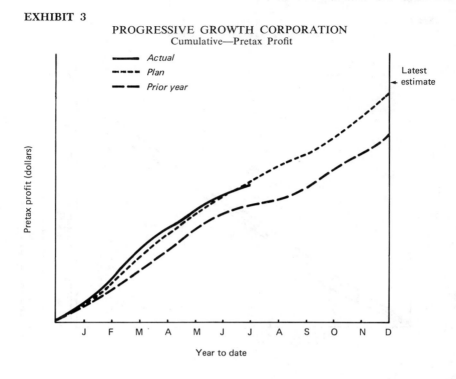

PROGRESSIVE GROWTH CORPORATION
Cumulative—Pretax Profit

Asset turnover as shown in Exhibit 5 represents another type of representation, as does the *collection period* shown in Exhibit 6. In both of these cases, the ratios might very well be planned to remain unchanged through the year and, therefore, the lines could be absolutely horizontal depending on whether or not the plan called for any improvement or worsening.

Another point should be made in connection with these two measures. Assets such as inventory are accumulated in support of shipments of the *forward* period. For top-level measurement and control the asset turnover is ordinarily measured in terms of the *past*—measured by comparing the average assets over a period with the sales of that same period.

Inventory would, of course, be compared with the cost of sales. In analyzing the plan and in controlling at the local level, consideration needs to be given to the activity in the period ahead of the time when the inventory exists. The plan, therefore, has considered the expected future activity; and, consequently, measurement of performance against the plan is made on a fair basis.

EXHIBIT 4

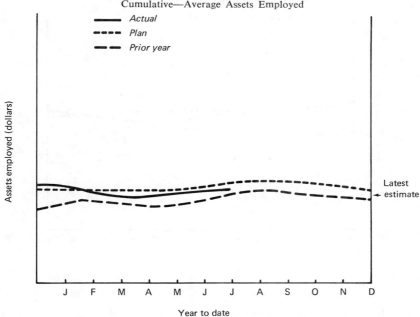

PROGRESSIVE GROWTH CORPORATION
Cumulative—Average Assets Employed

——— Actual
----- Plan
— — Prior year

Assets employed (dollars)

Latest
← estimate

J F M A M J J A S O N D

Year to date

EXHIBIT 5

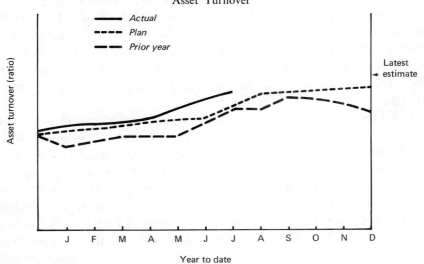

PROGRESSIVE GROWTH CORPORATION
Asset Turnover

——— Actual
----- Plan
— — Prior year

Asset turnover (ratio)

Latest
← estimate

J F M A M J J A S O N D

Year to date

EXHIBIT 6
PROGRESSIVE GROWTH CORPORATION
Collection Period

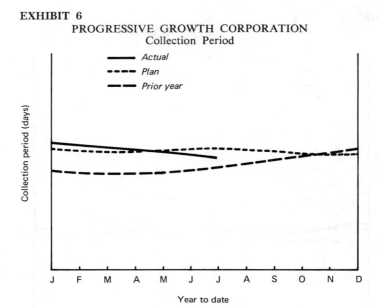

Furthermore, it avoids arguments which are bound to ensue if measurement of today's performance is based solely on an estimate of what tomorrow's results will be. The *collection period* measurement is less flawed, but arguments can be made that in the first part of the year the measurement should be related to the sales of the preceding period on the cumulative average basis. This tends to wash out after a few months, but if it is of substantial importance the measurement could be structured on a more precise basis. Here as in other instances one must find the balance between simplicity and precision which yields the optimum in understanding and usefulness.

Exhibits 7 and 8 illustrate two more factors and useful means of presenting them. *Cash flow* is a matter of importance in all businesses and, of course, *return on assets* is often considered the primary measure of performance. As used here we mean *total* assets. This asset base is unaffected by financial leverage and gives a better measure of operating results than does return on equity. Other asset bases have their usefulness. Total capital (equity plus debt) is a valid base, but means must be adopted to counter the possible tendency on the part of subordinate managers to offset asset growth

EXHIBIT 7

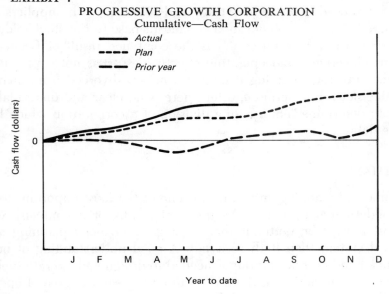

PROGRESSIVE GROWTH CORPORATION
Cumulative—Cash Flow

EXHIBIT 8

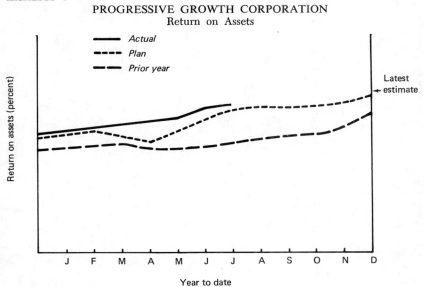

PROGRESSIVE GROWTH CORPORATION
Return on Assets

by inordinate increases in trade payables. The risk is that payments will be slowed and credit ratings and relations with suppliers be damaged. Equity is obviously a significant base to the stockholders, but since the return on equity is the combined result of financing means (leverage) and operating effectiveness, it is not a very useful measure for operating managers who are divorced from financing decisions. Furthermore, often there is no clear and unassailable way to determine "equity" in a division of a corporation which has some debt.

SUMMARY

Financial planning and control is one of the most important tools of modern management. The financial results of a company will almost always be better if there is a good financial planning and control system than if there is not. A good understanding of both financial and cost accounting is needed to design and operate such a system; but in addition, there is required a greater degree of operational understanding and ability to make judgments on operating feasibilities than is ordinarily required in the traditional accounting for past results.

Chapter 47

Managerial aspects of information systems

*C. A. Northrop**

ENVIRONMENT AND TRENDS

Computers have been put to work in many kinds of organizations and human endeavors. They are vital to space exploration and a key to control of air traffic. They monitor hospital patients and help the dairy farmer manage the herd. Athletic coaches use them in developing strategy. Anthropologists use them to help reconstruct man's history. And on and on. Many people feel the computer is one of the most important, if not the single most important, contributor to productivity improvement that has ever been invented.

We will confine ourselves here to a discussion of computers in the typical business or corporate organization. We will discuss information systems activities emphasizing the implications to financial executives. We will assume the reader has a basic understanding of computers, programming, and general data processing activities. Readers looking for fundamentals, perhaps before initially acquiring data processing equipment, will find help readily available from sources such as vendors, management seminars, or consultants.

We will use the term *information systems* in an all-encompassing way, referring to all use of computers in industry, the office, or any business. The term will also be used to refer to the organization that

---

* Controller, IBM Corporation.

operates the computer and designs, develops, and maintains the computer applications and programs.

Throughout the business community there is wide variation in the level of use and complexity of information systems. Consequently, the material presented here should be tempered to fit the reader's specific situation. In general we have attempted to present concepts and practices that have wide application. The manner in which these concepts and practices are implemented will naturally have to be tailored to the specific environment.

Historically, *financial departments* have been primary users of data processing services. In pre-computer days, terms like data processing and information systems were uncommon. Instead, punch card installations were frequently referred to as machine accounting or electric accounting machine departments. The implication was that the predominant, if not the sole, use of punch card equipment was for accounting applications. In many companies the machine accounting installation reported to accounting management.

We now find a much different environment. While the accounting applications were normally among the first to be converted to the computer, today, except for specialized financial institutions, these applications normally are a small part of the total computer workload. In some companies, for example, computer applications that directly support engineering design and product manufacturing operations now use more computer resources than do all the various administrative and financial applications. Accounting applications, furthermore, have frequently remained relatively stable while significant technological advancements have been made in computer applications supporting other areas of the business. Applications such as payroll, payables, and ledger processing frequently look the same today as when first programmed in the 1950s. In contrast, many applications such as order entry and production planning and control, as well as direct product support applications, have frequently introduced newer concepts such as the use of terminals for *on-line* or *real-time* interaction with the computer.

The last paragraph suggests two basic trends in the information systems area: *application expansion* and *interactive systems*. The first trend we will discuss is this growth of applications and expansion of the number of business functions supported by the computer installation. In some companies virtually every business area is dependent to some degree on receiving computer services from the information systems organization. This expansion, and especially the extension of computer applications into the mainline business functions such as engineering design and manufacturing, frequently has a significant impact on the information systems organization. Examples of ways this impact has become evident include:

1. Information systems seldom reports to accounting any longer, though it may still report to the financial organization. We find wide variations in the structure of the information systems organization. There may be a single systems department supporting the entire company or there may be multiple decentralized departments. There may be a purely line management structure or a combination of line and staff organizations. In some companies there is heavy, if not total, dependence on outside contracting and consultants' services for information systems activities.

2. The information systems manager and his or her people have frequently become involved in a new category of business decisions. Product plans and designs, product manufacturing schedules and costs, product marketing, and company organizational plans, for example, can now be significantly impacted by the effectiveness of the services from information systems. This, in turn, frequently means that it is necessary for information systems people to participate in the business planning process to a much greater degree than in the past. Some companies develop an information systems plan as part of the business plan.

The expanding list of computer applications has placed new demands on the financial organization to understand, measure, and evaluate information systems activities throughout the business. We will explore this thought further in the section entitled "Financial Role in Management of Information Systems."

The second and perhaps the most important trend in information systems activities is the movement *from batch to interactive systems.* This is one of the newer systems design concepts that is receiving rapidly expanding application. This trend is quite apparent because it typically requires the use of a physical machine, a computer terminal, in the user's work area. The terminal allows the user to work directly with the computer and its data files. In contrast, a batch system refers to the more traditional procedure wherein the user accumulates data—transactions—for a period of time—a day, a week, or a month—and then submits them to information systems for processing. Following the processing cycle predetermined output formats are returned to the user.

Examples of interactive systems abound. Terminals are used by administrative and clerical people to enter business transactions directly into the computer, or to inquire as to the status of an account. They are used by engineers to bring the power of the computer to their desks to solve complex design problems. The executive and his or her staff can use terminals to develop computer models of business conditions and test alternative actions before deciding on a specific course. The manufacturing or maintenance person can use the terminal to get step-by-step assembly or maintenance instructions, or to record data for use in inventory, payroll, and accounting systems. The programmer can use a terminal to help develop the programs that permit other people to use terminals.

In a typical interactive system many users may be interacting directly with the computer simultaneously. The two terms, *on line* and *real time*, are frequently used to describe some of the characteristics of an interactive system. The key characteristic is that the user processes data to the computer as an event occurs, or makes an inquiry of the computer as the need arises.

While the terminal is the physically obvious or visual part of an interactive system, there are other important but less apparent elements which should be understood.

The first of these is the *data files*. Typically they must be structured differently for interactive systems than for batch systems. A data file is a collection of records or information, usually concerning a single business area such as payroll, organized and coded so that it can be used in a computer. A *batch system* typically works with one or more data files. In contrast, an *interactive system* normally works with a data base, a collection of related computer data files organized to minimize duplicate information and to permit terminal activity, providing a single data source for a variety of computer applications.

Another element in an interactive system is *communications*. Terminals may be close to the computer and directly wired to it, or they may be thousands of miles away and connected to the computer by either dedicated or dial-up communication lines. Terminals, data bases, communication lines, and remoteness are all factors that generally make an interactive system much more complex than a batch system. In order to manage this complexity a further element must be considered. We refer to the use of *computer programs* to help manage the actions and interfaces between the other elements. Terms like *data base management* and *data communications networking* refer to the use of specialized programs and application design concepts that are usually required in these newer, more complex interactive systems.

Additional extensions to the concept of providing the user with the ability to work directly with computers are also emerging. One of these, generally referred to as *distributed processing,* provides for linking various computers and terminals together with different components, each performing part of the processing. In addition, certain applications sometimes can be most effectively processed on small stand-alone computers that are usually operated directly by the user.

In the following sections we will discuss the management implications of this expanding and changing information systems environment. First we will consider *finance's role* in managing and controlling systems activities. Then we will address *information systems activities* in support of the user. Finally, we will discuss some *general considerations* for insuring the benefits of these activities and for monitoring the overall information systems program. Emphasis throughout will be on *management.* What responsibilities should financial managers or executives have for information systems activities? What should they be able to expect from information systems?

FINANCIAL ROLE IN MANAGEMENT OF INFORMATION SYSTEMS

General responsibilities

The financial organization in many businesses has the responsibility of insuring that the company has a solid planning, control, and reporting system for financial reporting, management decision making, and performance measurement. This mission, in addition to finance's general responsibility for expense and profit management, requires the financial organization to have a broad role to play in the company. As we have seen, information systems may also be characterized by its pervasiveness. It impacts on many business functions.

Furthermore, this impact usually involves basic planning, control, reporting, and measurement activities. Recognizing these factors, many companies have concluded that finance has to be actively involved in the planning and control of information systems.

In some companies this involvement is accomplished by linking the information systems organization closely to the financial organization. Many of the responsibilities of finance can thus be implemented through direct management of the information systems mission. However, in those companies where information systems does not report to finance it is necessary for finance to handle its responsibilities indirectly.

Regardless of the organization, in order for finance to accomplish its overall responsibilities it may be desirable for it to have the following specific responsibilites in connection with information systems:

1. Maintain an *awareness of current information systems* to assure that they satisfy objectives at acceptable levels of performance and cost, and that they enforce sound business controls.
2. Insure that the anticipated expense of new systems or application development projects represents an *acceptable use of resources* and can be justified within the company's objectives.
3. Insure that new systems will be *manageable* and *auditable,* that they will provide adequate internal controls and security and privacy protections, and that they will be compatible with other systems and will not create duplication or operational conflicts.
4. Insure that mechanisms are established to *track the cost* of developing and implementing new systems, and to *monitor the benefits* after the systems have been implemented.

Planning and control of information systems

As information systems activities expand and become more complex they represent an increasing investment and require commensurate focus of management attention. Some companies have seen the need for establishing formal instructions or guidelines to insure planning and control of these activities. Finance should insure that adequate instructions are established and should participate in their effective implementation. The following are examples of subjects that lend themselves to *formal instructions:*

1. Information systems plan.
2. Data processing equipment justification.
3. Project control and accounting.
4. Phase reviews.
5. Information systems project audits.
6. Information systems operation audits.
7. Security and privacy.
8. Application auditability.
9. Performance measurements.

Each of these subjects can be thought of as an element in an overall management and control process for information systems activities. In the sections that follow these subjects will be discussed individually, giving indications to areas of possible financial involvement.

Information systems plan. It becomes increasingly more important for information systems to be involved in the planning process within the organization as their activities become more widespread and pervasive. Business planning processes vary widely, but a systems plan should be developed as an integral part, or functional subset, of whatever business planning process is in place. The scope and sophistication of the plan should increase as the resources and the decentralization of the information systems organization increase.

The basic *purpose of the plan* should be to provide a uniform vehicle for:

1. Stating plans needed to assure achievement of company objectives,
2. Assuring the integration of the information systems effort with business plans,
3. Providing goals and plans against which performance can be measured and evaluated, and
4. Seeking assessments and concurrence for plans.

Plans are normally prepared at the computer installation level and then summarized into larger aggregates if there are multiple installations.

The plans should have two basic orientations: a *time* orientation and a *project* orientation. The time part of the plan should focus on resources by period for current and future years. Resources commonly addressed include: *dollars,* for whatever cost elements are in

the manager's operating budget; *people,* by general job classifications; and *data processing equipment,* by system. Time periods
should be chosen to agree with the business planning cycle. A common practice is to show data in the plan for four years: the preceding year, the current year, and the next two years.

The *project* part of the plan should address key development
projects and other major activities, such as establishing a computer
center, developing a communications network, or installing additional equipment or otherwise upgrading the computer installation.
The project plans should cover the entire project cycle in terms of
objectives, schedules, expected benefits, and resource requirements.

A key ingredient in the planning process, the one that enforces and
disciplines the plan, is the *review and assessment* process. To the extent that the company business plan undergoes a formal approval
step, the information systems plan should be assessed as part of that
process.

Data processing equipment justification. The financial manager
at all levels in the organization should have a role to play in assessing proposed acquisitions of data processing equipment. The signature of the financial manager on the formal justification document
should indicate that in his or her judgment the justification is based
on a sound business proposition, that possible alternative solutions
have been adequately investigated, and that the financial and manpower resources required to support the equipment are covered
under approved financial plans.

Justifications are commonly based on one or more of the following
criteria: improved performance, economics, increased workload, alternative to other capital equipment, or as an integral part of a larger
business project. Regardless of the criteria, documentation supporting the justification should address such factors as cost, anticipated
cost distribution to the user, configuration, alternatives, applications,
manpower and training requirements, and performance and utilization factors. In many situations, the request for additional equipment
should properly trigger an effort to reevaluate and/or rejustify existing equipment as well.

In many companies a director or manager in each operating unit
headquarters is responsible for the proper use of data processing
equipment and for enforcing the justification procedures within the
unit. Focusing this responsibility in one person is an effective way of

insuring that operating efficiencies are realized whenever possible from such things as consolidation of people and equipment and enforcement of standard procedures.

Project control and accounting. Information systems projects need management attention comparable to that given project-oriented activities in other areas of the business. Project control begins with the establishment of plans and objectives, and continues with the measurement of performance and progress toward these objectives throughout the life of the project.

Essential *ingredients of control* include identification of the project, a breakdown of the project into phases, and a further breakdown of the phases into work assignment tasks. Each task should be identified so that plans, schedules, and progress can be tracked at the task level.

Some degree of project control should be maintained in all projects. The relative importance and complexity of the project should determine the comprehensiveness of the controls.

Project accounting provides management with the cost of each project. The cost history can be used to measure and control financial performance on a specific project, as well as serve as a basis for the construction of future financial plans. Items controlled by project include such things as headcount, man-months, and costs for salaries and benefits, installed data processing equipment, equipment services, travel, and contract programming fees. The accounting process should permit identification of costs with the various phases of a project.

Phase reviews. Phase reviews are conducted at major project milestones or checkpoints, at which time both project and user management have the opportunity to review the status of the project and consider problems or issues. Phase review meetings should result in a consolidated position and recommendation to management concerning the project's future. A convenient way of viewing the *life cycle* of a project is to break it into the following phases:

1.   Project selection and feasibility study.
2.   General design specifications and implementation plan.
3.   Detail design, programming, and testing.
4.   Pilot installation.
5.   Installation and use.

Phase reviews may fall into one of three categories:

1. A planned review at the completion of a specific project phase.
2. An interim phase review where a project phase is estimated to take longer than six months.
3. A default phase review wherein the original target date for a phase review cannot be met and a review is held to determine the causes for the delay and to establish new target dates.

Finance at the appropriate levels in the organization should be involved in phase reviews, either actively or as a reviewer of phase review summary reports. This is so regardless of the function of the business served by the system under development. Financial judgment is critical on matters dealing with return on investment and budgetary considerations, as well as the control implications of the project.

Some specific *objectives* of phase reviews include:

1. Insuring a comprehensive and timely review of the project and insuring that agreed upon objectives and results have been achieved.
2. Allowing for early identification of problems with the establishment of a corrective action plan.
3. Assessing the business risk involved in the project.
4. Reviewing plans and establishing or reconfirming objectives for the next phase.
5. Obtaining agreement by all interested parties with the level and direction of the continuing effort.

Just as in projects other than information systems, the project's importance and complexity should determine the degree of management involvement, as well as the comprehensiveness of the phase review. Projects consisting of multiple stages or subsystems should be reviewed by stage or subsystem when appropriate milestones are reached. During such reviews the relationship of the subsystem to the overall project should be considered in order to ensure overall system integrity.

Information systems project audits.   Major information systems projects frequently involve complex specifications and numerous interdependencies among several business functions. These projects may require significant resources for an extensive period of time. Implementation of other business activities may depend on having the project completed on time and according to specifications. Recognizing these complexities, some companies have established formal *project audit procedures* to help assure the successful completion of information systems projects.

The *objective* of a project audit is to provide management with the opportunity to focus on a specific area of concern, investigate all or part of a project, and secure an objective assessment of the risks and exposures to the planned course of action. Any facet of a system project may be a candidate for a formal audit. Each company should decide the appropriate level of management that can request an audit.

The audit should be conducted and controlled by personnel not directly concerned with the project. A report of the audit team's findings should be submitted to the operating unit responsible for the system as well as to the management which requested the review. Care must be taken to preserve the integrity of the team's findings in order to obtain maximum objectivity and benefit. A project audit would normally be called to examine areas of exposure or concern either preliminary to or following a phase review of the project—the difference being that a phase review is conducted by the project's participants.

To the extent that such audits become a normal part of the management process, a receptive climate for them can be created. If the size of the information systems community warrants, a small permanent review or audit department may be appropriate. The members of the department would serve as review leaders, and would be assisted by other employees with the skills needed for each specific audit.

Information systems operation audits. The computer operations department is normally a service function supporting many, if not most, of the other business functions. Management of the department in a manner that assures effective, yet efficient, service can be a complex process. Just as with information systems projects, some companies have seen the need to establish a formal auditing procedure for computer operations departments.

When an auditing procedure is established, a group within finance should be given the responsibility of auditing the computer installations throughout the organization. This function fits naturally with either the internal audit department or with that group responsible for conducting reviews of information systems projects.

The mission of this group should be to conduct audits of all significant-size computer installations on a periodic, routine basis. The scope of an audit should generally be all-encompassing, including such factors as:

1. Operating efficiency.
2. Management.
3. Objectives.
4. Data file and data base content.
5. Physical and data security considerations.
6. Equipment utilization and performance.
7. Personnel privacy considerations.
8. Applications auditability.
9. Program integrity and freedom from unauthorized program changes.
10. Relationships between the operations department and the various user and system development and maintenance departments.

An audit report requiring management response should be submitted to the installation manager and financial management at the location and at appropriate higher organization levels.

Security and privacy. High on the priority list of information systems matters in which finance should have a vital interest is the entire area of *security* and *privacy*. Computers, their programs, and the information in their storage devices are significant company assets. They demand the highest level of security attention. Vital company processes and operations are normally dependent on the availability and integrity of those assets. Likewise, information about a company's employees is frequently contained in computer files and needs to be made secure from invasion of privacy.

We can only begin to discuss security and privacy here. They have many facets and implications. The word *security* carries an implied image of protection from wilful disruption, damage, or compromise of the assets. An effective security program must focus on creating deterrents to the potential breaches of security. Effective deterrents have many and widely varied forms and include such things as: physical safeguards, division of responsibility, record and data classifications, input/output controls, application audit trails, rotation of personnel, program change controls, and terminal protection procedures.

The security program must also address the whole area of *pro-*

tection against and *recovery* from natural disasters, accidents, or mistakes. Experience suggests that unintentional mistakes are the most common security exposure, outweighing by far all wilfully created and disaster type problems. Emphasis here must be placed on recovery. Problems must be anticipated and a sound recovery procedure planned in advance. Some companies have established a regular program of simulating accidents or natural disasters as a means of assessing the recovery procedures. A few of the basic factors included in recovery are: retention of prior period master computer files, automated program restart procedures, off-site storage of vital records and programs, and formal emergency back-up computer arrangements.

Creating *security consciousness* should be a key function of many parts of the system control mechanism. Phase reviews, project and operational audits, and the plan process can all be used to focus attention on security. Many companies have established comprehensive security programs with extensive documented procedures and audits. Finance can play an important role in assuring that reasonable safeguards are prescribed and enforced.

Another financial role, deserving of more attention than it frequently gets, concerns the *economics of security*. Being secure costs money. Similarly, being secure has value. Equating the two, however, is complicated by the need to consider also for each type of security exposure the probability of a breach of security occurring and, at the same time, the relative degree of protection desirable. While no simple mathematical solutions to the economics of security are readily available, finance should insure that the economic factors are considered.

The process of insuring that information stored in computer data files about people is not misused is becoming more complex with the advent of such concepts as interactive systems, data bases, and distributed processing. Traditional approaches to protecting the individual's privacy have included such things as *file access security procedures* and design concepts that, first, *exclude unnecessary data* from the file design, and second, periodically purge dated material from the file. Both the enforcement of these procedures and the design of new procedures and protection concepts will continue to require increased attention.

Application auditability.   Closely related to the security subject, but worthy of separate discussion, is the area of *application auditability.* Information about many, if not all, of a company's assets is frequently stored in and processed by the computer installation. The emphasis in the previous section was on making the records of these assets secure and recoverable. Emphasis here is on the assets themselves.

Auditability involves protection against fraudulent manipulation of the records in a way that would compromise the assets. Deterrents such as division of responsibility and rotation of personnel are part of the protection process. In addition, a primary ingredient in this process is the formal audit as conducted by either the internal audit function or by professional auditing firms.

The introduction of computers into the record-keeping process means that computer programs as well as the procedures in the computer installation are major subjects for the auditor to address. The auditor is concerned about whether the programs do in fact always process the data according to specifications, and whether the procedures can be compromised without detection.

The application programs should receive major attention from the auditor. In the first place, the specifications must ensure that a sound audit trail is provided for. It may frequently be desirable to have the auditor review the specifications for a new application before the programs are written.

The auditor may also choose to process his or her own *test data* and records using the operational program. This can be a useful step in insuring that the programs themselves have not been compromised. This may require that the program specifications provide for this test. Care must be taken to keep the auditor's test data from affecting the operational records.

The auditor is also interested in insuring that adequate safeguards exist against *unauthorized changes* to the programs. Protection against fraud involving unauthorized program changes should involve assuring adequate control over the process whereby program changes are authorized, tested, and implemented.

Finance should have a primary responsibility for assuring that the company has a sound, effective procedure for periodically and formally auditing all sensitive computer applications, and especially those that process records about the company's assets.

Performance measurements. Effective management of a computer installation can be enhanced by a sound program of *usage and performance measurements*. An individual installation can benefit by measuring itself and comparing current and prior period statistics.

And if there are several computer installations in the business, added benefits can accrue from comparing and ranking them. This requires defining a set of standard performance criteria and establishing a recording and reporting procedure. Finance should play an active role in seeing that these steps are taken.

The first measurements to consider are simple *utilization statistics*. These are normally recorded by computer job or application as a means of telling the users the computer costs their work has incurred. Depending on the company and its organization structure, it may be desirable to treat the computer installation as a cost center for accounting and budgetary purposes. It would normally be finance's responsibility to implement an adequate charge-back procedure. If costs are not charged to the user, consideration should be given to providing the user with some periodic measure of computer use the user has generated.

Regardless of whether costs are actually charged to the user, utilization statistics are valuable tools for the installation manager. Comparing computer time required for a given application from one processing period to the next can give essential clues to operational and programming effectiveness.

Several techniques are available to record a number of other more detailed statistics about the computer operations. Various physical monitors can be attached to the computer. Or, as an alternative, computer programs can be used to record many operating facts such as:

1. Number of records processed.
2. Number of lines or records of output prepared.
3. Length of time each of the various computer components— storage, channels, central processing unit, and so on—are in use.
4. Number of program instructions executed.
5. Number of jobs being processed simultaneously.
6. Amount of storage being used by each job.

Sometimes measurements are recorded continuously; at other times a sampling or random measurement approach is satisfactory.

Ratios derived from the raw statistics are also useful. Commonly used ratios include such factors as:

1. Jobs per hour.
2. Program instructions executed per job or per hour or per shift.

3. Percent of available time actually used by the various computer components.

4. Busy time for a specific component, such as a channel, as a percentage of time used by the central processing unit.

Indications of trends, variations, or significant differences between computers can be a valuable tool for the installation manager to improve the operating efficiency of the computer facility. Measurements of this type can also be useful in supporting or challenging the need for additional computer capacity. It is in finance's interest to insure that an effective performance measurement program is established.

Consolidated versus decentralized activities

Advances in computers, programs, data communications, and application design concepts are made regularly. Some of these make consolidation of data processing facilities technically more desirable—others favor decentralization. Still others tend to minimize the difference between the two. Some large companies with multiple computer installations find simultaneous movement in both directions. There are apparent economic advantages from consolidation, and equally apparent, but sometimes hard to quantify, flexibility advantages of decentralization.

Many companies with multiple computer installations have witnessed an evolution along certain general lines:

1. During the 1950s and 1960s each computer center tended to process and maintain its own *locally developed applications.* Emphasis was placed on making sure that the many computer applications needed for each of the functions at the site, such as finance, personnel, and perhaps manufacturing, had sound interfaces and exchanged data with minimum file maintenance redundancy.

2. In time, frequently when it became necessary for a major redesign or rewrite of a given application, a *common program concept* was used. One location developed and maintained an application and made it available to other processing locations. Budgetary constraints frequently became so important that they overshadowed the concerns arising from any loss of local flexibility. There are obvious economic advantages to this com-

mon program approach. However, the concept imposes new and more strict disciplines on documentation, training, and program change controls, which in turn have their own economic considerations.

3. With advances in the power of computers and in data communications techniques, a frequent next step was for some applications to be *written, maintained, and processed centrally*. This does not necessarily mean central processing for the entire company. A central processing site frequently supports a specific organizational division of the company or a designated geographic area. Sometimes, this type of consolidation accompanies a similar consolidation of other functions. Perhaps multiple accounting departments are merged into a single department supporting several locations. Again the economics of centralization have to be balanced against the costs of the added disciplines imposed, and also against the added costs frequently incurred to interface the centralized systems with others which may have remained under local control.

A further evolutionary step is perhaps emerging now. Its impact has been seen in some companies. It involves some of the newer concepts we've discussed elsewhere such as interactive systems, data base management, and data communications management and networking. It also involves other concepts such as distributed processing and hierarchical systems, which concern linking a number of computers and terminals together with different components, each doing part of the processing within an overall structure of related applications and systems. Likewise, advances in smaller computers means that certain applications can sometimes be processed most effectively by these smaller machines, which are frequently operated directly by the user. The net effect of these concepts is that traditional approaches to organizing computer facilities are now being molded together into a complex and ever-changing combination of alternatives.

In summary, answering the question of how to organize the computer facilities often reduces to an evaluation of which structure best fits the company's organization structure, operating policies, and management style. Economics is always a factor, but in many situations the question is more related to management desires and concerns than it is to the sole issue of information system effectiveness and efficiency. Questions such as span of control, critical mass, manageability, risks of overconcentration of resources, and needs for emergency back-up facilities should all be considered. Financial management should be influential whenever the question of computer facility organization is addressed, not only because of their interest in the economics of the decision but also because of their interest in the related business operation and control factors that may be irrevocably tied to the decision.

INFORMATION SYSTEMS IN SUPPORT OF THE USER

Information systems' view of the financial system

This section will discuss the role that information systems plays in supporting finance, and especially the working relationships needed between the two organizations. It will be immediately obvious, however, that the material is equally applicable to other users of computer services.

Any company can illustrate or describe something they can call their "financial system." If it is drawn or written by a financial person it will probably look quite different than if it is prepared by an information systems person. The two will see the system from different backgrounds. Naturally, the illustration or description will vary widely from company to company. However, we can usually point to two separate although related parts of the *financial system:* the *accounting system* and the *financial reporting system.*

From a system person's point of view the financial system for a decentralized manufacturing company may look like the pyramid in Exhibit 1. A series of applications or subsystems is perceived linked together by common data flow and information file considerations to form an organized structure. Here the financial system is depicted as the sides of a pyramid, the left side the accounting system, the right side the financial reporting system. The base of the pyramid is divided into examples of the computer applications that may be found throughout most financial systems. In observing this illustration three points come to mind: (*1*) There are many pieces to any financial system; (*2*) they should be constructed to fit together into a solid, sound, aggregate structure without any unnecessary overlap, duplication, or redundant parts; and (*3*) the financial

EXHIBIT 1
Financial system

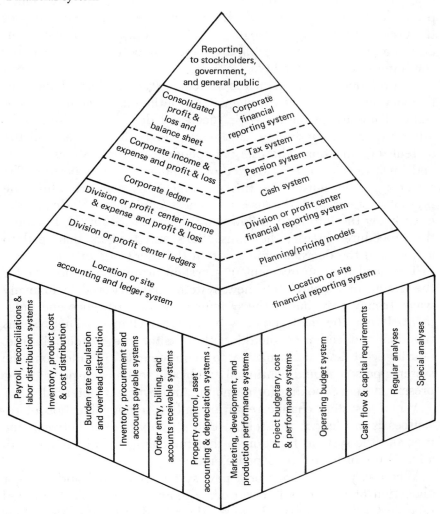

system does not stand alone but interfaces with and depends on systems supporting other parts of the business. These other systems can be thought of as represented by the hidden sides of the pyramid.

User-information systems working relationship

Implementation and operation of a sound, efficient information system require a blending of the efforts of the systems organization with the user organization. They require the systems function to bring to the user three distinct capabilities: a logical, disciplined problem-solving capability which must include an understanding of the user's business environment; a well-developed technical systems design and programming capability; and a smooth running, capable computer operations facility.

The relationship between the systems organization and the user is generally most effective when it is continuous. Systems are not static. They are dynamic. Their successful development and operation requires a continuing involvement of both the user and the systems organization. The user is dependent on the systems person, and must develop a high degree of confidence in this person. The systems person must earn this confidence by understanding the present systems and the user's business environment. He or she must know the information flows and their use within the function, the procedures in use, the transactions and triggers that lead to action, and the decision points within the user's organization.

The need for improvement in a system or an application, or for the design of a completely new system, may materialize in many ways. It may grow out of the systems person's experience and judgment. It may be made obvious by external changes. The systems function and the user should both monitor the systems in use, relating cost and performance to requirements. In addition, the systems person should continually audit the technical aspects of the present systems, looking for economic improvement potential.

When a system change requiring only a minor allocation of resources is needed, it is essential that a rapport exist between the user and the systems function so that the change can be made with a minimum of formality, expense, and delay.

When a system change or a new system is needed and a major allocation of resources is required, a more formal project-oriented relationship is necessary. However, the added formality this creates should not be permitted to lessen the attitude of cooperative teamwork. Effective project management requires regular and frequent exchanges between the systems organization and the user.

While a systems project should be broken up into specific phases, overlapping between the phases is common. Application specifications and processing logic tend to evolve through an iterative process and frequently are completed only as the programs themselves are developed and tested. Documentation, while essential, has a practical limitation. It cannot take the place of close teamwork. This must exist if the new system is to be satisfactorily implemented. Because of this close working relationship between information systems and the user, some organizations assign *application design and programming responsibilities to the user*. The obvious advantages of this approach must be measured against the effect of several disadvantages. First, the systems person or programmer in the user department is out of contact with his or her peers. This may be a handicap in his or her career and in keeping pace with a rapidly changing technology. Also, systems people in a user environment, while becoming specialists from an application point of view, tend to become technical generalists. Another disadvantage concerns critical mass. Many users cannot support a large enough systems group to provide for peak requirements.

Another approach, which is probably more widely used, is for the *user to employ a small group*—one to three people is typical—of dedicated systems interface or *liaison-type people*. These people, while maintaining their user orientation, take on a general responsibility for their function as the primary contact point with the information systems organization. They may interface not only for application design and program specification purposes but also for the daily input/output coordination with the computer operations department as well.

The following are a few suggestions as to the general responsibilities of the user and the information systems department.

User's general responsibilities

1. Define requirements and specifications for computer applications.
2. Continuously review present systems for adequacy and insure that systems are justified for current requirements.
3. Insure the integrity and accuracy of all system inputs and outputs on a continual basis.
4. Request, approve, and participate in all new systems development projects.
5. Participate in periodic phase reviews, insuring that resources are expended for a given phase only if user management approves the objectives for that phase.
6. Insure that existing and new systems give adequate attention to security, privacy, and auditability considerations.

7. Insure, through proper employee training and monitoring, that all system inputs and outputs are effectively used and understood.

Systems department's general responsibilities

1. Work with the user in defining his or her requirements for computer applications.
2. Design, program, test, and operate computer applications.
3. Insure overall systems integrity and auditability.
4. Insure integrity and security of all computer files and programs.
5. Insure that related systems effectively complement each other.
6. Take lead responsibility relative to system integration potentials.
7. Provide continuing surveillance of system performance, cost, and adequacy relative to the user's requirements, proposing and initiating improvement or corrective action when appropriate.
8. Provide a continuing technical evaluation of existing systems, proposing improvement action when appropriate.

System development task guideline

System development projects require the execution of many tasks. Some of these are done by the systems department, some by the user. Many involve both parties. Table 1 contains a nonexhaustive *checklist* of tasks showing which party normally would have the lead role. Some of these tasks may be combined and others expanded for a specific project. Similarly, the primary or lead responsibility may switch from one party to the other in a given situation. It is suggested, however, that an understanding of these lead responsibilities be documented in advance.

MANAGING AND MEASURING THE BENEFITS OF A NEW SYSTEM

System projects do not exist in a vacuum. Other business activities go on simultaneously: business volumes change, people change, missions change. All these tend to make the realization of system benefits and the measurement of them a complex managerial function. One step that is increasingly important is the need to determine, well in advance of system implementation, just what is likely to be involved in achieving the expected benefits.

TABLE 1
System development task guideline (P = primary role)

Task	Systems	User
A. Problem Identification		
1. Define problem to be addressed.		P
2. Conduct feasibility study of a systems solution.	P	
3. Conduct a feasibility study phase review.	P	
B. Develop General System Solution and Plan		
1. Develop general user specifications, implementation plans, and justification details.		P
2. Determine alternate technical approaches including pros, cons, and economics of each.	P	
3. Develop general systems specifications, project plan, and system justification (objectives, general specifications, economics, milestones and resources).	P	
4. Conduct a general design phase review.	P	
C. Develop Detail System Specifications		
1. Develop detail user specifications.		P
2. Develop and document detail system specifications.	P	
3. Match user and system specifications:		
a. Identify and evaluate trade-offs.	P	
b. Resolve trade-offs.		P
4. Coordinate as necessary with other functions.	P	
D. Develop Detail Technical System Design		
1. Define program modules and relationships.	P	
2. Define inputs/outputs/files.	P	
3. Define processing logic.	P	
4. Define systems flow and other technical matters.	P	
5. Coordinate as necessary with other functions.	P	
E. Develop the System		
1. Write and test programs.	P	
2. Develop administrative procedures for I/O, audits, tables, etc.	P	
3. Develop implementation plan.	P	
4. Develop implementation aids.	P	
5. Develop test data and conduct a systems test of all program modules.	P	
6. Review and concur with results of E 2-5.		P
7. Coordinate all aspects of system with other functions as necessary.	P	
8. Conduct a detail design phase review.	P	
F. Pilot Test		
1. Develop DP operating instructions.	P	
2. Develop user manual.		P
3. Train user personnel.		P
4. Review and concur with user manual and training plan.	P	
5. Coordinate as necessary with other functions.	P	
6. Convert or initiate files.	P	
7. Initiate new inputs from user function.		P
8. Initiate new inputs from other functions.	P	
9. Initiate use of systems output.		P
10. Evaluate data integrity and accuracy.		P
11. Initiate and follow through on corrective actions.	P	
12. Ensure user's understanding of systems outputs and procedures.	P	
13. Follow up with related functions.	P	
14. Conduct a pilot installation phase review.	P	

TABLE 1 (*continued*)

Task	Systems	User
G. Systems Installation, Operation, and Maintenance		
1. Ensure proper inputs from function area.		P
2. Ensure proper inputs from other areas.	P	
3. Evaluate and correct audit and edit errors.		P
4. Assure integrity and accuracy of outputs.		P
5. Distribute outputs.		P
6. Assure understanding of outputs.		P
7. Take action on specific systems, procedures, or input failures to ensure continued accomplishment of function mission.		P
8. Identify cause of systems, procedures, or input failure and take necessary follow-up action to ensure correction.	P	
9. Identify and request system changes to meet new requirements.		P
10. Identify and suggest system changes for improved system efficiency, economy, or performance when made possible by new technical capabilities.	P	
11. Identify and suggest system change as a result of requirements of other systems or functions.	P	
12. Decision point on system changes that affect input or output.		P
13. Decision point on system changes that do not directly affect the user.	P	
14. Conduct post-installation phase reviews at specified intervals following installation.	P	

Frequently, benefits will take the form of being able to handle increased business volumes with the existing workforce. Management should anticipate and establish necessary workload and performance measurements before the new system is implemented so that tracking can be continued throughout the implementation phase and for some months thereafter.

Other projects will have an objective of reducing the people needed by the function supported by the new system. But frequently this will take the form of reducing by some percentage the workload of each of a number of employees, rather than eliminating any specific positions outright. Management must, therefore, rearrange the workload in order to realize the savings. Failure to do this at the appropriate point in the implementation schedule can be critical—the workload gaps will refill quickly with something.

Frequently management must enter this arena and manage the benefits by the use of enforced budget changes, departmental remissioning, or organizational changes. *How to realize the benefits* should be a key topic for both the pilot test and post-installation phase review meetings.

Unfortunately for the manager, many of the benefits of today's system projects are difficult to track and measure. Some companies may be past the point where the majority of new systems are installed to realize a direct economic advantage, such as doing the job with fewer people. Rather, the objectives of today's system frequently include such things as: modeling various activities or business functions to test alternatives before making a decision, improving the accuracy and timeliness of customer invoicing, or offering a new service such as 24-hour banking and cash-dispensing from a sidewalk terminal. While the benefits may reduce ultimately to economics, there is frequently no ready measure to determine whether the objectives are being met. But that is not meant to suggest that management should not attempt to track and measure the benefits. The answer to this problem may lie in some form of *indirect measurement* such as customer or employee satisfaction surveys, customer complaints per thousand invoices, or employees required to generate a specified sales volume. Again, often the key is to plan the measurement process in advance so that a base measurement can be established before the system is installed.

MANAGING THE OVERALL INFORMATION SYSTEMS PROGRAM

We have approached information systems from a number of directions or points of view: from a discussion of the current environment, to a review of areas for possible financial involvement in managing information systems activities, to an exploration of the various relationships and responsibilities involved in developing a new system, and finally to a review of the process of managing to insure that the new system's benefits are achieved. In this final section we will examine the process of managing and coordinating the overall information systems program. While the material will be particularly aimed at those larger organizations that have multiple information systems departments and computer facilities, many of the thoughts should apply to the centralized and smaller organizations as well.

Computers are a powerful tool for improving productivity. Their value has been established in support of a growing list of business functions. A company's level of investment in information systems resources, as well as the prioritization of those resources, are matters for management concern and decision. Most large corporations, and a growing number of smaller organizations, have seen the need to designate an executive to monitor information systems activities throughout the company and to assist in making these decisions.

The role this information systems executive plays, the organizational status, and the makeup of his or her staff vary widely. We suggest however, that as a minimum the information systems executive's mission should include:

1. Insuring planning.
2. Monitoring key activities.
3. Giving technical and strategic guidance.
4. Identifying and tracking resources.

We have discussed the first two of these subjects, planning and key activities, at some length. The information systems executive's most important task may well be to provide a strong *coordinating and cohesive influence* over separately developed plans and activities. In order to provide the proper focus for the more important projects, some companies have found it beneficial to differentiate formally between the few key activities and the many lesser ones. Key activities might include those that meet one or more of the following criteria:

1. Cost more than a certain amount.
2. Take longer than a certain time to complete.
3. Support more than one location or operating unit.
4. Have significant interlocation dependencies.
5. Correct a significant company control exposure.
6. Embody new techniques or concepts for the first time.

The third key responsibility we stated for a company's information systems executive concerns providing *central guidance on technical and strategic matters.* Among the factors that make this desirable may be such things as:

1. Information systems dependencies—on the user, on other applications, on other installations.
2. The need to accommodate mission and organization changes.
3. The desire to maintain a degree of application mobility, perhaps for backup protection.
4. The interest in establishing certain standard practices and pro-

gramming methods to minimize training, assure people mobility, and maximize the advantages of new techniques.

Naturally the degree and form of this guidance varies, from ironclad standards on certain matters to "local-option" guidance on others. Information systems activities involve complex equipment and processes. To a large extent their effectiveness may well depend on the degree of technical and strategic guidance these activities receive. Naturally the form of this guidance must be chosen to fit the environment.

The last general responsibility we suggested for the information systems executive concerns tracking resources and the development and analysis of various ratios and indicators. We have already discussed measurements for individual computer installations and individual projects or key activities. Some companies also find it useful to track some additional factors that speak to the company's total information systems organization. Measurements that relate the size of the information systems effort to the size or work output of the total enterprise are sometimes used. Other more detailed measurements might include such factors as:

1. Information systems average cost per information systems person.
2. Information systems total costs as a factor against equipment costs.
3. Operational support people as a ratio to computer operators.
4. Application analysts and programmers as a ratio to equipment costs or total workforce.

Measurements and ratios of this type can be readily developed for each installation and for the company if the data is prescribed and collected as part of the information systems planning process. They make it possible to track each installation over time, to compare different installations, and to compare each installation against company averages. The value of such a measurement program lies first of all in the actions that can emanate from an *understanding of the factors causing differences* in the measurements. Some companies have also found that the discipline imposed by formalizing a measurement program can be a positive ingredient in an overall information systems management process.

 *Index*

Index

Authorities, accounting, 18
American Institute of CPAs, 817
Securities and Exchange Commission, 817
stock exchanges, 817
Avco, 758

B

Backer, Morton, 508, 585
Bankruptcy, corporate
accounting entity
business of debtor, 596
changes in, 596
conflict in, 596
contribution reporting, 597
estate under trustee, 596
nature, 595–96, 613
primary, 596
accounting requirements, 601–2
acts of, 591
administrative cost control, 607
basis of accountability, 595
capitalized value of future earnings, 597
Chapter X proceedings, 590, 601–13
Chapter XI proceedings, 590, 600–602
claim holders, 598
composition, 600–601
constitutional basis, 593–94, 613
creditor rights, 593
creditors' committee, 598
fair market value, 595, 597
fiduciary accountability, 596–97
fiduciary responsibility, 596
financing, 606, 608
going-concern versus liquidation, 587–88
going-concern value, 595
guidelines, 588
initiation, 591, 598–99
involuntary, 591–92, 599
lease of assets, 608
liquidation value, 595
personal bankruptcy versus, 595
plan of reorganization
absolute equity, 610
approaches, 610–11
capitalization of future earnings, 611, 613–14
classification of claims, 609
feasibility, 611–12
payment of claims, 611
priority claims, 609–10
secured claims, 610
source, 609
submission, 608–9
unsecured claims and interests, 610

Bankruptcy, corporate—*Cont.*
priority of claims
absolute equity, 606
administrative costs, 607
benefited interests, 607
proceedings, 597–98
adjudication as debtor, 600
commencement, 598–99
creditor meeting, 600
hearing for adjudication or dismissal, 599–600
initial phase, 598
petition, 598–600, 602
public interest, 594–95
receiver, 594–95, 598
referee, 597–98
rehabilitation, 602
pro forma balance sheet, 602
reporting requirements, 601–2, 613
full disclosure, 613
statement of affairs, 601–2
sale of assets, 608
stay of prepetition claims, 606
stockholder's rights
active, 593
passive, 593
transfer of property rights, 592, 612–13
trustee, 598
accounting responsibility, 614
audit, financial, 603
audit, management, 603
causes of financial distress, 605
claim evaluation, 603–4
election, 600
executory contracts, 604
fraud discovery, 604
insolvency or solvency, 605
inventory of assets, 603
mismanagement discovery, 604–5
operation of business, 605–6
purpose, 594–95, 613
qualification, 600
rehabilitation action, 605–6
rehabilitation prospects, 605
responsibilities, 603
trustee's certificates, 608
valuation, 597
voluntary, 591–92, 599
Bankruptcy Act
alternatives, 588–89
composition, 589
difficulties, 589
extension, 589
reorganization under creditor's committee, 589
reorganization in equity receivership, 589